Longman
Dictionary of
BUSINESS
ENGLISH

J. H. ADAM

Longman Dictionary of Contemporary English

The up-to-date learning dictionary – with 55,000 entries, easy-to-understand definitions and examples, new international pronunciation system, simple yet comprehensive grammatical coding, and many illustrations.

Longman Dictionary of English Idioms

A dictionary that explains all the most common idioms in use today, in language the learner can understand. Definitions are written in the 2,000-word vocabulary of the Longman Dictionary of Contemporary English, and there are up-to-date examples, historical explanations, and a full and clear cross-referencing system.

Longman Dictionary of Scientific Usage
A. GODMAN & E. M. F. PAYNE

A unique 'thesaurus' of scientific and technical terms – both a reference book and a practical aid. Its 10,000 entries are grouped in semantic sets, covering the most common terms used in General Science, Physics, Chemistry and Biology, and illustrated with over 300 drawings and diagrams.

Longman Lexicon of Contemporary English
TOM McARTHUR

The new vocabulary source book. It brings together words with similar meanings, listing them in sets and defining them in the 2,000-word Longman Dictionary of Contemporary English vocabulary. Full, clear definitions, examples *and* illustrations make it easy for students to understand the meanings of words and how they differ from others in the same set.

Longman
Dictionary of
BUSINESS
ENGLISH

J. H. ADAM

BSc(ECON) LONDON

Longman York Press

YORK PRESS
Immeuble Esseily, Place Riad Solh, Beirut.

LONGMAN GROUP LIMITED
Burnt Mill, Harlow, Essex

First published 1982
ISBN 0 582 55552 3
Printed and bound in Great Britain by
©ollins, Glasgow

Contents

To Alan Gilchrist
in grateful memory

Preface

THE AIM OF THIS DICTIONARY is to provide a useful reference book of the specialist and general vocabulary used in conducting business. The dictionary also aims to present that vocabulary in a clear and simple way which can be easily understood by the student of English.

Business consists of various forms of trade and the various services which are essential to trading. If a dictionary such as this is to be a useful tool for the business-man it must, therefore, deal with a number of independent but related fields of activity such as management, accounting and taxation, economic theory, banking and finance, computer technology, shipping and insurance, commercial law and the workings of the Stock Exchange. In making this dictionary, this full range of needs has always been kept in mind.

All of the words and phrases listed are defined in simple English, in a restricted vocabulary of about 2,000 words, based on Michael West's *A General Service List of English Words*, and complex grammatical structures have been avoided. This means that anyone who has studied English to intermediate level will be able to understand all of the definitions in this dictionary. Understanding is further aided by the use of example sentences to show how the words are used in context.

This dictionary is, however, more than just a list of words. It is fully cross-referenced so that related words and subjects can be studied for further information. In addition, the extensive appendices contain valuable information on weights and measures, conversion factors, and the countries of the world.

EPIGRAPH

No dictionary of a living tongue can ever be perfect, since while it is hastened to publication, some words are budding, and some falling away. – DR JOHNSON

Guide to the dictionary

Explanatory chart

THIS IS A QUICK GUIDE to the main features of the *Longman Dictionary of Business English*. These features are explained in more detail in the explanatory note on pages x to xiv. The numbers given in brackets after the descriptive labels on the right refer to the relevant paragraphs in the explanatory note.

agronomy AGR. agricultural economy; the theory and practice of crop and animal farming and soil management.	**main entries (1.1)**
break-even point ACCTS. the level of sales at which the income from goods sold is just enough to cover production, neither profit nor loss being made.	phrase (1.3)
Cie. (*French*, Compagnie) Company. **c.i.f., C.I.F.** cost, insurance, freight.	abbreviation (1.1)
Czechoslovakia a socialist federal republic in eastern Europe; pop. 15 million approx. (1973); capital, Prague, pop. 1.1 million approx.; languages, Czech, Slovak; currency unit, the koruna (crown), *pl.* koruny, divided into 100 haleru. Member, COMECON.	proper noun (1.1)
bridge SHIPG. the upper part of a ship used by the captain and officers, from which they control the ship. **air bridge** *see under* airline. **bridge deck** the highest deck of a ship. *Also* navigating bridge deck. **toll bridge** a bridge, usu. across a river, where a toll (charge) is made for permission to cross.	**sub-entries (1.2)**
alliance a union between two persons or groups of persons, and esp. an agreement between two or more countries to support each other.	**definitions (2.1)**
partition (1) division into parts or shares: *The partition of property among heirs.* (2) separation of parts: *The partition of India and Pakistan.* (3) a thing that separates, such as a light wall separating one office from another.	numbered definitions (2.2)
first-class *adj.* in the best class: *A first-class ticket/cabin/seat/hotel/passenger/compartment/saloon.*	**parts of speech (3.1)**

ahead (1) SHIPG. in a forward direction: *Full speed ahead.* (2) STK. EXCH. at higher prices: *Shares moved ahead,* were in demand and at higher prices.

field labels (4.1)

fox *v.* (1) (*colloq.*) to deceive by a trick: *He foxed me by pretending to be rich.* (2) to puzzle: *These figures fox me completely. Adj.* foxy.

examples (5.1)

fulfil to carry out: *This condition/clause has been fulfilled.* To complete; to perform: *He fulfilled his task/trust/responsibilities/obligations/duties.* (U.S.A., fulfill.)

oblique strokes (5.2)

airship *see under* aircraft.

cross-references (6.1)

air survey *see* aerial survey *under* survey.

see under (6.2)

Ajman *see* United Arab Emirates.

see (6.1)

biennial two-yearly; happening every two years: *The trade fair is biennial and is held only in odd-numbered years.* Cf. biannual.

cf. (6.4)

copy (1) matter to be set up in type or to be reproduced in print. (2) ADVTG. the words used in an advertisement. *See also* blind copy; carbon copy; fair copy; office copy.

see also (6.3)

lakh in the Indian subcontinent, one-hundred thousand, usu. of rupees, written Rs 1,00,000; one hundred lakhs make a crore, i.e. ten million rupees, written Rs 1,00,00,000. *Also* lac.

other information (7.1)
Also (7.1)

homeward *adj.* SHIPG. towards the home country: *Homeward freight. Homeward voyage. Syn.* inward. *Opp.* outward. *Adv.* homewards.

Syn./Opp. (7.2)

partial loss MAR.INSCE. a loss of part of the thing or goods insured, not the whole. *See* average (4). *Abbr.* P/L; P.L.

Abbr. (7.3)

moonshiner COM. (*colloq.*) a person who carries on an illegal trade, esp. by night.

colloq. (7.4)

abstract *n.* (1) a short account; information given in a shortened form: *The Statistical Abstract. Pron.* ábstrakt. (2) LAW *Abstract of title,* a legal document proving a person's right to possess certain property, giving a list in historical order of all deeds, claims, mortgages, etc. relating to the ownership.
v. LAW to steal; to turn to one's own use, money, securities, etc. belonging to another person; to take away secretly. *Syn.* embezzle, purloin. *Pron.* abstrákt.

pronunciation (8.1)

Explanatory note

Entries

1.1 main entry

The main entry is the word or words in **bold letters** at the beginning of each definition. This may be a single word, a phrase, a common abbreviation, the name of a person or place, or the title of a law or organization etc. The main entry begins with a capital letter only if it is a proper noun (that is, the name of a person or place) or the title of something (a government body, a principle of economic theory, for example).

The main entries are listed in alphabetical order.

1.2 sub-entry

Certain groups of words which have closely related but different meanings are shown under one general main entry. These sub-entries are printed in **small bold letters**. For example, **flight engineer**, **air hostess**, **air navigator**, **airline pilot** and **air steward** appear under the main entry **aircrew**.

Sometimes sub-entries will not begin with the same letter as the main entry. To help you find these sub-entries they are also listed as main entries with a cross-reference. If you look up **block grant** as a main entry you will find '**block grant** *see under* grant'.

1.3 phrases

If you are looking for a phrase you do not understand, you should look for it under one of the main words in the phrase, not necessarily under the first word. For example, the phrase **in account with** is explained under the main entry **account**; and **payable in arrear** is under the main entry **arrear**.

Definitions

2.1

The definition gives the meaning of the main entry in simple sentences or phrases. It is printed in roman letters (like these) and follows the main entry and – if they are shown – the part of speech and field-label (see below). All the definitions are written using a 2,000 word vocabulary based on West's *General Service List of English Words*.

2.2 numbered definitions

Under many of the entries in this dictionary you will find a series of definitions numbered (1), (2), (3) and so on. These numbers mean that the word has more than one meaning, and you should read them all to find the one you need. For example, two definitions are given in '**hold-up** (1) an armed robbery (2) a delay'.

Parts of speech

3.1

In this dictionary the part of speech of the main entry is only given where there is a risk of confusion about the way that the word or words in question are used to make sentences. The part of speech is given as an abbreviation in *italic letters*; for example, *n* for noun, *v* for verb (see the list of abbreviations on page xiv).

Field labels

4.1

Many of the definitions in this dictionary begin with a word or abbreviation in small capital letters, for example AGR., LAW, STK.EXCH. These are field labels, which show that the definition which follows belongs to a particular field of business: Agriculture, Law, the Stock Exchange etc. In some cases words or phrases have several meanings, each belonging to a separate field of business. These meanings are given as numbered definitions, each introduced by its own field label. A full list of field labels is given on page xiv.

Examples

5.1

With many of the definitions you will find examples, printed in *italic letters*, which show how the main word is used in a phrase or sentence. For example, under the main entry **particulars** you will find the definition 'detailed facts; full information' followed by the example *'Please give me full particulars of your new product'*.

Some examples show the special use of the main entry in a particular phrase or sentence, which may itself need further explanation. Thus in the second definition of the noun **mortgage** you will find: *'To raise a mortgage on (a house etc.)*, to borrow money by giving a mortgage on a house'.

5.2

Many of the main entries can be used in a variety of contexts. To show this range of use an oblique stroke (/) is employed in many of the examples to separate two or more words that might equally appear in this position. For example, under the main entry **daily**, you will find the following: *'A daily newspaper/meeting/delivery service'*. This means that you can say 'a daily newspaper', 'a daily meeting', and 'a daily delivery service'.

Cross-references

6.1

The cross-references show you where to look in the dictionary for a definition or a further explanation of a word or phrase. Most of the cross-references begin with the word *see*, and are followed by the word or phrase to which you should turn. Thus if you look up **Lady Day**, all you will find is: '**Lady Day** *see* quarter-day'. This means that Lady Day will be explained as part of the main entry **quarter-day**, where you will find a full definition and further details.

6.2

See under tells you to look at a sub-entry under a main entry. For example, if you look up **hard currency** you will find '**hard currency** *see under* currency'. This means that you should first find the main entry **currency**, and then look for the sub-entry **hard currency**. Similarly '**cyclical fluctuations** *see* trade cycle *under* cycle' means that you should first find the main entry **cycle** and then look for the sub-entry **trade cycle**.

6.3

Further information about a word is sometimes provided by telling you of other words on the same subject, introduced by *See also*. Thus after the definition and explanation given under the main entry **industrial medicine** you will find '*See also* industrial hygiene; industrial safety'. If you wish, therefore, to find out more about these aspects of industrial medicine you should look up **industrial hygiene** and **industrial safety** as main entries. In certain cases a special term relating to the word or phrase you have looked up may be found under a separate main entry. In such cases *See also* is used to direct you to this term. For example, under the main entry **ledger** you will find '*See also* self-balancing ledgers'. Thus you should look up **self-balancing ledgers** as a main entry to find its meaning.

6.4

A further form of cross-reference is introduced by Cf., meaning 'compare'. The comparison of the definition of one word with the definition of a related word will show how the meanings of these words are different or alike. Thus, following the definition for **mortgagee** you will find 'Cf. mortgagor', and under **civil commotion** 'Cf. riot'.

Other information

7.1

Other information about the main entries is given in a number of different forms.
   If there is more than one way to spell a word, or if a phrase has more than one form, the various forms are introduced by *or* or *also*. For example, you will find

affiliate *or* **affiliated company** as a main entry; and at the end of the definition and explanation of **laissez-faire** you will see '*Also* laisser-faire', this being an accepted alternative spelling.

7.2

Synonyms (words with the same or nearly the same meaning) and opposites are given at the end of certain definitions. These are introduced by the abbreviations *Syn.* and *Opp.* Thus, under **absolute monopoly**, you will find '*Syn.* pure monopoly; perfect monopoly'; and under **abundance** '*Opp.* dearth, scarcity'.

7.3

Where the main entry also has a common abbreviation, this is shown after the definition, explanation and examples, introduced by *Abbr.* Thus at the end of the entry on **Mountain (Standard) Time**, you will find '*Abbr.* M.S.T.'

7.4

Colloq., for colloquial, shows that a word or phrase is widely used in informal speech or writing, but is not suitable for formal use. *Colloq.* has also been employed to describe some words or phrases that should really be described as jargon or slang (words or phrases used only by persons belonging to certain professions, age-groups and other groups in society, and therefore not generally acceptable to the rest of society in formal speech or writing). Examples of this may be seen under **fudge**, **billet** and **bread and butter**.

Pronunciation

8.1

A guide to the pronunciation of a word is given only in unusual cases, or cases where the sound of word is altered according to its use. There are two forms in which this is shown, both introduced by the abbreviation *Pron.*, for pronunciation. First, where a word is not pronounced as you might expect from its spelling, the word is written in another form to show how the word might be spelled to sound as it is pronounced. For example, the sub-entry **puisne mortgage**, under **mortgage**, gives '*Pron.* pyooni' show how puisne is pronounced.

 Second, the meaning or use of a word sometimes changes when one part of the word is pronounced more strongly than another. In these cases the correct pronunciation is shown by a stress mark (´) placed over the part of the word which should be pronounced more strongly. For example, after the definition for the noun **contract** you will find '*Pron.* cóntract', and after the definition for the verb **contract** you will find '*Pron.* contráct'.

Field labels
(See Explanatory note, 4.1 on page xi)

ACCTS.	Accounts	IND. REL.	Industrial relations
ADVTG.	Advertising	IND. SFTY.	Industrial safety
AGR.	Agriculture	INSCE.	Insurance
BKG.	Banking	LAW	Law
COM.	Commerce	MAN.	Management
COMMOD. EXCH.	Commodity exchange	MAR. INSCE.	Marine insurance
		PUB. FIN.	Public finance
COMP.	Computers	QUAL. CONT.	Quality control
ECON.	Economics	SHIPG.	Shipping
ECON. HIST.	Economic history	STK. EXCH.	Stock exchange
ECON. THEORY	Economic theory	TAXN.	Taxation
FIN.	Finance	TOUR.	Tourism
IND.	Industry	TRANSPT.	Transport

Abbreviations used in the dictionary

Abbr.	abbreviation	*n.*	noun
adj.	adjective	*Opp.*	opposite
adv.	adverb	perh.	perhaps
approx.	approximately	*pl.*	plural
Cf.	compare	pop.	population
Colloq.	colloquial (used in informal speech or writing)	*prep.*	preposition
		Pron.	pronunciation
e.g.	for example	*sing.*	singular
esp.	especially	*Syn.*	synonym (a word with the same or nearly the same meaning)
etc.	et cetera, and so on, and the rest		
fem.	feminine	*usu.*	usually
fig.	figurative (using the word in some way other than its ordinary meaning)	*v.*	verb
		v.i.	intransitive verb
		v.t.	transitive verb
i.e.	that is to say		

Longman
Dictionary of
BUSINESS
ENGLISH

A

A Austria's international vehicle-registration letter.

A. ampere.

a. acre.

@ COM. at, a sign used in stating prices and quantities: *100 tonnes of coal @ £40 per tonne.*

A$ Australian dollar.

A1 (U.S.A., A 1) in the very best condition, of excellent quality. *A1 at Lloyd's, see* Lloyd's Register of Shipping.

a.a. always afloat; after arrival.

A.A.R. MAR. INSCE. against all risks.

A.B. able seaman.

ab. abridg(e)ment.

a/b airborne.

A/B. Aktiebolaget (*Swedish*, limited company).

a.B. auf Bestellung (*German*, on order).

abacus COM. a simple instrument for calculating, made up of a frame with rows of balls sliding on wires. *Pl.* abacuses. *Syn.* counting-frame.

abandon *n.* MAR. INSCE. the act of abandoning a ship or its cargo to the insurers.

v. (1) MAR. INSCE. to give up to the insurers one's rights of possession in a ship and its cargo when a total-loss insurance is paid. (2) LAW *To abandon an action*, to discontinue an action in the courts. (3) SHIPG. *To abandon ship*, to leave the ship unmanned and usu. in great danger. *See* derelict.

abandoned goods LAW goods having no owner.

abandonee MAR. INSCE. a person or organization to whom abandoned rights or property are given up; usu. the insurers.

abandonment (1) COM. giving up possession of rights or property to others: *Abandonment of goods in customs.*

product abandonment giving up, discontinuing to make or sell a product.

(2) MAR. INSCE. giving up possession of a ship and her cargo by the owners to the insurers when total-loss insurance is paid.

notice of abandonment written notice given by the insured to the insurer claiming for a total loss.

(3) TRANSP. the refusal by a consignee to accept delivery of goods badly damaged during carriage.

abandonment clause MAR. INSCE. a condition in a marine insurance policy that the owners of a ship may abandon it to the insurers if it becomes a total loss.

abandonment of action LAW *see* abandon, *v.* (2).

abatement (1) LAW legal action to put an end to a nuisance. (2) COM. a reduction in price; an amount taken off, a discount, esp. where there is a special reason, the goods perhaps being faulty, or arriving in a damaged condition. (3) TAXN. relief, reduction of tax.

abattoir a public building where animals are killed for food. *Syn.* slaughter-house.

abb., abbr., abbrev. abbreviation.

abbreviated address a shortened address used mainly for telegrams.

abbreviation a shortened form of a word or group of words made by writing only the first letter of the word or words, thus *B.A.* for *British Airways*; or by writing only part of a word: *Mon.* for *Monday.*

A.B.E.D.A. Arab Bank for Economic Development in Africa.

abeyance a state of being inactive, of not being in force: *The matter is in abeyance*, nothing is being done about it. *Many old laws and customs have fallen into abeyance*, have no longer any application.

abide to remain faithful to, to keep to, to hold to: *To abide by a decision, a rule.*

ability (1) COM. the state of being able to pay; having enough money to meet one's debts. (2) IND. REL. the basic idea that wages should be related to the profit-making power of the employer's business and thus to his ability to pay. (3) LAW having the right or power to act. (4) TAXN. the basic idea that the weight of taxes should be related to the income of the taxpayer in order to bring about equality of sacrifice.

aboard *adv. & prep.* SHIPG. on, in, or into a ship, train, plane or bus, etc.: *Passengers go aboard at noon.*

All aboard! a call to passengers and crew to board the ship, etc. quickly because it is about to go.

close aboard, hard aboard near the side of the ship, alongside.

abode LAW the place where a person lives or carries on his business, and may usu. be found.

abolition ECON. HIST. the movement which put an end to the international slave trade between about 1780 and 1880. *See* emancipation.

above *adv. & adj.* (in a document) mentioned earlier: *The above details. Refer to p. 3 above.* *Opp.* below.

above-mentioned a person or thing written about earlier in the document: *The above-mentioned debtors have paid. Abbr.* a/m.

above-named a person already mentioned by name.

above par STK. EXCH. (of a share) priced above its nominal or face value. Cf. at par; below par. *See* par.

above the line PUB. FIN. between 1947 and 1963 the budget accounts in Britain were presented in two parts: *above the line* were current expenditure and revenue (mainly taxes), while *below the line* were mostly capital items.

abr. abridge(d); abridg(e)ment.

abrasion of coin PUB. FIN. the loss of weight of coins by rubbing together in passing from person to person.

abridg(e)ment the act or result of shortening. A shortened form of a book.

abroad *adv.* away from the home country; in other lands, usu. across the sea: *He has gone abroad on business. We own property abroad.* *n. He has returned from abroad.*

abs. absent; absence; absolute; abstract.

A.B.S. American Bureau of Shipping.

abscond LAW to run away and hide for a dishonest reason: *The debtor absconded without paying his creditors. The cashier absconded with the cash. N.* absconder.

absence (1) the state of not being present: *Absence due to illness.* (2) time spent away: *During my absence.* (3) non-existence: *In the absence of information.*

absent *adj.* not present; staying away, esp. from work: *Mr Brown is absent from the office.* *Pron.* ábsent.
v. to stay away from: *He absented himself from the meeting. Pron.* absént.

absentee a person who stays away, esp. a worker who is often not at work or who stays away without good reason (a *voluntary absentee*) or because of sickness (an *involuntary absentee*).

absenteeism the practice by employees of frequently staying away from work, usu. without good reason.

absenteeism rate (1) the percentage of days lost out of the total number of days that could have been worked during a stated period. (2) the number of absentees per 100 workers on a certain day.

absentee landlord an owner of land who does not live in or near the property which he lets for rent to a tenant.

absentee ownership the state of being an absentee landlord.

absolute advantage ECON. the advantage that one country or part of a country possesses over others because it has natural supplies of raw materials, power, labour, etc. which enable it to make a certain product more cheaply. Cf. comparative advantage.

absolute interest LAW total and complete possession of, or ownership in, property.

absolute liability *see* strict liability.

absolute monopoly ECON. the theoretical situation which exists in a market where a single producer controls the whole of the supply of an article or service for which there is no substitute. *Syn.* pure monopoly; perfect monopoly.

absolute ownership *see under* ownership.

absolute privilege *see* privilege.

absolute title LAW a right of ownership that cannot be questioned, such as that of the owner of land registered under the Land Registration Act, 1925, which makes his right stronger than the right of any other person. Property registered 'with title absolute' has the advantage of having its ownership guaranteed by the State.

absolute value *see* intrinsic value.

absolve COM. to free from debt or from a responsibility: *You are absolved from further payments.*

absorption FIN. the uniting of one business with another, usu. smaller, business in order to make a single organization. *See* combination.

absorption costing ACCTS. the allocation of factory costs to each of the products and services making up the total output of the concern. *Syn.* full costing.

abstain to keep oneself from: *To abstain from strong drink;* to choose not to do: *To abstain from voting, from spending. N.* abstinence, abstention. *N. pers.* abstainer.

Abstinence Theory ECON. THEORY the theory expressed by Nassau Senior, English economist (1790–1864), that the supply of capital goods depended on the willingness of consumers to abstain from consumption by refusing to spend, thus freeing money for investing in capital goods. *Syn.* Agio Theory of Interest.

abstr. abstract.

abstract *n.* (1) a short account; information given in a shortened form: *The Statistical Abstract. Pron.* ábstrakt. (2) LAW *Abstract of title,* a legal document proving a person's right to possess certain property, giving a list in historical order of all deeds, claims, mortgages, etc. relating to the ownership.
v. LAW to steal; to turn to one's own use, money, securities, etc. belonging to another person; to take away secretly. *Syn.* embezzle; purloin. *Pron.* abstrákt.

abt. about.

Abu Dhabi *see under* United Arab Emirates.

abundance ECON. the theoretical situation when Man's wants are fully met. *Opp.* dearth, scarcity.

abuse of process LAW wrongful and unjust use of legal action in the courts by making foolish claims aimed at causing trouble and annoyance. *Syn.* frivolous action; vexatious action.

ac. acre.

A/C, A/c, a/c account (of money); account current.

a/c. bk. account book.

A.C. analogue computer.

a.c., à.c. (*French*: à compte) on account.

A.C.A. Associate of the Institute of Chartered Accountants in England and Wales. *See* chartered accountant.

A.C.A.S. Advisory, Conciliation and Arbitration Service.

acc. acceptance (of a bill of exchange); accepted; according to; account.

A.C.C.A. (certified accountant) Associate Member of the Association of Certified and Corporate Accountants.

accelerate (1) to increase speed; to cause to go faster: *The train service has been accelerated.*

(2) to increase in quantity: *Production is being accelerated to meet rising demand.*

accelerated depreciation TAXN. the practice of the tax authorities of allowing manufacturers to write off the cost of capital equipment, such as machinery, by larger amounts during the earlier years of its use than in the later years, and over fewer years than it is likely to be usable, in order to encourage investment.

acceleration LAW the happening of an event earlier than expected, or sooner than it would have happened, because of a change in the rights of other parties.

acceleration clause FIN. a condition in a bond, that if a party to the bond fails to make any payment by the due date, then all future payments immediately become due.

acceleration premium IND. an increasing rate of pay given to workers as their production increases, in order to urge them on to still higher productivity.

Acceleration Principle ECON. THEORY the idea developed by J.M. Keynes in his book *A General Theory of Employment, Interest and Money*, which relates consumption and investment by stating that changes in the demand for consumer goods bring about even greater changes in the demand for capital goods, such as machines, which make the consumer goods; and this fact explains why the demand for capital goods rises and falls at an accelerated, i.e. much faster, rate than the demand for consumer goods. *Syn.* Principle of Acceleration of Derived Demand. *See* accelerator; derived demand *under* demand. *Cf.* multiplier.

accelerator ECON. THEORY a shortened form of Acceleration Principle.

accept *v.* (1) to take, or agree to receive, something offered: *To accept a gift.* (2) to agree to, to say yes to an offer, proposal, suggestion, invitation, price, etc.: *I will accept £100 for it.* (3) to believe; to recognize; to take as being true and correct: *We must accept the facts. The members accepted the report.* (4) generally, to take as good or satisfactory: *The accepted method. I accept your opinion.* (5) to be received socially by one's fellows: *His colleagues accepted him.* (6) to make oneself responsible for performing a duty, for example making a payment.

to accept a bill of exchange COM. to promise by signing across the bill that it will be paid on the due date.

to accept on presentation to sign (a bill of exchange) as accepted when it is presented for the purpose.

an accepted bill a bill of exchange across which the drawee (debtor) has written 'accepted' and added his signature. *See* acceptance.

to accept a risk INSCE. to agree under a contract of insurance to be the insurer.

to accept service of a writ LAW to agree to recognize that the writ was properly delivered.

acceptable COM. of good enough quality for a particular purpose; not bad enough to be refused: *Printing of acceptable quality for paperbacks.*

acceptance (1) the act of accepting, taking what is offered or given.

acceptance of goods (*a*) COM. the position when the buyer *either* agrees to take them from the seller and willingly pays for them; *or* if after a reasonable time he has done nothing to refuse them, he is considered to have accepted them and is therefore bound to pay for them. (*b*) ADVTG. the willingness of consumers to buy a product. *See* brand acceptance; consumer acceptance.

acceptance of service LAW the act of a defendant's solicitor in agreeing to receive a writ of summons for his client. Once a solicitor has endorsed it, it need not be served personally on the defendant.

(2) the act of agreeing to an offer, invitation, proposal, and thus being bound to perform any duty it brings.

acceptance of offer LAW an agreement by one party to an offer put to him by another party. To become a contract the offer must be wholly accepted and the person making the offer must be informed.

acceptance of proposal INSCE. acknowledgment by an insurance company that it agrees to give the cover asked for, on payment of the premium.

acceptance sampling QUAL. CONT. the practice of choosing and examining only a small sample of articles being mass-produced, for it can be reasonably said that the quality of those samples reflects the general quality of the whole production and is a guide to the acceptability of the product.

acceptance trials SHIPG. a special voyage made to test a newly-built ship before it is accepted by its owners.

(3) the act of making oneself responsible for paying or bearing the cost, or performing duties, stated in a formal document. (4) BKG. the act of a person on whom a bill of exchange is drawn (the drawee) in writing on the face of the bill the word 'accepted' and his signature, so binding himself to pay the value of the bill when it is due.

acceptance against documents the position when the debtor or drawee is given the shipping documents at the time he accepts the bill.

acceptance by intervention the act of a third party who steps in and accepts a bill which has been protested for non-acceptance, i.e. has been dishonoured.

acceptance for honour the act of a person who is not a party to a dishonoured bill but who, as a kindness, accepts it in order to preserve the honour of the debtor.

acceptance supra protest the act of a person other than the debtor, who accepts a protested bill, usu. in return for a commission.

commission for acceptance the charge made by the acceptor, esp. a merchant banker, for accepting a bill and thus becoming responsible for its payment when it becomes due.

in default of acceptance in the event of a bill being refused when presented for acceptance.

non-acceptance refusal by the debtor to accept a bill when it is presented for acceptance, in spite of his having earlier agreed to accept it; dishonouring.

partial acceptance the act of accepting responsibility for paying only a part of the value of a bill, the balance being the responsibility of other acceptors.

present for acceptance to send a bill to the drawee for his acceptance.

procure acceptance to make arrangements for a bill to be accepted.

refuse acceptance to be unwilling to accept a bill when it is presented in spite of having earlier agreed to accept it; to dishonour.

term of acceptance (*a*) a condition made by the acceptor of a bill, e.g. that it shall be payable at a stated bank in a stated place; (*b*) the length of time between the date of acceptance of a bill and the date it becomes due for payment.

(5) BKG. a bill of exchange which has been accepted, presented to an acceptor who has written the word 'accepted' on the face of it, binding himself to pay the value of the bill when it becomes due. A bill of exchange generally.

acceptance account a record of business dealings in bills of exchange.

acceptance bill see *under* bill of exchange.

acceptance credit an exporter's bill of exchange which has been accepted by an accepting house and used as security for an advance or 'credit' by a bank, the exporter paying the discount. *Syn.* commercial credit. *See also* documentary acceptance credit *under* documentary.

acceptance house see accepting house.

acceptance market a section of the money market where accepted bills of exchange are bought and sold by discount houses and billbrokers.

accommodation acceptance see accommodation bill.

bank acceptance see bank bill.

blank acceptance see blank bill.

clean acceptance see general acceptance.

collateral acceptance an accepted bill of exchange lodged with a bank as security for a loan.

general *or* **clean acceptance** an accepted bill of exchange without special conditions. Cf. qualified or special acceptance *below*.

London acceptance credit a bill of exchange which has been accepted by an accepting house in London, whose name and reputation give added safety that the bill will be paid.

qualified *or* **special acceptance** a bill of exchange with special conditions as to when, where and how payment is to be made. Cf. general or clean acceptance *above*.

trade acceptance see trade bill.

uncovered acceptance (*a*) a bill of exchange which is open to risk of being dishonoured; (*b*) an accommodation bill, where one party receives no value.

accepted bill see bill of exchange.

accepting house BKG. a firm, usu. a merchant bank, which in return for a commission accepts bills of exchange drawn on certain trusted export merchants. Bills accepted by accepting houses are more easily and cheaply negotiated by the exporter because the high reputation of the accepting house greatly reduces the risk of non-payment. Accepting houses also act as bankers, esp. to many foreign companies. *Syn.* issuing house; merchant bank.

Accepting Houses Committee BKG. a group of the most important accepting houses and merchant banks in London. All members are of the highest reputation and bills of exchange drawn on them can be discounted at very favourable rates. *Abbr.* A.H.C.

acceptor BKG. a person who accepts, i.e. makes himself responsible for paying, a bill of exchange when due by signing his name on the face of the bill. A drawee becomes the acceptor when he accepts the bill.

acceptor for honour a person who accepts a dishonoured bill as a kindness, to preserve the honour of the debtor.

acceptor supra protest a person other than the debtor who accepts a protested bill.

access (1) a way by which a place, esp. property, can be reached or entered.

access road a road which gives access.

means of access: *The track is the only means of access to the farm.*

to allow access: *We cannot allow you access to our records.*

to bar access: *Access to the old mineshaft is barred.*

to gain access: *The firemen used a ladder to gain access to the roof.*

to give access: *That gate gives access to the garden.*

(2) a right of approach, of coming near to, of entry.

access to a market COM. the right or ability to sell goods freely into a market without breaking any laws or agreement. *Opp.* bar to a market.

legal access LAW a right allowed by law to certain persons to enter property, or to examine objects. A landlord enjoys access to his property at all reasonable times. Auditors have a legal right of access to the books and accounts of a company by whom they have been appointed auditors.

accessaries see accessories.

accessary see accessory.

accession (1) something added esp. to a collection, e.g. a book added to a library, investments added to a portfolio. Generally, an increase in a stock of anything.

accession of wealth the gaining possession of a stock of valuable things: *His main interest in life is the accession of wealth.*
(2) LAW additions to, or the improvement of, property.

accession rate MAN. the rate at which new employees have been added to the working force, expressed as a percentage of the average number of workers during a certain period.

accessories n. pl. COM. (1) parts which can be added to a machine, a car, a camera, etc. to make it more useful or more attractive. (2) extra things specially chosen to go well with a coat or dress, e.g. gloves, hat, shoes, handbag. *Also* accessaries.

accessory LAW a person who helps a criminal in breaking the law. *Syn.* accomplice. *Also* accessary.

access time COMP. (1) the time taken by a computer to find a piece of information in its memory or storage section and to use that information in its arithmetic unit. (2) the time needed to move a piece of information from the arithmetic unit to the memory.

accident LAW an unforeseen misfortune that is not caused by the carelessness or wrong-doing of the person applying for relief in the courts.

inevitable accident an accident which has results that were not intended and could not reasonably have been expected. *See* Act of God.

accident prevention IND. SFTY. measures taken to stop accidents from happening, esp. in factories and mines, on roads, railways, etc., and even in the home.

accident-prone said of a person who very often has accidents.

accident-repeater a person who is accident-prone, who repeatedly has accidents.

industrial accident an accident in which an employee is killed or injured while at work.

personal accident policy INSCE. *see under* policy of insurance.

marine accident *or* **accident of navigation** SHIPG. an accident causing loss or damage to a ship or ships at sea, esp. by collision.

accident frequency rate IND. SFTY. the number of accidents in which employees are killed or badly hurt, per million man-hours worked in a year.

accident insurance INSCE. any kind of insurance not included under the headings of marine, fire and life. *See* insurance, classes and kinds of; *also* insurance policy.

accidental (1) INSCE. happening by chance; unintentional; unexpected: *Accidental death, injury, loss.* Cf. negligent. (2) MAR. INSCE. *Accidental collision,* a collision which could not have been avoided. Cf. negligent collision.

acclamation loud, eager agreement; shouts of praise or approval: *The motion was passed with acclamation. The chairman was greeted with acclamation.*

accommodate (1) MAN. to make room for; to give lodging to: *The factory is too small to accommodate more machinery. Can you accommodate Mr Smith in your hotel?* (2) IND. (*with* to) to make a thing suitable for a special purpose: *This machine can be accommodated to making several sizes of product.* (3) SHIPG. to fit a ship for carrying a special class of passenger or cargo: *To accommodate a ship for transporting immigrants.* (4) FIN. to lend money, esp. as a kindness and usu. for only a short time: *I need to borrow £100 until tomorrow; could you please accommodate me?*

accommodation (1) MAN. lodgings; a place to stay or work; house-room, houses; rooms for use as offices, office space. (2) TOUR. *see* hotel accommodation. (3) SHIPG. the act of fitting out a ship or port to handle a special class of passenger or cargo. *See* accommodate (3); accommodation berth; passenger accommodation. (4) BKG. money lent, esp. when urgently needed; a short-term loan. *See* day-to-day accommodation.

to reach an accommodation COM. to come to an agreement, esp. about money matters.
(5) (in compounds) a thing made for a special purpose or having some special suitability. *See* accommodation land; accommodation road, etc.

accommodation acceptance *see* accommodation bill.

accommodation berth SHIPG. a berth reserved for use only by the ships of a particular shipowner. *Syn.* appropriated berth.

accommodation bill BKG. a bill of exchange which has been signed by a person as drawer, acceptor or endorser without his receiving any value but only to lend his name to help another person to negotiate the bill. *Syn.* accommodation acceptance; accommodation note; kite.

accommodation endorsement BKG. writing usu. on the back of a bill of exchange or other negotiable instrument by a person who signs the instrument as endorser, to lend his good name and reputation and to take responsibility for seeing that payment will be made on the due date, thus enabling the instrument to be more rapidly and more cheaply negotiated in the market. (In U.S.A., accommodation indorsement.) *See* endorsement.

accommodation land ECON. THEORY special farm land having a higher rental value than ordinary land because it is near a town or market centre and is therefore able to command an accommodation rent.

accommodation note *see* accommodation bill.

accommodation paper BKG. negotiable instruments which have an accommodation endorsement.

accommodation party BKG. a person or company of very good reputation who draws, accepts or endorses a negotiable instrument in order to make it more easily negotiable.

accommodation rent ECON. THEORY the extra rent or price that has to be paid for accommodation land.

accommodation road a road made specially for use by persons living in houses away from a public road. *Syn.* accommodation way.

accommodation unit used by local government housing officials to mean a house or a flat suitable as a home for a family unit, which could range from a single person to parents with several children.

accommodation way *see* accommodation road.

accompany to go with, in the company of.
accompanied by together with.
accompanied luggage/baggage that which travels with the passenger, not separately. *Opp.* unaccompanied.
accompanying documents/papers those which are to be found in the same cover or attached to this present letter, etc.

accomplice a helper in an unlawful act. Cf. accessory.

accordance agreement, esp. in phr. *in accordance with* (*the rules, etc.*), in keeping with, in agreement with, as required by.

accord and satisfaction LAW an agreement (the accord) between parties to an existing contract that, in return for the payment of a stated sum (the satisfaction) by one party, he is freed of his duties under the contract.

account *n.* (1) a counting up, a calculation: *Money of account. To be quick at accounts*, to be clever in making money calculations. (2) ACCTS. (*a*) generally, any counting and recording of money, esp. a statement of money received or paid: *You must keep an account of your expenses.* (*b*) a detailed record in orderly form of business dealings between parties who are debtor and creditor, and of the manner in which money is received, held, or spent.
in account with the heading of a statement or copy of the account kept by one party of dealings with another.
(*c*) the heading of a ledger sheet recording as debits and credits all dealings during a given period with a particular party, or relating to a

particular kind of asset, liability, receipt, expense, etc.: *We have opened an account in your name. Charge it to/put it on, my account. A payment on account*, a part-payment to be credited to an account. *See* accounts, *pl. below*.
(*d*) a customer, esp. one who has regular dealings with the business and therefore has a ledger account in his name, the balance being settled on presentation of a statement of account or at an agreed later date. (3) LAW an action in a court of law claiming 'an account', i.e. a true record of business dealings affecting the parties in disagreement. Thus a principal may claim from his agent a record, or account, of money received from the sale of the principal's goods; or one partner may claim from another a full statement, or account, of the business profits of the partnership. (4) a story, report, description, explanation: *An account of a conversation/a journey/negotiations.*
by all accounts from what one hears on all sides.
to call to account to make a person explain his actions, esp. when they appear to have been wrong.
to give a good account of oneself to succeed.
on this account for this reason.
on account of because; for the reason that.
on no account not for any reason; certainly not.
on his account for his sake; in his interest.
(5) consideration: *To take into account*, to take into consideration.
to take account of to take notice of; to give due weight to.
to leave out of account to take no notice of; intentionally not to include.
(6) importance: *A matter of little account. A man of no account*, of little or no importance.
v. (1) (*with* to) to explain, esp. how money has been received and spent: *I must account to him for the money he left with me.* (*with* for) to give reasons for: *Can you account for the loss on this order?* (2) to value: *We account him the best of our managers.*

Account, The STK. EXCH. one of the periods of credit, usu. of 14 days, allowed on dealings between members of the (London) Stock Exchange. Securities bought 'on account' during this time are either paid for 'at Settlement' at the agreed price, or the debt is 'carried over' or 'continued' to the next Account Day in return for a payment of interest called continuation or contango.

accountable *adj.* bound by duty to give an account or explanation of one's actions, esp. when one is responsible for the money or property of others: *The master is accountable to the owners for the safety of his ship.*
accountability *n.* the state of being accountable.

account agent *see* credit agent.

accountancy ACCTS. the keeping of accounts (called accounting in U.S.A.). The work and profession of an accountant: *He intends making a career in accountancy.*

accountant ACCTS. a person having special knowledge of commerce and of keeping of accounts in business and government organizations. *See* certified public accountant; chartered accountant; public accountant. Cf. bookkeeper.

chief accountant the highest-ranking officer responsible for the proper keeping of the accounts of a business or other organization.

cost *or* **management accountant** a person whose work is to give the managers of a business the information they require to control all forms of expense, including the cost of making products, providing services, deciding prices, and checking overheads.

account balance ACCTS. the difference between the totals of all the debit entries and all the credit entries in an account, i.e. the sum required to make one side of the account balance the other.

account books *see* books of account.

account current ACCTS. a statement, usu. headed *A in A/c with B* and made out in the form of a copy of the ledger account recording business dealings between the two parties during a given period. *Example:* a bank passbook. Cf. current account.

Account Day STK. EXCH. the last day of The Account and the fifth day of the periods of five days known as The Settlement, when brokers and their clients pay amounts due between them, when sums due between members are settled by cheque or are 'carried over' or 'continued', and when deliveries of stock are made to the buyers. *Syn.* Pay Day; Settling Day; Settlement Day. *See* contango.

account executive ADVTG. & COM. a business executive, esp. one in an advertising agency, who handles orders from customers having regular dealings with the business who have therefore had an account opened in their name.

accounting ACCTS. (1) in U.S.A., the same meaning as accountancy in Britain. (2) in Britain, a system of recording the money value of business dealings and income and expenditure accounts to enable the management of a concern to see the financial position at any time. *See also* cost accounting; management accounting; conservative accounting; current cost accounting.

accounting cost *see under* cost.

accounting equation ACCTS. the basic idea (or principle) on which all financial accounting depends, that the resources possessed by a business are equal to the sum of the sources from which those resources were obtained. In other words the capital (or sum supplied by the own-

ers) plus the liabilities (or amount owed by the business) together equal the assets (or resources), and is expressed in the equation: capital + liabilities = assets.

accounting machine ACCTS. strictly any machine intended to carry out at the same operation the entry, totalling of entries, and the balancing of accounts. More generally, the expression can also mean any machine which will prepare invoices, deal with pay-rolls or in any way be of use in keeping financial records.

accounting period (1) ACCTS. any period (or fixed length of time) usu. a year, at the end of which accounts are made up, balances are struck and a profit or loss figure is arrived at. *Syn.* financial year; accounting year. (2) STK. EXCH. the period for which an income distribution is due, usu. a year or half-year.

accounting procedure ACCTS. the orderly steps taken by accounts staff in keeping proper financial accounts.

accounting, social *see under* social.

accounting summary ACCTS. one of several short statements together forming the final accounts or financial reports of a business at the end of a given accounting period. These summaries are: the three profit statements (the trading account, the profit and loss account, and the appropriation account) and the balance sheet. The purpose of each summary is to show the financial position from a particular point of view. The expression accounting summary can also cover statements not included in the usual final accounts which are prepared for the information of the management, e.g. a funds flow statement.

accounting year *see under* year.

account, money of ACCTS. the standard unit of money of a particular country, in which all accounts are kept and all money values are measured. In Britain, the pound sterling; in U.S.A., the U.S. dollar; in France, the French franc; and so on. *Syn.* unit of account.

account payable ACCTS. an invoice that has yet to be paid, and therefore represents money owed by the business to somebody else. *Opp.* account receivable.

account payee BKG. words sometimes added to the crossing on a cheque in order to prevent dishonesty, to tell the paying banker to credit the amount of the cheque to the named payee's bank account and to no other. Sometimes the word 'only' is added: *account payee only. Abbr.* a/c payee.

account receivable (1) ACCTS. a sum of money due to be received from a customer in the ordinary course of trade but not yet paid. *Opp.* account payable. (2) *pl.* COM. the total of all the accounts receivable. This may be used by the business as security for a loan, or may be sold to a factor: *See* factoring. *Syn.* book debts.

account rendered ACCTS. words used in a statement of account to refer to an unpaid balance of account of which details have been given in an earlier statement.

accounts *n. pl.* ACCTS. a group or set of accounting records (each called an account) which, taken together, tell the owners and managers of a business how much it owes and how much it is owed; and after periodical balancing, how much profit and loss has been made. *See* interpretation of accounts *under* interpretation.

annual accounts a complete set of accounts required by law to be produced by all companies and most other business and administrative organizations, showing the results of trading and other operations during the accounting period, usu. of a year, and the state of affairs at the end of that period.

consolidated accounts those which must by law be prepared by a holding company, showing the results of trading and the financial position of all members of that group of companies in a combined form.

final accounts the official accounts of a company or other business concern, usu. the same as the annual accounts. *See also* directors' report.

group accounts the accounts of a holding company and of its subsidiaries presented together but not combined as in the case of consolidated accounts.

impersonal accounts any ledger accounts that are not personal accounts. Impersonal accounts may be subdivided into real accounts and nominal accounts, and are kept in the impersonal ledger. Cf. personal accounts *below*.

interim accounts those prepared by a company or group of companies to show the results of trading during only a part of the full accounting period, often for half a year, mainly to show progress and often not audited, being intended for information and guidance.

ledger accounts accounts forming the main part of the accounting system of a business organization, so called because they used to be written into a 'ledger' or large account book, but are often now kept on loose sheets or cards or in the files of a computer. They are in three groups as follows:

nominal accounts those ledger accounts which relate to revenue and expenditure.

personal accounts ledger accounts of debtors and creditors whose personal or business names are used as headings.

real accounts those ledger accounts which relate to the assets and capital of the business concern. The balances of the real accounts are the basis of the balance sheet.

account sales COM. a detailed statement sent by a commission agent to his principal, listing amounts obtained for goods sold for the principal and showing amounts to be taken off for selling-expenses, agent's commission, etc., the resulting balance being called 'net proceeds of sale'.

accounts clerk *see* book-keeper.

accounts, falsification of *see under* falsification.

accounts, interpretation of *see under* interpretation (1).

account stated COM. words used when referring to an account, the balance of which has already been agreed by the parties as being correct.

account, statement of *see* statement of account.

account terms COM. words used, esp. on a quotation or estimate, to point out that the goods to be supplied are to be debited to a credit account in the customer's name and are to be paid for at the usual time for such accounts to be settled. Cf. cash on delivery; cash with order.

account, unit of *see under* unit.

accred. accredited.

accredited COM. officially recognized. (of persons) highly trusted, of declared rank or position and holding formal power to represent. Officially declared to be of good quality: *Accredited milk.*

accredited agent *see* credit agent.

accredited parties persons to whom special powers have been given to act in certain stated matters, esp. bankers and brokers.

accretion ECON. an increase in value of an asset by natural growth, e.g. of land by a change in the coastline or in the course of a river; of forests by the growth of trees; of money by the adding of interest.

accrual (1) ACCTS. continual increase and growth; accumulation; the act of accruing. (2) LAW the gradual increase of a fund by additions.

accrual concept ACCTS. a basic accounting rule that when balancing costs against income to arrive at a profit or loss during a given period, the costs taken are 'accrued costs', i.e. of goods and services used up or employed during the period, whether paid for or not; and the income taken is accrued income, i.e. income earned during the period, whether actually received or not. *Syn.* (U.S.A.) accrual basis.

accrue COM. to increase gradually with time; to become larger by natural growth: *Interest accruing from 1 July. Arrears of rent accrued month by month. See* accrual.

accrued costs ACCTS. *see* accrual concept.

accrued expenses ACCTS. the same as accrued costs but limited to overhead expenses.

accrued income ACCTS. *see* accrual concept.

accrued interest (1) COM. interest earned during a certain period but which has not yet been paid, either because it is overdue or because it may not be due until a later event, e.g. the completion of a contract. (2) STK. EXCH. interest on gilt-edged securities which has been earned but is not yet due for payment. If a sale takes place at this stage, the seller and the buyer share the accrued interest.

acct. accountant; account.

accumulate to grow greater by regular or continual additions.

accumulated fund ACCTS. the balances in a group of accounts which, when totalled, show the liability of (i.e. the amount owed by) a non-trading concern, e.g. a club or society, to its members. Cf. the capital account in a trading concern.

accumulated dividends those on cumulative preference shares which have not been paid on the due date. *Syn.* accumulative dividends.

accumulated depreciation the total of all the yearly amounts so far written off the value of a fixed asset.

accumulated profits what remains in the profit and loss appropriation account after putting some profit to reserves and using some for dividends. The remaining unused balance, or accumulated profit, is carried forward and is available for use next year.

accumulation STK. EXCH. in U.S.A., the difference between the cost of a bond bought at a discount and its face value. This difference partly determines the yield at maturity.

accumulative dividends see accumulated dividends *under* accumulate.

accumulator COMP. that part of a computer in which the results of calculations are held until needed.

accumulator bet a bet on several horse or dog races, the original stake-money and any winnings being laid on the next race, and so on until at the end of the day the gambler either loses all or has big winnings.

accurate description COM. one, esp. in an advertisement, which is true and not misleading, otherwise it would be an offence under the fair trading laws: *This advertisement or catalogue gives an accurate description of the goods.*

acetate ribbon see carbon ribbon.

a.c.i. (*French*: assuré contre l'incendie) insured against fire.

acid test ratio FIN. a test used in deciding solvency, by relating a concern's most liquid assets (usu. its bank balance, money due from customers, cash, and quickly saleable investments) to its current liabilities. In U.S.A., quick asset ratio. Cf. liquid ratio test; current ratio.

ack. acknowledge.

ack'd. acknowledged.

ackers (*slang*) money.

ackgt. acknowledg(e)ment.

acknowledge (1) COM. to make known to the sender that a thing he has sent has arrived: *To acknowledge (receipt of) a letter, parcel, order, etc.* (2) LAW to recognize as legal, as having force: *To acknowledge a debt, a claim, an authority, ownership of copyright, a right of way, etc. Syn.* admit. *Opp.* disclaim.

acknowledg(e)ment COM. (1) a report to the sender that the thing he has sent has arrived: *We have had no acknowledgment of our letter.* (2) a formal document from a supplier to his customer accepting an offer such as a purchase order, and so making a contract to supply. (3) LAW a formal declaration by a person that the signature on a particular document is his own. (4) a statement recognizing another person's right or claim, e.g. of a debt.

acknowledg(e)ment of copyright COM. & LAW a note in a book or written article saying where a piece of copyright material has been taken from and usu. expressing thanks for permission to print it.

acknowledg(e)ment of debt COM. & LAW an admission in writing signed by a debtor that he owes the amount of the debt. This keeps the debt, 'alive' so that it does not become barred by limitation.

à compte (*French*, a payment on account) a part payment.

a/c payee see account payee.

acquaintance COM. some knowledge of a person or subject gained usu. through work: *I have an acquaintance with Spanish.*

business acquaintance a person one knows, but who is not close enough to call a friend.

acquiescence LAW assent by remaining silent; acceptance of an infringement of one's rights by raising no objection and so losing any right to relief as a plaintiff.

acquire COM. to become the owner of; to buy; to get possession of: *To acquire a property by purchase, by inheritance.*

to acquire a reputation for to get a name for being good at.

acquired for clients words on an estate agent's signboard making it known that he has negotiated the buying of the particular house for his clients.

acquired surplus FIN. a surplus that has been gained by means other than regular trading. An excess of assets over liabilities which has arisen from reorganizing the capital of one or more businesses, e.g. by a company changing the par value of its shares or stock, or by merging two or more businesses.

acquisition (1) the act of acquiring: *The acquisition of properties, of a business, of wealth. Opp.* disposal. (2) a thing acquired. Something newly added to an existing stock. *Recent acquisitions to a library*, books newly added.

acquisitive eager to acquire things; desiring to be wealthy. *The acquisitive society*, classes of people who greatly desire to possess material things and to have the means to buy them continually.

acquittance (1) COM. & LAW the settlement of a debt or other obligation or duty in full. *Syn.* quittance; quietus. (2) LAW a written document providing proof of the settlement of a debt or the performance of a duty. *Syn.* acquittal.

acre a measure of land (and sometimes of water) surfaces, 4840 sq. yds. = 1/640 sq. m. = 0.404686 ha, in general use in Britain and the U.S.A. The larger Scottish acre (6150 sq. yds.) and Irish acre (7840 sq. yds.) are not now used. *See also* customary acre.

acreage AGR. an area usu. expressed as a number of acres. *The barley acreage has doubled. Pron.* áykrij.

across the board including all persons and things in a group; words used to describe increases in wages or prices which are applied in the form of a standard or fixed amount or as a fixed percentage to every unit in a particular group, e.g. to the wages of each worker or to the price of each product in the group so that all are treated equally and there are no exceptions. *The increase in wages is limited to £6 per week across the board. An across-the-board increase of 5% on our list prices.*

across the counter COM. in the regular course of trade: *Sales made across the counter.* Cf. over the counter; under the counter.

act. acting; actuary.

A.C.T. advance corporation tax.

act *n.* LAW (1) the doing of something: *The thief was caught in the act of stealing.* (2) a thing done: *An act of kindness, of courtesy.* (3) a law decided by the governing body of a country which all citizens must obey. (Usu. with initial capital A: *Act.*) (4) any written agreement binding in law: *This is my act and deed*, words said when signing a binding legal instrument. *v.* (1) to do: *Think before you act. How soon can you act?* (2) (*with* for) to represent: *An agent acts for his principal; a solicitor acts for his client.* (3) to do some special work; to serve some special purpose: *The brakes act on the drum. Let me act as interpreter.*

acting performing the duties of another person for a short while: *The acting manager is doing the duties of the manager until a new man is appointed.*

acting partner COM. *see under* partner.

act in law LAW the making of a legal document, such as a contract or a will.

action LAW a case brought in a civil court to claim one's legal rights; a lawsuit. *Syn.* legal action. *See also* frivolous action; vexatious action.

actionable LAW providing good grounds for a legal action.

action in rem LAW a case brought in the Admiralty Court upon the arrest of a ship.

active (1) full of action; busy; alive. (2) STK. EXCH. of market conditions, much buying and selling of shares: *Active dealings took place in oils* (i.e. in oil shares). (3) COMMOD. EXCH. *The demand for copper is active*, many traders are wanting to buy copper.

active assets FIN. *see under* assets.

active balance ECON. (of payments, of trade) favourable. *Opp.* passive balance; unfavourable balance.

active bonds *see under* bond, *n.*

active circulation BKG. & PUB. FIN. bank-notes which are actively in use by the public as distinguished from stocks of notes which are held in reserve by the bank.

active file *see under* file.

active market *see under* market.

active money ECON. money actually circulating from person to person and being used by the public in buying and selling goods and services, as distinguished from inactive or idle money held in the form of bank balances.

active partner *see under* partner.

active trust LAW a trust of which the trustee actually performs certain duties in managing it. Cf. bare trustee.

act liability insurance INSCE. motor-car insurance which covers only those liabilities to other road users which must be insured under the law. *Syn.* third-party insurance.

act of bankruptcy LAW a thing done by a debtor which may give his creditors the legal right to have him made bankrupt, e.g. hiding or running away from his creditors.

Act of Congress LAW a law passed by Congress, the highest law-making body of the United States of America.

act of courtesy LAW a thing done out of kindness or courtesy, not because of any legal duty. *Syn.* act of grace.

Act of God (1) an event caused by natural forces which no human power could prevent, e.g. storm, earthquake. (2) SHIPG. when written on a bill of lading, neither party is responsible for loss so caused. Cf. force majeure.

act of grace (1) LAW a pardon given by Act of Parliament. (2) the same as an act of courtesy.

Act of Parliament LAW a law passed in those countries in which the name Parliament is given to the highest governing body. In Britain, an Act of Parliament cannot be overruled except by a further Act. *See* statute law.

act of war LAW an event caused by the use of force by one country upon another against the rules of international law and therefore leading, or likely to lead, to war. A warlike act.

actual *see* actual price.

actual loss INSCE. the exact value of the loss known to have been suffered, not merely a supposed or 'paper' loss.

actual price STK. EXCH. the price at which a jobber is agreeable to buy or sell; sometimes shortened to 'actual'.

actual total loss INSCE. where the thing insured is completely lost or is so badly damaged that it is not worth repairing. Cf. constructive total loss; presumed total loss.

actuarial calculation INSCE. the result of the work of an actuary, usu. in the form of tables showing the degree of chance or risk affecting some particular branch of insurance.

actuary INSCE. a professional person employed by an insurance company because he has special skills in calculating rates of insurance by using the mathematical laws of probability to measure risk. In England, actuaries are members of the Institute of Actuaries, and in Scotland, of the Faculty of Actuaries.

government actuary an official who makes forecasts about future movements and events, esp. of population statistics.

ad, ad. (*colloq.*) advertisement. *See also* small ads.

A/d., a.d. after date.

add. addenda; addressed.

added value *see* value added.

added value tax *see* value added tax.

adder (U.S.A.) an adding machine.

adding machine COM. & ACCTS. an office machine, usu. with keys like a typewriter, used for adding and subtracting figures. Cf. addlister; calculating machine.

additional premium *see under* premium.

addl. additional.

add-lister COM. & ACCTS. an adding machine that prints figures in the form of a list on a band of paper.

address *v.* (1) to write (on an envelope, parcel, etc.) the name of the receiver, usu. with the place where that person or company lives or works. (2) to speak to a person or group: *He addressed the meeting.* (3) COMP. a sign made up of letters or numbers which enables a digital computer to find the exact place in its memory where certain information is stored. The word is also used for the place itself.
n. (1) the number of the building, name of the street and town, etc. of a person or company. (2) such information written down, as on an envelope or parcel.

address book a book in which names and addresses are recorded, usu. in alphabetical order. Cf. address card.

address card one of a set of index cards used for recording names and addresses in alphabetical order. Cf. address book.

address commission SHIPG. a commission paid to the agent of the charterers for his work in arranging the loading of a ship.

addressee the person to whom a letter, telegram, parcel, etc. is addressed.

address, forms of *see under* forms.

addressing machine a machine which prints names and addresses on envelopes or letters by means of small printing plates or stencils.

Addressograph a well-known make of addressing machine.

addsd. addressed.

'add-to' system COM. an arrangement by which a customer gets a number of articles on hire-purchase but makes a down payment only on the first article.

adhesive stamp *see under* stamp.

adj. adjective; adjourned; adjustment.

adjective law LAW that part of the law which relates to practice and procedure, i.e. to the arrangements and rules by which the work of the courts is carried out in an orderly and proper manner. Cf. substantive law.

adjourn to put off until a later time or to another place. *The chairman adjourned the meeting until Monday. The adjourned hearing resumed today. The committee adjourned to the dining-room for lunch.*

adjournment sine die the adjourning or closing esp. of a meeting or a court case, without deciding on what day it will be reopened. (Sine die: *Latin*, without a day.)

adjudicate LAW to give judgment upon; to decide as a judge how a claim or quarrel be settled or how a legal question be dealt with.

adjudication order LAW a court order declaring a debtor to be bankrupt and arranging for his affairs to be managed by a trustee.

adjust (1) to put right: *The error in the account has been adjusted.* Syn. to correct; to rectify. (2) to make suitable for, or to fit, a particular purpose: *The book value of the stock has been adjusted to arrive at its true worth. The machine can be adjusted to make several different sizes of product.* (3) INSCE. to settle an insurance claim. *See* adjustment.

adjusted selling price ACCTS. one of the methods of valuing stock-in-trade for accounting purposes esp. in retail shops, i.e. reducing the selling price by taking off the expected profit and selling expenses.

adjuster INSCE. a person employed by an insurance company to value losses and to settle claims. *See* adjustment; average adjuster; claims adjuster; fire-loss adjuster.

adjustment (1) INSCE. the course of reaching an agreed settlement between insurer and insured regarding the amount of the claim. (2) MAR. INSCE. the actual amount of money due to the insured to repay his loss, after taking account of any allowances and deductions.

adjustment account *see* control account; total account.

adjustment bonds *see under* bond, *n.*

adjustment mechanism ECON. a means by which a country whose costs have become too high can regain a favourable balance of trade without suffering the pain of high unemployment to force wages down.

adjustment of average MAR. INSCE. *see* average adjuster; *also* general average, particular average *under* average.

adjustment of claims COM. the settlement of demands when goods are lost, damaged or delayed during carriage.

adm. admitted.

ad. man. advertising *or* advertisement manager.

admass *or* **ad-mass** ADVTG. (1) the systematic and excessive use of the mass media (television, radio, newspapers, etc.) by commercial and industrial firms for powerful advertising, with resulting bad effects on the life and happiness of the public. (2) the mass of people whom advertisers aim to reach in using the mass media. *See* advertising media.

Admin. Administration (Government).

admin. administrator; administratrix.

administered price *see under* price.

administration (1) MAN. the control, direction and management of a business or service. (2) LAW the work of an executor or administrator in managing and settling finally the affairs of a dead person.

Administration LAW (*with* capital A) (1) the government of a country, esp. in U.S.A. (2) in Britain, the ministers appointed by the Prime Minister to help him to govern the country: *Mr Callaghan's Administration.*

administration action LAW and action in the High Court by a creditor to obtain a court order for payment of money owing to him by a debtor who has died.

administration bond *see under* bond, n.

administration costs ACCTS the costs of controlling, directing and managing a business which cannot be directly charged to the production, distribution and selling of its products. *Syn.* administration expenses; administrative expenses; administrative overheads; establishment charges.

administration expenses *see* administration costs.

administration, letters of *see* letters of administration.

administration of estates LAW the work of settling the affairs of a dead person by his personal representatives, such as collecting and selling his assets, paying his debts and dividing up what is left among those persons having the right to receive it. *See* administrator; executor; letters of administration.

administration order LAW in the case of small bankruptcies, a court order for the quick administration, without further application to the court, of the affairs of a bankrupt who has died.

administrative control MAN. (1) a means of checking, testing and watching over the operations of running a business or public service in order to make it successful. (2) the power to direct, to make rules for the management and running of a business or service.

administrative expenses *see* administration costs.

administrative overheads *see* administration costs.

administrative tribunal one of a group of tribunals which have power to settle special problems of government administration, esp. in social and legal matters, e.g. industrial courts, rent tribunals, the Transport Tribunal and the Special Commissioners of Income Tax.

administrator (1) LAW a person appointed to manage the affairs of another, esp a person appointed by a probate court to settle the affairs of someone who has died without appointing an executor, or whose appointed executor has died or cannot or will not act. *See* personal representative. (2) MAN. a person having power to control, direct or manage a business or other organization.

administratrix LAW a female administrator.

Admiralty Court *or* **Court of Admiralty** LAW in Britain, a division of the High Court which has power to decide cases concerning ships and the sea.

admission (1) the act of allowing to enter: *Admission by ticket only. An admission ticket.* (2) the right to allow or refuse permission to enter: *Admission reserved,* (in a restaurant or bar) the management state that they have the right to admit or not to admit members of the public. (3) STK. EXCH. *Admission to quotation,* permission given by the Stock Exchange to a company for its shares to be dealt in by members of the Stock Exchange. *See* application for quotation.

admit (1) to allow to enter, to allow to join: *The shareholders were admitted to the meeting. He has been admitted a member of the Stock Exchange.* (2) to accept, to agree to be right: *We admit your claim.*

adopt (1) to approve, to accept: *The board adopted the recommendations of the committee.* (2) to pass or carry, esp. a resolution: *The meeting adopted the resolution proposed by Mr Smith.* (3) to choose formally, to support the work of: *Mr K. has been adopted as candidate for election to the council.* (4) to take up and act upon: *We must adopt a strong course of action to reduce expenses. He adopted a firm attitude.* (5) to take into one's care; to become responsible for: *The local authority has adopted this road,* has taken over responsibility for repairing it.

adoption of contract COM. & LAW the acceptance of a contract by one party as binding even though he has the right to be relieved of his duty under the contract.

adoptive Act LAW an Act of Parliament which does not operate as law until it is adopted, i.e. accepted and brought into force by a local authority or other body of persons who, under the provisions of the Act, are given special power to decide whether or not to bring it into effect.

A.D.P. automatic data processing.

ad referendum COM & LAW (*Latin*, to be further considered) words used to describe a contract which has been signed but which contains certain provisions of relatively little importance that remain to be further considered: *An ad referendum contract.*

ads. advertisements.

adulteration LAW & IND. the dishonest act of lowering the value of a substance by mixing it with impure matter so as to result in making the substance something different from and less pure than what it is intended or held out to be: *The adulteration of foodstuffs is illegal.* **adulteration of coinage** see debasement of coinage.

Adv. advance; advertisement; advice.

adv. advance; adverb; advisory.

ad val. ad valorem.

ad valorem COM. (*Latin*, according to value) words describing a duty or tax which is charged as a percentage of the value of the goods, as distinguished from a specific or fixed duty or tax. *See also* tariff; excise duty.

advance v. STK. EXCH. to move forward or upward: *Shares advanced in all sectors*, market prices were higher in all kinds of shares.
to advance money to pay money before it is due; to lend money.
n. (1) money advanced: *Pay him an advance of £20 on his wages.* (2) a payment of part of a sum due before receipt of the goods. *We require you to pay an advance of 50% of the price before supplying your order.* (3) BKG. a loan, esp. to a customer by a joint-stock bank in the form either of a bank overdraft or a bank loan; or by a finance company, esp. under a hire-purchase agreement. *See* advances, *n. pl.*

advance of royalties COM. a sum of money which a publisher pays to the writer of a book at an agreed time, usu. on signature of the publishing agreement or on the day of publication of the book, and which the publisher later takes back from the royalties due to the writer on sales of the book.

advance bill COM. a bill of exchange drawn before the goods are sent off.

advance freight SHIPG. & TRANSPT. freight paid in advance, i.e. before the goods are carried.

advance man COM. esp. in U.S.A., an employee or agent who travels to places in advance of a circus or theatrical company to arrange for lodgings, advertising, sale of tickets, etc. before the main party arrives.

advancement (1) LAW an arrangement by which a trustee under a will or settlement advances money in order to better the interests of the beneficiary, e.g. to pay for his education or to help him set up a business. (2) MAN. an increase in pay; an improvement in benefits; moving up to a higher rank: *To seek advancement to a higher grade. Syn.* promotion.

advances *n. pl.* BKG. & FIN. those assets of a bank which relate to money advanced to commercial and industrial companies and to private persons in the form of loans and overdrafts. Governments may control the freedom of the banks to make advances, because an increase in advances results in an addition to the country's money supply.

advances ratio BKG. & FIN. the proportion of total advances expressed as a percentage of the total deposits of a bank. This ratio is an instrument used by the Treasury and the Bank of England to measure conditions in the money market. Cf. liquidity ratio.

advb. adverb.

adventure (1) COM. in business, the taking of a commercial or financial risk. The action of a merchant who at his own risk sends goods abroad to an agent who will sell them at the highest price he can get. Cf. enterprise; speculation; venture. *See* joint adventure; bill of adventure. (2) MAR. INSCE. the time during which goods are at risk, whether insured or not.

adverse possession LAW illegal possession and use of land or property which, if allowed to continue for more than a certain length of time laid down by law, may give the illegal possessor the legal right to become the owner.

adverse trade balance ECON. the trade balance of a country is said to be adverse, passive, unfavourable or in deficit when the value of its visible imports is greater than the value of its visible exports. *Syn.* adverse balance of trade. *Opp.* active balance; favourable balance. *See* balance of trade; balance of payments.

advert. advertisement.

advertisement ADVTG. (1) a public notice usu. printed in a newspaper, of goods for sale or services offered; or of goods and services wanted. (2) a printed sheet bearing information about goods for sale, a poster.
classified advertisement (*colloq.* classified ad.) a small advertisement in a newspaper, usu. of only a few lines, placed with others of a similar kind under a heading such as Houses for Sale, Flats to Let, Situations Vacant, Situations Wanted.
keyed advertisement (*a*) one that is planned to give the advertiser a means of measuring the relative effectiveness of different newspapers or magazines for advertising. The public are asked in the advertisement to send a coupon,

or to write a letter to a coded address, such as 'Department AB', using different letters for each magazine or newspaper. (b) one that is shared by two advertisers whose products have some common demand or some other connection, e.g. biscuits and cheese.

small advertisement (colloq. small ad.) a small classified advertisement.

advertisement hoarding ADVTG. a large framed surface usu. of wood, on to which advertising posters are stuck. Syn. (U.S.A.) billboard.

advertisement rates ADVTG. a scale of prices charged by a newspaper, magazine or other advertising medium for including advertisements.

advertiser ADVTG. one who advertises; the particular person or organization who causes an advertisement to be put out to the public. The title of some newspapers which are specially intended to publish advertisements.

advertising (1) ADVTG. making a product or service known to the public, esp. in order to sell it, by using the various media, or means of spreading information, including newspapers, magazines, radio, television, street signs, hoardings, direct mail, etc. Syn. publicity.

direct mail advertising by letter addressed to possible buyers.

informative advertising to 'educate' the consumer by telling or reminding him that the particular goods or services exist, and to increase the total size of the market. Cf. product advertising.

mass advertising by radio, television, outdoor hoardings, posters and signs.

national advertising advertising a product all over the country.

persuasive or **combative** or **competitive** or **constructive advertising** to persuade consumers to buy the product or service of the advertiser rather than that of any other.

point-of-sale advertising by showcards, displays, etc. in retail shops, where the article can be bought on the spot.

product advertising advertising by different producers of a group of similar products, each producer competing to increase his share of the total market. Cf. informative advertising. Syn. competitive advertising.

publication advertising in magazines, newspapers and journals for specialists.

subliminal advertising see under subliminal.

(2) ECON. a selling cost which has to be borne in order to support sales, esp. under imperfect competition.

advertising agency ADVTG. a business which provides a skilled service to commercial and industrial concerns and other organizations by advising on the best way of advertising their products and services, and generally managing their advertising activities.

advertising agent ADVTG. a person who owns and runs an advertising agency.

advertising appropriation ADVTG. a sum of money set aside as an allowance to be spent on advertising during a budget period.

advertising budget ADVTG. a plan for the controlled spending of money on advertising during a given period.

advertising campaign ADVTG. a planned set of advertising operations spread over a given length of time and over a fixed range of media, with the object of having the strongest possible influence on the minds of consumers. Syn. advertising drive; sales drive.

advertising drive see advertising campaign.

advertising manager ADVTG. a person employed by a business concern to control and direct the work of advertising the products or services made or performed by the business.

advertising media ADVTG. the various means used by advertisers to tell the public about their products or services. The mass media include the press, radio and television; and the lesser media include direct mailing (of letters and circulars), street signs and hoardings, posters, etc. See admass.

advertising research see under research.

Advertising Standards Authority ADVTG. set up in Britain in 1962 to promote and enforce high standards in advertising. Abbr. A.S.A.

advice (1) MAN. opinion, esp. from an informed person, on how one should act: We must take expert advice. To seek legal advice. To act on a consultant's advice. Syn. counsel. (2) COM. a formal notice of a business transaction, e.g. an advice note. See railway advice.

advices pl. formal messages, usu. from abroad and particularly from an agent to his principal, giving up-to-date information on trading conditions.

advice, letter of see letter of advice.

advice note (1) BKG. a written notice from a banker informing a customer of sums credited to his account. (2) COM. a written notice from the sender of goods, giving the person who is to receive them details of the quantity and description of the goods and of when, and by what means of carriage they have been sent off. Sometimes shortened to 'an advice'. Cf. delivery note. Syn. letter of advice. (3) COM. an acknowledgment of receipt or arrival of money or goods. (4) TRANSPT. a notice from a rail or road carrier telling a consignee that his goods have arrived and are waiting to be collected.

advice of delivery COM. a notice sent by the Post Office telling the sender of a recorded-delivery letter or packet that it has been duly delivered. Cf. delivery note.

advice of despatch COM. in foreign trade, a letter, often a printed form, sent by the exporter advising (telling, informing) the buyer that goods ordered have been sent off.

advices *see under* advice.

Advisory, Conciliation and Arbitration Service (A.C.A.S.) IND. REL. a public body set up by Parliament to encourage the improvement of industrial relations in Britain and particularly the introduction of better systems of collective bargaining, and to work with unions and employers to settle disputes.

advisory service COM. & IND. in a business concern, a department having special technical knowledge and able to give advice to customers on how best to use the products or services of the business.

advocate LAW a lawyer, esp. in Scotland, who is qualified to help persons to put their case in a court of law. In England, called a barrister or solicitor, though both are called advocates when appearing in court. *Syn.* pleader.

advt. advertisement.

AE SHIPG. in Lloyd's classification, a ship of not very good class. *See* Lloyd's Register of Shipping.

A.E.A. Atomic Energy Authority.

aerial survey *see under* survey.

aerogram a message sent by radio; a telegram sent part of the way by telegraph and part by aeroplane. Cf. aerogramme.

aerogramme a special folded form for sending messages by airmail at a cheap rate of postage. *Syn.* air letter; airmail letter. Cf. aerogram.

a.f. advance(d) freight.

aff. affiliated.

affairs *n. pl.* business matters in general, but usu. of some importance: *The affairs of a company. A difficult state of affairs.*

man of affairs a person trained in business, esp. in the management of finances.

statement of affairs *see under* statement.

affidavit LAW a solemn declaration in writing, signed and sworn or affirmed by the person making it, and intended to be produced as evidence in a court of law.

affil. affiliated.

affiliate *v.* to enter into close relations; to become closely connected, esp. the relationship of one organization to a larger unit of organization, e.g. of a particular firm to an employers' association, or a trade union to the T.U.C. *n.* a person or organization who is affiliated, i.e. closely connected with a group of such persons or organization.

affiliate *or* **affiliated company** COM. a company which is partly or wholly owned by another company is said to be an affiliate of the owning or holding company and of all other companies in the group. Cf. associate(d) company; subsidiary company. *Syn.* related company.

affiliated societies IND. REL. friendly societies which join together to form federations so that

all their members may help each other in providing some form of insurance payments in sickness and old age.

affiliated trade unions IND. REL. trade unions which have a special relationship to a larger unit of organization such as the Trades Union Congress or the Federation of Trade Unions.

affiliation COM. the state of being affiliated, or closely connected; thus a parent company and its subsidiary are said to be *in affiliation* with each other, or (more simply) *affiliated. Syn.* association; alliance.

affirmation LAW a solemn declaration allowing a person to speak as a witness in court, or to sign certain documents such as an affidavit, without taking an oath (without swearing in the name of God).

affluence wealth; a state of being rich.

Affluent Society, The ECON. THEORY the title of a book by Prof. J.K. Galbraith, being a study of the economic and social conditions in the U.S.A. and many other countries during the 1960s. The expression 'affluent society' refers to the high standard of living of the peoples of wealthy countries and the new economic problems this brings.

affreight SHIPG. to hire a ship to carry freight (goods as cargo).

affreightment SHIPG. (1) the hiring of a cargo ship (a freighter). (2) a document, in the form either of a charter-party or a bill of lading, under which a shipowner agrees to carry goods by sea from one port to another for a stated price called freight. *Syn.* contract of affreightment; freighting.

afft. affidavit.

afghani the standard currency unit of Afghanistan, divided into 100 puli.

Afghanistan a republic in southern Asia, pop. 18 million approx. (1973); capital, Kabul, pop. 500,000 approx.; languages, Pashto and Farsi; currency unit, the afghani, divided into 100 puli.

A.F.L.–C.I.O. American Federation of Labor and Congress of Industrial Organizations (U.S.A.).

afloat (1) COM. (of a business) free of debt; able to finance its trading activities. (2) PROD. EXCH. a market price for goods still afloat, i.e. on a ship at sea. Cf. spot; futures.

aforesaid that which has already been mentioned earlier in the document.

A.F.R. accident frequency rate.

AFRASEC Afro-Asian Organization for Economic Co-operation.

afsd. aforesaid.

aft. after.

after date BKG. & FIN. words appearing on a bill of exchange or a promissory note, e.g. *three months after date pay...,* meaning that the length of time for which the bill or note is drawn must be calculated from the date on the document itself. Cf. after sight; on demand. *Syn.* from date.

after-hours dealings STK. EXCH. deals made between members after the official close of the Stock Exchange at 15.30 hrs. (in London). *Syn.* street dealings.

    after-hours price the price of a security in which after-hours dealings took place. *Syn.* street price; price after hours; price in the street.

after-market STK. EXCH. dealings in a recently-issued security during the time following its first appearance when its market price finds its own level according to supply and demand.

after-sales service COM. a service provided by the producer (or his agent) of a machine to keep that machine in good working order after it has been sold. Such service arrangements may include making regular checks, carrying out repairs, cleaning and greasing and keeping stocks of spare parts. Such service may be supplied under an agreement, called a *service agreement* or *maintenance agreement*, for which the customer usu. makes an annual payment.

after sight BKG. & FIN. words appearing on a bill of exchange or promissory note meaning that it is payable at a certain fixed time usu. 30, 60 or 90 days after the date on which it is accepted and dated by the drawee. Cf. after date; on demand. *Abbr.* A.S., A/S., a/s.

ag. agent; agreement; agriculture.

against FIN. (of rates of exchange) unfavourable: *The rate of exchange was against them.*

against all risks MAR. INSCE. words appearing in a marine insurance policy, meaning that the goods are insured against all generally-accepted risks. *Abbr.* A.A.R.

agcy. agency.

agd. agreed.

age admitted INSCE. words written by the insurer on a life assurance policy, meaning that the insurer has seen satisfactory proof of the age of the insured person.

age allowance TAXN. a special amount of tax-free income allowed at present in Britain to persons over 65 years of age, in addition to the normal allowances.

age limit MAN. the age at which an employee normally retires, at present 65 years for a man in Britain, and 60 years for a woman: *Mr X retires on 1 June on reaching the age limit.*

agency (1) COM. the work of an agent; the business run by an agent. (2) LAW the relationship brought about by one person (the principal) appointing another person (the agent) to act for him, e.g. to sell the principal's goods.

    exclusive agency *see* sole agency *below.*

    implied agency one which is accepted as a matter of course although not written, e.g. the power of a wife as her husband's agent in

buying things in his name that are necessary for their household. *See* agent.

    sole agency the business of an agent who is the only agent appointed in his area by his principal. *Syn.* exclusive agency.

agency bill BKG. a bill of exchange accepted by the London branch of a foreign bank.

agenda COM. a list of matters to be considered or decided at a meeting; the agenda is usu. sent out with the notice calling the meeting and forms the programme for dealing with the business at the meeting. *Syn.* agenda paper.

agent COM. a person or organization possessing power to act for another (the principal) in making business arrangements with third parties and in buying and selling goods. An agent is said to 'represent' his principal and must always perform his duties in the principal's interest and with care and skill; and he must give his principal a financial account when called upon.

    general agent one who has been given all the powers of his principal. *Syn.* free agent.

    special agent one holding only limited powers from his principal. *See* the following particular classes of agent: auctioneer; banker; broker; buying agent; commission agent; del credere agent; estate agent; export agent; factor; insurance agent; sole agent.

agent de change STK. EXCH. an officer of the Paris *Bourse* or Stock Exchange, who performs the same duties as a stockbroker in Britain. Cf. bureau de change.

agent of necessity COM. & LAW an agent who, without having any formal right, acts in the interest of another person only in conditions of extreme urgency which make it essential to act immediately, there being no time to refer to the principal, e.g. when the master of a ship may have to throw part of the cargo overboard in order to save the rest. In such cases the principal is bound to accept and approve any agreement or decision made by the agent in the principal's interest.

agents of production *see* factors of production.

aggregate analysis ECON. THEORY a branch of economic theory that studies the working of the economy as a whole, enquires what decides the total output of goods and services, the total use of resources, and what causes these totals to rise and fall. Aggregate analysis deals only with conditions in a complete economy. Cf. partial analysis. *Syn.* macro-economics; general equilibrium analysis.

aggregate demand ECON. THEORY the total demand for goods and services resulting from adding together all the spending-power of people in the complete economy of a country. The total level of economic activity is influenced by changes in aggregate demand. *See* aggregate analysis; aggregate demand & supply curves.

aggregate demand & supply curves ECON. THEORY in Keynes's *General Theory*, an *aggregate demand curve* shows, for various levels of employment, what will be the total (or aggregate) demand for the goods produced by all people employed. In the same way, an *aggregate supply curve* shows what all the mass of producers must expect to receive from the sale of the total (or aggregate) supply produced by the same number of people employed. Thus for each possible level of employment there is an aggregate demand price and an aggregate supply price.

aggregated rebates COM. several rebates added together, esp. when given by a supplier to a shopkeeper under a condition that the shopkeeper is compelled to sell only the products of the supplier, thus making sure of his custom as a sales outlet. *Syn.* deferred rebates.

aggregate supply *see under* supply.

aggregate supply price ECON. THEORY the total cost of producing the entire output made by a given number of workers employed in the whole economy. *See* aggregate demand & supply curves.

aggressive *adj.* (1) COM. daring, attacking, showing strength: *An aggressive sales policy.* (2) STK. EXCH. *Aggressive portfolio*, a collection of shares chosen and held in the expectation of a future increase in capital value rather than for the income they will bring in.

agio (1) ECON. (*a*) the amount by which the value of one metallic currency is greater than that of another, e.g. of a worn or debased currency. (*b*) sometimes, the difference in value between the metallic and the paper currency of a country. (2) BKG. the discount on a foreign bill of exchange. (3) FIN. a charge, usu. expressed as a percentage, made by a dealer in foreign currency for changing one currency into another, i.e. the difference between the dealer's buying and selling prices.

agiotage FIN. the business of taking the risk in buying and holding foreign currencies or stock-exchange securities in the expectation of making a gain when selling them later. *Syn.* money changing; stockjobbing; speculation.

Agio Theory of Interest *see* Abstinence Theory.

A.G.M. annual general meeting.

agora the fractional currency unit of the State of Israel. *Pl.* agorot. Since changing to the shekel, 100 new agorot = 1 shekel.

agr., agric. agriculture; agricultural.

Agrarian Revolution, The ECON. HIST. the name given to the great and far-reaching changes in farming methods in England in the second half of the eighteenth century.

agree *v.* (1) ACCTS. to make agree, to bring into accord: *To agree the books. To agree an account.* (2) to approve(of): *I have agreed your expense account. The manager agreed a list of*

assets. (3) to be in accord; to have the same meaning: *The books now agree. Syn.* to correspond. (4) BKG. *Words and figures do not agree*, a reason given by a bank for not paying a cheque, meaning that the amount stated in words on the cheque is not the same as the amount written in figures. The cheque is therefore referred back to the drawer. *See* refer to drawer. (5) to have the same idea(s); to hold the same opinion: *The members agreed that more capital was needed. The engineers agree that the machine is useless.* (*with on*) *To agree on a price.* (6) to accept; to be willing to do. (*with to*) *We agree to your plan.*

agreed COM. approved by all the parties: *An agreed price/payment/rate/sum, etc.*

agreed-value insurance *see under* insurance, classes and kinds of.

agreement (1) an agreeing, a state of accord, as when two or more persons are of the same opinion, or when two or more things have the same meaning: *The parties are in agreement. Your books are in agreement with ours. The words and figures on a cheque must be in agreement. See* gentleman's agreement. (2) LAW a spoken or written declaration by two or more persons or organizations (called the parties) who, having a common intention known to both or all of them, agree that each shall perform certain stated duties in the interests of both or all.

agreement to sell *see* contract to sell.

agricultural area AGR. (of a country) the total extent of land fit for ploughing, land under tree crops, and grassland.

agricultural bank AGR. & BKG. a bank set up specially to help in developing agriculture by making loans to farmers for longer periods than a commercial bank will do. *See* Agricultural Mortgage Corporation. *Syn.* land bank.

agricultural co-operative AGR. a producers' co-operative having as its main object the sale, through a single organization, of the produce of many small farmers; its members help to manage it and take a share in its profits.

agricultural economics AGR. & ECON. the branch of economics which deals with the production and distribution of goods grown on the land.

Agricultural Loans Fund AGR. & FIN. an amount of public money set apart by the government and controlled by the Ministry of Agriculture, for the purpose of making loans for improving farm land, but not for buying land.

Agricultural Marketing Board AGR. a public organization set up by the government in Britain to strengthen the weak bargaining-power of a large number of small farmers of a particular product, e.g. Milk Marketing Board.

Agricultural Mortgage Corporation Ltd. AGR. & FIN. a government-backed organization in

England and Wales which makes long-term loans to farmers against mortgages on their property and is the farmer's main source of mortgage finance. In Scotland, the service is provided by the Scottish Agricultural Securities Corporation Ltd.

agricultural show AGR. a public show of agricultural products and skills.

Agricultural Wages Board AGR. in Britain, a public organization set up by the government to look after the interests of farm workers by fixing minimum wage-rates and controlling conditions of work.

agriculture AGR. the skilled work of cultivating the soil for crops, bringing up animals, planting trees, managing forests, and fishing. *Syn.* farming; husbandry. *See also* extensive agriculture; intensive agriculture.

agro-industry AGR. agricultural industry; industry based on agricultural products.

agronomy AGR. agricultural economy; the theory and practice of crop and animal farming and soil management.

aground SHIPG. said of a ship that has run on to the shore in shallow water and is lying on the bottom but with part or all of her hull above the water. *Syn.* stranded.

Agt., agt. agent; against; agreement.

a.g.w. actual gross weight.

A.G.W.I. MAR. INSCE. Atlantic, Gulf, West Indies.

agy. agency.

A.H., A/H. MAR. INSCE. Antwerp–Hamburg coastal ports.

a.h. SHIPG. aft hatch *or* after hatch.

A.H.C. Accepting Houses Committee.

ahead (1) SHIPG. in a forward direction: *Full speed ahead*. (2) STK. EXCH. at higher prices: *Shares moved ahead*, were in demand and at higher prices.

aid (1) ECON. & FIN. help, esp. to a person, organization or country in difficulty: *Financial aid in the form of a subsidy. Foreign or overseas aid to developing countries. The Marshall Aid Programme. See also* foreign aid.

first aid IND. SFTY. immediate treatment given to an injured person with the aim of relieving pain and preventing his condition from getting worse before a doctor can attend to him.
(2) COM. something which helps, e.g. a tool, an instrument, a machine: *Household aids; kitchen aids; gardening aids; office aids.*

aids to trade COM. the activities of commerce which help to make its main activity, trade, both possible and profitable, esp. advertising, banking, insurance and transport. *Syn.* ancillaries to trade. *See* trade.

airborne (1) TRANSPT. in the air; flying: *The plane is airborne*, has left the ground and is actually flying. (2) COM. & IND. carried by air: *An airborne showroom/exhibition/test-bench/laboratory.*

air-bus *see under* aircraft.

air cargo *see under* air freight.

aircraft TRANSPT. aeroplanes and airships generally.

air-bus a very large airliner intended to carry passengers economically for short distances. *Syn.* (U.S.A.) air coach.

air coach (U.S.A.) an air-bus.

air freighter a plane used for carrying air cargo (air freight).

airliner a plane used for carrying passengers, and sometimes also goods, on regular services run by an airline.

airplane (U.S.A.) an aeroplane.

airship an aircraft that is lighter than air and driven by engines.

air-taxi a small plane, which may be hired like a taxi for short distances.

airworthy (of an aircraft) in good order and safe for flying.

aircrew TRANSPT. generally, specially-qualified persons employed in the work of flying and managing an aircraft.

air *or* **flight engineer** one specially qualified to manage the engines of an aircraft and to control the supply of fuel to them during flight.

air hostess a woman employed on an airliner to look after the needs of passengers. Cf. stewardess.

air navigator a person skilled in finding, checking and recording the position and course of an aircraft, for guiding the pilot regarding the correct course to steer, and for working the radio.

air pilot *or* **airline pilot** a person highly qualified to direct the flying of an aircraft by handling the controls and acting as leader of the aircrew.

air steward a man employed on an airliner to look after the needs of passengers. Cf. air hostess.

air cushion vehicle TRANSPT. (U.S.A., Canada) a hovercraft.

airdrome (U.S.A.) aerodrome. *See under* airport.

air engineer *see under* aircrew.

air freight TRANSPT. (1) goods carried by air. (2) a goods-carrying service run by commercial air carriers. *See* air cargo *below*.

air cargo goods carried by air either on scheduled or charter services, sometimes in the same plane as passengers (called all-traffic services), or in freight planes (known as all-freight services).

air consignment note *or* **air way-bill** a particular kind of consignment note or way-bill for use with air freight specially intended to reduce delays in delivering the goods to the consignee.

air freighter *see under* aircraft.

air hostess *see under* aircrew.

air letter *see* aerogramme.

airline TRANSPT. a regular commercial service for

carrying passengers and goods by air. A company running such services.

air bridge a regular public air service between two places.

air lane *or* **airway** the way or route which aircraft take when flying from one place to another, esp. routes or 'corridors' laid down by governments either in the interests of safety or for political reasons.

air service a system that meets public needs by providing regular journeys by aircraft, between places along a given route, to carry passengers and goods.

air shuttle a regular and frequent service of passenger-carrying planes which travel back and forth between large towns usu. a short distance apart.

air ticket a special form of passenger ticket used by airlines and giving more detail, e.g. concerning stops on the route, calculation of the fare charged, weight of baggage, etc., than is included on a road or rail ticket.

airway *see* air lane.

airways *pl.* an airline company running a number of air services: *British Airways*.

airliner *see under* aircraft.

airmail TRANSPT. letters, postal packets and parcels carried by air at higher postage rates than for surface mail. *Also* air mail.

first-class airmail the fastest service, bearing the highest rate of postage, is mainly intended for letters.

second-class airmail being a little slower but charged at a reduced rate, is intended mainly for business and printed papers (with which letters must not be included).

airmail letter *see* aerogramme.

airmail packets *or* **small air packets** (usu. up to 1 kg) bear a special rate of postage, may not contain letters, and must not be sealed.

air parcels (usu. over 1 kg and up to 10 kg) intended for any articles or goods too heavy for the air-packet service.

all-up airmail a special postal service from Britain to most countries in Europe which carries all first-class mail by air.

airmail transfer *see* bank transfer.

airplane (U.S.A.) an aeroplane.

airport TRANSPT. a large flat field provided with several hard strips (or runways) where large commercial aircraft can safely land, where proper arrangements exist for loading and unloading passengers and cargo, refilling with fuel and oil, and for repairs. *Syn.* aerodrome; airdrome.

international airport an airport specially intended to handle commercial air services to and from other countries, being able to handle the largest aircraft and providing customs and passenger-hotel arrangements.

airdrome (U.S.A.) an airport which may be used by both commercial planes and those of the armed forces.

airfield (*a*) a flat field with a hard strip (or runway) but without most of the arrangements found on an airport. (*b*) strictly, a word meaning that part of an airport actually used by aircraft for landing and taking off.

air station *see* air terminal.

air terminal *or* **air station** a special airline office building in the centre of a town where air passengers and freight beginning their journey are collected and taken by road to the airport; and to which air passengers and freight ending their journey are brought.

airship *see under* aircraft.

air survey *see* aerial survey *under* survey.

air-taxi *see under* aircraft.

airworthy *see under* aircraft.

Ajman *see* United Arab Emirates.

Aktb. (*Swedish*: Aktiebolaget) joint-stock company.

a.l. (*French*: après livraison) after delivery.

Ala. Alabama, U.S.A.

Alas. Alaska, U.S.A.

Albania a republic on the Adriatic Sea, in southeast Europe, pop. 2.4 million approx. (1973); capital, Tirana, pop. 160,000 approx.; language, Albanian; currency unit, the lek, divided into 100 qindars or qintars.

aleatory INSCE. depending on chance: *An aleatory contract*, a contract of insurance that covers the insured against loss arising from a chance event. Cf. wagering contract.

Algeria a republic in north-west Africa, pop. 16 million approx.; capital, Algiers (Alger), pop. 1 million approx.; languages, Arabic and French; currency unit, the Algerian dinar, divided into 100 centimes. Member, O.A.U.; Arab League.

Algol COMP. algorithmic language; a computer programming language using algebraic characters for making highly complicated calculations. Cf. Cobol; Fortran.

algorithm COMP. a number of rules applied in a strict order to a given set of numbers to solve certain kinds of problem. *See* Algol.

'A' licence TRANSPT. formal permission given under the Road Traffic Act 1960 in Britain to a road transport company to operate as general carriers, i.e. carrying the goods of other parties. A *'B' licence* is for those carriers who combine carrying their own goods with those of others. A *'C' licence* is for those carrying only their own goods.

alien foreign: *An alien*, a foreigner.

alliance a union between two persons or groups of persons, and esp. an agreement between two or more countries to support each other.

all-in rate *see* exchange rate.

all-loss insurance (U.S.A.) all-risk insurance.

all-moneys debenture *see under* debenture.

allocation FIN. & ACCTS. (1) the setting aside of money for a particular purpose; the sum of money so set aside: *An advertising allocation*, the amount of money set aside for advertising expenses for a given period. (2) the dividing-up of total cost into the separate kinds of costs of which it is made up, and then the charging of these separate costs to particular accounts: *The total cost of the project was found on allocation to be : materials £255, labour £570, machine-hire £175, total £1000.*

allocation of resources ECON. THEORY the choosing of the particular use to which a scarce resource (means of production) is put, e.g. whether to use water for electric power or for crops.

allocation of responsibilities MAN. in an office or factory, deciding who shall do each part of the work and then giving each employee a clear knowledge of what he or she is responsible for doing.

allonge BKG. & COM. a slip of paper fastened to and forming part of a bill of exchange to provide space for more endorsements to be added when there is no more room on the bill itself. *Syn.* rider.

allot to divide something up and share it out, giving a part to each of a number of persons or things: *Each man was allotted a piece of work to do. I have been allotted some money for research.*

allotment (1) STK. EXCH. allotting: *Allotment of shares*, the allotting of a new issue of shares in a company to persons or organizations who have applied for them. A number of shares so allotted.
(2) AGR. (*a*) the allotting, usu. by a local government organization, of a small piece of publicly-owned or leased land to a person living locally for the special purpose of growing food for himself and his family. (*b*) a piece of land so allotted.

allotment letter a letter from a company to a person who has applied for shares being newly issued, telling him the number of shares that he has been allotted. This letter is later exchanged for a share certificate. *Syn.* letter of allotment; share allotment form.

allotment money money due from a person or organization who has been allotted newly-issued shares in a company, and payable on allotment, i.e. before the shares can actually be made over. Cf. application money.

allotment note SHIPG. a document signed by a seaman arranging for his employers to send part or all of his pay direct to a named person, usu. his wife or other member of his family or to his bank.

allottee STK. EXCH. a person to whom an allotment has been made of newly-issued shares in a company.

allow (1) to give: *To allow a debtor more time to pay. A bank allows interest on deposit accounts. We allow a discount of 2½% for payment on delivery.* (2) to permit: *Smoking is not allowed in the factory. The company allows him the use of a car.* (3) INSCE. to accord as due: *The insurers have allowed your claim.* (4) TAXN. *The tax-inspector will not allow this expense*, will not let it be used in reduction of gross income when calculating taxable income.

allowable (1) that can be allowed; permitted by law; not forbidden. (2) TAXN. of an expense, one which the taxpayer may take off his gross income when calculating his taxable income: *An expense which is allowable for tax purposes.*

allowance (1) money given to a person regularly or from time to time for a special purpose: *A husband may give his wife a dress allowance each month.* (2) MAN. money paid to an employee for business expenses, such as for travel, entertainment, motor-car mileage, and subsistence. (3) COM. an amount or percentage given in order to reduce a payment, usu. for some special reason, e.g. for goods of substandard quality, for goods damaged or delayed while being carried. (4) money given in the form of an increased discount by a producer or wholesaler to a retailer who makes a special effort to sell the product. (5) TAXN. a stated amount of income allowed free of tax to a taxpayer in certain conditions. It may include: a personal allowance; a wife's earned-income allowance; and allowances for each child, a housekeeper, a dependent relative, a daughter's services, a blind person and an aged person. Certain expenses are also allowed to be deducted from gross income when calculating taxable income. (6) TOUR. & TRANSPT. *see* free allowance.

allowed time IND. & MAN. paid time allowed to a factory worker for certain necessary purposes, e.g. for rest, meals, care of tools and machines, during which time the worker is not actually producing any goods.

alloy (1) any mixture of metals. (2) PUB. FIN. in coinage, esp. a mixture of metals of high value with metals of lower value to make coins which are cheap to produce, yet are long-lasting and of good appearance. See cupro-nickel.

all-risk(s) policy *see under* insurance policy.

all risks whatsoever MAR. INSCE. words in a marine insurance policy which give even wider cover than the usual all-risks policy by not including any exceptions. Cf. all-risk insurance.

all-round price COM. an inclusive price; a special price which includes all charges usu. added as extras.

almighty dollar, the the power of wealth; the idea that money is the basis of all power. (Words of Washington Irving, American essayist, in the remark 'The almighty dollar, that great object of universal devotion throughout the land.')

almoner a person charged with the duty of giving out money or gifts to the poor.

alms *n. pl.* money given to the poor.

alms-deed LAW a deed which provides for gifts to the poor.

almshouse a house or group of houses where old and needy people are given lodging either free or at a very low rent.

alongside SHIPG. (1) (of a ship) tied up beside a quay or berth. (2) (of a barge, lighter, etc.) floating or tied up beside the ship: *To come alongside; to lie alongside. See* free alongside.

alphabetical filing *see under* filing system.

alphanumeric COMP. (of a computer) having both alphabetic and numeric characters, i.e. both letters and numbers, in its coding system, which may also include some other signs.

alt. alternate; alternative; altitude.

Alta. Alberta, Canada.

alternate demand ECON. THEORY (1) the demand for two or more products which are substitutes for each other, i.e. can replace each other, e.g. tea, coffee and cocoa as drinks. (2) the demand for factors of production which are interchangeable, i.e. which can be used in place of each other, e.g. coal, oil and natural gas for heating. *Syn.* composite demand; competing demand; rival demand.

alternate director COM. a person given power to act in the place of a named director of a company, but only in his absence. *Syn.* an alternate.

alternative (use) cost *see* opportunity cost *under* cost.

à l'usine (*French*) *see* ex works.

always afloat SHIPG. words expressing a condition in a charter-party that the charterer of the ship will make sure that there will always be not less than a stated depth of water under the ship so that she is 'always afloat' in order to protect her hull.

Am. America(n).

A.M. *French*: Assurance Mutuelle; airmail; assistant manager; associate member.

a/m above-mentioned.

amalgamation (1) COM. & FIN. the joining together of two or more businesses into one organization in order to improve their profit-making performance by, e.g. saving in management and administration costs, getting rid of competition, improving efficiency in production by obtaining the advantages of large-scale production, or widening the range of products. *Syn.* merger; combination; consolidation; integration; reconstruction; reorganization. *See also* absorption.

horizontal *or* **lateral amalgamation** the combining of companies within the same industry, e.g. two publishing houses.

vertical amalgamation the combining of companies performing different processes in the production of the same article, the product of one process becoming a raw material of another, e.g. a leather manufacturer and a shoe factory. (2) IND. REL. the joining of two or more trade unions into one, mainly in order to increase the bargaining-power of the group and to save administration expenses: *The Amalgamated Engineering Union (A.E.U.),* etc.

amalgamator MAN. a professional person, usu. an accountant, specially qualified in the work of amalgamating companies.

amanuensis a person employed to copy handwritten documents or to write down words dictated by another person. Sometimes now used to describe a copy-typist or a stenographer.

amass to pile up; to collect in large quantities: *He amassed a fortune. A miser amasses money. The Victorian industrialists amassed wealth.*

amateur a person who takes part in or performs some activity chiefly for pleasure and not to earn money: *He has been offered large sums of money to play tennis professionally but has chosen to remain an amateur.*

ambitious (1) said of a person who eagerly desires to do well, to succeed in life at all costs, e.g. by rising to high office or by making a large fortune. (2) of a course of action: *An ambitious programme of rebuilding,* a programme which can be completed only at great cost in effort and money. *N.* ambition.

A.M.C. Agricultural Mortgage Corporation.

amend (1) to correct something wrong; to change for the better, to improve, the wording of a document: *To amend an account. We have amended the faulty figures. I wish to amend my report. Cf.* emend. (2) LAW to change for the better: *The law has been amended.*

amendment (1) the act or result of amending. (2) MAN. a change (to a motion/resolution/proposal) put forward for consideration at a formal meeting, e.g. to add or take out certain words or to use different words: *To move (or propose) an amendment to the motion.* After discussion, the amendment is put to the vote and, if passed, causes the original motion to be changed accordingly before it, in turn, is voted on.

amenities *see* employees' amenities.

American Account countries BKG. certain countries, mainly in Central and South America, whose sterling held in accounts with banks in Britain is freely convertible into U.S. dollars. *Cf.* sterling area; transferable account.

American Bureau of Shipping SHIPG. & MAR. INSCE. the organization in the U.S.A. responsible for surveying, classifying and registering ships. *Cf.* Lloyd's Register of Shipping. *See* classification societies. *Abbr.* A.B.S.

American clause MAR. INSCE. a clause in certain marine insurance policies when the insured takes out two insurances on the same risk on the same property. The clause provides that the underwriter of the earliest-dated policy shall be the first to meet any loss, and that the insured may claim on the second underwriter only if the value of the loss is not fully covered by the first policy.

American Federation of Labor and Congress of Industrial Organizations (A.F.L.–C.I.O.) the parallel organization in the U.S.A. to the Trades Union Congress in Britain.

American Stock Exchange STK. EXCH. the next in size in the U.S.A. to the New York Stock Exchange, it deals particularly in stocks of new and smaller companies and of many foreign concerns. It publishes daily quotations and is based in New York City. It is sometimes still called the kerb (or curb) exchange by which name it was known before 1953 when it was a street (or kerb) market.

American ton see short ton under ton.

amidships SHIPG. in the middle part of a ship, about equal in distance from the bows and the stern.

amortize (1) FIN. to wipe out, to pay off a debt gradually over the years by setting aside money each year, usu. by means of a sinking fund. (2) to reduce a debt by periodic payments covering both interest and part of the principal until the whole debt has been paid off: *To amortize a loan. Syn.* to redeem.
amortizable *adj. An amortizable loan. A loan amortizable in 15 years.*
(3) ACCTS. to write off (reduce the value of in the books) an asset gradually over a period equal to its expected life. *Syn.* depreciate. (4) LAW to hand over property to a corporation or charity for ever. *N.* amortization; amortizement.

amount (1) a quantity; a sum; a total: *The dam will cost a very large amount of money. That milk contains only a small amount of cream. We suffered damage to the amount of £1000. The amount of a bill.* (2) ACCTS. the heading of a cash column; the total of an invoice, credit note, etc. Generally a sum of money: *Amount brought forward/brought down/carried forward/carried down; amount paid on account or in advance. An amount entered twice. You may pay in one amount or by instalments.* (3) FIN. in regard to a loan, the principal and interest added together. (4) BKG. the sum payable when a bill of exchange becomes due; the value of the bill.

amounts differ BKG. words written or stamped on a cheque which has not been paid because the amount expressed in words and the amount written in figures on the cheque do not agree. *See* words and figures do not agree.

ampere the unit of measurement of electric current in the metric system of SI units. *Abbr.* A; *also* amp. *Pron.* ampair.

a.m.t. airmail transfer.

amt. amount.

amusement industry IND. the industry which includes all business concerns providing the public with amusement, such as theatres, cinemas, sports centres, television and radio broadcasting companies, music recorded on tapes and discs, musical instruments, dance halls, bingo halls, amusement arcades, and the makers of machines and instruments for such firms.

amusement shares STK. EXCH. one of the headings under which stocks and shares are classified in the share-information lists published by the Stock Exchange. As a group, amusement shares include those of companies in the amusement industry, esp. cinemas, theatres and television broadcasting companies. *Syn.* entertainment shares.

analogue (or analog) computer COMP. *see under* computer.

analyse *or* **analyze** (U.S.A.) (1) to examine a substance or thing in detail to find out its qualities; to divide something up into the different parts or materials of which it is made. (2) ACCTS. *To analyse an account*, to separate and classify the various kinds of dealings recorded in an account in order to learn in what ways or on what things money has been spent, or to study what the dealings can tell us about the business. (3) COM. to sort numbers and other pieces of business information into various classes or categories in order to learn in what ways performance can be improved: *To analyse sales according to individual countries*, to separate out from a mass of sales information the value of goods sold into each of a given list of countries.

analysis (1) ACCTS. a statement or table setting out the results of analysing accounting records: *Analysis of expenses.* (2) the work of analysing sales accounting records: *Sales analysis.* (3) a table showing the results of this work.

analysis book a book in which the results of analysing accounting information are recorded usu. in the form of tables made up of columns of figures.

analysis column one of the divisions between upright ruled lines (a column) on analysis paper and in some analysis books making it possible to separate various kinds of expenses by entering each kind in its own column.

analysis paper paper specially divided into a number of spaces between upright lines (called columns) into which figures may be written one below another; any special paper used for analysing accounting records.
(4) IND. & MAN. *see* critical path analysis; job analysis. (5) ECON. *see* indifference curve.

analyst IND. a professional person skilled in the work of analysing. *See* public analyst; systems analyst.

analytical estimate ACCTS. & IND. the probable cost of a particular product, process or service, arrived at by dividing out the total costs so that each activity bears its own share.

analytical petty cash book ACCTS. a petty cash book which is ruled into a number of extra columns (i.e. upright divisions) to allow figures for various expenses to be written in different columns and totalled separately, thus giving an analysis of the various kinds of expense.

anch. anchored.

anchor SHIPG. a heavy, hooked weight lowered on a chain to the sea-bed to stop a ship from moving: *To cast, or drop, anchor*, to stop the ship by lowering the anchor. *To lie at, or ride at, anchor*, to be held by the anchor from moving. *To drag anchor*, to be pulling the anchor along the sea-bed because the anchor will not hold, causing a dangerous situation. *To weigh, or raise, anchor,* to pull the anchor up into the ship, ready to move away.

anchorage SHIPG. a place where ships may safely lie at anchor, sheltered from high winds and rough seas, out of the way of passing ships and having a firm sea-bed to hold their anchors.

anchorage charges *or* **dues** SHIPG. charges made to owners of ships by certain port and harbour authorities for permission to lie at anchor and for the use of the services provided by the port. Sometimes called simply anchorage.

anchor-and-chain clause MAR. INSCE. a clause sometimes included in marine policies freeing the insurers from the cost of getting back anchors and chains lost in bad weather.

AND Andorra's international vehicle-registration letter.

and Company *or* **& Co.** (1) COM. words forming part of the name of a business, e.g. Jones and Company (or Jones & Co.) meaning that Jones is not the only owner of the business, but shares its ownership with others. The words, without the addition of *Ltd.*, or *Limited*, usu. refer to a partnership; but if followed by *Ltd.*, or *Limited*, the business is a limited liability company. (2) BKG. words sometimes written on or near the crossing of a cheque, being the last words in the full business name of the collecting banker, although the name itself is often not stated. *See* crossed cheque *under* cheque.

and/or COM. an expression much used in business writings, it includes both an addition (the 'and') and an alternative (the 'or'): *The samples may go by road and/or air*, the samples may go either by road only, or by air only, or partly by road and partly by air.

Andorra a small principality in southern Europe, jointly ruled over by the President of France and the Bishop of Urgel, Spain; pop. 20,000 approx. (1973); capital, Andorra la Vella, pop. 2500 approx.; language, Catalan; currency unit, the French franc (Fr.), divided into 100 centimes. Spanish pesetas are also widely used.

and reduced *see* reduction of capital.

angel FIN. (*colloq.*) a person who is ready to support something, especially a play or a film, with loans of money in return for interest, or for a share in the profits, or both. *See* backer.

Angola a republic in west-central Africa, pop. 5.7 million approx. (1973); capital, Luanda, pop. 400,000 approx.; languages, Portuguese and tribal; currency unit, the kwanza, divided into 100 cents.

animal husbandry *see under* husbandry.

announcement effect PUB. FIN. & TAXN. the degree to which a consumer realizes that he is paying a tax; for example, since indirect taxes on spending are included in the final price to the consumer, he is less likely to realize that he is paying a tax and is less likely to notice, or object to, changes in the rate of tax; but if the amount of tax is stated separately from the price and is thus announced (made clearly known) to the consumer, he will be more likely to notice changes in the rate of tax and to resist any increase.

announcement of sale COM. a notice informing the public that a sale will be held. *See* sale.

annual *adj.* (1) happening every year, yearly: *The annual report of the directors. The annual general meeting.* (2) measured by the year: *An annual income of £5000.*
n. a book which comes out every year, usu. giving information about events during the year before; a yearbook.

Annual Abstract of Statistics COM. & ECON. a book produced once each year by the British Government giving figures collected, analysed and arranged in tables by the Central Statistical Office on important subjects concerning the nation, such as population, employment, production, trade, prices, etc.

annual accounts *see* accounts, *n. pl.*

annual charge ACCTS. (1) a charge made for services given for a whole year, e.g. a consultancy fee payable by one company to another. (2) an expense which is paid only once in a year, e.g. a subscription to a society, club, or association.

annual general meeting COM. & LAW a formal meeting of the members, shareholders and directors of a company, held by law once each year, at which they consider the accounts and directors' and auditors' reports on the year's activities, fix the auditors' pay, decide the amount of the dividend, and appoint or re-appoint the auditors and directors, as laid down in their Articles of Association. Annual general meetings are also held by clubs, societies, associations, trade unions and other, usu. non-profitmaking, organizations according to their rules. *Syn.* ordinary general meeting. *See also* company meeting. *Abbr.* A.G.M.

annual income (1) COM. & TAXN. the total amount of money that a person receives from all sources during a period of one year, often expressed thus: *£5000 per annum*, or *£5000 p.a.* (2) COM. the amount of money earned by an investment in a year: *This loan stock will produce an annual income of £500. His annual income from rents is £750.*

annual leave *see under* leave.

annual premium INSCE. an insurance premium payable only once a year. *See* premium.

annual report LAW & MAN. a report presented each year by the directors to the members and shareholders of a company, giving information about the company's trading activities and including certain documents which must be produced by law, namely the balance sheet, the profit and loss account and the auditors' and directors' reports.

annual return LAW & MAN. a formal statement made once a year, signed by a director and the secretary of a limited company, to the Registrar of Companies giving certain information laid down by law, including details about shares, debentures and mortgages, the members, shareholders, directors and secretary, and attaching copies of the balance sheet and other documents which have been put before the company during the period covered by the return.

annual value PUB. FIN. the value of a particular house-property which is taken as the basis for calculating the amount of rates (local taxes) payable by the owner or occupier. To arrive at the annual value, the gross value (i.e. the rack rent, which is the annual rent which could be got for the property if it were to be let) is reduced by taking off certain costs allowed by law such as repairs, insurance, etc., leaving a figure called the (net) annual value. *Syn.* rateable value.

annuitant INSCE. a person who holds or receives an annuity.

annuity INSCE. (1) a fixed sum of money paid or received once every year or at regular dates during the year, e.g. as a pension, and usu. during the rest of the life of the annuitant. (2) a loan of money which is repaid to the lender by equal annual amounts or at regular dates during the year, such payments usu. ceasing only on the death of the lender. *See* annuity insurance; annuity policies.

annuity bond *see under* bond, *n.*

annuity certain *see under* insurance policy.

annuity insurance *see under* insurance, classes and kinds of.

annuity policies, various *see under* insurance policies.

annuity system (1) ACCTS. a way of providing for the depreciation of an asset by means of regular annual charges, each consisting of two parts: first, a fixed amount arrived at by spreading the original cost of the asset equally over a given number of years; and second, an amount representing interest based on the value of the asset in each year; so that the annual amounts of interest gradually get smaller until they become nothing when the value of the asset is reduced to nothing. (2) FIN. a way of repaying a mortgage debt by making equal annual or monthly payments consisting partly of capital and partly of interest on the amount outstanding. *Syn.* annuity method.

ante-date BKG. & COM. to date back; to give a document a date earlier than the actual date on which it was signed, usu. to make it take effect from the earlier date: *The contract/bill of lading/cheque was ante-dated so as to run from 1 January. Also* antedate. *Syn.* fore-date; pre-date. *Opp.* post-date.

ante-dated cheque *see under* cheque.

ante-nuptial settlement *see under* settlement.

anticipate (1) to think of, realize, beforehand: *We anticipated their response to our letter*, we realized what they would say in reply. (2) to expect: *We anticipate a delay of three weeks in supplying your order.* (3) to act in advance: *Anticipating a rise in price, he bought 1000 shares. To anticipate a payment by one week*, to make the payment a week earlier than was arranged. *To anticipate demand*, to order or produce in advance.

anticipated prices ECON. the prices which the producer expects to pay for his raw materials, labour, etc., on the one hand, and the prices which he expects to receive for his finished products on the other, are matters which he must anticipate and take account of in planning his level of production.

anticipated profit INSCE. the profit which an insured person expects to make on a consignment of goods can be included in a policy of insurance on the grounds that if the goods are lost the expected profit will also be lost.

anticipation (1) COM. the act of anticipating: *In anticipation of your order, we have reserved stock for you. He bought gold in anticipation of a rise in price. Thanking you in anticipation*, a polite way of asking for co-operation. (2) ECON. one of the risks taken by the entrepreneur (producer) is that of causing goods to be produced in anticipation of demand, so that if the demand should grow less before the goods are ready to be sold, he is in danger of suffering a loss against which he cannot insure. (3) LAW the right of a person expecting to receive an income at some future date, to give or sell or raise money by pledging that right in advance.

anticipatory breach LAW under the law of contract, where one party has made it clear in advance that he will not perform his part of the contract (i.e. he intends to breach it) the other party may bring an action in the courts for damages for breach in anticipation.

Anti-Corn Law League ECON. HIST. a British political movement started in 1838 in Manchester by John Bright and Richard Cobden with the object of reducing the price of bread by removing the protective duty on imported corn. Their attack on the Corn Laws resulted in the Laws being done away with (repealed) in 1846 and was the beginning of a long period of free trade by Britain. *See* Corn Laws.

anti-dumping ECON. one form of action which may be taken by a government to protect industries from unfair competition, usu. by means of special import duties, to reduce or stop imports of goods for sale at a price lower than in the country in which they were manufactured. Protection may also be given (and less forcefully) by one government coming to an agreement with the other to limit the quantity of goods exported and even to put an export duty on them in order to make them dearer, and so less competitive, in the importing country's market. Cf. dumping.

Antigua an island state in the eastern Caribbean Sea, pop. 80,000 approx. (1975); capital, Saint John's, pop. 25,000 approx.; language, English; currency unit, the East Caribbean dollar (ECar$), divided into 100 cents. Member, (British) Commonwealth.

anti-inflation measures ECON. steps taken, esp. by the government of a country, to prevent prices and wages from rising too fast. *See* inflation.

Antipodes Day *see* Meridian Day *under* Meridian.

anti-trust laws LAW & COM. laws passed in the U.S.A. from 1890 onwards which made it illegal to form large combinations of existing commercial and industrial organizations or any new concerns having the effect of setting up monopolies which kill healthy competition. The laws also make it illegal to act in restraint of trade, i.e. to do anything to limit a person's freedom to carry on business as he wishes.

any other business usu. the last matter but one on the agenda of a meeting, meaning that at that point matters not listed earlier in the agenda may be put forward for consideration. *Abbr.* A.O.B.

A/o *or* **a/o** account of.

A.O.B. any other business.

a/or and/or.

'A' ordinary share *see* 'A' share *under* share.

A.P. (of bills of exchange) à protester (*French*, to be protested); additional premium; average payable.

app. appendix (to a book, report or other document).

apparel and tackle SHIPG. the instruments, working tools and fittings of a ship, including chains, anchors and boats; sometimes mentioned in a charter-party in which the charterers promise to keep the ship's apparel and tackle in good order.

apparent damage SHIPG. damage which is noticed at the time that the cargo is unloaded from the ship and which must be reported immediately to the carrier. *Opp.* hidden damage.

appeal LAW a formal request to a higher court to review a judgment earlier reached in a lower court. *See* Court of Appeal.

appeal bond *see under* bond, *n.*

Appeal Court *see* Court of Appeal.

appellant LAW a person who appeals to a higher court against a judgment.

append to join on; to add: *The lists appended to this letter. To append one's signature to a document.*

appendix a passage added to a book or paper, usu. at the end, intended to make it more useful or complete. *Pl.* appendices *or* appendixes.

applicant (1) COM. a person who applies for employment, for a situation: *Applicants for this post will be interviewed on Monday.* (2) STK. EXCH. a person or organization who applies for shares or stock in a company when a new issue is made: *Applicants will be informed of the number of shares allotted to them.*
(3) LAW a person applying to an authority for a licence, e.g. to keep a gun; to sell strong drink; to remove goods held by the Customs.

application (1) COM. a formal request: *You must make an application to the Post Office for a telephone connection.*
prices on application we shall give you our prices if you apply.
(2) MAN. a letter to an employer asking for employment. *One advertisement has brought in 30 applications for the post.*
payable on application STK. EXCH. to be paid when applying for shares or stock. *See* application money; letter of application.
(3) COM. a formal claim or demand: *An application for refund (repayment) of duty/tax/rail-fare, etc.*
final application the heading of a note to an overdue debtor threatening that, unless he settles the debt by a certain date, his supplies will be stopped and he will have an action brought against him in the courts; and that no more reminders or warnings will be given.
(4) IND. a putting to use. *Your invention can have no application to our factory processes,* cannot be put to any use in making our products.

application for quotation STK. EXCH. a formal application by a public company to the Quotations Committee of the London Stock Exchange for a 'stock-exchange quotation' so that the company's shares or stock may be dealt in on the Exchange. A quotation is given only after close examination of the company's financial position and of the reputation of its directors; and if all is found to be in order, the quotation is then included daily in the Official List.

application form MAN. a printed form provided by persons or organizations inviting applications of any kind. All applicants are expected to answer the questions printed on the form and may be asked to give additional information on some matters: *An application form for: a passport/shares in a company/planning permission for a new building/opening a bank account/employment, etc.*

application for shares see application money; letter of application.

application, letter of see under letter.

application money STK. EXCH. money payable by a person at the time of making application for a new issue or offer-for-sale of shares (or stock) in a company; the amount payable *on application* may be the full price of the share or it may be a lesser amount, the balance being payable later. *See* letter of application; allotment money; call money.

applied economics ECON. that part of the study of economics which uses the findings of theoretical economists to explain the causes and meaning of events reported by descriptive economists; it is basically concerned with the practical problems of commerce, industry and finance. Cf. pure economics.

applied research see under research.

apply (1) COM. to make a formal request. *See* application. *To apply as of right*, to make a demand for something that one has a right to receive. (2) to put to use: *To apply money in reduction of a loan. Apply your mind to your work.* (3) LAW to ask a court for a relief or remedy: *To apply for a court order.*

appoint (1) to choose a person for a post: *To appoint a manager.* (2) to fix, to decide on (a time, a place, a piece of work): *The appointed time is 3 o'clock tomorrow. We shall meet at the court appointed for the hearing. Your appointed task (piece of work) is to increase sales.* (3) to furnish, to provide with comforts: *The house/flat/hotel/ship is well appointed.*

appointee a person appointed to an office.

appointment (1) a time and place chosen and agreed upon for a meeting: *To make/arrange/keep/miss/an appointment.* (2) an office for which a person has been chosen: *He has been offered an appointment on the board. See* letter of appointment.

appointments *pl.* furniture, comforts, ornaments, esp. in a house, flat, hotel or ship.

apportion COM. to divide up and give out in fair shares according to rule: *Let us apportion the overheads according to the turnover of each department.*

apportionment (1) COM. & ACCTS. the charging of each item of expense to its proper account. (2) MAR. INSCE. the sharing-out between the parties of losses when a general average is declared. *See* general average. (3) LAW when property is sold, the sharing-out between buyer and seller of charges paid periodically, such as the half-yearly payment of rates, so that each party bears his fair share at the date on which the sale is completed.

appraise COM. to judge the value of; to give a professional opinion of the price, value or cost of something, usu. before a sale, or before a demand for tax or customs duty or for insurance. *N.* appraisal; appraisement.

appraiser (1) COM. a professional valuer, who serves the public by making valuations of goods or property. (2) TAXN. official employed by government authorities to make valuations for the collection of taxes and duties: *Tax appraiser. Customs appraiser. See* surveyor; valuer.

appreciation (1) COM. an increase in market value of a producer's stocks of goods in a period of rising prices. (2) STK. EXCH. (of securities) a rise in the market price. (3) BKG. & FIN. (of a currency) an increase in value as compared with other currencies. (4) ACCTS. an increase in market value of the assets of a business. *Opp.* depreciation.

appreciation surplus when the net worth of a concern is calculated, any surplus in the market value of its assets over the value shown in the books is the appreciation surplus and may be of some importance to a possible buyer or investor.

apprentice MAN. & IND. (1) a young learner in a skilled trade who has bound himself, by a contract called an indenture or articles of apprenticeship, to serve an employer for a stated number of years, usu. three, five or seven, during which the employer equally binds himself to teach the apprentice the skills of his trade. (2) generally, a young person learning a skilled trade. *Syn.* trainee; novice. *See* indenture; articles of apprenticeship.

apprenticeship MAN. & IND. (1) the state of being an apprentice. (2) the time served by an apprentice.

appro. approval.

appropriated berth see accommodation berth.

appropriated goods SHIPG. goods found in a ship's hold after unloading and having no known owner. Such goods may lawfully be given to a consignee in place of goods delivered short.

appropriated stamp see under stamp.

appropriation (1) COM. & ACCTS. the practice of setting apart an amount of money for a particular purpose: *An appropriation for a staff bonus. An advertising appropriation.* (2) COM. & BKG. the act of taking possession of something and treating it as one's own: *Appropriation of unclaimed deposits by a bank, or of unclaimed authors' royalties by a publisher.* (3) LAW the act of the personal representative of a dead person in applying the property of that dead person to paying his debts according to rules laid down by law. (4) PUB. FIN. the making legal of government spending of public money by passing an Appropriation Act each year.

appropriation account ACCTS. a part of the profit and loss account showing how the net profits of a business are used, e.g. by putting some profit to reserves, some to pay dividends, and the balance to be carried forward to the next year. *Syn.* outlay account.

appropriation fund FIN. a class of unit trust, the managers of which act as both agent and principal, i.e. they buy new securities on their own account and then arrange for them to be appropriated to the trust fund at market value. Thus the managers can make a profit or a loss in the deal. Cf. cash fund.

approval (1) the act of thinking well of; being favourable towards: *Approval of the annual report and accounts by the shareholders.*
on approval COM. in Britain goods supplied on approval are goods sent to an intending buyer on the understanding that, if he so wishes, he may return them without payment to the supplier within a fixed period or within a reasonable time if no time has been agreed. *Colloq.* on appro.
(2) permission: *The board have given their approval to the proposed course of action. This cannot be done without the owner's approval.*

approved accounts (1) ACCTS. accounts which have been formally accepted by the members of the company and made binding by law. (2) COM. customers who are given credit because the supplier is satisfied about their reputation and ability to pay.

approved place *see* bonded warehouse.

approved society *see* friendly society.

approx. approximate; approximately.

approximately (*with* a quantity of any kind) nearly, about; not exactly, but a little more or a little less: *There are approximately 100 shareholders. A shipment of approximately 300 tons of coffee. Abbr.* approx. *Opp.* exactly; precisely.

appurtenances SHIPG. & LAW all the things necessary for the proper operation of a ship, including tackle and furniture.

aptitude MAN. natural ability or cleverness suited to a particular kind of work or activity: *An accountant has an aptitude for figures.*

aptitude test a test intended to find out what kind of work would be best suited to someone's personal abilities, esp. of a young person leaving school to take up employment.

à quai (*French*) *see* ex quay.

Arab Bank for Economic Development in Africa (A.B.E.D.A.) set up by the Arab League in 1973 with its base in Khartoum, to provide the non-Arab countries of Africa with technical and financial help, esp. those with serious and urgent problems over their balance of payments. In 1976 A.B.E.D.A. was merged with S.A.A.F.A., the Special Arab Assistance Fund for Africa. Cf. Kuwait Fund for Arab Economic Development.

Arab Common Market an organization of some Arab states, Egypt, Iraq, Jordan and Syria, to help to develop trade between its members. Set up in 1964, it has not been as successful as its supporters hoped.

Arab Economic Unity, Council of *see under* Council.

Arab Fund for Economic and Social Development an organization set up by the Arab League to use funds from the wealthy Arab states for investment in the less wealthy states. *See* Arab League.

Arab League an important organization of Arab states formed in 1945 with its original base in Cairo and with the main purpose of promoting unity among Arab countries. The League has done much to support the setting-up of economic agencies such as the Arab Fund for Economic and Social Development, the Arab Monetary Fund and the Arab Bank for Economic Development in Africa.

arable land AGR. land fit for ploughing.

Arab Loan Fund for Africa *see* Special Arab Assistance Fund for Africa.

Arab Monetary Fund BKG. an organization set up by the Arab League similar to the International Monetary Fund (I.M.F.) to give help to Arab countries that suffer from problems of short-term liquidity.

ar., arrived.

a/r all risks.

arbitrage *or* **arbitraging** (1) COM. & BKG. the business of buying some commodity, currency or bill of exchange in one market centre and selling it in another almost at the same time, thus taking advantage of any difference in price or exchange rate between the two centres. When dealing takes place in several centres, arbitrage is said to be indirect or compound. *Syn.* arbitration of exchange. (2) STK. EXCH. in U.S.A., the difference in market price between two securities that are closely related, e.g. the stock of a holding company and of a subsidiary. Cf. shunting.

arbitrager *or* **arbitrageur** COM. a person carrying on the business of arbitrage.

arbitration (1) IND. REL. a way of settling disagreements without bringing a lawsuit or having a strike; the reference of an industrial dispute to a tribunal set up by Act of Parliament. Cf. conciliation; mediation. (2) LAW the reference of a dispute or disagreement to one or more independent persons specially chosen for their knowledge and fairness, called arbitrators, who may sometimes have power to make their decision binding on both parties. *See* award; dispute; mediation; Advisory, Conciliation and Arbitration Service.

arbitration agreement IND. REL. an agreement containing a clause providing for a dispute to be referred to arbitration.

arbitration of exchange *see* arbitrage (1).

arbitrator LAW a person, usu. highly qualified in the law, who is appointed to act alone or with others as a sort of judge in disputes referred to him for settlement. His decision is called an award and can be enforced by the courts. Cf. referee. *See* arbitration; mediation.

archaeology *see* industrial archaeology.

architect IND. a person whose profession is to make plans of buildings and to see that they are properly built.

    naval architect an engineer specially qualified to make plans of ships and to see that they are correctly built.

archives *n. pl.* a collection of documents that has been gathered together over a long period. A place where such documents are stored.

are the basic metric unit of area, being the area of a square with sides of 10 metres. *See* hectare (100 ares).

area (1) the extent of the surface e.g. of a piece of land or water. Area is calculated by multiplying length by breadth. (2) COM. part of a country which has been divided into areas for a particular purpose: *The northern area sales manager. Free delivery in the London area. Sales analysis by areas.*

area health authority under the National Health Service, Britain is divided into areas roughly equivalent to counties, each under an area health authority responsible for controlling the hospital services, medical practice and specialist services, and the local authority's health services.

Argentina a federal republic in South America, pop. 25 million approx. (1973); capital, Buenos Aires, pop. 8.3 million approx.; language, Spanish; currency unit, the Argentine peso (Ar.P.), divided into 100 centavos. Member, O.A.S.; L.A.F.T.A.

argosy ECON. HIST. & SHIPG. a large merchant ship with a valuable cargo, esp. of the sixteenth and seventeenth centuries.

ARIEL STK. EXCH. Automated Real-Time Investment Exchange Limited, a computerized channel for effecting very large share deals between certain big investing organizations without passing through the usual Stock Exchange system.

aristocracy government of a country by noblemen, i.e. persons of the highest rank and called the upper class; the members of this class, esp. the nobility.

arithmetical error ACCTS. & COM. a mistake in calculating.

arithmetic(al) progression MAN. & ACCTS. a series of numbers arranged in increasing (or decreasing) order, the difference between each number and the next being always equal, thus: 1, 2, 3, 4, the difference being 1; or 1, 7, 13, 19, the difference being 6. Cf. geometric progression; harmonic progression.

arithmetic mean an ordinary average arrived at by adding together the value of all the individual articles and dividing that sum by the number of articles. Cf. geometric mean; harmonic mean; quadratic mean; median; mode.

arithmetic unit COMP. the part of the central processor of a computer which performs calculations and such operations as comparing, sorting, choosing and making decisions.

Ariz. Arizona, U.S.A.

Ark. Arkansas, U.S.A.

Ar. P. the Argentine peso. *See* Argentina.

arr. arrive; arrived; arrival.

arrange (1) to set in order: *To arrange one's affairs/books/figures/papers.* (2) to prepare, to plan: *To arrange a meeting,* to call the persons together to meet at a fixed time and place. *Syn.* to convene (a meeting). (3) (*with* for) *To arrange for something to be done,* settle the details and cause the thing to be done. (4) COM. to agree: *Future deliveries at prices to be arranged. The house was sold at an arranged price. We have arranged to meet.* (5) LAW to settle: *They have arranged their differences in a friendly way.*

arrangement (1) an orderly setting-out: *The arrangement of the desks in the office. An arrangement of samples to show the range of our products.* (2) *pl.* plans, preparations: *What are 'the arrangements for the conference?* (3) COM. an agreement: *We have come to an arrangement to sell each other's products. See* barter arrangement. (4) COM. a settlement: *He has made an arrangement with his creditors,* has agreed with them either that he will pay in full but over a period of time or that he will be forgiven part or all of the debt. *See* deed of arrangement.

arrangement, deed of *see* deed of arrangement.

arrangement, scheme of *see* scheme of arrangement.

array MAN. & ACCTS. an arrangement of numbers in the order of their values, either from lowest to highest, e.g. 32, 54, 87, 96 or from highest to lowest, e.g. 96, 87, 54, 32.

arrd. arrived.

arrear *sing.* COM. (*with* in) at the end of a given period.

payable in arrear (of rent, interest, etc.) payable at the end of the period: *Rent payable monthly in arrear*, the January rent is payable on 31 January. *Opp.* in advance. *See* arrears, *pl.*

arrears *pl.* COM. money owing and overdue; esp. of rent, rates, taxes, dividends, subscriptions: *Your arrears of rent amount to £100. He is falling into arrears with his payments. To make up/pay off arrears*, to make good, to pay what was overdue.

arrears of work work that has fallen behind programme, that has accumulated: *To catch up on arrears of work*, to make good, to complete what had not been done in time.

arrest LAW to stop and hold a person or ship believed to have offended against the law: *The police arrested the thief. The ship is under arrest.*

arrival (1) TRANSPT. the act of arriving, of reaching a place: *On arrival you will report to the manager. What is the time of arrival of the train? The date of arrival is 16 April.*

arrival notice a notice sent by the carrier of goods to the consignee telling him that the goods have arrived.

arrival platform the part of a railway station reserved for trains arriving and unloading their passengers.

arrival station the actual station to which goods are being sent by rail. *Syn.* ultimate destination. *Opp.* departure station.

(2) COM. a trade term used in export contracts to mean the same as ex ship, i.e. the seller has to pay the freight and handling charges up to the point where the goods are ready for the buyer to collect from aboard the ship on arrival at the named port.

arrivals *n. pl.* persons or things that have arrived: *A list of new arrivals. The arrivals and sailings list*, a list giving names of ships and the dates of their arrival at a given port and of their leaving.

art. article.

artesian well AGR. & IND. a pipe sunk deep in the ground up which water rises by its own pressure to the surface. Such wells are effective only in certain areas called artesian basins. Cf. tube-well.

article *n.* (1) a particular thing; one separate object: *This is a luxury/essential/mass-produced/hand-made article. An article of clothing/dress/footwear.* (2) a written paper: *A newspaper article.*

leading article an important piece of writing, usu. by the editor of a newspaper, giving the paper's opinion on some subject of special public interest. *Syn.* (*colloq.*) leader.

(3) LAW (in a written agreement) one part or division (usu. given a number) which deals with a particular subject: *Article 15 lays down that....*

ship's articles *pl.* SHIPG. *see* articles of agreement.

v. (1) LAW to write down one by one in the form of articles, i.e. separate parts or divisions of a document each dealing with a particular subject: *To article an agreement/charges.* (2) LAW & COM. to bind by contract in order to train someone for a profession: *To article a young person to a firm of solicitors.*

articled clerk an office worker (the clerk) bound by a contract (the articles) to serve in his master's law office for a stated number of years in return for being taught the practice of the law as a profession.

articles of agreement SHIPG. a document setting out details of a contract of employment between the master of a ship and the crew (persons working on the ship). *Syn.* ship's articles; shipping articles.

articles of apprenticeship IND. a written agreement in which a learner promises to serve a master who, in turn, promises to teach him a craft or trade. *See* apprentice; apprenticeship. *Syn.* indenture.

Articles of Association LAW & MAN. an important document, essential by law, recording article by article the way in which a company shall be managed and giving the rules by which its internal affairs shall be dealt with. It covers matters concerning shares, formal meetings, the powers of the directors, the election of officers, and the approval of accounts. A copy of the Articles must be placed in the office of the Registrar of Companies for examination by any member of the public. Cf. Memorandum of Association.

Articles of Incorporation (U.S.A.) *see* Incorporation Charter.

articles of partnership *see* deed of partnership.

artificial harbour *see* harbour.

artificial person LAW a group or association of persons who together are given an imaginary personality, i.e. a character or existence separate from the living persons who form the group. Such artificial persons are called corporations and are treated for many legal purposes as though they were actual single human beings. *See* corporations aggregate; corporations sole. *Syn.* fictitious person; legal person.

artisan COM. & MAN. a person skilled in one of the industrial arts, esp. a workman who makes or does useful things with his hands, for example, a carpenter, a plumber, a mechanic. Cf. artist; craftsman.

artist COM. & MAN. a person who can make beautiful things or things which need much skill and imagination to produce. Cf. artisan; craftsman.

commercial artist an artist who is specially skilled in drawing or planning advertisements, labels, exhibitions, etc. as objects to help in selling a product.

arts, industrial *see under* industrial.

A.S., A/S., a/s. account sales; after sight; alongside.

A.S.A. Advertising Standards Authority.

a.s.a.p. as soon as possible.

as at ACCTS. on a certain date: *Balance as at 31 December 19__*, a balance sheet heading stating the date on which the assets and liabilities of the business were valued. *Value as at __*.

A.S.E.A.N. Association of South-East Asian Nations.

as from COM. from a certain date onwards: *As from 15 February all orders should be sent to our new address. Syn.* on and after.

'A' shares *see under* shares.

ashore SHIPG. on shore, not on the sea: *Passengers may go ashore at Bombay. The storm drove the ship ashore. Syn.* on shore.

Asian Development Bank BKG. & PUB. FIN. an international bank set up in 1967 by members of E.C.A.F.E. to help to provide money for development programmes in Asia. It is based in Manila, Philippines.

as is, where is COM. words sometimes used in an offer for sale of goods, meaning that the articles are offered in their existing condition and in the place where they are now lying, and suggesting that the articles are not perfect: *In an as is, where is, condition.* Cf. as seen.

ask *n.* (U.S.A.) a bid, an asked or asking price.

asking price *see under* price.

as per according to: *As per list enclosed/your letter.*

as per advice BKG. & COM. words sometimes written on a bill of exchange meaning that the drawee has been told that the bill is being drawn on him.

as per contra ACCTS. in accordance with, corresponding to, an entry on the opposite side of the account.

assay *v.* and *n.* FIN. & ECON. to test the purity of a metal; the result of such a test: *An assay would show whether the coin is false.*

assay master FIN. a government officer who declares the amount of precious metal in coin or bullion.

assay office FIN. in Britain, there are offices in London and certain other towns where things made of silver and gold are officially marked to show that the metal is of the purity laid down by law. *See* hallmark.

assayer IND. a person skilled in testing ores and alloys to find out the proportion of pure and precious metal in them.

as seen COM. (of goods offered for sale) in the condition in which the buyer sees (or has seen) them, the seller making no promise and bearing no responsibility concerning their condition; often used of goods sold at auction.

assemble (1) to bring together: *Please assemble the figures for the meeting.* (2) IND. to collect pieces and fit them together: *We buy the various parts and assemble them in our factory.* (3) to come together: *The directors have assembled in the boardroom.*

assembly (1) IND. the process of continually collecting and fitting together the various parts in order to make up a whole article. (2) IND. the result of such a process: *An exhaust-assembly,* various parts that have been assembled into one single exhaust-system ready for fitting to a motor car.

assembly line a special arrangement of work in a factory where the mass-produced articles being assembled move slowly along a line of workers each of whom adds a particular piece or does a particular operation until the finished product comes out complete at the end of the line. *See* automatic transfer machines. (3) a gathering of people.

assembly hall a large room in which many people may gather, as in a school.

assembly point a marked place where people are to assemble, in case of fire or other danger.

assembly rooms *pl.* a building consisting of a number of rooms intended for holding public meetings and entertainments.

assent LAW a document which hands over ownership of property from the personal representatives of a person who has died, to the person who has the right to receive it, e.g. to a beneficiary under a will.

assented bond *see under* bond, *n.*

assented stock *see under* stock.

assess (1) COM. & FIN. to judge an amount or value: *To assess the value of a crop/the weight of an animal/the speed of a car.* (2) INSCE. & TAXN. to fix a value for taxation or insurance: *The tax inspector has assessed my income at £3500. He assesses the loss at £1000.*

assessment INSCE. an official valuation of goods insured against loss or damage.

assessment insurance *see* mutual insurance *under* insurance, classes and kinds of.

tax assessment TAXN. (*a*) a document showing the amount of tax a person has to pay, usu. in relation to a particular tax year. (*b*) the amount itself.

self-assessment a system existing in some countries by which each taxpayer prepares his own tax assessment (the document showing the amount of tax he has to pay in relation to a particular tax year). In other countries a government tax official prepares the assessment from details supplied by the taxpayer in a document called a tax return.

assessor (1) INSCE. a professional person who assesses the amount of a loss or damage, esp.

for an insured person, when a claim is made. *See* adjuster. Cf. fire loss adjuster. (2) TAXN. in U.S.A., an inspector of taxes. (3) LAW a specially-qualified adviser who helps the judge in a court of law to reach a fair decision in civil cases where matters that demand special knowledge are raised.

nautical assessor one who helps to judge in certain cases in the Admiralty Court.

asset *sing.* (1) generally, any possession that has money value, esp. one that can be used to pay debts; any one of a person's goods, or the money owing to him. (2) (*colloq.*) something or someone useful or helpful. An advantage: *It is an asset to be near a port/post office/bus stop/ railway station. The new manager is a great asset to the business. See* assets, *pl.*

assets *pl.* (1) ACCTS. & COM. all things owned by a person or business and having some money value, esp. if they can be used to pay debts, produce goods, or in some way help the business to make a profit. Assets are of many kinds:

active assets assets that earn interest. *Syn.* productive assets.

available assets *see* liquid assets.

capital assets *see* fixed assets.

circulating assets *see* current assets.

contingent assets assets or gains which have not actually been taken into possession in the accounting period but which will come into possession upon the happening of an event.

current assets assets which may be consumed (used up) or turned into cash fairly soon in the ordinary course of business, e.g. stock-in-trade, raw materials, stores, book debts, etc. *Syn.* circulating assets; floating assets. *Opp.* fixed assets.

deferred assets the unused part of expenses which have been paid wholly or partly in advance.

fictitious assets assets which, to meet the needs of the system of double-entry book-keeping, have to appear on the assets side of a balance sheet but which do not have any real value and are therefore not really assets. *Syn.* nominal assets.

fixed assets possessions of a long-lasting and unchanging nature such as land, buildings, machinery, trade investments, etc., used for making and selling the products of the business and not intended for sale or to be turned into cash as long as they are useful to the business. *Syn.* capital assets; permanent assets. *Opp.* current assets.

floating assets *see* current assets.

frozen assets assets which cannot immediately be turned into cash, either because they have been put under some sort of limiting control, e.g. a court order, or because their sale would bring a severe loss.

hidden asset where an asset is given a value considerably less than its market value, the difference between its market value and its book value represents a hidden asset.

illiquid assets those that cannot be sold for cash at short notice.

intangible assets assets which are valuable in helping the business, but since they have no material form, are not easily turned into cash, e.g. goodwill, patents, copyrights, trademarks. Cf. tangible assets.

liquid assets possessions which consist of cash in hand, or cash with bankers, and anything which can be quickly turned into cash, e.g. bills receivable and marketable securities. *Syn.* available assets.

net assets (*a*) fixed assets plus current assets. (*b*) fixed assets plus the difference between current assets and current liabilities. The resulting figure is often called the capital employed. (*c*) the excess of assets over liabilities. *See* assets value.

nominal assets *see* fictitious assets.

operating assets those being used in the active operations of the business.

permanent assets *see* fixed assets.

productive assets *see* active assets *above*.

quick assets assets which are held in cash or can immediately be turned into cash without serious loss. *Syn.* realizable assets.

real assets property other than money, such as buildings, machinery.

realizable assets *see* quick assets.

slow assets assets that cannot be quickly sold for cash.

tangible assets assets which have material form and therefore can be turned into cash fairly quickly, e.g. securities, cash, cheques, etc. Cf. intangible assets.

wasting assets those fixed assets which are gradually used up in producing the products of the business, e.g. a mine, an oil-well, a sand-pit.

(2) LAW property which can be used for the payment of the debts of a dead person or of a person who cannot pay all he owes. In the legal sense, assets fall into several kinds:

equitable assets a special class of asset forming part of the property left by a person who has died, which can only be applied to the settlement of his debts after a court order has been obtained.

legal assets any assets forming part of the property left by a person who has died, other than equitable assets, which are therefore administered by his executor or an administrator.

personal assets any assets which are not real assets; esp. any movable property such as personal goods, and interests in leasehold land.

real assets assets which consist of real property, i.e. land and buildings and any similar immovable property.

asset and liability statement (U.S.A.) a balance sheet.

assets disposal account ACCTS. an account in which is recorded what happens when an asset is no longer used. The original cost of the asset is debited to the account, while the total amount of depreciation provided for during all the years of the use of the asset plus any cash received for it on being sold off, are credited. The resulting balance shows whether the provision for depreciation has been too much or too little. *Syn.* assets account.

assets side (of balance sheet) *see* balance sheet.

asset-stripping FIN. buying up cheaply companies that are showing poor results, then selling off the assets one by one at a profit and closing down the businesses. This practice may be bad because it can bring harm or even hardship to shareholders, employees, suppliers and creditors of a stripped company. *See* dividend-stripping.

assets value ACCTS. the total worth (value) of a business calculated by adding together the book values of all its assets. *See* revaluation of assets.

net assets value (of a company) the value of the net assets divided by the number of shares issued.

assign *v.* (1) MAN. to give or share out, esp. work or duties to a particular person or group of persons: *We have been assigned work on the new ship. Each family was assigned a plot of land.* (2) LAW & COM. to give formally by contract to another person (the assign or assignee) property, rights or interests, esp. patents, copyrights, insurance policies, usu. by a document called a deed of assignment, often shortened to: an assignment.
n. see assignee.

assignable debt *see under* debt.

assignat ECON. HIST. a bond (representing seized land) given out in large numbers by the revolutionary government in France and used as paper money from 1790 to 1796.

assignee LAW a person to whom a legal right or interest has been formally given, usu. by deed of assignment. *Syn.* assign. Cf. assignor.

assignee in bankruptcy *see* trustee in bankruptcy.

assignment (1) MAN. a particular piece of work or duty given to a person or group of persons to carry out: *Your assignment is to negotiate the order. He has been sent on special assignment to Japan.* (2) LAW the act of assigning, i.e. of giving rights or interests formally to another person. (3) the document which gives effect to this. *See* bargain and sale.

assignment clause MAR. INSCE. a provision in a marine insurance policy allowing the insured person to give away or sell his interest in the policy.

assignor LAW the person making an assignment of rights or interests to some other person, usu. under a deed of assignment. Cf. assign. *N.* assignee.

assistant MAN. & COM. (1) a helper; a low-ranking employee, esp. in an office or shop.

clerical assistant an employee who helps in an office with the letter writing and other paper work.

personal assistant an employee usu. with wider duties than those of a secretary, who gives personal help in an office to the manager or other officer of high rank, e.g. arranging his travel, interviews and meetings. *Abbr.* P.A.
(2) an employee who helps an official of higher rank by taking over and performing part of his duties.

assistant accountant ACCTS. an accountant who helps another of higher rank.

assistant manager MAN. an employee who helps the manager by doing some of the work for which the manager is responsible.

assisted areas places in Britain with a high level of unemployment, which receive government help in the form of tax allowances, low rents, training grants, loans, etc.; grants are also given for buying machinery and to provide working capital for new products. Projects which will increase employment in areas also receive grants from the European Regional Development Fund of the European Common Market. Assisted areas include special development areas and development areas.

Assn. *or* **assn.** association.

associate *v.* COM. & FIN. to join; be connected with: *He is associated with a transport company.*
n. sing. (1) COM. & FIN. a person joined or connected with others, esp. in a business or professional practice, e.g. that of architect or surveyor. *Syn.* partner.

associates *pl.* in a professional practice, the partners: *John Smith and Associates*, the full name of the partnership formed by Mr John Smith and some others of his profession. Cf. & Co.
(2) LAW two persons are considered by law to be associates if either has any financial interest in the business or property of the other; or if both have a common interest in any business or property; or if some third person has an interest in the business or property of both of them.

associated company COM. & FIN. a company of which at least 20% but not more than 50% of the equity is held by another company or group of companies. Cf. subsidiary company.

association MAN. an organization formed by persons having the same interests and held together by an orderly system of management. Most associations are non-profitmaking, existing only to carry out the aims and objects for which they were formed. Some are professional associations for doctors, lawyers, etc., others are for certain trades; there are associations for employers, employees, travellers, etc.

Association, Articles of *see* Articles of Association.

Association, Declaration of *see* Declaration of Association.

Association, Memorandum of *see* Memorandum of Association.

Association of British Chambers of Commerce COM. a central organization based in London to which over 100 local chambers of commerce are joined. It deals with matters of general commercial and administrative planning rather than problems of production and labour relations. *See* chamber of commerce.

Association of South-East Asian Nations (A.S.E.A.N.) a regional organization formed in 1967 for improving political, economic and social co-operation between its members — Indonesia, Malaysia, the Philippines, Singapore and Thailand. Its main offices are in Indonesia.

asst. assistant.

assumed bond *see under* bond, *n.*

assurance INSCE. in the British insurance business *assurance* means the insuring of human lives (and ·sometimes marine risks), while *insurance* is used for insuring other things. But nowadays, as in U.S.A., *insurance* is commonly used to include both lives and things. *See* insurance.

(life) assurance company a company that insures lives, i.e. agrees to pay a certain sum of money when a stated event happens in the life of the assured, e.g. on his 65th birthday, or on his death, in return for the payment either of a lump sum or by regular sums of money at stated dates. Cf. insurance. *See* life assurance; annuity policy.

assured, the INSCE. (1) the person who will receive from the insurers any money payable under a life insurance policy. (2) a person on whose life an assurance policy has been taken out. In both cases, usu. the person effecting the insurance. *Syn.* the insured.

assurer INSCE. a person or company who contracts to pay the assured if a stated event happens. Cf. underwriter; insurer.

astern SHIPG. in a backward direction: *Half speed astern. Moving astern*, going stern first; backwards. *Opp.* ahead.

at the fractional currency unit of Laos. 100 at = 1 kip.

at (a price) COM. expressing price: *Onions selling at 10p a pound. These shoes are priced at £5 a pair. At a profit/gain/loss. At a premium/discount. At cost/par/face value/valuation. Goods sent at our cost/owner's risk.* Sign: @: *5 oranges @ 7p ea. = 35p.*

at best STK. EXCH. at the most profitable price obtainable: *I ordered my stockbroker to buy/sell at best.* The broker will always buy or sell for his client at best unless given clear orders to do otherwise.

at call BKG. (of money on deposit with a bank) repayable immediately, on demand.

A.T.L. actual total loss.

Atl. Atlantic coast ports.

Atlantic, Gulf, West Indies Warranty MAR. INSCE. a condition in a marine insurance policy limiting the movement of the ship to the Atlantic coasts of North, Central and South America as far south as Surinam (Dutch Guiana).

Atlantic Time the time-zone of Eastern Canada, four hours behind Greenwich Mean Time.

Atomic Energy Authority IND. a public corporation responsible for the production and control of nuclear energy in Britain. It has built a number of nuclear power stations. *Abbr.* A.E.A.

Atomic Energy Commission IND. the equivalent in the U.S.A. of the Atomic Energy Authority.

atomistic competition *see* pure competition *under* competition.

at par STK. EXCH. (of a stock or share) having a market value equal to its nominal (face) value; thus when a share of 25p nominal value has a market value also of 25p, the share is said to be at par. *See* par.

at risk INSCE. (of insured goods) likely to suffer damage or loss caused by dangerous events insured against in the policy.

at sea MAR. INSCE. said of a ship that has left port and is on the sea; not in port.

at ship's rail SHIPG. *see* under ship's derrick. Cf. over ship's rail.

at sight BKG. & COM. words used on a bill of exchange meaning that the amount of the bill is payable on demand, i.e. as soon as the acceptor is presented with it. Such bills are known as sight bills.

att. attached.

attaché (1) an official on the staff of an embassy in a foreign country.
commercial attaché the attaché responsible for dealing with trade and commercial questions between the countries concerned.
(2) STK. EXCH. a person who introduces business to a member of the exchange and is given a share in the commission if a deal results.

attachment LAW (1) (of persons) where a person has disobeyed a court order or has offended the court in certain other ways, he may be arrested (seized) and put in prison until he has made matters right. (2) (of debts) where a judgment of the High Court has been given against a debtor and he does not pay, the creditor may obtain a court order that any money owed to the debtor by other parties shall be used (attached) to pay the judgment debt. (3)

COM. a slip of paper fastened to certain documents such as an insurance policy or a bill of lading and recording a special condition.

attend MAN. (1) to be present at: *He attended the meeting/show/lecture/interview/dinner, etc. The exhibition was well attended*, many people were present. (2) to deal with: *I must attend to my mail*, deal with letters. *Please attend to this customer*, please serve him.

attendance (1) MAN. the act of being present: *His attendance record is bad. There was a good attendance.* (2) personal service: *Rooms with attendance*, lodgings with service.

attendance book a book in which members' attendance at meetings is recorded by each member writing his signature. *Syn.* attendance register.

attendance money money paid to certain workers, e.g. dockers in Britain, for attending at their place of work even when there is no work for them to do.

attendance time the number of hours spent by an employee at his place of work for which he is actually paid, whether there was work for him to do or not. *Syn.* hours of attendance.

attendant MAN. (1) an employee usu. of low rank but one who is put in charge: *A lavatory/cloak-room/dining-car attendant.* (2) sometimes also a person of higher rank: *A medical attendant*, a doctor.

attest LAW to witness formally, esp. the signature of a document such as a will.

attestation LAW (1) a formal declaration in writing of having witnessed the signing of a deed or other document. (2) a part of a deed or will declaring that it has been written and signed in the presence of witnesses.

attested copy *see* certified copy.

attitude survey IND. REL. an enquiry made by the management of a concern to discover the cause of bad relations with the work force and to find out how best to improve the feelings of the workers towards the management.

attorney LAW (1) a person who has power to act in the place of another person and to represent him in legal matters. *Syn.* attorney in fact. *See* power of attorney. (2) a lawyer, esp. one acting for a person in a court of law. In U.S.A., attorney-at-law. Cf. advocate.

Attorney-General LAW the highest law officer in Britain, usu. a Member of Parliament, and a political appointment ranking as a minister.

attorney, letter of *see* power of attorney.

attorney, power of *see under* power.

attract to draw, to pull, towards: *A market attracts buyers and sellers. The prosperity of the industry attracts new capital from investors. These goods attract tax at 8%.*

attractive pleasing; attracting: *An attractive offer/post/salary/delivery date/price/personality/ secretary.*

attributable profit *see under* profit.

auction COM. a method of selling in public by letting intending buyers gather and compete with each other by making bids (offers of money); the sale is made to the person who makes the highest bid. The seller may state a reserve (or upset) price below which he will not sell. *See* Dutch auctions; mock auction; private treaty; hammer, *n. Syn.* (Scotland) roup; public sale.

auctioneer COM. a person who is licensed to hold a public auction sale, acting as agent of the seller until the goods are actually sold, after which he becomes the agent of the buyer. His is therefore a particular class of agency. He is usu. paid by commission. *See* agent.

audio-typist a person trained to use a typewriter to write down words from a sound recording. Cf. shorthand-typist; copy-typist.

audit ACCTS. an official examination and checking of the annual accounts of an organization by an independent qualified person, called an auditor, in order to make certain that they show accurately the true financial position and do not hide any dishonesty, and also that they are presented in proper form ordered by law.

continuous audit a method adopted in some large concerns, of carrying out a continuous check on the account books and records all through the financial year, the advantage being that the work is evenly spread over the year. *Syn.* internal audit.

completed audit the practice usually adopted of checking the accounts after they have been completed at the end of the financial year. *Syn.* general audit.

internal audit *see* continuous audit *above.*

Audit Office PUB. FIN. a British government department under the Comptroller and Auditor-General, an independent official who audits the accounts of government departments to see that public money is properly spent as ordered by law, and who reports any serious irregularities to the Public Accounts Committee of the House of Commons.

auditor (1) ACCTS. a person who audits accounts. *See* audit. (2) LAW every limited company must appoint an auditor at each annual general meeting to act until the next such meeting. He must be a member of an officially-recognized body of professional accountants. He must not be an officer or employee of the company. He has a legal right of access to the records and accounts of the company. His duty is to the shareholders who appointed him: to find out and state the true financial position at the time of the audit. To do this he must examine the books and records to see that they are properly kept, draw up a balance sheet, and on it, or attached to it, make an auditor's report. *See* access; auditor's report.

auditor's remuneration MAN. & ACCTS. the sum of money paid to an auditor for his services and expenses in auditing the accounts of a company or other organization. In a company, the amount is fixed either by the directors or by the shareholders at the annual general meeting, and must be shown in the accounts of a limited company.

auditor's report LAW a report by the auditor officially appointed by an organization to audit its accounts. The report, usu. written on the balance sheet or attached to it, must by law state: whether he has obtained all necessary information and explanations; whether the books of account have been properly kept; whether the balance sheet and profit and loss account agree with the books of account; whether in his opinion the profit and loss account gives a true and fair view of the profit or loss made during the financial year, and whether the balance sheet gives a true and fair view of the state of affairs at the end of the year; and whether the accounts as a whole are in accordance with the provisions of the Companies Acts.

au pair (*French*, as equal) words used for an arrangement by which a young person, usu. a girl wishing to learn a language, goes to stay in the home of a family in a foreign country, not as an employed servant but as an equal, helping with the housework and the children in return for her food and lodging and a little pocket-money. *An au pair girl. She is an au pair.*

aurar the fractional currency unit of Iceland. 100 aurar = 1 króna. *Also* aur.

AUS Australia's international vehicle-registration letter.

austerity ECON. an economic situation in which the public cannot afford to buy any unnecessary goods, bringing about a lack of comfort and satisfaction with life and work.
  austerity budget a national budget which aims to be deflationary by increasing taxes and thus reducing consumer demand.

Australia, Commonwealth of an independent federation of states covering the Continent of Australia between the Indian Ocean and the Pacific Ocean, pop. 13.5 million approx. (1975); capital, Canberra, pop. 140,000 approx.; language, English; currency unit, the Australian dollar (A$), divided into 100 cents. Member, (British) Commonwealth Colombo Plan; O.E.C.D.

Austria a federal republic in Central Europe, pop. 7.5 million approx. (1971); capital, Vienna, pop. 1.7 million; language, German; currency unit, the schilling, divided into 100 groschen. Member, E.F.T.A.; O.E.C.D.

Austrian School ECON. THEORY a school of thought which began in Austria in the later part of the nineteenth century with the writings

of the economists Karl Menger, Eugene von Böhm-Bawerk and Friedrich Wieser, and with those of Stanley Jevons in England and Léon Walras in Switzerland. They are sometimes known as the Marginal Utility School, because they started and developed the idea of marginal utility. *See* Hayek, F.A. von.

autarchy ECON. historically the word meant a system of government headed by a king or other ruler with complete and uncontrolled power (*see* autocrat) but it is now used with the same meaning as autarky.

autarky ECON. a planned ideal to make a country completely self-supporting in supplies of food and raw materials and thus to be totally independent of other countries. *Syn.* economic self-sufficiency.

author (1) the writer of a book or play. (2) the person who brings something into existence: *The author of a plan/proposal.*

authority (1) MAN. the power to decide, to command and to control: *A manager has authority over his staff. You had no authority to do this*, you had no power to do it. (2) an official organization having power to govern or to control: *A local authority*, an elected body of councillors who, with employed staff, carry out the local government of Britain. *The Port of London Authority*, an example of a public organization appointed to manage a port.

authority to negotiate BKG. (in financing foreign trade) the power given by an importer's bank to its branch in the exporter's country to negotiate (to obtain agreement on) a bill of exchange to be drawn by the exporter on the importer due for payment at the end of an agreed period from the date of presentation of the shipping documents. *Syn.* authority to purchase. Cf. authority to pay.

authority to pay BKG. (in financing foreign trade) the power given to the importer's bank's branch in the exporter's country to pay at sight a bill of exchange drawn on the branch by the exporter, on presentation of the shipping documents. Cf. authority to negotiate.

authority to purchase *see* authority to negotiate.

authorize MAN. (1) to give someone power to do something: *The board authorized the secretary to affix the company's seal to the contract.* (2) to give permission or approval for something to be done: *Our materials buyer has authorized payment of your invoice. Your journey has not been authorized*, you have not been given permission to make the journey.

authorized capital STK. EXCH. the amount of share capital that a company is allowed under its Memorandum of Association to issue, usu. expressed as a stated number of shares, each of a stated nominal (face) value, e.g. one million shares of 25p each. Capital in the form of shares actually issued is called issued or subscribed capital. The whole of the authorized capital need not be issued; any balance not yet issued is called unissued capital. *Syn.* authorized issue; authorized stock; nominal capital; registered capital; subscribed capital.

authorized clerk STK. EXCH. a stockbroker's clerk who has been given special power to do business in the Stock Exchange on behalf of his employer.

authorized depositary *see under* depositary.

authorized issue *see* authorized capital.

authorized stock *see* authorized capital.

auto an automobile (U.S.A.), a motor car.

autobahn (*German*) *see* motorway.

auto ferry TRANSPT. a boat which carries motor cars, lorries, etc. as well as passengers across a river or other narrow stretch of water. *Syn.* car ferry.

auto-financing COM. & FIN. (of a business) self-financing; able to raise enough money from its own earnings to pay the costs of present and future production and overheads without having to borrow money or to increase its capital. Cf. cash flow.

autograph book BKG. a book for collecting signatures, esp. one in which a bank records the cheque signatures of its customers as a check against dishonesty.

automat COM. (1) a system of selling goods by machine, esp. food in a restaurant, to customers who serve themselves by first choosing what they want from a number of articles to be seen behind locked glass windows, and by then putting coins into the machine, thus unlocking the chosen article for the customer to take away. (2) a restaurant using this system. *Syn.* slot-machine; vending machine.

automatic IND. (of machinery) working or moving by itself, without being made to do so by a driver or operator. *Examples*: the automatic gear change in some motor cars; an automatic telephone system; an automatic pilot in an aircraft; an automatic fire alarm.

automatic data processing COMP. the handling and treatment of information by computers.

automatic debit transfer BKG. & COM. a service provided by the National Giro in Britain which makes it possible for business organizations to collect money from a large number of customers at regular dates and at a very low administrative cost, provided each customer has a Giro account and agrees to this method of automatically debiting his account when a payment is due.

automatic stabilizers *see* stabilizers, economic.

automatic standard ECON. & PUB. FIN. a monetary system which manages itself without needing any action by the central bank. The amount of money and its value are left to settle their own level by the interaction of supply and demand for the precious metal (usu. gold or silver) or the foreign currency chosen to be the monetary standard.

automatic transfer machines IND. the machines on which the modern mass-production assembly line is based, esp. in the motor-car industry. The machines are placed at points along and beside a moving belt, and each machine delivers the right part to the right place at the right time, so enabling the whole line to keep flowing smoothly.

automation IND. a planned system of using automatic apparatus and machines, esp. computers, to replace human judgment, saving human effort and sometimes reducing the number of workers needed. *See* cybernetics; servo-mechanisms.

automobile (U.S.A.) a motor car or other vehicle that moves by its own power.

autonomous investment ECON. THEORY an increased level of investment made, not because of a short-run rise in the rate of interest, but for some deeper, longer-term reason, e.g. the effects of the accelerator and the multiplier. Cf. induced investment. *See* Acceleration Principle; multiplier.

autonomous port *see under* port.

autoroute (*French*) *see* motorway.

autostrada (*Italian*) *see* motorway.

aux. auxiliary.

Av., av. average; avenue; avoirdupois.

a/v. ad valorem (duty, tax).

avail (U.S.A.) COM. profit; what remains of a sum of money after taking off expenses. The word is not in modern use in Britain. *Syn.* net proceeds.

availability (1) COM. a state of being obtainable; being at hand: *The availability of capital for investment depends on the rate of interest. The availability of replacement parts for foreign cars is bad.* (2) TRANSPT. & TOUR. (of tickets, hotel accommodation) having force: *The availability of this air ticket is 90 days. We cannot promise the availability of your hotel reservation if you arrive after 8 p.m.*

available (1) COM. obtainable; ready at hand; ready for use: *We can buy the property from available funds*, from money at hand. *We have cash available for investment.* (2) TRANSPT. & TOUR. in force: *Return tickets are not available on this route*, cannot be obtained.

available assets *see* liquid assets *under* assets.

avdp. avoirdupois.

average (1) generally, a middle position between extremes. In mathematics, the middle value of a set of numbers. *Syn.* mean. *See* arithmetic mean; geometric mean; weighted average; moving average. (2) of an ordinary, common or usual kind in quality or amount: *Goods of average quality. We expect an average harvest this year.* (3) SHIPG. small gifts of money given by the master of a ship to persons performing certain services such as pilotage and towage to encourage them to take special care. These expenses are charged to the owners of the cargo on an average or sharing basis. *See also* petty average. (4) MAR. INSCE. (from *French*: avarie, damage) the sharing, among owners or insurers, of the cost of loss or damage at sea.

general average the sharing of a partial loss which has resulted from an extraordinary sacrifice made on purpose to prevent a total loss, e.g. when, in a situation of great danger, the master throws part of the cargo into the sea in order to save the ship and the rest of the cargo for the common good. It is an accepted rule of the sea that the master has the right to do this and 'that the loss should be shared by the various parties joined in the marine adventure. *Syn.* gross average. *Abbr.* g.a.; G/A; G.A.

gross average *see* general average.

particular average loss arising from an accidental happening, the cost of which is borne only by the owners of the particular thing or class of thing lost, i.e. of cargo, ship or freight. *See* with average.

(5) STK. EXCH. *see* averaging.

average adjuster MAR. INSCE. a person highly trained in the law of marine insurance and in valuing the losses under general average, who decides the amounts to be borne by the various parties. *See* average (4). *Syn.* average stater; average taker.

average agent MAR. INSCE. a person who, as an agent, arranges for assessments of claims and for surveys of damage to ships and goods.

average bond *see under* bond, *n.*

average clause (1) INSCE. a condition in a fire insurance policy that, in the event of a claim, the sum payable shall not be greater than the proportion that the face value of the property, i.e. the value stated in the policy, bears to its actual value. This is to make sure that the property is insured for at least its full actual value and that the premium is paid on this basis. *Syn.* pro rata condition. (2) MAR. INSCE. a part of a marine insurance policy which states what goods are expected from average.

average cost ECON. THEORY the cost per unit of output. Cf. average revenue. *See under* cost. *Syn.* unit cost.

average date COM. where several payments, e.g. for interest, become due to the same person at various dates, it is often convenient to combine them into one single payment on a date about half-way between the extremes of the due dates. *Syn.* equated time; average due date.

averager STK. EXCH. an investor who adopts the practice of averaging. *See* averaging.

average price *see under* price.

average rate *see under* rate.

average revenue ECON. THEORY under a system of perfect competition, the average revenue per unit of output sold, calculated by dividing total receipts by the number of units sold, must equal the price of the product, providing all units are sold.

average statement MAR. INSCE. the statement prepared by an average adjuster in the case of a general average claim, stating the amount to be paid by each of the parties whose goods have been saved. *See* general average *under* average.

average stater *see* average adjuster.

average stock COM. & ACCTS. in order to make comparisons, it is sometimes useful to know the average value of stock during the financial year. This is found by adding the values of opening and closing stock and dividing by two. *See* stock-turn.

average taker *see* average adjuster.

averaging STK. EXCH. a practice followed by some investors on the Stock Exchange of buying separate lots of the same share at different times at different prices. *See* speculation; pound/cost averaging.

averaging down buying more of a particular share when the market price is falling; this reduces the average price of one's existing holding, but increases one's overall loss, at least in the short term. Opinion does not favour this operation; it should be done only if the investor has a strong faith in an eventual rise in the market price; and if this happens, his profit will be greater.

averaging up buying more of a particular share when the market price is rising; this increases the average price of one's existing holding, but as long as the market price continues to rise the average price of the holding must always be below market price, so that one is covered against loss.

aviation IND. & TRANSPT. (1) the science and practice of flying aircraft. (2) aircraft manufacture.

aviation broker an agent who buys, sells, charters and insures aircraft and arranges airfreight transport.

aviation insurance *see under* insurance, classes and kinds of.

avoidable costs *see* supplementary costs.

avoidance *see* tax avoidance.

avoir. avoirdupois.

avoirdupois weight a system of weights in general commercial use in Britain and the U.S.A. Britain is now changing to the metric system. *Abbr.* avoir; avdp. *See table on page 478.*

award IND. REL. a decision of an arbitration tribunal giving its view of the facts and its recommendations for settling the claims of the parties in disagreement. *See* arbitration.

awareness ADVTG. (of a product, by consumers)

knowing the existence of; conscious of the qualities of: *Consumer awareness.*

axe to take strong action to reduce expenses; to put an end to, in order to save money: *Our plans for a new factory have been axed. To get the axe*, to be dismissed from a post.

B

b. born, e.g. *b. 1885.*

B Belgium's international vehicle-registration letter.

B., b. bag, bale.

B.A.A. British Airports Authority.

Babeuf François-Émile (1760–97), French revolutionary and writer on ideas which influenced the rise of modern socialism. He demanded public ownership of all land and industry.

back *n.* see backwardation.

v. (1) to support, esp. by providing money: *To back a new project/scheme/development/enterprise.* (2) BKG. & COM. to take the responsibility for paying a bill of exchange by endorsing it: *To back a bill.*

back bond see under bond, *n.*

back country see hinterland.

backdate (1) to put an earlier date (on a document) than the real date, in order that the document takes effect as. though it had been made on the earlier date. (2) to provide for payments to apply from a certain date in the past: *A pay rise backdated to 1 January.*

backed bill see under bill of exchange.

backed note SHIPG. a receiving note from a shipbroker to the master of a ship giving him permission to take on board goods brought in barges or other boats. In making this note the shipper becomes bound to pay the freight.

backer (1) COM. & FIN. a person who supports another, esp. with money in a commercial venture. *Syn.* financier. See angel. (2) BKG. & COM. a person who takes the responsibility for paying a bill of exchange by endorsing it.

back freight see under freight.

backhander (*colloq.*) a bribe.

backing (1) help and support, esp. with money or influence: *With your backing, he should get the job.* (2) PUB. FIN. gold and government securities which support a country's bank-note issue. Originally the British note issue was backed almost wholly by gold. Until 1931 a pound note could be exchanged for gold at the Bank of England. That part of the note issue not backed by gold, the fiduciary (in faith) issue, is backed by government securities and has increased to the point where today the entire note issue is fiduciary and is unbacked by precious metal.

back letter SHIPG. a letter sometimes given by the shipper to the shipping company when goods are loaded in poor condition, agreeing to make good all loss suffered by the carrier if any claims arise from a foul bill of lading, i.e. one recording some fault in the goods or in the packing. The shipping company may then be willing to give the shipper a clean bill of lading which will make it easier for him to collect payment from the bank. *Syn.* backward letter; letter of indemnity.

back load TRANSPT. a load for a road-transport vehicle to carry on its return journey. *Syn.* return load.

backlog an accumulation of work (orders to supply, letters to write, etc.) needing to be dealt with quickly.

back pay pay which is overdue. It may have been extra pay for work done in the past, or it may have accumulated because of an agreement allowing an increase in pay dating back to a past date.

backsheesh see baksheesh.

back spacer a key on a typewriter which, when pressed, moves the carriage back one space.

backwardation (1) STK. EXCH. a charge made by a buyer of stock on a seller who has bound himself to deliver it on Settling Day but cannot do so, and who thus arranges with the buyer to delay delivery until the next Settling Day. *Syn.* backwardization; back. *See* contango. (2) COMMOD. EXCH. the amount by which the spot price is higher than the forward price.

backward integration IND. & MAN. the practice of increasing the size or the profitability of a business by gaining control of organizations which supply it with its raw materials. *See* integration.

backwardization see backwardation.

backward letter see back letter.

bad (1) not good; poor.

to the bad in a state of loss; out of pocket: *After this venture I am £1000 to the bad. Syn.* worse off. *Opp.* to the good.

(2) LAW wrong; not good in law: *A bad claim.*

bad book STK. EXCH. a jobber would say that he 'had a bad book' in a certain security if he had bought a quantity and the price had then fallen, leaving him with the choice either of holding his stock in the hope of a rise in price or of selling now at a loss.

bad coin see debasement of coinage.

bad debt COM. & ACCTS. debts which are likely never to be paid and must be treated as worthless by being entered as *written off* in a bad debts account.

bad debts account a nominal account (since bad debts are an ordinary business expense) to which are debited all bad debts. The total is later debited in the profit and loss account and has the effect of reducing the profit (or increasing the loss) for the accounting period.

bad debts insurance *see* credit policy *under* insurance policy.

bad debts policy *see* credit policy *under* insurance policy.

bad delivery STK. EXCH. stocks or shares which, when delivered by the jobber to the broker or by the broker to the client, are found to have some fault.

bad faith dishonesty; deceit; insincerity; disloyalty: *To act in bad faith.*

badly off (*colloq.*) poor. *Opp.* well off.

bad money *see* debasement of coinage.

bad paper BKG. bills of exchange which have been, or are likely to be, dishonoured.

bag cargo SHIPG. goods packed and carried in bags or sacks. *Syn.* bagged cargo.

Bagehot Walter (1826–77), English economist, banker and writer. He was editor of *The Economist* from 1860 until his death. He wrote widely on economic subjects, esp. finance and banking. A critic of the Classical School of economists, he offered an explanation of the trade cycle based on the swings of opinion and outlook in the business world.

baggage the bags or cases containing clothing and personal things belonging to a passenger. In Britain usu. called *luggage*, but both *baggage* and *luggage* are words in everyday use. *See also* unaccompanied baggage.

baggage declaration TOUR. a form made out by a passenger in order to obtain customs clearance of his baggage.

baggage master SHIPG. on a ship, a member of the crew who is in charge of the passengers' baggage.

baggage policy *see under* insurance policy.

baggage room TRANSPT. & SHIPG. (1) in U.S.A., a place, usu. in a railway station, where baggage may be left for short periods on payment of a small charge. *Syn.* left-luggage office. (2) in Britain, a part of a ship reserved for passengers' baggage.

baggage sufferance *see* bill of sufferance.

bagged cargo *see* bag cargo.

Bahamas a group of islands in the West Indies, a self-governing state since 1964, pop. 187,000 approx. (1973); capital, Nassau, pop. 113,000; language, English; currency, the Bahamian dollar (Ba$), divided into 100 cents.

Bahrain an independent island sheikhdom in the Arabian Gulf off the coast of Saudi Arabia, pop. 235,000 approx. (1973); capital, Manama, pop. 62,000 approx.; languages, Arabic and Urdu; currency, the Bahraini dinar, divided into 1000 fils. Member, Arab League.

baht the currency unit of Thailand, divided into 100 satang.

bail LAW money given, or promised in a bond, as surety that a person who has been arrested, and is being set free until his trial, will appear in court at the proper time: *His father went/*

stood bail for him. The son was out on bail/released on bail/admitted to bail. He surrendered to his bail, appeared in court at the proper time. *The accused jumped his bail,* failed to appear in court; absconded. *The accused thief was refused bail.*

bail bond *see under* bond, *n.*

bailee LAW a person to whom goods are entrusted by the owner (the bailor) to be held for a stated purpose and on condition that they shall be returned to the owner when he asks. Thus the bailee takes possession of the goods for a time but the bailor keeps the ownership.

bailiff LAW an officer of a court of law who makes people obey the orders of the court. He makes arrests, and seizes property, esp. furniture, to obtain payment of debts which the court has ordered to be paid. *See* process-server.

farm-bailiff AGR. in Britain, a person employed by the owner of a large area of land to manage the work of farming and forestry.

bailment LAW the temporary delivery of goods by their owner (the bailor) to another person (the bailee) to whom they are entrusted for a stated purpose, on condition that they remain the property of the bailor and will be returned to him or otherwise dealt with according to his wishes. The delivery may be, e.g. for hire; or as an act of kindness such as a loan; or as security for money borrowed by the bailor; or as goods to be carried or repaired or stored, etc.

bailor LAW a person who entrusts another person (the bailee) with possession of his goods for a stated purpose, but without losing his ownership of the goods. *See* bailee; bailment.

bail, paper *see under* paper.

baiza the fractional currency unit of Oman. 1000 baizas = 1 rial Omani.

baker's dozen *see* dozen.

baksheesh in the Indian subcontinent and the Middle East, a tip; a small gift to the poor. In Britain (*colloq.*), anything got for nothing. *Also* backsheesh; bakshish.

bal. balance.

balance *n.* (1) ACCTS. the sum required to make one side of an account equal to the other side, i.e. the difference between the total of all the debit entries and the total of all the credit entries in an account. This amount, esp. whether it is a debit or a credit, expresses the financial position of the particular account at the time the balance is struck.

balance b/d balance brought down. *See* balance c/d.

balance b/fwd balance brought forward. *See* balance c/d.

balance c/d balance carried down, the amount required to balance the account, i.e. to make both sides equal, is entered in the proper column at the end of the fixed period when the accounts are balanced. The same amount is entered in the opposite side of the account, using the words balance b/d or balance brought down, to begin the new fixed period.

balance c/fwd balance carried forward. *See* balance c/d.

balance in hand *or* **on hand** usu. money in notes and coin, held in ready form for making payments.

bank balance the balance to the credit or debit of a customer's account with a bank. *Syn.* balance at bank.

cash balance (a) the amount of money, in notes and coin, held at any particular time in the cash-box or till of a business. (b) the amount standing to the credit of the current account of a person or business, often called 'cash at bank'.

closing balance the balance of an account at the end of the accounting period; this balance becomes the opening balance of the next accounting period.

credit balance a balance on the credit (right-hand) side of an account.

debit balance a balance on the debit (left-hand) side of an account.

opening balance the balance of an account at the beginning of an accounting period; this balance is the same as the closing balance at the end of the accounting period just completed.

trial balance *see under* trial.

(2) the rest; what remains; what is left. *Our terms are: 50% cash with order, balance to be paid within 30 days. We have supplied most of your order; the balance will follow after the holidays. You have not paid all you owe; I shall sue you for the balance.*

v. ACCTS. to calculate the sum required to make one side of an account equal to the other.

to balance off *or* **balance up** (a set of accounts) to carry out the work of balancing each of the accounts in order to arrive at the difference between all the debit and all the credit entries in the entire set of accounts and to arrive at a figure of profit or loss.

balanced account an account which balances or which has been balanced off.

balance certificate STK. EXCH. a certificate or written declaration given by a company to a shareholder who has sold only a part of the shares shown on an earlier share certificate, stating that he is the registered owner of the balance of the shares detailed in it. The certificate is given in exchange for a balance receipt or balance ticket. *See* balance receipt.

balanced budget *see* budget (1).

balance for official financing *see* balance of payments.

balance of indebtedness *see* balance of payments.

balance of payments the balance of a national account in which are recorded all international

dealings resulting in payments of money during a certain period. Unlike the balance of trade, which includes only visible dealings (articles of trade, and gold and silver bars and coins), the balance of payments takes note of invisible imports and exports (payments for banking, insurance, transport, and other services), interest payments and movements of capital. (*See also* current balance.) The balance is said to be in deficit, adverse, passive or unfavourable if it shows that the country pays or owes more than it receives or is owed; and in surplus, active or favourable if the opposite is true. Cf. balance of trade.

balance of payments on capital account the difference in the money values of the capital flowing into and out of the country.

balance of payments on current account this combines visible and invisible items and is the difference between the money values of exports (visible and invisible) and of imports (visible and invisible).

balance of trade ECON. & PUB. FIN. the difference between the money values of the visible exports and the visible imports of a country. In Britain, exports are taken at f.o.b. prices, and imports at c.i.f. prices. *See* adverse trade balance; active balance; invisible balance. *Syn.* trade balance.

balance receipt STK. EXCH. a temporary document given by a company to a shareholder who has sold only a part of the shares detailed on an earlier share certificate. When the transfer of shares has been formally recorded, he gives the receipt back to the company in exchange for a balance certificate. *Syn.* balance ticket. *See* balance certificate.

balance sheet ACCTS. a statement showing the financial position of a business at a certain date, usu. the end of the financial year; it contains the balances of the ledger accounts separated into liabilities (mainly capital invested, creditors, reserves, e.g. for future taxation, and provisions, e.g. for staff pensions) and assets (mainly land and buildings, machinery, stock-in-trade, cash, investments, and amounts receivable from debtors). Balance sheets are presented in one of two forms:

account-form balance sheet in two columns with liabilities on the left and assets on the right.

report-form balance sheet the more modern form listing assets, liabilities and ownership capital one under the other.

balances, idle *see under* idle.

balance ticket *see* balance receipt.

balboa the currency unit of Panama, divided into 100 centesimos.

bale a large package of soft goods, e.g. cotton, skins, wool, usu. compressed, wrapped in sacking and bound by rope, wire or metal bands. *Syn.* bundle.

bale cargo cargo consisting entirely of bales, usu. of standard size (30 in. × 15 in. × 15 in.). *Syn.* baled cargo.

bale cubic capacity (of a ship) the amount of space that can be used for carrying bales, boxes and bags. Cf. grain capacity.

ball. ballast.

ballast (1) SHIPG. any heavy material, e.g. stones, sand, put into the bottom of a ship or boat to keep her steady.

ballast passage a voyage without cargo, the ship carrying only ballast and therefore earning no freight. *Opp.* cargo passage.

in ballast carrying no cargo only ballast. (2) TRANSPT. stony material used to make a hard base for a road or railway track.

ballot (1) any method of secret voting. (2) COM. a small bale weighing 70–120 lb.

Baltic Exchange COMMOD. EXCH. & SHIPG. sometimes known as 'The Baltic', its full name is the Baltic Mercantile and Shipping Exchange, in the City of London. Originally the market for produce from the Baltic countries, it is now an association of (*a*) shipowners and ship-brokers forming the world's largest international shipping market for the chartering, buying and selling, and the insurance of ships and the chartering of aircraft; (*b*) merchants and brokers forming a commodity market specializing in grain but also dealing in coal, timber and oilseeds. The Baltic is important for its earnings from invisible exports.

Baltic ice warranty MAR. INSCE. a condition in an insurance policy on the hull of a ship, that the ship will not be taken into certain parts of the Baltic Sea during times of the year when the sea is frozen.

ban an official order of disapproval forbidding someone to do something.

overtime ban an official order by a trade union forbidding its members to work overtime; a means of putting pressure on an employer to agree to the union's demands. Cf. go slow; strike action; industrial action; work to rule.

Banca d'Italia BKG. the central bank of Italy.

banco BKG. bank value; the standard unit of money in which a bank keeps its accounts, e.g. sterling, U.S. dollars, as distinguished from the currency of any country in which it may be doing business.

Bancogiro *see under* Giro.

bancor BKG. & FIN. the name given to a world currency unit suggested by Lord Keynes and the British Treasury at the Bretton Woods Conference (1944) as an international medium of exchange. Although it was not accepted by the conference, an idea very like it was introduced by the International Monetary Fund in 1970, known as special drawing rights.

banging the market STK. EXCH. the sudden offering for sale of large quantities of stocks or shares on the open market, without thought for the dangerous fall in prices which must result.

Bangladesh an independent republic (formerly East Pakistan) between India and Burma on the northern shore of the Bay of Bengal; pop. 76 million (1974); capital, Dacca, pop. 1.6 million approx.; language, Bengali; currency unit, the taka, divided into 100 poisha. Member, (British) Commonwealth.

bani the fractional currency unit of Romania. 100 bani = 1 leu.

bank *v.* BKG. (1) to pay money, cheques, etc. into a bank, usu. for safe-keeping: *A wise man banks his savings.* (2) to keep money in, to have an account with, a bank: *We bank with the Midland (Bank).* (3) to carry on the work of a banker; to trade in money. (4) (*colloq.*) (*with* on) to depend on; to rely on: *We are banking on you to deliver the goods on time.* *n.* BKG. a business organization, usu. a limited company, which trades mainly in money, receiving and holding deposits and paying sums out of them by order of the customer, lending money at interest, discounting bills of exchange, moving money from one place to another, acting as customer's agent in buying and selling securities, serving as trustee or executor, and performing various extra services for customers, e.g. arranging travel and insurance, and advising on tax and investment. *See* banking system; foreign trade.

Bank, The (in Britain) the Bank of England.

in the bank BKG. said of a discount house when it has to borrow from the Bank of England.

bankable asset BKG. any asset that a bank will receive or handle or accept as security for a loan: *Bankable securities/bills/paper. See* bank bill.

bank acceptance *see* bank bill.

bank account BKG. an arrangement between a bank and a customer under which the customer pays in or deposits with the bank a sum of money which may be added to from time to time, and has the right to cash cheques and to draw cheques on his account in favour of other parties. A customer may arrange to have more than one account with the same bank, in which case they are usu. numbered No. 1 account, No. 2 account, etc. Bank accounts are usu. one of three kinds in Britain.

current account (demand deposits in U.S.A.) on which the commercial bank customer receives no interest and may in fact pay bank charges unless a certain minimum average balance is kept in the account; and it is on his current account that a customer cashes and draws cheques. Trustee savings banks, however, pay some interest on current accounts. *Syn.* cheque a/c; drawing a/c.

deposit account (time, or notice, deposit in U.S.A.) a bank account in which money paid in or deposited by a customer earns interest at a rate which varies with the bank's base rate; the customer usu. has to give seven days' notice before he can take his money out of his deposit account, and he cannot draw cheques on this account though he can transfer sums from it to his current account after due notice. Deposit accounts are often used as a reserve into which money not immediately needed can be put to earn interest; they can include fixed deposits, which are loans by the customer to the bank at a fixed rate of interest for a fixed length of time. *Abbr.* D.A.; D/a.

drawing account *see* current account *above.*

savings account a bank account into which personal savings are paid and on which the bank usu. pays a slightly higher rate of interest than on ordinary deposit accounts. Small sums can be drawn out on demand but due notice must be given before taking out larger sums. In Britain such accounts are held not with the commercial banks but with the National Savings Bank and the building societies. *See also* dead account; joint account; public account.

bank advances *see* advances, *n.pl.*

bank balance *see under* balance.

bank bill BKG. (1) in Britain, a bill of exchange that has been drawn, accepted or endorsed by a bank; such a bill can be more easily and more cheaply discounted in the money market because of the high reputation of the bank. In U.S.A., a bankable bill. *Syn.* bank acceptance; bank draft; banker's bill. Cf. banker's draft. (2) in U.S.A., a bank-note.

bank book *see* bank pass-book.

bank certificate ACCTS. & BKG. a declaration signed by a responsible official of a bank, made on the formal request of a company's auditors, stating the amount of the balance in the company's bank account at a certain date. This document provides a check on the company's own accounts and on the honesty of its employees responsible for dealings with the bank.

bank charges BKG. charges made by a bank on a customer for the work of keeping a current account and for certain other services. Some banks charge a commission on current accounts of an eighth to a quarter per cent on the total value of all cheques debited, while others base their charge on the number, not the value, of all cheques drawn and credits made to the account, during a given period, usu. of six months. Most banks, however, make no charge if the average credit balance in the account is kept above an agreed minimum figure. *Syn.* bank commission; commission on current accounts; ledger fees.

Bank Charter Act, 1844 BKG. & ECON. HIST. a law passed by Parliament after a series of bank failures, and mainly intended to make the Bank of England responsible for controlling the issue of bank-notes by the other banks and gradually to become the only note-issuing bank in England and Wales. The Act also gave the Bank of England the duty of making public a balance sheet in the form of a weekly bank return.

bank cheque *see* bank draft.

bank circulation *see under* circulation.

bank clearing *see* clearing house.

bank clerk BKG. a person employed in a bank, esp. one who deals with the customers, receiving and paying out money and carrying out ordinary everyday business. Cf. bank manager. *Syn.* teller; cashier.

bank commission *see* bank charges.

bank credit ECON. & BKG. money lent by banks to their customers. This money is 'created', i.e. brought into existence, by the banks and has great economic importance because of its effect on the total supply of money.

bank deposits BKG. (1) money deposited with a bank by its customers. (2) the total sum of money owed by a bank to all its customers, either received and held as deposits or credited to their accounts as interest or as overdrafts. This total sum represents claims by customers and is therefore a liability of the bank. Cf. bankers' deposits. *See* deposit. (3) ECON. the total of all bank deposits in a country's economy is important because they are a form of money (called deposit money) and make up the largest part of the total money supply in the economy.

bank discount *see* banker's discount.

bank, discount *see* discount bank.

bank draft *or* **banker's draft** BKG. (1) a cheque payable on demand drawn by a bank on itself and signed by one of its responsible officials. Since no bank is likely to refuse payment of such a cheque it is regarded as cash. In practice, a debtor buys a bank draft and uses it to pay a creditor who will not accept a personal cheque. *Syn.* bank cheque; banker's cheque. *Abbr.* B/D.; B/Dft. (2) a bank bill (British).

banker BKG. (1) a person or body of persons, now usu. a limited company, who, by arrangement: on the one hand accepts money deposited by customers to be held safely for them or to be paid out by honouring cheques drawn by them on current account; and, on the other hand lends money in return for interest, always keeping enough of the depositors' money on hand to meet any demands for cash that they may make. *See* bank; banking. The ordinary legal position between banker and customer is that of debtor and creditor depending on who owes money to the other; but when the banker pays out money for his customer, he becomes the customer's agent. (2) loosely, any person who is in the banking business. *See* investment banker *under* investment; industrial banker *under* industrial.

bankers' bank BKG. the Bank of England, with

which each of the clearing banks keeps a de-·
posit. This allows the clearing bank to receive
or pay money from the other banks without
handling cash. *See* clearing banks; Clearing
House.

banker's call rate BKG. the rate of interest which
discount houses, bill-brokers, stockbrokers
and jobbers have to pay to the commercial
banks for loans of money 'at call and short
notice'. *See* call money *under* call.

banker's card *see* cheque card.

banker's cheque *see* bank draft.

banker's clearing house *see* clearing house.

banker's credit *see* letter of credit.

bankers' deposits BKG. the credit balances of
the joint-stock banks held by the Bank of England and considered to be part of their cash
reserves. These deposits are used by the government as a measure of the state of the economy and as a means of controlling (through
the Bank of England) the supply of money. Cf.
bank deposits.

banker's discount BKG. the difference between
the face value of a bill of exchange or promissory note bought by a bank from a customer,
and the amount credited to that customer's
account with the bank. This difference is the
discount deducted by the bank and is the interest for the time the bill of exchange or
promissory note has to be held until it becomes
payable, plus a varying charge for the degree
of risk involved.

banker's draft *see* bank draft.

banker's enquiry *see* banker's reference.

banker's lien *see under* lien.

banker's opinion BKG. a service offered by most
banks is that of giving a customer, on request
and in the strictest confidence, information
about the financial reputation of a person or
business organization. *See* banker's reference.
Syn. credit information.

banker's order BKG. an order in writing by a
customer to his bank to pay a stated sum of
money to a named party at certain stated dates
until further orders. This is a service offered by
banks to their customers in return for a small
charge for each payment and is much used for
paying fixed amounts which fall due on known
dates such as insurance premiums, rents, subscriptions, etc. *Syn.* standing order.

banker's reference BKG. where a customer gives
the name of his banker as a reference, e.g. to a
new supplier, the supplier may ask his own
bank to obtain the opinion from the customer's
bank concerning that customer's financial
reputation. Banks always express such opinions
in a very general and guarded way, and give
them only to their own customers or to another
bank in the strictest confidence. *See* reference.
Cf. banker's opinion. *Syn.* banker's enquiry.

banker's transfer *see* bank transfer.

Bank for International Settlements BKG. & PUB.
FIN. started in 1930 in Basle, Switzerland by the
League of Nations. It acts as an international
banker to all the central banks of Western
Europe and of Japan and Canada, in settling
debts resulting from trade between members
of the O.E.C.D. and the European Monetary
Agreement. It also acts as a centre for the exchange of information and ideas among central
banks. Most of the original duties are now performed by the International Monetary Fund.
Abbr. B.I.S.

Bank Giro *see under* Giro.

bank guarantee BKG. (1) a formal promise by a
bank to a creditor to pay him a sum of money if
the debtor does not pay by a certain date. (2) a
written promise by a bank to open a commercial credit, subject to certain conditions. (3) a
formal promise to a bank to repay a loan made
by a bank to a third party if that third party
should fail to repay it.

bank holiday (U.S.A.) BKG. the closing of banks
by government order for a limited period in
order to prevent frightened depositors from
drawing out their funds and hoarding them.
See bank run. Cf. bank holidays (Britain).

bank holidays *pl.* (Britain) certain weekdays in
the year that are by law public holidays on
which all banks, post offices, business houses
and government offices are officially closed.
The bank holidays are: in England and Wales
and the Channel Islands, New Year's Day (1
January), Good Friday, Easter Monday, May
Day, late Spring Holiday, late Summer Holiday, Christmas Day (25 December) and Boxing Day (the first weekday after Christmas
Day); in Northern Ireland, all the English holidays and in addition St. Patrick's Day (17
March), Easter Tuesday, and the Com-
memoration of the Battle of the Boyne (12 July); in Scotland, all the English holidays except
Easter Monday and Boxing Day. *See also* non-
business days.

Banking Department BKG. one of the two main
departments of the Bank of England. *See* bank
return.

banking BKG. the business of running a bank, of
being a banker, i.e. trading in money.

Banking School ECON. HIST. & BKG. a group of
bankers and economists who, during a period
of bank failures from 1825 onwards, demanded
that banks be free to issue notes, and expressed strong opinions against the views of the
Currency School who wanted the government
to control and limit the note issue. The Currency School's views became generally accepted
and were built into the Bank Charter Act,
1844.

banking system BKG. the arrangements under
which a country's banking services are organized. These vary in different countries.

in Britain they consist of: the *Bank of England* acting as the central bank; a small number of *joint-stock banks* (also called *commercial* or *deposit banks*) most with a large number of branches; the *savings banks*; and other banking concerns including *merchant banks*, *discount houses* and the *National Giro*.

in U.S.A. the central banking organization is the *Federal Reserve System* which controls the *commercial banks* and *trust companies*. In addition there are *investment banks, savings banks,* the *Export-Import Bank, finance companies* and *credit unions.* The commercial banks are either: *state banks*, of which there are very many, since they are not allowed to open branches outside the state (sometimes even the town) in which they are based; or *national banks* which have by law to be members of the Federal Reserve System.

bank interest BKG. (1) interest paid by a bank to a customer on money deposited with the bank. (2) interest paid by a customer to a bank on an overdraft or a loan.

bank, joint-stock *see* joint-stock bank.

bank loan BKG. an agreed sum of money lent by a bank to a customer for a fixed period, usu. 6–12 months, against an approved security. A special loan account is usu. opened on which the customer can draw cheques, and to which the interest on the whole sum for the whole period is debited, whether the customer draws or pays out the whole loan or not. Cf. bank overdraft. *Syn.* advance.

bank personal loan a service offered by some banks to customers who do not qualify for overdrafts. Loans are mainly for buying goods for furnishing the home and are usu. made without security and therefore at a higher rate of interest than for overdrafts. The interest is added to the loan at the start, and the whole is repaid by equal monthly instalments. Cf. bank overdraft.

bank manager *see under* manager.

bank money BKG. & ECON. that part of the deposits held by banks which is on current account and can be used as money by drawing cheques. *Syn.* (U.S.A.) deposit currency.

bank-note BKG. printed paper money issued by a bank, usu. the country's central bank. The Bank of England issues notes of four denominations at present — £1, £5, £10 and £20. A bank-note is a form of promissory note and carries a promise to pay the bearer on demand a stated sum of money. In Britain, by the Currency and Bank-Notes Act of 1954, the Bank of England is the only bank having the right to issue notes in England and Wales, but certain banks in Scotland and Northern Ireland have limited rights to do so. In U.S.A. bank-notes are issued only through the Federal Reserve System.

Bank of America BKG. in spite of its name and the fact that it is the largest of the American branch banks, all its 700 branches in the U.S.A. are in the State of California. It is *not* the central bank of the U.S.A. *See* Federal Reserve System.

bank of deposit BKG. a bank which receives deposits from the public but does not issue currency notes. Cf. bank of issue.

Bank of England BKG. the central bank of the United Kingdom, is state-owned and works closely with the Treasury in carrying out the financial aims of the government, controlling the note issue and the volume of credit, managing the national debt, administering the exchange control and exchange equalization account, guarding the nation's gold and silver reserves, and acting as banker to the government and to the joint-stock and other banks. It is the only bank having power to issue notes in England and Wales. *See* central bank; bank return. *Abbr.* B.E.; B/E.

Bank of England minimum lending rate *see under* minimum.

bank of issue BKG. a bank having power by law to issue currency notes payable to bearer (the holder) on demand. Cf. bank of deposit.

bank overdraft BKG. an agreed sum of money which by arrangement a bank allows a customer to overdraw his account, i.e. to run into debt to the bank by drawing more than the amount standing to his credit in the account. The customer can make use of this money when he wishes, and for an agreed length of time. Interest is payable only on the amount overdrawn at the end of each day, but the bank may make an additional charge for agreeing to the arrangement, and will usu. demand that the customer should deposit easily saleable stocks and shares as security for repayment of the debt. Cf. bank loan.

bank paper (1) BKG. a general name for bills of exchange that have been drawn, accepted or endorsed by a bank. *See* bank bills. Cf. trade paper; trade bills. (2) a general name for thin writing-paper.

bank-paper BKG. currency notes which have been paid out by banks and are in circulation, i.e. in the hands of the public and not held in reserve by the banks.

bank pass-book *or* **passbook** BKG. a small book supplied by a bank to a customer, in which payments in and out of his account are recorded in handwriting as they take place, so giving the customer a copy of his ledger account with the bank. Pass-books are now used only for savings accounts, having been replaced for all other kinds of account by loose-leaf statements printed by computer. *See* bank statement.

bank, private *see* private banks.

bank rate BKG. & FIN. replaced since October 1972 by the minimum lending rate, it was the lowest rate at which the Bank of England would discount approved bills of exchange. Made public weekly, it was taken by all the other banks as the basis for their interest rates for deposits, loans and discounts. It was used by the Bank of England as an instrument for controlling the volume of credit and, in the days of the gold standard, as a means of protecting the nation's gold reserves.

bank reconciliation statement ACCTS. a statement, usu. written in red ink in the cash book of a business, showing exactly what entries make up the difference at any one time between the bank balance shown in the cash book and that shown in the bank statement. This difference is made up of (*a*) cheques drawn but not yet presented, to be set against (*b*) cheques paid in but not yet credited, plus various special matters, e.g. bank charges not yet entered in the cash book. The object is to explain the difference and to correct any mistakes at an early stage.

bank reserves BKG. a stock of money in the form of bank-notes and coin, and also of securities which can very quickly be sold for money, held by a bank for the purpose of meeting demands from its customers who wish to draw money out of their accounts.

bank return BKG. the short name for the weekly balance sheet (a statement of assets and liabilities) made public by the Bank of England as ordered by the Bank Charter Act, 1844. The return consists of two balance sheets, one for each of the Bank's departments. One is for the *Issue Department*, which is responsible for the note issue, and gives on the left as a liability the value of notes issued and, on the right, the assets which support the note issue, being government and other securities, gold coin and bullion. The other is for the *Banking Department*, which does general banking business, and shows on the left the Bank's liabilities, consisting of its own capital (as owned by its original stockholders), its reserves of undistributed profits, and deposits by government departments, banks, etc.; and on the right its assets which are mainly government and other securities, advances mainly to other banks, and its stock of notes and of gold and silver coin. *Syn.* weekly return. *See also* proportion, the.

bank run (U.S.A.) BKG. very heavy and urgent demands by the customers of a bank for repayment of their deposits, caused usu. by fear that the bank may be in financial trouble. *Syn.* (Britain) a run on the bank. *See* bank holiday (U.S.A.).

bankrupt *adj.* LAW declared by a bankruptcy court to be a bankrupt. *See* bankrupt, *n.*; bankruptcy. Cf. insolvent. *To go bankrupt*, to become a bankrupt. *To be declared/adjudged/made/bankrupt.*
v. LAW & COM. to cause a person to become or to be declared a bankrupt.
n. LAW a debtor who has been declared by a bankruptcy court to be insolvent, i.e. unable to pay his debts in full, and whose affairs have by court order been put in the charge of a trustee in bankruptcy who becomes his personal representative until the debtor is discharged from bankruptcy. A company unable to pay its debts cannot be made bankrupt; instead it can be *put into liquidation*, i.e. its assets are sold for cash, which is used to settle its debts. *See* bankruptcy.

certificated bankrupt a bankrupt person who, on being discharged from bankruptcy, has been given a certificate of misfortune by the court, stating that his bankruptcy was caused by misfortune and not by any wrongful act of the bankrupt.

undischarged bankrupt a bankrupt who has not been discharged, i.e. released by the court from the limits placed upon him under the law. While a bankrupt he may not obtain much credit, nor own any property (except the tools of his trade and a few clothes); nor may he be a company director; he is barred from holding most public offices; and his right to enter into contracts is severely limited.

bankruptcy LAW the state of being bankrupt. The bankruptcy laws aim at: relieving the honest debtor from a hopeless position where he may never be able to settle his debts; forcing the dishonest debtor to meet the just claims of his creditors; and dividing the debtor's property fairly among the creditors. The legal process starts with a *petition in bankruptcy*, presented to the High Court either by a creditor owed more than £50 (called the *petitioning creditor*) or by the debtor himself. The Court then makes a receiving order giving the Official Receiver power to take possession of the debtor's entire property (except tools of his trade and a little clothing) and to get a list of all his assets and debts. The creditors and the debtor may then agree to a *deed or scheme of arrangement* or *composition* by which each creditor may be paid wholly or in part, in which event the debtor is not made bankrupt. But if an arrangement is not agreed, the Court must declare the debtor bankrupt and appoint a *trustee in bankruptcy* who, as his personal representative, will share out the debtor's property justly among his creditors in a manner fixed by law. Once this has been done, the debtor may be discharged, i.e. released from the limits laid on him, provided that it is clear to the Court that he has done everything reasonably possible to settle his debts, any amounts still unpaid being usu. wiped out. *See* bankrupt.

bank statement BKG. (1) a loose-leaf sheet or sheets supplied by a bank to each customer, giving details of all debits and credits made, esp. to his current account, during a given period, and showing the opening and closing balances. This document, prepared by computer, has now replaced the handwritten bank pass-book except for savings accounts. (2) in U.S.A., a report on the financial position of a bank made to a controlling authority.

bank transfer BKG. a simple system for making international credit transfers, used mainly for personal payments such as salaries of overseas employees, pensions and allowances, earnings from investments, and royalties from patents and copyrights. The bank is told to pay a stated sum to a named person abroad. The bank debits the sum, plus bank charges, to the drawer's account and makes payment through its branch, agent or correspondent in the payee's country. A bank transfer is usu. made by airmail but, in cases of urgency, instructions can be passed by telegraph, esp. by cable or by telex, at slight extra cost. *Syn.* banker's transfer. *See* telegraphic transfer.

Banque de France the central bank of France. *Abbr.* B.F.

b.à.p. (*French*: billets à payer) bills payable.

b.à.r.(*French*: billets à recevoir) bills receivable.

bar. barrister; barrel.

bar v. (1) COM. to forbid: *To bar a market.*

barred market a market (e.g. a foreign country) to which, by law or by agreement, the export of a particular product is forbidden. (2) LAW to destroy, to put an end to, to make ineffective: *To bar a right.*

barred by limitation *see* limitation.

bar.-at-law barrister-at-law.

Bar, the LAW in Britain, the profession of a barrister; the body of lawyers who practise as barristers.

to be called to the Bar to be made a member of the Bar.

to read for the Bar to study law in order to become a barrister.

Barbados an independent island state in the Eastern Caribbean; pop. 250,000 approx. (1973); capital, Bridgetown, pop. 12,500 approx.; language, English; currency, the Barbados dollar (Bds$), divided into 100 cents. Member, (British) Commonwealth; O.A.S.

bar chart *see under* chart.

bareboat charter *see under* charter.

bare contract *see* nude contract *under* contract.

bare trustee LAW a trustee who has no other duty than to hold property and to pass it on to someone else at the proper time. Cf. active trust.

barg. bargain.

bargain v. (1) COM. to discuss and agree on a price before making a business deal: *They bargained all day about prices. I shall bargain with the trader. Syn.* to haggle, to higgle; to negotiate a price. (2) (*with* away) to sacrifice as part of a deal: *He bargained away his independence in return for a directorship.* (3) (*with* on) to depend on: *I am bargaining on your support.* (4) (*with* for) to expect: *We did not bargain for his resignation, we were surprised by his resigning.*

n. (1) an agreement about price: *To make/ strike a bargain. To drive a hard bargain,* to make severe conditions. *See also* Dutch bargain *under* Dutch. (2) something bought cheap: *You've got a bargain,* you have got good value for your money. (3) something offered at a cheap or specially-reduced price: *This week's bargain.*

bargain-basement the part of a department store, usu. below ground level, where one can buy cheap goods.

bargain-counter a long table in a shop at which one can buy cheap goods.

bargain-hunter a person who searches for things he can buy cheaply.

bargain price a specially low price.

bargain sale (in a shop) a selling of unwanted or leftover stock at especially low prices. (4) STK. EXCH. a deal in securities between members of the Stock Exchange. If it is not profitable, it is called a bad bargain.

bargain book a book in which a stockbroker records all the deals he has made in buying and selling securities.

bargain for the account a deal agreed to be settled at the next Account Day (*see* Account, The).

bargains done the number of separate deals that took place on a particular day on the Stock Exchange, used as a measure of business activity on that day.

time bargain a contract to deliver shares on a fixed future date. Cf. option.

bargain and sale LAW a contract by which the ownership of real or personal property is given by one party to another for a consideration. *Syn.* assignment.

bargaining IND. REL. *see* collective bargaining.

bargaining power the power that one person or group of persons has when negotiating prices, wages, working conditions, etc. with another. The bargaining power of labour as a factor of production is largely directed by the trade unions in negotiating with employers, esp. producers.

Bargaining Theory of Wages ECON. a general view taken by certain economists that the level of wage rates is decided by the relative bargaining power of the workers and the employers; and that the range of wage levels will be limited at the lower end by subsistence (the bare cost of keeping alive) and at the upper end by the point at which producers will be unwilling to produce. *See* bargaining power.

barge SHIPG. & TRANSPT. a slow-moving, flat-bottomed boat for carrying goods, esp. large amounts of loose material, e.g. coal, sand, stone, on rivers and canals. *Syn.* lighter.

dumb barge one that has no sails or engines, so has to be pushed or towed (pulled along).

power(ed) barge one that can move by its own power.

bargee a member of the crew of a barge. *Syn.* bargeman.

barge hire SHIPG. the charge made for the use of barges, esp. for loading and unloading ships in a barge port. *Syn.* lighterage.

bargeman *see* bargee.

barge port *see under* port.

barometer stock STK. EXCH. one of a few widely-held securities the market prices of which are considered by investors to be a measure of the condition of the market. Cf. business barometer.

baron IND. & FIN. a businessman at the head of a large industrial or financial organization, esp. a person who exercises great power: *A press baron. Syn.* magnate.

barr. barrister.

barrage a large wall built across a river to hold back the water. Barrages are important in the economy of some countries and are built for a variety of purposes: to store water for use in homes, farms, factories and irrigation; to increase the depth of water for shipping; to control floods; and to provide water-power, esp. for making electricity. *Syn.* dam.

barratry (1) SHIPG. & MAR. INSCE. any serious failure of duty, whether on purpose or from extreme carelessness by the master and crew of a ship, resulting in loss to the shipowners or charterers, the owners of the cargo or the insurers, e.g. stealing or destroying the cargo, trading with an enemy, smuggling, or causing the wrecking or sinking of the ship. The word is used in bills of lading, charter-parties, and policies of marine insurance. *See* scuttling. (2) LAW the offence of causing repeated trouble by frequently starting quarrels and bringing annoying lawsuits.

barrel (1) a round wooden or metal container with flat ends and outward-swelling sides, used usu. for holding liquids. *Syn.* cask. Cf. hogshead, pipe, puncheon. (2) a unit of volume of various values, e.g. a barrel of ale, 32 (imperial) gallons; of beer, 36 gals.; of unrefined petroleum, 35 gals.; of Bordeaux wine, 50 gals.; also by weight when used for dry goods, e.g. of flour (U.S.A.) 196 lb; of butter, 224 lb; of soap, 256 lb; and by numbers of fishes, esp. cured herrings, about 1000 fishes;

red herrings, 160 fishes; fresh herrings, 660 fishes. *Abbr.* brl.; bl.; *in pl.* bbl.

barrel cargo one consisting of goods packed in barrels.

slack barrel one for carrying dry goods.

tight barrel one for carrying liquids.

barrier anything that bars or stops progress or prevents persons or things from passing or entering.

barrier to entry ECON. a market situation which prevents new producers from entering an industry, e.g. government controls, insufficient demand, high capital investment costs, patent rights. The cost of overcoming such barriers can be taken to be the height of the barrier and determines the point to which existing producers may raise their prices without encouraging new producers to enter the industry. A reduction of barriers will bring in more producers, increase competition and reduce prices.

barrier to trade any action by the government of a country to limit or prevent the free flow of goods in and out of that country, e.g. duties on imports and exports, quotas, embargoes. *See also* trade restrictions.

barrister-at-law LAW a lawyer, esp. in England, who has been 'called to the Bar' by one of the four Inns of Court in London, and has thus become a member of that branch of the legal profession which alone has the right to speak and argue for others in any of the higher courts. *See* advocate; counsel. Cf. solicitor. *Abbr.* Bar.-at-Law.

barrow TRANSPT. a handcart, usu. with two wheels, used by street-traders.

barrow-boy a street-trader. *Syn.* costermonger, hawker.

barter COM. trade by the direct exchange of goods for other goods without using money or other medium of exchange: *Barter was the earliest form of trade.*

barter arrangement an agreement providing for certain products of one country to be exchanged for certain products of another country at stated rates, but without any money being paid. *Syn.* barter agreement.

base *adj.* of little value. *Base coins,* false coins made of metals of low value by dishonest persons who pass them as real ones. *See* debasement of coinage. *Syn.* counterfeit coin; forged coin; debased coin. *Base metals,* non-precious metals, esp. copper, lead, zinc and tin, or alloys of these.

based COM. set up (in a place): *The head office of the company is in Cairo; it is a Cairo-based company.*

basement *see* bargain-basement *under* bargain, *n.* (3).

base period *see* index numbers.

base rate BKG. the advertised rate of interest on which a clearing bank bases its lending rate for advances and its borrowing rate for deposits. The rate charged for advances will be from ½% to 5% higher than the base rate, depending on the nature of the advance, the bargaining power of the borrower, and the degree of risk that he will not repay the advance. The rate given for deposits at seven days' call is usu. 1½% lower than the base rate. Although each bank is free to decide its base rate, in practice, whenever there is a change in the Bank of England's minimum lending rate, the clearing banks very soon adopt a new common base rate.

base year *see* cost-of-living index.

basic industry *see under* industry.

basic needs ECON. the things Man must have if he is to live: food, clothing and shelter. *Syn.* subsistence.

basic rate MAR. INSCE. a premium rate for a standard kind of risk, on which actual rates are based, depending on the different circumstances affecting the risk to be insured. *See* standard rate.

basic research *see under* research.

basic wage-rate IND. REL. the agreed standard rate of wages paid to a class of ordinary workers for a given period of work — hourly, daily or weekly. This rate forms the basis to which may be added other payments aimed at rewarding special skills and abilities and at encouraging hard work, e.g. incentive bonuses and overtime pay. Cf. minimum wage.

basin (1) SHIPG. a harbour shut in by land; an area of enclosed water surrounded by places where ships can be tied to the shore, esp. for fitting-out, repair, loading and unloading.

building basin a basin in which ships are built.

dock basin a place where a river or canal has been widened so that ships or boats can be tied to the shore.

tidal basin a basin or harbour where the tide flows in and out.

(2) a hollow area of land, where the surface or the underground rock system slopes inwards from the sides to the centre.

artesian basin *see* artesian well.

coal basin an area where deposits of coal are found in layers of rock which dip inward from the sides to the centre.

river basin an area of land drained by a river.

basis (*fig.*) (1) the base on which some idea, thought, or law is built: *The basis of an agreement, a claim, a forecast.* (2) a given point or number on which calculations are based: *We take last year's actual expenses as the basis of our budget.* (3) an agreed arrangement: *We hire our machinery on a long-term basis*, we arrange to hire it for a long time.

basis price *or* **basis rate** COM. where an article or service is sold with or without extra things or special additions, the basis price or rate is that

of the article or service only, and does not include any extras. *See* basic rate; basic wage-rate.

batch IND. a group of things of the same kind, or a quantity of some material or substance, esp. when made at one time: *A batch of loaves of bread; a batch of invoices/orders/letters for posting.*

batch costing the calculation and control of the cost of making batches of a product, including finding out the size of batch which is most profitable in a given set of conditions.

batch production a system of producing in batches, as compared with a continuous production process.

battery (1) IND. a group of machines of the same kind: *A battery of printing presses/lathes/drills/ typewriters.* (2) AGR. a group of many cages specially arranged for keeping large numbers of chickens in a small space and needing only a few workers to care for them and to collect the eggs; a battery farm. *See* factory farming.

battery hen a hen kept in a battery. *Opp.* free-range.

b.à.v. (*French*: bon à vue) a sight draft. *See under* bill of exchange.

bazaar (1) a market-place, esp. in eastern countries. (2) in western countries, a shop selling many small cheap things. (3) a sale of various unwanted things in order to obtain money to give to the poor or for some other good purpose.

b.b. bearer bond(s).

bbl. barrels.

b.c. blind copy.

B.C. bank clearing; bankruptcy court; bills for collection; British Columbia (Canada).

b.c.c. blind carbon copy.

B.C.E. Board of Customs and Excise.

B.C.M. British Commercial Monomark.

bd. board; bond; boulevard; bound.

b.d. bill discounted.

B/D. bank draft.

b/d. brought down.

B/Dft. bank draft.

b.d.i. both days inclusive.

bdls. bundles.

BDS Barbados's international vehicle-registration letters.

B.E. Bank of England.

b.e. bill of exchange.

B/E. Bank of England; bill of entry; bill of exchange.

beaconage SHIPG. (1) a system of marks used to guide seamen. (2) charges made by a port to pay the cost of providing beacons, buoys, etc.

beam SHIPG. the width of a ship at its widest part. *On one's beam ends*, (*colloq.*) in a financially hopeless condition.

bean (*colloq.*) money: *He hasn't a bean*, he has no money.

bear *v.* (1) to carry: *This floor will not bear the weight of the machinery.* (2) to have; to show: *The cheque bears his signature.* (3) to be responsible for: *I will bear all the expenses.* (4) to produce: *A bond which bears interest at 10%.* (5) STK. EXCH. to force prices down: *To bear the market.*
n. STK. EXCH. a dealer in the stock market who, believing that prices will fall, sells for delivery on a future date securities which he does not at the time possess, but which he expects to buy at a lower price by the date he has to deliver them. The difference between his selling and buying prices is profit. Cf. bull. *See* covered bear.

bear campaign STK. EXCH. action by dealers aimed to drive prices down by selling securities, usu. in small lots so that these securities may be bought back later at a lower price. *Syn.* bear raid (U.S.A.); bear tack. Cf. bull campaign.

bearer (1) BKG. & COM. the holder of a document: *Please hand the goods to the bearer of this letter.* (2) BKG. & COM. the person in possession of a cheque, bank-note, bond or bill of exchange which is stated as payable to bearer.

bearer bill BKG. a bill of exchange that is made payable to a named party or bearer, meaning that the money may be paid to anyone who presents the bill for payment.

bearer bond *see under* bond, *n.*

bearer cheque BKG. a cheque that bears the words *Pay (name of payee) or bearer*, meaning that the bank may pay the money to anyone who is in possession of the cheque and who presents it for payment. Cf. order cheque. *Syn.* cheque to bearer.

bearer debenture *see under* debenture.

bearer paper BKG. any negotiable instrument payable to bearer, i.e. to the person presenting it for payment.

bearer scrip STK. EXCH. a temporary document given to a person who has been allotted government bonds or a new issue of company debentures and has paid the first instalment. *See* definitive bond *under* bond. When all the instalments have been paid, the bearer scrip will be exchanged for a bearer bond or for a registered bond or for a scrip certificate.

bearer security STK. EXCH. a security for which an official record (registration) of ownership is not needed, the legal owner being the person actually in possession of the security. Such securities are negotiable instruments and ownership in them can be freely passed from one person to another without formality. *Syn.* bearer share; bearer stock; floater.

bearer share *see under* share.

bearish STK. EXCH. of market conditions, having a tendency to falling prices; expecting share prices to fall; expressing an unfavourable outlook.

bear market *see under* market.

bear position STK. EXCH. the trading situation of a bear in the stock market who finds that he has contracted to deliver more securities than he possesses. Cf. bull position.

bear raid *see* bear campaign.

bear squeeze *see* squeeze (2).

bear tack *see* bear campaign.

bear transaction *see under* transaction.

beat down COM. to argue with somebody to make him lower his price: *I beat him down from £8 to £5.*

Bedaux system IND. one of a number of wage systems which, by measuring exactly the amount of human effort needed to make an article, aims to pay each worker not only a fair wage for work done, but also an incentive, i.e. some extra money to encourage greater production. *Syn.* Bedaux point system.

Beds. Bedfordshire, England.

beds. bedrooms.

bed-sit. bed-sitting room.

beggar *n.* (1) a person who makes a living by begging (asking for gifts of money, food, etc.). (2) a poor person, esp. one needing help or understanding. *Poor beggar!* poor fellow. *Beggars can't be choosers*, beggars have no choice, so must take what they are given.
v. to make poor; to ruin: *He beggared himself and his family by gambling.*

beggar-my-neighbour policy used to describe the policy adopted by many countries during the economic depression in the 1930s. Ways of increasing employment, such as import restrictions and devaluation, were introduced by many countries regardless of the effect on others. This led to a sharp fall in international trade, from which all countries suffered.

behind (1) late, esp. in making regular payments such as rent or instalments: *You are behind in/with your rent.* In debt. *Syn.* in arrears. (2) supporting with money or influence: *A financier is behind the venture.*

Belgium a kingdom in north-west Europe, pop. 10 million approx. (1973); capital, Brussels, pop. 1.1 million approx.; languages, French and Flemish; currency unit, the Belgian franc (B.F.), divided into 100 centimes. Member, O.E.C.D.; E.E.C.; Benelux.

Belgium-Luxemburg Economic Union (B.L.E.U.) an economic association begun in 1921 and still in existence, although the two countries have since joined with the Netherlands to form Benelux. Both are members of the E.E.C.

Belize formerly British Honduras, a republic in Central America, pop. 150,000 approx. (1973); capital, Belmopan, pop. 6,000 approx.; principal town, Belize City, pop. 40,000 approx.; languages, English and Spanish; currency unit, the Belize dollar (B$), divided into 100 cents. Member, (British) Commonwealth.

below par STK. EXCH. (of a share) priced below its nominal or face value. Cf. at par; above par. *See* par.

below the line *see* above the line.

benefice (1) a place where a priest is employed by a church. (2) the money he receives from the church. *Syn.* living.

beneficial owner LAW (of property) the person who has the right to live in a property, to use it as he wishes, and to receive and use any income or produce it may bring in, although he may not actually possess the full ownership, e.g. in the case of leasehold property. *See also* beneficial ownership *under* ownership.

beneficiary LAW & INSCE. a person or object (e.g. a charity) intended to benefit from a will, trust or insurance policy, as distinguished from executors or trustees who only hold the trust property for the good of the beneficiary and not for their own profit. *Syn.* cestui que trust.

benefit (1) something to one's advantage, interest or profit: *The benefit of a university education. The rate of exchange was to my benefit*, in my favour. Something done that is for the good of a person or thing: *A trustee holds property for the benefit of the beneficiaries*. (2) MAN. something given to an employee in addition to his salary or wages, to save tax or to encourage hard work. *Syn.* employees' amenity; fringe benefit; perquisite. (3) INSCE. money, usu. an allowance, paid under an insurance policy for some kinds of losses, or given by the government to people who cannot earn by working, such as disability, industrial injury, maternity, sickness, unemployment and death benefits. (4) a theatrical performance or game at which the money collected is given as a present to an actor or player who is retiring.

benefit club a non-profitmaking organization, esp. in the U.S.A., that provides its members with mutual insurance in the event of sickness or accident, and with help in old age. *See* friendly society. *Also* benefit association; benefit society.

benefit in kind MAN. something extra given to an employee, other than money, in return for his services, such as free meals, the use of a house or car, or a luxury holiday. *Syn.* fringe benefit.

Benelux a customs union formed in 1947 by Belgium, the Netherlands and Luxemburg. Internal tariffs no longer exist and there are common external tariffs, free movement of capital and labour and a common aim to combine financial and monetary systems. The Benelux countries joined the E.E.C. in 1958.

Benin People's Republic of, *see* Dahomey.

Bentham Jeremy (1748–1832), English philosopher, lawyer and economist of the Classical School. He was the first to advance the idea of utilitarianism: that Man's economic and politic-al behaviour is influenced by pleasure and pain, both of which can be measured, and that the utility (usefulness) of an institution such as a law or a custom depends on how far it produces 'the greatest happiness of the greatest number'. His main works were: *Defence of Usury* (1787), *Principles of Morals and Legislation* (1789) and *Manual of Political Economy* (1825), in which he sees laissez-faire (freedom of action) as the best form of economic organization. His writings and teachings resulted in many changes for the better in the law and in government administration.

Bentley's telegraphic code *see* code (4).

bequest LAW personal property given to somebody under a will. *Syn.* legacy. *See* beneficiary.

Berks. Berkshire, England.

berth SHIPG. (1) a space in a harbour where a ship may lie, either at anchor or, more usu., tied up at a quay, dock or wharf. *A ship on the berth*, unloading, ready to unload. *See also* accommodation berth; appropriated berth; quay; wharf. (2) a narrow bed or other sleeping-space in a ship or train: *A two-berth cabin. A first-class berth. Syn.* bunk; couchette; sleeper (train only). (3) (*colloq.*) a situation as an employee: *He has found a good berth as sales manager.*

berthage SHIPG. a charge made to shipowners by a port for the use of a berth; sometimes a charge for the use of a barge. *Syn.* dockage; berth charge. Cf. groundage.

berth bill of lading *see under* bill of lading.

berth cargo SHIPG. cargo carried at cheap rates to fill up empty space in a ship.

berth charge *see* berthage.

berth charter SHIPG. a charter which does not state the kinds of cargo to be carried.

berth clause SHIPG. a clause in a charter-party stating that the hire of the ship shall not start until the day that loading begins, thus avoiding payment for days when the ship has to wait for her turn to berth. *Syn.* twin-berth clause.

berth freight *see* berth rates.

berth owner SHIPG. a shipowner who offers to carry goods as a common carrier for anyone offering cargo. *Syn.* berth shipowner. *See* berth cargo.

berth rates SHIPG. freight rates charged by regular shipping lines for carrying goods as cargo. *Syn.* berth freight; berth terms; liner rates.

bespoke COM. made to order, not mass-produced. *Syn.* custom-made.

best buy COM. & IND. a product which has been carefully tested and has been recommended by a consumer organization as giving the best value for money among competing brands.

best price *see under* price.

bet *v.* to risk one's money against another person's on the result of a race or other happening that has not yet taken place. *Syn.* to wager.

n. the making of an agreement to bet; the amount of money so risked. *Syn.* wager.

beta factor STK. EXCH. a measure of the performance of a security from the point of view of risk and the steadiness of its market price. A beta of unity (i.e. 1.00) is given to a share of which the price changes exactly according to the market; a share having a beta of greater than unity (e.g. 1.25) is an above-average performer; and one with a beta less than unity (e.g. 0.80) shows a performance below the average.

betterment LAW & COM. an increase in the value of property caused by public improvements in the neighbourhood or by commercial development.

betterment levy a charge made by government on owners of property which has risen in value because of public improvements or because it has been commercially developed.

Beveridge Sir William (1879–1963), English economist and social reformer. He greatly influenced government action in dealing with unemployment and produced a plan in 1942 on which was based the present British national insurance system, started in 1947. Director of the London School of Economics, 1932–7; Liberal Member of Parliament, 1944–5.

B.F. Banque de France; Belgian francs.

B/f., b/f. brought forward.

BG Bulgaria's international vehicle-registration letters.

B/G., b/g. bonded goods.

bg., bgs. bag, bags.

B/H bill of health.

B'ham Birmingham, England.

B'head Birkenhead, England.

Bhutan a small monarchy (kingdom) in south Asia, pop. 1.2 million approx. (1975); capital, Thimphu, pop. 10,000 approx.; language, Bhutanese (a form of Tibetan); currency unit, the ngultrum, equal to 2 tikchung or 100 Indian paise.

biannual half-yearly; happening twice in a year. *Interest is payable biannually on 1 January and 1 July.* Cf. biennial.

bid *n.* (1) an offer to buy something at a stated price, esp. at an auction sale: *To make a bid. To enter a bid.* A bid can be taken back at any time before a buyer has formally told the seller that he accepts it: *To invite bids. To revoke, withdraw a bid. See* counter-bid; sealed bid. (2) the actual price stated in making an offer to buy: *My bid of £5.50 was higher than yours of £5.25.*

takeover bid *see* takeover.

Code on Bids *see under* code.

v. (1) to make a bid, or offer to buy at a stated price, an article being sold at an auction sale: *To bid £5 for a silver dish.* (2) *To enter a bid,* to make an offer, usu. in writing so that it is recorded, when bargaining for property.

bidders' ring COM. a group of persons, usu. dealers, who secretly agree to act together at an auction sale to avoid competition in bidding. The purpose is for one of the group to get an article at a low price, to the seller's loss. The article is usu. then sold elsewhere and the ring shares the profit. This practice is illegal. *Syn.* bidding ring. *See* knock-out agreement.

bid price STK. EXCH. (1) the price at which an intending buyer is willing to buy a stock or share, being the lower of two prices (bid price and offer price) quoted by a stockjobber. (2) of trust units, the price at which the management company will buy back units from unit-holders. *Syn.* buying price.

biennial two-yearly; happening every two years: *The trade fair is biennial and is held only in odd-numbered years.* Cf. biannual.

Big Four, The BKG. the four largest joint-stock or commercial clearing banks in Britain. They are: Barclays, Lloyds, the Midland, and the National Westminster.

bilateral contract *see under* contract, *n.*

bilateralism ECON. a system, believed by some economists to be the very best way of organizing international trade, by which each country balances its trade with every other country. *See* bilateral trade agreements. Cf. multilateralism.

bilateral monopoly *see under* monopoly.

bilateral trade agreements COM. attempts made by national governments after the depression of the 1930s to make the foreign trade with each individual country balance. The result was close to a system of barter and it greatly reduced the level of international trade. After the Second World War, multilateral agreements under G.A.T.T. replaced the bilateral agreements as one of the means of removing hindrances to world trade, but bilateral agreements still largely govern trade between the Western and the communist-bloc countries. Cf. multilateral trade.

bilingual able to speak and write two different languages well: *A bilingual secretary.*

bilk COM. (*colloq.*) dishonestly to avoid paying a debt; to run away from one's creditors; to cheat: *We have been bilked of our money. Syn.* swindle.

bill *n.* (1) a word which has many meanings in commerce and the law, but always basically a formal written or printed document of some kind, its nature usu. being given by a word or words which go with it: *Bill of health, bill of lading, bill of exchange, way-bill, money bill.* (2) a note or list of charges for supplying goods or services: *Waiter! Please bring me the bill. He pays his bills promptly. Let me settle the bill. See* invoice; account; cash memo. (3) COM. & BKG. a written order to pay money: *A bill of exchange.* (4) a notice; an advertisement: *A bill of fare. Stick no bills. See* handbill; billboard.

(5) a certificate (i.e. a written declaration): *A bill of health.* (6) BKG. in U.S.A., a bank-note: *A dollar bill.* (*colloq.*) $1.00. (7) LAW in a lawsuit, a short form of *bill of particulars* (details), being a written statement of exactly what the plaintiff is claiming. (8) LAW (often with capital B) in Britain, the plan of a proposed new law which after being considered and passed by both Houses of Parliament, and after receiving the royal assent, becomes an Act of Parliament.

money bill a bill dealing with the collecting of money by taxes and the spending of money for public purposes. Such a bill can have its origin only in the House of Commons and, if passed by the Commons, becomes law whether or not the House of Lords passes it.

v. COM. (1) to advertise by public notice or bill: *Actor X is billed to play Hamlet.* (2) (U.S.A.) to perform the act of making and sending out bills (invoices) stating charges due for goods or services supplied: *Please bill me for these articles. To bill goods.*

billboard (U.S.A.) ADVTG. a large board in a public position on which bills, i.e. advertisements, are pasted. *Syn.* hoarding. *See* bill, *n.* (4).

bill book ACCTS. an account book in which are recorded details of all bills of exchange, both receivable and payable by a business, esp. in a trade or industry in which bills are frequently used as a means of payment.

bill-broker BKG. & COM. a dealer in bills of exchange, who buys bills from traders and either sells them to bankers and discount houses or holds them until they mature (become due for payment). In these deals his profit is the difference in the discount he gives and receives. He may also act as a *running broker*, i.e. as an agent between sellers and buyers of bills of exchange, arranging for bills to be negotiated and receiving a commission for his services. In recent years bill-brokers have become main dealers in Treasury bills and short-dated government bonds. *See* acceptance market *under* acceptance (5). *Syn.* discount broker.

bill, due *see* due bill.

billet COM. (*colloq.*) a job; a situation as an employee. *Syn.* berth.

billfold (U.S.A.) a folding pocket-case for carrying bank-notes, esp. dollar bills. *See* bill, *n.* (6). *Syn.* (Britain) wallet; note-case; pocket-book; purse.

billhead (1) COM. a printed form with a heading giving the name and address, etc. of a business and used for bills, i.e. for charging customers for goods or services. (2) the heading itself. Cf. letterhead.

billing COM. the American word for invoicing: *A billing department.*

billing clerk *see* invoice clerk *under* clerk.

billing machine a special typewriting machine which can produce up to ten carbon copies, used esp. for export invoices.

Billingsgate COM. the main fish market, in the City of London.

billion 1,000,000,000, a thousand million or milliard (10^9).

billionaire a person who possesses assets worth a billion pounds, dollars, francs, etc.

bill market *see* discount market.

bill of adventure COM. & SHIPG. a written declaration by a merchant that goods shipped in his name are owned by another person, who is in fact bearing the risks of the adventure.

bill of costs LAW & ACCTS. the detailed account of charges made by a solicitor for the work he has done for his client and of sums of money he has paid out for him esp. in court fees, counsel's fees and witnesses' expenses.

bill of entry COM. a written declaration by an importer or exporter giving details of goods which are being 'entered' at the Custom House for examination, etc. *Syn.* customs declaration; customs entry. *Abbr.* B/E.

bill of exchange BKG. & COM. a written order telling one person to pay a certain sum of money to a named person on demand or at a certain time in the future. Formerly much used as a means of payment in home trade, bills of exchange are now used mainly in foreign trade. *See also* acceptance. *Syn.* draft. *Abbr.* B/E; b.e.

acceptance bill one which is presented for acceptance, not for payment. Cf. payment bill *below*.

accepted bill one across which the drawee (debtor) has written 'accepted' and added his signature, thus accepting responsibility for paying it when due. *Syn.* acceptance. *Opp.* unaccepted bill.

accommodation bill *see under* accommodation.

advance bill *see under* advance.

backed bill one which has been endorsed by a third party, usu. a bank or finance house, which thus makes itself responsible for paying it if the drawee fails to do so. *Syn.* guaranteed bill.

bank bill *see under* bank.

banker's bill *see* bank bill.

bearer bill *see under* bearer.

blank bill (1) one which does not mention the name of the payee. (2) one which does not mention the amount for which it is drawn, the acceptor leaving the figure to be added later by the drawer. *Syn.* blank acceptance.

clean bill one which has no special conditions or any documents joined to it, esp. one which is a bank bill (accepted by a bank). Cf. documentary bill.

commercial bill one which is a payment for the sale of goods. *Syn.* mercantile bill; trade bill; commercial paper; mercantile paper.

currency bill one drawn in foreign currency.

D/A bill *see* documents-against-acceptance bill *below.*

date bill *see* time bill *below.*

demand bill *see* sight bill *below.*

discounted bill one which has been bought by a bank (or discount house or broker) for a price that is lower than the value of the bill when it becomes due for payment. The difference is the banker's discount or discounting charge which is the price that the person discounting the bill pays for getting his money early instead of waiting for payment on the due date. The rate of discount depends on the degree of risk that the bill will not be paid when due and on the length of time before payment is due.

dishonoured bill one which the drawee (the debtor on whom it is drawn) has refused to accept, or which the acceptor (the person who has agreed to pay it) fails to pay when it is due. *See* dishonour (1).

documentary bill one which is fastened to shipping documents such as a bill of lading, insurance policy, invoice, dock warrant, etc. Cf. clean bill. *Syn.* document bill.

documents-against-acceptance bill a bill of exchange which the drawee must accept before the bank will give him the documents he needs in order to get possession of the goods. Cf. documents-against-payment bill *below. Abbr.* D/A bill.

documents-against-payment bill a bill of exchange which the drawee must pay before the bank will give him the documents he needs to get possession of the goods. Cf. documents-against-acceptance bill *above. Abbr.* D/P bill.

domestic bill (*a*) in U.S.A., one which is payable in the state in which it has been drawn. Cf. foreign bill; external bill. (*b*) in Britain, one which is payable in the country in which it is drawn. *Syn.* home bill; inland bill.

domiciled bill one which is payable only at a particular place.

drawn bill in Britain, a foreign bill that has been negotiated (transferred by endorsement) by the drawer to the London branch of a foreign bank. Cf. made bill.

external bill (U.S.A.) one which has been drawn in one country and is payable in another. In Britain such a bill is called a foreign bill.

finance bill (*a*) one which is not drawn for value received (e.g. to pay for goods) but which only promises to pay a stated sum of money on a certain day. Cf. promissory note. (*b*) a bill drawn by a government, esp. by the British Government as a means of borrowing money from the public and known as a *Treasury bill. See under* Treasury. (*c*) a bill drawn by a bank or finance house in order to borrow money, usu. from a bank or finance house in another country. *Syn.* bank acceptance; bank bill; banker's bill.

fine bank bill *see* fine trade bill *under* fine.

fine trade bill *see under* fine.

foreign bill in Britain, one which is *either* drawn by a person who does not live permanently in the British Isles, *or* is drawn by a person who does live permanently in the British Isles upon a person who lives permanently abroad and is payable abroad. *See also* drawn bill *above*; made bill *below.* Cf. inland bill. *Syn.* long draft. In U.S.A., one which is drawn in one state and payable in another state. Cf. domestic bill; home bill; external bill.

gilt-edged bill a bill that has been drawn, accepted and endorsed by a firm of the highest credit.

guaranteed bill *see* backed bill *above.*

home bill *see* inland bill *below.*

hot bill (*a*) a bill of exchange which will become payable within the next few days. (*b*) a Treasury bill which has only just been bought and therefore has a relatively long time to go before it matures (becomes payable).

house bill a bill drawn by a foreign branch of a firm or company on its head office. Thus the drawer and acceptor are the same person or organization. *Syn.* house paper.

incomplete bill *see* inchoate instrument.

inland bill (Britain) one which is both drawn and payable in the British Isles or is drawn in the British Isles upon a person living permanently in the British Isles. Any other bill is a foreign bill. Cf. domestic bill; external bill; foreign bill. *Syn.* home bill.

investment bill one which the owner has bought at a discount with the object of holding it as an investment until it becomes due for payment. The profit made is the amount of the discount.

long-dated bill one which is drawn to be payable after a long period, usu. of three or more months. *Syn.* long-dated paper.

made bill in Britain, a foreign bill that has been negotiated (transferred by endorsement) to a London banker or correspondent. Cf. drawn bill.

mercantile bill *see* commercial bill *above.*

original bill one that has been discounted before being endorsed.

overdue bill one which has not been paid on the due date; if it is payable on demand it is considered to be overdue when it has been in existence for an unreasonable time. *Syn.* past-due bill.

paid bill one that has been paid by the due date.

past-due bill *see* overdue bill *above.*

payment bill one which is presented for payment, not for acceptance. Cf. acceptance bill.

period bill *see* usance bill *below.*

prime bill one which is regarded as being a first-class credit risk, i.e. the chances of its being dishonoured are so small as to be not worth considering.

renewed bill a new bill that is accepted in place of one maturing, to give more 'time for payment. Cf. re-draft.

respectable bill *see* fine bill *under* fine.

retired bill one which has not been held until it matures (becomes due for payment) *either* because it has been paid early *or* because it has been replaced by one or more new bills, e.g. when the period of credit has been extended.

short bill one payable at sight, on demand or within ten days.

sight bill one payable 'at sight', i.e. on presentation to the debtor, regardless of the date on which it was drawn. *Syn.* sight draft; demand bill; demand draft. Cf. time bill or draft.

sole bill *see* sola.

term sight bill *see* time bill *below*.

time bill one which is payable at a fixed or stated time; if payable at a stated number of days after the date the bill was drawn, it is called a *date bill* or *date draft*; if it is payable a stated number of days after presentation it is called a *term sight bill* or *draft*.

trade bill one used in trade, i.e. in paying for goods bought. *Syn.* commercial bill. *See* fine trade bill *under* fine.

Treasury bill *see under* Treasury; *also* finance bill (*b*) *above*.

usance bill one which is payable 'after sight', i.e. a stated number of days after it is first presented to the debtor. Cf. sight bill. *See* usance. *Syn.* period bill; term bill.

bill (of exchange) in a set BKG. & COM. foreign bills of exchange are usu. drawn in a set of two or three parts numbered 'First of Exchange', 'Second of Exchange', etc., all of which bear the same wording except that each mentions the other(s). Payment is made on presentation of any one of these parts, the other parts then ceasing to have any effect. *See* duplicate of exchange; second via; sola.

bill of Exchequer FIN. a promissory note issued by the British Government until the 1870s, but now replaced by the Treasury bill. *Syn.* Exchequer bill.

bill of fare a list of dishes served in a restaurant, showing prices. *Syn.* menu; tariff.

bill of health SHIPG. a written declaration signed by a Consul or port official and given to the master of a ship before leaving a port, recording the health conditions there at the time, as well as the health of persons on the ship. *Abbr.* B/H.

clean bill of health one which records that the port and the persons on the ship were free of infection.

foul bill of health one which records the existence of infectious disease in the port or on the ship.

suspected *or* **touched bill of health** one which records an uncertain situation, e.g. when there is common talk of an infectious disease being present.

bill of lading (b/l) SHIPG. & BKG. a shipping document given by a shipowner or his agent or the master of a ship to the shipper acknowledging receipt of goods, recording their condition, and promising to deliver them in the same condition to the person named as consignee or according to his order. The b/l also states the conditions under which the goods are carried, the amount of the freight and other details. The consignee uses the b/l to prove his title, i.e. his right to take possession of the goods. The shipper or consignor may use the b/l as security when discounting a bill of exchange. The b/l thus serves three important purposes, being a receipt for goods carried, a contract to carry, and a documentary proof of title. *Abbr.* b/l.; B/L.

berth b/l one issued by a liner (a ship owned by a commercial shipping line and running a regular service) as distinguished from a ship working under a charter-party. *Syn.* liner b/l.

blank b/l one which makes no mention of the name of the consignee; in such a case the goods are delivered to 'bearer', i.e. to any party in possession of the document.

claused b/l *see* dirty b/l *below*.

clean b/l one which acknowledges that the goods were received by the shipowners in apparent good order and condition. Cf. dirty b/l.

combined transport b/l *see* container b/l *below*.

container b/l a special kind of through b/l for use in shipping goods in containers (large sealed boxes transported by road, rail and ship without being opened). *See* through b/l *below*. *Syn.* combined transport b/l.

custody b/l a special kind of b/l used in the cotton trade and issued by shipowners or their agents to shippers while the goods are held in safe keeping at the port before the arrival of the ship.

dirty b/l one into which the shipowners have put a clause stating that the condition of the goods or packing when received was unsatisfactory. *Syn.* claused b/l; foul b/l; unclean b/l.

foul b/l *see* dirty b/l *above*.

groupage b/l one which groups together a number of small shipments consigned to a number of separate consignees at the port to which the ship is going; a document used esp. by a forwarding agent and addressed to his correspondent in the country to which the goods are being shipped.

inland waterways b/l one used for transport by boat on canals, rivers or lakes. Cf. ocean b/l. *Syn.* river bill.

inward b/l one relating to goods arriving in the country.

liner b/l *see* berth b/l *above*.

ocean b/l the most usual kind of b/l used for consignments of goods carried by ocean-going ships, as distinguished from ships making voyages only on rivers, canals and lakes. Cf. inland waterways b/l. *Abbr.* Oc. B/L.

on-board b/l *see* shipped b/l *below*.

order b/l one which is made out 'to the order' of the shipper, or of the consignee, or of a bank, and can therefore be endorsed by any of these in favour of another party. Cf. straight b/l.

outward b/l one relating to goods leaving the country.

port b/l one signed by a responsible person acknowledging that he has received the goods at the port.

railroad b/l (U.S.A.) one used for transport by railway.

received b/l one which acknowledges goods which have been received for shipment but have not yet been loaded into a ship.

river b/l *see* inland waterways b/l *above*.

shipped b/l one which relates to goods already loaded into a ship. *Syn.* on-board b/l.

straight b/l one which is not an order b/l but is issued to the consignee only, thus preventing it from being endorsed in favour of another party. Cf. order b/l.

through b/l one relating to a shipment which has to be handed over from one carrier to another during the journey.

unclean b/l *see* dirty b/l *above*.

bill-of-lading freight SHIPG. the freight paid by the shipper to the carrier for carrying goods for which a bill of lading exists (as distinguished from chartered freight). A bill of lading will state that freight is payable either in advance or at destination, i.e. at the end of the voyage. If payable in advance, the bill of lading will not be given by the carrier until the freight has been paid; if payable at destination, the goods will not be handed over to the consignee until the freight has been settled. Cf. chartered freight.

bill of materials IND. a document stating in detail all the materials, parts, etc. including the number or quantity of each, and its price, which are necessary to manufacture a particular product. *Abbr.* b.o.m. Cf. bill of quantities.

bill of quantities IND. a document stating in detail all the materials, parts, etc. including the number or quantity of each and its price, and the labour costs, which are necessary for the building of a structure, e.g. a house, factory, bridge, etc., or the making of any engineering works. It is drawn up by a *quantity surveyor* and is used to obtain prices from contractors. Cf. bill of materials.

bill of sale (1) a document by which the owner of personal property (the grantor) transfers it to another party. *Abbr.* b.s.

absolute b.s. one where the grantor hands the property over without any right ever to repossess it.

conditional b.s. one where the grantor has a right to reclaim possession of the property once he has met certain stated conditions, esp. repayment of money advanced to him by the grantee.

(2) SHIPG. & MAR. INSCE. a legal document which records the change of ownership when a ship is sold; it is a document which is accepted internationally as proof of ownership. It is the nautical equivalent of a conveyance. *Syn.* ship bill of sale.

bill of sight COM. a document given to the Customs by an importer who cannot complete the customs entry papers because he lacks a proper description of goods sent to him from abroad. When the goods have been landed, the importer is allowed to examine them and, having now had a sight of them, is able to complete the entry papers by making a full description. This is known as *perfecting the sight*. *Syn.* bill of view; sight entry. Cf. sight bill. *Abbr.* B/St.

bill of store COM. in Britain, a document giving permission of Customs to re-import, free of duty, goods that have been exported from Britain less than five years before the date of re-importation. Cf. bill of stores, *pl.* (U.S.A.).

bill of stores SHIPG. in U.S.A., a document given by the Customs allowing a merchant ship to carry stores of food, etc. for the voyage free of duty. Cf. bill of store, *sing.* (Britain).

bill of sufferance SHIPG. & COM. a document giving the permission of the Customs to land goods, esp. baggage, or to hold articles on board, esp. ship's stores of dutiable goods, without producing detailed entry papers, but open to customs examination at any time. *Syn.* a sufferance; baggage sufferance. Cf. bill of sight.

bill of victualling *see* victualling bill.

bill of view *see* bill of sight.

billposter a person employed in sticking bills or posters on hoardings, etc. *Syn.* billsticker.

bill rate BKG. the rate of discount paid by banks, discount houses, etc. on bills of exchange. The rate varies partly according to the degree of risk of the bill not being met (Treasury bills having the lowest rate of discount, followed by bank bills and fine trade bills) and partly according to the current market rate of interest.

bills for collection BKG. bills of exchange which are left by a customer with his bank to be collected when they mature (become due for payment). The bank keeps a record of such bills and credits the customer's current account only when the amount of the bill has been collected. *Syn.* short bills.

bills payable (1) BKG. & COM. bills of exchange which, to the debtor, are those which he will have to pay when they mature (become due for payment). Cf. bills receivable (1). (2) ACCTS. the heading of an account in which a record is made of all bills of exchange which will have to be paid when each matures. Cf. bills receivable (2).

bills receivable (1) BKG. & COM. bills of exchange which to the creditor (the person who is to receive money for the bills) are those which he is holding while they mature (become due for payment). Cf. bills payable (1). (2) ACCTS. the heading of an account in which a record is made of all bills of exchange which are being held until they mature or have been discounted (bought by a bank or discount house). Cf. bills payable (2).

billsticker see billposter.

B.I.M. British Institute of Management.

bimetallism ECON. & FIN. a monetary system having both gold and silver as standard metals for the coinage, with a fixed rate of exchange between the two metals, both being legal tender for an unlimited amount. The system was adopted in U.S.A. and on the continent of Europe during the nineteenth century but became difficult to manage when the world prices of the two metals changed greatly. The use of paper money in the present century made unnecessary the use of metals as a standard basis for the coinage. Cf. monometallism.

bin (1) in a shop, a container for storing things, esp. loose foodstuffs, e.g. corn, flour, tea, etc. (2) in an industrial concern, an enclosed space, large box or shelf for storing parts of products or the products themselves. (3) a container for rubbish: A dustbin.

bin card a record card kept in or near a bin containing stock of an article, and on which receipts and issues of the article are recorded, together with the running balance and notes on when to re-order.

bin number in a warehouse containing many bins, each bin is given a serial number; and the bins are arranged in bays which are lettered or numbered. Thus the bin number gives the position of any article stored in the warehouse so that it can be found quickly.

binary system COMP. a numbering system, ideal for computers, which uses only two marks, 0 and 1, and deals with powers of 2 (rather than powers of 10 in the decimal system). Thus:

decimal	32	16	8	4	2	1
binary	2^5	2^4	2^3	2^2	2^1	2^0

bind v. LAW to put under a legal duty: A contract binds the parties making it. An agreement is not always binding in law. See bound, adj.

binder LAW & INSCE. a temporary form of contract intended to be a record of agreement while the formal contract document is being prepared. It binds e.g. an insurance company to cover the risk, and is later replaced by the policy.

binding in honour only see contract binding in honour.

birth certificate an official copy of the entry in the register of births in Britain recording the date and place of birth and the parentage of a particular person. This document is usually accepted, e.g. by insurance companies, as proof of the person's age.

birth control see family planning.

birth rate the number of births per thousand of the population, in a particular place or region, in a stated year.

B.I.S. Bank for International Settlements.

bit (1) a piece, esp. a piece of money, a coin: A fivepenny/tenpenny bit. (2) in U.S.A., a coin of value 12½ cents or one eighth of a dollar. A two-bit newspaper, one of no importance. (3) COMP. the standard measure of computer information.

bite n. COM. (colloq.) the showing of interest in an offer; acceptance of an offer: His house is for sale but he has not had a single bite, no one has shown any interest in buying it (a comparison to a fish taking the bait — a tempting piece of food — on the hook of a fishing-line).

v. to deceive; to cheat: Once bitten, twice shy, a person who has been deceived will be cautious in future.

biz (colloq.) business, esp. show biz, the entertainment industry.

bk. backwardation; bank; book.

bkg. banking.

bkge. breakage.

bkrpt. bankrupt.

bks. books.

bl. bale; barrel.

B.L. bill lodged; bill of lading.

B/L bill of lading.

b.l., b/l bill of lading.

black adj. IND. REL. (of goods) forbidden by a trade union to be handled by its members in any way: Company X's products have been declared black by the unions.

v. IND. REL. to order all members of a trade

decimal figure		binary figure	decimal figure		binary figure	decimal figure	binary figure	
1	1	2^0	7	111	$2^2 + 2^1 + 2^0$	64	1000000	2^6
2	10	2^1	8	1000	2^3	128	10000000	2^7
3	11	$2^1 + 2^0$	9	1001	$2^3 + 2^0$	256	100000000	2^8
4	100	2^2	10	1010	$2^3 + 2^1$	512	1000000000	2^9
5	101	$2^2 + 2^0$	16	10000	2^4			
6	110	$2^2 + 2^1$	32	100000	2^5			

union to stop handling goods and performing services for an employer whose workers are on strike: *The union has decided to black the products of the company.*

black-coated workers IND. REL. workers in shops, offices, etc. who do not work with their hands, e.g. Civil Servants and local government employees, shop assistants, teachers, technicians, as distinguished from manual, industrial or factory workers. *Syn.* blackcoat; white-collar worker.

Black Country IND. a crowded industrial area in the West Midlands of England, in the past made black by smoke from factory chimneys.

black diamonds coal.

black economy ECON. (*colloq.*) work or services supplied usu. between private individuals, and paid for in cash. These dealings avoid income tax and are not recorded in official income statistics. *See* moonlighting.

blackleg (1) IND. REL. an impolite name given by trade unionists to: an employee who refuses to stop working during a strike; or to a person who does the work of a striker; or to a worker who refuses to be a member of a trade union; or, being a member, acts against the union's interests. *Syn.* strike-breaker; scab; fink. (2) a person of very bad character; a swindler esp. on a race-course.

blacklist *or* **black list** (1) COM. a secret list of persons or organizations reported to be dishonest or not otherwise trustworthy with whom traders are advised to deal cautiously or not at all. (2) IND. REL. a secret list of persons who are ·known to be active trade unionists. The list is usu. made and kept by an employers' association as a way of making sure that persons on the blacklist are not given employment. (3) a list of business and industrial organizations whom the trade unions consider to be bad employers. *See* boycott.

blackmail LAW the crime of demanding money by threats of injury or dishonour. Cf. extortion.

black market *see under* market.

black marketeer a person who trades in a black market.

black money FIN. money that has been made unlawfully and has been stored away, usu. in currency notes.

Black Sea berth terms SHIPG. a contract under which a ship chartered to carry a cargo of grain or seeds may, if the charterers so wish, carry general cargo.

blank plain; wholly or partly bearing no writing; an empty space for words or figures to be written in: *A blank sheet of paper. A form with spaces left blank. A blank space.*

in blank (of a form or document) left with spaces to be written in.

blank acceptance *see* blank bill of exchange *under* bill of exchange.

blank bill of exchange *see under* bill of exchange.

blank bill of lading *see under* bill of lading.

blank cheque (U.S.A. check) BKG. one which the drawer signs but in which he leaves the amount blank, trusting the payee or some other authorized person to write in the proper figure when it has been decided.

blank credit BKG. a letter of credit which does not mention any fixed amount of money. *See* letter of credit.

blank endorsement *or* **indorsement** *see under* endorsement.

blanket bond *see under* bond, *n.*

blanket insurance *see under* insurance, classes and kinds of.

blanket mortgage *see* mortgage.

blank transfer STK. EXCH. & LAW a share transfer form which the registered owner of shares has signed but in which he has left the spaces for the name of the transferee and the date of transfer blank. Blank transfers are often deposited with a bank when shares are used as security for a loan. They are also given to the real owners by a person who holds shares as a nominee. The holder of a blank transfer can simply complete the blank spaces in the form and thus become the registered owner of the shares. *See* stock transfer *under* transfer. *Syn.* transfer in blank.

bldg. building.

bleed COM. to get money from someone by wrongful means, e.g. threats: *To bleed a person white*, to ruin him by wrongfully getting all his money.

blend COM. a mixture of two or more substances or commodities so that it becomes impossible to separate them, e.g. of tea, of coffee, of tobacco, of wine, of spirits.

B.L.E.U. Belgium-Luxembourg Economic Union.

'B' licence *see* 'A' licence.

blind copy a carbon or other copy of a letter sent to someone for his information and without the knowledge of the addressee. *Abbr.* b.c.c.; b.c.

blk. black; blank; bulk.

bloc ECON. & FIN. (1) a group of countries which are united in having the same economic interests or in using the same or similar methods, esp. of managing their currency. *See* dollar bloc, sterling bloc. (2) any group of persons banded together for a common purpose, e.g. the farm bloc in the U.S. Congress.

block *n.* (1) STK. EXCH. a large number of shares in the same company, usu. sold as a single unit. *Syn.* lot; parcel (of shares). (2) a large building. (3) (U.S.A.) part of a town, esp. a group of buildings, enclosed on all sides by streets. (4) a metal printing plate for letterpress printing. (5) a group of things forming a unit, e.g. a block of seats in a theatre, etc.

blockade SHIPG. & COM. the situation when the government of a country which is at war forbids all trade by sea with the enemy. International law allows this right to any country at war, and ships of neutral countries have to obey or suffer capture. *Blockade-runner* a person or ship attempting to pass through a blockade.

blocked account BKG. a bank account in a country which has a blocked currency. Money in a blocked account can be spent only in the country in which the bank keeping the account is situated.

blocked currency BKG. & FIN. one which, by government order (usu. in wartime), may be spent only within the home country and cannot be exported or changed into any other currency. *Opp.* free currency. *Syn.* blocked exchange.

blocked exchange *see* blocked currency.

block grant *see under* grant.

block insurance *see under* insurance, classes and kinds of.

block offer STK. EXCH. a special offer by managers of a unit trust to sell units to the public at a price which remains fixed for a limited period.

block vote IND. REL. in Britain, the system of voting at Trades Union Congress where delegates do not vote as single individuals but as representatives of the number of members of their branch.

blood money (1) money paid to a person for killing someone. (2) money paid for giving information leading to the arrest of a criminal. (3) a payment which a murderer was at one time forced to make to the family of the person killed.

bloodsucker (1) an evil person who lives by another person's earnings. (2) a person who unjustly obtains money from another. *Syn.* sponger.

blower (*colloq.*) a telephone.

blow-up ADVTG. a much-enlarged photograph, esp. one used when arranging a show of goods, e.g. at an exhibition.

bls. bales; barrels.

blue *v.* (*colloq.*) to waste money by unwise spending: *He blued a fortune on idle living.*

blue book *see* Central Statistical Office.

blue chip STK. EXCH. a commercial or industrial share of the highest class among investments. A blue-chip company must be well known, have a large paid-up capital, a good record in paying a high rate of dividend in good times and bad, a highly-skilled and progressive management, and must provide a safe investment. Cf. gilt-edged securities.

blue-chip rate *see* prime rate.

blue-collar workers IND. factory workers (in reference to their blue working clothes). Cf. white-collar workers.

blueprint (1) a photographic print of a drawing or diagram, which appears as white lines on a blue background, used esp. by builders and engineers for their plans. (2) (*colloq.*) any detailed plan of future action: *An economic blueprint*, a plan for managing the economy.

blue-sky laws LAW in U.S.A., certain state laws which are intended to protect investors from buying valueless securities ('pieces of blue sky').

bluff *v.* to mislead by purposely deceiving a person: *He was bluffed into thinking that the business was worth buying. You can't bluff me!* To behave in an insincere or deceitful manner.

n. the act of bluffing: *I called his bluff*, called upon him to carry out his threat.

blurb (1) ADVTG. a publisher's short notice or advertisement printed on the cover or jacket of a book. (2) any piece of writing which praises someone or something unjustly.

Blvd. Boulevard.

B.M. British Monomark.

b.m. board measure (in shipping timber).

B.N. bank-note.

bnkg. banking.

b.o. branch office; broker's order; buyer's option; broker's option.

b/o. brought over.

board *v. & n.* (1) to go on board: *To board a ship/train/bus/coach/aircraft.*

by the board over the ship's side, esp. of cargo or parts of the ship thrown or lost *overboard. To go by the board*, to be thrown away as useless.

on board on or in a ship, plane, train or bus: *To go on board*, to go into or on to a ship. *Syn.* on shipboard.

(2) to provide meals for someone: *She boards students. She runs a boarding house. People board with her.* (3) to take one's meals (with): *He boards with his aunt. He boards out*, takes his meals in a place away from where he lives.

board and lodging an arrangement for accommodation for living and sleeping, with meals provided.

full board all meals provided, usu. three a day.

half board breakfast and one main meal, usu. dinner, provided.

boarding card SHIPG. & TRANSPT. a card given to passengers who have satisfied Customs and other formalities and therefore have permission to board a ship or plane. Cf. landing card. *Syn.* boarding pass.

boarding house a house where lodging and meals are supplied. Cf. guest-house.

board measure (U.S.A.) SHIPG. a unit of space taken by a cargo of timber; 1 board foot = 1 in. × 12 in. × 12 in. = 144 cu. in.; 12 board feet = 1 cu. ft; 100 board feet = 1 mille or $83\frac{1}{3}$ cu. ft. *Abbr.* b.m.

Board of Customs and Excise TAXN. in Britain, the government department that runs the customs service and collects customs and excise duties and the value added tax. Its offices are in London. *Abbr.* B.C.E. or B.O.C.E. Cf. Board of Inland Revenue.

board of directors MAN. the group of persons elected by the members (shareholders) of a company to carry on the management of the company; often called simply *the board.*

board meeting MAN. a meeting of the board of directors of a company. *Syn.* directors' meeting.

board minutes a record of discussions and decisions at meetings of the board of directors.

boardroom a special room in which a board of directors holds its meetings.

local board a board of directors appointed with limited powers to manage a part of a company's business in a particular area away from the company's head office.

Board of Inland Revenue TAXN. in Britain, the government department that collects direct taxes on income and capital and the stamp duties. Cf. Board of Customs and Excise.

Board of Trade formerly the government department in Britain dealing with trade, now become the Department of Trade and Industry. *Abbr.* B.O.T., B.o.T., BoT.

boatage SHIPG. a charge made to the owners of a ship by a port for the services of a boat, e.g. for taking ropes ashore when the ship is being tied up. *Syn.* boat hire; boatman charge.

boat-deck SHIPG. the second highest deck in a ship, where the lifeboats are kept and usu. where the most expensive cabins in a passenger ship are situated. *See* deck.

boat-harbour a harbour for small boats. *Syn.* boat haven; marina.

boat-load SHIPG. (1) the amount of cargo that a ship can carry when fully loaded: *A thousand tons of coal will just make a boat-load.* (2) the kind of goods making up a ship's cargo: *We are expecting a boat-load of skins. Syn.* ship-load.

boat-train TOUR. & SHIPG. a special train to and from a port for the convenience of passengers travelling by ship.

bob (*colloq.*) in Britain, a shilling, a former name of a coin, now the equivalent of five pence or one-twentieth of a pound.

B.O.C.E. Board of Customs and Excise.

body corporate a group of persons who have formed themselves by law into a corporation. *See* corporation.

bogus appearing to be good but in fact totally bad. *Syn.* sham; fraudulent.

bogus company one that is said by dishonest persons to exist but which is in fact only an excuse to persuade people to part with their money by buying bogus shares in it.

bogus shares shares which appear real but are worthless because e.g. they are in a company that does not exist or is concerned in a deceitful trick to take money from people.

bogus transaction a deal in which one party uses deceit to get money from the other.

B. of E. Bank of England.

Böhm-Bawerk Eugene von (1851–1914), statesman and leader of the Austrian School of economists, noted esp. for his theory of capital, of marginal utility in relation to interest, and of 'time preference'. His main works were *Capital and Interest* (1884) and *Positive Theory of Capital* (1889). Several times Finance Minister of Austria, he became Professor of Economics in Vienna in 1904. *See* Austrian School.

boiler-room (U.S.A.) an illegal organization using the telephone and other direct methods of persuasion to sell risky or valueless securities to the public.

bol., Bol. bolivar.

bolivar the standard currency unit of Venezuela, divided into 100 centimos. *Pl.* bolivares.

Bolivia a republic in South America, pop. 5.6 million approx. (1975); capital, La Paz, pop. 560,000; language, Spanish; currency unit, the Bolivian peso, divided into 100 centavos. Member, O.A.S.; Rio Pact.

bolshevism the teachings and beliefs of the Russian Communists. The system of government which resulted from the Revolution of 1917, the State having central control of economic production and distribution, the whole being based on the soviets, social organizations run by the workers. *Adj.* bolshevik. *N. pers.* Bolshevist. Cf. communism.

b.o.m. bill of materials.

bona fide *adv.* (*Latin*, in good faith) honestly, truthfully, with good intentions: *He acted bona fide.*
adj. (with hyphen) *A bona-fide offer. Opp.* mala fide.

bona fides *n.* honesty: sincerity; truthfulness: *I do not accept his bona fides*, I believe he is not acting in good faith.

bonanza good fortune, great success in business: *The new product proved to be a bonanza.* (U.S.A.) a mine rich in ore, hence wealth.

bond *n.* (1) COM., FIN. etc. a formal document promising to pay a sum of money (called a *common money bond*) or acknowledging the existence of a debt. The person bound by the bond is the *obligor*, the person receiving it is the *obligee*. If the bond makes no conditions about payment, it is called a *single bond*; but if it carries one or more conditions, e.g. the performance (or non-performance) of certain acts which will cause the document to be no longer binding, it is called a *double* or *conditional bond*. (2) STK. EXCH. a document issued by a government or a company borrowing money from the public, stating the existence of a debt and the amount owing to the holder of the document, called a bondholder, who must use the document to obtain repayment of the loan.

See bonds, *n. pl.* (3) COM. the holding and storing under guard by the Customs and Excise of goods on which duty will have to be paid before they can be removed from the warehouse for use or sale. Goods so held are said to be *in bond* or *under bond* or *bonded goods*. *See* customs bond *below*; bonded warehouse.

active bond a bond which bears a fixed rate of interest which is paid from the date when the bond is first put on the market. Most negotiable bonds are active. Cf. passive bond; deferred bond.

adjustment bond in U.S.A. a bond resulting from the reorganization of a concern; called in Britain a reorganization bond.

administration bond a bond which must be entered into by a person applying to the court for letters of administration to administer the estate of someone who has died without making a will. The bond promises that the administrator will carry out his duties according to the law, under the punishment of losing double the value of the estate if he fails.

annuity bond a bond which has no stated maturity date and on which, therefore, interest is payable for ever, e.g. Consols. *Syn.* irredeemable bond or stock; perpetual bond.

appeal bond a bond which has to be entered into by an appellant to make sure that all costs and damages will be paid if he loses his appeal. *Syn.* judgment bond.

assented bond a bond in the conditions of which the holder has agreed to accept a change. *Syn.* enfaced bond.

assumed bond a bond issued by one borrower but later becoming the responsibility of another who has assumed, i.e. taken over, the liability to pay it. *Syn.* endorsed bond, indorsed bond.

average bond a formal document prepared by the master of a ship and signed by the consignee(s) before taking delivery of a shipment of goods, agreeing to bear a fair share of a general average suffered by the ship, as soon as the amount is known. *See* average (4).

back bond a bond given to a surety, i.e. a person who makes himself responsible for the performance of a duty by another person, promising to make good any loss he may suffer as a result of the other person failing to perform his duty. *See* indemnity bond; surety bond *below*.

bail bond a bond which must be entered into by a prisoner awaiting trial if he is to be set free until his trial. The bond promises payment by himself and perh. others if the prisoner fails to appear in court at the proper time. *See* bail.

bearer bond a bond which states that it is payable to the bearer, i.e. a bond which is not registered (formally recorded) in the name of the holder. A bearer bond is a negotiable instrument. Cf. registered bond. *Abbr.* b.b.

blanket bond an insurance contract protecting an employer in the event of loss caused by any act of dishonesty or failure to perform duties by any of his employees. Cf. fidelity bond; fiduciary bond; indemnity bond; surety bond.

bottomry bond the formal document recording the conditions of a bottomry agreement on the mortgage of a ship.

callable bond a bond which may be repaid whenever the borrower wishes, on his giving notice. *Syn.* redeemable bond. Cf. called bond.

called bond one which has been called in on the proper date for repayment, no interest being payable after that date. Cf. callable bond.

chattel mortgage bond (U.S.A.) a bond in which the borrower gives his chattels, i.e. movable property, as security for a loan of money.

clean bond a government bond of which the price needs no adjustment to allow for accumulated interest, the interest having just been paid and no more having yet accumulated. Cf. dirty bond.

collateral trust bond (U.S.A.) a bond issued by one corporation but having as security its holding or investment in another corporation.

common money bond one containing a promise to pay a sum of money.

conditional bond one which makes one or more conditions. *Syn.* double bond. Cf. single bond.

consolidated bond one issued for the purpose of consolidating, i.e. combining, several other issues of bonds. *Syn.* unified bond; unified stock.

continued bond a bond the holder of which may present it for payment either on its maturity date or at a later date.

contract bond *see* performance bond.

convertible bond a bond, esp. one issued by a government, which may be exchanged, if the holder so wishes, for another kind of loan stock at the date of maturity instead of being repaid. Cf. convertible loan stock.

coupon bond a bond, usu. a bearer bond, joined to a set of coupons, one of which the bondholder gives up in exchange for the interest payment due on the date stated on the coupon. *See also* registered coupon bond *below*. Cf. registered bond.

currency bond (*a*) in Britain, a bond which will be repaid in the currency of the country in which the bond was issued. (*b*) in U.S.A., a bond which can be repaid in the currency of any country.

customs bond a formal document given to the Customs and Excise by an importer when goods are placed on arrival in a bonded warehouse, promising to pay the import duty at the proper time. *See* bonded warehouse.

debenture bond the formal document issued to the holder of debentures in a company or other organization. *See* debenture.

deferred bond one that pays a rate of interest which is low at the start, but gradually increases until after a stated time it reaches its full rate, when the bond becomes an active bond paying a fixed interest.

definitive bond a permanent document given in exchange for a bearer scrip when all the instalments have been paid. *See* bearer scrip *under* bearer.

dirty bond a government bond, the price of which needs to be adjusted to allow for accumulated interest. Cf. clean bond.

discount bond a bond sold at a discount, i.e. at a price less than its face value or its value at maturity. Interest is payable, not annually, but in one sum at maturity.

double bond *see* conditional bond *above*.

drawn bond bonds which are chosen for repayment by drawing lots.

endorsed bond *see* assumed bond *above*.

enfaced bond *see* assented bond *above*.

escalator bond a dated loan stock of which the rate of interest varies according to market conditions.

extended bond one of an issue of bonds, the holders of which, as a group, have agreed that the original maturity (repayment) date be changed to a later date.

fidelity bond an insurance contract protecting an employer against loss caused by any act of dishonesty or failure to perform duties by an employee, e.g. a cashier. Cf. blanket bond; fiduciary bond; indemnity bond; surety bond.

fiduciary bond a surety bond which a trustee (or other person in a position of trust or confidence) bringing a lawsuit has to enter into with an insurance company which promises to pay any damages or losses caused by a failure of the trustee, etc. to perform his duties. Cf. fidelity bond.

first-mortgage bond (U.S.A.) a kind of debenture, being a loan at a fixed rate of interest for a fixed length of time on the security of the borrower's assets. First-mortgage bondholders have first claim to be repaid out of those assets if the borrower cannot pay his debts.

general mortgage bond (U.S.A.) a mortgage bond for which the whole of the property of the company is given as security.

gold bond a bond, usu. issued by a government, of which the interest and repayment are payable in gold.

guaranty bond a special form of surety bond giving protection against loss arising from the failure of a named person to perform a stated duty.

heritable bond in Scotland, a bond given by a debtor for a loan for which the security is a conveyance of land.

income bond *see* income debenture *under* debenture.

indemnity bond the description given to all those kinds of bond which provide for payment of money in the event of loss caused by dishonesty or by the failure of another party to perform certain duties. *See* blanket bond, fidelity bond *above*; surety bond *below*.

indexed bond a bond of which the rate of interest and the repayment sum are based on changes in the cost-of-living index, so that the bond maintains its value in actual buying-power. *Syn.* stabilized bond.

indorsed bond *see* assumed bond *above*.

instalment bond (U.S.A., installment bond) a bond of which the repayment is by a number of instalments over a stated number of years. *See* instalment.

interchangeable bond one that carries the right of being exchanged for another bond if the holder so wishes.

interest bond a bond that is offered in payment of interest when the borrower cannot pay the interest in cash.

interim bond a certificate given to a bondholder to prove his ownership while the bond document is being prepared.

irredeemable bond *see* annuity bond *above*.

joint and several bond a bond which is supported by two or more guarantors, i.e. persons who accept, both together and separately, full responsibility for paying the debt if the debtor fails to pay. *See* joint and several.

judgment bond *see* appeal bond *above*.

life bond a document showing proof of the existence of an annuity contract.

mortgage bond a formal document acknowledging a debt and making land and property the security for its payment. *See* mortgage.

municipal bond one issued, mainly in U.S.A., by a local government authority.

option(al) bond a bond which can be repaid by the borrower at his option, i.e. when he so wishes.

participating bond *see* profit-sharing bond *below*.

passive bond one on which no interest is payable. Cf. active bond.

penalty bond one which provides that a stated sum of money (the penalty or punishment) is to be paid if a certain named party fails to perform a promised duty, e.g. to complete a building by the promised date.

performance bond an insurance protecting the insured against the risk of a contractor failing to perform his contract. *Syn.* contract bond.

perpetual bond *see* annuity bond *above*.

post obit bond a bond promising to repay a loan, with interest, on the death of a certain named person who is expected to leave the borrower money in his will.

premium bond *see* premium savings bond *under* premium.

profit-sharing bond a bond which not only bears interest at a fixed rate but also earns a share in the profits of the borrowing concern, usu. if the ordinary shareholders' dividend is greater than a certain fixed amount. *Syn.* participating bond.

property bond a bond issued by a life insurance company, the premiums being invested in a property fund.

redeemable bond *see* callable bond *above.*

refunding bond a new issue of bonds to raise money to repay an earlier issue.

registered bond a bond of which the holder's name is registered, i.e. recorded, by the issuing concern. Such bonds do not usu. have coupons, but *see* registered coupon bond *below.*

registered coupon bond a bond of which the name of the owner is registered (officially recorded) by the issuing concern but which has coupons payable to bearer. *See* coupon bond *above.*

removal bond one promising to pay any duty that may be chargeable on imported goods removed from a customs warehouse for manufacturing or processing before being reexported.

reorganization bond *see* adjustment bond *above.*

replevin bond *see under* replevin.

savings bond *see under* savings.

single bond one which makes no conditions about payment. Cf. conditional bond; double bond.

stabilized bond *see* indexed bond *above.*

sterling bond a bond issued by a foreign country but payable in sterling currency.

surety bond a formal agreement by a person (called a guarantor) to pay a stated sum of money if a certain party fails to perform a duty he owes to another party, e.g. to pay a debt by a stated date. Such bonds often take the form of an insurance contract, the insurance company being the guarantor.

transferable bond usu. a bearer bond the ownership of which can be freely transferred, i.e. passed from one person to another without the change of owner being recorded by the organization that issued the bond.

Treasury bond (*a*) (U.S.A.) a bond issued by the U.S. Treasury. (*b*) any bond held by the organization that issued it and kept in its treasury, either because it has not yet been sold or because it has been bought back by the organization. Cf. Treasury bill.

unified bond *see* consolidated bond *above.*

yearling bond *see* local (authority) loans.

v. to put (goods) into bond. *See* bond, *n.* (3).

bond certificate STK. EXCH. a temporary document of acknowledgment given to a person who has bought bearer bonds. It will be ex-

changed later for the bond itself when the bond is ready.

bond creditor COM. & FIN. a creditor (a person to whom money is owed) who has been given a bond signed by the debtor promising to pay the debt. The holder of such a bond is said to have his debt 'secured' by the bond. *Syn.* bondholder.

bonded carman a carrier specially licensed by the Customs and Excise to carry goods which are in bond. *See* bond, *n.* (3).

bonded factory IND. & TAXN. a factory which has been licensed by the government to stock and handle dutiable goods used in processes of manufacture, the duty being paid only when the goods leave the factory. Such factories are kept under close control by customs and excise officers. In U.S.A., called bonded manufacturing warehouses. Cf. bonded warehouse.

bonded goods COM. goods held in a bonded warehouse. *See* bond, *n.* (3). *Abbr.* B/G; b/g.

bonded manufacturing warehouse *see* bonded factory.

bonded stores SHIPG. ship's stores needed for use on a voyage and placed in bond with the Customs at a port. By special arrangement such stores can be moved from the bonded warehouse to the ship without payment of duty. Cf. bonded goods.

bonded vaults COM. & TAXN. a special bonded warehouse, usu. underground, for storing wines and spirits on which import or excise duty has not been paid, i.e. which are in bond.

bonded warehouse COM. & TAXN. a building in which dutiable goods may be stored under the control of customs and excise officers until duty has been paid. Many importers and producers use such warehouses in order not to have to pay the duty until the goods are required for production or are about to be sold. Bonded warehouses may be privately-run concerns the owners of which have given a bond to the government promising to do their duties correctly; or they may be publicly owned, in which case they are called government-bonded or customs warehouses. *See* bond, *n.* (3). *Syn.* bonded store. Cf. bonded factory; bonded vaults.

bonder COM. a person who gives the Customs a bond when putting goods into a bonded warehouse, promising to pay any duty and charges which may become due.

bondholder (1) COM. & FIN. a person who holds a bond given by a debtor as security for the debt. *See* bond creditor. (2) STK. EXCH. the holder of bonds issued by a government or commercial organization as fixed-interest loan stock.

bonding *n.* COM. the putting of goods into bond. *See* bond, *v.*

bond market STK. EXCH. the market for government securities.

bond note a note signed by a customs and excise officer allowing goods to be removed from a bonded warehouse or factory. *See* bond, *n.* (3). *Syn.* customs warrant; trans-shipment note.

bond of credit *see* cash credit.

bonds *n. pl.* STK. EXCH. in the plural, an accepted word for bearer bonds, esp. those issued by governments. Any securities payable to bearer.

bondsman LAW & COM. a person who is bound by a bond, esp. one who has become surety for another person.

bond warrant COM. a formal acknowledgment that certain goods are being held in a bonded warehouse. Such a document is negotiable, i.e. it can be passed from one owner to another by endorsement. Cf. warehouse-keeper's receipt. *Syn.* warehouse warrant; (in U.S.A.) negotiable warehouse receipt.

bons STK. EXCH. any document, esp. bonds issued by the French Government, on which appear the words 'bon pour' followed by a stated sum in francs, thus 'bon pour 1000 francs', meaning the bond is 'good for 1000 francs'.

bonus (1) COM. an extra allowance, over and above the usual discount, offered by producers to dealers for placing large orders esp. for a new product. A bonus is usu. expressed as a percentage of the value of goods bought, and the amount per cent may vary according to the size of the order. Cf. quantity discount. (2) IND. REL. & MAN. something extra; a special payment to employees over and above what is regularly due, usu. to encourage better work, or as reward for dangerous or unpleasant work, or to share out an excess of money.

cost-of-living bonus *see under* cost of living.

efficiency bonus a special reward for performing duties well.

incentive bonus any kind of bonus which makes employees want to work harder; any extra pay for working well.

merit bonus a special reward for doing very good work, beyond the call of duty. *See also* merit increase.

premium bonus a bonus based on the time that the employee saves over the standard time allowed for doing the work. *Syn.* time-saving bonus.

production bonus the payment of piecework rates for production above a fixed level, in addition to a daily wage.

productivity bonus extra money given to a worker to encourage increased production.

task bonus a bonus paid if a task (piece of work) is completed in a fixed time.

time-saving bonus *see* premium bonus *above*.

bonus, insurance INSCE. an extra payment of a share of the profits of a life insurance company or society to holders of 'with-profits' life insurance policies. A bonus may be paid either with the sum insured when it becomes due, or periodically. *Syn.* dividend.

cash bonus *see under* cash.

compound bonus one that is calculated on the sum insured added to any bonuses already declared at valuations made at regular intervals, e.g. every three years.

interim bonus one that will apply only until the next valuation.

no-claim bonus a bonus given by an insurer if the insured has made no claim during the past several years; it is particularly important in motor-vehicle insurance. *Abbr.* N.C.B. *See* no-claim discount *under* discount.

reversionary bonus the usual kind of bonus, i.e. one which is not paid every year but is added to the sum insured and paid when it becomes due.

simple bonus one which is expressed as a simple percentage of the sum insured.

special *or* **capital bonus** one which is paid out of an expected gain and is not likely to be repeated.

terminal bonus one that is given only in the last year of the life of the policy.

bonus issue *see* bonus shares; scrip issue *under* issue of securities.

bonus shares STK. EXCH. new shares issued by a company to its existing members (shareholders) free of payment by the members as a means of capitalizing (turning into capital) some of the accumulated profits and reserves of the company. Bonus shares are usu. issued in the proportion of one bonus share for every two, three or four, etc. shares held by a shareholder. *See* capitalization issue; capitalization of reserves. *Syn.* bonus issue; scrip issue.

bonus stock (U.S.A.) STK. EXCH. stock in a corporation issued free to attract sales of other stock.

book *v.* (1) to enter or record (esp. in a book): *To book an order*, to accept it and note it in an order-book. (2) to reserve or order for future use: *To book tickets for a journey/seats at a theatre or in a train, coach, plane, etc./a passage on a ship or plane/a room at a hotel/freight or cargo space for goods/a hall for a meeting/advertising space in a paper*. *See* double booking. *Syn.* reserve. (3) to make a firm and binding arrangement in advance: *To book the services of a speaker/an appointment with a lawyer, doctor. I am fully booked this week, I am not free to make any new appointments*.

book debt ACCTS. an amount owing to a business for goods sold, as shown in the account books.

book debts *pl.* the total amount owing to the business for goods sold. Book debts are sometimes used as a means of obtaining a loan, by being assigned to the lender as security. *Syn.* accounts receivable.

book entry ACCTS. an entry made only for the purpose of adjusting the account books, e.g. to correct a mistake.

bookie (*colloq.*) a bookmaker.

booking clerk in Britain, a person who sells tickets in a booking office, esp. an employee doing this on a railway.

booking fee a small charge made by some travel agents and most theatre-ticket agencies for arranging the booking of tickets and the reservation of seats.

booking hall part of a railway or motor-coach station or airline office where there are a number of windows or counters at which tickets for journeys can be bought and seats or places can be reserved.

booking office in Britain, a place where the public can buy tickets for travel or for the theatre, etc. *Syn.* (U.S.A.) ticket office.

book-keeper *or* **bookkeeper** ACCTS. a person employed to keep, i.e. to make records of business dealings in, the account books of an organization. Cf. accountant. *Syn.* accounts clerk.

book-keeping *or* **bookkeeping** ACCTS. the keeping of business accounts. That part of accounting by which an orderly record is made in books of account of the money value of all the business dealings of a particular organization. These records provide the basic information from which a profit and loss account and balance sheet are prepared at the end of the accounting period, usu. once each year. The main records are the journal (a book of first or original or prime entry in which the dealings are recorded in the order in which they take place) and the ledger (a book of final entry in which all individual accounts are kept). *See also* double entry; single entry.

booklet *see* brochure.

bookmaker a person whose profession it is to receive money from persons making bets on a horse or dog in a race, and who promises to pay according to the chances of their chosen animal winning. He keeps a record in a book of all the bets he receives. *Syn.* turf accountant; (*colloq.*) bookie.

book profit ACCTS. a profit which exists only on paper, i.e. as shown in the account books but not realized in money, e.g. the supposed increase in value of an asset over its original cost or over its book value.

books of account ACCTS. the set of books in which the accounts of a business are kept. In a double-entry system they consist of books of first or prime entry and of final entry, as well as certain memorandum books. *Syn.* financial books; account books.

books of final entry ACCTS. in a set of account books, the ledgers, in which are finally entered the debits and credits first recorded in the books of first or prime entry. *See* book-keeping. Cf. books of first entry.

books of first entry ACCTS. a set of account books, often called journals (or day books), in

which all business dealings of the concern are first recorded in the order in which they take place. From these journals, entries are posted, i.e. written into, the proper ledger accounts. A concern will have several journals, the most frequently used being a cash book, a bill book, a sales day book, a purchases book and a general journal. *See* book-keeping. Cf. books of final entry. *Syn.* books of original or prime entry; subsidiary books of account.

books of original entry *see* books of first entry.

books of prime entry *see* books of first entry.

bookseller the owner or manager of a bookshop.

book token *see under* token.

book trade COM. & IND. all those businesses which together are concerned with the manufacture, distribution and sale of books including booksellers, publishers and those printers and binders specializing in the production of books. *See also* Net Book Agreement; publisher.

book value ACCTS. the value of an asset or group of assets of a business as shown in its account books. This value is not necessarily the same as the actual market value, it being the usual custom to value stock at cost or market value whichever is the lower, and other assets at cost less amounts written off for depreciation. *See* hidden asset *under* assets, *pl*.

boom (1) ECON. a period of increasing business activity when a rising demand for all commodities causes industrial production to expand, prices and wages to rise, and unemployment to fall. *See* trade cycle *under* cycle. *Syn.* prosperity. *Opp.* depression; recession; slump. (2) STK. EXCH. a period when the demand for most securities reaches the highest level, with much buying and selling and high market prices. A boom may also exist in the market for a single security or group of securities.

boomlet ECON. & STK. EXCH. a small boom which does not continue for long.

boost *v.* (1) to increase forcefully: *To boost production/sales/prices*. (2) ADVT. to make popular by giving much praise. *Syn.* (U.S.A.) (*colloq.*) shove, hoist.

boot (*colloq.*) dismissal: *To get the boot*, to be dismissed from employment. *To give someone the boot*, to dismiss him. *Syn.* kick; push; sack.

bootlegger (*colloq.*) a person trading illegally, esp. in forbidden products (e.g. wines and spirits in a country in which there is prohibition).

bordereau INSCE. a list, schedule, memorandum or account, esp. one joined to a policy or contract document. *Pl.* bordereaux.

booth COM. a small shop, usu. of a temporary nature, e.g. in a market or fair. *Syn.* stall.

borrow-all policy *see under* insurance policy.

borrowing powers FIN. & LAW powers given to the directors of a company, as one of the objects set out in the Memorandum of Association, to borrow money, usu. up to certain limits stated in the company's Articles. If no limits are stated, the directors' powers are controlled by the Companies Acts.

boss *n.* (*colloq.*) a person in charge; one who controls the work in an organization; a master, head or chief.
v. (*colloq.*) to be the master or person in charge: *To boss people about*, to give orders to people in a commanding manner. *To boss the show*, to put oneself improperly in control over others.

bot. bought; bottle.

B.O.T., B.o.T., BoT Board of Trade (now Department of Trade and Industry).

Botswana a republic in southern Africa, formerly Bechuanaland, pop. 700,000 approx. (1973); capital, Gaborone, pop. 18,000 approx.; languages, English and Tswana; currency unit, the pula, divided into 100 cents. Member, (British) Commonwealth; O.A.U.

bottleneck (1) IND. any difficulty which slows down production by preventing easy and regular working in a factory, mine or other productive unit. (2) ECON. anything which hinders the production of a particular commodity or service to the point where the demand cannot be satisfied and a shortage arises.

bottom SHIPG. (1) a ship, esp. one for carrying cargo. *Goods carried in British/American/foreign bottoms.* (2) the underside of a ship, the part below the water-line: *A dirty bottom*, one which needs to be cleaned of weeds, etc. and painted. (3) STK. EXCH. (of prices of securities) the lowest level: *Prices have touched bottom. The market is bumping on the bottom*, prices have reached their lowest point. *The shares are at rock bottom*, they have reached a level below which the price may fall no further. *The bottom has fallen out of the market*, prices have fallen to unexpectedly low levels because no one is willing to buy however low the price.

bottomry SHIPG. & FIN. the mortgage of a ship; the borrowing of money by the master of a ship to pay for repairs and other necessary expenses to get the ship back to its home port. The ship itself is given as security for the loan, but if the ship is lost before the loan is repaid, the lender loses the money advanced.
bottomry bond *see under* bond. Cf. respondentia.

bought and sold note *see* contract note.

bought book *see* purchases day book.

bought day book *see* purchases day book.

bought journal *see* purchases day book.

bought ledger *see* ledgers.

bought note STK. EXCH. a stockbroker's note to a client who has given him an order to buy a security, recording full details of the particular deal. *See* contract note. *Opp.* sold note.

Bought of *or* **Bot. of** COM. the formal heading of an invoice sometimes used in place of *Dr* (*to*), meaning that the sum of the invoice is owing for goods or services bought from the supplier.

Boul. Boulevard.

boulevard a broad main street or avenue usu. planted with trees, esp. in a city.

bounce (1) BKG. (*colloq.*) (of a cheque) to be dishonoured; to fail to be paid by the bank on which it is drawn: *His cheque has bounced*, it has been returned unpaid by the bank because there is no money in his account, i.e. the cheque has been dishonoured. (2) STK. EXCH. (of a share) to make a sudden jump in price: *Standard Oil bounced higher after news of increased earnings.*

bouncer BKG. (*colloq.*) a cheque which has bounced, i.e. has been dishonoured. *Syn.* dud.

bound (1) SHIPG. (*with* for) ready to go to; on the way to: *The ship is bound for Alexandria. Outward bound* or *outbound*, on a voyage starting at the home port. *Homeward bound*, or *inward bound* or *inbound*, on a voyage ending at the home port. *Fog-bound, storm-bound*, temporarily unable to continue the voyage because of fog, storm. *London-bound*, going to London. (2) LAW tied by a promise or a legal duty: *An apprentice is bound to serve his master. I am bound by my word/the contract/terms of service/the rules of the society. See* bind.

bounty (1) a reward offered to encourage the performance of some stated act. (2) money given to the poor.
export bounty money paid by the government to producers of certain goods to encourage exports.
forces and services bounty money paid to members of the forces for serving for a certain number of years.
prize bounty money paid to the crew of a warship for seizing an enemy ship, also called prize money.

bourgeois *adj.* (1) a French word which means *belonging to the middle class*, as distinguished from the proletariat or wage-earning or working class on the one hand, and the capitalist or land-owning class on the other hand. (2) in the view of Marxists, any person who makes unfair gains from the work of the wage-earning class.

bourse STK. EXCH the French word, in general use on the continent of Europe, for a stock or commodity exchange or money market. The Bourse usu. means the Paris Bourse, the main stock exchange of France.

boxcar (U.S.A.) TRANSPT. a railway goods wagon which is completely closed in. *Syn.* (Britain) box wagon.

box file *see under* file.

box number ADVTG. a number forming part of the address to which replies to a newspaper advertisement should be sent. Cf. P.O. box.

box-office (1) a place in a theatre where seats can be reserved and tickets bought by the public. (2) the amount of money received from the sale of tickets at a box-office.

box wagon TRANSPT. a railway goods wagon which is completely closed in. *Syn.* (U.S.A.) boxcar. *Opp.* open wagon.

boycott organized refusal by a group of persons, e.g. a trade union, to have dealings of any kind with a person, firm or country who is considered to have offended against the rules of behaviour supported by the group, as a means of forcing the offender to change his ways: *To boycott a person/an organization/a product/the goods of another country*.

B.P., b.p., b/p. bills payable.

Br. British.

br. branch.

B.R. British Rail.

b.r. bank rate.

B.R., b.r., b/r. bills receivable.

brain drain *see* drain.

branch *n.* (1) a local office or shop of a business, e.g. a bank or a chain-store, or of some other organization, e.g. a public library service, under the control of a central or head office which is usu. situated in some other place. *Syn.* a branch office; branch house. Cf. head office; central office. (2) IND. REL. a small local division or unit of a trade union at the meetings of which all members have the right to be present.

v. COM. (*with* out) to extend one's business by making or selling new products; to widen one's activities: *A bookshop branching out as a newsagent*.

branch manager *see under* manager.

brand COM. & IND. originally an owner's mark, made by burning, on cattle, etc. but now a maker's name, trade-mark or sign, usu. officially registered and protected, put on goods to make it easy for buyers to recognize the make or quality. *Local brand*, a brand of product sold locally, usu. in the area in which it is manufactured. *National brand*, one sold all over the country. *Own-brand, see under* own; *also* house brand.

brand acceptance ADVTG. the willingness of consumers to buy one brand as compared with other brands of what are essentially the same product. *Syn.* consumer acceptance.

branded goods COM. goods marked with the name of the producer or some other brand name chosen by him, and usu. put in special packaging before leaving the factory. The object is to make the particular brand of goods easily recognizable and distinguishable from other brands in the shops. *See also* house brand. *Opp.* unbranded goods.

brand image ADVTG. the image (mental picture) of a particular branded product which a consumer carries in his mind. By advertising, a producer tries to improve the brand image of his product so that more and more consumers prefer his brand to the other brands.

brass (*colloq.*) money: *He has plenty of brass*.

brassage FIN. (1) the charge made by a government for manufacturing coins out of metal. (2) the actual cost of the coin. *See* seigniorage. *Syn.* mintage.

Brazil a federal republic in the eastern part of South America, pop. 100 million approx. (1975); capital, Brasilia, pop. 550,000 approx.; language, Portuguese; currency unit, the cruzeiro, divided into 100 centavos. Member, O.A.S.; L.A.F.T.A.

brch. branch.

breach of confidence failure to keep secret some information that one has been given as a secret. *Syn.* breach of security.

breach of contract LAW failure to perform a duty accepted by a person under a contract, thus giving the other contracting party a right to claim damages in a court of law.

partial breach one where only some of the duties under the contract have not been performed. If the failure is so serious that an essential part of the contract has been broken, the party harmed may treat the contract as no longer being in force.

total breach a situation where one party to a contract shows intention not to perform any part of it, or makes it impossible, or entirely fails to perform it. *See also* anticipatory breach; breach of warranty; essence of a contract.

breach of security *see* breach of confidence.

breach of trust (1) LAW failure by a trustee to perform his duty to a trust, e.g. by acting wrongly or by neglecting to do something he ought to do, with the result that loss is caused to the trust. (2) (*colloq.*) failure by any person to perform a duty which he was trusted to do. *Syn.* defalcation; embezzlement; fraudulent conversion.

breach of warranty LAW failure to perform a duty which forms part of a contract but not an essential part. If there is a failure by one party to perform a warranty, the other party cannot treat the contract as no longer having any force, but can claim damages in a court of law. *See* breach of contract.

bread and butter (*colloq.*) (1) the way in which a person earns his living: *Selling houses is his bread and butter*. (2) the most important of two or more ways by which a person earns his living: *He is a fine artist but he makes his bread and butter by teaching languages*.

breadline a line of very poor people waiting to be given free food: *To be on the breadline*, to be so poor as to have only enough income to pay for the bare necessities of life.

breadwinner a person who earns a living for himself and his dependants.

break *n.* (1) STK. EXCH. a sudden and severe fall in market prices. (2) ADVTG. a short pause in a television programme to show advertising films. (3) INDUS. a short interval for refreshment: *We stop work for 15 minutes for a coffee-break in the morning and for a tea-break in the afternoon.* (4) (*colloq.*) a change from bad to good fortune: *A lucky break*, a chance to do better than in the past.
v. (1) FIN. to ruin (someone) financially: *The bad harvest broke him.* *To break the bank*, at a gaming table, to win so much money that the person running the game has to stop payment. (2) (*fig.*) to make very large gains at other people's expense.
to break bulk SHIPG. & TRANSPT. (*a*) to open large packages or containers in order to sell or to carry in smaller quantities, e.g. action taken by a wholesaler. (*b*) to begin unloading a ship.
to break one's journey to stop on the way; to interrupt one's journey.

breakages COM. & ACCTS. charges made for things broken while on hire or on loan; the cost of broken china, glass, etc. used in a business, e.g. a hotel or restaurant.

break down *v.* (1) to set out as separate parts, esp. figures, so that they may be studied: *Please break this sum down to show how it was arrived at.* (2) to stop working or running; to fail to work properly: *The car/machine broke down. His health will break down unless he takes a holiday.*

breakdown *n.* (1) ACCTS. a statement of various small sums which together make up a bigger sum, for the purpose of study: *Give me a breakdown of expenses.* (2) a failure in a machine or a system to work properly: *Trains are late because of a breakdown on the line.*
adj. We are sending our breakdown van to repair your car.

breakdown clause SHIPG. a condition in a chartering contract that the hirers of the ship will not be charged for time during which the ship was broken down, i.e. could not continue working properly. *Syn.* off-hire clause.

break even *v.* (1) in Britain, to be in a situation where income from sales equals the expenses of production, so that neither profit nor loss is made. (2) in U.S.A., to earn from sales not only just enough to pay all expenses but also enough for a moderate dividend.

break-even analysis ACCTS. a method of studying the profitability of a business or of a single product by showing at what level of production costs are just covered by income, neither profit nor loss being made; and thus to calculate the effect on profit of changes in the amount of goods produced, the costs of production, and the selling price.

break-even chart a graph which shows the management the results of a break-even analysis. *Syn.* profitgraph.

break-even point ACCTS. the level of sales at which the income from goods sold is just enough to cover production, neither profit nor loss being made.

break up (1) SHIPG. of a wrecked ship, to fall to pieces; to be destroyed: *The vessel on the rocks has broken up.* (2) to take or cut to pieces (a now useless thing) in order to sell or re-use the material: *The old ship is to be broken up. Syn.* to scrap; to demolish.

break-up value ACCTS. (1) the value of an asset when it is no longer of any practical use but will bring in some money if it is broken up and the material sold or re-used. (2) the total value of the assets of a business if each asset is sold separately, as distinguished from the value of the business as a whole if sold as a going concern.

breakwater SHIPG. a strong wall built across part of a harbour to provide shelter for ships. *See* artificial harbour. Cf. mole; jetty; quay.

b. rec. bills receivable.

Bretton Woods Agreement ECON. the result of a conference of 44 nations held in 1944 at Bretton Woods, U.S.A., to plan better co-operation in world trade and currency matters. The International Monetary Fund and the International Bank for Reconstruction and Development (the World Bank) were started under the control of the United Nations, with the aim of raising world incomes, encouraging international trade and investment, and making steadier the exchange rates between currencies.

bribe a reward of money or goods given secretly to influence a person to do something. In most countries it is a criminal offence to offer or give a bribe to a public servant or to an agent; and for a public servant or an agent to accept or receive a bribe. *Syn.* secret commission.

bribery the act or practice of giving and receiving bribes. *Syn.* corruption; illegal gratification.

bricks and mortar (*colloq.*) property in the form of buildings, i.e. houses, offices, factories. *He invested his money in bricks and mortar.*

bridge SHIPG. the upper part of a ship used by the captain and officers, from which they control the ship.
air bridge *see under* airline.
bridge deck the highest deck of a ship. *Also* navigating bridge deck.
toll bridge a bridge, usu. across a river, where a toll (charge) is made for permission to cross.

bridging loan BKG. a loan made by a bank for a short period to help the borrower to bridge the gap in time between buying, e.g. a new house, and selling, e.g. the old house. *Syn.* bridging advance; bridging finance.

brief *n*. (1) LAW a document prepared by a solicitor for the use of a barrister who is presenting their client's case in court. The brief states all the known facts and the law relating to the case, and usu. has other documents fastened to it such as copies of letters and formal statements of witnesses. (2) a short statement giving information needed by a person having to perform a certain piece of work or to gain a certain object: *The sales manager gave each salesman a brief about the new product.*
v. (1) LAW to give directions to a barrister by means of a brief: *The solicitor has briefed counsel.* (2) generally, to give someone advance information on a particular subject or for a particular purpose, e.g. to the captain of an airliner about the weather. *The sales manager briefed the representatives on the new product.*

briefcase a flat case, usu. of leather, with a handle, for carrying papers, books, etc. *Syn.* dispatch case.

bright STK. EXCH. (of securities) in good demand: *Mogul Oil shares were bright at 196 pence. The market showed a brighter turn*, there was a better demand for securities.

Bright John (1811–89), British Liberal statesman and economist who, with Richard Cobden in Manchester in 1838, started the Anti-Corn Law League. Entering Parliament in 1843, he succeeded in obtaining the repeal (ending) of the Corn Laws in 1846, an event which began a long period of free trade by Britain.

bring-and-buy sale COM. a means of collecting money for those in need. Each person brings something to sell, and each person buys something to take away. Cf. sale of work.

brisk STK. EXCH. active: *Business is brisk. There was a brisk demand for engineering shares.*

Brit. Britain; British.

British Commercial Monomark *see* Monomark.

British Commonwealth *see* Commonwealth of Nations.

British Funds FIN. & STK. EXCH. a short name for fixed-interest government stocks which are strictly part of the funded debt of the British Government, with no fixed date for repayment, e.g. Consols; but the words are often used in a more general way to include all fixed-interest stocks issued by the British Government and the nationalized industries guaranteed by the government, whether dated or undated. *See* funded debt, unfunded debt *under* national debt. *Syn.* gilt-edged securities; the Funds.

British savings bonds *see* savings bonds.

British South Africa Company formed in 1889 by royal charter for trade and commerce in south-central Africa. In large areas it was made responsible for the administration as agent for the British Government, esp. in Northern and Southern Rhodesia from 1900 to 1924, when these countries became self-governing under the British Colonial Office. The Company's commercial activities continued until 1965.

British Standards Institution an independent body in Britain, supported by the government, which lays down standards of quality in engineering, building, chemical and household products, etc. Manufacturers are not forced to use these standards, but many do. *See* kite-mark.

British thermal unit the quantity of heat needed to raise one pound of water by one degree Fahrenheit. *Abbr.* B.T.U.

British ton *see* long ton *under* ton.

brl. barrel.

BRN Bahrain's international vehicle-registration letters.

Bro., Bros. Brother, Brothers.

broad gauge *see under* gauge.

brochure a small book consisting of a few pages in a paper cover, esp. advertising material in this form. *Syn.* booklet; pamphlet.

brokage *see* brokerage (1).

broke *adj*. (*colloq.*) having no money; bankrupt: *He is broke*, he is penniless. *I am stony-broke/flat broke*, completely without money.
v. (*colloq.*) to run a business as a broker: *He brokes in insurance*, he is an insurance broker.

broken amount STK. EXCH. an irregular amount, e.g. 67 shares, as distinguished from a regular marketable amount, which might be a lot or parcel of 50 or 100 shares. Broken amounts are not so easy to sell or to buy, and therefore call for a special price.

broker generally, a particular class of agent who is employed by his principal to buy or sell the principal's goods or services, usu. in return for payment of a brokerage or commission calculated as a percentage of the amount of business done. The broker does not become the owner of the goods and cannot act in his own name but only in the name of the principal. A bill-broker and some commodity brokers are exceptions. A broker usu. deals in a special kind of business, e.g. as a foreign-exchange broker, a ship-broker or an insurance broker. Cf. jobber; factor.

brokerage COM. (1) the payment received by a broker for his services. It is usu. a commission calculated as a percentage of the value of business done by him but may also take the form of a fixed fee. *Syn.* brokage; courtage. (2) the business carried on by a broker.

broker's lien INSCE. & LAW the right given by law to a broker to hold an insurance policy and not to deliver it to the insured party until that party has paid the premium. This right protects the broker from loss from his client's failure to pay, for once the broker has placed (arranged) an insurance he is responsible for paying the premium, whether his client pays him or not.

broker's return SHIPG. a list, sent usu. daily to the ship-brokers by the persons loading a ship, noting all the goods that have been put on board.

broking COM. the profession of a broker.

broking house a firm (partnership) or company that carries on the business of brokers.

bronze FIN. the metal of which in many countries coins of lower values are made, an alloy (mixture of metals) consisting of 95% copper, 4% tin and 1% zinc. In Britain, three bronze coins are issued: the twopence or twopenny piece (2p); the penny (1p) (*pl.* pennies *or* pence); the halfpenny (½p). The weight of each coin is proportional to its face value. Bronze coins are legal tender to the value of 20p.

Brookings Institution an organization for advanced study in economics and government. Set up in Washington in 1927.

broom (1) a large brush with a long handle, used for sweeping. (2) SHIPG. a broom at the masthead of a ship is a sign that she is for sale.

Bros. Brothers.

brot. brought.

brot. fwd. brought forward.

brought down ACCTS. words written usu. in shortened form, e.g. B/d.; b.d., at the beginning of an account to show a total that has had to be brought down from an earlier account which ended higher up on the same page of the account book. Cf. carried down; brought forward.

brought forward ACCTS. words written, usu. in shortened form, e.g. B/f.; bt. fwd., at the top of an account to show a total which has had to be carried forward from the last account or from an earlier page in the account book. Cf. carried forward; brought down.

B.R.S. British Road Services.

Brunei a constitutional monarchy (kingdom) in south-east Asia, ruled by a sultan under British protection, pop. 150,000 approx. (1975); capital, Bandar Seri Begawan, pop. 40,000 approx.; languages, Malay, English and Cantonese; currency unit, the Brunei dollar (Br$), divided into 100 cents.

Brussels (Tariff) Nomenclature COM. & FIN. an international system of naming and classifying all goods in international trade for the purpose of standardizing customs tariffs, signed at a convention held in Brussels in 1950. *See also* Standard International Trade Classification. *Abbr.* B.T.N.

bs. bags; bales.

B.S. balance sheet; bill of sale; British Standard; building society.

B/S. bill of store; bill of sale.

b.s. balance sheet; bill of sale.

B.S.C. British Steel Corporation.

b.s.g.d.g. (*French*: breveté sans garantie du gouvernement) patented without government guarantee.

bsh. bushel.

'B' share *see* multiple voting share *under* share.

B.S.I. British Standards Institution.

Bs.L. *or* **Bs/L.** bills of lading.

B.S.S. British Standard Specification.

B/St. bill of sight.

B.S.T. British Summer Time.

b.t. berth terms *see* berth rates.

bt. fd., bt. fwd. brought forward.

bth. bath(room).

B.T.N. Brussels Tariff Nomenclature.

B.T.U. Board of Trade unit (one kilowatt hour); British thermal unit.

bu. bushel(s).

bubble COM. unreasonable and excited buying of shares in a company that is financially weak, with the effect of raising the market price of the shares far higher than their true value. *See* South Sea Bubble.

buck *v.* COM. (*colloq.*) to resist; to fight against: *To buck the trend*, to succeed in resisting the unfavourable effects of a slump in business; to do well when other businesses are doing badly. *n.* (U.S.A. *colloq.*) a dollar: *The book cost ten bucks*, ten dollars.

bucket shop (*colloq.*) a share- or commodity-broking concern run by dishonest persons who are not members of any stock or commodity exchange. They arrange deals in worthless or non-existent shares and commodities, and by these and other tricks cheat the public of their money. *See* share-pushing; share-hawking.

Bucks. Buckinghamshire, England.

buckshee *adj.* (*colloq.*) free of cost; got for nothing. *Syn.* gratis.

budget (1) FIN. & ACCTS. an account of probable future income (money coming in) and expenditure (money going out) during a stated period, usu. a year, used as a guide in making financial arrangements. *See* cash budget; financial budget; variable budget.

balanced budget one in which income roughly equals expenditure.

deficit budget one in which income falls short of expenditure.

surplus budget one in which income is greater than expenditure.

unbalanced budget one that is in deficit.

(2) PUB. FIN. *The Budget*, the British Government's formal plan for future national revenue and expenditure which is put before Parliament by the Chancellor of the Exchequer usu. once each year, making proposals for changes in taxation which later become law in the yearly Finance Act. *Syn.* national budget; (U.S.A.) national accounts budget. *See* capital budget.

(3) MAN. an account of the probable cost of carrying out a plan or programme for a special purpose: *An advertising budget*; *a capital budget*; *a research budget*. The amount of

money set aside for a special purpose. *See* allocation. We *have used up/spent our promotional budget.*

budget account (1) BKG. an arrangement with a bank by which the bank pays a customer's main household bills when they become due, but debits the customer's current account with a fixed monthly sum calculated by dividing the total yearly value of the bills by 12. The customer is thus able to budget for (plan) his expenses. *Syn.* personal loan. (2) COM. an arrangement with a shop, esp. a department store, by which the customer pays the store a fixed sum every month and is able to buy goods at any time up to a value of (say) 12 times the monthly sum being paid. *Syn.* budget-plan.

budgetary control MAN. a system of management control by making detailed comparisons of actual income and expenditure with budgeted income and expenditure in order to make sure that plans are being kept to, and to learn where those plans may need changing in order that a profit will be made.

budgetary policy *see* fiscal policy.

Budget Day FIN. the day, usu. in late March or early April, on which the British national budget is presented to the House of Commons by the Chancellor of the Exchequer.

budget-day value TAXN. the value of an asset on 6 April 1965, used in calculating capital gains tax in Britain.

budgeted MAN. & ACCTS. included in, allowed for, provided for in a budget: *The actual costs exceed the budgeted figure by £100.*

budgeting MAN. & ACCTS. the process of preparing budgets as an aid to planning and controlling the financial management and direction esp. of a business or other organization.

budget-plan *see* budget account (2).

buffer stock ECON. & IND. a stock of raw material, food, parts of finished products or other goods, which has been bought when supplies are plentiful and cheap and then stored for use when supplies are short and would therefore be dear to buy. Buffer stocks are one way of reducing wide variations in market prices and are sometimes employed by governments to make the supply of certain goods roughly equal to the current demand for them. *Syn.* safety stock.

builder's certificate SHIPG. an official document given by the Customs to the builders of a newly-built ship allowing the vessel to leave the shipyard for trials at sea without the usual customs formalities.

builders' policy *see* shipbuilders' policy *under* insurance policy.

building basin *see* basin (1).

building lease *see under* lease.

building port SHIPG. the port where a particular ship was built.

building society FIN. a financial organization formed for the purpose of helping people to build or buy houses. By issuing shares and accepting deposits from small investors, it collects money which it lends to borrowers on mortgage, i.e. against the security of the borrowers' property. These loans are usu. repayable over many years by the annuity system, i.e. equal periodical payments consisting partly of capital and partly of interest on the amount outstanding.

building-society interest FIN. (1) the interest received from a building society by an investor who has taken shares in the society or who has placed money on deposit with it. (2) the interest payable by a mortgagor, i.e. a person who has borrowed money on mortgage from a building society.

built-in stabilizers *see* stabilizers, economic.

Bulgaria a communist republic in south-eastern Europe, pop. 8.7 million approx. (1973); capital, Sofia, pop. 870,000 approx.; languages, Bulgarian and Turkish; currency unit, the lev (*pl.* leva), divided into 100 stotinki. Member, COMECON.

bulk a large mass, volume or quantity.

break bulk *see under* break, *v.*

in bulk (*a*) in large amounts: *By producing in bulk we can sell at low prices. See* laden in bulk. (*b*) loose, not packed in containers: *Cargoes of grain are loaded/carried in bulk.*

bulk buying buying in large quantities in order to obtain a low price, thus gaining an advantage over those persons who buy only in small quantities.

bulk cargo cargo consisting entirely of one kind of loose substance that does not need any packing, such as coal or wheat. Cf. general cargo.

bulk carrier SHIPG. a ship intended for carrying cargoes of loose materials such as coal, ore, grain, which are not packed in containers.

bulkhead SHIPG. one of the strong steel walls across the inside of a ship dividing it into several watertight compartments.

bull STK. EXCH. a dealer in the stock market who, believing that prices will rise, contracts to buy many shares in the hope of selling them at a profit before he has to pay for them on Settling Day. The word is also used to mean any person who buys shares which he intends not to keep, but to hold only long enough to make some profit by selling them at a higher price. Cf. bear, *n.*

bull account *see* bull position.

bull campaign STK. EXCH. action by dealers aimed to push prices up by buying securities, influencing others to buy too. When demand exceeds supply, the bulls sell at a profit. Cf. bear campaign.

bullion FIN. gold and silver of official quality in the form of bars, not coins, and valued by its weight as merchandise, not by its value as coin. *See* assay master *under* assay. Cf. specie.

bullion broker COMMOD. EXCH. one of a small number of firms of brokers in the London bullion market who act both as agents for buyers and sellers of gold and silver bullion, and as dealers buying and selling in their own name.

bullish STK. EXCH. (1) tending towards a rise in prices: *There was a bullish trend in the market.* (2) hopeful; cheerful; expecting good business: *The business outlook is bullish.*

bull market *see under* market.

bull position STK. EXCH. the trading situation of a bull in the stock market who finds that he has contracted to buy more shares than he can pay for on Settling Day. He therefore arranges to have his account carried over to the next Settling Day, paying contango as the price. *Syn.* bull account.

bull transaction *see under* transaction.

bunce (*colloq.*) an extra payment, in the form *either* of an unexpected profit *or* of commission.

bundle *see* bale.

bunk SHIPG. one of the narrow beds in a ship, usu. arranged in rows like shelves one above another to provide sleeping places for a number of persons in the least space possible.

bunker SHIPG. (1) a place, esp. in a ship, for storing fuel for the engines. (2) the fuel itself. (3) the supply of fuel in bulk.

bunkering arrangements at a port for ships to load fuel into their bunkers.

bunker port a port that has bunkering arrangements.

buoy SHIPG. a firmly-anchored floating mark for ships to tie up to (a *moving buoy*), or for use by seamen as a guide marking a channel or dangerous places such as rocks, sandbanks, wrecks, etc. (a *navigational buoy*).

buoy dues *see* buoyage (2).

buoyage SHIPG. (1) the provision of a system of buoys in a port or waterway. (2) the charges which a ship's owners have to pay to the port for keeping the system of buoys in good order. *Syn.* buoy dues.

buoyant *adj.* STK. EXCH. of prices, tending to keep high: *Oils were buoyant*, prices of oil-company shares were high. *There was a buoyant market in chemicals. Opp.* depressed.

buoy dues *see* buoyage (2).

buqshah former fractional currency unit of Yemen (San'a). 40 buqshahs = 1 Yemeni riyal.

BUR Burma's international vehicle-registration letters.

burden (1) COM. & LAW a duty that one is bound by a promise to perform: *The burden of a contract.* (2) ACCTS. general or indirect expenses of production (rent, rates, etc.) as distinguished from direct costs (material, labour, etc.). *Syn.* overheads; overhead cost; oncost; fixed cost.

(3) SHIPG. the weight in tons of the load that a ship can carry: *A ship of 1000 tons burden*; but the ton is taken to be 40 cu. ft instead of the normal tonnage measure of 100 cu. ft per ton. *Syn.* burthen. Cf. registered tonnage.

burden of proof LAW the duty to prove the truth of formal statements made in court about facts or events. When one party in a court case states formally that a certain fact is true, the court will accept it and treat it as true unless the other party can prove that it is untrue. This is called *shifting the burden of proof. Syn.* onus of proof.

bureau (1) an office, esp. one doing business direct with the public: *An information/enquiry/employment/tourist bureau. Citizens' Advice Bureau.* (2) a government department (or part of one) esp. in U.S.A.: *The Federal Bureau of Investigation (F.B.I.), the Bureau of the Mint, the Bureau of Standards, the American Weather Bureau.* (3) INSCE. *see* Lloyd's Policy Signing Bureau *under* Lloyd's policy.

bureaucracy rule by a class of people in offices, esp. by paid officials appointed by the government, who do not understand the wish of the ordinary man to be free to earn his living in the way he chooses and to take risks if he chooses, and who think that they know best how the economy should be managed. The word is also used of those very large companies and industrial concerns which show the same trend towards impersonal administration.

bureau de change COM. & TOUR. (*French*, exchange office) an office or shop run by a dealer in foreign exchange, where the public may change foreign currencies into the local money and local money into foreign currencies. *Syn.* foreign-exchange office.

Bureau of Customs (U.S.A.) the division of the U.S. Department of the Treasury which is responsible for collecting customs duties; the equivalent of the British Board of Customs and Excise.

Bureau Veritas SHIPG. & MAR. INSCE. the French Register of Shipping and the organization responsible in France for checking the safety and fitness of ships and for classifying them. The French equivalent of Lloyd's Register of Shipping. *See* classification societies. *Abbr.* B.V.

burglary LAW breaking a way by force into, and actually entering, a house for the purpose of serious crime. Cf. housebreaking.

burglary insurance *see* theft insurance *under* insurance, classes and kinds of.

Burke Edmund (1729–97), British statesman and economist. He taught the theory of society known as individualism, which believes that the best economic order is that in which there is no central direction, each individual producer being left free to compete with others to serve the public good. He entered Parliament in 1766, supported the fight of the American colonies for independence (1775–83), led the impeachment (accusing and trial) of Warren Hastings, Governor-General of India, and opposed the slave trade and the French Revolution.

Burma a republic in south-eastern Asia, on the eastern shore of the Bay of Bengal, pop. 29 million approx. (1973); capital, Rangoon, pop. 1.8 million approx.; languages, Burmese, Chin, Karen and Shan; currency unit, the kyat, divided into 100 pyas. Member, Colombo Plan.

burn (1) to destroy by fire. (2) COM. (*fig.*) *To burn a hole in one's pocket*, to make one want to spend (money) carelessly, foolishly, wastefully. *He has money to burn*, far more than he needs. *To burn one's fingers*, to suffer some financial loss through careless or ill-judged action.

bursar FIN. (1) a treasurer or trusted financial official esp. of a college. (2) in Scotland, a college student who receives a bursary.

bursary FIN. an allowance of money paid to a student to help him during the period of his studies. *Syn.* scholarship.

burthen *see* burden (3).

Burundi a small republic in Central Africa, pop. 3.8 million approx. (1973); capital, Bujumbura, pop. 70,000 approx.; languages, Kirundi, French and English; currency unit, the Burundi franc (Bur Fr.), divided into 100 centimes. Member, O.A.U.

bus. business; bushel.

bush. bushel.

bushel a unit of measuring dry goods esp. grain and fruit by volume: 8 gals. or 4 pk. or one-eighth of a qr., 2219.36 cu. in. (36.37 litres) in Britain, the imperial bushel; (2150.42 cu. in., the Winchester bushel, in U.S.A.). A bushel of barley weighs 48 lb; of maize 56 lb; of oats 34 lb; of wheat 60 lb; of flour 56 lb. Also used as a measure of fish: 1 bushel = 56 lb. *See* corn and dry measure *table on page 477. Abbr.* bsh.; bu.; bush.

business (1) a person, firm, company or other organization which makes or produces a product, buys and sells goods or provides some kind of service, usu. for the purpose of making a profit: *Ours is a profitable business; it is a butcher's business. He owns a share in the family business. She intends to buy a business. They have started up a business. See* one-man business. (2) trading generally; the practice of commerce: *We are in business together*, we are partners. *I shall be happy to do business with you. Business is good. Business as usual*, we are carrying on in spite of difficulties. (3) matters for discussion or decision, esp. at a meeting: *Business to be transacted. Any other business*, words appearing on the agenda for a

meeting, to allow those persons attending to raise matters not already listed in the agenda. *See* order of business; order of the day. (4) generally, something that has to be done; something with which one is closely concerned: *Let us get down to business*, let us start work on the matters needing attention. *Mind your own business*, don't interfere in matters that do not concern you. *Business is business*, in business life one must not allow personal feelings to influence one's judgment.

business agent (1) in Britain, a person who represents another and has powers to act for him in business matters. (2) in U.S.A., an employee who represents a labour union in business matters.

business barometer STK. EXCH. (1) anything which acts as a pointer for businessmen, esp. investors, to changes in market conditions. *See* barometer stock. *Syn.* economic indicator; leading indicator. (2) an average of various index numbers each dealing with a particular field of economic activity, the aim being to give investors a general idea of changes in the economic climate.

business card COM. a small piece of card printed with one's name and the name and address of one's business, used when making business visits.

business cycle *see* trade cycle *under* cycle.

business day *see* non-business day.

business economics COM. the study of the production, supply and distribution of goods and services, now usu. called commerce.

business economist *see* economist.

business entity concept ACCTS. a basic rule in accountancy that a business firm, being a corporation, has an existence of its own, separate from the persons who own or run it, and that therefore the only dealings entered in the firm's account books are those that relate to the business itself and must not include the personal affairs of its owners.

business interruption policy *see* consequential loss policy *under* insurance policy.

business law *see* commercial law.

business-like practical; methodical; using care, skill and common sense; clever at business; being a good manager. *The office manager is very business-like. This is a business-like system. You must be more business-like in your work*, use more care and skill.

businessman COM. & IND. a man who works, or is employed, in business, esp. a man who owns, or holds a high post in, a large or important business. *Pl.* -men. *Fem.* businesswoman: *pl.* -women.

business manager COM. (1) a person employed to manage the business affairs of a professional person, e.g. a musician, in order to leave that person free to carry on his profession. (2) an employee in a commercial or industrial concern who is responsible for administrative and financial matters.

business premises policy *see under* insurance policy.

business reply service COM. an arrangement with the Post Office by which an advertiser who has been duly licensed can send out publicity material in a special form and invite members of the public to send him replies at no cost to themselves, the postage being paid by the licensee when he receives the reply.

bust (*colloq.*) (1) to go bankrupt; to become ruined, a failure: *His firm has gone bust.* (2) to break; to bankrupt; to ruin: *A bad harvest can bust many farmers.* Cf. broke.

bust-up (*a*) a violent disagreement; a quarrel: *A bust-up in the boardroom*, a quarrel among the directors. (*b*) a bankruptcy; a business failure.

busy (U.S.A.) (of a telephone line) in use; engaged: *The number is busy, so please try again in a few minutes.*

butt (1) a very large barrel containing beer or sherry (usu. 108 gals.) or wine (usu. 126 gals). (2) a unit of volume for liquids (varying from 103 to 108 gals.); two hogsheads. *See* cask. *Syn.* pipe.

butty (*colloq.*) a small contractor, esp. in coal-mining, who is paid by the mine-owners to get certain work done by a group of men, known as a butty-gang, whom he employs and with whom he shares the profit. The arrangement is called the butty system.

butut the fractional currency unit of Gambia. 100 butut = 1 dalasi.

buy *n.* COM. (*colloq.*) a bargain: *A good buy. The best buy*, the article or product which gives the best value for money when compared with its competitors.

v. (1) to obtain, to get possession (of something) by paying a price, either in money or in goods or services: *To buy a house for £20,000. I bought a car at an auction sale. Syn.* to acquire; to purchase; to procure. *Opp.* to sell. (2) (*sometimes with* over) to bribe: *We suspect that he has been bought* (*over*), that he has been bribed. *I will not be bought*, I will not take bribes.

buy a bull STK. EXCH. to buy shares in the hope or expectation of a rise in price. Cf. sell a bear.

buy a pig in a poke COM. to buy something without first examining it to see that it is good value: *The machine which I bought in a hurry has proved to be a pig in a poke*, it does not work.

buy a pup COM. (1) to buy something which proves to be useless and without value. (2) to be cheated.

buy earnings STK. EXCH. to invest money by buying shares in a company which at present give a low yield but have a good record of growth in earnings which is expected to continue and to lead to an increased yield and therefore to a higher price, giving the investor a capital gain. *Syn.* to buy growth.

buyer (1) a person who buys, as opposed to one who sells. *Syn.* purchaser. Cf. seller. (2) an agent or employee of a business, esp. a department store or chain-store, who is responsible for buying the stocks of goods sold by the business. *See also* materials buyer; special buyer.

buyer's interest INSCE. the interest that an insured person must have in the property he is insuring. Thus a buyer of goods obtains an insurable interest, here called a buyer's interest, as soon as he becomes the legal owner of the goods. *See* buyer's risk (2) *Syn.* consignee's interest.

buyers' market *see under* market.

buyer's monopoly *see* commercial monopoly *under* monopoly.

buyer's option to double *see* call-of-more option *under* option.

buyers over STK. EXCH. words used of a market when there is an excess of buyers over sellers, or when there are no sellers at all, resulting in some intending buyers being unable to find anything to buy: *Yesterday there were buyers over*, there was little offered for sale. Cf. sellers over.

buyer's risk (1) COM. goods offered for sale *at buyer's risk* carry no warranty (promise of quality or fitness for a particular purpose). The intending buyer must satisfy himself that the goods are acceptable before buying them. The seller has no responsibility once a sale has taken place. *See* caveat emptor. (2) INSCE. where ownership of goods is passed from one party to another under a contract of sale, the point at which the buyer's risk of loss or damage in transit (during carriage) begins usu. depends on who pays the carriage. If the goods are supplied *carriage paid*, the buyer's risk begins when the goods are delivered to the buyer; and if supplied *ex-factory* or *ex-warehouse* or *ex-wharf*, the buyer's risk begins when the supplier hands the goods to the carrier appointed by the buyer.

buyer's surplus *see* consumer's surplus.

buy in COM. (1) at an auction sale, to buy back for the owner if there are no buyers at the reserve price. (2) to buy materials, parts, etc. in order to accumulate a stock to use in the business, not for immediate resale. (3) FIN. action by a government to buy its own currency to prevent a fall in value or to cause an increase in value when compared with other currencies. (4) STK. EXCH. *see* buying-in.

buying agent one who buys goods for his principal. *Syn.* purchasing agent. Cf. selling agent.

buying forward *see* forward buying.

buying-in STK. EXCH. action taken by an official broker of the buying-in department of the London Stock Exchange to help a member who cannot deliver stock on a promised date. The department buys the necessary stock in the market and charges the cost to the member. *Opp.* selling-out.

buying long STK. & COMMOD. EXCH. the action of a dealer who buys and holds securities or commodities in the expectation of a rise in price. *See* bull; long.

buying-power *see* purchasing power (2).

buying round COM. (1) buying direct from a manufacturer or exporter instead of buying from wholesale agents and other middlemen. (2) any system of obtaining goods or of getting them more cheaply by avoiding ordinary channels of supply.

buy into FIN. (1) to buy a share in the capital of a business. (2) to obtain an interest in any investment, including a government loan.

buy off to pay somebody money to give up a claim or to stop being a nuisance.

buy out FIN. to buy the entire interest in a business: *To buy out the other shareholders.*

buy over to bribe.

buy turnover COM. to obtain a high volume of sales, but at the expense of making little or no profit.

buy up (1) STK. EXCH. to buy as many shares in a particular company as one can get, usu. to obtain control of it or to force up the market price. *He bought up most of the shares in John Smith Ltd. and is now its chairman.* (2) COMMOD. EXCH. to buy as much of a commodity as one can in order to control its supply: *We intend to buy up every ton of coffee in the market.*

b.v. book value.

B.V. Bureau Veritas.

B.W. bonded warehouse; British Waterways.

bx., bxs. box; boxes.

By ACCTS. in respect of: *By cheque £5*, a bookkeeping entry showing that a cheque for £5 has been received and is now credited to the account of the person who sent the cheque; the opposite of *To*, used to show debit entries.

by-law *or* **bye-law** LAW (1) a law of less importance than a main law such as statute law or the rules contained in the constitution of an organization. (2) one of a set of detailed laws made by a local government authority or a public corporation, e.g. the railways, using powers given by Act of Parliament. Such by-laws are examples of delegated legislation. (3) one of a set of detailed rules made by an organization such as a club or society in addition to the main rules in its constitution. *See* standing orders. (4) in U.S.A., one of a set of rules made by the body of members of a corporation, in addition to the rules in its corporation charter, for the proper running of its affairs.

by-product IND. some useful but less important substance or thing which happens to be produced in the course of manufacturing a more important or main product. Cf. end-product.

C

C Cuba's international vehicle-registration letter.

C. Cape; the Roman numeral for 100; C19, the nineteenth century; Celsius; centigrade.

© copyright, *see* copyright notice.

c. cent(s); centime(s).

c., ca. *circa*, about.

C.A. chartered accountant; commercial agent; commission agent; Consumers' Association; credit account; current account.

C/A. capital account; credit account; current account.

cab TRANSPT. (1) a taxi. (2) the driver's cabin of a truck or locomotive.

cabin SHIPG. & TOUR. (1) a private room in a ship: *A two-berth cabin. The captain's cabin.* Cf. saloon.

 cabin baggage bags, suitcases, etc. which a passenger needs during the voyage and keeps in the cabin. Cf. hold baggage.

 cabin class a class of passenger-ship accommodation, lower in comfort than first class but higher than tourist class.

 cabin passenger one travelling cabin class.

 cabin ship a ship carrying only cabin-class passengers.

(2) the space for passengers in an aeroplane. (3) a hut or small building used esp. as sleeping accommodation by visitors, e.g. in the grounds of a hotel or holiday camp: *A lake-side cabin.*

cabinet (1) the group of chief ministers who govern a country. (2) a piece of office furniture with drawers or trays for keeping papers, etc.: *A filing/card-index cabinet*; or with shelves: *A drinks/display cabinet.*

cable *n.* (1) SHIPG. the rope or chain by which a ship is anchored. *Cable's length*, a unit of length used by seamen, 100 fathoms or approx. 200 yds. (Britain), 240 yds. (U.S.A.). (2) a metal line running over or under the ground or under the sea for sending messages, pictures and sounds by electricity. (3) a message sent by this means to or from a place across the sea; an overseas or foreign telegram sent by underwater cable, not by radio. Cf. radiogram.
v. to send a message by cable: *To cable the latest market information. Please cable instructions.* Cf. telegraph; radio-telegraph.

cable address a shortened address, recorded at the Post Office, to which cables and telegrams may be sent. *Syn.* telegraphic address.

cable code *see* codes, telegraphic.

cable company one which provides the public with a service by sending cables (messages by submarine cable) between countries separated by sea. Most submarine cables are now owned by governments but some are still owned by commercial concerns. In Britain, cables go mainly through Cable and Wireless Ltd., a company wholly owned by the British Government since 1946.

cablese the special kind of language used by writers of cables and telegrams, using as few words as possible, e.g. *unreceived* for *not received*. Unnecessary articles (*a, an, the*) and polite expressions (*please, thank you*) are omitted; some words are combined or adapted; *comma, colon* and *full stop* are spelt out, and so are important numbers. Cf. journalese; officialese.

cablegram a message sent by submarine cable. *Syn.* cable. Cf. telegram.

cable rate BKG. in foreign-exchange dealings, the rate of exchange for cable or telegraphic transfers. Cf. cheque rate; sight rate.

cable transfer BKG. & COM. a quick way of sending money to a place in a foreign country by cable or telegraph. The service is performed by banks on the orders of the customer. *Syn.* telegraphic transfer (*abbr.* TT). Cf. mail transfer. *Abbr.* CT.

cableway *see* ropeway.

cabotage SHIPG. (1) coastal shipping, usu. by small or medium-sized ships making short voyages between ports in the same country. (2) the action of some governments in forbidding ships of foreign countries to make such voyages within the coastal waters of the home country.

ca'canny IND. REL. a Scottish expression meaning 'act cautiously', used of workers who intentionally work slowly in order to improve their bargaining-power with their employers. *Syn.* go-slow.

c.a.d. cash against documents.

cadastre LAW & TAXN. a detailed register (official record) of the ownership of land, mainly for the purpose of collecting taxes, made with the help of a large-scale map called a *cadastral survey, see under* survey.

cadge to beg for money; to borrow money or small things without having any intention of repaying: *Don't lend to him for he is a cadger. Syn.* (*colloq.*) to touch.

c.a.f. (*French:* coût, assurance, fret); cost, insurance, freight. *See* c.i.f.

Cairene a native or citizen of Cairo.

Cairnes John Elliot (1823–75), Irish economist, Professor of Political Economy in Galway and London Universities. Cairnes was the last of the Classical School of economists, whose ideas and teachings he restated in his book *Some Leading Principles of Political Economy*

Newly Expounded (1874). His work on monetary theory, imperfect competition and monopolies was important. His examination of the economics of slave labour greatly influenced opinion in Britain to favour the North in the American Civil War of 1861–5.

Cal., Calif. California, U.S.A.

cal. calendar.

calculating machine *see* calculator.

calculator any instrument or machine which determines the answers to questions by mathematics quickly and accurately. *Syn.* calculating machine. Cf. computer.

calendar a table arranged to show the days of the week for each of 12 months in a particular year.

  calendar day a day of 24 hours from midnight to midnight.

  calendar month a month of 28, 29, 30 or 31 days as it is given in the calendar. Cf. lunar month.

  calendar year a year of 365 or 366 days from 1 January to 31 December as given in the calendar for the year. Cf. financial year.

calendar-line *see* date-line.

Calif. California, U.S.A.

call *n.* (1) BKG. a demand by a lender for payment of money that has been advanced on condition that the lender can claim its immediate repayment *at call*, or *on call*, i.e. without notice and at any time he wishes. (In practice 24 hours or more may be allowed to the borrower.) (2) SHIPG. a short visit to a port: *The ship is making a call at Alexandria. Port of call*, a port where ships regularly stop to get fuel, stores and repairs. (3) STK. EXCH. a demand by a company for payment of money due by a shareholder who has been allotted shares in a new issue in which the shares are not fully paid. The total price of the share may be divided into several payments or instalments: the first on application; the next on allotment; a further payment on first call and the remainder by one or more calls which are the second or third (or more) calls, the last being the final call. The calls are usu. made several months apart by call letter. The shares are said to be paid up when the final call has been paid. Failure to pay a call may mean that the shareholder will lose his right to the share and to any money he has already paid. *Call letter*, a letter to a shareholder from a company calling for payment of the balance, or part of the balance of money due for shares. *See* called-up capital. (4) a telephone conversation or connection.

v. (1) to invite notice or help: *To call attention to a mistake. To call the police/the fire brigade/an ambulance.* (2) to telephone somebody: *He called me from Beirut.* (3) to cause to come or to happen: *He called a meeting. Call the next case,* in a court of law. (4) to regard as; to consider: *Let us call it a deal*, consider the bargain as completely agreed. *I call that cheating*, I consider that dishonest. (5) to demand, e.g. payment: *To call loans*, to demand that debtors pay what they owe. *I called his bluff*, demanded proof that he was not deceiving me.

call in (*a*) to demand payment of debts; to collect money due: *The bank called in his overdraft/advance*. (*b*) to take back from circulation: *The publishers have called in all copies of the book for correction. All £50 notes have been called in by the Bank of England.*

call off to cause something to stop or not to take place: *The union has called off the strike*, has ordered its members to return to work. *The meeting has been called off*, will not now take place. *Call it off*, go no further with the matter.

call on *or* **upon** (*a*) to demand that money owing be paid or that some promised action be taken: *We call (up)on you to pay your debt. They called (up)on him to increase their wages.* (*b*) to make a short visit to: *Our sales representative will call on you.*

call out to order or to direct workers to strike: *The union leaders called out the dockers.*

callable bond *see under* bond , *n.*

callable preferred stock (U.S.A.) a fixed-interest stock, e.g. debentures, which may be repaid at a stated price or replaced by another stock at any time that the borrowing organization may decide. *Syn.* redeemable stock.

call birds COM. (*colloq.*) goods sold by a shopkeeper at a very low price in order to tempt buyers into his shop where they may be charged high prices on other goods. Cf. loss leader.

call-box a small box-like building, or enclosure in a building, containing a coin-operated telephone for use by the public. *Syn.* coin-box; phone-box (*colloq.*); telephone kiosk.

call deposit BKG. money left with a bank by its customers which is repayable at call, i.e. without notice. *See* call rate.

called bond *see under* bond, *n.*

called-up capital STK. EXCH. & FIN. that part of the issued share-capital of a company which has been called up, i.e. partly paid by instalments on application, on allotment or by one or more calls, but not the final call, there being still a balance to be called. After the final call has been paid, the shares are no longer called-up capital, but fully-paid capital.

caller COM. (1) a visitor; a person who makes a short visit. *Callers welcome*, (in advertisements) you are welcome to visit our shop/office/factory. (2) the person who originates a telephone call (causes it to happen). *Syn.* calling subscriber.

calling a profession, business or employment; the kind of work one does for a living: *What is your calling? Let him follow his calling.*

calling card a small printed card with one's name (and perh. address) on it, used when calling on (visiting) people. *Syn.* visiting card. Cf. business card.

call loan FIN. & BKG. a loan that is repayable at call.

call money (1) BKG. the total of all advances made by a bank at call at any one time. *See* money at call and short notice. (2) STK. EXCH. *see under* option.

call of more *see* option.

call option *see under* option.

call, port of *see* port of call.

call rate BKG. the rate of interest paid by a bank on customers' call deposits. This rate is lower than that paid on e.g. seven-day and thirty-day deposits.

call, telephone *see under* telephone.

calls in arrears (1) FIN. money owing to a company by shareholders who have failed to answer one or more calls for payment on shares issued to them. *See* call, *n.* (3). (2) ACCTS. the heading of an account recording the sums owing by shareholders who are in arrears in paying calls. The total is the difference between called-up capital and paid-up capital. *See* forfeited shares *under* shares.

camber SHIPG. (1) a small dock (enclosed water) where ships can be tied up to load, etc. (2) a track or road sloping down into the water for pulling boats on land. *Syn.* slip; slipway.

cambist COM. (1) a dealer in bills of exchange and foreign currencies. A professional person with special knowledge of foreign exchanges. (2) a book or list giving information about foreign currencies, weights and measures.

Cambodia *see* Kampuchea.

Cambridge School ECON. THEORY a school of economic thought set up mainly by Alfred Marshall (1842–1924), Professor of Political Economy at Cambridge from 1885 to 1908, and built up by a group of followers during the last years of the nineteenth century. Sometimes called the Neo-Classical School, its members aimed at restating the ideas and teachings of the classical economists but brought scientific methods into economic analysis in order to measure the results of human behaviour in a price-system. Alfred Marshall and his followers, esp. A.C. Pigou, also a professor at Cambridge, introduced the theory of equilibrium in an economic society, and developed the Quantity Theory of Money. They advanced the ideas of quasi-rent, consumer surplus and elasticity; and they produced a detailed analysis of monopoly conditions. They greatly influenced the study of economics. *Syn.* Marshallian School; Neo-Classical School.

Cambs. Cambridgeshire, England.

cameralism ECON. HIST. the system of management of state finances in central Europe, esp.

Germany and Austria, during the seventeenth and eighteenth centuries. It was a form of mercantilism but in addition to encouraging active foreign trade, it aimed at building a strong economic and monetary system on which to base the rule of the State. *Also* kameralism.

Cameroon a democratic federal republic in West Africa, pop. 6 million approx. (1973); capital, Yaoundé, pop. 180,000 approx; languages, English, French and tribal; currency unit, the C.F.A. franc (CFA Fr.), divided into 100 centimes. Member, O.A.U.; O.C.A.M.M.; E.E.C. (Associate).

campaign COM. any planned operation or group of activities which aims to obtain a particular result, e.g. *An economy campaign*, to reduce expenses; *A sales campaign*, to sell more goods. *See* advertising campaign.

camp(ing) site TOUR. an area of enclosed land where people on holiday may camp, usu. for a week or two, in return for payment which includes the cost of services such as a supply of water and perh. also baths, kitchens and arrangements for playing games.

Can. Canada.

can *n.* IND. & COM. a metal airtight container for preserving small quantities of goods, esp. foods, which need to be kept away from the atmosphere. *See* tin.
v. to preserve by packing in cans: *the canning industry. Canned foods*.

Canada a large parliamentary democracy in North America, with a Governor-General representing the British Queen as head of state, pop. 22½ million approx. (1973); capital, Ottawa, pop. 500,000 approx.; languages, English and French; currency unit, the Canadian dollar (Can $), divided into 100 cents. Member, (British) Commonwealth; O.E.C.D.

canal a man-made watercourse for the passage of boats or ships or as a channel for a supply of water. *Canal boat*, a narrow barge or boat specially intended for use on canals, sometimes called a narrow boat on certain canals in Britain. *Canal tolls*, charges which owners of canal boats or ships have to pay for using canals.
ship-canal a large canal able to allow passage to ocean-going ships. The most important are: Gota (Sweden) approx. length 115 m.; Kiel (West Germany) 61 m.; Manchester (Britain) 35 m.; Panama (Central America) 50 m.; St Lawrence Seaway (N. America) 140 m.; Suez (Egypt) 100 m.; Welland (Canada) 27 m.

cancel (1) LAW to draw lines across words in a document, e.g. a lease, in order to stop it from having legal effect. A document, e.g. a contract, may also be cancelled if the word *cancelled* is written across it and the signatures of the parties are added. A postage stamp is cancelled by stamping a mark on it to prevent it from being used again. *See* cancelled cheque *under*

cheque. (2) COM. to destroy the force of; make no longer effective: *Please cancel my order*, do not act upon it. *I wish to cancel my booking of a room in your hotel/a passage on your ship/a seat in an airliner or theatre. The meeting is cancelled*, it will not now take place. *Syn.* annul; countermand.

c. and d., c. & d. collection and delivery.

candela the basic SI unit of luminous intensity (strength of light). *Abbr.* cd.

c. and f., c. & f. cost and freight.

c. and i., c. & i. cost and insurance.

candidate (1) a person who offers himself for, and tries to get, a job, an elected post or membership of an organization, e.g. a society or club. *He is a candidate for the post of sales director. She is a candidate for the Writers' Society.* (2) a person taking an examination.

Candlemas *see* quarter-day.

candle-power a unit of measurement of the strength of light, esp. of the light given by a lamp. *Abbr.* c.p.

Cannan Sir Edwin (1861–1935), British economist, Professor at the London School of Economics, London University. He was particularly interested in the growth of economic ideas. His book *Wealth* (1914) showed that he was less critical of classical economists than he had earlier been. He regarded economics as the study of material welfare.

Cantab. Cambridge (*Latin*: Cantabrigiensis) esp. relating to Cambridge University, e.g. M.A. (Cantab.).

canteen a restaurant for the workers in a factory or office. *Syn.* staff restaurant.

Cantillon Richard (d. 1734), British economist, born in Ireland, ran a banking business in Paris but later moved to London. His *Essai sur la Nature du Commerce en Général*, published in 1755 but written about 30 years earlier, was one of the first to analyse the nature of wealth, the uses of currency, and the basis of agricultural economics. It greatly influenced the writings of the physiocrats.

Canton system ECON. HIST. the organization and controlling of foreign trade in a place or region by bodies of merchants. The system takes its name from Canton, China, where from about 1760 to 1842 the Chinese Imperial Government appointed a *cohong* or body of 13 Chinese merchants or hongs to control all foreign ships coming to Canton. The *cohong* made the British East India Company responsible for the behaviour of all British ships and men. The two governments did not deal directly with each other.

canvasser a person who canvasses, i.e. goes from house to house asking people to buy his things, or asking their opinion of a product, idea, political party, etc.

cap. capital; capital letter; foolscap.

C.A.P. Common Agricultural Policy of the European Economic Community.

capacity (1) IND. the amount that a factory or process can produce in a certain time: *The capacity of this plant is 100 tons a day. Installed capacity*, the highest amount that can be expected if the plant is fully used. *Utilized capacity*, the amount actually produced when the plant is not being fully used; the part not being used is *excess capacity* or *over-capacity* or *surplus capacity*. *Capacity factor*, the percentage of utilized capacity to installed capacity. *Syn.* plant factor; load factor. (2) the amount that anything can hold: *Cubic capacity. The deadweight capacity of a ship*, the weight of cargo, fuel, stores, etc. that a ship can carry when fully loaded. (*See* deadweight tonnage.) *The capacity of the dock is 17 ships*, it does not have room for more. *The hall was filled to capacity*, it was full of people.

capacity to contract LAW the power of a person to be a party to a contract, i.e. his legal capacity, meaning that he is not legally prevented by, e.g. bankruptcy or insanity (madness).

Cape Verde Islands an island republic under Portuguese protection, off the coast of West Africa, pop. 300,000 approx. (1973); capital, Praia, pop. 6,000 approx.; languages, Portuguese and tribal; currency unit, the Cape Verde escudo, divided into 100 centavos.

capital (1) ECON. THEORY in economics, accumulated wealth or property used in the production of further wealth; one of the factors of production (the others being land and labour). *Human capital*, labour as a factor of production. (2) in business, capital is the value, measured in units of money, of real assets, i.e. assets in the form of property other than money, e.g. machinery, buildings and stocks of materials. The capital of a company is the money which its shareholders have put into the concern to buy the real assets it needs to start up and carry on the business; it is usu. calculated to be its net worth (the value of its assets *less* the amount it owes to its creditors). *Syn.* share-capital. (3) the capital of a private person is the total value of the property he owns, including land, buildings, machines, tools, investments, goods such as jewels, pictures, furniture, cash, money in the bank and money owing to him *less* money owed by him. (4) the capital of governments and public authorities is the land, machinery, buildings, etc. they own *less* their share of the national debt.

authorized capital *see under* authorized.

called-up capital of a company *see under* called-up.

current capital *see* working capital *below*.

dead capital capital which is held in some unproductive investment or lying uninvested. *Syn.* dead money.

debenture capital *see* loan capital *below*.

equity capital that part of the capital of a company that consists of ordinary, deferred, deferred ordinary or founders' shares, all of which together, in effect, carry the right of ownership (the equity) in the business. *Syn.* junior capital.

fixed capital that part of the capital of a business which is represented by the value of producer goods, i.e. goods held and used to produce the products which the business sells. *Syn.* fixed assets. *See* capital expenditure.

floating capital *see* working capital *below*.

free capital capital held in the form of money.

impaired capital of the subscribed capital of a company, that part which is not represented by assets and which therefore has no backing if the company goes into liquidation.

invested capital *see* capital structure.

issued capital the total amount of capital actually issued in shares to the members (shareholders) of a company. Cf. paid-up capital; subscribed capital.

junior capital *see* equity capital *above*.

liquid capital *see* working capital *below*.

loan capital a debt owed by a company to one or more creditors who have lent money to it. Such capital is not part of the owners' share-capital and is usually called debenture capital. *See* debentures; debenture stock.

money capital capital held in the form of money, with which a business intends to buy real assets. Cf. real capital.

national capital the total value of all capital owned in a particular country. *Syn.* national wealth.

ordinary capital that part of a company's capital issued in the form of ordinary shares. These have a right to receive a dividend out of net profits remaining after the company has paid the fixed dividends on preference shares. Cf. preference capital.

paid-in capital *see* paid-up capital *below*.

paid-up capital of a company, the total amount actually paid up on the issued capital. This amount is equal to the amount of the issued capital *less* the value of calls in arrears. *Syn.* (U.S.A.) paid-in capital.

preference capital that part of a company's capital issued in the form of preference shares. These have a right to receive a fixed rate of dividend out of net profits before the ordinary shares receive any dividend, i.e. they have a claim to preference over the ordinary shares. Cf. ordinary capital.

real capital the actual property of all kinds (except money) belonging to a business. Cf. money capital.

refugee capital *see* hot money *under* money.

reserve capital *see* uncalled capital *below*.

risk capital capital open to considerable risk of

loss. Cf. security capital. *Syn.* venture capital.

security capital capital that is safely invested, with little risk of loss. Cf. risk capital.

share-capital *see* capital (2).

specific capital a special kind of fixed capital, consisting of a capital asset which can be used only for one particular purpose, e.g. a machine for making only one kind of paper.

split capital *see under* split.

subscribed capital of a company, that part of the issued capital that is issued for cash and not for consideration other than cash, such as for property or for shares in another company. *Syn.* subscriber capital. *See also* authorized capital.

trading capital the combined value of the fixed and current assets of a business.

uncalled capital of a company, that part of the issued capital which has not yet been called up. Cf. called-up capital; unissued capital. It is called reserve capital if it is intended to be called up only in the event of the company being wound up (brought to an end).

unissued capital of a company, that part of the authorized capital which has not yet been issued. Cf. uncalled capital.

venture capital *see* risk capital *above.*

working capital the stock of money needed by a business in order to keep trading or to carry on production. It consists·of stocks and liquid resources (cash and things that can quickly be turned into cash); and it is equal to the difference between the current assets and the current liabilities. *Syn.* circulating capital; floating capital; liquid capital; liquid assets; current assets; circulating assets; (U.S.A.) current capital.

capital account ACCTS. a ledger account in which all dealings between the owners and the business are recorded; it is so called because it records the amounts of capital which the owners invest in or pay to the business, and any amounts they take out of it.

capital accumulation ECON. THEORY the practice by consumers of increasing their stock of wealth by not consuming it now; instead, some of it is used (or is set aside to be used in the future) to increase the supply of capital goods (goods such as machinery and buildings needed to produce further goods). To increase output a country must accumulate new capital at a faster rate than it uses up its existing stock of capital goods. *Syn.* capital formation.

capital allowances TAXN. a certain amount of profit allowed free of tax to a business to cover the cost of replacing the wear and tear of its fixed assets, esp. machinery and industrial buildings. Capital allowances may be more favourable than the depreciation allowance used by the business in its accounts. For example, to stimulate investment, a government may allow a business to write off the whole cost

of an asset against tax in one year. *Syn.* investment allowances.

capital appreciation COM., FIN. & STK. EXCH. an increase in the market value of an investment esp. in shares or in property.

capital assets *see* fixed assets *under* assets, *pl.*

capital bonus *see* special bonus *under* bonus, insurance.

capital budget (1) FIN. that part of the national budget of a country that relates to receipts and payments mainly of a capital nature met by borrowing by the State rather than from taxation. *See* above the line; budget (2). (2) MAN. & ACCTS. a budget showing probable future receipts and payments of a capital nature, such as in buying and selling fixed assets, during a stated period, e.g. a year; perh. also showing how these receipts may be employed and how these payments may be met. *See* budget (3).

capital charges FIN. & ACCTS. the cost to a business of paying interest on loan capital (money it has borrowed) and of providing (setting profits aside) for depreciation of fixed assets and repayment of capital when due.

capital consumption *see under* consumption.

capital duty TAXN. the stamp duty that has to be paid by a limited company on any shares that it issues.

capital employed FIN. & ACCTS. the amount of money that is being effectively used in a business, that is, the difference between the total value of all the assets and the total value of all the liabilities. It is equal to the balance of the capital account, and is called the net assets. Cf. capital invested. *Syn.* capital owned.

capital equipment ACCTS. & COM. machinery, instruments, vehicles, tools, etc. owned and used by a business to produce its finished product or to supply the services it provides. *Syn.* fixed assets. *See* accelerated depreciation.

capital expenditure ACCTS. & MAN. money spent by a business on buying a fixed asset, e.g. machinery or a building, and on stocks of materials to be used for producing the finished products of the business.

capital, flight of *see* flight of capital.

capital formation *see* capital accumulation.

capital gain TAXN. an increase in the money value of a capital asset such as buildings, land, or shares in a company. The gain may be realized, i.e. turned into money, when the asset is sold, but until then it remains an unrealized gain. Cf. capital loss.

capital gains tax *see under* tax.

capital gearing *see* gearing.

capital goods *see under* goods (7).

capital grant *see under* grant.

capital-intensive IND. of an industry, needing a large amount of capital per employee to produce its products, e.g. the petroleum industry, the electricity industry. Cf. labour-intensive.

capital invested FIN. & ACCTS. the total amount of actual money and the money value of any property other than money, brought into a business by its owner(s). This amount is not affected by any profits made or losses suffered by the business, nor by the amount of any liabilities. Cf. capital employed.

capital investment see under investment.

capitalism ECON. pure capitalism is, in theory, an economic system in which capital, representing the means of production, is owned by private persons, who are free to carry on business, to make profits, and to work, as they wish, without any interference from the State. In practice in advanced economies, the State has to interfere in order to put right the weaknesses of the system, e.g. by controlling the supply of money, by financing and managing public utilities and nationalized industries, by limiting monopolies, and by helping private industry where needed. This form of capitalism is known as a mixed capital(ist) economy. Syn. capitalist economy; free enterprise; private enterprise. See also state capitalism.

capital issue STK. EXCH. the issue of shares in a company. The action of a company in allotting shares to those persons or organizations who have applied for them.

capitalist ECON. (1) a person who provides capital of his own or organizes the collection of capital belonging to others, in order to set up and operate a business. (2) a person who possesses great wealth, esp. wealth which is invested, and is thus powerful in the economic life of the country. (3) a person who believes a capitalist system is the best form of economic organization. Cf. Communist, Socialist, etc.

capitalist economy see capitalism.

capitalization STK. EXCH. (1) see capital structure. (2) the total market value of a company's capital, called the market capitalization. This is measured by multiplying the number of shares issued by the market price of a share.

capitalization of reserves STK. EXCH. an issue of bonus shares, free of cost and only to existing shareholders, using part of the company's reserves. The purpose is either to increase the amount of the capital to be more in accord with the company's assets or to take the place of a dividend when the company is short of cash. See bonus shares. Syn. bonus issue; scrip issue.

capitalize (1) STK. EXCH. to take money out of the reserves of a company and turn it into capital by giving it to the shareholders in the form of extra shares, usu. called bonus shares. See bonus issue; scrip issue. (2) FIN. to sell an asset and thus obtain its capital value. (3) FIN. to calculate the present value of an asset, esp. one which brings an income. See capital value. (4) FIN. to provide money to be used as capital in a business concern.

capitalized value FIN. & STK. EXCH. a way of calculating the value of a business by dividing the annual profit by a figure equal to the present market rate of earnings of businesses with the same kind of risks. Syn. capital value.

capital levy TAXN. a special tax on the capital, i.e. the total value of the property and possessions, of private persons. Such a tax usu. has to be paid out of capital. It is only applied once and then usu. in a sudden and serious situation such as a war or an event of great natural misfortune; but in some countries a capital levy has been used as a means of redistributing wealth. See capital taxation.

capital loss ACCTS. & FIN. a loss arising from the sale of a fixed asset. Cf. capital profit.

capital market FIN. a place, e.g. a large city, which is a centre for raising the long-term capital needed by commercial and industrial concerns, the central and local governments and other organizations. The money is supplied by investors, who may range from private savers to large insurance companies, pension funds, etc. The raising of new capital is usu. arranged by issuing-houses, who are in touch with large investors, and the stock exchanges provide a market once the shares and loans have been issued. Cf. money market.

capital movements FIN. the flow of capital between one country and another. A capital inflow consists of money coming into the country from loans, repayments of loans and sales of investments made abroad. An outflow takes place in the opposite direction, when money leaves the country. Syn. capital transfers.

capital owned see capital employed.

capital profit see under profit.

capital redemption policy see under insurance policy.

capital redemption reserve fund ACCTS. & FIN. a reserve fund (stock of money set aside from profits) which must by law be set up by a company that has issued redeemable preference shares. The fund is used to repay the holders of these particular shares. Money that has been set aside for this purpose cannot be used for paying dividends. See capital reserve.

capital, reduction of see under reduction.

capital reserve see under reserves.

capital stock (U.S.A.) STK. EXCH. the entire shares of a joint-stock corporation (company), the holders of which together form the ownership of the concern.

capital structure FIN. & STK. EXCH. the different kinds of shares, stock, etc. which together compose a company's capital. Syn. capitalization; invested capital.

capital sum INSCE. the amount of money payable by an insurance company to the insured person on the happening of a stated event. e.g. his reaching a certain age.

capital surplus see capital profit.

capital taxation TAXN. a system of taxing a private person on the total value of his property and possessions as opposed to his income. There are several forms: an annual capital tax; a capital levy; death or estate duty; an inheritance tax; a capital transfer or gift tax; a capital gains tax. See capital tax under tax.

capital transfers see capital movements.

capital transfer tax TAXN. a tax introduced by the British Government in 1975 to replace estate duty. It is usu. payable by the person who transfers (i.e. gives) money and other forms of wealth to other persons during his lifetime and, by his personal representatives, on his death. No tax is payable on gifts to the transferor's spouse (a wife or husband), or on a basic amount transferred, or on certain kinds of gifts, esp. to charities. The rate of tax increases by steps as more and more money has been given by the transferor. Abbr. C.T.T. Syn. gift tax.

capital turnover FIN. & STK. EXCH. the proportion which the total figure of annual sales of a business bears to its issued share-capital; this proportion shows how many times the capital has been turned over (used again) during the year. Thus, if sales in the year totalled £25 million and the share-capital was £10 million, the capital turnover was 25:10 or 2.5:1, meaning that the share-capital was turned over 2½ times during the year. Syn. investment turnover.

capital value FIN. the sum one would have to pay to buy an investment, e.g. a property or security, which will bring in a given annual income. The sum will depend mainly on the current market rate of interest; if this is 5% per annum, the capital value will be $\frac{100}{5} = 20$ times the annual income, e.g. if a property gives an annual income (rent) of £200, its capital value is £200 × 20 = £4000. Other considerations also affect the value, such as the certainty of the income continuing into the future, or changes in the nature and usefulness of the thing invested in. Syn. capitalized value.

capitation fee FIN. a charge based on an equal amount being payable by each person in a group, e.g. the annual charge for membership of a society.

capitation grant see under grant.

capitation tax see under tax.

capt. captain.

captain SHIPG. the officer in command of a merchant ship. Syn. master. Abbr. capt.

captain's copy (of a bill of lading) SHIPG. an extra copy of a bill of lading which is given to the captain with the ship's papers.

captain's entry SHIPG. as no cargo can be landed from a ship without the Customs being given a bill of entry for each consignment, it may happen that the captain will make a temporary customs entry if the importer has failed to make one, or when the captain decides that all the cargo must be unloaded at that port.

captain's protest MAR. INSCE. & SHIPG. a formal declaration signed by the captain of a ship which has suffered an accident resulting in damage to her cargo. The document gives details of the accident and damage, and is made when the ship reaches port. Syn. ship's protest.

captive audience ADVTG. any group of people who, whether they like it or not, find themselves unable to escape from seeing or hearing advertisement material, e.g. when watching some television programmes.

captive market ECON. a market in which one single supplier holds a monopoly or near-monopoly, i.e. he alone has the power to control supplies to the market. Because consumers can buy only from him, he may be said to hold the market captive (prisoner).

captive outlet see under outlet.

car. carat.

car TRANSPT. a vehicle on wheels, esp. one for carrying people.

motor car a road vehicle driven by an engine using petrol or fuel-oil and intended to carry only a few people. Cf. coach; bus. Syn. (U.S.A.) automobile.

Pullman car a railway carriage providing the highest level of comfort.

railcar in Britain, a railway carriage that can move by its own power. In U.S.A., any railroad car.

railroad car (U.S.A.) (a) a railway carriage or wagon. (b) a boxcar.

tramcar (a) an electrically-driven passenger vehicle that runs on rails in the streets. Syn. (U.S.A.) streetcar. (b) a wagon running on rails for carrying ore in a mine.

carat (1) FIN. the measure of the amount of pure gold in a gold alloy (a mixture of gold and other metals). Pure or fine gold is 24 carat; gold eleven-twelfths fine is 22 carat, and so on. (2) a measure of the weight of precious stones (diamonds and other gems). 1 carat is 3.17 troy grains or 200 mg. Syn. karat.

caravan TRANSPT. a covered vehicle fitted with beds, tables, etc. usu. drawn by a car, and used as a temporary home, esp. by holidaymakers. Syn. (U.S.A.) trailer.

caravan site TOUR. an area of enclosed land where people on holiday may put their caravans, usu. for a week or two, in return for payment which includes the cost of services such as a supply of water. Syn. caravan park; (U.S.A.) trailer park. Cf. camp(ing) site.

carbon copy a copy of a typewritten or handwritten document made by using carbon paper. Sometimes shortened to carbon. Abbr. c.c.

blind carbon copy see blind copy. Abbr. b.c.c.

carbon paper sheets of very thin paper coated with a wax-like substance, used for making copies of typed or handwritten documents.

carbon ribbon a special ribbon, used esp. on electric typewriters, which gives an excellent finish to typewritten work but which can be used only once. *Syn.* acetate ribbon.

carboy INDUS. a large bottle protected by a cage of metal or basketwork and used for carrying liquid chemicals, e.g. acids.

card-carrying IND. REL. (of an employee) carrying a membership card, esp. of a trade union or political party, usu. suggesting that the person is an eager and active supporter of his union or party, not just a sympathizer: *John Smith is a card-carrying member of our party/union.*

card index system a method of storing information on cards of equal size and shape, arranged usu. alphabetically in drawers or on trays. *Syn.* index cards.

cards (*colloq.*) in Britain until recently an employee's official national insurance record cards were kept by his employer who had to put stamps on them regularly. When the employee left the service of that employer, his cards had to go with him. The system has been changed and the stamping of cards discontinued but these expressions are still in use: *To ask for one's cards*, to leave one's employer. *To be given one's cards*, to be dismissed.

care and maintenance basis INDUS. an official expression for keeping in good repair a ship, a building, machinery, etc. which is no longer in active use but may have to be brought back into use quickly in the future: *The airfield has been put on a care and maintenance basis. Abbr.* c. & m.

care, duty of LAW every member of the public has a duty of care to other persons, to make sure that they are not harmed and that they do not suffer loss. For example, an employer must provide his employees with a safe system of work, i.e. the work must be so organized and arranged that it is safe; a householder has a duty of care towards anyone lawfully visiting his house. A failure to perform this duty gives the harmed person good reason to claim damages in a court of law.

career (1) the profession or employment at which a person works to earn a living: *He chose accounting as his career. He has made a career in banking.* (2) one's progress through life: *He has had a successful career as a director.* **career woman** one who is more interested in making a career in a profession or business than in staying at home as a housewife or mother. *Syn.* career girl.

care of (*abbr.* c/o) words meaning *at the address of* (a named person or organization) to which a letter may be sent for someone not usu. living there. *Syn.* (U.S.A.) in care of.

caretaker a person employed to take care of a building by keeping it clean, by seeing that its services are working properly, e.g. electricity, water, telephones and heating, and by protecting it from destructive persons. *Syn.* (U.S.A.) janitor.

Carey Street a street in central London, near the law courts, where the Bankruptcy Court is situated. *To be in Carey Street* (*colloq.*), to be bankrupt.

car ferry *see* auto ferry.

cargo TRANSPT. & SHIPG. the goods carried in a ship or aircraft in return for payment of freight. *Pl.* cargoes.
air cargo goods carried by air. *See under* air freight.
barrel cargo *see under* barrel.
berth cargo *see under* berth.
bulk cargo *see under* bulk.
deadweight cargo *see under* deadweight.
deck cargo *see under* deck.
general cargo cargo consisting of various kinds of goods, not of any particular kind, nor full cargoes of a single commodity.

cargo boat SHIPG. a ship built and arranged for the carriage of goods, as opposed to a passenger ship. *Syn.* cargo vessel; cargo steamer.

cargo book SHIPG. (1) a book kept by shipbrokers in which details of all shipments of cargo are recorded. (2) a book kept by the master of a coasting ship, i.e. one not visiting foreign ports, recording details of the ship's movements and of the cargoes carried. The book must be shown to the Customs at any time if demanded. Cf. transire.

cargo, discharge of *see under* discharge.

cargo insurance policy *see under* insurance policy.

cargo liner a cargo ship which makes regular voyages between certain known ports carrying cargo which is ready and waiting for loading at each port. Cf. tramp (ship).

cargo passage SHIPG. a voyage carrying cargo and therefore earning freight. *Opp.* ballast passage.

cargo syndicate MAR. INSCE. a group of Lloyd's underwriters formed for the special purpose of underwriting cargoes.

cargo ton *see* freight ton *under* ton.

cargo tonnage *see under* tonnage.

cargo underwriter MAR. INSCE. *see* cargo syndicate.

cargo-worthy clause MAR. INSCE. a clause in a cargo insurance which states that the insurance will apply only if the vessel is suitable for the safe carriage of the cargo.

carman TRANSPT. the driver or the man in charge of a car, truck, lorry, etc. carrying goods by road: *Please pay the carman.*
licensed carman a carrier who has signed a bond promising the government that goods re-

leased from customs bond for re-export will be duly exported and not dealt with otherwise.

Caroline Islands see Pacific Islands, Trust Territory of the.

car park TRANSPT. in Britain, a place where a car may be parked (left when not in use). *Syn.* (U.S.A.) parking lot.

multistorey car park one consisting of a building with several floors.

underground car park one below the level of the street.

carpetbagger (U.S.A.) COM. a disrespectful word for a person who comes to a place with so few possessions that they can easily be contained in a carpet bag for carrying tools, his intention being to take unfair advantage of local people in order to get rich or famous quickly, used esp. of a political candidate.

carr. fwd., Carr. Fwd. carriage forward.

carriage (1) TRANSPT. the act of carrying goods, esp. for payment. Inland transport and freight. *Syn.* cartage. (2) COM. & ACCTS. the cost of having goods carried from place to place; the charge made by the carrier.

carriage forward COM. means that, at the price quoted, the buyer has to pay the cost of carriage. *Abbr.* carr. fwd.

carriage free COM. means that, at the price quoted, the seller will deliver the goods using his own transport system at no extra charge to the buyer.

carriage inwards ACCTS. payments for carriage on goods bought by a business, being part of the cost price of the goods and shown on the debit side of the trading account. *Syn.* freight inwards; return freight.

carriage outwards ACCTS. payments for carriage on goods sold by a business, being part of its expenses and shown on the debit side of the profit and loss account. *Syn.* freight outwards.

carriage paid COM. means that, at the price quoted, the seller pays all carriage charges up to an agreed delivery point at the place of destination, e.g. a local railway station. From this point the buyer has to bear all charges for carriage. *Syn.* freight paid; fret payé or port payé (France). *See* Incoterms.

carriage paid home COM. means that, at the price quoted, the seller will bear the cost of carriage on the goods up to their delivery at the address of the buyer.

(3) TRANSPT. any kind of cart or machine for carrying people and goods from one place to another on land: *A horse and carriage. A carriage and pair* (of horses). *A railway carriage*, a passenger-carrying vehicle on the railway. *A horseless carriage*, one which moves by its own force, such as the early steam locomotives. (4) any part of a machine which carries or supports another, esp. a moving part: *The carriage of a typewriter*, the part which travels across the machine and which carries the platen and the paper-feed. *The carriage lever*, the handle or bar used to move the carriage of a typewriter.

carried down ACCTS. words written, usu. in shortened form, e.g. *c.d.*, at the end of an account to show a total which has had to be carried down to the beginning of the next account lower down the same page of the account book. Cf. brought down; carried forward.

carried forward ACCTS. words written, usu. in shortened form, e.g. *cd. fwd.*, at the foot of an account to show a total which has had to be carried forward to the next account or to a later page in the account book. Cf. brought forward; carried down.

carried over ACCTS. words written, usu. in shortened form: *c/o*, at the foot of an account to show that a total has been carried to the top of the next page. *Syn.* carried forward.

carrier TRANSPT. a person or organization whose business it is to carry goods from one place to another for a price called hire.

common carrier a person or organization providing a service to the public and bound to carry any goods offered by the public for collection and delivery at any places on the carrier's regular routes (lines of places visited) provided he is paid the hire charges. He is responsible for any loss of goods entrusted to him, and in Britain he has to have a public carrier's licence from the government. *See* 'A' licence.

contract carrier a carrier who arranges special contracts with a number of producers, dealers, etc. for the carriage of their goods. He may, if he wishes, refuse to carry the goods of anyone else. Cf. common carrier. *Syn.* haulier; public carrier; haulage contractor; cartage contractor.

limited carrier a carrier who carries goods only of certain kinds for hire, e.g. provides only tankers for carrying liquids; for this in Britain he must have a 'B' licence. *See* 'A' licence.

private carrier a carrier who uses goods vehicles to carry only his own goods; for this in Britain he must have a 'C' licence from the government. *See* 'A' licence.

public carrier see contract carrier *above*.

carrier bag a bag for carrying things bought while shopping. *Syn.* shopping bag.

carrier's lien TRANSPT. & LAW if the freight on the goods is payable on delivery by the consignee (buyer), the carrier has a lien on the goods, i.e. the right to hold them as security for the payment of the freight and any other charges such as storage, that may become payable. *Syn.* shipowner's lien.

carrier's risk TRANSPT. any loss of or damage to goods while being carried *at carrier's risk* must be paid for by the carrier; and for this he gets a higher rate of freight. *Syn.* company's risk. Cf. owner's risk.

carry-over STK. EXCH. the practice of delaying the settling of an account from one Account Day to the next. *See* Account, The; Account Day. *Syn.* continuation.

cartage (1) TRANSPT. the act of carrying goods by road, formerly in a hand-cart or cart drawn by a horse, but now usu. in a motor vehicle. Carriage over short distances.

cartage contractor *see* contract carrier *under* carrier.

cartage port *see* barge port *under* port.

cartage service *see* common carrier *under* carrier.

(2) TRANSPT. & ACCTS. the price paid to a carter or carrier for his services. *Syn.* carriage; freight. *Abbr.* ctge.

cartage note (*a*) a bill of charges payable for the cartage of goods. *Syn.* cart note. (*b*) a note giving written permission to a carter or carrier to remove goods which have been cleared by Customs.

carte blanche (*French*, blank paper or card) full power to decide and act on one's own judgment or to spend unlimited sums of money: *The board gave him carte blanche to negotiate the contract*, he was free to do what he thought was best. Originally a written order leaving out certain important words or names so that the person to whom it was written would use his own judgment in writing in the missing words. *Syn.* free hand.

cartel COM. & IND. (1) a group of manufacturers and dealers in the same trade who combine to form a joint selling organization, called *a syndicate*, with the aim of avoiding competition between themselves and of increasing their profits. The syndicate controls prices and output and, by allotting quotas to its members, it shares the market demand among them. (2) the word cartel is also used more generally for any association of producers and suppliers that controls prices, output and selling arrangements. Cf. trust.

international cartel (*a*) one consisting of members in different countries. (*b*) one formed for the purpose of expanding foreign trade.

cartload as much as a cart can carry: *A cartload of soil*; a measure of volume, in Britain, about half a cubic yard.

cart note *see* cartage note *under* cartage (2).

cartogram a simple diagram, sometimes coloured, based on a map and intended to show geographically certain kinds of statistical information (facts expressed in numbers): *A cartogram showing the density of population. Syn.* diagrammatic map.

cartography the production of maps and charts.

carton IND. a light, strong container made of cardboard or strawboard, usu. in the form of a box, and closed by glued tape, metal staples (pieces of wire), or bands of steel or plastic.

case (1) a strong box, usu. made of wood, enclosing something: *A packing case*, one used to protect goods while they are being carried or shipped. *A case of wine*, usu. 12 bottles. *Goods shipped in cases, not bales.* Cf. carton; bale. *Abbr.* c., *pl.* c/s. (2) the stiff cover of a book. (3) a tray holding printer's type: *Upper case* for capital letters; *lower case* for small letters. *See also* briefcase; note-case; show-case; suitcase. (4) LAW an action in a court of law: *I shall bring a case against you. You should defend the case. I shall win and you will lose the case.* (5) LAW a legal statement of facts on which a court action is based: *To prepare a case for counsel.*

case law LAW that part of English law which has been built up from past decisions made by judges and not by laws passed by Parliament. Decisions of the House of Lords are binding on all courts except itself; those of the Court of Appeal are binding on itself and on all courts except the House of Lords; and decisions of the High Court bind all courts below it. *Syn.* judicial precedent. Cf. statute law.

case of need BKG. a note written by the drawer or an endorser on a bill of exchange giving the name of a person, called *a referee in case of need*, whom the holder may ask to pay the bill if the drawee (borrower) fails to pay it. The note usu. states: *In case of need apply to* (e.g.) ---- *Bank Ltd., Glasgow*, or *In need with* ---- *Bank, Glasgow.*

case-rate discount *see under* discount.

cash *n.* money in the form of coin and bank-notes, and perh. cheques and negotiable instruments that can be quickly and easily exchanged for coin and bank-notes.

buy for cash *see* pay cash *below*.

hard cash coin and bank-notes.

pay cash to pay either in coin and notes or by cheque at the time of delivery, not taking the goods on credit. A discount may be given for cash payments. *See also* pay cash *under* pay; crossed cheque *under* cheque.

ready cash coin and bank-notes held ready for immediate use. *Syn.* ready money.

prompt cash payment in cash within a few days of delivery.

spot cash in dealings on certain commodity exchanges, the quoting of a price *spot cash* means immediate delivery and immediate payment, as distinguished from e.g. futures. In commerce generally: *Our terms are spot cash*, we do not allow any credit. *Syn.* cash on delivery. *v.* to obtain or to give cash in exchange for something, e.g. a cheque, a postal order, a money order. *Syn.* encash.

to cash a cheque (*a*) to get money in cash from a bank, by drawing (writing) a cheque made payable to *cash* or *self* and presenting it at the bank. (*b*) to obtain money in cash from a person in return for a cheque made payable to him: *Could you please cash me a cheque?* (c) to give a person money in cash in return for a cheque which he has made payable to you.

to cash in (a) to exchange for cash; to sell an investment for cash: *I must cash in these shares to pay my debts.* (b) in U.S.A., to retire from a business deal, or risky activity, like a gambler who cashes in his gaming chips (tokens) at the end of the game.

to cash in on (*colloq.*) to seize an opportunity and turn it to one's financial advantage: *Let us sell now to cash in on the present high prices.*

to cash up of shopkeepers and cashiers, to count up the cash received during the day.

cash account (1) ACCTS. in a set of accounts, that account in which are recorded all cash receipts and payments. The cash account is combined with the bank account in one book called the cash book. (2) COM. & ACCTS. in arrangements for payment by customers, a cash account is one which is settled promptly in notes or coin when presented, as distinguished from a credit account. (3) BKG. in England, a current account at a bank, but in Scotland, the account of a customer who has been allowed a cash credit.

cash accounting ACCTS. that part of the work of accounting which deals with financial records, as distinguished from other branches such as cost accounting, management accounting.

cash against documents, BKG. a means of getting payment for export shipments, by which the exporter or his agent sends the shipping documents to a bank at the port of destination (i.e. where the goods are to be unloaded) with an order to hand the documents to the consignee (buyer) or his agent only when the bill of exchange has been paid. Thus, since the consignee cannot get possession of the goods from the master of the ship without presenting the bill of lading (which is one of the shipping documents) he must first pay the bill of exchange. *Abbr.* c.a.d., or c.v.d. *Syn.* documents against presentation; documents against cash; documents against payment.

cash agent, INSCE. an insurance agent who is not allowed credit by the insurance companies he represents, i.e. he has to pay premiums before the policies are issued to him. Cf. account agent; accredited agent; credit agent.

cash and carry, COM. a wholesaler, esp. in the grocery trade, who sells goods at a discount on condition that buyers pay cash and themselves collect and carry away the goods, no credit being given. *A cash-and-carry store.*

cash at bank BKG. & ACCTS. (1) money held by a bank to the credit of a current account of a customer. (2) a heading on the assets side of a balance sheet, usu. next to a heading *cash in hand*, or combined with it thus: *cash in hand and at bank.* Cf. cash in hand.

cash balance, *see under* balance, *n.* (1).

cash basis, TAXN. in Britain, the basis on which some taxpayers carrying on a profession or vocation are taxed, i.e. the tax will be based on cash received. Cf. earnings basis.

cash book ACCTS. a part of a set of accounts which is both a book of prime entry in which is recorded all cash received and paid (cash here including cheques and money in the bank) and at the same time a ledger account. Sometimes it may for convenience be divided into two, a *cash received book* and a *cash paid book.* A *two-column cash book* has columns for cash and bank on both the debit side and the credit side. A *three-column cash book* has an extra column for discounts.

cash bonus (1) STK. EXCH. a cash payment to a shareholder who has chosen to accept cash instead of receiving bonus shares in a company which is making a bonus issue to capitalize some of its profits. Cf. share bonus. (2) INSCE. a bonus on a life policy paid in cash at the time it is earned or declared. Cf. reversionary bonus.

cash-box ACCTS. & FIN. a strong metal box with a good lock for storing cash.

cash budget MAN. & ACCTS. a financial statement intended to show the management of a business the expected cash position at the end of each of a series of equal periods ahead, e.g. weekly, monthly, quarterly. For each period the statement shows the probable opening figure of cash, the expected cash receipts and payments and the closing figure of cash. Cash here includes not only notes and coins but also amounts in current and deposit accounts at the bank. Cf. funds-flow statement. *Syn.* cash flow; cash forecast.

cash capital STK. EXCH. capital consisting of shares issued for cash, as distinguished from shares issued for a consideration other than cash, e.g. vendor's shares. *Syn.* cash shares.

cash card *see* cash dispenser.

cash column ACCTS. in the cash book, the column in which cash amounts are entered, as distinguished from the bank column. *See* cash book.

cash credit BKG. an arrangement made by banks in Scotland by which a customer may draw on a special credit up to an agreed sum against the security of a *bond of credit* signed by the debtor customer and by one or more sureties called cautioners.

cash crop AGR. one grown mainly for sale in order to obtain cash, as distinguished from a subsistence crop, i.e. one grown for the farmer's own consumption. *Syn.* ready-money crop.

cash department ACCTS. in a business organization, the department responsible for looking after money. The cashier or chief cashier, a highly-trusted officer, is at its head. It receives and pays cash and cheques, records all deals in the cash book and bill book, pays money into and draws money out of the account at the bank, and holds the petty cash. To prevent dishonesty, the cashier and his staff are normally not allowed to make entries in any of the ledger accounts except the cash book and bill book. Cf. cash desk. *Syn.* counting-house.

cash-deposit ratio *see* cash ratio.

cash desk COM. a desk at which a person, usu. called a cashier, receives money from customers in a shop, restaurant, etc. *Please pay at the cash desk.* Cf. cash department. *Syn.* (esp. U.S.A.) checkout.

cash discount COM. an allowance, or reduction of the price, offered or given by a seller for prompt payment by the buyer: *Our terms: 2½% cash discount for payment within seven days. Syn.* settlement discount. Cf. trade discount.

cash dispenser BKG. a machine from which the customer of a bank can obtain cash in banknotes up to a certain value at any time of day or night. The machines are operated by putting a special numbered card, called a *cash card*, into the machine and giving a personal number by pressing numbered keys. *Syn.* (U.S.A.) cashomat.

cash down COM. paid for in cash immediately the goods are delivered, no credit being allowed. *Syn.* cash on delivery; collect on delivery; spot cash.

cash float ACCTS. *see* imprest system; float (1) and (2).

cash flow ACCTS· & FIN. (1) the amount of cash made by a business during a specified period which it can use for investment; it can be calculated from the accounts of a business and is a means of measuring its financial strength. To the net profit (after taxation) are added depreciation and any sums put to reserves; the resulting sum, after taking away the expenses of running the business shows the ability of the business to earn cash. *See also* funds-flow statement. *Syn.* cash generation; flow of funds; funds flow. Cf. discounted cash flow. (2) the information provided by a cash budget.

cash forecast *see* cash budget.

cash fund FIN. a type of unit trust, the managers of which must use cash paid by new holders of units in the trust fund to buy new shares, i.e. the managers may not buy new securities on their own account and then arrange for them to be appropriated to the trust fund. Thus the managers cannot themselves make a profit (or a loss) on such deals. Cf. appropriation fund.

cash generation *see* cash flow.

cashier COM. & ACCTS. (1) in the accounts department of a business, the employee who is responsible for the care of all money received and paid, both in cash and in cheques; issuing receipts; recording all cash deals in the cash

book(s) and all bills of exchange receivable and payable in the bill book(s); paying money and cheques into the bank and, when necessary, drawing cash out of the bank; and taking charge of the petty cash. (2) any person employed to receive cash at the cash desk, e.g. in a shop or restaurant or at a checkout in a supermarket.

petty cashier a junior cashier who makes small payments from the petty cash and enters them in the petty cash book.

(3) BKG. an employee of a bank whose work is to receive and pay out money. *Syn.* bank clerk; teller.

cashier's cheque *see under* cheque.

cash in hand ACCTS. money held by a business in the form of notes and coin as distinguished from money in a bank account.

cash-in-transit policy *see under* insurance policy.

cash market *see under* market.

cash memo COM. a memorandum or note, usu. handwritten on a printed form, given by a shopkeeper to a customer as a record of the sale for cash of an article or service and as an acknowledgment of the receipt of the price paid.

cashomat (U.S.A.) *see* cash dispenser.

cash on delivery COM. a condition made by a supplier when advertising his goods, meaning that he will send goods which have been ordered by post if the buyer agrees to pay the postman or carman at the time of delivery the full price of the goods and any delivery charges. *Abbr.* C.O.D. *Syn.* (U.S.A.) collect on delivery; payment on receipt of goods.

cash order *see under* order, *n.* (4).

cash paid book *see* cash book.

cash, petty *see* petty cash.

cash price COM. the price at which the seller is willing to sell on condition that payment is made immediately. Cf. hire-purchase price.

cash ratio BKG. the relation between a bank's total cash reserves of notes, coin, etc. and its total deposit liabilities, i.e. the amount it owes to its customers, esp. on current and deposit accounts. Cash reserves must be held to meet the demands of depositors, but since these reserves earn no interest and so are unproductive, bankers try to keep them as small as possible, usu. at about 8% of deposit liabilities. *See* fractional banking. Cf. advances ratio; liquidity ratio. *Syn.* cash-deposit ratio; reserve ratio.

cash received book *see* cash book.

cash refund annuity *see under* insurance policy.

cash register COM. a special machine used in shops, etc. with a drawer for receiving money, which shows the value of each sale, at the same time recording the sale and keeping a running total of sales made, and sometimes calculating change. It may also print the details of the sale on a strip of paper which is given to the customer as a receipt.

cash sale COM. a deal in which the seller is willing to sell at a certain price on condition that the buyer pays immediately. Cf. credit sale; hire-purchase agreement. *See also* cash price.

cash settlement STK. EXCH. the condition on which a deal in gilt-edged securities is usu. done; the buyer will pay on the next day and not on the next Stock Exchange Settlement Day.

cash shares *see* cash capital; *also under* share.

cash statement ACCTS. a statement prepared by a cashier each day to show that the cash he holds (*cash in hand*) is right, or if it is wrong, to show by what sum it is short or in excess.

cash surrender *see* surrender value.

cash voucher ACCTS. & COM. a written or printed record of money paid in cash for goods and services, e.g. for an article bought for cash in a shop; also a receipt for a stated sum of money. In a business these vouchers are numbered and carefully kept as proof of sums spent, the voucher number being recorded in support of each entry in the account books. *Syn.* receipt.

cash with order COM. a condition made by a supplier when advertising his goods, meaning that he will only supply if he receives payment in some acceptable form with the order and that he will not allow any credit, nor will he send the goods *on approval* (to be paid for later if approved). *Abbr.* c.w.o. *Syn.* payment with order.

casino a building or hall where games of chance are played for money (gambling).

cask COM. a barrel-like container for liquids, used esp. in the ale and beer trades, and of various sizes: a butt or pipe, 108 to 126 gals.; a hogshead, 51½ or 54 gals.; a kilderkin, 18 gals.; a firkin, 9 gals.; a pin or keg, 4½ gals. Used also in the wine trade. *Abbr.* ck.; csk.

Cassel Gustav (1866–1945), Swedish economist, Professor of Political Economy at Stockholm University (1904–33), author of *Theory of Social Economy* and other works. He is best known for his studies of the trade cycle, the theory of interest, and for his work in international monetary economics.

cast *v.* (1) ACCTS. (*with* up) to add up (a column of figures). *Syn.* to total; to tot up (*colloq.*).

cross-cast to add together figures set out horizontally.

casting error a mistake made in adding figures, as distinguished from a posting error. (2) SHIPG. to throw over the side.

cast anchor to anchor a boat or ship.

cast away (*a*) to throw (cargo, etc.) into the sea, esp. in a situation of great danger. *Syn.* to jettison. (*b*) to be shipwrecked or abandoned at sea.

casting vote the right to an extra and deciding vote given to the chairman or other person

officially in charge of a meeting, and used only when the voting for and against a proposal is equally divided.

casual (1) happening by chance; accidental; not intentional.

casual profits profits made by chance events, e.g. from an unplanned and unexpected order or from a rise in prices.

casual vacancy an office or position in employment the holder of which has left unexpectedly and which now needs filling.

(2) irregular, not continuous.

casual labour workers employed only irregularly, i.e. whenever needed and not continuously.

casual leave *see under* leave.

casualty INSCE. an accident or chance happening, esp. one which causes loss or damage.

casualty insurance *see under* insurance, classes and kinds of.

casualty report service MAR. INSCE. & SHIPG. a service provided by Lloyd's to anyone willing to pay for it, giving details of casualties, i.e. accidents to ships and cargoes, immediately the information is received. These details are published in Lloyd's *Weekly Casualty Reports*.

cat. catalogue; category.

catallactics ECON. the study of exchange of goods and services; thus another and more exact word for economics or political economy.

catalog *see* catalogue.

catalogue COM. a list, usu. in the form of a book, of goods for sale, with prices, or of objects shown, e.g. in a collection or an exhibition, or of things stored or held, e.g. of books in a library or documents in archives. *Syn.* (U.S.A.) catalog.

classified catalogue one which groups things of the same class together, e.g. in a publisher's catalogue books on the same subject or in the same language.

descriptive catalogue one which contains descriptions in some detail of the items listed.

illustrated catalogue one with pictures.

catalogue price *see* list price *under* price.

catastrophe an event causing ruin or great suffering. The types of catastrophe usu. recognized by insurers are: earthquake, fire, flood, riot and various kinds of storm. *Catastrophe risk*, a risk of very heavy losses if a catastrophe happens.

catch a cold STK. EXCH. (*colloq.*) to lose money in an unprofitable business affair: *Having caught a cold in the recent bank crisis, investors are cautious.*

catch-crop AGR. a crop grown by catching the opportunity to use land for a short time, e.g. while it is not being used for main crops, or where a main crop has failed, or by making use of ground between rows of other crops. Cf. cash crop.

catchpenny COM. any article which, by catching (attracting) the eye of a customer also catches his money. Such articles are always cheap and, although attractive, are usu. of poor quality, made only to sell quickly, and of no lasting value.

caterer (1) COM. a person or organization who, as a business, provides meals and drink, esp. in places of amusement. (2) a person employed to arrange the supply of food and drink in large organizations, e.g. hospitals, schools, universities, hotels, etc.

cattle (1) animals of the bovine race (the ox), used generally of cows, bullocks, etc. kept on farms. (2) LAW in law, the word cattle includes: asses (donkeys), goats, horses, mules, pigs and sheep as well as bovine animals.

caught short see under short.

cauri the fractional currency unit of Guinea. 100 cauris = 1 syli.

cause LAW an action in the courts. Syn. civil proceeding.

cause of action the facts which, together, make a good reason in law for bringing an action in the courts.

commercial cause see under commercial.

cautioner LAW a Scottish word for a surety. See cash credit.

caution money COM. (1) money deposited in advance with some person or organization, e.g. a landlord, a university, as security for good behaviour. (2) money paid as security for proper performance of duties under a contract. (3) a deposit of money by a person proposing to buy, e.g. a house, to show his good faith and his intention to complete the deal. (4) LAW the repayment of the expenses of a person called as a witness in a court action. Syn. conduct money.

caveat LAW (Latin, let him beware) a warning notice given to officers of the law that the caveator, i.e. the person giving the warning, has an interest and claims the right to be given official notice before certain steps can be taken by other parties which might affect that interest. To enter a caveat, e.g. at the Probate Registry, so that no one can be officially made the legal representative of a dead person without due notice to the caveator.

caveat emptor LAW & COM. (Latin, let the buyer beware) an ancient common-law rule that the buyer of goods must be careful to find out for himself any faults in them, or suffer the results; and that the seller (the vendor) is not bound to make these known, though he too must take care not to be guilty of misrepresentation (giving false information or a misleading description).

Cayman Islands a British colony in the Caribbean Sea, pop. 11,000 approx. (1971); capital, Georgetown; language, English; currency unit, the Cayman Island dollar (Cay.I.$), divided into 100 cents.

C.B.A. cost-benefit analysis.

C.B.D. cash before delivery; central business district.

C.B.I. Confederation of British Industries (formerly F.B.I.)

C.C. civil commotion; collision course.

c.c. carbon copy.

C.C.A. current cost accounting.

C.D. certificate of deposit; Corps Diplomatique or Diplomatic Corps.

C/D. consular declaration.

c.d. cum (with) dividend.

c/d., C/d. carried down.

cd. fwd., Cd/Fwd. carried forward.

CDN Canada's international vehicle-registration letters.

C.D.V. current domestic value.

C.E. Council of Europe.

c.e. caveat emptor.

cedi the standard currency unit of Ghana, divided into 100 pesewas.

ceiling an upper limit placed on a price or quantity: A ceiling on incomes/bank loans.

price-ceiling the highest price allowed by law, or that can be obtained in the market. A ceiling price. Cf. price-floor.

wage-ceiling the highest wage that an employer is allowed by law to pay a particular class of worker when income-controls are in operation.

cellarage COM. (1) charges for storing goods esp. wine in a cellar (an underground room or space). (2) space in a cellar for storing goods.

Celsius a scale of temperature in which water freezes at 0° and boils at 100°. Cf. Fahrenheit. Syn. centigrade.

census an official count of the number of people in a country, where they live and how they are divided into different groups such as sexes, ages, professions and employments, etc. and known as a population census. Such a census is taken every five years in some countries, every ten years in others. A large amount of useful statistical information is thus obtained.

distribution census an official count, made usu. every five years, of the wholesale and retail trades and certain service industries, giving details of sales, numbers of persons employed, etc.

production census an official count of the output and other details of all the main manufacturing industries, made every three or four years, with a sample census in the years between.

traffic census an official count of the number and types of road vehicles using given stretches of road, to provide information for planning new roads.

cent in various currencies, a coin of low value, one-hundredth part of a dollar. In Malta, one-hundredth part of a pound. Abbr. c. or ct. Sign: ¢.

cent a hundred (*Latin*: centum).
per cent (%) so much for each hundred: *A commission of 5%*, £5 for every £100 of value. *An insurance premium of £1.50 per cent*, £1.50 for every £100 of the insured value. *Cent per cent*, one hundred per cent, i.e. £100 for each £100 of value.
cental COM. a measure of weight, esp. of corn, being 100 lb avoirdupois. (Now rarely used.)
centavo the fractional unit of several currencies, being always one-hundredth part of a larger unit, e.g. of: a cordoba in Nicaragua; a colón in El Salvador; a cruziero in Brazil; an escudo in Angola, the Cape Verde Islands, Guinea-Bissau, Mozambique, Portugal, and São Tomé & Principe; a lempira in Honduras; a peso in Argentina, Bolivia, Colombia, Cuba, the Dominican Republic, Mexico and the Philippines; a quetzal in Guatemala; a sol in Peru; and a sucre in Ecuador.
centesimo the fractional unit of several currencies, being always one-hundredth part of a large unit, e.g. of: a balboa in Panama; a lira in Italy; and of a peso in Uruguay. *Pl.* centesimi or centesimos.
centi- the *prefix* in the metric system meaning one-hundredth; thus, e.g. a centimetre is one-hundredth of a metre, and a centilitre is one-hundredth of a litre.
centigrade *see* Celsius.
centime in various countries, a small unit of currency, being one-hundredth part of a franc.
centimo in various countries, a small unit of currency, being one-hundredth part of a peseta in Spain and Equatorial Guinea, of a bolivar in Venezuela, of a colón in Costa Rica and El Salvador, and of a guarani in Paraguay.
Central African Republic a landlocked country in central Africa, pop. 2.6 million approx. (1973); capital, Bangui, pop. 300,000 approx.; languages, French and Sangho; currency unit, the C.F.A. franc (CFA Fr.), divided into 100 centimes. Member, French Community; O.A.U.; O.C.A.M.M.; Associate, E.E.C.
central bank BKG. a bank officially appointed by law to work closely with the government of the country and to perform the duties of issuing and managing the country's currency, holding its gold reserves, controlling the volume of credit and acting as banker to the government and to the commercial and other banks. The central bank in Britain is the Bank of England; in the U.S.A., the Federal Reserve System; in France, the Banque de France; in Italy, the Banca d'Italia, etc.
central business district (U.S.A.) COM. the heart of any American city, where most of its commercial activities take place. *Syn.* downtown (U.S.A. *colloq.*). *Abbr.* C.B.D.
Central European Time the local time one hour ahead of Greenwich Mean Time, adopted by

international agreement by the countries on the continent of Europe lying in a zone roughly between the meridians of 7½° W. and 22½° E. The zone includes Spain (but not Portugal) in the west, and Poland (but not Finland and Greece) in the east. In this zone, when it is noon (12.00 hrs.) G.M.T., local time or Central European Time is 13.00 hrs. *See* time-zones.
centralization the placing of a high degree of control with officials at the centre of an organization, e.g. the government of a country or the management of a business concern, leaving little freedom of action to officials at local levels. *Syn.* centralism. *Opp.* decentralization; dispersal; dispersion.
central processor COMP. in a computer, the centre of the machine, where the control unit, memory and the arithmetic unit are placed.
central registry *see under* registry.
Central Statistical Office ECON. & FIN. a British government department responsible for collecting, sorting, arranging and publishing detailed information in tables of figures relating to the national economy. One of its most important publications is *National Income and Expenditure*, commonly known as the blue book, which appears annually and gives detailed figures for the past ten years. *Abbr.* C.S.O.
Central Time a time-zone in North America, six hours behind Greenwich Mean Time, one hour behind Eastern Time.
centre (1) COM. & FIN. a place which is important because it attracts some special activity: *A centre of trade/commerce. A business/commercial/financial/shopping centre. See also* central business district. (2) TOUR. a place which attracts tourists because it provides for some special interest or sport: *A ski centre; a yachting centre.*
cereal *see* corn.
cert. certificate.
certain (1) LAW fixed and settled without a doubt: *A sum certain*, a fixed amount of money e.g. £500, not 'about £500', nor '£500 plus freight as charged'. (2) BKG. & FIN. in foreign currency dealings, *to quote certain exchange*, or a *certain rate*, is to quote a price in a home currency for providing foreign currency at a future date, thus fixing the exact exchange rate in advance. *Syn.* fixed exchange; direct exchange.
certain annuity *see* annuity certain *under* insurance policy.
certain rate *see* certain (2).
certificate a document signed usu. by a person in authority (in a position of control or power) formally declaring that a certain fact is true. For example birth, death and marriage certificates are issued by the registrar and are declared by him to be a true copy of the entry in the register of births, deaths and marriages. *See* share certificate.

certificated bankrupt *see under* bankrupt.

certificate of analysis IND. & COM. a document signed by a public analyst declaring officially that the stated composition of a product is true and correct.

certificate of damage INSCE. one given by a port official declaring that certain goods have been landed in a damaged state from a ship. The document is needed by the importer to support his claim on an insurer or the shipowners.

certificate of deposit BKG. a document given by a bank to a depositor who agrees to leave a stated sum of money with the bank for a fixed period. Such certificates, being payable to bearer or to order, are attractive to some investors because they can be easily negotiated. A special form of time deposit. *Abbr.* C.D. Cf. memorandum of deposit.

dollar C.D. a certificate issued by a London branch of an American bank to a depositor who has placed a certain sum in dollars with the bank's New York office for an agreed period, usu. of one to twelve months. The bank repays the amount, with interest, in dollars in New York.

sterling C.D. a certificate issued by certain banks in Britain to a depositor, usu. a large institutional investor, who has placed a sum of at least £50,000 for a fixed period of from three to five years at a rate of interest a little below that for fixed deposits.

Certificate of Incorporation LAW a document issued by the Registrar of Companies to an association of persons forming a new limited liability company, declaring that all the provisions of the Companies Acts have been met and that the company has been incorporated. Until this certificate has been given, the company does not legally exist and cannot start trading. *See* incorporation. *Syn.* Corporation Charter (U.S.A.).

certificate of inscription STK. EXCH. in the case of inscribed stock, a document noting or acknowledging that the holder's name and the amount of stock he owns have been recorded at the Bank of England. *See* inscribed stock *under* stock.

certificate of insurance INSCE. a short document issued by an insurance company to an insured party, declaring that an insurance contract exists, that it covers the insured against certain stated risk(s) and mentions the essential conditions of the policy. A *marine certificate of insurance* relating to goods shipped by sea forms part of the shipping documents. A *motor-vehicle certificate of insurance* must be carried by the driver of any vehicle while using the roads, as proof that the vehicle is insured.

certificate of inward clearance *see* jerque note.

certificate of manufacture COM. (1) a document signed by an exporter declaring that goods have been manufactured to the order of the overseas customer and await shipment. (2) a document signed by an exporter in Britain declaring that goods being shipped or about to be shipped are of British manufacture. *Syn.* certificate of origin.

certificate of misfortune *see* certificated bankrupt *under* bankrupt.

certificate of origin COM. a formal declaration stating the name of the country in which certain goods, usu. those covered by an export invoice, have been manufactured. Such certificates are signed either by the exporter or by an organization officially appointed to do so, e.g. a chamber of commerce, according to the demands of the importer's country. *Syn.* certificate of manufacture.

certificate of posting COM. a signed paper given by the Post Office as proof that a letter or parcel has been posted by ordinary, i.e. not registered, post at the time and place stamped on the paper to a particular addressee.

certificate of pratique SHIPG. a paper signed by the health officer of a port to the master of a ship allowing him to use the port provided that he either shows a clean bill of health or obeys the quarantine rules. The ship is then said to be admitted to pratique.

certificate of registry *see under* registry.

Certificate of Secondary Education (C.S.E.) a certificate given to persons who have passed a course of general education at a secondary school in Britain, but at a lower level than the Ordinary level of the General Certificate of Education (G.C.E.).

certificate of transfer *see under* transfer.

certificate to commence business STK. EXCH. & FIN. a document given to a public limited company declaring that the company has completed certain legal formalities and is free to begin trading.

certified accountant ACCTS. & MAN. in Britain, a member of the Association of Certified Accountants either as a Fellow (F.C.C.A.) or Associate (A.C.C.A.) and so qualified by law to be an auditor of a company. Cf. chartered accountant. In U.S.A., the equivalent is a certified public accountant (C.P.A.), a member of the Institute of Certified Public Accountants who holds a licence from the State to practise accounting.

certified cheque *see under* cheque.

certified copy LAW a copy of a document which has on it a formal declaration signed by an official that it is a true copy. *Syn.* attested copy.

certified invoice *see under* invoice.

certified public accountant *see* certified accountant.

certified transfer *see* transfer.

certify to declare formally that a certain stated fact is true: *I/We hereby certify that...*

cert. inv. certified invoice.

cess TAXN. a special form of tax, esp. one of a local nature or applying to a particular product: *A rubber cess; a tea cess; the Irish land cess.*

cesser LAW the ending, e.g. of a lease after the agreed number of years, or of a mortgage when the last of the payments is made.

cession LAW & COM. the act of giving up property, esp. when done willingly, as by a debtor to his creditors.

cestui que trust LAW a legal expression meaning the person or object for whose benefit, i.e. interest and advantage, a trust has been set up. *See* beneficiary.

C.E.T. Central European Time.

Ceylon *see* Sri Lanka.

c.f., c/f carried forward; cubic feet; cost and freight.

Cf., cf. compare (*Latin:* conferatur).

C.F. compensation fee.

C.F.A. Communauté Financière Africaine.

c.f.i., C.F.I. cost, freight and insurance (*see* c.i.f.).

C.F.P. Communauté Financière du Pacifique.

cge. carriage.

C.G.H. Cape of Good Hope (S. Africa).

cgo. cargo.

C.G.T. Confédération Générale du Travail (*French,* General Confederation of Labour).

CH Switzerland's international vehicle-registration letters.

C.H. Clearing House; Custom(s) House.

ch. chain (22 yards); chapter; charge(s).

ch. fwd. charges forward.

ch. pd. charges paid.

ch. ppd. charges prepaid.

c.h. central heating.

c.h.w. constant hot water.

Chad a republic in west-central Africa, pop. 4 million approx. (1974); capital, N'Djamena, formerly Fort Lamy, pop. 130,000 approx.; languages, French, Arabic and tribal languages; currency unit, the C.F.A. franc (CFA Fr.), divided into 100 centimes. Member, O.A.U.; F.C.; O.C.A.M.M.; Associate, E.E.C.

chaf. chafage.

chafage INSCE. & TRANSPT. damage to goods caused by chafing, i.e. rubbing against other cargo, etc. during the journey or voyage.

chain a unit of length on the ground. When used by surveyors, a surveyor's or Gunter's chain 66 ft long; and by engineers, 100 ft long.

chain of command *see* line of command.

chain of distribution COM. the line of persons, each like a link in a chain, who play a part in distributing, i.e. in sending out, supplying in all directions, the products of manufacturers to the retailers or shopkeepers who sell them to the public. The line may well be: manufacturer — wholesaler — agent — exporter — shipper — importer — agent — shopkeeper — public. *Syn.* channels of distribution.

chain-store COM. one of a group of shops under the same ownership and management, all selling more or less the same range of goods at the same prices and being supplied from a central warehouse. *Syn.* multiple store/ shop.

chair the position held by the chairman, the highest officer of an organization or the person elected or appointed to be president at a formal meeting: *Mr J. Smith is now in the chair of Smith Transport Ltd., he is now the chairman. Mr T. Jones took the chair at the committee meeting. You must always address the chair,* at a formal meeting you must speak only to the chairman and not to other persons.

chairman (1) man or woman in charge of, president at, a formal meeting. His duties are to keep order, to see that the rules are obeyed, to prevent talk that has nothing to do with the subject and to see that voting on motions and amendments is properly done. He has certain powers, e.g. to decide and settle arguments, make disorderly persons leave, and may have a casting vote to use when voting is equal. (2) the chairman of the board of directors. *Syn.* (U.S.A.) president.

chaldron a dry measure used for coal: 36 bushels.

chalk up COM. (*colloq.*) to record: *They chalked up big sales last month. Chalk it up,* make a note of it; add it to what I already owe you.

challenge ACCTS. as part of an audit and to uncover any dishonesty, to make a careful check of the cash and securities held in the charge of employees of a business.

chamber of commerce COM. an association of local businessmen, esp. employers, and including manufacturers, merchants and traders, with the aim of discussing subjects of common interest, of improving trading conditions and of encouraging business generally. Cf. chamber of trade. *See also* Association of British Chambers of Commerce.

Chamber of Shipping SHIPG. a combination of British shipowners' associations.

chamber of trade COM. an association of local traders formed to discuss matters of common concern and to act generally in the interests of its members. Cf. chamber of commerce.

chambers LAW (1) part of a law courts building consisting of rooms where judges attend to legal business which does not have to be done in court: *A judge sitting in chambers,* not sitting in court. (2) in England, the private office(s) of a barrister.

champerty LAW the offence of interfering in legal actions that do not concern one; as e.g. a person who, having no interest in a lawsuit and without lawful reason, encourages a party, perh. by supplying money, to bring or defend, the suit, in order to gain some share of any damages that may be offered. *See also* maintenance (4).

chance n. (1) the probability of a particular event happening: *The chances are in favour of/against a profitable outcome. There is an even chance of success*, the chances for and against are equal. *By chance*, unexpected. *He has an eye to the main chance*, looks for any opportunity to make money. *To take a/one's chance*, to trust one's luck in running a risk. *We do not stand a chance*, there is no possibility of our succeeding. (2) COM. the element of risk always present in certain business activities, and accepted by the entrepreneur.
v. COM. (*colloq.*) to accept a risk: *To chance it*, to risk it. *To chance one's arm/luck*, to attempt to do something in spite of the probability of failure.
adj. unexpected; not regular: *A chance gain, a chance meeting.*

Chancellor of the Exchequer the British cabinet minister in charge of the country's financial affairs. He prepares the yearly budget and presents it to the House of Commons, and guides the Treasury and the Bank of England in controlling the monetary system. *See* budget; Exchequer.

Chancery, Court of LAW in Britain, the Chancery Division of the High Court of Justice, the court of equity ruled over by the Lord Chancellor. It deals with all civil (not criminal) cases except probate, divorce and Admiralty cases.
ward in chancery a (usu. young) person placed by order of the Court under the care of the Lord Chancellor, e.g. if the parents are dead or missing.

chancy (*colloq.*) risky; uncertain: *A chancy affair/business/venture/investment.*

chandler COM. originally one who made candles, but later a trader; a dealer: *A corn-chandler*, one who deals in corn. *Ship's chandler, see under* ship.

change n. COM. (1) money in the form of coins: *Please give me change for a pound note*, coins to the value of £1.
change machine one that delivers coins of low value in exchange for a larger coin, e.g. ten 5p coins for one 50p coin.
small change coins of low value: *You will need some small change for the journey.*
(2) money returned to a buyer by the seller as the difference between the price of the goods sold and a larger sum given by the buyer, e.g. if I buy goods for 60p and pay with a £1 note I am given change for the difference of 40p. *No change given*, customers must pay the exact amount, e.g. the exact fare on entering a bus.
v. BKG. & COM. to exchange one thing for another: *To change a traveller's cheque*, to exchange it for money in the local currency. *To change a £1 note*, to exchange it for coins. *To change my pounds into rupees. To get no change out of someone* (*colloq.*), to fail to get

help from him; also to fail to get an advantage over him. *To change hands*, to pass, or be passed, from one person to another, esp. from one owner to another. *To ring the changes* (*colloq.*), to put false money in place of good.

Change STK. EXCH. & COM. a meeting-place for merchants. (Sometimes wrongly written 'Change.) An exchange, esp. a stock exchange: *On Change*, on the Stock Exchange.

channel SHIPG. (1) a waterway fit for the passage of ships or boats in a river, harbour or through shallow waters at sea; such channels are usu. marked by buoys or beacons. (2) a narrow area of water between two land areas, e.g. the English Channel, the Bristol Channel. *Syn.* strait. (3) AGR. a canal for irrigation (bringing water for growing crops). (4) MAN. (*fig.*) in management and administration, the course through which commands are given, business is carried on, and goods and supplies are obtained: *We get our supplies through the usual channel(s)*, from our usual supplier(s).

Channel, The the English Channel, between Britain and France.

Channel Ports the ports on the English Channel along the south coast of England and the north coast of France, esp. those which are used by regular cross-channel ferry-boat services. They are: in England, Dover, Folkestone, Newhaven, Portsmouth, Southampton, Weymouth, Plymouth; and in France, Dunkirk, Calais, Boulogne, Dieppe, Le Havre, Cherbourg, St. Malo, Roscoff. Cf. Cinque Ports.

Channel Tunnel TRANSPT. a proposed railway tunnel about 20 miles long under the English Channel between England and France. *Syn.* (*colloq.*) Chunnel.

chapel IND. REL. an association of workers (like a branch of a trade union) in a printing works, whose president is called the father of the chapel and whose position is much the same as that of a shop steward.

char *see* charwoman.

character (1) MAN. a formal description, by an employer, of the working ability, behaviour and moral nature of a former employee: *I can give him an excellent character. Syn.* reference. (2) SHIPG. a figure consisting of a number and letters which together state the classification of a ship, e.g. 100 A1. *See* classification societies; Lloyd's Register of Shipping. (3) COMP. a number, letter or special sign (e.g. $, %, *, etc.) used in forming the machine-language by which a computer is controlled.

charge n. (1) a responsibility, esp. for controlling or caring for somebody or something: *To take charge/to be in charge/of persons or things*, to be responsible for. (2) ACCTS. a debit: *A charge on the profit and loss account.* (3) COM. a sum of money that has to be paid as a price, esp. for services: *What is your charge for a haircut/cleaning a coat?* An *admission charge*, for admitting, allowing someone to enter. *A delivery/service/collection charge.* Cf. price. (4) COM. & IND. an expense or liability which a business has to bear, such as rent, rates, taxes, interest, e.g. on debentures and mortgages: *An overhead charge is part of the cost of running the business.* (5) LAW in the law of property, the right of a creditor to be paid from a stated fund or accumulation of money set aside for a particular purpose, such as money received from selling the property. A mortgage. (6) LAW in criminal law, a formal act accusing a person of a crime. *He faces a charge of stealing. A copy of the written charge is given to the accused person.* (7) LAW the address by a judge to a jury directing them on points of law and giving his opinion on the value of what the witnesses have stated in court.

charge account (U.S.A.) COM. & ACCTS. an arrangement between a supplier, esp. a retail store or shop, and a customer, by which the customer is allowed to pay at the end of an agreed period, e.g. one month, for all the goods that he has bought (and that have therefore been charged to his account) during that period. *Syn.* (Britain) credit account.

Charge Certificate *see* title-deeds *under* deed.

chargee LAW a person who has power to force a debtor to pay a debt which is charged, e.g. a mortgagee.

charge hand INDUS. the leader of a group of workers, but below the rank of foreman.

charge nurse a nurse in charge of a section of a hospital.

charges, bank *see* bank charges.

charges forward TRANSPT. charges will be paid by the consignee (buyer).

charges on assets LAW & STK. EXCH. in a limited company, debts owing to creditors, e.g. debenture-holders, who have as security the right to receive payment from the company's assets if the company fails to pay the debt when due. *See* register of charges.

fixed charge the right of the creditor is limited to certain stated assets only, e.g. a building.

floating charge the creditor's right extends to all the company's assets.

prior charge *see under* prior.

charges prepaid TRANSPT. charges paid by the consignor (seller).

charges register LAW in Britain, part of the main records of the Land Registry. A detailed record of the charges, e.g. mortgages and restrictive covenants, which exist in relation to a particular property. Cf. register of charges.

charges, register of *see under* register.

charging lien *see under* lien; *also* charging order.

charging order LAW an order given by a court of

law to a judgment creditor charging (mortgaging) the assets of the judgment debtor so long as the debt is unpaid. If after six months the debt remains unpaid, the creditor may take possession of the assets to satisfy the debt and the interest on it. *See* charges on assets.

charitable trust LAW a trust for relieving poverty, for the advancement of education or religion, or for the good of the public in other ways. Such trusts do not have to pay income tax but in most cases must be registered with and guided by the Charity Commissioners, a body of persons responsible to Parliament. *Syn.* public trust; charity.

charity (1) kindness and generosity to those persons who are poor or are in need of help. *Charity begins at home*, provide well for your family before you give money to others. (2) an organization formed for the purpose of giving help to those who are poor or for doing good to the public in other ways. *See* charitable trust.

Charity Commissioners *see* charitable trust.

chart (1) SHIPG. a map, esp. of the sea and coastlines with depths of water to guide sailors: *An Admiralty chart*, an official map of sea areas published by the British Government. *Syn.* sea-chart. (2) COM. & MAN. a diagram or graph, used as a method of presenting information, esp. of figures, e.g. movements in the prices of commodities or shares, progress of work, etc. *Syn.* graph.

bar chart a diagram consisting of a series of bars or thick lines set on a base line, each of a length proportional to a given value, making it possible to compare the values of different items in a group. *Syn.* band chart; histogram; staircase chart.

flow chart *see under* flow.

organization chart a diagram showing the work and responsibilities of each of the various parts of an organization and how the parts are related to each other and to outside organizations. *Syn.* table of organization.

pie chart a circular chart divided into sectors (the area between two straight lines drawn from the centre of a circle to the circumference), the size of each sector being in proportion to a given value (like slices of a circular pie or cake); used esp. to show how various percentages make up the total of a given group of values. *Syn.* circular chart; sector chart; pie diagram.

progress chart a horizontal bar chart, usu. consisting of two lines of different colour or thickness, the first showing budgeted or planned progress through a period of time, the second showing the actual progress.

charter *n.* (1) LAW a document by a state formally giving certain special rights and powers to a person or organization, e.g. the royal charter given by the King or Queen to a chartered company such as the British, French and Dutch East India Companies and the British South Africa Company. See Chartered Bank. (2) (U.S.A.) the articles of a corporation. Certificate of Incorporation; Corporation. See Charter.

charter member one who has been a member of an organization since it was first incorporated.

(3) SHIPG. & TRANSPT. a contract by which an owner agrees to hire a ship or aircraft to a person or organization called the charterer. The document containing the conditions of the contract is called a charter-party.

bareboat charter a time charter under which the shipowner hires only the ship, leaving the charterer to employ the master and crew, provide fuel and stores, and bear all the cost and responsibility of operating the ship, including insurance cover. Syn. bare-pole charter; bare-hull charter; demise charter.

charter by demise a time charter which in effect gives the charterer a demise (lease) of the ship, so that during the second period of the charter he has full possession and control of the ship. See demise charterer under charterer.

charter flight TRANSPT. one by an aircraft hired for that particular journey. Cf. scheduled flight.

demise charter see bareboat charter above; also charter by demise.

full charter one by which the whole of the cargo space of a ship or aircraft is hired by the charterer. Cf. partial charter below.

open charter one which allows the charterer to use the ship or aircraft to carry any kind of cargo to any port he wishes.

partial charter one by which only part of the cargo space of a ship or aircraft is hired by the charterer. Cf. full charter above.

time charter one by which the ship or aircraft is hired for an agreed period of time during which the charterer may use the ship or aircraft as he wishes, paying a monthly rate of hire based on the deadweight tonnage of the ship. The ship is operated by the owners, but the charterer pays the cost of fuel and stores consumed during the period of the charter. Cf. voyage charter. See bareboat charter above.

voyage charter one by which the ship or aircraft is hired for a single voyage between certain agreed ports, to carry a stated cargo at a fixed rate of freight. The owner bears all the expenses of the voyage and is responsible for operating the ship. Cf. time charter above.

v. TRANSPT. to hire or let a ship or aeroplane for the carriage of goods or passengers: To charter a ship. That aircraft has been chartered.

charterage (1) the chartering of a ship or aircraft. (2) the price of such chartering.

charter by demise see under charter..

chartered accountant ACCTS. in Britain, a member of one of the institutes of chartered accountants in England and Wales, in Scotland and in Ireland. To become a member a person must first serve a period articled to a practising accountant, and then pass the institute's examinations, which deal with a range of subjects from accounting and auditing to taxation, law and management. When qualified, a chartered accountant may put the initials A.C.A. or F.C.A. after his name. The letters C.A. are used only in Scotland.

Chartered Bank (Canada) BKG. one of nine banks formed under the Bank Act, which together run about 6000 branches in Canada. See charter, n. (1).

chartered corporation see under corporation.

chartered freight see under freight.

chartered secretary MAN. in Britain, a member of the Institute of Chartered Secretaries. To become a member he must pass the Institute's examinations and have obtained up to six years' professional experience. See company secretary.

charterer TRANSPT. a person or organization agreeing to hire a ship or aircraft from its owners under an arrangement called a charter and recorded in a document called a charter-party. See charter, n. (3).

demise charterer one who takes over entire responsibility for manning, operating and controlling a ship under a bareboat charter. See charter, n. (3).

charterer's freight see chartered freight under freight.

charter market or **chartering market** TRANSPT. the chief international market for chartering ships and aircraft is in London. See Baltic Exchange.

charter-party or **charter party** SHIPG. a formal document recording the detailed conditions of a contract between an owner who agrees to hire his ship or aircraft or part of the cargo space in it, and a charterer who agrees to charter it, for a fixed period of time or for a stated number of voyages between named ports, for a sum of money or a rate of hire called freight. Such contracts are usu. arranged by shipbrokers. See affreightment; Baltic Exchange; charter, n. (3). Abbr. C/P. Syn. charter agreement (U.S.A.). Cf. bill of lading.

chartists STK. EXCH. professional market analysts (skilled examiners) who, after studying present market conditions, preparing charts, drawing up tables of figures and weighing the effect of new influences, claim to be able to tell the future course of prices on the Stock Exchange.

charwoman a woman employed by the hour or by the day to do housework or office cleaning, now more politely called a cleaner. Syn. char (colloq.); cleaner; daily woman.

chattel LAW property of any kind other than freehold land (esp. in the phrase *goods and chattels*).

chattel personal movable possessions including personal and household articles (*choses in possession*), and rights such as copyrights and patents (*choses in action*). *Syn.* pure personalty.

chattel real a leasehold interest in land, i.e. immovable property other than freehold.

chattel mortgage FIN. a mortgage in which the security for payment of the debt consists of chattels, i.e. personal possessions other than freehold land.

chattel mortgage bond *see under* bond, *n.*

cheap (1) of low price; costing little: *Milk is cheap in summer. A cheap meal in a café. Cheap labour*, workers who are paid low wages; also who are willing to work for low wages. *To do something on the cheap* (*colloq.*), at as little cost as possible. (2) asking low prices: *A cheap hotel/restaurant/shop.* (3) good value for money; at a bargain price: *These goods are dirt cheap*, astonishingly cheap. *Something going cheap*, being offered at a bargain price. *Cheap at the price*, well worth the money asked. (4) of poor quality: *Those clothes are cheap and nasty. A cheap Jack*, a street-seller offering cheap articles of low quality. *See* cheap money *below. Syn.* inexpensive.

cheap money FIN. & BKG. in the money market, money is said to be cheap when it is easy to borrow at low rates of interest usu. because the minimum lending rate is low. Cf. dear money. *Syn.* easy money.

cheat *n.* a deceitful person who lives by getting money or goods by trickery. *Syn.* fraud; swindler.

v. to deceive; to steal by a trick; to obtain money or goods by false pretences: *He cheated me out of my money. To cheat at cards/in an examination. It does not pay to cheat the Customs. Syn.* to defraud; to swindle.

check *n.* (1) a stop or holding back: *To keep someone in check*, to hold him back esp. from acting foolishly or wrongly. *To keep expenses in check. To keep a check on expenses*, to watch them carefully in order to limit them. *To put a check on smoking at work*, to control or stop it, esp. if forbidden. (2) a sudden interference or interruption: *His accident was a check to his career. The factory fire is a serious check to production. A check to profits caused by high interest rates.* (3) a control for the purpose of making sure of the correctness of information, esp. of figures: *A trial balance is an essential check of the accounting system. A check of the day's takings*, a counting of the cash received, esp. in a shop. *See also* management control *under* control.(4) a system of preventing or uncovering dishonesty: *A sudden check of the stock showed that some had been stolen. A cus-*

toms check is aimed at preventing smuggling. I suspect that cashier, so keep a check on him, watch him for signs of dishonesty. (5) (U.S.A.) a cheque. (6) (U.S.A.) a bill, esp. in a restaurant. (7) (U.S.A.) a receipt or ticket for luggage or for clothes left in a cloakroom: *A baggage check. A hat check.* (8) (U.S.A.) a mark used when checking, thus √, i.e. a tick. (9)(U.S.A.*colloq.*)Yes;Iagree;youarecorrect.

v. to examine in order to find out whether something is correct; to make sure that something is as it should be.

check in (U.S.A.) (*a*) to leave or to accept something for safe keeping in a checkroom (a cloakroom or a left-luggage office in Britain). (*b*) to take a room in a hotel and sign the register on arrival. (*c*) to record one's arrival for work, esp. in a factory. *Syn.* clock in; clock on.

check off to mark an item (e.g. in a list) with a tick, √, to show that it is correct.

check out (U.S.A.) (*a*) to pay one's bill on leaving, e.g. a hotel, a restaurant, a supermarket: *Sorry, sir, Mr Jones checked out yesterday*, left the hotel yesterday. *A queue of customers waiting to check out* (of the supermarket). (*b*) to record one's leaving a factory or office after work. *Syn.* clock out; clock off.

check up on to examine for the purpose of making sure that all is in order; to look into some matter to see whether certain statements or claims are true or honest: *You must check up on his character*, find out whether he is honest, etc. *In checking up on his claim, I find it is false.*

check with to be in agreement with; to correspond to: *The invoice checks exactly with the dispatch note.*

checkbook (U.S.A.) BKG. a cheque book.

checker (1) a person who checks that things are correct, e.g. the contents of an invoice, order, list, account, etc. (2) in U.S.A., a cloakroom attendant. (3) in U.S.A., a cashier in a supermarket.

checking account (U.S.A.) BKG. a current account, i.e. one on which cheques (checks) can be drawn.

checklist *or* **check list** MAN. a specially-prepared list of things, names, subjects, steps in a process, etc., arranged in a certain order and intended to help in checking and comparing.

checkout COM. in a supermarket, the desk at which one pays for goods bought. *Syn.* cash desk; checkout point.

checkroom (U.S.A.) TOUR. a left-luggage office; a cloakroom.

check trading (U.S.A.) COM. & FIN. a system of payment by which a shopkeeper sells a cheque (check) to a customer who later repays the amount with interest and usu. by instalments, i.e. regular part payments spread over a period. Cf. hire-purchase agreement.

cheerful STK. EXCH. happy, expecting business to be good: *The tone of the market was more cheerful*, share prices were higher and there was more business to be done.

cheeseparing (*colloq.*) excessively and foolishly unwilling to spend money: *An owner too cheeseparing to keep his property in good repair.*

chef (de cuisine) TOUR. the chief male cook in charge of the kitchen of a restaurant or large private house.

cheque BKG. legally, a bill of exchange drawn on a banker, payable on demand. In practice it is a direction in writing to a bank to pay a stated sum of money on demand to a named person or organization, or to his or their order, or to bearer. *Syn.* check (U.S.A.).

ante-dated cheque one which has been given a date earlier than the date on which it was signed, in order to make it appear that it had been drawn earlier and had been delayed in delivery. Cf. post-dated cheque.

bank cheque *see* bank draft.

banker's cheque *see* bank draft.

bearer cheque *see under* bearer.

blank cheque *see under* blank.

cancelled cheque one which has been paid and so cancelled by being marked with a paid date-stamp by the bank on which it was drawn. It is used as a voucher until the amount has been debited and is sometimes later sent, with any other paid cheques, to the customer with his next bank statement. *Syn.* paid cheque.

cashier's cheque/check (U.S.A.) a cheque drawn by a cashier of a bank on the same bank. *Syn.* bank draft (Britain).

certified cheque/check (U.S.A.) one that has been formally declared by a bank to be good and will be paid from money which the bank has set aside. *Syn.* marked cheque (Britain).

crossed cheque one with two parallel lines drawn across it, usu. by the drawer or his agent, e.g. his bank. This crossing, without any other words, or with only the words 'and Company' or '& Co.' between the lines (*see* and Company (2)) is called a *general crossing* and is a direction that payment of the cheque can be made only to a bank, who will then credit the amount to the account of the customer; it will not be paid in cash over the counter. Crossing a cheque lessens the risk of loss by dishonesty. Any holder of a cheque may cross it. If the name of the bank is written between the lines, it is a *special crossing*, and the cheque can be paid only to the named bank. The words 'not negotiable' may be written across the cheque by the drawer or by any person who becomes the holder of the cheque; this is to guard against payment being made to a person who has no right to possess it (*see* not negotiable). The words 'account payee' or 'a/c payee' written across the cheque are a direction to the bank that the amount is to be credited to the account only of the named payee and no one else (*see* account payee). A crossed cheque may be *uncrossed* or *opened* by the drawer by writing the words 'pay cash' against the crossing and adding his initials. *Opp.* open cheque.

dishonoured cheque *see* dishonour (2).

gift cheque *see under* gift.

house cheque one drawn on and presented for payment at the same bank, possibly at a different branch. Such cheques are not put through the clearing house.

limited cheque in dealings in foreign currencies, a cheque drawn in a foreign currency and marked in the margin with a sum in the drawer's own currency, to show that the cheque is limited to the equivalent of not more than that sum.

manager's cheque a cheque drawn by a bank on itself and signed by one of its managers. Such cheques are used by a bank when acting on directions from a customer, esp. one who has temporarily gone abroad, to pay certain bills when sent to the bank. Cf. bank draft.

marked cheque a cheque to which the banker on whom it is drawn has added a note, or mark, that the cheque is good and will be met. In Britain this practice is not favoured and has been largely replaced by using a banker's draft. *Syn.* certified check (U.S.A.).

memorandum cheque a post-dated cheque given by a debtor to a creditor who will use it only if the debt is not repaid by the due date.

negotiable cheque one which is made payable to order or to bearer, thus allowing the holder to transfer it (pass the ownership of it) to another party simply by delivering it. See negotiable instrument.

open cheque one that has not been crossed.

order cheque one which is payable to a named person or order: *Pay John Brown or order, Tom Smith*, the wording of a cheque drawn by Tom Smith directing his bank to pay the amount of the cheque to John Brown or to his order. Cf. bearer cheque.

out-of-date cheque *see* stale cheque.

overdue cheque one which, for the purpose of negotiation, has been in circulation for an unreasonable time. What period is unreasonable is a question of fact in each case, but up to 12 days is probably right, although a longer period would apply to a cheque from abroad. Not to be confused with a stale or out-of-date cheque.

paid cheque *see* cancelled cheque *above.*

personal cheque one drawn by a private person, not a firm or organization.

personalized cheque one on which the issuing bank has printed the number and name of the account in the bottom right-hand corner before issuing it to the customer.

post-dated cheque one bearing a date later than the day on which it was drawn.

returned cheque one on which payment has been refused and which has been returned to the branch of the bank that presented it for payment. Cf. dishonoured cheque *under* dishonour (2).

rubber cheque/check (U.S.A. *colloq.*) a dishonoured cheque that bounces back to the payee. *See* bounce; bouncer.

self cheque *see* self.

stale cheque one which has not been presented for payment within six months of the date when it was drawn. Such a cheque is returned unpaid with a note written or stamped on it saying 'out of date'. *Syn.* out-of-date cheque.

stock cheque *see under* stock.

stopped cheque one of which the payment has been stopped by the drawer by giving a direction to his bank, either by word of mouth or in writing, not to pay it. The banker returns the stopped cheque unpaid to the person who presented it for payment with a note written or stamped on it saying 'payment countermanded (cancelled) by the drawer' or 'orders not to pay'. If the bank pays a cheque in spite of a stop order, the bank must bear the loss. *See also* countermand (1).

traveller's cheque a special kind of cheque issued by a bank to a traveller who can get payment in local currency at sight, i.e. on presenting it, with proof of his signature, at a bank, store, hotel, etc. almost anywhere. Such cheques are usu. paid for at the time they are issued; if they are lost, the issuing bank will repay or replace the missing cheques unless the traveller has been guilty of carelessness. *Syn.* traveler's check (U.S.A.).

cheque account BKG. a current account, *see under* bank account.

cheque book *or* **chequebook** BKG. a book of printed cheque forms for use in drawing cheques on a bank. The form is in two parts, the cheque itself, which is torn out, leaving a counterfoil or stub as a record of what was written on the cheque itself. *Syn.* checkbook (U.S.A.).

cheque card BKG. a card supplied by a bank to a customer, stating that the bank binds itself to honour any cheque up to a stated value, e.g. £50, drawn by the customer (whose signature appears on the card) provided that the number of the card is written on the back of the cheque. *Syn.* banker's card. Cf. credit card.

cheque rate BKG. in foreign-exchange dealings, the rate at which a foreign-exchange dealer will buy a cheque or sight draft payable in another country. *Syn.* sight rate; cable rate; short rate.

cheque requisition ACCTS. & MAN. a printed form prepared by an employee who in the course of his work needs a cheque signed by or for his employers in order to make a business payment. The form gives the necessary details for the cheque to be drawn, after the payment has been approved by a person having power to do so.

cheque-writing machine BKG. a kind of typewriter that cuts letters and figures into the paper, making it impossible to change them. Such machines are used esp. for preparing cheques and other negotiable instruments in order to prevent dishonesty.

cherry-picking COM. (*colloq.*) words used by shopkeepers to describe the practice of those shoppers who go from shop to shop buying a particular article in the shop where it is cheapest, and buying nothing else there (as might a bird fly from tree to tree eating only the ripest fruit).

Ches. Cheshire, England.

ch. fwd. charges forward.

chge. charge.

chiao fractional currency unit of China, divided into 10 fen. 10 chiao = 1 yuan or People's Bank dollar. *Also* jiao.

chicken-feed (1) (*colloq.*) a sum of money so small as to be not worth considering; something worth very little: *His income from writing books is chicken-feed.* (2) in U.S.A., small change; coins of low value.

chief executive in U.S.A., the President of the United States of America. In Britain, the highest official of an organization, the person charged with the responsibility for seeing that it is properly and profitably run. The name is gradually replacing the words *managing director.*

chief-rent LAW in Britain, a small sum of money, usu. only a few pounds a year, payable by the owners of some freehold properties, e.g. to the lord of the manor. It was formerly payable for ever but it can now be redeemed (paid off by a lump sum) if the holder of the property so wishes. Cf. ground rent. *Syn.* rent-charge.

child *or* **children's allowance** TAXN. in Britain, a personal allowance or amount of money by which a taxpayer who supports children may reduce his taxable income.

child benefit in Britain, a sum of money paid weekly to a mother for each of her children below the age of 16. This is paid by the government out of general taxation.

child's deferred policy *see under* insurance policy.

Chile a republic on the west coast of South America, pop. 9 million approx. (1973); capital, Santiago, pop. 3 million approx.; language, Spanish; currency unit, the peso, divided into 100 centavos. Member, O.A.S.; L.A.F.T.A.

China a people's (communist) republic in eastern Asia, pop. 839 million approx. (1975); capital, Peking (Beijing), pop. 7.5 million approx.; language, Chinese; currency unit, the yuan or

Chinese People's Bank dollar, divided into 10 chiao or jiao, each of 10 fen. Member of no international organizations except the U.N.

Chinese auction *see* Dutch auction.

chip (1) small round piece of bone or ivory in imitation of a coin, used in playing certain card games. (2) bad feeling against somebody, esp. in the expression: *He has a chip on his shoulder*, has bad feelings against, is angry with, other people in general; is offended. (3) STK. EXCH. a share. *See* blue chip.

chips *pl.* a ship's carpenter.

chisel (*colloq.*) to cheat; to obtain money or goods by dishonest tricks. *N.* a chiseller.

chit (1) any short handwritten note; a formal demand-note. (2) a note signed by a customer agreeing to pay later for food or drink served in a club or hotel. (3) a letter giving an opinion of a person's character and qualifications.

chn. chairman.

choice *n.* ECON. THEORY the basic truth which governs all economic action is that people must frequently make a choice between two or more courses in deciding how best to satisfy their wants. They tend to choose the course which makes the best use of the limited supply of materials, etc., at their command, i.e. to choose the cheapest course, thus introducing the idea of a system of prices. Economic theory studies the ways in which people choose to act in a society in which a price system exists. *adj.* specially chosen; of high quality: *Choice fruit.*

chon the fractional currency unit of South Korea. 100 chon = 1 won or hwan.

chop COM. (1) in the East, esp. India and China, a stamp or mark giving approval; thus a signed permit or licence or more general permission to perform a certain activity. (2) a brand or trade-mark applied to goods to distinguish them from those of other manufacturers or importers.

chopper (1) COM. (*colloq.*) a used motor car taken in part-exchange. (2) TRANSPT. (*colloq.*) a helicopter.

chose in action LAW a personal right to bring an action in a court of law against another party in order to obtain payment of a debt, or to get damages for breach of contract or for some other personal wrong or harm suffered. Cf. chose in possession. *Pron.* sho-. *See* chattel personal.

chose in possession LAW any actual object or thing personally possessed, e.g. furniture, a motor car, as distinguished from a right to something, e.g. to damages for breach of contract, or repayment of a debt. *Pron.* sho-. *See* chattel personal.

ch. ppd. charges prepaid.

chq. cheque.

Christmas *see* quarter-day.

chuck (*colloq.*) dismissal: *To get the chuck*, to be dismissed. *To give* (*someone*) *the chuck*, to dismiss.

Chunnel *see* Channel Tunnel.

CI the Ivory Coast's international vehicle-registration letters.

C.I. Channel Islands.

C.I.D., CID Criminal Investigation Department, in Britain.

Cie. (*French*, Compagnie) Company.

c.i.f., C.I.F. cost, insurance, freight.

c.i.f. and c. cost, insurance, freight and commission.

c.i.f. and c. and i. cost, insurance, freight and commission and interest.

c.i.f. and e. cost, insurance, freight and exchange.

c.i.f.c.i. cost, insurance, freight, commission and interest.

Cinque Ports ECON. HIST. an eleventh-century grouping, originally of five ports in the southeast of England, Sandwich, Dover, Hythe, Romney and Hastings, to which were later added Rye and Winchelsea. The purpose of the grouping was to provide ships and men to defend England and the short crossing of the English Channel. Most of the harbours became silted up (filled with sand, etc.) or eroded (eaten away by the sea). Only Dover is now a port of some size.

C.I.O. *see* American Federation of Labor and Congress of Industrial Organizations (A.F.L.–C.I.O.).

cipher (1) a secret method of writing words. (2) the key to this. *Also* cypher.

circular ADVTG. & COM. a printed notice or advertisement sent to a wide circle of people.

circular letter a circular in the form of a letter, often typewritten or printed to look like an ordinary letter sent only to the addressee, but in fact sent to many people.

circular letter of credit *see under* letter of credit.

circular ticket *see under* ticket.

circulating assets *see* current assets *under* assets, *pl.*

circulating capital *see* working capital *under* capital.

circulating medium ECON. money as a means of exchange, i.e. for buying and selling goods and services. It includes not only bank-notes, coins, and gold and silver bars but also cheques, bills of exchange, and any other instruments used instead of money. *Syn.* currency; medium of exchange.

circulation the movement of such things as goods, money, ideas, news.

bank circulation BKG. of a note-issuing bank, the total value of notes which it has issued and which are in circulation, i.e. in the hands of the public. Such notes are payable on demand.

coin circulation BKG. the number and value of coins in the hands of the public. Of these only a few are kept in pockets and purses for everyday use for buying things — in Britain about 20%. Most coins are locked or stored away and are not being actively used, e.g. stocks in banks (about 20%), lying in meters and slot machines (about 15%), or held in the home as savings (about 20%); the balance of 25% is either lost or cannot be accounted for.

currency circulation see under currency.

money circulation BKG. & ECON. money which is in the hands of the public, such as coins, notes, cheques, bills of exchange, etc. and being used to pay for goods and services. See velocity of circulation.

newspaper circulation ADVTG. the average total number of copies actually sold of each issue of a particular newspaper (or magazine) during a stated period. Cf. readership circulation *below*.

readership circulation ADVTG. the number of persons who are believed to read any one issue of a newspaper or magazine. Cf. newspaper circulation *above*.

City desk see under desk.

City editor in Britain, the head of a staff of persons employed by one of the larger newspapers to report on commercial and financial news, esp. of business activities in the City (i.e. of London). See City desk under desk.

City, The the City of London, an area of about one square mile on the north bank of the River Thames in the heart of Greater London. It is one of the world's leading financial and commercial centres. Its highly-developed financial systems are based on the Bank of England, the large joint-stock banks and advanced capital and discount markets. Its famous Stock Exchange provides a world market for all types of investments. Its many insurance companies, led by Lloyd's, form an insurance market of great international importance. The City has many of the world's largest commodity exchanges and shipping companies. Cf. Wall Street. *Syn.* The Square Mile.

civil commotion INSCE. violent disturbance of the public order, esp. when it causes harm to lives and property. It is a risk which is covered only by special insurance arrangements. Cf. riot.

civil law LAW (1) in Britain and U.S.A., etc. the law relating to the rights and duties of private persons, as distinguished from criminal law. *See* common law. (2) on the continent of Europe, the law based mainly on Roman, German, church, commercial and other systems of law. Such civil law is found also in areas governed in the past by European nations other than the British. *Syn.* Roman law. (3) the law of a particular nation, as distinguished from international law.

Civil List see crown land.

Civil Service the body of government employees, called Civil Servants, who deal with the administration of the country, other than those who are members of the armed services.

ck. cask; check (cheque).

c.k.d., C.K.D. completely knocked down.

CL Sri Lanka's international vehicle-registration letters.

cl. clause.

claim *n.* (1) a piece of land to which one has a legal right of ownership: *To stake a claim*, to mark out the boundaries of the land which is claimed. *A mining claim*, a claim to the right to mine on a piece of land. (2) INSCE. a demand made by an insured party on the insurer for payment under an insurance policy. (3) INSCE. the policy itself when the event insured against has happened. *See also* exaggerated claim. (4) LAW a demand for something due as a right: *A claim for damages for breach of contract.*

v. (1) to demand something that is due by right: *To claim payment of a debt/of damages/ of the sum insured/a share in the profits. To claim one's possessions/goods/land/lost property/rights, etc.* (2) to declare, to state as a fact: *He claimed to be a professional accountant. I claim that he stole the money.* (3) to need, to deserve: *These papers claim my attention/immediate action.*

claimant LAW & INSCE. a person who claims, makes a claim, e.g. under a will or an insurance policy. *Syn.* claimer.

claimer see claimant.

claims adjuster INSCE. a person employed by an insurance company to settle claims under policies issued by the company. See adjuster.

claim, statement of see under statement.

clandestine secret, done under deceit: *Clandestine trade*, forbidden trade, e.g. with an enemy country in time of war.

Clark John Bates (1847–1938), American economist, professor at Columbia University. His *Philosophy of Wealth* (1885) restated in a clear and well-ordered but critical manner the teachings of the classical economists. In his *Distribution of Wealth* (1899) he developed his theory of production and distribution and was the first to put forward the idea of marginal productivity.

Clark John Maurice (1884–1971), American economist, like his father, John Bates Clark, also professor at Columbia University. He is best known for his study of overhead costs and for first putting forward the idea of the Acceleration Principle.

class TOUR. & TRANSPT. a division according to quality or price: *High-class accommodation; the low-class district of a town. First-/second-/ economy-/tourist-class/ticket, etc. Single-class ship*, one that carries only one class of passenger. *First class*, the best.

classical economics the ideas and teachings of the British economists from about 1776 to 1890. *See* Classical School.

Classical School ECON. THEORY a school of thought, also called the English School of Classical Political Economy, which may be said to have given birth to economics as a separate subject for study. It began in 1776 with the publication of Adam Smith's *An Enquiry into the Nature and Causes of the Wealth of Nations*, the first full and well-ordered book on economics. In 1819 David Ricardo published his *Principles of Political Economy and Taxation*, a critical examination of Adam Smith's work but also greatly developing the use of a reasoned argument, esp. in regard to the advantages of international trade and the Law of Comparative Costs. In 1848 John Stuart Mill in turn published his *Principles of Political Economy*, a critical restatement of Ricardo's work. The basic teaching of the Classical School was that in any organized economic system there is a natural tendency towards equilibrium (a state of balance) caused by the continuous action upon one another of the factors of production: land, labour and capital. Other important economists in this school were: Jeremy Bentham, John Elliott Cairnes, John Ramsey MacCulloch, Thomas Malthus, James Mill, Nassau Senior, and Robert Torrens. From about 1890 the Cambridge or Neo-Classical School led by Alfred Marshall, followed and developed the work of the classical economists.

classification of ships SHIPG. & MAR. INSCE. the survey (close examination) and placing of ships in classes according to certain rules relating to the quality and safety of their hulls, engines and apparatus such as steering, boats, anchors, chains and cables. This work is done by specialists. *See* classification societies.

classification societies SHIPG. & MAR. INSCE. organizations that are recognized by their governments in various countries and given powers to see that ships are as safe as possible. The societies employ surveyors who make sure that the ships are properly built, of good materials and that they are kept in good and safe working order. The societies make safety rules which shipowners and masters must follow. Each ship is classified according to its level of safety, thus pointing out the degree of risk accepted by the marine insurers of the ship. The main classification societies are: Lloyd's Register of Shipping (*see under* Lloyd's) in London, the leading society; the American Bureau of Shipping in U.S.A.; Bureau Veritas, originally in Belgium but now in Paris; Norske Veritas in Norway; Registro Italiano Navale in Italy; Polski Rejestr in Poland; and Germanischer Lloyd in Germany. Most of these work in co-operation with Lloyd's Register of Shipping.

classified advertisement *see under* advertisement.

classified catalogue *see under* catalogue.

classified common stock (U.S.A.) STK. EXCH. stock (in a corporation) which has been issued in two classes, 'A' stock, the holders of which have no right to vote, and 'B' stock, the holders of which have a right to vote. *Syn.* (in Britain) voting and non-voting shares.

classified directory *see under* directory.

class struggle (1) ECON. THEORY the basic idea of the Marxists, that in a capitalist system, where the means of production are owned by private persons or organizations aiming to make as much profit as possible, there is a continual struggle between those who own the means of production (the capitalists) and the workers they employ (the proletariat). (2) social struggle between the aristocracy (ruling class of noblemen) and the commoners. *See* Marx, Karl.

clause (1) LAW a sentence or paragraph, complete in itself, forming part of a legal document. Clauses are usu. numbered. (2) INSCE. in a formal insurance document, e.g. in the policy or joined to it, a part consisting of a sentence or paragraph which contains one or more conditions or warranties. *Syn.* proviso.

claused bill of lading *see* dirty b/l *under* bill of lading.

claw-back TAXN. in Britain, the money which the government takes back from the public by higher taxes after giving increased tax allowances and higher regular payments by the State, such as retirement pensions.

cld. cleared (through Customs).

clean *v.* to make clean; to remove anything unwanted.

to clean someone out (*colloq.*) to take all his money.

to be cleaned out (*colloq.*) to have nothing, esp. no money.

to clean up (*colloq.*) to make a profit, usu. on a single transaction: *He sold his business and cleaned up a million pounds.*

clean acceptance an accepted bill of exchange without special conditions. *See* general acceptance *under* acceptance. Cf. qualified or special acceptance.

clean bill of exchange *see under* bill of exchange.

clean bill of health *see under* bill of health.

clean bill of lading *see under* bill of lading.

clean bond *see under* bond, *n.*

clean credit *see under* credit (3).

clean hands LAW a rule of equity that a person who asks for the help of a court of law must 'come with clean hands', i.e. his own behaviour and actions must be faultless.

clean ship SHIPG. one that is not in quarantine, or is no longer in quarantine.

clear *v.* (1) COM. of goods, to sell off, get rid of: *To clear*, for sale at a cheap price to get rid of old stock. (2) *To clear one's costs/expenses*, to make neither a profit nor a loss.
to clear someone out to take, use up, all his money.
(3) to clear Customs, *see* clearance. (4) BKG. *To clear a cheque*, to pass it through a clearing house. (5) SHIPG. to complete all the steps necessary to allow a ship to sail, esp. getting the ship's papers passed by the Customs. *See* clearance. *adj.* full, complete: *A clear week's notice is needed*, at least a week's notice of seven full days excluding the date of issue of the notice and the date of the event it relates to, such as a meeting. These are known as *clear days*.

clearance (1) COM. the formalities necessary to satisfy the customs officers before they will allow goods to be cleared (removed) from customs for dispatch or delivery elsewhere. The work is usu. done by a clearing agent for imported goods and by a shipping agent for goods being exported. (2) SHIPG. a customs document given to the master of a ship, allowing him either to unload (*clearance inwards*) or to leave the port (*clearance outwards*). Clearance is given only after examining the records carried by the ship concerning her cargo, her crew, their state of health, etc., and payment of port dues. *See* jerque note; inward clearing bill; certificate of inward clearance.
clearance agent *see* clearing agent.
clearance papers documents given by the Customs to the master of a ship allowing him to unload or to sail.

clearance sale COM. a special selling of goods at reduced prices to clear (get rid of) remaining stocks quickly in order to make room for new stocks. Cf. end-of-season sale, closing-down sale, *under* sale.

clearers BKG. (*colloq.*) the clearing banks.

clearing BKG. a process adopted by members of the banking system of a country, of exchanging cheques and drafts and settling only the balances at the end of the day. *See* Clearing House.

clearing agent COM. & SHIPG. one specially skilled in completing the formalities needed to clear imported goods through the Customs. He is paid usu. by a small commission. *Syn.* clearance agent; customs agent.

clearing agreement FIN. & ECON. a form of bilateral trade agreement between two countries, one or both of which are suffering from severe difficulties in their balance of payments. To make trade easier, all payments for imports are made through the central bank of the country concerned. Exporters receive payment from this bank at certain dates during the year.

clearing banks BKG. in England and Wales, those larger joint-stock banks which are members of the London Bankers Clearing House: the Big Four, i.e. Barclays Bank, Lloyds Bank, the Midland Bank and the National Westminster Bank, and also Coutts & Co., Williams & Glyn's Bank and the Co-operative Banks. Banks which are not members of a clearing house are called *non-clearers*; they have accounts with the clearing banks. In Scotland and Northern Ireland banks have separate clearing arrangements which work in connection with the London Clearing House. *Syn.* (*colloq.*) clearers.

Clearing House BKG. the London Bankers' Clearing House, an association formed by the larger commercial banks to carry out the process of sorting and exchanging cheques and drafts and settling differences at the end of the day by cheque drawn on the members' accounts at the Bank of England.

clerical *adj.* of or relating to a clerk; dealing with office work: *A clerical error*, a clerk's mistake. *Clerical staff*, employees working in an office, as distinguished from those working in a factory, etc. *Clerical work*, office work. *Clerical worker*, a clerk; an office worker. *Clerical assistant*, see assistant.

clerk (1) a person employed in an office or shop, to deal with business papers, letters, orders, bills, etc. and to keep accounts. *Adj.* clerical. (2) in U.S.A., a person who serves customers in a shop. (3) an officer responsible for the administration esp. of a government organization: *The clerk of the council. A justice's clerk.*
booking clerk *see under* booking.
filing clerk *see under* filing.
invoice clerk *see under* invoice.
ledger clerk *see under* ledger.
order clerk *see under* order.
wages clerk *see under* wages.
See also articled clerk; authorized clerk.

clerk of the works IND. a person in charge of the work on a new building.

'C' licence *see* 'A' licence.

client (1) a person who employs or uses the services of a professional adviser (other than a doctor or dentist) esp. of a lawyer, architect, stockbroker. (2) a customer, a person who buys or is likely to buy from a seller.

clientele all the clients or customers, esp. those who are in the habit of using the services of a professional adviser or businessman: *The clientele of a hotel. Pron.* -tel.

clinch COM. to settle (an argument, bargain, business deal); to bring to a successful result: *To clinch a deal/sale.*

clip-joint COM. & TOUR. (*colloq.*) a restaurant, esp. a night-club, which robs its customers by charging prices that are far too high.

clipped coin FIN. a coin that has had its edges cut

away, thus reducing its intrinsic value, i.e. its value as a piece of metal. *See* debasement of coinage.

clipper ship SHIPG. & ECON. HIST. a very fast sailing ship, specially built to bring the first cargoes of tea and wool every season from the East Indies and Australia to Britain and America during the nineteenth century.

cloakroom TOUR. & TRANSPT. (1) a place where coats, hats and luggage may be safely left for short periods on payment of a small charge called a cloakroom fee. *Syn.* left-luggage office. (2) in Britain, a lavatory, esp. in a public building.

clock *v.* IND. to record the time (of an event).

to clock in/on to record the time of one's arrival at work on a card by putting it into a time-clock.

to clock out/off to record the time of one's leaving work in the same way. *Syn.* (U.S.A.) to check in/out.

close *n.* STK. EXCH. the end of the day's trading; the close of business: *At the close, share prices were steady after earlier falls.*

v. (1) COM. & FIN. *To close down*, to stop trading; to shut down: *The shop/factory/branch office/business, etc. has closed down.* (2) in U.S.A., *To close out*, to try to get rid of goods by selling at reduced prices.

close company *see under* company.

close price *see under* price.

closed case TRANSPT. a completely-closed packing-case. Cf. crate.

closed-end trust *see under* trust.

closed indent *see under* indent.

closed market *see under* market.

closed shop IND. REL. a factory or other industrial or business concern where only trade unionists are employed, usu. the result of the unions being strong enough to reach an agreement with the employers that no person who is not a member of a trade union will be employed. Cf. open shop. *Syn.* union shop.

closing (1) STK. EXCH. the end of business for the day: *The closing price* of a security is the market price late in the afternoon of the particular day. (2) COM. the time at which shops, offices, restaurants, public houses, etc. close their business, usu. for the day: *Closing time. Early closing, see under* early. (3) ACCTS. the end of an accounting period: *Closing stock*, the value of stocks of materials and finished products at the end of the accounting period, as compared with the opening stock.

closing-down sale *see under* sale.

closing entry ACCTS. a journal entry transferring a balance from a nominal account to the profit and loss account as part of the work of closing the books of account at the end of each accounting period. *See* closing balance *under* balance, *n.* (1).

club accounts ACCTS. accounting systems which are simpler than those of commercial organizations because clubs, societies and associations are non-profitmaking. They have no trading or profit and loss accounts and often have nothing more than a receipts and payments account, sometimes called an income and expenditure account. If the organization owns assets it will also have a balance sheet. *See* summary book.

cm centimetre.

C.M.E.A. Council for Mutual Economic Assistance (COMECON).

cml. commercial.

C/N credit note; cover-note; consignment note.

C/O cash order; certificate of origin.

C/o care of; carried over.

Co. Company; county.

CO Colombia's international vehicle-registration letters.

coach TRANSPT. (1) in Britain, a bus, usu. with a single deck, used for long-distance journeys: *A motor coach. A coach station.* (2) a railway wagon built for carrying passengers.

coal basin *see* basin (2).

coal-ship *see* collier.

co-assurer *or* **co-insurer** INSCE. one of a group of insurers among whom a large insurance may be divided.

coaster SHIPG. a small cargo-carrying ship which makes short voyages between home ports along the coast without visiting foreign ports. *Syn.* coasting ship; coasting vessel.

coasting trade SHIPG. the business of carrying goods by coaster or coasting ship/steamer/vessel from one port to another port in the same country, i.e. without visiting a foreign country. *Syn.* coastwise trade; coasting.

Cobden Richard (1804–65), English businessman, politician and economic reformer. In 1838, with John Bright, he formed the Anti-Corn Law League in Manchester. He became a Member of Parliament in 1838 and his work was rewarded in 1846 by the repeal (ending) of the Corn Laws. With Bright he was a leader of the Manchester School of Economists, who believed in free trade and freedom from interference by government in economic matters. *See* Anti-Corn Law League.

Cobol COMP. Common Business Oriented Language. A standard system of putting a computer programme into machine language that can be used on a large number of different computers. Cf. Algol; Fortran.

C.O.D. cash on delivery (Britain); collect on delivery (U.S.A.).

code (1) LAW a complete collection of laws relating to a particular subject, e.g. the Bills of Exchange Act, 1882, which brought together in one statute (Act of Parliament) all the earlier laws on bills of exchange. (2) STK. EXCH. the *Code on Bids*, a guiding document issued by the takeover panel of the London Stock Exchange. (3) ADVTG. the *Code of Practice for Advertisers*, a guiding document issued by the Advertising Standards Association. (4) COM. a system of words and figures used in sending telegrams and cables, with the purpose of saving costs by reducing the number of words in a message. *See also* postcode. (5) COMP. a system of letters and figures forming a machine-language that can be used in a computer. *Syn.* coding system. *See* alphanumeric. (6) TAXN. under the pay as you earn (P.A.Y.E.) system in Britain each employee is given a code number that is determined by the income-tax allowances to which he has a right and which must be approved by the tax authorities. The higher the tax code number the higher the allowances. The employer can read from the tax table the total tax-free pay, and thus calculate the taxable pay from which tax must be taken and paid to the government.

codicil LAW a document added to a will and becoming part of it, making changes to one or more parts of the will.

coffer (1) a strong box for storing valuable articles. (2) a place for storing money, securities, bullion: *The coffers of a bank/the State.*

cohong *see* Canton system (of trade).

coin *n.* FIN. a piece of money made of a fixed weight of a particular metal, issued by the government of a country for use as a means of making small payments: *Gold/silver/cupro-nickel/bronze/copper coins.* Metal money generally: *Payment in coin. False/base/bad coin. Standard coin, token coin, see* coinage. Cf. note issue.
v. to make pieces of money from metal. *Syn.* to mint.

to coin money to make a fortune quickly.

coinage FIN. (1) a system of coins issued and controlled by the government of a country through its central bank for use as money. Cf. note issue. *See also* debasement of coinage. (2) the manufacture of metal money. (3) the right to manufacture it. *See* brassage; seigniorage.

decimal coinage *see* decimal currency *under* currency.

free coinage formerly a service offered by the State, which made no charge for manufacturing coins. *Syn.* gratuitous coinage.

standard coinage the former system of issuing coins with a face value equal to their intrinsic value, i.e. the value of the metal in them.

token coinage the present system of issuing coins having only a token value, i.e. their intrinsic value is much less than their face value.

coin-box *see* call-box.

coin circulation *see under* circulation.

coiner a criminal who makes false coins. *Syn.* forger; counterfeiter.

COINS Computerized Information System.

co-insurance *see under* insurance, classes and kinds of.

col. column.

Col., Colo. Colorado, U.S.A.

cold *see* catch a cold.

cold store (1) a place where goods, esp. food, furs, etc., can be stored at low temperature in order to preserve them. *Syn.* refrigerated warehouse. (2) (*colloq.*) *To put a matter/plan/project into cold storage*, to put off for consideration at a later time.

coll., colln. collision.

collaborate to work closely with another person, esp. in the writing of a book, the preparation of a plan or project of joint interest: *Let us collaborate in this research*, let us work together. *Syn.* co-operate.

collapse (1) of a company, to fail in business, usu. suddenly. *Syn.* crash. (2) STK. EXCH. a heavy and sudden fall in prices.

collateral BKG. & FIN. a security given for the repayment of a loan. *Syn.* collateral security.

collateral acceptance *see under* acceptance (5).

collateral loan BKG. one covered by collateral security.

collateral note FIN. a special kind of promissory note that includes a list of securities or other valuable things that the debtor has pledged to the creditor as security in case the promise to pay is not kept.

collateral security FIN. & BKG. extra security provided by or for a borrower to support his intention to repay a loan. The security may be in the form of documents giving a right to property of some kind, such as the title-deeds of a house, government bonds, notes, etc. *Syn.* collateral.

collateral trust bond *see under* bond, *n.*

colleague a fellow worker, esp. one of equal importance and in the same profession or organization: *I must ask my colleagues on the board* (*of directors*). *He is liked/accepted by his colleagues.*

collect (1) COM. & TAXN. to obtain payment of money, e.g. of debts, subscriptions, donations, taxes, cheques, bills of exchange, esp. from a number of people. (2) BKG. as a banker, to present a cheque to the banker on whom it is drawn and thus to collect the amount for credit to the customer's account.

collecting banker one who collects cheques either for himself or for his customers, i.e. he presents cheques to other bankers for payment. He must use proper care while acting as collecting agent for his customer and must tell the customer if any cheque handed in for collection is returned unpaid.

(3) COM. & TRANSPT. to take away, remove, goods from a particular place: *We will collect your waste twice weekly. The goods are ready for you to collect. See* freight collect.

collecting commission *see* collecting note.

collecting note INSCE. a document signed by an insured person who has made a claim under an insurance policy, giving power to an insurance broker to collect money due to the insured under the claim. For his services the broker receives a *collecting commission*.

collection FIN. & ACCTS. obtaining payment of a debt, e.g. a bill, cheque, etc.

charity collection the collecting of money to give to the poor.

collection and delivery a charge appearing on invoices to meet the cost of collecting and delivering. *Abbr.* c. & d.

postal collection the clearing of post office letter-boxes.

collections *pl.* COM. & FIN. money collected or received.

collective agreement IND. REL. the formal contract between an employer or group of employers and a trade union representing employees, recording the agreed rates of wages and the hours and conditions of work of the employees. *See* collective bargaining.

collective bargaining IND. REL. the work of trade unions and similar organizations representing employees in bargaining with employers in order to settle by formal agreement the level of wages, and the hours and conditions of employment.

collective farm AGR. in socialist countries, a farm owned by the State and run by the persons who work on it, as distinguished from farms in non-socialist countries which are owned and run by private persons. Each worker on a collective farm usu. has a small plot of land which he can cultivate privately, but most of the land is farmed collectively.

collective goods ECON. THEORY goods owned by the public as a whole, not by private persons or organizations, such as roads, public buildings, parks, hospitals, etc.

collective policy *see under* insurance policy.

collectivism ECON. any form of social organization which supports state planning of the economy and public ownership of all the means of production. The word first applied to the ideas of Socialists who disagreed with Marxism and communism; but it now refers loosely to state socialism, which opposes co-operation and guild socialism but allows private persons some limited freedom to own personal property. Collectivism is the opposite of individualism and liberalism.

collectivist ECON. a person who supports the ideas of collectivism.

collect on delivery *see* cash on delivery.

collector a person employed to collect or gather in sums of money such as rents, rates, taxes, debts , subscriptions, gifts, etc. *Abbr.* collr.

collector of taxes in Britain, a local official of the Department of Inland Revenue whose duty it is to receive taxes from the public. Cf. inspector of taxes.

collier (1) IND. a coal-miner. (2) SHIPG. a ship for carrying coal.

colliery IND. a coal-mine. *Syn.* pit.

collision INSCE. the violent striking together of one vehicle, ship or aircraft with another or with some other object: *The van was in collision with a lorry. The two ships are on a collision course*, and will run into each other if one or the other does not change course. *See* marine accident *under* accident; negligent collision *under* negligent. *Collision clause*, a special set of conditions put into a marine insurance policy covering the owner of a ship against risk of liability to the owner of another ship which may be in collision with his. *Syn.* running-down clause.

Colombo Plan ECON. an organization first suggested at a meeting of commonwealth foreign ministers at Colombo, Sri Lanka (Ceylon), in 1950 and put into effect in 1951 for the purpose of providing technical and financial help to the less-developed countries of south and southeast Asia, esp. in planning the work of government in developing health services, training in agriculture and technology, and scientific research. Money is provided mainly by the International Bank for Reconstruction and Development. The original members, Australia, Ceylon, Great Britain, India, New Zealand and Pakistan were later joined by Japan and the U.S.A. as well as a number of Asian countries. There are now 24 member countries.

colón the currency unit of both Costa Rica and El Salvador, divided into 100 centimos (100 centavos in El Salvador). *Pl.* colones or colóns.

colonialism ECON. the view that trade between the advanced and the less-developed countries is always to the advantage of the advanced countries. Cf. neo-colonialism.

colophon COM. the special mark or sign of a publisher, printer or author (writer) of a book.

colourable (1) COM. (of a copy) good enough to

colloquial in common use in the conversation of ordinary people. Not formal. *Abbr.* colloq.

collusive tendering COM. & IND. the practice of several firms coming to a secret understanding when sending in tenders to do work or to supply goods, so that the party calling for the tenders is misled into thinking that the tenderers are in honest competition. *Syn.* dummy tendering; level tendering. *See also* common price *under* price.

Colo. Colorado, U.S.A.

Colombia a democratic republic in the northwest of South America, pop. 23 million approx. (1973); capital, Bogota, pop. 2.3 million approx.; language, Spanish; currency unit, the peso, divided into 100 centavos. Member, O.A.S.; L.A.F.T.A.

deceive: *A colourable imitation*, something that is not really what it appears and is claimed to be. (2) LAW in U.S.A., tending to support a statement of fact: *A colourable title*, one supported by facts or events which make it likely to be true. *Syn.* colorable (U.S.A.).

colours SHIPG. the flag flown by a ship to show the country in which it is registered: *A ship sailing under Panamanian colours*, flying the flag of Panama.

Columbia see District of Columbia.

column ACCTS. (1) figures set one under another so that they may be easily added up. (2) a space enclosed by upright lines within which figures may be written one under another. *See* analysis column *under* analysis; folio column *under* folio. (3) ADVTG. the upright rows of printed matter running from top to bottom of a page in a newspaper or magazine.

column-inch the unit used in measuring space in a newspaper, on which advertisement rates are usu. based. Cf. lineage.

columnar account books ACCTS. when it is desired to analyse the sales, expenses, etc. between various classes of goods or between departments or areas or in any other way, the day book is provided with extra columns called analysis columns. *See under* analysis.

com. commercial; commission; communication.

combative advertising see advertising.

combination (1) IND. REL. & ECON. HIST. a name given in the eighteenth and nineteenth centuries to an association of workmen at a time when such associations were against the law. The Combination Laws were brought to an end in 1824. *See* freedom of association; trade union. (2) ACCTS. *see* absorption. (3) IND. & STK. EXCH. the combining of two or more independent companies or groups of companies to make one single organization under a common control. *Syn.* amalgamation; absorption; consolidation; integration; merger; rationalization.

horizontal combination *see* horizontal integration *under* integration.

vertical combination *see* vertical integration *under* integration.

combine IND. a combination.

combined certificate of value and origin *see* customs invoice *under* invoice.

combined policy *see under* insurance policy.

combined transport bill of lading *see* container bill of lading *under* bill of lading.

COMECON Council for Mutual Economic Assistance (C.M.E.A.) an organization set up in 1949 by six communist countries of Eastern Europe, namely the U.S.S.R., Poland, Czechoslovakia, Hungary, Romania and Bulgaria, to help forward the economic development of the member countries, who were later joined by the German Democratic Republic

(1950), the Mongolian People's Republic (1962), Yugoslavia (1964) and Cuba (1969). The organization aims to improve mutual trade and investment, to provide technical assistance, and to bring about a greater degree of industrial integration and specialization among its members. With its help, the International Bank for Economic Co-operation was formed in 1963 to provide investment finance and a means of settling trade payments between members.

comfortably off *see* well off.

comfort letter BKG. & FIN. a letter to a bank or other lender of money in which the writer supports a person who wishes to borrow money, and recommends that a loan be given to him.

comm. commerce.

command COM. & FIN. to be able to obtain: *He can command a high salary. This product commands a high price.*

command economy ECON. the type of economy now existing in certain socialist countries such as Communist China and the U.S.S.R., in which all planning and direction of economic activity is done by a central body and not left to private enterprise and the price system. It has proved to be an effective system in some less-developed countries. *Syn.* controlled economy; planned economy; statism.

commanditaire *see* commandite partnership *under* partnership.

commence to begin; to start: *To commence business/trading/loading/operations/proceedings. Opp.* to cease; to end; to terminate.

certificate to commence business *see under* certificate.

commencement COM. of a commercial letter, the opening words, called the salutation or greeting, such as *Sir(s)* or *Dear Sir(s)*, or, in U.S.A., *Gentlemen*.

commerce (1) COM. & ECON. in its wide sense, the exchange of goods and services for money or for other goods and services by way of trade, and all the various business operations, such as banking, insurance, transport and communications, that make such exchange possible. In the narrow sense, commerce means trading between buyers and sellers in different countries, i.e. foreign or overseas trade.

passive commerce goods being imported and exported by a country in ships that are owned by other countries.

(2) a subject of study and research in many universities and commercial colleges. It includes courses in economics, business, commercial law, management, etc. Many schools teach children commerce to prepare them for business life. *Syn.* business economics.

commerce, chamber of *see under* chamber.

commerce clause LAW in the U.S. Constitution, Article 1, section 8, which gives Congress power 'to regulate Commerce with foreign nations and among the several States and with Indian tribes'. The courts have ruled that this clause gives Congress power to regulate business, labour and agriculture when these form part of interstate commerce. *See* interstate commerce.

commercial *adj.* COM. concerned with the buying and selling of goods and services by way of trade.
n. (1) ADVTG. a short picture or sound programme on radio, television or in a cinema, advertising a product or service. (2) COM. (*colloq.*) a commercial traveller; a travelling representative or salesman. *Syn.* traveller. (3) COM. (*colloq.*) a hotel providing food and lodging at low prices for commercial travellers rather than for tourists. (4) STK. EXCH. *see* commercials.

commercial agent COM. a person or organization, usu. appointed by a manufacturer under an agency agreement to sell the principal's products in return for a commission on the value of the business he gets. Cf. commercial agency; commission agent.

commercial agency COM. a business organization which gives advice on the financial position of persons or companies, esp. on whether they can be trusted to pay. *Syn.* credit agency.

commercial art ADVTG. a branch of the graphic arts which provides material for advertising, books, magazines and newspapers in the form of pictures and designs, including the presentation of matter set up in type. *Syn.* industrial art.

commercial artist *see* artist.

commercial attaché *see* attaché.

commercial banks *see* joint-stock banks.

commercial bill *see under* bill of exchange.

commercial cause LAW a case brought in a civil court concerning a business claim; a lawsuit relating to commercial matters. *See* cause.

commercial code *see* code.

commercial college COM. & MAN. a school for higher education which provides courses in business subjects.

commercial correspondence COM. the letters and other documents which are used in business and which make it possible for people at a distance from each other to make their ideas and wishes known. These papers also form the records of the agreements and dealings of the business.

commercial counsellor COM. an official working in an embassy whose duty it is to advise on commercial matters.

Commercial Court LAW in Britain, part of the Queen's Bench Division of the High Court in which only commercial cases are tried, by a single judge either alone or with a special jury.

commercial credit COM. & FIN. (1) any arrangement which provides for goods to be bought and sold without immediate payment. (2) the length of time agreed or allowed between the date of charging the goods and the date the payment becomes due, called the credit period. *Syn.* mercantile credit. (3) BKG. an exporter's bill of exchange, *see* acceptance credit *under* acceptance (5).

commercial credit company COM. & FIN. in Britain, one that makes loans to manufacturers and traders against the security of their book debts (accounts receivable). *Syn.* sales finance company. In U.S.A., a discount house.

commercial education *see* commerce (2); commercial college.

commercialese COM. (*colloq.*) the strange language of business letters during the nineteenth and early twentieth centuries, now happily replaced by ordinary everyday English. It mainly consisted of formal meaningless expressions based on excessive politeness: *Your esteemed favour to hand*, we have received your letter. *Syn.* commercial jargon. *See also* date.

commercial geography that part of geography which deals with the commodities and products of world trade, and their transport and distribution to the consumer markets. *See also* economic geography.

commercial invoice *see under* invoice.

commercial jargon *see* commercialese; jargon.

commercial law LAW & COM. the law of a country as applied to any kind of business activity. It includes among its many branches: the law of agency, banking and bankruptcy; company and partnership law; the law of contracts, import and export, insurance, copyrights, designs, patents and trade-marks, and the sale of goods. *Syn.* mercantile law; law merchant.

commercial letter of credit *see under* letter of credit.

commercial monopoly *see under* monopoly.

commercial manager *see under* manager.

commercial paper COM. & BKG. (1) in U.S.A., various kinds of short-term negotiable instruments used by business concerns in making payments, including bills of exchange, esp. trade acceptances, and promissory notes. (2) sums advanced as loans by banks to finance the buying of goods. Cf. commodity paper; financial paper. *Syn.* mercantile paper.

prime commercial paper promissory notes payable in from four to twelve months, issued by large American business concerns of good reputation and sold to the public through brokers in the commercial-paper market.

commercial radio and television COM. & ADVTG. broadcast programmes paid for by advertisers who are charged according to the length of time that their advertisement lasts. *Syn.* independent radio/television.

commercial sale rooms COM. rooms, usu. in a hotel, which can be hired by commercial travellers for showing examples of their goods to retailers. *Syn.* stock-rooms; salesroom(s).

commercial services COM. the services of persons concerned with buying and selling goods and commodities, and with business operations such as banking, insurance, transport and communications.

commercial set COM. & BKG a set of four essential shipping documents needed when sending goods abroad: bill of exchange, bill of lading, certificate of insurance, and invoice. The exporter usu. sends the buyer at least two separate sets of shipping documents, posted on different days.

commercial traveller COM. (1) in Britain, a person employed by a manufacturer or wholesale dealer to travel to different places to obtain orders from retailers, now usu. called a sales representative. *Syn.* representative. (2) (U.S.A.) traveling salesman.

commercial treaty COM. & FIN. an agreement signed by two or more countries recording special arrangements for trade between them, including the making of payments, the fixing of import or export duties, etc. *Syn.* trade agreement.

commercial vehicles TRANSPT. trucks, lorries, vans, etc. used for purposes of trade, as distinguished from private and public-service vehicles.

commercials STK. EXCH. shares of commercial companies esp. those making or selling consumer goods, as distinguished from industrials.

commissary (U.S.A.) COM. a special shop run by the government, where government employees such as diplomats and soldiers may buy food, drink, clothing and other goods at controlled prices.

commission (1) LAW an official document giving a person or group of persons some special power or authority such as is given to officers of the armed forces and of the police, and to a Justice of the Peace. (2) a group of persons of high rank and with special knowledge who are appointed by the State to serve the public in some special way, either as a permanent body of officials such as the Civil Service Commission, or the Monopolies and Mergers Commission, or temporarily to examine and report on some social problem, such as the Royal Commission on Taxation, or on Population, or on the Press. *See* commissioners. (3) a method of paying to employees such as sales representatives, shop assistants and others, some extra money, called a sales commission, over and above their normal wage or salary to encourage them to sell as much as possible. (4) COM. & INSCE. payment to agents and others for their services, usu. in buying and selling goods, and calculated as an agreed percentage of the amount of business done or introduced.

banker's commission a charge made by a bank for certain services, esp. a charge made for keeping a current account when the average balance in the account is small and the amount of work done by the bank is large. The commission may be a percentage of the total value of cheques debited to the account, or be based on the number of cheques drawn and cheques paid in. A charge, often called commission, is also made for each payment of standing orders, credit transfers, etc.

buying commission payment made at an agreed rate to an agent, esp. to a commission agent, based on the total value of the goods he buys for his principal. *Syn.* buyer's commission. Cf. selling commission.

insurance commission the payment made by insurers to insurance agents and brokers for their services in selling insurance. It is usu. expressed as a percentage of either the premium income or the sum assured. *Syn.* brokerage.

overriding commission (*a*) a very special commission, one that is more important than, and over and above, all other commissions or discounts. Such a commission is usu. allowed by a manufacturer or exporter to an agent to cover his extra overhead expenses in selling the product in his market. (*b*) STK. EXCH. a special commission charged by brokers who arrange for a new issue of shares to be underwritten.

selling commission the payment made at an agreed rate to an agent, esp. a sales or selling agent, based on the total value of the goods he sells for his principal.

commission agent COM. in foreign trade, an agent who, in return for an agreed rate of commission, buys or sells goods in one country according to the directions of a principal who is in another country.

export commission agent a buying or purchasing agent acting for an overseas importer. The agent buys and exports goods according to the principal's orders, called indents. *Syn.* confirming house; commission merchant; commercial agent.

import commission agent a firm with special knowledge of the home market, often having its own warehouses and sales organization, who acts for foreign manufacturers, arranges for goods to be consigned to it, sells the goods in the home market and sends the money so obtained to the principal after keeping back its own commission and other agreed charges.

commission broker STK. EXCH. in U.S.A., a stockbroker.

commissioner for oaths LAW a solicitor officially appointed by the government to witness the swearing on oath, or the affirmation, of legal documents such as affidavits.

Commissioner, Parliamentary *see under* Parliamentary.

Commissioners of Customs and Excise LAW & TAXN. in Britain, a body of officials appointed by the State and given the duty mainly of collecting customs duties, excise duties, and value added tax. Cf. Commissioners of Inland Revenue.

Commissioners of Inland Revenue LAW & TAXN. in Britain, a body of officials appointed by the State and given the duty mainly of collecting income tax, capital gains tax, capital transfer tax, and stamp duties. Cf. Commissioners of Customs and Excise. *Syn.* tax commissioners.

commissioner, trade *see under* trade.

commission merchant COM. (1) a merchant or middleman who never holds any goods in stock, buys on credit only enough goods to supply his customers' immediate orders, and sells usu. only to wholesalers by showing samples and by using his powers of persuasion. *Syn.* commission salesman. (2) a commission agent.

commission on current accounts *see* bank charges.

commission salesman *see* commission merchant.

commit to promise; to bind (oneself) to do something: *I have committed myself to lending him money. The company is committed to paying a staff bonus. You are fully committed,* you are forced to do what you agreed to do.

commitment a promise; something to which one has committed oneself, which one is bound to do; a payment which one is bound to make: *We have heavy commitments next month,* we shall have much expense to meet. *This is a firm commitment,* a promise which we are bound to keep. *Without commitment on my part,* without making a firm promise. *He is unable to meet his commitments,* unable to pay his debts.

Committee of Public Accounts PUB. FIN. in Britain, a group of members of the House of Commons appointed to examine the report of the Comptroller and Auditor-General on the spending of money by government departments, in order to make sure that the sums voted by Parliament have been properly used. *See* Audit Office.

Committee of Ways and Means *see under* ways and means.

commodity (1) ECON. economic goods are useful and scarce things wanted by buyers, and are divided by economists into two classes: commodities and services. Thus a commodity is any useful but scarce article or substance, but the name is given esp. to a basic foodstuff or material such as wheat or raw cotton that needs a manufacturing process before it is ready for the consumer. (2) ECON. THEORY goods which are perfect substitutes for each other.

commodity broker COMMOD. EXCH. a broker who acts as agent for buyers and sellers in one of the commodity markets, receiving a brokerage for his services. But in certain trades brokers may buy and sell for themselves, thus being dealers. In commodity markets other than metals, brokers are sometimes called *produce brokers*.

commodity exchanges COMMOD. EXCH. centres in commodity markets where, except for auction sales, all dealings are either in *actuals* or in *futures*. A trader in actuals may deal in spot (immediate) delivery or in forward supplies (delivery some time ahead). A trader in futures contracts to buy or sell a standardized class of commodity at a stated price at some fixed time in the future; the main purpose is to hedge (reduce) his risk of price changes. To do this he will sell futures when he buys actuals, and buy futures when he sells his stock. His gain or loss on his actuals dealings will roughly balance his gain or loss on his futures dealings.

commodity market COMMOD. EXCH. one in which commodities are bought and sold, esp. food and raw materials forming part of international trade, such as wheat and wool. The main markets are grouped in large cities, London and New York being the largest centres. Buying and selling is by brokers representing users and producers. Goods are usu. classified according to agreed standards of quality and variety so that dealing can take place without the commodity being seen. Some commodities are sold in public auction, but most are exchanged as actuals or futures. *See* commodity exchanges; produce exchange.

commodity money ECON. HIST. in former times many commodities such as cattle or shells or grain have been used as money. These were gradually replaced by precious metals, esp. gold and silver in the form of bars and coins. Later even these forms of commodity money were replaced by token money and notes. *See* cowrie; commodity standard *under* standard.

commodity paper COM. & BKG. in U.S.A., negotiable instruments such as bills of exchange, promissory notes, drafts, etc. held as security for loans made to finance imports, esp. of commodities. Cf. commercial paper; financial paper.

commodity standard *see under* standard.

common LAW in Britain, an area of land which belongs to the public. All members of the public have the right to use common land for air and exercise as long as they obey certain rules which the government has power to make. In some areas the public has the right also to cut wood, to fish in streams and to put animals to feed on the grass. *Syn.* common land.

common adventure MAR. INSCE. any group of things which are open to the same risks, such as a ship, its cargo and the freight earned in carrying it.

Common Agricultural Policy AGR. & COM. the system set up by the European Economic Community, partly to introduce and support free trade within the Community, and partly to protect the incomes of farmers producing foodstuffs in the member countries. Protection is given by fixing from time to time for each commodity a set of prices, esp. a target or desired price usu. above the market price, and by applying variable import levies and subsidies. The aim is to keep home prices at or near the target price. If E.E.C. production of a commodity is greater than consumption, the authorities will buy the surplus for storage or for export at a subsidized price. *See* target price, threshold price, support price, *all under* price. *Abbr.* C.A.P.

common average MAR. INSCE. *see* particular average *under* average (4).

common carrier *see under* carrier.

common customs tariff ECON. & TAXN. the customs duties charged by the members of the European Economic Community (E.E.C.) on imports from countries who are not members of the Community.

common employment LAW & IND. a rule under common law, that an employer is not responsible to his employee for injury caused by the carelessness of a fellow employee, unless the employer failed in his duty to take care in choosing his employees and in arranging for their safety. However, this rule is not always applied by the courts nowadays, because it tends to favour the employer.

common law LAW that branch of the law of England that has developed from ancient custom, i.e. the rules of society, and from the decisions of judges. *See* case law. Cf. civil law; equity; statute law.

Common Market, The European *see* European Economic Community.

common money bond *see* bond, *n.*

common ownership *see* ownership in common.

common pricing COM. (1) an agreement (usu. illegal) among competing business organizations to sell at exactly the same prices, the aim being to avoid a price war when one competitor lowers his prices and others have to do the same. (2) an agreement (usu. illegal) by several contractors to quote exactly the same price when tendering for a large engineering contract. *Syn.* level tendering; collusive tendering; dummy tendering.

common seal MAN. & LAW (1) a special mark pressed or stamped into the paper of a formal document issued by a limited company; it is the official equivalent of a signature. Every limited company must have such a seal bearing the name of the company, and it may be used only by authority of the board of directors. A seal book must be kept to record details of all docu-

ments on which the company's common seal has been stamped. (2) the instrument which applies the seal to a document. *Syn.* company seal.

common share *see* common stock/shares.

common stock/shares STK. EXCH. the words used in Canada and U.S.A. for ordinary, or equity, stock or shares.

Commonwealth Development Corporation an official organization set up by the British Government to give financial and technical help to the dependent territories of the Commonwealth so that they may develop their own skills and products.

Commonwealth of Australia *see under* Australia.

Commonwealth of Nations sometimes called *the British Commonwealth* or more loosely *the Commonwealth*. A free association of the United Kingdom and most of the independent nations which were formerly part of the British Empire, with the Queen recognized by all as head of the Commonwealth. They are united for political, commercial and cultural reasons.

commonwealth preference *see under* preference.

communal (1) public; owned in common by all: *A communal kitchen.* (2) belonging to a community; relating to groups of people having the same religion or occupation: *Communal beliefs*, beliefs shared by people belonging to the same community or religion.

communal agricultural organization *see* co-operative farm.

communicate (1) to pass to another person news, information, a request, etc.: *To communicate by cable/letter/telephone/telex, etc.* (2) to be connected to or with: *Communicating rooms in a hotel. Offices which communicate.*

communication COM. the act of communicating: *To be in communication with someone*, to be in touch, speaking or writing to one another. Something which passes messages or information, such as a letter: *We have received your communication of yesterday*, your letter . . .

communications *pl.* ways of moving goods, of travelling, and of sending messages, etc. between places.

communism an advanced socialist system and a form of government in which all economic power is in the hands of a classless society of workers, and all main means of production and distribution are publicly owned and used for the good of all. The ideas of modern communism came mainly from Karl Marx and Friedrich Engels in the nineteenth century. The two most important communist countries are the U.S.S.R. and Communist China. The aim of communism is, in the end, the total abolition of the State. *See* command economy; Karl Marx. Cf. bolshevism.

Communist one who believes communism to be the best form of political, social and economic organization.

community (1) a group of people living in one place or having common interests: *A rural/urban/village/farming/fishing/community*. (2) an organization of countries for the purpose of developing or controlling a common activity: *The European Coal and Steel Community*; *the European Economic Community*.

community investment investment in goods and services needed for the good of the community (schools, hospitals, etc.) and not for financial gain.

Community preference see under preference.

commutation (1) INSCE. the right of holders of certain life assurance policies to receive at retirement a tax-free lump sum instead of the whole or part of an annual pension. (2) the right generally to receive cash immediately by giving up a right to receive annual payments in the future.

commuter TRANSPT. (*colloq.*) a person who regularly travels some distance by public transport between his home in one place and his place of work in another. *Syn.* a season-ticket holder.

commuter-bélt the outlying parts round a city, where commuters live.

companies, group of see under group.

Companies Registry the office, formerly in London but now in Cardiff, of the Registrar of Companies, a government official responsible for keeping the register (official list) of companies and for recording detailed information about them, such as their accounts, their directors and any charges and mortgages on their assets.

company (1) a formal association of persons for business purposes, esp. a corporation or group of persons legally incorporated under company law. *Syn.* (U.S.A.) corporation. (2) in U.S.A., a general word for any business, whether it is a sole proprietorship, or a partnership or a corporation.

affiliate, affiliated company see under affiliate.

associated company see under associated.

banking company in Britain, a company carrying on the business of banking, to which certain sections of the Companies Acts relate which do not apply to other kinds of company.

blue-chip company see under blue chip.

bogus company see under bogus.

chartered company a joint-stock company incorporated by charter. *See* charter, *n*. (1).

close company a company of which the share-capital is held or controlled by five or fewer persons, or by persons who are all directors of the company. A close company must either pay out a large part of its profit as dividend or be classed for tax purposes as a private person. *Syn.* (U.S.A.) close corporation.

commercial company a limited company of which the main activity is commerce, i.e. buying and selling. *Syn.* trading company.

commercial credit company see under commercial credit.

controlling company see holding company below.

daughter company a company which is a subsidiary company of a parent or holding company. Cf. sister company.

defunct company one which is no longer carrying on business and has been struck off the register of companies. *See* dead book.

finance company see finance house.

foreign company see under foreign.

hire-purchase company see finance house.

holding company in Britain, a company that has been formed for the special purpose of holding the whole, or more than half, the share-capital of one or more other companies called subsidiary companies. In U.S.A. this is called a *pure holding company*, while an *operating holding company* is a company which operates a business, i.e. trading, and also holds more than half the capital of one or more other companies. Cf. controlling company; parent company; shell company (*colloq.*).

investment (trust) company a limited company that uses its capital to buy securities as investments, hoping to make a profit from dividends and interest received and from capital gains on sales of securities. Such companies are often called *investment trusts*, although they are seldom real trusts.

joint-stock company (*a*) in Britain, a form of business organization called a corporation, which has its capital divided into many small units of stock or into shares of low face value so that they may be bought by small and large investors. (The expression often has the same meaning as limited company.) Joint-stock companies are set up by (i) royal charter (*see* chartered company *under* charter, *n*. (1)); or (ii) Act of Parliament (*see* statutory company, e.g. the early railway and canal companies); or (iii) by registration under the Companies Acts (*see* registered company *under* company). (*b*) in U.S.A., a business organization having its capital divided into small units of stock, but the liability of its members is unlimited, as in a partnership.

limited liability company a joint-stock company, the financial liability of whose members is limited by law. If the company is *limited by shares*, the liability of each member is limited to the amount unpaid on his shares, and he may have to lose the cost of his shares, but no more, if the company goes into liquidation because of its debts. If the company is *limited by guarantee*, the liability of each member is limited to the amount he has personally guaranteed (promised) to pay if necessary in the event of liquidation. *See* private limited company; public limited company. Cf. unlimited company *below*.

livery company in the City of London one of a number of chartered companies, mostly very ancient (being descended from the craft guilds of the Middle Ages), whose members have the right to wear livery (special highly-decorated clothing). Although they are not trading companies, they are very rich and use their wealth in supporting schools and other activities for the public good.

management company a company that manages one or more unit trusts.

marine insurance company a special kind of limited company which carries on business as an underwriter of marine insurance, the liability of which is limited to the value of its declared assets and not by shares.

no-liability company (Australia) certain mining companies that may, by law, allow their shareholders to choose whether to pay calls upon their shares or to forfeit them. *See* forfeited share *under* share.

nominee company *see under* nominee.

one-man company *see under* one-man.

overseas company one incorporated outside Great Britain but having a place of business within Great Britain. *Syn.* foreign company.

parent company *see* subsidiary company *below*; group of companies.

private limited company a limited company which must not invite the public to subscribe for its shares or debentures, and does not allow its members to transfer their shares without the agreement of the other shareholders. It must have at least two but usu. not more than fifty members. Cf. public limited company. In India and some other countries the word 'Private' must by law form part of its name, usu. abbreviated to Pte, thus Desai & Co. Pte. Ltd.

property company *see under* property.

proprietary company (*a*) a holding company. (*b*) a company that owns land suitable for mining. (*c*) in Australia and South Africa, a private limited company; the word 'Proprietary' must by law form part of the name, usu. abbreviated to Pty.

public limited company a limited company which can offer its shares and debentures to the public; there is normally no limit to the right of its members to transfer their shares to other persons. There is no limit to the total number of members except that there must be at least seven.

public utility company a limited company which enjoys a monopoly for supplying essential services to the public, such as gas, electricity, water, transport and many others. It is under government control in fixing prices and

in obtaining money for expansion and development, and is often partly or wholly owned by the government.

related company *see* affiliate.

sales finance company *see* commercial credit company.

shell company (*colloq.*) a holding company.

sister company one of two or more subsidiary companies in the same group, or under the same holding company. Cf. daughter company.

statutory company a public utility company incorporated by Special Act of Parliament.

subsidiary company a company of which more than half the share-capital is owned by another company, called either a holding company or a parent company. The subsidiaries of the same parent or holding company are said to be affiliates. Cf. associated company.

sub-subsidiary company a company that is a subsidiary of a subsidiary of a holding company.

trading company (*a*) a limited company which is actively trading, i.e. buying and selling products and services for profit, unlike a nontrading company such as a holding company. (*b*) a company of which the business is that of a trader, i.e. buying other producers' products and selling them for profit, as distinguished from e.g. a manufacturing or mining company or a company offering services such as banking, insurance, etc. *Syn.* commercial company.

trust company (*a*) in Britain, an investment trust company. (*b*) in U.S.A., a corporation which performs the services of a trustee for the property of persons who have died, or for property in trust for living persons, and also advises on investments, etc.

unlimited company a company of which the liability of the members is unlimited, i.e. each member has to pay his full share of the debts of the company if it is brought to an end.

Company, The (in India, Pakistan, etc.) the (British) East India Company, 1600–1858. *Syn.* John Company.

company director MAN. a person who is a member of the board of directors of a company. *See* director.

company doctor *see under* doctor.

company formation LAW & STK. EXCH. the work of bringing into existence a new company. In Britain the first step is to send a written application, along with the Memorandum of Association, Articles of Association, Statutory Declaration and, in the case of a public company, certain other documents relating to the directors, to the Registrar of Companies. If everything is correct, the Registrar will issue the Certificate of Incorporation and a certificate to commence business, and the new company may start trading. *See* company promoter; formation expenses.

company law LAW that branch of law mainly contained in the Companies Acts, which govern the forming, registration and operation of companies of all kinds.

company limited by guarantee see limited liability company *under* company.

company limited by shares see limited liability company *under* company.

company meeting a meeting of the members (shareholders) of a company. The holding of these meetings is governed by law: every meeting must be properly convened (called) by giving due notice to everyone having a right to be present; it must be properly constituted (composed) with a quorum (minimum number) of members and a chairman. There are several kinds of company meeting. *Syn.* shareholders' meeting.

annual general meeting see *under* annual.

extraordinary general meeting an extra meeting called by the directors of a company to deal with matters which cannot be held over until the next annual general meeting.

ordinary general meeting see annual general meeting *under* annual.

statutory meeting a company meeting that must by law be held not earlier than one month nor more than three months after a company commences business; at this meeting the members (shareholders) consider the statutory report on the forming of the company and discuss related matters such as the share-capital, cash position, etc.

company officer LAW any official, such as a director, company secretary, manager, solicitor and auditor, who is concerned with the management of a company's affairs at its head or central office. The importance of distinguishing a company officer is that by law, esp. in a case of liquidation, the courts may examine the behaviour of the company officers and get back any money that they may have illegally obtained.

company promoter STK. EXCH. a person who, alone or with others, organizes and helps in the forming of a new company. He prepares a formation scheme, gets a board of directors together, obtains the services of solicitors, accountants, bankers and stockbrokers, pays the expenses of drawing up and issuing a prospectus and generally makes himself responsible for starting the company. *See also* company formation; formation expenses.

company seal see common seal.

company secretary MAN. in Britain, in a public company, a professionally-qualified person appointed by the board of directors to carry out the legal duties of the company such as keeping certain records, sending certain information to the Registrar of Companies, and generally to manage the administration of the company. In a private company the person appointed must be 'suitable' but need not have professional qualifications. All limited companies must appoint a company secretary.

company's risk see carrier's risk.

company, ship's see ship's company.

company union IND. REL. an association of workers in a factory or other industrial or commercial concern, often encouraged by employers and having no connection with the trade union movement. *Syn.* house union.

comparative advantage see Comparative Cost Principle.

Comparative Cost Principle ECON. a basic idea in the Theory of International Trade, that the highest world production of all kinds of goods and services will be reached if each country and region puts most of its effort into producing the things for which it has a comparative advantage over the other countries, i.e. the things which it is best fitted to produce. *See* bilateralism; multilateralism. *Syn.* Law of Comparative Cost(s); comparative advantage.

Comparative Cost(s), Law of see Comparative Cost Principle.

compartment TOUR. & TRANSPT. a separate division or small room in a larger structure, such as in a railway carriage: *A seat in a first-/second-class compartment on the morning train to Glasgow. A smoking/non-smoking compartment. A reserved compartment.*

compassionate leave see *under* leave.

compensating error ACCTS. a mistake in bookkeeping which tends to remain hidden because it is exactly balanced by another mistake on the other side of the trial balance, e.g. if interest receivable account was added up £100 too much and bank charges account was also added up £100 too much. *See also* reversal of entries.

compensation a payment to make good a loss: *He received £10,000 in compensation for the loss of an eye. Compensation is paid to a landowner if his property is taken by the government. Syn.* consideration; quid pro quo.

workmen's compensation a payment which an employer is bound by law to make to an employee or his family for personal injury or death caused by an accident at work, and for injury to his health caused by an industrial disease. This liability is largely covered by the National Insurance (Industrial Injuries) Act.

compensation fee (C.F.) see parcel post *under* post.

Compensation Fund STK. EXCH. a fund into which members of the Stock Exchange pay their share, and which is used to make good losses suffered by investors when a member firm cannot pay its debts.

compensation stocks STK. EXCH. British Government guaranteed stocks, such as British electricity, gas and transport stocks, given to the shareholders as compensation when certain industries were nationalized (brought under state ownership).

compensatory finance *see* deficit financing.

compete COM. to try to win or to obtain business for oneself against one's rivals: *Our product has to compete with theirs. We are competing for a larger share of the market. See also* competition.

competence (1) FIN. enough money income to live comfortably. (2) LAW legal power to do something, such as being of age (over 18 years in Britain), of sound mind (not mad) and legally free, e.g. to make a contract, a will, a marriage, etc. (3) LAW the legal power of a court of law to try a particular case. *Syn.* competency.

competent *adj.* of a person, having the skill, knowledge and ability to do something: *He is a competent manager/accountant/doctor, etc. Opp.* incompetent.

competition COM. rivalry between business concerns in the same market, usu. in selling at the lowest price or in giving better quality or generally offering better value for money.

atomistic competition *see* perfect competition *below.*

fair competition *see* healthy competition *below.*

free competition ECON. an economy in which there is complete freedom from interference by the State, and in which prices are free to move according to the forces of supply and demand. *Syn.* free economy.

healthy competition COM. competition that is clean, free of unfair practices. *Syn.* fair competition. *Opp.* unfair competition.

imperfect competition ECON. THEORY a state of competition in a market in which there is neither pure competition nor pure monopoly, i.e. buyers and sellers have an imperfect knowledge of the market, there is a lack of freedom of movement of factors of production from one industry to another, and there are limiting transport costs. *Syn.* monopolistic competition. *Opp.* perfect competition. *See* differentiation.

monopolistic competition ECON. THEORY (*a*) a state of competition in a market in which there are only a few producers, who can force buyers to accept their prices. (*b*) that form of competition where sellers can influence buyers by differences in the quality or appearance of the goods they produce. *Syn.* imperfect competition. *Opp.* pure competition; perfect competition.

non-price competition COM. a market situation where rival sellers are competing for trade not by price but by offering attractions such as better quality of product and packaging, free installation, servicing, etc.

perfect competition ECON. THEORY a state of competition in which the price of a good is the same throughout the market because buyers and sellers have a perfect knowledge of market conditions, there is complete freedom of movement of factors of production from one industry to another, and there are no transport costs. *Syn.* pure competition; atomistic competition. *Opp.* monopolistic competition; imperfect competition.

pure competition ECON. THEORY *see* perfect competition *above. Syn.* atomistic competition. *Opp.* monopolistic competition.

unfair competition COM. competition that is dishonest, or not in accord with accepted business behaviour, such as giving secret discounts, making false claims about the quality of the product, or employing under-paid workers.

competitive COM. comparing favourably in price and quality with other products of the same kind. Able to attract buyers away from rival products in the market: *A competitive price*, one which is lower than that of rivals, or which gives better value for money.

competitive advertising *see* advertising.

competitive demand *see under* demand.

competitive examination one in which the candidates compete for a limited number of jobs.

competitive market ECON. THEORY one in which: there is only one price for a given commodity at any one time; all buyers and sellers know the condition of the market; and the price of a given commodity is at a level which results in the sale of the whole quantity offered.

competitive supply *see under* supply.

competitor a rival in business.

competitor analysis COM. & IND. the practice of many producers and wholesalers of examining very carefully the competing products in the market, comparing them with their own and finding out in what ways their own products can be changed or improved so as to obtain a larger share of the market. This forms a branch of market research.

compilation (1) the act of compiling. (2) a thing that has been compiled.

compile to collect and arrange information, figures, ideas, opinions, etc. in a form fit for study or examination: *To compile statistics/a dictionary/a report/a list.*

compiler a person who compiles.

complain COM. to express dissatisfaction: *He complains that we are charging him too much. We wish to complain about your service. They complain about the food in the canteen. Please stop complaining.*

complainant LAW *see* plaintiff.

complaint (1) LAW a first statement of the facts on which a person bases his action in a civil court. (2) COM. an expression of dissatisfaction, esp. by a customer or consumer: *I wish to make/lodge a complaint. You have cause for complaint. We get many complaints about our service. Your complaint is justified.*

complaints book/box a book or box in a restaurant, hostel, hotel, etc. where written complaints to the management may be placed.

complementary demand *see under* demand.

complementary supply *see under* supply.

completed audit *see* audit.

completely knocked down (c.k.d.) COM. & IND. goods, esp. machines, offered for sale or quoted c.k.d. and supplied in separate parts which the buyer must put together at his cost: *Our ex-works price for the printing press is £10,000 c.k.d.*, in parts not put together.

completion LAW in the sale of property, the point where the contract is completed, the vendor (seller) having conveyed (handed over) the property, and the purchaser (buyer) having accepted it and paid the purchase price.

completion statement an account drawn up by the seller's solicitor showing the exact amount of money the seller claims from the buyer at completion of the contract, such as the purchase price, the deposit and the apportionment of rates, etc.

compliance, declaration of *see under* declaration.

complimentary close (of a letter), the usual ending of formal business letters such as *Yours faithfully*; but in less formal and more personal letters, *Yours sincerely* or *Yours truly*.

compliments *pl.* an expression of friendly greeting: *With compliments. Please accept this book with our compliments*, meaning that it is offered free of charge. *The compliments of the season*, greetings fit for the occasion, such as at Christmas and the New Year.

compliments slip a printed slip of paper bearing the words *With the compliments of* followed by the name and address of the person or organization sending it. Such slips are enclosed with other material to show who has sent it, and are used only when there is no need to enclose a letter.

composite demand *see* alternate demand.

composite supply *see under* supply.

composition LAW an agreement between a debtor and all his creditors about settling his debts by paying a smaller sum instead of the whole amount owed, i.e. a part payment, called a composition or dividend, usu. expressed as so much in the pound: *He has made a composition of 65p in the £1.* *Syn.* compounding. *See* scheme of arrangement; dividend (2).

scheme of composition as a course taken to avoid being made bankrupt, a debtor may propose a plan, to be formally recorded in a registered deed, by which he pays only a part

of the whole amount that he owes. The plan, or scheme, must be approved by the Bankruptcy Court and by creditors representing three-fourths of the total value of unpaid debts. *Syn.* scheme of arrangement.

composition for stamp duty TAXN. & LAW a sum of money paid to the tax authorities before they will stamp documents for duty.

compositor IND. a skilled employee who sets up type in a printing works; a typesetter.

compound *v.* LAW to accept a composition: *To compound with creditors. See* composition.

compound bonus *see under* bonus, insurance.

compound entry ACCTS. in book-keeping, a journal entry which includes postings to several accounts.

compounding *see* composition.

compound interest FIN. interest upon interest; interest which is payable not only on the original capital sum but also on sums of interest as they accumulate. Thus £100 at 10% per annum compound would be worth £100 + £10 = £110 after one year; £110 + £11 = £121 after two years; £121 + £12.10 = £133.10 after three years, and so on. Cf. simple interest.

compound tariff *see under* tariff.

comprehensive policy *see under* insurance policy.

compromise (1) LAW an agreement to settle a lawsuit out of court. (2) IND. REL. the settlement of a dispute by agreeing that each side gives way on some of its demands, with the result that neither side gets all it wants. *To agree to/accept/suggest/put forward/arrive at/ reach/a compromise.*

comptometer a fast adding machine.

comptroller FIN. & ACCTS. a title given to a controller, esp. of accounts and finance: *The Comptroller and Auditor-General. Syn.* controller.

Comptroller and Auditor-General *see* Audit Office.

compulsory acquisition *see* compulsory purchase.

compulsory purchase LAW the taking away of the ownership of property, without the present owner's agreement, by a government organization under powers given by Parliament, e.g. to allow a whole street to be redeveloped. There are rules for payment of compensation. *Syn.* compulsory acquisition. Cf. requisition.

compulsory saving *see under* saving.

compulsory winding-up LAW & STK. EXCH. the forced ending of the existence of a company by order of the court. Cf. voluntary winding-up. *See* winding-up.

compute to calculate; to determine by counting: *We compute the cost at £1 million. To compute a bill*, to calculate the date on which a bill of exchange will mature (become due for payment).

computer COMP. a very fast electronic calculating

machine that can make decisions by comparing numbers, can store in its memory very large amounts of information in the form of numbers and letters, and can answer complicated questions in a few seconds. It can print information on paper, record it on magnetic tape or send it over long distances by telegraph, cable or radio. Because it can choose instantly between various paths, it can be used by industry to control machines (*see* automation). Computers are widely used by research scientists for calculations; by commercial concerns for such work as accounting, the preparation of payrolls, sales and stock records, stock exchange and commodity-market prices; and by government offices for a variety of purposes.

analogue computer the kind of computer mainly used for scientific calculations and based on the idea of making a mechanical or electrical likeness (an analogue) of the problem to be solved. *Syn.* (U.S.A.) analog computer.

digital computer the kind of computer in most common use, which counts and calculates. It is so named because it uses only digits (numbers 1 to 9 and 0), usually in the binary system, which are represented by a group of pulses (short increases in electric current).

computer file *see* file, *n.* (3).

computerize COM. & IND. to provide with computers: *Computerized accounts systems have replaced manual accounting.* To control by computer: *All airline booking in Britain is computerized.*

Con. Consols; Consul.

con. contra (*Latin*, against). *See* pro.

concealment (1) LAW the offence of hiding something, of not making something known that ought to be made known, such as the concealment of assets by a bankrupt. (2) INSCE. a failure of an insured person to make known facts that the insurers ought to be told about, so making the insurance have no effect.

concentration of industry IND. the tendency for certain industries to gather together in certain areas or places, for one or more of the following reasons: nearness to supplies of energy, raw materials, labour (skilled and unskilled); markets; transport; weather. *Syn.* location of industry.

concept an idea: *The accrual concept*, the thought that comes to one's mind when one considers accrual.

concern COM. & IND. a business; a commercial or industrial organization, usu. a limited company. *Syn.* undertaking; enterprise.

concession COM. & IND. (1) a right given formally by a government to use an area of land for a stated purpose: *A mineral/mining/oil/railway/canal/concession.* (2) the area of land so affected. (3) a right given by the manufacturer of a product to a business organization, called

a *concessionaire*, to be the only sellers of that product in a particular area or country. (4) TAXN. an allowance given to certain taxpayers for a special reason, such as to encourage exports, increase employment and reduce overcrowding in certain places: *A tax concession.*

concessionaire *see* concession (3).

conciliation IND. REL. the settlement of industrial disputes by employers and trade unions being brought into willing agreement by the efforts of a third party called a *conciliator*. Cf. arbitration; mediation. *See* Advisory, Conciliation and Arbitration Service.

conclude (1) to arrange; to settle: *To conclude an agreement/a bargain/contract/treaty/ deal.* (2) to bring or come to an end: *The meeting concluded with a vote of thanks to the chairman.* (3) to reach an opinion, a decision, a judgment, by the use of reasoning: *After reading your report, I conclude that you are in favour of the proposal.*

con. cr. contra credit.

condition LAW in the law of contract, an essential duty, failure to carry out which will allow the other party to treat the contract as ended. Cf. warranty.

condition precedent one which becomes effective only on the happening of some future event, e.g. the rebuilding of a house if it is destroyed by fire.

condition subsequent one which continues to be effective until some future event happens, such as the payment of a sum of money annually to a person until his death. Thus a condition subsequent will in fact bring the contract to an end.

express condition one which is clearly expressed in the contract, as distinguished from an implied condition.

implied condition one which is accepted as being effective and binding although it is not actually stated in the contract, e.g. that the seller has the right to sell the goods and that the goods are as described in the contract.

conditional COM. dependent on; containing some condition(s): *A conditional offer*, one which is not firm, being dependent, e.g. on the goods being still in stock when the offer is accepted, or on the buyer accepting it by a certain date. *A conditional acceptance*, where a buyer accepts an offer on condition that some demand of his is met, e.g. that he gets an extra discount, or that delivery is made by a certain date. *Opp.* unconditional.

conditional bill of sale *see under* bill of sale.

conditional bond *see under* bond, *n.*

conditional endorsement *see under* endorsement.

conditional sale *see under* sale.

conditions of sale COM. & LAW in contracts for the sale of goods, the arrangements on which the seller is willing to sell his goods and which usu. appear in his printed price-lists or in documents acknowledging orders. *See* condition.

conduct to lead or guide; to manage: *To conduct a business. To conduct negotiations. To conduct a party on a tour of the factory.*

conducted tour TOUR. one on which a guide travels with the party of tourists to look after arrangements for the journey and to point out and explain the interesting sights.

conduct money *see* caution money (4).

conductor TRANSPT. (1) a person employed to collect fares (the cost of travel) on a bus. (2) (U.S.A.) a person in charge of people being carried on a public vehicle, esp. a train, or employed as a guide on a sightseeing tour. *See* conducted tour. *Syn.* guard (Britain).

Confédération Générale du Travail (C.G.T.) IND. REL. (*French*, General Confederation of Labour) the French equivalent of the Trades Union Congress (T.U.C.).

Confederation of British Industry IND. a large association of industrial and commercial companies, trade associations and publicly-owned industries which represents employers and management in dealings with the government and trade unions on industrial problems.

confer (1) to discuss; to get advice: *To confer with one's lawyers. We have been conferring on the subject*, talking together. (2) to give; to allow: *To confer a degree on a university student/a knighthood on the chairman of the company. To confer the status of sole stockist on a customer.*

conference a more or less formal meeting or series of meetings attended by persons who talk to each other, discuss or settle matters of common interest and perh. reach decisions on action to be taken: *We are in conference. A press conference.*

conference lines owners of shipping lines who have formed a shipping conference.

shipping conference *see under* shipping.

confidence (1) a feeling of trust: *I have confidence in him*, I trust him. *My confidence was misplaced*, I was wrong to trust him. *I lost confidence in them when they did not pay.*

confidence trick *see* con-man.

(2) a secret told to another person: *We exchanged confidences about our employers. He told me in* (strict) *confidence that . . . He took me into his confidence*, told me his secret(s).

abuse/breach of confidence the breaking of a promise to keep a secret. *See under* breach.

(3) belief in oneself: *She is full of self-confidence.* (4) ECON. trust in the present and future economic situation by businessmen, investors: *We must await the return of confidence before buying another ship.*

confidential *adj.* secret; told in confidence and expected to be kept a secret: *I have received*

confidential information. *A confidential talk/letter/file/communication.* A document marked confidential must not be shown to persons who do not need to see it. *Adj.* confidentially.

confidential clerk/secretary a person who can be trusted not to give away secret information.

confirm (1) to make firm; to settle: *We are able to confirm that the goods will be delivered on 1 December. Please confirm the dates of your visit to Alexandria. The minutes of the meeting have been confirmed*, approved, declared correct. (2) to make certain or binding: *We now confirm our acceptance of your quotation. He has confirmed his order. A confirmed credit*, one that is binding. *His appointment as manager has been confirmed.*

confirmed irrevocable credit BKG. & COM. in foreign trade, a banker's credit that is irrevocable (cannot be changed or recalled) and against which the banker must accept bills of exchange drawn by the exporter, usu. on condition that the bill has with it the shipping documents endorsed in blank. For this reason such credits are called documentary credits. Cf. confirmed letter of credit.

confirmed letter of credit *see under* letter of credit.

confirming house *see* commission agent.

confiscation the seizing of private property by a government without compensating the owner, esp. in time of war or as the result of a serious crime by the owner, e.g. confiscation of forbidden or smuggled goods, of the fish caught and the nets of a vessel found fishing in forbidden waters.

conflict of laws *see* international law.

confrère a fellow member of a group of persons in the same profession, such as doctors and lawyers. A colleague.

congestion TRANSPT. the state of excessive fullness or crowding: *Traffic congestion is bad during the rush-hour. Congestion at the port of Calcutta will delay delivery. There is severe congestion in the warehouse.*

conglomerate (1) a mass composed of different materials or things. (2) STK. EXCH. a group of companies resulting from a conglomerate merger: *A banking and publishing conglomerate.*

conglomerate merger a merger or combination of a number of commercial or industrial companies which are completely different in nature, usu. for the purpose of diversification, i.e. to spread business risks. Cf. horizontal merger; vertical merger.

Congo (Brazzaville) a republic in west-central Africa, pop. 1.3 million approx. (1974); capital, Brazzaville, pop. 136,000 approx.; languages, French and tribal; currency unit, the C.F.A. franc (CFA Fr), divided into 100 centimes. Formerly, the French Congo. Member, O.A.U., O.C.A.M.M.; Associate, E.E.C.

Congress (1) LAW the elected law-making body of the U.S.A. consisting of the Senate or upper chamber and the House of Representatives or lower chamber. (2) the name given to the Senate and Chamber of Deputies in Mexico. (3) in India, one of the main political parties.

con. inv. consular invoice.

con-man (*colloq.*) a man who uses a confidence trick to get money; a confidence trickster; a dishonest person who gains one's confidence, persuades one to hand over money or valuable articles, and then disappears.

Conn. Connecticut, U.S.A.

connection *or* **connexion** TOUR. the position where one form of travel connects with another, e.g. a bus arrives at a place in time for its passengers to leave without much delay by another bus or by e.g. a train: *To catch/to miss/one's connection. Is there a good connection between train and plane at Cairo?*
connections *or* **connexions** *pl.* COM. in business, relations with suppliers, customers, bankers, etc. *He has good connections in the City. The firm has excellent business connections. We have built up useful connections in foreign markets.*

connoisseur a person who is a good judge in matters of taste; a person having special knowledge of objects of beauty or of wines, cigars, etc. *He is a connoisseur of antique books/china/silver/paintings/prints, etc.*

conscience money TAXN. a sum of money paid to the government by a person with a tender conscience who has acted dishonestly in the past by not paying enough tax.

consensual contract *see under* contract.

consensus ad idem (*Latin*, agreement about the same thing) LAW in the law of contract, the common understanding between the parties which is essential to make any contract binding.

consent (1) agreement: *He gave his consent to our crossing his land. A contract needs the consent of both parties. They have, by mutual consent, ended their long partnership. I now give my formal consent, in writing. He gave his tacit consent, shown but not stated in words.* (2) LAW in the law of contract all parties must willingly agree to the making and conditions of the contract, otherwise the courts cannot force obedience to it. There must have been no duress (use of force or excessive influence), deceit, or other dishonesty by any of the parties.

consent decree LAW an order of the court putting an end to a lawsuit in which the defendant admits the plaintiff's charges and agrees to the remedy proposed.

consequential damages *see under* damages, *n. pl.*

consequential loss policy *see under* insurance policy.

conservative *adj.* cautious; moderate: *A conservative estimate. To adopt a conservative policy. A conservative investment,* running little risk.

conservative accounting ACCTS. a guiding rule in accounting that caution and moderation must always be used. When an accountant has to make a choice between figures, he will take that which results in understating rather than overstating the profit. He will be certain to take account of all losses, but he will not bring into account profits that have not yet been made.

conservator in U.S.A. (1) LAW a person appointed by a court to protect the interests and to manage the affairs of a person who cannot do so himself. *Syn.* a guardian; a custodian. (2) LAW a person appointed by the court to close down a bankrupt business. *Syn.* liquidator. (3) an official in charge of, or employed in, a museum (a collection of articles of interest to students of history, science, etc.), whose work is to conserve (keep safe, preserve) the objects in it.

conservators of the peace LAW officials appointed by the State to preserve law and order and the public peace, such as judges and Justices of the Peace.

consgt. consignment.

consideration (1) LAW something of material value given or sacrificed by a party to a contract in return for some duty taken upon himself by the other party. To have legal force, all contracts (except those made under seal, i.e. deeds) must provide that whatever is gained by one party shall be in exchange for some gain (valuable consideration) to the other party. Consideration may be in the form of a payment of money, a delivery of goods, a performance of services or promises to do or make any of these. *Syn.* quid pro quo; compensation. (2) STK. EXCH. the amount paid for a security bought on the stock or share market, not including stamp duty or brokerage.
consideration for sale the sale price; the amount of money which the buyer has to pay.
executed consideration something of value already given as part or the whole of the consideration due by a party to a contract.
executory consideration something of value to be given in the future as part or the whole of the consideration due by a party to a contract.
good consideration that which does not possess material value and which represents no real sacrifice, such as natural love and affection. Good consideration is not valuable consideration.
illegal consideration payment under an illegal contract.
past consideration that which has taken place in the past and before the making of the con-

tract. It is, legally, no consideration and the contract containing it has no legal force.

valuable consideration that which has some material value such that when given it represents some real sacrifice by the giver. Cf. good consideration.

consign v. COM. & TRANSPT. to send off goods from one place to another, esp. for delivery to a customer or to an agent for sale: *Your order has been consigned by rail today.*

consignee COM. & TRANSPT. a person to whom goods are consigned (sent), esp. an agent to whom the goods sent are on consignment. *See* consignor. *Syn.* addressee; recipient.

consignee's interest INSCE. *see* buyer's interest.

consignment COM. (1) a set or group of goods or articles consigned at one time: *The articles formed part of the consignment sent last month.* (2) goods sent by the owner to an agent for sale on commission, the consignor keeping the ownership of the goods until the agent has sold them. Goods sent under these conditions are said to be sent *on consignment. Abbr.* consgt.

consignment account ACCTS. a special form of account in the nature of a combined trading and profit and loss account made for each consignment sent to an agent for sale on commission. The cost of the goods, of transport, duty, dock and warehouse charges, and agent's commission are debited to the account, and the sum received from sales is credited; the difference, being profit or loss, is transferred to the profit and loss on consignment account.

consignment invoice *see under* invoice.

consignment note *see* way-bill.

consignor COM. & TRANSPT. (1) a person or organization that consigns goods. Cf. consignee. *Syn.* sender. (2) the owner of goods who sends them to an agent (the consignee) who has agreed to receive, store and sell them for the owner. *See* consignment.

consolidate STK. EXCH. & FIN. to unite; to merge; to bring together as one for the purpose of making stronger: *To consolidate several companies. See* consolidation.

consolidated accounts *see under* accounts, *n. pl.*

Consolidated Annuities *see* Consols.

consolidated bond *see under* bond, *n.*

Consolidated Fund FIN. in Britain, that part of the money received by the government in taxes, from which are paid certain expenditures approved by Parliament, such as the cost of running the armed forces and the Civil Service, and the interest on the national debt. The Fund is kept by the Bank of England, under the orders of the Treasury, in an account called the Exchequer account. *See* Exchequer.

Consolidated Stock *see* Consols.

consolidating Act LAW a law bringing together various laws passed earlier by Parliament.

consolidation STK. EXCH. (1) the bringing together and uniting of two or more companies. *Syn.* a merger. (2) a change in the face value of a company's shares, usu. to increase the face value by combining a number of low-value shares into one higher-value e.g. ten 10p shares may be consolidated into one £1 share: *A consolidation of capital.* (3) LAW the combining of two or more laws into one new statute.

Consols STK. EXCH. & FIN. Consolidated Annuities or Consolidated Stock, interest-bearing securities or bonds issued by the British Government which have no maturity (repayment) date. *See* annuity bond. The present bonds are the result of the consolidating or merging of several loans raised at different times and at different rates of interest. The interest on them is backed by the whole of the Consolidated Fund of the government.

consortium IND. & FIN. a combination, usu. of two or more large international companies, formed for a special and limited common purpose, such as to act as one in bargaining for a contract for very big building works, nuclear power stations, dams, etc. *Syn.* syndicate. *Pl.* consortiums or consortia.

conspiracy LAW a secret agreement or plan by two or more persons to do an unlawful act.

constant-ratio investment plan *see under* investment.

constant cost *see under* cost.

constituted having legal form: *A properly (or regularly) constituted meeting,* one which, to be legally effective, must have been properly called in accordance with the Articles, must have the right person as president or chairman, and a proper quorum (sufficient number of members) present.

constitution LAW (1) the way in which the government of a country is constituted, i.e. made up or organized. Britain has an unwritten constitution which is continuously changing, while the U.S.A. has a written constitution which is slow to change. *Adj.* constitutional. (2) the laws which government and people regard as basic to the orderly running of society. (3) the document containing these basic laws.

construction policy *see* shipbuilders' policy *under* insurance policy.

constructive dismissal IND. REL. & MAN. an act of improper behaviour by an employer, e.g. victimization, which is so serious as to give an employee the right to resign and still claim payment for wrongful dismissal, on the grounds that the employee could no longer suffer the treatment he was receiving.

constructive possession *see under* possession (3).

constructive total loss MAR. INSCE. where a ship or her cargo are so badly damaged that the cost of repair would be greater than the market value, they are treated as totally lost, and the insurers are bound to pay the total sum for which the damaged ship or cargo was insured. Cf. actual total loss. *Abbr.* C.T.L.

constructive trust *see under* trust.

constructive trustee *see under* trustee.

Consul a government official sent to work in a foreign town to act as local representative of his government, protecting the interests of its citizens visiting or living there; to report on trade and economic conditions; and to carry out certain commercial duties such as signing consular invoices (*see under* invoice). His office is called a *consulate*. *Adj.* consular.

Consul General a Consul of the highest rank.

Vice-Consul a consular official next below a Consul in rank.

consular agent a person who does the work of a Consul, usu. at a place of less importance than those having Consuls.

consulage *see* consular fees.

consular agent *see under* Consul.

consular fees COM. & SHIPG. charges by consular offices abroad for the services they perform, esp. in signing documents and issuing certificates. *Syn.* consulage; consular charges.

consular invoice *see under* invoice.

consulate *see* Consul.

consult (1) to get advice, usu. from a professionally-qualified person: *To consult a lawyer/doctor/accountant/architect, etc.* (2) to get information from: *To consult a document/book/dictionary/directory.* (3) to show concern for a person's feelings, interests or rights: *You must consult the owner before you drive your cattle across his land.*

consultant a person or organization selling professional advice: *An advertising/business/engineering/industrial/management/marketing/medical/mining/tax consultant. A firm of architectural consultants. A consultant surgeon.*

consulting room(s) a room or set of rooms where sick or injured people come to be examined and treated by a doctor. Cf. surgery.

consume, propensity to *see under* propensity.

consumer ECON. a person whose wants are satisfied by producers; a person who consumes (uses or uses up) the products and services that he buys, and who does not resell them. Opp. producer.

consumer acceptance *see* brand acceptance.

consumer credit BKG. & FIN. the lending of money, or a right to money, to members of the public by banks, finance houses, pawnbrokers and money-lenders, for the purpose of buying consumer goods, the goods themselves often being taken as security for the loan. For various forms of consumer credit *see* hire-purchase agreement; deferred payment agreement; monthly account; budget account; credit card; charge account.

consumer demand ECON. THEORY the amount of a commodity or service that consumers are willing to buy at a given price during a stated period. It is not the amount that the consumers would like to have but the amount that they are willing to pay for, i.e. demand in the economic sense. Cf. market demand.

consumer durables COM. & ECON. consumer goods that are intended to be used over a period of time, such as household refrigerators and washing machines. In certain theories of the trade cycle, the state of the industries producing consumer durables is considered to be a pointer to a downward or upward swing. *See also* durable goods. Cf. consumer non-durables. *Syn.* hard goods; white goods (U.S.A.).

consumer goods *see under* goods (7).

consumer group COM. a small group of people living in the same place who study the prices and examine the quality of consumer goods being sold in local shops, and make the information known to the public.

consumer investment *see under* investment.

consumer non-durables COM. & ECON. those consumer goods that are consumed, or used up, soon after they are bought, such as food, drink and tobacco, most clothes, household cleaning materials, newspapers and magazines (not books). Cf. consumer durables. *Syn.* single-use goods; soft goods.

Consumer Price Index ECON. & COM. in U.S.A., the index of retail prices produced by the government, to which many wage agreements in America are related; the equivalent of the Index of Retail Prices in Britain.

consumer research *see under* research.

consumers' co-operative *see under* co-operative.

consumer services *see under* services.

consumer's surplus ECON. THEORY the difference between the price which a buyer is willing to pay for a thing rather than not have it, and the price he actually does pay. *Syn.* buyer's surplus; surplus value. Cf. producer's surplus.

consumption (1) the act of consuming, of using, of using up. (2) an amount consumed: *The petrol consumption of a car*, the distance it will run on a given amount of petrol, e.g. 30 miles per gallon, or the amount of petrol it will use to run a given distance, e.g. 9.4 litres per 100 kilometres. (3) ECON. the amount of money that the entire public spends on consumer goods in a given period.

capital consumption in economic analysis, the amount of capital goods used up in the process of producing consumer goods and further capital goods.

conspicuous consumption the buying of goods and services not for one's own use but just for show.

home consumption (*a*) goods consumed in the country in which they are made. (*b*) foreign goods held in a bonded warehouse until they are needed for consumption.

induced consumption increased spending on consumer goods as a result of increased investment. Cf. induced investment *under* investment.

consumption function *see* propensity to consume.

consumption goods *see* consumer goods *under* goods (7).

consumption tax TAXN. a tax which governments have sometimes used, esp. in time of war or economic trouble, in order to discourage the public from spending money on certain kinds of goods which have become scarce but which cannot be fairly rationed (shared out to everyone). The aim of the tax is not to bring in money but rather to act as a means of economic control. Cf. expenditure tax.

Cont. Continent (of Europe).

cont. continued; content(s); container.

contacts COM. persons one knows who may be useful or helpful in getting business: *He has good contacts in local government circles. We have no business contacts in Greece. I have not had time to make any contacts.*

container (1) anything such as a box, barrel, bottle, etc. used for holding something. (2) TRANSPT. a large metal case, of standard shape and size, for carrying goods by specially-built road vehicles, railway wagons and ships. Containers are 8 ft (2.4 m) wide, 8 ft (2.4 m) high and either 20 ft (6.1 m) or 40 ft (12.2 m) long and weigh from 3 to 12 tons when loaded. Their standardized form greatly helps in handling and transporting them quickly and cheaply. *Syn.* lift-van.

container crane a large crane specially planned and built to lift and move containers at a container depot or port.

container depot a place specially arranged for loading, unloading and storing containers.

container ship a large, fast ship specially planned and built to carry containers filled with cargo. *Syn.* van ship.

container traffic the movement of goods by using containers.

container train a fast freight train made up of railway wagons specially planned and built to carry containers. The British railways run a service of fast container trains between all the larger cities and ports, called freightliners.

container truck a road or railway vehicle specially planned and built to carry containers.

transcontainer a container planned and built specially for transporting one kind of product, e.g. soft fruit.

contamination MAR. INSCE. the spoiling of a ship's cargo, esp. by sea-water.

contango STK. EXCH. the payment of interest made by brokers for 'carrying over' or 'continuing' a debt from one Account to the next. *See* continuation; Account, The.

contango day the day on which contango rate is fixed, being the first of the Stock Exchange Settling Days. *Syn.* continuation day; making-up day; Settlement Day; Account Day.

contemptuous damages *see under* damages, *n. pl.*

contg. containing.

contests ADVTG. an aid to selling goods, by holding a competition for valuable prizes for those persons who write the best answers to questions or who make up the best slogan (clever saying for use in advertising).

continent one of the seven largest land masses in the world: North and South America, Europe, Asia, Africa, Australasia and Antarctica.

The Continent (*colloq.*) the mainland of Europe (usu. excluding Scandinavia) as distinguished from the British Isles. *Adj.* continental.

subcontinent a large land area forming part of a continent, such as the Indian (or Indo-Pakistan) subcontinent.

continental cover INSCE. the insurance by British insurers against risk of accident to motor cars and goods vehicles while in stated countries on the continent of Europe. *See* green card.

continental shelf the belt of shallow sea bordering a continent and extending to a depth of 100 fathoms (600 ft or about 183 m). This shelf has become important in regard to international claims to catch fish and to sink oil-wells in these waters.

contingency (1) an uncertain and usu. unwelcome event which, if it happens, will need sudden and immediate action: *To be prepared for/ guard against/all contingencies.* (2) ACCTS. & FIN. an expense of an unknown nature that has to be provided for, e.g. by setting up a reserve fund: *A contingency fund.*

contingency account *see* contingency reserve.

contingency insurance *see under* insurance, classes and kinds of.

contingency reserve ACCTS. a reserve fund set up to meet a contingency such as a loss that would be suffered if a large overseas market were suddenly closed. *Syn.* contingency account; contingency fund.

contingent annuity *see under* insurance policy.

contingent assets *see* assets.

contingent liabilities ACCTS. & FIN. possible debts which will come into existence only on the happening of a contingency (uncertain event), e.g. the liability of a guarantor.

contingent *or* **survivorship policy** *see under* insurance policy.

continuation STK. EXCH. *see* Account, The.

continuation clause (1) INSCE. a condition in an insurance policy which binds the insurer to continue to give cover after the ending of the period of the policy until a renewal is arranged and paid for. (2) MAR. INSCE. a condition in a marine policy which binds the insurers to keep a ship covered by insurance until she gets back to her home port if her return is delayed for any reason beyond the ending of the period of the policy.

continuation day see contango day under contango.

continue see Account Day.

continued bond see under bond, n.

continuous audit see audit.

continuous disability policy see permanent health policy under insurance policy.

continuous inventory see under stocktaking.

continuous stationery printed forms such as invoices or headed notepaper joined together as an unbroken strip of paper, so that they can be fed continuously into a typewriter or invoicing/billing machine or computer print-out machine without the troublesome work of reloading.

continuous stocktaking see under stocktaking.

contour on a map, a line joining points that are at an equal height above sea-level.

contra ACCTS. (1) an entry made on the opposite side of an account from that of an entry or entries made earlier. The purpose is to balance or cancel (make ineffective) the earlier entry or entries.

contra credit an amount credited to an account in order to cancel (make ineffective) a previous debit.

(2) an entry made in the cash book to record cash paid into or taken out of the bank account.

contraband COM. & LAW goods which are illegally brought into or taken out of a country. Syn. smuggled goods.

contraband of war any goods which a country at war forbids other countries, including neutrals, to supply to the enemy.

contract n. LAW any legally binding agreement between two or more parties. To be effective according to law, it is essential that the parties to a contract have legal capacity (power) and freedom of contract; they must intend it to be binding; they must be agreed on the purpose of the contract and the purpose must not be illegal; there must be valuable consideration, i.e. some payment or service or sacrifice must be promised by each party; and the meaning of the agreement must be clear enough to be understood. It need not necessarily be in writing unless it is of a nature that must by law be in writing or under seal. Pron. cóntract.

aleatory contract see under aleatory.

bare contract see nude contract below.

bilateral contract a contract between two par-

ties which binds each party to perform some duty for the other party.

consensual contract one which exists only because both parties have consented (agreed) to it, without putting it into a written document.

executed contract one that has been completely performed.

executory contract one that has not yet been performed.

formal contract see specialty contract below.

gaming contract a special kind of wagering contract, being one which relates to a bet on the result of a game. See wagering contract below.

hire-purchase contract see hire-purchase agreement.

illegal contract one that is for a purpose which is an offence against the law, or against the national interest, etc. All illegal contracts are void. See void contract below.

implied contract one which is not expressed but is taken by law to exist, judging by the behaviour and intentions of the parties, such as when both parties clearly intend that goods and services provided by one party shall be paid for by the other party.

infant's contract one made by a person under the age of 18 years. Except for contracts for necessaries and for contracts of service which are to his advantage, no contract made by an infant has force in a court of law. See void contract; voidable contract below.

moneylending contract one made by a professional moneylender and a borrower, to which certain special rules under the Moneylenders Acts apply, such as an upper limit on the rate of interest and on the length of time during which the lender may take action in the courts to obtain repayment of the loan.

naked contract see nude contract below.

nude contract an agreement which provides for no consideration and which is unenforceable unless it is made a contract under seal. Syn. nudum pactum; bare contract; naked contract.

onerous contract one that is severe and unjust, because the duties of one of the parties are so hard that he cannot get any advantage from it.

open contract a simple contract which is written. See simple contract below.

option contract one which gives one party, in return for the payment of a certain sum of money, the right to buy or to sell something, such as a number of shares, at a fixed price within a stated period of time. See option.

parol contract a simple contract which is oral, by word of mouth, not in writing. See simple contract below.

quasi-contract a duty for which no formal contract has been made but which comes into existence in certain circumstances. Thus, a person has a right to be repaid his expenses in looking after a neighbour's unguarded property. *See also* salvage.

sale contract *see under* sale.

simple contract one which, although legally binding, has not been formally drawn up as a deed under seal. If it is written it is called an **open contract**, and if oral (made by word of mouth, not written) it is called a **parol contract**. Cf. specialty contract.

specialty contract one which is in the form of a deed, i.e. under seal and therefore a very solemn promise. Contracts made under seal are necessary in cases such as: a promise to give without consideration; transfers (changes of ownership) of land; leases of more than three years; transfers of shares in ships. Cf. simple contract. *Syn.* contract under seal; contract by deed; formal contract.

unenforceable contract (*a*) one to which the courts cannot force obedience, only because of some unimportant detail such as the absence of a document. (*b*) one where the right of action is barred by limitation.

unilateral contract one in which one of the parties has already completed or partly completed his duties under the contract before it is signed. Such a contract must be under seal.

valid contract one that is correct according to law.

void contract one which will not be recognized by the courts and which is therefore not a contract at all. It may be a contract which is illegal, either because it is forbidden by law, e.g. to steal, or because it is against public policy, e.g. not to compete with a former employer; or it may be one made by an infant (a young person under 18 years of age) agreeing to repay loans or to pay for goods; or where the parties were, by mistake, not thinking of the same thing.

voidable contract a contract which may be avoided, being one that gives *one* of the parties the right to bring it to an end when he wishes, but until he does so, the contract is fully effective in law. Such contracts usu. relate to the rights of infants (young persons under the age of 18 years in Britain). Cf. void contract.

wagering contract one which relates to any kind of bet, not only on the result of a game. The courts will not hold any wagering contract to be binding. *See* gaming contract *above*. Cf. aleatory contract.

v. COM. & LAW (1) to bring into existence a liability: *To contract a debt/a duty/a loan/an obligation.* (2) to enter into an agreement; to bind oneself: *An infant has no power to contract. I have contracted to buy a house. They contracted with the manufacturer for a regular supply of parts. Pron.* contráct.

contract 'binding in honour only' LAW an agreement which states clearly that the parties intend it not to have legal force, in order to avoid a legal relationship between them. Such agreements are not legal contracts, and no court would support them. *Syn.* contract 'not subject to legal jurisdiction'.

contract bond *see* performance bond *under* bond, *n.*

contract, breach of *see under* breach.

contract by deed *see* specialty contract *under* contract.

contract carrier *see under* carrier.

contract, discharge of *see under* discharge.

contract, frustration of *see under* frustration.

contracting out (1) LAW giving up a legally-held right in exchange for some other advantage. Thus, an employer may contract out of a state pension scheme if he has set up an occupational pension scheme that is at least as good to the employees as the state scheme. (2) ECON. & IND. the practice of some groups of manufacturers to put work out to contract, i.e. to buy certain products and processed materials from subcontractors instead of manufacturing them themselves. *See* disintegration.

contraction (1) ECON. a reduction in size or scale, esp. the lessening of business activity which happens during periods of economic depression: *A contraction of market demand/investment/credit. See* trade cycle *under* cycle. (2) IND. the reduction in the size and output of an industry usu. caused by a lessening world demand or by greater world competition: *The contraction of the Lancashire cotton industry.* (3) a reduction in the scale of production of an industrial unit: *The contraction in the output of our factory will lead to a contraction in the size of our work force. Opp.* expansion; increase; growth.

contract labour *see* indentured labour *under* labour.

contract note STK. EXCH. the document sent to a client by a stockbroker for each deal he makes, in which are recorded full details of the stocks or shares he has just bought or sold for the client, and the price, commission, duty paid, etc. *Syn.* bought and sold note.

contract 'not subject to legal jurisdiction' *see* contract 'binding in honour only'.

contract of employment LAW & MAN. a contract of service or of apprenticeship, whether it is express or implied, oral or in writing.

contract of insurance INSCE. one in which, in return for the payment of a charge called a premium, an insurer agrees to pay to the insured on the happening of a stated event, a fixed sum of money, or the equivalent value of something lost or damaged. *Syn.* insurance policy.

contract of marine insurance MAR. INSCE. a contract of insurance which relates to marine losses, i.e. those caused by an event or events at sea. *Syn.* contract of sea insurance; marine insurance policy.

contract of record LAW a contract connected with the work and rules of a court of law and entered in its records, such as a binding promise by an accused person to keep the peace, to be of good behaviour, to appear for trial at the proper time.

contract of service LAW & MAN. one between employer and employee; the employee agrees to serve continuously under the control and direction of the employer in return for remuneration (payment of wages or salary) or other reward. Cf. contract of services.

contract of services LAW & MAN. an agreement between employer and employee: the employee is employed as an independent contractor, not continuously and not under the control of his employer, to whom he owes no duty of obedience. He is thus not a servant. Examples are doctors, lawyers, architects, and also accountants when employed for audit purposes. Cf. contract of service.

contractor one who contracts to do something; one of the parties to a contract, esp. one who agrees to supply goods or to perform services at a fixed price for a stated period.
building contractor one who builds houses, etc. under a contract.
subcontractor one who contracts to supply goods, such as materials, or to perform services, that are needed for the performance of a separate contract made by another contractor. E.g. a carpenter may be a subcontractor to a builder who has himself contracted to build a house.

contractor's indemnity policy see under insurance policy.

contract policy see under insurance policy.

contracts, exchange of see exchange of contracts.

contract supplies COM. goods ordered in large quantities under a contract between the buyer and the supplier, e.g. a manufacturer.

contract to sell COM. & LAW an agreement in which one party promises in advance to sell, and another to buy, some stated thing, when a certain future event takes place; such as the sale of a house or ship, now being built, when it has been completed, or the sale of next year's harvest. Cf. sale contract. *Syn.* agreement to sell.

contractual LAW relating to, in the nature of, a contract: *A contractual duty/obligation/payment/liability*, one accepted by one party to a contract, to the benefit of the other party. Cf. legal liability.

contractual rent see under rent.

contract under seal see specialty contract *under* contract, *n.*

contribute (1) to give, with other persons, for a common purpose, esp. to a good cause, such as to help the poor. (2) to give or pay one's share:

To contribute to the expenses/the cost of research. (3) to be partly the cause of some happening or event: *His carelessness contributed to the accident/the loss of the ship.* (4) to write for, to share in the writing of, a book or magazine: *She regularly contributes an article to our journal.*

contribution (1) something contributed (given, with others, for a common purpose). (2) something paid as a share in the cost of a common expense or loss. (3) INSCE. the share of a loss which will be borne by each insurer in proportion to the face value or sum assured on their policies.
general average contribution MAR. INSCE. the share that each of the various parties joined in a marine adventure has to bear in a partial loss resulting from an extraordinary sacrifice made on purpose to prevent a total loss. See average (4).
national insurance contribution see under national insurance.
voluntary contribution that of a voluntary contributor. See under contributor.

contributor one who contributes, who makes a contribution. Cf. contributory.
voluntary contributor one who contributes freely, without being forced; esp. a person who is not forced to pay national insurance contributions in Britain but who does so of his own free will, usu. in order to qualify for a retirement pension.

contributory *n.* LAW & STK. EXCH. (1) a member (shareholder) in a company. (2) the holder of fully-paid shares in a company. (3) any person bound by law to contribute (give with others) towards the assets of a company in the event of its being wound up, usu. a shareholder who is liable to pay only the uncalled balance on the shares he holds. See call, *n.* (3).

contributory negligence LAW in an action claiming damages for negligence, the plaintiff's own failure to take reasonable care, resulting in partial responsibility for damage or injury to himself. The effect is to reduce the amount of damages in proportion to the extent to which the court decides that the plaintiff is to blame.

contributory pension scheme one in which the employee, as well as the employer, contributes to the financing of the pension. Cf. noncontributory pension scheme.

control (1) STK. EXCH. the power that belongs to the holder(s) of more than 50% of the voting-power in a company, and so the power of being able to direct the plans and activities of that company. (2) MAN. any system for checking and, if necessary, for correcting the performance of a business or of any part of its organization, such as budgetary, progress, production, quality and stock controls, as described below:
budgetary control see under budgetary.

inventory control see stock control below.

management control any system which makes it possible for the management of a business or other organization to check whether their plans and courses of action are being carried out. The system will also show where action is necessary to correct any movement away from a planned course. The actual controls must vary according to the type of organization, but will usu. include budgetary control, audit or accounting control, personnel or staff control, and quality and production controls. The main methods used are observation, examination and reporting. Syn. management checks.

personnel control see under personnel.

production control a control system for seeing that plans for production are carried out and that the supply of materials is sufficient for the needs of the organization. See progress control below.

progress control a control system for checking that work is completed according to plan and for showing where action is necessary to avoid any delays or difficulties that may upset plans for production. See production control above.

quality control a system for checking and measuring the quality of materials used and of the finished products of a manufacturing organization, so that comparisons can be made with fixed standards and action can be taken to correct any movement away from those standards.

staff control see personnel control under personnel.

stock control a system of checking the stock of goods and materials held by an organization, to see that it is correct according to the stock records, that stock is not being lost or stolen, that early action is taken to obtain more stock when needed, and that the quantities held are reasonable. Syn. inventory control.

control account ACCTS. a system of checking and proving the correctness of the accounts in a particular ledger, such as the bought ledger, by listing all the debits and credits made during a given period. Mistakes in posting are quickly discovered, the work of preparing the trial balance is made much easier, and in addition the management know at any one time the total of debtors and creditors. Syn. adjustment account; total account.

controlled economy see command economy.

controller see comptroller.

controlling company see holding company under company.

controlling interest see holding company under company.

control systems IND. various kinds of instruments and machines, esp. electronic and hydraulic, for checking and automatically operating the controls of production processes and activities. See cybernetics; servo-mechanisms.

conurbation a group of towns, formerly separate but now combined by growth into a continuous large urban area. In Britain such areas are: Greater London, S.E. Lancashire, Merseyside, W. Midlands, W. Yorkshire, Tyneside, Clydeside, etc.

convene to call people, esp. members of an association, together for a meeting: To convene a meeting. To be properly convened, according to the law, sufficient written notice must be given of any formal meeting, such as that of members (shareholders) of a company, to every person having a right to attend.

convenience, flag of see flag of convenience.

convenience goods COM. consumer goods which command a higher price because they are specially produced or packed so as to save work. Many kinds of food sold already prepared or cooked and ready to eat are convenience goods (or convenience foods). Syn. (U.S.A.) fast foods.

conversion LAW wrongfully selling or giving away another person's property without his permission. Cf. detinue. Syn. trover.

conversion stock one issued with the intention that it should replace a stock issued earlier and soon due to be redeemed (paid back). See convertible bond under bond, n. (1); convertible loan stock.

convertibility FIN. & BKG. of currency, originally the right of the holder of notes and coin of a certain currency to exchange them for gold. Nowadays it is the right of the holder to convert (change) a currency freely into other currencies.

full convertibility when both residents and non-residents are free to convert at all times.

limited or restricted convertibility when only non-residents can convert, or when convertibility exists only in regard to some special kinds of payment, such as for imports.

convertible bond see under bond, n.

convertible currency FIN. one that can be freely exchanged for all other currencies at the rates of exchange existing in the market.

convertible loan stock STK. EXCH. loan stock in a company, i.e. stock which will earn a fixed, regular rate of interest, but which can, at a stated date, be converted, i.e. exchanged for shares in the same company if the stockholder wishes. It will be to his advantage to use his option to convert if the dividend on the shares is likely to be higher in the future than the interest on the loan stock, or if the price of the shares is likely to rise. See convertible bond.

convertible money/paper (1) FIN. paper money, esp. bank-notes, which can be exchanged for coin at the office of the bank issuing the paper money. (2) paper money which can be freely exchanged for gold or silver when the holder wishes.

convertible term insurance *see* term policy *under* insurance policy.

conveyance LAW (1) the transfer (passing) of ownership rights in land from one person to another. (2) the document recording the transfer. *See* deed of conveyance.

conveyancer LAW a person, esp. a solicitor or a barrister, whose main work is to draw up conveyances.

conviction LAW a formal finding of guilty in a criminal court. A person found guilty and sent to prison is called a *convict*.

cook ACCTS. (*colloq.*) to deceive dishonestly by making accounts or other figures false or incorrect: *He was caught cooking the accounts*, dishonestly making them untrue or incorrect. *Their profit figures have been cooked in order to hide the real financial situation.*

coomb a British corn and dry measure, = 4 bushels = 32 gallons = 145.47 litres.

co-op. co-operative.

co-operative COM. a business organization owned and run by a society of persons or of groups of persons whose aim is not to make a profit but to give benefits to the members. *Syn.* co-operative society. *Colloq.* co-op.

agricultural co-operative *see under* agricultural.

consumers' co-operative a co-operative society that buys goods from a co-operative wholesale society and sells them in a retail store. The members hold shares on which a fixed rate of interest is paid. Any trading surplus or profit is paid to the members as a dividend according to the value of the goods each has bought. *Syn.* retail co-operative; retail distributive society.

credit co-operative a co-operative society which collects money from its members and lends it at low rates of interest, usu. to farmers. Such co-operatives carry out much of the financing of agriculture in many countries of the world, but have had little success in Britain. *Syn.* credit bank; credit society; co-operative bank.

marketing co-operative an agricultural co-operative which runs an organization for marketing (selling) the produce of its members. Cf. producers' co-operative.

producers' co-operative a co-operative society whose members are usu. small manufacturers who thus combine to obtain the advantages of bulk buying and other services such as jointly-owned buildings and machinery. Cf. marketing co-operative.

retail co-operative *see* consumers' co-operative.

wholesale co-operative a co-operative society owned by a number of consumer (retail) co-operatives to act as a supplier, to its member societies and to other co-operatives, of goods which it has had the advantage of buying in

bulk or of having itself manufactured. The profit is shared according to the value of goods each society has bought, those societies which are shareholders getting a higher rate of dividend than those which are not. *Syn.* co-operative wholesale society.

co-operative advertising ADVTG. an arrangement by which two or more businesses co-operate to save advertising costs.

co-operative bank *see* credit co-operative *under* co-operative; *also* Co-operative Wholesale Society Bank.

co-operative farm AGR. a large farm jointly run by a group of farmers and their families as a co-operative organization, sometimes with associated industries, such as food-packing and preserving factories under the same management. *Syn.* communal agricultural organization.

co-operative marketing an arrangement by which a number of producers co-operate or work together to set up a jointly-owned organization to put their goods on the market.

co-operative society *see* co-operative.

co-operative shop *or* **store** COM. one run by a co-operative society.

co-operative wholesale society *see* wholesale co-operative *under* co-operative.

Co-operative Wholesale Society Bank BKG. one of the British clearing banks, which acts as the central financing organization supplying capital to the co-operative movement generally. It is also used by local authorities and trade unions and has a relatively small number of private customers.

co-ownership of industry IND. the practice of giving the employees a share in the ownership of the business that employs them. *Syn.* co-partnership; worker participation.

co-ownership of land *see* joint ownership; ownership in common.

co-partnership *see* co-ownership.

copeck a small copper coin, the smallest currency unit of the U.S.S.R., one-hundredth part of a rouble. *Also*, kopeck.

copper (1) any coin of low value made of copper or bronze. (2) (*colloq.*) a policeman.

copper-bottomed financially safe: *Shares in a copper-bottomed company.*

coppers *pl.* STK. EXCH. copper shares.

copy (1) matter to be set up in type or to be reproduced in print. (2) ADVTG. the words used in an advertisement. *See also* blind copy; carbon copy; fair copy; master copy; office copy.

copy order COM. a document sent by a supplier to a buyer who has ordered goods, telling him exactly what items are being supplied, at what prices and on what conditions. *See* invoice; bill.

copyright LAW a legal right, possessed by no one else, of publishing or reproducing a literary (of books and writing), artistic or musical work, and of preventing anyone else from doing so. The first owner of a copyright is the person who creates the work (brings it into existence), e.g. the writer of a book or article. Copyright can be assigned, but only in writing. It normally lasts for the life of the person who creates the work and for 50 years after his death. Cf. patent.

copyright notice the sign ©, followed by the name of the owner of the copyright and the year of first publication, appearing usu. on the back of the title-page, in all books claiming copyright protection.

copy-typist a person trained to use a typewriter to type from handwritten, typewritten or printed matter, but who does not use shorthand or a tape-recording. Cf. steno-typist; shorthand-typist.

copywriter ADVTG. a person writing material for advertisements.

córdoba the standard currency unit of Nicaragua, divided into 100 centavos.

Corn. Cornwall, England.

corn (1) in Britain, a collective word for the cereal food-grains, i.e. those obtained from grass-like plants, esp. wheat, oats, barley, rye, maize. (2) in U.S.A. the word means maize only.

corn and dry measure (Britain) a measure of volume used for non-liquid substances. Cf. liquid measure. *See table on page 477.*

corn chandler COM. a dealer in corn, i.e. wheat, oats, barley, rye, maize, etc. as food-grains.

corner v. (1) COM. & STK. EXCH. to obtain control of the price of an article, commodity, stock or share, by buying up all supplies and stocks of it in the market, thus forcing dealers who have contracts to meet to buy from the person who has *cornered the market.* (2) generally, any action which will raise prices by bringing a monopoly into existence. *See also* engross (2); forestalling.
n. To form a corner in (a certain share or commodity).

Corn Laws ECON. HIST. in Britain, a series of laws which controlled the international trade in corn, esp. those that prevented free imports into England during the eighteenth and early nineteenth centuries. The law of 1815 put an import duty on wheat when its price fell below 80s. a quarter, as a way of keeping prices high to protect home farmers. The high price of bread caused much misery. The struggle of the Anti-Corn Law League resulted in the repeal (ending) of the Corn Laws in 1846. *See* Anti-Corn Law League.

corporate planning *see under* planning.

corporate saving *see under* saving.

corporate seal *see* common seal.

corporate sector ECON. in a mixed economy, that part of the economy that is owned and operated by corporate organizations such as publicly-owned corporations and privately-owned companies. Cf. personal sector; private sector; public sector.

corporate state ECON. a system of government under which all economic power is held by large state corporations, such as existed in Fascist Italy under Mussolini. *Syn.* corporative state.

corporation (1) LAW a group of persons in Britain who have formed themselves into an association which itself has by law a separate legal existence or artificial personality quite different from the persons who compose it. The law allows it to continue to exist indefinitely although its members (shareholders) may change. It has a name and can express its will by fixing its common seal on written documents. *Syn.* body corporate.
chartered corporation one brought into existence by royal charter.
statutory corporation one brought into existence by Act of Parliament.
(2) in U.S.A., a business organization equivalent to a limited company in Britain.

corporation aggregate LAW a corporation that consists of a number of persons, not just one single person. Cf. corporation sole.

corporation sole LAW in Britain, the holder of one of certain public offices, such as the Crown, the public trustee, and a bishop or priest, who is treated by law as having an artificial personality separate from his real personality. Thus any contracts he may make are not binding on him after he retires but are binding on those persons who follow him in the office. Cf. corporation aggregate.

corporation stock *see under* stock.

corporation tax TAXN. a tax in Britain on the profits of business corporations, i.e. companies. *See under* tax.

corporative state *see* corporate state.

corporeal hereditament *see under* hereditament.

correct v. ACCTS. to put right: *We have corrected the mistake in our ledgers.* *Syn.* rectify; adjust. *N.* correction.

correspond (1) ACCTS. of figures, to be in agreement: *The entries in the cash book correspond with the vouchers.* *Syn.* check (U.S.A.). (2) to exchange letters, cables, etc. with somebody.

correspondence COM. (1) the writing, receiving and answering of letters: *He is good at correspondence.* (2) letters being received and answered: *Have you any correspondence for me? You must attend to your correspondence more promptly.*

correspondence clerk an office employee who deals with the writing, receiving, answering and filing of letters and other documents.

correspondent (1) BKG. a bank which is an agent for another bank, esp. one which acts as agent in a foreign town, of a bank which has no branch there. (2) COM. a person from whom one receives news, information, reports: *A newspaper correspondent.* (3) a person or organization with whom one has regular business relations, usu. in a foreign country.

corruption LAW bribery.

'corset' BKG. & FIN. the popular name for controls put by the British Government on the total amount of bank credit (the amount that the banks may lend to their customers), thus limiting the amount of money in circulation when inflation tends to be rising.

cost (1) COM. the price paid for something: *At cost*, at the bare price paid, with nothing added for profit, etc. (2) ECON. the real effort and sacrifice needed to produce goods and services. *See also* costs, *pl.* (3) ACCTS. the value given for accounting purposes to the stock of an article or commodity at the end of an accounting period. In a retail business the cost is usu. taken to be prime cost, i.e. the price paid to the supplier, but other amounts to cover storage and transport are sometimes added. In a manufacturing business the cost is usu. prime cost or production cost.

accounting cost ECON. the cost, expressed in units of money, of making or obtaining goods or services, as distinguished from economic cost.

alternative-use cost *see* opportunity cost *below*.

average cost (*a*) ECON. *see under* average. (*b*) ACCTS. the total cost of goods held in stock divided by the number of the goods or units of goods. *Syn.* unit cost.

current cost *see* replacement cost *below*.

direct cost one which is directly related to the production of a particular article or unit of output, and which therefore varies in proportion to the number of articles or units produced. *Syn.* variable cost. Cf. fixed cost.

economic cost the economist's view of cost as compared with the accountant's view. It is usu. greater than the accounting or money view because it includes opportunity cost, not taken notice of by the accountant. It thus represents what is really sacrificed. The accountant counts up only the actual sums of money spent on the factors of production used in making a given quantity of a given product. If the producer uses his own capital for this, the accountant will not include interest charges because none were paid. But the economist would take note of the sacrifice that the producer has made in using his own capital and would include in his economic cost an interest charge equal to the amount of interest the producer would have received if he had lent his capital out at interest. *See* opportunity cost *below*.

extra cost *see* marginal cost *below*.

first cost *see* prime cost *below*.

fixed cost one that does not vary with output (the volume of goods produced); a cost that has to be paid whether anything is produced or not. *Syn.* indirect cost; oncost; burden; (U.S.A.) period cost.

flat cost *see* prime cost *below*.

historic(al) cost the original cost of an asset. *See also* current cost accounting.

implicit cost the cost that is extra to main costs and is usu. unrecorded or hidden, such as the cost of the services performed by the owner of a business in managing it.

incremental cost *see* marginal cost *below*.

indirect cost *see* fixed cost *above*.

landed cost the c.i.f. price and all other charges including import duty.

marginal cost in economics, the extra cost of increasing the output (or volume of goods produced) by one more unit. *Syn.* extra cost; incremental cost.

opportunity cost in economic theory, the cost of something that one has decided not to take an opportunity to buy. Because the supply of economic goods is limited, a person has continually to make choices, to satisfy one want and to leave another (or alternative) want unsatisfied; to buy e.g. an overcoat and to do without buying a radio. The real or opportunity cost of the overcoat is the cost of the radio that the person has sacrificed the opportunity of possessing. Similarly, a manufacturer will decide to produce one kind of article and not to produce another. The real or opportunity cost of the article he produces is the article he would have produced if he had not sacrificed his opportunity to use his factors of production differently. The concept of opportunity cost is of great importance in economics because it influences every decision in which a scarcity of means and a choice between alternatives play their part. *See* economic cost *above*. *Syn.* real cost; alternative-use cost; transfer earnings.

overhead cost the expenses of running a business; those costs that cannot be directly related to the separate products produced, or bought and sold, by the business. *See* overheads.

period cost *see* fixed cost *above*.

prime cost IND. & COM. (*a*) the amount spent on materials, labour and other expenses in actually manufacturing a product. Cf. production cost. (*b*) the price paid by a trader for what he buys. *Syn.* first cost; flat cost; shut-down cost.

production cost IND. the prime cost added to the factory overhead expenses. Cf. prime cost.

real cost *see* opportunity cost *above*.

replacement cost the present market price of a similar partly-used asset to replace an old unuseable asset. *Syn.* current cost.

shut-down cost *see* prime cost *above.*

single cost IND. the cost of production per unit of output.

total cost IND. & COM. the production cost added to the expenses of selling and distributing the product and of the administration of the business.

unit cost *see* average cost.

variable cost *see* direct cost *above.*

cost accountant *see* accountant.

cost accounting ACCTS. the keeping of special accounts to record the cost of making and selling the products of a business and of running it. The work of a cost accountant. *See also* current cost accounting *under* current.

cost and freight (c. & f.) COM. words used in foreign trade contracts meaning the price paid to the seller includes packing and freight to a named port of destination, but does not include insurance, the cost of which must be borne by the buyer. If the goods are sold *c. & f. landed,* the seller has to bear the cost of getting the goods unloaded from the ship, including wharfage and lighterage charges. Cf. c.a.f.; c.i.f.

Costa Rica a republic in Central America, pop. 1.9 million approx. (1973); capital, San José, pop. 200,000 approx.; language, Spanish; currency unit, the colón (*pl.* colones), divided into 100 centimos. Member, O.A.S.

cost-benefit analysis a systematic method of examining and valuing a planned course of action, esp. one needing investment of large sums of money, such as a new motorway or airport, to decide whether it is worth the cost. This is done partly by discounting the future expected costs to obtain the probable present value (*see* discounting (2)), and partly by an attempt at measuring the money value of the social advantages, such as the saving in time, petrol, human lives, and the social disadvantages such as noise, smoke, dirt, loss of farm land, etc. *Abbr.* C.B.A.

cost concept ACCTS. the basic guiding rule in accounting, that assets are normally recorded at the cost price or market value, whichever is lower, and that increases in the value of assets are usually not taken notice of.

cost-effective MAN. & ACCTS. in planning future investment of money in a business, the management will choose to spend the money in such a way as to get the highest possible returns from it, i.e. to make the investment as cost-effective as possible.

coster COM. a street-trader, usu. of fruit and vegetables, from a hand-cart. *Syn.* costermonger; hawker; barrow-boy.

cost inflation *see under* inflation.

costing ACCTS. & IND. finding out the cost of making and selling a product or of performing a service.

batch costing *see under* batch.

full costing *see* absorption costing.

job costing *see under* job.

cost, insurance, freight (c.i.f.) COM. in foreign trade contracts the seller's price includes all charges and risks up to the point where the ship carrying the goods arrives at the port of destination. From that point the buyer has to bear all charges and risks, including unloading costs, lighterage and wharfage, unless these have been included in the freight or collected by the shipowners when the freight was paid. If the contract states that the goods are sold *c.i.f. landed,* the unloading costs, lighterage and wharfage are borne by the seller. *Syn.* (*French*) c.a.f.

cost, insurance, freight and commission (c.i.f. and c.) as c.i.f. but the price also includes the commission payable to the exporter when acting as a buying agent for the foreign buyer.

cost, insurance, freight and commission and interest (c.i.f. and c. and i.) as c.i.f. and c. but the price also includes interest charged by the seller's bank for negotiating the bill of exchange relating to the goods.

cost, insurance, freight and exchange (c.i.f. and e.) as c.i.f. but the price also includes exchange, which may mean *either* that the price will stay unchanged in spite of future movements in the rate of exchange, *or* that the price includes banker's commission, i.e. the same as c.i.f. and c.

cost of control ACCTS. & FIN. the cost of gaining control of the assets of a company, i.e. another name for goodwill.

cost of goods sold ACCTS. the difference between the total of the opening stock, plus purchases during the period, and the total value of unsold stock at the end of the period, which can only be calculated after stocktaking. *Syn.* cost of sales; cost of merchandise sold.

cost of living ECON. the amount of money paid by a person or family for food, clothing and other things necessary to be able to live at a certain standard of living.

cost-of-living bonus COM. & IND. a bonus (extra money) paid in addition to ordinary pay, the amount depending on movements in the cost-of-living index.

cost-of-living index ECON. a means of measuring changes in the cost of living by using index numbers. *See* Index of Retail Prices; Consumer Price Index; index numbers.

cost of merchandise sold *see* cost of goods sold.

Cost of Production Theory of Value ECON. THEORY the idea argued by some of the later classical economists of the nineteenth century, that in the absence of monopoly, and in the long run, value in exchange, or price, is dependent on the cost of production. Modern economists do not accept this view because it is much too simple; it takes no account of the effect of supply and demand or of the scale of production. Cf. Labour Theory of Value.

cost of sales *see* cost of goods sold.

cost-plus COM. of a contract price, a promise to supply at cost plus an agreed percentage of the cost, or at cost plus an agreed fee. Such agreements are made only when the cost is not known at the time when the agreement is made.

cost price *see under* price.

costs (1) LAW the amounts which the party who wins a lawsuit is ordered by the court to be paid by the losing party to meet the actual expenses of bringing or defending the action: *Judgment was entered, with costs, for the plaintiff.* (2) ECON. payments to the factors of production.

avoidable costs *see* variable costs *below.*

constant costs *see* fixed costs *below.*

Decreasing Costs, Law of *see under* decreasing.

distributive costs *see under* distributive.

fixed costs those that do not vary with output (the volume of goods produced); costs that have to be paid whether or not anything is produced. *Syn.* constant costs; permanent costs; sunk costs; supplementary costs; unavoidable costs.

Increasing Costs, Law of *see* Diminishing Returns, Law of.

overhead costs variable costs that are not directly related to a particular article produced, but are costs which are common to a number of other articles. *Syn.* overheads; running costs.

permanent costs *see* fixed costs *above.*

prime costs *see* variable costs *below.*

recurrent *or* **recurring costs** *see* variable costs *below.*

running costs *see* overhead costs *above.*

selling costs *see under* selling.

standard costs *see under* standard.

sunk costs *see* fixed costs *above.*

supplementary costs *see* fixed costs *above.*

unavoidable costs *see* fixed costs *above.*

variable costs costs such as materials, labour, power, which vary in proportion to the output or volume of goods produced by a business. *Syn.* avoidable costs; prime costs; recurrent *or* recurring costs.

cottage industry IND. an industry which is carried on in the worker's home, such as pottery, weaving, and the making of toys, watches and clocks. *Syn.* home industry. *See* domestic system.

couchette (1) TOUR. a sleeping-berth on a train or ship. (2) a compartment containing one or more sleeping-berths. *See* berth.

cough up (*colloq.*) to hand over, to pay money unwillingly.

Coulisse STK. EXCH. in the Paris Bourse, a group of unofficial dealers in stocks and shares. Cf. Parquet.

Council for Mutual Economic Assistance (COMECON or C.M.E.A.) ECON. an organization of socialist countries started in 1949, with its central office in Moscow. It is the equivalent of the European Common Market (E.E.C.) and it aims to carry forward and strengthen the economic development of its member countries, which are: Bulgaria, Czechoslovakia, Cuba, East Germany, Hungary, Mongolia, Poland, Rumania, and the U.S.S.R. Yugoslavia is an associate member. Generally known as COMECON, it is also abbreviated to C.M.E.A.

Council of Arab Economic Unity an organization that sets up and supports Arab companies running joint ventures in mining, medical products, agriculture and food production, tourism and general investment in industry.

Council of Ministers the decision-making body of the European Economic Community (E.E.C.), consisting of a representative of each member country, and acting on the proposals made by the European Commission.

counsel LAW a professional advocate in a court of law in England, commonly given the title 'barrister-at-law' or 'King's/Queen's Counsel'. *Pl.* counsel. In Scotland, advocate.

counsel's opinion *see under* opinion.

counter in a shop or bank, a long flat table or board on which goods are placed or on which business is done, usu. with the customer on one side and the shopkeeper or assistant on the other. *See* bargain-counter; trade counter.

across/over the counter in the ordinary course of trade; said of consumer goods being sold in shops. *Across-the-counter sales*, retail sales.

over-the-counter market *see under* market.

under the counter hidden from sight; said of scarce or forbidden goods sold secretly only to favoured customers.

counter-bid COM. a bid made against another bid, esp. at an auction sale. *See* bid.

counter check BKG. in U.S.A., a cheque or receipt signed by a bank customer when drawing cash out of his account over the bank counter.

counter-claim LAW a claim for damages made by a defendant against the claim(s) of the plaintiff in a lawsuit.

counterfeit made in imitation of the real thing, but with intention to deceive: *A counterfeit cheque/bank-note/coin.* *See* base coins *under* base. *Syn.* forged. *See* counterfeit money *under* money.

counterfoil COM. & BKG. that part of a leaf which is kept in a book when the other part of the leaf (containing a cheque, receipt, order or other document) is torn out. *Syn.* stub; butt; heel.

counter-jumper (*colloq.*) a salesman or shop assistant serving customers at a counter.

countermand (1) BKG. to direct one's banker to stop payment of a cheque. The banker is liable if he fails to obey the drawer's direction, unless the cheque has already been certified or marked at the drawer's request. *Syn.* to stop. *See* stopped cheque *under* cheque. (2) COM. to cancel (an order for goods). *See* cancel.

counterpart (1) LAW an exact copy of a document such as a lease or contract, each party having his own copy which has been signed by the other party. (2) MAN. *see* opposite number.

counter-productive IND. & COM. resulting in lower production; acting against what is desired; producing a result opposite to that which is desired: *To employ more workers is sometimes counter-productive*, they may, e.g. get in one another's way.

countersign COM. & BKG. to sign on the other side or in addition to a signature by someone else, in order to give a document, such as a cheque, more authority than it would have if signed by only one person.

countervailing credit *see under* credit (3).

countervailing duty TAXN. & COM. an import duty aimed to protect an industry from foreign competition, esp. when a foreign country pays its exporters an export bounty. *Syn.* countervailing tariff; matching duty.

counting-frame *see* abacus.

counting-house ACCTS. *see* cash department.

country *adj.* (in India & Pakistan) locally made; produced in the country, not foreign: *Country boat/craft*, small fishing-boats. *Country liquor*, locally-made strong drink.

county court LAW in England, a local court of civil, not criminal, law, lower in importance than the High Court, meeting in the larger towns for the trial of claims in contract and tort arising in the local district. It tries cases concerning payment of small debts, ownership of land, disputes about wills and disputes between landlord and tenant, and makes orders for winding up small companies. Cases relating to sums above a certain figure (e.g. £750) have to be tried in the High Court; appeals from county courts go to the Court of Appeal.

coupon (1) STK. EXCH. one of a number of slips of paper that are separated from a bearer bond or bearer debenture and used to claim payment of interest on the date when it becomes due. (2) STK. EXCH. the rate of interest paid on a fixed-interest security (*see* high coupon). *Cum coupon, see under* cum. (3) ADVTG. a ticket, label or other slip of paper that can be used by a consumer to obtain something either free or at a reduced price, for example cigarette/gift coupons.

coupon bond *see under* bond, *n.*

courier TOUR. a person employed to travel with parties of tourists and to make arrangements for their comfort. Cf. guide.

Cournot Antoine-Augustin (1801–77), French mathematician and economist, who first introduced mathematics as a means of solving economic problems, esp. that of price equilibrium under monopoly, duopoly and perfect competition.

courtage *see* brokerage.

courtesy *adj.* COM. (of something supplied) free of charge; given as a favour: *Please accept the enclosed courtesy copy (of a book)/courtesy tickets (for the theatre).*
n. something given or done without charge: *We shall be happy to extend you this courtesy*, to do this for you free of charge.

Court of Admiralty *see under* Admiralty.

Court of Appeal LAW since 1966 the Court of Appeal in Britain has consisted of two divisions — criminal and civil. The *criminal division* hears appeals in criminal cases from the Crown Court. The *civil division* hears civil appeals from the High Court and county courts. Appeals from the Court of Appeal go to the House of Lords. *Syn.* Appeal Court.

Court of Queen's Bench LAW in Britain, a division of the High Court of Justice. *Syn.* King's Bench. *Abbr.* Q.B.

court order *see* order (5).

covenant LAW (1) a solemn agreement in the form of a deed, binding the parties to perform some stated duty or duties (*positive covenant*) or not to perform certain acts (*restrictive* or *negative covenant*) or to pay money. *See also* deed of covenant. (2) one of the conditions or duties contained in such a deed.

covenanted employee/servant one bound by a covenant to serve in a position of special trust.

cover *n.* (1) an envelope or wrapper: *We are sending (something) under separate cover*, in a separate envelope or wrapper.
registered cover an envelope sent by registered post.
(2) BKG. & FIN. security for money lent or against a possible loss. *Syn.* collateral. (3) BKG. the amount of notes and coin needed by a bank to meet the demands of its customers. *Syn.* cash requirement. (4) INSCE. in Britain, protection by insurance against risk of loss: *To take out cover*, to arrange an insurance. *The policy gives cover against burglary.* (5) INSCE. the range or scale of protection given to the insured under an insurance policy: *The policy gives cover against storm damage but not against frost. We must increase the amount of insurance cover to include our new machinery. Syn.* (U.S.A.) coverage. *See also* open cover *under* open. (6) STK. EXCH. the relation between a company's net earnings and its dividend payments; this is a measure of the basic strength of the company's shares. *The dividend is twice covered if half the net earnings are distributed.* (7) STK. EXCH. a deposit of money or

securities required by a stockbroker to protect him against loss in carrying on market dealings as agent for a client, esp. if the dealings are risky.

v. INSCE. to insure: *To hold covered*, to declare to an insured person that he is covered by insurance although the cover-note and the policy documents have not yet been prepared. *We confirm that we hold your house covered against fire risks for £20,000.*

to cover oneself to protect oneself, e.g. by demanding a security for a loan or a liability.

coverage (U.S.A.) *see* cover, *n.* (5).

cover-charge TOUR. in some restaurants, a charge of so much for each cover (place laid for a person at a table) is added to the bill.

covered bear STK. EXCH. a bear (investor who sells shares in expectation of a fall in price) who possesses enough securities to meet his contracts without risk of having to buy in a rising market in order to do so. *Syn.* protected bear.

covering *see* hedging.

covering letter a letter that is sent with something explaining why the thing has been sent: *Send him a sample of our new product with a covering letter.* Cf. compliments slip.

cover-note INSCE. an acknowledgment in writing from an insurance company proving that a certain insurance contract exists. It is a temporary document intended to be used until the policy itself has been drawn up and issued to the insured. In motor insurance, a cover-note acts as a temporary certificate of insurance.

cowrie FIN. the very hard, smooth shell of a small sea-snail used as money in some parts of Africa and Asia, esp. Thailand. *Syn.* cowry. *Pl.* cowries. *See* commodity money.

cp. compare.

C.P. carriage paid; charter-party.

C/P. charter-party.

c.p. candlepower.

C.P.A. certified public accountant (U.S.A.); claims payable abroad; critical path analysis.

CR cash receipts; also Costa Rica's international vehicle-registration letters.

C.R. current rate; company's risk; carrier's risk.

Cr. credit.

craft (1) SHIPG. any small boat or ship such as a lighter, barge, launch.

aircraft *see* aircraft.

marine craft a boat.

(2) IND. a means of earning a living by doing skilled work by hand as well as by machine, and needing some taste and cleverness. *Syn.* handicraft.

craft guild *see* guild.

craft port SHIPG. a port where ships cannot tie up at a wharf so have to unload their cargo into lighters or other small craft. *Syn.* overside port; surf port. *See* barge port *under* port.

craftsman IND. a skilled workman in a craft. *Syn.* artisan; handicraftsman. Cf. artist. *Pl.* -men.

craftsmanship IND. the quality of something made by a craftsman: *The furniture is of excellent craftsmanship.*

craft union IND. REL. a trade union, usu. a small union, whose members all practise the same craft or trade, esp. one needing a long training and much skill, such as printing. Members of such unions usu. work for various employers. By controlling the rate of entry, esp. by limiting apprenticeship, and thus keeping low the supply of skilled labour, these unions are often very powerful. Cf. industrial union.

cran COM. a unit of measurement for herrings, expressing the quantity of fresh fishes that will fill a barrel.

cranage SHIPG. charges that have to be paid to a port authority for the use of cranes.

crane a machine for lifting and moving heavy loads, esp. on building sites, ships and in harbours. *Syn.* derrick; hoist.

crash FIN. the sudden and severe financial failure of a business, or fall of prices on the stock and commodity exchanges: *A bank crash. The crash on Wall Street. A crash in coffee prices. Syn.* collapse.

crate TRANSPT. an open wooden packing-case having a strong frame to which strips of wood are fixed with spaces between, leaving the contents well protected from knocks but not fully enclosed. Cf. closed case. *Abbr.* ct(s).

create to bring into existence; to make for the first time.

to create credit BKG. to make or increase purchasing power by allowing overdrafts and making loans.

to create reserves FIN. to put aside some of the profits of a business to form a reserve either for a special purpose, such as buying a new asset, or for distributing later as a return of capital to the shareholders.

to create a trust *see* trust, *n.* (5).

credentials (1) one or more letters and other documents which prove that a person is what he says he is. (2) a letter supporting a person's character and ability.

credit *n.* (1) BKG. any arrangement with a bank by which the bank will accept and pay bills of exchange for the customer. (2) a letter of credit. (3) BKG. any sum of money advanced by a bank and held in a bank account ready for the borrower to draw upon, in return for a promise to pay at some future date. *See* bank credit *below.*

acceptance credit *see under* acceptance (5).

bank credit bank loans and overdrafts, i.e. credit created by the banks, which is of great economic importance.

clean credit a credit arrangement with a bank under which foreign buyers can draw bills of exchange which the bank agrees to accept on conditions stated in the credit document. The credit is said to be clean because no documents are joined to the bills drawn upon it. Only firms of the highest reputation are allowed such credits. *Syn.* open credit.

confirmed credit *see under* confirmed.

countervailing credit an arrangement in foreign trade by which a finance house advances money to a foreign buyer to help him pay for goods supplied by a foreign seller.

documentary credit an arrangement between a bank and an exporter by which the bank will accept bills of exchange drawn by the exporter on the named overseas customer up to an agreed total amount on condition that the bills have certain shipping documents with them.

fixed credit a bank credit against which can be drawn one or more amounts up to a fixed sum; when this sum has been reached, the credit is completely used up and is finished. *Opp.* revolving credit.

irrevocable credit one that cannot be changed or cancelled. *Opp.* revocable credit.

London acceptance credit *see under* acceptance.

open credit *see* clean credit *above.*

paper credit *see under* paper.

revocable credit one that can be changed or cancelled at any time. *Opp.* irrevocable credit.

revolving credit a bank credit against which an unlimited amount can be drawn at any time; or a limited amount can be drawn at any *one* time but with no limit on the total; or a limited total amount that is automatically renewed as soon as debts are paid off. *Opp.* fixed credit.

(4) COM. a system of trading on trust, the seller allowing payment to be made later. (5) the length of time given by a seller to a buyer for payment for goods sold on trust: *To buy or sell on credit.*

extended credit *see under* extended.

open credit unlimited credit, esp. where a supplier allows a trusted customer to buy as many goods as he wants without immediately paying for them, but on the understanding that payment will be made after an agreed time. Cf. credit limit.

trade credit the time which a supplier gives his customer to pay for goods supplied. *Syn.* supplier credit. *See also* instalment credit.

(6) FIN. the trust or confidence placed in a person with whom one deals: *John Gilpin was a citizen of credit and renown*, everybody trusted him and he was very well known. *His credit is worthless*, he cannot be trusted to pay.

at his credit (money) ready to be called upon on demand.

personal credit a person's power to obtain goods on credit, i.e. to be paid for in the future.

(7) ACCTS. an entry on the creditor (right-hand) side of an account recording a payment received. *Opp.* debit. *Credit side* of an account, the creditor (right-hand) side, as compared with the debit (left-hand) side. (8) TAXN. *see* tax credit.

v. ACCTS. to enter on the creditor (right-hand) side of an account: *We are crediting you with the value of goods returned. Please credit my account with interest on the loan. Opp.* to debit.

credit account COM. an arrangement with a shop, esp. a department store, by which the customer can buy goods up to an agreed value every month and is allowed to pay for them at the end of an agreed period, usu. monthly or quarterly. *Syn.* open account; (U.S.A.) charge account.

credit agency COM. a commercial organization that, for a fee, supplies information about the financial strength of, and the degree of trust that can be placed in, business concerns. *Syn.* mercantile agency; mercantile credit agency; credit bureau; enquiry agent; status enquiry agency. Cf. debt collection agency.

credit agent INSCE. an insurance agent who is allowed credit by the insurance companies he represents, paying them usu. at the end of each quarter. *Syn.* account agent; accredited agent. Cf. cash agent. *See* credit (4).

credit balance *see under* balance, *n.* (1).

credit bank *see* credit co-operative *under* co-operative.

credit bureau *see* credit agency.

credit card COM. & BKG. a form of consumer credit, being a card issued by a bank or other finance organization which allows the customer to get credit at most shops, restaurants, garages, hotels, etc. He shows the card and signs the bill, which is then paid by the concern issuing the card. The card-holder receives an account, usu. monthly, with all the bills for the period, and he has to pay this within a fixed number of days, after which interest at a high rate becomes payable. In Britain the main credit cards are: Barclaycard (issued by Barclays Bank); Access; American Express. A number of other clearing banks also issue credit cards. *See* credit (1).

credit control (1) FIN. & BKG. in U.S.A., action by a government, working through the banking system, to control the volume of credit, esp. the making of loans and allowing of overdrafts by the banks to the public. *Syn.* in Britain, monetary control. (2) COM. & ACCTS. in Britain, a department of a business under a *credit controller* responsible for preventing bad debts and for keeping the amount of overdue debts as small as possible; thus helping the business to make the greatest use of its working capital. *See* credit gap.

credit co-operative *see under* co-operative.

crédit export BKG. & FIN. in Belgium, an organization that advances money to exporters.

crédit foncier BKG. & FIN. in France, an organization that makes loans of money, esp. in the building industry, against security of land and buildings, repayable by annual sums over a number of years. Cf. crédit mobilier; crédit hotelier.

credit freeze *see under* freeze.

credit gap COM. the gap or basic difference of interest between the buyer, who always desires to delay paying for goods as long as he can, and the supplier, who always wishes to get his money as early as possible. In foreign trade the instrument most useful in bridging this gap is the bill of exchange.

crédit hotelier BKG. & FIN. in France, an organization making loans to the hotel, catering and tourist industry.

credit information *see* banker's opinion.

credit instrument *see under* instrument.

credit, letter of *see* letter of credit.

credit limit COM. & ACCTS. the amount of credit that is allowed by a supplier to a particular customer. The limit applies both to the value of the goods which the customer may receive without immediately paying for them, and to the time allowed him to pay. *See* credit control. Cf. open credit. *Syn.* (U.S.A.) credit line.

credit line (1) COM. & ACCTS. the U.S.A. equivalent of credit limit in Britain. (2) an acknowledgment, printed in a book, magazine or newspaper, of the use made of copyright material.

credit memorandum (U.S.A.) *see* credit note.

crédit mobilier BKG. & FIN. in France, an organization making loans of money to manufacturers and traders on the security of movable property. Cf. crédit foncier.

credit money BKG. (1) money in a bank account. (2) bank credit, i.e. purchasing power created by banks in making loans or allowing overdrafts to their customers. (3) bank-notes that cannot be exchanged for gold or other metal.

credit note ACCTS. an acknowledgment (usu. printed in red) given by a supplier when a customer has been overcharged on an invoice, or has returned goods or containers for which he has the right to a credit. The credit note states the quantity and value of the goods concerned and the reason for the credit. *Abbr.* C/N. *Syn.* (U.S.A.) credit memorandum; credit memo.

creditor a person or organization to whom money is owing.

creditors *pl.* all those to whom a business owes money.

general creditor in a case of bankruptcy, a creditor who is not a preferential creditor or a secured creditor. *Syn.* unsecured creditor; ordinary creditor.

judgment creditor a creditor who has obtained a judgment in a court of law against a debtor for the payment of a debt.

petitioning creditor *see* bankruptcy.

preferential creditor a creditor who by law is paid first when the assets of a bankrupt are distributed. *See* preferential payments. *Syn.* preferred creditor (U.S.A.).

secured creditor a person holding a mortgage charge or lien on some or all of the property of the debtor as a security for a debt owing by the debtor. *See* unsecured creditor *below*.

unsecured creditor a person who is owed a debt by a debtor but who holds no security if the debtor is made bankrupt. When a bankrupt's property is shared out among his creditors, the unsecured or general creditors will not be paid anything until all the preferential and secured creditors' debts have been paid in full. *Syn.* general creditor.

creditor nation ECON. & FIN. in international trade, a nation that is owed more by other nations than it owes to them.

creditors' meeting *see under* meeting.

credit policy *see under* insurance policy.

credit rating COM. a system of classifying customers and possible future customers according to their financial strength and the degree of trust that a supplier can place in them. *Syn.* credit status; credit standing.

credits, frozen *see under* frozen.

credit sale COM. a sale for which payment will be made later, either as a lump sum on a certain date or by regular instalments over a period. Goods bought in this way become the property of the buyer as soon as they have been delivered to him. Cf. hire-purchase sale.

credit slip *see* paying-in slip.

credit society *see* credit co-operative *under* co-operative.

credit squeeze ECON. & FIN. in Britain, the placing of a limit by the government on the amount of credit that banks can give to their customers as part of a policy to reduce total demand in the economy through control of the money supply. *Syn.* credit freeze.

credit standing *see* credit rating.

credit, standing *see* standing credit.

credit status *see* credit rating.

credit, tax *see* tax credit.

credit transfer BKG. in Britain, a method of payment which makes it possible for any person to pay money into a clearing bank for the credit of the account of any customer of the banks operating the system. In 1967 the name of the credit transfer was changed to Bank Giro, with which was also merged the direct debiting system.

credit union FIN. an association of persons with a common interest, such as their work or the place where they live, who agree to save money regularly to build up a fund from which the members may borrow at a much lower rate of interest than that charged by banks, finance companies and other commercial lenders.

credit voucher see paying-in slip.

creditworthy adj. deserving of trust; certain to pay debts promptly, and therefore worthy of being allowed credit. N. creditworthiness.

Creole a language which began as a lingua franca or pidgin and has become the mother tongue of a particular group of people, such as the French spoken in Louisiana, U.S.A.

Cres. Crescent.

crew SHIPG. specially-qualified persons employed in working a ship, sometimes except the officers: *The officers are Egyptians and the crew are Scotsmen.* Cf. aircrew; ground crew.

crew list SHIPG. one of the ship's papers; a list of the names and other details of every member of the crew of the ship and of her officers. *Syn.* muster roll.

crime LAW an act which is of serious harm to the public and punishable under the law of the State. Cf. offence.

criminal law LAW that part of public law which controls acts which are harmful to the whole community, i.e. crimes.

crisis a time of difficulty and anxiety, esp. in the economic life of a country: *A financial/economic/business crisis. A crisis of confidence. Pl.* crises. *See* trade cycle *under* cycle.

critical path analysis IND. & MAN. a method of planning a highly complicated operation such as the building of a bridge or a motorway. The whole work is divided into many separate steps each of which is represented on a chart by an arrow having a time value. The result is a series of parallel chains which come together at certain points. The chain taking the longest time is the 'critical path' because it determines the total length of the work. The chart shows the points at which various materials, tools, etc. will be needed, just when each step must be begun and completed, and by whom. *Abbr.* C.P.A. *Syn.* network analysis; critical path method (C.P.M.)

croft AGR. a small farm, usu. on poor land, in the Highlands and Western Isles of Scotland. The farmer, called a *crofter*, is the tenant of a few enclosed arable fields surrounded by common land where his cattle and sheep and those of his neighbours can graze (eat the grass).

crook (*colloq.*) a dishonest person; one in the habit of breaking the law: *Do not trust him, for he is a crook.*

crooked (*colloq.*) not straight; dishonest; not to be trusted: *Every deal he makes proves to be crooked.*

crop (1) AGR. the produce from cultivated land, such as grain, fruit and vegetables. (2) the amount harvested: *A season's crop of apples/corn/potatoes, etc. See also* cash crop; main crop.

crore in the Indo-Pakistan subcontinent, ten million (usu. of rupees) written as Rs. 1,00,00,000, being one hundred lakhs each of Rs. 100,000. *A crore of rupees.*

cross v. BKG. to draw two parallel lines across the face of a cheque to direct the banker not to pay the value of the cheque in cash but only as a credit to a customer's bank account. *See* crossed cheque *under* cheque.

cross-cast see under cast.

crossed cheque see under cheque.

cross-examination see under examination.

cross exchange see cross rate.

cross rate FIN. the rate of exchange between two currencies, calculated by reference to a third currency. When the exchange rate between currencies is not the same as the cross rate there is a chance of obtaining some arbitrage. *Syn.* (U.S.A.) cross exchange; (Britain) indirect parity.

Crown (1) in Britain, the head of the State in the person of the king or queen acting as a corporation sole, i.e. a body having an existence separate from that of the person who is its only member. Thus the Crown, represented by the monarch or sovereign (the king or queen), is the highest branch of the government. (2) FIN. in Britain, a large cupro-nickel coin worth 25 pence. (3) the English name for the standard unit of currency in Czechoslovakia (koruna), Denmark (krone), Norway (krone), Iceland and Sweden (krona).

Crown Agents for Overseas Governments and Administrations (short title: Crown Agents) a British government organization that acts as agent for many foreign governments and other public services in buying goods and services, advising on financial and technical matters, and acting as bankers and investment managers.

crown court LAW in England, a local branch of the Supreme Court of Judicature with High Court judges trying cases in the main towns. Most of its work is on criminal cases but some is civil; all the criminal cases it tries come to it from the magistrates' courts. Appeals from the crown court go to the Court of Appeal.

crown debt see under debt.

crown land in Britain, land owned by the Crown, the income from which is given to the government in return for an annual payment to the monarch under an Act called the Civil List.

crude adj. (1) IND. raw; untreated: *Crude sugar/rubber/oil.* (2) ECON. uncorrected.

crude death rate the actual number of deaths per thousand of the population, no allowance being made for the proportion of very young or very old people in the population.

n. IND. crude, untreated, petroleum oil: *The tanker is carrying crude.*

cruise TOUR. a voyage by ship from place to

place for pleasure: *A Mediterranean/Baltic/ round-the-world/summer/winter, etc. cruise. A cruise liner/ship. See* fly-cruise.

cruzeiro the currency unit of Brazil, divided into 100 centavos.

CS Czechoslovakia's international vehicle-registration letters.

C.S. Civil Service.

c/s. cases.

C.S.E. Certificate of Secondary Education.

csk. cask.

C.S.O. Central Statistical Office.

Cstms. Customs.

ct. cent.

CT. cable transfer.

Ctge. cartage.

cts. crates; cents.

C.T.L. constructive total loss.

C.T.T. capital transfer tax.

cu., cub. cubic.

Cuba an island republic in the Caribbean, pop. 9 million approx. (1975); capital, Havana, pop. 800,000 approx.; language, Spanish; currency unit, the peso, divided into 100 centavos. Member, COMECON.

cubic *or* **solid measure** measurement of volume in cubic units, i.e. length multiplied by breadth multiplied by height. 1728 cubic inches = 1 cubic foot and 1000 cubic millimetres = 1 cubic centimetre. *See table on page 477.*

cuisine TOUR. & COM. (1) cooking arrangements: *The owner's wife looks after the cuisine.* (2) way of cooking: *We prefer French cuisine,* food cooked the French way. (3) quality of cooking: *Claridges (Hotel) is famous for its cuisine,* for the quality of its meals.

cultivated land AGR. land ploughed or otherwise prepared for growing crops.

culture (1) the development of the human body, mind and spirit. *Adj.* cultural. (2) AGR. the growing of crops.

cum. cumulative.

cum STK. EXCH. (*Latin,* with) when the price of a security is quoted e.g. *cum div.* it means that the price includes the right to receive the next dividend or other benefit soon to fall due. *Opp.* ex (*Latin,* without).

cum all with all benefits soon due.

cum bonus with bonus shares soon to be issued.

cum coupon (of a bond) with the coupon soon due for payment.

cum distribution (*Abbr.* cum dist.) with the next income distribution or dividend.

cum dividend (*Abbr.* cum div.) with the next dividend.

cum drawing (of bonds soon to be drawn) with any rights that may come with the drawing, such as profit or premium.

cum interest (*Abbr.* cum int.) with the next interest payment.

cum new *see* cum rights *below.*

cum rights with the rights issue soon due. *Syn.* cum new; with rights.

Cumb., Cumbria Cumberland, now part of Cumbria, England.

cum. pref. cumulative preference (shares).

cumulative dividend *see under* dividend.

cumulative preference share *see under* share. *Abbr.* cum. pref.

cupro-nickel FIN. an alloy of copper with 25% nickel, used for the so-called 'silver' coinage at present in use in Britain and many other countries. *See* nickel.

cur. currency.

currency (1) BKG. of a bill of exchange, the length of time that has to pass before the bill becomes due for payment. The currency of a bill drawn *after sight* starts to run from the date on which the bill is accepted. (2) FIN. any kind of money that is in general use as cash, passing from person to person, such as coin and banknotes. (3) any generally accepted means of payment; anything used as a medium of exchange such as coin, bank-notes, cheques, bills of exchange, promissory notes, and any document that can be used in place of money. (4) the money of a particular country: *The French franc/Dutch guilder/Italian lira/U.S.A. dollar, etc. Abbr.* cur.; cy.

blocked currency *see under* blocked.

convertible currency *see under* convertible; *see also* convertibility.

decimal currency one based on the decimal system, using a number scale of ten and generally counting in sets of ten or in tenths. Nearly all nations of the world have decimal currencies, Britain being one of the last to change, in 1971. *Syn.* decimal coinage.

domestic currency that of the home country: in Britain the pound sterling. Cf. foreign currency.

floating currency one of which the rate of exchange is allowed to rise and fall according to the market demand and supply, with as little interference as possible by the authorities, usu. the central bank.

foreign currency in Britain, any currency other than sterling.

fractional currency coins which are each a fraction of the standard unit of currency of a country, such as a penny, which is one-hundredth of a pound.

full-bodied currency one entirely of gold and silver.

green currencies *see under* green; *also* green pound.

hard currency that of a country which has a strong balance of payments and a currency that is unlikely to fall in value. It is, therefore, much in demand. Its price is high, esp. in exchange for soft currency. Cf. soft currency.

inconvertible currency one which cannot be freely exchanged for other currencies. *Syn.* irredeemable currency. *Opp.* convertible currency.

international currency one that is recognized and accepted in payment of debts in most countries of the world. Before the Second World War, sterling was in world-wide use; after the war, the U.S.A. dollar became the most important. *Syn.* key currency; leading currency.

irredeemable currency *see* inconvertible currency *above*.

key currency *see* international currency *above*.

leading currency *see* international currency *above*.

managed currency one of which the rate of exchange is controlled by the government, usu. through the central bank. This is done by using means such as varying the minimum lending rate, and by buying and selling in the foreign-exchange market. *Syn.* managed money.

metallic currency coins made of gold, silver, cupro-nickel, nickel and bronze, as distinguished from paper currency.

mixed currency (*a*) one that consists of coin of various metals, and paper money in the form of bank-notes. (*b*) formerly, a currency that consisted of coins of two precious metals, usu. one of gold, the other of silver.

paper currency bank-notes. Cf. paper money.

reserve currency one which is held as part of their official reserves by the governments of other countries, because these governments have confidence in its value remaining high and in its usefulness in settling future international debts. The two main reserve currencies are the U.S.A. dollar and the pound sterling.

scarce currency one for which the demand on the foreign-exchange market exceeds the amount offered for sale at the usual rate of exchange. If this situation continues for long, members of the International Monetary Fund may bring exchange control restrictions (limits) against the scarce currency.

soft currency that of a country which has a weak balance of payments and therefore a currency for which there is relatively little demand. It can usu. be bought cheaply, esp. in exchange for hard currency.

trading currency in international trade, a currency which importers and exporters all over the world generally use for settling debts, esp. the U.S.A. dollar and the pound sterling. In certain regions where there is a common currency, such as in parts of Africa using the C.F.A. franc, this regional currency is usu. used for trading.

currency appreciation *see* appreciation (3).

currency bill BKG. a bill of exchange drawn in a foreign currency.

currency bond *see under* bond, *n*.

currency circulation BKG. & FIN. in Britain, the value of the notes issued by the Bank of England (and by the Scottish and Irish banks of issue) and considered to be circulating (passing from person to person) or otherwise held by the public. It is shown as a liability of the Issue Department in the Bank of England's weekly return. *See* bank return. *Syn.* notes in circulation; notes issued.

currency deflation *see under* deflation.

currency depreciation *see* depreciation (3).

currency notes FIN. notes issued as money by the British Treasury during the war of 1914–18 and after, of two values, £1 and 10s. later amalgamated (1928) with Bank of England notes. *Syn.* Treasury notes.

currency rate *see under* exchange rate.

Currency School ECON. HIST. & BKG. a group of financiers and economists who, during the period of great swings from very good to very bad economic conditions between 1825 and 1860, demanded that the power of the banks to issue notes should be strictly controlled by the government by keeping the amount of paper money within a fixed proportion of the amount of gold held by the banks. Their fight for a change in the law led to the passing of the Bank Charter Act of 1844. The Currency School's ideas were opposed by the Banking School, who wanted banks to have complete freedom to issue notes. *See* Torrens, Robert.

current *adj.* in general use; not out of date: *Current coin*, coin which still has value as money. *The guinea, farthing, half-crown and sixpence are no longer current. The Churchill crown is current but rare.* Not past or future but happening or existing now; relating to the present: *Current trading results. Current opinion/reports/views*, now being expressed. *Please send us your current price-list. The current week/month/year/period. What is the current rate of premium/of exchange? See* current assets; current account, etc. *Opp.* obsolete; past.

current account *see under* bank account.

current assets *see under* assets, *pl*.

current balance ECON. & PUB. FIN. that part of the balance of payments account that records payments for imports and exports, both visible and invisible, but not movements of capital.

current capital (U.S.A.) *see* working capital *under* capital.

current cost accounting ACCTS. an important modern development in accounting method that aims to show better than the usual historic-cost method the true effect of price changes on the trading results of a firm. In the usual system, profits are calculated after valuing assets (including stocks) at cost or market value, whichever is the lower. But this historic-cost valuation makes no adjustment for price changes in the period between buying an asset and replacing it. To obtain a really fair view in a time of rapidly rising prices, it is important to take account of the cost of replacing each class of asset at current price-levels. Accounts prepared on the usual historic-cost basis may show the firm to be trading profitably, but current cost accounts for the same period may well show it to be selling goods at a price which is hardly enough to cover the cost of replacing its stocks. *Abbr.* C.C.A.

current debt *see under* debt.

current liabilities *see under* liabilities.

current money *see under* money.

current ratio ACCTS. & FIN. ratio (relation) between current assets and current liabilities. A ratio used as a test of solvency. *See* acid test ratio.

current yield *see under* yield.

curt. current.

curtail to reduce, to cut, to make less than was earlier intended: *To curtail one's activities/expenses/output/holiday.*

custodian a person who has custody (care); a guardian (one who guards the safety of someone or something) esp. of public property.

custodian trustee *see under* trustee.

custody *see* safe custody.

custody bill of lading *see under* bill of lading.

custom (1) COM. the support given to a business by its regular customers, i.e. the people who regularly buy from it: *We greatly value your custom. We cannot afford to lose his custom.* (2) LAW an ancient rule of behaviour or an activity that has long been practised and now has the force of law, such as a local custom giving fishermen the right to spread nets on part of the shore owned by someone else. Much general custom now forms part of common law but some commercial and professional customs still exist.

customary acre LAW the area of land that a man and his horses could plough in one day. *See* acre.

customer (1) COM. & BKG. a buyer, esp. a person who buys at a shop or restaurant, or stays at a hotel, or has an account with a bank: *A regular customer. Syn.* (of a bank) client; (of a hotel) guest; (of a restaurant) patron. (2) (*colloq.*) An *awkward/queer/customer*, a peculiar person, difficult to handle.

customers' ledger *see under* ledger.

Custom(s) House TAXN. the offices, usu. in a port, of the customs service, where duty on imports or exports and certain other taxes are paid.

Custom-House broker *see* clearing agent.

Custom-House report SHIPG. a document signed by the master of a ship on arrival at a port, giving the customs authorities details of the passengers and cargo on board the ship.

custom-made (U.S.A.) IND. & COM. made specially to the order of a particular customer, not part of regular production. *Syn.* bespoke.

Customs (1) TAXN. in Britain, Her Majesty's Customs, the group of government officials responsible for collecting customs duties and for controlling the import and export of forbidden goods. *Syn.* H.M.Customs. *Abbr.* Cstms. (2) import duties generally.

customs agent *see* clearing agent.

Customs and Excise, Board of TAXN. the British government department which is responsible for collecting all indirect taxes, i.e. taxes which are collected from some person or organization, who passes the charge on to the final consumer. Cf. Inland Revenue, Board of.

customs bills of entry COM. & SHIPG. daily information published by the Customs and Excise about ships entering or leaving British ports and about their cargoes.

customs bond *see under* bond, *n.*

customs clearance *see* clearance.

customs debenture TAXN. & COM. a document given by the Customs to an exporter who has the right to claim back duty paid on goods that he earlier imported under drawback. The debenture is a negotiable instrument.

customs declaration *see* declaration (2).

customs drawback *see* drawback.

customs duty *see under* duty.

customs entry COM. & TAXN. the act of entering and recording with the Customs the import or export of a consignment of goods. This is done by means of a bill of entry; *see under* bill. *Also see* declaration (2).

captain's entry *see under* captain.

entry for free goods a document signed by an importer and handed to the Customs if no duty is payable. A copy, signed by a customs officer and called a *duplicate warrant*, is given to the importer as a permit to take the goods away. Cf. entry for home use.

entry for home use ex ship a document signed by an importer and handed to the Customs if duty is payable and if the goods are to be sold immediately in the home market. On payment of the duty the importer is allowed to take the goods away. Cf. entry for free goods.

entry in a customs entry of an import.

entry out a customs entry of an export.

free entry *see* entry for free goods *above*.

over-entry certificate a note given by the Customs to an importer allowing him to obtain payment of a return of money overpaid on prime entry. Cf. post entry.

perfect entry a bill of sight that has been perfected. *See* bill of sight.

post entry a document issued by the Customs to an importer calling for payment of more duty because not enough was paid on prime entry. Cf. over entry.

prime entry the first customs entry made when imported goods arrive in a country and on which any import duty is paid. Cf. post entry; over entry.

transit entry a customs entry for goods in transit, usu. to another country.

warehousing entry a document signed by an importer and handed to the Customs if duty is payable. If the goods are to be stored for a time the Customs will give the importer a *landing order* allowing the goods to be removed to a bonded warehouse, the payment of duty being postponed until they are needed for sale or use.

customs examination *see under* examination (2).

customs invoice *see under* invoice.

customs permit *see under* permit.

customs specification SHIPG. & COM. in Britain, a document which every importer and exporter must complete for the Customs, recording the value of the goods and the country of origin or destination. The details are used for calculating the balance of trade.

customs tariff COM. an official printed table issued by the government showing the rate of customs duty that has to be paid on goods imported into the country issuing the tariff.

customs union ECON. a union of two or more independent countries to form a single customs area within which there are no customs duties or other limiting controls on trade between the member countries; common customs duties are charged on all goods imported into the union from other countries. *Examples:* the E.E.C., Benelux, and COMECON. Cf. free trade area.

customs warehouse *see* bonded warehouse.

cut *n.* (1) COM. a reduction: *A cut in price(s). A cut in wages/salary/commission/discount/output, etc. A cut in the minimum lending rate.* See cut-price shop. (2) (*colloq.*) a share in some profit or commission: *He got a cut of 5% for introducing the customer.*
v. COM. (1) to reduce: *To cut prices/discounts/ interest rates. To cut back production. To cut back on expenses/investment. To cut down expenses.* (2) to stop; to put an end to: *To cut one's losses,* to stop some unprofitable activity in order not to lose more money. *To cut off supplies/services. To cut out unnecessary expense.*

cut price *see under* price.

cut-price shop COM. a shop that sells at unusually low prices, well below those of any competitors. *Syn.* discount house; discount store.

cut-throat competition COM. & ECON. the severest possible form of competition, existing usu. when there are few suppliers in the market and where supply exceeds demand. A cruel price war results, which is of no benefit to any of the suppliers and often causes some of them to be put out of business.

c.v.d. cash against (versus) documents.

c.w.o. cash with order.

C.W.S. Co-operative Wholesale Society.

cwt. hundredweight.

cy. currency.

CY Cyprus's international vehicle-registration letters.

cybernetics MAN. & IND. a new branch of science that studies methods of communication and control of actions both in nature, e.g. the nerve-systems of animals and Man, and in modern industry and commerce. In practice, cybernetics is mainly concerned with automation of industrial processes by self-regulating (self-controlling) mechanisms and with the presentation of data for decision-making. *See* automation; servo-mechanism.

cycle a period of time in which a series of events happening in a certain order is completed, and then happens again and again with the events coming each time in the same order and generally within a similar length of time.

business cycle *see* trade cycle *below.*

trade cycle a cycle in time during which trade moves from a state of high activity (boom, prosperity) through a running-down period (contraction, downswing, recession, slump, downturn) to a state of low activity (depression, stagnation, trough), then upward again when business improves (expansion, recovery, revival) until there is a return to high activity once more. The whole cycle then begins again. *Syn.* business cycle (U.S.A.); cyclical fluctuations; economic fluctuations; industrial fluctuations. *See* trade-cycle theories *below.*

trade-cycle theories attempts, of which there have been many, to explain the causes of trade cycles in a variety of ways: natural causes such as the effects of weather and sunspots on harvests; the mental outlook of businessmen; over-investment in capital goods; over-production with under-consumption of consumer goods; savings being out of balance with investment; bad judgment in lending by banks, and insufficient control by governments of the money supply.

cyclical fluctuations *see* trade cycle *under* cycle.

cypher *see* cipher.

Cyprus an island republic in the eastern Mediterranean; pop. 650,000 approx. (1971); capital, Nicosia, pop. 115,000; languages, Greek, Turkish; currency unit, the Cyprus pound (C£), divided into 1000 mils. Member, (British) Commonwealth.

Czechoslovakia a socialist federal republic in eastern Europe; pop. 15 million approx. (1973); capital, Prague, pop. 1.1 million approx.; languages, Czech, Slovak; currency unit, the koruna (crown), *pl.* koruny, divided into 100 haleru. Member, COMECON.

D

D West Germany's international vehicle-registration letter; the Roman numeral for 500.

d. date; dime; dollar; (old) penny or pence (denarii); died, e.g. *d.* 1937.

℔ delete.

D.A. deposit account; deed of arrangement; documents (against) acceptance; dearness allowance.

D/A days after acceptance; documents against acceptance.

D/a. deposit account; discharge afloat.

d/a. days after acceptance; documents against acceptance.

D/A bill *see* documents-against-acceptance bill *under* bill of exchange.

Dahomey or the People's Republic of Benin in West Africa, pop. 3 million approx. (1973); capital, Porto Novo, pop. 85,000 approx.; largest town, Cotonou, pop. 120,000 approx.; languages, French and tribal languages; currency unit, the C.F.A. franc (CFA Fr), divided into 100 centimes. Member, O.A.U.; O.C.A.M.M.; Associate, E.E.C.

daily *adj.* appearing or happening every day: *A daily newspaper/meeting/delivery service.*
adv. every day: *The service runs twice daily.* *Abbr.* dly.
n. (*colloq.*) a part-time employee who comes in each day for a few hours to do cleaning work in a home or office. *Syn.* cleaner; char-(woman); daily woman.

dairy farm AGR. a farm that keeps cattle for the sale of milk and milk products such as butter and cheese. *See* milch cattle.

dak (in India & Pakistan) the mail; the postal service.
dak-bungalow a rest-house for travellers, one of many formerly run by the postal service.

dal. decalitre.

dalasi the standard currency unit of Gambia, divided into 100 butut.

dam. decametre.

dam INDUS. & AGR. a high wall or bank of earth built to hold back river-water in a reservoir where it is stored for use in various ways: making electricity; and supplying water to people's houses and to farms for watering crops.

damage *n.* (1) harm; loss of value caused by being broken or spoilt: *Damage by fire/storm/water/flood, etc.* (2) (*colloq.*) cost, expense: *What's the damage?* What do I owe you? *See also* apparent damage; hidden damage; malicious damage; damages, *pl.*
v. to harm; to break; to cause loss: *Damaged goods. Goods damaged in transit,* broken or spoilt while being carried from one place to another. *His reputation has been damaged.*

damage certificate *see* certificate of damage.

damage claim INSCE. a claim for partial loss.

damages *n. pl.* LAW where a person has suffered a wrong, the amount of money which he has the right to obtain from the party responsible for wronging him. The amount may be paid by agreement without there being a lawsuit, or it may be paid by order of the court.

action for damages a lawsuit claiming damages.

consequential damages damages to compensate for injury, such as loss of profits, that is a direct consequence (result) of failure to perform the contract. *Syn.* indirect damages.

contemptuous damages a very small sum, perh. only a halfpenny, the smallest coin in Britain, ordered by a court to be paid in cases where the plaintiff has suffered little or no financial loss and where the court thinks that the case ought never to have been brought. Cf. nominal damages.

exemplary damages extra damages ordered by a court as a punishment where the wrong suffered has been made worse by the bad behaviour of the party responsible for the wrong, e.g. acting with unreasonable hatred or bad temper or showing a desire only to do harm.

general damages the damages that the law accepts will result from every breach of contract or of legal rights. In his claim, the plaintiff need not put a value on general damages, but only on other forms such as special damages. *Syn.* ordinary damages; substantial damages. Cf. special damages.

indirect damages *see* consequential damages *above.*

liquidated damages damages which can be exactly calculated or valued and the amount agreed by both parties in an action for breach of contract.

mitigated damages damages that the court has made less severe because the wrongdoer has acted correctly by doing all he could to reduce the harm to the plaintiff, or because he has shown some other reason why he should be treated with mercy.

nominal damages a small sum, perh. £1 in Britain, ordered to be paid by a court when the plaintiff has suffered no financial loss, to recognize the fact that a wrong has been done. Cf. contemptuous damages.

ordinary damages *see* general damages *above.*

real damages the total amount of damages due by law to the wronged party including both general and special damages.

special damages those of a nature which cannot be obtained by law unless actually claimed, proved and argued in court, such as loss of earnings, medical expenses, etc.

substantial damages *see* general damages *above.*
unliquidated damages *see* damages at large.

damages at large LAW damages for which no actual sum of money has been mentioned by the plaintiff in his claim, it being left to the court to decide what sum is fair. *Syn.* unliquidated damages.

dandy note SHIPG. a delivery order made by an exporter and approved by a customs officer, authorizing a shipping agent to remove goods from a bonded warehouse to a ship for loading.

danger money *see under* money.

d.a.p. documents against payment.

d.a.s. delivered alongside ship.

data facts that are known; information accepted as true or correct for the purpose of argument or reasoning.

data bank COMP. a collection of facts stored in a computer and kept ready for use as may be necessary, such as for commerce, industry, medical and scientific research, and for government administration. *Syn.* data base.

data base *see* data bank.

data processing COMP. the recording, re-arrangement, and organization of large quantities of data put into a computer so that it may produce the calculations, lists, accounts, controls, etc. which the system has been planned to provide. *Abbr.* D.P. *Syn.* electronic data processing (E.D.P.)

date the day of the month and year as appearing on documents to show on exactly which day the document was signed. This also distinguishes a document from others. On letters it is British custom to write the day of the month first, then the name of the month, and then the year: *15 September 1978*; but in U.S.A. and in many other countries the name of the month is put first, then the day of the month, and then the year: *July 22, 1978*. A shorter form is sometimes used, giving the number of the month instead of its name and only the last two figures of the year, thus 15/9/78 (in Britain) and 7/22/78 (in U.S.A. etc.). Old-fashioned expressions such as: *ult.* or *ultimo* for last month; *prox.* or *proximo* for next month; and *inst.* or *instant* for this month, are to be avoided. *See* commercialese. *Abbr.* d.

after date *see under* after.

average date *see under* average.

due date the date on which some debt, such as an interest payment or a bill of exchange, becomes due to be paid.

from date *see* after date *under* after.

out of date *adv.* old-fashioned; no longer useful: *Their machines are out of date. His ideas are out of date.*

out-of-date *adj. These out-of-date figures are useless.*

redemption date the date on which a dated security, such as a debenture or loan, is due to be redeemed (repaid).

to date until today; to this day: *We have not received your cheque to date,* at the time of writing.

up to date *adv.* up to the present time: *To bring the filing/records/invoicing up to date. Let me bring you up to date.*

up-to-date *adj. An up-to-date edition of a book.*

vesting date *see under* vesting.

dated security STK. EXCH. a loan or debenture which bears a date on which it will be redeemed (repaid). Cf. undated security.

date-line, international an internationally-agreed line on the map mainly along the meridian of 180° from Greenwich. As one crosses this line the date changes by one day: going westwards one loses a day, e.g. Monday suddenly becomes Tuesday; but going eastwards one gains a day, e.g. Monday becomes Sunday. *Syn.* calendar-line.

date-stamp *see under* stamp.

daughter company *see under* company.

day *see* legal day; non-business days.

day book ACCTS. in book-keeping, one of the books of prime entry in which are recorded day by day all purchases and sales of goods on credit. *See* purchases day book; sales day book. *Abbr.* D.B.

Daylight Saving Time *see under* time.

days after sight *see* after sight.

days lost *see* lost days.

days of grace LAW in Britain, a number of days allowed by law or by custom for certain payments to be made after the day they become actually due. Three days are allowed for promissory notes and bills of exchange other than those payable on demand or at sight. Insurance companies usu. allow 14 days for renewal of fire insurance, 30 days for renewal of life assurance premiums.

days, running *see under* running.

day-to-day accommodation STK. EXCH. & BKG. loans borrowed from banks by stockbrokers, bill-brokers and others for one day only but renewable from one day to the next if both parties agree. *Syn.* day-to-day loan.

day-to-day option *see under* option.

D.B. day book.

d.b.a. doing business at.

dbk. drawback.

dble. double.

D.C. documents (against) cash; District of Columbia, U.S.A.; direct current (or d.c.).

D/C. deviation clause.

D.C.F. discounted cash flow.

dcg. decigram(me).

dcl. decalitre.

dcm. decametre.

dd. dated; delivered.

D.D. demand draft; damage done.

D/D. delivered at docks; demand draft; dock dues.

D/d. days after date; delivered.

d.d. days after date; delivered dock; demand draft; dry dock.

D.D. & Shipg. dock dues and shipping.

D.D.D. deadline delivery date.

D.D.R. Deutsche Demokratische Republik (German Democratic Republic or East Germany).

D.D.R. Mark the standard currency unit of the D.D.R., divided into 100 pfennig. *Syn.* G.D.R. Mark; East Mark; Östmark.

dd/s. delivered sound.

d.e. double entry.

dead account BKG. (1) the balance in the account of a dead person. (2) an account that is no longer at all active.

dead book STK. EXCH. (*colloq.*) the register of defunct (dead) companies.

dead capital *see under* capital.

dead file *see under* file.

dead freight *see under* freight, *n.*

deadhead in U.S.A., (*colloq.*) a person who wrongfully avoids paying for his ticket on a bus or in a theatre.

Dead Letter Office *see* Returned Letter Office.

deadline a time fixed in a contract or by a person in authority for some work or activity to be completed: *The deadline for sending in our budget is next Tuesday. A deadline delivery date (D.D.D.).*

dead loan BKG. one which was a temporary advance but has become a permanent loan because the borrower could not repay it when it became due. Bankers avoid putting their money in dead loans.

dead loss a complete loss.

dead money *see* dead capital *under* capital.

dead rent (1) rent which is being paid for the hire of an unproductive asset such as buildings which are not at present being used. (2) in mining, the fixed rent which is paid whether any ore is produced or not, as distinguished from royalty rent, which varies with the output or profitability of the mine.

dead season TOUR. a time of year when the demand for travel, tours and accommodation is at its lowest.

dead security BKG. certain industrial properties such as mines, iron-workings, quarries, etc. which have little value when they stop working and therefore do not provide good security for loans.

dead stock (1) AGR. farm machinery, plant and buildings. Cf. livestock. (2) COM. goods which are difficult to sell, which produce no part of the turnover of a business and are therefore unprofitable.

dead weight (1) TRANSPT. in U.S.A., the weight of a road or rail truck without any load. *Syn.* (Britain) tare; kerb weight. (2) SHIPG. heavy goods such as mineral ores, coal, stone, etc. carried in the bottom of a ship to make the vessel steadier. *See* deadweight cargo.

deadweight cargo SHIPG. certain kinds of cargo on which freight is charged by weight, not by volume, such as mineral ores, coal, stone, etc. *See* dead weight (2).

deadweight (carrying) capacity *see* deadweight tonnage *under* tonnage.

deadweight debt *see under* national debt.

deadweight tonnage *see under* tonnage.

deal *n.* COM. (1) a piece of business, esp. of buying and selling; a bargain: *We have come to/done/made/arrived at/concluded/a deal with a customer. This is a cash/credit deal. Syn.* transaction. (2) a large amount: *He has made a (great) deal of money.* (3) an arrangement; a settlement: *A square deal,* a fair and reasonable arrangement, fair treatment. *A raw deal,* a very unfair arrangement. (4) ADVTG. a special effort, lasting only a short time, to attract buyers by a temporary price reduction or by providing a gift with each article sold. *Syn.* premium; special offer.

v. COM. (1) to do business; to trade (buy and sell): *We have dealt with him for many years. They deal in cotton.* (2) to act in some necessary way towards someone or something: *The law deals with offenders,* punishes them. *We must deal with this problem,* take the action required to solve it. (3) to be concerned with: *The article/report/paper deals with labour relations.*

dealer (1) COM. a person who, at his own risk, buys commodities to sell at a profit, usu. to consumers. *Syn.* trader. (2) BKG. a person or organization buying and selling bills of exchange, called a discount house. (3) one who buys and sells foreign currency, called a foreign-exchange dealer. (4) STK. EXCH. a person buying and selling securities on the Stock Exchange, esp. a stockjobber doing business as a principal, i.e. for himself and not as an agent or broker. (5) COMMOD. EXCH. a trader in an organized commodity exchange, esp. a merchant or wholesaler.

dealer aids ADVTG. advertising material, such as samples, models, showcards, catalogues, brochures, price-lists, stands, shelves, bookcases, supplied free by manufacturers or importers to shopkeepers to help them to show goods attractively in the shops.

dealer's brand *see* own-brand.

dealing COM. doing business; trading: *They have a reputation for honest dealing.*

dealings *pl.* business relations: *Business dealings. We have had dealings with them for many years.*

dear COM. (1) expensive: *Your goods are too dear,* your prices are too high. *Buy cheap and sell dear. My mistake cost me dear.* (2) precious: *His reputation is very dear to him.*

dear money FIN. & BKG. in the money market, money is said to be dear when interest rates are high and loans from banks are difficult to obtain. *Opp.* cheap money.

dear-money policy ECON. & FIN. in Britain, when the government, through the Bank of England, decides to hold back spending, it makes money dearer to borrow by raising the interest rates, esp. the Bank of England minimum lending rate.

dearness allowance FIN. in some countries, esp. India, Pakistan, etc., a cost-of-living allowance paid to employees in times of rising prices. *Abbr.* D.A.

Dear Sir(s) the usual greeting or salutation (polite form of opening) for a business letter in Britain. In U.S.A. *Gentlemen* is preferred, but *Dear Sir(s)* (followed by a colon:) is often used. *See* greeting.

dearth COM. lack; scarcity, esp. a painfully short supply, rather than a complete absence. *There is a dearth of apples this year. A dearth of food. Syn.* shortage; scarcity. *Opp.* plenty; excess; abundance.

death benefit INSCE. a lump sum paid by the national insurance scheme in Britain to representatives of an employee who has died as a result of an accident while at work. Cf. funeral benefit. *See* death grant.

death duties TAXN. in Britain, certain kinds of taxes which are usu. payable on the estate (property) of a person who has died. The former estate duty has been replaced since 1975 by the capital transfer tax (C.T.T.). Capital gains tax (C.G.T.) is also payable in some cases. *See also* death-duties policy *under* insurance policy. *Syn.* (U.S.A.) death tax.

death grant INSCE. in Britain, a sum of money paid towards funeral expenses by the national insurance scheme and by friendly and burial societies to the representatives of a person who has just died. *Syn.* funeral benefit. Cf. death benefit.

death rate the number of deaths per thousand of the population in a given year. The actual or crude figures for any one area are adjusted to allow for variations in the expectation of life and in the way the population is divided into age groups which differ in different parts of the country. *Syn.* mortality rate.

death tax *see* death duties; estate tax *under* tax.

deb. debenture; debit.

debasement of coinage ECON. HIST. in past times when the value of the metal in a coin was expected to equal its face value, dishonest persons reduced the weight of coins by rubbing or clipping (cutting) bits of metal from them or by sweating (using chemicals). Governments, too, sometimes put less valuable metal, esp. silver, into newly-made coins. Gradually this led to a fall in the buying-power of the coins and therefore to severe rises in prices. *Syn.* adulteration or depreciation of coinage. *See* Gresham's Law.

debenture STK. EXCH. an acknowledgment of a debt, usu. in the form of a deed (document under seal) by a company or public organization and secured by a trust deed protecting the rights of the debenture-holder. A debenture represents a separate debt of a fixed sum of money. Cf. debenture stock. *Abbr.* deb.

all-moneys debenture one given to a bank, with an arrangement that the amount of the loan can be increased without the formalities necessary when increasing a fixed-sum debenture.

bearer debenture one which is payable to bearer. It is a negotiable instrument transferable by delivery, i.e. ownership of it can be passed from one person to another simply by handing it over, without any formalities regarding registration (recording) in the borrower's office. Cf. registered debenture.

customs debenture *see under* customs.

fixed debenture one for which the security is some particular asset of the borrower, such as a machine, building, etc. Cf. floating debenture.

fixed-sum debenture one given to a bank for a certain sum under an agreement which provides that the bank may hold the debenture as security for all money owed by the borrower to the bank now or in the future, with the rate of interest rising and falling with the bank's base rate. Cf. all-moneys debenture; fixed debenture.

floating debenture one which has as security all the assets of the borrower, not any particular asset. Cf. fixed debenture.

guaranteed debenture one of which the payment of interest is guaranteed (firmly promised) by another company or body.

income debenture one that allows that payment of interest and principal shall be made only out of the income or profits of the borrower. *Syn.* income bond.

irredeemable debenture one which has no arrangement for the repayment of the sum borrowed. Repayment will be made only if the borrower-company goes into liquidation. *Syn.* perpetual debenture.

mortgage debenture a debenture which promises to repay a certain sum borrowed at interest and also gives the debenture-holder the right to receive payment if necessary out of certain funds (stocks of money) or from the sale of some or all of the property of the borrower.

naked debenture a simple acknowledgment of a debt; a debenture which is not secured on any of the borrower's property. *Syn.* unsecured debenture.

perpetual debenture *see* irredeemable debenture *above*.

prior-lien debenture a debenture issued with the agreement of the existing debenture-holders, that carries a first claim to payment of interest and repayment of capital.

redeemable debenture one which, under the conditions of the loan, may be redeemed (repaid) by the borrower either at a fixed date, or at any time provided that proper notice is given. Cf. irredeemable debenture.

registered debenture the usual kind of debenture of which the holder's name is registered or recorded in the offices of the borrower as being the party to be paid. Cf. bearer debenture.

secured debenture one which has as security a right to be paid out of the assets of the borrower. *Syn.* mortgage debenture.

unsecured debenture *see* naked debenture *above.*

debenture bond *see under* bond, *n.*

debenture-holder STK. EXCH. the holder of a debenture, i.e. the person to whom the principal and interest of a debenture are payable. If he is a registered holder, his name will be recorded in the offices of the borrower-company and he will usu. receive interest by cheque or warrant when due. If he holds a bearer debenture he will usu. have to send a coupon to the company to claim payment of interest at the due date. If the interest is not paid, the debenture-holders may sue the company for the amount owing, or may appoint a receiver to run the business for them, or may put the company into liquidation. *See* register of debenture-holders.

debenture stock STK. EXCH. borrowed capital of a company or other organization, with all or some of the borrower's property promised as security by a trust deed. A debenture-stock certificate represents part of one large debt, and thus differs from a debenture. Debenture stock is usu. not redeemable and is registered in the owner's name. The stockholder has the right to be paid *debenture interest* before any dividends are paid on the equity capital (shares). Cf. debenture; debenture bond; loan stock. *Abbr.* D.S.

debenture trust *see under* trust.

debit *n.* ACCTS. an entry on the debtor (left-hand) side of an account. *Opp.* credit. *Abbr.* Dr.; deb.

debit side of an account, the debtor (left-hand) side, as distinct from the credit (right-hand) side.

v. to enter on the debtor (left-hand) side of an account: *We are debiting the cable charges to your account. Please debit me with the cost of the repairs. Opp.* to credit.

debit balance *see under* balance, *n.* (1).

debit, direct *see* direct debit.

debit note (1) COM. & ACCTS. a note in a form similar to an invoice but used where an invoice would not be right for the purpose. The debit note usu. relates to charges, such as freight, extra to amounts already invoiced for goods, and is also used to correct mistakes such as an amount undercharged in an invoice. *Abbr.*

D.N.; D/N. (2) INSCE. a note sent by insurers to the agent or proposer of a new insurance to show the amount of the premium to be paid. Cf. invoice.

debt COM. & ACCTS. an amount, usu. of money, owed by one party to another; a duty to pay, usu. in money, goods or services: *To be in (someone's) debt. To get into/run into debt. To contract/incur/owe/run up a debt. To be out of/ get out of debt. To clear/discharge/meet/pay/pay off a debt.*

assignable debt one in such a form that it can be assigned (formally given) to another party, such as any negotiable instrument.

bad debt *see under* bad.

bad debts account *see under* bad debt.

crown debt one owing to the Crown.

current debt a debt due to be paid in a short time, usu. within a year.

deadweight debt *see under* national debt.

doubtful debt(s) a debt which possibly may not be paid. In accounting, allowance is made for such debts, usu. by charging against gross profit a percentage of the total of all debts due. The percentage is decided by experience. Cf. bad debt.

external debt *see under* national debt.

fixed debt *see* funded debt *under* national debt.

floating debt *see under* floating.

funded debt *see under* national debt.

gaming debt money owing to someone as the result of playing a game of chance. Payment of such debts cannot be obtained by action in the courts. *Syn.* wagering debt. *See* debt of honour.

judgment debt one which a court of law has ordered to be paid.

living debt *see under* national debt.

national debt *see under* national.

ordinary debt *see* unsecured debt *below.*

preferential debt in a case of bankruptcy, a debt that is paid in full before other debts: i.e. one year's rates and taxes, four months' salaries and wages due to employees; also unpaid workmen's compensation and national insurance contributions. *See also* preferential payments. *Syn.* preferred debt; privileged debt.

productive debt *see under* national debt.

public debt *see* national debt.

secured debt one for which some security (property) has been given or deposited to make sure that the lender does not lose his money if the borrower fails to repay the debt.

specialty debt in law, one brought into existence by a deed (formal document under seal).

unfunded debt *see under* national debt.

unsecured debt one for which no security has been given. Cf. secured debt. *Syn.* ordinary debt.

wagering debt *see* gaming debt *above.*

debt-collection agency COM. & FIN. an organization, usu. a commercial firm or a society, which, in return for a fee or commission, uses its special knowledge and experience to obtain payment of overdue debts. *Syn.* trade-protection society. Cf. credit agency.

debt-collection letter COM. a letter asking or demanding that a customer pays an overdue debt.

debt collector FIN. a person employed by a business to collect its overdue debts.

debt, discharge of *see under* discharge.

debt of honour one that has no force in law but is morally binding, such as wagering or gaming debts relating to bets or games of chance.

debtor a person owing money to another, as distinguished from a creditor, a person to whom money is owed.

judgment debtor a debtor who has been ordered, by a court of law, to pay a debt. If he should fail to pay, the judgment creditor may cause the debtor's property to be seized and used in payment of the debt.

sundry debtor one who is not a trade debtor but who owes money for a reason not connected with trading, such as an employee or a trade association which has been lent money by the business.

trade debtor a customer who has not yet paid for goods or services sold to him.

debt servicing FIN. the payment of interest on a debt. *Syn.* (U.S.A.) debt service.

Dec. December.

dec. deceased; decimal; declaration; declare; decrease.

deca- the *prefix* used in the metric system of SI units to mean ten times: a decagram = ten grams; a decalitre = ten litres, etc. *Also* deka-.

decd. deceased.

deceased *n.* a person who has died.
adj. dead: *Mr T. Smith, deceased. Abbr.* dec.; decd.

deceit LAW making a false statement with the dishonest intention that if it is acted upon, someone will suffer loss. *Syn.* deception; fraud; misrepresentation.

decentralization the placing of a large amount of responsibility with officials situated away from the centre of a large commercial or industrial organization such as regional boards of the nationalized public utilities in Britain.

deception *see* deceit.

deci- the *prefix* used in the metric system of SI units to mean one-tenth: 10 decimetres = 1 metre; 10 decilitres = 1 litre.

decim. decimetre. *See* deci-.

decimal currency *see under* currency.

decipher (1) to work out the meaning of secret writing: *To decipher a message in code.* (2) (*fig.*) to discover the meaning of very bad handwriting.

deck (1) SHIPG. one of the horizontal divisions in ships which correspond to floors in houses.

Starting from the bottom, most large ships have: the lower, main and upper decks, usu. running the entire length of the ship; the bridge and poop deck in the stern, and the forecastle deck at the same level in the bows; the boat deck and, highest of all, the navigating-bridge deck. The freeboard deck is the highest continuous deck of a ship, and the tonnage deck is the upper deck in ships having less than three complete decks; in any other ship it is the second deck from the bottom of the ship. *See* main deck; 'tween deck. *Abbr.* Dk. (2) TRANSPT. *see* double-decker.

deck-cargo SHIPG. & INSCE. cargo carried on the uncovered deck of a ship. When there is greater risk of damage by rough weather, etc. insurance rates on deck-cargo are higher than for cargo carried below decks. *Syn.* deck-load.

deck-gear SHIPG. machinery placed on the deck of a ship for loading or unloading cargo, etc.

decl. declaration; declared.

declarant a person making a declaration, such as for Customs.

declaration (1) a solemn statement. *Abbr.* dec.; decl. (2) TAXN. a statement made to the Customs listing goods on which duty will have to be paid: *You must make a customs declaration.* (3) INSCE. a statement or notice by the insured party to the insurers, giving details of the shipment being insured. *See* declaration policy *under* policy of insurance. (4) INSCE. a statement signed by a person asking for insurance, promising that details given in the proposal form are true and correct.

declaration day STK. EXCH. the last date on which the holder of an option may declare whether he takes it up (accepts it) or not. Always the day before Account Day. *See* option; Account Day.

declaration insurance *see under* insurance, classes and kinds of.

Declaration of Association LAW the last part of the Memorandum of Association consisting of a declaration by seven or more persons, called *subscribers to the memorandum*, asking to be formed into a company and listing the number of shares each subscriber has agreed to take.

Declaration of Compliance LAW one of the documents which must be sent to the Registrar of Companies when a new limited liability company is formed. It is a statement signed by a solicitor or by a director or the secretary declaring that all action required by the Companies Act concerning registration has been taken.

declare (1) STK. EXCH. to make publicly known; to announce: *The company has declared a dividend of 20%,* announced that it would pay this to the shareholders. *The declared profits of the company,* those given in the published accounts. *To declare an option,* to state whether one is taking it up (accepting it) or not. *See* declaration day. *Abbr.* dec.; decl. (2) MAN. to make known formally (esp. in a formal meeting): *The chairman declared the motion carried/the meeting closed. Mr Smith declared his (financial) interest in the matter being discussed. Syn.* disclose. (3) TAXN. to make a full statement to a government department such as the Customs, of goods liable to duty, or to the Inland Revenue of income, capital gains, etc. liable to tax.

declared value TAXN. the figure declared to the Customs as being the value on which any duty or tax payable should be based.

decline (1) to refuse: *To decline an offer/help/an invitation.* (2) to grow weaker: *Prices have declined. It is a declining industry.*

Decreasing Costs, Law of ECON. THEORY the situation which exists when an increase in the quantity produced of a commodity results in a decrease in the cost per unit. *Syn.* Increasing Returns, Law of.

decreasing term assurance *see* term assurance *under* life assurance.

decree (1) LAW an order made by a court of law after the trial of a civil action. (2) in some countries, a law made by a person or group of persons in high authority: *A president ruling by decree.*

deducing title LAW the work of a solicitor acting for a buyer in satisfying himself that the vendor (seller) of a property has a clear right to sell.

deduct to take off; to take away from, esp. one figure from another. *Syn.* to subtract. *Opp.* to add. *N.* deduction.

deductions from pay MAN. amounts which an employer must by law deduct from the pay of an employee and hand to the government in regard to income tax and national insurance contributions; other amounts which may by agreement with the employee also be deducted from pay, such as pension fund contributions, trade union dues, and national savings. The employer must by law give the employee, with his pay, a statement listing all deductions made from pay.

deed LAW an agreement in the form of a written document which has been properly signed, sealed and delivered (formally handed over). If made by only one party it is sometimes called a *deed poll*, and if by two or more parties, an *indenture.* Certain agreements have no force in law unless they are in the form of a deed, such as conveyances (changes of ownership) of land, leases of seven years or more, and agreements made without consideration (payment). *To execute a deed*, to make it effective by signing, sealing and delivering it. *See* delivery (2).
mortgage deed *see under* mortgage.
notarial deed a deed drawn up by a notary.
title-deeds *pl.* deeds and other legal documents which transfer, or prove, ownership of land.

They usu. include every deed transferring ownership of the land during the last 30 years or more and any mortgage deeds; but where the title to the property is registered at the Land Registry, a Land Certificate replaces the title-deeds. If there is a mortgage, the Land Certificate is replaced by a Charge Certificate.
trust deed *see under* trust.

deed of arrangement LAW a formal agreement made by a debtor with his creditors, under which (*a*) the debtor assigns (gives the ownership of) his property to a trustee to be sold and the money to be divided among his creditors, and (*b*) the creditors agree to accept payment of a reduced sum instead of the full amount of the debts. Cf. letter of licence. *See* composition; arrangement (4); bankruptcy. *Syn.* deed of assignment; private arrangement. *Abbr.* D.A.

deed of assignment *see* deed of arrangement.

deed of conveyance LAW a formal document under seal conveying (passing ownership of) property or an interest in property from one person to another.

deed of covenant LAW a formal document, usu. under seal, in which a person covenants (agrees) to pay an annual sum for seven years to some association, charity, etc. which, with the approval of the income tax authorities, can claim back the tax paid by the covenanter. *See also* covenant.

deed of gift LAW a formal document under seal, being a conveyance (change of ownership) of property as a gift, i.e. without consideration. *See also* gift.

deed of partnership LAW a written agreement, made under seal, stating the rights of the partners in a partnership firm as agreed between themselves. *See* partnership. *Syn.* articles of partnership; partnership deed.

deed of transfer STK. EXCH. a formal document under seal by which the legal ownership of securities is passed from one party to another. It is used mainly for transfers of stocks or shares of those companies of which the Articles of Association demand that transfers shall be by deed. Transferable securities held by persons whose names have been recorded in a register may, under the Stock Transfer Act, 1963, be transferred by a simpler system. *See* stock transfer *under* transfer. *Syn.* transfer deed; instrument of transfer.

deed poll *see* deed.

deep (1) extending far down: *Deep sea, the deep*, the ocean. *Deep-sea ship/vessel/captain/diver. Deep-water canal*, deep enough for ships. (2) (*colloq.*) *In deep water*, in trouble, esp. in financial difficulty.

de-escalate *see* escalate.

def. defence; defendant; deferred; deficit.

def. a/c. deferred account.

deface FIN. & BKG. to spoil the face (of something): *Defaced coin or notes*, those which have had some marks or words stamped or printed on them. The notes remain legal in use but the coins are no longer legal tender and the person who is found guilty of defacing them can be punished by law. *A defaced cheque*, one in which the writing has been changed or made unreadable. A banker is not forced to pay a defaced cheque.

de facto (*Latin*, in fact) in reality; in actual existence; holding a certain position, whether legally or not. *The de facto government/head of state. Britain has granted him de facto recognition.* Cf. *de jure*.

de facto corporation in U.S.A., one which according to law has not been properly incorporated but which is allowed to remain in existence as if it had been legally formed.

defalcation the stealing or dishonest use of money by a person who has been specially trusted to look after it. *Syn.* misappropriation.

default *n.* (1) LAW failure to perform a duty, such as to appear in court, in which case a *judgment by default* may be given against the defaulter. (2) failure to pay a debt at the right time: *Default in the repayment of a loan. To be in default*, to be guilty of failing in one's duty. *In default of*, in the absence of: *In default of directions from you, I shall act as I think best.*

v. LAW to fail to perform a duty, esp. in paying a debt at the right time: *The country has defaulted on its loan.* *N.* defaulter.

defaulter (1) STK. EXCH. in Britain, a member of the Stock Exchange who is unable to pay his debts or otherwise perform his contracts. Under the rules, official assignees are appointed to settle his debts and to wind up his business, usu. without his being made bankrupt. (2) FIN. & LAW one who defaults, esp. a person who fails to perform a legal duty or to pay a debt when it is due.

defective title *see under* title.

defective-title policy *see under* insurance policy.

defendant LAW a person against whom an action is brought in a court of law. Cf. plaintiff.

defer to put off until later; to postpone: *To defer payment of interest.*

deferred account INSCE. an agreement under which an insured person is allowed to pay a premium by instalments. *Abbr.* def. a/c.

deferred annuity *see under* annuity.

deferred assets *see under* assets.

deferred bond *see under* bond, *n.*

deferred credits ACCTS. sums received for goods to be supplied or for services to be performed in the future. Money thus held is shown on the liabilities side of the balance sheet. *Syn.* deferred income.

deferred delivery STK. EXCH. an agreement by a buyer of shares that he will not press for deliv-

ery but will allow extra time for the jobber to obtain the shares ordered.

deferred interest certificate STK. EXCH. a document given by a company to holders of its loan stock such as debentures when the payment of interest is being deferred (postponed). *Syn.* deferred interest warrant; deferred interest scrip.

deferred liabilities *see under* liabilities.

deferred ordinary share *see under* share.

deferred-payment agreement COM. & FIN. a form of consumer credit, being a contract to pay for an article by instalments over a stated period, the ownership of the article passing to the buyer at the time of delivery. The retail seller usu. arranges for the agreement to be made between his customer and a finance house, but some retailers finance such sales themselves. Cf. hire-purchase agreement.

deferred premium *see under* premium, *n.* (6).

deferred rebates *see* aggregated rebates.

deferred share *see under* share.

deficiency *see* deficit.

deficit (1) an amount that is lacking, that is insufficient to meet a particular need: *A 5000-ton deficit in the year's harvest*, the harvest is so much less than our needs. *We shall supply/make up the deficit later.* *Syn.* deficiency; shortfall. *Opp.* excess; surplus. *Abbr.* def. (2) FIN. an amount by which a sum of money is smaller than a desired sum: *At the end of the year the society had a deficit of £500*, received so much less than it spent, *or* owed so much more than it could pay. *See* deficit financing. (3) ACCTS. a loss, shown by a debit balance in the profit and loss account. (4) ACCTS. an excess of liabilities over assets. *Opp.* profit; surplus.

balance of payments deficit when the total value of imports is greater than the total value of exports. *Syn.* external deficit; trade deficit.

budget deficit when income is insufficient to pay for expenditure. *See* deficit financing.

deficit financing FIN. intentional action by the government of a country, when faced with a trade depression, to spend more money than it receives in revenue from taxes, etc.; the difference, called a *budget deficit*, is made up by borrowing on a large scale from the public. The deficit is obtained by reducing taxes and by increased spending, esp. on productive public works. More money is thus put into the economy, economic activity is increased, unemployment is reduced and, it is hoped, the downward path of the depression is stopped. *Syn.* compensatory finance; deficit spending; (U.S.A.) pump-priming.

deficit spending *see* deficit financing.

definite COM. clear beyond any doubt: *A definite date for delivery. A definite price*, one that will not be changed. *Syn.* firm. *Opp.* uncertain; provisional.

definitive bond see under bond, n.

deflation ECON. & FIN. a decrease in the supply of money, usu. produced intentionally by a government in order to reduce demand and check rising prices. It results in a reduction in money incomes and in the buying-power of the public, so that there is too little money to buy the goods and services that can be got. Nowadays deflation rarely leads to a lowering of the price-level, but rather to a reduction in the standard of living. Opp. inflation.

currency deflation an intentional reduction in the money supply for some special purpose, such as was made by the British Government in 1925 with the aim of reducing the price-level so that the currency could return to the gold standard at the same parity-rate as it was in 1914. Syn. monetary deflation.

deflationary adj. tending to cause deflation. Cf. disinflation; reflation.

defraud LAW to take away something that another person has a right to possess, esp. by making false statements or by deceitful behaviour: To defraud the Customs/one's creditors. See fraud. Syn. to cheat; to swindle.

defray COM. & FIN. to pay; to bear the cost: We shall defray your expenses, we shall pay them. All charges to be defrayed by you.

deft. defendant.

defunct company see under company.

deg. degree.

degressive tax see under tax.

de jure (Latin, by right) with the support of law. Cf. de facto.

deka- see deca-.

Del. Delaware, U.S.A.

del. delete; deliver(ed).

del credere agent COM. a particular class of agent who is employed by his principal to sell goods for him but on the condition that the agent bears all risk of non-payment by customers; in return for bearing the risk, the agent usu. receives an extra commission.

deld. delivered.

delegate v. (1) LAW & MAN. to give power to a trusted person to do certain acts, such as managing part of a business. (2) to appoint as one's representative.
n. a person acting for one or more others, such as a representative to a meeting or an organization.

delegated legislation LAW in Britain, rules and orders having the force of law made, not directly by Parliament, but by government ministers under powers given to them by Acts of Parliament. Such powers are delegated (given to trusted persons)mainly because Parliament has neither the time nor the special knowledge to make some very detailed laws itself. As an example, see by-law (2). Syn. statutory instruments.

delivered see delivery.

delivered price COM. a price which includes all charges such as freight and packing to the place of delivery. See also free delivered.

deliver the goods (colloq.) to complete a contract; to do what had been agreed or promised.

delivery (1) BKG. of a bill of exchange, the act of transfer (handing-over) of possession of the bill. Thus a bill which has been drawn but has not yet been actually passed to another party is not legally effective because it has not been delivered. (2) LAW the solemn declaration 'I deliver this as my act and deed', spoken by a person making a deed which he has signed, sealed and delivered. The deed is effective in law only from the date of delivery.

delivery note COM. & TRANSPT. a note prepared by the consignor (sender) and delivered with goods. It gives details of the goods and, when signed by the consignee (receiver), provides proof of delivery. Cf. delivery order; advice note.

delivery order COM. & TRANSPT. a written direction from the owner of goods to a person who holds them, e.g. in storage, to deliver or to hand them over to a named party or to bearer. The document can become a negotiable instrument when it is joined to a dock warrant and is accepted by a bank as security for an advance. Cf. delivery note. Abbr. D.O.; d/o.

delivery receipt COM. & TRANSPT. a delivery note that has been signed by the consignee (receiver) on delivery of the goods.

delivery time see lead time.

delv. delivered.

dely. delivery.

dem. demand; demurrage.

demand (1) BKG. & FIN. a request, usu. for payment of money, made by a person having a legal right to make it. Abbr. dem.

on demand any instrument payable on demand is payable as soon as payment is asked by the person who has the legal right to receive it.
(2) COM. the quantity needed of a commodity to supply orders already received or expected: The demand from our customers is about 500 tons. We have a steady demand for 100 copies a year, we regularly sell that number. (3) the wants of buyers in the market: This article is much in demand, many people want to buy it. There is no demand for knife-polish, no one wants to buy it. (4) ECON. THEORY in economics, not just the desire of a person to have or to own a thing, but his desire to get it by paying a price for it. See effective demand below. (5) ECON. the amount of a commodity that the public will buy at a certain price. See also elasticity of demand.

alternate demand see under alternate.

competitive demand the situation where two or more products are competing to satisfy the market demand. Thus the demand for two products which are possible substitutes for one another is said to be competitive if an increase in demand for one product will result in a reduction in demand for the other. *Syn.* substitute demand; rival demand.

complementary demand a demand for two commodities that are jointly needed, such as bread and butter, or toothbrushes and toothpaste, the one giving little or no satisfaction without the other. *Syn.* joint demand.

composite demand where a commodity is in demand for several different uses, the total of all these demands added together.

consumer('s) demand *see under* consumer.

derived demand the demand for a commodity, esp. a factor of production, that is wanted, not for itself but for something derived or obtained from it. Thus the demand for iron-ore is derived from the demand for iron and steel. The demand for labour is derived from the demand for the goods produced by that labour. Cf. direct demand.

direct demand the demand for a commodity that is wanted for its own qualities, not for what can be derived (obtained) from it. Most consumer goods are produced to satisfy a direct demand. Cf. derived demand.

effective demand demand which has some effect, produces some result. In economics it is the desire of consumers to spend money to buy a commodity at a certain price.

elastic demand *see* elasticity of demand.

excess demand a situation in which, at a certain price, the amount of a particular product demanded by buyers is greater than the amount supplied by the industry. If the price is a full-cost price, i.e. one which includes a satisfactory profit, producers may raise the price temporarily to discourage demand while they arrange to increase their output; but in the long run the price is likely to return to and stay at the full-cost level, with the demand satisfied by the increased output.

individual demand the demand of one single consumer. In a particular market, all the individual demands added together form the market demand.

inelastic demand *see* elasticity of demand.

joint demand *see* complementary demand *above*.

market demand *see* individual demand *above*.

rival demand *see* competitive demand *above*.

substitute demand *see* competitive demand *above*.

demand bill *or* **draft** BKG. a bill of exchange that is payable immediately the payee or holder demands payment; usu. a bank draft. *Syn.* sight bill. *Abbr.* D.D.; D/D.; d/d.

demand curve *see* demand schedule.

demand deposit *see under* deposit.

demand draft *see* demand bill.

demand, extension of *see* extension of demand.

demand inflation *see under* inflation.

Demand, Law of ECON. THEORY a basic rule in economics that the amount demanded increases when the price falls and reduces when the price rises. Stated another way, the lower the price the greater the quantity demanded, and the higher the price the smaller the quantity demanded. *See also* Supply and Demand, Laws of.

demand note BKG. a written promise to pay on demand a stated sum of money.

demand price ECON. THEORY the price at which a given quantity of a commodity will be demanded: *The quantity ordered is 20,000 kg at a demand price of £1.50 per kg. See* demand schedule.

demand-pull *see* demand inflation *under* inflation.

demand rate (of exchange) *see* short rate *under* exchange rate.

demand schedule ECON. THEORY a table showing the quantities of a commodity that buyers will demand at varying prices. The figures in this table can be used to draw a graph called a demand curve.

demarcation dispute IND. REL. a strong disagreement among members of different trade unions about which workers shall do certain classes of work. In Britain, the Demarcation Disputes Tribunal has been set up to avoid the many strikes that once troubled the economy.

demise (1) LAW to let property; to grant a lease of land and buildings. (2) to hire out a ship on charter.

demise charter *see* charter by demise *under* charter.

demise charterer *see under* charterer.

democracy (1) a system of government based on rule by the people through their elected representatives, who form a law-making body that controls the power of the government in running and managing the affairs of the country. (2) a country governed under such a system. *See also* industrial democracy.

democrat (1) a person who believes in democracy, in the right of the people to govern their country through elected representatives. (2) a member of the U.S. Democratic Party. *Adj.* democratic.

demography the study of population, esp. of statistics relating to births, deaths, age and sex distributions. *Adj.* demographic.

demonetize FIN. to put an end to the use of a coin or note as money; to cause a note or coin to be no longer legal tender. In Britain, the farthing was demonetized in 1961, the old half-penny in 1969 and the half-crown in 1970. *Syn.* (U.S.A.) demonitize. *Opp.* to monetize. *N.* demonetization; *Opp.* monetization.

demonstration ADVTG. & COM. a method of selling by showing and explaining the use of a product, usu. in the actual place where it is intended to be used, such as a factory, workshop or home, with the aim of persuading interested persons to buy the product.

demonstration effect ECON. THEORY an idea expressed by Prof. Duesenberry after the Second World War, that many families spend money on things they would not normally buy because their neighbours buy them. They wish to make a good showing before their neighbours. Also known as *keeping up with the Joneses*.

demonstrative legacy *see under* legacy.

demurrage (1) SHIPG. & TRANSPT. unreasonable delay in keeping a ship, barge or railway wagon beyond the time agreed or allowed. (2) money paid to a shipowner in accordance with a charter-party if the charterer delays the sailing of the ship. *Opp.* despatch money. *See* lay days.

Den. Denmark.

denkli *see* shaduf.

Denmark a parliamentary democracy and constitutional monarchy (kingdom) in northern Europe, pop. 5 million approx. (1971); capital, Copenhagen, pop. 850,000 approx.; language, Danish; currency unit, the krone, *pl.* kroner, divided into 100 örer. Member, O.E.C.D., E.E.C.

denomination a class or unit based on quantity, value, or measure: *Notes/coin of small denomination*, of small values. *Stamps issued in denominations of 1p, 2p, 5p, etc.*

Dep. department; deposits; depot; deputy.

dep. depart; deposit.

depart (1) TRANSPT. & TOUR. to go away; to leave; to start (on a journey): *The noon train to Glasgow will depart from Platform 5. Your plane departs from Cairo at 07.00 hrs. and arrives at Rome at 10.00 hrs. Abbr.* dep. *Opp.* arrive. (2) (*with* from) to change: *He departed from his plan*. To fail to follow: *You have departed from your orders*, you have failed to carry them out.

department one of the separate divisions which together form a large organization: *A government department*, with (in Britain) a minister as its head, such as the Department of Trade. *A university department*, with a professor as its head, such as the Department of Business Administration. *A department of a business*, with a manager at its head, such as the men's clothing department in a large shop or department store. *Abbr.* Dep.; Dept. *Adj.* departmental.

Department of Health and Social Security *see under* health.

department store *see under* store.

departure TRANSPT. & TOUR. the act of departing, of going away, of starting on a voyage or journey: *A port/place/station of departure. A departure port/platform. Opp.* arrival.

dependant *or* **dependent** *n.* (1) INSCE. a person, usu. the wife (or widow), a child or a parent of the assured person, who depends or has depended on the assured person. (2) TAXN. a person, usu. a near relation, who is partly or wholly supported by a taxpayer and for whom the taxpayer receives a *dependent relative allowance*.

depletion IND. using up until little or nothing remains: *Depletion of stocks/reserves/resources*.

provision for depletion ACCTS. the practice of gradually writing down (reducing) the book value of a wasting asset such as a coal-mine or oil-well until its value is taken as nothing when it has been totally depleted (used up). *See* endowment policy system *under* endowment.

deponent LAW a person who makes a solemn statement in the form of an affidavit, or as a witness under oath or affirmation in a court of law. *See* deposition.

deposit (1) COM. & FIN. the amount of money that the buyer of an article under a hire-purchase agreement has to pay as the first payment, usu. at the time he takes possession of the article. *See* hire-purchase agreement. (2) COM. & FIN. a sum of money given in part-payment of the price of something bought or to be bought in the future. (3) IND. any material in the ground which has been brought and laid down by natural means, such as by rivers, seas and winds: *Important mineral deposits have been found*. (4) BKG. money or its equivalent deposited (left with) a person or organization, esp. a bank, for safe-keeping, or as security, or to bear interest.

on deposit (money) credited by a banker to a customer's deposit account, which bears interest.

call deposit *see under* call, *n.* (1).

certificate of deposit *see under* certificate.

demand deposit (U.S.A.) money placed with a bank on current account, on which cheques can be drawn. Cf. time deposit.

fixed deposit a deposit of a sum of money with a bank for a fixed length of time at a fixed rate of interest. Such deposits earn a higher rate of interest than that paid on call deposits.

memorandum of deposit *see under* memorandum.

special deposit *see under* special.

time deposit (*a*) (U.S.A.) money placed with a bank in a deposit account earning interest and needing at least 30 days' notice of withdrawal. Cf. demand deposit. (*b*) any deposit that needs notice of withdrawal.

deposit account *see under* bank account.

deposit banks *see* joint-stock banks.

deposit, certificate of *see under* certificate.

deposit currency *see* bank money.

deposit insurance BKG. in U.S.A. each bank must insure the balances of its depositors up to a stated limit against the risk of the bank failing to meet its debts. Insurance is arranged with the Federal Deposit Insurance Corporation (F.D.I.C.) which is under government control.

deposit, memorandum of *see under* memorandum.

deposition LAW a written record of a solemn statement made in a court of law by a witness under oath or on affirmation. *See* deponent.

depositor BKG. a person who deposits money, etc. with a bank, esp. a person who has a deposit account with the bank.

depository FIN. & BKG. a person or organization in whose care money or other valuable things such as securities have been deposited for safekeeping. *Also* depositary.

authorized depository a person or concern of good reputation, such as a solicitor, banker or broker, authorized by the Bank of England to hold foreign securities for the owners who, if living in Britain, used to be forbidden by exchange-control rules to hold them themselves.

deposit premium *see under* premium.

deposit receipt (1) BKG. a written acknowledgment by a bank that a certain sum of money is being held on deposit by the bank, repayable at an agreed date. The document has to be presented to the bank when the depositor wishes to take the money out of the bank account. Deposit receipts are not negotiable but may be assigned to another party. *Abbr.* D/R. (2) MAR. INSCE. a receipt for money given as a part-payment when a general average has been declared. *See* average (4).

deposit slip *see* paying-in slip.

deposit warrant *see* dock warrant.

depot (1) COM. a place where goods are collected and stored, esp. before being distributed to shops. *Syn.* warehouse. (2) TRANSPT. in Britain, a garage to and from which bus and other road transport services run. In U.S.A., a railway station. *Pron.* British: deppo; U.S.A.: deepo.

depreciate ACCTS. to lose value gradually over a period of time. All fixed assets except land and perh. some buildings tend to lose value or to depreciate, because they gradually wear out or are replaced by more modern and efficient things. *Opp.* appreciate. *See* depreciation.

depreciation (1) ACCTS. the gradual loss of value of fixed assets such as buildings, plant and machinery, etc. because they wear out or decay (*physical* or *internal depreciation*) or are replaced by more modern and efficient things (*external depreciation* or *obsolescence*). This is one of the costs of running a business and must be charged against the profits. *See* depreciation methods. *Opp.* appreciation. (2) FIN. of the coinage, *see* debasement of coinage. (3) FIN. & BKG. in foreign-exchange business, there is depreciation of a country's currency (the exchange rate falls) if the demand for it is small in relation to the supply offered on the market. Im-

ports into that country thus become dearer and its exports cheaper when measured by other currencies.

depreciation account ACCTS. a real account in which the amount allowed as depreciation on an asset is entered on the debit side and the amount is also credited to the account of the asset concerned. The value of the asset is thus reduced to a proper amount each year.

depreciation allowance a tax allowance to companies on the money spent on new machinery, vehicles, etc. spread either over the life of the asset, or over a shorter period when it is called *accelerated depreciation. See* capital allowances; accelerated depreciation.

depreciation fund system ACCTS. a method of providing for depreciation, by debiting the profit and loss account each year with a fixed amount equal to the depreciation of an asset, and crediting the amount to a depreciation fund account. At the same time gilt-edged securities are bought to an equal value. With interest being reinvested and more securities being bought each year for the number of years that the asset is expected to be useful, the fund grows to provide an investment with a value roughly equal to the original cost of the asset. Thus, there is money ready to be spent on a replacement when needed. *Syn.* amortization; amortizement.

depreciation methods ACCTS. in accounting, depreciation of an asset is charged against profits by writing off part of its value every year during its expected life. The aim is to make sure that the cost of the asset is charged in a fair and reasonable way. Certain problems occur in times of rising prices, when the cost of replacing an asset may be far higher than the original cost. The more usual depreciation methods are: the *annuity system* (*see under* annuity); the *depreciation fund system* (*see under* depreciation fund); the *endowment policy system* (*see under* endowment); the *fixed instalment system* (*see under* fixed instalment); the *reducing balance method* (*see under* reducing balance); and the *straight line method* (*see under* endowment policy system).

depressed ECON. low in spirit; dull; inactive.

depressed area ECON. a region which is suffering from a severe economic depression, with high unemployment, much poverty, low standards of living, poor public services and a lack of confidence in the minds of businessmen and industrialists. Such areas may receive special help from the government in attracting new industries, in retraining schemes for the unemployed and in overcoming poverty. *See* assisted areas.

depressed market conditions in a market when prices are falling because supply is greater than demand. *Syn.* flat market.

depressing news STK. EXCH. any news which is bad for investors and leads to falling prices because there are few buyers and possibly many wanting to sell.

depression ECON. that part of the trade cycle (*see under* cycle) that is marked by a large fall in output, high unemployment, low prices, low business activity, and by low spirits and lack of confidence in the minds of businessmen and industrialists. *Opp.* boom. *Syn.* trade depression; slump; recession; stagnation; trough. *See also* Great Depression.

Dept. department.

deputy MAN. a person who is given power to do the work or business of another, or to act for another: *The deputy chairman; a deputy manager.*

Derbys. Derbyshire, England.

derelict (vessel) SHIPG. & MAR. INSCE. a ship that has been abandoned by her crew. Anyone who helps to save her or her cargo has the right to salvage, i.e. money as compensation.

de-requisitioning *see* requisitioning.

derivative lease *see* under-lease *under* lease.

derived demand *see under* demand.

derrick *see* crane.

derv fuel-oil used in heavy road vehicles (from diesel-engined road vehicle).

desalination IND. the process of taking the salt out of sea-water to make fresh water.

description (1) COM. an account in words giving information about something or somebody: *The police have issued a description of the stolen goods/the thief. The storm damage is beyond description*, so bad that no words can properly describe it. *See esp.* trade description; sale by description. (2) (of a person) his profession or occupation: *Description: chartered accountant/merchant/publisher.* (3) sort; kind: *We do not sell goods of that description.*

descriptive catalogue *see under* catalogue.

descriptive economics ECON. that part of the study of economics that collects and examines facts about the working of an institution or organization, such as the Bank of England, the Common Agricultural Policy of the E.E.C. or any particular industry. Cf. economic theory; applied economics.

design *n.* IND. an outline, plan or drawing made in advance, esp. of something to be manufactured: *We are making/preparing/drafting a design for a new model. An article of the most modern design.* *Syn.* plan.

industrial design the planning of the appearance of the products of industry. In Britain, the Council for Industrial Design is financed by the government to advise on and encourage improved design in industry. It runs the Design Centre in London and organizes exhibitions to show examples of good design.

registered design in Britain, a design which the owner has caused to be registered (recorded) with the designs department of the Patent Office. This gives protection against persons who copy the shape or form of the article, but not against copying its mechanical operation (the way it works), which can only be protected by a patent.

v. IND. to plan in advance what a product or a work of art shall look like, how it should be made, how it will work, etc.: *An architect designs buildings. This car is designed to do 150 m.p.h.*

designate *adj.* appointed to take up an office when the present holder leaves it: *Mr Jones is chairman-designate of the board.*

Design Centre *see* industrial design *under* design.

desk a kind of table, usu. with drawers, intended to be used for reading, writing or doing business: *A reading/writing/cash desk.*

City desk in a newspaper office, where the financial news is dealt with, under the control of the City editor.

desp. despatch(ed).

despatch *see* dispatch.

despatch money SHIPG. a sum of money allowed by the shipowner when the charterer gets the loading or unloading of the ship done in less than the time stated in the charter-party. *Opp.* demurrage. *See* lay days.

destination (1) TRANSPT. & TOUR. the intended end of a voyage or journey; the place to which something is sent: *The destination of this bus/train/ship/plane is Alexandria. The ship has reached its destination*, the end of its voyage. *Port of destination. Abbr.* destn.; dstn. (2) MAR. INSCE. the place at which a marine adventure ends. *See* adventure.

destitute *adj.* lacking the things necessary to live; penniless; extremely poor and needing immediate help: *Bankruptcy left him destitute.*

destitution *n.* extreme poverty.

destn. destination.

detached not joined: *A detached house*, one not joined to another. *A semi-detached house (colloq.* a semi), one joined to another on one side only.

deterioration COM. & INSCE. loss of quality without any apparent outside cause, such as in goods which go bad if kept long. *See* perishable goods.

physical deterioration that caused by wear and tear, rusting, rotting and decay from climate and weather.

determine (1) LAW to bring or come to an end: *To determine a contract.* (2) LAW to reach a decision, a judgment, in a lawsuit.

detinue LAW the tort (civil wrong) done by a person who holds goods which he agrees are owned by another person but wrongfully refuses to deliver to him. Cf. conversion.

Deutsche Bank BKG. the main commercial bank of West Germany. Cf. Deutsche Bundesbank.

Deutsche Bundesbank BKG. (German Federal Bank) the central bank of West Germany. Cf. Deutsche Bank.

Deutsche Mark FIN. the standard currency unit of West Germany, divided into 100 pfennig. *Abbr.* DM; D-Mark.

devaluation ECON. & FIN. (1) the act of a government in reducing by law the exchange value of a country's currency in units of gold or as compared with other currencies. This step is taken when the balance of payments is unfavourable for a long period, usu. because of high inflation at home. On devaluation the change in exchange rates makes exports cheaper for foreign buyers, but imports are dearer for home buyers. Devaluation should thus improve the country's balance of payments. (2) intentional devaluation by a government occurs only where a country has a *fixed exchange rate*; with a *floating exchange rate* devaluation takes place automatically, as reduced demand for a country's currency causes the exchange rate to fall without government intervention. Britain and most other countries moved from a fixed to a floating exchange rate in 1972. *See* floating exchange rate.

developing countries *see* under-developed countries; economic development.

development COM. & IND. making use of the results of research to produce new and improved products. *See also* research and development; property development; redevelopment.

development aid *see* foreign aid.

development areas IND. one of several areas in Britain with high unemployment in which the government has taken special measures to attract new industries. *See* assisted areas; retraining.

development certificate *see* Industrial Development Certificate.

development corporation FIN. in Britain, an organization financed by the government to control the building of the new towns such as Harlow and Milton Keynes.

development economics *see under* economics.

deviation (1) a change of route. (2) MAR. INSCE. turning aside by a ship from the usual or direct course stated in the insurance policy. Unless this change is made in order to avoid some danger, the policy no longer has any force.

devise *n.* LAW a gift of land or buildings by will. The person receiving the gift is a *devisee*, the person making it is the *devisor*. *Syn.* legacy. Cf. bequest.
v. to make a gift of real property by will.

Devon. Devonshire, England.

df. draft.

d.f. dead freight.

dft. defendant; draft.

dg. decigram(me).

dhow SHIPG. an Arab sailing-ship with one or two masts and lateen (triangular) sails, used by coastal traders along the shores of the Arabian Gulf, the Red Sea and the Indian Ocean.

D.H.S.S. Department of Health and Social Security.

Di. dinar(s).

dia. diameter.

diagrammatic map *see* cartogram.

diam. diameter.

diary a book for recording daily notes of things done or to be done. *I carry a pocket-diary/personal diary.*

    bill diary ACCTS. a forward diary in which only bills of exchange are entered.

    forward diary ACCTS. one in which are recorded in proper order the dates on which payments are due to be made or received.

diazo process *see* dyeline process.

dibs pieces of bone or metal used instead of money when playing card games; so (*colloq.*) money: *I have no dibs with me.*

dict. dictation; dictated.

dicta. dictaphone.

dictaphone a machine for recording the voice on a wax cylinder or magnetic tape for a typist to type on paper what has been said.

dictate (1) to speak words which are recorded *either* by a person who writes them down, usu. in shorthand, *or* by a machine such as a dictaphone, so that what has been said may be typewritten on paper: *To dictate a letter/report/message.* N. dictation. (2) to speak or act in a commanding manner: *Their chairman dictates the policy of the board*, it is he who commands what the policy shall be. *To dictate terms*, to command, to rule, what the terms shall be.

dictating machine one of a number of machines or instruments used in offices for recording the voice on magnetic tape, discs, cylinders or belts made of plastic, etc. The words spoken can be played back by a typist (called an audio-typist) who then types them out on paper as letters, reports, memoranda, etc. *See* dictaphone; tape recorder.

dictatorship of the proletariat ECON. in Marxist theory, a middle stage between the abolition by revolution of the capitalist system and the final stage of complete communism. During the middle stage, absolute ruling power (dictatorship) would be in the hands of a classless society of workers (the proletariat), who would practise socialism, develop all forms of industry, esp. heavy industries, and a system of distribution freed of the profit motive.

Dictum meum pactum (*Latin*, my word is my bond) the motto (a saying adopted as a rule of behaviour) of the London Stock Exchange.

diddle (*colloq.*) to cheat, esp. in small things. *Syn.* to swindle. N. diddler.

diff. difference.

difference STK. EXCH. the amount payable to, or due to be paid by, a person who has ordered his stockbroker to buy and then to sell a security within the period of a single Stock Exchange Account. This practice is known as *trading in differences*. *Abbr*. diff.

differential duty *see under* duty.

differential pay IND. & IND. REL. the difference in wage-levels of similar grades of workers in different industries; or between different grades within the same industry, such as between skilled and unskilled workers. Differentials tend over the years to become smaller because trade unions fight more to raise the wages of the lower-paid workers than of the higher-paid.

differential prices COM. the practice of manufacturers and traders of charging different prices for the same product in different markets, such as the home and overseas markets; or in different rooms in a restaurant or public house. *Syn*. split prices.

differential rent *see under* rent.

differentiation ECON. & IND. making one's product as different as possible from its competitors by means of brand names, attractive packaging, etc. so that buyers may recognize and buy the product of their choice. To the economist such products are not perfect substitutes (replacements) for each other and the competition between them is therefore imperfect.

difficulties FIN. a state of difficulty: *In financial difficulties*, short of money and perh. unable to pay what is owing. *There are supply difficulties*, the goods are difficult to obtain. *Difficulties of communication*, of making each other understood because of language differences or a failure of postal, telegraph and transport services.

dig. digit(al).

Diggers STK. EXCH. Australian gold-mining shares.

diggings (*colloq.*) lodgings. *Syn*. digs.

digit one of the ten numbers 1 to 9 and 0.

digital computer *see under* computer.

digs *see* diggings.

dilapidations LAW the things that a tenant of unfurnished property has to repair at his expense at the end of his lease.

diligence MAR. INSCE. the duty that falls on the owners of a ship to do everything reasonably possible to make sure of the safety of the ship, her crew and cargo, and to avoid causing damage to others.

dilution of equity STK. EXCH. where the ordinary share-capital (the equity) of a company has been increased without a similar increase in assets or in profit-earning power, the equity is said to be diluted and suffers a reduction in market value.

dilution of labour IND. REL. the employment of unskilled labour to do work usu. done by skilled people.

dim. dimension.

dime in U.S.A. and Canada, a coin worth 10 cents or one-tenth of a dollar. *Abbr*. d.

dimension COM. & TRANSPT. measurement in a particular direction such as length, breadth or height: *The dimensions of a container are 2.4 m × 2.4 m × 12.2 m*. *Abbr*. dim.

Diminishing Marginal Productivity, Law of *see* Diminishing Returns, Law of.

Diminishing Returns, Law of ECON. THEORY a basic law of economics, relating to the combining of factors of production in varying proportions. It states that if, in the production of a commodity, one factor of production is increased by stages while the other factors are kept unchanged, the stage will sooner or later be reached where each further addition to the increasing factor will produce a smaller and smaller increase in output. For example, if the number of men working with a fixed amount of machinery is increased, then sooner or later the addition of each further man will bring in a smaller and smaller increase in output. *Syn*. Law of Variable Proportions; Law of Diminishing Marginal Productivity; Law of Increasing Costs.

Diminishing Utility, Law of ECON. THEORY a basic law of economics relating to the utility or satisfaction obtained from increases in the supply of a commodity. The law states that as more and more units are added to a consumer's stock of a commodity there will come a point at which he will get less and less satisfaction from each unit added, until the stage will be reached when he will have enough, and will get no satisfaction from an additional unit. For example, if a man's supply of oranges is increased by one orange at a time, after a certain point each additional orange will bring him less and less satisfaction until he will reach the stage where he will have enough (or even too many) and will not want any more. *Syn*. Law of Diminishing Marginal Utility; Law of Satiable Wants.

din. dinner; dining-car; dining-room.

dinar an ancient Arab gold coin; nowadays the standard currency unit of Algeria (= 100 centimes), Bahrain (= 1000 fils), Iraq (= 1000 fils), Jordan (= 1000 fils), Kuwait (= 1000 fils), Libya (= 1000 dirhams), South Yemen (Aden) (= 1000 fils), Tunisia (= 1000 millimes), Yugoslavia (= 100 paras). The dinar is also the fractional unit of the currency of Iran (1 rial = 100 dinars). *Abbr*. Di.

diner (1) a person who dines (eats dinner). (2) in U.S.A., a railway dining- or restaurant car.

dinghy a small rowing-boat, sometimes fitted with a mast and sail.

dining-car TRANSPT. a railway restaurant car. *Syn.* diner. *Abbr.* din.

dip STK. EXCH. to go down and then perh. up again: *Share prices dipped.*

Dir. dirham.

dir. direct(ion); director.

direct action IND. REL. any way other than talking used by organized workers to press demands on their employers for better pay and conditions. Direct action may include strikes, working to rule, and banning (refusing to work) overtime.

direct cost *see under* cost.

direct debit BKG. & COM. in Britain, a way of making payments. A customer arranges for his bank to pay money to certain organizations, usu. suppliers of good reputation, when they present (produce) their bills direct to the bank, and to debit the amounts to his account. This saves the customer the work of paying cash or of writing cheques, the expense of postage, etc.

direct demand *see under* demand.

direct exchange BKG. & FIN. the exchange between two countries is direct if one of their currencies is quoted in units of the other, and not in units of a third country. *See* foreign exchange.

direct expenses ACCTS. those sums spent in actually manufacturing a particular product or in performing a certain service, rather than expenses of a more general nature such as management costs which relate to a number of products and services. Cf. direct labour (2); indirect expenses.

direct exporting COM. selling goods direct to a consumer in a foreign country without using the services of a middleman. Cf. indirect exporting.

directive MAN. a written paper from someone in authority giving directions about what is to be done: *Treasury directive*, one telling the Bank of England, e.g., to reduce the money supply.

direct labour (1) IND. workers who are employed by an organization or local government authority in Britain to do certain work, such as building or repairing houses, directly under the control of the organization, and not through a contractor. (2) ACCTS. the cost of labour which is employed in actually manufacturing a particular product or in performing a service. Cf. direct expenses; indirect labour.

direct letter of credit *see under* letter of credit.

direct (mail) advertising *see under* advertising (1).

director FIN. & LAW of a company, a person elected by the members (shareholders) to control for them the day-to-day management of the business and to decide its general policy. *See* board of directors; rotation of directors *under* rotation.

company director a director of a limited liability company, not of a government department or other non-commercial organization.

divisional director a person in charge of a division of a company. He is not necessarily a member of the board of directors.

executive director a member of the board of directors who also has the authority and responsibility of managing a certain part of the work of the company, such as the sales director, finance director, etc. Cf. non-executive director.

guineapig director a non-executive director who does nothing for the company but attend meetings of the board of which he is a member, usu. as a nominee director. Such directors were formerly paid a few guineas (gold coins) for each meeting that they attended; and a guineapig is a small unimportant animal kept as a pet.

local director a member of a local board of directors.

managing director a company director who holds special powers under the company's Articles of Association to manage the day-to-day affairs of the company. He is usu. next in importance to the chairman. If there is more than one managing director, each is called a *joint managing director.*

nominee director one appointed to the board of a company to represent a principal stockholder or group of shareholders, such as a parent company.

non-executive director a director who, as a member of the board of directors, helps to plan and decide the policy of the company but who has no responsibility to execute (carry out) that policy. Cf. executive director.

outside director one who is not employed by the company and usu. a non-executive director.

directorate (1) MAN. the place where a director has his office. (2) the post held by a director. (3) a body of persons who are directors. *See* interlocking directorates.

Director of Public Prosecutions LAW in England, a high government officer responsible for advising the government on legal matters and for bringing actions in the courts in the case of certain difficult or important crimes. *Syn.* in other countries: Public Prosecutor; Fiscal. *See also* Procurator-fiscal.

directors, board of *see under* board.

directors, register of *see under* register.

directorship (1) LAW & STK. EXCH. the position of a company director: *He has been offered a directorship.* (2) the period served as a director: *During your directorship the company made a profit.*

directors' report LAW & STK. EXCH. a written or printed report made by the board of directors and usu. signed by the chairman, to the members (shareholders) of a company, and presented together with a set of final accounts, at each annual general meeting. *Syn.* chairman's report; company report.

directors' share *see under* share.

directors' shareholdings, register of *see under* register.

directory a book listing, usu. in alphabetical order, names and addresses and other information about persons or organizations in an area, or in certain trades or occupations: *The telephone/telex directory. A street/trade directory.*

classified directory one in which the information has been grouped under headings which are arranged in an orderly system, e.g. in a *trade directory* firms' names and details are grouped according to their trades, and the trades themselves grouped according to industries and again according to countries. The *classified telephone directory* is known colloq. as the Yellow Pages.

direct production *see under* production.

direct sale/selling (1) COM. the practice of a manufacturer or importer in selling goods direct to shopkeepers without using the services of a wholesaler or distributor. (2) the practice of a wholesaler or distributor in selling goods direct to the public without using the services of a retailer (shopkeeper).

direct services IND. services that are performed personally by many kinds of workers who deal direct with members of the public and are not connected with trade or commerce; they include the work of doctors, lawyers, hairdressers, government employees, etc. Cf. commercial services; industrial services.

direct tax TAXN. one which has to be paid by the taxpayer direct to the government, such as income tax, capital gains tax, capital transfer tax, and not through some other party such as a shopkeeper. *See* Board of Inland Revenue. Cf. indirect tax.

dirham an ancient Arab silver coin, nowadays the standard currency unit of Morocco, divided into 100 Moroccan francs. In Libya, one-thousandth of a dinar. In the United Arab Emirates, one-hundredth of a Qatar or Dubai riyal. *Abbr.* dir.; Dir.

dirt cheap price *see* knock-out price *under* price.

dirty bill of lading *see under* bill of lading.

dirty bond *see under* bond, *n.*

dis. discharge; discount; distribute.

disability *see* disablement.

disablement the state of being disabled, unable to use one's limbs. *See also* Remploy; handicapped persons. *Syn.* disability.

disablement benefit in Britain, an allowance paid under the national insurance scheme to persons during the time that they are unable to work because they cannot use their limbs. *Syn.* disability benefit.

disablement pension in Britain, a pension paid under the national insurance scheme to a person who is permanently disabled because of an injury received while at work. *Syn.* disability pension.

disallow to refuse to accept: *The insurers have disallowed your claim. The manager will disallow an expense if it is too high.*

disaster (1) a great natural misfortune, usu. sudden and causing much damage and suffering, such as *an earthquake/storm/flood disaster.* (2) a serious accident to a train, plane or ship, called a *rail/air/marine disaster.* (3) FIN. a financial crash: *The company is heading for disaster,* in danger of going out of business, of being wound up.

disbs. disbursements.

disbursements FIN. payments of cash, esp. by a professional person such as a solicitor who pays money on behalf of, and has the right to be repaid by, his clients. *See* out-of-pocket expenses. *Abbr.* disbs.

disc., disct. discount.

disc a thin round plate, esp. one used in a machine for recording the voice or for storing data for a computer. *Also* disk.

discharge INSCE. on payment of a claim, a combined form of receipt and acknowledgment by a claimant that he has no further claim against the insurer.

discharge from bankruptcy *see* petition in bankruptcy *under* bankruptcy.

discharge from employment to dismiss; put an end to someone's employment: *When the factory closed, the workers were discharged. He was honourably discharged from the Army. To discharge the crew of a ship.*

discharge of cargo TRANSPT. & SHIPG. the unloading of goods carried as cargo in a ship, plane, etc.
v. to unload: *The ship is discharging grain at London docks.*

discharge of contract LAW the ending of the duties and responsibilities of the parties to a contract. This can happen in several ways: by the carrying out of their duties by both parties (performance); by agreement between the parties to end the contract (waiver); by one party breaking the contract (breach); by performance becoming impossible (impossibility); or by the passing of time making the contract no longer legally effective (limitation).

discharge of debt COM. payment of the whole of a debt, so that nothing is still owing: *To discharge a bill of exchange/customs bond/promissory note. A receipt proves discharge of a debt.*

discharge port *see* lading.

disclaimer LAW a giving up of rights or duties, esp. the formal refusal, recorded in a deed, to accept the powers and duties of a trustee.

disclosure (1) INSCE. the duty of an insured person to make known to the insurers every fact of any importance relating to the insurance. *See* utmost good faith. (2) BKG. the supplying by a bank of information about a customer's accounts, to any outside organization such as the Inland Revenue or the police. Banks have the right to refuse to disclose such information except where ordered to do so by a court of law. (3) LAW & FIN. the duty of a company director to make known to other directors details of any interest he may have in a contract in which his company is concerned.

discount (1) BKG. a sum of money allowed for immediate payment of a sum due at a later date. If the sum is secured by a bill of exchange, the party who buys the bill and receives the discount is said to discount the bill. **banker's discount** *see under* banker's.
(2) COM. a reduction from list price or catalogue price or marked price, such as a trade discount, quantity discount, etc.
case-rate discount a form of quantity discount, where the discount varies according to the number of cases of goods ordered: *A discount of 20% for up to 100 cases, 25% beyond.*
at a discount at a price below par or face value. *Opp.* at a premium.
cash discount *see under* cash.
functional discount *see* trade discount *below.*
incentive discount any discount which urges the buyer to buy before a certain date or to buy more goods.
quantity discount a trade discount which varies with the quantity of goods demanded in a single order: the larger the quantity, the higher the rate of discount. The aim is to encourage the buyer to place as big an order as he can in order to get the highest possible rate of discount. *Syn.* quantity rebate. *See also* case-rate discount *above.*
settlement discount *see* cash discount *under* cash.
trade discount a discount, usu. a percentage of the list or catalogue price, allowed by a manufacturer or wholesaler to a retailer in the same trade. *Syn.* functional discount.
true discount *see under* true.
(3) STK. EXCH. the amount by which the market price of a share stands below its paid-up price, or par value or face value. (4) INSCE. a reduction in the premium to allow for the special nature of the risk.
no-claim discount one given to a motorist who has made no claim in immediate past years. *Syn.* no-claim bonus.
(5) MAR. INSCE. an allowance for prompt payment of a premium.
discount bank BKG. a bank which includes among its business activities the discounting of bills of exchange and promissory notes.

discount bond *see under* bond, *n.*
discount broker *see* bill-broker.
discounted bill *see under* bill of exchange.
discounted cash flow FIN. a way of finding out whether or not an investment, e.g. in a new asset, is worth making. The *net present value method*: the income expected from the asset during each year of its future life is discounted, i.e. reduced, to allow for the delay in receiving that income, using a rate of interest based on the current market rate and the degree of risk. If the total of these discounted annual amounts is greater than the capital sum needed to buy the asset now, the investment may be considered profitable. The *yield method* is to calculate at what rate of interest the total discounted annual amounts of income would be exactly equal to the capital sum needed to buy the asset now. If this rate of interest, or yield, is greater than the market rate, the investment may be regarded as profitable. *Abbr.* D.C.F.
discount house (1) BKG. a commercial banking firm or company that discounts bills of exchange which have been accepted by the accepting houses, and also discounts bank bills and Treasury bills, besides dealing in short-term securities of the central and local governments and public corporations and in certificates of deposit. Such houses usu. borrow 'at call' from the joint-stock banks but when they cannot do this they go to the Bank of England as 'lender of last resort'. *Syn.* (U.S.A.) commercial credit company. (2) COM. a retailer esp. of durable consumer goods at low prices, sometimes near wholesale prices. *Syn.* cut-price shop/store; discount store.
discounting (1) BKG. in return for a discount, buying, or advancing money on, a negotiable instrument, such as a bill of exchange, which is due for payment some time in the future. The discount is in fact interest calculated at the market rate for the number of days that the bill has yet to run until due for payment plus a varying element for the risk involved. (2) FIN. calculating the present value of a future sum of money, allowing for interest. The present value must be less than the future amount because of the delay in getting and using the future amount. The present value or discounted value is the capital sum which, if invested at a certain rate of interest compound, will increase to equal the future amount after a given number of years. *Syn.* discounting back.
discount market FIN. in Britain, a section of the money market consisting of a small number of discount houses and bill-brokers who borrow money for short periods from banks and other large lenders and with the money buy (or discount) Treasury bills and bills of exchange generally. By arrangement, if the loans are called in (have to be paid immediately) the bor-

rowers can go to the Bank of England for help, using as security the bills that they have discounted.

discount rate (1) BKG. the rate of interest which banks are charging for discounting bills of exchange. In Britain the rate varies from time to time according to the Bank of England's current lending rate; the rate will also vary according to the financial reputation of the acceptor of the bill. *Syn.* market rate of discount. (2) in U.S.A., the minimum lending rate, i.e. the rate of interest charged by the Federal Reserve Banks on loans to other banks in the federal system.

discount store *see* discount house.

discount tables COM. a book of tables of figures which make it easy for buyers and sellers to know quickly the answers to calculations concerning discounts and prices.

discrepancy ACCTS. of figures, totals, balances, a failure to agree, showing that some mistake has been made, such as in adding or in posting. *Syn.* error; mistake.

discretion freedom given by one businessman to another, such as by a client to his broker, or by an employer to an employee, to act as he thinks best in certain clearly-stated matters; but he must generally keep within the limits of his orders or directions: *You have discretion to allow an extra discount up to 5%. I leave the matter to your discretion*, to your judgment.

discretionary income *see under* income.

discretionary order STK. EXCH. an order by a client to a stockbroker with a sum of money, directing him to buy securities to the value of that sum and giving him discretion (freedom) to decide which securities to buy.

discretionary spending ECON. & COM. the spending of money by consumers on things that are not essential to living, but which can be bought (or not bought) at the discretion, or choice, of the consumer. *See* discretionary income *under* income.

discretionary trust LAW & FIN. a trust of which the trustees are allowed to use their discretion or judgment in managing it and in distributing its income, and in some cases its capital, among the beneficiaries.

discriminating duty *see under* duty.

discriminating monopoly *see under* monopoly.

discriminating tariff *see* multiple tariff *under* tariff.

discrimination (1) treating some people or things differently from others esp. in distinguishing good from bad: *She shows discrimination in choosing her friends*. (2) IND. REL. showing prejudice in treating some persons more favourably than others: *The employers promised that there would be no discrimination against the strikers*, they would not be treated differently from other employees.

racial discrimination treating people unfavourably because of their race.
(3) ECON. treating one market or country differently from another: *Price discrimination*, charging different prices for the same commodity in different markets. *See* discriminating monopoly *under* monopoly. *Trade discrimination*, in foreign trade, showing favour to some countries and disfavour to others by the use of exchange controls, quotas, tariffs, etc.

discriminatory tax *see under* tax.

diseconomies of scale ECON. & IND. increases in average costs as an industrial unit expands. Increases of efficiency and a lowering of costs per unit of output usu. result from increasing the scale of production but only up to a point. Decreases in efficiency and rising costs then set in, caused either by internal difficulties of managing the bigger unit, with more and more managers needed to run it, or by external difficulties caused by increased demand for materials, labour, etc. Cf. economies of scale.

disembarkation SHIPG. the act of going on shore, or of putting on shore passengers and cargo from a ship or boat: *Disembarkation of passengers at Beirut will begin at 10.00 hrs. from the main deck. Syn.* landing.

disencumber LAW to free (somebody) from a charge or liability such as a mortgage. *N.* disencumbrance.

disequilibrium ECON. THEORY an unbalanced state in an economy when market forces, such as changes in supply and demand, cause a stable or steady situation, esp. in the price-level, to be disturbed. Unsteadiness will normally continue until a new position of equilibrium (or state of balance) is reached. *Opp.* equilibrium.

disguised unemployment *see* hidden unemployment *under* unemployment.

dishoarding ECON. bringing idle money-balances or stored goods back into economic use after being hoarded, i.e. kept in a state of unproductiveness. *Opp.* hoarding. *Pron.* dis-hor-.

dishonest handling *see* handling (3).

dishonour BKG. & COM. (1) of a bill of exchange, failure by the person on whom a bill is drawn (the drawee or debtor) to accept it on presentation, called *dishonour by non-acceptance* or, having accepted it, failure to pay it at maturity, called *dishonour by non-payment. Pron.* dis-on-or. *Syn.* (U.S.A.) dishonor.

notice of dishonour notice that must be given immediately by the holder of a bill of exchange to the drawer and to each endorser when the bill has been dishonoured. The return of the dishonoured bill to the drawer is by law sufficient notice of dishonour. (2) of a cheque, refusal by a bank to pay a cheque because there is not a sufficient credit balance in the drawer's account. This is usu. done by the bank marking the cheque *Refer to drawer* and returning it to the payee through his bank.

dishonoured bill *see under* bill of exchange.

dishonoured cheque *see* dishonour (2).

disinflation ECON. & FIN. planned action taken by a government, as a gentle form of deflation, to slow down or stop the rate of inflation without causing high unemployment. The aim is to reduce monetary demand and to increase the supply of goods and services without raising the level of incomes. The measures taken may include: rationing and price controls on scarce commodities, controls on consumer credit and hire-purchase, and fairly high interest-rates. Cf. deflation; reflation. *Opp.* inflation.

disintegration ECON. planned action by a group of industrial units to stop producing certain products and instead to buy them from outside producers. *See* contracting-out; subcontracting. *Opp.* integration.

disinvest ECON. (1) to reduce stocks of commodities, esp. after a boom period when they will have risen above the normal level. (2) to reduce a stock of capital equipment by not replacing items when they wear out. *Opp.* to invest.

disinvestment ECON. & FIN. a reduction in the total amount of capital goods in an economy, usu. after a severe trade depression during which capital goods wore out or became out of date and were not replaced, or because they were sold for foreign currency to pay for the expense of a war. *See also* inventory investment *under* investment. *Opp.* investment.

dismal science, the ECON. the name given in the first half of the nineteenth century to economics (then called political economy) after Malthus and the Classical School had written so miserably about the future standard of living of the people of Britain. *See* Malthus, Thomas Robert.

dismissal *see* constructive dismissal; wrongful dismissal.

dispatch (1) to send away to a certain place: *We have dispatched the goods by rail today.* (2) quick, prompt settlement of business: *He acted with dispatch.* (3) a report: *A dispatch-box, dispatch-case,* for keeping or carrying dispatches. *Syn.* despatch.

dispatch, advice of *see under* advice.

dispatch-case *see* briefcase.

dispatch note COM. & TRANSPT. a written notice from the sender of goods telling the person who is to receive them that they have been dispatched (sent away). *Syn.* advice note.

dispenser *see* cash dispenser.

displ. displacement.

displacement tonnage *see under* tonnage.

display (1) COM. an arrangement of goods in a shop to attract the eye of the public: *A window/counter/shelf display. Display packaging,*

containers such as boxes, tins, bottles, attractively produced in order to make a good display in shops. *Display material,* posters, showcards, etc. intended to be displayed with goods in shops or shop windows. *Display cabinet,* a glass-enclosed cupboard or tray for showing goods. (2) ADVTG. the special use of printer's type and artist's designs to produce an attractive arrangement of words esp. in an advertisement (called a *display advert.*). *Display-face,* a type-face used for displays and headings rather than for setting the pages of a book, called a book-face.

disposable goods COM. consumer goods that are intended to be used only once and then be disposed of (thrown away), such as towels, plates, cups and clothing made of paper, and knives, forks and spoons made of plastic. *Syn.* disposables.

disposable income ECON. the total income which all people in the economy have left for spending after paying direct taxes, such as income tax, and contributions that must be made by law, such as for national insurance.

disposal the act of getting rid of (something): *Disposal of property,* by selling it. *Disposal of business,* at a meeting, by discussing or settling it. *Disposal of assets, securities.*

at one's disposal for use as one wishes: *I put my car at your disposal,* for you to use as you wish.

government disposals *pl.* goods no longer needed by the government and therefore sold cheaply to the public.

dispossession *see* expropriation.

dispute (1) a strong disagreement. (2) IND. REL. a heated argument with one side struggling to make the other yield: *A trade/industrial dispute,* one between employer or management on one side and employer or trade union(s) on the other about wages and working conditions. *Matters under/in dispute,* being argued or discussed. *See also* demarcation dispute.

disruption of markets, seriously disturbed conditions making trading difficult or impossible: *Disruption of business caused by the war/the general election. Syn.* disturbance.

dis-saving ECON. the opposite of saving; the using up of past savings by spending. The situation in an economy when total consumption is greater than total income.

dissolution LAW (1) of a company, the end of its existence, when it has been wound up or when it has been made a defunct company by the Registrar of Companies. (2) of a partnership, when it has been brought to an end by the retirement, death or bankruptcy of any one of the partners, or by common agreement of all the partners, or by order of a court of law.

dissolve to bring to an end; to break up; *To dissolve a partnership/association/company. N* dissolution.

dist. distant; district; distinguish.

distance freight *see under* freight.

distant (1) far away: *The distant subscriber*, the person being telephoned by the caller. (2) TRANSPT. of a place, far or the furthest away: *The station is five miles distant. The distant port*, that which is furthest away.

distr. distribution.

distrain LAW to seize goods, esp. goods belonging to a tenant in order to get payment of rent in arrear. *See* distress. *N.* distraint.

distrainor LAW a person who distrains.

distress (1) LAW the act of seizing goods by permission of a court of law, esp. by a landlord to obtain payment of rent in arrear. Also by a rate-collector or tax-collector to obtain payment of arrears, and by an officer of the court to obtain payment of unpaid fines. *Syn.* distraint; levy. (2) SHIPG. great difficulty or danger: *A ship in distress. Port of distress*, one at which a ship calls only because it has been in difficulty and needs shelter or repairs. *Distress signals*, calling for help from other ships, rescue services, etc.

distress selling COM. selling which is forced and often therefore at a low price, such as the stock of a bankrupt business in liquidation, or on the death of the owner of property or, by court order, to pay debts. Cf. distrain.

distress warrant *see under* warrant.

distributable profit ACCTS. what is left of the net profit of a business (including any balance brought forward from last year) after allowing for transfers to reserves. *Syn.* earnings.

distribution (1) the dividing up, sending out, spreading or scattering of something among a number of people or places. (2) COM. the arrangements and activities needed for getting goods from the manufacturer or importer to the consumer through the *channels of distribution* which are usu. the wholesalers and retailers. Activities include the storage of stocks, the spreading of supplies among retailers, the handling of orders, the transport of the goods, relations with customers and credit control. *See* chain of distribution; distributive trades. (3) ECON. THEORY one of the main branches of economics, often called the Theory of Distribution or of Income Distribution. It examines and explains the prices (incomes) paid out of the national income to owners of the factors of production, i.e. rent for the use of land, wages for labour, interest for the use of capital, and profits as the reward for enterprise, esp. the taking of risks. It studies particularly the influences that determine these factor-prices under various market conditions. It also studies how the national income is divided among the different classes and occupations of the people, esp. to assess the degree of inequality of income. (4) IND. of industry, the general pattern of the places or regions in which industries have come to exist in a country. In areas where the older industries are dying, governments attempt to reduce the resulting high unemployment and poverty by attracting new industries and by providing for the retraining of the unemployed workers. (5) LAW the division of the personal assets of a bankrupt person among his creditors according to the law. (6) LAW the division of the property of an intestate (a person who has died without leaving a will) among his next-of-kin according to the law. (7) STK. EXCH. the division of a part or most of the net profit of a company, usu. once or twice a year, among its members (shareholders) in the form of dividends. (8) the amount of dividend paid on each share or the amount paid on loan capital such as debentures: *The next distribution is due on 31 June*.

cum distribution *see under* cum.

total distribution the total of the interim and final·dividends declared by a company. *See* final dividend *under* dividend.

distribution census *see under* census.

distribution, chain of *see under* chain.

distributive costs COM. & IND. the cost of getting goods from the place of production to the consumer including storage, transport and selling costs.

distributive trades COM. all those business organizations, large or small, that play a part in commercial distribution, i.e. bringing goods from producer to consumer. They consist broadly of: traders, such as wholesalers, retailers, shopkeepers, self-service stores, supermarkets, hotels, restaurants and caterers; commercial and financial services, such as banks, discount and finance houses, lawyers, advertising agencies and printers; and transport services by rail, road, sea and air.

distributor COM. a retailer who has arranged with one or more suppliers to sell a product or range of products. Where he is the only seller in a particular place or area he is known as the *sole distributor*. He is often said to have a *sole agency* or *exclusive agency*, but he is strictly not an agent because he buys and sells for himself and not as the representative of another party. *See* exclusive sales agreement.

district manager *see under* manager.

District of Columbia an area in U.S.A. in which the federal capital, Washington, is situated. The District is ruled by Congress, and belongs to no state. *Abbr.* D.C.

distringas notice LAW & STK. EXCH. a special kind of notice which, with the approval of the court, can be served on a company, forbidding dealings in certain of its stocks and shares for a limited period without first giving information to the person serving the notice. Distringas notices usu. arise in distress cases.

disturbance *see* disruption.

disutility ECON. THEORY the opposite of utility; the dissatisfaction, inconvenience or pain that is suffered by having too much of a commodity, such as the discomfort from too much food, or the nuisance of having so much furniture that it gets in the way.

D.I.T. double income-tax (relief).

ditto the same; sometimes represented by the sign „. *Abbr.* do.

Div. dividend.

div. divide; division; dividend.

diversification (1) STK. EXCH. the placing of one's investments in a wide range of companies in order to spread the risk of losing one's money if a company fails. To small private investors this is the special attraction of unit trusts as an investment. (2) COM. & IND. the production of a number of widely differing products, or the running of a number of completely different commercial activities, in order to reduce the risk of losses when business is bad.

diversion TRANSPT. a change from the normal route travelled by road, rail, ship or plane. *The tanker made a diversion to repair her engines. A diversion on the Oxford road to avoid floods.*

divi. (*colloq.*) dividend.

dividend (1) strictly, an amount to be divided, such as the total sum to be paid out of profits or as interest on a loan. Its commercial meaning is: one of the parts into which an amount has been divided and shared out, esp. to stockholders or shareholders of a company, or to the creditors of a bankrupt. A dividend is expressed *either* as a percentage, *or* as a part of a pound/dollar, etc.
national dividend *see* national income.
(2) LAW a part-payment of a number of pence in each pound made to creditors of a bankrupt or of a company in liquidation, after the assets have been sold for cash. (3) COM. a share of the trading surplus of a co-operative society expressed as a percentage of the amount spent in the co-operative store during a certain period and paid to each member after the end of the period or returned in the form of trading stamps. Strictly, this is a return of money overpaid on goods bought. *See* consumers' co-operative *under* co-operative. (4) INSCE. a share of the profits of a life insurance company that is paid to holders of 'with profits' policies. *See* bonus, insurance. (5) INSCE. the share of the 'profits' paid to policy holders of a mutual insurance company. Strictly, this is a return of money overpaid on the premiums. (6) STK. EXCH. that part of a company's profits which is divided among the members (stockholders or shareholders). It can only be paid out of profits, not out of capital or reserves, and may not be greater than the amount recommended by the directors. Dividends are expressed

either as a percentage of the face value of the stock or share on which they are paid, or as a fixed sum per share: *The company has declared a dividend of 20% or 5p per share of 25p face value. See also* cum; ex.
cum dividend *see under* cum.
(7) STK. EXCH. incorrectly, a periodical payment of interest on the loan stock of a company such as debentures or on a government security. Strictly, this is interest payable on a loan, not a division of profit.
accumulated dividend arrears of dividends on cumulative preference stock or shares, which have not been paid when due.
cumulative dividend one payable on cumulative preference shares, which, if not paid annually, will accumulate from year to year; the accumulation has to be paid before any ordinary dividends become payable.
debenture dividend an inaccurate expression for debenture interest. *See* debenture stock.
final dividend where an interim dividend has been paid earlier in the financial year, a final dividend is that declared by the members (shareholders) of the company at their annual general meeting. It is an addition to the interim dividend, and the two dividends, interim and final, together are known as the *total distribution.*
final interim dividend the last of several interim dividends.
interim dividend a partial dividend that may be declared by the directors usu. half-way through the financial year, and before the full profits are known. The amount must be confirmed (approved) at the next annual general meeting before the final dividend is declared.
ordinary dividend that payable on the ordinary stock or shares of a company.
preference dividend that payable on preference stock or shares in a company.

dividend cover *see* cover (6).

dividend limitation FIN. the placing by the government of an upper limit on the rate of dividend that a company may pay perh. as part of a policy to hold down incomes and reduce inflation. *Syn.* dividend restraint.

dividend mandate *see under* mandate.

dividend off (U.S.A.) STK. EXCH. without the next dividend payment. *Syn.* (Britain) ex dividend (ex div.). Cf. dividend on.

dividend on (U.S.A.) STK. EXCH. including the next dividend payment. *Syn.* (Britain) cum dividend (cum div.). Cf. dividend off.

dividend options INSCE. the choices given to the holder of a 'with-profits' life assurance policy concerning the way he wishes the insurers to pay his dividend, whether in cash, or to be held by the insurers to earn interest, or to be used towards payment of the next premium, or to be used to buy more insurance.

dividend-price ratio (U.S.A.) STK. EXCH. the relation between the current dividend rate and the market price of a security. Cf. price-earnings ratio.

dividend-stripping FIN. any practice by which one company buys control of another company and arranges matters so that income is received in such a way that tax is evaded (dishonestly avoided). Cf. asset-stripping.

dividend warrant BKG. in Britain, an order similar to a cheque by a company to its bank to pay a stated sum to a named stockholder or shareholder. Unless stated otherwise on its face, the warrant is a negotiable instrument. A *tax voucher* is attached to it showing how the sum was calculated and the amount of tax that has been held back by the company. This voucher is used by the stockholder or shareholder in supporting any claim he may make for a return of tax by the Inland Revenue.

dividend yield see under yield.

division one of the more or less independent units into which a large commercial, industrial or governmental organization has been divided for purposes of management: *The plastics division of Imperial Chemical Industries. The book-publishing division of H.M. Stationery Office.*

divisional director see under director.

division of labour ECON. THEORY & IND. the basic system of obtaining economies in production and increasing the total output of the economy by organizing the manufacture of an article so that each worker gives all his time and attention to performing a single operation (called specialization) instead of performing the many different operations needed to produce the article. Advantages include: greatly increased output at lower cost, development of special skills and machinery, and saving in time because operation is continuous. Disadvantages are that the work becomes uninteresting, quality of workmanship may be lower, administration becomes more complicated and business risk is increased. *Syn.* specialization.

divs. dividends.

divvy. (*colloq.*) dividend.

D.I.Y. do it yourself.

DK Denmark's international vehicle-registration letters.

dk. dock; deck.

dkg. decagram(me).

Dk. L. deck load; deck loss.

dkl. decalitre.

dkm. decametre.

dkyd. dockyard.

dl. decilitre.

dld. delivered.

D.L.O. Dead Letter Office.

d.l.o. dispatch loading only.

dlvd. delivered.

dly. daily.

dm. decimetre.

DM Deutsche Mark.

D-Mark Deutsche Mark.

D.N., D/N debit note.

do. ditto.

D.O. deferred ordinary (shares); delivery order; direct order.

d/o. delivery order.

do (*colloq.*) (1) to cheat; to obtain by a trick: *I have been done*, cheated. *Be careful that he does not do you.* (2) to visit and look at, as a tourist: *To do the Pyramids/the Cairo Museum/ the Valley of the Kings.* (3) to work for, as a cleaner: *Mrs Mop does for me.* (4) to help: *What can I do for you?* (5) *do down*, to cheat: *He will try to do you down.* (6) *do for*, to destroy; to ruin; to become useless: *The ship on the rocks/this old machine/the defendant's career is done for.* (7) *do with*, to need: *We could do with a new car. This town could do with a supermarket. You could do with a haircut. See also* do it yourself.

Doc. document(s); Doctor.

dock (1) SHIPG. in Britain, an area of enclosed water where ships can tie up to the shore and use the machinery and services provided by the port while loading and unloading passengers or cargo. (2) a place where ships are built or repaired. *See* docks; dry dock; floating dock; graving dock. (3) (U.S.A.) a pier, jetty or wharf itself, not necessarily in enclosed water. *Abbr.* dk.

to be in dock to be undergoing repair, esp. of ships but also of road vehicles: *My car is in dock today.*

dock company one that owns and runs or manages a dock or system of docks for commercial gain.

dock dues see dockage.

dockage SHIPG. charges based usu. on net register tonnage payable by a shipowner when the ship enters or leaves dock, for the use of the arrangements provided. *See* tonnage dues. *Syn.* dock dues.

dock basin see basin (1).

docker SHIPG. a worker employed in loading and unloading ships in the docks (port area). *Syn.* (U.S.A.) longshoreman.

docket (1) a short note on the outside of a folded document or packet of papers stating its contents. Dockets were formerly much used when papers were stored in pigeon-holes, but are not now needed with modern filing systems. (2) LAW in U.S.A., a list of cases coming up for trial in a court of law. (3) COM. a cash memo.

dock receipt TRANSPT. a receipt for goods held or handled in the course of carriage, by the owner or manager of a dock-side warehouse. *Syn.* wharfinger's receipt.

docks *n. pl.* the port area of a town.

dockside *see* quay.

dock warrant SHIPG. a formal receipt handed to the owner of goods stored in a dock warehouse or to his agent, giving him the right to get possession of the stored goods or to transfer that right to another party by endorsement. *Syn.* warehouse warrant; deposit warrant; wharfinger's warrant. *See also* delivery order. *Abbr.* D.W.; d.w.

dockyard SHIPG. a shipyard with machinery and supplies where ships are built or repaired. *Abbr.* dkyd.; Dyd.; D.Y.

doctor (1) a person holding the highest degree given by a university: *A Doctor of Philosophy/Civil Law/Economic Science, etc.* A learned teacher. (2) a doctor of medicine, the title *doctor* being given by custom to physicians (persons practising medicine) but not to surgeons. **company doctor** a professional medical man employed by a company to advise the management on medical matters and to attend to the health of its employees. **company-doctor** a person with special knowledge of how to rescue unprofitable companies from going into liquidation. He may be employed as a consultant to advise, or he may be given wide powers to reorganize the staff and activities of the company.

document *n.* (1) a written or printed paper, esp. one which records important information and provides proof of some fact. *Abbr.* Doc. (2) LAW legal and official papers; any paper that can be used as evidence (proof of a fact). (3) BKG. & COM. shipping documents, *see under* shipping.
v. to provide with documents; to record in a document: *The case has been well documented.*

documentary acceptance credit BKG. & COM. an acceptance credit (*see under* acceptance) that has been granted to an importer with an arrangement that the exporter's bill of exchange will be accepted by a bank in the exporter's country on presentation of the shipping documents.

documentary bill *see under* bill of exchange.

documentary credit *see under* credit (3).

documentary draft *see* documentary bill *under* bill of exchange.

documentary letter of credit *see under* letter of credit.

document bill *see* documentary bill *under* bill of exchange.

document of title LAW a document which gives the holder a right to deal with the property to which the document relates as though he owns the property. Bills of lading, export invoices and dock warrants are documents of title.

documents against acceptance BKG. a means of getting payment for export shipments, by which the exporter or his agent sends the shipping documents to a bank at the port of destination (i.e. where the goods are to be unloaded) with an order to hand the documents to the consignee or his agent only when the bill of exchange has been accepted by the consignee. Cf. cash against documents. *Abbr.* D.A.; D/A.; d/a.

documents-against-acceptance bill *see under* bill of exchange.

documents against cash *see* cash against documents.

documents against payment *see* cash against documents.

documents-against-payment bill *see under* bill of exchange.

documents against presentation *see* cash against documents.

documents for collection *see* cash against documents; documents against acceptance.

dodger TAXN. a person who illegally avoids paying taxes: *A tax-dodger needs to be clever.*

dodgy (*colloq.*) risky; difficult; possibly dangerous: *A dodgy situation/transaction/venture.*

dogsbody (*colloq.*) an unskilled and usu. overworked employee who is given the unpleasant and uninteresting jobs to do.

do it yourself COM. the practice of an unskilled person who carries out repairs, etc. to his own house or makes things himself in his spare time, partly to save money by not employing professional workers, and partly because he enjoys doing the work himself. A *do-it-yourself* shop sells the materials and tools needed by such persons. *Abbr.* D.I.Y.

dol. dollar.

doldrums STK. EXCH. a calm period of trading during which there is little movement in prices: *Shares were in the doldrums.* The name of an area near the equator where there is often no wind, so that sailing ships could not move.

dole (*colloq.*) an allowance paid for a limited period to unemployed persons, called officially unemployment benefit: *He is on the dole*, is receiving unemployment benefit. *A dole queue*, a line of unemployed people waiting to get the dole.

dollar the standard monetary unit of many countries, the most important of which are the U.S.A., Canadian, East Caribbean, Australian and New Zealand dollars, all subdivided into 100 cents. The name dollar is also used in the currencies of: the Bahamas, Barbados, Belize, Bermuda, Cayman Is., Ethiopia, Fiji, Guyana, Hong Kong, Jamaica, Liberia, Malaysia, Singapore, Taiwan, Trinidad and Tobago, and Zimbabwe. *Sign:* $. *Abbr.* d.; dol. **Australian dollar** is used in Australia, Christmas I., Cocos (Keeling) Is., Gilbert Is., Nauru, New Hebrides, Norfolk I., Solomon Is. *Abbr.* A$. **East Caribbean dollar** is used in Antigua, Dominica, Grenada, Montserrat, St. Kitts-

Nevis-Anguilla, St. Lucia, St. Vincent. *Abbr.* ECar$.

New Zealand dollar is used in New Zealand, Cook Is., Nieue, Tokelau Is. *Abbr.* NZ$.

U.S.A. dollar (also called U.S. or American dollar) is used in U.S.A., American Samoa, Guam, Johnston I., Midway Is., Panama Canal Zone, Puerto Rico, Turks & Caicos Is., Wake I., Virgin Is. *Syn.* buck (*colloq.*). *Abbr.* US$. *Sign*: $. *See also* almighty dollar, the; Maria Theresa dollars; petrodollars; Eurodollars.

dollar area (1) FIN. & BKG. the area of the world where the U.S. dollar is used as standard currency. (2) the American Account countries and Canada.

dollar pool FIN. & STK. EXCH. the total amount of U.S. dollars and dollar securities held by people resident (living permanently) in Britain.

dollar premium FIN. & BKG. the extra cost of buying U.S. and Canadian investment dollars in Britain before the removal in 1979 of exchange controls that forbade the changing of sterling into dollars for investment in U.S. securities except through the dollar pool.

dollar stocks STK. EXCH. U.S. or Canadian securities.

dols. dollars.

DOM the international vehicle-registration letters of the Dominican Republic.

dom. domestic.

domestic (1) relating to the home, the private house or other place where one lives: *Domestic servant/service. Domestic animal*, one that is kept at home, is not wild. (2) relating to the home country: *The domestic market*, that existing at home, not abroad. *Domestic value*, the cost of goods in the home country. *Abbr.* dom.

domestic bill *see under* bill of exchange.

domestic currency *see under* currency.

domestic investment *see* private investment *under* investment.

domestic port *see under* port.

domestic system ECON. HIST. the system of economic development which came before the factory system. Most articles and commodities were made in small workshops in or near the worker's home. These workers had to depend often on travelling merchants to 'put out' or supply them with materials such as wool for spinning or weaving, and to collect and sell the finished product. *Syn.* putting-out system; homework.

domestic trade *see under* trade.

domicile (1) LAW the country in which a person has his permanent home and, if he is away, the place to which he intends to return in old age. *Domicile of origin* is the country in which a person is born. *Domicile of choice* is the country to which a person goes to live in and intends to stay, it not being the country in which he was born. *Also* domicil. (2) BKG. the business house or bank where a bill of exchange is made payable. The bill is said to be domiciled there. *See* domiciled bill *under* bill of exchange.

domiciled bill *see under* bill of exchange.

Dominica an independent island state in the Caribbean Sea, pop. 75,000 approx. (1975); capital, Roseau, pop. 10,000 approx.; language, English; currency unit, the East Caribbean dollar (ECar$). Member, (British) Commonwealth.

Dominican Republic the eastern two-thirds of Hispaniola, an island in the Caribbean, pop. 4.3 million approx. (1972); capital, Santo Domingo, pop. 820,000 approx.; language, Spanish; currency unit, the peso, divided into 8 reales or 100 centavos. Member, O.A.S.

donation a gift, esp. of money given to some work for the public good, such as to the Red Cross.

donee (1) a person who receives a gift from a donor. (2) LAW a person to whom a donor, grantor or principal has granted a power of attorney. *Syn.* grantee; attorney.

dong the standard currency unit of Vietnam, divided into 10 hao or 100 xu.

donor (1) one who gives, a giver: *A blood donor*, a person who gives his blood for others who need it. (2) LAW a person giving a power of attorney to a donee. *See also* settlor. *Syn.* grantor; principal.

door-to-door salesman *see* salesman; canvasser.

door-to-door service TRANSPT. an arrangement by which a carrier collects goods, possibly packed in a container, from the sender's factory or warehouse and delivers to the address of the consignee.

Dorchester Labourers *see* Tolpuddle Martyrs.

dormant balance BKG. money lying in a dead account.

dormant partner *see* sleeping partner *under* partner.

dormitory a place for sleeping: *Dormitory town/city*, a place in which most of its citizens seem only to sleep, because they travel daily to another town or city to work. *Dormitory suburb*, an area just outside a town, where many people live who work in the town itself.

Dors. Dorset, England.

doss-house (*colloq.*) a cheap, low-class lodging-house. *Syn.* flop-house (U.S.A. *colloq.*)

dossier a collection of papers relating to a certain subject or to a certain person.

double-bedded TOUR. of a hotel room, with one double bed. Sometimes, a room with two single beds, but this is usu. called a twin-bedded room.

double bond *see under* bond, *n.*

double booking TOUR. the accepting of two (or more) bookings for the same room in a hotel, seat in a plane, train, etc. to make sure that there will be no loss by cancellation. *See* book, *v.* (2).

double-cross (*colloq.*) disloyal or deceitful behaviour such as that of a dishonest person acting as agent for both sides in a deal; or giving secret information to business rivals. *N.* double-crosser.

double dealing deception; cheating; dishonest dealing esp. in promising to do one thing and doing another. *Syn.* duplicity.

double-decker (1) TRANSPT. a bus with two decks. (2) a ship with two decks above water-level.

double endowment insurance *see* endowment policy *under* insurance policy.

double entry ACCTS. the basic system of modern book-keeping by which each account has two sides, a debit side and a credit side, and each transaction (business deal) is entered twice, as a debit in one account and as a credit in another. The rule is: debit the receiver, credit the giver. Every debit must have a corresponding credit and every credit a corresponding debit. If all the entries have been correctly made, the total of all the debits must at any time equal the total of all the credits. By this simple check, mistakes can be quickly found and corrected. Cf. single entry. *Abbr.* d.e.

double income-tax relief TAXN. to avoid making taxpayers pay income tax in two countries on the same income, the tax authorities in most countries give relief where tax has already been paid in another country. Some countries have signed double taxation relief agreements to make this practice official. *Abbr.* D.I.T. relief. *Syn.* double taxation relief (D.T.R.).

double insurance INSCE. the practice of arranging to insure a certain object by means of two (or more) policies. This is quite proper so long as the combined value of the sums insured is not greater than the value of the object insured.

double liability *see under* liability.

double option *see under* option.

double pricing COM. the showing by some shopkeepers of two prices on an article, the higher price being crossed through to make customers believe that it has been reduced. Governments are against this practice, for if the higher price shown is a false one, the customer is being tricked into thinking that the article is a good bargain.

double standard *see under* standard.

double taxation relief *see* double income-tax relief.

doubtful debt(s) *see under* debt.

dough (*colloq.*) money.

Dow-Jones Industrial Average STK. EXCH. one of a number of averages or indexes issued by Dow Jones & Company, a firm providing a financial news service. This average is probably the world's best known index of the movement of prices and yields of common stock (ordinary stocks or shares) on the New York Stock Exchange. It is based on 30 of the leading industrial companies in the U.S.A. Cf. Financial Times Industrial Ordinary Index.

down (1) in a low or lower state or position: *Down and out*, (*colloq.*) in a state of poverty. *A down-and-out(er)*, a person in that condition. *Down on one's luck*, suffering a period of misfortune and poverty. *Down at heel*, looking poor. (2) COM. & FIN. immediate payment: *Cash down*; *Money down*, paid or to be paid at the time of buying. *Down payment*, the first payment under a mortgage or hire-purchase agreement. *£50 down, the balance by instalments*. (3) IND. & IND. REL. *To down tools*, (*a*) to stop work for the day. (*b*) to refuse to work; to go on strike, usu. suddenly and without warning. (4) STK. EXCH. of securities, lower in price: *Industrials were marked down on fears of a strike*. (5) COMMOD. EXCH. of commodities, lower in price: *Zinc was down £10 per ton*. (6) TRANSPT. of railways, in a direction away from the capital or important railway centre: *The down line/ down train. Down platform*, that from which down trains start. *Opp.* up.

downhill COM. & FIN. *To go downhill*, to get into a worse financial condition.

down-market COM. of a shop or store, a tendency to supply what is wanted by buyers in the poorer sections of the market: *That dress shop has moved down-market*, is selling cheaper goods of lower quality than before. *Opp.* up-market.

down payment *see* down (2).

downswing *see* trade cycle *under* cycle.

downtime *or* **down time** (1) IND. (*a*) time during which a worker is paid but is unable to do any useful work, perh. for lack of materials or directions. (*b*) time during which no use is made of machinery. *Syn.* lost time. (2) COMP. the time during which a computer is not being used because it is not working properly, expressed as a percentage of the time that it has been planned to operate. Cf. uptime.

downtown *see* central business district.

down train *see under* train; *also* down (6).

downturn *see* trade cycle *under* cycle.

downward(s) STK. EXCH. towards a lower position: *A downward tendency in oils*, prices of oil shares tended to fall.

doz. dozen(s).

dozen COM. a set or group of 12 things. In some trades, esp. *A baker's dozen* or *long dozen*, 13 charged as 12. *Cheaper by the dozen*, the price per unit is lower if you buy not less than 12 at one time.

dozen *pl.* three dozen eggs; *but* dozens of eggs (if no number of dozens is stated).

D.P. delivery point; documents against payment; duty paid; data processing.

D/P. documents against payment.

d.p. direct port.

D.P.B. deposit pass book.

D/P bill *see* documents-against-payment bill *under* bill of exchange.

dpt. department; deposit; depot.

Dr. debit; debtor; director; Doctor; drachma; drawer.

dr. debit; debtor; drachm; drachma; dram; draw(n).

D/R. deposit receipt.

drachm (1) *see* dram. (2) a drachma. *Abbr.* dr.

drachma (1) a dram. (2) FIN. the standard currency unit of Greece, divided into 100 lepta. *Pl.* -ae. *Pron.* drakma. *Abbr.* Dr.; dr.

draft (1) formal document which is used to draw (extract) money from a source of supply. *Abbr.* df.; dft. (2) BKG. a bill of exchange, esp. any bill before it has been accepted, or a bank bill, or a sight bill, or an inland bill. Any written order to pay money; the money so paid. *See* bill of exchange. (3) a document in an early or rough form while it is being prepared: *This is the first draft of my report. The final draft of the accounts is ready.* V. to draft a document.

draft terms COM. conditions of sale which provide for the exporter drawing a bill of exchange or draft on his customer or on a bank.

dragoman TOUR. a local guide and interpreter (a person who can speak several languages), esp. in the Middle East.

drain an outflow; an opening through which something runs away and is lost: *The brain drain*, the loss of highly skilled and clever persons who are attracted abroad by higher pay and better conditions of work. *A drain of capital/gold/money, etc. from the country.*

dram (1) a small weight, one-sixteenth of an ounce avoirdupois, 1.772 g; or one-eighth of an ounce apothecaries' weight, 3.885 g. *Also* drachm, *pron.* dram. (2) a small quantity of liquid, esp. of strong drink. *Abbr.* dr.

draught (1) SHIPG. of a ship, the distance from the bottom of the ship to the water-line at which the vessel is actually floating. The least depth of water needed by a ship to float.

laden draught the draught when loaded, as opposed to *light draught*.

load draught the distance from the bottom of the ship to the load water-line, i.e. the limiting line to which a ship is allowed to load according to the rules of classification or the conditions under which she is operating. *See* load-line.

(2) TRANSPT. of animals, used for pulling carts, ploughs, etc.: *A draught-horse*. Cf. pack-horse. (3) (*colloq.*) *To feel the draught*, to suffer the discomfort of unfavourable economic conditions: *The shipbuilding industry is feeling the draught of world depression. Retailers felt the draught when V.A.T. was raised. Pron.* draft. *Syn.* (U.S.A.) draft.

draw *n.* COM. (*colloq.*) something that attracts the interest of shoppers and encourages them to spend money. *Father Christmas is a great draw in the toy department. The giving of double trading stamps on Tuesday is a draw. Abbr.* dr.

v. (1) to attract; to pull: *A horse-drawn waggon. To draw someone's attention to something*, to bring it to his notice. *To draw a large audience/many customers/adverse comment/criticism/praise.* (2) to extract; to take out: *To draw cash/interest/profits/salary/expenses/allowances*, etc. *To draw on stocks/reserves/one's savings. To draw lots*, to decide a question or choice by chance, by taking something (e.g. a name or number) out that is hidden from sight in a container. (3) to make out, write out: *To draw up a document/plan/programme/list/agenda/itinerary*, etc. *To draw the line (at)*, to set a limit. (4) BKG. to write out and sign a cheque, bill of exchange, etc. The person who draws is called *the drawer*; the person who is called on to pay is *the drawee*; the person who is to receive the money is *the payee. Syn.* to draft.

drawback (1) COM. & TAXN. a repayment of customs duty when goods or materials on which import duty has been paid are later exported. (2) the document authorizing such a repayment, sometimes called a customs debenture. *Syn.* customs drawback. *See* customs debenture. *Abbr.* dbk.

drawee BKG. *of a cheque*: the named bank on whom the cheque (or order to pay) is drawn. *Of a bank draft*: the bank named in the order to pay. *Of a bill of exchange*: the named person to whom the bill is addressed and who is expected to accept it and to pay it when it matures. He becomes the acceptor when he accepts the bill. Cf. drawer.

drawer BKG. *of a cheque*: a person who draws (writes out and signs) a cheque ordering his bank, called the drawee, to pay a sum of money on demand. *Of a bill of exchange*: a person who signs a bill ordering another person, the drawee, to pay a stated sum of money at a stated time. Cf. drawee.

drawing account BKG. a current account, *see under* bank account.

drawing, cum *see* cum drawing.

Drawing Rights FIN. the original rights of countries who are members of the International Monetary Fund, and who have a temporarily adverse balance of payments, to buy limited supplies of foreign currencies from a reserve collected and managed by the Fund. This original system of rights, called *Ordinary or Regular Drawing Rights*, was found to be in some ways lacking and was enlarged and strengthened in 1968 by *Special Drawing Rights* (S.D.R.s) a new international reserve currency system. The amount, which is fixed for each country each year, can be used along with gold for settling debts between governments without having to be exchanged into any particular currency. *See* International Monetary Fund.

drawings account ACCTS. in a privately-owned business, a personal account of the owner, in which are recorded all drawings (sums of money drawn by him). If he takes goods from the stock of the business, their value too is entered in the drawings account.

drawn bill *see under* bill of exchange.

drawn bond *see under* bond, *n.*

drift STK. EXCH. of prices, to move slowly, usu. downwards: *Equities continued to drift lower.*

drifter SHIPG. a fishing vessel that uses a drift-net, i.e. a net that hangs upright in the water and is left to drift (move slowly with the tide). Cf. trawler.

drilling rig INDUS. a tower-like structure with machinery for making holes deep in the earth for getting oil or natural gas. An *offshore drilling rig* is one specially made for drilling in the sea-bed.

drive *v.* COM. to force: *To drive a (hard) bargain,* to make severe conditions. *To drive sales away. To drive prices up or down.* *n.* (1) a planned effort: *A sales drive,* to increase sales. *An advertising drive. Syn.* campaign. (2) in a person, energy and will-power in getting things done: *A manager with plenty of drive.*

driver TRANSPT. the person in control of the movement of a train or of a road vehicle. *The engine-driver,* man in control of a railway engine (locomotive). *A bus-/taxi-/car-driver.*

drive-in bank BKG. esp. in U.S.A., one having service counters where customers may do business without leaving their motor cars.

drive-up store COM. esp. in U.S.A., a retail shop or store where customers can do their shopping without leaving their motor cars. *Syn.* drive-in store.

droop STK. EXCH. of prices, to sink lower: *Chemicals drooped, then rose.*

drug (1) any substance used as a medicine or in making medicines. (2) (*colloq.*) any article or commodity that shopkeepers find very difficult to sell, usu. because the market has been oversupplied: *A drug on/in the market.*

drugstore (U.S.A.) COM. a chemist's shop that not only sells medicines but also toilet articles, newspapers, magazines, stationery, etc., and sometimes serves light meals.

drum *n.* COM. a container in the shape of a cylinder, usu. of metal for carrying liquids, or of wood or cardboard for carrying powders.

to drum up *v.* to go out to get business: *To drum up business/sales.*

drummer (U.S.A.) COM. a travelling salesman.

drunkard (1) a person who is unable to think clearly because he frequently drinks too much strong drink. A drunk (*colloq.*). (2) LAW a contract to which a drunkard is a party is voidable if he so wishes, if he can prove that when he signed it he was unable to understand it and that the other party knew this.

dry dock SHIPG. a dock which can be made watertight, i.e. all the water in it can be pumped out and kept out by movable gates at one end, and in which ships can be built or repaired. After the work is completed, the dock is flooded, the gates are opened and the ship is floated out. *See also* floating dock; wet dock. *Syn.* graving dock. *Abbr.* d.d.

dry farming AGR. farming under conditions of water shortage when irrigation cannot be used. Special methods used aim at preserving moisture in the soil and preventing evaporation.

dry goods (1) COM. mainly in U.S.A., cloth and clothing as articles of trade. *Syn.* drapery; mercery. (2) in Britain, sometimes dry foodstuffs such as corn and other grains, tea, coffee, sugar. *Opp.* wet goods.

dry measure *see* corn and dry measure.

dry ship *see* general ship *under* ship.

D.S. debenture stock.

D/S, d.s. days after sight; days' sight.

D.S.T. Daylight Saving Time.

dstn. destination.

d.t.b.a. date to be advised.

D.T.I. Department of Trade and Industry.

D.T.R. double taxation relief.

dub up (*colloq.*) to pay, usu. unwillingly: *He could not pay the bill, so I had to dub up.*

Dubai *see* United Arab Emirates.

ducat (1) FIN. any of several gold and silver coins formerly in use as currency in many European countries, esp. in Venice from the thirteenth to the eighteenth century. (2) a measure of weight of gold and other precious metals and gems in Austria and Germany, 53.873 grains = 3.491 g. (3) (*modern colloq.*) money, esp. coin.

dud BKG. (*colloq.*) false; worthless: *A dud cheque,* one that is not honoured by the paying banker because there is insufficient money in the drawer's account. Cf. bouncer.

due *adj.* (1) (of money) owed; payable: *The rent/ wages will become due tomorrow. Interest/instalment payments fall due today.* (2) (of time) expected: *The train is due at 10.00 hrs.,* is expected to arrive then. *When is it due to depart from here and to arrive in Aswan? The ship is due (to arrive, to call) at Port Said on Thursday.* Cf. overdue. (3) right; proper: *With due care,* with proper care. *After due consideration/ thought. In due course/time,* at the proper time. (4) as a result of; because of: *The delay was due to an accident,* was caused by.

adv. of directions by the compass: north, south, east and west exactly, directly: *Steer due east*, not north-east or south-east but exactly east. *The wind is due west*, blowing directly from the west. *The compass needle points due north*, towards the north (magnetic) pole.
n. that which is due or owing by right: *Give him his due*, be fair to him. *One must claim one's due*, demand what is owing.

due bill (U.S.A.) COM. a written acknowledgment of a debt.

due course *see* holder in due course *under* holder.

due date *see under* date.

dues *pl.* (1) FIN. money which is due to be paid: *Club dues; Union dues*, sums payable by members. *We must pay our dues promptly.* (2) SHIPG. charges paid by shipowners for the use of ports, harbours, etc.: *Harbour/dock/port/ anchorage/dues.* Any payment for services. (3) COM. advance orders which are received before the goods are received into stock and which are due to be supplied later. Such orders are recorded in a *dues book* or on *dues cards*.

dukawallah COM. (*from Hindi*: dukanwallah) an Asian shopkeeper in East Africa.

dull STK. EXCH. of market conditions, inactive, there being few buyers and few bargains made: *A dull day. Business was dull at the beginning of the Account. Syn.* inactive.

duly properly, carefully: *Duly noted*, with special care. *Duly authorized*, properly. *I duly received your parcel*, in proper time.

dumb unable to move by its own power. *A dumb barge*, one without sails or engine. *A dumb waiter*, a stand of shelves or revolving trays for serving food at table.

Dumf. Dumfries and Galloway, Scotland.

dummy (1) a person who lends his name to a business deal in order to hide who the real buyer or seller is: *A dummy shareholder/director. Syn.* prête-nom. (2) an imitation of something, esp. for showing in a shop or shop-window: *A tailor's dummy*, of a human body, to show suits and dresses. *Dummy packages*, e.g. of cigarette packets. *Publisher's dummy*, a book consisting of pages of unprinted paper in a binding case to show what a new book will look like.

dummy tendering *see* collusive tendering.

dumping COM. in international trade, the practice of a producer or supplier, usu. a monopolist, who sells a product at a lower price in a foreign country than in the home market. If the higher home price subsidizes the export price, he enjoys an unfair advantage over producers in the foreign country and other exporters. Some countries practise or encourage dumping for the special purpose of getting a supply of certain foreign currencies. Cf. anti-dumping.

dun. dunnage.

dunnage SHIPG. loose material such as brushwood, mats, cloth, used in a ship's hold to protect cargo from damage by chafing (rubbing) or by water during the voyage. *Abbr.* dun.

duopoly ECON. THEORY the form of imperfect competition that exists in a market in which there are only two producers or sellers of a product or service. Cut-throat competition is the likely result; and this can only be stopped by the two sellers agreeing to share the market or to keep prices above a certain level. Cf. monopoly; oligopoly.

duopsony ECON. THEORY the form of imperfect competition that exists in a market in which there are only two buyers. Cf. monopoly; oligopsony.

dup. duplicate.

duplicate *n.* of a document, plan, etc., an exact copy; a second copy: *In duplicate*, two copies exactly the same *or* an original document with a (carbon) copy. Cf. triplicate, quadruplicate, etc. *Abbr.* dup.
v. (1) to make a duplicate, or to make several copies of a document, etc. (2) to cause something to be done twice, usu. wastefully: *To duplicate the work*.

duplicate book a book usu. of blank forms bound in sets of two, the original or top copy, when written up, being torn out and sent away, leaving the second or carbon or duplicate copy in the book to serve as a record. Cf. triplicate, etc. book. *Syn.* manifold book.

duplicate of exchange BKG. & COM. a second of exchange, the second copy of a bill of exchange drawn only in two parts. *See* bill (of exchange) in a set.

duplicate warrant *see* entry for free goods *under* customs entry.

duplicating machine *see* duplicator.

duplicating system ACCTS. a system of bookkeeping in which the ledger sheets are not kept in loose-leaf books but are stored in deep boxes or drawers. Entries are made direct to the ledger sheet, and a carbon copy is made on a journal or control sheet. This system is fast and accurate and can be adapted to give many other useful documents.

duplication (1) the act of duplicating. (2) the causing of something to be done twice over, usu. wastefully: *Duplication of effort/work/records*.

duplicator an office printing machine for duplicating letters and other documents. *Syn.* duplicating machine. *See* photocopier.

duplicity *see* double dealing.

Dur. Durham, England.

durable goods ECON. THEORY goods that are intended to be used over a period of time. They are of two kinds: capital or producer's goods, and consumer's goods. Changes in the demand for these types of goods are used in some theories of the trade cycle to explain the upswings and downswings in economic activity. *See also* consumer durables. *Opp.* nondurables.

duration the length of time during which something continues or lasts: *The duration of a lease/an emergency. A visit of short duration.*

duress LAW the use of force, or threats of force, of dishonour or other injury, to make a person do something. Normally, an act done, such as the signature of a contract, under duress has no legal effect and will not be supported by a court of law.

dust (*colloq.*) money.

dust bowl AGR. any area, but esp. one in western U.S.A., where drought (lack of rain), duststorms and bad farming methods have made the soil very poor.

Dutch auction COM. a kind of auction sale in which the auctioneer (seller) begins by calling a high price and gradually lowers it until he reaches a price at which someone is willing to buy. *Syn.* Chinese auction.

Dutch bargain COM. a deal in which one side gets all the advantage.

Dutch party a gathering of people for a meal or entertainment at which each person pays his own share of the cost. *Syn.* Dutch treat.

dutiable goods TAXN. & COM. goods on which duty, esp. customs duty, has to be paid. *Opp.* duty-free goods.

duty (1) something that every person is morally bound to do or not to do: *A citizen's duty to obey the law, to help the police, to pay his taxes. His duty not to disturb the peace, not to make a nuisance, etc. It is the duty of all parents to supervise the welfare of their children.* (2) something one owes to somebody that arises from one's position or employment: *An employer's duty to his employees. The directors' duty to the shareholders. A servant's duty to his master. The duties of a manager/cashier/guard, etc. On duty, actually working. Off duty, not officially working.* (3) TAXN. a government tax on certain goods and commodities such as a wide range of imports and some exports, called *customs duty, import duty, tariffs*; on some home-produced things such as drink and tobacco, petrol and fuel oil, called *excise duty. See* dutiable goods.

ad valorem duty *see* ad valorem.

countervailing duty *see under* countervailing.

customs duty a government tax on imports and exports of commodities in order partly to raise money for the expenses of government and partly to protect home industries from foreign competition. This duty is collected by the Customs at ports and airports and at customs posts on land frontiers. *See* import duty; tariffs; antidumping.

death duty *see under* death.

differential duty a rate of customs duty which differs on goods imported from one country, as compared with another, often the result of trade agreements. Cf. discriminating duty.

discriminating duty an import duty with a variable rate depending on the country of origin of the goods. Cf. differential duty.

estate duty *see* death duties.

excise duty *see* excise (2).

export duty a duty or tax charged on goods when leaving a country.

fixed duty *see* specific duty *below.*

import duty *see under* import.

matching duty *see* countervailing duty *under* countervailing.

primage duty in some countries, esp. Australia, a customs duty on certain classes of imports.

protective duty an import duty aimed at controlling the amount of imports of a particular commodity to protect home producers from foreign competition. *Syn.* protective tariff.

specific duty a tax based on a fixed sum of money for each unit of quantity or weight: *A duty of £1 per gallon of wine.* Cf. ad valorem duty. *Syn.* fixed duty.

stamp duty a tax on certain documents, such as the conveyance of a property. The tax is paid to the Inland Revenue, who then stamp the document.

transfer duty *see under* transfer.

duty-free COM. & TAXN. of goods, on which no duty is charged: *Duty-free cigarettes/wines/spirits/perfumes, etc.,* goods allowed into a country in small quantities duty-free if carried by a traveller for his own use. *Opp.* dutiable.

duty-free shop a shop selling duty-free goods to travellers, usu. at airports, ferry-ports or frontier posts and under close customs control.

duty of care *see under* care.

duty paid COM. in foreign trade price quotations in which, at the price quoted, the exporter is responsible for paying the import duty.

duty-paid value the total landed cost of imported goods after all charges and import duty have been paid.

D.W. dock warrant.

d.w. dead weight; delivered weight; dock warrant.

d.w.c. deadweight capacity.

dwt. pennyweight (in troy weight).

d.w.t. deadweight tons/tonnage.

DY Dahomey's international vehicle-registration letters.

dy. delivery.

D.Y., Dyd. dockyard.

dyeline process a cheap method of making copies of single-sided, transparent plans, etc. on to chemically-treated paper under a very strong light. *Syn.* diazo process.

dynamic economics ECON. THEORY a branch of economic science that examines and explains economic change and growth, not only of the national income but also of population or the work force, of capital accumulation and of technical (scientific and industrial) progress. Cf. static economics.

DZ Algeria's international vehicle-registration letters.

E

E Spain's international vehicle-registration letter.

E. East.

E£ Egyptian pound(s).

ea. each.

E.A.C. East African Community.

eagle a former gold coin of the U.S.A. of face value ten dollars. There were also: a *double eagle* ($20), a *half eagle* ($5) and a *quarter eagle* ($2.50). All bear the figure of an eagle.

EAK Kenya's international vehicle-registration letters.

e. & e. each and every.

E. & O.E. ACCTS. & COM. errors and omissions excepted, letters commonly printed at the foot of invoices to warn the customer that any mistakes or omissions may later be corrected.

e.a.o.n. except as otherwise noted.

early closing COM. in Britain, many shops are closed to customers by 13.00 hrs. on one week-day every week. The day of the week is fixed by the local government authority and may differ for different kinds of shops, different districts or different seasons of the year.

earmark COM. to set something aside for a special purpose: *To earmark goods in stock to meet an expected order. The money collected is earmarked for helping old people.*

earn COM. (1) to get something, esp. by working: *To earn a wage/a salary/ a living/ one's keep/ a livelihood.* Of a business or investment, to bring in a monetary gain: *His business earns him a good profit. My bonds earn me 5% interest. These shares earn a good dividend. The company earned less profit last year.* (2) to receive what one deserves, as reward or punishment: *His hard work earned the respect of his colleagues. The cheat earned the punishment he received.*

earned *adj.* that which has been worked for; deserved: *Earned leave. Earned income.*

earned income TAXN. in Britain, the income which, for tax purposes, one receives as a reward for work, and includes one's salary or wages; pension or retirement annuity; profits received from one's trade or profession and from an active partnership; royalties from patents and copyrights if one created them one-self. Most other income is treated as unearned and is usu. taxed more heavily than earned income. Cf. investment income; unearned income.

earned income allowance, wife's *see under* wife's.

earner a person who earns money by working: *A wage-earner.*

earnest *or* **earnest-money** COM. & IND. money given to the seller as a first payment by the buyer to show that he agrees to the contract of sale and intends to honour it; and the seller, too, by accepting the earnest, shows his agreement to be bound by the contract. A formal contract may allow the seller to keep the money if the buyer fails to perform his part. *Syn.* earnest-penny; handsel; token payment.

earning rate STK. EXCH. the rate at which a company earns profits, found by calculating the net profit as a percentage of the paid-up capital. This is not the same as the dividend rate.

earnings (1) COM. & IND. the total of the sums of money earned by an employee during a regular pay period such as a week or a month, including additional pay for overtime, bonuses, etc. (2) STK. EXCH. *see* distributable profit.

earnings basis TAXN. in Britain, the basis on which a taxpayer carrying on a trade is taxed, i.e. the tax will be based on sales, not on actual receipts of money in payment for those sales. Cf. cash basis.

earnings of management *see* wages of management.

earnings rule FIN. & TAXN. in Britain, a law by which the amount of the state retirement pension paid to men between the ages 65 and 70 and to women between the ages 60 and 65 whose earnings from employment are more than a certain figure per week, is reduced by £1 for every £1 earned, until at a certain level of earnings no pension at all is payable.

earnings yield *see under* yield.

earthquake (1) a natural shaking of the ground caused by movements in the earth's surface or by volcanic explosions, sometimes causing terrible damage and loss of lives. (2) INSCE. one of the special perils (risks) against which protection is given by an *earthquake clause* in most fire-insurance policies.

ease STK. EXCH. of prices, to become rather lower; to fall slightly: *Equities opened strong but some eased later.*

ease off, ease up to become much less: *The rush for mining shares has eased off/up lately.*

easement LAW a right which one person enjoys over the land of another, such as a right of way, or a right to a flow of water. A *positive easement* is a right to do something on another person's land. A *negative easement* is a right to prevent the owner of the land from doing something. Cf. profit à prendre.

East African Community (E.A.C.) an association of three countries, Kenya, Tanzania and Uganda, to form a customs union, to co-operate in the industrial development of the region, and to share the advantages of common services, such as airlines and railways. For political reasons, the Community has not proved to be the success that its members had hoped for.

East(ern) European Time the standard time in the time-zone of Eastern Europe, two hours ahead of Greenwich Mean Time and one hour ahead of Mid-European Time. The zone consists of Bulgaria, Finland, Greece and Turkey. *Abbr.* E.E.T.

Eastern (Standard) Time (E.S.T.) the time in the Eastern time-zone in North America, five hours behind Greenwich Mean Time and one hour ahead of Central Time.

Eastern Time the time in a time-zone in South America 4½ hours behind Greenwich Mean Time, consisting of Venezuela and Curaçao I.

East Germany *see under* Germany, German Democratic Republic.

East India Company, British ECON. HIST. a joint-stock company formed by royal charter in 1600 with a monopoly in trade with India and the East Indies. Dutch resistance in what is now Indonesia caused the British company to trade mainly with India, where it gradually got political and economic control of a great part of the country. The British Parliament took control of the company's political activities in 1784 and ended the monopoly in 1813. By 1834 the company had become the administrative agent in India of the British Government, but after the so-called Indian Mutiny in 1857 and the setting-up of the Indian Empire, the company lost all power and its existence ended in 1873.

East India Company, Dutch ECON. HIST. *in Dutch, Vereenigde Oostindische Compagnie (V.O.C.)*, formed in 1602 with a monopoly in trade in the Indian Ocean area. Well supported by the Dutch Government, it defeated the British and Portuguese in the East Indies, but its commercial power grew less and less until by the eighteenth century it was heavily in debt. It closed down in 1799.

East India Company, French ECON. HIST. *in French, la Compagnie des Indes Orientales*, formed in 1664 as the political and commercial agency of the French Government for the French colonies in India. Its attempts to defeat the power and influence of the British East India Company totally failed during the Seven Years' War (1756–63) and, abandoned by the French Government, it ceased to exist during the French Revolution of 1789.

East Mark *see* D.D.R. Mark.

easy not difficult; comfortable: *Easy money, money that is not difficult to earn. An easy-*

money policy, see cheap money. *Prices were easy,* slightly lower. *The market is easy,* supplies (of a commodity) are not difficult to get because there are few buyers. *Easy terms,* hire-purchase. *To be on Easy Street, (colloq.)* to have a pleasant, well-paid job.

EAT, EAZ international vehicle-registration letters of Tanzania (formerly Tanganyika and Zanzibar).

EAU Uganda's international vehicle-registration letters.

ebb tide SHIPG. the flow of the tide as it falls. *See* flood tide.

EC Ecuador's international vehicle-registration letters.

E.C. European (Economic) Community; East Central; East Coast; East Caribbean.

E.C.A. Economic Commission for Africa; European Co-operation Administration.

E.C.A.F.E. Economic Commission for Asia and the Far East.

ECar$ East Caribbean dollar.

E.C.E. Economic Commission for Europe.

E.C.G.D. Export Credits Guarantee Department.

E.C.L.A. Economic Commission for Latin America.

econometrician ECON. a person having special knowledge of econometrics, usu. employed in statistical departments of large financial, commercial and industrial organizations.

econometrics ECON. a relatively new branch of economics which scientifically measures economic facts and tests economic theories, using mathematics and statistical methods. With the help of computers, masses of economic data (facts) are analysed and the results are applied to financial problems in business such as forecasting, market research and industrial planning. *Syn.* mathematical economics.

economic ECON. (1) having to do with the production, distribution and consumption of wealth and income: *Economic development/planning/power/policy. The economic system.* (2) relating to the science of economics or to commerce and industry: *Economic activity/theory. The economic effects of taxation.*

economical saving money or expense wherever possible; careful, esp. with money or materials: *An economical cook/housewife/production process/budget.*

economic analysis *see* economic theory.

economic and monetary union (E.M.U.) ECON. the aim of the European Economic Community (E.E.C.) to have a single European currency, a single central bank and one body in control of monetary affairs.

Economic and Social Council (Ecosoc) a division of the United Nations that directs and encourages economic, social and cultural activities. Helping it are four regional Commissions,

E.C.A., E.C.A.F.E., E.C.E., E.C.L.A. and three functional Commissions serving special purposes: the Economic Commission, the Social Commission and the Commission on Human Rights. Cf. Economic and Social Committee (of the E.E.C.).

Economic Commission for Africa (E.C.A.) a regional agency of the United Nations, formed in 1958 with its central office in Addis Ababa, Ethiopia.

Economic Commission for Asia and the Far East (E.C.A.F.E.) an agency of the United Nations, formed in 1947 with its central office in Bangkok, Thailand.

Economic Commission for Europe (E.C.E.) a regional agency of the United Nations, formed in 1947 with its central office in Geneva.

Economic Commission for Latin America (E.C.L.A.) a regional agency of the United Nations, formed in 1948 with its central office in Santiago, Chile, and a branch office in Mexico City.

economic co-operation *see* O.E.C.D.

economic cost *see under* cost.

economic development ECON. the process of raising the income per head of the people of a country, esp. of an under-developed country, by increasing their production of goods and services.

Economic Development Committees *see* National Economic Development Council.

economic efficiency *see under* efficiency.

economic fluctuations *see* fluctuations; trade cycle *under* cycle.

economic geography ECON. a branch of study which deals with the geographical influences on the production, distribution and consumption of wealth. *Syn.* geonomics.

economic goods *see under* goods (7).

economic growth ECON. the rate at which the national income of a country increases.

economic history ECON. that branch of economics that deals with the various ways which Man has developed to satisfy his needs, esp. in regard to the growth of production, distribution and consumption of goods and services. It attempts to explain the growth of economic institutions such as banking, stock and commodity exchanges, transport and communications, insurance, international trade, and the effects of inventions and trade cycles.

economic indicator *see* business barometer.

economic nationalism *see* self-sufficiency.

economic planning *see under* planning.

economic rent *see under* rent.

economics ECON. the study of the natural laws governing the production, distribution and consumption of wealth. It examines and explains that part of Man's social and personal behaviour that is directed towards the satisfaction of his wants. *Syn.* political economy.

development economics a branch of economics that examines and explains the process of economic growth and the human and social organizations that make this growth possible.

home economics *see under* home.

institutional economics *see under* institutional.

Keynesian economics *see under* Keynesian.

managerial economics *see under* managerial.

new economics *see* Keynesian economics.

pure economics *see* economic theory.

welfare economics a branch of economics that studies and explains economic activity as a means of raising the standard of living and general social well-being of the people and is particularly concerned with economic efficiency. *See* Pigou, A.C.

economic sanctions *see under* sanctions.

economic system ECON. the particular way in which the economic activity in a country is organized, such as capitalism (the private-enterprise system) and socialism (a centrally-planned system). In between these there are the mixed economies.

economic theory ECON. that part of the study of economics that examines and explains the working of an economic system and how it is influenced by human behaviour, by the natural forces of the world, and by man-made institutions such as markets, laws, and governments. Cf. descriptive economics; applied economics. *Syn.* economic analysis; pure economics.

economies of scale ECON. & IND. the advantages to be got from large-scale production, esp. that of lower unit costs which make it possible to compete better in the market, to conquer a larger share of the market, and thus perh. to get some monopolistic control over prices. Cf. diseconomies of scale.

external economies those that affect a large part or the whole of a particular industry.

internal economies those that can be introduced within a single production unit such as a factory or a farm by better use of the factors of production, and by spreading over a larger number of articles produced the costs of managing, marketing, financing and developing the business.

economist ECON. a social scientist with special knowledge of economics, such as a teacher or writer on the subject or a person called a *business economist* who is employed by a business organization to forecast movements in prices and in the market demand for various products and services.

Economist, The a weekly journal published in London since 1843, known for the high quality of its articles on economic problems by leading economists.

économistes, les *see* Physiocrats.

economize (1) to use or spend as little as possible: *We must all economize on (in the use of)* *petrol/electricity/energy*, we must avoid waste. (2) to cut down expenses in order to save for the future: *By economizing, they saved the money to buy a house.*

economy ECON. (1) an organized system for the production, distribution and consumption of wealth (the needs of society): *A capitalist/socialist/free/market/mixed economy. An agricultural/industrial/expanding economy.* (2) the science of the management of natural resources and man-made economic organizations such as the business, trade and industries of a country: *The national economy.* See political economy *under* political. (3) taking care to avoid waste, to save money or material: *By exercising/practising strict economy he saved enough money to retire early. Economy of effort/words.* A particular act of saving money: *If we make these economies we shall soon pay our debts.* Syn. thrift.

economy class TRANSPT. & TOUR. the cheapest class of travel by air and sea, with lower standards of comfort than in the first class.

Ecosoc Economic and Social Council.

E.C.S.C. the European Coal and Steel Community.

Ecuador a republic in the north-west of South America, pop. 6.4 million approx. (1971); capital, Quito, pop. 650,000 approx.; language, Spanish; currency unit, the sucre, divided into 100 centavos. Member, O.A.S.

ed. edition; editor; edited by.

E.D. ex dividend.

E.D.C. Economic Development Committee.

edge (1) STK. EXCH. to advance slowly; to move forward gradually: *Prices edged up about a quarter of a point.* (2) COM. (*colloq.*) an advantage: *To have the edge on somebody*, to have a competitive advantage.

Edgeworth Francis Ysidro (1845–1926), Irish mathematician and economist, Professor of Political Economy, London University and later at Oxford University. His mathematical ability applied to problems in economic theory led him to introduce the idea of indifference curves, set out in his work *Mathematical Psychics* (1881). His *Theory of Monopoly* (1897) and *Theory of Distribution* (1904) further built up his reputation as an advanced thinker in statistical and mathematical method in the study of economics.

edit to prepare, check, correct and arrange written matter, photos, etc. for a book, magazine or newspaper. To check and arrange recorded material on magnetic tape or film for the radio, television and cinema.

edition a word that has several meanings even within the book trade: (1) one of several printings of a book, etc. printed at different times each with some substantial changes or additions. (2) one of several printings which are exactly the same, more properly called impressions. (3) a particular form in which a book, etc. is produced: *The quarto editions of Shakespeare. A thin-paper edition of the Bible.* (4) of a newspaper, one of several printings made at different times during a day or a night: *The early/provincial/late/final editions.*

editor a person who edits written or recorded matter. Of a book, a person responsible for collecting, choosing and preparing articles (contributions) written by a number of writers (contributors). Of a newspaper or magazine, the editor who is in charge of and is responsible for the contents; he is sometimes called the editor-in-chief, controlling other editors such as the *sports/literary/art/fashion editors.* See City editor *under* City.

sub-editor an assistant editor.

E.D.P. electronic data processing.

educational policy *see under* insurance policy.

education, commercial *see* commerce; commercial college.

E.E. errors excepted.

E.E.C. European Economic Community, the Common Market.

E.E.T. East(ern) European Time.

effect *n.* (1) a result, esp. one produced by a cause or agency. *Cause and effect.* Power to produce a result: *Efforts to save the company were of no effect.* (2) the state of being in operation: *The new law took/came into effect on 1 January. In effect*, in operation *or* in reality, in truth. *With effect from . . .*, on and from (a certain date).

effects *pl.* goods; personal, movable property: *Personal effects. Movable effects. To leave no effects*, to die leaving nothing.

no effects BKG. words written or stamped by a banker on a dishonoured cheque.

v. (1) to make: *To effect a payment.* (2) INSCE. to be bound by: *To effect a policy of insurance.* (3) IND. REL. to bring about, produce: *To effect a compromise.*

effective *adj.* having an effect: *Our advertising is effective in increasing our sales. To become effective*, to begin to have an effect. *Effective date*, the date on which something begins to operate, e.g. a new law, or a new set of prices.

cost-effective *see under* cost.

effective demand *see under* demand.

effective tax rate TAXN. in Britain, the average rate at which a person pays income tax on his gross (total) income after allowing for tax-free allowances.

effects not cleared BKG. words written or stamped on a cheque which the drawer's bank is returning unpaid because, although the drawer has paid cheques into his account to a sufficient value, these have not yet been cleared and the balance in the account is not enough to meet the cheque.

efficiency ECON. the ability of a person or organization to produce a desired result. A way of working that is satisfactory. *See also* tax efficiency *under* tax.

economic efficiency the ability of a manufacturing plant to produce at a low unit cost or market value, as distinguished from technical efficiency, which is effectiveness of a different kind. Things that are technically perfect may be economically inefficient because few buyers can afford their prices.

industrial efficiency the ability of an industry or a part of an industry, to produce goods at an economic price, i.e. a price that the public is prepared to pay. To compare the efficiency of units within an industry, checks are continually made of such pointers as output per worker, and profit per pound of capital invested.

technical efficiency the ability of a manufacturing unit, such as a machine, to produce an article or commodity of high quality, without regard to the cost of production. Cf. economic efficiency.

efficiency bonus *see* bonus (2).

efficient able to work well, to get things done quickly and with good effect.

E.F.T.A. European Free Trade Association.

e.g. (*Latin*: exempli gratia) for example.

Egypt an Arab republic in north-eastern Africa, pop. 36 million approx. (1973); capital, Cairo, pop. 5.5 million approx.; language, Arabic; currency unit, the Egyptian pound (E£), divided into 100 piastres or 1000 millièmes. Member, O.A.U., Arab League.

E.I.B. European Investment Bank.

Eire *see* Ireland.

ejection *see* expulsion.

ekpwele the standard currency unit of Equatorial Guinea, divided into 100 centimos. *Also* peseta Guineana.

elastic demand *see* elasticity of demand.

elasticity ECON. THEORY a concept (basic idea) of great importance in economic analysis; it concerns the amount by which one variable will change as the result of a change in another variable. If a change of one per cent in the second variable results in a change of *more than* one per cent in the first variable, the effect is *elastic*. If it is *less than* one per cent it is *inelastic*. *See* elasticity of demand; elasticity of supply.

elasticity of demand ECON. THEORY the degree to which the demand for a commodity is sensitive to, or affected by, a change in price. If a small change of price results in a large change in demand, demand is said to be *elastic*; if a large change in price leads to only a small change in demand, demand is said to be *inelastic*.

elasticity of substitution ECON. THEORY the degree to which one economic good can be substituted for (used in place of) another. For ex-

ample, in producing a certain commodity, if the price of labour increases and the price of capital (interest) remains unchanged, it may be possible to increase the amount of machinery used and to reduce the amount of labour employed. The extent to which one factor (in this case capital) can be substituted for the more expensive factor (labour) will depend on how quickly the advantages of doing so are outweighed by such disadvantages as having too many machines and not enough labour. *See* marginal productivity.

elasticity of supply ECON. THEORY the degree to which the supply of a commodity is sensitive to, or affected by, a change in price. If an increase in price of one per cent results in an increase in supply of more than one per cent, the supply is said to be *elastic*. If the supply increases by less than one per cent, it is said to be *inelastic*.

elect *v.* (1) to choose, esp. by vote, for an office: *To elect a chairman/director(s) of a company/officer(s) of a society. I was elected a shop steward.* (2) to decide in favour of, to choose, a course of action: *He elected to go to prison rather than pay a fine. He elected to join the family business.*

adj. chosen to be the next holder of a (high) office when the present holder retires from it: *The chairman-elect; the President-elect* (the word elect follows the name of the office).

election the choice of a person by vote to hold an office: *The election of officers. Parliamentary/local elections.*

electronic data processing *see* data processing.

eleemosynary to do with the giving of money to the poor.

elevator (1) (U.S.A.) a lift. (2) special buildings and machinery for storing and handling grain, such as wheat, in very large quantities: *A grain elevator.*

eligible desirable; worthy of trust: *An eligible bachelor*, an unmarried man who would be a good husband.

eligible paper BKG. bank bills and fine trade bills (of exchange), i.e. bills of the highest trustworthiness and therefore fit to be discounted by the Bank of England.

eliminate to remove completely: *To eliminate competition/errors (mistakes).*

élite (1) the best persons in a group or in society: *A government chosen from the élite of the party.* (2) a size of type on some typewriters, having 12 letters to the inch, each letter being 10 points (0.139 in.) high. Cf. pica.

El Salvador a republic on the Pacific coast of Central America, pop. 3,500,000 approx. (1971); capital, San Salvador, pop. 350,000 approx.; language, Spanish; currency unit, the colón, *pl.* colones, divided into 100 centavos. Member, O.A.S., O.C.A.S., Rio Pact.

E.M.A. European Monetary Agreement.

emalangeni the fractional currency unit of Swaziland. 100 emalangeni = 1 lijangeni.

emancipation the act of setting people free from some cruel or illegal treatment: *The emancipation of slaves. The emancipation of women. Catholic emancipation. See* abolition.

embargo (1) COM. a government order forbidding the import or export of certain goods. (2) SHIPG. an order by a government when it expects war to begin soon, preventing ships of possible enemy countries from entering or leaving its ports. (3) IND. REL. action by a trade union for political reasons, forbidding its members to handle goods imported from or to be exported to a foreign country. *Pl.* -oes.

embark (1) SHIPG. *v.i.* to go on board a ship: *Passengers will embark at 11.00 hrs.*; (2) SHIPG. *v.t.* to put or take on board a ship: *The ferry embarked 50 cars and 200 passengers. Opp.* disembark. *N.* embarkation. (3) to start some special activity: *He embarked on a risky venture/a banking career.*

embassy (1) a group of persons, headed by an ambassador, sent to represent the government of one country in another country. (2) the office in which they work. (3) the house in which an ambassador lives. *The British/Egyptian/Syrian Embassy.* Cf. legation.

embezzlement LAW the crime of an employee in a trusted position who dishonestly puts to his own use money intended for his employer. *Syn.* defalcation; misappropriation; breach of trust; fraudulent conversion; peculation.

emboss to cause (writing, type, a pattern, etc.) to have a raised surface, esp. by pressing: *To emboss the company's seal on a deed. Embossed notepaper*, having the printing on it raised, not flat.

emend to remove mistakes from: *To emend a document.*
  emendation *n.* the act of emending; also the actual corrections or alterations. Cf. amend.

emergency (1) a sudden and unexpected danger; a serious situation needing immediate action.
  emergency reserve(s) FIN. money held ready for use in an emergency, usu. in the form of cash or balances in banks and building societies.

emerging countries *see* under-developed countries.

emigrant a person who emigrates: *An emigrant ship*, one that is intended to carry emigrants as passengers. Cf. immigrant.

emigrate to leave one's own country to settle permanently in another country. Cf. to immigrate.

emigration the act of emigrating. *Emigration officer*, a person representing an overseas country who finds and helps emigrants to settle in the country which he represents. Cf. immigration. *Emigration society*, one of several organizations formed to encourage people to emigrate from Britain, esp. to Australia, New Zealand and Canada.

emirate a country ruled by an Emir (Muslim ruler).

emolument(s) FIN. usu. in *pl.*, the financial rewards earned for their services esp. by persons in the professions and in government office, such as the fees received by a lawyer or doctor, the pay and other benefits of a public official, and the earnings of company directors who are not employees of the companies concerned. Cf. salary.

employ *v.* (1) to use (something): *We employ modern tools in our factory. How much capital is employed in the business? You must employ more skill in your work. How do you employ your time?* (2) to use a person's services; to put someone to work, esp. for payment: *They employ 20 salesmen. The labourers are employed in/on ploughing/sowing/reaping. There is not enough work to keep them employed.*
  n. employment; the state of being employed: *I was once in his employ*, I worked for him.

employee (1) a person employed, esp. as a regular worker; a person who works for another for money (called salary or wages). (2) LAW a person under a contract of service or apprenticeship.

employee participation IND. REL. & MAN. giving a place on the board of directors of a company to one or more representatives of its employees so that the workers may have a part in the direction of the company's operations and plans.

employees' amenities IND. REL. extra rewards given by an employer to employees in addition to wages and salaries, such as free or cheap meals, arrangements for sports and games, and transport to and from work. Cf. fringe benefits.

employer a person or organization who regularly employs one or more persons to work for a money payment.

employers' liability policy *see under* insurance policy.

employers' organizations IND. REL. associations of employers mainly for the purpose of bargaining with trade unions on wages and conditions of work, and also to represent employers in discussions with public organizations and the government. *See* Confederation of British Industries. *Syn.* trade associations.

employer's surplus *see* producer surplus.

employment (1) the state of being employed, of having paid work to do. *Opp.* unemployment. (2) the kind of work on which a person is, or can be, employed: *What employment are you looking for? My employment as a waiter is seasonal.*

employment agency *or* **bureau** COM. & IND. a business which provides a service to employers by introducing persons suitable for employment. The agency receives a fee from the employer if the introduction results in a person being employed.

employment, contract of *see under* contract.

employment, discharge from *see under* discharge.

employment exchange *see* job centre.

employment, full *see* full employment.

employment, security of *see* security (1).

Employment Theory ECON. THEORY that branch of economics that studies and explains the causes of changes in the level of employment in the economy. *See* full employment.

emporium COM. (1) an important trading centre, usu. a town such as London, Frankfurt, Paris. (2) a large shop selling many different kinds of goods. *Syn.* mart.

empower to give power (to somebody) to act: *I empowered an agent to sell my house. He was empowered by the board to act for the company.*

empties empty containers which are to be used again.

E.M.S. European Monetary System, *see* Snake.

E.M.U. Economic and Monetary Union.

encash FIN. & BKG. to change (a cheque, postal order, etc.) into cash. To receive money in the form of cash in exchange for giving up a claim to money. *Syn.* to cash. *Adj.* encashable.

encashment FIN. & BKG. the act of encashing.

encashment credit an arrangement that makes it possible for a customer with a bank account in one place to encash cheques up to an agreed amount at a bank in another place.

encl., enclo. enclosure; enclosed.

enclosure (1) a thing enclosed in (put inside) a letter. (U.S.A.) inclosure. (2) ECON. HIST. & AGR. the practice, which had important effects on the agricultural system, of enclosing and taking possession of areas of land formerly considered to be common land. In England this process was used first in the fifteenth and sixteenth centuries to obtain more pasture (grassland) to support the wool trade, and again in the eighteenth and nineteenth centuries to form fields that were larger and more economically cultivated.

encumber to hinder with difficulties: *She is encumbered with too much luggage/debt. His estate is encumbered with mortgages. He encumbered his property with mortgages.*

encumbrance LAW a charge or liability on property such as a mortgage: *Free of all encumbrances,* there are no mortgages or other charges on the property referred to. *Also* incumbrance.

Encyclopédistes ECON. HIST. a group of social thinkers led by Diderot and d'Alembert in France in the mid-eighteenth century who wrote articles for the great French Encyclopedia using scientific argument and refusing to accept many old ideas and teachings. They were very much attacked by the Roman Catholic Church and by the French King and Government, but greatly influenced the new schools of thought that were developing before and during the French Revolution.

end *n.* (1) the last part; the furthest limit: *The end of the risk/road/a journey/contract/period of time.* To make (both) ends meet, to manage with difficulty to live within one's income. (2) STK. EXCH. *The end of the Account,* the last day of one of the credit periods allowed on dealings between members of the Stock Exchange. *See* Account, The. *Syn.* Account Day; Settlement, The. (3) an aim; a purpose: *The end of all business activity is to make a profit. He uses the company's property for his own ends,* for his own purposes and advantage.

ends *pl.* ECON. the various purposes for which the factors of production (land, labour, capital) can be used. The ends being unlimited in number and the factors of production being relatively scarce, the producer has to choose ends on which to use the factors he can employ.

end-consumer COM. the person who actually uses and consumes a product. *Syn.* end-user.

end-of-season sale *see under* sale.

endorse to sign one's name on the back (of a cheque, bill of exchange, etc.). *Syn.* indorse (esp. in U.S.A.).

endorsing stamp a rubber stamp used for printing by hand (using an *endorsing pad* and *endorsing ink*) such information as numbers, dates, receipts, addresses, and directions.

endorsee BKG. the person in whose favour, or to whose advantage, a cheque, bill of exchange, bill of lading, etc. is endorsed. Cf. endorser. *Syn.* indorsee.

endorsement (1) LAW a signature needed on a document to make it effective in law. (2) LAW a short account of the contents written on the outside of a folded document. (3) LAW a note made on a driving licence officially recording that the holder has been convicted (found guilty) of a motoring offence. (4) INSCE. any writing added to a policy or cover-note which records a change in the conditions or adds a new condition to those in the main document. (5) BKG. & COM. writing signed by the holder on the back of a bill of exchange or a cheque which has been drawn as payable to order, making it payable to the holder who has signed it. If there is more than one endorsement, it is payable to the holder who signed last. *Syn.* indorsement; (Scotland) indorsation.

accommodation endorsement *see under* accommodation.

blank endorsement on a bill of exchange, an

endorsement which does not state that it must be paid to, or to the order of, any named party. It will therefore be paid to the person who presents it. *Syn.* general endorsement; endorsement in blank. Cf. special endorsement.

conditional endorsement on a bill of exchange, an endorsement in which the endorser makes a condition such as 'Pay Thomas Smith or order, on his arrival in London'. The paying bank will usu. take no notice of the condition and will pay the bill when normally due, as if the condition did not exist.

general endorsement *see* blank endorsement *above.*

qualified endorsement one by which the endorser limits or refuses his personal liability. *See* without recourse.

restrictive endorsement on a bill of exchange, an endorsement which forbids further negotiation of the bill, such as 'Pay Thomas Smith only', or 'Pay John Brown for the account of Richard Green'.

special endorsement on a bill of exchange, an endorsement which states the name of the person to whom, or to whose order, the bill is payable.

endorsement in blank *see* blank endorsement *under* endorsement.

endorser BKG. the person who, as payee, endorses (writes his name on the back of) a cheque or bill of exchange. Cf. endorsee. *See* endorsement. *Syn.* indorser.

endowment FIN. money or property given upon trust so as to produce a regular and permanent income for the person or organization to whom it is given. Such gifts are often made to charity or to a widow or daughter.

endowment policy *see under* insurance policy.

endowment policy system (of depreciation) ACCTS. a method of providing for depreciation by arranging with an insurance company for a policy which will produce a payment equal to the original cost of the asset, this payment being due when the asset is expected to become no longer useful. This method is esp. used for wasting assets.

straight line method this charges each year an equal sum calculated by dividing the original cost of the asset (less any expected scrap value) by the number of years of the expected useful life (past and future) of the asset. It is the most usual method in U.S.A. and Britain.

reducing balance method *see under* reducing balance.

end-product IND. the main article or commodity that results after the last of a series of processes or operations. Cf. by-product.

end-user *see* end-consumer.

enemy (1) a person or country with whom one is at war: *The Queen's enemies* (in bills of lading) those countries on which Britain has declared

war. (2) MAR. INSCE. any countries which are at war with each other, not necessarily with one's own country.

enfaced bond *see* assented bond *under* bond, *n.*

Eng. England; English; Engineer(ing).

engage (1) to arrange to employ: *To engage staff/a secretary.* (2) to hire accommodation, a vehicle, etc.: *I have engaged a bus/taxi/hotel room/hall.* (3) to employ (oneself) in: *He engages in business/politics/sports/crime. The factory is engaged in secret work.* (4) to promise; to bind oneself: *He engaged to serve me as an apprentice for five years. She is engaged to be married.* (5) to be in use: *The (telephone) line/ toilet is engaged,* being used temporarily by somebody else. *Syn.* (U.S.A.) busy.

engagement, without *see* without engagement.

Engel's Law ECON. a basic idea first put forward by Ernst Engel, a German statistician (1821–96), that poor families spend a higher proportion of their income on food than richer families.

engineering insurance *see under* insurance, classes and kinds of.

engineer surveyor *see* Lloyd's surveyor.

England, Bank of *see* Bank of England.

English ton *see* long ton *under* ton.

engross (1) LAW to write or type a document, such as a deed, in a form ready for execution, i.e. ready to be made effective by being signed, sealed and delivered. (2) COM. esp. in U.S.A., to obtain monopolistic control of a market by buying up the whole supply of a commodity. *Syn.* corner. *See* forestalling.

engrossment LAW the actual copy of a document, such as a deed, that has been made ready for execution. *See* engross.

enhance to increase, esp. in value or appearance: *Dry weather has enhanced the price of vegetables. Designers enhance the attractiveness of products. N.* enhancement.

enjoyment LAW the use of a legal right: *Enjoyment of peaceful possession of one's property.*

enquire (1) to ask for information: *Enquire who he is/how he is. Enquire about/after his health. Enquire for this brand of goods in the shops,* ask for, try to find. *Enquire into an accident,* look into and examine the causes. (2) STK. EXCH. of a security, *enquired for,* asked about, looked for, in demand. *Syn.* inquire.

enquirer a person who enquires, who asks for information. *Syn.* inquirer.

enquiries before contract LAW the questions on a number of matters to which a solicitor has to obtain answers before his client, the buyer of a house, can safely sign the contract of sale. The most important questions relate to the seller's title or right to sell the house. *Syn.* preliminary enquiries.

enquiry (1) the act of asking for information: *I found out by enquiry,* by asking. *On enquiry,* *he obtained our address*, when he asked. (2) a question; a request for information: *We are receiving many enquiries about our tours/products/prices.* *A public enquiry*, a formal examination by persons in authority of (*a*) the causes that led to an event of public importance or (*b*) a proposed new development such as a major road. (3) COM. a request for a quotation, i.e. a request to be told the price and conditions of delivery, etc. before placing an order for the goods. *Syn.* inquiry.

enquiry agent *see* credit agency.

enquiry office *see under* office.

ensilage *see* silage.

entail LAW a condition placed on the holder of land that the ownership shall pass only to a stated line of persons, usu. the eldest son of the eldest son, so that the land shall always stay in the family. *See* fee tail *under* fee.

entd. entered.

enter (1) to go or come into: *To enter a building.* (2) to join: *He entered the firm in 1930.* (3) to put one's name down for an examination or a competition. (4) to make a record in a book or list, esp. an account book: *To enter an amount in the ledger account. To enter up an account,* to bring it up to date; to make it complete. (5) to become bound by: *To enter into an agreement.* To start; to carry on: *He entered into/upon negotiations for the sale of the business. To enter bids,* in bargaining. (6) to present formally, esp. to some authority: *To enter an action/writ/plea in the courts. To enter goods with the Customs.*

enterprise (1) the quality (in a businessman) of commercial energy and daring, and a willingness to take financial, esp. uninsurable, risks. It is considered by many economists to be one of the factors of production, along with land, labour and capital. (2) an industrial or commercial organization. (3) an economic system which allows a degree of freedom to the private businessman.

free enterprise an economic system in which private persons are free to own capital and to organize their businesses as they wish on condition that they obey certain laws intended to protect society from harm by dishonest or greedy people. *Syn.* capitalism; private enterprise.

private enterprise an economic system in which private persons are entirely free to own all kinds of property and to carry on any commercial or industrial activity, the state interfering as little as possible in the running of the economy. *Syn.* capitalism; free enterprise.

public enterprise a publicly-owned commercial or industrial organization that performs some essential service, such as transport, or produces some essential commodity, such as coal, that could be (and in the past often was) per-

formed or produced by privately-owned organizations. *Syn.* state enterprise.

state enterprise *see* public enterprise *above.*

enterpriser *see* entrepreneur.

enterprising possessing the qualities of energy, daring and readiness to take financial risks in a commercial or industrial activity: *An enterprising builder/trader/manufacturer.*

entertainment COM. & IND. in business, the giving of food, drink and amusement to guests, esp. to special customers, suppliers and visitors from abroad, for the purpose of making business deals easier to complete.

entertainment account ACCTS. the account to which the costs of entertainment are charged.

entertainment allowance MAN. a sum of money given regularly to an employee from which to pay for the entertainment of his employer's business guests.

entertainment expenses *see under* expenses.

entertainment shares *see* amusement shares.

entrepôt *n.* COM. (*French*) a warehouse; a commercial or trading centre where goods are collected, temporarily stored and then sent out by land, sea or air, to be sold in other markets. Usu. a town or a district having a port. *Adj. An entrepôt port. Entrepôt trade. Pron.* ontrepo.

entrepreneur (1) ECON. THEORY a person who organizes the factors of production, land, labour and capital, to produce and sell goods, often in anticipation of demand, in the expectation of receiving a profit. He is a basic concept (idea) in economics, being the planner and risk-taker, and is considered by many economists to form a fourth factor of production called *enterprise*, without which the other three cannot be effective. *Pron.* Ontreprenur. *Syn.* enterpriser. *See* enterprise. *Adj.* entrepreneurial. (2) MAN. a person, usu. the owner, who organizes, finances and manages a commercial or industrial organization in the expectation of making a profit.

entrust to put, place (something) in somebody's care: *I entrust my money to my bankers. He entrusted me with the job of reorganizing the factory. Also* intrust.

entry (1) ACCTS. *see* double entry; single entry; closing entry. (2) LAW the act of entering a property for the purpose of claiming and defending one's rights in it.

entry, bill of *see* bill of entry.

entry, captain's *see under* captain.

entry, customs *see* customs entry.

entry visa *see under* visa.

eq. equal; equivalent.

equality of sacrifice TAXN. a basic idea in the theory of taxation, that in charging taxes there should be equal sacrifice by all.

equalization fund *see* exchange equalization account.

equalization grant *see* rate-deficiency grant *under* grant.

equal pay IND. the guiding rule that men and women should earn equal pay for work of equal value. The equal-pay movement started after the Second World War, and in 1970 a law was passed by the British Parliament making it an offence for an employer to pay a person of one sex more than a person of the other for doing the same kind of work.

equated time *see* average date.

equation of exchange *see* Fisher Equation.

Equator on the map, a line round the earth through points or places that are an equal distance from the North and South Poles, latitude 0°. *Syn.* The Line (*colloq.*)

Equatorial Guinea a small republic on the west coast of Central Africa, pop. 305,000 approx. (1974); capital, Malabo (formerly Santa Isabel) on the island of Fernando Po, pop. 20,000 approx.; language, Spanish; currency unit, the ekpwele or peseta Guineana, divided into 100 céntimos. Member, O.A.U.

equilibrium ECON. THEORY a basic concept (idea) much used in economic argument: a state of balance, when all the economic forces present in a situation have an equal influence and there is no tendency to change. Thus, the price of a commodity is in equilibrium when the total demand is just satisfied by the total supply. This price is called the *equilibrium price*; and so long as the total demand and the total supply of the commodity remain equal, the equilibrium price will remain unchanged. *See* Cambridge School. *Opp.* disequilibrium.

general equilibrium a state of balance in all the many markets that make up the economic system. Economic theory studies the effect that e.g. a change of price of one commodity may have on the prices of other commodities before a state of general equilibrium is reintroduced.

partial equilibrium a state of balance in the market for a particular commodity. Economic theory studies the effect of a change e.g. of price, in that particular market only, supposing that no changes take place in other markets. *Syn.* particular equilibrium.

particular equilibrium *see* partial equilibrium above.

Equi-Marginal Returns, Law of *see* Substitution, Law of.

equipment things needed for a special purpose: *Fire-fighting equipment. Office equipment.*

equitable assets *see* assets (2).

equitable lien *see under* lien.

equitable mortgage *see under* mortgage.

equities STK. EXCH. ordinary shares in limited liability companies, so called because they carry a right to a share in the equity of the company. *See* equity of a company. *Syn.* ordinary shares.

equity LAW a branch of English and American law consisting of rules based on the idea that fairness and justice are more important than common law. Thus, in the settling of legal actions, if there is a disagreement between the rules of law and equity, equity must be the stronger, and the courts will decide accordingly.

equity capital *see under* capital.

equity-linked policy *see under* insurance policy.

equity of a company (1) STK. EXCH. the right possessed by the holders of ordinary shares or stock in a limited liability company to receive a part of the balance remaining of the accumulated profits and total assets of the company after paying all prior charges, such as creditors, debenture-holders and preference shareholders. (2) ordinary stock or shares in a company.

equity of redemption FIN. the right of a mortgagor (borrower) to regain possession of his property when he has repaid the money lent, after giving reasonable notice to the mortgagee (lender).

equity of taxation LAW & TAXN. a basic legal rule that taxes should be charged on members of the public as fairly and justly as possible, and that they should be based on equality of sacrifice and ability to pay. *See* equality of sacrifice.

equity, owners' *see* net worth.

equity share *see under* share; *also* equity of a company.

equiv. equivalent.

equivalent *adj.* equal in some respect, such as in value, effect, importance: *A distribution/dividend/yield equivalent to 10%. One pound is equivalent to 100 pence.*

n. that which is equal: *One kilogram is the equivalent of 2.2 pounds avoirdupois.*

eraser (1) a piece of special rubber or plastic for rubbing out writing or typewriting. *We stock and sell pencil/ink/typewriter erasers.* (2) a knife used for scraping away writing.

erasure (1) writing or typewritten matter that has been rubbed out or scraped away. *Erasures are not allowed in account books. Corrections and erasures must be initialled.* (2) removal of recorded material from magnetic tape, etc.

ergonometrics IND. the scientific measurement of the amount of work done by a worker in a factory, mine, etc.

ergonomics IND. the study of the ways in which human beings do their work and the means by which those ways may be improved to make work more productive. In large production units these improvements consist mainly in giving the worker pleasant and comfortable surroundings, more interesting jobs to perform and special tools, equipment and training to make the work easier to do. *Syn.* human-factor engineering.

E.R.N.I.E. Electronic Random Number Indicator Equipment. *See* premium savings bond.

error a mistake: *An arithmetical error. An error of addition/calculation/judgment/navigation. Human/clerical error. To correct/adjust/rectify an error. In error*, by mistake; wrongly: *We regret that the article was sent/dispatched/invoiced/debited/credited/returned in error.*

posting error *or* **error of posting** ACCTS. one of several kinds of error made in book-keeping: *Error of commission*, when the wrong account or the wrong amount has been debited or credited. *Error of omission*, when an entry has been omitted entirely from the books. *Error of principle*, when an entry has been made in an entirely wrong kind of account, such as a liability entered as a profit. *See* trial balance; reversal of entries.

errors and omissions excepted *see* E. & O.E.

escalate to increase in quantity or value, like the upward movement of an escalator (moving staircase). *The turnover of his business is escalating. His pension escalates by 3% per annum. Our costs, and therefore our prices, are escalating in this period of inflation.* Cf. rise, *v.*; rocket. *Opp.* de-escalate.

escalator bond *see under* bond, *n.*

escalator clause COM. in a contract, a clause that provides for the price to be adjusted (changed) under certain stated conditions, such as an increase in the cost of labour and materials. Such a clause is often included in a contract in times of rapid inflation.

escape clause LAW in a contract, a clause that, in certain stated conditions, allows one party to be free of certain of his duties under the contract, or to be no longer bound at all by it.

escrow LAW a written agreement such as a contract, deed or bond that has been formally delivered by one of the parties to an independent person to be held in trust and to be delivered to the other party only when he has performed some stated duty, such as the payment of a sum of money. While the document is held in trust by the independent person it is said to be *in escrow*. *Pron.* escro.

escudo (1) the standard currency unit of Portugal and of some present or former Portuguese territories such as the Cape Verde Islands and São Thomé & Principe, divided into 100 centavos. (2) the standard currency unit of Chile, divided into 100 centesimos.

Esq. Esquire.

Esquire in Britain, strictly a title given to gentlemen next in rank below a knight; but now used only in abbreviated form Esq. placed after the name and as a polite custom instead of Mr, Dr, etc. *Address letters to him as: John Smith, Esq., Barrister-at-Law; but when you speak to him call him Mr Smith.*

Ess. Essex, England.

essence of a contract LAW the essentially important condition, being the main purpose of the contract. If such a condition is broken, the party harmed may treat the contract as no longer being in force and may bring an action in the courts for damages for breach of contract. *See* breach of contract.

E.S.T. Eastern Standard Time.

establish to set up in permanent form; to begin building or forming: *A business established in 1724 is an old-established business. He established himself in banking*, became a successful banker. *To establish good/friendly/cordial relations with customers/staff/suppliers/one's bank manager. Syn.* to found.

establishment (1) COM. & IND. a business organization, esp. a large successful concern employing many people. (2) the administrative organization such as staff, buildings and services, needed to support the work of a business concern. *Establishment charges*, the expenses of running such an organization. *Syn.* overheads. (3) a large private household employing a number of servants: *A large private establishment.* (4) the act of establishing: *The board decided on the establishment of a branch in Cairo.*

Establishment, The in Britain, a broad combination of persons in high positions who tend to be an unofficial ruling class and are considered by many to have too much influence in public affairs.

estate (1) LAW an interest in, or ownership of, land. *Syn.* legal estate.

freehold estate land owned totally and completely, without a fixed limit in time.

leasehold estate land held for a fixed number of years under a lease, sometimes renewable for further periods.

life estate an interest in land for the owner's lifetime only.

personal estate *see under* personal.

real estate *see under* real.

(2) LAW the property (considered as a whole) of a person who has died, or of a bankrupt. (3) an area of land which has been planned and developed by building houses (*a housing estate*), or factories (*an industrial estate*), or warehouses and offices (*a trading estate*). *Syn.* industrial park (U.S.A.). (4) AGR. a large area of land where useful trees are grown: *A tea/ rubber estate. Syn.* plantation. (5) an area of land forming a single property: *He owns an estate in Scotland.*

estate agent COM. a person who acts as agent for another in buying, selling, letting and renting land and buildings and who, for a fee or commission, provides certain services such as managing leased property, collecting rents, making surveys and valuing properties. *Syn.* house agent; land agent; (U.S.A.) realtor.

estate duty *see* death duties.

estate manager *see* land agent (2).

estate tax *see under* tax.

esteem *v.* (1) to set a high value on; to regard with favour: *I esteem him highly. Thank you for your esteemed order*, a polite expression now little used. (2) to consider; regard: *We esteem your complaint unjustified.*
n. great respect: *He was held in (high) esteem by his colleagues.*

estimate *n.* (1) a probable figure of size, cost, time, etc. arrived at by any method, from guessing to careful calculation. (2) a statement of probable cost of supplying certain stated goods or services, made in the hope of getting an order. *Syn.* a quotation; a quote.
v. to work out, to arrive at a probable figure: *The builders estimate a delay of three weeks. I estimate that you owe me £75. The estimated cost of production is £2 per article.*

estimator IND. & COM. a person who prepares estimates, esp. of costs of production.

estoppel LAW a rule of evidence which prevents a person from saying that a formal statement which he made earlier is untrue, or from claiming that facts which he formerly said were true are untrue. He is said to be estopped from denying (saying the opposite to) what he said earlier.

estuarine port SHIPG. a port at the mouth of a river.

ET Egypt's international vehicle-registration letters.

et al. (*Latin*: et alii *or* alia) and others.

etc. (*Latin*: et cetera) and the others; and the rest; and so on.

ethical goods ADVTG. certain medical goods that are advertised only in medical magazines and newspapers and not to the general public. Such goods are usu. the products of companies that have patents to manufacture them.

ethics (1) the study of right and wrong behaviour. (2) a set of moral rules, esp. those that guide members of a profession or of an organized group of businessmen, such as stockbrokers, to deal honestly and responsibly with the public and with each other. *Professional/ legal/medical/business ethics.* Cf. etiquette.

Ethiopia (formerly Abyssinia) a socialist republic in eastern Africa, pop. 27 million approx. (1974); capital, Addis Ababa, pop. 650,000 approx.; language, Amharic and local languages; currency unit, the Ethiopian birr (Br), divided into 100 cents.

etiquette the rules of social behaviour, usu. based on custom and morality and serving as a guide esp. to groups of persons in business and in the medical and legal professions, on how to behave correctly in various situations. Accepted rules governing correct manners in polite society. *It is not etiquette to ask a lady her age/ask a man his income. Medical etiquette forbids a doctor from attracting patients away from another doctor. Legal etiquette prevents solicitors or barristers from giving away the secrets of their clients.* Cf. ethics.

et seq. (*Latin*: et sequentes *or* et sequentia) and the following; and what follows.

Eurailpass TOUR. a pass or ticket which allows a tourist to travel at reduced cost on railways of most countries on the continent of Europe.

Euratom the European Atomic Energy Community.

Eurobond FIN. & BKG. a type of bond issued by non-European banks, usu. American, and sold to investors in Europe in return for Eurodollars. The issuing banks thus obtain a supply of long-term capital. Trading in the various bonds takes place in what is called the *Eurobond market.*

Eurocapital FIN. & BKG. capital raised in the money markets of the European Economic Community, usu. by the activities of the London merchant banks. *See* Eurocurrency.

Eurocheque FIN. & BKG. a cheque drawn on a British bank, which can be cashed at certain other banks in Europe.

Eurocurrency FIN. & BKG. currencies other than dollars used in the same way as Eurodollars. *See* Eurodollars.

Eurodollars FIN. & BKG. U.S. dollars that have been deposited with banks outside the U.S.A., not necessarily in Europe, and lent to borrowers outside the U.S.A. These deposits and loans of dollars are not subject to the same regulations as dealings in domestic currencies, and have grown rapidly in importance as finance for international trade.
Eurodollar market the market for Eurodollars, consisting of banks mainly in London and other European cities which accept deposits and offer loans in Eurodollars.

Euromarket a short name for the European Common Market or E.E.C.

Euromoney *see* Eurocurrency.

European Atomic Energy Community (Euratom) set up in 1958 to develop the industrial production and use of nuclear energy for peaceful purposes on a European scale. In 1967 the controlling bodies of Euratom and the E.C.S.C. were combined with that of the E.E.C. to form the present Council of Ministers and the Commission of the European Communities.

European Coal and Steel Community (E.C.S.C.) an organization set up in 1952 to develop and control the production and distribution of coal and steel in the six countries that later (1957) formed the E.E.C.: West Germany, France, Belgium, Holland, Luxemburg and Italy. Its controlling body was later (1967) combined with those of Euratom and the E.E.C. to form the present Council of Ministers and the Commission of the European Communities.

European Commission one of the governing organs of the E.E.C. It is the body which puts proposals to the Council of Ministers for decision and sees that the members carry out their duties under the Treaty. It consists of two members from each of the larger countries, Germany, France, Italy and Britain, and one each from the other countries.

European Common Market *see* European Economic Community.

European Co-operation Administration *see* Marshall (Aid) Plan.

European Council *see* Council of Ministers.

European Court of Justice LAW one of the main organs of the E.E.C.; it is responsible for explaining and deciding the meaning of the provisions of the Treaty of Rome and for trying actions brought by any member state or by corporations or private persons. Its decisions have greater power than those of any of the national courts. It meets in Luxemburg. Cf. International Court of Justice of the U.N.

European Economic Community (E.E.C.) an association of western European countries formed under the Treaty of Rome in 1957 to bring by stages a state of complete economic unity and a common market among its members. At the start there were six members: West Germany, France, Belgium, Holland, Luxemburg and Italy. These were joined in 1973 by Britain (the United Kingdom), Ireland and Denmark and in 1980 by Greece and Spain. There are a number of associate members, *see* Lomé Convention. Unity was to be gained by steps leading to: the removal of all hindrances to trade and free competition, and to mobility of labour, capital and enterprise between and within the member countries; the adoption of a common trading policy with non-member countries; the adoption of common agricultural and economic policies and the co-ordination (causing to work together) of transport systems. The main organs that govern the E.E.C. are: the Council of Ministers; the European Commission; the European Court of Justice; and the European Parliament. There are also a European Development Fund, a European Social Fund, a European Investment Bank, and a European Regional Development Fund.

European Free Trade Association (E.F.T.A.) ECON. an economic grouping of seven European countries — Austria, Finland, Iceland, Norway, Portugal, Sweden and Switzerland — who, by the Stockholm Convention of 1959, formed a free trade area by gradually removing all import duties on goods (except agricultural produce) made in any E.F.T.A. country. Be-

fore joining the E.E.C. in 1970, the United Kingdom and Denmark also were members of E.F.T.A. Unlike the E.E.C., E.F.T.A. has no common trade policy towards non-members, each member being free to charge what import duties it wishes.

European Fund *see* European Monetary Agreement (E.M.A.).

European Investment Bank BKG. & FIN. a bank formed in Brussels in 1958 by the European Economic Community to help to finance economic development within the Community.

European Monetary Agreement (E.M.A.) ECON. an association of European countries set up in 1958 under the management of the O.E.C.D. to replace the European Payments Union as their currencies became convertible. The aim of the E.M.A. is to encourage and develop international trade and convertibility of currencies between its members. Through the European Fund, which it operates, it arranges monthly settlements of debt between members and provides them with short-term loans when needed. Membership of E.M.A. consists of members of the E.E.C., E.F.T.A. and some other countries.

European Regional Development Fund a body of the E.E.C. which gives loans and grants to develop backward areas of the Community.

Europort SHIPG. & COM. any of the more important ports in the European Economic Community, but esp. Rotterdam, in Holland.

Eurosterling FIN. & BKG. amounts of sterling (the currency of Britain) that have been deposited with and lent by banks in the European money market outside Britain. Cf. Eurodollars.

evade to escape (from paying) with dishonest intentions: *To evade one's responsibilities/ obligations. He evaded his creditors. He is good at evading taxes.*

evaluate to find out, calculate or measure the value (of something). *N.* evaluation, the act of evaluating. *See* job evaluation.

evasion TAXN. using illegal means of avoiding payment of a tax. The crime of reducing the tax payable by making false tax declarations. Cf. avoidance.

even *adj.* (1) unchanging: *The quality of our product is even*, never changes. *Our prices remain even all through the year.* (2) equal; the same: *An even account*, one with both sides totalling the same, leaving no debit or credit balance. *Even money; even odds; evens*, in betting, equal chances of winning or losing. *Your letter of even date*, of today's date. *To break even, see under* break. (3) fair; just: *An even bargain/ deal/game*, fair to both sides, not favouring one or the other. (4) of numbers (*a*) that can be divided exactly by two, with nothing left over, e.g. 2, 4, 6, 8, etc. *The even-numbered houses are on one side of the street, the odd numbers* *are on the other. Opp.* odd. (*b*) in whole numbers, without fractions, or to the nearest ten, hundred, thousand, etc. *For simplicity we count in even tens/hundreds/thousands. Syn.* in round figures.

v. to make even or equal: *To even (up) an account*, to balance, to make both sides equal. *To even out difficulties*, to examine and get over them.

eviction LAW the act of regaining possession of land and buildings by a court order forcing persons to leave who have no right to be there.

evidence LAW something placed before a court that tends to prove a fact, or that makes a fact or thing clear: *He gave evidence in court*, made a solemn statement. *These documents provide all the evidence we need.* Evidence may be *oral*, spoken; *documentary*, written; *direct*, seen or felt by the witness himself; *indirect*, *circumstantial or hearsay*, not actually seen or felt by the witness; *prima facie*, accepted as proof unless disproved by other evidence.

ex. excluding; examined; exchange; executed.

ex (1) COM. out of; from; at. When a seller quotes a price, e.g. *ex works*, he means that that is the price at the place stated, in this case the works or factory; and that the buyer bears all risks and expenses relating to the goods from that place to wherever the buyer has them moved. **ex bond** out of bond. *Opp.* in bond.

ex dock the price includes all costs up to delivery on land at the named port, including unloading, and customs duty. *Syn.* ex quay; ex wharf. Cf. ex ship.

ex factory *as* ex works *below. Abbr.* X factory.

ex mill(s) *as* ex works *below*, but collection is at the mill(s). *Abbr.* X mill(s); X ml.

ex quay *see* ex dock *above*.

ex ship the price includes all costs up to delivery *at ship's rail*, i.e. still on board the ship, at the agreed port, the buyer being responsible for bearing all risks and costs from that point, including unloading charges, such as lighterage if the ship cannot be tied up at a wharf, and customs duty. Cf. ex dock. *Syn.* ex steamer; free overside. *Abbr.* X ship; X shp; X sh.

ex steamer *see* ex ship *above. Abbr.* ex ss.; X ss.

ex stock from present stock, not from some future production or from goods not yet in stock. *Abbr.* ex stk; X stk.

ex store *as* ex works *below* but collection is from the seller's store. *Abbr.* ex stre; X store; X stre.

ex warehouse *as* ex works *below* but collection is at the seller's warehouse. *Abbr.* ex whse; X whse.

ex wharf *see* ex dock *above. Abbr.* ex whf; X whf.

ex works the price is for delivery at the works (factory). The buyer has to arrange for the collection of the goods at the works and is re-

sponsible for all expenses such as loading, cartage, carriage, insurance, etc. *Syn.* ex factory; ex mill(s); ex store; ex warehouse. *Abbr.* X wks.

(2) STK. EXCH. without. When the price of a security is quoted, e.g. *ex div.*, it means that the price does not include the right to receive the next distribution or benefit (e.g. dividend) soon falling due, which will belong to the seller. *Abbr.* x. *Opp.* cum; with.

ex all without any of the benefits soon due. *Abbr.* x.a.

ex bonus without the bonus shares soon to be issued. *Syn.* ex capitalization; ex scrip. *Abbr.* x.b.

ex capitalization *or* ex cap. without the capitalization shares about to be issued. *Syn.* ex scrip; ex bonus. *Abbr.* x.c.

ex claim *see* ex rights *below*.

ex coupon *or* ex cp. (of a bond) without the interest on the coupon soon due for payment. *Abbr.* x cp.

ex dist. without the next income distribution or dividend. *Abbr.* x.d.

ex div. without the next dividend soon due. *Abbr.* x.d.

ex drawing (of a bond) without any benefit that may come from a drawing soon to take place.

ex interest *or* ex int. without the next interest payment soon due. *Abbr.* x. in.

ex new *see* ex rights *below. Abbr.* ex n.; x. new.

ex repayment without the repayment of capital about to be made.

ex rights without the rights issue soon due. *Syn.* ex claim; ex new. *Abbr.* x. r.

ex scrip without the scrip issue about to take place. *Syn.* ex bonus; ex capitalization.

exact *v.* to demand and force payment esp. of taxes or debts, or the giving of time, labour or attention: *To exact payment from a debtor/taxpayer/ratepayer.*

exacting *adj.* difficult, demanding special attention or treatment. *An exacting job/journey/manager/market.*

exaction *n.* (*a*) the act of exacting (money, etc.). (*b*) something exacted, esp. money which somebody has been unreasonably forced to pay.

exaggerated claim INSCE. an insurance claim that has been stated to be much greater than it ought to be: *He exaggerated the value of the damage done by the fire.* Where an insured person dishonestly exaggerates the amount of a claim the insurers may treat the contract as breached (broken) and refuse to pay anything.

ex all *see under* ex (2).

examination (1) LAW the formal questioning of a witness in court usu. under oath or affirmation. There are three stages.

examination-in-chief the questions put by, or for, the party calling the witness.

cross-examination further questioning by, or for, the other party to check and if possible destroy or reduce the effect of the examination-in-chief.

re-examination still further questioning by, or for, the party calling the witness, with the aim of mending any unfavourable impression left by the cross-examination.

(2) TAXN. by customs officers, the act of closely looking at goods being imported or exported, including where necessary the taking of samples for testing, in order to check that the goods are as described in the customs entry (declaration) and to determine the amount of duty, if any, to be paid. *Syn.* inspection.

examination, public *see* public examination.

ex bond COM. out of bond. *Opp.* in bond.

ex bonus *see under* ex (2).

excambion (Scotland) LAW a contract for the exchange of property.

ex capitalization *see under* ex (2).

exceed (1) to go beyond a certain limit: *He exceeded his instructions/orders. Our sales have exceeded all expectations. They have exceeded their credit limit.* (2) to be greater than: *Demand exceeds supply.*

excepted perils TRANSPT. & INSCE. in the carriage of goods, risks which are expressly not covered by an ordinary insurance policy and for which the carriers are not liable. *See* Act of God; inherent vice; negligence; Queen's enemies.

exception INSCE. an event or risk specially excluded (kept out) and so stated in the policy. *See* excepted perils.

exception principle *see* management by exception.

excess (1) the amount by which one quantity exceeds another, or is above a certain limit. *An excess of receipts over expenses. Syn.* surplus. (2) INSCE. in an insurance policy, an agreed amount that the insured will himself bear each time a claim is made, such as the first £25 of accident damage to a motor car. The insurer is bound to pay only for damage in excess of the agreed amount. Such a condition in a policy discourages the making of small claims and results in a reduction in the premium. (3) TOUR. an extra amount of money that has to be paid.

excess fare (*a*) money paid by a passenger who wishes to change from a lower class of accommodation to a higher. (*b*) money paid by a passenger who has a ticket for only part of the journey but wishes to travel a longer distance.

excess baggage money paid by a passenger whose baggage is heavier or larger than the free allowance.

excess capacity *see* capacity.

excess demand *see under* demand.

excess profit *see* super-profit *under* profit.

excess profits tax *see under* tax.

excess share(s) *see under* share.

excess supply *see under* supply.

exch. exchange; exchequer.

exchange *v.* (1) to accept one thing for another: *They exchanged cattle for horses.* (2) to give and receive: *We exchanged correspondence/letters/gifts. See* exchange of contracts; exchange of shares. (3) BKG. to change the money of one country for that of another: *To exchange currencies/traveller's cheques/pounds for dollars/francs, etc.*

n. (1) the act of exchanging: *We agreed on an exchange of shares. He gave his car in exchange for her motor boat.*

part-exchange the act of paying for something partly in money and partly in some article of which the value has been agreed.

(2) the process of giving and receiving by common agreement: *An exchange of information/views/know-how/ideas.* (3) the changing of the money of one country into that of another. *See* foreign exchange; direct exchange; indirect exchange. (4) the value of one currency expressed in units of another. *See* exchange rate. *Abbr.* exch. (5) the commission received by a money-changer or dealer in foreign currencies. Any profit made in changing money. (6) COMMOD. & STK. EXCH. a place, esp. a building or market-place, where goods and services are exchanged, usu. for money. *Abbr.* exch.

commodity exchange *see under* commodity.

employment exchange *see* job centre.

labour exchange *see* job centre.

Stock Exchange *see under* Stock.

telephone exchange *see under* telephone.

(7) ECON. the act of giving a commodity or service in return for another commodity or service or for money. Economics studies the systems which Man has developed in order to obtain the advantages of specialization, which are possible only if there exists a system for exchanging the products of specialization. *See* exchange economy; value in exchange.

exchangeable COM. of goods, supplied on condition that if they are found by the buyer not to suit his purpose, he may return them either for credit, or for exchange for an equal value of other goods.

exchange, bill of *see under* bill.

exchange broker *see* foreign-exchange broker.

exchange control FIN. government rules limiting freedom of movement of money to other countries and on the buying and selling of foreign currencies, in order to prevent a flight of capital to other countries and to protect the external value of the country's currency. In Britain the controls were removed in 1979.

exchange dealer *see* foreign-exchange dealer.

exchange, duplicate of *see under* duplicate.

exchange economy ECON. an organized system for the production of wealth which has developed such a degree of specialization that products must be exchanged, a process made easy by the wide use of money.

Exchange Equalization Account FIN. & BKG. in Britain an account at the Bank of England, controlled by the Treasury, which is used by the government as a fund with which to buy and sell gold and foreign currencies, whenever necessary, to protect the external value of sterling against large upward or downward swings. It is a most important part of the country's exchange-management system.

Exchange, First of, Second of *see* bill (of exchange) in a set.

exchange, foreign *see under* foreign.

exchange jobber BKG. & FIN. a dealer, usu. a bank, who buys large amounts of foreign currencies and sells to smaller buyers and sellers such as other banks, brokers or merchants. Cf. foreign-exchange broker.

exchange, medium of ECON. & FIN. any article or substance which, like money, is widely used, not for its own natural qualities, but because it forms a convenient and commonly acceptable means of payment when goods are exchanged, bought and sold. *The main use of money is as a medium of exchange. See* currency (3).

exchange of contracts LAW the important stage in the transfer of property, when the buyer signs the contract of sale and sends it to the seller who also signs it. Thus both parties become legally bound to complete the transfer.

exchange of shares STK. EXCH. the simplest method of effecting a combination joining two or more companies, by an exchange (giving and receiving) of each other's shares.

exchanger FIN. & BKG. a dealer in foreign exchange; a money-changer.

exchange rate *or* **rate of exchange** BKG. the amount which one currency will buy of another currency at a particular time: *Today's exchange rate is $1.95 to the pound sterling.*

all-in-rate *see* tel quel rate.

cable rate *see under* cable.

certain rate *see* certain (2).

cheque rate *see under* cheque.

currency rate a rate that in Britain is quoted by stating the number of foreign units that are obtainable for one pound sterling: *$1.95 to £1* or *£1 = $1.95.* Cf. pence rate.

demand rate *see* short rate *below.*

floating rate *see* floating exchange rate.

forward rate the rate or price of foreign currency which is bought or sold for delivery at some future time. The rate is expressed as a premium or discount above or below the spot rate (that for telegraphic transfers); for example, if today the Paris/London T.T. rate is 9.32 sellers, 9.37 buyers; and if delivery three months ahead is quoted at 15 centimes discount, the three-month forward rates will be

9.47 selling, and 9.52 buying. *See* forward exchange.

free rate *see* floating exchange rate.

long rate the rate for bills of exchange payable at 30, 60 or 90 days. Cf. short rate.

multiple rate a rate that varies according to the purpose to which the foreign currency is put, such as specially favourable rates to importers of certain kinds of goods, or to tourists to encourage tourism.

official rate the standard rate of exchange that the government has fixed for a particular foreign currency.

parallel rate in markets where there are two rates of exchange, the unofficial rate.

par rate *see* mint par of exchange; par (3).

pence rate a rate that is quoted by stating the number of pence (sterling) that are needed to buy one, or a stated number, of foreign units: *$1 = 51p.*

short rate the rate for cheques, and bills of exchange payable on demand or at sight or with eight or fewer days until maturity. *Syn.* demand rate; cheque rate; sight rate; cable rate.

sight rate *see* short rate *above.*

spot rate the rate for telegraphic transfers (T.T.s).

tel quel rate a rate used by a bank when buying a foreign-currency bill of exchange that has some time to run before reaching maturity (becoming due for payment). The rate is based on the T.T. (spot) rate, adjusted with reference to the long rate, the time to wait to get payment and the cost of various collection charges. *Pron.* tel kel. *Also* tale quale. *Pron.* tahli kwa-li. *Abbr.* t.q.; T.Q.

T.T. rate the telegraphic transfer rate, *see* spot rate *above.*

unofficial rate a market rate that is different from the official rate fixed by the government for its own foreign deals.

exchange, telephone *see under* telephone.

Exchequer, The FIN. in Britain, the department of the Treasury in charge of the country's revenues. These are all paid into the *Exchequer Account* at the Bank of England and form the Consolidated Fund. From this account is paid all government expenditure authorized by Parliament. Each week the Treasury makes public a statement, called the *Exchequer Return*, giving details of revenue and expenditure. *Abbr.* Exch.

Chancellor of the Exchequer *see under* Chancellor.

Exchequer bill *see* bill of Exchequer *under* bill.

excise TAXN. (1) in Britain, the group of government officials, called excisemen, responsible for collecting excise duty and certain other taxes. *See* Customs and Excise, Board of. (2) a duty or tax, often called *excise duty*, charged on certain goods and services produced and sold within the country, such as tobacco, beer, wines and spirits. *See* duty (3).

excise permit *see under* permit.

excise tax *see* excise (2).

excited STK. EXCH. of the state of the market, very active, with strong demand for stocks and shares, supplies lacking and prices rising rapidly.

excl. excluding; exclusive (of).

ex claim *see* ex rights *under* ex (2).

excluding not including; not counting: *A party of 20, excluding the guide.*

exclusive sales agreement COM. an arrangement between a manufacturer or supplier and a local trader. In return for the manufacturer agreeing not to supply any other trader in that area, the trader promises to buy all his supplies of that kind of product from that manufacturer and from no other. The nature of the agreement will vary according to whether the trader is appointed an exclusive (or sole) agent or exclusive distributor or exclusive stockist.

ex coupon *see under* ex (2).

excursion TOUR. a short pleasure trip to a place of interest and back, usu. at reduced cost, called an *excursion fare. See also* excursion ticket *under* ticket.

excursionist *n.* a person travelling on an excursion.

exd. examined.

ex-directory (of a telephone number) not listed in the telephone directory, because the subscriber (hirer of the line) wishes his number to be kept secret from the public.

ex dist. ex distribution.

ex distribution *see under* ex (2).

ex div. ex dividend.

ex dividend *see under* ex (2).

ex dock *see under* ex (1).

ex drawing *see under* ex (2).

exec. executive; executor.

execute (1) to carry out; to put into effect: *To execute a plan/order/contract.* (2) LAW to give effect to a law, judgment, court order, etc. (3) LAW formally to sign, seal and deliver a deed in the presence of witnesses (*see* deed). (4) LAW to carry out the directions contained in a will (*see* executor). *N.* execution.

executed consideration *see under* consideration.

executed contract *see under* contract, *n.* LAW.

executed trust *see under* trust.

execution, writ of *see under* writ.

executive (1) a person or body of persons given responsibility and power to put into effect certain laws, or of carrying out the decisions and orders made by some higher authority. (2) in U.S.A. esp., the branch of the government led by the President that carries out the laws and decisions of Congress and that administers and manages the affairs of the nation. (3) MAN. in a business organization, a person given responsibility for making important decisions, and power to manage a part or the whole of the affairs of the organization.

executive director *see under* director.

account executive *see under* account.

Chief Executive the highest administrative officer of a business or other organization.

senior executive a responsible officer of high rank in a business organization.

executor LAW a person named as executor in a will and trusted by the testator who made the will to be his personal representative in carrying out its provisions. The executor's main duties are: to bury or otherwise dispose of the body; to prove (obtain probate) of the will; to collect and, if necessary sell, all property; to settle the debts, in the proper order; to pay any taxes and legacies, and to give what is left to the person or persons who have a legal right to it. Solicitors are usu. employed to do this work under the general direction of the executor. *Abbr.* exor.

executory consideration *see under* consideration.

executory contract *see under* contract, *n.* LAW.

executory trust *see under* trust.

executrix LAW a female executor. *Abbr.* exrx.

exemplary damages *see under* damages.

exemption, tax *see* tax exemption.

exercise to use; to employ (a thing or activity): *He exercised his powers as chairman and closed the meeting. I intend to exercise my option to buy the business.* To *exercise a profession*, to carry on.

exes. expenses.

ex factory *see* ex works *under* ex (1).

ex gratia (*Latin*, as (an act) of grace (kindness)) as a favour. *An allowance made ex gratia*; *An ex gratia payment*, a payment made out of kindness or thankfulness, not because the payer was bound by law to pay, or because the recipient had any legal right to the payment.

exhaust to use up, consume completely: *Our stocks are exhausted*, all sold. *That coal-mine is exhausted*, can no longer be profitably worked. *He exhausted his energies/himself*, became weak from overwork.

exhibit (1) ADVTG. to place on view or on show: *We are exhibiting our products at the trade fair.* *Syn.* display; show. (2) LAW an object such as a document exhibited in court because it is referred to by a witness.

exhibition ADVTG. a placing of goods on show to the public, esp. for advertising purposes.

exhibitor *n.* one who exhibits.

Eximbank *see* Export-Import Bank.

ex int. *see* ex interest *under* ex (2).

ex interest, ex int. *see under* ex (2).

existing-use value *see under* value.

ex mill(s) *see* ex works *under* ex (1).

ex new *see* ex rights *under* ex (2).

ex officio (*Latin*) by reason of one's office: *He is a member ex officio. An ex-officio chairman,* a person who is chairman because he holds some other, usu. higher, office.

exor(s). executor(s).

exorbitant COM. beyond all reasonable limits: *Exorbitant terms. An exorbitant price. Syn.* excessive; inordinate.

expand ECON. to cause to become larger: *He greatly expanded the business. We need to expand production to meet demand. An expanding industry,* one that is increasing in size and output. *Opp.* declining industry.

expansion (1) ECON. a growing larger, wider; growth: *The expansion of (foreign) trade. The expansion of the economy,* the growth of total output and the increase of the national income. (*See* trade cycle *under* cycle.) *Expansion of the firm,* growth, by reinvesting profits, or by increasing the capital or by combining with one or more other firms. *Expansion of the currency,* official action in putting more bank-notes into circulation. (2) AGR. increasing crop production by improving the output of existing cultivated land (*vertical expansion*), and by bringing new land into use (*horizontal expansion*).

expatriate esp. a business employee, who has chosen to work and live in a place away from the country of which he is a national, such as an Iraqi national working and living in Britain.

expectation of life INSCE. the average number of years that a group of persons of the same age and sex will continue to live. This information is of great importance to life assurance companies in fixing premium rates. In most countries women tend to have an expectation of life three to four years longer than men, but in a few countries, esp. India and Pakistan, men tend to live rather longer than women. Cf. life expectancy.

expectations (1) ECON. what most businessmen, farmers, industrialists and government officials believe is going to happen in the economy in the future; it is sometimes called the state of public confidence. Keynes taught that expectations greatly influence the level of investment. (2) LAW chances of inheriting, at some future date, money or property at present enjoyed by another person during his lifetime.

expected TRANSPT. considered likely to happen: *Expected time of arrival/departure.* Due to arrive: *The ship is expected at Port Said today.*

expected to rank LAW of a bankruptcy, the total value of those debts that are expected to qualify for payment out of the assets.

expel to prevent a person from continuing his membership of an organization: *He was expelled from school/a society/trade union/political party/meeting. N.* expulsion.

expendable of stores, stationery, small tools, etc., considered to be consumed in use or not returnable for re-use, and therefore not to be kept account of after having been issued. *Syn. not durable; throw-away (colloq.). Opp.* accountable; returnable; re-useable, *also* reusable.

expenditure FIN. the spending of something having value, such as time or money; an amount of money spent. *Opp.* income. *Syn.* outlay.

capital expenditure money spent on fixed assets or on improvements to fixed assets.

productive expenditure money spent by the State for public services and on roads, buildings, etc.

public expenditure money spent by the government on the needs of the country, public services, interest on the national debt and the building of roads, schools, hospitals and houses.

revenue expenditure money spent on running a business, without adding to the value of fixed assets.

expenditure tax TAXN. a tax charged on the total amount of money spent by a person on consumer goods and services during a given year. Such a tax has been introduced with limited success in India and Sri Lanka. *Syn.* consumption tax.

expense FIN. money spent; the cost of things bought. *Your mistake has put me to much expense,* has caused me to spend much money. *You will bear the expense,* you will pay. *I had to go to the expense of a taxi. See* expenses.

expense account ACCTS. (1) an account in which are recorded the expenses of running a business. (2) an account of the amounts spent by a businessman in the interest of his business, such as on travelling and entertainment. Such amounts are repaid to him by the business and are usu. allowed as a business expense by the tax authorities.

expense ratio (1) COM. the relation between the total expenses of running a business and its turnover (total sales), usu. expressed as a percentage. (2) INSCE. the relation between an insurance company's expenses and its premium income.

expenses *pl.* ACCTS. & MAN. sums of money spent on the running of a business in such a way that they do not add to the value of its assets. Thus money spent on rent, rates (local taxes), electricity, insurance, advertising, wages, salaries etc. are expenses; while money spent on buildings, machinery, raw materials are classed as capital expenditure, not expenses, as they relate to the assets of the business. Cf. expenditure. *Abbr.* exes.; exs.

direct expenses *see under* direct.

entertainment expenses money spent on giving food, drink and amusement to customers, suppliers, etc. in the interests of the business. *See* entertainment; expense account (2).

factory expenses see under factory.

fixed expenses those that remain the same, or nearly the same, year after year, whatever the sales or output of the business, such as rent, rates (local taxes), lighting, heating.

formation expenses see under formation.

general expenses see overhead expenses below.

handling expenses (a) the extra expenses of buying and selling goods, other than the cost of the goods themselves, such as freight, cartage, loading and unloading, cranage, inspection, surveys, insurance. (b) money spent by an agent for his principal while the goods are passing through the agent's hands, such as receiving, carting, storing and selling the goods.

incidental expenses sums that have to be spent from time to time but not regularly.

operating expenses see overhead expenses below; also under operating.

out-of-pocket expenses money paid out in cash, usu. in small amounts. Syn. disbursements.

overhead expenses the cost of running a business; all sums of money spent other than the cost of the goods produced or sold and money spent on increasing the value of assets. Syn. general expenses; operating expenses; working expenses; overheads.

preliminary expenses see formation expenses under formation.

promotion expenses see formation expenses under formation.

removal expenses sums spent in moving a home, office or business from one address to another.

selling expenses any expenses relating only to the selling of a product, such as advertising, catalogues, wages and expenses of sales representatives, free samples, exhibitions.

travelling expenses sums spent in travel in the interest of the business. They include fares paid for road, rail, air and steamer journeys, baggage and porterage, hotel charges, the cost of meals and refreshment, telephones, telegrams, postage, necessary personal expenses of the traveller, such as tips, the cleaning and clothes, and the entertainment of customers.

variable expenses those that change with the total sales or output of the business, but not necessarily at the same rate, such as telephone, postage, delivery charges.

working expenses see overhead expenses above.

expensive (1) dear; costing much money; needing great expense: Long-lasting machinery is expensive. (2) high priced; priced higher than the proper value: That fur coat is too expensive. He works in an expensive office. (3) charging very high prices: Expensive shops in Bond Street.

experience INSCE. (1) as a check on the profitability of a certain class of insurance, the difference between the total premiums received

and the total claims paid during a given period. (2) the past history of the claims made by an insured party; this may result in a reduction in premium if the insured has a good record, or an increase if his record is bad.

expert n. a person with very special knowledge or great skill, usu. as the result of long experience: We must call in a financial/legal/tax expert to advise us. He is acknowledged to be a great marketing expert. A body/panel/committee of experts.
adj. To obtain expert opinion/advice. To make an expert examination.

expertise see know-how.

expertness see know-how.

expiration see expiry.

expiry (1) ending; coming to an end: Date of expiry, of an option/a permit/licence/tenancy/ travel ticket, etc., the date on which it becomes no longer effective. Expiry of a term of office. Syn. expiration. (2) INSCE. the ending of the cover given by a policy. (3) INSCE. the ending of a risk, e.g. when an insured article is broken up or sold.

exploit (1) COM. & IND. to obtain the greatest possible commercial advantage from some source of wealth: To exploit an oilfield/a discovery of gold/an invention. (2) sometimes a word of moral disapproval, esp. when associated with monopoly and unjust disadvantage to the public: He exploited his neighbours by charging for water during the drought. Exploiting workers by paying low wages. N. exploitation.

export v. to send out of the country as an act of trade: We export merchandise of all kinds to many countries. The British export machinery in return for foodstuffs. Opp. import.
adj. The export trade is essential to the nation.
n. a thing or class of things sent and sold to another country: Goods for export. See exports, pl.; direct exporting; indirect exporting.

export agent COM. a commission agent who represents a home manufacturer in a stated foreign market, often being appointed that manufacturer's sole agent in that market.

exportation (1) COM. the act of exporting; export. (2) (U.S.A.) a thing exported.

export bounty see under bounty.

export commission nouse see commission agent.

Export Credits Guarantee Department (E.C.G.D.) INSCE. & COM. in Britain, a government department responsible for encouraging exports by providing British concerns with export credit insurance. It charges premiums in the normal way for insurance against certain stated risks, esp. of non-payment by overseas buyers. E.C.G.D. does not lend money or in any way finance business. Cf. Export-Import Bank (U.S.A.).

export documents *see* shipping documents.

export duty *see under* duty.

exporter COM. (1) one who exports, esp. a merchant or agent with special knowledge of, and influence in, two markets, the one where the goods are produced, the other where they are sold; and who is also able to attend to all the customs and transport formalities that are special to export trade. (2) an exporting country: *India is a big exporter of tea. Egypt is a leading exporter of cotton.*

Export-Import Bank (Eximbank) BKG. & COM. in U.S.A., a government organization for encouraging exports by helping to finance payments and insuring U.S. exporters against risk of non-payment. It guarantees loans made by commercial banks to U.S. exporters, working closely with the Foreign Credit Insurance Association. Cf. Export Credits Guarantee Department (Britain).

exporting *see* direct exporting; indirect exporting.

export invoice *see under* invoice.

export licence COM. a document obtained from the government giving permission to export certain goods. In Britain export licences are needed for very few goods, such as certain works of art and antiques (things of historical interest), and certain arms and military stores. *Syn.* export permit.

Export List, The *see* Official Import and Export List.

export manager *see under* manager.

export merchant COM. a person or organization whose business is to buy goods made in his home country, ship them abroad to another country and sell them there, paying all expenses and keeping all the profit. *Syn.* export agent; merchant shipper.

export permit *see* export licence.

export restitution FIN. the subsidies paid to exporters of food products from the E.E.C. countries to make it possible for the exporters to compete in world markets.

exports *pl.* COM. goods and services sold to other countries.

invisible exports exports in the form of services performed for, and paid for by, persons abroad, esp. services such as transport, banking, insurance, advertising and investment income. Cf. visible exports.

prohibited exports exports of goods that are forbidden by law.

visible exports exports in the form of goods having a material form or substance, as distinguished from services performed for, and paid for by, persons and organizations in other countries. Cf. invisible exports. *See also* re-exports.

export sales *see under* sales.

export tax relief *see under* tax relief.

export trade *see under* trade.

expose COM. to show, to put on view, esp. for the purpose of selling: *Goods exposed for sale.*

exposition COM. & ADVTG. an exhibition, esp. one held by a government to show the products of art, industry and commerce of the nation.

express *v.* (1) to show or to tell in words: *He expressed his thanks in a letter. We must express our views at the meeting.* (2) to send off by the fastest possible means: *We are expressing the goods to you today.*

adj. (1) LAW clearly stated in words, esp. in a document: *An express condition,* one fully stated, not just implied. *Express warranty,* one stated fully in an insurance policy. *Opp.* implied. (2) TRANSPT. fast: *An express train/messenger/parcel/cleaning service. Express freight. Express letter,* one sent by special delivery.

expressage (U.S.A.) (1) the business of moving goods, money, parcels and letters quickly, by express services. (2) the charge for these services.

expressed trust *see under* trust.

expressway (U.S.A.) a road specially made for high-speed traffic. In Britain, a motorway. *Syn.* freeway; superhighway.

expropriation LAW any action by a government that takes away a person's right to property. Such action is usu. taken in the public interest, and compensation is usu. paid. *Syn.* dispossession.

expulsion the act of expelling, driving out, removing or sending away. The chairman of a meeting has power to order the expulsion (removal) of a disorderly person, by force if necessary. *See* expel.

expunge to wipe or rub out words, names, etc. in a document: *Agreed that the matter be expunged from the minutes/record. Expunge his name from the list.*

ex quay *see* ex dock *under* ex (1).

ex repayment *see under* ex (2).

ex rights *see under* ex (2).

exrx. executrix.

exs. expenses.

ex scrip *see under* ex (2).

ex-serviceman *see under* serviceman.

ex ship *see under* ex (1).

ex steamer *see* ex ship *under* ex (1).

ex stock *see under* ex (1).

ex store *see under* ex (1).

ext. extension.

extend (1) to make longer, wider: *They are extending their factory,* making it bigger. *We agree to extend your credit period from three to four months. To extend a bond, a bill of exchange.* (2) to give; to offer: *To extend an invitation/hospitality/a welcome.* (3) to use to the fullest amount: *Our factory staff are fully extended. Their capital resources are extended,* entirely invested. (4) ACCTS. in book-keeping.

to carry a figure, such as a balance, to the next column or to another column in the account. (5) in preparing an invoice, debit note or credit note, to calculate the total price of a quantity of the same article, e.g. 20 copies of Smith's *Commercial Dictionary* at £1.50 per copy = £30.00, less 20% discount (−£6.00) = £24.00.

extended bond *see under* bond, *n*.

extended credit COM. & FIN. credit given for a longer period than that earlier agreed, or than is usual.

extension (1) a lengthening; an enlargement: *An extension to our printing works. A factory extension*. (2) a telephone line extending the outside or exchange line through a private branch exchange (switchboard) to an instrument in a room in an office building, hotel, etc. *Abbr*. ext.

extension of demand ECON. of a commodity, the larger quantity that is demanded as the result of a reduction in price. This is not the same as an increase in demand, which is what happens when a larger quantity is demanded although there has been no change in price.

extensive agriculture AGR. farming by cultivating very large areas of land with the least possible expenditure of work and money on the land, so that the yield per acre or hectare is small. *Opp*. intensive agriculture.

external ECON. (1) foreign: *External trade*, trade with foreign countries. (2) outside a particular firm, industry or group: *External economies*. (3) INSCE. coming from, caused by, some outside force: *External means*, some means coming from outside, e.g. a collision causing a car to catch fire, as compared with the car catching fire because of some internal fault. *See* personal accident policy *under* policy of insurance.

external account BKG. a sterling bank account held by a person resident outside the sterling area. The money in these accounts is called external (account) sterling.

external bill *see under* bill of exchange.

external convertibility *see* limited convertibility *under* convertibility.

external debt *see under* national debt.

external deficit *see* balance of payments deficit *under* deficit.

external economies *see under* economies of scale.

external liabilities *see under* liabilities.

external sterling *see* external account.

external surplus *see under* surplus.

external trade COM. & ECON. the activity of a merchant who buys goods in one foreign country and sells them in another, the goods being transported direct without ever entering the merchant's home country. His profit on the deal will, however, form part of his country's invisible trade. Cf. entrepot trade. *Syn*. foreign trade; international trade.

extinguish to put out, to wipe out: *To extinguish a fire/a light/a debt*.

extortion LAW (1) the offence of obtaining something by force or threats from a person. (2) the offence done by a public official who wrongly uses his office to obtain money or other property from a person. Cf. blackmail.

extra *adj*. COM. (1) more than normal: *Extra pay for night work. Extra quality*, better than the usual. (2) in addition: *Packing and freight (charged) extra. No extra charge for alterations* (to clothes).

n. (1) an additional thing, esp. an expense: *A cover-charge is an extra*.

extras *pl*. extra charges, esp. on a bill. (2) an additional employee (U.S.A.): *A film extra*, a low-paid daily worker employed in crowd scenes in a film studio.

extra cost ECON. *see* marginal cost *under* cost.

extract (1) to take out, obtain, using either force or persuasion: *To extract money from a client. To extract metal from ore. N. An extract of coffee*. (2) to copy out and present separately, esp. in a document: *To extract a paragraph from the committee's report*.

an extract *n*. a part of a document/book/report copied and printed in another.

extractive industry *see under* industry.

extractor ECON. a primary producer who extracts wealth from natural surroundings by farming, mining, etc. and sells his products to manufacturers as raw material.

extraordinary general meeting *see under* company meeting.

extraordinary reserve *see under* reserve.

extraordinary resolution *see* resolution.

extra premium *see under* premium (6).

extravagant (1) spending beyond proper limits; wasteful: *An extravagant manager/cook. Extravagant tastes*. (2) extremely high, esp. of prices or costs: *Extravagant hotel extras/car-hire charges/entertainment expenses*. (3) of demands, ideas, beyond reasonable limits: *The shop stewards' demands are not extravagant. He has extravagant ideas about furnishing his office. N*. extravagance.

extrinsic value COM. & ECON. value that comes from outside, that exists for an outside reason. A cheap watch may have great extrinsic value because it once belonged to a famous person. Cf. intrinsic value.

ex warehouse *see under* ex (1).

ex wharf *see* ex dock *under* ex (1).

ex works *see under* ex (1).

eyewash (*colloq.*) deceit; misleading talk or behaviour to persuade someone that a bad thing is good.

eyewitness LAW a witness who was present at some happening and can therefore give a statement from his personal knowledge.

F

F France's international vehicle-registration letter.

F. Fahrenheit; franc.

f. franc; folio; foot; following (page).

F$ Fiji dollar.

f.a. free alongside.

F.A.A. free of all average.

Fabian Society ECON. a group of moderate Socialists calling themselves Fabians, formed in London in 1883–4 with the aim of gradually introducing a democratic socialist state in Britain. They argued against the more forceful ideas of the Marxists. Their main activity today is in educating the public by issuing books and pamphlets, holding public discussions, and generally spreading socialist ideas, particularly among the educated middle classes.

fac. facsimile.

f.a.c. as fast as can (be).

F.A.C.C.A. Fellow of the Association of Certified and Corporate Accountants.

face-lift (1) COM. improved appearance, esp. of buildings, shops, or packaging of products: *The banks propose to give their high street branches a face-lift.* (2) improved financial structure: *The reorganization of Smith & Co. Ltd. gives their balance sheet a face-lift.*

face value FIN. the value on a bank-note or stamped on a coin. The nominal value of a stock or share, as distinguished from the market value.

facilitate to make easy; to make easily possible: *Stock Exchanges facilitate the placing of small investments.*

facility (1) the ability to do something easily: *He has a facility in commercial design/foreign languages/salesmanship.* (2) a special arrangement: *A credit facility of up to £2000.*
facilities *pl.* arrangements that allow or make some activity easy: *The town has good shopping/banking/transport facilities. The company offers good facilities for training/sports/travel.*

facsimile an exact copy or reproduction of an original object, made by photography, some printing process or other means. *Facsimile signature*, a printed copy of a signature made to look like the original handwritten one. *Pron.* faksimili.

factor (1) anything that helps to produce, causes or influences a result: *Hard work is the main factor of his success. Skilled labour is the most important factor in the manufacture of machinery.* See factors of production. (2) COM. in Britain, a particular class of agent who is employed by his principal to sell the principal's goods or services usu. in return for payment of a commission, called factorage, calculated on the amount of business done. Unlike the brok-

er, the factor takes possession of the goods and acts in his own name in making bargains to sell them. The principal is bound to honour such bargains. Cf. broker. *Syn.* mercantile agent; (in some trades) wholesaler; factoring agent. (3) FIN. in U.S.A., a person or organization that finances the production, esp. of textiles, by taking responsibility for all risk of non-payment by customers. See factoring. (4) AGR. in Scotland, the farm-bailiff of a large area of land, responsible for managing the work of farming and forestry. *Syn.* land-agent; steward; estate manager. (5) ECON. HIST. a European employed by the East India Company to run one of its factories or trading stations.

factorage COM. the commission and other earnings of a factor for selling his principal's goods. See factor (2).

factor cost ECON. THEORY (1) the price paid for the use of the factors of production: rent for land and natural supplies; wages and salaries for labour; interest for capital; and profits for enterprise. (2) the total costs of the factors of production used in producing an article and making up the price paid for it by the consumer. If a subsidy has been paid to the manufacturer, that will be added; and if the consumer has paid a tax, such as V.A.T. or excise duty, that will be taken off. In other words, it is the part of the price paid by the consumer that represents the true cost of the factors of production. This factor cost, rather than the market price, is used as the basis for calculating the national income. See gross national product.

factoring FIN. an arrangement between a supplier, esp. an exporter of textiles, and a special kind of finance house called a *factor* or *factoring company*, by which the supplier sells to the factor the right to collect amounts payable to the supplier by approved customers at some future date. Thus the supplier receives payment immediately he supplies the goods, the factor taking full responsibility for collecting the accounts and bearing all losses from bad debts. The factor's charges consist of a fee based on the rate of discount for bills of exchange and an added small percentage for collecting the accounts. In Britain, factoring companies are owned by commercial banks, merchant banks and some export houses. Some factoring companies also lend money to suppliers for short periods. *Syn.* factorizing.

factoring agent see factor (2).

factor price see under price.

factorship COM. the office or position held by a factor who acts as a commercial agent.

factor's lien see under lien.

factors of production ECON. THEORY in economic theory, the basic things that are used by Man, esp. land, labour, capital and enterprise to produce economic goods. *Land* includes a usable and scarce materials provided by Nature; *labour* includes the human energy, mental skill and judgment applied in producing economic goods; *capital* includes stores of unconsumed wealth and stocks of assets in the form of tools, machinery and raw materials, and also money to finance work in progress of manufacture and for further investment; and *enterprise* or *organization* consists of the organizing ability of the entrepreneurs and their willingness to bear financial risks. Each factor has its price, or factor cost, that for land being rent, that for labour being wages or salaries, that for capital being interest and that for enterprise being profit. *Syn.* agents of production.

factory (1) IND. officially, any place or building in which one or more persons are employed as workers in any process for making, altering, repairing, ornamenting or preparing for sale by way of trade or gain any article; or where animals are killed for food, or electricity is made or distributed, etc. The various factory laws in Britain control the conditions of factory workers, protect their health and safety, and prevent employment of women and children in certain kinds of work that would be harmful to them. (2) ECON. HIST. a trading station in wild or foreign country, e.g. Canada, India, where factors, esp. those representing large trading companies, bought, sold or exchanged goods. *See* factor (5).

factory expenses ACCTS. & IND. any expenses that relate to the factory which cannot be directly connected with the actual products being manufactured, such as rent, rates, heating, lighting, power, cleaning, wages, and some management salaries. *Syn.* factory overheads.

factory farming AGR. a way of farming in which animals and birds are kept in small cages inside large buildings and made to grow or produce milk, eggs, etc. very quickly. *See* battery (2).

factory-hand IND. an ordinary worker in a factory.

factory inspectors IND. in Britain, government officials who have the responsibility for visiting factories and for checking that the rules of the Factory Acts are being obeyed.

Factory, Letter of LAW in Scotland, a document similar to a Power of Attorney, giving one person power to act for another.

factory system ECON. HIST. the system of economic development that followed the domestic system, by which people were employed to work together in factories under the direction of the owner. Large power-driven machines and suitable buildings for them and the workers operating them needed much capital and called for commercial and technical specialization. The great change from the domestic to the factory system was called the Industrial Revolution.

Fahr. Fahrenheit (temperature scale).

Fahrenheit a scale of temperature in which water freezes at 32° and boils at 212°. Cf. Celsius.

fail (1) to be unsuccessful: *We must not fail to get the contract/to increase sales. Unless you work harder you will fail your examination.* (2) COM. & LAW to be unable to pay one's debts; to be insolvent or bankrupt or to go into liquidation: *The business/bank/company has failed.* (3) COM. to neglect or omit to do some duty: *They failed to pay the bill/to deliver the goods/to honour the contract. Failing prompt settlement of your account we shall stop supplies. He failed to write.* (4) to be lacking at some essential point: *One engine failed on take-off. Our crops have failed.*

failing MAN. a weakness of character: *Drink is his failing,* he takes too much strong drink.

failure (1) lack of success: *Our failure to get the order. He is a failure in business.* (2) inability to pay debts; insolvency, bankruptcy or liquidation: *A bank failure.* (3) neglect of duty: *Failure to deliver/to honour a bill/to acknowledge a letter.* (4) non-performance, esp. at some essential point: *Engine failure. Crop failure.*

fair *adj.* (1) just; honourable: *A fair share of the market. Fair dealing. To see fair play. A fair deal/bargain/arrangement.* Reasonable: *To charge fair prices.* (2) satisfactory; reasonably good: *A fair sample,* one of fair quality. *A car in fair condition. We have done a fair amount of business with them. To make fair profits/provision for depreciation.* (3) of weather conditions: *It remained fair throughout the voyage/the bank holiday. The fair weather has brought a glut of vegetables.* (4) clean; faultless: *He has a fair name for honesty,* an honest reputation. *See* fair copy.

n. (1) a local market, held at regular times, and esp. for farm produce: *A cattle/vegetable fair. A fair-ground,* a place where fairs are held. (2) a large commercial and industrial exhibition where buyers and sellers of a particular group of commodities meet to do business, such as The Frankfurt Book Fair, The London Antiques Fair. Such gatherings are called *trade fairs* or *sample fairs.* (3) a collection of amusements, sporting shows, etc. usu. held in connection with a trade fair or local market and called a *fun fair.*

fair average quality COMMOD. EXCH. words used to describe the standard quality of wheat, esp. that from the Argentine, on the London Corn Exchange. *Abbr.* f.a.q.

fair competition *see* healthy competition *under* competition.

fair copy LAW of a document, a clean copy of a corrected draft, without mistakes or corrections, for study or careful consideration before the engrossment (final copy) is prepared. *Abbr.* f.co.

fair trade (1) COM. & ECON. a system of international trade in which certain countries agree not to charge duties on imports of certain goods but are free to charge duties on imports for which no such agreement exists. *Syn.* reciprocity. (2) (*colloq.*) smuggled (illegally imported) goods.

fair-trade agreement see resale price maintenance.

fair trading see Office of Fair Trading.

fair wages clause IND. REL. in Britain, a clause included by law in all contracts made by central government departments and local authorities, by which the contractor must keep to the rates of pay and hours of work ruling in the trade and in the area where the work is done; he must allow his workers to organize themselves as trade unions; and must accept that any unsettled dispute shall be referred to arbitration. See fair wages *under* wages.

fairway SHIPG. a channel of deep water used by ships in a harbour or river, usu. marked by buoys.

fair wear and tear see wear and tear.

faith *n.* COM. trust, confidence: *We have faith in our cashier/bankers/employees. A good salesman has faith in his product*, believes it to be good. *We made the bargain in good faith*, with honest intentions. *See* bona fide. *In bad faith*, intending to deceive; not sincere. *See* mala fide. *adj.* faithful: *A faithful servant.*

faithfully loyally; truly; in good faith: *Yours faithfully*, the usual closing words of a formal business letter, esp. when the writer and the person to whom he is writing do not know each other. Cf. yours sincerely; yours truly.

fake (1) a thing that is made to appear real but is only an imitation; an imitation or copy intended to deceive: *The story was a fake*, was untrue. *The diamond proved to be a fake.* (2) a person who deceives others by making false claims. *Syn.* (*colloq.*) fudge.

falaj see qanat.

Falkland Islands a British colony in the south Atlantic Ocean, near the coast of Argentina, pop. 2000 approx. (1972); capital, Stanley; language, English; currency unit, the Falkland Islands pound (FI£). divided into 100 pence.

fall *v.* to go lower; to drop: *Prices are falling.*
fall away to fail to support: *His customers fell away.* To become smaller: *Business has fallen away badly this year. Sales have fallen away to nothing.*
fall back of prices, to become lower again: *Gilts fell back after news of poor trade figures.*
fall back on to go to a person or thing for help or support: *If we run short of money we can fall back on the bank for an overdraft.*
fall behind to go too slowly; to be unable to keep up with: *We have fallen behind in our payments/work/orders.*

fall down (*colloq.*) to fail: *He fell down on the job/on his mortgage payments.*
fall due to become payable: *The rent falls due tomorrow.*
fall foul of (*a*) of ships, to come into collision: *The tanker and the container-ship fell foul of each other.* (*b*) to quarrel with: *I fell foul of the manager when I demanded more pay.*
fall in with to agree with others in some joint activity: *We fell in with their plans.*
fall off to become smaller: *Production is falling off because of labour trouble. Bad weather caused holiday bookings to fall off.*
fall on evil days/hard times to suffer bad fortune.
fall on one's feet to be successful: *He lost his job but soon fell on his feet selling old cars.*
fall through to fail; to come to no result: *Negotiations for the merger have fallen through. Our plans nearly fell through.*
fall under the hammer to be sold by auction.
n. (1) the act of falling: *A fall in prices/orders/demand/supply.* (2) an amount by which something falls: *A fall of 25p during the day.* (3) in U.S.A. & Canada, the autumn: *In the fall of next year.*

fall-back price see reserve price (*c*) *under* price.

fall guy (U.S.A. *colloq.*) (1) a person who is easily deceived and made to suffer by dishonest persons. (2) one who is unjustly blamed for a wrong he did not do.

fall money (U.S.A. *colloq.*) a store of money used by one or more criminals to pay legal costs.

fallow land AGR. land on which no crop is being grown because the soil is being rested or is being specially treated with fertilizers or weedkillers. Such land is said to be *lying fallow.*

false *adj.* (1) wrong; not correct; untrue: *A false figure/value/step/alarm/calculation.* (2) intending to deceive; not loyal; misleading: *A false declaration. False weights/jewels/witness/papers. A false bottom*, in a box, to hide things in. *A ship flying a false flag*, to deceive other ships. (3) artificial: *False teeth.*

false pretences LAW the offence of obtaining money or goods dishonestly by pretending that something is true when it is not, such as falsely pretending to be the payee of a cheque, or paying for goods with a worthless cheque. *Syn.* obtaining property by deception; fraud.

false representation see fraud.

falsification of accounts LAW & ACCTS. the offence of an employee who dishonestly makes a false entry in an account or destroys, or makes changes in, an account book or document, with the intention of obtaining money or goods by deceit.

family (1) parents and their children: *Our family consists of father, mother and three children* (2) children only: *They have a family of ten* *children.* (3) persons who are descended from the same line: *Charles Darwin's family includes many famous names.*

family allowance *see* child benefit.

family business COM. one owned and run by one or more members of the same family.

family butcher/grocer COM. a shopkeeper who aims to provide everything that a family needs, and who will sometimes deliver goods to the homes of his customers.

family doctor one who practises general (not special) medicine and perh. some surgery and who treats his patients in their homes and at his surgery. *Syn.* general practitioner. Cf. specialist; consultant.

family hotel COM. & TOUR. a hotel that offers special services and charges lower rates for families with children. Cf. commercial (hotel).

family income policy *see under* insurance policy.

family planning controlling the size of one's family by using medical means to prevent children from being produced. This practice has been the main cause of the fall in the birth-rate in most countries. *Syn.* birth control.

family reunion fare *see under* fare (2).

famine an extreme lack of food causing many people to die of hunger.

fancy goods (1) COM. small articles of trade that attract buyers by their pleasing or interesting appearance. (2) cloth material of bright colours or gay patterns.

F. & A.P. fire and allied perils.

f. & d., F. & D. freight and demurrage.

f.a.o. for (the) attention of.

F.A.O. Food and Agriculture Organization (of the United Nations).

F.A.P. (*French*) franc d'avarie particulière; equivalent to F.P.A., free of particular average.

f.a.q. fair average quality; free alongside quay.

F.A.R. *see* F.C.A.R.

fare (1) TOUR. food served at table. *See* bill of fare *under* bill. (2) TRANSPT. the price of carrying a person from one place to another by plane (air-fare), ship (steamer-fare *or* passage money), train (train-fare *or* rail-fare), bus (bus-fare), etc. The price of hiring a taxi, which may pay for several persons (taxi-fare).

family reunion fare a specially low-cost return fare charged by airlines for journeys on scheduled (ordinary) services by passengers visiting members of their family (and sometimes friends) in far-away countries. Such fares usu. vary according to the season and are conditional upon the passenger staying away at least 45 days and not more than 180 days.

high- or low-season fares the fares charged for a journey at different times of the year, according to the demand for travel. The price is higher in those months when many passengers want to travel (the high season), and low in those months (the low season) when lower fares

attract some people to travel who would not otherwise do so.

off-peak fare fares for travel at times of the day when the public demand for rail and road travel is at its lowest. Full fares are charged when demand for travel is high (at a peak).

return fare the price of travelling from one place to another and back. *Syn.* (U.S.A.) round-trip fare. Cf. single fare.

single fare the price for making a single journey only. *Syn.* (U.S.A.) one-way fare. Cf. return fare. (3) a passenger who has hired a taxi.

Far East the countries of Asia eastwards from Malaysia and Singapore, and esp. China and Japan.

farm *n.* AGR. (1) an area of agricultural land owned or held and managed by a person, called a farmer, or group of persons, such as a farm co-operative, who run it commercially for growing crops, raising animals, or making dairy products: *An arable/dairy/poultry farm.* (2) the house where a farmer lives and carries on his work: *We live at Strawberry Farm.* (3) a place situated on water where fish are raised: *A fish/oyster farm. See also* co-operative farm. *v.* (1) to cultivate land, grow crops, raise animals, fish, birds, etc. as a commercial activity. *N.* farming. (2) *To farm out taxes,* a method of collecting money by letting out areas of land for a fixed price to persons who then collect and keep the taxes from the people who live there. (3) *To farm out work,* to arrange for work to be done by a contractor instead of doing it in one's own factory.

farm-bailiff *see under* bailiff.

farmer AGR. a person who carries on the activity of cultivating land and raising animals; a person who owns or runs a farm. *Gentleman farmer,* a person who farms land for pleasure rather than for profit. *Tenant farmer, see under* tenant.

farm-hand AGR. an unskilled worker on a farm; a farm-labourer.

farming AGR. *see* dry farming; subsistence farming.

farm-labourer *see* farm-hand.

farmstead AGR. a small farm and its buildings.

farthing FIN. a small coin worth a quarter of an old penny, formerly in use in Britain. It was demonetized in 1961. The word is still used for any very small sum of money: *This article is not worth a farthing.*

f.a.s. free alongside ship/steamer.

Fascism the political and economic systems set up by the fascist movements in Italy, Germany and Japan between the two great wars, and later in Argentina. Fascism based its strength on extreme nationalism, the power and greatness of the nation, and on the absolute authority of the leader. Highly centralized state corporations controlled each main industry, some units of which were privately owned. Strikes were totally forbidden by law. The desire for military power led to very great production of arms rather than consumer goods because the living standard of the people was of little importance. Fascism allowed the people little freedom and no voice in everyday government; it brought unbelievable cruelty and mass murder to millions of Jews and others.

fashion (1) a way of making or doing something: *We do it/make it in this fashion.* (2) a way e.g. of dressing that is popular, that it is the custom to imitate, at a particular time. *Fashions change. Smart people keep up with the fashions. Today's fashions. Paris leads the way in ladies' fashions. Waistcoats are the fashion/in fashion/ out of fashion.* Syn. vogue.

fashionable *adj.* in line with fashion; of a place, used or visited by the rich or the upper classes.

old-fashioned in a way that is now not in fashion; having an appearance that was formerly fashionable.

fashion goods COM. those that supply the public demand esp. for clothes, that must continually change in appearance to keep up with changing fashions.

fashion shares STK. EXCH. shares which are for some reason much in demand by investors for a short time and are then forgotten.

fast *adj.* (1) that moves or travels quickly: *A fast boat/train. The fast line*, on the railway, the track used by fast trains. *Opp.* slow. (2) tightly held; fixed: *The ship was (held) fast on the rocks. Make fast the boat*, tie it tightly to something. *Opp.* loose. (3) permanent: *Fast colours/ dyes*, that will not fade. *A fast friend.*

fast foods (U.S.A.) *see* convenience goods.

fat (*colloq.*) money.

father of the chapel *see* chapel.

fathom (1) SHIPG. a unit of measurement of depth of water and the length of rope, also sometimes of distance. 1 fathom (fm.) = 6 ft or 1.8288 m. 100 fathoms = 1 cable. *Abbr.* fm.; fth.; fthm. (2) a unit of measurement of timber (wood for building) 1 fathom being the volume of a pile 6 ft × 6 ft × 6 ft = 216 cu. ft = 6.1165 cu. m.

favour an old-fashioned and excessively polite word for a letter, esp. a business letter: *Your favour of yesterday*, a way of saying that the writer has done you a favour by writing to you.

by favour of...(name) words written for politeness on the cover of a letter which is being delivered personally by the named person.

in favour of... (*a*) on the side of: *The judge decided the case in favour of Mr Jones.* (*b*) to the advantage of; in the interest of: *He made a will in favour of his brother. The exchange was in our favour.* (*c*) BKG. payable to: *To draw a cheque, etc. in favour of John Smith.*

favourable balance *see* active balance.

F.C.A. Fellow of the Institute of Chartered Accountants.

f'cap., f/cap. foolscap.

F.C.A.R. free of claim for accident reported. *Also* F.A.R.

F.C.C.A. Fellow of the Association of Certified and Corporate Accountants.

F. chgs. forwarding charges.

F.C.I.A. Foreign Credit Insurance Association.

F.C.I.I. Fellow of the Chartered Insurance Institute.

fco. franco (free).

f. co. fair copy.

fcp. foolscap.

fcs., Fcs. francs.

F.D.,f/d. free delivery; free delivered at docks.

F.D.O. for declaration (purposes) only.

feasibility study a careful analysis of the scientific and mechanical details of a proposed new process or product, followed by an examination of the expected income, probable capital expense and running costs, to see whether the plan is likely to be commercially successful.

feather-bedding (1) IND. the action of a government in protecting a home industry by charging duties or placing quotas on imports (*see* protection) or by giving subsidies. (2) IND. REL. action by a trade union to force employers to employ as many workers as possible, esp. by opposing the introduction of labour-saving machines or demanding that new machines be overmanned. *A feather-bed rule*, a trade-union rule ordering its members to work slowly when there is a shortage of work, in order to avoid dismissals.

feature something that particularly strikes the attention, that is specially remarkable or important: *A feature advertisement/article/book review/display/film/act* (part of a show). *Excited buying of industrials was the feature of the day. A feature of the final accounts is the large bank loan.*

Fed. (U.S.A. *colloq.*) (1) the federal government of the U.S.A. (2) the Federal Reserve System (of banks) in the U.S.A.

Federal Deposit Insurance Corporation *see* deposit insurance.

Federal Reserve System BKG. & FIN. in U.S.A., a group of 12 local Federal Reserve Banks that together form the central banking authority of the nation under the centralized control of the powerful Federal Reserve Board in Washington, now very like a government department. All national banks and most state and other banks deposit certain reserves with their local Federal Reserve Bank which, in turn, acts as a banker's bank, issuing banknotes and coins, making loans, discounting bills, advising on government policy, etc. *Abbr.* Fed.

federal tax *see under* tax.

Federal Trade Commission ADVTG. & COM. in U.S.A., a central government agency responsible for stopping unfair competition, and esp. for protecting the public from false and deceitful claims in advertising.

federal union a form of political organization adopted by many nations, in which a number of states have agreed to form a united whole, each state keeping its full independence in internal (home) matters such as public health and education but giving up some of its powers, such as foreign affairs, defence and communications, to the central government. Brazil is an example of a federal union of states. *Syn.* federation (of states).

federation (1) a central organization formed by a number of societies or associations whose members have a broad common interest: *The British Federation of Master Printers. Abbr.* F. or Fed. *See* affiliated societies. (2) of states, *see* federal union.

fee (1) FIN. & COM. a payment for a piece of professional advice or for some special service(s): *An architect's/dentist's/doctor's/solicitor's/barrister's/accountant's fees. Syn.* honorarium. (2) a charge made for giving permission to use or do something: *Permission/reproduction/copyright fee. Entry/entrance/admission/parking/cancellation fee.* (3) a charge for recording something: *A reservation/registration/booking fee. See also* scale fee. (4) LAW an inherited interest in land.

fee simple land inherited with complete freedom to pass it to whom one wishes. Freehold.

fee tail land inherited with freedom to pass it to a limited class of persons, such as to one's eldest son. *See* entail.

(5) *in pl.* money paid for a course of study or for education: *School/college/tuition/examination/sports fees.*

feed *n.* AGR. any kind of food for farm animals: *Chicken/cattle/pig feed.* Cf. fodder; forage.

feeder TRANSPT. a branch or local road, railway line, air route, etc. that brings traffic from surrounding areas to the main road, line, etc.

feeler COM. a quiet suggestion or enquiry intended to find out what others are thinking, or to get information about their intentions: *To put out a feeler/feelers in the hope of getting an order.*

feet *see* foot.

feint-ruled paper writing-paper machine-ruled with the lightest weight of line. (An old spelling of faint.)

fellah AGR. in Egypt and Syria, a farm-worker (*from Arabic*). Pl. fellahs; fellahin; fellaheen.

felony LAW a word that nowadays has no exact meaning. A felony is one of the broad classifications of criminal offences, next in seriousness below treason but above misdemeanour.

In Britain felonies are considered to be the more serious crimes that must be tried by a judge and jury and that may be punished by imprisonment for five years or more. They include murder, manslaughter, rape, bigamy, and serious theft.

felon *n.* a person who is guilty of a felony.

felonious *adj.* relating to felony: *With felonious intent*, intending to commit a felony. *Felonious tort*, a civil wrong that may also be a criminal offence such as armed assault or some forms of libel.

felucca SHIPG. a small coastal sailing-ship with triangular sails and sometimes with oars, carrying cargo between ports in the Mediterranean.

fen a fractional currency unit of China. 100 fen = 10 chiao = 1 yuan.

fence (1) a person who is a professional receiver and seller of stolen goods. *Syn.* receiver. (2) the place where he carries on his business.

feoffee to uses *see* trustee.

ferry (1) TRANSPT. a ship or boat, usu. specially planned and built, for carrying people, goods and vehicles, usu. for short distances, e.g. across a river or other narrow stretch of water. (2) the service provided by regular crossings by one or more ferry-boats. (3) the legal right to run a public ferry service charging a toll for persons, animals and vehicles carried.

auto ferry *see under* auto.

car ferry *see* auto ferry *under* auto.

rail ferry *see* train ferry *below*.

roll-on ferry a ship specially built with openings at both ends so that vehicles can drive on at one end and off at the other. *Syn.* roll-on/roll-off ship; drive-on/drive-off ship.

train ferry a ferry specially built to carry a railway train complete with goods and passengers.

vehicle ferry *see* auto ferry *under* auto.

fertile (1) AGR. of land, able to produce much: *The soil on the banks of the Nile is very fertile.* (2) of the human mind, producing many good ideas. (3) of Man and animals, able to reproduce sexually; able to produce young: *Chicks hatch out from fertile eggs.*

Fertile Crescent, The ECON. & AGR. a region of naturally fertile land in the Near East, shaped like a new moon. From one point in Upper Egypt it curves northwards along the valley and delta of the River Nile, along the coastal strip of Palestine, Lebanon and Syria and then eastwards to include the great river basin of the Tigris and Euphrates in Iraq, to the other point at the head of the Arabian Gulf. It is generally thought that in this region Man first practised agriculture at least 10,000 years ago.

fertility rate the rate at which a population reproduces itself, expressed as the number of births per thousand women of child-bearing age, i.e. between 15 and 45.

fertility rent *see under* rent.

feudal system the ancient social and economic system that existed in continental Europe from the ninth to the fourteenth century and was brought to England in the eleventh century by the Normans. The king was the true owner of all land; he divided his kingdom between a number of lords to whom he gave protection and who had the use of his land in return for their declared loyalty, military support and other services. The smallest unit was the manor, held by a lord, who allowed the peasants, called villeins or serfs, to hold and cultivate some of his land, and who gave them his protection in return for their part-time labour and for certain payments in the form of produce. There was also common land which all could use for feeding animals. The system gradually came to an end when the peasants were paid wages for their work and, as tenants, paid rent for the land they used. *Syn.* manorial system; feudalism. *See also* open-field system.

ff. folios; following (pages).

f.f.a. free from alongside.

ffy. faithfully.

f.g. fully good.

F.G.A., f.g.a. foreign general average.

f.g.f. fully good, fair.

F.H. fore hatch; forward hatch.

F.H.A. Finance Houses Association.

FI£ Falkland Islands pound.

F.I.A. Fellow of the Institute of Actuaries; full interest admitted.

fiat LAW (*Latin*, let it be done) a formal order made by a person in authority; a command; formal permission.

fiat money FIN. paper money or coins of little or no intrinsic (material) value in themselves and not convertible into gold or silver but made legal tender by fiat (order) of the government, such as the paper Marks issued in Germany after the First World War.

fiat standard *see under* standard.

f.i.b. free into barge; free into bunker.

fictitious not existing in reality; imaginary: *Fictitious names/employees/visits to customers.*

fictitious assets *see under* assets.

fictitious payee *see under* payee.

fictitious person *see* artificial person.

fiddle *v.* (*colloq.*) to obtain some small advantage by illegal and deceitful means: *To fiddle one's expense account/tax return.*
n. (*colloq.*) a dishonest trick to get money: *The collection for charity was a fiddle. To be on the fiddle.*

fiddler (*colloq.*) a person who obtains some small advantage by deceitful means; a cheat on a small scale.

fidelity MAN. (1) faithfulness; honesty; loyalty; truthfulness: *Fidelity is essential in a cashier. We have confidence in his fidelity.* (2) accuracy: *He has written a report of the meeting with perfect fidelity,* has recorded it with accuracy.

fidelity bond *see under* bond, *n.*

fidelity insurance *see under* insurance, classes and kinds of.

fiduciary *n.* LAW a person holding a position formally recognized by law as being one of special confidence, usu. a person such as a trustee or executor to whom property has been given to hold and manage, not for his own profit, but for the benefit (advantage) of someone else. Such a person is said to hold the property *in a fiduciary capacity.*

fiduciary bond *see under* bond, *n.*

fiduciary loan FIN. one made entirely on trust, without any security, the lender having confidence in the honour of the borrower.

fiduciary money *see* fiduciary note issue.

fiduciary note issue FIN. & BKG. in Britain, formerly that part of the note issue that was not backed (supported) by gold, and which obtained its value from the trust the public had in the issuing bank. Today, the amount fixed by Parliament of notes issued by the Bank of England on the authority of the Treasury and backed by securities (government debt, government and other safe stocks) which are held by the Bank of England as cover or backing for the fiduciary issue. Cf. fiat money. *Syn.* fiduciary money.

field staff COM. persons employed by a business to work in areas away from the office, such as travelling salesmen or representatives under a field sales manager. *Syn.* field workers; field personnel.

fieri facias LAW (*Latin*, see that it is done) a writ (order of a court of law) directing an officer to seize and sell the goods of a judgment debtor up to the amount of the debt. *Abbr.* fi. fa.

fi. fa. fieri facias.

F.I.F.O. first in, first out.

fifty-fifty (*colloq.*) in equal shares; fifty per cent each: *We share the profits fifty-fifty/on a fifty-fifty basis,* we each take half. *Let me go fifty-fifty with you on the expenses,* let me pay half. Having equal chances: *There is a fifty-fifty chance of success. Syn.* half-and-half.

fig. figurative(ly).

Fig. figure(s).

figure *n.* a sign for a number, as distinguished from a letter; an amount expressed in numbers: *The figure on the cheque is illegible,* the number written on it cannot be read. *He set its value at a very high figure.*

figures *pl.* numbers used in calculating and recording: *She is good at figures. Look into the figures,* examine them. *In legal documents, quantities are expressed in words and figures. Words and figures don't agree,* note written or stamped on a returned cheque pointing out the drawer's mistake.

Fiji a group of many islands in the south-central Pacific formed into an independent parliamentary state within the (British) Commonwealth, pop. 560,000 approx. (1973); capital, Suva, pop. 54,000 approx.; language, English; currency, the Fiji dollar (F$), divided into 100 cents.

filch to steal, esp. small things of little value. *Syn.* pilfer.

file *v.* (1) to put (papers, etc.) into a file in order to preserve them in a methodical system for later reference. (2) LAW to bring before a court of law: *To file an action for breach of contract.* (3) to register (a document) with a registrar: *The return has been filed with the Registrar of Companies.*
n. (1) any cover in which letters or other papers are kept together in proper order. (2) a collection of such covers kept in an orderly arrangement. *On file*, kept or held as a record. *File copy*, see office copy.

active file one that is in active use and is frequently being added to and referred to. Cf. dead file.

box file a cardboard or wooden box with a lid, for storing papers which must be kept free of dust.

dead file one that is no longer in use because it relates to a subject (person, activity, problem) that is not now active. Such files are usu. put in transfer or storage cases and stored for a certain number of years in a place away from the active files. Cf. active file.

individual file a folder or cover containing papers relating only to one subject such as one particular customer or supplier or employee. Cf. sundries *or* miscellaneous file.

miscellaneous file *see* sundries file *below*.

sundries file a folder or cover in which papers relating to several or many subjects such as customers, suppliers, etc. are filed, esp. when the correspondence with each is not frequent. All papers relating to one subject are kept together, and the various subjects are put into alphabetical or any other order that may have been decided, such as numerical, geographical. *Syn.* miscellaneous file.
(3) a complete division of a computer storage unit in which items of information, already arranged or classified in a planned order, are held ready for a particular purpose, such as producing data for inventory or pay-roll.

filing basket in an office, a basket or tray into which are put letters and other papers that are to be filed. *Syn.* filing tray.

filing cabinet a piece of office furniture, usu. made of steel, for storing files. *See* cabinet (2).

filing clerk a person employed in an office to look after the filing of letters, papers, etc.

filing system any methodical arrangement for keeping letters and other papers in proper order so that they may be quickly found when needed for reference.

alphabetical filing the usual method of keeping files, in alphabetical order (A, B, C, etc.) of subjects.

geographical filing a method of filing papers according to the areas or places to which they relate. It is adopted esp. where it is advisable to have customers of one country or city grouped together because they are visited by the same sales representatives.

lateral suspension filing an arrangement by which each file cover is kept in its own pocket hanging from a shelf, either in a cupboard or on a wall. This system takes the least space, and is now very much used in modern offices.

numerical filing a method adopted when a very large number of files have to be kept, esp. of persons such as patients in a hospital or customers of a large bank, many of whom will have the same name. Each person is given a number which is recorded on a card index. The folders containing the papers relating to each person are filed in numerical order.

subject filing the method of filing usu. adopted when the subject-matter of the paper is more important than the name of the person who wrote it or the place he wrote it from. All papers relating to one subject are kept together, and the subjects are then arranged in alphabetical order. Some subjects may be subdivided into several sub-headings, each with its cover filed alphabetically under the subject.

vertical suspension filing an arrangement by which each file cover is kept in its own hanging pocket in the drawer of the filing cabinet. Cf. lateral suspension filing *above*.

filing tray *see* filing basket.

fill to make full: *The packers fill the boxes. The goods fill the warehouse. A well-filled order book.* To fill a vacancy, to find and employ a person for a job: *The job/position/post/situation/vacancy is still unfilled. To fill the bill (colloq.)* to be satisfactory.

fill in to complete a document, esp. a form with blank spaces to write in.

fill up to fill completely, e.g. a petrol tank. Also as *fill in: To fill up a form.*

filler the fractional currency unit of Hungary. 100 filler = 1 forint.

filmsetting the setting of typematter on film, instead of in printer's metal.

fils the fractional unit of the currency of Bahrain, Iraq, Jordan, Kuwait and South Yemen (Aden): one-thousandth part of a dinar.

filthy lucre (*colloq.*) money, esp. when obtained dishonestly.

final (1) the last of a number of things coming one after another: *The final examinations. A final instalment/mortgage payment. This is our final notice/demand/warning,* we shall not ask again, but will take legal action unless you pay now. *Final port*, the port of destination, the end of the voyage. (2) replacing something temporary or incomplete or unsettled: *This final invoice replaces our earlier provisional/ estimated/pro-forma invoice. .A final date for delivery*, a firm date, or at last acceptable date.

final accounts *see* accounts, *n. pl.*

final application *see* application (3).

final distribution *see* distribution (7).

final dividend *see under* dividend (6).

final entry *see* books of final entry.

final invoice *see under* invoice.

final money *see under* money.

final utility *see* marginal utility.

finance *n.* FIN. (1) the management of money matters: *Public/business/company/private finance*. The controlling of money, esp. as an economic activity, such as investment. *The chairman is expert at finance. A director of finance. See* high finance. (2) the provision of money for a particular purpose such as capital to build a factory, or a loan to a farmer to help him to carry on until he sells his harvest.

finances *pl.* a supply of money from an accumulation or from revenue (money coming in). *The finances of the business are in a bad state.* *v.* FIN. (1) to provide or arrange means of payment: *He will finance the venture*, will put up the necessary capital. (2) to work in the business of providing money.

Finance Act *see* Finance Bill.

finance bill *see under* bill of exchange.

Finance Bill FIN. & LAW in Britain, a plan for a new law which the government presents to Parliament every year and which, when passed, becomes the Finance Act for that year. It gives the government power to obtain money, e.g. by taxation, and to spend money in certain approved ways.

finance company *see* finance house.

finance house BKG. & FIN. in Britain, a company of which the main business is the financing of hire-purchase. It does this by buying for cash, at a discounted price, the right to receive the regular part-payments, called instalments, under hire-purchase agreements between traders and buyers. For this purpose, finance houses borrow large sums from the commercial banks and attract large deposits from the public by paying higher rates of interest than those banks. They are therefore sometimes called secondary banks, but they do not have the legal position of a bank. The larger finance companies, many of which are controlled by the commercial banks, are members of the Finance Houses Association. *Syn.* finance company; secondary bank; industrial banker; hire-purchase company.

Finance Houses Association BKG. & FIN. an organization formed in London in 1945 by all the main British finance houses esp. to represent their interests to the government. Its members effect over 85% of all hire-purchase finance in the country.

finance market *see under* market.

financial advisers FIN. in Britain, a firm of merchant bankers who look after the interests of a company and of its shareholders during a takeover.

financial analysis FIN. the study of the present financial situation of a company, industry or country, using statistical information about the immediate past and taking note of present market tendencies, such as consumer demand and government spending. From such a study, a skilful analyst will produce a forecast of future movements of prices of securities and commodities, rates of interest, consumer spending, the cost of living, etc.

financial books *see* books of account.

financial budget MAN. & ACCTS. a statement or plan made after a study of the cash budget, intended to show to the management of a business (*a*) the amount of money that will have to be borrowed from time to time to meet any lack of cash and the source of such borrowings and (*b*) the amount of any excess of money that may accumulate from time to time and how it is to be employed. Cf. cash budget.

financial investment *see under* investment.

financial paper FIN. & BKG. in U.S.A., short-term loans made by banks for some purpose not connected with the buying or selling of goods. Cf. commercial paper; commodity paper.

financial position *see* financial statement (3).

financial standing COM. a person's or company's position and reputation, esp. in regard to ability to pay. *A firm of good financial standing can be trusted to pay bills promptly.*

financial statement (1) FIN. in Britain, a document giving detailed figures referred to in the budget speech which the Chancellor of the Exchequer makes in the House of Commons in March or April each year. The statement shows the changes in taxation and in certain other matters that will result if the budget proposals are made law. (2) LAW & STK. EXCH. in Britain, a document issued to shareholders before the annual general meeting of a company, containing the company's final accounts, the directors' report and sometimes the chairman's statement. (3) ACCTS. any document that shows the state of the finances or financial position of a person or organization, usu. listing assets and liabilities as in a balance sheet, or giving an account of profit and loss.

Financial Times, The FIN. the leading British daily newspaper dealing mainly, but not entirely, with business and financial matters, esp. the Stock Exchange, money market and commodity exchanges.

Financial Times-Actuaries Share Indexes STK. EXCH. a set of over 50 indexes calculated by computer with the help of the Institute of Actuaries in London and the Faculty of Actuaries in Edinburgh and published daily except Monday in the *Financial Times* newspaper. These indexes record movements in the market price of the shares of the more important companies, and are divided into sectors for capital goods, consumer goods, etc., and subdivided into the various industries. They are much used by investors.

Financial Times Industrial Ordinary Share Index STK. EXCH. the average price of 30 leading shares considered to represent the whole of British Industry. The index is published by the *Financial Times* newspaper in London twice each working day, at noon and at the close of business on the Stock Exchange and is regarded by investors as the best barometer of the state of the market for British securities. It is the equivalent of the Dow-Jones Industrial Average (U.S.A.). *See* business barometer. *Syn.* Thirty-Share Index; The Index.

financial year ACCTS. an accounting period, usu. of one complete year, such as from 1 January to 31 December. In Britain, however, the Companies Act defines it as the period covered by a company's accounts, which may not necessarily be one year. Cf. fiscal year.

financier FIN. (1) a person whose business it is to arrange finance, such as a banker. (2) a person, perh. an employee, with special knowledge of financing business ventures. *See* Lombard Street. (3) a person who finances a particular deal or venture by backing it with his money. *Syn.* backer. *See* angel.

fine (1) LAW a sum of money paid as a punishment by persons found guilty of breaking the law. (2) money demanded by trade unions from members who have been judged guilty of breaking the rules of the union.

fine bank bill *see* fine trade bill.

fineness FIN. of gold, of a standard of purity used for the former metal currencies of many countries. In Britain, the gold sovereign was made of eleven parts of pure gold and one part of other metals needed to harden the alloy. In U.S.A., the gold eagle ($10) was made of nine parts of pure gold and one part of other metals. Gold that is of the correct fineness according to the law is called *fine gold*.

fine paper BKG. & FIN. bills of exchange, cheques and promissory notes drawn on, or accepted or endorsed by, banks or other financial houses of first-class reputation. *Syn.* first-class paper; white paper. *Abbr.* f.p.

fine rate (of interest) *see* prime rate.

fine trade bill BKG. a bill of exchange of the highest class, and one which meets the qualifications demanded by the Bank of England for

bills which the Bank will accept from other banks as collateral security or for rediscounting. Such bills must have been accepted by a bank or by other financial houses of first-class reputation. *See* bank bill *under* bank; trade bill *under* bill of exchange. *Syn.* fine bank bill; respectable bill.

finish STK. & COMMOD. EXCH. the closing of the day's trading: *At the finish, gilts became active.*

fink (U.S.A. *colloq.*) a strikebreaker; a worker who acts against the orders or interests of his trade union. *Syn.* blackleg; scab.

Finland a republic in north-eastern Europe, pop. 4.6 million approx. (1972); capital, Helsinki, pop. 550,000 approx.; languages, Finnish and Swedish; currency unit, the Finnish mark or markka, *pl.* markkaa, divided into 100 pennia, *sing.* penni. Member, O.E.C.D.

Finnish mark *see* markka.

F.I.P.A. Fellow of the Institute of Incorporated Practitioners in Advertising.

fir. firkin.

fire MAN. (*colloq.*) to dismiss (an employee): *He was fired the next day. A hire-and-fire employer,* one who is merciless in dismissing his employees for the slightest reason.

fire insurance policy *see under* insurance, classes and kinds of; *also under* insurance policy.

fire loss adjuster INSCE. a person employed by a fire insurance company for his special knowledge of the valuing of losses by fire and for his skill in settling claims for such losses. *Syn.* claims adjuster.

fire office INSCE. an insurance company or society that insures property against fire and similar risks. Cf. life office.

firkin (1) an old liquid measure still used in the beer and ale trade, a small barrel of 9 imperial gallons. (2) a barrel of soap, 64 lb, and of butter, 56 lb. *Abbr.* fir.

firm *adj.* (1) STK. EXCH. of market prices, steady, with a tendency to rise: *Chemicals remained firm.* (2) STK. EXCH. of a bargain, fixed, settled, as compared with conditional or optional: *A firm price.* (3) COM. of a quotation, not to be changed: *This price is firm for seven days,* you can be sure that during that time the price will not change and the goods will be reserved for you, but not for any longer. *A firm price/offer,* one that is fixed, that the offerer is not willing to change. *Abbr.* F.O. *A firm order,* one that is settled and is not conditional.

adv. STK. EXCH. & COM. at a fixed or agreed price: *To buy firm,* to place an order at a fixed price for delivery now or at an agreed date, as compared with an option deal.

n. (1) ECON. THEORY the basic controlling unit the members of which bring together and direct the factors of production and cause distribution and trade to take place. It represents the decision-makers, the persons who direct what happens when changes take place in demand and supply. The firm forms part of an industry and controls one or more productive units or plants. *Syn.* entrepreneur. (2) ECON. THEORY in economic analysis, a single production unit, owned by one person, the entrepreneur, producing only one product, the price of which does not change. The entrepreneur behaves rationally, i.e. reasonably and with common sense, produces his product as cheaply as possible and tries to make as much profit as possible. This image of a firm is used as a tool in analysing basic situations relating esp. to production. Cf. consumer. (3) LAW an association of two or more persons who have formally agreed to work together as partners. A partnership. (4) COM. any business organization, or commercial house, whether it is a partnership or not, often a company. (5) (*colloq.*) any group of people who regularly work or play together.

firm sale *see under* sale.

first aid *see under* aid.

first call *see* call (3).

first class *n.* TRANSPT. & TOUR. the most comfortable and expensive class of accommodation for passengers on ships, trains, aircraft, and sometimes on buses and trams. Cf. second/third/tourist/economy class.

first-class *adj.* in the best class: *A first-class ticket/cabin/seat/hotel/passenger/compartment/saloon.*

first-class mail *see under* mail.

first-class paper *see* fine paper.

first cost *see* prime cost *under* cost.

first entry *see* books of first entry.

first-half *adj.* STK. EXCH. & ACCTS. relating to the first half of the financial year: *First-half profits were 40% up but the full-year figure showed little change.*

first-hand *adj.* COM. of goods, direct from the manufacturer, importer or shop. New and unused by anyone else. Cf. second-hand.

first in, first out (F.I.F.O.) ACCTS. & FIN. a method of valuing stocks by basing the value on the cost of the oldest items received into stock, in the belief that the items received first were also sold or used first. Cf. last in, first out (L.I.F.O.).

First Lord of the Treasury *see under* Treasury.

first mortgage *see under* mortgage.

first mortgage bond (U.S.A.) *see under* bond, *n.*

First of Exchange *see* bill (of exchange) in a set.

first officer *see* mate.

first premium *see under* premium.

first rate of the highest and best class; excellent. *Business is first rate*, extremely good.

first-rate *adj. This is of first-rate quality. First-rate investments.* Cf. second-rate.

fiscal *n.* LAW in some countries, a public official whose duty it is to take action against offenders in a court of law. A public prosecutor. In Scotland, a Procurator-fiscal.

adj. FIN. of or related to public money, taxes, debts, etc. *See* fiscal policy; fiscal year.

fiscal monopoly *see under* monopoly.

fiscal policy FIN. the plans made and followed by a government in raising and spending money. It raises money mainly by taxation, changes in which can affect personal incomes and the demand for goods. Changes in the way the government spends money can also affect the economy. *Syn.* budgetary policy.

fiscal year FIN. the government's financial year. In Britain, from 6 April in one year to 5 April the next. In the U.S.A., from 1 July to 30 June. *See* financial year. *Syn.* tax year.

Fisher Irving (1867–1947), American mathematician and economist, Professor of Political Economy at Yale University. His *Nature of Capital and Income* (1906), *Rate of Interest* (1907), *Purchasing Power of Money* (1911), and *Theory of Interest* (1930) had great influence particularly on the growth of mathematical method in economics and on the development of econometrics. *See* Fisher Equation.

Fisher Equation ECON. THEORY $MV = PT$, Irving Fisher's way of explaining the Quantity Theory of Money by introducing the two (then new) concepts (ideas) of the velocity of circulation of money (V) and the total volume of goods and services (T) where M is the quantity of money and P the general price-level. *See* Quantity Theory. *Syn.* Equation of Exchange; Quantity Equation; Transactions Equation.

fisherman one who catches fish as the main way of earning a living. Cf. fishmonger.

fishery (1) AGR. any organized activity aimed at catching fish, esp. as a commercial venture. (2) a place where fish are caught. *Pl.* fisheries.

fishmonger COM. a trader who buys and sells fish. Cf. fisherman.

fishy FIN. (*colloq.*) financially doubtful; causing a feeling of distrust; not entirely to be trusted: *The whole deal seems fishy to me.*

f.i.t. free of income tax.

fit to fit out, to supply with the necessary machinery, instruments, furniture and comforts. *To fit out a ship. To fit out a factory. We fitted him out with working clothes/tools.*

a fitting-out basin a piece of enclosed water where new ships are fitted out or where old ships are repaired.

fitting (1) one of a number of combinations of size and shape, esp. in clothing, boots and shoes: *A wide/narrow fitting. Shoes are made in three fittings for each size of foot.* (2) in tailoring, the operation of trying on new clothes to make sure that they fit properly. (3) LAW *see* fixtures and fittings.

fiver (*colloq.*) a five-pound note, or a five-dollar bill.

f.i.w. free in (or into) wagon(s).

fixed (1) settled, not changing or varying: *Fixed prices/rates of interest/charges.* Opp. flexible. (2) (*colloq.*) secretly arranged, usu. deceitfully or dishonestly, such as by bribery or unfair influence: *Our rivals had fixed the deal beforehand by bribing the negotiator.*

fixed assets *see under* assets, *pl.*

fixed capital *see under* capital.

fixed charge *see under* charges on assets.

fixed charges ACCTS. & FIN. business expenses that are likely to continue unchanged so long as the business remains in existence, such as debenture interest. Any expense that does not vary with size of output or total sales.

fixed costs *see under* costs (2).

fixed credit *see under* credit, *n.* (3).

fixed debenture *see under* debenture.

fixed debt *see* funded debt *under* national debt.

fixed deposit *see under* deposit.

fixed duty *see* specific duty *under* duty (3).

fixed expenses *see under* expenses.

fixed income *see under* income.

fixed instalment system ACCTS. a way of providing for the depreciation of an asset by writing off each year a fixed percentage of its original cost until its book value is equal to its scrap value at the end of its useful life. *See* depreciation methods.

fixed-interest securities STK. EXCH. in Britain, securities that bear a fixed rate of interest, which are called *creditor securities* or *debentures* when issued by joint-stock companies and *government stocks* when issued as government loans. In addition, many companies issue *preference shares* which bear a fixed rate of interest; these are not creditor securities, but their holders have a claim to the company's assets before the holders of ordinary shares, but after the debenture-holders. In U.S.A. the fixed-interest securities issued by stock corporations are called *corporate bonds*, and those issued by government agencies are *U.S. Government bonds*, *state bonds* and *municipal bonds*.

fixed investment *see under* investment.

fixed liabilities *see* deferred liabilities *under* liabilities.

fixed penalty bond *see* penalty bond *under* bond, *n.*

fixed price *see under* price.

fixed-sum debenture *see under* debenture.

fixed supply *see under* supply.

fixed trust *see under* trust.

fixture SHIPG. in chartering ships, a firm arrangement for a ship to be ready to load cargo on a fixed date and at a port convenient to the charterers.

fixtures and fittings (1) LAW things fixed or fastened to a house by permanent fastenings such as nails, screws, cement, etc. and therefore considered to be part of the house itself when sold, unless it is agreed otherwise. By contrast, any articles not permanently fixed to the house are not included as part of the house. (2) ACCTS. one of the fixed assets of a business, so far as they continue to be owned and enjoyed by the business.

FL Liechtenstein's international vehicle-registration letters.

fl. florin (Dutch guilder).

Fla. Florida, U.S.A.

flag a piece of coloured cloth, usu. with distinguishing marks on it, used to show a country or organization to which the user belongs. Each nation has its own flag, and so have airlines, shipping lines, etc., so that nationality and ownership can be easily recognized. Flags are also used to make signals, to show rank, and to mark places and special occasions: *A ship sailing under the Egyptian flag.* *A house flag,* a special flag flown by vessels of a particular shipping line or airline. *See* flag of convenience.

flag of convenience SHIPG. the national flag of certain small countries, esp. Panama, Liberia, Honduras and Costa Rica (collectively known as 'Panlibhonco') who are willing to register ships owned by nationals of other countries. These owners are attracted by the 'conveniences' offered which include: cheap registration; low standards of safety equipment; low rates of pay and poor quality of living accommodation for the crew; and above all, a means of avoiding heavy taxation. *Syn.* flag of necessity.

flag of necessity *see* flag of convenience.

flat *adj.* STK. EXCH. of market conditions, in low spirits, with prices falling because there is insufficient demand. *Syn.* depressed.
n. (1) COM. a set of rooms in which people live, usu. all on the same floor of a building called a *block of flats.* *Syn.* (U.S.A.) apartment. (2) TRANSPT. any flat vehicle without sides such as a railway wagon, truck or lorry; also a barge with flat deck.

flat broke (*colloq.*) completely without money; penniless.

flat cost *see* prime cost *under* cost.

flat rate *see* flat yield *under* yield.

flat-rate tariff COM. a method of charging small users of electricity, at a fixed sum per unit consumed.

flat yield *see under* yield.

fleece to rob someone of all his money. *Syn.* to skin.

fleet (1) SHIPG. a group of ships or boats sailing together, esp. as a fishing fleet. (2) SHIPG. all the ships owned by one shipping company. (3) SHIPG. the ships owned by a particular country, esp. its fleet of warships. (4) TRANSPT a group of cars, lorries or other road vehicles belonging to a particular owner.

fleet rating INSCE. specially low premium rates charged by an insurer to cover a fleet of ships, cars, trucks, etc. belonging to one owner.

fleet terms special discounts given by a car dealer to a company owning a fleet of cars, usu. provided that it agrees to buy all its cars from that dealer.

Fleet Street an important street in the City of London in and near which most of the main British daily newspapers have their offices. It has thus become a name for the newspaper world generally.

flexible that can be bent or changed or adapted: *A flexible budget*, one that can be varied from time to time. *Flexible tariffs*, a scale of import duties that can be changed at short notice to deal with such problems as dumping. *Opp.* fixed.

flexible trust *see under* trust.

flight (1) the act of flying. (2) TRANSPT. a journey by aeroplane: *A direct/non-stop flight*, without stopping on the way. *A night flight*. (3) a regular air trip or journey on a fixed route at a fixed time daily, weekly, etc., bearing a *flight number* and called a *scheduled flight*. *There are ten flights daily to Cairo*.

flight of capital BKG. & FIN. a movement of capital on a large scale away from one country in time of economic difficulty, usu. caused by fear that the currency will very soon lose value in relation to other currencies. Such flights of capital can only make the situation more difficult still.

flimsy very thin paper used when typing several carbon copies at one time.

flit (*colloq.*) to leave one's home secretly, without giving notice, to avoid paying what one owes: *To do a moonlight flit*, to run away during the night leaving rent owing to one's landlord. *Also, To shoot the moon*.

float *n.* (1) ACCTS. the sum of money held in an imprest account. *See* imprest system. (2) COM. the opening balance of coins and notes in a shopkeeper's till (drawer for holding money). *Syn.* cash float. (3) TRANSPT. a low flat wagon or truck for carrying goods: *A milk float*, an electric vehicle used in Britain for delivering milk. *An advertising float*, a flat wooden floor on wheels, for carrying an advertisement display through the streets.

v. FIN. & STK. EXCH. to start a business: *To float a company*, to provide the capital and make the necessary arrangements to form the company. *See* company promoter.

floatation *n. see* flotation.

floater (1) INSCE. *see* floating policy *under* policy of insurance. (2) IND. a worker, esp. a docker, who prefers casual (irregular) employment and to choose jobs that he thinks will bring him the most money.

floaters BKG. & STK. EXCH. (1) government bearer bonds which are given by bill-brokers to a bank as security for money lent to them at call. *See* bearer bonds. (2) *see* bearer security *under* bearer. (3) local authority stocks that have a rate of interest that floats, i.e. that is liable to be changed, usu. every six months according to changes in the general level of interest.

floating assets *see* current assets *under* assets.

floating capital *see* working capital *under* capital.

floating charge *see under* charges on assets.

floating currency *see under* currency.

floating debenture *see under* debenture.

floating debt (1) *see under* national debt. (2) a debt that may have to be repaid at short notice, such as money borrowed at call.

floating dock SHIPG. a movable dock which, by means of a system of tanks and pumps, can be lowered in the water to allow a ship to enter, and can then be raised, lifting the ship out of the water for repair. Cf. dry dock.

floating exchange rate FIN. an exchange rate that is allowed to move up and down according to the conditions of supply and demand in the foreign-exchange market. *See* exchange rate. *Syn.* free-exchange rate.

floating insurance *see under* insurance, classes and kinds of.

floating money *see under* money.

floating mortgage *see under* mortgage.

flog (*colloq.*) to sell, usu. something that has been dishonestly obtained: *The youth flogged his mother's jewellery*.

flood (1) INSCE. an overflowing of water; one of the special perils (risks) against which protection is given in most fire insurance policies. (2) COM. a rush; a very large number, e.g. of orders/complaints, etc.

flood tide SHIPG. the flow of the tide as it rises, a period of about six hours, followed by the ebb: *The ship sailed on the flood tide*. *Syn.* the flow. *Opp.* ebb tide.

floor (1) the lowest part of a room; the bottom surface on which one stands or walks. *Floor space*, the area of building that can be used for productive activity, usu. expressed in square feet or square metres.

price-floor the lowest point below which a controlled price is not allowed to fall. Cf. price-ceiling.

shop floor (*a*) the main space in a factory or workshop where the goods are produced. (*b*) the main body of ordinary workers. *To rise from the shop floor*, to progress from being an ordinary worker to holding a post of responsibility.

wages floor the lowest amount of wages that may by law be paid. *Syn.* minimum wage.

(2) a set of rooms or space taking up the whole of one level of a building: *The ground floor*, level with the ground outside, at street level; in

U.S.A. this is called the first floor. *The first floor*, in Britain, the floor next above the ground floor, but in U.S.A. this is called the second floor, and so on. *To be in/come in/be let in/on the ground floor (colloq.)*, to take part in a venture from the beginning. *To be on the floor*, to be very poor, to have no money. (3) the hall in which members of the London Stock Exchange meet to do business.

flop COM. of a business venture, a failure: *His new book/film/play/was a flop. Our advertising campaign has proved to be a flop.*

flop-house (U.S.A. *colloq.*) a cheap, low-class lodging-house. *Syn.* doss-house.

florin FIN. (1) an ancient gold coin originally from Florence, but made part of the British gold coinage in the fourteenth century. Since 1849 a silver or cupro-nickel coin worth one-tenth of a pound, i.e. two shillings, now ten pence. (2) a name given to the guilder or gulden of the Netherlands. *Abbr.* fl.

flotation FIN. & STK. EXCH. the act, or work, of starting a business, esp. a company. *The flotation of shares*, the issue of a new company's shares esp. to the public. *Also* floatation.

flotel TOUR. a floating hotel, esp. a former passenger liner now used for this purpose.

flotsam SHIPG. & LAW cargo goods floating on the sea after a shipwreck. In British waters, they become the property of the Crown if not claimed within a year and a day. Cf. jetsam.

flow (1) movement in a stream: *The oil is now on flow/has come on flow. There is a speedy flow of goods going out/money coming in/orders/ complaints/enquiries.* (2) the rising tide, *see* flood tide.

flow chart FIN. & IND. any diagram intended to explain a process or operation step by step. *Syn.* flow diagram; flow process chart.

flow of funds *see* cash flow.

flow production *see* mass production.

fluctuate to move up and down; to rise and fall continually: *Prices fluctuated widely all day.*

fluctuations ECON. upward and downward movements in the economic system. *Economic fluctuations* are booms and slumps when industrial activity rises and falls, also called *trade fluctuations* and *industrial fluctuations. See* trade cycle *under* cycle. *Market fluctuations, price fluctuations*, periods of rising and falling market prices.

fluff COM. (*colloq.*) to take dishonest advantage of a customer by giving him the wrong change, in the expectation that he will not notice. *Syn.* to short-change.

fluidity of labour *see* mobility of labour.

fluid measure *see* liquid measure.

flush (*colloq.*) having plenty of money; rich.

flutter COM. a small bet or wager; a small commercial venture.

fly a kite *see* kite-flying *under* kite.

fly-back (*colloq.*) a worthless cheque.

fly-by-night (1) a debtor who runs away from his creditors secretly at night. (2) an irresponsible person, more interested in enjoying himself than in doing any work. (3) a person or business that is not firmly established but interested only in making quick profits, esp. by slightly dishonest methods.

fly-cruise TOUR. a sea-cruise by ship starting and ending at a foreign port, to and from which air travel is arranged.

fly pitch COM. a temporary shop or stand for selling goods in a street-market or market-place.

fm. fathom.

F.O. firm offer.

fo. folio.

f/o. for orders.

f.o.b. free on board.

fob off to sell someone an article of poor quality by making him think it is good; to cheat; to deceive: *He fobbed me off with an imitation jewel. They always fob one off with promises which they never keep.* Cf. foist.

F.O.C., f.o.c. free of charge; free of claims.

foc's'le *see* forecastle.

F.O.D. free of damage.

fodder AGR. food for farm animals. esp. if dried and stored, such as hay. *Fodder crop*, a crop grown only to be dried as food for animals. Cf. feed; forage.

foist to persuade a person to buy bad goods by pretending that they are good: *To foist a useless article on a customer. I have been foisted off with a bad machine.* Cf. fob.

fol. folio.

folder (1) a cover for papers, usu. a piece of stiff paper or card folded in two. (2) a folded sheet of printed paper giving information about a product to help to sell it. (3) a machine for folding letters, leaflets, etc. before they are put into envelopes. (4) a machine for folding the sheets of printed books in the process of bookbinding.

fold up COM. of a business or company, to come to an end; to stop trading; to go into liquidation.

folg. following.

folio (1) a leaf of a book or handwritten paper numbered only on one side. (2) used by printers to refer to the page number of a book. *Abbr.* f.; fo.; fol. (3) ACCTS. the number of a single page in a journal, or of a pair of facing pages in a ledger.

folio column in an account book, a column into which the book-keeper writes the number of the folio or page of another account book where the corresponding entry is to be found.

follow (1) to employ oneself in: to engage in, a profession or trade: *To follow a calling/occupation. He follows the sea*, is a sailor. *I follow the law*, am a lawyer. (2) to act in agreement with;

to accept: *To follow advice/directions/instructions/precedent*. (3) to keep up with; to keep in line with: *To follow the fashions/latest news/scientific developments*.

to follow up to cause one action to be followed by another in order to get a result where the first action has failed or is not complete, such as sending out a *follow-up letter* to customers who have made an enquiry but have not yet placed an order.

food (1) any material that is eaten: *Farmers grow food for human beings and for animals. Fish are caught for food*. (2) dry or solid substances that are eaten, rather than liquids that are drunk: *Our shop sells food and drink*. (3) a particular product that is eaten, esp. if prepared for a particular purpose: *Canned/frozen/dog/cat food*. See convenience goods.

Food and Agriculture Organization a specialized agency of the United Nations with its central office in Rome, having responsibility for organizing agricultural development programmes in accordance with a world plan to end hunger and improve nutrition (feeding habits). *Abbr*. F.A.O.

foodgrains AGR. & COM. the seeds of grasses that are used as food, such as wheat, maize and rice.

foodstuff any substance regularly used as food, such as grain, sugar and meat.

foolscap (1) a standard size of printing paper: in Britain, 17 in. × 13½ in. (432 mm × 343 mm); in U.S.A., 16 in. × 12 in. (406 mm × 305 mm). (2) in Britain, also a size of writing paper, 16½ in. × 13¼ in. (419 mm × 337 mm). *Abbr*. f'cap.; f/cap.; fcp.; cap.

foot *n*. a standard unit of length in Britain, U.S.A. and other countries, 12 inches or one-third of a yard. One foot = 0.3048 metre exactly. *Abbr*. ft. *Sign*: ': *A table 3' wide*.

feet *pl*. (but foot when used with inches): *Six feet. Five foot ten inches*.

foot rule a straight-edge one foot long, usu. marked in inches and divisions of an inch, for measuring and for drawing straight lines.

v. (*colloq*.) *To foot up*, to add up a column of figures. *To foot the bill*, to pay, to bear the cost.

footage COM. a length expressed in feet; a rate of payment by the foot; an amount of money paid for material or work measured by the foot: *Footage for digging a 300-foot trench at £50 per 100-foot run = £150*.

footgear *see* footwear.

footwear COM. a trade name for boots and shoes. *Syn*. footgear.

f.o.q. free on quay.

f.o.r. free on rail.

for. foreign.

forage AGR. food for farm animals, esp. if eaten by grazing or browsing or fed fresh, not dried.

Forage crops, grown as food for animals, such as maize for silage (preserving in a silo). Cf. fodder; feed.

force *n*. (1) strength or power; effect: *The forces of nature. Winds of gale force. There is no need to use force*, be gentle. *The force of circumstances*, effects outside one's control. *The force of public opinion. Market forces. The forces of supply and demand*. (2) LAW operation; effect: *This law is in force/has come into force/no longer has (any) force*. Strength: *The force of law*. (3) INSCE. a policy is *in force* between the time of its acceptance by the insurer and the time it expires (ends) or is cancelled.

forced labour *see* slavery; serfdom.

forced sale *see under* sale.

forced saving *see under* saving.

forced selling *see under* selling.

force majeure LAW (*French*, superior force) a cause or event which neither party to a contract can control such as action by a government in time of war, or strikes, lockouts and Acts of God. If a contract states that it is 'subject to *force majeure*', either or both parties may be excused from performing their part of the agreement in such an event.

forces and services bounty *see under* bounty.

forecast (1) an account of what may be expected to happen in the future, usu. by looking at conditions that lie ahead: *Plans are based on forecasts. A forecast of sales/expenses/profits. A weather forecast*. (2) ECON. any methodical attempt to tell the nature, extent and direction of future changes in the economic system, such as a change in the size of the population. Such forecasts, called projections, are essential aids when deciding government policy.

forecastle SHIPG. the raised forward part of a merchant ship, often containing the seamen's quarters. *Also written* fo'c'sle. *Pron*. foak-sl.

foreclosure LAW the action of a mortgagee (lender) in exercising his right to obtain a court order, called a *foreclosure nisi*, against a mortgagor (borrower) who has failed to repay a debt by the due date. The court order will fix a new date by which the mortgagor must pay the debt. If he fails to do so he loses his equity of redemption (his right to regain possession of the mortgaged property) and the mortgagee has permission to sell the property. *V*. to foreclose.

fore-date *see* ante-date.

foreign aid ECON. & FIN. money, goods and services given by the government of one, usu. developed, country to help the people of another, usu. poor country. Such help may be in the form of: *technical aid*, to improve scientific and industrial skills; *development aid*, aimed to raise real income and living standards; relief after a single disaster (sudden misfortune) such as a severe earthquake; and sometimes *military aid*, to help a weak country to defend itself from attack. The effects of foreign aid on international economic relations are of great importance.

foreign balance *see* balance of payments.

foreign banks BKG· in Britain, the branches of banks incorporated (formally set up and registered) outside Great Britain. Branches of banks with their head offices in the (British) Commonwealth are sometimes called British overseas banks.

foreign bill *see under* bill of exchange.

foreign company LAW in Britain, a company incorporated (formally set up and registered) outside Great Britain, but having a place of business within this country. A foreign company must, within 30 days of setting up a place of business in Britain, give certain information about itself to the Registrar of Companies. It must also state its name and the country in which it is incorporated on all its letterheadings, bill-heads, notices, advertisements and other official documents. *Syn.* overseas company.

Foreign Credit Insurance Association (U.S.A.) INSCE. & COM. an organization that insures U.S. exporters against commercial credit risks while the Export-Import Bank insures against political risks; together they correspond to the British Export Credits Guarantee Department. *Abbr.* F.C.I.A.

foreign currency *see under* currency.

foreign exchange BKG. & FIN. (1) the currency of a country other than one's own: *My bankers will supply me with foreign exchange for my trip abroad: French francs, lire and Egyptian pounds.* (2) the exchanging of the currency of one country for that of another. (3) the practice of buying and selling the money of other countries. *See* direct exchange.

foreign-exchange broker BKG. & FIN. a professional agent for the buying and selling of foreign exchange. He may represent the government or any of the foreign-exchange dealers (mostly commercial banks) but not the general public; he is paid for his work, of bringing buyers and sellers together, by a commission on each deal, called *exchange brokerage*. *Syn.* exchange broker.

foreign-exchange dealer BKG. & FIN. a professional dealer in the money of other currencies; usu. an official of one of the commercial banks who has been authorized by the exchange control department of the Bank of England to buy and sell foreign exchange for his bank and its customers. *Syn.* exchange dealer.

foreign-exchange market BKG. & FIN. in Britain, a group of exchange dealers, mostly representing the commercial banks, and the exchange brokers. The market has two main divisions, the *spot market*, in which deliveries are made

and paid for on the spot (immediately), and the *forward market*, in which deals are arranged for future deliveries, to be paid for on agreed dates on or after delivery. Deals must be in accordance with the directions of the exchange control department of the Bank of England.

foreign-exchange office *see* bureau de change.

foreign investment *see under* investment.

foreign money order *see* overseas money order *under* money order.

foreign trade *see* international trade.

foreign (trade) zone *see* free port *under* port.

foreman (1) IND. a man in charge of a number of workers. Cf. forewoman. (2) LAW a member of a jury chosen by other members to speak for all of them.

foreshore (1) LAW that part of the seashore that lies between the high-water and low-water states of the tides. In Britain, this land belongs to the Crown (the State). (2) any strip of land between the edge of the sea and the nearest farmland or buildings. (3) land facing the sea.

forest (1) a large area of land now covered, or formerly covered, mainly by trees. Cf. woodland. (2) ECON. an area of land on which large numbers of trees are grown for commercial gain.

forester a person employed in looking after forests.

forewoman IND a woman in charge of a number of workers, who may be either men or women.

forestalling ECON. & COM. the ancient, and sometimes illegal, practice by some merchants of buying the entire harvest of an important agricultural product, or the entire output of an industry, before it reached the market, with the intention of wiping out competition and gaining monopolistic control of the market price. *Syn.* regrating; engrossing.

forestry (1) AGR. the science and work of managing forests. (2) an area of land covered by forests.

forfeited share *see under* share.

forfeiture LAW loss of a right to some property as a punishment for a crime or wrong-doing, such as a fine, or as a penalty for failure to perform a duty, such as shares forfeited (lost) because the issuing company's calls for payment have not been met.

forge *v.* to perform the act of forgery: *He forged her signature on the will. They were caught forging bank-notes. This is a forged document. He gave me a forged cheque.* *Syn.* to counterfeit.

forger *n.* one who forges.

forgery LAW (1) the common-law offence of making or altering (changing) any document with the intention of causing harm to another person's rights. (2) making a false document in order that it may be used as genuine (the real thing) such as false bank-notes or cheque signatures. (3) deceitfully making an imitation of a seal. (4) any false thing that has been made in order that it may be used as the real thing: *This bank-note/that signature is a forgery. Syn.* a counterfeit.

forgive COM. & FIN. to give up all claim to: *To forgive (someone) a debt.*

forint the standard currency unit of Hungary, divided into 100 filler.

fork-lift truck a small industrial truck, usu. driven by electric batteries, for lifting and carrying loads on pallets (small trays or platforms) from one part of a factory to another. *Syn.* materials handling truck; industrial truck.

fork out (*colloq.*) to pay, usu. unwillingly: *They made me fork out £15 for the meal.*

forlorn hope COM. a commercial or other venture that has little possibility of success.

form *n.* (1) a shape; an appearance: *A trademark in the form of a ship. Publicity in the form of circular letters.* (2) a kind; a sort: *Different forms of industrial combination/advertising/ partnership.* (3) a model to be followed esp. for documents: *A legal form. A form of words. See* forms of address. (4) a printed document with spaces left in which answers to questions or other information may be written or typed: *A form of application* or *an application form. A cheque form. An order form.*
v. (1) to give shape or existence to; to set up; to organize: *To form a company/trade association/cartel/partnership. Have you formed an opinion?* (2) to make up; to be: *The company forms part of a large group. Groceries form the basis of our business. The cash book forms part of the books of account.*

formal (1) according to accepted rules: *A formal meeting/dinner/occasion. Formal proceedings of the court. Opp.* informal; casual. (2) giving necessary authority: *Formal permission/authorization,* usu. in writing. *A formal order,* recording in writing one given by word of mouth. *A formal denial/refusal/acceptance,* a solemn expression of denial, etc.

formal contract *see* specialty contract *under* contract.

formal incidence *see* impact (3).

formality (1) something that has to be done because a rule has to be obeyed: *Legal/customs formalities.* (2) unnecessary attention to custom and etiquette (rules of behaviour).

format the general appearance and form of an object, esp. a book: its size, shape, kind of binding, quality of paper, typographic design and general arrangement.

formation expenses ACCTS. & MAN. amounts of money advanced by the promoters of a new company before it is incorporated and can start trading, such as legal and accounting fees, stamp duty and registration charges. Such

amounts are usu. repaid by the company once it is in existence and they are written off in the first year of trading. *Syn.* promotion expenses.

formation of a company *see* company formation; company promoter.

former of earlier times. *The former,* the person or thing first mentioned.

formerly in past times.

for money STK. EXCH. of deals, to be paid for in cash immediately, not on the next Settling Day. Cf. for The Account.

Formosa *see* Taiwan.

forms of address by custom, the correct ways of addressing persons of different rank and profession, such as: in addressing an envelope, Mr, Mrs, Messrs, Esq., Dr, etc.; in the salutation or the beginning of the letter, Dear Sir, Dear Madam, Sirs, Gentlemen, etc.; in closing the letter, Yours faithfully/sincerely/truly.

formula a set form or list of words or numbers intended to be followed as a guide to doing or making something, or to human behaviour: *A secret formula for making medicine/paint. Mathematical/algebraic/geometrical formulae. Courtesy formulas,* such polite expressions as 'Good morning', 'How do you do?', 'Excuse me'. *Pl.* formulas *or* formulae. *Pron.* -las *or* -lee. *See* Fortran.

formulate to express very exactly; to state clearly, as a formula to be followed: *To formulate a plan/policy/claim/problem. N.* formulation.

for The Account STK. EXCH. of deals, to be paid for at the next Account Day. Cf. for money.

fortnight *n.* two weeks; a period of 14 days: *Some workers are paid every fortnight. The factory is inspected once a fortnight. Adv.* fortnightly: *We advertise fortnightly in the national papers. Adj. A fortnightly magazine/steamer service/bank statement/account.*

Fortran COMP. a machine language, called in full Formula Translation, used for scientific and algebraic computer programs. Cf. Cobol; Algol.

fortuity MAR. INSCE. an accident; any chance event causing loss or damage which was not inevitable, i.e. which was not certain to happen. *Adj.* fortuitous.

fortune (1) great wealth, esp. a large accumulation of money; success in making money: *To make/seek/possess a fortune. To come into a fortune,* to inherit much money. *There is a fortune to be made in stockbroking. A fortune-hunter,* a man looking for a rich woman to marry. (2) luck; chance: *I wish you good fortune To try one's fortune,* to take a risk in business *A fortune-teller,* a person who claims to tell future events.

fortunes *pl. He suffered a decline in fortunes* luck turned against him. *The fortunes of war* chances of good and bad luck, of success an failure in wartime.

fortunate *adj.* having good fortune; favoured by good luck; successful.

fortunately *adv.* luckily; happily; by good fortune.

forward *adv.* (1) towards the front; ahead: *Prices moved forward*, rose steadily. (2) SHIPG. in the front part of the ship: *The seamen's quarters are forward*. *Pron.* forrard. *adj.* (1) in the front: *The forward hold*, nearest the front of the ship. (2) in the future: *A forward contract*, one for performance in the future. *Forward delivery*. See charges forward. *v.* (1) to cause to move ahead; to dispatch; to send: *To forward a consignment of goods by rail*. See forwarding agent. (2) to re-address and send on by post a letter or parcel that has arrived for someone who has gone to another address: *Please forward*, note on letters, etc. where this may be necessary. *He arranged for his mail to be forwarded*. *Syn.* redirect. (3) ACCTS. see brought forward; carried forward.

forward buying COM. & IND. buying stocks of materials well in advance of having to use them, partly to make sure of supplies being ready when needed, and partly to increase one's profit when prices are rising. *Syn.* stockpiling.

forward dealings see commodity exchanges.

forwarder see shipping and forwarding agent.

forward exchange see forward rate *under* exchange rate; *also* foreign-exchange market.

forwarding agent see shipping and forwarding agent.

forward integration see *under* integration.

forward market see foreign-exchange market.

forward price COM., STK. & COMMOD. EXCH. the price of an article or commodity for delivery at an agreed date in the future, as distinguished from the current or spot price for immediate delivery. If the forward price is higher than the current price, it is said to be *at a premium*; if the opposite is the case, it is said to be *at a discount*.

forward rate see *under* exchange rate.

f.o.s. free on ship/steamer/station.

f.o.t. free on truck(s).

F.O.T. free of tax.

foul SHIPG. to crash into; to come into violent contact with: *The vessel fouled the jetty*.

foul bill of health see *under* bill of health.

foul bill of lading see dirty bill of lading *under* bill of lading.

found *v.* to set up on a firm basis; to bring into permanent existence: *To found a business/industry/society*, etc. *The business was founded in 1724*. *Syn.* to establish.

founder (1) a person who founds something: *The founder of the business was John Smith. I am a founder-member of the club*, one of the founders. (2) SHIPG. to become filled with water and sink.

founders' share see *under* share.

fourth estate the press; newspapers and the journalists who write and edit them. In Britain, any powerful group, outside the government and the church, that can influence the affairs of the nation.

fourth market see *under* market.

f.o.w. free on wagon; first open water.

fox *v.* (1) (*colloq.*) to deceive by a trick: *He foxed me by pretending to be rich*. (2) to puzzle: *These figures fox me completely*. *Adj.* foxy.

foyer a hall or public room in a hotel or theatre where people can meet.

f.p. fine paper; fully paid (shares).

F.P. fire policy; floating policy.

F.P.A. free of particular average.

F/R folio reference.

F.R. freight release.

Fr. franc; France; Friday.

fr. franc; from.

fractional banking BKG. a practice, in some countries demanded by law, by which banks keep their cash reserves at a fixed percentage of their deposit liabilities (the amount owed to customers). See cash ratio.

fractional certificate STK. EXCH. (1) a share certificate for a fraction (part) of a share, a need arising esp. when two companies are merged (become one) and there is an exchange of shares in unequal proportions, such as four shares of one company for three of the other. (2) see deferred interest certificate.

fractional currency see *under* currency.

fractional money see *under* money.

franc a former gold coin of France, now the name of the standard monetary unit of a number of countries; they include the French, Belgian, Swiss, Luxemburg, New Hebrides, Burundi, Malagasy Republic, Mali, Rwanda, Djibouti, C.F.A. and C.F.P. francs, divided into 100 centimes, but having different values. The Moroccan franc is an exception; *see below*.

C.F.A. franc the standard monetary unit of the Communauté Financière Africaine, used in: Cameroon, Central African Republic, Chad, Comoro Is., Congo (Brazzaville), Dahomey, Gabon, Ivory Coast, Niger, Réunion, Senegal, Togo, Upper Volta, all former French colonies or protectorates. *Syn.* African franc. *Abbr.* C.F.A. Fr. *or* Fr. C.F.A.

C.F.P. franc the standard monetary unit of the Communauté Financière du Pacifique, used in: French Polynesia, New Caledonia, and the Wallis and Futuna Is., all former French colonies. **French franc** the franc used in France, Andorra, French Guiana, Guadeloupe, Martinique, Monaco, and St. Pierre and Miquelon. *Abbr.* F.; fr.; Fr.

Moroccan franc the fractional currency unit of Morocco. 1 dirham = 100 Moroccan francs.

Swiss franc the franc used in Switzerland and also in Liechtenstein.

France a republic in western Europe, pop. 52 million approx. (1973); capital, Paris, pop. 8 million approx.; language, French; currency unit, the French franc (f. *or* F., fr. *or* Fr., frs. *or* Frs., fcs. *or* Fcs.), divided into 100 centimes. Member, E.E.C.; O.E.C.D.

franchise (1) COM. an arrangement by which a monopoly producer (the franchisor) gives another producer or trader (the franchisee) by formal licence the exclusive right, i.e. a right held by no one else, to manufacture or sell the products of the franchisor in a certain area such as a town, county or country. The franchisee may pay the franchisor by a royalty on the number of units produced or on the number sold, and he may agree to buy all his supplies only from the franchisor. (2) MAR. INSCE. an amount of loss below which in certain conditions the insurers are not bound to pay anything, but above which they are bound to pay in full. The purpose is to discourage very small claims. Cf. excess (2).

franco COM. (*French*, free) a foreign-trade price quotation which includes the cost of the goods and all risks and charges up to a stated point. Where no point is stated, franco means delivery free of expense to the buyer's warehouse as the English f.o.b., f.o.r., etc. *Syn.* rendu.

franco à bord *see* free on board.

franco domicile *or* **franco domicilium** delivered free of expense to the consignee's address. *Syn.* free delivered.

franco frontier delivered free to the frontier (border) of the exporting country.

franco invoice *see under* invoice.

franco quay *see* free alongside ship.

franco wagon *see* free on rail.

frank (1) to put an official mark on a letter, parcel, etc. instead of postage stamps, to show that the postage has been paid by a special arrangement with the Post Office. *See* franking machine. (2) to mark a postage stamp on a letter, parcel, etc. to prevent it being used again. *See* postmark. *Syn.* cancel.

franked investment income FIN. & STK. EXCH. income on which tax has already been paid, such as dividends from preference shares. To a company having money to invest, it would be more attractive to buy such an investment because the company would not have to pay tax on the dividends; on the other hand, if the company were to invest in loan stock (debentures) it would have to pay tax on the income received in the form of interest.

franking machine MAN. & ACCTS. a relatively fast machine for franking envelopes and labels with the correct postage without the use of gummed postage stamps. The machine has a meter in which the value of the franking is recorded and the amount payable to the Post Office is determined. *See also* stamping machine.

fraud LAW the gaining of some material advantage by dishonest means. A court will order an offender to pay damages if it is proved that he has used deceit with the intention that the plaintiff (the person bringing the case) should act upon the deception, that the plaintiff did act upon it and suffered damage as a result. *See* deceit; holding out; misrepresentation. *Syn.* false representation. *Adj.* fraudulent. *V.* to defraud. *Syn.* cheat; swindle.

fraudulent conversion *see* defalcation.

fraudulent misrepresentation *see* misrepresentation.

fraudulent preference LAW any payment of money by a debtor to one or some of his creditors to the disadvantage of the other creditors during a period of three months before he becomes bankrupt. Such payments are considered a fraud on the other creditors and the trustee in bankruptcy can demand repayment of the money.

free *adj.* (1) at liberty: *The arrested man is now free. I am free to see you now. I am not free to give you the figures/information. You are free to choose/act.* (2) not bound by rules: *Free trade/ port/vote/zone.* (3) without charge: *Free samples/gifts. Admission/estimates/alterations (to clothes) free. I got it free/(U.S.A.) for free.* (4) not hindered or spoilt: *Land free of/from weeds/pests. Property free of charges/mortgages. To be free of debt.* (5) STK. EXCH. *Free of stamp duty and fee:* (*a*) a condition made when a small lot of a stock or a share is sold, meaning that the seller will pay these costs. (*b*) when a new security is sold *free of stamp* after allotment but before registration.

v. to make free: *To free a house/estate/business from mortgage/debt. To free someone from his bond/promise.* To rid: *To free a farm of pests.* To set free: *He was freed from prison.*

free agent (1) *see* general agent *under* agent. (2) any person who is completely free to act on his own decisions and is not responsible or accountable to anyone for what he does.

free allowance TOUR. & TRANSPT. the amount of baggage that a passenger is allowed to take with him by bus, train, ship or aeroplane without charge, usu. expressed as a weight, such as 20 kg. If more is taken the carrier has the right to make a charge. *See* excess baggage *under* excess (3).

free alongside ship/steamer (F.A.S. or f.a.s.) COM. in foreign-trade contracts, the seller's price includes all charges and risks up to the point where the goods are placed alongside the ship ready to be taken on board. Thus the buyer must pay for the loading of the goods, but if the ship cannot enter the port or tie up to the shore, the seller must arrange and pay for lighters. *See* Incoterms. *Syn.* free on quay; franco quay (France); free at wharf.

free at wharf *see* free alongside ship.

freebee (U.S.A.) COM. (*colloq.*) something given free, without charge, to attract customers, such as a free dish in a restaurant. *Syn.* freebie.

freeboard SHIPG. the distance from the highest continuous deck to the centre of the disc marked on the side of the ship to show the load water-line in summer.

freeboard deck *see under* deck.

free capital *see under* capital.

free competition *see under* competition.

free delivered COM. a foreign-trade price quotation which includes the cost of the goods and all risks and charges for delivery to a stated place, point or address such as 'free delivered Alexandria'. If no place is stated, delivery must be to the consignee's address. *Syn.* franco domicile; franco domicilium.

free delivery COM. & IND. a service given free of charge by a supplier to his customers, of carrying the goods they have bought and delivering them to their own premises, if within a certain area, called a *free-delivery area*.

free docks COM. a foreign-trade price quotation which includes the cost of the goods and all risks and charges up to the point of delivery to the docks at the port where the goods are to be loaded on to the ship.

free economy *see* free competition *under* competition.

free enterprise *see under* enterprise.

free entry *see* entry for free goods *under* customs entry.

free-exchange rate *see* floating-exchange rate.

free goods *see under* goods (7).

free hand complete freedom and authority, without any limiting conditions: *We gave him a free hand to reorganize the business.*

free-handed (*colloq.*) ready to give away money; generous; spending money freely.

freehold *n.* LAW a legal right to hold land as the absolute owner, free of payment or duty to others. Cf. leasehold.
adj. held by freehold. *See* freehold estate *under* estate.

freehold property *see under* property.

free house COM. a business, esp. an inn or public house, that is run personally by its owner who is free to buy from any supplier and is not bound to one particular supplier. Cf. tied house.

free insurance *see under* insurance, classes and kinds of.

freelance COM. a professional skilled worker esp. a writer or artist, who does not work as an employee but is free to work for anyone who wishes to use his services in return for a fee.

Free List COM. & TAXN. the official list of goods that may be imported into Britain free of customs duty.

free market *see under* market.

free of all average MAR. INSCE. a condition in a marine policy that the insurance is against total loss only, and that claims for partial loss (average) are not covered. *Abbr.* F.A.A.; f.a.a.

free of income tax STK. EXCH. on some British government stocks, interest is paid in full, without any deduction for income tax. This is of special interest to persons with very small incomes who pay no income tax and therefore do not have the trouble of claiming a refund (repayment) of tax. *Abbr.* f.i.t.

free of particular average MAR. INSCE. a condition in a marine policy that the insurance is against total as well as partial loss. *Abbr.* F.P.A.

free on board (1) COM. in foreign-trade contracts, the seller's price includes all charges and risks up to the point where the seller delivers the goods on board the ship named by the buyer at the named port of shipment. From that point, all charges and risks have to be borne by the buyer. *See* Incoterms. (2) in U.S.A., 'free on board' may mean 'free on anything', such as a truck or a building site. *Syn.* franco à bord (France). *Abbr.* f.o.b.

free on quay *see* free alongside ship.

free on rail COM. in foreign-trade quotations, the seller's price includes all charges and risks up to the point where the seller delivers the goods to the railway at a named place ready for the railway to take away or convey to the buyer or to a place ordered by the buyer. From that point all charges and risks have to be borne by the buyer. *See* Incoterms. *Syn.* free on truck (f.o.t.) (U.S.A.); franco wagon (France). *Abbr.* F.O.R.; f.o.r.

free on truck *see* free on rail.

free overboard *see* free overside.

free overside COM. in foreign-trade quotations, the seller's price includes all risks and charges up to the point where the goods are discharged (unloaded) from the ship; from that point the costs must be borne by the buyer, including any lighterage and customs duty. *Syn.* ex ship; free overboard.

free pay TAXN. that portion of a taxpayer's income on which he pays no income tax.

freephone COM. a service offered by the British Post Office to commercial organizations by which a member of the public who wishes to answer an advertisement by telephone can do so by calling a certain number at the expense of the advertiser. Cf. freepost.

free port *see under* port.

freepost COM. a service offered by the British Post Office to commercial organizations by which a member of the public who wishes to send a letter in answer to an advertisement may address it to a certain address and post it without paying postage. The Post Office collects the postage from the advertiser on delivery of the letter. Cf. freephone.

free-range AGR. of poultry, kept in the open air and allowed to run about. Cf. battery hen *under* battery.

free trade ECON. THEORY international trade that is completely free of hindrances to the movement of goods such as tariffs (customs duties) and quotas (limits on quantity). The classical economists' view was that world-wide free trade would be good for all countries because of the comparative advantages of specialization. *See* Comparative Cost Principle. But many later economists, from Adam Smith to the present day, favour some degree of protection for essential industries. *See* free trade association.

free trade area *see* free trade association.

free trade association ECON. & COM. an agreement between two or more countries to unite in charging no duties on goods moving between the member countries. Examples are: Benelux; the European Free Trade Association (E.F.T.A.) and the European Economic Community (E.E.C.). *Syn.* free trade area.

free-trader ECON. a person who supports the idea of free trade.

freeway (U.S.A.) an expressway that is free of toll charges. In Britain, a motorway.

freeze *n.* the fixing by law of wages, prices, rents, etc. at present levels.

credit freeze government action to control the amount of money in circulation, by severely limiting bank lending. Cf. credit squeeze. *See also* frozen credits.

pay freeze *see* wage freeze *below*.

price freeze action by government to control prices in times of inflation to prevent the cost of living from rising, esp. during a wage freeze.

rent freeze action by government to fix rents esp. of private houses and flats, at their present level, usu. at a time of serious housing shortage.

wage freeze action by government, usu. in times of inflation, by which all wages and salaries are fixed at their present level. *Syn.* pay freeze.

free zone *see* free port *under* port.

freight TRANSPT. (1) the carrying of goods, esp. by water (*sea freight*) or by air (*air freight*) but, in U.S.A., also by rail or road. *Abbr.* Frt. (2) the amount charged or money earned for carrying goods, usu. expressed as a price per ton weight but for sea-cargo often per ton of cubic space filled. *Syn.* freightage. (3) goods, cargo, carried in return for payment of freight. *Syn.* freightage. (4) MAR. INSCE. the profit made by a shipowner on the freight his ship earns by carrying cargoes. (5) the charge, called *charter(ed) freight*, paid for hiring a ship or aircraft for carrying goods.

air freight *see under* air; *also* freight (1) *above*.

back freight a charge for freight which has to be paid by the owner to get back goods which a ship has overcarried, i.e. has been unable, from causes beyond the master's control, to land at the port of destination and has had to bring back to the port where they were loaded.

bill-of-lading freight *see under* bill.

charter(ed) freight money paid for hiring a ship or plane. *Syn.* charterer's freight.

dead freight charges that a shipper has to pay for space reserved for cargo which he has failed to ship, i.e. payment for space ordered in advance but not used. *Abbr.* d.f.

distance freight a freight charge which is proportional to distance, such as £5 per ton per mile.

return freight *see* carriage inwards *under* carriage.

sea freight *see* freight (1) *above*.

freight account MAR. INSCE. a record kept by a shipowner of all freight earned by a ship during a voyage so that it may be claimed from insurers if a loss is suffered.

freightage (1) TRANSPT. the charge made for carrying goods. (2) the goods carried in return for payment of freight or freightage. *Syn.* freight.

freight car (U.S.A.) TRANSPT. a railway goods wagon; a luggage van.

freight collect (U.S.A.) TRANSPT. freight to be paid by the consignee when the goods are delivered at the destination. *Syn.* (Britain) freight forward.

freighter TRANSPT. (1) a ship or plane that mainly carries goods as freight; a cargo boat; air freighter. (2) a person or business organization that charters cargo boats, accepts and transports goods, or forwards goods by other carriers.

freight forward TRANSPT. freight to be paid by the consignee on delivery of the goods at the destination. *Syn.* (U.S.A.) freight collect. *Abbr.* Frt. fwd.

freighting *see* affreightment.

freight inwards *see* carriage inwards *under* carriage (2).

freightliner TRANSPT. a railway train, consisting entirely of wagons carrying containers packed with goods, running on a regular fast service between important towns, industrial areas, ports, etc. Freightliner service, *see* container train *under* container.

freight note SHIPG. a note sent by the shipowner to the shipper showing the amount of freight payable on a certain cargo.

freight outwards *see* carriage outwards *under* carriage (2).

freight paid *see* carriage paid *under* carriage (2).

freight policy *see under* insurance policy.

freight prepaid TRANSPT. words written on a bill of lading by the shipowner to record that the freight has been paid in advance. *Abbr.* Frt. ppd.

freight rates TRANSPT. the charges for freight. *Sea freight* is charged either by weight or by measurement, whichever the master of the ship decides. *See* freight ton *under* ton. *Air freight* is usu. charged on the basis of 1 kg or 1000 cu. cm.

freight release SHIPG. a document issued when the freight has been paid, authorizing the person in charge of the goods, usu. a ship's officer or a warehouseman, to release them, i.e. to allow them to be taken away. *Abbr.* F.R.

freight ton *see under* ton.

freight train (U.S.A.) TRANSPT. a goods train.

French East India Company *see under* East India Company.

French Guiana an overseas department of France on the north coast of South America, pop. 58,000 approx. (1974); capital, Cayenne, pop. 25,000 approx.; language, French; currency unit, the French franc, divided into 100 centimes.

frequency the number of times something happens during a given period. *Frequency of flights/sailings, etc.* The number of flights that take place per hour, day, week or month. *The frequency of service is: three trains per hour/two flights per day/one sailing per week/one cruise per month. See also* accident frequency rate.

fresh money *see under* money.

fret payé *see* carriage paid *under* carriage (2).

friction ECON. THEORY the interference caused by outside influences that prevent the normal operation of economic laws, such as a lack of knowledge by producers of the size of demand, or limits placed on the movement of workers.

frictional unemployment *see under* unemployment.

Friendly Islands *see* Tonga.

friendly society FIN. in Britain, one of the 7000 or more non-profitmaking associations of persons, originally groups of friends, who pay regular subscriptions with the object of giving economic support to members and their families when they are ill or have grown old, and to their widows and fatherless children. Some societies provide an insurance service, some run working-men's clubs. By adopting certain rules and registering as an *approved society* with the Registrar of Friendly Societies, certain rights and powers are gained, esp. in borrowing, investing and lending money. Many trade unions started as friendly societies. *See also* industrial and provident society. *Syn.* (U.S.A.) benefit club; benefit society; benefit association.

fringe benefit any reward given to an employee in addition to normal wage or salary, such as a pension, the use of a company car or house, free or cheap meals, loans at low rates of interest, and private medical treatment. *See also* benefit in kind *under* benefit.

fringe market *see under* market.

frivolous action *see* abuse of process.

F.R.O. fire risk only.

from date *see* after date.

front (*colloq.*) an apparently honourable person or organization that is made to act as a screen to hide some illegal or dishonest activity: *His company is only a front for tax-evasion.*

frontage (1) the front of a piece of land. (2) the length of the front that lies along the line of a road, street or river.

frontager an owner of land lying along a road, street or river.

frontier (1) that part of a country that borders another country. (2) the boundary-line between two countries. (3) in U.S.A., the furthest limit of a country's settled or developed area: *The frontier moved westwards to the Rocky Mountains.*

frozen assets *see under* assets.

frozen credits FIN. & BKG. credit balances in bank accounts which, by government order, cannot be transferred to their owners, usu. persons or organizations based in other countries. *See* blocked account.

Frs., frs. francs.

Frt. freight.

Frt. fwd. freight forward.

Frt. ppd. freight prepaid.

fruiterer a shopkeeper who sells fruit.

frustration of contract LAW the discharge (ending) of the duties and responsibilities of the parties to a contract where some outside causes, not thought of at the time of making the contract, have since arisen and make it impossible to perform. *See* discharge of contract.

F.T. *Financial Times* (newspaper).

F.T.-Actuaries Share Indexes *see under* Financial Times.

ft foot; feet.

fth., fthm. fathom.

fudge (*colloq.*) to cheat, esp. to change dishonestly: *He fudged the accounts. Syn.* falsify; fake.

Fujairah *see under* United Arab Emirates.

fulfil to carry out: *This condition/clause has been fulfilled.* To complete; to perform: *He fulfilled his task/trust/responsibilities/obligations/duties.* (U.S.A., fulfill.)

full whole; complete: *Full name/address/fare/price/value. Full board*, sleeping accommodation and all main meals. *Full house*, in a theatre, all places filled. *Full-time worker*, one present during the whole of normal working hours.

full-bodied currency *see under* currency.

full costing *see* absorption costing.

full-cost price *see under* price.

full employment ECON. THEORY in economic analysis, an ideal situation in which unemployment is at the lowest possible level, with the supply of labour meeting the demand for it at a given level of wages. Even under full employment there will always exist some kinds of unemployment. *See* unemployment. A different view of full employment is given in the Beveridge Report of 1942, which describes it as a situation in which the number of vacancies (unfilled jobs) is greater than the number of persons unemployed, i.e. the supply of labour is less than the demand. Some economists call this *over-full employment*, which is a main cause of inflation; and they believe that inflation can only be avoided if the ideal aim of full employment is replaced by a lesser aim of keeping a 'high and stable level of employment' without full employment.

full-line forcing COM. a condition forced by some suppliers on their customers, of having to buy certain products from that supplier only. Cf. tied house.

fully-fledged fully-qualified: *A fully-fledged accountant/engineer/barrister.*

fully-paid share *see under* share.

fully-subscribed *see* oversubscribed.

function *n.* (1) what a person or thing has to do; a natural or proper activity; a reason for existence; a purpose: *The main function of the board of directors is to decide the policy of the company. The function(s) of a manager/secretary/foreman, etc.* (2) a social gathering: *A dinner/office/afternoon/evening function.*
v. to carry out a duty or activity: *The machine/system functions perfectly.*

functional discount *see* trade discount *under* discount.

functionary an official; a government servant.

fund *n.* FIN. & ACCTS. a stock of money, esp. one set aside for a special purpose: *A sinking/reserve/pension/benevolent/charity fund. See also* funds, *pl.*
v. (1) to put money into a fund or store to accumulate esp. for a certain purpose, such as to provide a pension, or to help the poor, or to pay off a debt. (2) FIN. to replace a short-term floating debt by an issue of permanent or long-term bonds bearing a fixed rate of interest. (3) STK. EXCH. to invest money in The Funds (British government stocks).

fundamental disequilibrium ECON. the condition that exists when the balance of payments of a country with a fixed exchange rate gets so bad that only a devaluation of its currency or an internal deflation of its economy will bring back a state of equilibrium.

funded debt *see under* national debt.

fund, guarantee *see* guarantee fund.

funding (1) FIN. replacing a short-term debt by an issue of long-term or perpetual (permanent) bonds. (2) the issue of debentures by a company for the purpose of paying off a large bank overdraft.

funds *pl.* FIN. (1) a stock or supply of money generally, but esp. money being used as working capital in a business. (2) cash, i.e. notes, coin and credit balances at the bank. (3) all the financial resources (possessions), consisting of cash, fixed assets, and investments belonging to a business. (4) BKG. a credit balance in a customer's account. *See* 'no funds'. (5) ACCTS. & FIN. *Flow of funds, see* cash flow; funds flow statement. (6) COM. *To be in funds*, to possess money or to hold money for another person. *Opp.* to be out of funds. *To put someone in funds*, to give him a supply of money to pay one's expenses, as to a solicitor to pay court fees, etc. (7) (*colloq.*) money.

Funds, The FIN. & STK. EXCH. British government stocks; gilt-edged securities. *See* British Funds.

funds flow statement ACCTS. & FIN. a financial statement of flows (movements) of funds into and out of a business. Sometimes called a *funds statement*, or a *statement of source and application of funds*, and in U.S.A., a *statement of changes in financial position*.

funeral benefit *see* death grant.

fun fair *see* fair, *n.* (3).

funk money *see under* money.

funny business COM. (*colloq.*) an affair or dealings of a suspicious or dishonest kind.

fur. furlong.

furlong a measure of distance, one-eighth of a mile or 220 yards = 201.168 metres. *Abbr.* fur.

furn. furnished.

furnish (1) to provide with furniture such as tables, chairs, beds: *A furnished house*, one let for rent, with all necessary furniture. *Abbr.* furn. (2) to supply: *To furnish documents/evidence/statistics/information. To furnish someone with money/capital.*

furnisher *n.* one who furnishes; a dealer in (new) furniture.

furniture (1) COM. movable articles needed for use in a home, called *domestic furniture*, such as tables, chairs and beds; or for an office, called *office furniture*, such as desks, chairs and filing cabinets. (2) SHIPG. the movable equipment of a ship, including everything needed to operate her, such as anchors, boats, machinery, ropes and cables, but not her stocks of food and fuel. *See* appurtenances.

fuse FIN. & STK. EXCH. of two or more companies, to combine to form one unit. *The companies decided to fuse to meet competition. Syn.* to amalgamate; to merge.

fusion *n.* combination; merger; amalgamation.

fut. futures.

futures *see* commodity exchanges.

futures market *see under* market.

future value *see under* value.

f.v. fishing vessel.

fwd. forward.

f.w.t. fair wear and tear *see* wear and tear.

G

G. German; Germany; Gulf.

g gram(me).

Ga. Georgia, U.S.A.

g.a., G/A., G.A. general average.

G.A.B. General Arrangements to Borrow.

Gabon a republic in west-central Africa, pop. 950,000 approx. (1970); capital, Libreville, pop. 75,000 approx.; language, French; currency unit, the C.F.A. franc, divided into 100 centimes. Member, O.A.U.; O.C.A.M.M.; Associate, E.E.C.

gaffer (*colloq.*) the owner; the person in charge; the foreman or boss. *Syn.* guv'nor (governor).

gage FIN. an article given as security for the payment of a loan or for the keeping of a promise; a pledge. *See* mortgage; pawn.

gain *n.* (1) an increase of wealth; profit: *He lives/works/only for gain. See* capital gain. (2) STK. EXCH. an increase, advance in price: *Oil shares showed a gain of five points.*

gains *pl.* (*a*) winnings, profits: *Ill-gotten gains*, wealth obtained dishonestly. *It is time to count your gains*, to pause to reconsider. (*b*) those shares that show an increase in price: *Gains included I.C.I. but British Oxygen were among the losses*, I.C.I. shares were some of those that showed an increase in price, but British Oxygen shares were among those that showed a reduction.

v. (1) to get or obtain something wanted: *To gain experience/knowledge/time/control of a company.* (2) to win, to obtain in competition: *He gained the advantage/victory/prize.* (3) to get money as profit: *He gained £1000 in selling his house.* (4) to advance; to progress: *Shares gained* (*ground*) *before the close*, prices rose.

gain and loss account *see* profit and loss account.

gainful *adj.* bringing in money or some other valuable substance or service; paid: *She is in gainful employment. A gainful occupation*, such as that of a shopkeeper. *Adv.* gainfully, *Gainfully employed.*

gains tax *see* capital gains tax *under* tax.

gal., gall. gallon.

Galbraith J.K. (1908–), American economist, public servant and highly popular writer, well known, first, for his argument in his book *American Capitalism* (1951) that in capitalist economies there is a degree of self-regulation which he calls *countervailing power* (power resisting equal power) because the economic strength of the great corporations is checked by the strength of organized labour, the trade unions. His book *The Affluent Society* (1958), which has had a remarkable sale, calls for greater attention to be given to the development of public services and less to production by pri-

vate industry, much of which is wasteful and extravagant (unreasonably costly). He was American Ambassador to India, 1961–3.

gallon the standard unit of measurement in Britain and U.S.A. for liquids. In Britain, the imperial gallon is the volume of 10 pounds (avoirdupois) of water, 277.42 cu. in. = 4.546 litres. In U.S.A., the American gallon is the volume of 8⅓ pounds of water, 231 cu. in. = 3.785 litres. *Abbr.* gal.; gall.

gals. cap. gallons capacity.

Gambia, The a small republic in West Africa, pop. 524,000 approx. (1975); capital, Banjul (formerly Bathurst), pop. 39,000 approx.; language, English; currency unit, the dalasi, divided into 100 butut. Member, (British) Commonwealth; O.A.U.

gamble *v.* (1) to risk money in the hope of making a profit: *He gambled his fortune on buying a farm but lost everything when the crop failed. They gamble on the Stock Exchange.* (2) to play a game of chance with money; to bet on sporting events: *To gamble at cards/on horse-races/in the casino. A gambling debt, see* gaming debt *under* debt. *See* debt of honour; gaming; wagering.

n. any risky course of action: *Investing in equities is a gamble.*

game any form of play for amusement, esp. in competition with other persons: *Outdoor games*, such as football, cricket, tennis. *Indoor games*, such as bridge, billiards, basketball. *A game of chance*, one in which luck is more important than skill. *A game of skill. A management game*, one played by managers in training, based on imaginary business situations. *A game not worth the candle*, a risk that is not worth taking, or an unprofitable plan.

gaming LAW the playing of a game of chance for money. *Gaming contract, see under* contract. *Gaming debt, see under* debt. *To plead the Gaming Act*, to take advantage of the law in refusing to pay one's gaming debts. *Syn.* gambling; wagering.

gangway SHIPG. & TOUR. (1) a movable bridge which connects a ship and the shore, and by which people can enter or leave the ship when she is tied up at a port. (2) a movable ladder in the form of a light stairway down the side of a ship for persons entering or leaving the ship while she is at anchor. *Syn.* gangway ladder. *See* accommodation ladder.

gap *see* trade gap; inflationary gap.

garage (1) a building where motor vehicles are kept when not in use. (2) in Britain, a workshop where motor vehicles are repaired and where petrol and oil may usu. be bought.

garnishee order LAW a judge's order obtained by a person who has been declared by the court a judgment creditor. It is sent to persons, called *garnishees*, who owe money to the judgment debtor or who hold money belonging to him. The order directs them not to pay the money to the judgment debtor but to pay it either into court or to the judgment creditor. One of the garnishees is often the banker who holds money in the judgment debtor's bank account. Such orders provide a means of making sure that a debtor's money is used to pay his creditors and not put to his own use. *Syn.* garnishment.

gas (U.S.A.) *abbr. of* gasolene, petrol.

gate (1) money paid for admission to a sports ground such as a football ground: *Gate money.* (2) the number of persons that paid or the total sum paid: *There was a record gate.* (3) *Gate pass*, in a factory or warehouse, written permission to take stated objects or goods away from the place.

G.A.T.T. General Agreement on Tariffs and Trade.

gauge *v.* to measure; to judge: *To gauge the contents of a cask/of a water or petrol tank*, using a gauging-rod. *Also* gage. *Pron.* gayj.
n. (1) a standard measure of weight, size, etc. to which objects can be compared. (2) an instrument for measuring, esp. pressure, dimension and quantity: *A rain/pressure/wire gauge.* (3) TRANSPT. on a railway, the distance between the inside faces of the rails. Because narrow-gauge lines are cheaper to build than broad-gauge, many railways in under-developed countries were built to narrow gauges. About 60% of the total length of the railways of the world are of standard gauge, 4ft 8½ in. (1.44 m). Countries that have not adopted the standard gauge, in whole or in part, are listed below under broad gauge and narrow gauge.
broad gauge any of a number of gauges that are broader than standard gauge: 5 ft 6 in. (1.68 m) Argentina (part), Chile, India (part), Pakistan, Portugal, Spain, Sri Lanka (Ceylon); 5 ft 3 in. (1.60 m) Australia (part), Ireland; 5 ft 0 in. (1.54 m) Finland, U.S.S.R.
narrow gauge any of a number of gauges that are narrower than standard gauge: 3 ft 6 in. (1.06 m) Australia (part), Indonesia, Japan, Mozambique, New Zealand, Nigeria, Rhodesia, S. Africa, Sudan, Taiwan, Zaire, Zambia; metre (3 ft 3⅜ in.) Argentine (part), Bangladesh, Brazil, Burma, Chile, India (part), Kenya, Malaysia, Switzerland (part), Tanzania, Thailand, Tunisia, Uganda; 2 ft 6 in. (0.76 m) and 2 ft 0 in. (0.61 m) India (part).
standard gauge 4 ft 8½ in. (1.44 m) railways in all countries not listed under broad gauge or narrow gauge *above.*

gazette (1) a newspaper. (2) a government paper published regularly, giving official information: *The London Gazette.*

gazump COM. (*colloq.*) when selling a house in Britain, to demand a higher price after a price has already been agreed.

GB Great Britain's international vehicle-registration letters, with which are connected the following: GBA, Alderney; GBG, Guernsey; GBJ, Jersey; GBM, Isle of Man; GBZ, Gibraltar.

g.b.o. goods in bad order.

GCA Guatemala's international vehicle-registration letters.

G.C.E. General Certificate of Education.

Gdns. Gardens.

G.D.P. gross domestic product.

G.D.R. German Democratic Republic (East Germany).

G.D.R. Mark *see* D.D.R. Mark.

gear *see* deck-gear.

geared to (1) BKG. closely connected with; moving with: *The rate of interest on overdrafts is geared to the minimum lending rate.* (2) COM. made to meet certain conditions: *A factory geared to batch production. Discounts geared to price-competition. The number of people we employ is geared to our highly seasonal trade.*

gearing FIN. (1) borrowing money at a fixed rate of interest and investing it to yield (produce) more than enough to pay the interest on the loan. (2) of a company's capital, the relation between the amount of its loan capital (money borrowed at a fixed rate of interest) and its ordinary-share capital. Gearing is said to be high when there is a large proportion of fixed-interest capital to ordinary-share capital and low when the opposite is true. *Syn.* (U.S.A.) leverage.

gelt (*colloq.*) money; profit.

general acceptance *see under* acceptance (5).

general agent *see* agent.

General Agreement on Tariffs and Trade (G.A.T.T.) an international organization started by an agreement signed by 23 nations in Geneva in 1947 and now having over 80 member nations. It aims to encourage and develop multilateral trade between nations by obtaining lower tariffs and the abolition of quotas and other limiting rules that show favour to some countries and disfavour to others. It holds international conferences and has been very active in negotiating reductions in tariffs on many articles and commodities. It has introduced an important international code of commercial behaviour. *See* Kennedy Round.

General Arrangements to Borrow (G.A.B.) FIN. the name of a document containing an agreement made in 1961 by ten countries (*see* Group of Ten) to provide standby credits extra to those obtainable under the standby arrangements of the International Monetary Fund. Such credits are ready for use in an emergency and they form one of the means by which members of the I.M.F. can be helped if they get into temporary difficulty with their balance of payments.

general audit see completed audit under audit.

general average see average (4).

general average bond see average bond under bond.

general average contribution MAR. INSCE. a sum of money paid by a consignee to a ship-owner when a general average has been declared. The money is held in a general average fund until the adjustment of the average has been made.

general cargo see under cargo.

General Certificate of Education in Britain, a certificate given to persons who have passed an examination, usu. at secondary schools in England and Wales, at any of three levels, Ordinary, Advanced and Scholarship. The examination is set and controlled by boards of the universities and covers a wide choice of subjects. Abbr. G.C.E. at O-level or A-level or S-level.

General Conference on Weights and Measures see International Bureau of Weights and Measures.

general creditor see under creditor.

general crossing see crossed cheque under cheque.

general damages see under damages, n. pl.

general delivery (U.S.A.) see poste restante.

general endorsement see blank endorsement under endorsement.

general equilibrium see under equilibrium.

general equilibrium analysis see aggregate analysis.

general expenses see overhead expenses under expenses.

general grant see rate support grant under grant.

general ledger see under ledger.

general legacy see under legacy.

general level of prices see price-level.

general lien see under lien.

general management trust see flexible trust under trust.

general manager see under manager.

general meeting see company meeting.

general mortgage bond see under bond.

general offer see under offer.

general partner see acting partner under partner.

general partnership see under partnership.

general power see under power; power of attorney.

general practitioner see family doctor. Abbr. G.P.

general-purpose having many uses; not limited to a particular use or purpose: A general-purpose tool/machine/fertilizer/insecticide/metal polish.

general reserve see under reserves.

general ship see under ship.

general store COM. a shop, usu. in country areas, where many different kinds of goods can be bought, such as food and drink, clothing, tools and materials for cleaning and repairing houses, toilet articles, medicines, magazines, newspapers and stationery.

general strike see under strike.

General Theory of Employment, Interest and Money ECON. THEORY the book by J. M. Keynes, published in 1936, that completely changed world thought on the causes of the trade cycle. Keynes pointed particularly to the importance of: the national income and level of employment; the quantity of money; the rate of interest; the levels of investment, saving and consumption; and liquidity preference. See Keynes, J.M.

general union see industrial union under trade union.

general warrant see under warrant.

gentleman (1) formerly, in Britain, a man of good family, ranking below noblemen but above yeomen, esp. a person who did not need to work for his living. A gentleman of leisure. (2) nowadays, a man of polite manners, who has consideration for others and high moral character. He is a perfect gentleman, an honourable man. (3) any person of the male sex: The gentleman over there. Gentlemen's hairdresser/tailoring/lavatory/toilet/cloakroom. **Gentlemen** pl. a greeting or salutation (polite form of opening) (a) for a business letter, esp. in U.S.A. Cf. Dear Sir(s). (b) at a meeting: Gentlemen, please be seated. Ladies and gentlemen, (may I have) your attention, please.

gentleman's agreement an informal agreement, considered to be binding in honour but not in a court of law. Syn. gentlemen's agreement (U.S.A.).

gentleman farmer see under farmer.

geographical filing see under filing system.

geographical mile see under mile.

geography (1) the study of the earth. (2) a book dealing with this subject. (3) the natural and other surroundings of an area or place: He knows the geography of Cairo better than I do, can find his way better. See economic geography; commercial geography; physical geography. Adj. geographical.

geology the study of the earth's crust (hard outside covering), esp. of the rocks of which it consists. Adj. geological.

geometric average see geometric mean.

geometric mean a kind of average that is specially suitable for calculating index numbers because it is not influenced by extreme quantities to the same extent as the arithmetic mean. It is always less than the arithmetic mean and is found by calculating the nth root of the product of the quantities, where n is the number of quantities. Thus the geometric mean of three quantities 3, 9 and 37 is the third or cube root of $3 \times 9 \times 37 = \sqrt[3]{999} = 9.9967$. The arithmetic mean $\left(\dfrac{3 + 9 + 37}{3} = \dfrac{49}{3}\right)$ is 16.3333.

Syn. geometric average.

geometric(al) progression quantities are said to be in geometric progression when each is equal to the one before it multiplied by a constant number called the common ratio: 1, 3, 9, 27, etc., common ratio 3; or 16, 8, 4, 2, 1, common ratio ½. *See* Malthus, Thomas Robert. *Cf.* arithmetic(al) progression; harmonic(al) progression.

geonomics *see* economic geography.

geophysical surveying the work of examining the earth's crust (hard outer covering) for the purpose of finding minerals.

George Henry (1839–97), American writer and economist. Having little education, he worked as clerk, seaman, printer and journalist. His argument was that land was the only factor of production that did not increase in quantity, and as labour and capital increased in productivity, landlords had an undeserved advantage. Rent was the cause of business cycles. His book *Progress and Poverty* (1879) called for a single tax on all land, that would take away from the landlord all economic rent (the income from the use of the basic land but not from improvements made to it) and for all other taxes to be abolished. His plan was never put into effect but his ideas made economists re-examine the classical theory of rent.

Germanischer Lloyd SHIPG. the German organization for surveying and classifying ships, corresponding to Lloyd's Register of Shipping in Britain. *See* classification societies. *Abbr.* GL.

Germany, Federal Republic of (West Germany) in western Europe, pop. 62 million approx. (1975); capital, Bonn, pop. 300,000 approx.; language, German; currency unit, the Deutsche Mark (DM), divided into 100 pfennig. Member, E.E.C.; O.E.C.D.; W.E.U.; U.N.E.S.C.O., (not U.N.).

Germany, German Democratic Republic (East Germany) a socialist republic in eastern Europe, pop. 17 million approx. (1973); capital, East Berlin, pop. 1.2 million approx.; language, German; currency unit, the DDR Mark (M) (*also* Östmark), divided into 100 pfennig. Member, COMECON. *Abbr.* G.D.R.; D.D.R.

g. gr. great gross.

GH Ghana's international vehicle-registration letters.

Ghana a republic in West Africa, pop. 9½ million approx. (1973); capital, Accra, pop. 700,000 approx.; languages, English and tribal; currency unit, the cedi, divided into 100 pesewas. Member, (British) Commonwealth; O.A.U.

gharry TRANSPT. in the Indian subcontinent, a cart or carriage drawn by an animal; a motor car or lorry; a railway coach or wagon. *Syn.* vehicle. *Gharry allowance*, a sum of money paid monthly by an employer to an employee who uses his own car for his employer's business. *Syn.* car allowance.

ghost writer a little-known professional writer who writes articles or books that are sold as the work of other writers.

to ghost *v.* to act as a ghost writer.

G.I. (U.S.A.) (1) government issue (property). (2) (*colloq.*) an enlisted soldier (below officer rank) in the U.S. Army.

Gib. Gibraltar.

Gib£ Gibraltar pound.

Gibraltar a small self-governing colony of the United Kingdom, in southern Europe, at the southernmost point of Spain, pop. 28,000 approx. (1970); languages, English and Spanish; currency unit, the Gibraltar pound (Gib£), equal to the pound sterling, divided into 100 pence.

Giffen good *see* Giffen's paradox.

Giffen's paradox ECON. THEORY a paradox (strange truth) pointed out by Sir Robert Giffen in the nineteenth century, that when consumers, esp. those in the poorer classes, spend a very high proportion of their incomes on one commodity, such as bread, an increase in the price can lead to an increase in demand for the commodity. This is because the dearer bread causes a great fall in real incomes and greatly reduces the amount that consumers spend on more expensive foods such as meat, so they eat more bread in spite of its higher price. Similarly, if the price of bread falls, real incomes rise; consumers prefer to buy the more expensive foods and to eat less bread, in spite of its relative cheapness. Such a commodity is called a *Giffen good* or an *inferior good*. *Syn.* Giffen effect; negative income effect.

gift LAW property given as a present, i.e. without consideration (payment of any kind). To be recognized by law, there must have been a clear intention to give, and a clear act of giving, either by personally delivering the property or by otherwise making a permanent transfer of ownership, such as by a deed of gift. *Syn.* donation.

gift cheque BKG. a cheque printed in decorative form issued for a small extra charge by some banks for use by customers who wish to give presents of money on special occasions.

gift, deed of *see* deed of gift.

gifts inter vivos LAW & TAXN. gifts between living persons. In Britain, such gifts are liable to capital transfer tax unless they are between spouses (persons married to each other) or are below certain limits allowed by law.

gift tax *see* capital transfer tax.

gift token COM. a printed card or ticket, representing a stated sum of money, given as a present to someone who may use it instead of money to buy goods in a shop. *Syn.* gift voucher.

gift-wrapping COM. (1) ornamental paper, string, ribbon, labels, etc. for wrapping parcels containing gifts. (2) a service offered by retail shops of specially wrapping gift-parcels usu. in return for a small extra charge.

giga- the *prefix* used in the metric system of SI units to mean a thousand million times: 1 gigawatt (gW) = 1 000 000 000 watts (W).

gild *see* guild.

gill a unit of liquid measure in Britain, a quarter of a pint, 5 fluid ounces or 0.142 litres. *Pron.* jill. *Abbr.* gl.

gilt-edged bill *see under* bill of exchange.

gilt-edged securities (1) STK. EXCH. & FIN. fixed-interest securities issued or guaranteed by the British Government. (2) more generally, securities of the highest class, considered by investors to be without any financial risk. *Syn.* gilts. *See* British Funds; Funds, The.

gilts STK. EXCH. gilt-edged securities collectively.

gimmick COM. (*colloq.*) any clever or unusual idea or trick intended to attract the attention, esp. as a method of selling something. *Gimmickry*, the use of gimmicks as a way of increasing sales. Advertisements that show a lack of good taste.

girl Friday a girl employee who types letters and generally helps in an office. Cf. man Friday.

g.i.p. glazed imitation parchment.

gip *see* gyp.

Giro BKG. originally intended to be a cheap and simple means of making payments of money for persons who have no bank account, the Giro systems on the continent of Europe, in Japan and more recently (1968) in Britain, have developed a number of additional services that give them some advantage over commercial banking systems.

Bancogiro a simple system used on the continent of Europe, allowing a payment by one customer of a bank to another customer of the same bank, by making only book entries debiting the payer's account and crediting the payee's account, no notes or coins being used. This method differs from the cheque system in that the payee's account is almost immediately credited. Cf. Bank Giro.

Bank Giro a free service offered by commercial banks in Britain by which a customer can make any number of payments by credit transfer to other parties who have bank accounts, and also, on payment of a small charge, to persons who have no bank account. The Bank Giro has no central organization but is run by the many branches of the banks. Cf. Bancogiro.

National Giro in Britain, the government-backed Giro system operated by the Post Office. All records are kept at a computerized Giro Centre at Bootle, Lancs. Having opened an account by depositing at least £20 at any of the 21,000 post offices in Britain, an account-holder can transfer sums from his account to any other account-holder's account by completing a transfer form; or he may send money to a non-account-holder by means of a Giro cheque that can be cashed or paid into a bank account. Cheques, etc. are posted to the Centre for credit. Cash is paid into, and can be withdrawn from, any post office. Extra services include standing orders, personal and bridging loans, cash cards and traveller's cheques, but not overdrafts. No interest is paid on deposits.

give on (1) STK. EXCH. to pay contango. (2) to lend stock to a broker in return for interest. Cf. take in.

giver on *n.* a broker who lends stock to another broker. *Pl.* givers on. Cf. taker in.

giver (1) STK. EXCH. a person who buys an option, so called because he gives money for it. (2) a buyer who arranges to delay paying for shares by giving interest to the seller.

gl. gill.

GL Germanischer Lloyd.

glassine a greaseproof paper which, when treated, produces a transparent sheet used for wrapping goods and for windows in envelopes. *Syn.* glazed transparent grease-proof.

glazed imitation parchment a kind of paper much used for wrapping food and tobacco. *Abbr.* g.i.p.

glazed transparent greaseproof *see* glassine.

G.L.C. Greater London Council.

glebe land land owned by a church, usu. having been bequeathed (given by will) to provide an income for the parish priest.

globe-trotter TOUR. (*colloq.*) a person who travels frequently to places all over the world for the purpose of sight-seeing. Cf. rubberneck (U.S.A.).

Glos. Gloucestershire, England.

glut *v.* (1) to eat too much. (2) to feed (an animal) too much. (3) *To glut the market*, to cause a glut by supplying far more of a commodity than is likely to be demanded, thus causing prices to be unreasonably low.

n. AGR. & COM. a great excess, caused by over-production, in the supply, esp. of perishable goods (those likely to go bad quickly), such as foodstuffs.

G.M.T. Greenwich Mean Time.

gm gram(me).

gm², g/m² grams per square metre; metric method for measuring weight of paper.

g.m.b. good merchantable brand.

g. mile geographical mile.

g.m.q. good merchantable quality.

gn(s). guinea(s).

Gnomes of Zürich (*colloq.*) Central-European, esp. Swiss, financiers, many of whom have banks in Zürich, Switzerland; they are sometimes held to be responsible for bringing political influence to bear secretly in difficult international financial situations, such as sudden flights of capital from one market centre to another.

G.N.P. gross national product.

go *n.* a success: *We must make a go of it.*
v. to move, esp. away or along. *To go back on one's word/promise,* to fail to keep. *To go under,* to fail financially.

go-ahead *adj.* active; eager to get ahead in business. *Syn.* enterprising.

g.o.b. good ordinary brand.

go-between a person who acts as agent or representative between two other persons, esp. in the course of negotiations. *Syn.* intermediary; middleman.

God, Act of *see under* act.

godown in India and the Far East, a storehouse or storeroom. *Syn.* warehouse.

go-getter (*colloq.*) a determined person who is always ready to fight for what he wants.

going concern a business that is trading steadily and profitably and is likely to continue to do so, being in no danger of becoming insolvent (unable to pay its debts). Such a business, if sold, will attract an extra sum of money known as goodwill, in addition to the value of its fixed assets.

going rate the rate current in the market: *The going rate of interest/yield is 6%. The going rate of pay for freelance typists is £1.50 per hour.*

gold bars *see* bullion.

gold bond *see under* bond, *n.*

gold-brick (1) (*colloq.*) a dishonest imitation; a worthless article sold by a dishonest person who pretends that it is valuable, such as a brick that appears to be of solid gold but is in reality lead with a thin coat of gold. (2) (U.S.A. *colloq.*) an idle person who avoids work.

gold bullion standard *see under* gold standard.

gold digger (1) a miner who digs for gold on or near the surface. (2) (*colloq.*) a woman who uses her charms to persuade men to spend money on her.

golden handshake MAN. (*colloq.*) a sum of money, usu. large, paid as compensation for loss of employment by a company to a high employee who is being forced to retire early or to leave his employment.

gold exchange standard *see under* gold standard.

goldfield an area where gold is mined.

gold, fine *see* fineness.

gold-mine (1) a mine from which gold ore (rock containing gold) is obtained. (2) (*colloq.*) any property that produces much profit. *He wrote a book that soon became a gold-mine,* brought him a large income. *The business is a gold-mine,* is highly profitable.

gold point FIN. under a gold standard system, when there exists a free market in gold, the limit of the amount by which the rate of exchange between the currencies can vary from the mint par of exchange. This variation can only be between two points, called gold points, one just below and one just above the par rate, the difference being fixed by the costs of transporting the metal from one country to another. Outside these limits it would be more profitable to export or import gold than to pay or be paid by a bill of exchange. *Syn.* specie point.

gold reserve(s) *see under* reserves.

gold-rush a rush of miners and others to an area where gold has just been discovered.

gold standard FIN. a monetary system formerly used by many countries, under which the value of the standard unit of currency was by law made equal to a fixed weight of gold of a stated fineness. Thus the rates of exchange between various gold-standard countries remained fixed, which helped international trade, but the system limited the power of the monetary authorities to control the supply of money in fighting inflation and unemployment. Under a full gold-standard system, such as existed in Britain from the 1870s to 1914, gold coin and bullion (bars of gold) could be freely imported and exported; gold coins circulated freely; and the central bank bought and sold gold in any quantity at the fixed price. The system was set up again by 1928 in a limited form but it broke down in the 1930s. After the Second World War some countries in Europe agreed to make their currencies freely convertible into gold for international payments only, thus forming a gold standard that was entirely external. Variations of the gold standard are:

gold bullion standard a limited form of gold standard such as existed in Britain from 1925 to 1931, under which the Bank of England would sell gold bars in return for bank-notes; imports and exports of gold were controlled, gold coins were not in circulation, and single notes were not convertible into gold on demand. *Syn.* limited gold standard.

gold exchange standard a limited form of gold standard used from 1925 to 1931 by some of the smaller countries, esp. the group of Scandinavian countries, under which the central bank would exchange the currency of its own country for a fixed amount of the currency of a particular country which was on the gold standard, and not for gold. Gold coins did not circulate, and reserves were held, not of gold but of the particular gold-standard currency chosen.

good *to the good*, in a state of profit: *After this contract I shall be £1000 to the good.* Syn. better off. *Opp.* to the bad.

good average quality *see under* quality.

good, economic *see under* goods (7).

good faith honest intentions: *We acted in good faith, not knowing that we were risking your money.* See utmost good faith; bona fides.

good, Giffen *see* Giffen's paradox.

good, inferior *see* Giffen's paradox.

good merchantable quality *see under* quality.

goods (1) LAW & COM. all personal movable property other than money and certain claims to money: *Goods and chattels,* personal possessions. (2) any article or commodity that is the subject of manufacture or trade: *The goods we make. The trade in leather goods. Duty-paid goods. Goods of high quality.* Syn. merchandise. (3) TRANSPT. things carried by rail; rail freight: *A goods train,* one for carrying things, not passengers (U.S.A. freight train). *Goods depot/yard/wagon/truck/lift.*

goods in transit merchandise that is in the course of being carried by rail, ship, air, etc.

measurement goods *see under* measurement.

(4) MAR. INSCE. in marine insurance policies, cargo consisting of merchandise (things bought or sold) and excluding deck cargo, live animals, personal effects of the crew and passengers, and stocks of food and materials for use on the voyage. (5) TAXN. *see* dutiable goods. (6) COM. & IND. *see* dry goods; fancy goods; soft goods; wet goods. (7) ECON. THEORY commodities and services that have a price, i.e. that are useful and scarce. *See* economic goods *below.*

capital goods all goods that are made with the intention of using them to produce other goods. They themselves do not satisfy Man's wants directly but are necessary for making goods which do, e.g. machines, industrial buildings and raw materials. Cf. consumer('s) goods. *Syn.* producer('s) goods; production goods; investment goods.

consumer('s) goods goods in everyday use, such as food, clothing, household goods, and personal services, such as those of doctors, dentists, hairdressers; goods that directly satisfy the needs of the public. *Syn.* consumption goods; hard goods. Cf. producer('s) goods; investment goods; capital goods. *See* consumer durables; consumer non-durables.

convenience goods *see under* convenience.

durable goods *see under* durable.

economic goods goods and services that are both useful and scarce and therefore have a price. They are of two kinds, producer's goods and consumer's goods. No other goods are of interest to the economist. Cf. free goods.

ethical goods *see under* ethical.

fancy goods *see under* fancy.

fashion goods *see under* fashion.

free goods 'gifts of nature' that have utility (usefulness) and give satisfaction but are not scarce. They have no exchange value and no price and for this reason are of no interest to the economist. An example is the air around us. Cf. economic goods. *Syn.* original goods.

hard goods *see* consumer durables.

household goods *see* household.

impulse goods *see* impulse buyer.

inferior goods *see under* inferior.

intermediate goods goods that are in course of manufacture and are still unfinished.

investment goods *see* capital goods *above.*

original goods in economic theory, the free gifts of nature. *See* free goods *above.*

piece-goods *see under* piece.

poor man's goods *see* inferior goods *under* inferior.

prestige goods *see* prestige.

producer('s) goods *see* capital goods *above.*

production goods *see* capital goods *above.*

prohibited goods *see* prohibit.

(8) (*colloq.*) *The goods,* (*a*) the real thing, not an imitation: *These pearls are the goods.* (*b*) just what is wanted or expected: *He gave us the goods,* what was needed. *To deliver the goods, see under* deliver.

goods in progress (U.S.A.) *see* work(s) in progress.

goods-in-transit policy *see under* insurance policy.

goods train *see* goods (3).

goodwill (1) COM. the advantage possessed by an established business over a new business. The attractive force that brings in customers. (2) LAW the right to use and to profit from the established name and connections of a business. (3) FIN. the capital value of an intangible asset, that is the right to receive the extra profits which an established business may be expected to earn, over and above the normal earnings for a similar business. *See* intangible assets *under* assets; cost of control; going concern. *Also* good will (U.S.A.).

goon IND. REL. in U.S.A., a person hired to make trouble between employers and employees.

go-slow IND. REL. a situation where, instead of striking, the employees of a factory or other organization work very slowly and find every excuse they can to slow down production or the speed of service. *Syn.* ca'canny; work to rule; (U.S.A.) slow-down.

Gosplan in U.S.S.R., the central planning authority, responsible for carrying out the economic policy of the government. The word is a short form of *Gosudarstvennyy Planovy Komitet* or State Planning Committee.

gourde the standard currency unit of Haiti, divided into 100 centimes.

Gov., gov. government; governor.

governed economy *see* mixed economy.

government actuary *see under* actuary.

Government Broker FIN. & STK. EXCH. in Britain, the stockbroker officially appointed broker to the National Debt Commissioners; his duty is to buy and sell government securities on the Stock Exchange as directed by the Bank of England, usu. buying stock in order to support the price and selling later when support is no longer needed. Cf. special buyer.

government investment *see* public investment *under* investment.

government securities FIN. & STK. EXCH. fixed-interest loan stock issued by the government of a country. In Britain such securities are known as gilt-edged. *Syn.* government stock.

government security *see under* security.

government stock *see* government securities.

governor (1) MAN. a person placed in charge of the management of an organization: *The Governor of the Bank of England*. (2) one of a group of persons forming a governing body or *board of governors*, in control of an organization such as a school. *Abbr.* Gov.; gov.

Govt., govt. government.

G.P. general practitioner.

Gp. group.

GR Greece's international vehicle-registration letters.

Gr., gr. gross; gram(me); grain.

grace *see* days of grace.

grade crossing (U.S.A.) a railway level-crossing.

grading COMMOD. EXCH. the accurate classification of a commodity, such as wheat, into standards (groups) according to quality, in order to make buying and selling possible without having to examine the stock of the commodity itself. The quality of some commodities, such as tea, is so variable that grading is not possible without examining samples of each shipment before buying, which in this case is usu. by auction.

grading, labour *see* job evaluation.

graduate (1) in Britain, a person who has taken a university degree. (2) in U.S.A., a person who has received a diploma at a school or college.

graft (1) (*colloq.*) gaining an unfair or dishonest advantage by influence or by bribery. *Graft and corruption*. (2) honest work: *Hard graft*, in Australia and New Zealand, hard or difficult work.

grain *n.* (1) a small unit of weight, originally a dried grain of wheat, and the smallest unit of the troy measure, equal to 1/480 of an ounce troy, or 0.648 decigrams (dg). (2) AGR. the seed of any of the grasses that are grown for food, such as barley, maize, oats, rice, rye and wheat. *Syn.* (in Britain) corn. (3) collectively, such seeds in general: *The grain harvest/trade. A grain broker. Abbr.* gr.

grain capacity (of a ship) the total cargo-space that can be used for carrying grain. Cf. bale cubic capacity. *Syn.* grain cubic capacity.

grain elevator AGR. & COM. (1) a mechanical arrangement for lifting grain into a building for storage. (2) the building itself. Cf. granary.

grain silo AGR. & COM. *see* granary.

gram a unit of weight in the metric system, one-thousandth part (0.001) of a kilogram or 0.03527 oz. avoir. It equals the mass of one cubic centimetre (cm³) of water at 4°C. *Also* gramme. *Abbr.* g; gm; gr.

granary COM. & AGR. a special building for storing grain. *Syn.* grain silo; grain elevator; grange.

grand (*colloq.*) in Britain, one thousand pounds (£1000). In U.S.A., one thousand dollars ($1000).

grande vitesse TRANSPT. (*French*, high speed) in Europe, by fast goods train or passenger train, as distinguished from *petite vitesse* (P.V.), ordinary goods train or slow train. *Abbr.* G.V.

grange AGR. (1) a granary. (2) a country house with farm buildings, often the home of a gentleman farmer.

grant (1) LAW the conveyance (formal transfer of ownership) of land. (2) FIN. a sum of money given usu. by the government for a particular purpose such as a *student's grant*, on which he can live while studying. (3) in Britain, money provided by the central government to local government authorities to be spent on the services which they provide for the public in their areas:

block grant in Britain, a sum of money given annually by the central government to a local government authority to cover its expenses in connection with a particular service or activity, such as the police. Cf. capitation grant; general grant.

capital grant in Britain, money provided by the central government to a local government authority for an approved project, usu. for new roads, street lighting, land drains.

capitation grant in Britain, an annual payment by the central government to a local government authority, usu. for a special purpose, based on an equal amount of money per head (for each person), such as a grant for school libraries of an amount for each schoolchild. Cf. block grant; rate-support grant.

equalization grant *see* rate-deficiency grant *below*.

general grant *see* rate-support grant *below*.

investment grant *see under* investment.

rate-deficiency grant in England and Wales, an annual grant paid by the central government to the poorer local government authorities in order to reduce inequalities in the amount collected as rates on property. In Scotland it is called an *equalization grant*.

rate-support grant in Britain, the largest of the grants made annually by the central government to the local government authorities. It is calculated mainly according to size and density of population, the number of schoolchildren, the proportion of old or very young persons, and the amount of money that the local authority can obtain from rates on property in its area. *Abbr.* R.S.G. *Syn.* general grant.
specific grant *see* block grant *above*.

grantee LAW a person to whom a grant is made. Cf. grantor. *Syn.* donee.

grant-in-aid (1) FIN. money provided by a government to a colony or dependent country to be spent on local public services. (2) in Britain, all grants made by the central government to local government authorities other than the rate-support grant. *Pl.* grants-in-aid.

grantor LAW a person who makes a grant, esp. a conveyance of land. Cf. grantee. *Syn.* donor; principal.

graph *see* chart (2).

graphic arts COM. & ADVTG. those which use lines, shading, type, etc. to express ideas on flat surfaces. They include drawing, painting, engraving and typography but not sculpture, modelling, etc. *See* commercial art.

grass *To put someone out to grass*, (*colloq.*) to cause a person to retire because he has reached the age-limit.

grassland (1) AGR. land on which grass is grown, either as pasture or as grazing, on which the animals eat the grass as it grows, or as a crop of hay for fodder. (2) land on which the natural plant cover is grass, with few trees. Cf. forest; pasture.

gratification something that pleases; a reward or tip. *Illegal gratification*, a bribe; bribery.

gratis for nothing; free of cost; without payment: *Catalogues/price-lists/samples supplied gratis.*

gratuitous LAW given free and without asking for any consideration (payment in return): *Gratuitous help/advice/relief*. *Gratuitous coinage*, *see* free coinage *under* coinage.

gratuity (1) a tip. (2) a sum of money given to a retiring employee for long service, or to a member of the armed forces at the end of a fixed period of service.

graving dock *see* dry dock.

gravy (*colloq.* mainly U.S.A.) (1) things given by an employer to an employee extra to his normal pay. (2) money that is easily earned: *To be on the gravy train*, to have a well-paid but easy job. To be very rich.

grazier AGR. a farmer who keeps animals on grassland in order to fatten them for market.

grazing AGR. land on which farm animals graze, i.e. eat the growing grass. *Syn.* grassland; pasture.

grease (*colloq.*) *n.* a bribe; money paid in advance for services that would not otherwise

be given, or that should not be given. *Syn.* palm-grease; palm-oil.
v. (1) to bribe: *To grease someone's palm.* (2) to help by removing difficulties or by providing money: *To grease the wheels of industry by raising government spending.*

greaseproof a kind of paper made specially for wrapping small quantities of greasy foods.

Great Britain *see* United Kingdom.

Great Depression ECON. the period from about 1929 to 1935 which was marked by very low economic activity and extremely high unemployment in most countries of the world, causing much poverty and suffering. *See* depression; trade cycle *under* cycle.

great gross *see under* gross, *n.*

great hundred *see* hundred.

Greece a republic of south-eastern Europe, pop. 9 million approx. (1973); capital, Athens; language, Greek; currency unit, the drachma, divided into 100 lepta. Member, O.E.C.D.; E.E.C.

greenback BKG. & FIN. (*colloq.*) in U.S.A., a bank-note issued by the U.S. Government, usu. printed in green on one side.

green belt an area of open country in Britain, usu. surrounding a town, in which new building is strictly controlled.

green card TOUR. & INSCE. a document carried by a motorist touring in a foreign country, declaring that in the event of an accident he is insured against claims by third parties (persons who are not parties to the insurance contract).

green currencies FIN. under the Common Agricultural Policy of the European Economic Community, the artificial rates of exchange used to protect farm prices in all member countries from wide variations. These rates of exchange are expressed in units of account. *See* green pound.

greengrocer COM. a shopkeeper who sells vegetables and fruit. Cf. grocer.

green pound FIN. under the Common Agricultural Policy of the European Economic Community the popular name given to the British pound sterling expressed in units of account. This value is used for calculating payments due by Britain to the Common Agricultural Fund, and by that Fund to Britain whenever the market rate of exchange of the pound differs from its value as fixed in units of account. *See* green currencies.

Green Revolution AGR. the very great increase that has taken place in several less-developed countries since about 1960 in the production of foodgrains, made possible by using new, improved varieties of high-yielding seeds, mainly of wheat, maize and rice. Among the countries that have so far shown the greatest progress are Mexico, the Philippines, India, Pakistan and Sri Lanka.

Greenwich Mean Time (G.M.T.) by international agreement, the time accepted as the standard on which all measurements of time throughout the world are based. It is the time of day at Greenwich, a town near London on 0° longitude. Thus Greenwich Mean Time is the time shown on a clock at Greenwich at any instant of local time anywhere in the world. *Syn.* Greenwich Standard Time; Greenwich Time; West(ern) European Time.

Greenwich Time-Zone a standard time-zone using Greenwich Mean Time and consisting of: in Europe, the Faroe Is., Great Britain, Ireland and Portugal; in Africa, Algeria, Ghana, Morocco, Sierra Leone and various other West African countries but not Nigeria. *Syn.* West(ern) European Time.

greeting in a letter, the polite or friendly opening words. In a business letter, usu. *Dear Sir,* or *Dear Madam* to a person (sometimes, in a circular letter *Dear Sir or Madam*); to a firm or company, *Dear Sirs,* or (esp. in U.S.A.) *Gentlemen.* In a personal letter, *Dear Mr Smith, Dear Mrs Jones, Dear Miss Robinson,* are more formal than *Dear John,* etc. For close friends many use *My dear James,* and for a relation, *Dearest James. Syn.* salutation.

Grenada an island state in the Caribbean, pop. 100,000 approx. (1975); capital, St George's, pop. 30,000 approx.; language, English; currency unit, the East Caribbean dollar (ECar$), divided into 100 cents. Member, (British) Commonwealth of Nations.

Gresham's Law FIN. a natural tendency, wrongly supposed to have been first stated by Sir Thomas Gresham, financier and founder of the London Stock Exchange in the sixteenth century, that 'bad money drives out good money, but good money can never drive out bad money'. Where two kinds of coin or currency of unequal values exist together in the same country, the more precious will be hoarded (stored secretly), or be melted down, or be spent on foreign exchange, leaving the less precious in circulation.

grey market *see under* market.

grievance (1) a real or imaginary reason to complain against a wrong: *To have a grievance against someone.* (2) IND. REL. a disagreement between an employer and a worker who feels that he has been treated unjustly. In most countries that have a system of collective bargaining, employers' associations and trade unions have reached agreement on the process, called *grievance procedure,* by which such disagreements may be settled.

grind *n.* (*colloq.*) uninteresting and tiring work. *Syn.* drudgery.

v. COM. (*colloq.*) to drive a hard bargain; to force a seller to accept a low price: *To grind someone down.*

grocer COM. a shopkeeper who sells groceries, i.e. food, esp. sugar, dried fruits, tinned and packaged foods, and also materials for cleaning, such as soap. Cf. greengrocer.

grocery the trade of a grocer: *He runs a grocery business,* sells groceries.

groschen (1) in the currency of Austria, one-hundredth part of a schilling. (2) (*colloq.*) in Germany, a ten-pfennig nickel coin.

gross *adj.* COM. & ACCTS. a quantity or a sum of money, whole; entire; without anything deducted: *Gross weight,* the full weight of a package before taking off any allowance for packing, etc. *Gross interest/income/yield,* the full amount receivable before allowing for income tax. Cf. net. *Abbr.* Gr.; gr.; Grs.

n. COM. a unit of 12 dozen or 144 articles. *Abbr.* gr. *Great gross,* 12 gross, or 1728 articles. *Abbr.* g. gr.

gross average *see* general average *under* average (4).

gross domestic product (G.D.P.) ECON. THEORY that part of the gross national product (G.N.P.) remaining after taking away the country's net income from abroad. It is a measure of the total of incomes received by residents only for production carried out within the country. As with the G.N.P., the G.D.P. may be calculated at constant prices, at market prices or at factor cost. *See* gross national product.

gross equivalent COM. & FIN. a net amount plus an amount needed to bring it up to the original gross amount before any deduction was made. *See* grossing-up.

gross income *see under* income.

grossing-up COM. & FIN. the calculation of the gross equivalent of a net amount, i.e. a calculation that puts back a percentage deduction so as to change a net figure into a gross figure. *Example: To gross up,* i.e. to calculate the gross dividend G from a tax-free dividend N paid net of 30% tax or 30p in the £.

$$G = N \times \frac{100\text{p}}{100\text{p} - 30\text{p}} = N \times \frac{100}{70}$$

If $N = £100$

$$G = £100 \times \frac{100}{70} = £142.86$$

Opp. netting-down.

gross interest *see under* interest.

gross investment *see under* investment.

gross loss *see under* loss.

gross margin COM. the difference between the retail and the wholesale price, i.e. the retailer's gross profit usu. expressed as a percentage of sales. Cf. net margin. *See* margin (5).

gross national product (G.N.P.) ECON. THEORY the total wealth earned or brought into existence in a particular year by a country. It is the total value of all the goods and services produced by the country during that year includ ing net income from abroad, before allowing for depreciation and for any reduction in the stock of capital goods. The G.N.P. is calculated in three different ways: *at constant prices*, adjusted to allow for changes in the value of money over a period; or *at market prices* for comparison with similar figures for other countries; or *at factor cost*, for use when measuring the part played by the various factors of production. *Syn.* gross product. Cf. net national product.

gross output *see under* output.

gross product *see* gross national product.

gross profit *see under* profit.

gross receipts ACCTS. & FIN. the total amount of money received, before taking away anything for expenses. Cf. net receipts.

gross (register) tonnage *see under* tonnage.

gross sales ACCTS. the total value of all sales made by a business before taking off amounts allowed to customers as credits for goods returned, goods over-invoiced, etc. Cf. net sales.

gross ton *see* long ton *under* ton.

gross tonnage *see* gross register tonnage *under* tonnage.

gross value TAXN. of a property, the annual value, a figure based on the annual rent which a tenant might be expected to pay for the property, if he pays the rates and taxes, and the landlord bears the cost of repairing and insuring it. In Britain, the gross value is the basis for calculating the rateable value of premises (the value on which rates are determined).

gross wage *see under* wage.

gross yield *see under* yield.

groszy the fractional currency unit of Poland. 100 groszy = 1 zloty.

Gro. t. gross tons/tonnage.

ground (1) STK. EXCH. of stock and share prices. *To gain ground*, to rise, advance in price. *To lose/give ground*, to go down, become lower in price. (2) SHIPG. the bottom of the sea, esp. under and in the area around a ship. *See* grounding.

groundage (1) SHIPG. a charge made to shipowners by a port for the space used by a ship when it is anchored within the limits of the port. Cf. berthage. (2) harbour dues generally.

ground crew TRANSPT. persons employed to keep aircraft in good repair, such as mechanics; or to manage the running of an airline, such as ground hostesses, whose duties do not normally require them to fly. Cf. aircrew.

ground floor *see* floor (2).

grounding (1) SHIPG. & MAR. INSCE. the running of a ship on to the ground, where it is held, usu. for only a short time. Cf. stranding. (2) TRANSPT. an order preventing an airman, esp. a pilot, from flying or an aircraft from being flown. (3) STK. EXCH. of stock and share prices, touching the bottom: *Prices will be grounding*

soon, reaching their lowest level, after which they will rise.

ground landlord *see under* landlord.

ground rent *see under* rent.

group accounts *see* accounts, *n. pl.*

groupage SHIPG. the practice, by forwarding agents, of grouping together several small consignments in one bill of lading. *See* groupage bill of lading *under* bill of lading.

  groupage rates freight rates for small consignments grouped together in a single bill of lading, as distinguished from rates for large shipments. *Syn.* grouping.

grouping *see* groupage.

group insurance *see under* insurance, classes and kinds of; *also* insurance policy.

group of companies STK. EXCH. a combination of companies that are legally independent but which make up a group consisting of a parent company and one or more subsidiary companies or affiliates each of which the parent company controls because it holds more than half its share-capital. *Abbr.* Gp.

Group of Ten FIN. ten relatively rich industrial countries which have agreed to lend money to the International Monetary Fund (I.M.F.) when required. The ten members are: Belgium, Canada, France, Italy, Japan, the Netherlands, Sweden, West Germany, the United Kingdom and the U.S.A. *See* General Arrangements to Borrow. *Syn.* The Paris Club.

group pension policy *see under* insurance policy.

growth, economic *see under* economic.

growth share *or* **stock** STK. EXCH. a security that is much favoured by investors because it is likely to increase its earnings in the future at a faster rate than other securities, thus increasing its market price and bringing the present investor a capital gain.

Grs. gross.

grs. grains.

G.R.T. gross register tonnage.

Gr. T. gross ton.

grub-stake (*colloq.*) money given to an author (writer) so that he may live while writing a book.

Grub Street formerly a street in London where poor writers lived and worked. The words now mean undistinguished writers in general. *adj.* grub-street *writing/prose*, of low quality. *A grub-street hack*.

gr. wt. gross weight.

gs. guineas.

g.s.m. grams per square metre; (of) good, sound, merchantable (quality).

G.S.M. general sales manager.

gt. great.

gua. guarani.

guar. guarantee(d).

guarani the standard currency unit of Paraguay, divided into 100 centimos. *Abbr.* gua.

guarantee (1) a promise given by a manufacturer or other supplier in writing, that the article sold is of good quality and that he will make good any faults for which he is responsible, if claimed within a stated period, usu. a year. Cf. indemnity. *Syn.* warranty; maker's guarantee; guaranty; surety. *Abbr.* guar. (2) LAW a promise by a third person who is not a party to a contract to become liable if one of the parties fails to perform his duty under the contract. (3) LAW a person to whom a guaranty is made or given. (4) BKG. *see* bank guarantee. (5) BKG. & COM. one of certain bank guarantees (*see under* bank) that exporters must arrange when tendering to foreign customers, esp. government departments.

performance guarantee one required by the customer, usu. in the form of a bond for 5% to 10% of the value of the contract, to be effective until the contract is completed.

tender guarantee one demanded by the customer for a small percentage, such as 2% to 5% of the total value of the contract, the purpose being to test the financial reputation of the exporter, and to protect the customer if the exporter fails to sign the contract if it is awarded to him.

guarantee, company limited by *see* limited company *under* company.

guarantee fund STK. EXCH. a fund of money kept by the London Stock Exchange for paying members of the public who suffer losses when a member of the Stock Exchange fails.

guaranteed annuity *see under* insurance policy.

guaranteed bill *see* backed bill *under* bill of exchange.

guaranteed debenture *see under* debenture.

guaranteed income bond *see* single premium policy *under* insurance policy.

guaranteed prices AGR. certain minimum prices for various farm products, such as corn and cattle, which a government has promised to farmers in order to encourage production. If the market price falls below these guaranteed prices, the farmers receive the difference in the form of a subsidy.

guaranteed stocks STK. EXCH. in Britain, stocks issued by the nationalized industries, the interest on which is guaranteed by the government. They are therefore gilt-edged securities.

guaranteed wage *see under* wage.

guarantor LAW & BKG. a person who binds himself by an agreement with a banker or other creditor to be responsible for paying the debt of another person if he fails to pay when it is due. *Syn.* a surety.

guaranty LAW a legal form of the word guarantee. *Syn.* suretyship.

guaranty bond *see under* bond, *n.*

guardian LAW a person possessing the legal right and duty to protect another person who cannot manage his personal affairs, such as an infant (in Britain, a person under 18 years of age) or someone who is mad.

Guatemala a republic on the Pacific coast of Central America, pop. 5½ million approx.; capital, Guatemala City, pop. 800,000 approx.; language, Spanish; currency unit, the quetzal, divided into 100 centavos. Member, O.A.S.

guest-house a house where paying guests may stay; a high-class boarding house where the owner personally looks after the guests. Cf. boarding house; hotel; motel.

Guiana *see* French Guiana.

guide (1) a person employed to show travellers, esp. tourists, the way and to point out and describe places of interest. Cf. courier. (2) a guide-book, a book that gives information for travellers esp. about places of interest.

guide price *see under* price.

guil. guilder(s).

guild ECON. HIST. one of the many associations, religious, commercial and professional, that played an important part in the economic organization of Europe, esp. in the twelfth and thirteenth centuries. The powerful *guilds merchant* or *merchant guilds*, consisting of international traders, gradually developed into *craft guilds* of skilled master craftsmen and specialist traders. These craft guilds largely controlled industry, introducing periods of apprenticeship, setting standards of workmanship and fair trading, protecting the interests of their members and taking a large part in local government. They lost their importance with the rise of large-scale industry, but some still exist, mainly as charities. *Also* gild.

guilder a former gold coin but now the standard currency unit of the Netherlands and Surinam, divided into 100 cents. *Syn.* florin; gulden. *Also* Dutch guilder; Surinam guilder. *Abbr.* guil.

guild socialism ECON. HIST. a movement calling for a special form of socialism based on bringing back the self-governing craft guilds (*see* guild) that controlled industry in Europe in the Middle Ages. The idea was first put forward in 1906 and led to much discussion; after the 1914 –18 war some working guilds appeared at first to be having some success; but the movement had failed by 1925, mainly because of lack of interest by the workers and the difficult financial situation of the times.

guinea a former British gold coin first issued in the seventeenth century, made of gold from Guinea, and originally worth 20 shillings. Its value later varied much but by 1717 settled at 21 shillings. In 1821 it was replaced by the sovereign worth 20 shillings. As a unit for charg ing some professional services and for pricing some luxury goods, the guinea remained in use until recently. *Abbr. g.; gn.; gu.*

Guinea a republic in West Africa, pop. 4¼ million approx. (1973); capital, Conakry, pop. 120,000; languages, French and tribal; currency unit, the syli or suli or sily, divided into 100 cauris. Member, O.A.U.

Guinea-Bissau (formerly Portuguese Guinea), a republic in West Africa, pop. 500,000 approx. (1973); capital, Madina do Boé, pop. 120,000 approx.; languages, Portuguese and tribal; currency unit, the peso, divided into 100 centavos. Member, O.A.U.

guinea-pig director *see under* director.

gulden *see* guilder; florin.

Gulf MAR. INSCE. in marine insurance, the Gulf of Mexico.

Gunter's chain *see* chain.

guv'nor (*colloq.*, governor) (1) in Britain, a title of respect used by some persons when speaking to a person of higher rank or position: *Good morning, guv'nor. Syn.* (*colloq.*) gaffer. (2) (*with* the) the person in charge, esp. of a workshop or factory: *Let me speak to the guv- 'nor.* (3) father: *My guv'nor has financed me.*

Guyana a republic on the northern coast of South America, pop. 750,000 approx.; capital, Georgetown, pop. 200,000 approx.; language, English; currency unit, the Guyana dollar (Guy $), divided into 100 cents. Member, (British) Commonwealth of Nations.

G.V. grande vitesse.

gyp *v.* (U.S.A. *colloq.*) to cheat; to rob by deceit. *Also* gip. *Pron.* jip.
n. in Britain, a college servant at Cambridge University.

gypper a cheat, a robber.

H

H Hungary's international vehicle-registration letter.

habeas corpus LAW (*Latin*, if you have the body) a court order directing that a person who is being held in prison shall be brought before the court to determine whether his imprisonment is legal. *Pron.* haybyas corpus.

haberdasher COM. (1) in Britain, a shopkeeper who deals in small articles connected with dress, such as ribbons, tapes and buttons. The trade is called *haberdashery.* (2) in U.S.A., a shopkeeper who sells men's clothing.

habitant (*French*, an inhabitant) a French settler in Canada or U.S.A. *Pron.* abiton.

hacienda AGR. (*Spanish*, landed property) in Latin America, a large country house with land that is usu. extensively farmed to raise cattle. *Syn.* ranch. *Pron.* athyenda *or* asyenda.

hack an undistinguished and unoriginal writer who writes only what he is told to write or bases his work on that of other people. Cf. ghost writer. *See* Grub Street.

hackwork the work of a hack; unoriginal writing done to order.

hackney-carriage TRANSPT. in Britain, originally a horse-drawn carriage kept for hire. Now, any vehicle which plies for hire, i.e. is driven round the streets looking for hirers. *Syn.* taxi; cab; taxi-cab.

had (*colloq.*) *To be had,* to be deceived, cheated: *I have been had by that cheat. See* have.

haggle COM. to bargain to excess before agreeing to buy or sell. *Also* higgle.

Hague Rules LAW & SHIPG. since 1921, a set of internationally accepted rules governing the carriage of goods by sea, esp. the rights and duties of carriers in relation to bills of lading.

Haiti a republic, the western third of Hispaniola, an island in the Caribbean, pop. 5 million approx. (1973); capital, Port au Prince, pop. 450,000 approx.; language, French; currency unit, the gourde, divided into 100 centimes.

halalah the fractional currency unit of Saudi Arabia. 100 halalah = 1 Saudi riyal.

haleru the fractional currency unit of Czechoslovakia. 100 haleru = 1 koruna.

half a bar (*colloq.*) half a pound or 50 pence.

half a century (*colloq.*) fifty pounds (£50).

half-and-half *see* fifty-fifty.

half a ton (*colloq.*) fifty pounds (£50).

half-commission man STK. EXCH. a person who, though not himself a broker, introduces clients to a stockbroker and receives half the broker's commission as payment. *Syn.* remisier.

half-dollar a silver coin of U.S.A., 50 cents.

half-dozen half a dozen, six.

halfpenny the smallest British coin, made of bronze. *Pron.* haypni. *Pl.* halfpence, *pron.* haypens.

halfpennyworth an amount that can be bought for a halfpenny. A very small amount. *Pron.* haypeth.

half-title (1) a page bearing the title of a book, sometimes in shortened form, placed before the title page. (2) a page bearing only the title of a part or subdivision of a book.

halftone a printing-block or other means of reproducing photographs or other pictures, in which various tones (degrees of shading or colour) are obtained by dots of varying sizes.

hallmark (1) in Britain, an official mark or marks that must by law be stamped on gold, silver and platinum articles to show that the metal has been assayed (tested) and that it is of the right purity. *See* assay office *under* assay. (2) generally any mark of good quality: *Our name on an article is the hallmark of excellence,* shows that it is of the highest quality.

halt *n.* TRANSPT. & TOUR. a temporary stop; a stopping-place.
v. STK. EXCH. to stop: *The upward movement of prices was halted by news of a miners' strike.*

halves *To go halves*, to share equally: *Let us go halves on the expenses/losses/profits.*

hamlet in England, a group of a few houses in the country, too small to be called a village, often without a shop, bank or bus service.

hammer *n.* COM. the instrument used by an auctioneer when he strikes his desk to mark the close of the auction, the article being sold to the last person to bid before the hammer falls. *To come/go under the hammer*, to be sold by auction.
v. STK. EXCH. (1) until 1970, to announce formally in public, by blows of a hammer to call attention, that a named member of the Stock Exchange could not pay his debts. The member was said to be hammered. He had to stop trading until his debts were at least partially paid and he obtained permission to start trading again. (2) *To hammer the market*, to sell large quantities of a security at one time, thus causing a rapid fall in price.

hamper (1) a large box-like basket with a lid, used esp. as a container for storing or transporting clothing. (2) a box or basket containing a gift of a collection of good food and drink: *A Christmas hamper.*

hand (1) IND. a manual worker (one who works with his hands): *A factory-/farm-/mill-hand. We employ 100 hands*, 100 persons. (2) SHIPG. one of the crew of a ship: *All hands on deck!* the entire crew. *The vessel was lost with all hands. A deck-hand.* (3) COM. *Hand-picked*, carefully chosen. *Living from hand to mouth*, having to spend money as soon as it is received. *Hand-to-mouth buying*, buying only as much as is immediately needed. *First-hand, second-hand, see under* first, second. *Note of hand*, a promissory note. *To have (something) on hand*, to have it ready for immediate use. *To have (something) on one's hands*, something one is trying to sell. *To shake hands on a bargain/deal*, to express agreement that it is binding. (4) ACCTS. *Cash/balance/stock in hand*, actually held; ready for use; possessed.

handbill ADVTG. a printed sheet of paper bearing a notice or an advertisement, usu. given out or delivered by hand.

handbook (1) a small book giving directions on how to use or repair something, such as a machine. (2) a guide-book.

handful (*colloq.*) five pounds (£5).

handicapped persons persons suffering from some bodily disadvantage, such as the loss of a limb or an eye, or from a nervous illness, such as epilepsy. In Britain, government help is given in training such persons for employment in factories and offices. *Syn.* disabled persons.

handicraft any skilled work done mostly by hand, such as making pottery. *Handicraftsman*, a person who practises a handicraft. *Syn.* craft.

handle (1) COM. to deal in, as an article of trade: *We do not handle medical books*, we do not stock or sell them. *We handle spare parts for motor cars.* (2) to hold or move with the hands: *A printer employs men to handle paper from one machine to another. Cashiers handle money. Do not handle the goods*, don't touch. (3) to attend to, to manage, to deal with a matter: *He is handling this problem. I handle only staff matters. She is good at handling the boss.*

handling (1) COM. & IND. the work of receiving, storing, packing and sending away goods: *Our staff are skilled in handling heavy goods. See* materials handling.
handling charge a charge made for packing and dispatching goods, esp. for small orders when labour costs are a high proportion of the value of the order.
(2) TRANSPT. the moving of goods from one means of transport to another, or to the place where they are to be delivered. *See* arrival (2).
unitized handling the transport of goods by container.
(3) LAW *Dishonest handling*, the crime of receiving and selling stolen property.

handling expenses *see under* expenses.

hand-out (1) a printed or typed statement handed to press reporters as news. (2) ADVTG. a free sample. (3) anything given away, such as food to the poor.

handsel *see* earnest.

handshake *see* golden handshake.

hands, show of when voting at a meeting, the act of each person in raising his hand to show whether he votes for or against a motion (proposed course of action). The chairman is able to judge by the number of hands raised whether the motion is won or lost. Cf. poll.

handy (1) convenient: *A handy pack or package*, easy to use, open, or carry, esp. in the pocket or handbag; of convenient size. (2) skilful with the hands: *He is handy about the house.*
handyman a person employed to do repair jobs, often needing some skill with the hands.

hangar TRANSPT. a large building for sheltering aeroplanes on an aerodrome.

Hansard the name given to the official printed record of the members' speeches and decisions in the British Parliament.

Hanseatic League, The ECON. HIST. a union (Hanse) of certain towns (numbering over 70 at times) in northern and central Germany, formed in the thirteenth century to help one another in defence and in trading in the Baltic. It became most powerful and, by the fourteenth and fifteenth centuries, was controlling all trade in northern Europe. Its importance in history lies in its development of orderly commerce, its improvements in shipbuilding, and its system of mercantile and maritime law. It slowly declined in the sixteenth century and came to an end in 1699.

Hants. Hampshire, England.

hao a fractional currency unit of Vietnam, equal to 10 xu or one-tenth of a dong.

harbour a safe place of shelter for ships. If it also provides a safe landing-place for people and goods, and facilities, such as docks, wharves, cranes, for loading and unloading ships, it is called a port. *Syn.* haven. (U.S.A., harbor.)
a harbour of refuge a harbour with no port facilities.
artificial harbour one made by man, usu. by building walls called breakwaters out from the land.
natural harbour a place that provides shelter for ships without needing man-made breakwaters.

harbourage (1) the shelter given to ships by a harbour. (2) a harbour.

harbour dues SHIPG. money payable by the owner of a ship for the use of a harbour and the ·services provided there, usu. based as a charge per ton on the ship's net register tonnage. *See* tonnage. (U.S.A., harbor dues.)

harbour master SHIPG. the head official responsible for the orderly working of a harbour or port, esp. in seeing that the rules regarding the mooring and berthing of ships are obeyed. (U.S.A., harbor master.)

hard *n.* SHIPG. a beach, foreshore, or bed of a river where the ground is hard enough to lay up a ship. A landing-place for boats.

hard cash *see under* cash.

hard currency *see under* currency.

harden STK. & COMMOD. EXCH. of prices, to rise steadily: *Shares hardened towards the end of The Account. Copper hardened during the day.*

hard goods ECON. *see* consumer durables.

hard money *see under* money.

hard selling ADVTG. the use of unpleasantly powerful methods of advertising and selling a product, by continually repeating its name and good qualities. *Syn.* high-pressure selling. *N.* (*colloq.*) a hard sell.

hard up (*colloq.*) poor; short of money.

hardware (1) metal articles for use in the home or workshop, such as pots and pans, tools, locks, nails, screws, and instruments for measuring. (2) COMP. in data processing by computers, the computer itself, with its mechanical, electronic and electrical parts, as distinguished from the programs that decide and control the working of the computer. Cf. software.

harmonic mean an average arrived at by adding together the reciprocals of all the individual quantities, dividing by the number of quanti-

ties and taking the reciprocal of the result. *Example*: to find the harmonic mean of 3 + 5 + 7: Add the reciprocals: $\frac{1}{3} + \frac{1}{5} + \frac{1}{7} = 0.333 + 0.200 + 0.143 = 0.676$; $0.676 \div 3 = 0.225$, reciprocal of which is 4.44 = harmonic mean. The harmonic mean is always less than the arithmetic mean, which in this case is 5.00. The harmonic mean is useful in comparing average speeds over various distances and in solving statistical problems in transport.

harmonic(al) progression a set of numbers is said to be in harmonic(al) progression if the reciprocals of the numbers form an arithmetic progression. *Example*: $\frac{1}{3}, \frac{1}{5}, \frac{1}{7}, \frac{1}{9}$. Cf. arithmetic(al) progression; geometric(al) progression.

Harrod Sir Roy Forbes (1900–78), English economist, follower of J.M. Keynes and teacher of economics at Oxford University. His most important works were his theory of economic growth, relating Keynesian teaching to the passing of time, as expressed in his book, *Towards a Dynamic Economics* (1948); and his part in developing the Harrod-Domar model of economic growth, a mathematical analysis of the causes of trade cycles.

hatch SHIPG. (1) an opening in the deck of a ship to allow cargo to be loaded into and unloaded from one of the ship's holds. (2) a cover for such an opening. *Aft/forward hatch. Pl.* hatches. *Syn.* hatchway.

hat money *see* primage.

Hatton Garden the street in the City of London in which is situated one of the world's main markets in diamonds and other jewels.

haul *v.* TRANSPT. to drag; to pull or move with force; to transport, esp. heavy goods, by road, rail or canal. *An engine/locomotive hauls a train. Trucks hauling coal.*
n. (1) the act of hauling: *A lorry ready for the haul across Europe.* (2) a distance over which a load is hauled: *A long/short haul.* (3) a quantity obtained by hard work: *A haul of fish.* (4) valuable articles stolen by a thief: *The burglar got away with his haul.*

haulage TRANSPT. (1) the moving of heavy loads by road, rail or canal: *The haulage industry. A haulage contractor.* (2) the charge made for hauling, esp. by railway, canal or port authorities, for moving trucks and wagons for shipowners.

haulage contractor *see* contract carrier *under* carrier.

haulier *see* contract carrier *under* carrier.

hauling stock TRANSPT. on the railways, vehicles such as engines, locomotives that are provided with power to haul carriages and wagons. Cf. rolling stock.

have (*colloq.*) to cheat: *To have a person*, to cheat him. *See* had.

haven *see* harbour.

hawk COM. to sell goods in the streets, usu. from a cart or from door to door. Cf. peddle.

hawker COM. a street-seller; one who sells small cheap articles which he carries about the streets on a cart, calling from door to door or selling at the side of the road. Cf. peddler; pedlar. *Syn.* street-trader.

share-hawker STK. EXCH. *see* share-pushing.

Hawtrey Sir Ralph George (1879–1975), English economist, high Treasury official and later professor at the Royal Institute of International Affairs (Chatham House). He wrote on currency, banking, employment, and the trade cycle; *Currency and Credit* (1919), *The Art of Central Banking* (1937), *Capital and Employment* (1937), *The Balance of Payments and the Standard of Living* (1950) are among his main works.

hay and straw measure 1 truss = 56 lb old hay, or 60 lb new hay, or 60 lb straw. 36 trusses = 1 load.

Hayek F.A. (1899–), Austrian economist, writer and teacher; Nobel prizewinner, 1974. As a member of the Austrian School of economists, he has argued strongly for free enterprise and against interference by the State in economic life. His most important work has been on the theory of the trade cycle. His books include: *Monetary Theory and the Trade Cycle* (1929), *Prices and Production* (1931), *The Pure Theory of Capital* (1941), *The Road to Serfdom* (1944).

hazard INSCE. anything which may cause, or increase the probability of, a loss from a particular peril (great danger), e.g. the carrying of petrol in leaking containers in a car is a *fire hazard*.

moral hazard the possibility of dishonest behaviour or carelessness by the insured or by his employees which would increase the risk of a loss arising.

occupational hazard *see under* occupational.

adj. hazardous, depending on chance; risky: *A hazardous adventure/speculation/undertaking.*

H & C, h & c hot and cold (water supply).

H/C, h/c held covered (insurance).

Hd. head (headland).

head *n.* (1) a person or animal: *We charge £1 per head. He owns 4000 head of sheep/cattle. A head tax, see* capitation tax *under* tax. (2) the chief person, leader, of an organization: *The head of the firm*, the senior partner. *Heads of department/division*, or *Divisional/departmental heads.* (3) the front part of a ship: *Down by the head*, the front of the ship lower in the water than the back.

headed letter-paper paper printed with a heading, usu. the name of the business or other organization, its address, telephone and telex numbers, and other information. *Syn.* headed notepaper. *See* letterhead.

headhunt *v.* (*colloq.*) to search for persons to join an organization as executives, i.e. employees carrying fairly high responsibility, such as managers. *Syn.* recruitment of senior staff. *n.* the operation of headhunting.

head office the chief or central office of a business organization, from which controlling directions are given to its branch offices: *The bank has its head office in Cairo and twenty branches in other parts of Egypt. Abbr.* H.O.

head tax *see* capitation tax *under* tax.

headword (1) a word that heads, or begins, a paragraph or chapter. (2) in a dictionary, the first word of an entry or article: *A dictionary containing 10,000 headwords.*

health *see* industrial hygiene.

Health and Social Security, Department of (D.H.S.S.) the British government department that administers the National Health Service and the national insurance and industrial injuries scheme. It also directs the welfare and public-health services that are run by local government authorities. *See* National Health Service; national insurance.

health, bill of *see under* bill.

health insurance *see* national insurance; private health policy; medical expenses policy *under* insurance policy.

Health Service *see* National Health Service.

hearing LAW a trial in a court of law.

heavy industry *see under* industry.

heavy lift SHIPG. a piece of cargo that is too heavy to be handled by the ship's derricks, and needs special cranes or hoists to lift it.

heavy-lift ship a ship provided with special cranes or other arrangements for lifting very heavy loads on to or off the vessel.

heavy market STK. & COMMOD. EXCH. a condition in the stock or commodity markets when prices are falling and buyers are slow to buy.

hectare (ha) a metric measure of area, 100 ares, or 10,000 m², or 1/100th of a square kilometre. 1 ha = 2.471 acres; 1 acre = 0.405 ha.

hecto- the *prefix* used in the metric system of SI units to mean one hundred times: 1 hectolitre = 100 litres; 1 hectogram = 100 grams; but note 1 hectare = 100 ares.

hedge fund STK. & COMMOD. EXCH. in U.S.A., a fund formed by a group of persons, often personal friends, for the purpose of investing in risky ventures in the stock and commodity markets.

hedging (1) COMMOD. EXCH. an operation adopted by merchants and others in the commodity markets who deal in futures to protect themselves against risk of loss, caused by future changes in price. Thus a merchant who has bought a quantity of a commodity will sell futures to an equal value so that he is certain of a fixed price when the time comes to sell his goods. A buyer, such as a manufacturer, however, will buy futures in order to make sure of a fixed price for his future supply of materials. Both these operators are hedging. *Syn.* covering. *See* commodity exchange. (2) FIN. & STK. EXCH. operations similar in purpose to those described above for commodity markets are carried out in the foreign-exchange and stock and share markets. Thus when an investor, in times of inflation, buys equities (ordinary shares) at a lower return than he can get from fixed-interest securities, he is hedging against inflation because he expects the market value of equities to rise faster than the fall in the value of money.

heel *see* counterfoil.

heir LAW one who inherits (receives by right) the land and property of a person who has died, either under a will made by the dead person or, if there is no will, then because they are related, e.g. father and son, husband and wife, brother and sister. *Fem.* heiress, a female heir.

heirloom an article, such as a picture, that has long been possessed by members of one family and passed down, e.g. from father to son, again and again.

helicopter TRANSPT. a special kind of aircraft or flying machine which can lift itself straight up from the ground, hover (stay still in the air without moving in any direction) and come straight down gently without running along the ground. *Syn.* (*colloq.*) chopper; copter.

helipad *see* heliport.

heliport TRANSPT. a place where helicopters may regularly land and take off. *Syn.* helipad.

Hellenic Register of Shipping SHIPG. the Greek society responsible for checking the safety and fitness of ships registered with the society and for classifying them. The Greek equivalent of Lloyd's Register of Shipping in Britain.

hereditament LAW real property, i.e. land and buildings.

  corporeal hereditament one that actually exists in the form of earth, bricks, etc.

  incorporeal hereditament a right to an income or benefit from a corporeal hereditament without having the rights of ownership.

  industrial hereditament *see under* industrial.

heritable bond *see under* bond, *n.*

Herts. Hertfordshire, England.

hhd. h'hd. hogshead.

Hicks Sir John Richard (1904–), English economist, taught economics at the Universities of London (Lecturer, L.S.E. 1926–35), Manchester (Professor, 1938–46), and later at Cambridge and Oxford. Nobel prizewinner (1973) for his work on the theory of equilibrium in an economic system. He has also done valuable work in carrying further the ideas of J.M. Keynes on the economics of growth. Among his many books are: *Value and Capital* (1939); *A Contribution to the Theory of the*

Trade Cycle (1950); *A Revision of Demand Theory* (1956), *Capital and Growth* (1965). He makes frequent use of mathematical methods.

hidden asset *see* assets.

hidden damage SHIPG. damage which is not noticeable at the time when the cargo is unloaded from the ship, but which is discovered when a close examination is made. *Opp.* apparent damage.

hidden inflation *see under* inflation.

hidden reserve *see under* reserve.

hidden tax *see under* tax.

hidden unemployment *see under* unemployment.

higgle *see* haggle.

high STK. EXCH. of prices, a high point or level; a situation in the market when prices are relatively high. *To reach an all-time high*, to rise to the highest price ever. *Opp.* low.

High Commissioner the chief representative of one member state in the (British) Commonwealth of Nations to another, equivalent to an ambassador. His office is called a High Commission.

high coupon STK. EXCH. a fixed-interest security that pays a high rate of interest.

High Court of Justice LAW in Britain, the lower branch of the Supreme Court of Judicature that consists of: the Queen's Bench Division; the Chancery Division; the Family Division. Appeals are heard by the Court of Appeal, the upper branch of the Supreme Court.

Higher National Certificate (H.N.C.) in Britain, a certificate given to students who have passed the Ordinary National Certificate examination and have completed a further two-year part-time course at one of the higher educational institutions. Among the many subjects for which the certificate is granted, is business studies. Cf. Ordinary National Certificate (O.N.C.)

higher-rate tax *see* income tax *under* income.

high finance FIN. the control by rich and powerful financiers of lending and investment deals on a large scale, often of a highly complicated and sometimes risky nature.

high-rise building a very tall building for offices or flats.

high seas SHIPG. & LAW any part of the seas and oceans which is not under the ruling power of any country; the open sea outside territorial waters, where all persons are free to come and go as they please, provided that they obey the rules of international law.

high-season fare *see under* fare.

High Street (1) often the actual name of the main street in a town or village. (U.S.A. Main Street.) (2) words used to describe the sort of shops found in most shopping centres in Britain, esp. in towns: *A plan to give high street co-operative stores a new appearance.*

high water SHIPG. high tide; the highest level that the sea reaches in a single swing (rise and fall) of the tide. *Opp.* low water. *Abbr.* H.W.

highway TRANSPT. in law, any road or track along which the public have the right to pass and repass. In general, a road, esp. a main road, fit for motor traffic.

Highway Code in Britain, a set of rules published by the government to guide persons using the highway; esp. drivers of vehicles.

high-yielders STK. EXCH. stocks and shares that give a high yield and are sometimes, but not always, more risky than other securities. *Syn.* high-income shares.

hike TOUR. to walk long distances, usu. for pleasure; to tour on foot. Cf. hitch-hike. *N.* a hike; a hiker.

hill-station TOUR. in hot countries, a place high in the mountains to which people go, esp. in summer to escape from the heat of the plains, such as: Simla, Darjeeling, Ootacamund in India; Murree in Pakistan.

hinterland COM. & TRANSPT. (1) the area served by a trading centre such as an inland city. (2) an inland area of which the greater part of the trade passes through a single port. *Syn.* back country.

hire *v.* (1) to employ (a person); to pay wages for a worker's services: *A hired man/woman*, a person who helps in the home. *We have hired 50 additional mill-hands.* (2) to pay money for the temporary use of something: *A hired car. To hire a horse/taxi/bus/ship.* Cf. rent. *See* hire-purchase.

n. the wages or money paid for somebody's services or for the use of something. *A good labourer is worth his hire. Plant-hire,* money paid for the use of plant (machines, equipment and buildings for manufacturing things). *For hire. A car-hire firm.*

hire-and-fire *see* fire.

hire-purchase agreement COM. & FIN. a form of consumer credit, being a contract to hire an article with the right to buy it, i.e. become its owner only when the last instalment has been paid. Until then the article remains the property of the hirer/seller although used by the buyer. The agreement (which must always be in writing) is usu. made between the customer and a hire-purchase finance house which buys the article from the shopkeeper and hires it to the customer, but in some cases the finance house advances the money to the shopkeeper, using as security the shopkeeper's hire-purchase agreement with the customer. Cf. deferred-payment agreement. *Syn.* easy terms.

hire-purchase company *see* finance house.

hire-purchase price COM. the total price that the buyer of an article by hire-purchase will have to pay, consisting of the cash price of the article, all interest and other charges. Cf. cash price.

hire-purchase sale *see under* sale.

histogram *see* bar chart *under* chart.

historic(al) cost *see under* cost.

hitch-hike TOUR. (*colloq.*) to travel by getting a free ride in passing motor cars or lorries. This is illegal in some parts of the United States. Cf. hike.

hive off MAN. & IND. (1) to arrange for the manufacture by another company, of some part of one's product. *Syn.* subcontract. (2) to separate a part of a business organization to make it into a separate business, such as forming a branch, or group of branches, into a subsidiary company.

HK Hong Kong's international vehicle-registration letters.

H.M.G. Her Majesty's Government.

H.M.S. Her Majesty's Ship/Service.

H.M.S.O. Her Majesty's Stationery Office.

H.N.C. Higher National Certificate.

Ho. house.

H.O. head office.

hoard *n.* ECON. a secret store of money, valuable goods or food that has been saved or collected for use in the future: *A hoard of gold and silver.*

v. to make or keep a hoard: *To hoard up,* to save and store for future use. *Hoarded money is idle for it produces nothing.*

hoarder a person who hoards.

hoarding (1) ECON. THEORY a tendency by the public, esp. under conditions of uncertainty, to hold economically idle cash rather than a productive form of wealth. Hoarding may greatly affect the economy because the sale of assets to get cash for hoarding causes prices of securities to fall and interest rates and the quantity of money to rise. Investment is slowed down, money incomes are reduced and unemployment rises. *See* liquidity preference; saving. *Opp.* dishoarding. (2) ADVTG. *see* advertisement hoarding.

hock (*colloq.*) to pledge or pawn: *In hock,* pawned. *To be in hock to the bankers,* to be heavily in debt to them.

hogshead (1) a large cask or barrel. *Abbr.* hhd.; h'hd. (2) a varying unit of volume, 51½, 54 or 63 imperial gallons; 234, 245 or 286 litres.

hoist *n.* a machine for lifting heavy loads; a goods lift (or elevator in U.S.A.).

v. (1) (*colloq.*) to make popular by giving much praise. *Syn.* shove; boost. (2) (*colloq.*) to shoplift (to steal goods offered for sale in shops).

hold SHIPG. that part of the space inside a ship in which the cargo is carried.

holder BKG. & COM. the person who holds, or lawfully has in his possession, a bill of exchange or other document. He may be the payee, or the indorsee or the bearer.

holder for value a person holding a bill of ex

change on which value has been given, e.g. goods have been supplied in return for the expected payment of the bill. Cf. holder in due course.

holder in due course a person who has in good faith and for value taken a bill of exchange before it was overdue and having had no notice that it had been dishonoured; such a person has an absolute right, which no one else has, to receive the value of the bill when in due course he presents it for acceptance and payment.

holding (1) AGR. a small farm. *Syn.* smallholding. (2) a group of several farms managed and run as a single unit. (3) STK. EXCH. a quantity of a security held by one owner: *A shareholding. A large holding of shares in your company.*

holding company *see under* company.

holding out LAW falsely allowing oneself to be accepted as having a certain position, esp. as a partner in a firm. A form of false representation. *See* fraud.

hold-up (1) an armed robbery. (2) a delay: *A hold-up in the rail service. A production hold-up.*

holiday (1) a day on which, by law or custom, no business dealings take place, and only employees of essential services are required to work: *A bank/public/statutory holiday. A religious/Muslim/Christian/Hindu/Jewish holiday. See* bank holiday (U.S.A.); *also* bank holidays (Britain). *Tax holiday, see under* tax. (2) (*often pl.*) a period of rest and freedom from work: *Our employees get 20 working days' annual holiday. He spends his holidays in Egypt. Did you have a good holiday? The school holidays. The manager is on holiday this week. Syn.* leave; furlough; vacation.

holiday camp a permanent set of buildings, usu. by the sea, where many people on holiday can be fed and accommodated and kept fully amused with organized games, sports, music and dancing.

Holland *see* Netherlands, The.

holograph *adj.* of a document, entirely in the handwriting of the person who has signed it. Handwritten. *A holograph letter/will. n.* any handwritten document. *In holograph,* handwritten, not typed or printed. *Syn.* manuscript; longhand.

home bill *see* inland bill *under* bill of exchange.

home consumption *see under* consumption.

home economics the study of the activity of making and running a home for a family. *Syn.* domestic science.

home industry *see* cottage industry; domestic system.

home loan FIN. a loan of money on mortgage by a building society to the buyer of a house, esp. to an owner-occupier. *See* building society.

homeowner's policy *see* comprehensive policy *under* insurance policy.

home port SHIPG. the port of registry of a ship.

home sales *see under* sales.

home service insurance *see* industrial life insurance *under* insurance, classes and kinds of.

homestead (1) AGR. a house, usu. a farmhouse, with land and farm buildings, owned by the farmer. (2) land given to a settler in newly-developing country on condition that he builds a house and farms the land.

home trade *see under* trade.

homeward *adj.* SHIPG. towards the home country: *Homeward freight. Homeward voyage. Syn.* inward. *Opp.* outward. *Adv.* homewards.

homeward bound *see* bound (1).

homework *see* domestic system.

Hon. Honourable; honorary.

hon. honorary.

Honduras a republic in Central America, pop. 2½ million approx. (1973); capital, Tegucigalpa, pop. 250,000 approx.; language, Spanish; currency unit, the lempira, divided into 100 centavos. Member, O.A.S.; Caribbean Common Market.

honest broker (*colloq.*) a trusted person who represents both parties in a dispute or in negotiations of a financial nature.

hong (1) a member of a cohong. *See* Canton system. (2) in China, (*a*) a warehouse. (*b*) a foreign-merchant firm or company.

Hong Kong a British crown colony in the Far East, pop. 4· million approx. (1973); capital, Victoria, pop. 1 million approx.; languages, English and Chinese; currency unit, the Hong Kong dollar (HK $), divided into 100 cents.

honorarium FIN. payment for professional services, such as those of a lawyer, accountant, architect. *Syn.* fee.

honorary of a position, office, title, held for the honour only, not for monetary gain or payment. *The honorary secretary (Abbr.* Hon. Sec.) an unpaid secretary, usu. of a society or other non-profitmaking organization. *Honorary member,* a member who has been given the honour of free membership, usu. for life, of a club or society.

honour *v.* (1) BKG. to pay a cheque, bill of exchange, or promissory note when it becomes due. *Opp.* to dishonour. *Also* (U.S.A.) honor. (2) to carry out a promise or to meet a liability: *Businessmen must honour their obligations. n.* a special favour: *I have the honour to inform you,* usu. a polite expression when writing to a person of higher rank. *A point of honour,* a moral duty.

hoof AGR. *On the hoof,* of animals, esp. cattle, still alive, not slaughtered (killed).

hopper SHIPG. a barge or boat with hinged doors in its bottom to allow material such as earth and sand, brought up from the bed of a river or harbour by a dredger, to be dropped out at sea.

horizontal amalgamation *see under* amalgamation.

horizontal combination *see under* combination.

horizontal expansion *see* expansion (2).

horizontal integration *see under* integration.

horizontal trust *see under* trust.

horse (*colloq.*) a five-pound note.

horse-box TRANSPT. a vehicle specially built for transporting horses by road or rail.

horse latitudes SHIPG. a belt of calms or very light variable winds lying north of the north-east trade winds in the South Atlantic, roughly in lat. 20° to 35°S.

horsepower a unit of measurement of power, i.e. the rate at which a machine works; 1 hp is the power needed to lift 550 lb a height of 1 ft in 1 sec. In metric measure, 1 hp = 0.7457 kW. *Abbr.* hp; h.p.

horse-trading COM. sharp and hard bargaining. Thus *horse-trader*, a person who makes a hard bargain or is difficult to bargain with.

horticulture AGR. the cultivation of plants in gardens, esp. a system of farming giving a high yield per acre applied to market gardens and glasshouses growing flowers, fruit and vegetables for sale in the market.

hosiery COM. originally, hose (stockings), but nowadays all kinds of knitted goods and underclothing.

host (1) a man who receives guests and entertains them in his home or some other place such as a restaurant. (2) the landlord of an inn.

hostel a building, usu. not run for profit, where students, nurses, etc. can obtain cheap board and lodging. Cf. hotel.

hostelry an old word for an inn.

hostess (1) a female host. (2) a woman who helps to entertain guests in a club or restaurant. (3) *air hostess*, *see under* aircrew.

hot bill *see under* bill of exchange.

hot money *see under* money.

hotel (1) a building run as a business, in which persons, esp. travellers or holidaymakers, are given lodging and usu. food. *See* commercial hotel; family hotel. Cf. hostel. (2) in India, Pakistan, a tea-room, a restaurant.

hotel accommodation TOUR. lodgings in a hotel for tourists and other travellers, usu. hired by the day with or without meals. Cf. motel; guest-house.

hotelier TOUR. & COM. a hotel-keeper.

hourly rate COM. & IND. in those trades where workers are paid by the hour, the amount paid for each hour worked.

hours of attendance *see* attendance time *under* attendance.

house (1) a home, a place to live in: *To keep house*, to run a home, esp. for one's family. (2) a business, esp. a large organization: *The House of Longman. House journal*, a magazine produced by the management and given free to employees, containing news and information about the organization and its employees.

House, The (1) The House of Commons. (2) BKG. The Clearing House. (3) STK. EXCH. The London Stock Exchange.

house agent *see* estate agent.

house bill *see under* bill of exchange.

house brand *see* own-brand.

housebreaking LAW forcing a way into a building for a criminal purpose and then forcing a way out. *See* burglary.

house cheque *see under* cheque.

house flag *see* flag.

household *n.* all the persons who live in a house; members of the family and any others, such as guests, lodgers and servants.
adj. having to do with a household: *Household expenses. Household goods/effects*, the usual contents of a home, linen, furniture, curtains, carpets, etc. but not clothes.

householder the person who holds the right to live in a house, either as owner or tenant. Often, the head of the family.

household policy *see* comprehensive policy *under* insurance policy.

housekeeper a person, usu. a woman, who is paid to run a house, perhaps directing the work of other employees.

housekeeping money money provided usu. by a husband to be spent by his wife on food and household goods.

House of Commons LAW the lower house of the British Parliament, consisting of 635 elected members called Members of Parliament (M.P.s). Cf. House of Lords.

House of Lords LAW the upper house of the British Parliament, consisting of hereditary peers (noblemen whose titles are passed down from parent to child) and life peers appointed by the government for life only. It is also the highest court of appeal for the United Kingdom, acting through its Judicial Committee of Law Lords (Lords of Appeal in Ordinary) and other peers who are or have been judges, all under the direction of the Lord Chancellor. Its decisions are binding on all courts in Britain.

house-purchase policy *see under* insurance policy.

house union *see* company union.

Houses of Parliament the House of Lords and the House of Commons which together form the Parliament of the United Kingdom. The Palace of Westminster in London, where the two Houses meet, is also popularly known as the Houses of Parliament.

housing the provision of houses for the public.

housing association FIN. in Britain, co-operative organizations formed to help members to build their own houses by making loans and giving advice.

hovercraft TRANSPT. & SHIPG. a vehicle that travels over land and water, close to the surface, on a cushion of air.

H.P. hire-purchase; Houses of Parliament.

hp, h.p. horsepower.

H.Q. headquarters.

HR Hellenic Register (of Shipping).

hrs. hours.

huckster (1) COM. a street-seller, either a hawker or a pedlar. (2) any person trading on a very small scale.

Hudson's Bay Company ECON. HIST. a company of adventurers, formed in 1670 to trade in the Hudson Bay region of Canada and to look for a north-west passage to the Pacific. The company long had a monopoly of trade in parts of Canada and also administered great areas of the country. In 1859 it lost its monopoly position but continued to trade, esp. in furs. It now has many general retail stores, and is one of the largest business concerns in Canada. Full name: Hudson's Bay Trading Company Ltd.

hull (1) SHIPG. the body of a ship, consisting of a frame, an outer covering or shell and decks, but excluding masts and engines and any cargo. (2) MAR. INSCE. the whole ship as distinguished from its cargo: *Hull insurance*, covers the ship, its engines and other machinery and equipment but not any cargo: *Hull policy/risk/ underwriter*.

human capital *see under* capital (1).

human-factor engineering *see* ergonomics.

Hume David (1711–76), Scottish philosopher, historian and economist. He is believed to have greatly influenced Adam Smith, 12 years younger than Hume, esp. in his criticism of mercantilist policies. He was one of the earliest well-informed writers on subjects such as the supply of money, rates of interest and the importance of one country's natural advantages over those of others in developing international trade. He welcomed industrialization as a way of progressing beyond a mainly agricultural economy. His main book dealing with economics is *Political Discourses*, being Part 2 of his *Essays, Moral, Political and Literary* (1752).

hundi BKG. in India, Pakistan and Bangladesh, a credit instrument similar to a promissory note or banker's draft, much used by the many private bankers who finance internal commerce.

hundred (1) a number, 100. (2) COM. a *great hundred* or *long hundred*, sometimes used in commerce, consists of 120 articles. (3) (*colloq.*) a hundred pounds, £100.

hundredweight a unit of weight. (*a*) in Britain, 112 lb avoirdupois (50.80 kg), one-twentieth of a U.K. (long) ton of 2240 lb and divided into four quarters of 28 lb. (*b*) in U.S.A., 100 lb (45.36 kg), being one-twentieth of a short ton of 2000 lb. *Abbr.* cwt.

Hungary a socialist republic in eastern Europe, pop. 10.5 million approx. (1973); capital, Budapest, pop. 2 million approx.; language, Magyar; currency unit, the forint, divided into 100 filler. Member, COMECON.

Hunts. Huntingdonshire, now part of Cambridgeshire, England.

husband v. to economize; to save; to use carefully: *To husband one's resources*, to consume one's stock of money or goods carefully, economically. *See also* ship's husband.

husbandman AGR. a farmer.

husbandry AGR. the management of a farm; the practice of farming: *Good/bad husbandry*, the management of affairs generally.

animal husbandry a branch of farming which is concerned with the management and breeding of animals, esp. cattle, sheep, horses and pigs, and includes dairy-farming and the production of raw wool and other animal products.

hush-money *see under* money.

hwan *see* won.

H.W. high water.

H.W.M. high water mark.

H.W.O.N.T. high water ordinary neap tides.

H.W.O.S.T. high water ordinary spring tides.

hydel *see* hydro-electricity.

hydraulic IND. worked or driven by water or other liquid such as oil: *Hydraulic control system*, one using water or oil under pressure, as compared with one using electricity.

hydro-electricity IND. electricity produced by water-power. *Abbr.* hydel.

hydrofoil SHIPG. a very fast boat provided with a set or sets of foils (surfaces) used to hold or lift the boat up when moving through the water so that, above a certain speed, it is sliding fast along the surface with its hull out of the water.

hygiene *see* industrial hygiene.

hyper-inflation ECON. an extreme form of inflation; the situation that exists in an economy when the money supply is being increased very rapidly, resulting in an increase of over 20% in the annual growth of the money supply or of the price-level. *See* inflation. *Syn.* runaway inflation.

hypermarket COM. a very large supermarket.

hypothecate BKG. & COM. (1) (when a bill of exchange is drawn) to agree to the goods being given as security for the payment of the bill.

letter of hypothecation a document in which the drawer of a bill agrees that the goods shall be sold and the money used to pay the bill if it is dishonoured. *Syn.* an hypothecation.
(2) (when an advance is being obtained from a bank) to agree to certain stated goods, e.g. stocks of materials and finished products, or book debts, being treated as security for the repayment of the advance. Such goods are said to be *hypothecated goods*.

I

I Italy's international vehicle-registration letter.

Ia. Iowa, U.S.A.

I.A.S. Indian Administrative Service, formerly the Indian Civil Service (I.C.S.).

I.A.T.A. International Air Transport Association.

i.b. in bond.

ib., ibid. (*Latin*: ibidem) in the same place.

I.B. invoice book; in bond; International Bank (for Reconstruction and Development); Institute of Bankers; industrial business.

I.B.E.C. International Bank for Economic Co-operation.

I.B.I. invoice book inwards.

I.B.O. invoice book outwards.

I.B.R.D. International Bank for Reconstruction and Development.

i/c. in charge.

I.C.A.O. International Civil Aviation Organization.

I.C.C. International Chamber of Commerce.

icebreaker SHIPG. a ship specially built for use in forcing a way for other vessels through the ice.

Iceland an island republic off northern Europe, pop. 200,000 approx. (1973); capital, Reykjavik, pop. 80,000 approx.; language, Icelandic; currency unit, the króna, *pl.* kronur, divided into 100 aurar. Member, O.E.C.D.

I.C.F.T.U. International Confederation of Free Trade Unions.

I.C.S. Institute of Chartered Shipbrokers; Indian Civil Service; International Chamber of Shipping.

I.C.W.A. Institute of Cost and Works Accountants.

id. (*Latin*: idem) the same.

Id. Idaho, U.S.A.

I.D.A. International Development Association.

I.D.B. illicit diamond-buying.

idle STK. EXCH. of market conditions, showing total inactivity, no business being done.

idle balances ECON. money held in current accounts with banks, earning no interest and therefore a form of hoarding. *See* dishoarding; hoarding. *Syn.* inactive money.

idle money *see under* money.

i.e. (*Latin*: id est) that is to say.

I/F. (on a dishonoured cheque) insufficient funds.

i.f. in full.

I.F.C. International Finance Corporation.

IL Israel's international vehicle-registration letters.

Ill. Illinois, U.S.A.

illegal LAW forbidden by law: *An illegal act*, one which breaks the law. Cf. unlawful. *Opp.* legal.

illegal consideration *see under* consideration.

illegal contract *see under* contract.

illegality LAW an unlawful act or quality: *The illegality of certain contracts.*

illegal partnership *see under* partnership.

illegible *adj.* of writing, esp. of a signature, not clear enough to be read; unreadable. *Illegible handwriting/carbon copies/printing.* Type so small as to be illegible. N. illegibility.

illicit not allowed; illegal; unlawful: *Illicit trading*, trading without a licence. *Illicit distilling*, making alcohol secretly and without a licence, usu. to avoid paying excise duty. *Illicit gain*, money or profits made unlawfully. *Illicit diamond-buying*, in South Africa, trading in diamonds without a government licence. *Abbr.* I.D.B.

illiquid assets *see under* assets.

illustrated catalogue *see under* catalogue.

I.L.O. International Labour Organization.

I.L.U. Institute of London Underwriters.

im- *prefix* a variation of in-, used before the letters b, m, p, as in *imbalance, immigrant, impersonal. See* in-, *prefix*.

image ADVTG. (1) the picture that comes to the mind of the public when it thinks of a particular manufacturer or his product. (2) the favourable view or opinion about a product that is put into the mind of the public by active publicity and public relations. *See* brand image.

I.M.C.O. Inter-Governmental Maritime Consultative Organization.

I.M.F. International Monetary Fund.

I.M.F. quota FIN. the amount which a member country of the I.M.F. has to subscribe to the Fund in the form of gold and of its own currency, in order that the Fund can lend to countries that are temporarily in difficulty with their balance of payments.

immediate annuity *see under* insurance policy.

immediate possession *see* possession (3).

immigrant a person who comes into a country to settle permanently. *Opp.* emigrant.

immigrant remittances money sent back to their families in the country from which the immigrants came. In countries where there are many immigrants, these remittances can form a large part in the balance of payments as an invisible payment.

immigration the coming into one country of settlers from another country with the intention of living there permanently. *Opp.* emigration.

net immigration the amount by which the number of immigrants exceeds the number of emigrants.

imminent peril *see under* peril.

immobility ECON. THEORY of the factors of production (land, labour and capital), the state of not being easily movable from one kind of use or employment to another, or from one place to another. *See* mobility of labour.

immobilize FIN. of capital, to make no longer mobile (movable) by, e.g. replacing circulating capital by fixed capital.

immovable LAW of property, land and anything that is permanently on the land such as trees and buildings; real, as compared with personal, property.

impact (1) ADVTG. & COM. the effect that a certain advertising or sales-promotion activity has upon the public demand for a product: *Good advertising is making an impact on sales of their cars.* (2) ECON. THEORY the immediate effect of an increase in demand when it is not possible to increase the supply until some time later, known as the *impact effect.* (3) TAXN. (*a*) the effect that a tax may have on the market for a particular product. (*b*) the level at which a tax is first paid to a government, also called the *formal incidence* of a tax.

impaired capital *see under* capital.

impecunious always poor; having little or no money and tending to borrow from, or live on, others: *He has to help his impecunious relations.* N. impecuniosity.

imperfect competition *see under* competition.

imperfect market *see under* market.

imperial bushel *see* bushel.

imperial gallon *see* gallon.

imperialism ECON. the policy of an economically advanced country of extending its influence in one or more under-developed countries in order to provide its businessmen with opportunities for overseas investment, export markets for its products and cheap supplies of certain commodities for its home market. The word imperialism is usu. used in a critical sense, in the belief that the poorer, under-developed country always suffers to the advantage of the advanced country.

imperial preference ECON. HIST. the policy adopted by member countries of the British Empire, at the Ottawa Conference in 1932, of favouring other members of the Empire by fixing specially low rates of import duty on goods passing between them. A large increase in trade among Empire countries resulted, but after the Second World War, the setting up of G.A.T.T., and the intention of all countries to reduce hindrances to world trade, led to a gradual lessening of imperial (later commonwealth) preference. This system ceased in Britain when the E.E.C. tariff was applied in full in 1977.

imperial ton *see* long ton *under* ton.

imperilled INSCE. of insured property, laid open to a peril (danger) against which the property is insured. A ship may be imperilled by being in a severe storm and in danger of being lost, without any loss actually occurring.

impersonal accounts *see under* accounts.

impersonal ledger *see under* ledger.

impersonal payee *see under* payee.

implicit cost *see under* cost.

implicit rent *see under* rent.

implied LAW not written in a contract but understood by both parties to be binding as if it were so written: *An implied condition/contract/ obligation/warranty.* Opp. express. *See* implied contract *under* contract.

implied trust *see* constructive trust *under* trust.

import v. COM. to bring in, esp. goods from another country, usu. for sale as merchandise: *We import tea from Sri Lanka.* Opp. to export. *n.* (1) a thing or class of things imported from another country: *Visible/invisible imports. A prohibited (forbidden) import.* (2) the act of importing: *The import of foreign-made cars.* Syn. importation. *See also* imports, *pl.*

Import and Export List COM. in Britain, a list published once a year by the government, showing the official classification of all goods. This classification must be used by all importers and exporters when preparing forms for the Customs.

importation COM. (1) the act of importing. (2) anything that is imported.

import broker COM. usu. a produce broker who acts as agent for other brokers or exporters in foreign countries in finding a buyer for cargoes, either as a whole or in smaller lots. He charges a commission, called brokerage, for his services.

import commission agent *see under* commission agent.

import duty TAXN. a tax on goods coming into a country, for the purpose of raising money, or protecting industry against foreign competition, or reducing imports to help to correct an unfavourable balance of payments. *See also* duty (3).

importer COM. (1) one who imports goods from abroad: *We are importers of raw cotton from Egypt.* (2) a country that imports more of a commodity than it exports: *Britain is a large importer of foodstuffs.*

independent importer *see* import merchant.

import gold point *see* gold point.

import levy *see under* levy.

import licence COM. a document obtained from the government giving permission to import certain stated goods. Import licensing is sometimes used as a means of exchange control, for without such a licence an importer will not be allowed to pay for the goods. Also, goods to which an import quota applies can only be imported if an import licence has first been issued to the importer. Syn. import permit.

import merchant COM. an importer who buys foreign goods for himself, stocks them and sells them to buyers in his home country, thus taking all the risk. Syn. independent importer.

import permit *see* import licence.

import, propensity to *see under* propensity.

import quota COM. a stated quantity fixed by the government as the total amount of a commodity that may be imported into the country in a certain period. Importers of a commodity to which an import quota applies must first obtain an import licence. Import quotas are used by governments to limit the amount of foreign exchange leaving the country, or to protect a home industry, or as a means of bargaining with a foreign country.

imports *pl.* COM. goods and services bought from other countries.

invisible imports imports in the form of services performed by persons abroad, esp. services such as transport, banking, insurance, advertising and payments to foreign investors. Cf. visible imports.

protected imports goods on which there is a protective duty.

visible imports imports of goods having a material form or substance, as distinguished from services. Cf. invisible imports.

import surcharge TAXN. & FIN. an extra tax on imports, in addition to ordinary customs duties, as a temporary means of discouraging imports, usu. applied by the government of a country that is in difficulties with its balance of payments.

import trade *see under* trade.

impose LAW & TAXN. to put or place a load or charge on, esp. a duty that one is bound by law to perform, such as the registration of title to (ownership of) land; or a tax or duty on a commodity: *To impose a tax on sugar.* N. imposition.

to impose upon to take unfair advantage of (somebody).

impost TAXN. a tax, esp. a customs duty on imported goods.

impostor a person who dishonestly pretends to be someone else, or that he is something, e.g. a rent-collector, which he is not.

impound LAW (1) to seize (cattle and other property) and keep as security for a debt. (2) by court order, to obtain and keep documents, etc. to be used as evidence in a court of law. (3) to enclose and store water in a reservoir (artificial lake).

impressed stamp *see under* stamp.

impression *see* edition (2).

imprest account *see* imprest system.

imprest system ACCTS. the method usu. used in running the petty cash arrangements in an office. The petty cashier is advanced sufficient money to pay the expected expenses for a given period. He keeps an account called an *imprest* or *petty cash account* of all he spends, and at the end of the period he is given a sum in cash equal to the amount he has spent; his cash in hand (the cash he holds) is thus brought up to the amount he originally started with. The fixed sum held at the beginning of each period is called a *cash float*.

imprint a note appearing in a book, magazine or newspaper, giving the name, and sometimes the address, of the publisher and printer.

improve STK. EXCH. of prices of stocks and shares, to rise: *Prices improved after an earlier fall.* N. improvement.

improver IND. a person learning a trade who agrees to work for low wages or no wages at all in order to improve his skill.

impulse buyer COM. a person who buys a thing, not because he has planned to buy it, but because when he sees it he gets a sudden desire to possess it. Goods sold in this way are called *impulse goods*, and their sale *impulse sales*.

impute (1) to place a probable value on something, where the actual value is not known. N. imputation. (2) ECON. THEORY some nineteenth-century economists argued that the value of the factors of production, taken together, could be imputed from the value of the product; and that since the proportion in which the factors are combined was known, the value, and therefore the imputed or notional price, of each factor could be calculated. (3) ACCTS. where a company occupies its own buildings, an accountant may fix an imputed or notional rent at a figure equal to the rent which the company could get if it leased the buildings to somebody else, i.e. the opportunity cost.

in. inch; inches.

in- *prefix* (1) in; into; on; towards; against: *inland/income/input/inquire/inspect/inflation/inshore.* (2) expressing a negative; not: *inactive/inequality/infertile.*

inactive STK. EXCH. (1) of market conditions, showing little or no activity, there being few buyers and few sellers. *Syn.* dull. (2) of a security, one that is not often bought or sold.

inactive money *see* idle money *under* money.

in bond *see* bond, *n.* (3). *Abbr.* i.b.; I.B.

in-bond price in foreign-trade quotations, the buyer has to pay all charges arising from getting the goods released from a bonded warehouse (including payment of customs duty), the cost of loading on to the ship and of transshipment.

inbound *see under* bound (1).

inc. including; inclusive (of); increase.

Inc. Incorporated.

incalculable INSCE. unable to be calculated (worked out by mathematics). *An incalculable risk. Incalculable loss(es)/damage.*

incentive (1) IND. something that gives an employee a desire to work harder, such as the payment of a bonus if his output is greater than an agreed amount. *See* incentive bonus *under* bonus. Various other schemes to encourage productivity are found in industry, such as profit sharing, commission on sales, and piecework. (2) COM. some extra allowance offered by a supplier to a customer to encourage him to increase the amount of goods he buys. *See* incentive discount *under* discount.

Inception INSCE. the beginning of the period for which an insurance policy is effective.

Inch a unit of length in common use in Britain, U.S.A. and some other English-speaking countries; one-twelfth of a foot. One inch = 25.40 millimetres. *Abbr.* in.; ins. *Sign*: ": A 6" nail.

inchoate instrument LAW & BKG. an incomplete or unfinished negotiable instrument, esp. a blank bill of exchange form that has been signed only by the drawer, who has then given it to another person to complete. The person left to complete it has legal power to do so in any way he thinks fit, but he must keep within the general directions given him by the person who has signed it. *Syn.* incomplete bill.

incidence TAXN. of a tax, esp. an indirect tax on a commodity, the liability to pay it. The method of collecting the tax will depend on whether the liability falls on the supplier or on the consumer or partly on both. *Syn.* impact.

incidental expenses *see under* expenses.

incl. including; inclusive.

'in' clearing BKG. cheques, bills of exchange, etc. received by a bank after clearing at the clearing house. Cf. 'out' clearing.

inclosure (U.S.A.) *see* enclosure.

including counting: *A party of 21 passengers, including the guide. Abbr.* inc.; incl.

inclusive (1) containing or including everything, or many things: *An inclusive charge.* (2) of a price or charge, including other costs that are often paid separately: *The rent is £10 inclusive of heating. Inclusive of tax* or *tax-inclusive. Opp.* exclusive.

Income ECON. & TAXN. money of all kinds coming in regularly, esp. to a person, family or organization, such as salary or wages from employment, rent from property, profits from business, and fees for professional services. Income is usu. expressed as an amount *per annum* (in a year), but sometimes also *per mensem* (in a month) or even per week. *See also* national income.

accrued income *see* accrual concept *under* accrued.

deferred income *see* deferred credits.

discretionary income ECON. THEORY that part of a person's income that he can spend on things that are not essential. *See* discretionary spending.

disposable income *see under* disposable.

earned income *see under* earned. Cf. unearned income.

fixed income an income that does not increase with time or with changes in the cost of living, such as the income for a life annuity, or from property let on a long lease.

franked investment income *see under* franked.

gross income TAXN. the total income of a person before taking off allowances or tax. Cf. taxable income; net income.

investment income TAXN. *see* unearned income *below.*

life income an income that a person will receive for the rest of his life, usu. from a life insurance contract which will give him a life annuity, or from rents which he has the right to receive from property until he dies.

money income ECON. the amount of actual money received by a consumer during a stated period. Cf. real income.

national income *see under* national.

net income TAXN. a taxpayer's total income that remains after paying direct taxes and social-security contributions. Cf. taxable income; gross income.

notional income ECON. THEORY & TAXN. an income that represents some gain received, but in the form neither of money nor of goods and services. Thus, a person living in a house which he himself owns receives no rent but gains the valuable advantage of being able to live in it without paying.

per capita income the average annual income for each member of the population of a country. (*Latin*, by heads.)

permanent income ECON. the income that a consumer expects to earn from his work, and to receive from his capital assets such as investments. Cf. transitory income.

personal income ECON. that part of the national income that is received by private persons, not public authorities, companies, etc.

premium income *see under* premium.

real income ECON. THEORY the amount of goods and services that a consumer can buy with his money income. Cf. money income.

taxable income TAXN. the net amount that is left of a taxpayer's gross income after taking off the tax-free allowances, such as personal, children's or old-age allowances. The amount on which tax has to be paid. *Syn.* net income.

tax-free income TAXN. (1) any income on which no tax is payable, such as money won on bets on horse-races. (2) that part of a taxpayer's income that is within his personal or other allowances.

transfer income ECON. & FIN. income received by persons who give no goods or services in return, such as retirement pensions, social security and unemployment benefits. Such payments are transfers of money from one part of the community to another. Also included are interest payments on the national debt, and subsidies paid by the government to farmers and others.

transitory income ECON. income that a person cannot be sure of earning or receiving regularly in the future, such as royalties earned by the writer of a book, of which the sales may be good during the first year but then fall to little or nothing. Cf. permanent income.

unearned income TAXN. income from property (rents) and investments (interest, dividends). *Syn.* investment income. Cf. earned income.

income and expenditure account ACCTS. an account prepared by a non-trading organization that owns assets, the purpose being to show not only the cash position but also any additions to the organization's capital during the period. It is the equivalent of the profit and loss account of a trading concern, expenses being debited and receipts being credited in the account. A credit balance in the account is called surplus of income over expenditure; and a debit balance excess of expenditure over income. The balance is carried to a balance sheet. Cf. receipts and payments account.

income bond (1) *see* income debenture *under* debenture. (2) *see* single-premium policy *under* insurance policy.

income debenture *see under* debenture.

income effect ECON. THEORY the result of a change in a consumer's income. When prices in a market remain unchanged, the effect of an increase in the consumer's income, known as an income effect, is to make him buy more of the things he wants. Similarly, if his income bècomes less, the effect will be to make him buy less of the things he wants. Cf. substitution effect; price effect.

income in kind income that is received, not in money, but in goods and services, such as that of a farm-worker who gets a rent-free house, free vegetables and milk, etc.; or that of a manager who gets the free use of a car belonging to his employers.

income, national *see* national income.

income profit *see under* profit.

income, redistribution of *see under* redistribution.

income stock STK. EXCH. a high-yielding security, either a stock bearing a fixed rate of interest or an ordinary share that is likely to produce a steady rate of dividend every year.

income tax TAXN. in Britain, a tax on personal incomes which is the main means of obtaining money by the government for use in running the public services. It is reimposed annually by the Finance Act and is assessed and collected by the Board of Inland Revenue. It is charged at a rate known as the standard rate, to which are added graded increases of rate, called the *higher rates*, for higher taxable incomes. An extra rate is added for investment (or unearned) income above a certain level. Persons receive certain allowances which reduce the amount of tax that they pay.

income-tax schedules *see* Schedules A to E *under* schedules, tax.

incoming invoice *see* purchase invoice *under* invoice.

inconvertible currency *see under* currency.

incorporate LAW & STK. EXCH. in Britain, to form and register a company in the manner required by the Companies Acts. When this has been done, the Registrar of Companies issues a Certificate of Incorporation.

incorporated (Inc.) in U.S.A., when placed after the name of a company, the word means that the company is a legal personality called a corporation, usu. with limited liability. The equivalent of *Limited* (*Ltd.*) in Britain.

incorporation LAW the formal act of a group of persons combining together to become a single body with its own legal personality, such as a limited liability company. *See* Certificate of Incorporation.

incorporeal hereditament *see under* hereditament.

incorporeal possession *see under* possession (3).

Incoterms COM. a set of international rules published by the International Chamber of Commerce, Paris, for deciding the exact meaning of the chief terms (expressions) used in foreign-trade contracts, such as f.o.b. The object is to avoid disagreements caused by differences in trading practices in various countries by describing clearly the duties of the parties. Merchants using these rules need only state that their contracts are 'governed by the provisions of Incoterms'. *Syn.* trade terms.

increasing annuity *see under* insurance policy.

Increasing Costs, Law of *see* Diminishing Returns, Law of.

Increasing Returns, Law of *see* Decreasing Costs, Law of.

increment MAN. the amount by which a person's salary increases each year, usu. according to a salary scale. *See also* unearned increment.

incremental cost *see* marginal cost *under* cost.

incumbrance *see* encumbrance.

incur to bring upon oneself: *He has incurred expenses while travelling. To incur a risk.*

IND India's international vehicle-registration letters.

Ind. Indiana, U.S.A.

indebted (1) owing money: *I am indebted to the bank for a loan of £1000.* (2) owing thanks: *He is indebted to his father for teaching him his trade.*

indebtedness (1) a sum owed: *The amount of your indebtedness to me is £150, you owe me £150.* (2) debts in general: *Britain's international indebtedness is being reduced.* (3) a state of owing money: *A period of indebtedness.* (4) balance of indebtedness, *see* balance of payments.

indemnify (1) to pay someone money to make good a loss; to compensate. (2) to give some thing as a security against some possible future damage or loss. (3) INSCE. to pay money to an insured person when he has suffered a loss; to settle a claim.

indemnity (1) INSCE. a basic idea in all branches of insurance (except life and personal accident) that the insured should be in the same position after a loss as he was immediately before it, i.e. neither richer nor poorer as a result of the loss. (2) BKG. a promise to indemnify or compensate a person for expense or loss.

letter of indemnity a letter in which the person issuing it promises to compensate the party to whom it is addressed, such as a bank, against loss.

indemnity bond see under bond, n.

indent n. (1) COM. an order from an importer to a shipper or commission agent, esp. an indent house, to buy and ship certain stated goods. (2) any export order.

closed or **specific indent** one which states exactly the make of the goods to be shipped, leaving the agent no choice.

open indent one in which the agent is left free to decide the brand or make of goods to be supplied.

to indent for v. to order; to place an order for the supply of something.

indent house (U.S.A.) COM. an importing business with special knowledge of foreign suppliers, that accepts indents (orders) from customers in the home country for goods manufactured abroad.

indenture LAW a former practice, now long discontinued, of writing two copies of a deed on the same parchment and cutting them apart along an indented or wavy line. The two copies, called counterparts, were known to be true and correct if they fitted together. Nowadays an indenture is any deed, but esp. one between master and apprentice. See apprenticeship; also articles of apprenticeship.

indenture deed see deed.

indentured labour IND. workers who are bound by a contract, called indentures, to serve an employer, usu. in a far country, for a given number of years to repay the cost of the journey, a house, tools, etc. Such contracts, often very unfair to the worker, were much used to bring European labourers, mainly British, to North America in the eighteenth and nineteenth centuries, and Indian and Chinese labourers to other parts of the world. Syn. contract labour.

independent importer see import merchant.

independent means FIN. a private income, usu. from land or securities. A person is said to be independent or of independent means when he does not need to work for a living.

index, The STK. EXCH. see Financial Times Industrial Ordinary Share Index.

indexation a way of making some payments rise and fall as the general level of prices rises and falls. It applies to pensions, tax allowances, income from some investments and the capital value of some investments. When prices are rising fast, it is used to keep the real value of pensions and loans at a steady level. See indexed bond under bond; indexed pension under pension.

index cards see card index system.

indexed bond see under bond, n.

indexed pension see under pension.

indexes, share see under Financial Times; Dow-Jones.

index number(s) ECON. a number or set of numbers that represent changes in values. These may be the prices of commodities and securities or the cost of living. The index number compares values at certain times with a value at a chosen point in time, which is taken as 100.

price index one that shows variations in the prices of a group of specially-chosen commodities, for example the (British) Index of Retail Prices.

quantity index one that shows variations in the quantity or volume of a group of variables such as the Index of Industrial Production, or of Imports and Exports. Syn. volume index.

value index a combination of price index and quantity index showing the total effect of changes, esp. in real income. Syn. real-value index.

volume index see quantity index above.

weighted index one in the calculation of which some items are given a higher value than others because they are more important. See weighted average.

Index of Industrial Production ECON. & IND. in Britain, a set of monthly index numbers calculated by the Central Statistical Office to show variations in the volume of industrial production in the entire British economy as well as for each main industry.

Index of Retail Prices ECON. in Britain, the official monthly index, based on government statistics, which measures changes in the prices of certain goods and services chosen because they represent the things bought by the families of most wage-earners and moderate salary-earners. See cost-of-living index. Syn. in U.S.A., Consumer Price Index.

Index of Weekly Earnings ECON. & IND. in Britain, a set of index numbers issued by the government twice each year to show variations in the payments made for labour in all the manufacturing and some other main industries, esp. in workers' earnings, hours of work, overtime, short time and payments for piecework, as well as changes in the level of absenteeism.

India a federal republic in south Asia, pop. 600 million approx. (1977); capital, New Delhi, pop. 4 million approx.; languages, Hindi, English and regional languages; currency unit, the Indian rupee (Re., *pl.* Rs.). divided into 100 paise, *sing.* paisa. Member, (British) Commonwealth; Colombo.Plan.

Indiaman ECON. HIST. a large sailing ship used by the British East India Company for trading with India and the East Indies during the eighteenth and nineteenth centuries.

Indian Standard Time (I.S.T.) a standard time-zone covering India, Nepal and Sri Lanka, 5½ hours ahead of Greenwich Mean Time.

indication, letter of *see* traveller's letter of credit *under* letter of credit.

indicator, economic *see* business barometer; money supply.

indices *pl.* of index. *Also* indexes. *See* index number(s).

indictment LAW a document telling an accused person exactly what crime(s) he is accused of. *Pron.* indite-.

indifference curve ECON. THEORY a curved line drawn on a graph to represent various combinations of two commodities that give to a consumer an equal amount of satisfaction, i.e. he is indifferent about which combination to choose because they are all of equal interest to him. Because indifference curves point out what human behaviour will be in certain known economic conditions, they are much used by economists to analyse many economic problems, esp. that of consumer demand; such use is called *indifference analysis. See also* preference curve.

indigenous (1) born or belonging locally; native: *The indigenous inhabitants of a country. Indigenous language(s).* (2) locally made or grown; not foreign: *Indigenous production. Syn.* domestic; home.

indigent of a person, reduced to a state of poverty and lacking normal comforts. *Syn.* needy.

indirect arbitrage *see* arbitrage.

indirect cost *see* fixed cost *under* cost.

indirect damages *see* consequential damages *under* damages, *n. pl.*

indirect exchange BKG. & FIN. the exchange between two countries expressed not in units of each other's currencies (direct exchange) but in units of a third country. Cf. direct exchange.

indirect expenses ACCTS. expenses of a general nature such as management and distribution costs that cannot be directly related to a particular product or service. Cf. direct expenses.

indirect exporting COM. supplying goods to foreign markets through middlemen in the supplier's country, such as export agents, export commission houses, export merchants and export shippers. Cf. direct exporting.

indirect labour ACCTS. the cost of labour which is employed on work which is not directly related to a particular product or service, such as

cleaning and repairing buildings, running offices and canteens. Such costs are charged to the various products and services by using a sensible system of allocation. Cf. direct labour; direct expenses.

indirect parity *see* cross rate.

indirect production *see under* production.

indirect tax *see under* tax.

individual demand *see under* demand.

individual file *see under* file.

individualism *see* Burke, Edmund.

Indonesia a republic in south-east Asia, pop. 130 million approx. (1977); capital, Djakarta, pop. 5 million approx.; languages, Indonesian (similar to Malay), English; currency unit, the rupiah, divided into 100 sen. Member, A.S.E.A.N.; Colombo Plan.

indorsation *see* endorsement (5).

indorse *see* endorse.

indorsed bond *see* assumed bond *under* bond *n.*

indorsee *see* endorsee.

indorsement *see* endorsement.

indorser *see* endorser.

induced consumption *see under* consumption.

induced investment *see under* investment.

inducement (1) COM. something that persuades or influences someone to do something: *Hopes of high profits act as an inducement to take risks. You must offer him some inducement to obtain his services. Syn.* incentive. (2) LAW *Inducement to break a contract,* the tort (civil wrong) of unlawfully influencing a person to break a contract, or of unlawfully hindering him in his attempts to perform it.

in due course *see* holder in due course.

industrial IND. relating to, concerned with, industry: *Industrial development/organizations/workers/shares. See also* industrials, *pl.*

industrial accident *see under* accident.

industrial action IND. REL. any action taken by employees, usu. members of a trade union, with the intention of forcing the employers to agree to demands for higher wages or better conditions of work. Such action may take the form of a go-slow, a ban on overtime, or a strike.

industrial and provident society IND. & FIN. in Britain, one of a number of special friendly societies formed for the purpose of carrying on a trade or industry on a co-operative basis, mainly to improve the living conditions of members of the working classes. Such societies have limited liability.

industrial archaeology ECON. HIST. the study of former industrial activities as shown by the remains of machines, tools, etc.

industrial arts IND. (1) the processes and methods used in a manufacturing industry such as woodworking, metalworking and building construction. (2) the study of these in industrial schools.

industrial banker BKG. a special kind of finance house that accepts long-term deposits which it uses for paying traders for goods sold under hire-purchase agreements. *See* finance house.

Industrial Court IND. REL. in Britain, an administrative tribunal that has power to settle industrial disputes if the employers' association and the trade union concerned both agree to bring the case to it. *See* arbitration.

industrial democracy ECON. & IND. any economic system under which the workers take part in managing industries and in making industrial decisions. Various forms have been suggested, including syndicalism, guild socialism, and worker directors on the boards of nationalized and private industries.

industrial design *see under* design, *n.*

industrial development certificate IND. in Britain, a certificate which every industrial concern must obtain from the Department of Industry before starting to build a new factory or an extension to an existing factory above a certain size. The Department is more likely to grant a certificate if the development is to take place in a development area, thus influencing the siting (situation) of new industries. *See* development areas.

industrial dispute *see* dispute.

industrial efficiency *see under* efficiency.

industrial espionage *see* industrial spying.

industrial estate *see* estate (3).

industrial fluctuations *see* fluctuations; trade cycle *under* cycle.

industrial health *see* industrial hygiene.

industrial hereditaments LAW land and buildings used for industrial purposes, and business premises.

industrial hygiene IND. that branch of medical science that deals with protecting the health of industrial workers. *Syn.* industrial health. *See also* industrial medicine; industrial safety.

industrial inertia IND. & ECON. an unwillingness on the part of owners of industries to move away from the place where their industries were originally set up, although the conditions that caused them to be placed there have greatly changed.

industrial injuries insurance *see under* insurance, classes and kinds of; benefit (3).

industrial·life insurance *see under* insurance, classes and kinds of.

industrialism ECON. an economic and political system under which great importance is given to large-scale industry.

industrialist IND. (1) a person who owns or runs an industrial concern, esp. a large industrial company. (2) a person who believes in industrialism.

industrialization ECON. the development of the economy of a country or region by setting up large-scale industries.

industrial medicine IND. the branch of medical science that deals with the protection and improvement of the health of people while they are at work. It aims to prevent accidents by making tools and machines safe to use, and dangerous substances safe to handle; and to prevent diseases caused by smoke, dust, gases, poisons, noise, heat and cold, etc. *Syn.* occupational medicine. *See also* industrial hygiene; industrial safety.

industrial momentum IND. a tendency of industries that were originally set up in places where certain special conditions existed, to continue to grow in importance long after those special conditions have lost their effectiveness.

industrial park (U.S.A.) IND. an industrial estate.

industrial property LAW patents, industrial designs and trade-marks. *See* International Convention for the Protection of Industrial Property.

Industrial Production, Index of *see under* Index.

industrial psychology IND. the study of human behaviour in working surroundings, and of relations between workers, managers, employers and trade unions. *Syn.* occupational psychology.

industrial relations IND. REL. relations between employers and employees (*individual relations*) and between employers' associations and trade unions (*collective relations*). *See* collective bargaining. *Syn.* labour relations.

Industrial Revolution ECON. HIST. the name given by economic historians to the period of great changes in economic and social organization that took place, first in Britain from about 1750 to about 1850, and later in some countries on the continent (from 1830) and in U.S.A. (from 1860), Japan (1870) and Russia (1900). During this period the domestic system was replaced by a factory system. It began in Britain with the invention of many kinds of machines, the introduction of steam-power, the division of labour, and the development of road, rail and canal transport. The period saw the rise of trade unionism, the laissez-faire teachings of Adam Smith, Malthus and Ricardo, the opening up of overseas markets, a much higher output per worker and a generally higher standard of living.

industrials STK. EXCH. stocks and shares of industrial companies, esp. those producing non-consumer goods, i.e. machine tools and other capital goods, as distinguished from commercials. *Syn.* industrial stocks and shares.

industrial safety IND. that part of industrial medicine that is concerned with the safety of people while at work, esp. from moving machinery, cranes, lifts, etc., and from dangerous substances. *See* industrial medicine.

industrial services IND. the services performed by the many persons employed in all forms of industry. Cf. commercial services; direct services.

industrial spying IND. the dishonest practice of obtaining industrial secrets belonging to one's competitors by employing spies or secret agents who work in the competitors' offices and factories.

industrial truck *see* fork-lift truck.

industrial union *see under* trade union.

industrious hard-working; taking great care to work well.

industry ECON. & IND. (1) work done for gain. (2) the production of useful goods by the organized use of capital and labour: *Commerce depends on industry*. (3) any organized activity using capital and labour to produce a particular product or class of product: *The shipbuilding/ aircraft/chemical/iron and steel industries*.

basic industry a heavy industry of great economic importance to other industries or to a nation, such as the iron and steel and the chemical industries. Cf. local industry. *Syn*. key industry.

capital-intensive industry *see* capital-intensive.

cottage industry *see under* cottage.

extractive industry one that extracts (takes out) minerals from the earth, such as the coalmining, petroleum and iron-ore industries.

heavy industry one that produces capital goods of a heavy or bulky nature usu. from heavy or bulky raw materials and needing heavy machinery, such as the iron and steel, shipbuilding, and engineering industries.

home industry *see* cottage industry *under* cottage.

infant industry a new industry which, in the opinion of some economists, should be helped by receiving some protection in the form of an import duty on similar goods imported from foreign countries.

labour-intensive industry *see* labour-intensive.

light industry one that produces relatively small or light articles made from materials that are not heavy or bulky, such as the clothing, pharmaceutical and printing industries.

linked industry an industry that produces a finished product which consists of many separate materials or parts usu. manufactured by many producers, as in the automobile and aircraft industries.

local industry one that tends to serve only nearby markets, i.e. the service industries such as hairdressers, garages, suppliers of fuel, food and drink, road transport, such as buses, taxis and carriers of local goods, and builders of houses and roads. Cf. basic industry.

manufacturing industry one that changes raw materials into finished products.

primary industry one that is concerned with

collecting and bringing in materials that exist in nature, such as farming, fishing and mining. Cf. secondary industry; tertiary industry.

secondary industry any industry that uses the materials gathered in by primary industries to produce commodities that Man can use either as capital goods or as consumer goods. Cf. primary industry; tertiary industry.

service *or* **servicing industry** *see* tertiary industry.

tertiary industry any industry that does not produce an article or commodity but performs a service, such as trade, banking, insurance, transport, administration, the professions and also personal services. Cf. primary industry; secondary industry. *Syn*. service *or* servicing industry.

inelastic demand *see* elasticity of demand.

inelastic supply *see* elasticity of supply.

inertia *see* industrial inertia.

inertia selling COM. a method of marketing or selling by which the article to be sold is sent to a person by post without his having asked for or ordered it, and in some countries he has either to return it or pay for it.

infant LAW in Britain, a person under the age of 18 years. *Syn*. minor.

infant's contract *see under* contract.

infant industry *see under* industry.

inferior good ECON. THEORY a good for which the demand falls when the price falls. *See* Giffen's paradox. *Syn*. poor man's goods.

inflate *v*. (1) to increase; to cause to grow in size or amount. (2) ECON. to cause prices or the level of economic activity to rise, esp. by increasing the supply of money.

inflation ECON. & FIN. a rise in the general level of prices caused by an excess of demand over supply and related to an increase in the supply of money, both as bank-notes and in the form of bank credit. If the rise in prices is very large and rapid the condition is known as hyperinflation. Cf. disinflation; reflation. *Opp*. deflation.

cost inflation the kind of inflation that is caused by rising costs of labour and materials, not by increased demand. Cf. demand inflation. *Syn*. cost-push inflation.

demand inflation the kind of inflation caused by an excess of demand over supply resulting in a rise in the price-level and thus in a decrease in the value of money. Cf. cost inflation. *Syn*. demand-pull inflation.

hidden inflation the lowering of the quality of products in general in order to prevent, and so to hide, an increase in price.

hyper-inflation *see under* hyper.

repressed inflation *see* suppressed inflation below.

runaway inflation *see* hyper-inflation *under* hyper.

suppressed inflation inflation that would be much greater if the government were to remove controls on prices and wages, such as has existed in Britain in time of war. *Syn.* repressed inflation.

inflation accounting ACCTS. a system of accounting that tries to allow for the effects of inflation; various methods are possible including valuing assets at their current value instead of at cost. *See* depreciation.

inflationary gap ECON. THEORY (1) in a state of inflation, the difference between the total of private and government spending and the level of spending needed just to support full employment; that is, the excess of total demand over total supply. (2) that part of government spending which is not covered by taxes or borrowing from the public, but is met by borrowing from the banks, etc. or by issuing new paper money, and thus adding to total demand.

inflationary spiral ECON. a state of inflation that gets worse and worse, because higher prices result in demands for higher wages; and higher wages increase costs and so cause higher prices. *Syn.* wage-price spiral.

influx FIN. a flowing in, esp. of large amounts of money coming into a country: *An influx of foreign capital.* Also of persons: *An influx of unskilled workers.*

influence *n.* power to produce an effect, such as to persuade someone to do some act: *He used his influence to obtain an overdraft from the bank/an order from the government/a job for his son/money for the poor. Adj.* influential.
v. to have an effect on, esp. in an indirect or hidden manner: *You cannot influence him by bribery. Do not be influenced by him.*

informative advertising *see under* advertising.

infraction the breaking of a law or rule.

infrastructure large-scale public services, such as water and power supplies, road, rail and air transport systems, telephone, telex and radio communications, needed to support economic activity, esp. industry, trade and commerce. In modern conditions such services need very large amounts of capital which only governments can provide.

infringement LAW any breach or interference in the rights of other persons, esp. copyrights and patents.

ingot FIN. a bar of metal cast in a mould, for use in some further process.

in-hand foods COM. foods that are eaten in the shop or very soon after they are bought, such as ice-cream, as opposed to take-home foods (foods that are taken away from the shop and eaten at home).

inherent vice INSCE. & TRANSPT. the risk or tendency of certain goods to go bad, to spoil, as in the case of many foods, such as fish, meat, fruit and vegetables, during a journey unless special steps are taken to preserve them. The carrier of such goods will not be held liable for their poor condition unless he has been told of the risk so that he could take special care. In insurance policies covering goods while being carried, this risk is one of the *excepted perils. Syn.* vice propre.

inherit LAW to receive property, rights, etc. as a gift under a will or, if there is no will, by intestate succession.

inheritance LAW any inherited property.

inheritance tax *see under* tax.

initial *adj.* at the beginning; the first: *The initial capital of a company,* the capital when the company was first formed. *The initial bid at an auction,* the bid at which the auction begins. *An initial letter,* the first letter of a word, esp. of a name or of the first word in a chapter.
v. to sign a document with one's initials to show that one has seen, read or approved of it.

initials *n. pl.* (1) a shortened signature, consisting of the first letter of each of a person's or organization's names: *G.B.S.* for George Bernard Shaw; *U.S.A.* for United States of America. (2) in an abbreviation: *V.A.T.* for value added tax.

inject to put or force into: *To inject new capital/ideas/energy into a business. N.* injection.

injunction LAW an order of a court of law telling a person that he must do, or not do, a certain thing. If the person does not obey, the court will punish him for contempt of court. *Syn.* (Scotland) interdict. *See also* interlocutory injunction.

injury harm suffered by a person, such as a hurt to his body, or a wrong suffered, such as an injustice.

inland *adj.* relating to the part of any region or country away from the coast. *Inland waterways,* rivers, canals, lakes. *Inland postal services,* those serving places within the country, as opposed to foreign or overseas services.

inland bill *see under* bill of exchange.

inland invoice *see under* invoice.

inland marine insurance MAR. INSCE. a class of insurance that covers risks to small ships, barges, bridges, wharves, etc. on inland waterways such as rivers, lakes and canals. *Syn.* inland transit insurance.

inland port *see under* port.

Inland Revenue *see* Board of Inland Revenue.

inland waterways TRANSPT. rivers, canals and lakes used by ships, lighters or barges for transporting bulk cargoes, when speed is less important than low cost.

inland waterways bill of lading *see under* bill of lading.

inn COM. & TOUR. a hotel or public house, esp. one that provides food and lodging for travellers. *Syn.* hostelry.

inner reserve *see* hidden reserve *under* reserve.

innkeeper COM. & TOUR. a person who manages an inn and is ready to provide food and lodging to travellers. *Syn.* landlord; host.

innkeeper's lien *see under* lien.

innovation ECON. & IND. any new invention or improved method of producing goods. Any change in methods of production that gives the producer who first introduces it an advantage over his competitors that may amount to a temporary monopoly. Cf. invention.

Inns of Court LAW in London, four ancient societies, formerly schools of law, that have the right of admitting properly-qualified persons to practise at the Bar, i.e. as barristers. The Inns are Gray's Inn, the Inner Temple, the Middle Temple and Lincoln's Inn.

inoperative having no effect; not in operation. *Inoperative clause*, in an agreement, a clause that for any reason has no effect.

inputs ECON. the factors of production (land, labour and capital, including materials) that are put into a business to produce its output, either as a commodity or as a service.

input tax *see* value added tax *under* tax.

input unit COMP. part of an electronic computer that is used to feed data (information) either into a storage system or memory or direct into the central processor. Cf. output unit.

inquire *see* enquire.

inquirer *see* enquirer.

inquiry *see* enquiry.

inquiry agent *see* credit agency.

inquiry office *see* enquiry office *under* office.

ins. inches; insurance.

insane person LAW a mad person, one whose mind is so disordered that he does not know whether his actions are right or wrong. A contract made by an insane person, although valid (effective), may be voidable (treated as having never existed) if he so wishes, but it must be shown that the other party to the contract knew of his madness. A will made by a person while in a state of madness will not be supported in a court of law.

insce. insurance.

inscribed stock *see under* stock.

insertion ADVTG. (1) the act of putting an advertisement into a newspaper or magazine. (2) the advertisement itself: *Our rate for three insertions is £30*, we charge £30 for printing an advertisement in three issues of our paper.

insider trading STK. EXCH. unfair secret buying and selling of shares by company directors and high officials who take advantage of their special knowledge of the affairs of their companies which other investors do not receive until later.

insolvency LAW the state or condition of being insolvent. Cf. solvency.

insolvent *adj.* unable to pay one's debts when they become due. A person is said to be insol-vent when he declares that he cannot pay what he owes. A business is insolvent if its liabilities are greater than its assets or, in the case of a company, if its debts cannot be paid within 12 months, the time allowed for selling all its assets.

n. a debtor who is insolvent.

inspection *see* examination (2).

inspector (1) INSCE. an official of an insurance company responsible for increasing the company's business or for settling claims. (2) BKG. a high officer of a bank, responsible for making sure that its branches are properly run. (3) TRANSPT. an official of a transport service responsible for making sure that the fares are collected (*ticket inspector*) and that the service is properly run. (4) IND. a government official responsible for seeing that the laws concerning safety and health in factories are obeyed (*factory inspector*). *See* factory inspectors.

inspector of taxes TAXN. a local official of the Department of Inland Revenue whose main duty it is to obtain and inspect (examine) returns of income from all persons and organizations who have an income, and to decide how much tax they must pay. Cf. collector of taxes. *Syn.* (U.S.A.) tax assessor.

inst. instant, *see* date.

inst. institute.

installation IND. (1) apparatus and machinery used for a special purpose: *A heating/plumbing/air-conditioning installation*. (2) sometimes, buildings serving a special purpose: *Port installations*, wharves, warehouses, cranes, etc. for loading and unloading ships and storing goods. *Oil-storage installations. Syn.* plant.

installed capacity *see* capacity (1).

instal(l)ment bond *see under* bond, *n.*

installment note (U.S.A.) COM. a special kind of promissory note used when paying for goods bought on an instalment plan.

instalment (1) COM. one of a series of regular payments, made under an agreement, in order to settle a debt, esp. to buy an asset. The buyer expects to pay more if he buys by instalments than he would if payment were made in one cash sum because of the need to reward the seller for the cost of collecting the instalments and the interest he loses by having to wait for his money; but the buyer has the advantage of having possession and use of the asset while it is being paid for: *Payment by weekly/monthly/quarterly instalments. Also* (U.S.A.) install-ment. *See* hire-purchase. (2) STK. EXCH. one of a series of payments made by the buyer of a newly-issued security, usu. consisting of application money, allotment money and one or more further payments at later dates.

instalment credit COM. & ECON. the time that a supplier gives to a customer who has arranged to pay for goods by instalments.

instalment trading COM. an arrangement between buyer and seller which allows the buyer to become the owner of the goods immediately, although he pays for them by a series of weekly or monthly instalments. *See* hire-purchase.

instant (1) COM. of a food, quickly made; requiring little or no preparation; ready to be eaten or drunk immediately: *Instant coffee/tea/soup.* (2) *see* date.

institute clauses MAR. INSCE. in British marine insurance policies, certain clauses that mainly relate to cargoes and have the approval of the Institute of London Underwriters.

Institute of London Underwriters MAR. INSCE. an association of insurance companies in London which carry on marine insurance business. Sometimes its members compete with Lloyd's, but more often the two organizations work in co-operation with each other. The Institute helps its members by appointing agents to settle claims, by issuing certificates of insurance, by approving clauses in policies and the wording of marine policies themselves, and generally by looking after the interests of marine insurers. *Abbr.* I.L.U.

institution (1) LAW a rule of conduct or social behaviour set up by custom, i.e. by having long been accepted with approval by society, and thus becoming part of the law of the country: *Marriage is an institution, and so are the family and inheritance.* (2) ECON. a group of people united for a common purpose, with an organization or system that has been set up to carry out this purpose: *A charitable/educational/research/financial institution.* (3) FIN. & COM. a large and important unit in the business system such as the Bank of England, Lloyd's, the money market.

institutional economics ECON. THEORY the study of the part played in the economic system by the main institutions, i.e. social organizations that take collective action, such as employers' associations, trade unions, companies, cartels, and trade associations, rather than by single persons acting alone. *See* Veblen, Thorstein. *Syn.* institutionalism.

institutional investors STK. EXCH. large organizations such as insurance companies, unit trusts, pension funds and trade unions, that have large sums of money to invest and are therefore much more powerful in influencing financial policy than single private investors.

institutionalism *see* institutional economics.

institutionalist ECON. a person who believes in the importance of having powerful institutions to develop and run the economic and social system. *See* institutional economics.

institutional monopoly *see under* monopoly.

instruct (1) LAW to give directions, esp. as a client to a solicitor, or as a solicitor to a barrister: *We have instructed our solicitor to bring a court action and he will instruct counsel. The judge instructed the jury on difficult points of law,* he explained them. (2) BKG. to give an order to one's bankers to do something: *You should instruct your bank to stop the cheque.*

instruction (1) an order, direction or command telling somebody to do something: *We await your instructions,* please tell us what you wish us to do. (2) training in some subject by an instructor (teacher): *Instruction in credit control.* (3) COMP. a word or group of letters or numbers that directs the computer to perform a particular operation.

instructions *pl.* directions on how something is to be done or used: *Read the instructions on the box carefully before using this instrument.*

instrument LAW a legal name for a formal document; a document drawn up in legal form, e.g. a deed; a bond.

credit instrument any of a number of documents that result in money being transferred from one person to another, such as cheques, promissory notes, drafts, letters of credit, and postal and money orders.

inchoate instrument *see under* inchoate.

negotiable instrument *see under* negotiable.

insurable interest INSCE. & LAW a direct monetary interest in an object or person being insured. It is a ruling condition of insurance that the person who benefits from an insurance contract must himself be liable to suffer a loss that can be valued in units of money if the insured object is damaged or lost, or the insured person is injured or dies. If this condition is not met, the interest is not insurable and the contract would not be supported in a court of law.

insurable risk *see under* risk.

insurance INSCE. (1) the practice of sharing among many persons, risks to life or property that would otherwise be suffered by only a few. This is effected by each person paying a sum of money called a *premium* which, with those paid by all the others, is put into a 'pool' or *insurance fund,* out of which money is paid to the few who suffer loss. *See also* assurance. *Abbr.* ins.; insce.; insur. (2) the business of insuring lives and property against harm, damage or loss in return for the payment of a sum of money (the *premium*) according to the degree of risk. (3) a written or printed contract, called a *policy of insurance* or *insurance policy.* *See* insurance policy. (4) the amount for which a life or thing is insured, called the *sum insured: When he died, his widow received the £5000 insurance. With the insurance I got on my wrecked car, I bought a boat.* (5) the premiums paid for insuring a life or thing: *It is the landlord's responsibility to pay the insurance on his property. My employer pays the insurance on my life.*

insurance agent INSCE. (1) a person who introduces insurance business to an insurance company in return for a commission. (2) the name given to an insurance employee who looks after a group of policy holders.

insurance broker INSCE. a middleman or broker with special knowledge of the insurance market who, not being a direct employee of any insurance company, is free to offer advice to his clients and, as their agent, to negotiate the most favourable insurance contracts for them with the insurers. He is usu. paid by commission or fee from the insurers. In Britain, *associated brokers* are those who are members of the Association of Insurance Brokers; *incorporated brokers* are those who are members of the Corporation of Insurance Brokers; and a *Lloyd's broker* is a member of Lloyd's and is the only kind of broker through whom the public can insure with Lloyd's underwriters.

insurance certificate *see* certificate of insurance.

insurance, classes and kinds of INSCE. There are many kinds of insurance contract, all of which fall within one or other of the four main classes: accident, fire, life and marine. (For names of various policies *see under* insurance policy.)

accident insurance includes a wide variety of policies dealing mainly with loss of property other than by fire and lightning and with property other than ships and their cargoes. One of the biggest sections is theft insurance, formerly called burglary insurance. It also includes a wide range of liability insurance.

agreed-value insurance in the case of a non-marine insurance, any insurance that provides that in the event of a total loss, the sum insured will be payable, no allowance being made for appreciation or depreciation. In the case of a marine insurance, the value of the goods is agreed at the start of the policy and will be the basis of payment by the insurers in the event of any loss, whether total or partial.

aleatory insurance *see* aleatory contract *under* aleatory.

annuity insurance a group of life insurance contracts under which a fixed sum of money is payable by the insurer to the party named to receive it (the *annuitant*), for a stated number of years (*terminable annuity*), or during the life of the annuitant (*life annuity*), or during his life and that of another person (*joint annuity*). (A perpetual annuity is not an insurance contract: *see under* perpetual.) The right to receive an annuity can be bought, usu. from a life insurance society or company, either for a single premium (i.e. a single sum in cash) or by instalments (fixed regular payments) over a number of years. The price paid for a life annuity is based on the annuitant's expectation of life at

the age at which the payments by the insurers are due to begin, and the price is higher for women because they usu. live longer than men.

assessment insurance *see* mutual insurance *below.*

aviation insurance an important section of accident insurance that includes policies insuring an aircraft itself, its cargo and legal liability to passengers and crew and to airport authorities, etc. Some marine insurance offices also offer aviation policies.

blanket insurance (*a*) any insurance that covers a group of different kinds of risk, such as fire, theft, storm, etc. (*b*) an insurance that covers property in a number of different places. *Syn.* (U.S.A.) package insurance.

block insurance any insurance that covers risks of several kinds on goods being sent in many small lots by various means of transport. Such policies usu. make conditions, e.g. that goods to not more than a certain value shall be sent in the same vehicle.

burglary insurance *see* theft insurance *below.*

casualty insurance all classes of insurance except fire and life insurance. *Syn.* (U.S.A.) property and liability insurance.

co-insurance the sharing of a risk by two or more insurers within a single insurance contract. An under-insured claimant is considered to be a co-insurer for the amount of the under-insurance, i.e. he has to bear that part of the risk himself. In certain cases an insurer may make it a condition that the insured shall be a co-insurer for part of the risk. *See* under-insurance *below.*

contingency insurance an important section of accident insurance that includes policies insuring against loss from a variety of risks, such as breach of trust, defects in title, missing documents, etc.

declaration insurance any insurance that provides that the insured will declare to the insurers at regular intervals, e.g. monthly, details such as the value of goods held in stock or in transit and covered under a fire or loss-in-transit policy, and details of journeys made by persons covered under a personal accident group policy; and at the end of the year, the premium is adjusted according to the amounts declared. *Syn.* stock declaration policy; floating policy (marine).

deposit insurance *see under* deposit.

engineering insurance a section in the accident insurance class, by which the insurers provide an inspection (examination) service by skilled surveyors, and insurance cover for: lifts and lifting gear such as cranes; boilers and other pressure plant; electrical machinery and apparatus; and engines of all kinds.

fidelity insurance (*a*) a section in the accident

insurance class including policies that insure against breaches of fidelity, such as loss resulting from an employee's dishonesty. (*b*) policies that provide insurance against breach of contract.

fire insurance one of the four main classes of insurance; it includes a number of risks as well as fire.

floating insurance (*a*) any insurance that covers property in more than one place, or the fidelity of more than one employee. (*b*) in marine insurance, a kind of declaration policy, the insurer receiving a premium for an agreed sum insured; this sum is reduced by the value of each cargo declared by the insured. *Syn.* floater; open insurance.

free insurance any insurance contract under which premiums are no longer payable, e.g. when the policy has been fully paid.

group insurance the insurance under a single policy of a group of persons, such as employees of the same employer, or members of a club.

health insurance *see* national insurance *under* national; private health insurance *below*; medical expenses insurance *below*.

hull insurance *see* hull.

industrial injuries insurance in Britain, a government insurance scheme that provides for payment of benefits to industrial workers who are injured or disabled or made seriously ill at work. Special death benefits are also paid to the representatives of persons who may be killed, or develop a serious disease, at work.

industrial life insurance a special group of life insurance contracts aimed to attract industrial workers with relatively low incomes. Premiums are collected in small amounts weekly, fortnightly or monthly, usu. by agents visiting the homes of the policy holders. Policies may be *whole-life, endowment* or *recurring endowment* policies, these last being for five, seven or ten years, giving the policy holder the option (choice) of putting the cash received at the end of the period into further insurance for a larger sum insured. *Syn.* home service insurance; industrial business.

liability insurance a group of policies in the accident insurance class, that protect the insured person against his liability to pay compensation for bodily injury, sickness or death, or for damage to property. Such liability may arise esp. in the use of motor vehicles, the exercise of a profession (such as medicine and the law), the running of a business (employer's liability, etc.) and in private life.

life insurance *or* **assurance** (*a*) one of the four main classes of insurance which includes all insurances that relate to an inevitable event, i.e. one that must happen at some time, such as a person's death, or the date he reaches a certain age. (*b*) a way of providing for money to be paid by an insurance company or society either to oneself at some fixed date, such as on one's retirement, or to one's representatives after one's death. The main kinds of life insurance policy are *whole-life, term, endowment* and *annuity*.

marine insurance the oldest of the four main classes of insurance, dealing with a variety of policies that give cover to owners of ships, their cargoes, and of other marine property against damage or loss caused by maritime perils, i.e. accidents that may happen at sea, in harbour or on inland waterways. Some marine policies cover liabilities to third parties (persons not party to the contract), and also cover loss of earnings from freight. *Abbr.* mar. insce.

motor insurance a special section in the accident insurance class covering the owner of a motor vehicle against damage or loss due to an accident, fire, theft, etc. and also his legal liability to third parties, usu. other road users. *See* third party. *Syn.* (U.S.A.) automobile insurance.

mutual insurance insurance by a non-profitmaking organization usu. called a mutual insurance company or society. The members are its policy holders, who share any profits; but they do not have limited liability and therefore have to pay extra contributions if the society's claims and expenses are greater than its income from premiums and contributions. In marine insurance, special mutual insurance associations exist to protect shipowners. Cf. proprietary insurance *below*. *Syn.* assessment insurance; (U.S.A.) participating insurance; reciprocal insurance.

national insurance *see under* national.

open insurance *see* floating insurance *above*.

package insurance (U.S.A.) *see* blanket insurance *above*.

paid-up insurance a whole-life or endowment insurance which, at the request of the insured person, has been changed so that no further premiums are payable and the sum insured is reduced in the proportion that the number of premiums paid bears to the total of premiums that would be payable if the original contract had continued unchanged. The date when the sum insured is payable remains unchanged, i.e. on the maturity date originally agreed or on the earlier death of the insured person.

participating insurance *see* mutual insurance *above*.

pluvius insurance *see under* pluvius.

property and liability insurance *see* casualty insurance *above*.

proprietary insurance insurance by a commercial profit-making company, not a mutual insurance.

reciprocal insurance *see* mutual insurance *above*.

reinsurance the sharing of a large risk among two or more insurers, each of whom takes responsibility for a fixed part of any loss, and receives a like proportion of the premiums. *Also* re-insurance (with hyphen). *Abbr.* R.I.

social insurance *see* national insurance *under* national.

theft insurance an important section of accident insurance that includes policies insuring against loss where the main risk is from stealing, such as all-risks policies, money policies, and sometimes policies for business premises and private houses. Formerly called burglary insurance.

under-insurance the position of a person who is insufficiently insured under a policy, e.g. when the sum insured is not sufficient to rebuild the insured property in the event of a total loss by fire. *See* co-insurance *above*.

weather insurance an insurance against the risk of some event, such as a sports meeting, being cancelled by bad weather. *See* pluvius insurance *under* pluvius.

insurance commission *see under* commission.
insurance, double *see under* double.
insurance fund *see* insurance (1).
insurance market *see* Lloyd's.
insurance policy INSCE. a written or printed contract by which the insurer, in return for a payment called a *premium*, binds himself to pay the person named in the policy, called *the insured*, a certain sum of money, called *the sum insured*, when a stated event happens. This event may be the death or injury of the insured, or of some other named person, or damage or loss to the insured's property by fire, by theft or other forms of dishonesty, by accident, or from dangers at sea. There are many variations of insurance policy; the most frequently met are given below. *See also* insurance, classes and kinds of. *Syn.* policy of insurance.

all-risks policy a policy within the theft section of accident insurance (because the main risk is stealing) that insures the policy holder against loss from a very wide set of risks while in certain stated countries or the whole world. This kind of insurance is important for persons who have clothing, personal possessions and other valuable property that is often taken away from home or moved from place to place. The premium rate is high.

annuity certain a life insurance annuity policy that provides for the payment of an annuity in fixed amounts at stated dates, usu. for a fixed number of years. These payments are not affected by the death of the annuitant or of any other person. Cf. life annuity. *Syn.* certain annuity; terminable annuity.

bad debts policy *see* credit policy *below*.

baggage policy a policy, usu. in the class of accident insurance, but sometimes arranged by marine insurers, that insures passengers' baggage and personal things against most of the risks likely to be met on a journey, the dates and places of the journey being stated in the policy. Such insurance is often combined with medical expenses and loss-of-deposits insurance. *See* traveller's policy *below*.

borrow-all policy a life insurance contract that gives the insured person the right to borrow enough money each year from the insurance company to pay the annual premiums.

builders' policy *see* shipbuilders' policy *below*.

business interruption policy *see* consequential loss policy *below*.

business premises policy a policy in the fire insurance class that insures business premises including buildings, contents and rent against loss by fire and lightning, aircraft and explosion, earthquake, riot and civil disturbance, storm, burst pipes or tanks, and impact (striking) by vehicles or animals.

capital redemption policy a life insurance policy by which a sum of money is paid on a fixed date, whether or not the insured person is alive or dead on that date. *Syn.* sinking fund policy.

cargo policy a marine insurance policy that covers a ship's cargo, as distinguished from a policy that covers the hull. *See also* cargo syndicate.

cash-in-transit policy a money policy in the theft section of accident insurance, that covers the insured against loss, esp. by theft, of sums of cash, e.g. for wages being carried between a stated bank and the insured's offices and also, in the case of some businesses receiving large amounts of cash from sales, such as a department store, between their premises and the bank. (In transitu: *Latin*, on the journey.)

cash-refund annuity a life insurance annuity contract that provides for the payment at the death of the annuitant of a sum in cash equal to the difference between the capital sum paid by the annuitant for the annuity and the total of the sums paid to him up to his death.

child's deferred policy usu. an insurance on the parent's life for a period until the child is aged 18 or more when a lump sum will be payable to the child. (There are a number of variations.) *Syn.* children's policy; junior policy; threshold policy; child's policy.

collective policy a policy that is issued where co-insurance exists. *See* co-insurance *under* insurance, classes and kinds of.

combined policy a marine insurance contract between a group of insurers and the shipowners, which covers a number of vessels against a number of risks.

comprehensive *or* **household policy** a policy in the fire insurance class that insures the building and contents of a private house against fire, flood, storm, explosion, theft, malicious damage, certain accidental breakages, and liabilities to third parties. *Syn.* householder's policy; house-owner's policy; (U.S.A.) home-owner's policy.

comprehensive motor policy a motor-car policy in the accident insurance class, that covers several kinds of risk, such as accidental damage to, or loss of, the car, accidental injury to, or death of, the driver and passengers, medical expenses, loss of possessions by accident, theft or fire, third-party liability, etc.

consequential loss policy a policy in the fire insurance class that protects the insured from loss of profit and the additional cost of working following interference with, or interruption of, the business caused by fire or by any other risk insured against. *Syn.* business interruption policy; loss-of-profits policy; profits policy; (U.S.A.) use and occupancy policy.

construction policy *see* shipbuilder's policy *below.*

contingent annuity a life insurance annuity policy that provides for payments to begin when a certain event takes place, e.g. the death of a named person who is not the annuitant.

contingent or survivorship policy a life insurance policy by which the sum insured is payable only if the person whose life is insured dies while a named other person is still alive.

continuous disability policy *see* permanent health policy.

contract policy one of the medium-term policies issued to British exporters by the Export Credits Guarantee Department (E.C.G.D.) of the government to provide insurance cover if the foreign buyer should fail to perform his part of the contract.

contractor's indemnity policy a policy in the accident insurance class, insuring a building-contractor's property against loss or damage, and covering his liability to third parties. *Syn.* contractor's all-risks policy.

credit policy a policy in the accident insurance class that protects the insured seller of goods against loss due to the insolvency of the buyer. Such policies are often given in connection with bills of exchange. *Syn.* bad debts insurance. Cf. contract policy.

death duties policy a life insurance policy of which the sum insured is intended to pay capital transfer tax on the death of the insured person.

defective-title policy a contingency policy in the accident insurance class, arranged by a buyer of land and buildings when the seller cannot prove a perfectly clear title to the property. The buyer is protected against loss if some other person successfully claims a better title. *Syn.* title policy.

deferred annuity a life insurance annuity policy that becomes payable at a stated date in the future, usu. when the annuitant reaches a certain age. Cf. reversionary annuity.

earthquake policy *see* earthquake.

educational policy a special kind of endowment insurance on the life of a parent, the sum insured being payable by instalments over a number of years during which the cost of a child's education has to be paid.

employers' liability policy a policy in the accident insurance class protecting an employer against his liability to pay compensation if there is an accident caused by his failure to perform a duty owed to his employees. In Britain, every employer of labour must by law have this insurance.

endowment policy a life insurance policy by which the sum insured is payable at the end of a fixed period of ten or more years or on the earlier death of the person insured. *Double endowment policy*, an arrangement by which the sum insured will be doubled if the insured person lives to the end of the fixed period. *Pure endowment policy*, an arrangement by which no life is insured, payment of the sum insured being due at a fixed date; if the insured person dies before that date, the contract ends, with or without any return of the premiums. *Recurring endowment policy*, an industrial insurance producing a cash sum payable at intervals of five or seven years.

equity-linked policy a life insurance policy of which the sum insured varies according to the performance of equity, or ordinary, shares, on the Stock Exchange. Some insurers have investment trusts which they use, while others invest the premiums in existing unit trusts under skilled management. Such policies are more risky, and may therefore not be attractive to the man with a family to provide for, but may give some hedge (protection) against inflation.

family-income policy a temporary life insurance policy; if the person dies within the term of the policy, an income is payable from the date of death to the end of the term. If the person insured is still alive at the end of the term, the policy comes to an end and he receives nothing.

fire policy a contract by which an insurer, in return for a premium, agrees to pay to the insured the cost of any damage or loss caused by fire. In Britain, the *standard fire policy* insures not only against fire but also against lightning and explosion of gas and household boilers; and for an extra premium other risks may be included such as damage by burst pipes, storm, flood, earthquake, riot and civil commotion. *See also* comprehensive or householder's policy; business premises policy; profits policy. *Abbr.* F.P.

floating policy *see* floating insurance *under* insurance, classes and kinds of. *Abbr.* F.P.

flood policy *see* flood.

freight policy a marine insurance contract that protects the insured against loss of freight (payment for carrying a cargo).

goods-in-transit policy a policy in the accident insurance class, that covers damage or loss to goods while they are being transported (carried), from the moment they are loaded on to a vehicle until they are unloaded at the end of the journey; or from dispatch to delivery in the case of postal parcels.

group life policy a single policy that insures the lives of many or all the employees in an organization; the sum insured for each separate employee is based on an agreed number of times his salary or wages.

group pension policy a single life insurance policy to provide each of a number of employees with a retirement pension for life, either by using a number of deferred annuities or by buying immediate annuities with money received from endowment insurances. *See also* retirement policy.

guaranteed annuity (*a*) an annuity which must be paid for a certain number of years whether or not the person insured has died. (*b*) an annuity which will continue until all the purchase money has been paid back.

homeowner's policy (U.S.A.) *see* comprehensive policy *above*.

household *or* **householder's** *or* **house-owner's policy** *see* comprehensive policy *above*.

house-purchase policy a life insurance policy that is either: a *term insurance*, when a mortgage is repaid by annual payments, the life cover getting less and less as the unpaid balance of the debt is reduced, but being always enough to settle the unpaid balance if the insured should die before the end of the term; or an *endowment insurance*, which will repay the loan on maturity or in the event of the death of the insured before maturity. *Syn.* mortgage protection policy.

hull policy a marine insurance policy on the hull of a ship.

immediate annuity a life insurance annuity policy by which the annuity payments begin either immediately it has been bought or six months later. Cf. deferred annuity.

increasing annuity a life insurance annuity policy that provides for an increase in payments at a stated percentage rate, either annually or after agreed periods such as every five years; it is intended to help the annuitant to meet increases in the cost of living in times of inflation.

investment-linked policy a life insurance contract by which part of the premiums are used by the insurers to buy investment trust units, either with an equity or a property portfolio. *See also* equity-linked policy *above*. *Syn.* unit-linked policy.

joint annuity a life insurance annuity policy that provides for payment of an annuity on the lives of two persons; it continues during the life of the person who lives the longer.

joint life and survivor annuity a life insurance annuity policy similar to a joint annuity except that the payments are at a reduced rate from the time that the first person dies. *Syn.* joint and survivorship annuity.

joint life endowment policy an insurance on the lives of two persons, the sum insured being payable on the maturity date or on the death of the first to die if that happens before the maturity date.

joint whole-life policy an insurance on the lives of two persons, the sum insured being payable on the death of the first to die.

junior insurance policy *see* child's deferred policy *above*.

last-survivor policy an insurance on the lives of two persons, the sum insured being payable on the death of the last to die.

life annuity a life insurance annuity policy that provides for payment of an annuity only during a life or lives. Cf. annuity certain.

Lloyd's policy *see under* Lloyd's.

loss-of-profits policy *see* consequential loss policy *above*.

medical expenses policy a policy in the accident insurance class that insures a person against the risk of accident or illness, esp. when abroad, resulting in heavy medical expenses. Such policies are often combined with baggage and loss-of-deposits policies. *See* traveller's policy; private health policy *below*.

mixed policy a marine insurance policy that insures a ship for a fixed period during which she is making voyages between two stated places; a mixture of time policy and voyage policy.

mortgage protection policy *see* house-purchase policy *above*.

non-profit policy *see* without-profits policy *below*.

open policy *see* floating insurance *under* insurance, classes and kinds of.

partnership policy a special life insurance contract intended to provide the remaining partners of a firm with a capital sum of money on the death of any one of their fellow partners. This payment helps to overcome the disturbance caused by the dead partner's capital being taken out of the firm by his representatives.

permanent health policy an extension of a personal accident insurance with sickness cover for an agreed number of years, usu. until the insured person reaches a certain age; the insurer agrees to continue the policy during that period provided the premiums are paid however many claims the insured person may make. *Syn.* continuous disability policy.

perpetual annuity *see under* perpetual.

personal accident policy an insurance contract under which an agreed sum of money is paid in the event of death or loss of eyes and limbs as the result of an accident caused by violent external and visible means, with weekly payments during the time that the insured person cannot work. *See also* traveller's policy *below*. Some personal accident policies also insure against sickness of all kinds or against certain stated diseases. The amount of the premium differs widely according to the occupation of the insured person.

pluvius policy *see* pluvius insurance.

private health policy a special kind of contract with an insurance company or a non-profitmaking society, often in the form of a group insurance, by which, in return for a regular premium, the insured person is repaid, up to an agreed figure, certain stated expenses such as doctor's and surgeon's fees, hospital charges for room, board, nursing and laboratory service, and the cost of medicines. In many countries private health insurance exists in addition to, or as part of, national health services run by the government. *See* National Health Service, *under* national; medical expenses policy *above*.

professional indemnity policy a policy in the accident insurance class, protecting a professional person, such as a doctor, lawyer, or architect, if claims are made against him for damages for negligence or mistakes. *Syn.* public liability policy.

profits policy *see* consequential loss policy *above*.

public liability policy *see* professional indemnity policy *above*.

refund annuity a life insurance annuity policy that provides for the payment on the annuitant's death of a lump sum (the *refund*) to his representatives, based on the difference between the original price paid for the annuity and the total amount paid to the annuitant up to his death. This lump sum is sometimes replaced by regular payments to a named person.

reinstatement policy a fire or accident policy in which the insurer promises to pay claims based on the cost of rebuilding or replacing the insured goods, buildings, machinery, etc. with new goods or articles.

retirement annuity a deferred annuity policy that provides for payment of a pension to the annuitant from the date of his retirement, (usu. at the age of 60 or 65, until his death. There are a number of variations.) *See also* group pension policy *above*.

reversionary annuity a life insurance annuity

policy that provides for payments to begin on the death of an insured person to a named person and to continue for life; but if the named person dies first, the contract comes to an end and nothing is payable.

shipbuilders' policy a marine insurance policy that covers certain risks when building a vessel. *Syn.* construction policy; building risk policy; builders' policy.

shipment policy in Britain, one of the medium-term policies issued to British exporters by the Export Credits Guarantee Department (E.C.G.D.) of the government to provide insurance cover if the foreign buyer should fail to perform his part of the contract. *See* E.C.G.D.

single-premium policy a life insurance policy for which only one premium is paid, in a single payment at the beginning of the agreed period of the insurance, usu. two to five years. Such policies are sometimes called *guaranteed income bonds*; during the agreed period the insured person receives an income, usu. paid half-yearly, of an agreed percentage of the original premium, this income being net of basic-rate income tax. At the end of the agreed period, the insurers must return to the insured person a sum equivalent to the original premium.

sinking fund policy *see* capital redemption policy *above*.

storm policy *see* pluvius insurance.

survivor policy *see* contingent or survivorship policy *above*.

survivorship annuity a life insurance annuity that continues to be paid after the annuitant's death to a named person, e.g. his widow.

temporary annuity a life insurance annuity payable for a fixed period of years; but it stops if the annuitant dies before the end of that period.

temporary policy *see* term policy *below*.

term policy a life insurance contract for a fixed term (period of time) e.g. five or ten years; the sum insured becomes payable if the insured person dies within this period. If he is alive at the end of it, the policy comes to an end and he receives nothing. A *convertible term policy* is an arrangement by which the insured person may convert (change) at any time to a whole-life policy, or to an endowment policy. A *decreasing term policy* is one under which the sum insured gets smaller every year; such a policy is usu. used to provide life cover when the insured person is buying a house on a redeemable mortgage. Another form of term policy is a family-income policy, *see above*.

terminable annuity an annuity certain that is payable for a stated number of years. Cf. perpetual annuity.

threshold insurance policy *see* child's deferred policy *above*.

time policy a marine insurance policy insuring a ship for a stated period of from one month to one year.

title policy see defective-title policy *above*.

traveller's policy a personal accident policy combined with insurance of baggage, medical expenses and loss of deposits.

unit-linked policy see investment-linked policy *above*.

unvalued policy see *under* unvalued.

use and occupancy policy (U.S.A.) see consequential loss policy *above*.

valued policy see agreed-value insurance *under* insurance, classes and kinds of.

variable annuity a life insurance annuity policy under which the amount of the payments to the annuitant vary according to the income from the stocks and shares in which the purchase price has been invested. It is intended to protect the annuitant in time of inflation.

voyage policy a marine insurance policy insuring a ship for a stated voyage. Cf. time policy.

wager policy see *under* wager.

whole-life policy a policy that provides that the insured person pays the premiums (weekly, monthly, or yearly) for the rest of his life, and that the insurers will pay the sum insured only on his death. This is called a *straight life policy*. It is, however, usual to arrange that premiums are no longer paid when the insured person reaches retirement age (60 or 65), this being called *whole life with limited payments policy*.

with-profits policy a life insurance policy which carries with it the right to receive a share in the profits made by the life fund of the insurance company. The premium is higher than in the case of a without-profits policy. The profits are added to the basic sum insured in the form of bonuses declared by the company out of its profits for a given period. Cf. without-profits policy.

without-profits policy a life insurance policy in which the sum insured is fixed from the start of the contract, and there is to be no share in the profits of the insurance company. Cf. with-profits policy. *Syn.* non-profit policy.

insurance premium see premium (6).

insurance surveyor see *under* surveyor.

insure INSCE. to make sure, esp. to arrange by paying money to an insurer that one will be paid an agreed sum if one suffers loss caused by an uncertain happening such as accident, fire or theft; or that an amount will be paid on a certain date or on one's death or the death of another person. Generally, to give or obtain an insurance policy. *To insure against*, to arrange insurance covering a particular risk, such as fire. *Insured peril*, one of the dangers stated in the policy. *Insured value*, the value of the goods insured in the policy. *Insured vessel*, the ship insured in the policy.

insured, the INSCE. the person or organization whose life or property is insured under an insurance contract given or issued by the insurers. *Syn.* the assured.

insurer(s) INSCE. the party or parties, usu. an insurance company or a Lloyd's underwriter, who take upon themselves the risk of paying for losses in accordance with the conditions of an insurance contract. Cf. insured, the; assurer.

int. interest.

intangible assets see *under* assets.

integration IND. & ECON. THEORY the combining under one management of two or more manufacturing concerns. There are various forms of integration in industry. *Syn.* combination. Cf. interlocking directorates.

backward integration see vertical integration *below*.

circular integration a form of integration that is partly vertical and partly horizontal.

diagonal integration a form of integration that takes place when a producer buys control of a business that performs services that are useful for the main activity of the producer, such as a vehicle-repair works integrated with a road-transport company.

forward integration see vertical integration *below*.

horizontal integration that form of integration by which an individual concern obtains control of competing businesses carrying out the same stage in the production process or producing the same or similar products. *Syn.* lateral integration.

lateral integration see horizontal integration *above*.

vertical integration that form of integration by which an industrial concern obtains control of the business that supplies most of its materials (called *backward integration*) or of the business that buys most of its products, i.e. its customers (called *forward integration*).

integrity honesty; goodness of character: *Business/commercial/professional integrity. A man of the highest integrity*, having very high standards of honesty and responsibility, esp. in a position of trust. *Syn.* probity.

intensive agriculture AGR. a method of farming in which by investing large amounts of capital, labour and fertilizer in a relatively small area of land, a high rate of crop-production is obtained. It is carried on esp. in countries where the price of farm land is high. *Opp.* extensive agriculture.

intent, letter of see *under* letter.

inter alia *Latin*, among other things.

interchange (1) of correspondence, ideas, information, a giving and receiving, esp. by turns: *There has been an interchange of letters/ ideas between the two companies*. (2) TRANSP.

a place where special bridges, etc. have been built so that road vehicles can safely change from one main road, esp. a motorway, to another without crossing lines of vehicles at the same level.

interchangeable bond *see under* bond, *n.*

intercourse dealings between people or countries. *Commercial intercourse*, trade between nations.

interdict LAW in Scotland, an injunction.

interest ECON. THEORY (1) the price paid for the use of money such as by a borrower to a lender of money; the money earned by a lender as a reward for allowing the borrower to use his money and for waiting for the repayment of the loan. *Abbr.* int. (2) the extra amount earned, or expected to be earned, by a capital asset, after paying for its capital cost. (3) in the teaching of classical economists, the supply price of capital, a price that is influenced by the effects of supply and demand for capital. (4) in Keynes's liquidity preference theory, the reward for suffering loss of liquidity by lending one's money. (5) FIN. rights of ownership in a business or of a substantial share in a business: *Mr Jones has a large interest in this business. He has many business/commercial/industrial/financial/property interests.* (6) a business of which a certain person is owner or part-owner. *See* minority interests. (7) LAW the possession of rights, esp. in land. *See* life interest. *Syn.* estate. (8) INSCE. the thing that is the subject of an insurance policy, such as the ship in a marine hull policy, or its cargo in a cargo policy. *See also* insurable interest.

accrued interest *see under* accrued.

building society interest *see under* building society.

compound interest *see under* compound.

cum interest *see under* cum.

debenture interest *see* debenture stock.

ex interest *see under* ex.

gross interest ECON. THEORY the total interest received by the lender of capital. This interest may be considered to consist of two parts, one being the lender's reward for taking the risk and suffering the trouble of making the loan, and the other, the *pure* or *net interest*, being a hire charge paid by the borrower for the use of the money.

net interest *see* gross interest *above.*

nominal interest the rate of interest payable on a security based on its par value, such as 13% Treasury Stock 1997. Cf. yield. *Syn.* money rate of interest; nominal coupon.

ordinary interest *see* simple interest *below.*

pure interest *see* gross interest *above.*

simple interest interest calculated only on the principal (capital sum), not on any accrued interest. *Syn.* ordinary interest.

interest bond *see under* bond, *n.*

interest rate FIN. (1) the relation between the payment received by a lender of money and the amount of money lent, expressed as a percentage per period of time: *5% per annum,* the lender receives from the borrower £5 per year for every £100 borrowed. (2) the main financial rates of interest in Britain are: the minimum lending (formerly bank) rate; the Bank of England loan rate; the market rate of discount; the London banker's deposit rate; and the bankers' call rate and seven day rate. *See also* prime rate.

interest tables a book containing a set of tables showing the amount of interest at various rates per cent for various numbers of units and various lengths of time. One can quickly see from these tables, for example, that at 6% per annum the interest on a loan of £150 for three months is £2.25.

interest warrant *see under* warrant.

Inter-Governmental Maritime Consultative Organization (I.M.C.O.) SHIPG. a specialized agency of the United Nations, with its central office in London and responsibility for setting up rules for international shipping, encouraging the highest standards of navigation and safety at sea, and the removal of unfair practices among shipping organizations.

interim accounts *see* accounts, *n. pl.*

interim bond *see under* bond, *n.*

interim bonus *see under* bonus, insurance.

interim dividend *see under* dividend.

interlocking directorates STK. EXCH. several separate and apparently independent companies that are in fact in close association because they each have a number of the same persons as directors. These directors can thus influence the companies to adopt a common policy to get rid of competition, fix prices, resist wage demands, etc. Cf. combination; integration.

interlocutory injunction LAW a temporary order made by a court of law during the course of a civil action and before the court can reach a decision. *See also* injunction.

intermediary COM. & FIN. a person who acts as an agent in business dealings between other persons or organizations. *Syn.* middleman; broker; go-between.

intermediate goods *see under* goods.

internal debt *see* national debt.

International Air Transport Association (I.A.T.A.) a non-government organization to which most international airlines belong. Its main purpose is to keep passenger fares and freight rates at an economic level.

International Bank for Economic Co-operation (I.B.E.C.) FIN. a banking organization set up in 1963 by eight communist countries: Bulgaria, Czechoslovakia, East Germany, Hungary, Mongolia, Poland, Romania, and the U.S.S.R. It helps its members by giving credits when needed to correct a temporary adverse trade balance, makes international settlements in roubles and provides other banking services. Its governing body consists of representatives of its member countries.

International Bank for Reconstruction and Development (I.B.R.D.) popularly known as the *World Bank*, an organization under the control of the United Nations. Like the International Monetary Fund, it was set up as a result of the Bretton Woods Agreement in 1944 and began to operate in 1946. Until 1949 it made loans for reconstruction (rebuilding) in those countries that had suffered most in the Second World War, but it then began making long-term loans to its member nations for the development of production and for the growth of international trade. Its capital is subscribed by its member nations and it operates by lending direct to governments, or to private concerns if the government guarantees the loan; and it guarantees loans made by commercial and private investors to approved borrowers who are thus able to get their loans at a low rate of interest.

International Bureau of Weights and Measures COM. & IND. an organization started in 1875 to bring a unified system of weights and measures and to carry out scientific work needed to set up standards (approved examples or models for comparison). It organizes a General Conference on Weights and Measures every six years at which is elected the International Committee of Weights and Measures, the controlling authority for the SI (système internationale) system of international units.

International Chamber of Commerce (I.C.C.) COM. a federation of business organizations and businessmen from all over the world. It represents the business community in international affairs and has its offices in Paris.

International Chamber of Shipping (I.C.S.) SHIPG. an organization formed by shipowners in 1921 with its offices in London. It is concerned with looking after the interests of the shipping industry, and in giving advice on scientific and technical problems, esp. in regard to standards of safety.

International Civil Aviation Organization (I.C.A.O.) TRANSPT. an organization set up in 1947, with its main office in Montreal, to control the licensing of aircraft and aircrews, and to encourage international co-operation for weather services, communications, and systems for controlling aircraft in flight. It gives technical help, esp. to under-developed countries as part of the U.N. Development Programme.

International Confederation of Free Trade Unions (I.C.F.T.U.) IND. REL. a world-wide organization of trade-union federations in non-communist countries. Formed in 1949 with its offices in Brussels, it aims to encourage co-operation among free and democratic trade-union movements throughout the world. Cf. World Federation of Trade Unions.

International Convention for the Protection of Industrial Property LAW an agreement signed in 1883 to give protection under international law to owners of patents, industrial designs and trade-marks.

International Court of Justice LAW the main judicial branch of the United Nations, based on The Hague, in Holland. The Court has 15 judges, all from different nations, who hear and decide disputes between states. All member states agree, on joining the U.N., to accept and obey the decisions of the Court. Cf. European Court of Justice (of the E.E.C.).

international currency *see under* currency.

international date line *see* date line.

International Development Association (I.D.A.) FIN. an organization set up in 1960 as part of the multilateral aid programme of the World Bank. The I.D.A. makes loans almost free of interest and for long periods (called 'soft' loans) to the less-developed countries for economic development. It receives most of its funds from the 18 wealthiest nations.

International Finance Corporation (I.F.C.) FIN. an organization set up in 1956, in close association with the World Bank, to provide capital for private concerns in countries where enough private capital cannot be raised. It makes loans for five to fifteen years and does not demand a government guarantee that loans will be repaid.

International Labour Organization (I.L.O.) IND. REL. a specialized agency of the United Nations, with its main offices in Geneva. It has about 120 member states, each represented at an annual conference by persons from employers' and workers' organizations as well as by government officials. Its main purpose is to improve conditions of labour and standards of living all over the world; this it does by guiding and encouraging the introduction of good labour laws, training officials, collecting and publishing statistics and, in recent years, protecting human rights, esp. in the less-developed countries.

international law LAW the legal rules concerning relations between states, sometimes called the *law of nations*. These rules have been internationally accepted. They deal with such subjects as: the freedom of the seas, of navigation and commerce; the rules of war and neutrality diplomatic law; and the protection of nationals abroad. International law means *public international law*. *Private international law* is a separate group of rules, sometimes called the *con* *flict of laws*, which concerns differences between the internal laws in different countries, and questions of the jurisdiction of courts in civil cases of an international nature.

international liquidity *see* liquidity, international.

international load-line *see* load-line.

International Monetary Fund (I.M.F.) FIN. a fund set up in 1944 at the Bretton Woods conference as a specialized agency of the United Nations, mainly to encourage monetary co-operation between nations and to increase international trade. Its offices are in Washington and its members number more than 120 states. Each member deposits, mainly in its own currency, an amount determined by the size of its national income, international trade and currency reserves. (*See* I.M.F. quota.) A member in temporary difficulty with its balance of payments may use its Regular and Special Drawing Rights (*see* Drawing Rights) and can get further help if necessary (*see* standby arrangements; *also* General Arrangements to Borrow). The Fund is essentially a bank from which a borrower uses its own currency to buy the foreign currency it needs. Credits are for short periods of only three to five years. The work of the Fund in rebuilding confidence in currencies that are in temporary difficulty has been valuable.

international money order *see* overseas money order *under* money order.

international nautical *or* **air mile** *see under* mile.

international postal reply coupon a coupon or slip of paper that can be bought at main post offices and sent to a person in a foreign country, who uses it to buy stamps to a value sufficient to cover the postage on a reply.

International Price Index ECON. a statistical comparison, using index numbers, of the gross national product of each country, calculated and published twice yearly by the United Nations.

International Settlements, Bank for *see* Bank for International Settlements.

International System of Units IND. the SI system (*French:* système internationale d'unités, international system of units). This system has been universally accepted and is being adopted in all countries. *See* SI system; International Bureau of Weights and Measures.

international trade COM. the exchange of goods and services across national boundaries; buying and selling between different countries. International trade differs from home or internal trade because of differences in laws, languages and standards of living, while currency differences need the use of foreign-exchange rates and the making of special payment arrangements. *Syn.* foreign trade; external trade; overseas trade.

interpretation (1) explaining the meaning of: *The interpretation of statistics/technical data/plans.*

interpretation of accounts the act of examining and analysing a set of accounts to know whether they show a satisfactory or an unsatisfactory state of affairs.

(2) giving the meaning of words, usu. spoken, in another language; translation.

interpreter TOUR. & MAN. a person who translates speech or conversation from one language into another immediately after the words have been spoken. Cf. translator.

interstate commerce LAW in the U.S.A., the commerce that takes place between persons or organizations in different states and therefore, by the U.S. Constitution, a matter under the control of the federal government. Commerce includes trade (buying and selling), transportation (carriage of people and goods), and communications such as radio, television, telephone and telegraph. *See* commerce clause.

intervention (1) the act of coming between, of interfering in, some activity. (2) ECON. action by a government, called *state intervention*, to control the economic system, ranging from the provision of laws for the protection of weaker groups of workers such as women and children, low-paid employees, those doing dangerous or unhealthy work, to state ownership of entire industries. (3) LAW the act of a person who, to protect his own interests and with the permission of the court, makes himself a party to a civil lawsuit that has already been begun between other parties.

interventionist *n.* ECON. a person who supports the idea that the State should interfere in economic matters. *Adj. Sweden's interventionist policy in industry.*

intervention price ECON. the price at which the E.E.C. authorities under the Common Agricultural Policy will buy up all supplies of a farm product in the market for storage in order to stop prices falling so low as to be unprofitable to the farmers. The intervention price is a little lower than the threshold price and is intended to help producers to sell at the target price. *See* threshold price and target price *under* price.

interview *n.* a meeting, esp. of two, or of only a few, persons, to do business, or to decide whether one of the persons is fit for a post, or to obtain a person's views, such as in a television interview: *Please ask for/seek/arrange/grant an interview with* (someone).

to interview *v.* to give an interview to; to have an interview with: *I interviewed him for the post of manager.*

interviewee a person who is interviewed.

interviewer a person who interviews.

inter vivos *Latin*, between living persons. *See* gifts *inter vivos*.

inter vivos trust *see under* trust.

intestacy LAW the condition of having died intestate (without having left a will).

intestate LAW *adj.* (of a dead person) not having left a will. *See* administrator (1). *Opp.* testate. *n.* a person who has died intestate.

intestate succession (*a*) the right by which certain persons inherit the property of an intestate. (*b*) the group of laws relating to such rights.

in trans. in transit.

in transit TRANSPT. (*Latin:* in transitu) in course of being transported; on the way.

intrinsic value the value possessed by a thing because of its own nature or the matter of which it is composed. Thus the intrinsic value of a coin depends on the market value of the metal(s) it contains. *Syn.* absolute value. *Opp.* extrinsic value.

introduction STK. EXCH. a way of issuing shares in a private company that is about to become a public company, by which a broker or issuing house buys the shares, not in large numbers but often in small lots as may be needed to supply clients' orders. Cf. placing.

intrust *see* entrust.

inv. invoice.

invalid *adj.* LAW not valid; having no legal force or effectiveness: *An invalid insurance policy,* one that is not accepted as evidence in a court of law, e.g. if no insurable interest exists. *An invalid cheque/marriage/will/claim/bill of exchange.*

invalidate to make or declare invalid.

invalidity the state of not being valid, of not having legal force.

invaluable that cannot be valued; of the very greatest value; beyond value: *Your services were invaluable in obtaining the order.*

invention any machine, instrument or process that has not been made or produced before. The economic effect of inventions is to reduce labour costs by permitting one man to do the work of many. Cf. innovations.

inventory (1) a detailed list of things; an agreed list, given by the owner to a tenant, of furniture and articles provided by the owner of furnished property. (2) ACCTS. a U.S. expression for stocks held by a business for sale to its customers, but now widely used in English-speaking countries as a synonym for stock in hand. (3) the process of taking stock. *See* stocktaking.

continuous inventory *see* continuous stocktaking *under* stocktaking.

ship's inventory a list of the movable things permanently carried by a ship. *See* furniture (2).

inventory control *see* stock control *under* control.

inventory investment *see under* investment.

inventory valuation *see* stock valuation *under* valuation.

inverted takeover *see under* takeover.

invest (1) to use money in such a way that it will produce an income or profit. *See* investment.

to invest in to spend one's money on buying an investment: *To invest in property/equities/gilt-edged securities/an annuity.*

(2) (*colloq.*) to spend money on, put money into buying, a very useful article: *To invest in a motor car. The accountant invested in a pocket calculator.*

invested capital *see* capital structure.

investible that can be invested: *Investible funds,* funds that are intended to be lent to others. *Syn.* loanable.

investigation LAW & STK. EXCH. in Britain, an examination of the books and accounts of a company by government officials called inspectors, in cases where the Department of Trade suspects that the company is not being run in accordance with the law, that the company's creditors are being defrauded or that the directors are guilty of misfeasance (improper performance of acts that are not in themselves unlawful).

investment (1) the act of investing, of using money to obtain income or profits: *The choice between spending and investment. Opp.* disinvestment. (2) money invested: *He lives on income from investments.* (3) a particular security, or class of security, or other thing, in which money is invested: *Oil shares are a good investment. Those shares proved to be the best investment of last year.* (4) ECON. THEORY capital assets consisting of goods that are not intended for immediate consumption (called *investment goods* or *capital goods* or *producer goods*) but are for use in the production of consumer goods and further capital goods. (5) FIN. & STK. EXCH. the buying of securities and the lending of money to banks, building societies, etc. to obtain an income from interest or dividends or a profit on a future sale.

autonomous investment *see under* autonomous.

capital investment investment in capital goods, i.e. new assets such as factories, machinery and vehicles needed to produce further goods.

community investment *see* real investment *below.*

constant-ratio investment (plan) STK. EXCH. a system by which a sum of money is divided into two funds, one being used for buying various stocks and shares, the other to provide liquid cash. Thus, by selling securities on a rising market and buying on a falling market, the ratio between the funds can be preserved.

consumer investment spending by consumers on assets having a long life, esp. on buying houses.

domestic investment *see* private investment *below*.

financial investment investment in claims on wealth, i.e. stocks and shares, bonds, mortgages, etc. rather than on wealth in the form of real assets. *Syn.* personal investment. Cf. real investment; community investment.

fixed investment money spent by a government on new houses, roads, hospitals, etc., and by privately-owned concerns on new buildings, ships, aircraft and vehicles, all being capital goods, not consumer goods. *See* infrastructure.

foreign investment money that has been invested by the government and the public of one country in real assets and securities in other countries.

government investment *see* public investment *below*.

gross investment in economic analysis, the total amount of new capital goods added to the existing stock of those goods in the economy during a given period. Cf. net investment.

induced investment investment resulting from an increase in private and public spending, i.e. from a rise in consumption. Cf. autonomous investment; induced consumption.

inventory investment the amount of money spent by a business in adding to its stock-in-trade and work-in-progress during a stated period. If the real value of these assets has fallen during the period, there has been *inventory disinvestment*.

involuntary investment the money invested in unplanned increases in producers' stocks resulting from an unexpected reduction in demand.

legal investments trustee securities.

net investment in economic analysis, the net addition to the stock of capital goods in an economy during a given period. It is the gross investment reduced by the amount of capital consumption.

non-monetary investment money spent by the public on rare or precious objects such as a work of art, antique (very old) silver and glass objects, and diamonds, in the expectation of a rise in the market value either in the near or the more distant future.

overseas investment *see* foreign investment *above*.

personal investment *see* financial investment *above*.

private investment in economic analysis, the total amount of capital goods bought by persons and organizations other than the government and publicly-owned concerns such as nationalized industries and public utilities. *Syn.* domestic investment.

public investment money spent by the government on fixed investments. *Syn.* government investment.

real investment investment in goods and services needed for the good of the community (schools, hospitals, etc.) and not for financial gain. *Syn.* community investment.

speculative investment the use of money to buy a security or commodity with the intention of selling it at a profit. Cf. true investment.

tax-free investment one that produces a tax-free income or a tax-free capital profit, such as savings certificates and premium savings bonds.

trade investments *see under* trade.

true investment the use of money to bring in a regular income of reasonable amount as interest or dividend. Cf. speculative investment.

trustee investment *see under* trustee.

investment allowances *see* capital allowances.

investment analysis STK. EXCH. & FIN. the making of forecasts of stock and share prices, based on detailed study of the trading outlook for each company. Persons skilled in making such forecasts, called *investment analysts*, are employed by large organizations concerned with trading in securities, such as stockbrokers, banks, insurance companies and pension funds.

investment bank(er) BKG. & STK. EXCH. in U.S.A., a financial organization that, alone or with a group of others called a syndicate, buys from a corporation (company) an entire new issue of bonds or stock and sells in smaller units to the public. Investment bankers thus take over the risk and responsibility for the financial success of the new issue. In this sense they are often called underwriters. They sometimes also arrange mergers and reorganizations of companies and act as advisers on the raising of capital and on financial matters generally. In Britain, the merchant banks perform the same services.

investment bill *see under* bill of exchange.

investment currency *see under* currency.

investment goods *see* capital goods *under* goods (7).

investment grant FIN. & IND. money paid by the government to encourage certain industries to invest in new machinery, buildings and other fixed assets. Such grants are paid whether the company makes a profit or a loss.

investment income *see* unearned income *under* income.

investment income surcharge TAXN. in Britain, an extra rate of income tax that is payable on unearned (investment) income above a certain amount. *Syn.* special investment surcharge.

investment-linked policy *see under* insurance policy.

investment portfolio *see* portfolio (2).

investment (trust) company *see under* company.

investment turnover *see* capital turnover.

investor STK. EXCH. a person who invests money.

institutional investors *see under* institutional.

private investor a person who, acting only for himself and his family, invests money, esp. his savings, by buying stocks and shares, or by lending money to a bank or building society.

invest, propensity to *see under* propensity.

invisible balance ECON. & PUB. FIN. the difference between the money values of the invisible exports and the invisible imports of a country. This invisible balance, with the visible balance (called the balance of trade), together form the balance of payments.

invisible exports *see under* exports, *pl.*

invisible imports *see under* imports, *pl.*

invisibles (*colloq.*) invisible exports and imports.

invitation the act of inviting; a polite or formal request, either written or spoken, asking that one should do a particular act, such as to come to dinner, to make a bid, etc.

invitation to make an offer *see under* offer (2).

invitation to subscribe *see under* subscribe.

invitation to tender *see* sealed-bid tender *under* tender.

invitation to treat *see* offer (2).

invite *v.* to request formally or politely: *He invited me to dinner. We invite your comments*, please tell us what you have to say. *To invite applications*, to ask people to apply, esp. for a job or for a new issue of shares. *To invite offers/bids/tenders/quotations/donations(gifts)*, to make it known that one wishes to receive these.

an invite *n.* (*colloq.*) an invitation.

invoice *v.* ACCTS. & COM. (1) to prepare an invoice: *Orders waiting to be invoiced*, waiting to have invoices prepared for them. *Syn.* (U.S.A.) to bill. (2) to send (a customer) an invoice, charging the amount to his account if he is an account customer, or demanding payment if he is not: *We are invoicing you for the extra quantity you are taking.* (3) to include in an invoice: *Is this item to be invoiced or are we supplying it free?*

n. ACCTS. & COM. a bill relating to the sale of goods or services. A separate document, sent by the seller to the buyer, for each sale, giving details of the goods sold. An invoice may be a record of a credit sale (*see* payment on statement), or a demand for payment (*see* payment on invoice), or a paper giving information (*see* pro-forma invoice). Every invoice must give certain basic information: the names and addresses of the seller and the buyer; the dates and numbers of the invoice and the order; a description of each kind of goods bought, the quantity, price per unit and total price of each kind; the total price of the goods; the discount allowed; the total amount of the invoice. De-

pending on its purpose, an invoice may also give: the number of packages, their nature (bales, cases, cartons, etc.) and their marks; responsibility for insurance of the goods while being carried, etc. Export invoices usu. need special treatment. *Syn.* bill; account. *Abbr.* inv.

certified invoice an export invoice bearing, usu. on the back, a printed and signed certificate of origin concerning the goods.

commercial invoice the usual kind of export invoice sent by the seller to the buyer, either direct or through a bank, recording a sale of goods; it also tells the buyer that the amount of the invoice has been debited in the buyer's account in the seller's ledger. Cf. pro-forma invoice; customs invoice; consular invoice.

consignment invoice an export invoice which relates to goods sent to an agent abroad to be sold on commission and at the risk of the exporter, i.e. for goods sent *on consignment*.

consular invoice an export invoice which has been legally attested (formally signed by) the Consul of the country to which the goods are being sent. Such invoices are accepted by the Customs in the buyer's country as a true basis for charging import duty.

customs invoice one prepared by an exporter specially for customs purposes on an official form and giving more information than in an ordinary invoice, such as the value of the goods in the exporting and the importing country. The invoice usu. has to be signed and witnessed. *Syn.* combined certificate of value and origin.

export invoice one that is part of a set of export and shipping documents and which gives extra details such as shipping marks, freight, insurance, dock charges, etc. special to export trading. It is a document of title. Cf. inland invoice. *See also* certified invoice; consignment invoice; consular invoice; customs invoice; franco invoice.

final invoice one which follows or replaces a provisional invoice sent earlier.

franco invoice a special export invoice planned to help the customer who does not understand English. The price of the goods includes all costs of delivery to the buyer's premises. Often, esp. for sales to countries in continental Europe, franco invoices are expressed in the language of the buyer, prices are given in his local currency and measurements are in metric units.

incoming invoice *see* purchase(s) invoice below.

inland invoice one relating to goods etc. sold in the home market. Cf. export invoice.

invoice inwards *see* purchase(s) invoice below.

original invoice (*a*) the original or top copy of an invoice as distinguished from a carbon c other copy. (*b*) an invoice which has later been followed by a supplementary invoice.

outgoing invoice *see* sale(s) invoice *below*.

payment on invoice *see under* payment.

pro-forma invoice (*a*) in the home trade, an invoice sent to a buyer, usu. a stranger who has to pay for the goods before they are sent off to him. (*b*) in export trading, a sample invoice to give a possible buyer information about prices, discounts, charges and conditions of sale if he places an order. A way of making a quotation. (*c*) a sample invoice sent by a business to its branches and agents to give them information which they need to fix local selling prices.

provisional invoice one which is intended to serve for the present only and which will be followed or replaced by a final invoice.

purchase(s) invoice the name given to an invoice by the buyer of the goods referred to in it. *Syn.* incoming invoice; invoice inwards. *Opp.* sale(s) invoice.

sale(s) invoice the name given to an invoice by the seller of the goods referred to in it. *Syn.* outgoing invoice. *Opp.* purchase(s) invoice.

supplementary invoice one which supplements or adds to charges included in another invoice, e.g. a supplementary invoice for freight and insurance charges on a shipment of goods for which an invoice has been sent earlier.

invoice clerk ACCTS. & COM. an office employee responsible for, and having special knowledge of, preparing invoices, usu. as a member of the invoicing department of a business. *Syn.* (U.S.A.) billing clerk.

invoice price *see under* price.

invoice typist *see under* typist.

invoicing department ACCTS. & COM. the department of a business in which invoices are prepared, produced and sent to customers, etc. *Syn.* (U.S.A.) billing department.

involuntary absentee *see* absentee.

involuntary investment *see under* investment.

involuntary saving *see under* saving.

involuntary unemployment *see under* unemployment.

inward SHIPG. coming in, as opposed to going out: *Inward cargo*, being imported. *Inward port*, at which a ship or a cargo arrives. *Inward charges*, those payable when a ship enters a port. *Inward bill of lading*, *see under* bill of lading. *See also* carriage inwards *under* carriage; clearance (2). *Opp.* outward.

inward bound *see under* bound (1).

inward clearing bill *see* jerque note.

I.O.M. Isle of Man.

I.O.U. FIN. (meaning 'I owe you') letters which, when written on a piece of paper stating the amount owed, and then signed and dated, form a simple acknowledgment of a debt, being both a receipt for the money and an acceptance of the duty to pay it back. The cre-

ditor keeps the I.O.U. as proof of the debt and may show it in a court of law as evidence. An I.O.U. is not negotiable. It is not a promissory note.

I.O.W. Isle of Wight.

ipso facto *Latin*, by the mere fact: *A director who is declared bankrupt ipso facto cannot continue to hold that office.*

IR Iran's international vehicle-registration letters.

I.R. Inland Revenue.

ir- *prefix*, a variation of in-, used before the letter r, as in *irregular/irrigate/irrelevant*.

Iran a republic in south-central Asia, pop. 32 million approx. (1973); capital, Tehran, pop. 3.5 million approx.; languages, Farsi (Persian), French and English; currency unit, the rial, divided into 100 dinars. Member, R.C.D.; Colombo Plan.

Iraq a republic in south-west Asia, pop. 10.5 million approx. (1973); capital, Baghdad, pop. 3 million approx.; language, Arabic; currency unit, the Iraqi dinar, divided into 1000 fils. Member, Arab League.

Ireland (Éire), a republic in northern Europe to the west of Great Britain, pop. 3 million approx. (1971); capital, Dublin, pop. 600,000 approx.; languages, Irish (Erse) and English; currency unit, the Irish pound (£) or punt, divided into 100 pence. Member, E.E.C.; O.E.C.D.

IRL Ireland's international vehicle-registration letters.

I.R.O. Inland Revenue Office.

iron (*colloq.*) money. *To have many irons in the fire*, to have interests in many business concerns.

ironmongery articles made of iron and other non-precious metals, such as tools, hinges, locks, knives and cooking pots sold by an *ironmonger*. *Syn.* ironware; hardware. *Pron.* -gri.

Iron Law of Wages *see* Subsistence Theory of Wages.

IRQ Iraq's international vehicle-registration letters.

irrecoverable that cannot be got back, such as business losses or certain expenses, e.g. freight. Of a debt, that will never be paid. *Syn.* non-recoverable.

irredeemable bond *see* annuity bond *under* bond, *n*.

irredeemable currency *see* inconvertible currency *under* currency.

irredeemable debenture *see under* debenture.

irredeemable money *see* inconvertible currency *under* currency.

irredeemable preference share *see under* share.

irredeemables STK. EXCH. in Britain, government and other loan stock such as debentures, for which there is no provision for a date for redemption (repayment). *Syn.* annuity bonds;

irredeemable bonds; irredeemable stock; irredeemable debentures; undated stock.

irredeemable stock *see* annuity bond *under* bond, *n.*

irrevocable (letter of) credit BKG. & COM. in foreign trade, a credit that cannot be called back, changed or cancelled after it has been opened. It may or may not be confirmed. *See* confirmed irrevocable credit. Cf. revocable credit.

irrigation AGR. the bringing, storing and supplying of water to grow crops in areas where the rainfall is either insufficient or too irregular for good cultivation. The two main types are: *annual* or *basin irrigation*, by which the waters of a river are led by canals to basins or compartments and thus to the crops only when the river is in flood; and *perennial irrigation* by which the water is caught by dams and is stored in artificial lakes, called reservoirs, from which it can be led by channels or pipes to the crops at all times of the year. As more dams and canals are built, and because they provide a regular supply of water, the area under perennial irrigation is being increased while that under annual irrigation is being reduced.

pump irrigation irrigation by using mechanical pumps to raise water from wells.

tank irrigation a method of irrigation much used in India and Sri Lanka, by which tanks or small artificial lakes are built. These catch water esp. during the rainy season and store it for use during the dry season.

well irrigation irrigation by digging wells deep enough to collect underground water, which is then raised by pumps and led by channels to the crops.

IS Iceland's international vehicle-registration letters.

iso- *prefix* equal in value.

isobar on a map, a line that joins places where the barometric pressure is the same, either at a particular time, or on average during a given period.

isobath on a map, a line joining places at the bottom of the sea that are at an equal depth below sea-level; a submarine contour.

isohyet on a map, a line joining places receiving an equal amount of rainfall.

isopleth on a map, a line joining places where the value of any particular measurable thing is the same; for example, isobars and isotherms are isopleths of pressure and temperature.

isotherm on a map, a line joining places having an equal temperature.

Israel a republic in south-west Asia, on the eastern shore of the Mediterranean Sea, pop. 3.3 million approx. (1973); languages, Hebrew and Arabic, with English also widely used; currency unit, the shekel (IS), divided into 100 new agorot (*sing.* agora).

iss. issue.

issue *v.* (1) to put forth, send out for use, esp. to the public: *To issue securities/debentures/banknotes/cheques/bills of exchange.* (2) to publish (to print for sale or distribution): *To issue a book/report/paper/notice/advertisement/information sheet/instructions/prospectus.* (3) to distribute food, clothing, tools, etc. esp. to workers or soldiers: *Protective clothing/uniforms/tools were issued to the men.*

n. (1) the act of putting forth, sending out for use, esp. to the public: *An issue of shares/debentures/postage stamps/notes.* (2) the act of publishing (printing for sale and distribution): *The date of issue. The first day of issue,* of a new postage stamp. *The office of issue,* of a postal order or passport. *Abbr.* iss.

issue broker STK. EXCH. a stockbroker or firm of stockbrokers actively supporting a company that is making a new issue of securities. *See* issue of securities.

issue by tender STK. EXCH. a method of making a new issue of shares or loan stock in a company through an issuing house by asking applicants to tender, i.e. to state a price that they are willing to pay. The highest bidder is allotted the shares or stock. (This method of issuing shares is not often used.) Cf. public issue; placing; offer for sale; introduction.

issued capital *see under* capital.

Issue Department BKG. one of the main departments of the Bank of England. *See* bank return.

issue house *see* issuing house.

issue of securities STK. EXCH. the practice of making a new issue of equity shares or loan stock in a company that has already been granted a Stock Exchange quotation, or of issuing existing capital of a private company which is in process of becoming a public company and is requesting a quotation. For the methods used to make new issues, *see* public issue *below*; offer for sale; placings; issue by tender; introduction.

bonus issue *see* scrip issue *below.*

junior issue an issue of shares or debenture that are lower in rank than other securitie issued by the same company. Thus ordinar shares come below preference shares for right to dividends or for repayment of capital if th company is wound up.

public issue a method of making a new issue c equities or loan stock in a company, by invitin the public, through advertisements in th newspapers, to apply for the number of share or the amount of stock that they wish to buy, a the price fixed by the company. Cf. offer fc sale; issue by tender; placings.

rights issue an offer by a company to its preser shareholders to participate in a new issue c shares in the company, thus giving these shar holders rights not enjoyed by other investors. (A shareholder is free to sell his rights in the new issue to some other person.) The new shares are offered in proportion to each shareholder's existing holding, and usu. at a specially low price.

scrip issue an issue of shares free of charge to existing shareholders, the shares being brought into existence by the capitalization of the company's reserves. *See* capitalization of reserves. *Syn.* bonus issue; capitalization issue.

issue price STK. EXCH. the price of a new issue of a security. For public issues and offers for sale of equities, the issue price is that given in the prospectus. For placings, it is the price fixed by the issue broker negotiating the sale of the issue to his clients. For issues by tender, it is the price bid by the highest tenderer.

issuing house *or* **issue house** BKG. & STK. EXCH. in Britain, a merchant bank or other financial concern that specializes in finding buyers for new shares, or other kinds of long-term capital issued by their customers. Sometimes the whole of a new issue of shares is allotted to, and paid for by, an issuing house which will then sell the shares to the public through an offer for sale. In this way the issuing company is sure that the whole of the issue will be sold. *See* underwriting. Issuing houses also act as advisers to governments, local authorities, public utilities and companies, on the best methods of raising long-term capital.

I.S.T. Indian Standard Time.

I.T. income tax.

i.t. in transit.

Italy a republic in southern Europe, on the northern coast of the Mediterranean Sea, pop. 55.5 million approx. (1974); capital, Rome, pop. 3 million approx.; language, Italian; currency unit, the lira (*pl.* lire), divided into 100 centesimi (*sing.* centesimo). Member, E.E.C.; O.E.C.D.; Council of Europe.

item (1) a single article or class of articles in a list, account, inventory, etc.

news item a separate piece of news in a newspaper or radio or television broadcast.
(2) COMP. a single unit of information stored in a computer, such as all necessary information about a particular employee included in a computerized pay-roll.

itemize to record or state things item by item; to write down every detail in a list. *To itemize an account. An itemized bill.*

itinerant travelling from place to place: *An itinerant salesman*, any dealer in goods who has no settled place of business but moves about selling his goods, such as a pedlar.

itinerary TOUR. a plan for travel from place to place, usu. with dates and times of arrival and departure and perh. other details such as hotel bookings, places of interest to visit, or names and addresses of persons to be seen.

I.V., i.v. invoice value.

Ivory Coast a republic in West Africa, pop. 4.7 million approx. (1973); capital, Abidjan, pop. 400,000 approx.; languages, French and tribal; currency unit, the C.F.A. franc (CFA Fr.), divided into 100 centimes. Member, O.A.U.; O.C.A.M.M.; Associate, E.E.C.

J

J. joule; judge; Justice.

J.A. joint account.

Jam. Jamaica.

Jamaica an island parliamentary democracy in the Caribbean Sea, pop. 2.2 million approx. (1973); capital, Kingston, pop. 600,000 approx.; language, English; currency unit, the Jamaican dollar (Jam $), divided into 100 cents. Member, (British) Commonwealth; O.A.S.

Jan. January.

j. & w.o. jettison and washing overboard.

janitor *see* caretaker.

Jap. Japan(ese).

Japan an island constitutional monarchy (kingdom) off east Asia, pop. 108 million approx. (1973); capital, Tokyo, pop. 11.5 million approx.; language, Japanese; currency unit, the yen, divided into 100 sen. Member, O.E.C.D.

Japanese Marine Corporation SHIPG. the Japanese organization for surveying and classifying ships. *Also* Nippon Kaiji Kyokai. *See* classification societies.

jargon (1) language, written or spoken, that is difficult or impossible for an ordinary person to understand because it is full of words known only to specialists: *The jargon of economists/ computer analysts/industry.* (2) language that uses words that are unnecessarily long and that is badly put together.

jd. joined.

jerque note SHIPG. a certificate given to the master of a ship by a customs officer called a jerquer, who has searched the ship and examined her papers and is satisfied that all cargo for that port has been properly entered and discharged (landed) and that all formalities in connection with the inward clearance have been completed. *Syn.* certificate of inward clearance; inward clearing bill.

jerry-built of a house, cheaply and badly built. A person or firm building such houses is called a *jerry-builder.*

jetsam SHIPG. & LAW (1) popularly, goods jettisoned from a ship and washed ashore. (2) in law, cargo that has been jettisoned and remains under water, not floating. Cf. flotsam.

jettison SHIPG. & MAR. INSCE. the act of throwing into the sea part of the cargo, etc. of a ship, in an attempt to save her when in great danger by making her lighter. *Syn.* cast away.

jetty SHIPG. & TRANSPT. (1) a breakwater. (2) a structure built out from the shore into the water to provide a landing-place for boats. *Syn.* pier.

Jevons William Stanley (1835–82), English economist, Professor of Political Economy at Manchester and later at London. In his *Theory of Political Economy* (1871), he put forward new thoughts on the theory of value and, with Walras and Menger, was among the first to think out and expand the idea of marginal utility. He was a member of the group known as the Austrian School of economists.

j.g. junior grade.

jitney (U.S.A. *colloq.*) (1) a car carrying passengers for a cheap fare. (2) a five-cent coin.

JJ. Justices. *See* justice (4).

jnc. junction.

Jnr. Junior.

job *n.* (1) a piece of work: *He is paid by the job*, he is paid a separate amount of money for each piece of work. *Odd jobs*, various small pieces of work needing little skill, done by an *odd-job man*. *Job lot*, a collection of different articles, apparently of little value, offered for sale together and usu. bought in the hope that it contains something valuable. *Jobbing work*, small orders that are paid for as soon as done; piecework. *A jobbing printer*, one who accepts small orders only. *A jobbing gardener*, one who works by the hour or day. (2) a position, a post, as an employee: *He has found a good job. She is out of/without a job*, unemployed. *Part-time job*, employment for less than the full working day or week. *Opp.* full-time job. *On the job*, working. *Syn.* billet; berth. (3) (*colloq.*) an act of dishonesty such as burglary, or robbery: *They were sent to prison for the job they did at/on the bank*, for robbing the bank. *An inside job*, theft done with the help of a person working in the place where the crime took place.

v. (1) to do small pieces of work; to accept and carry out small orders only. *To job off*, to get rid of slow-selling stock or unwanted material by selling it cheaply. *To job out*, to give out work to a number of workmen or contractors. (2) to carry on a business as a jobber, buying and selling commodities wholesale or securities on the Stock Exchange. *He is jobbing in the City*, he is a stockjobber on the Stock Exchange.

job analysis MAN. an examination of the work of an employee in detail to discover and record the processes, methods and operations by which he does the work, the tools, instruments and other apparatus he needs to do it, the working conditions, and the relation of his work to that of other workers in the factory or office. *Syn.* job study.

jobber a person who buys and sells.

commodity jobber COMMOD. EXCH. a wholesaler or middleman, esp. in the grain and meat trades, who buys in large quantities from importers and sells in smaller quantities to retail shopkeepers.

exchange jobber FIN. *see under* exchange.

a stockjobber STK. EXCH. a member of the Stock Exchange who deals in securities, buying for himself from, and selling to, brokers and other jobbers, stocks and shares of the particular class or classes in which he specializes. Jobbers are sometimes called dealers. They are not allowed to have direct dealings with the public but must always work through a broker. Cf. broker.

jobber's turn STK. EXCH. the profit made by a jobber, i.e. the difference between his buying or offer price and his selling or bid price. *Syn.* turn of the market.

jobbery the dishonest gaining of money by a public servant.

jobbing (shop) production IND. a system of production that usu. exists in small engineering workshops and other small factories where each order is for a different product, and the quantity to be produced is not large enough for batch production or mass production.

job centre in Britain, a government service with a branch called a job centre in most towns, which finds employment for those who are out of work; helps employers who want to employ workers; and arranges training in those trades in which there is a shortage of skilled workers. Job centres have replaced the former employment exchanges and labour exchanges.

job costing IND. & ACCTS. the process of allocating all costs to the job (piece of work) to which each item of cost relates.

job description MAN. a short account giving the title of the job and stating the work the particular employee is expected to do. Cf. job specification.

job evaluation MAN. finding out how much pay a job is worth. *Syn.* labour grading.

jobless without a job; unemployed.

job specification MAN. a careful and detailed description of the work that an employee is paid to do, the degree of skill, knowledge and experience needed to do it, and any personal qualities that are demanded for its successful performance. Cf. job description.

job study *see* job analysis.

John Company ECON. HIST. the (British) East India Company, 1600–1873.

joint *adj.* (1) shared by, belonging to, two or more persons: *Joint owners/proprietors/tenants of a business/property. A joint account.* (2) held by two or more persons: *A joint directorship.* *Abbr.* Jt.

n. (*colloq.*) a restaurant or night-club, esp. one with a bad reputation for dishonesty or immorality. *See* clip-joint.

joint account (1) BKG. a bank account existing in the names of two or more persons, often husband and wife. Any or all of them must have the power to operate the account, either alone or with the others. Partnership, executor and trustee accounts are special forms of joint accounts. *Abbr.* J.A. (2) STK. EXCH. *shares held on joint account,* shares owned by two or more persons or firms. (3) ACCTS. an account of the business dealings of a joint venture that is owned and financed by two or more persons or firms. *See* joint venture.

joint adventure *see* joint venture.

joint and several LAW words that are used to mean that when two or more persons sign a document promising jointly and severally to pay any money or to perform some action, they are all bound, both together as a group and separately as independent persons. A creditor has better rights in law when debtors or guarantors are jointly and severally liable than when they are only jointly liable. *Adv.* jointly and severally.

joint and several bond *see under* bond, *n.*

joint-and-survivorship annuity *see under* insurance policy.

joint annuity *see under* insurance policy.

joint demand *see* complementary demand *under* demand.

joint life (endowment) policy *see under* insurance policy.

joint managing director *see* managing director *under* director.

joint ownership LAW of land, the owning of freehold or leasehold land by two or more persons, called co-owners or joint tenants, each having rights in the whole of the land. Cf. ownership in common. Before 1926 in Britain, when one joint tenant died the whole of the property was owned by the joint tenants who survived (continued to live); and the land could be left to somebody by will only by the tenant who survived all the others. The law was then changed, and now all joint tenants have a right to a share in the money obtained from the sale of the property; and such rights can be given by will. *Syn.* joint tenancy; co-ownership.

joint-stock banks BKG. also called *commercial banks* and *deposit banks,* form the largest class in the whole banking system. They are profit-making concerns, usu. with many branch offices serving the ordinary banking needs of the public, and are either members of, or are associated with, the clearing-house system. (*See* clearing banks.) In Britain they include

the London clearing banks and their equivalents in Scotland and Northern Ireland, the National Giro, and the Banking Department of the Bank of England. Joint-stock banks accept customers' money on current account, deposit account and savings account. They pay and collect customers' cheques, deal in foreign money, move money from one place to another, deal with documentary credits, and advance credits in the form of overdrafts, short-term loans and personal loans, for all of which they charge interest. They offer a wide range of services including: paying customers' standing orders; operating the Bank Giro, the direct debiting and credit card systems; advising on, and buying and selling, securities for their customers; acting as executor and trustee; keeping customers' valuable possessions locked up in strong-rooms; arranging travel and insurance; making credit-status enquiries and giving bankers' opinions and references. Most of the larger British joint-stock banks have branch offices overseas. There are also a number of British overseas joint-stock banks most of whose branches are in other countries, and there are many commonwealth and foreign banks which have branches in Britain. The relationship between banker and customer is generally that of debtor and creditor, but in some matters, esp. the bank's action in collecting customers' cheques, the relationship is that of agent and principal. *Abbr.* J.S.B.

joint-stock company *see under* company.

joint supply *see* complementary supply *under* supply.

joint tenancy *see* joint ownership.

joint tenant *see* joint ownership.

joint tortfeasor *see* tortfeasor.

joint venture FIN. (1) a partnership, usu. temporary but sometimes becoming permanent, formed by two or more persons or companies co-operating in some special business activity in which there is some risk of loss, but a reasonable hope of profit. The parties in the venture share the costs and the profits in agreed proportions. This arrangement exists in banking, insurance and publishing. (2) the expression is also used for a company formed jointly by two or more other companies.

joint whole-life policy *see under* insurance policy.

jon the fractional currency unit of North Korea. 100 jon = 1 won.

JOR Jordan's international vehicle-registration letters.

Jordan a constitutional monarchy (kingdom) in south-west Asia, pop. 2.5 million approx. (1973); capital, Amman, pop. 500,000 approx.; language, Arabic; currency unit, the Jordanian dinar, divided into 1000 fils. Member, Arab League.

jouissance share *see under* share.

joule (J) the SI unit of energy, including work and quantity of heat.

journal (1) originally a daily newspaper, but nowadays it means any periodical from weeklies to monthlies and quarterlies. (2) a daily record of events or business deals, such as the general journal (*see* book-keeping). Of a ship, the log or logbook.

journalese the poor manner of writing of some journalists, containing many colloquial words, and expressions that are too often used, or used in a careless way; and often showing that the report or article has been too hastily written.

journalism the work or profession of a journalist.

journalist (1) a professional writer for newspapers and other journals. (2) a person employed in editing and producing newspapers, and periodicals.

journalize ACCTS. in book-keeping, to make an entry in the journal, esp. one correcting an earlier mistake, or recording a transfer from one ledger account to another, i.e. any entry that cannot be put into a book of prime entry.

journey order COM. an order given personally by a retailer to a manufacturer's sales representative when he visits the retailer's shop. In some cases the retailer buys the goods *on journey account*, paying the traveller when he makes his next visit. Some manufacturers allow an extra discount, called *journey discount* or *journey terms*, on such orders, to encourage the retailer to receive the traveller who, by persuasive talk, may succeed in selling him more goods.

journeyman (1) IND. a worker in a craft or trade who has served an apprenticeship and is qualified for employment at the journeyman's rate of pay; this rate is above that of an apprentice but below that of a master craftsman. (2) TRANSPT. (*colloq.*) in the taxi trade, a driver of a taxi belonging to his employer(s). Cf. master.

J.P. Justice of the Peace.

Jr. Junior.

J.S.B. joint-stock bank.

Jt. joint.

judge LAW a public officer (in Britain, appointed by the Crown) to decide cases, either civil or criminal, in the court of law of which he is president.

judge's order LAW an order made by a judge of the High Court or a county court, giving directions. *See* charging order; garnishee order.

judg(e)ment LAW (1) a decision made by a court of law in a civil case, or a sentence in a criminal case. (2) the speech made by a judge in which he gives his reasons for reaching his decision. (3) the document or certificate in which is recorded the decision made by a court of law.

judgment bond *see* appeal bond *under* bond, *n*.

judgment by default *see* default.

judgment creditor *see under* creditor.

judgment debt *see under* debt.

judgment debtor *see under* debtor.

judgment note FIN. a special kind of promissory note that gives the holder power to have judgment declared against the debtor in a court of law, if his promise to pay is not kept. This arrangement is intended to make a formal lawsuit unnecessary.

judicial LAW having to do with the administration of justice, esp. by judgments in courts of law; relating to a judge or magistrate; bearing the authority of a court: *Judicial precedent. Judicial separation.*

Judicial Committee of the House of Lords *see* House of Lords.

Judicial Committee of the Privy Council *see* Privy Council.

judicial precedent *see* case law.

judiciary LAW (1) the system of courts of law in a country. (2) the judges as a group of persons responsible for the administration of justice.

jug (*colloq.*) prison: *He is in jug. The thief was jugged for two years*, sent to prison.

Jugoslavia *see* Yugoslavia.

Jul. July.

jumble sale *see under* sale.

jump (1) STK. EXCH. to. move suddenly upward: *Share prices jumped.* (2) LAW *To jump one's bail*, to fail to keep one's promise to appear in court at the proper time. *See* bail; *also* bail bond *under* bond, *n*. (3) SHIPG. *To jump ship*, being a member of the crew, to leave a ship without permission.

Jun. June; Junior.

Junc. junction.

junction TRANSPT. (1) a place where two or more roads, railway lines, etc. meet, join or cross: *A road/railway junction.* (2) a railway station at a place where lines join: *Clapham Junction.* *Abbr.* Junc.; jnc.

jungle (1) uncultivated land covered thickly with wild trees, bushes or grass, esp. in hot countries. (2) STK. EXCH. (*a*) the Jungle, part of the Stock Exchange where West African securities are dealt in. (*b*) West African shares generally.

junior LAW (1) a barrister who is not a Queen's Counsel. (2) of legal rights, claims and mortgages, of lower rank to those that have higher preference, such as junior capital (ordinary shares). (3) MAN. a young clerk or other employee at the lowest rank, esp. an *office junior*, a young person learning office work while helping with simple duties in an office.

Junior the younger: *Thomas Jones Junior*, the son of Thomas Jones Senior. *Abbr.* Jnr.; Jr.; Jun.

junior capital *see under* capital.

junior insurance policy *see* child's deferred policy *under* insurance policy.

junior issue see under issue of securities.
junior partner see under partner.
junior share see ordinary share under share.
junk (1) SHIPG. a Chinese wooden sailing-ship having a flat bottom, a high stern (back part) and fan-shaped sails on two or three masts. (2) COM. a mixed variety of old or unwanted objects of little value, sold by a *junk dealer* in a *junk shop* or *junk yard*.
junking (U.S.A. *colloq.*) IND. getting rid of old, worn-out or unproductive machinery that has been replaced by newer and better machines. *V.* to junk.
jurisdiction LAW (1) the legal power of a court of law, or of a judge, to try a particular case. (*See* competence.) *This court has no jurisdiction in the matter.* (2) the limits of the area within which a court's orders and judgments can be put into force, called *territorial jurisdiction.* That of the High Court of Justice, in London, is limited to England and Wales.
juror LAW a person serving on a jury or who is one of a panel (list of persons) chosen to serve on juries. (*See* jury.) Every person owes a duty to serve on a jury unless excused because he is under 18 or over 65 years of age or for certain other reasons. Jury service is unpaid, but compensation for loss of earnings and travelling expenses may be claimed.
jury *adj.* SHIPG. temporary; replacing something lost or broken in a situation of great danger: *A jury mast/rudder. A jury-rigged ship*, a ship with temporary ropes, chains and other apparatus.
n. LAW in cases being tried in a court of law, a group of ordinary men and women, called jurors, usu. 12 in number, chosen by ballot and sworn to answer what they honestly believe to be the truth on questions of fact in accordance with the evidence put to them. In criminal cases in England, except when a person admits that he is guilty, all cases in the crown courts are tried before a jury who, guided by the judge, decides whether the accused person is guilty or not guilty. In certain civil lawsuits in the High Court, either party has the right to ask for the case to be tried before a jury, who may sometimes have to decide not only questions of fact but also the amount of any damages. In coroner's courts, *coroner's juries* of from seven to eleven persons, with the coroner's guidance, decide the facts under which a person met his death.
justice LAW (1) the quality of being just; moral rightness; fairness. (2) the administration of law, through a system of courts with magistrates and judges as presidents, who support rights and punish wrongs according to the law in force. (3) a judge or magistrate. (4) the title given to all judges of the High Court in Britain: *Mr Justice Smith*, and sometimes, esp. in law

reports, *abbr.* J. or *pl.* JJ. placed after the name: *Smith J.* or *Brown and Jones JJ.* (Judges of lower courts are given the title *Judge* placed before the name: *Judge Robinson.*) (5) the title given to a Justice of the Peace, *abbr.* J.P. placed after the name: *Mrs Mary Jones J.P.*
Justice, European Court of (E.E.C.) *see under* European.
Justice, International Court of *see under* International.
Justice of the Peace (J.P.) LAW in England, one of a number of unpaid magistrates, chosen from persons of good reputation and social position but without much legal training. They are appointed by the Crown to keep the peace in a certain district, mainly by administering justice in the lower courts, esp. the magistrates' or justices' courts, sometimes called Petty Sessions or police courts. J.P.s are helped by the Clerk of the Court who is a solicitor or barrister. *See* justice (5); magistrates' courts.
justices' court *see* magistrates' court.
'just' price *see under* price.
juvenile *adj.* relating to, intended for, young people: *Juvenile offenders*, children (under 14) and young persons (over 14 and under 17) who have broken the law. *Juvenile court*, a special court for trying children and young persons who have offended against the law or who are needing care and protection. *Juvenile labour*, children and young persons who work in shops and factories; in many countries their hours and conditions of work are strictly controlled by law. *Juvenile literature*, books and magazines written for the young.
Jy. July.

K

K the international vehicle-registration letter of Kampuchea.
K kelvin.
k kilo-.
kA kiloampere.
Kaffirs STK. EXCH. (1) shares in South African companies, esp. in gold mining. (2) *Kaffir market, Kaffir circus*, that part of the floor of the Stock Exchange where dealers in these shares are grouped.
Kaldor Nicholas, Lord Kaldor (1908–), British economist, born in Hungary; professor at Cambridge University. He has made important contributions to the economics of growth, esp. in his book *Capital Accumulation and Economic Growth* (1964). As adviser to British and other governments he has influenced public policy on managing the economy.
Kameralism *see* Cameralism.

Kampuchea (Cambodia), a republic in southeast Asia, pop. 7.6 million approx. (1973); capital, Phnom Penh, pop. 1.5 million approx.; languages, Khmer (Cambodian) and French; currency unit, the riel, divided into 100 sen. *Also* Khmer Republic.

Kan. Kansas, U.S.A.

kangaroo court IND. REL. an irregular court set up without legal authority by members of a trade union to judge other members accused of disobeying union rules.

Kangaroos STK. EXCH. (*colloq.*) shares in Australian companies, esp. in mining, land and tobacco.

karat *see* carat.

Katar *see* Qatar.

k.d., K.D. knocked down.

k.d.c., K.D.C. knocked down condition.

keel SHIPG. (1) the main part of the frame of a boat or ship, being a strong straight beam of steel, wood, etc. extending the full length of the bottom of the vessel and supporting the rest of the structure. (2) a barge or lighter used for carrying coal, esp. in the ports on the river Tyne in north-east England. (3) the weight of coal (about 21 tons) needed to fill such a barge.

keelage SHIPG. charges payable by a ship while it is in a harbour or port.

keelboat SHIPG. a lighter or barge used esp. in ports in western U.S.A.

keen COM. of prices, competitive, and therefore very low: *Our price is the keenest in town.*

keep *v.* (1) to own and manage for profit: *To keep a shop/an inn* as does *a shopkeeper/an innkeeper.* (2) to hold in stock for sale: *We do not keep shoe-polish.* (3) to make a continuous record in writing: *To keep books of account,* as does *a book-keeper. To keep a diary.* (4) to manage household affairs in a hotel or private house: *To keep house,* as does *a housekeeper.* (5) to own and support: *To keep a family/a horse/cattle.* (6) to earn sufficient money: *To keep out of debt. To keep one's head above water. To keep the wolf from the door.*
n. the cost of food, shelter and other necessities for living: *To earn one's keep. She works in return for her keep.*

keeper a person who keeps, owns, manages or supports. *See* keep, *v.* for examples.

keeping safe keeping, *see* safe custody.

keeping up with the Joneses (*colloq.*) trying always to have a standard of living as high as that of one's friends and neighbours. *See* demonstration effect.

keg *see* cask.

kelvin the basic SI unit of temperature. *Abbr.* K.

Ken. Kentucky, U.S.A.

Kennedy Round a series of meetings suggested in 1963 by the American President, John F. Kennedy, with the aim of removing hindrances to international trade. Under arrangements made by G.A.T.T., the meetings were held from 1964 to 1967 in Geneva, with over 50 countries taking part. The negotiations resulted in agreements for a general reduction in tariffs by 1972 of up to 50%, esp. on industrial products.

Kenya a republic in East Africa, pop. 12 million approx. (1973); capital, Nairobi, pop. 550,000 approx.; languages, Swahili, English and tribal; currency unit, the Kenyan shilling (KSh), divided into 100 cents. Member, O.A.U.; E.A.C.; Associate, E.E.C.

kerb broker STK. EXCH. a stock and share broker who is not a member of the Stock Exchange. *Syn.* kerb-stone broker.

kerb exchange *see* American Stock Exchange.

kerb market STK. EXCH. (1) an unofficial market in which securities are bought and sold after hours, i.e. after the Stock Exchange has closed for the day. (2) a market for securities that are not quoted or dealt in on the Stock Exchange. *Syn.* street market.

ketch SHIPG. a small two-masted, strongly-built sailing vessel used mainly for short coastal voyages.

keyboard *n.* (1) a set of keys or levers by which a typewriter and a typesetting machine are operated. (2) the keys or notes on a musical instrument such as a piano and accordion.
v. to work the keyboard of a machine.

key currency *see* international currency *under* currency.

keyed advertisement *see under* advertisement.

key industries IND. the chief or basic industries; those that are so important that, if they stopped production, many other industries, and the whole country, would suffer badly.

key money COM. a payment of premium, over and above the rent, that a new tenant may agree to pay to the owner of a property before being given the key and thus being allowed to enter and use it.

Keynes John Maynard, Lord Keynes (1883–1946), English economist. After lecturing at Cambridge under Alfred Marshall, editing the *Economic Journal* and being secretary of the Royal Economic Society, he joined the Treasury during the 1914–18 war. His book *The Economic Consequences of the Peace* (1919) described how he resigned when the allied countries at the Paris Peace Conference refused to adopt his advice on how Germany should be treated financially. Advanced study at Cambridge led to the writing of his *General Theory of Employment, Interest and Money* (1936). This book had far-reaching effects on world economic thought, called by some the Keynesian Revolution. During the Second World War he again worked in the Treasury and prepared the Keynes Plan for reorganizing the monetary system of the world; but this plan was replaced at the Bretton Woods Conference in 1944 by another setting up the International Monetary Fund and the World Bank. *See also* Keynesian Economics.

Keynesian Economics ECON. THEORY called by some the Keynesian Revolution or the New Economics, the entirely new explanation of the trade cycle and the ways of controlling it, presented in J.M. Keynes's book *General Theory of Employment, Interest and Money* (1936). He and his followers argued that: the government of any country has the power and the duty to keep employment always at the highest possible level; that this can be done by influencing the demand for goods and services by adjusting taxation and public spending; and that private investment can be influenced by monetary controls, esp. the level of interest rates and the quantity of money. Other important matters in Keynesian economic theory are: the national income; liquidity preference; and the levels of consumption and saving. *See also* Keynes, John Maynard.

K.F.A.E.D. Kuwait Fund for Arab Economic Development.

kg kilogram(me).

Khmer Republic *see* Kampuchea.

khoum the fractional currency unit of Mauretania. 5 khoums = 1 ouguiya.

kick (*colloq.*) dismissal: *To get the kick*, to be dismissed from employment. *Syn.* boot; push; sack.

kickback (U.S.A. *colloq.*) (1) money that is sometimes demanded secretly from a worker by a foreman, manager or employer. (This practice is, of course, unlawful.) (2) any money paid in order to receive a favour.

kil., kild. kilderkin.

kilderkin *see* cask.

kilo kilogram(me).

kilo- the *prefix* used in the metric system of SI units to mean one thousand: 1 kilogram = 1000 grams; 1 kilometre = 1000 metres; 1 kilovolt = 1000 volts; 1 kilowatt = 1000 watts.

kina the standard currency unit of Papua New Guinea, divided into 100 toeas.

kind *see* income in kind; payment in kind.

kingpin (*colloq.*) the most important person in a group of persons. *Mr Jones, the chairman, is the kingpin of the company. Young Smith is the kingpin of our sales team.*

king-size COM. an extra large size (esp. of cigarettes).

king's shilling ECON. HIST. *To take the king's shilling*, to join the (British) army (from the shilling (5p) coin given to a newly-joined soldier in the nineteenth century). It became the *queen's shilling* when the monarch was a queen.

kiosk a small hut with one or more sides open when used for selling newspapers, tobacco,

ice-cream, sweets, etc. *Telephone kiosk, see* call-box.

kip the standard currency unit of Laos, divided into 100 at.

kit (1) a traveller's clothes and personal property carried with him in his luggage or baggage. (2) a set of tools: *A tool kit is supplied free with a new car.* (3) a complete set of materials and parts, sometimes with tools also, needed to make something, such as a toy, a piece of furniture, or a machine.

kite (1) BKG. (*colloq.*) a worthless cheque or accommodation bill of exchange. *Kite-flying*, a dishonest trick practised on banks: an accommodation bill (*see under* bill of exchange) is drawn on a person and is quickly discounted at the bank; it is then found that the person on whom the bill was drawn fails to honour it because he has received no consideration (goods or money in return). *Syn.* kiting. (2) TRANSPT. (*colloq.*) an aircraft.

kite-mark IND. & COM. a mark, in the form of a kite, placed by manufacturers on goods approved by the British Standards Institution.

kiting BKG. (*colloq.*) kite-flying, *see* kite.

kitty (1) money collected from each of a group of persons to be held and used later for an agreed common purpose, such as a pleasure trip to the seaside or the theatre or a supply of good food for a feast day. *Syn.* pool. (2) money collected from each of a group of persons at the beginning of a game, to be given to the winner(s). *Syn.* stake-money. (3) generally, any money that has been accumulated, such as personal savings. (4) the general state of a person's or organization's finances: *He has plenty in the kitty. The club has very little in the kitty*, has very little capital to spend.

km kilometre.

Kiwi (*colloq.*) a New Zealander (the name of the flightless bird which is used as a national emblem (sign)).

knock down at an auction sale, the action of the auctioneer in knocking his table with a small hammer to declare that an article has been sold to the last bidder.

knock-down price a very low price, esp. one reduced (knocked down) from a much higher price.

knocked down condition *see* completely knocked down. *Abbr.* k.d.c.; K.D.C.

knock-for-knock agreement INSCE. an agreement among a group of insurers, esp. of motor vehicles, that each insurer in the group bears his own loss by paying the claim of his own policy holders whatever their liability, instead of going to the trouble and expense of making claims against, and settling the claims of, other insurers' policy holders.

knocking copy ADVTG. any wording in an advertisement that is critical of a rival product.

knock off (1) (*colloq.*) to stop work for the day: *We knock off at five o'clock.* (2) to deduct; to make a simple price by deducting something: *We shall knock off the pence.* (3) (*colloq.*) to steal.

knock-out agreement COM. a secret (an illegal) agreement by a group of dealers at an auction sale not to bid against each other, so that an article may be sold to one of them at an unfairly low price. *See* bidders' ring.

knock-out price *see under* price.

knot SHIPG. (1) incorrectly, a sea mile of 6080 ft in English-speaking countries. *Syn.* nautical mile; geographical mile. Cf. statute mile. (2) correctly, a unit of speed of one sea (or nautical) mile per hour used in navigation (fixing a ship's position and course).

know-how (*colloq.*) special knowledge or skill; knowing how to do something difficult, esp. in planning and starting something new, such as a new process, or new machinery; or in overcoming some difficulty, such as stopping a fire in an oil-well. *Syn.* expertise; expertness.

kobo the fractional currency unit of Nigeria. 100 kobo = 1 naira.

kopeck *see* copeck.

Korea *see* North Korea; South Korea.

koruna the standard currency unit of Czechoslovakia, divided into 100 haleru. *Pl.* koruny; korun. *Syn.* crown.

kr. krona, *pl.* kronor (Sweden); krona, *pl.* kronur (Iceland); krone, *pl.* kroner (Denmark and Norway).

Kraft COM. a kind of strong paper much used by shopkeepers for packing parcels.

krona the standard currency unit of Sweden, divided into 100 örer. *Pl.* kronor. *Abbr.* kr. *Also* of Iceland, divided into 100 aurar. *Pl.* kronur. *Syn.* crown. *Abbr.* kr.

krone the standard currency unit of Denmark and of Norway, divided into 100 örer. *Pl.* kroner. *Syn.* crown. *Abbr.* kr.

krugerrand FIN. an unofficial coin containing one ounce of pure gold, issued in the Republic of South Africa by the Chamber of Mines, but never used as currency. Krugerrands are bought in those countries where the public may not buy gold bullion (bars) but may buy gold coins. There is a good demand for them from persons wishing to possess gold as a hedge (protection) against inflation. Their market price varies with the price of gold.

kurus the fractional currency unit of Turkey. 100 kurus = 1 Turkish lira. *Syn.* Turkish piastre.

Kuwait a constitutional emirate at the head of the Arabian Gulf, pop. 1.1 million approx. (1977); capital, Kuwait City, pop. 350,000 approx.; language, Arabic; currency unit, the Kuwaiti dinar, divided into 1000 fils. Member, Arab League.

Kuwait Fund for Arab Economic Develop- ment (K.F.A.E.D.) an organization set up in 1961 to use oil revenues to improve social conditions, esp. in countries of the Arab world. Generally known as the Kuwait Fund, it is also doing much by providing technical and financial help in the developing non-Arab countries of Africa. Cf. Arab Bank for Economic Development in Africa (A.B.E.D.A.).

kV kilovolt.

kVA kilovolt-ampere.

kW kilowatt.

kwacha the standard currency unit of Malawi, divided into 100 tambala. *Also* of Zambia, divided into 100 ngwee.

kWh kilowatt-hour.

KWT Kuwait's international vehicle-registration letters.

Ky. Kentucky, U.S.A.

kyat (1) the standard currency unit of Burma, divided into 100 pyas. (2) a Burmese unit of weight. 16.33 g = 0.564 oz. avoir.

L

£ sign for the pound sterling.

L Luxemburg's international vehicle-registration letters; the Roman numeral for 50.

L£ Lebanese pound(s).

La. Louisiana, U.S.A.

Lab. Labrador, Canada.

labor (U.S.A.) *see* labour.

laboratory *see* language laboratory.

labor union (U.S.A.) IND. REL. a trade union.

labour (1) work, esp. human work needing the use of strength of body or skill and effort of mind, usu. done for gain: *It is the hope of reward that sweetens labour.* (2) the whole class of persons who work for their living: *The organization of labour.* See organized labour. (3) ECON. THEORY one of the main factors of production, the human energy and mental skill and judgment applied in producing economic goods. The return to, or price of, labour is called *wages* and depends on supply and demand. The supply of labour is affected by the size of the population, its geographical distribution, its level of education and training, its organization, and its composition by age and sex. The demand for labour is a 'derived demand', needed only for the products it produces; and the employer will employ more labour until he reaches the point where the cost of employing one more worker will just equal the amount of revenue that the worker will bring in, i.e. when the marginal revenue equals the marginal cost.

casual labour *see* casual (2).

contract labour *see* indentured labour *under* indentured.

direct labour *see under* direct.

indentured labour *see under* indentured.

indirect labour *see* indirect.

labour, division of *see under* division.

labourer an unskilled worker, esp. one doing outdoor work that needs strength rather than skill or training: *An agricultural/builder's labourer. A day labourer*, one employed and paid by the day.

Labourers, Statute of ECON. HIST. a law passed by the English Parliament in 1351 in an attempt to stop the sharp rise in wages and prices caused by the shortage of labour that followed the Black Death (1347–50), a terrible illness that killed more than a third of the population of Europe.

labour exchange *see* job centre.

labour, fluidity of *see* mobility of labour.

labour force *see* manpower.

labour grading *see* job evaluation.

labour-intensive IND. of an industry, needing a large amount of labour per unit of output, i.e. one in which wages form a high proportion of the costs of production.

labour market *see under* market.

labour, mobility of *see under* mobility.

labour relations *see* industrial relations.

Labour Theory of Value ECON. THEORY the idea argued by the English economists Adam Smith (1723–90) and David Ricardo (1772–1823) and later developed by Karl Marx (1818–83), that the value of a good is equal to the cost, in wages, of all the labour used in producing it. Many economists have pointed out that this theory takes no note of the part played by other factors of production, such as land and capital, or of the cost of using these factors — rent and interest; nor does the theory consider the effect of variations in the productivity of workers. *Syn.* Labour Value Theory. Cf. Cost of Production Theory of Value.

lac *see* lakh.

laches LAW neglect or unreasonable delay in claiming the remedy of a legal wrong. The law demands that the owner of a right shall take action to protect the right within a reasonable time of being wronged; and states that if he does not, and without complaining allows himself to be wronged over a long period, he will get no remedy in a court of law.

laden (1) TRANSPT. loaded: *Laden weight*, weight (of a vehicle) when fully loaded. *Opp.* unladen. (2) SHIPG. *Laden draught, see under* draught. *Laden in bulk*, (of a ship) loaded with a cargo that is loose, not placed in any kind of containers.

lading *n.* (1) SHIPG. & TRANSPT. (the act of) loading: *The lading of a ship*.

lading port *adj.* the port at which a ship loads her cargo, as opposed to the discharge port, where she unloads it.

(2) a load or cargo; freight. *See* bill of lading *under* bill.

Lady Day *see* quarter-day.

L.A.F.T.A. Latin-American Free Trade Association.

lagan SHIPG. goods lost or thrown overboard that have sunk to the bottom but are marked, e.g. by a buoy, to help to find them. *Also* lagin *or* ligan.

laid up (1) TRANSPT. & SHIPG. taken out of use and stored until needed to be used again: *Three of our ships are laid up. Abbr.* l/u. (2) (*colloq.*) of a person, ill and unable to work: *To be laid up with influenza*.

laissez-faire ECON. THEORY *French*, allow to do, i.e. 'leave people free to act as they wish'. The words express the strong belief that the economy is best left alone and that the best results are obtained when each person is free to act as he wishes. This policy of non-interference by the State in economic affairs was supported by various groups of economists from the mid-eighteenth-century Physiocrats in France and the Classical School from Adam Smith and John Stuart Mill onwards to the Cambridge School under Alfred Marshall. By the end of the nineteenth century, most supporters of the policy came to accept the need for some degree of government control, but many still believe that such control should be as little as possible. *Also* laisser-faire.

lakers SHIPG. ships employed in carrying cargoes on the Great Lakes and connected canals and waterways of Canada and U.S.A.

lakh in the Indian subcontinent, one hundred thousand, usu. of rupees, written Rs 1,00,000; one hundred lakhs make a crore, i.e. ten million rupees, written Rs 1,00,00,000. *Also* lac.

lame duck (1) FIN. & IND. (*colloq.*) a popular British expression for inefficient, unprofitable producers who cannot continue in business without help from the government. (2) (U.S.A. *colloq.*) a high official who, because he is soon to retire or be replaced, no longer has enough authority to act effectively. (3) STK. EXCH. a member of the Stock Exchange who will soon be hammered because he cannot pay his debts. *See* hammer, *v.* (1).

Lammas *see* quarter-day.

Lancs. Lancashire, England.

land *n.* (1) ECON. THEORY one of the factors of production, called 'natural resources', being the gifts of Nature in the form of useful materials of all kinds in or on the earth, including surface space, soil, rocks, minerals, water, winds and weather. The return to, or price of, land is called rent, and depends on supply and demand. The supply of land is relatively limited and cannot easily be increased to meet an increase in demand. Land itself has no cost of production, so that its earnings, rent, depend on the degree of scarcity and on the demand for it. (2) LAW any part of the earth that can be possessed as property, and any interest in a part of the earth, such as mining rights.

landed *adj. Landed property. Landed gentry*, a class of persons owning land.
v. (1) to put persons or goods on to the land: *The ship has landed her passengers and cargo.* (2) of aircraft, to come down to the earth's surface: *The plane landed at Cairo.* (3) (*colloq.*) to obtain; to gain: *He has landed a good job/a big order/a contract/the first prize.* (4) *To be landed with*, to become responsible for carrying a burden such as an unprofitable asset or somebody else's debts: *The merger has landed us with some unsaleable stock. His father's death has landed him with heavy debts to settle.*

land agent COM. (1) an agent who acts for buyers and sellers of land. *Syn.* estate agent. (2) a manager employed by the owner of a large estate to let farms and houses, to collect rents, to keep accounts, and generally to make the estate as profitable as possible. *Syn.* estate manager; steward.

land bank *see* agricultural bank.

Land Certificate *see* title-deeds *under* deed.

Land Charges Registry in Britain, a government office responsible for recording all charges such as mortgages, on land to which the title is *unregistered*, i.e. not yet recorded at the Land Registry. Cf. register of charges.

landed cost *see under* cost.

landfall TRANSPT. & SHIPG. (1) the first sight of land after a sea or air voyage. (2) the place on the coast which is first seen from the sea or air.

landing *see* disembarkation.

landing card SHIPG. & TRANSPT. a card given to passengers who have satisfied customs and other formalities and therefore have permission to land from a ship or plane. Cf. boarding card.

landing charges COM. charges that have to be paid when cargo is landed at the port of destination.

landing craft SHIPG. a special vessel with a flat bottom and a front part that can be lowered to let men and vehicles land on a beach.

landing order *see* warehousing entry *under* customs entry.

landing stage SHIPG. a wharf, pier or jetty where people may land on the shore from boats or ships.

landlady COM. (1) a woman who keeps an inn or a boarding house or lets rooms in her house to one or more lodgers. (2) the wife of an innkeeper, *see* landlord (3).

landless COM. esp. of poor farmers, not owning any land; having to cultivate land owned by others.

landlord (1) a landowner. (2) LAW the owner of a property who allows a tenant to use his land or

house in return for payment of rent, usu. as stated formally in the lease. (3) COM. an innkeeper. *Fem.* landlady.

ground landlord the owner of land which has been leased to a person for a fixed period (usu. 99 years) on condition that he builds a house or other things on the land. *See* ground rent *under* rent.

landlord and tenant LAW a branch of the law that deals with the rights and duties of landlords, the owners of property, and tenants, who lease property from them in return for payment of rent.

land, marginal *see* marginal land.

Land Registry LAW in Britain, a government department responsible for recording information about all property in England and Wales that has a registered title, i.e. is in an area of the country in which changes of ownership in land must be registered. These areas are being gradually extended. Information about each property is recorded in its own register, which consists of three parts: a *charges register*, a *property register*, and a *proprietorship register*. (*See* all these.) Cf. Land Charges Registry.

Lands Tribunal LAW in Britain, a special court with power to determine what compensation shall be paid to owners of land that has been taken for public use, called *compulsory purchase*, if the question cannot be settled by negotiation.

land tax *see under* tax.

language a system of words by which human beings speak or write to each other: *To learn a foreign language. See also* mother tongue; pidgin.

computer language *see* machine language *below*.

indigenous language the language of the people who are descended from the original native people of a region.

language of instruction the language used in the schools and universities of a country. *Syn.* medium of instruction.

machine language one of the special systems of letters, numbers and signs adopted by computer programmers to give instructions to the computer on the exact details of the operations it is to perform. *See* Algol; Cobol; Fortran. *Syn.* computer language; programming language.

native language *see* mother tongue.

official language the language used by the government of a country in its law-making councils, law courts and public offices.

programming language *see* machine language *above*.

second language a language which a person has learnt and can use in addition to his mother tongue. Here second means extra, for a person may have several second languages, e.g. a person who lives in Beirut, whose mother tongue is Arabic, may well have English and French as second languages.

world language a language used very widely in the world, e.g. English, French.

language laboratory a room provided with special sound-recording apparatus for teaching foreign languages.

LAO Laos's international vehicle-registration letters.

Laos a republic in south-east Asia, pop. 3.3 million approx. (1975); capital, Vientiane, pop. 180,000 approx.; language, Lao (Laotian); currency unit, the kip, divided into 100 at.

lapse INSCE. an insurance contract which has not been renewed and is no longer effective. *Syn.* lapsed policy.

lapse of time LAW one of the several ways by which a contract may be discharged (come to an end), esp. if the contract is for a stated period and that period has passed. If there is delay by both parties in performing the contract it may be ended by common agreement. If one of the conditions of the contract is that 'time is of the essence', i.e. that the time of performance is essentially important, the contract is not ended by the failure of the party to perform the condition and he remains liable. In Britain, lapse of time may, under the Limitation Acts, make a contract unenforceable, i.e. impossible for a court of law to support, and it becomes statute barred.

L.A.P.T. London Association for the Protection of Trade.

larboard SHIPG. the old word for port, the left-hand side of a ship when facing forward. *Opp.* starboard.

larceny LAW the offence of stealing. *See* theft.

large-scale (1) in an intensive manner: *Large-scale production*, producing a commodity in large quantities, needing the employment of many workers and use of large amounts of capital. (2) of a map, drawn to a large scale, i.e. a unit of length on the map represents relatively few of the same units on the ground.

lascar SHIPG. an Asian seaman, esp. one from India or Pakistan.

last (1) a unit of volume used for measuring corn, 640 gallons = 2909. 5 litres. *See* corn and dry measure *table on page 477.* (2) a unit of weight used for measuring wool, 12 sacks of 364 lb = 4368 lb (1981.3 kg). (3) ship's cargo.

lastage SHIPG. the cargo-space in a ship.

last in, first out (L.I.F.O.) ACCTS. & FIN. a method of valuing stocks by valuing them all at the cost of the newest items received into stock, in the belief that items received last were sold first. In time of rising prices, L.I.F.O. reduces profits compared with the F.I.F.O. method. Cf. first in, first out (F.I.F.O.).

last-survivor policy *see under* insurance policy.

lat. latitude.

lateral filing *see under* filing system.

lateral integration *see* horizontal integration *under* integration.

Latin American Free Trade Association (L.A.F.T.A.) a regional organization formed in 1961 by Argentina, Brazil, Chile, Colombia, Ecuador, Mexico, Paraguay, Peru, Uruguay and Venezuela. It aims to encourage trade between its members and to set up a Latin American Common Market at a later stage; and tariffs have been partially reduced. In 1969 a new group, the Andean Pact, was set up by several of the member countries.

latitude the distance of a place north or south of the equator, measured in degrees, minutes and seconds, e.g. 51° 07′ 40″ (Dover), of an angle at the centre of the earth. Thus, the equator is lat. 0°; the North Pole lat. 90°N; the South Pole lat. 90°S. *High latitudes* are those near the poles, *low latitudes* are those near the equator, and *mid-latitudes*, those between. *Parallels of latitude* are lines drawn on a map through points or places of equal latitude. These lines are of course parallel with the equator. *See also* horse latitudes. Cf. longitude. *Abbr.* lat.

launch *n.* SHIPG. a small passenger vessel with an engine, used for short journeys on rivers or in harbours: *A motor launch.*
v. (1) SHIPG. to float a newly-built ship. (2) STK. EXCH. to start a new company. (3) COM. & ADVTG. to put a new product on the market.

launderette a room, usu. in a retail shopping centre, in which the public can use coin-operated machines for washing, drying (and sometimes also dry-cleaning) clothes. *Syn.* washeteria; (U.S.A.) laundromat.

laundry (1) a room or building provided with machinery and apparatus for washing and ironing clothes. (2) clothes that need to be, or have just been, washed and ironed.

law LAW (1) a rule of correct behaviour, made by the government or law-making body of a country, that must be obeyed by every member of society. These rules are kept in force by the power of the courts and certain other authorities to order offenders to be punished: *The law of copyright/theft. International law.* (2) the whole body or system of accepted rules and basic ideas that guide the State and its officials in administering justice: *Common law. The law of equity.* (3) the profession of those persons trained in the accepted rules of public behaviour and the administration of justice: *He has chosen the law as a career.* (4) (*colloq.*) the police, a policeman: *Here comes the law,* a policeman. *The arm of the law,* the police. *See also* by-law.

lawful LAW (1) allowed by law; that does not go against the law: *It is lawful to sell food on a Sunday. Stealing is not lawful. Opp.* unlawful;

illegal. (2) having a right or rights given by law: *He is my lawful heir. She is my lawful wife. I am the lawful owner of my house.* Cf. legal.

lawful money *see under* money.

law merchant *see* commercial law.

law of nations *see* international law.

law of property *see* property, law of.

laws, conflict of *see* international law.

Law Society LAW in England and Wales, the professional organization, based in London, that controls all practising solicitors (but not barristers). It has legal power and responsibility for the training, examining and admission of new entrants to the profession, for keeping a roll or list of working solicitors; for seeing that they work to very high standards of honesty and discipline; and for performing certain other services for the profession and the public such as administering the Legal Aid Scheme.

lawsuit LAW (1) the making of a claim in a court of law. (2) any civil action in a law court.

lawyer LAW a professional person, trained in the law and authorized to advise clients on legal business and to represent them in courts of law. In England and Wales, lawyers are either barristers-at-law (also called counsel) or solicitors. In Scotland, lawyers are either advocates or writers. In the U.S.A., lawyers are either counsellors or attorneys-at-law.

lay days SHIPG. the number of days allowed in the charter-party for the loading and unloading of the ship. *See* demurrage; despatch money. *Syn.* lay time.

lay off IND. *To lay off workers*, temporarily to stop employing them, usu. because there is no work for them to do.

lay out (1) *To lay out money*, to spend money, esp. large sums according to a plan or system: *The company has laid out £1 million on research.* (2) *To lay out goods*, to place them on show so that they are easily seen.

layout (1) ADVTG. the arrangement of words, pictures, etc. in printed matter. A diagram showing this. (2) IND. of a factory, offices, etc., the way the building and its contents are arranged. A drawing or diagram showing this.

lay time *see* lay days.

lay up *see* laid up.

lazaret SHIPG. (1) a building in a port, set apart for goods needing fumigation, i.e. treatment by smoke or gas to destroy the causes of disease and kill harmful insects. (2) a space in a ship set aside for persons who are being kept in quarantine. *Also* lazaretto.

lb pound (weight), pounds.

L.C., L/C, l.c., l/c, lc. letter of credit.

l.c. lower case (small letters, not capitals).

L.C.C. London Chamber of Commerce; London County Council.

L.D. London Docks.

Ld. Limited.

ldg. loading, landing.

lds. loads.

Le leone.

leadage IND. & TRANSPT. (1) the distance that coal has to be carried from a mine to the nearest railway or port. (2) the cost per ton of carrying the coal over this distance.

leader (1) STK. EXCH. a leading stock or share; a security that is usu. bought and sold in larger numbers than are other securities. (2) COM. an article or commodity that a shopkeeper sells mainly to attract customers and to tempt them to buy other goods.

loss-leader a leader that is sold below its cost.

leading indicator *see* business barometer; economic indicator.

lead time (1) IND. time needed to obtain supplies, from the date of placing an order until the date that delivery can be expected. *Syn.* delivery time. (2) MKTG. time needed to encourage a consumer to take a decision to purchase.

leaflet a single sheet of printed paper, sometimes folded to form several pages, containing matter either advertising a product or giving directions on how to use it. Cf. brochure.

leakage COM. (1) an escape of liquid from a container. (2) an allowance made for natural loss in the quantity of a liquid, by various causes such as evaporation. *Abbr.* lkge.

leap year *see under* year.

lease LAW an agreement in writing by which one person gives another the right to use property, usu. for a fixed number of years, in return for either a single sum of money called a premium or a series of regular payments called rent. The person giving the lease is called *the lessor*, the person to whom it is given is *the lessee* or *tenant. Syn.* tenancy. *To grant a lease*, to give (a person) a lease. *To take a lease*, to become the lessee (of a property). *To take on lease*, to arrange to have the use (of property) by paying a premium or rent. *See* let, *v*.

building lease a lease of land which binds the lessee to build certain stated buildings, to keep them in good repair during the period of the lease, usu. 99 years, and to pay a stated rent (called ground rent). At the end of this time the buildings belong to the lessor.

derivative lease *see* under-lease *below*.

head-lease a lease given by an original lessor who is the freeholder of the property, as distinguished from an under-lease.

long lease in Britain, under the Companies Acts, a lease that has at least 50 years left before it ends. Cf. short lease.

occupational lease a lease that allows the lessee to occupy (live in or take possession of) the property as a tenant for a stated number of years.

repairing lease one in which the tenant must pay for repairs.

short lease a lease that has less than 50 years left before it ends. Cf. long lease.

sub-lease see under-lease below.

under-lease a lease that is given by a person who is already the lessee of the property under a head-lease. Syn. sub-lease; derivative lease.

lease-back FIN. a practice adopted by an owner of property to obtain cash for use as capital. He sells the property on condition that he can lease it back at an agreed rent for a fixed number of years.

leasehold n. LAW the right, given in a lease to a person called the leaseholder or lessee or tenant, to own and use land and buildings for a stated period in return for payment of a premium or rent. See leasehold estate under estate.

adj. (of land and buildings) held on lease. Cf. freehold.

leasehold mortgage see under mortgage.

leasehold property see under property.

leave (1) permission to be absent from work: To give/grant/allow an employee leave of absence. To overstay one's leave, to fail to return promptly at the end of a period of leave. To be absent without leave. (2) a holiday: To go on/be on leave. Our employees get three weeks' annual leave. He works in Singapore and gets six weeks' home leave, so that he can visit his home country.

annual leave days of leave with pay that an employee has the right to take each year by law or under his contract of service, esp. for a rest from work or for a holiday. Syn. privilege leave; paid leave; paid holiday; holiday with pay.

casual leave extra days of leave with pay that some employees have the right to take, i.e. above their annual leave, in order to deal with unexpected happenings such as attendance at marriages, burials and similar ceremonies.

compassionate leave days of leave with pay that are allowed by an employer as an act of kindness or pity for an employee who has suffered some serious misfortune, such as the loss of his home by fire or flood, or the serious illness of his wife or family. Such leave is usu. extra to annual or casual leave.

privilege leave see annual leave above.

sabbatical leave a period of leave, with or without pay, allowed to some teachers for study, research, or travel. Such leave is often for periods as long as one year, known as a sabbatical year.

sick leave days of leave with pay that an employee has the right to take if he is too ill to work. Under the law of some countries or under the employee's contract of service, leave on full pay is allowed for up to a fixed period, e.g. 30 days in any one year; after that, sick leave on half pay is allowed for up to a further

period, e.g. 30 more days; and beyond this, sick leave without pay may be allowed.

leave and licence see licensee (2).

Lebanon a republic in south-west Asia on the eastern shore of the Mediterranean Sea, pop. 2.5 million approx. (1975); capital, Beirut, pop. 550,000 approx.; languages, Arabic, French, English; currency unit, the Lebanese pound (L£), divided into 100 piastres. Member, Arab League.

ledger ACCTS. in double-entry book-keeping, one of a set of main account books, or books of final entry. In the ledgers, the debits and credits of all business dealings of a particular organization are recorded. (See double entry; accounts n. pl.) A set of ledgers has two parts: the first contains the real and nominal accounts and is called the impersonal ledger or general ledger or nominal ledger; the other contains the personal accounts and is called the personal ledger. The personal ledger is itself divided into two parts: the first contains the accounts of suppliers and is called the bought ledger or purchases ledger; the other contains the accounts of customers and is called the sales ledger or customers' ledger. The cash book is also a ledger combining the cash account and the bank account. Ledgers were formerly kept as bound books but are now usu. loose-leaf or on special cards for use with book-keeping machines. See also self-balancing ledgers.

ledger account see accounts, n. pl.

ledger clerk ACCTS. an employee in the accounts department whose work is to enter items in the ledger accounts.

ledger fees see bank charges.

lee, leeward SHIPG. on the side of the ship that is away from the wind and is therefore the more sheltered side. A lee shore, a shore towards which the wind blows from the sea, and therefore dangerous to nearby ships in a storm. A lee tide is a tide flowing in the same direction as the wind. Opp. windward; weather.

left-luggage office see cloakroom.

left out see short shipment.

leg. legal.

legacy LAW personal property given by a person under his will, including leaseholds (but not freeholds), money, securities, furniture, etc. See legatee.

demonstrative legacy a legacy of money that must be paid only out of a particular fund in the estate.

general legacy a legacy usu. of money, that can be paid only out of the general assets of the estate, and not from any particular fund.

residuary legacy a legacy consisting of all the assets in an estate that remain after specific legacies have been settled. Such a legacy may be shared out in stated proportions among two or more legatees, called residuary legatees.

specific legacy a legacy that must be paid out of a stated part of the assets of the estate.

legal *adj.* (1) concerning or connected with the law: *A legal action/opinion. The legal profession.* (2) allowed by, or according to, the law; lawful: *It is legal to possess gold coins but not bullion (bars). Opp.* illegal. *Adv.* legally.

legal access *see* access (2).

legal action *see* action.

legal advice LAW the written or spoken opinion of a lawyer about a client's legal rights and duties or about the action he should take in a legal matter.

legal aid LAW in Britain, a government scheme by which a person with little money gets help from the State towards the cost of legal expenses. This help is intended to make it possible for anyone accused of a crime to be represented in a court by a lawyer; and also to help a person to bring or to defend an action in a civil court.

legal assets *see* assets (2).

legal capacity *see* capacity to contract.

legal charge *sing.* LAW a mortgage.

legal charges *pl.* LAW the charges made by a solicitor for his professional services to his client.

legal day LAW a full day lasting until midnight. Thus, if a debt has to be paid on a certain day, the debtor has until midnight on that day in which to pay; and he cannot be held to be a defaulter unless that hour has passed without his having paid.

legal estate LAW the ownership of an interest in land, either as a freehold or as a leasehold.

legal investments (U.S.A.) FIN. & LAW trustee securities.

legalize *v.* LAW to make legal, lawful: *Certain local lotteries have been legalized by the Gaming Act. N.* legalization.

legal monopoly *see under* monopoly.

legal mortgage *see under* mortgage.

legal person LAW a person or group of persons recognized by law as having a separate legal existence with his or its own rights and duties. A legal person is either a *natural person*, i.e. a human being, or an *artificial person*, i.e. a corporation. *See* artificial person.

legal remedy *see* remedy.

legal right *see under* right.

legal tender FIN. & COM. that form of money in which a person has a right by law to pay a debt, and which the creditor must by law accept in settlement of the debt. In Britain, Bank of England notes have *unlimited legal tender*, i.e. must be accepted as payment of debts up to any amount. Coins, however, have only *limited legal tender*; a creditor is bound to accept, in one payment, bronze coins (½p, 1p, 2p) only up to a total of 20p, silver and cupro-nickel 5p and 10p coins up to £5, and 50p coins up to £10.

legatee LAW a person who receives a legacy, i.e. a gift of personal property by the will of a person who has died. The person who receives all the property that is left after all the legatees have received their legacies is called the *residuary legatee.*

legation (1) a group of persons, headed by a minister, sent to represent the government of one country in another country. (2) the office or building in which they work. *The British Legation.*

legislation LAW (1) the act of making laws. (2) laws, esp. statute laws, i.e. Acts of Parliament in Britain, Acts of Congress in U.S.A., etc.

lei *see* leu.

Leics. Leicestershire, England.

leisure (1) ECON. THEORY time spent not working, but in enjoyment, amusement, and personal interests. Since leisure is part of a worker's standard of living, it is an economic good. When his wages are increased he may decide to work fewer hours in order to have more time to spend on leisure, i.e. he shows a marginal preference for leisure.

leisure industries LAW those making products or performing services demanded by the public for use in enjoying leisure, from books, music, games equipment, amusements such as the theatre and television, to sports and travel.

lek the standard currency unit of Albania, divided into 100 qindars or qintars.

lempira the standard currency unit of Honduras, divided into 100 centavos.

lender of last resort BKG. & FIN. the central bank of a country in its responsibility for controlling the country's banking system. In Britain, the Bank of England is always ready to lend money to the leading discount houses to which it acts as banker, but only on its own conditions. Thus when the commercial banks need money, they call in loans from the discount houses, who then have to borrow from the Bank of England as lender of last resort, i.e. they have no other means of borrowing. The Bank uses its special position to charge a high rate of interest (called the minimum lending rate) for these loans, and this rate is its main instrument in controlling the banking system.

leone the standard currency unit of Sierra Leone, divided into 100 cents. *Abbr.* Le.

lepton *pl.* lepta, the fractional currency unit of Greece. 100 lepta = 1 drachma.

Lesotho (formerly Basutoland) a constitutional monarchy (kingdom) in southern Africa pop. 1 million approx. (1973); capital, Maseru pop. 15,000 approx.; languages, Sesotho, English; currency unit, the loti (*pl.* maloti), divided into 100 lisente. Member, (British) Commonwealth; O.A.U.

less (before a number or quantity) decreased or reduced by; made less by: *10 less 2 = 8.*

gross income of £5000, less income tax of £1000, leaves a net income of £4000. *Syn.* minus. *Sign:* – (10 – 2 = 8; £5000–£1000 = £4000).

less-developed countries *see* under-developed countries.

lessee LAW the person to whom the lease of a property is granted (given) on certain conditions by the owner or lessor. *Syn.* tenant; nominee.

lessor LAW the person who grants (gives) a lease. Cf. lessee. *Syn.* landlord.

let *v.* of property, to lease: *I have let my house to Mr John Smith for five years at £1000 per annum. House to let*, the house may be taken on lease for rent.
n. (*colloq.*) property that is let; a lease: *A good let*, a property that brings in a good rent. *A long/short let*, a long or short letting or lease.

letterhead(ing) the heading printed, usu. at the top of the notepaper on which letters are written or typed, giving the full name and address of the person or organization, telephone and telex numbers, cable and telegraphic addresses, and other useful information. *See* headed letter-paper.

letter of advice COM. & BKG. (1) a letter sent by the drawer of a bill of exchange ahead of the bill itself, to the drawee to advise (inform or warn) him that the bill has been drawn so that he may be ready to accept or pay it when it arrives. (2) any letter from a supplier to a customer esp. one abroad, giving information on matters of common interest, such as names and addresses of the supplier's agents and bankers in the customer's country.

letter of allotment *see* allotment letter *under* allotment.

letter of application STK. EXCH. a letter, usu. on a printed form, from a person who intends to invest in a company when shares are first issued, requesting to be allotted a stated number of shares. If the company accepts his application, he will receive a letter of allotment, but if not, he will be sent a letter of regret.

letter of appointment MAN. a formal letter from an employer telling a new employee that he has been appointed to (chosen to fill) a certain post, the date on which his service and right to receive pay will begin, the amount of salary or wages, and the hours of work and other conditions of service.

letter of attorney *see* power of attorney.

letter of credit BKG. & COM. a letter from one party, usu. a bank, to another party, usu. also a bank, by which a third party, usu. a customer named in the letter, is given the right to obtain the money, credit or goods he may need, up to a stated value, for which the writer of the letter takes responsibility. *Abbr.* L.C.; L/C; l.c.; l/c; lc. *Syn.* a credit.

blank L/C *see under* blank.

circular L/C one which is addressed to all branches, correspondents and agents of the issuing bank. Cf. direct L/C.

commercial L/C in foreign trade, one that records a business arrangement between an importer and a bank by which the bank pays the seller of the goods in a foreign country as soon as certain stated conditions have been met; the bank is repaid by the importer. Such L/Cs are usu. irrevocable, i.e. cannot be cancelled.

confirmed L/C one which carries a promise by the paying bank that it will be responsible for any credit given in connection with the L/C, and will pay the amount due if the issuing bank fails to honour it. *See* irrevocable L/C *below*; confirmed irrevocable credit.

direct L/C one which is addressed by the issuing bank to one particular branch, correspondent or agent. Cf. circular L/C.

documentary L/C one to which a number of documents such as a bill of lading, insurance certificate, consignment note, consular invoice, certificate of origin, have to be joined by the exporter to get payment from the bank.

irrevocable L/C one which cannot be revoked (cancelled) without the agreement of the party to whom payment is to be made. *See* confirmed L/C. To be really safe, L/Cs should be both irrevocable and confirmed.

limited L/C a circular letter of credit that can be used by the payee in only a limited number of places.

revocable L/C one that can be cancelled or changed.

traveller's L/C a document in the form of a letter which a banker gives to a traveller to carry with him, introducing him to the banker's branches, agents and correspondents abroad, directing them to advance money or credit to him up to a stated value. Each time a payment or an advance is made, it is recorded on the back of the L/C, and when the whole amount has been paid or advanced, it is sent back to the issuing bank. The traveller also carries separately a *letter of indication*, sometimes called a *letter of identification*, which bears a sample of his signature and the number of the L/C; this he must produce with the L/C itself each time he asks for a payment or an advance.

unconfirmed L/C one in which the bank gives no promise that it will accept bills drawn upon it. Cf. confirmed L/C.

letter of deposit *see* memorandum of deposit.

letter of hypothecation *see under* hypothecation.

letter of identification *see* traveller's L/C *under* letter of credit.

letter of indemnity *see under* indemnity.

letter of indication *see* traveller's L/C *under* letter of credit.

letter of intent a formal letter declaring it to be the writer's firm intention to follow a certain stated course of action if or when a particular event takes place. The document records what is in the writer's mind at the time of writing it; it does not amount to a promise, but shows the writer's willingness to negotiate some important deal or arrangement.

letter of licence COM. & FIN. a document recording that the creditors of an insolvent debtor agree not to press him for payment for a stated period, to give him time, e.g. to reorganize his business. Cf. deed of arrangement.

letter of lien BKG. & COM. a document signed by a debtor, giving to his creditor, often a bank, power to sell the debtor's goods held by a third party, if the debt is not paid when due.

letter of regret STK. EXCH. a formal letter from the directors of a company to a person who has applied for an allotment from a new issue of shares, telling him politely 'with regret' that no shares are being allotted to him.

letter of renunciation a form, usu. printed on the back of a letter of allotment, which the allottee can fill in and sign if he wishes to renounce (refuse) his claim to the shares he has been allotted so that they may be allotted to one or more other persons.

letter post see under post.

letterpress a method of printing from a raised surface such as from type or printing blocks, as distinguished from methods which use a flat surface as in lithography, or a groove or hollow as in intaglio printing.

letter-punch see punch.

letters of administration LAW in Britain, a document issued by the Probate Court appointing a person to be the administrator of the estate of a person who has died. See administrator (1); administration bond under bond. n.

letters patent see patent.

letting LAW & TAXN. a property that is let, usu. furnished, to a tenant: Income from furnished lettings.

leu pl. lei, the standard currency unit of Romania, divided into 100 bani.

lev pl. leva, the standard currency unit of Bulgaria, divided into 100 stotinki, sing. stotinka.

Levant the countries of the East, but esp. those of the eastern Mediterranean Sea, including Lebanon and Syria. Adj. Levantine.

levee a high bank, usu. of earth and stones, built along a river to prevent flooding.

level crossing TRANSPT. a place where a road and a railway cross on the same level. Syn. (U.S.A.) railroad crossing; grade crossing.

level off STK. EXCH. of prices, etc., tending to become steady, not rising or falling much: Interest rates are levelling off after a period of rapid rise.

level of living (U.S.A.) standard of living.

level tendering see collusive tendering; common pricing.

leverage (U.S.A.) see gearing.

levy v. TAXN. (1) to introduce by law the payment of a tax to the government of a country: To levy a tax on motor vehicles. Syn. to impose. (2) to collect a tax. (3) LAW to seize, take possession of property by order of a court of law. See distress.

n. the amount of tax collected. See capital levy; betterment levy.

import levy under the Common Agricultural Policy of the E.E.C., the main instrument for keeping home prices at a level fair to the farmer. It is a charge, similar to a customs duty, on imports of most farm products into the community. It is variable, going up or down with the landed cost, and is fixed periodically by the C.A.P. authorities at an amount equal to the difference between the landed cost and the threshold price.

L Fr. the Luxemburg franc.

lg. large (size).

liabilities pl. ACCTS. the debts owed by a business to its creditors and to its owner(s). See balance sheet.

contingent liabilities see under contingent.

current liabilities those payable on demand or at short notice, or in the near future, such as trade creditors (suppliers of goods and materials). Syn. short-term liabilities.

deferred liabilities those which, by arrangement with the creditors concerned, do not have to be paid for a relatively long time (usu. more than one year), such as goods bought on long credit, or money borrowed against a mortgage. Syn. non-current liabilities; fixed liabilities; long-term liabilities.

external liabilities the debts owed by a company to persons or organizations other than its ordinary and preference shareholders. Thus, sums owing to debenture-holders, the Inland Revenue (for taxes), banks (for loans and overdrafts) and trade creditors, are external liabilities.

fixed liabilities see deferred liabilities above.

long-term liabilities see deferred liabilities above.

non-current liabilities see deferred liabilities above.

liability sing. LAW & FIN. (1) the state of being bound by law to settle a debt or to make good possible loss or damage. (2) the debt itself, or the amount of the loss or damage. Opp. exemption; immunity. (3) ACCTS. an amount owing by a business or other organization to other persons or concerns; debts of all kinds. See liabilities, pl. Cf. asset. (4) MAN. a person or thing bringing loss rather than gain: An inefficient manager can be a liability to his employers.

double liability (U.S.A.) the liability that stockholders of some U.S.A. banks formerly had to suffer, of risking up to double the amount of their stockholding in the bank if it went into liquidation.

limited liability see limited liability company under company.

single liability (U.S.A.) limited liability, by which members of a corporation (company) are liable to lose only the amount they have invested in it. Cf. double liability.

strict liability see under strict.

unlimited liability the liability of a private owner of a business, or of a member of a partnership or a company that is not registered as a limited liability company.

liability insurance see under insurance, classes and kinds of.

liable LAW & FIN. (with for) responsible; legally bound to pay: A husband is liable for his wife's debts. (With to) tending to attract or suffer from, or to do, something that is not desired: Capital gains are liable to tax. He is liable to act without authority.

liberalism ECON. THEORY the belief of many economists of the eighteenth and nineteenth centuries that the driving force of economic life is self-interest; that competition and the price mechanism in a free market are the best means of obtaining economic growth and social progress; and that the State should help this activity by not interfering except to operate essential services that need collective support.

Liberia a republic in West Africa, pop. 1.7 million approx. (1975); capital, Monrovia, pop. 100,000 approx.; languages, English and tribal; currency unit, the Liberian dollar (L$), divided into 100 cents. Member, O.A.U.

Libya a republic in North Africa, on the southern shore of the Mediterranean Sea, pop. 2.3 million approx. (1975); capital, Tripoli, pop. 330,000 approx.; language, Arabic; currency unit, the Libyan dinar, divided into 1000 dirhams. Member, Arab League; O.A.U.

licence n. LAW (1) formal permission in writing, from an authority recognized by law, to perform an act which, without that permission, would be unlawful: An import/export/driving/building licence. Syn. permit. (2) authority given by an owner to enter or use his property or to exercise some right, such as to cross his land or to fish in his river, acts which would be wrongful without his licence. (3) permission given by the owner of a copyright to reproduce an article, such as a book or work of art; or by the owner of a patent, to use a process or to produce an article under licence. Also (U.S.A.) license.

export licence see under export.

import licence see under import.

open general licence see under open.

licence, letter of see under letter.

licence v. LAW to give formal permission to someone to do something, to grant (give) a licence. See licence n. Also (U.S.A.) licence.

licensed victualler COM. a person who holds a licence to sell strong drink, usu. the landlord of an inn or public house, or the manager of a restaurant.

licensee n. (1) COM. in Britain, a person to whom a licence has been issued, esp. the owner or manager of an inn or public house. (2) LAW a person to whom permission has been given, esp. to enter and use premises. Such a person has a good answer to a charge of trespass (wrongful entry into premises) if he can show that he has the owner's permission, known legally as 'leave and licence'.

licensing hours LAW & COM. in Britain, the hours during which a licensed innkeeper or other licensee is allowed to sell strong drink.

licensor LAW a person granting a licence.

Liechtenstein a small constitutional principality (country ruled by a prince) in western Europe between Switzerland and Austria, pop. 23,000 approx. (1975); capital, Vaduz, pop. 4000 approx.; language, German; currency unit, the Swiss franc (SFr), divided into 100 centimes.

lien LAW strictly, a bond or tie. In practice, a legal claim; the right to hold anything as security until the claim of the holder has been satisfied; e.g. a letter of hypothecation gives the buyer of a bill of exchange a lien on the goods against which the bill is drawn until the bill has been paid. A lien is usu. lost when possession of the property held is given up.

banker's lien a form of general lien, giving a banker the right to hold all property belonging to his customer that comes into the banker's possession in the course of banking business, unless that property is related to a contract that clearly shows that it is not subject to a lien, such as securities left with the banker to sell through a stockbroker, or articles left with the banker for safe custody.

broker's lien see under broker's.

carrier's lien see under carrier's.

charging lien the right of a creditor to charge with the payment of the debt property belonging to a debtor but held by another person. See charging order.

equitable lien a right to keep someone else's property to meet a loss or expense, such as trust property kept by a trustee to pay his expenses in managing the trust. Cf. possessory lien.

factor's lien the right of a factoring agent to hold goods belonging to his principal until the principal has paid him his commission or factorage.

general lien a form of possessory lien giving a creditor the right to hold a debtor's property as security for all debts resulting from the same kind of deal between the parties. Thus, a ship-owner may hold any cargo belonging to the same cargo-owner until all freight and other costs have been paid; and a solicitor may hold any or all papers belonging to a client until all his fees have been paid. Cf. particular lien.

innkeeper's lien the right of an innkeeper under common law to hold the baggage of a customer as security for payment for goods supplied and services performed.

maritime lien any lien that results from a contract for the carriage of goods by sea, or from loss or damage caused by collision, etc. Persons who may have a lien on a ship or its cargo are: members of the crew for unpaid wages; holders of a bottomry bond; owners of another ship or of other property damaged or lost in a collision. The lien may be either a possessory or a charging lien.

mechanic's lien esp. in U.S.A., the right of labourers and others who in addition to their work also supply materials, to hold the property on which they have been working until all payments due to them have been paid. A form of particular lien.

particular lien a form of possessory lien giving a creditor the right to hold a debtor's property as security only for one particular debt, such as the right of a garage-owner to hold a customer's car until repairs done have been paid for. Cf. general lien. *Syn.* mechanic's lien.

possessory lien the right of a creditor to keep property belonging to a debtor until payment of a debt is made. Cf. equitable lien. A possessory lien may be a *particular lien* or a *general lien*.

salvor's lien *see under* salvor.

seaman's lien the right of a seaman to hold a ship for non-payment of wages.

shipowner's lien *see* carrier's lien *under* carrier's.

solicitor's lien *see under* solicitor's.

vendor's lien the right of a vendor (seller) to hold the property sold so long as the price remains unpaid. *Syn.* seller's lien.

warehouse-keeper's lien *see* warehouse-keeper.

lienee LAW a person who owns property on which another person has a lien. Cf. lienor.

lien, letter of *see* letter of lien.

lien on shares STK. EXCH. & LAW the right that most companies have, under their Articles of Association, to take possession of and to sell the shares of any of its members (shareholders) who owe the company money, up to the amount owed.

lienor LAW a person who has a lien on somebody else's property. Cf. lienee.

life annuity *see under* insurance policy.

life assurance *or* **insurance** *see* life insurance *under* insurance, classes and kinds of.

life assured *or* **insured** INSCE. (1) in life insurance, the person on whose life the insurance contract has been made, and on whose death the sum assured becomes payable by the insurer. (2) the person named in an endowment policy whose life continues after a fixed date on which payment is due to be made, or instalments are due to begin, under the policy.

life estate *see under* estate (1).

life expectancy INSCE. the average age to which a class or group of persons will live. The figure varies for different classes and groups, being influenced by the kind of work done, the standard of living and esp. of feeding, their sex, and the qualities handed down from parents to children. Cf. expectation of life.

life fund INSCE. a fund (stock of money) set aside by an insurance company or society to meet future claims of policy holders. The money is invested in a wide range of fixed-interest and equity securities and in property. *Also* life and annuity fund.

life income *see under* income.

life insurance *see under* insurance, classes and kinds of.

life insured *see* life assured.

life interest LAW an interest in land and buildings but only for the life of the owner, esp. a right to receive an income from property for life; the property passes, on death, to other persons.

lifeless STK. EXCH. of market prices, lacking any change, there being very few buyers and sellers, and little or no business being done.

life office INSCE. an insurance company or society that insures lives. In Britain, most life insurance companies belong to the Life Offices' Association. Cf. fire office.

life tables INSCE. tables prepared from statistics on the age at death of a large number of persons of different occupations in different places, which show the expectation of life at various ages and on which the price of an annuity largely depends. *Syn.* mortality tables.

life tenant LAW the owner of a life estate. *See* life interest; tenant for life.

L.I.F.O. last in, first out.

lift an apparatus for carrying people or goods upwards or downwards from one floor of a building to another. *See* heavy lift. *Syn.* (U.S.A.) elevator. Cf. hoist.

lift-van *see* container.

ligan *see* lagan.

light *adj.* (1) SHIPG. & TRANSPT. unloaded, empty of cargo or goods: *The ship/lorry/aircraft was travelling light. Light draught*, the draught of a ship when unloaded. (2) STK. EXCH. of market conditions, little business being done: *Trading was light at 9 million shares*, only 9 million shares were bought and sold that day. (3) COM. less than the proper measure: *Some traders give light weight*.

light-dues SHIPG. money collected from masters of ships entering a port, and used for keeping lighthouses, buoys, light-vessels, marks and beacons on the coast and in harbours in good repair. In Britain, this work is done by Trinity House.

lighter SHIPG. a flat-bottomed open boat, usually without engines, used to carry cargoes over short distances, esp. between ships and the shore. *Syn.* barge. *Abbr.* ltr.

lighterage SHIPG. (1) the cost of hiring lighters or barges. (2) the charge made for carrying goods by lighter or barge.

lighterman SHIPG. a person who owns, or is in charge of, a lighter. A *licensed lighterman* is one who has signed a document promising that goods released from a bonded warehouse for re-export are properly guarded and are delivered as directed in a bond warrant.

lighthouse SHIPG. a tower built on a rock or headland or at the entrance to a harbour, showing a bright light at night to guide ships. Lighthouses usu. also have a foghorn which is sounded in misty weather, and some make radio or radar signals to warn ships of danger.

light industry see under industry.

lightning strike see under strike.

lightship see light-vessel.

light-vessel SHIPG. a floating lighthouse; a vessel permanently anchored near a rock or sandbank, showing a bright light to guide ships. *Syn.* lightship.

lightweight tonnage see under tonnage.

lijangeni the standard currency unit of Swaziland, divided into 100 emalangeni.

Limey n. (U.S.A. *colloq.*) (1) a British ship or sailor. (2) a Britisher. *adj.* British.

limit (1) STK. EXCH. an order by a client to a stockbroker to buy securities below a stated highest price, or to sell above a stated lowest price. Such an order is called a *limited order* or *limit order*. Cf. market order. (2) COM. & FIN. *To go to the limit*, to risk all one's money on a business venture.

limitation LAW (1) the placing of a limit to the amount payable by a contractor for loss or damage, e.g. by a carrier of passengers and goods. (2) certain periods allowed by law for action to be taken in the civil courts to enforce (give force to) a legal right; beyond these periods the right of action in the courts becomes *barred by limitation* or *statute-barred* or *time-barred*. In Britain, the periods during which action must be begun are: *12 years* for damages for breach of specialty contracts, for regaining possession of land and personal property, for obtaining payment of mortgages on land, and claims against personal estates of dead persons; *6 years* for damages for simple breach of contract and in tort (breach of duty);

3 years for damages for personal injuries; *1 year* for obtaining payment of moneylenders' loans and interest. *See* unenforceable contract *under* contract. (3) dividend limitation, *see under* dividend.

Limited (Ltd.) LAW & STK. EXCH. in Britain, the word that must by law be placed as the last word of the name of a limited liability company. The abbreviations Ltd. or Ld. may also be used. It means that the liability of each of its members (its shareholders) is limited. *See* limited liability company *under* company. It is illegal for any person or company other than a limited liability company to include the word Limited or the abbreviations Ltd. or Ld. in the name. *See also* reduction of capital. The U.S.A. equivalent is *Incorporated. Abbr.* Inc.; the French, Société Anonyme. *Abbr.* S.A.

Limited (U.S.A.) TRANSPT. & TOUR. a fast, very comfortable train or motor coach that stops at only a limited number of places and carries only a limited number of passengers.

Limited and Reduced see reduction of capital.

limited carrier see under carrier.

limited cheque see under cheque.

limited company see limited liability company under company.

limited legal tender see legal tender.

limited letter of credit see under letter of credit.

limited liability company see under company.

limited market see under market.

limited order see limit (1).

limited partner see limited partnership under partnership.

limited partnership see under partnership.

limousine TRANSPT. & TOUR. a large and very comfortable motor car, esp. one with a sheet of glass separating the driver from the passengers.

Lincs. Lincolnshire, England.

line (1) a particular kind of business or work: *What line are you in? I am in the export/banking/grocery/bricklaying line. This job is not my line*, does not suit me. (2) COM. a particular class or kind of article or commodity dealt in by a business: *Carbon paper is one of our best-selling lines. We have a new line in men's hats*, a new kind of hat. (3) COMP. *Line or on-line computer*, one connected to the telephone system and thus able to serve a number of separate businesses which operate it by telephone. (4) SHIPG. *see* liner. (5) STK. EXCH. a large quantity of one particular security being either bought or sold by a single investor, usu. an institution. Dealings in a line are usu. arranged to take place over a length of time to avoid seriously disturbing the market price.

Line, The (*colloq.*) a popular name among seamen for the equator, esp. in the expression: *Crossing the Line*.

lineage ADVTG. a charge made by newspapers for

advertisements, based on an amount of money for each line or space taken up. *Also* linage. Cf. column inch.

line and staff management *see under* management.

linear measure measurement of length, in one direction only. *Syn.* long measure. *See table on page 475.*

line, assembly *see under* assembly.

line manager *see under* manager.

line of command MAN. a system of management by which orders and directions are passed down from one manager to the next below him in the line to the lowest manager. *Syn.* chain of command. *See* line and staff management *under* management.

liner SHIPG. a ship that makes regular voyages, on dates made known in advance, between certain ports, as opposed to a tramp that keeps to no regular route or timetable.

liner bill of lading *see* berth bill of lading *under* bill of lading.

liner rates *see* berth rates.

lingua franca any common language widely used among groups of people of different languages, such as: English and Hindi in India; Swahili in East Africa; French and English among diplomats (persons representing governments in foreign affairs). *See also* pidgin.

linked industry *see under* industry.

Linotype a machine with a keyboard, used by printers for the rapid composing (putting together) and casting of metal type, one line at a time, each line being produced in the form of a bar called a *slug*. Cf. Monotype.

L.I.P. life insurance policy.

liquid FIN. existing in the form of cash, or easily and quickly turned into cash: *Liquid assets.*

liquid assets *see under* assets.

liquidate FIN. & ACCTS. (1) to pay off (a debt): *I have liquidated all my debts.* To settle: *The company has liquidated all claims made against it.* (2) to sell for cash: *To liquidate one's property and investments*, e.g. before emigrating. *Syn.* realize. (3) to go into liquidation. *Syn.* be wound up. (4) to put into liquidation. *Syn.* to wind up.

liquidated damages *see under* damages, *n. pl.*

liquidation FIN. & ACCTS. the act or process of ending the existence of a company. *See* winding-up. A company is said to be *in liquidation* when a liquidator has been appointed to wind it up. A person unable to pay his debts can be made bankrupt but a company cannot; instead it can be *put into liquidation*, i.e. its assets will be realized (sold for cash) and the money used for settling its liabilities (debts).

liquidator LAW, FIN. & ACCTS. a person appointed to wind up (bring to an end the existence of) a company. *See* winding-up. A liquidator is appointed by a court in a compulsory winding-up, by the members (shareholders) of a company in a members' voluntary winding-up, and by the creditors in a creditors' voluntary winding-up. His duties are: to obtain possession of all the company's assets and to sell them for cash at the best price he can get; to share out this money between the creditors of the company according to the law; and if any money remains, to divide it among the members of the company as repayment of capital.

liquid capital *see* working capital *under* capital.

liquidity FIN. (1) the quality of being liquid, esp. of assets. (2) of a company or other business, the cash and those liquid assets that are left after meeting current liabilities. (3) the degree to which a business has ready cash or can find it by quickly selling its assets. Its liquidity is said to be high if its liquid assets form a large proportion of its total assets.

liquidity, international FIN. the valuable quality possessed by gold and the currencies of a few countries, such as the U.S. dollar and the pound sterling, of being always accepted by businessmen and easily obtained in all parts of the world for settling international debts. *See* international currency *under* currency.

liquidity preference ECON. THEORY the desire of the public to hold money in the form of cash or current bank accounts, as a means of short-term hoarding. It is the demand for *money to hold*, not to spend or to lend, and it expresses the preference of the public for liquidity, i.e. money immediately ready to be spent or invested. J.M. Keynes argued that an increase in liquidity preference must lead to a temporary fall in demand for goods and services, and that this would cause producers to produce less and to employ fewer people. *See* hoarding.

liquidity ratio BKG. the relation between a bank's total liquid assets, i.e. cash and possessions which can be quickly turned into cash, and its total deposit liabilities, i.e. the amount it owes to its customers, esp. on current and deposit accounts. Bankers usu. aim to keep the proportion of liquid assets at about 30% of total deposit liabilities. Cf. advances ratio; cash ratio.

liquid measure a measure of volume for liquid substances. Cf. corn and dry measure. *See table on page 478.*

liquid ratio test *see* acid test ratio.

lira the standard currency unit of Italy, divided into 100 centesimi. *Pl.* lire. *Also* of Turkey, divided into 100 kurus or piastres; or 4000 para.

list *n.* (1) COM. a document, written, typed or printed, that records information such as names, articles, ships, etc. in a desired order **black list** *see under* black.

Lloyd's List *see under* Lloyd's.

Official List *see* Stock Exchange Daily Official List.

passenger list a list of all persons carried as passengers on a ship or plane.

price-list a printed list showing the retail prices fixed or recommended (*a*) by a manufacturer or wholesaler as a guide to retailers or (*b*) by a retailer as a guide to his customers among the public. *See* list price *under* price.

stock list a list of all the different kinds of articles stocked by a business at any time during the accounting year, for use by employees when stocktaking, and later by the managers when making the stock valuation.

(2) SHIPG. one of several documents that are part of a ship's papers, such as a *cargo list, crew list, passenger list.*

sailings list a list issued by a shipping line giving future dates of arrival and sailing of their ships at and from various ports. *See also* Lloyd's List; Lloyd's Loading List; sailing card.

(3) STK. EXCH. *see* Stock Exchange Daily Official List.

v. SHIPG. of a ship, to lean to one side, because the cargo has shifted (moved) or the ship is taking in water on one side. *N. A* list to port/ starboard.

listed securities STK. EXCH. securities that have been admitted (accepted) by the Quotations Committee of the Stock Exchange and, after close examination of the company's financial position and reputation, have been included in the Official List of securities dealt in by members of the Stock Exchange. *Syn.* quoted securities.

listless STK. EXCH. of market conditions, lacking activity, with nobody showing any interest in buying securities: *A listless session left most prices unchanged at the close.*

list price *see under* price.

literature *see* sales literature.

litho *see* lithography.

lithographer IND. a printer using the offset lithographic method of printing, sometimes called photolitho offset. *See* lithography.

lithography IND. originally a method of printing from a flat piece of stone, using the natural tendency for grease and water not to mix. Later the stone was replaced by a metal plate. The system of *direct lithography*, by which the paper receives the ink direct from the plate, has been replaced by *offset lithography*, by which the text is first printed on a rubber surface and then 'offset' on to the paper. *Syn.* photolitho offset. *Abbr.* litho; offset litho.

litigant LAW a person who is a party in a civil action before a court of law.

litigate LAW to be concerned in, to carry on, a lawsuit, either as plaintiff or as defendant in a civil court of law.

litigation LAW a lawsuit; the action of litigating.

litigious LAW tending to litigate excessively; too ready to bring a lawsuit in the courts.

litre a metric unit of volume, one cubic decimetre (dm^3) or 1000 cubic centimetres (cm^3). 1 U.K. gallon = 4.546 litres; 1 U.S. gallon = 3.785 litres. *See* liquid measure *table on page 478.*

'Little Neddies' *see* National Economic Development Council.

livelihood a way of earning money to pay for the necessities of life: *He makes a livelihood as a builder. Cf. living.*

lively STK. EXCH. of market conditions, full of life and action, with many buyers and sellers and much business being done.

livery COM. the business of running a stable in which horses are kept and fed or are hired out.

livery stable the building in which a livery business is run.

livery company *see under* company.

liveryman (1) a person who owns, or is employed in, a livery stable. (2) a member of a livery company in the City of London. *See* livery company *under* company.

livestock AGR. live animals kept for profit, such as cattle, sheep, horses and other farm animals. *Cf.* dead stock. *Syn.* stock.

live weight AGR. the weight of a live farm animal.

living (1) the money needed to pay for the necessities of life: *To earn/get/make a living: One makes a bare living by writing books*, one makes just enough to live. *A living wage*, enough money to support oneself and one's family, but at a low standard. *Cf.* livelihood. (2) the position and pay of a parish priest in the Church of England. *Syn.* benefice.

living, cost of *see* cost of living.

living debt *see under* national debt.

living standard *see* standard of living.

lkge. leakage.

Llds. Lloyd's.

Lloyd's INSCE. a leading international insurance market. It began in 1689 when shipowners, mariners and merchants met at Mr Edward Lloyd's coffee-house in the City of London to arrange insurances. In 1774 the insurers formed a body which, in 1871 by Act of Parliament, became the present Corporation of Lloyd's, ruled by a Committee and often called *Lloyd's of London*. This is an association of underwriters (insurers) and insurance brokers interested in both marine and non-marine risks. Lloyd's itself does no trading but acts as a governing body, making rules for its members and providing arrangements to help them in business. All trading is done by the members, working either singly or in groups called *syndicates*, and together forming a highly competitive market. *See* Lloyd's broker; casualty report service; Lloyd's underwriter; Lloyd's associates. *Abbr.* Lld.

Lloyd's agent MAR. INSCE. a person appointed to manage the business of the members of the

Corporation of Lloyd's. A Lloyd's agent is stationed in every important port in the world. He keeps Lloyd's informed of shipping movements, accidents, etc., arranges for surveys of damage to ships and cargoes, deals with the settling of marine insurance claims, and helps masters of ships when in trouble.

Lloyd's associates INSCE. persons such as lawyers, accountants, assessors who, although not directly working in insurance, need to visit underwriters in the Underwriting Room and are made associate members of Lloyd's for this purpose.

Lloyd's broker INSCE. a member of the Corporation of Lloyd's who acts as an agent of the insured in placing insurance contracts with an underwriting member, agreeing the rate, sending his client a cover-note, preparing a Lloyd's policy and getting it signed by Lloyd's Policy Signing Office. The broker receives a commission which he takes from the premiums paid to him by the insured and passed on to the underwriter.

Lloyd's List and Shipping Gazette INSCE. a daily newspaper published by the Corporation of Lloyd's giving news of movements of ships and aircraft and information about accidents, etc. of interest to the insurance world.

Lloyd's Loading List SHIPG. a weekly paper published by Lloyd's in London, listing ships that are, or soon will be, loading cargoes at British and continental ports, stating the ports to which each ship is going and the closing date for loading cargo. This list is useful to exporters.

Lloyd's policy INSCE. a policy issued by Lloyd's underwriters, who still use an eighteenth-century form of wording. Lloyd's policies differ from company policies in several ways, esp. in the fact that they provide for disagreements to be settled by judgment in a court of law instead of by arbitration.

Lloyd's Policy Signing Office also known as *The Bureau*, an office set up and authorized by the Committee of Lloyd's to prepare and sign for the underwriters all Lloyd's policies. *Abbr.* L.P.S.O.

Lloyd's Register of British and Foreign Shipping SHIPG. a book published annually containing details of all ships classed by Lloyd's Register of Shipping and, so far as possible, of all other ocean-going ships over 100 tons in the world. *Syn.* Lloyd's Register Book; the Book.

Lloyd's Register of Shipping SHIPG. & MAR. INSCE. the world's oldest and leading classification society, being an association dating from 1760 of shipowners, shipbuilders, marine engineers, merchants, underwriters, etc., for the main purpose of setting and keeping up standards for the building, operating and repair of ships; and of surveying and classifying them

according to the degree of safety of their hulls, engines and apparatus. The society also provides a service that gives technical advice and help. *Abbr.* L.R.

Lloyd's Room MAR. INSCE. also known as *The Room*, a hall at Lloyd's in the City of London, where Lloyd's underwriters meet marine insurance brokers and shipbrokers to do business.

Lloyd's surveyor SHIPG. one of a number of highly-qualified employees of Lloyd's Register of Shipping who watch over the building and repair of ships, examine and report on the state of a vessel and on the extent of any damage to it and to stores and cargo insured by Lloyd's underwriters. Lloyd's *ship surveyors* deal with hulls, steering and safety apparatus; *engineer* or *marine* surveyors deal with engines and machinery generally.

Lloyd's underwriter INSCE. an insurer who is a member of the Corporation of Lloyd's. He is so called because his name is written under the insurance policy as a party to the contract. Lloyd's underwriters deal with the public only through Lloyd's brokers, whom they reward by paying commission on the premiums paid by their clients. *See* syndicate.

Lloyd's Weekly Casualty Reports *see* casualty report service.

load (1) TRANSPT. & SHIPG. an amount, often a weight, of goods that is, or can be, carried: *A cart-load; lorry-load, train-load, plane-load, ship-load*; or of human beings: A car-load, bus-load. *See also* payload.

return load a load arranged for a lorry or plane to bring back after delivering another load, in order to avoid its having to travel empty. *Syn.* back load.

unit load a load of goods packed for handling as a single unit, such as a container, a lift-van, a pallet.

work load the amount of work which a person or organization has to do, or is responsible for getting done.

(2) AGR. a measure of corn, *see* corn and dry measure *table on page 477. Also* of hay, 36 trusses; of timber, 40 cu. ft rough, 50 cu. ft sawn; of earth, 27 cu. ft or 1 cu. yd.

load draught *see under* draught.

loaded (1) TRANSPT. & SHIPG. carrying a load: *loaded weight*, weight when fully loaded. *Syn.* laden weight. (2) FIN. (*colloq.*) of a person, very rich.

loaded price *see under* price.

loader (1) SHIPG. a ship that is taking aboard a load of cargo or passengers: *A Pacific loader*, a ship loading cargo for Pacific ports. (2) a man employed to handle loads. *See also* low-loader.

load factor (1) TRANSPT. the percentage of all seats or berths in a vehicle that are actually used by fare-paying passengers. (2) IND. *see* capacity factor *under* capacity (1).

loading INSCE. an extra amount added to a basic amount such as a life insurance premium, to cover management expenses.

load-line SHIPG. a set of markings painted on both sides of a cargo ship half-way along its length, showing the limit to which the vessel may safely be allowed to settle in the water when loaded. Several horizontal lines, each marked with letters, apply according to the kind of water in which the ship is floating: TF = tropical fresh; F = fresh; T = tropical (sea); S = summer (sea); W = winter (sea); WNA = winter North Atlantic. *Syn.* Plimsoll line/mark; international load-line; load-water-line.

load-shedding IND. stopping the electricity supply for a short period in certain areas by turn in order to relieve an excess demand on power stations.

loan *v.* to lend; to make a loan.
n. (1) the act of lending, esp. on condition that the thing lent will be returned. (2) FIN. something lent, esp. money, on condition that interest will be paid at an agreed rate and that the amount lent will be repaid in an agreed time or in an agreed manner.

bank loan *see under* bank.
bottomry loan *see* bottomry.
bridging loan *see under* bridging.
call loan *see* call money *under* call.
collateral loan *see under* collateral.
consumption loan (U.S.A.) a personal loan.
day-to-day loan *see* day-to-day accommodation.
dead loan *see under* dead.
fiduciary loan *see under* fiduciary.
home loan *see under* home.
local loan in Britain, a loan issued by a local government authority to pay for capital expenditure.
mortgage loan *see* local authority loans.
personal loan money lent by a bank to a private person for the purpose of personal expenditure, such as payment of household bills or for buying consumption goods such as a motor car, boat, furniture, etc. Such loans are usu. repayable by instalments in less than two years and are often made without security; the rate of interest is therefore high. *Syn.* (U.S.A.) consumption loan.
secured loan a loan against which certain assets have been handed by the borrower to the lender as security for the repayment of the loan and interest. Cf. fiduciary loan.
term loan a bank loan repayable by an agreed number of instalments.
time loan a bank loan repayable after a stated time.
unsecured loan a loan made without any security, i.e. a fiduciary loan.
◆anable *see* investible.
◆an account BKG. *see* bank loan.

loan capital *see under* capital.
loan club FIN. a private club whose members, usu. low-paid workers in a factory or office, pay regular amounts into a fund from which short-term interest-bearing loans are made to members who request them during the year. Fines are charged for late repayment, and interest is paid to members who deposit money with the club. On a certain date each year, usu. just before Christmas (25 December), the entire fund is shared out among the members. *Syn.* slate club; loan society.
loan market FIN. (1) that part of the capital market that is concerned with the provision of medium-term and long-term loans to governments, commercial houses and industrial companies. (2) the money market for very short-term loans.
loan office FIN. (1) an office where members of the public may pay money for government loans. (2) a moneylender's or pawnbroker's office.
loan stock *see under* stock.
loan value *see* surrender value *under* surrender.
L.O.B. Location of Offices Bureau.
local *adj.* in or relating to a particular place: *Local transport services*, bus and train services in and around a place. *A local newspaper*, not a national newspaper. *The local job centre. A local call*, a telephone call to a nearby place, usu. within a few miles. *Local brand, see under* brand.
n. (*colloq.*) the inn or public house serving the people living near it.
local authority in Britain, the elected local government organization and its paid employees who have legal power and duty to provide and administer many local services on which rates (local taxes) are spent, such as schools, roads, public health, police, and planning.
local authority loans FIN. & STK. EXCH. in Britain, borrowing by a local authority to finance capital expenditure on public services. Long-term borrowing is by issuing stock on the Stock Exchange. Shorter-term loans may be obtained by *mortgage loans* from the public at a fixed rate of interest for one, two or more years, and from *yearling bonds* or *yearlings* (so called because they are repayable in one year) which can be bought either direct from the borrowing authority or through the Stock Exchange.
local board *see under* board of directors.
local director *see under* director.
local industry *see under* industry.
localization of industry ECON. HIST. the tendency in the past of certain industries to group themselves in certain districts, usu. because production costs were lowest there, and there were many advantages, such as specialization by producers, a supply of trained workers, etc.

The greatest disadvantage was that when local industry suffered in a trade depression, there was very high local unemployment. For this reason, some governments cause new industries to be more widely placed. *See* location of industry.

local loan *see under* loan.

local tax *see under* tax.

local time TRANSPT. the time at a particular place or in a particular country, usu. calculated from local noon (midday), i.e. the moment when the sun reaches its highest point in the sky. Cf. Greenwich Mean Time. *Abbr.* l.t.

location of industry ECON. HIST. & IND. the places in which industries are first located (set up). The choice of place was largely influenced by the aim of the industrialist to keep costs as low as possible. In Britain, before the nineteenth century, industries tended to rise on banks of fast rivers that supplied water-power for machines. In the nineteenth century the introduction of steam-power caused the coalfields to attract many industries, esp. if other raw materials, such as iron, were cheaply obtainable nearby. Other locating influences were nearness to supplies of skilled labour, to canals and ports, and to markets for the product; and in some industries, such as cotton, a favourable climate. These locating influences became less and less important with the development of transport and the distribution of gas, electricity and oil as sources of power. *See* industrial inertia; localization of industry.

Location of Offices Bureau COM. & IND. in Britain, a government office that advises and encourages businesses to move their offices away from central London to other parts of the country. *Abbr.* L.O.B.

lock TRANSPT. & SHIPG. an enclosed space of water in a canal, dock or river, with gates at both ends, arranged so that the water and any vessels in it can be raised or lowered from one level to another.

lockage TRANSPT. (1) a system of locks for changing the levels of the water in different parts of a canal, river or docks. (2) the charges payable by owners of vessels passing through locks.

lock-keeper TRANSPT. a person employed to look after a lock on a canal or other waterway. *Syn.* lockman.

lockman *see* lock-keeper.

lock-out IND. REL. the action of an employer who refuses to employ workers unless they accept his conditions, esp. a lower rate of pay, or longer hours of work. Cf. strike.

lock-up *n.* (1) COM. a shop or garage or structure that is locked up and not guarded at night. (2) STK. EXCH. (*colloq.*) any long-term investment, esp. a security that is not expected to rise in price but is worth buying for the regular income it will produce.

lock up *v.* to invest (money, capital, etc.) in an investment that cannot be quickly sold: *He has all his money locked up in business ventures/ mortgages/unfurnished properties.*

loco COM. (*Latin*, in that place) in foreign trade, a price quoted as, e.g., *loco Glasgow* means that the price is for goods that are at Glasgow at the time of quoting, and that the buyer must bear all costs and risks of moving the goods to another place. Such a quotation is called a *loco price.*

loco. TRANSPT. a locomotive or railway engine.

locum (*Latin:* locum tenens) a person acting temporarily in place of another person, usu. a doctor or parish priest.

locus sigilli LAW (*Latin*, the place for a seal) usu. printed as *abbr.* L.S. in a circle on a formal document that needs to be sealed, such as a deed, to show where the seal is to be placed.

lodge *n.* (in India & Pakistan) a lodging-house, a boarding house.

v. (1) to live in another person's house, paying rent. *See* lodger. To take someone into one's house as a lodger. (2) to place formally, to deposit, documents or securities with some person or office authorized to hold or receive them: *These stocks must be lodged with the bank as security. To lodge a document with the Registrar of Companies. To lodge a complaint/ information with the police.*

lodger a person who pays for, and lives in, a room in another person's house. *Syn.* (U.S.A.) roomer.

lodging COM. a place to live, esp. a furnished room or rooms in another person's house for rent. Often *pl.* lodgings. *Syn.* rooms; apartments (Britain).

a lodging-house a house, other than a hotel or inn, where rooms can be hired, usu. without meals. Cf. boarding house.

log SHIPG. (1) an instrument for measuring the speed and distance travelled by a ship at sea. (2) the official daily record, called a *ship's log* kept by the master of a ship, of all important events and of the ship's progress during a voyage. It forms part of a ship's papers. (3) TRANSPT. a record of a journey by a road vehicle or aircraft. (4) in Britain, a registration document, called a log book, recording the ownership and other details of a road vehicle.

logging AGR. & IND. in forestry, the work of cutting down trees, sawing them into logs and moving them to a sawmill. *Syn.* lumbering.

logic COMP. a non-mathematical data-processing operation performed by a computer, such as sorting, choosing, comparing values and making decisions.

logogram IND. & COM. a single sign or picture representing a whole word, esp. a name, often used as a trade-mark. *See* colophon. *Syn.* logograph. *Abbr.* logo.

lolly (*colloq.*) money.

Lombard Street FIN. & BKG. (1) the popular name for the London money market; many discount houses, bill-brokers and commercial banks have their main offices in or near this street in the City of London. (2) financiers as a group.

Lomé Convention FIN. & COM. an arrangement made in 1975 at Lomé, capital of Togo, West Africa, between the relatively rich countries of the E.E.C. and 46 of the less-developed countries of Africa, the Caribbean and the Pacific (the A.C.P. countries). The E.E.C. countries agreed to help the A.C.P. countries by: allowing duty-free imports of many of the A.C.P. countries' products; by providing financial and technical help in developing their industries; and by supporting a plan called Stabex that aims to stabilize (keep steady) the earnings of A.C.P. countries from certain exports to the E.E.C., esp. of bananas, cocoa, coconuts, coffee, cotton, groundnuts, iron ore, leather, sisal, palm oil, tea and timber.

London acceptance credit see *under* acceptance.

London Association for the Protection of Trade FIN. & COM. an association that keeps records of all hire-purchase deals in Britain and advises its members about the creditworthiness of any hire-purchase customer. *Abbr.* L.A.P.T.

London Bankers Clearing House see clearing banks.

London Chamber of Commerce COM. the largest chamber of commerce in Britain, with over 9000 members from all branches of commercial activity. Besides offering the usual services provided by chambers of commerce, it is an important examining authority on commercial subjects. *Abbr.* L.C.C.

London Clearing Bankers Association BKG. the organization that operates the London Bankers Clearing House. *See* clearing banks.

London Commodity Exchange COMMOD. EXCH. in Britain, the building called Plantation House in Mincing Lane in the City of London, which forms the main commodity market (popularly known as Mincing Lane) for important commodities, mostly from tropical countries. It deals with certain foodstuffs such as cocoa, coffee, pepper and spices, soya beans, sugar, tea and vegetable oils; some raw fibres such as jute and wool, and certain other raw materials such as rubber and shellac. *See* commodity exchanges.

London Gazette an official weekly paper giving information about government matters, appointments of persons to important official positions, bankruptcies, winding-up orders, the ending of partnerships, changes in company names and any matters which must, by

law, be published in the *Gazette*. In Scotland, the equivalent is the *Edinburgh Gazette*.

London School of Economics (L.S.E.) in the University of London, one of the world's leading centres for study and research in the social sciences. It was founded by Sidney Webb in 1895 and has an excellent library — the British Library of Political and Economic Science.

London Stock Exchange see Stock Exchange, The.

long. longitude.

long STK. EXCH. holding a quantity of a particular security usu. in the expectation of a rise in price: *To be long* (in a certain stock or share). *A long position*, of a dealer, holding more of a particular security than he needs for supplying the quantities he has contracted to deliver. *Syn.* bull position. *See also* buying long.

long-dated bill see *under* bill of exchange.

long-dated paper see long-dated bill *under* bill of exchange.

long-dated securities see longs.

long-distance call (U.S.A.) a trunk call on the telephone.

long dozen see dozen.

long draft see foreign bill of exchange *under* bill of exchange.

longer STK. EXCH. *To go longer*, in the market for fixed-interest securities, to sell short-dated stocks and use the money to buy medium-dated or long-dated stocks. *Syn.* switching.

long exchange BKG. in foreign exchange, bills of exchange that will not mature (become payable) for 60 or 90 days. *See* long rate *under* exchange rate.

long firm FIN. a firm or company set up for the dishonest purpose of obtaining goods on credit, with the intention of never paying for them.

longhand ordinary handwriting, with words written in full, as compared with typing or shorthand: *Applications are invited in longhand*, in the applicant's own handwriting. *Syn.* manuscript; holograph.

long hundred see hundred.

longitude the distance of a place east or west of the standard meridian of Greenwich (0°), measured in degrees, minutes and seconds, e.g. 1° 19′ 35″ E (Dover), by the angle which the meridian of the place makes, at the centre of the earth, with Greenwich meridian. Cf. latitude. *Abbr.* long.

long lease see *under* lease.

long measure see linear measure.

long period see long run.

long position see long.

long rate see *under* exchange rate.

long run ECON. THEORY (1) the time taken for a change in demand to be balanced by a change in supply. It is the time needed by a firm to change all the factors of production and so vary output to meet the new level of demand in the most efficient way possible. It is not a fixed length of time and may be different for each firm and industry. *Syn.* long period. *See* short run. (2) the time needed for all the economic factors in a situation to reach a new equilibrium with no further tendency to change.

longs STK. EXCH. in Britain, gilt-edged and other fixed-interest securities repayable in more than 15 years from the present time. *Syn.* long-dated securities. Cf. shorts.

longshore along and close to the shore: *Longshore fisheries/fishing*.

longshoreman (U.S.A.) a docker; a harbour-worker or stevedore, employed in loading and unloading ships, or in fishing from the shore.

long-term liabilities *see* deferred liabilities *under* liabilities.

long ton *see under* ton.

look up improve: *Business is looking up*, is improving.

loose-leaf *adj.* of a book, having a system of binding arranged so that any leaf or page can be taken out and replaced, or new leaves added, in any order at any time. *A loose-leaf ledger/address book/catalogue*. The cover is called a *loose-leaf binder*.

loot (1) anything obtained dishonestly or by force: *The thief escaped with his loot*. (2) (*colloq.*) money.

lorcha SHIPG. a small ship built with a European shape of hull and fitted with sails shaped like those of a Chinese junk.

Lord (High) Chancellor LAW in Britain, the head of the judiciary. He is usu. a cabinet minister and is Speaker (Chairman) of the House of Lords.

loro account BKG. (*Italian*, their account) the account of a third party. An expression used e.g. by one bank when telling another bank to transfer money to the account of a third bank. Cf. nostro account; vostro account.

lorry TRANSPT. a large motor vehicle for carrying goods by road. *Syn.* truck (esp. U.S.A.).

lose out (on) to suffer a loss or disadvantage; to become a loser, esp. as the result of a business deal or an administrative change of arrangements. *We lost out on the company merger/joint venture/export deal*.

loss (1) ACCTS. & FIN. the financial harm or disadvantage resulting in business from any of a number of causes, such as: inability to obtain payment from debtors for goods supplied; selling goods below cost; overheads (the costs of running the business) being greater than the gross profit from sales; the destruction or wearing-out of assets. *Syn.* deficit. *Opp.* profit; gain; surplus.

dead loss *see under* dead.

gross loss the financial result when the cost of goods sold is greater than the amount received from their sale.

net loss the financial result when the costs of running the business are greater than the gross profit from sales.

paper loss a loss that has been suffered but has not been realized, i.e. has not been paid out in cash. Thus if the value of a security falls it will show a paper loss, but this loss will be realized in the form of a loss of cash only if the security is sold. Cf. paper profit.
(2) INSCE. (*a*) an event resulting in a claim under a contract of insurance. (*b*) the amount which an insurer is bound to pay to the insured on the happening of an event insured against. (*c*) the money value of the harm suffered by the policy holder as the result of the event insured against. A loss is either total or partial.

actual loss *see under* actual.

actual total loss *see under* actual.

constructive total loss *see under* constructive.

general average loss *see under* average (4).

gross average loss *see under* average (4).

partial loss *see under* partial.

particular average loss *see under* average (4).

total loss *see under* total.

loss-leader *see under* leader.

loss-of-profits policy *see* consequential loss policy *under* insurance policy.

loss ratio INSCE. the proportion between the total amount of premiums received by an insurance company or society, and the total losses suffered, during a particular period.

lost days IND. REL. (the number of) working days lost by industrial disputes in a particular factory or industry or area.

lost time *see* downtime.

lot (1) any group or collection of things offered for sale together as one deal. *See also* job lot; odd lot. (2) a particular article or group of articles taken together, forming one of a number of deals each numbered and sold by a separate auction during an auction sale: *Lot No. 23 was sold for £10*. (3) (U.S.A.) a piece of land, esp. in a town: *A parking lot*, a car park. (4) the act of choosing something or someone, or of deciding a question, by chance, usu. by taking one of several articles of different sizes and marks, called *casting lots* or *drawing lots*. (5) STK. EXCH. a number of shares in the same company offered for sale together as one deal. *See* odd lot.

lot money COM. an auctioneer's charge for each lot sold by him during an auction sale.

lottery a game of chance, usu. for raising money for charity, in which numbered tickets are bought by the players and mixed together in a container, from which a few are drawn out to decide by chance which players are the winners of the prizes.

Low Countries an area of lowland in northern Europe containing Belgium, Luxemburg and the Netherlands (Holland).

low-loader TRANSPT. a vehicle specially built with a low floor for carrying by road or rail tall loads that would not pass under bridges, etc. if carried on an ordinary vehicle.

low-season fare *see under* fare.

low water (1) SHIPG. low tide; the lowest level that the sea reaches in a single swing (rise and fall) of the tide. *Opp.* high water. *Abbr.* L.W. (2) (*colloq.*) unsatisfactory finances: *To be in low water*, to have very little money; to be doing badly in business.

L.P.S.O. Lloyd's Policy Signing Office.

L.R. Lloyd's Register (of Shipping).

L.S. locus sigilli (*Latin*, the place for a seal).

l.s. lump sum.

L.s.d. (1) pounds, shillings and pence (from *Latin*: librae, solidi, denarii). (2) (*colloq.*) money.

L.S.E. London School of Economics (and Political Science).

l.s.t. local standard time.

l.t. long ton; local time.

Ltd. Limited (liability company).

ltr. lighter.

l/u. laid up; lying up.

lucrative profitable; earning much money: *Banking is a lucrative trade/business. He has a lucrative post/position/situation*, one that is very well paid.

lucre riches, money, esp. if obtained by some undesirable means: *Filthy lucre*, money accumulated by someone whose main desire is to get rich.

luggage *see* baggage.

lull STK. EXCH. & COM. a period when business is temporarily quiet: *After a rather busy day yesterday, there was a lull in trading today.*

lumber (1) IND. (U.S.A. & Canada) timber, esp. wood sawn into boards. (2) in Britain, articles put aside because they are no longer of use but in too good a condition to throw away.

lumberer *see* lumberman.

lumbering *see* logging.

lumberjack *see* lumberman.

lumberman (1) IND. (U.S.A. & Canada) a person employed in cutting down trees in a forest and in moving them to a saw-mill. *Syn.* lumberer; lumberjack. (2) a dealer in timber.

lump sum (1) FIN. & COM. money paid all at one time, not, e.g., by instalments. *Abbr.* l.s. (2) INSCE. a sum of money paid to an insured person, usu. on retirement, as well as his regular pension.

lump, the IND. (*colloq.*) in Britain, a popular name given to a class of workers in the building industry who, to avoid paying taxes, do not work as regular employees of building firms but prefer to be self-employed and to work as subcontractors.

lunar month *see under* month.

lunar year *see under* year.

luncheon voucher a printed ticket that will buy a meal in a restaurant, or food in a grocer's or other shop, to a stated value. Some employers who do not provide a staff canteen or restaurant serving cheap meals use these vouchers as a means of giving their employees a small tax-free advantage. The employer buys the vouchers from a voucher company that later pays the restaurants or shops that accept them as payment. *Abbr.* l.v.

Lutine Bell INSCE. & SHIPG. a bell sometimes rung at Lloyd's in London to signal that important news is to be made known about a ship in trouble or about some other disaster.

Luxemburg a small constitutional monarchy in western Europe, bordered by France, Germany and Belgium, pop. 350,000 approx. (1975); capital, Luxemburg, pop. 78,000; languages, French and German; currency unit, the Luxemburg franc (L Fr), divided into 100 centimes. Member, Benelux; E.E.C.; O.E.C.D.

luxury *n.* (1) very great comfort: *He lives a life of luxury. I am accustomed to live in luxury.* (2) a most enjoyable thing that is expensive and not necessary: *A Rolls Royce (motor car) is a luxury we cannot afford.*
adj. providing very great comfort: *A luxury cabin/flat/hotel/restaurant. A luxury article*, an expensive and unnecessary thing that only rich people buy. *The luxury trade*, the trade in luxury articles.

luxury tax *see under* tax.

l.v. luncheon voucher.

L.W. low water.

L.W.O.S.T. low water ordinary spring tides.

M

m minim; *prefix* milli- (10^{-3}); metre.

m. male; married; mile(s).

M motorway; the Roman numeral for 1000.

M. Monsieur; mille (1000).

M₁, M₂, M₃ *see* money supply.

M$ Malaysian dollar.

M£ Maltese pound.

MA Morocco's international vehicle-registration letters.

MacCulloch John Ramsey (1789–1864), Scottish economist, statistician and writer, and Comptroller of H.M. Stationery Office. He produced special editions, with notes, of Ricardo's and Adam Smith's main works and, in 1824, wrote one of the first histories of economic thought. In 1832 he published a commercial dictionary.

machine IND. a power-driven apparatus or instrument for doing work of a particular kind: *A printing/binding/paper-making/drilling/sewing machine. Abbr.* m/c., *pl.* m/cs.

calculating machine see calculator.

duplicating machine see duplicator.

machine language see under language.

machine loading IND. in a factory, deciding what work will be done by each machine, usu. the responsibility of the production control office.

machine-made IND. made by machinery, as distinguished from handmade.

machinery IND. (1) machines collectively: *It pays to buy the best kind of machinery. The factory contains a million pounds' worth of machinery. Machinery for printing books.* (2) the working or moving parts of a machine: *Dangerous machinery must be properly fenced. The machinery of a clock. Abbr.* mchy. (3) MAN. any organized system or process for getting something done or made or for obtaining desired results: *The machinery of banking/government/administration/the courts.*

office machinery all kinds of machines for use in offices, such as typewriters, duplicators, calculators, and copying machines.

machine shop IND. (1) a place, esp. in a factory, where machines are made or put together or repaired. (2) a place where things are made by machine.

machine-tool IND. any fixed power-driven machine used for cutting and shaping metal and other materials. Machine tools include lathes, drills, and grinding, milling and planing machines.

machinist (1) a person who works a machine esp. a sewing machine. *Syn.* operative; operator. (2) a mechanic or mechanical engineer (esp. U.S.A.).

macro-economics ECON. THEORY that branch of economics that examines and explains economic facts in the aggregate, i.e. in totals for the whole community or nation, such as the total volume of employment, investment, money supply, production, consumption, etc. *See* aggregate analysis. Cf. micro-economics.

Madagascar see Malagasy Republic.

Madam a polite form of spoken address or greeting used for an unmarried as well as a married woman. *Dear Madam*, the formal opening or greeting in a letter to a woman.

Madame the polite form of address, both spoken and written, for a Frenchwoman who is married, and often for any married woman other than one from an English-speaking country: *Madame Dubois, the French Ambassador's wife, was speaking to Madame Li of the Chinese consulate. Abbr.* Mme.

made bill see under bill of exchange.

Mademoiselle the polite form of address, both spoken and written, for an unmarried Frenchwoman. *Abbr.* Mlle.; Melle.

mag. magazine.

magazine ADVTG. a paper-bound collection of articles or stories by various writers, published every week or every month, usu. containing advertisements. *Abbr.* mag.

magistrate LAW in England, a justice (judicial officer appointed by the Crown) with power to try criminal cases in the lower or magistrates' courts. Magistrates are either unpaid part-time Justices of the Peace or, as in certain large cities, paid full-time stipendiary magistrates.

magistrates' courts LAW in England and Wales, the lowest level of criminal court held by Justices of the Peace or a stipendiary magistrate. They deal with the less serious criminal cases at all stages; and they also hear more serious cases in their early stages only, and certain cases concerning children and young persons. Cf. crown court.

magnate COM. & IND. a person of great wealth, power and importance in business and industry: *A newspaper/property/shipping magnate. Syn.* baron.

magnetic ink character recognition (M.I.C.R.) BKG. a modern system of printing a mark consisting of letters or numbers in a special style of type, in magnetic ink on cheques, credits and other documents. By this means, the documents are rapidly sorted and listed by automatic machines, and the information on them is fed into a computer that makes debits and credits to the accounts concerned.

magnetic tape see under tape.

Maghreb the countries in the western part of the Arab World, i.e. Morocco, Algeria, Tunisia and sometimes Libya. *Also* Maghrib.

maid a female servant in a home or hotel.

mail (1) letters, packets and parcels sent or received by post: *My secretary opens my mail. Syn.* post. (2) the postal system of a country, called in Britain the royal mail; in U.S.A., the U.S. mail. *Syn.* post.

air mail see airmail.

direct mail see under advertising (1).

first-class mail in Britain (*a*) a fast inland postal service for carrying and delivering letters or packets, for which a higher rate of postage is paid than for the slower second-class mail. (*b*) letters and packets sent and received by the faster service.

sea mail mail carried entirely by ship. *See* surface mail *below.*

second-class mail in Britain (*a*) the ordinary inland postal service for carrying and delivering letters or packets. It is cheaper and slower than first-class mail. (*b*) letters and packets sent and received by this ordinary service. *See* first-class mail *above.*

surface mail mail that is carried by sea or over land, not by air. *See* sea mail.

v. (esp. in U.S.A.) to post; to send by mail.

mailboat see packet-boat.

mailing-card (U.S.A.) a postcard.

mailing list ADVTG. a list of names and addresses

of persons and organizations to whom advertising material such as notices, leaflets, offers and other sales information is regularly sent.

mailing machine an electric office machine that prepares letters for sending by post; it seals (sticks down) envelopes, stamps them and arranges them in piles.

mail order COM. an order for goods to be sent direct to the customer by post. *Abbr.* M.O.

mail order house a company selling a wide variety of goods, sending them by post direct from its warehouse to the customer. Orders are collected or obtained, with the help of an illustrated catalogue, by agents who are paid by commission. Prices are kept low by avoiding the cost of running retail shops, and by buying in bulk. Payment is accepted by instalments, usu. without extra charge.

mail room *see* post room.

mail steamer *see under* steamer.

mail train *see under* train.

mail transfer *see under* transfer.

main crop AGR. the chief or leading crop grown by a farmer to provide most of his income. Cf. cash crop; catch-crop.

main deck SHIPG. in a ship with only two decks, the upper deck; in a ship with more than two decks, the next deck below the upper deck.

Main Street *see* High Street.

maintain (1) to support; to keep provided with what is needed: *To maintain a family/home*, to provide money, food, shelter, etc. needed for living. *To maintain a fund*, to cause it to receive a regular income. (2) to keep in proper repair, in good order: *To maintain a vehicle/road/railway.*

maintenance (1) the act of maintaining or of being maintained. *See* care and maintenance. (2) the provision of things necessary to support a person. (3) LAW the provision of income under a deed of settlement by a man to his separated or divorced wife, to support her and children of the marriage. (4) LAW the civil offence of interfering in a lawsuit in the result of which one has no personal interest. If the intention is that the maintainer will share in any gain received from the action, the offence is called champerty. *See also* barratry (2).

maisonette a flat on more than one floor, usu. only part of a house.

major greater in importance than others: *A major road/advertiser/producer. Opp.* minor.

majority (1) LAW the state of being no longer a minor or infant (child or young person) but a person of full legal age. In many countries the *age of majority* or *coming of age* is 18, and in others it is usu. 21 years. (2) MAN. when a vote is taken, the greater number of voters voting for one person or thing. (3) the number of votes by which those voting one way exceed those voting another way.

make *n.* (1) manufacture; production: *Our own make of shoe polish. A well-known make of camera. Syn.* brand. (2) a quantity made. *Syn.* batch; making.

make out to write, esp. a form, such as a cheque or paying-in slip: *Please make out an application form.*

make up ACCTS. to complete: *Accounts are made up to the end of June.*

making-up day *see* contango day.

making-up price *see under* price.

makuta the fractional currency unit of Zaïre. 100 makuta = 1 zaïre.

maladminister MAN. to administer or manage badly, esp. inefficiently or perh. dishonestly. *N.* maladministration.

mala fide *adv.* (*Latin*, in bad faith) intending to deceive; not sincere. *Opp.* bona fide. *See* faith.

mala fides *n.* dishonesty; insincerity; untruthfulness.

Malagasy Republic (formerly Madagascar) an island republic in the Indian Ocean, pop. 7 million approx. (1973); capital, Atananarivo, pop. 367,000 approx.; languages, French and Malagasy; currency unit, the Malagasy franc (Mal Fr.), divided into 100 centimes. Member, O.A.U; French Community; O.C.A.M.M.; Associate, E.E.C.

Malawi (formerly Nyasaland) a republic in East Africa, pop. 4.8 million approx. (1973); capital, Lilongwe; languages, English and Chinyanja; currency unit, the kwacha, divided into 100 tambala. Member, (British) Commonwealth; O.A.U.

Malaysia a constitutional monarchy (kingdom) in south-east Asia, pop. 11.6 million approx. (1973); capital, Kuala Lumpur, pop. 500,000 approx.; language, Malay; currency unit, the ringgit or Malaysian dollar (M$), divided into 100 cents. Member, (British) Commonwealth; A.S.E.A.N.

Maldives a small island republic in the Indian Ocean, pop. 126,000 approx. (1973); capital, Male, pop. 14,000 approx.; language, Divehi; currency unit, the Maldivian rupee, divided into 100 paise.

Mal Fr. Malagasy franc.

Mali (formerly French Sudan) a republic in western Africa, pop. 5.4 million (1973); capital, Bamako, pop. 200,000 approx.; languages, French and tribal; currency unit, the Mali franc (M Fr.), divided into 100 centimes.

malicious damage INSCE. damage done on purpose, from a desire to cause suffering or loss to somebody. *Abbr.* M.D.

malicious prosecution LAW the civil offence of wrongfully causing a person to be accused of a crime or to be made bankrupt, or of wrongfully causing a company to be put into liquidation, out of a desire to cause suffering or loss.

Malta an island republic in the central Mediterranean, pop. 320,000 approx. (1973); capital, Valletta, pop. 14,000 approx.; languages, Maltese and English; currency unit, the Maltese pound (M£), divided into 100 cents or 1000 mils. Member, (British) Commonwealth; Council of Europe; Associate, E.E.C.

Malthus Thomas Robert (1766–1834), English economist of the Classical School, and country priest. His *Essay on the Principle of Population* appeared in 1789 but was rewritten in 1803. It presented a fearful picture of the future because the population of the world would grow in geometrical progression, much faster than the supply of food, which would increase only in arithmetical progression. Overpopulation would force wages down so low that people would only just be able to exist. Natural checks such as disease, wars and famine would not be effective enough; and the preventive check, i.e. self-control in having children, would only have effect when wages and the standard of living had fallen to a miserably low level because 'Man is both comfort-loving and philo-progenitive [has a natural desire to have children].' Malthus's theory of population seemed very true in the terrible social conditions of his time and it had a great influence not only on the studies and writings of his fellow economists but also on the government, resulting in great social changes in Britain. Events proved, however, that there was no real basis for his fears. As wealth and education increased in the industrial countries, people tended to have smaller families; but in the industrially less-developed countries, overpopulation remains the most serious social problem.

Malthusianism belief in the teachings of Thomas Malthus on the need for population control.

Man. Manitoba, Canada.

man v. to provide with men: *To man a ship*, to arrange for a ship to have officers and men to work it.

manage MAN. to direct, control, take charge of (a business or other organization). *Syn.* to administer.

managed currency see under currency.

managed money see managed currency *under* currency.

management MAN. (1) the board of directors of a company. (2) the group of persons who control a business, including both directors and high-ranking managers. (3) the governing body of any organization. *Management committee*, a group of persons, either appointed or elected, to manage the affairs of an organization such as a village hall. *Syn.* administration.

general management the directors and one or more high-ranking managers called general managers who are responsible for the higher management of the business or other organiza-tion and who control a number of departmental and service managers.

higher management *see* top management *below.*

line and staff management a system by which a business or other organization is controlled by two chains of command: one, the *line management*, consists of *line managers* responsible for policy on the main product, service or activity of the concern; the other, the *staff management*, is responsible for supporting the line management with services such as warehousing, transport, accounting, secretarial work and technical advice.

middle management the group of managers immediately below, but working closely with, top management. Many of the responsibilities of the highest officers are delegated (passed down) to middle managers to carry out. A middle manager (in U.S.A. a junior administrator) has charge of a number of supervisors or foremen. Together they run the detailed parts of the organization.

top management the group of persons who are the highest officers of an organization. They are usu. led by the chief executive and his deputy who work closely with the board of directors, and include the heads of the various divisions or departments. Immediately below them are the middle management. *Syn.* higher management; upper management.

management accountant see accountant.

management by exception MAN. a method of managing the work of an organization by setting up controls that show up exceptions, i.e. things that are not normal. These are given the attention they need from the managers, while normal things carry on without using management time. *Syn.* exception principle.

management checks see management control *under* control.

management company see *under* company.

management consultant MAN. a person or firm selling professional advice on management questions, such as administration, organization, the use of capital and manpower, the employment of managers and workers, industrial relations and marketing policy.

management control see *under* control.

management ratio MAN. (1) the number of managers employed for every 1000 employees in a business or other organization. (2) any of a number of ratios that are of use to the management as measures of the efficiency of the business, such as those showing the relation between sales and stocks, sales and overhead costs, current assets and current liabilities.

management share see *under* share.

management, wages of see *under* wages.

manager MAN. a person employed to manage, i.e. to control or direct part or all of the work of other employees in a business, industrial concern or other organization. He is usu. under the orders of a director. *Abbr.* mngr. *Fem.* manageress.

bank manager the name given by customers to the manager in charge of a branch of a bank. Up to a fixed limit, he may lend money without reference to the head office. He is officially called a branch manager.

branch manager a responsible person placed in charge of a branch, i.e. a local division, of a business or other organization. The branch manager of a bank is also called a bank manager. Cf. district manager.

business manager *see under* business.

commercial manager one who is responsible for the successful control of the commercial activities of an organization, i.e. buying and selling so as to produce a profit.

district manager in a large concern, a manager who has the responsibility for a district in which there are several branches of the business or other organization. He is usu. under the orders of the general manager and controls a number of branch managers.

estate manager *see* land agent (2).

export manager the manager responsible for the exporting activities of a business. He is usu. under the orders of the sales manager.

factory manager *see* works manager *below*.

general manager a chief manager who controls the work of a number of other managers.

line manager *see* line and staff management *under* management.

middle manager *see* middle management *under* management.

office manager a manager in charge of an office, esp. a departmental office in a business or factory; he has special responsibility for dealing with documents, records and the passing of information such as reports and returns needed not only by the higher management but also by the other managers, foremen and ordinary workers.

personnel manager a manager responsible for all matters concerning the employment of factory workers, office and travelling staff. He is usu. under the direct orders of the general manager or the personnel director. *Syn.* staff manager.

sales manager a manager who is responsible for the work of a sales department. He controls the work of the office staff, the home sales manager, the export manager and the sales representatives or travellers. In a large organization he is under the orders of the sales director.

staff manager *see* personnel manager *above*.

station manager the official in charge of a large railway station.

under-manager an assistant manager, of lower rank than a manager.

works manager the manager responsible for controlling a factory. He is usu. under the direct orders of the general manager. *Syn.* factory manager; production manager.

manageress MAN. a female manager.

managerial MAN. relating to management or to a manager: *The managerial class. At managerial level.*

managerial economics the use of the laws and ideas of economic theory in planning business activities and in making business decisions.

manager's cheque *see under* cheque.

manager's share *see* deferred share; *also* management share *under* share.

managing agent MAN. an agent appointed by the owner(s) of property or of a business to manage it in return for a fee or commission based on the amount of the turnover or of the profits or of both. The owners of a block of flats might appoint an estate agent to manage it. The owners of a number of tea estates in India have appointed managing agents to control and run the estates.

managing director MAN. *see under* director.

managing owner SHIPG. where a ship has several joint-owners, the one appointed by the others to manage the affairs of the ship.

managing partner *see under* partner.

Manchester School (of economic thought) *see* Cobden, Richard.

mandamus LAW (*Latin*, we command) in Britain, a High Court order of the greatest power and authority, commanding some person or organization, esp. a government department, to perform a public duty which it owes to the complainant. Such orders are rare and are issued only when all other means of obtaining justice have failed.

mandant LAW a person who gives a mandate. Cf. mandatory. *Syn.* mandator.

mandate *n.* BKG. & LAW a direction, command or request, esp. a formal written authority by one person, called the *mandant* or *mandator* giving another person, called the *mandatory*, power to act for him in certain stated matters, such as to sign cheques or to operate a joint account. **dividend mandate** an order by a shareholder to the company of which he is a member, to pay his dividends to another party, such as a bank. *v.* to put (a place) under a mandate.

mandator *see* mandant.

mandatory *n.* LAW the person to whom a mandate has been given. *adj.* that must necessarily be done. *Syn.* obligatory.

man Friday a male employee who is willing to do any kind of work. Cf. girl Friday.

man-hour IND. a unit of measurement of human work; the amount of work done by one man in one hour: *This wall will take 100 man-hours to build. Also,* similarly, man-day.

manifest SHIPG. & TRANSPT. a detailed official list of goods carried as cargo in a ship or aircraft, signed by the master or captain and delivered to the Customs after loading and before departure and again before unloading. The manifest is one of the ship's papers.

passenger manifest a list of all the passengers on board a ship or aircraft, given to the Customs by the master or captain on arrival. *Syn.* passenger return; passenger list.

manifold to make many copies (of a document). **manifold book** *see* duplicate book; triplicate book.

manifold paper very thin typing paper used with carbon paper for making many copies on a typewriter.

manilla a strong, light brown paper made partly or entirely from the fibres of manilla hemp, much used for commercial envelopes.

manipulate STK. EXCH. to cause a change to take place to one's advantage by clever use of hidden influence, unfair trading or other deceitful means: *To manipulate the market/share prices*, to cause prices to change by, e.g. buying and selling in order to make the market appear more active than it really is. *See also* bear campaign; bull campaign. *Syn.* to rig.

manning agreement IND. REL. an agreement between management and labour (usu. a union) on how many men are needed to carry out a certain piece of work.

man of affairs *see* affairs, *n. pl.*

man of business LAW a person who has been given power to act for another in legal matters and to manage his private legal affairs. Cf. man of affairs.

man-of-war SHIPG. a warship; a ship forming part of the armed forces of a country.

manorial system *see* feudal system.

manpower ECON. & IND. the whole labour force, male and female, of a country or region or industry, esp. considered in relation to employment in industry. If there are more people ready to work than there are jobs for them, there is a *manpower surplus*; if there are more jobs than people to fill them, there is a *manpower deficit*.

manual *adj.* IND. of, done by using, the hands: *Manual labour*, work needing strength and perh. some skill with the hands. Done by hand, not by machine: *A manual exchange*, a telephone exchange that is not automatic but is worked by persons called operators.
n. (1) a book giving information on a special subject, such as the care of a machine or vehicle. (2) a book giving directions on how some work or process is to be done, such as a manual of administration.

manufactory IND. a factory.

manufacture IND. the systematic making of goods from raw materials. Originally manufacture was the making of something by hand, but now includes making by machinery.

manufacture, certificate of *see under* certificate.

manufacturer (1) IND. a person or organization making goods from raw materials. (2) ECON. THEORY an employer of labour and capital to make useful goods for sale in the market.

manufacturer's agent COM. a commission agent who has been given the franchise to sell a particular manufacturer's goods in a certain district or country for an agreed period. Such agents, usu. look for customers who will place contracts for large regular supplies, such as other manufacturers or wholesalers.

manufacturing industry *see under* industry.

manuscript handwritten or typed matter (not printed), esp. an author's copy before publication. *See* holograph; longhand. *Abbr.* MS., *pl.* MSS.

mar. marine.

margarine a substance similar to butter, made from oils obtained from plants or animals.

margin (1) an edge; a border; an area on or round the border of a space: *The margins on a page*. (2) an allowance: *A margin of error*, a number of mistakes or a degree of inaccuracy that is allowed or accepted. (3) ACCTS. & COM. the relation between profit and selling price, the *profit margin*, expressed either as a fraction, e.g. $\frac{1}{4}$, or as a percentage, e.g. 25%. Cf. mark-up. If the mark-up is known, the margin (of profit) can be found: e.g. if the mark-up is $\frac{1}{3}$, the margin is $\frac{1}{3+1} = \frac{1}{4}$ or 25%; again, if the margin is $\frac{2}{7}$, the mark-up is $\frac{1}{7+2} = \frac{1}{9}$ or 11.11%. Similarly, if the margin is known, the mark-up can be found, e.g. if the margin is $\frac{1}{5}$, the mark-up is $\frac{1}{5-1} = \frac{1}{4}$ or 25%; again, if the margin is $\frac{3}{8}$, the mark-up is $\frac{1}{8-3} = \frac{1}{5}$ or 20%. Cf. mark-down. (4) BKG. the difference between the amount of a bank loan and the market value of the security given by the borrower. The bank usu. demands that the value of the security shall be greater than the amount lent to allow for a fall in the market value of the security. (5) COM. the difference between the cost or buying price and the selling price, i.e. gross profit. *Pl. margins*, or *profit margins*, the rate of profit generally made in selling an article or commodity: *Margins on groceries are higher than last year. See* gross margin; net margin. (6) STK. & COMMOD. EXCH. (*a*) the difference between the broker's buying and selling prices. (*b*) any amount owed by one broker to another and due to be settled at the end of The Account, or trading period. (7) ECON. THEORY that unit of a commodity that the consumer hesitates whether to buy or not, because he is 'on the margin (edge) of doubt' whether the satisfaction he will get from buying that unit will be worth the money spent on it. If he buys it, it is a *marginal purchase*, only just worth buying. (8) ECON. THEORY the point at which the return (gain) to a producer from producing one more unit only just exceeds the cost of production. (9) STK. EXCH. money or securities deposited by a client with a stockbroker as security against the client's failure to pay for deals (called *deals on margin*) about to be made for him by the stockbroker. (10) STK. EXCH. a deal in which both the client and the stockbroker share the outlay and the profit.

marginal cost *see under* cost.

marginal land ECON. THEORY land that is only just worth cultivating at current prices; land that produces a crop the value of which is just sufficient to pay the cost of production. Marginal land will be put to use in years when the farmer expects prices to rise; but will go out of use when he expects them to fall, unless production costs can also be expected to fall.

marginal productivity *see under* productivity.

Marginal Productivity, Law of Diminishing *see* Diminishing Returns, Law of.

Marginal Productivity Theory of Wages ECON. THEORY a theory that wages, being the earnings of the factor of production called labour, tend to equal the value of the marginal product of labour, i.e. the addition to the value of the output resulting from the addition of the last or marginal worker. At this point, it would be unprofitable to employ any more workers because their wages would be greater than the value of their output; and to employ fewer workers would mean losing the opportunity of making some profit. All the workers therefore tend to be paid a wage equal to the marginal productivity of the last worker. Cf. Subsistence Theory of Wages; Wages-Fund Theory.

marginal rate TAXN. the percentage rate of income tax paid by a taxpayer on that part of his income that is taxed the most.

marginal relief TAXN. a reduction in the rate of income tax when income slightly exceeds a level at which a higher rate is payable.

Marginal Returns, Law of *see* Diminishing Returns, Law of.

marginal revenue ECON. THEORY the addition to his total receipts that a producer will earn from selling one more unit of his product.

marginal significance *see* marginal utility.

Marginal Theory of Value ECON. THEORY the idea generally accepted by most modern economists, replacing the Labour and the Cost of Production Theories of Value, that price, or value in exchange, depends on the relation of demand and supply. More exactly, it depends on the behaviour of the marginal purchaser

and the marginal producer; the marginal purchaser will not pay more than the marginal utility of the article, and the marginal producer will not produce the article if its price is lower than its marginal cost of production.

marginal utility ECON. THEORY the satisfaction obtained from that unit of a commodity that a consumer finds is only just worth obtaining. *See* Diminishing Utility, Law of. *Syn.* marginal significance.

Marginal Utility School *see* Austrian School.

Mariana Islands *see* Pacific Islands, Trust Territory of the.

Maria Theresa dollars FIN. silver coins originally issued in Austria in the eighteenth century and all dated 1780, although minted in many places down to the present day; they are still accepted as trading currency in many parts of North Africa and the Middle East, but are not legal tender anywhere.

marina SHIPG. & TOUR. a dock or basin specially arranged as a harbour for small pleasure boats with shops, clubs, hotels and other services such as fresh water, fuel and repairs. *Syn.* boat harbour; boat haven.

marine *adj.* (1) of or relating to the sea: *Marine products. Marine navigation*, fixing one's position at sea. Intended for use at sea: *Marine instruments*, special instruments for use at sea, such as compasses, sextants, and radar apparatus. (2) of or relating to ships: *Marine engineering*, the science of making and operating ships' engines and other machinery. (Cf. naval architecture.) *Marine craft*, a boat. *Abbr.* mar. *n.* (1) sea-going ships generally: *The Merchant Marine*. (2) a class of soldier serving at sea as well as on land: *The Royal Marines*.

marine accident MAR. INSCE. an accident at sea, usu. to a ship or to her crew and cargo.

marine insurance *see under* insurance, classes and kinds of.

marine insurance broker MAR. INSCE. a broker who has special knowledge of insurance against the risks of the sea. He is the agent of the insured party (usu. the owner of the ship or cargo) and not of the insurance company.

marine insurance company *see under* company.

marine insurance survey *see under* survey.

marine insurer(s) MAR. INSCE. a marine insurance company or Lloyd's underwriters.

marine law *see* maritime law.

mariner SHIPG. (1) a seaman; anybody employed on board a ship. (2) a person skilled in operating and navigating a ship.

    master mariner (*a*) a seaman qualified to take charge of a ship. (*b*) the captain or master of a merchant ship.

marine superintendent *see* superintendent.

marine surveyor *see* Lloyd's surveyor.

marine syndicate MAR. INSCE. a group of Lloyd's

underwriters who specialize in marine insurance.

marine underwriter *see* underwriter (4).

maritime close to, relating to, the sea: *Britain is a maritime nation/power. A maritime climate*, a climate with cool summers and gentle winters, found in regions near the sea. *Syn.* oceanic.

maritime law LAW & SHIPG. a branch of commercial or mercantile law that deals with ships, their operation, navigation and trading activities. *Syn.* marine law.

maritime lien *see under* lien.

maritime mortgage *see under* mortgage.

mark (1) FIN. the standard currency unit of: Finland (*see* markka); East Germany (*see* D.D.R. Mark); West Germany (*see* Deutsche Mark). *See also* Reichsmark; Östmark. *Abbr.* Mk. (2) STK. EXCH. an official record of a deal in securities, sometimes used as a measure of business activity on the Stock Exchange: 'Today's marks were over 3000 lower than on last Monday.' (3) IND. *see* hallmark. (4) LAW & COM. *see* trade-mark.

mark-down COM. a reduction in price, usu. to encourage a quick sale. The amount of the mark-down may be expressed as a percentage *either* of the former price, e.g. a reduction from £1 to 75p is a 25% mark-down; *or* of the reduced price, here 33⅓%. Cf. mark-up.

marked cheque *see under* cheque.

marked notes FIN. & LAW bank-notes marked by the police to catch a thief.

marked price *see under* price.

marked share *see under* share.

market (1) COM. a place where buyers and sellers come together to trade in goods; the building, open space or town where they meet to trade; and the persons, buyers and sellers, who form a group to buy and sell a particular commodity. (2) the total public demand for an article or commodity. *To be in the market*, wanting to buy. *To be/to come on (to) the market*, to be for sale; able to be bought. *To put on the market*, to offer for sale. *See* market town; downmarket; up-market. *Syn.* mart. *Abbr.* mkt. (3) ECON. THEORY an organized group of buyers and sellers of a particular economic good who are sufficiently in touch with each other personally or by telephone for all to know the current conditions of demand and supply, so that there is only one price, called the *market price*, for the good. (4) the present or possible future demand for a commodity. (5) STK. & COMMOD. EXCH. the organized group of professional buyers and sellers who trade together in securities or commodities, such as the London money market, the Liverpool grain and cotton markets. *To buy/sell at the market*, at the best price obtainable. *To make a market*, to bring into existence an active market for a new issue of a security by exciting public interest in it. *To*

play the market, to speculate (to buy and sell for immediate gain, not for regular income).

active market STK. EXCH. (*a*) the market that exists for certain popular stocks and shares which are frequently changing hands and can therefore always be bought. *Syn.* free market. *Opp.* limited market. (*b*) a market that is in a state of activity, with much business being done.

bear market STK. EXCH. a market in which prices are tending to fall. One in which there are many bears. Cf. bull market.

black market COM. unlawful trading in goods that are scarce, either because supplies are officially rationed or forbidden, or because prices are controlled by government order. *Black marketeer*, a person who trades in the black market, esp. one who makes his living thus. Cf. open market; grey market.

bull market STK. EXCH. a market in which prices are tending to rise. One in which there are many bulls. Cf. bear market.

buyers' market ECON. a market in which the supply of goods is plentiful; buyers can therefore influence sellers to compete with each other in forcing down prices. Buyers' markets that exist for a long time are a sign of economic slump. *Also* buyer's market. Cf. sellers' market.

capital market *see under* capital.

cash market COMMOD. EXCH. the dealings that take place on a commodity exchange on condition that the buyer pays cash immediately or as soon as he gets the documents which give him the right to possess the goods. *Syn.* spot market. Cf. futures market.

closed market COM. a country or area which a monopolist, such as the owner of a copyright or patent, has declared to be closed to all producers and sellers except himself or his licensee.

commodity market *see under* commodity.

Common Market *see* European Economic Community.

depressed market *see under* depressed.

discount market *see under* discount.

finance market FIN. one of several markets where money is dealt in as a commodity, where people who can provide money meet others who need to use it and are willing to pay for its use. *See* capital market; discount market; foreign-exchange market; money market; securities market.

foreign-exchange market *see under* foreign exchange.

forward market *see* foreign-exchange market.

fourth market (U.S.A.) STK. EXCH. the market in which unlisted securities are traded privately between brokers and clients without using the more normal trading methods, such as the national stock exchanges. Cf. third market.

free market (*a*) ECON. a market in which buyers and sellers are free of interference and control and are therefore able to determine the market price according to the forces of supply and demand. *Syn.* open market. (*b*) BKG. in the foreign-exchange market, a situation where the rate of exchange between two currencies is free to rise or fall according to the forces of supply and demand. (*c*) STK. EXCH. the market for a security that is always active, there being many people interested in buying or selling the security, and the amount offered being enough to satisfy a relatively large demand. Cf. limited market. *Syn.* active market.

fringe market COM. any market that exists for a commodity in addition to its main market. For example, the market for small containers of liquid gas for filling cigarette lighters is a fringe market for industrial gases.

futures market COMMOD. EXCH. the market for futures (contracts to buy or sell a commodity at a stated price at some future time). *See* commodity exchanges.

grey market COM. lawful trading in goods that are scarce at a particular time and therefore command a much higher price than is normal. *Also* gray market (mainly U.S.A.). Cf. black market.

heavy market *see under* heavy.

imperfect market ECON. THEORY a market in which conditions of imperfect competition exist. *See* imperfect competition *under* competition.

insurance market *see* Lloyd's.

kerb market *see under* kerb.

labour market ECON. the market for the services of workers, i.e. labour considered as one of the factors of production. The labour market is a very general concept (idea), being the arrangements by which the demand for, and the supply of, labour are brought together. It consists of large groups of persons, one group wanting the services of workers of all kinds, and the other wanting employment for their own services.

limited market STK. EXCH. a market for a particular security for which it is difficult to find buyers and sellers. Cf. free market; active market.

loan market *see under* loan.

money market FIN. the market for short-term loans, in which the commodity is credit, in which the buyers are bill-brokers, discount and acceptance houses, and the sellers are the banks. *See also* Lombard Street.

narrow market *see under* narrow.

new issue market *see under* new.

off-board market *see* over-the-counter market *below*.

open market COM. (*a*) *see* free market (*a*) *above*. (*b*) a country or area in which by agreement, several manufacturers or their agents are free to compete with each other in selling their products. Cf. restricted market; closed market; black market; grey market. *See* market-sharing. (*c*) *see* market overt.

organized market one where business is controlled by rules set by the body to whom all principal buyers and sellers belong, such as stock and commodity exchanges.

over-the-counter market STK. EXCH. a market run by dealers mainly in securities that are unlisted and are therefore not dealt in on the stock exchanges. *Syn.* (U.S.A.) off-board market; unlisted market.

perfect market ECON. THEORY a market in which perfect competition exists. *See* perfect competition *under* competition.

piece market *see under* piece.

produce market any commodity market other than one dealing in metals.

ready market one in which goods are quickly and easily sold.

reserved market *see* restricted market *below*.

restricted market COM. a market into which a producer has agreed with one or more other producers to restrict (limit) his selling, in order to avoid competition. *Syn.* reserved market. *See* market-sharing.

securities market *see* stock exchange; *also* kerb market *under* kerb.

sellers' market ECON. a market in which there is a scarcity in the supply of goods, and sellers can therefore influence buyers to compete with each other in forcing up prices. *Also* seller's market. Cf. buyers' market.

speculative market a market in which speculation regularly takes place.

spot market *see* cash market *above*; *also* foreign-exchange market *under* foreign exchange.

stock market a stock exchange; the business of dealing in stocks and shares.

street market (*a*) STK. EXCH. *see* kerb market *under* kerb. (*b*) COM. an open-air market held in a street, not in a market square or market hall, where a variety of goods is sold.

terminal market COMMOD. EXCH. in Britain, a market in which dealings are mainly in futures, esp. in such commodities as rubber and sugar.

third market (U.S.A.) STK. EXCH. the market in which listed securities are traded privately between brokers and clients, using neither the national stock exchanges nor the market in unlisted securities. Cf. fourth market.

unlisted market *see* over-the-counter market *above*.

marketable able to be sold easily and quickly. *N.* marketability.

marketable security *see under* security.

marketable title *see under* title.

market capitalization *see* capitalization (2).

market day *see* market town.

market demand ECON. the total demand from all consumers. *See* consumer demand. *Syn.* individual demand.

market fluctuations *see* fluctuations.

market garden a piece of land on which vegetables and fruit are grown for sale in a nearby market, not mainly for use in the grower's home. *Syn.* (U.S.A.) truck farm.

marketing (1) COM. (esp. U.S.A.) shopping; buying goods in a market, esp. fresh food, groceries and other goods needed for a household. *He goes marketing twice a week. Mother does the marketing every morning.* (2) COM. & ADVTG. activities intended to make and attract a profitable demand for a product by means such as advertising, sales promotion, pricing, carrying out market research, and developing and testing new products.

marketing boards COM. & IND. producers' organizations set up with government support to help producers of a commodity to distribute and sell their product. In Britain, such boards have been set up for, e.g. eggs, milk, potatoes, tomatoes and wool. *See* agricultural marketing boards.

marketing co-operative *see under* co-operative.

marketing mix ADVTG. in a sales campaign, the relative amounts of money to be spent on the various methods of attracting the interest of consumers, such as on the advertising media, free gifts and competitions.

market order *see under* order (6).

market overt COM. (1) a public market where goods are openly offered for sale. (2) one of several markets in England where by ancient custom special legal protection is given to a buyer of goods, such as allowing him the legal right to keep possession of any goods he buys, even if they were stolen; but he must have acted in good faith, honestly and without deceit, when he bought them, and the thief must have been caught and convicted.

market penny (*colloq.*) a secret commission which used to be given by some shopkeepers to servants of wealthy households who bought goods from them.

market-place COM. an open space, usu. in a town, where a market is regularly held. *Syn.* market square. *Also* marketplace; market place.

market, playing the *see under* playing; market (5).

market price *see under* price.

market rate (of discount) *see* discount rate.

market rate (of interest) *see* interest rate.

market report any report that gives detailed information about the state of a market, esp. the stock and commodity exchanges and the money market. Such reports give current prices, rates of discount and interest, etc. and a general account of present and possible future trends. Such reports appear daily in the City pages of the main daily newspapers.

market research MAN. the work of finding out what kind of goods consumers want, what they are willing to spend and how to persuade them to buy. This information is used by manufacturers before producing a new product and putting it on the market. The work is done by *market researchers* who make a *market survey*, using various methods such as questioning large numbers of possible consumers and retailers, and *market tests*, testing the market by selling the product in a small area. *See also* competitor analysis; canvasser.

market share COM. the proportion of the total demand (for a product) that is supplied by a particular manufacturer or brand.

market-sharing COM. an arrangement between two or more producers to avoid competition between them by sharing the market for their product. Each producer sells his product only into one particular area or country called a *restricted* or *reserved market* and not into any other. For example one producer may sell only into South America while the other may sell only into North America, and so on. Any area into which they agree that both may sell is called an *open market*. Cf. closed market.

markets, playing the *see under* playing.

Markets, Say's Law of *see* Say, Jean-Baptiste.

market survey *see* market research.

market town a town in which one or more markets are regularly held on fixed *market days* in a building (a *market hall* or *market house*) or an open space (a *market-place* or *market square* or *street market*) specially reserved by the town authorities and arranged for selling certain products, e.g. a *cattle market* or *corn market* or *hay market*.

market value ACCTS. the sum of money that could be obtained for an asset if it were sold in the market at a certain time; it is usu. the market price (the price current in the market) at that time.

marking STK. EXCH. the official record kept of every deal and the price at which it was made. The details are written on a *marking slip* by a *marking clerk*.

markings *pl.* the official number of deals taking place in any one day's trading.

markka the standard currency unit of Finland, divided into 100 pennia. *Pl.* markkaa. *Abbr.* Mk. *Syn.* Finnish mark.

Mark Lane COMMOD. EXCH. a street in the City of London in which many corn- and grain-brokers have their offices. For this reason the name is popularly used to refer to the corn and grain market.

marks (1) COM. & SHIPG. special marks painted on crates and packing-cases sent by ship so that the persons handling the cargo can recognize to whom they belong. The marks usu. consist of the consignee's initials within a square, circle or diamond. The mark appears also on the export invoice, the bill of lading, and other shipping documents relating to the shipment. (2) COM. & IND. trade-marks. (3) LAW see merchandise marks.

mark, standard *see* standard mark.

mark-up *see* margin (3).

marriage settlement *see under* settlement (4).

Marshall (Aid) Plan ECON. HIST. economic help given by the U.S.A. mainly to countries in Europe to help to rebuild their economies after the Second World War. The three-year plan was administered in the U.S.A. by the E.C.A. (European Co-operation Administration) and in Europe by the O.E.E.C. (Organization for European Economic Co-operation). The help was in the form of money, goods and technical advice, and was directed to increasing industrial and agricultural production, rebuilding internal finances and encouraging international trade. *Syn.* European Economic Recovery Programme.

Marshall Alfred (1842–1924), English classical economist, Professor of Political Economy at Cambridge (1885–1908). His most famous book, *Principles of Economics* (1890), introduced a number of entirely new concepts (ideas) that had a great influence on the study of economics and made him the leading authority of his time. He was the first to put forward the idea of consumer's surplus, elasticity of demand, quasi-rent, and the representative firm; and he drew attention to the important part played by time in the decisions made by the entrepreneur. His other books include *Industry and Trade* (1919) and *Money, Credit and Commerce* (1923). He set up the Cambridge or Neo-Classical School. *See* Cambridge School.

Marshallian School (of economic thought) *see* Cambridge School.

Marshall Islands *see* Pacific Islands, Trust Territory of the.

mart COM. (1) a busy trading and commercial centre, usu. a large town, esp. a port. (2) an auction room; also a shop or store: *The Car Mart.* (3) an old-fashioned word for market, market-place.

Martinique an island in the eastern Caribbean that is an overseas territory of France, pop. 350,000 approx. (1974); capital, Fort-de-France, pop. 100,000 approx.; language, French; currency unit, the French franc (Fr.), divided into 100 centimes.

Martinmas *see* quarter-day.

Marx Karl (1818–83), German economist, sociologist and political writer, founder of the Marxist movement and modern socialism. After studying at Bonn and Berlin, and working as a journalist in Paris and Brussels, he settled in London to write his *Critique of Political Economy* (1859) and later his famous book *Capital* in four volumes published over the years 1867 to 1910. Moved by a strong desire for justice for the poor and suffering, he attacked the immoral spirit of the businessmen who ruled the capitalist commercial system of his times; and he held out socialism as the road to improvement. His economic argument depends on the Labour Theory of Value and his Theory of Surplus Value, the surplus that enriches the capitalist at the expense of the worker. He called for revolution (overthrow of the government by force) to get rid of the few owners of the means of production, and the setting up of a dictatorship of the proletariat, to be followed by a fully socialist system with a classless society.

Marxian *see* Marxist.

Marxism the political, social and economic teachings of Karl Marx and his followers, esp. Friedrich Engels. *See* Marx, Karl. Marxian economic teaching is mainly based on the Labour Theory of Value.

Marxist *n.* a supporter of Marxism. *adj.* of, relating to, supporting, Marxism. *Syn.* Marxian.

Mass. Massachusetts, U.S.A.

mass advertising *see under* advertising.

mass media *see* advertising media; admass.

mass production IND. & ECON. organized and rapid production of very large quantities of a standard article or commodity, using all possible means to keep down the unit cost, such as fast machinery, special tools, continuous processes and a high degree of division of labour.

master *n.* a person, usu. male, who employs, controls or commands others such as servants and other workers. The head of a family. *See* master (of a ship). *adj.* (1) of a skilled worker, qualified to work without supervision and to teach apprentices: *A master craftsman.* (2) very highly skilled in the arts and sciences: *A master musician.*

Master and Servant, Law of LAW a branch of the law that deals with the special relationship between employer and employee, also called the Law of Service. This relationship exists when one person, the master, has the right to control the way in which another person, the servant, shall act. Thus, besides domestic servants, any employee who is paid a wage or salary, such as a clerk, waiter or factory-worker, is legally the servant of his employer; and both master and servant have duties and responsibilities towards each other. Doctors, lawyers, architects and free-lance artists are not legally servants but independent contractors who are not subject to the Law of Master and Servant.

master builder IND. a building contractor.

master copy the original copy of a document from which more copies are prepared on duplicators or by some photocopying processes.

master mariner see under mariner.

master (of a ship) SHIPG. the officer who commands a merchant ship. He is responsible to the owners for the management, safety, and navigation of the ship, and has special powers over the crew and cargo. He is allowed by custom the title of captain. Cf. shipping-master. See captain.

master porter SHIPG. an employee of a dock company who is responsible for controlling the unloading, sorting and removal of cargo from a ship.

matching duty see countervailing duty.

mate SHIPG. a high-ranking officer on a ship, next in rank to the captain or master. Syn. first officer. On large ships there are several such officers, called first mate, second mate, and so on.

mate's receipt a receipt given to a carrier and signed by, or for, the mate of a ship for goods delivered direct to the ship and not through a warehouse. A mate's receipt is a temporary document of title for use until the bill of lading is complete.

material fact (1) INSCE. any important fact which must by law be declared by a person making a proposal for an insurance, in order that the underwriter may properly decide whether to accept the risk and, if so, what the rate of premium and other conditions shall be. (2) STK. EXCH. important information about the company, that must by law be made known by a company issuing a prospectus. (3) LAW in a lawsuit or criminal trial, facts given by a witness that are so important that they could influence the decision of the court.

materials, bill of see bill of quantities.

materials buyer IND. an employee in a factory, who is responsible for buying the materials needed for production. It is his duty to buy materials at the lowest price and yet of acceptable quality, and to make sure that they arrive in good time and in the right quantities. See materials control. Syn. procurement officer; purchasing officer.

materials control (1) IND. a system of controlling the amount of each material held in stock, with the aim of avoiding locking up capital in unnecessary stocks, yet making sure that enough of the right materials is available for production when needed. Syn. stock control; inventory control. (2) a system of checking the quality of materials bought.

materials handling IND. the movement of materials from one part of a factory to another, or from one factory to another factory within the same organization.

matériel French, MAN. all the material things necessary for the running of a business, as opposed to personnel, i.e. human beings.

maternity benefit INSCE. in Britain, a sum of money paid, under the national insurance scheme, to a mother on the birth of each child.

mature v. BKG. & COM. in business, esp. regarding bills of exchange or insurance policies, to become due for payment.

maturity BKG., INSCE., STK. EXCH. the date on which a bill of exchange, promissory note, insurance policy, debenture or loan stock becomes due for payment or repayment.

Maundy money see under money.

Mauritania a republic in north-west Africa, pop. 1.3 million approx. (1974); capital, Nouakchott, pop. 55,000 approx.; languages, French and Arabic; currency unit, the ouguiya, divided into 5 khoums. Member, Arab League; O.A.U.; Associate, E.E.C.

Mauritius an independent island state in the Indian Ocean, pop. 860,000 approx. (1973); capital, Port Louis, pop. 150,000 approx.; languages, English, French and Hindi; currency unit, the Mauritius rupee (Mau Re., pl. Rs.), divided into 100 cents. Member, O.C.A.M.M.; Associate, E.E.C.; (British) Commonwealth.

Mau Re. the Mauritius rupee.

max. maximum.

maximize to make as big or as numerous as possible: To maximize profits/output. Opp. to minimize.

maximum the greatest possible quantity, value or degree. The maximum retail prices of milk and bread are fixed by the government. Opp. minimum. Abbr. max. Cf. optimum.

maximum price see under price.

m.b., m/b., M.B. motor boat; motor barge.

MC Monaco's international vehicle-registration letters.

m/c. motor cycle; machine

M.C.A. monetary compensatory amount.

mchy. machinery.

m/cs. machines.

Md. Maryland, U.S.A.

M/d months (after) date.

M.D. memorandum of deposit; malicious damage; doctor of medicine; managing director.

M.D.H.B. Mersey Docks and Harbour Board.

mdise. merchandise.

mdnt. midnight.

mdse. merchandise.

Me. Maine, U.S.A.

mean adj. selfish; unwilling to give or spend money: He is too mean to buy me a drink. Syn. stingy.

n. an average quantity or number. See arithmetic mean; geometric mean; harmonic mean; quadratic mean. Syn. average. Cf. median; mode.

v. to intend: To mean to write to him.

to mean business (*colloq.*) to intend to act firmly in a difficult situation.

mean price STK. EXCH. the market price of a security calculated by taking the average of the jobber's buying and selling prices. *Syn.* middle market price.

means FIN. the amount of a person's wealth, in the form of income and assets: *He is a man of means*, he is rich, wealthy. *I have no private means*, I have no income other than my pay.

means test FIN. an examination of the income and assets of a person and his family to determine whether he may rightfully be given certain allowances or benefits.

measurement goods SHIPG. goods that are light but bulky (take up much space), such as wood pulp, and are therefore carried as cargo on payment of a freight rate based on a measurement ton of 40 cubic feet. *See* freight ton *under* ton.

measurement ton *see* freight ton *under* ton.

measures *see* weights and measures.

mechanic's lien *see under* lien.

med., Med. medium (size); (*colloq.*) Mediterranean sea.

media *pl.* ADVTG. means of spreading information. *See* advertising (1); advertising media; admass. *Sing.* medium.

media analysis ADVTG. the scientific study of the relative effectiveness of the various advertising media, esp. in making a particular product more widely known to the public. *Syn.* media research.

median in a set of variables arranged in increasing or decreasing order of value, the value of the variable in the middle, i.e. that divides the set into two equal parts, with an equal number of values below it and above it. In a set of eleven variables so arranged, the median will be the sixth, there being five values below and five above it. If there is an even number of variables in the set, the median is the arithmetic mean of the two middle numbers. The median being the middle value, half-way between the lowest and the highest, its usefulness depends entirely on its position in the set. Cf. mode; quartile.

mediate possession *see under* possession (3).

mediation IND. REL. the act of a person, called a *mediator*, who brings together the two parties to an industrial dispute with the aim of settling their differences. If he has power to make the parties obey his decision, he is called an *arbitrator* and the process is *arbitration*. If he can do no more than suggest a settlement, he is a *conciliator* and the process is *conciliation*. *See* arbitration; conciliation; Advisory, Conciliation and Arbitration Service.

medical certificate MAN. a note signed by a doctor formally declaring that a certain person, e.g. an employee, is unable to work, or is able to perform only light duties, because of illness or injury.

medical examination an examination of a person by a doctor to decide the state of the person's health. Cf. medical inspection.

medical expenses policy *see under* insurance policy.

medical inspection a close and critical examination by a doctor or health official of a place, building, ship, etc. to see whether it is in a healthy condition for human beings to work or live in. Cf. medical examination.

medicine *see* industrial medicine.

medium-dated securities *see* mediums.

medium of exchange *see* exchange, medium of.

medium of instruction *see* language of instruction *under* language.

mediums STK. EXCH. in Britain, gilt-edged and other fixed-interest securities repayable in five to fifteen years from the present time. Cf. longs; shorts.

meet (1) to settle: *To meet a bill/debt/instalment/interest payment*, to pay it when due. (2) to satisfy: *This new product meets a need/demand*.

meeting *see* company meeting; board of directors.

meeting of creditors LAW (1) in the case of a debtor against whom a receiving order has recently been made, a meeting of his creditors called by the official receiver and presided over by him, at which the creditors and the debtor decide whether to accept a scheme of arrangement or whether the debtor shall be declared bankrupt. *See* bankruptcy. (2) in the case of a company in liquidation, a meeting of the company's creditors called by the official receiver to decide whether to apply to the court to appoint a liquidator in place of the official receiver. If a liquidator is appointed, he may call further general meetings of the creditors. *See* winding-up.

mega- the *prefix* used in the metric system of SI units to mean one million times: 1 megawatt = 1,000,000 watts; 1 megatonne = 1,000,000 tonnes.

mem. memorandum. *See* memo.

member bank BKG. (1) in U.S.A., a commercial bank that is a member of the Federal Reserve System. (2) in Britain, a commercial bank that is a member of the London Bankers' Clearing House; a clearing bank.

member of a company STK. EXCH. a shareholder in a company. The persons signing the Memorandum of Association of a company become its first members. Any persons allotted or coming into possession of shares in the company become members as soon as their name is recorded in the company's register of members or share register.

membership (1) the state of being a member of an organization such as a society, club, partnership, company. (2) the whole group of members of an organization: *The trade union has a membership of 200,000*, it has 200,000 members.

members, register of *see* register of members.

members' voluntary liquidation *see* winding-up.

memo. memorandum.

memorandum (1) (a note of) something to be remembered, esp. for future action: *Travellers keep a memorandum of their daily expenses and write out a claim every month.* (2) a short informal note or report on some deal or event or conversation. (3) an informal written or typed message to someone in the same office or organization, sent in place of a letter. *Pl.* memoranda; memorandums. *Abbr.* memo.; mem.

memorandum cheque *see under* cheque.

Memorandum of Association LAW & MAN. an important and essential document in which the persons associating together to form a new company set down in detail the objects of the company, its name, and the country in which its registered office will be, whether the liability of its members will be limited, the amount of its authorized capital and the number and value of its shares. The Memorandum is one of the documents sent to the Registrar of Companies in Britain with the application for a Certificate of Incorporation. Cf. Articles of Association.

memorandum of deposit BKG. a document signed by a person who deposits stocks, shares and other negotiable instruments as security for a loan from a bank. The document records in detail the conditions on which the loan is made and gives the bank the powers it needs to sell the things deposited if the loan is not repaid when due. Cf. certificate of deposit. *Syn.* letter of deposit. *Abbr.* M.D.

Memorandum of Satisfaction LAW a formal notice sent to the Registrar of Companies by a company whenever any mortgage or other charge, such as debentures or debenture stock, has been satisfied, i.e. paid off, wholly or partly.

memory COMP. in a computer, the central storage unit that holds data (information) in machine language, on magnetic cores, tapes, discs or drums, in such a form that the data can later be quickly found and used.

Menger Karl (1840–1921), Austrian economist, Professor of Political Economy at Vienna (1873–1903). He became famous as leader of a group of teachers and writers known as the Austrian School. He developed a Theory of Value based on utility and consumer satisfaction, and at about the same time as Jevons and Walras, although working independently, he produced the Theory of Marginal Utility. *See* Austrian School.

mentioned *see* above-mentioned.

menu COM. & TOUR. a list of dishes served in a restaurant, showing prices. *Syn.* bill of fare.

mercantile COM. commercial; relating to merchants and trade: *A mercantile bank.*

mercantile agent *see* factor (2).

mercantile credit *see* commercial credit (2).

mercantile credit agency *see* credit agency.

mercantile house COM. & IND. any business organization carrying on some industrial or commercial activity, such as manufacturers, wholesalers, retailers, merchants, brokers and factors.

mercantile law *see* commercial law.

mercantile marine SHIPG. a country's merchant ships and the men who serve in them. *Syn.* merchant navy. *Abbr.* M.M.

mercantile paper BKG. negotiable instruments of a commercial nature, such as commercial bills of exchange, promissory notes. *Syn.* commercial paper.

mercantilism ECON. HIST. a name first given by Adam Smith in his *Wealth of Nations* (1776) to the economic system current in much of Europe from the sixteenth to early eighteenth centuries following the gradual end of the feudal system. The mercantilists favoured the mercantile (trading) classes and gave the highest importance to international trade rather than to agriculture; money alone was wealth, and gold and silver were essential forms of wealth; a surplus balance of trade was necessary to increase the country's stock of gold; exports of manufactured goods were encouraged but wages had to be kept low; imports were kept low by protective and other import duties. All this required much public control over prices, wages, exports, imports, etc. Mercantilism was strongly attacked by the classical economists (*see* Classical School) and was gradually replaced by laissez-faire systems during the eighteenth century. *See also* cameralism.

mercantilist ECON. a person who believes in, supports, mercantilism. *Adj.* mercantilistic.

mercer COM. a seller of cloth, esp. of expensive silk and woollen materials. The goods he sells are called *mercery*.

merchandise *n.* COM. goods, esp. manufactured articles, that are intended for sale, not for the personal use of the present owner: *Goods imported as merchandise, not as a traveller's personal effects. Abbr.* mdise.; mdse. *Pron.* -ize. *v.* to buy and sell; to trade (in). *See* merchandising.

merchandise broker COM. a broker who acts as a middleman or agent for a manufacturer or importer, esp. in finding buyers interested in large quantities of a product. The goods are not at any time the property of the broker.

merchandise marks (1) COM. & IND. trademarks. (2) LAW *Merchandise Marks Acts* (from

1887) a number of laws that prevent the sale in Britain of merchandise bearing dishonest marks intended to mislead the consumer. If a foreign-made article carries the name or trademark of a person or firm in Britain, or the name of a place in Britain, it must also be marked with its country of origin.

merchandiser COM. a trader.

merchandising COM. (1) the active planning and organization of various ways of attracting the public to buy a particular product in the shops such as displays, free samples, free gifts, competitions. (2) the planning and development of new products. Cf. marketing; merchanting.

merchant *n.* COM. (1) a trader who buys and sells goods or commodities in large quantities, usu. at his own cost, to sell in smaller quantities, esp. in foreign trade: *A commodity/commission/general/paper merchant. See* export agent; export merchant; import merchant. *Syn.* a trader; a wholesale dealer; a wholesaler. (2) a shopkeeper; a retailer: *A coal merchant.*
adj. relating to trade or commerce. *See* merchant bank; merchant guild, etc.
v. to buy and sell; to trade. *See also* merchanting.

merchantable (1) COM. fit for sale: *Made merchantable*, (of damaged goods) repaired and made saleable. (2) LAW *Of merchantable quality*, in the law relating to the sale of goods, of a quality sufficiently good to satisfy the purpose for which the buyer intends to use the goods, or for which the seller intends that they should be used. If the goods are not good enough for the intended purpose they are not, in law, merchantable and ought not to be sold.

Merchant Adventurers ECON. HIST. a company of English merchants who had a monopoly in the export trade in woollen cloth to the Low Countries and later to Germany between 1407 and 1806. It had important trading centres on the continent, esp. in Antwerp and Hamburg.

merchant bank BKG. any of a number of banks in Britain that formerly acted as financiers to foreign governments but are now mainly commercial organizations specializing in the financing of international trade by accepting bills of exchange, and in servicing (arranging and managing) home and overseas loans. *See* accepting house. Merchant banks accept some deposits from the public, deal in foreign exchange and bullion, arrange Euromarket loans, act as confirming houses for overseas buyers of British products, raise capital for companies by acting as issuing houses, keep the share registers of certain companies, act as financial advisers, manage investment trusts and unit trusts, and may themselves own and deal in securities. Cf. merchant banker.

merchant banker *see* merchant bank.

merchant guild *see* guild.

merchanting COM. buying and selling; trading. *Merchanting house*, a commercial organization trading with foreign countries in large quantities of goods, with activities that include importing, exporting, shipping, banking and insurance. Cf. merchandising.

merchantman SHIPG. a merchant ship, esp. a cargo vessel.

merchant marine *see* mercantile marine.

merchant navy *see* mercantile marine.

merchant prince COM. a very powerful and wealthy merchant.

merchant service *see* mercantile marine.

merchant ship SHIPG. a ship used in commerce; a cargo vessel or passenger liner, *not* a man-of-war. *Syn.* merchantman.

merchant shipper *see* export merchant.

merchant shipping *see under* shipping.

merger (1) LAW the ending of an interest in a property when the owner becomes the owner also of a larger interest in the same property. Thus, e.g. when a leaseholder buys the freehold, the leasehold interest is merged (joined, combined) in the freehold and no longer has a separate existence in law. (2) LAW a simple contract is said to be merged when its provisions have been contained in a specialty contract, i.e. one in the form of a deed. (3) one of two particular forms of combination: (*a*) in one form the ownership of two companies, often about equal in size, is combined to form one new company, the shareholders of both the old companies being given shares in the new and (*b*) in the other form, one company, usu. the larger, obtains the ownership of the other, which then becomes a subsidiary company and may or may not keep its name.

conglomerate merger *see under* conglomerate.

horizontal merger *see* horizontal amalgamation *under* amalgamation.

vertical merger *see* vertical amalgamation *under* amalgamation.

meridian (1) a great circle (one having its centre at the centre of the earth) that passes through the North and South Poles. (2) the line of longitude of a place.

Meridian Day the name given to the whole day that is gained when a ship crosses the international date line from west to east, thus avoiding having, e.g., two Mondays in one week. The second is called Meridian Day. *Syn.* Antipodes Day.

merit MAN. a quality deserving reward or praise: *A merit increase*, a special increase in pay given to an employee as a reward for excellent work, or for services performed beyond the call of normal duty. Cf. merit bonus.

merit bonus *see under* bonus.

Messieurs (*French*, gentlemen) a form of address to a firm, esp. a partnership. In English correspondence it is never written in full.

but always as the abbreviation Messrs. In France, the abbreviation is MM.

Messrs. Messieurs.

messuage LAW a house where people live, with the gardens and buildings that go with it.

metallic currency *see under* currency.

meter *n.* an instrument for measuring the amount of some substance passing through it, such as a *gas, electricity* or *water meter*, or for measuring the passing of time, such as a *parking-meter*. A *coin meter*, a meter operated by coins. *Syn.* slot-meter.
v. to measure (something) with a meter.

method study MAN. & IND. the recording and examining of ways of doing work, with the aim of determining whether it can be done more cheaply and effectively. Cf. work study; work measurement; organization and method.

métier *French*, a person's trade or profession; the work he has been trained to do or is accustomed to do. *Pron.* may-tiay.

metre the standard unit of length in the metric system of SI units. It is one-thousandth of a kilometre and consists of 100 centimetres. 1 metre = 1.0936133 yards. *Abbr.* m.

metric system of SI units the modern system of weights and measures that has replaced the older metric system first introduced into France during the French Revolution. The SI system is based on the metre (length), kilogram (mass), second (time), ampere (electric current), kelvin (thermodynamic temperature), and candela (luminous intensity). All other units are obtained by multiplying these basic units by factors of ten.

metric ton *see* tonne. *Abbr.* m.t.

metropolis the chief city of a country or region, esp. the centre of government or of commerce and finance. In Britain, Greater London.

MEX Mexico's international vehicle-registration letters.

Mexico a federal republic in North America, pop. 55 million approx. (1973); capital, Mexico City, pop. 8 million approx.; language, Spanish; currency unit, the peso, divided into 100 centavos. Member, O.A.S.; L.A.F.T.A.

mfg. manufacturing.

M Fr. Mali franc.

M.H.W.S. mean high water springs (tides).

Mich. Michigan, U.S.A.

Michaelmas *see* quarter-day.

M.I.C.R. magnetic ink character recognition.

micro- in the metric system of SI units, the *prefix* meaning one-millionth (10^{-6}): 1 second (s) = 1,000,000 micro-seconds (μ s). *Sign:* μ.

micro-economics ECON. THEORY that branch of economics that examines and explains the behaviour of human beings and things in small units: e.g. a particular firm, household, or person, a single commodity, one person's wage. Cf. macro-economics; partial analysis.

Middle East the countries on the eastern and southern shores of the Mediterranean and extending eastwards to include Iran and the Arabian peninsula.

middleman COM. & ECON. a businessman or commercial organization that plays a part in the channels of distribution, by which goods pass from producer to consumer. Middlemen are useful in buying in bulk from producers, often anticipating demand, in stocking the goods in places near the market, in breaking bulk, in informing producers of the wants of consumers, in sharing risks with producers. The following may be classed as middlemen: agents, brokers, dealers, factors, jobbers, merchants, retailers, warehousemen, wholesalers. *Syn.* intermediary; go-between.

middle management *see under* management.

middle market price *see under* price.

Middx. Middlesex, once a county, now part of Greater London.

Mid-European Time *see* Central European Time.

Midsummer Day *see* quarter-day.

migrant *n.* a person who has moved from his own country to settle in another. He is called an *emigrant* in his original country and an *immigrant* in the country in which he settles.
adj. A *migrant worker*, a worker who migrated from another region or country. *Syn.* migratory worker.

migrate to move from one region or country to live or settle in another.

migratory *see* migrant, *adj.*

mil the fractional currency unit of Cyprus. 1000 mils = 1 Cyprus pound (C£).

milage *see* mileage.

milch cattle AGR. cows kept for producing milk.

mile a unit of distance in common use in Britain, the U.S.A., and some other, esp. English-speaking, countries; and also in general use by navigators everywhere.

Admiralty measured mile a sea mile of 6080 feet = 1853.18 metres, used by the British Admiralty until 1970, when it was replaced by the international nautical mile (*see below*).

air mile *see* international nautical mile *below.*

geographical mile a (U.K.) nautical mile, being the length of one minute of latitude at 48°, standardized at 6080 feet. *Abbr.* g.mile.

international nautical mile since 1970, the standard measure of distance used by sea and air navigators, replacing the U.K. nautical mile. It is the length of one minute of latitude at 45°, standardized at 1852 metres exactly, or 1.50779 statute miles, or 6076.1131 feet. *Also* air mile.

land mile *see* statute mile *below.*

nautical mile the standard measure of distance formerly used by sea and air navigators; sometimes called the *U.K. nautical mile*, it is the length of a minute of latitude at 48°, standardized at 6080 feet exactly, or 1853.18 metres. Since 1970, this unit has been mainly replaced by the *international nautical mile* (*see above*). *Also* geographical mile.

sea mile the basic unit of measurement of distance at sea, being the length of a minute of latitude. A sea mile has no standardized length: because the earth is not a true sphere but is flattened towards the two Poles, the length of a minute of latitude varies from 1842 metres at the Poles to 1861 metres at the Equator. Navigators measure distances from the latitude scales printed on charts; the scales allow for variations in the length of a minute at different latitudes. These distances are sometimes incorrectly called nautical miles.

statute mile in Britain, the U.S.A., and some other English-speaking countries, a unit of distance on land equal to 8 furlongs or 1760 yards or 5280 feet or 1.609344 kilometres exactly. *Syn.* land mile.

Swedish mile a unit of distance on land still used in Sweden, equal to 10 kilometres.

mileage TRANSPT. (1) a number of miles covered, such as during a journey or the life of a vehicle: *A low-mileage car*, one that has run relatively few miles. (2) a distance expressed in miles: *The mileage from London to Glasgow by road is 401.* (3) a charge payable for each mile travelled; a rate per mile. (4) the average number of miles that a motor vehicle will run on one gallon of petrol. *Also* milage.

military aid *see* foreign aid.

milk STK. EXCH. *To milk the profits*, to draw out, extract, drain a company of its profits by taking unfair advantage of voting power to pay unreasonably high salaries to the directors, or by declaring excessive dividends instead of building up reserves. *To milk stocks*, to reduce stocks, usu. to free capital for other uses.

mill IND. (1) a factory, esp. one in which cloth or paper is made by machinery: *A woollen/cotton mill.* (2) a place or machine for grinding substances into powder: *A flour mill*; or for shaping metals: *A rolling mill.*

Mill James (1773–1836), Scottish historian, philosopher and economist. He wrote an important textbook *Elements of Political Economy* (1821) based largely on David Ricardo's teachings. A member of the Classical School, he brought to the study of economics the mind of a radical philosopher, i.e. one who searches for the origin and causes of events in order to make a better world.

Mill John Stuart (1806–73), English philosopher and classical economist, son of James Mill (*see above*). He served many years with the East India Company in London and later became a Member of Parliament. Of the many books he wrote, his *Principles of Political Economy* (1848) was a most important and clearly-

written survey of the economics of his times; it was basically a restatement of the teachings of Ricardo but it also contained much original thought. *See* Classical School.

miller IND. a person who owns or operates a mill, esp. a flour mill.

milli- in the metric system of SI units, the *prefix* meaning one-thousandth (10^{-3}): 1 metre (m) = 1000 millimetres (mm). 1 litre (l) = 1000 millilitres (ml).

milliard in Britain, a thousand million, 1,000,000,000 or 10^9. In U.S.A. and some other countries, this number is called a billion.

millième the fractional currency unit of Egypt, the Sudan and Libya. 1000 millièmes = 1 Egyptian pound, 1 Sudanese pound and 1 Libyan dinar.

millime the fractional currency unit of Tunisia. 1000 millimes = 1 Tunisian dinar.

millionaire a person who possesses one or more millions of a certain currency: *A dollar millionaire.* Any very rich person. If he is known to possess many millions, he is said to be a *multimillionaire.*

mill ream *see* ream.

Mimeograph *n.* the name of a make of duplicator using a typewritten or handwritten wax stencil.

min. minimum; minute; mining; minim.

Mincing Lane COMMOD. EXCH. the popular name for the London Commodity Exchange at Plantation House in Mincing Lane, in the City of London.

minim the smallest unit in the system of liquid measure commonly used in Britain, the U.S.A. and some other countries, esp. by pharmacists (makers of medicine). 1 fluid ounce (fl. oz.) = 480 minims (min.). *See* liquid measure *table on page 478. Abbr.* m.; min.

minimize to make as small as possible: *To minimize a loss. Opp.* to maximize.

minimum the smallest quantity, value or degree possible or allowable. Cf. maximum. *Abbr.* min.

minimum lending rate BKG. in Britain until 1981, the lowest rate at which the Bank of England would discount approved bills of exchange. In theory, it had to be kept within certain limits based on the current average discount rate on Treasury bills, but at times, esp. under the influence of the government, the Bank fixed the rate within a range set by other money rates. Like the former bank rate which it replaced in 1972, the M.L.R. influenced most other interest rates in the money market. *See* base rate; managed currency *under* currency. *Abbr.* M.L.R.

Minimum-of-Existence Theory of Wages *see* Subsistence Theory of Wages.

minimum price *see under* price.

minimum wage (1) LAW in those industries or

trades in which wages are low because the workers lack bargaining-power, the lowest wage that an employer may legally pay to an employee. (2) most trade unions settle by agreement with employers what shall be the lowest, or minimum, wage paid to their members.

minister (1) in Britain, a person who holds high office under the Crown, usu. as head of a government department. *A cabinet minister* is a minister who is a member of the cabinet, a group of leading ministers under the Prime Minister, who together govern the country. (2) a high government officer sent to represent his country in a foreign country. He is next in rank below an ambassador and is usu. in charge of a legation. (3) a priest (usu. not of the Church of England) called a *minister of religion* if he is authorized to lead worship in a church or similar religious institution. *Syn.* pastor.

Minn. Minnesota, U.S.A.

minor LAW *see* infant.

minority interests STK. EXCH. in a subsidiary company that is not wholly owned by the holding company, those shareholders who together own the shares not held by the holding company. *Syn.* minority shareholders.

mint FIN. *n.* a government factory for making coins: *The Royal Mint.*
v. to make coins by stamping them in metal.

mintage *see* brassage.

mint par of exchange FIN. the rate of exchange between two currencies that are on the gold standard, i.e. when the gold value of their standard currency unit has been fixed by law. The rate between any pair of gold-standard currencies is always directly related to the amount of gold in a unit of each currency. *Syn.* par rate of exchange; mint parity of exchange. *See* par (3).

mint ratio FIN. under bimetallism, the relation between the values of the two standard metals, usu. gold and silver.

minus *see* less.

minute (1) one-sixtieth part of a degree, a unit used in measuring angles. (2) one-sixtieth part of an hour. 1 minute = 60 seconds. *Abbr.* min. *Sign*: ': *1' = one minute.* (3) a written or typed note; a memorandum.
minutes *pl.* (of a meeting) an official or typed record of business done, including decisions reached, at the meeting. Minutes, usu. recorded in a *minute book*, are read at the beginning of the next meeting and, if confirmed (approved) by those present, are signed by the chairman as a correct record of what took place. *See also* board minutes *under* board of directors.

M.I.P. marine insurance policy; monthly investment plan.

misappropriation *see* defalcation.

misc. miscellaneous.

miscarriage (1) SHIPG. & TRANSPT. (*a*) incorrect carriage of goods, esp. when not as arranged or provided in a contract. (*b*) loss in transit (on the journey). (2) LAW a failure: *Miscarriage of justice*, failure of a court of law to reach a fair decision; an injustice.

miscellaneous consisting of different kinds; various; mixed: *Miscellaneous goods/articles/objects. See* miscellaneous file *under* file. *Abbr.* misc.

misdemeanour (1) LAW a criminal offence that is less serious than felony and treason. (2) generally, any kind of misbehaviour. *Also* (U.S.A.) misdemeanor.

miser a person who lives a poor and miserable life because of an excessive desire to save and store up money.

Mises Ludwig Edler von (1881–1973), Austrian (later American) economist and a leading member of the Austrian School; Professor of Economics at Vienna (1931–8), Geneva (1934–40) and New York (1945–69). In many books and articles, esp. his *The Anti-Capitalistic Mentality* (1956), he attacked socialism and all who opposed a free market as the essential basis for economic success. He also did important work on the theory of the trade cycle in relation to bank credit, and on the place of marginal utility in the theory of money.

misfeasance LAW the performance in a wrongful manner of a lawful act, such as doing something negligently (very carelessly) or failing to do it when it ought to have been done. Cf. non-feasance.

misfortune, certificate of *see* certificated bankrupt *under* bankrupt.

misleading description *see* misrepresentation.

misprision LAW the offence at common law of unlawfully hiding, covering up, the fact that someone has done a criminal act.

misrepresentation LAW & COM. a statement which gives false information or a misleading description and is intended to deceive is called a *false* or *fraudulent misrepresentation* and gives a wronged party good reason for bringing an action for damages in the courts. Any contract is voidable at the wish of the party who has been harmed if misrepresentation by the other party can be proved. *Syn.* deceit; deception; fraud; misstatement.

Miss. Mississippi, U.S.A.

mission *see* trade mission.

misstatement *see* misrepresentation.

mistake *see* operative mistake; error.

mix *see* marketing mix; sales mix.

mixed currency *see under* currency.

mixed economy ECON. an economic system in which some industries are owned by the State and others are owned by private persons as shareholders of industrial companies. *Syn.* governed economy; mixed capitalist economy.

mixed farming AGR. farming in which both arable crops and livestock are important.

mixed policy see under insurance policy.

Mk. mark.

mkt. market.

ml millilitre.

M.L. motor launch.

Mlle. Mademoiselle.

M.L.R. minimum lending rate (of the Bank of England) abolished in Britain in 1981.

M.L.W.N. mean low water neap (tide).

M.L.W.S. mean low water spring (tide).

MM Messieurs (Gentlemen).

mm millimetres.

M.M. mercantile marine.

m.m. made merchantable.

Mme. Madame.

Mmes. Mesdames.

mn. midnight.

M.N. merchant navy.

mng. managing.

mngmt. management.

mngr. manager.

Mo. Missouri, U.S.A.

M.O. money order; mail order; medical officer.

mo. month.

m.-o. months old.

mobile shop COM. a shop in a motor van making regular visits esp. to new housing areas and to country villages not well served by shops, to sell groceries, household goods and sometimes clothing.

mobility of labour ECON. THEORY the degree to which workers are able and willing to move from one place to work in another (*geographical mobility*), or to change from one kind of work to another (*occupational mobility*). A lack of mobility of labour has an important effect on the supply of labour and may increase unemployment. *Syn.* fluidity of labour.

mock auction COM. an auction at which the auctioneer or the seller of an article dishonestly arranges for bids to be made that are not serious but intended only to force up the price.

mode (1) in a set of variables, the value that happens most frequently. Thus in the set 5, 3, 9, 5, 8, 6, 5, 10, 5, 8, 3, the value 5 is the mode because it happens four times, more frequently than any of the other values. It is also called the position of greatest density, and is much used in commerce, e.g. in determining which are the most popular sizes of shoes and clothing to stock in a shop. Cf. median; mean. (2) a manner; a method used: *The mode of payment*, the form in which payment is made, by cheque, cash, etc. (3) fashion, esp. in dress: *She dresses in the latest mode.*

modify to make changes in the form of something: *This machine can be modified to print on cloth instead of on paper. The architect modi-fied the design of the building to give more light to the offices. We have modified our demands*, we have changed them. *N.* modification.

modiste COM. a maker or seller of women's fashionable clothes, esp. hats.

module IND. one of a number of standard units of which a building or furniture may be made up. *Adj.* modular.

M.O.H. medical officer of health.

mohur a former gold coin of India and Persia, worth 15 rupees; a unit of value of 16 rupees, still sometimes used in India when fixing professional fees of doctors, lawyers and architects. *Syn.* gold mohur.

moiety LAW a half, esp. one of two equal instalments.

mole a long sea wall or pier protecting the entrance to a harbour when the weather is rough.

momentum see industrial momentum.

Mon. Monmouthshire, a former county in Wales, now part of Gwent.

Monaco a small principality (country ruled by a prince) in western Europe on the shores of the Mediterranean, pop. 23,000 approx. (1974); capital, Monte Carlo; language, French; currency unit, the French franc (f., fr., Fr.), divided into 100 centimes.

monarch a person who is the hereditary holder of the office of head of state, such as a king or queen, emperor, prince, sultan. Cf. Crown. *Syn.* sovereign.

monarchy a system of government in which the head of state is a monarch. *Syn.* kingdom.

monetarists ECON. THEORY economists who believe that the economy can and should be controlled by limits placed by the government on the total supply of money, esp. on bank credit. *Syn.* Monetary School.

monetary FIN. (1) relating to, consisting of, money: *A monetary reward*, a reward paid in money. *For a monetary consideration*, for a sum of money. *Syn.* pecuniary. (2) relating to the coinage, currency and financial arrangements of a country: *Monetary policy. The monetary system.*

monetary compensatory amount ECON. under the European Economic Community's Common Agricultural Policy, the expression that relates to subsidies and taxes on farm products used to support the green currencies. *Abbr.* M.C.A.

monetary deflation see currency deflation under deflation.

monetary economy FIN. an economy in which goods are exchanged for money, compared with a barter economy in which money is not used.

monetary policy FIN. the control, by the government, of a country's currency and its system for lending and borrowing money, esp. through the supply of money.

Monetary School *see* monetarists.

monetary standard *see* standard (4).

monetary system FIN. (1) the entire system that exists in a country to provide industry, commerce and the public with money of all kinds, such as coins, bank-notes, bank credit and deposits. (2) the methods and institutions used by the government to control the supply of money and near-money, such as hire-purchase borrowing, trade credits and deposits with building societies and finance houses that re-lend money but are outside the banking system. (3) the kind of convertibility adopted by a government for its currency, whether freely into gold as under the gold standard, or into paper of some kind, as under a paper standard.

monetary theory (of the trade cycle) *see* trade-cycle theories *under* cycle.

monetary unit FIN. the standard unit of the currency of a country: *The dollar is the monetary unit of the U.S.A.*

monetize FIN. (1) to coin money from (a metal or alloy). (2) to fix the official money value of a metal or alloy when used as money. *Opp.* demonetize. *N.* monetization. *Opp.* demonetization.

money (1) any article or commodity that is generally acceptable by law and custom as a means of payment, as a measure of value, and as a store of wealth. Various forms of money have developed, from the *commodity money* (such as cattle and cowrie shells) that replaced the barter system, to *hard money* made of precious metals, esp. gold and silver bars and coins, and *token money* of other metals; later, *paper money*, also called *soft money* or *representative money* was introduced, followed by the great development of the use of *substitute money* consisting of bank deposits and credits transferable by cheque, bills of exchange and Treasury bills that now make up the most important form of money in most countries. (2) wealth generally, calculated in units of the currency, but including all kinds of property: *He is worth a lot of money*, he is rich. *Money's worth*, reasonable value for the price paid. *To make money*, to get rich, be rich. *To mint/coin money*, (*colloq.*) to get rich quickly. *To put money into*, to invest in, support with money. *To be in the money*, (*colloq.*) to be rich. *To put money down*, to pay cash immediately. *Money for jam/for old rope* (*colloq.*) (*a*) money that is easily (perh. too easily) earned; (*b*) money that is certain to come in, or profit that is certain to be made. *To put one's money on*, to risk one's money on a horse in a race or on a business venture likely to succeed. *For money, see under* for.

active money *see under* active.

allotment money *see under* allotment.

application money *see under* application.

bank money *see under* bank.

call money *see under* call, *n.* (1).

caution money *see under* caution.

cheap money *see under* cheap.

commodity money *see under* commodity.

conduct money *see* caution money (4).

convertible money *see under* convertible.

counterfeit money bad money, both coin and bank-notes, made in imitation of real, or good, or genuine money with intention to deceive. *Syn.* false money.

credit money *see under* credit.

current money coins and bank-notes that are currently legal tender, as opposed to those that are no longer so because they have been demonetized.

danger money extra pay for doing dangerous work.

dead money *see* dead capital *under* capital.

dear money *see under* dear.

despatch money *see under* despatch.

earnest money *see under* earnest.

fall money *see under* fall.

false money *see* counterfeit money *above*.

fiat money *see under* fiat.

fiduciary money *see* fiduciary note issue.

final money all forms of bank deposit or bank credit that can be transferred by means of cheques.

floating money money temporarily held by bankers for which they cannot find any profitable use other than to put it on deposit with the Bank of England until it can be better invested.

fractional money coins of values less than the standard unit of currency: in Britain, the 50p, 10p, 5p, 2p, 1p, ½p coins; and in U.S.A., the 50c, 25c (quarter), 10c (dime), 5c (nickel) coins. Cf. standard money. *Syn.* fractional currency.

fresh money additional capital, esp. loan capital, as opposed to old money, which is existing capital.

funk money BKG. & FIN. money that is moved in a hurry, and sometimes secretly, from a country where economic or political conditions are bad, to another country where they are good, because the owner is frightened. Cf. hot money.

gate money *see under* gate.

hard money metal coins, not paper money. *See also* hard currency *under* currency. *Syn.* specie; cash; change.

hat money *see* primage.

hot money attracted from abroad by high interest rates or to find a relatively safe place in a time of political trouble. Since it may be quickly transferred elsewhere, it can greatly upset a country's balance of payments. Cf. funk money. *Syn.* refugee capital.

housekeeping money *see under* housekeeping.

hush-money money paid to a person as a bribe for not telling anyone about a crime, or for not giving information or evidence in a trial. A payment for secrecy.

idle money money held in the form of cash or held in idle balances, i.e. bank balances that are used to store money without bringing in any income. *Syn.* inactive money.

inactive money *see* idle money *above*.

inconvertible money *see* inconvertible currency *under* currency.

irredeemable money *see* inconvertible currency *under* currency.

key money *see under* key.

lawful money any money that is legal tender.

lot money *see under* lot.

managed money *see* managed currency *under* currency.

Maundy money specially-minted silver coins given personally to the poor on the Thursday before Easter by the British king or queen.

near money an asset which can be used almost as if it were money although it is not. For example, a bill of exchange is transferable and can be used to pay a debt although it is not money in the way that bank-notes, cheques and coins are. *Syn.* quasi-money. *See* money supply.

non-physical money *see* substitute money *below*.

old money *see* fresh money *above*.

option money *see* option.

paper money bank-notes; sometimes also cheques, bills of exchange, promissory notes and other documents that can be used as money in business, although not legal tender.

passage money *see* passage.

pin-money (*a*) a regular allowance given by a man to his wife or daughter to spend as she wishes, esp. on dress or dressmaking materials. (*b*) money saved by a woman from her housekeeping money. (*c*) money received by a married woman under a marriage settlement. (*d*) generally, any small sum regularly received as a reward for services. Cf. pocket-money.

pocket-money a small regular allowance made by a parent to a child, usu. weekly.

prize money (*a*) money paid to a winner in a competition or lottery. (*b*) in time of war, money paid to the crew of a ship that seizes an enemy vessel. *Syn.* prize bounty.

promotion money money paid to the promoters of a new company for their services in arranging and managing the operation.

purchase money the sum of money required to buy something, esp. a house.

quasi-money *see* near money *above*.

quick money money invested in such a way that it can be withdrawn on demand.

rag money (*colloq.*) paper money.

ready money cash; money, esp. coin and bank-notes, actually in hand, held ready for immediate payments: *I shall pay in ready money*, I shall pay in cash and I do not want credit.

real money money in the form of coin and bank-notes, not substitute money.

representative money paper money that is convertible into gold and silver, or that is fully backed by gold and silver stocks held by the issuing authority.

retention money an amount retained (held back) from a payment to a contractor in case he does not complete the contract by the agreed date, or in case his work is not properly done.

short money money lent for a short period at a fixed rate of interest.

slush-money money given as a bribe. *See* slush fund.

soft money paper money, not coins. *See also* soft currency *under* currency.

spending money money for personal expenses; pocket-money.

standard money the main unit of currency of a particular country. Cf. fractional money.

substitute money documents such as bank deposits or bank credit that can be transferred by cheque, commercial bills of exchange, trade credit and Treasury bills; these are not legal tender but are generally acceptable as money within certain business circles. *Syn.* non-physical money. Cf. near money; real money.

temporary money commercial bills of exchange and also Treasury bills, both of which can be discounted and made payable to other parties before they mature.

tight money *see* dear money *under* dear.

token money *see under* token.

world money any kind of money or medium of exchange that is very widely accepted for the settlement of international debts, usu. gold, the U.S. dollar and the pound sterling. *Syn.* international currency.

money at call *see* call money *under* call, *n.* (1).

money at call and short notice BKG. very short-term loans made by a bank, usu. to discount houses, bill-brokers, stockbrokers and jobbers. Such loans are for periods of from one to fourteen days and form an important part of a bank's liquid assets.

money-bags (1) bags for money. (2) (*colloq.*) a rich person, esp. someone who has a great desire for wealth.

money bill *see under* bill (8).

money-box (1) a closed box with a lock or seal and a small opening for putting in coins and notes, used for collecting contributions to charity or for storing small savings. (2) any closed object with an opening for putting in small savings, such as a china animal.

money-broker BKG. & FIN. (1) in Britain, a broker in the money market who arranges short-term loans by banks to discount houses and to dealers in government securities. (2) in U.S.A., a dealer in foreign exchange.

money capital *see under* capital.

money-changer FIN. a person whose business is to exchange the currency of one country for that of another. *Syn.* changer.

money circulation *see under* circulation.

moneyed *adj.* having money; rich; wealthy: *My stockbroker is a moneyed man.*

money-grubber (*colloq.*) a person who is much too interested in accumulating money.

money had and received LAW money that has been paid to a person who unjustly fails to give a promised consideration in return; such money can be recovered in an action in the courts by the person who paid it.

money illusion ECON. THEORY the false idea that money has a fixed and unchanging purchasing power. The expression was first used in 1927 by Irving Fisher, the American economist, who described it as 'a failure to perceive [understand] that the dollar or any other unit of money expands and shrinks in value'.

money income *see under* income.

moneylender LAW & FIN. in Britain, any person or organization whose business is to lend money, *other than*: a friendly society, a building society, a·pawnbroker, a banking or insurance business, or an organization, such as a local authority, given powers by a special Act of Parliament to lend money. Moneylenders must be registered and must obtain a licence each year from the government to carry on the business of moneylending. *See* consumer credit.

moneylending contract *see under* contract.

money-maker FIN. & COM. (1) a person who is successful in earning or gaining money. (2) a profitable business or commercial venture.

money market *see under* market.

money-measurement concept ACCTS. the basic rule in accounting, that the value of things and events can be measured only in units of money.

money of account *see* account, money of.

money on call *see* call money *under* call, *n.* (1).

money order FIN. a method of making small payments through the Post Office. In Britain, inland money orders for sending by post are no longer issued, but inland telegraph money orders are issued at certain post offices that are both money-order and telegraph offices. Cf. postal order. *Abbr.* M.O.

crossed money order one that has been crossed like a cheque; it can only be paid to a bank for credit to an account with that bank. *See* crossed cheque *under* cheque.

inland money order one payable to a payee in the country in which the order is issued.

international money order *see* overseas money order *below. Abbr.* I.M.O.

overseas money order one payable to a person in another country; such money orders may be limited by the exchange controls of the sender's country. *Abbr.* O.M.O. *Syn.* international money order.

telegraph(ic) money order one that is arranged urgently by telegraph, at an extra charge to cover the cost of the telegram. *Abbr.* T.M.O.

Money, Quantity Theory of *see under* Quantity Theory.

money rate of interest *see* nominal interest *under* interest.

money-spinner COM. (*colloq.*) a highly profitable product, business or property, such as a best-selling book, a highly successful film or play, or a shop selling a product much in demand.

money stock *see under* stock.

money supply FIN. & ECON. THEORY the total of all the money held by all persons and organizations in a country at a particular time; the whole of a country's existing stock (or supply) of money to hold as a liquid asset. In Britain, there are three measures, called *indicators of the money supply*:

M_1 the most limited, consists of only notes and coins in circulation, and private-sector current and sterling deposit accounts that can be transferred by cheque. It does not include non-sterling or public-sector accounts and deposits.

M_2 is broader, consisting of notes and coins in circulation, all private-sector sterling current accounts at commercial banks, and private-sector deposit accounts with deposit banks and discount houses. It is less used than M_1 and M_3.

M_3 is the broadest-based indicator, consisting of M_2 plus all other term deposits including non-sterling deposits, deposits with all banks and discount houses, and all public-sector deposits. There is a variation called *Sterling M_3* which is M_3 without the non-sterling deposits.

money wages *see under* wages.

monger COM. a retail trader; a dealer; a shopkeeper. Usu. combined with the name of a commodity: *A fishmonger/ironmonger. A costermonger*, a street seller, usu. of fish or fruit and vegetables.

möngö the fractional currency unit of the Mongolian Republic. 100 möngös = 1 tugrik.

Mongolian Republic a communist republic in north-east Asia, pop. 1.4 million approx. (1973); capital, Ulan Bạtor, pop. 250,000 approx.; languages, Mongolian and Russian; currency unit, the tugrik, divided into 100 möngös. Member, COMECON.

monkey (*colloq.*) five hundred pounds (£500).

monometallism ECON. & FIN. a monetary system in which only one standard metal is coined and is legal tender for unlimited amounts. A more useful variation, called a *composite legal tender* *system*, uses also freely-convertible paper money and token money consisting of coins of baser metal, with legal tender for a limited amount. *See* gold standard. Cf. bimetallism.

Monophoto *see* Monotype.

Monopolies and Mergers Commission IND., COM. & LAW in Britain, a commission with responsibility for examining, reporting and recommending whether a monopoly in the supply, manufacture or export of goods is in the public interest. In this case, monopoly means one supplier, or group of suppliers acting together, who can control at least one-third of the total supply of the article or commodity. The commission also acts similarly in regard to certain restrictive practices. After the commission has reported, the government can use its powers under the law to prevent new monopolistic mergers from forming, and to break up existing monopolies that are not in the public interest.

monopolist ECON. THEORY (1) a supplier who has a monopoly. (2) a person who believes in monopolies. Cf. monopsonist.

monopolistic competition *see under* competition.

monopolize COM. to obtain a monopoly; to get complete possession or control of something.

monopoly ECON. THEORY strictly the situation in a market in which there is only one supplier of a commodity and he therefore faces no competition (*pure monopoly*). Since there will usu. be some competition, such as from other goods, a monopoly is accepted by economists as being the situation in which one supplier or a group of suppliers acting together can control the market price. Cf. monopsony.

absolute monopoly *see under* absolute.

bilateral monopoly ECON. THEORY an imaginary situation in a market where there is only one buyer and only one supplier of a particular commodity or service. Thus both buyer and supplier are monopolists.

buyer's monopoly *see* monopsony.

commercial monopoly a monopoly that exists in a market for a commodity when one buyer or one supplier is in a position to determine the price. *See* monopsony; oligopsony. Cf. legal monopoly.

discriminating monopoly a monopoly that exists when a monopolist sells exactly similar articles or units of a commodity at different prices. *Syn.* price discrimination. *See* dumping.

fiscal monopoly a monopoly held by the State of the production and sale of certain popular commodities, mainly in order to obtain the highest possible amount of revenue from consumers, e.g. the monopolies in tobacco and matches in France. Cf. public monopoly. *Syn.* state monopoly; government monopoly.

institutional monopoly a partial monopoly that

exists when the owner of a trade-mark uses it to distinguish his product from other similar products in the market and, by means such as advertising and special packaging, persuades consumers that because his product is well known, it is the best one to buy.

legal monopoly a monopoly that exists by law, such as a copyright or patent, as opposed to a commercial monopoly.

natural monopoly a monopoly that exists because the entire demand for a product can be supplied by one producer producing on the smallest scale that is commercially possible.

perfect monopoly *see* pure monopoly *below*.

public monopoly a monopoly that by law belongs to the government, usu. a public service such as the postal, telegraph and telephone services, and the main means of transport such as the railways. Cf. fiscal monopoly.

pure monopoly the situation in a market in which there is one producer or supplier of a commodity and there are no near substitutes and therefore there is no competition. A pure or perfect monopoly is not likely to exist in practice but has some theoretical use in economic analysis. *Syn.* perfect monopoly; absolute monopoly.

sellers' monopoly the monopoly that exists in a market in which a commodity is scarce, allowing sellers to force buyers to compete with each other to raise prices. *Also* seller's monopoly. *Syn.* oligopoly.

monopoly price *see under* price.

monopoly profit *see under* profit.

monopsonist ECON. THEORY the one and only buyer of a commodity in the market. Cf. monopolist.

monopsonistic *adj.* A *monopsonistic firm*, the only firm buying a particular commodity.

monopsony ECON. THEORY the condition in a market where there is only one buyer of a commodity. *Syn.* buyer's monopoly.

Monotype a machine with a keyboard, used by printers for rapid composing (putting together) and casting of metal type, each letter or figure being produced separately but in its proper order. Cf. Linotype. *Monophoto* is a similar machine that produces photographic film bearing the matter to be printed, usu. by photolitho offset.

Mont. Montana, U.S.A.

month (1) one of 12 unequal divisions (of 28 to 31 days) called a *calendar month*, into which a (western) calendar year is divided. (2) a period of four weeks (or 28 days) often called a *lunar month*, the time roughly between one full moon and the next (more correctly about 29½ days). In commerce, a month always means a calendar month unless a lunar month of 28 days is clearly stated. *Adj.* and *adv.* monthly. *Abbr.* m.; mo.; mth.

monthly account COM. a form of consumer credit, being an arrangement with a retail shop or store that the customer's purchases are debited to his account up to an agreed fixed credit limit each month. The customer pays within an agreed period after receiving the statement of account from the retailer. Cf. budget account.

moonlight flit see flit.

moonlighting IND. (*colloq.*) having two jobs, one being a regular full-time job, the other only part-time, usu. in the evenings. The worker may be paid in cash and may not declare it to the tax authorities to avoid payment of income tax on this part of his income. *See* black economy.

moonshiner COM. (*colloq.*) a person who carries on an illegal trade, esp. by night.

moor SHIPG. to fasten a ship or boat by ropes or cables to a firmly-fixed object on land or on the bed of the sea, or to a floating buoy that is itself fastened by cables to the bottom.

moorage SHIPG. money charged for the use of moorings.

mooring SHIPG. a place where a ship or boat may be moored.

moorings *pl.* the ropes, cables, buoys, etc. by which a ship or boat is moored.

moral hazard see under hazard.

moratorium LAW & FIN. (1) a law allowing debtors to delay payment of debts, esp. at a time of national emergency. (2) an agreement between a debtor and a creditor that more time shall be allowed for payment of a debt. *Pl.* moratoria; moratoriums.

Morocco a constitutional monarchy (kingdom) in North Africa, pop. 16.3 million approx. (1973); capital, Rabat, pop. 450,000 approx.; languages, Arabic and French; currency unit, the dirham, divided into 100 Moroccan francs. Member, Arab League; O.A.U.

mortality rate see death rate.

mortality tables see life tables.

mortgage *n.* LAW & FIN. (1) a contract by which the owner of land (the mortgagor) borrows money, giving the lender (the mortgagee) an interest in the land as security for the loan. In Britain, by law a mortgage is either a legal mortgage or an equitable mortgage (*see these below*). A ship or yacht may also be mortgaged (*see* maritime mortgage *below*). A mortgage may also be given on goods and chattels (*see* chattel mortgage *under* chattel). (2) the document or deed recording a mortgage contract. *To raise a mortgage on* (*a house, etc.*), to borrow money by giving a mortgage on a house, etc. *To redeem/pay off a mortgage*, to repay the loan under a mortgage contract and so regain the property. (3) the thing given as security. *Syn.* gage; pawn.

v. to borrow money by giving a mortgage. *Syn.* to charge; to hypothecate. *Pron.* mor-gij.

blanket mortgage (*a*) in Britain, a mortgage that combines and replaces a number of existing mortgages. (*b*) in U.S.A., a mortgage in which the borrower gives all his fixed assets as security, rather than any particular assets.

chattel mortgage see under chattel.

equitable mortgage one of the two main kinds of mortgage (*see also* legal mortgage *below*); under it the mortgagor (borrower) gives the mortgagee (lender) the title-deeds of the property but without any document that gives the creditor complete control if the debt is not repaid when due. If the lender desires to sell the property in order to obtain repayment of the loan, he has to apply to a court of law for power to sell, or to gain possession, or to appoint a receiver.

first mortgage the original mortgage first given by the mortgagor of a property. *See* second and subsequent mortgage(s) *below*.

leasehold mortgage (*a*) in Britain, the mortgage of a property of which the mortgagor (borrower) owns the leasehold, not the freehold. (*b*) in U.S.A., a mortgage under which the mortgagor gives a lease of the property to the mortgagee as security for the loan.

legal mortgage one of the two main kinds of mortgage (*see also* equitable mortgage *above*); under it the mortgagee (lender) has complete control of the property if the mortgagor (borrower) fails to repay the debt when due; and he does not need to apply to a court of law for power to sell or take possession of the property or to appoint a receiver.

maritime mortgage a mortgage on a ship or yacht.

open-ended mortgage see open-ended.

option mortgage a mortgage arranged under the British Government's Option Mortgage Scheme, begun in 1968, by which persons borrowing money under mortgage contracts have the option (choice) of either obtaining income-tax relief on the interest paid on the loan or paying a rate of interest that is reduced by a government subsidy but does not qualify for tax relief.

puisne mortgage in Britain, a legal mortgage that is not registered in the local deeds register and is not protected by the deposit of the title-deeds to the property. *Pron.* pyooni.

second and subsequent mortgage(s) one or more further mortgages, called second, third, etc. mortgages, given by a mortgagor (borrower) after he has given a first or original mortgage on the same property. The number shows the order in which the interest of each mortgagee (lender) ranks if the property is sold, the first or original mortgagee having a higher claim than the second, and so on.

sub-mortgage the mortgage of a mortgage. The action of a mortgagee (lender) who himself borrows money by mortgaging the property to another mortgagee, called the sub-mortgagee, usu. for a period of a few days shorter than that of the original mortgage.

mortgage bond see under bond, n.

mortgage debenture see under debenture.

mortgagee FIN. a person or organization that lends money under a mortgage contract, e.g. a bank or building society lending money on the security of a house. See mortgage. If the borrower fails to pay the debt, the mortgagee has the right to take possession of the mortgaged property, or he can foreclose (see foreclosure), or he can bring an action in the courts for breach of contract, or he can sell the property if allowed under the mortgage contract, or he can appoint a receiver to collect income from the property and use it to reduce the debt. Cf. mortgagor.

mortgage-protection policy see house-purchase policy under insurance policy.

mortgage repayment see annuity system (2).

mortgagor FIN. a person or organization that borrows money under a mortgage contract, e.g. a house-owner who borrows money on the security of his house from a bank or building society. He has the right by law of redemption, i.e. of regaining his property by repaying the debt to the mortgagee. See equity of redemption. Cf. mortgagee.

mos. months.

most-favoured-nation clause COM. in a commercial treaty (agreement between countries), a clause by which each country agrees to give the other the same favourable benefit that it may give to any other country in the form of reduced tariffs.

motel TOUR. a motor hotel, i.e. a hotel esp. for motorists.

mother tongue the first language that a person learns, i.e. as a child from its mother, and thus the language spoken in the ordinary homes of a region or country. Syn. native language.

motion MAN. a proposal put forward for discussion at a formal meeting. If it is put to the vote (voted upon) and is agreed to by a majority of votes, it becomes a resolution. A dropped motion is one that is not put to the vote.

motion study see time and motion study.

motivate to give (a person) a strong reason or purpose for acting in a certain way, such as giving employees an extra reward for working hard, or giving customers something attractive to persuade them to buy a particular item.

motivational research ADVTG. & COM. a branch of market research that examines the reasons why people choose to buy one brand of goods rather than others.

motor hotel see motel.

motor insurance see under insurance, classes and kinds of.

motors STK. EXCH. stocks or shares of motor-manufacturing companies.

motor ship see motor vessel.

motor vessel SHIPG. a ship driven usu. by diesel motors (engines which run on fuel oil). Cf. sailing ship/vessel; steamship. Abbr. M/V or m.v. Syn. (U.S.A.) motor ship (M/S).

motorway TRANSPT. a main road specially made to allow traffic to travel safely at high speeds. Syn. in U.S.A., expressway, freeway, superhighway; in France, autoroute; in Italy, autostrada; in Germany, autobahn. Abbr. M.

mountain a very large stock, esp. of a farm product such as butter or meat, bought as a result of the Common Agricultural Policy of the European Economic Community. See intervention price.

Mountain (Standard) Time a time-zone in North America, seven hours behind Greenwich Mean Time and one hour ahead of Pacific Time. Abbr. M.S.T.

movable property LAW personal property in the form of goods and chattels, not real (immovable) property in the form of land and buildings.

movables pl. movable property such as money, securities, negotiable instruments and any valuable personal assets. A ship is, in law, not movable but real property.

move v. MAN. to put forward a proposal at a formal meeting; to propose a motion for discussion with the intention that, if voted upon and accepted, it should be adopted.

mover n. a person who moves, puts forward, proposes, a motion.

moving average a method used to show the trend (general tendency to rise or fall) of a set of values related to regular periods of time, such as the total monthly sales of a business. For example, a 12-month moving average would start in December of the first year with the average of the monthly sales in the 12 months January to December of that year; the next month's figure (for January) is the average of the past 12-month period February to January; the next (for February) is the average for March to February, and so on. This method greatly reduces the effect of temporary and seasonal variations, and shows clearly the general direction of the sales of the business. The same method can be adopted using moving annual totals instead of averages.

Mozambique a republic in east-central Africa, pop. 10 million approx. (1975); capital, Maputo (formerly Lourenço Marques), pop. 260,000 approx.; languages, Portuguese and tribal; currency unit, the metical (pl. meticais), divided into 100 centavos.

M.P. Member of Parliament.

m.p.g., mpg. miles per gallon.

m.p.h., mph. miles per hour.

Mr, Mr. a polite title given to a man and placed before his name or position: *Mr John Smith, Mr Chairman. Pron.* mister.

M.R., M/R mate's receipt.

Mrs, Mrs. a polite title given to a married woman and placed before her name: *Mrs Robinson. Also* (sometimes) *Mrs Henry Robinson,* to show that the woman is the wife of Mr Henry Robinson. *Pron.* misiz.

ms., MS. manuscript.

M/S., M.S. motor ship (U.S.A.); mail steamer.

m/s, M/s months after sight.

m.s. mail steamer.

M.S.C. Manchester Ship Canal.

m.s.l. mean sea level.

mss., MSS. manuscripts.

M.S.T. Mountain Standard Time.

Mt. mount; mountain.

MT mail transfer.

M.T. Mean Time; motor transport; mechanical transport; motor tanker.

m.t. metric tons.

multi- a *prefix* meaning many: *A multi-storey car park,* one having many storeys (floors). *A multi-millionaire,* a man who possesses many millions of pounds, dollars or other money units. *Multilingual secretary,* one able to speak and write many (usu. at least three) languages.

Multigraph a small printing machine used as a duplicator in offices; it uses a curved plate of type-metal fixed to a revolving drum.

multilateralism ECON. THEORY in the Theory of International Trade, an ideal system favoured by some economists (called multilateralists), by which there is complete freedom from any kind of hindrance to trade between nations; people in all countries are free to buy where they wish, all currencies are freely convertible, and there are no tariffs, quotas or exchange controls. *See* Comparative Cost Principle. *Syn.* free trade.

multilateral trade *see under* trade.

Multilith a small offset-litho printing machine used as a duplicator in offices.

multiple pricing COM. a practice adopted by some producers and traders of charging different prices for the same basic product in different markets, higher prices being charged in places where the customers tend to be rich.

multiple rate (of exchange) *see under* exchange rate.

multiple shop *see* chain-store.

multiple store *see* chain-store.

multiple tariff *see under* tariff.

multiple taxation *see under* taxation.

multiple voting share *see under* share.

multiplier ECON. THEORY a concept (idea) developed by Keynes in his book *General Theory of Employment, Interest and Money* (1936) and of great importance in modern economic thought. The multiplier is the name given to the proportion by which both the national income and the level of employment are affected by an increase in investment. A given increase in investment causes an increase several times as big in income, this proportion being called the *income* or *investment multiplier;* similarly a given increase in investment causes an increase several times as big in employment, this proportion being called the *employment multiplier.* But if there is already full employment, an increase in investment causes an increase in prices rather than in real incomes. Cf. Acceleration Principle.

mun. municipal.

municipal *adj.* of or relating to local government, esp. of a city or town: *Municipal services. A municipal enterprise,* a business owned and operated by the local government authority. *Abbr.* mun.

municipality *n.* a city or town having its own local government authority.

municipal bond *see under* bond, *n.*

municipal tax *see under* tax.

mushroom organization COM. & IND. a firm or company that has grown very fast and has so far made no reputation for honest dealing.

muster roll *see* crew list.

mutatis mutandis (*Latin,* having changed the things that had to be changed), the necessary changes having been made.

mutilated damaged; torn; made imperfect: *A mutilated document/bank-note.*

mutual held in common; shared by two or more persons forming a group: *A mutual interest,* one that is shared by two or more persons. *By mutual consent,* by agreement between the parties. *A mutual cancellation,* a cancellation agreed to by all parties. Cf. reciprocal.

mutual funds (U.S.A.) STK. EXCH. unit trusts.

mutual insurance *see under* insurance, classes and kinds of.

mutual savings bank *see under* savings bank.

M.V. merchant vessel.

M/V, m.v. motor vessel.

N

N Norway's international vehicle-registration letter.

N. North.

NA Netherlands Antilles (Dutch West Indies) international vehicle-registration letters.

N.A. North America.

N/A., N/a. new account; no account; not applicable; not available; no advice; non-acceptance.

n.a.a. not always afloat.

nab (*colloq.*) (1) to steal. (2) to arrest.

nabob COM. formerly, an Englishman who had worked for the East India Company and had made a large fortune in India. Now (*colloq.*) a rich and important businessman.

nail *Payment on the nail*, (*a*) immediate payment; (*b*) punctual payment.

naira the standard currency unit of Nigeria, divided into 100 kobo.

naked contract *see* nude contract *under* contract.

naked debenture *see under* debenture.

name *see* surname.

Name Day STK. EXCH. the second day of the five-day periods known as The Settlement, during which accounts between members and clients are paid. On this day stockbrokers give name-tickets, showing the names of the buyers, to sellers. *Syn.* Ticket Day. *See* name-ticket.

name-ticket STK. EXCH. a printed form given by a stockbroker on Name Day to a seller of securities, giving the name and other details of the buyer. *Syn.* ticket.

Namibia (formerly south-west Africa) an independent state in southern Africa, pop. 750,000 approx. (1973); capital, Windhoek, 60,000 approx.; languages, Afrikaans, English, German and tribal; currency unit, the South African rand, divided into 100 cents.

nano- the *prefix* used in the metric system of SI units to mean one thousand millionth, i.e. one billionth, 10^{-9}, or 0.000 000 001. 1 nanometre (nm) = one billionth of a metre.

Naoero *see* Nauru.

nap (1) a card game. (2) COM. & FIN. *To go nap*, to risk all one's money on a venture.

narration ACCTS. a short note explaining an entry made in the journal (*see* book-keeping), such as 'Sale of London factory', or 'Purchase of motor car'. *Syn.* narrative.

narrative *see* narration.

narrow boat *see* canal boat *under* canal.

narrower-range investments *see* trustee investments.

narrow gauge *see under* gauge.

narrow market STK. EXCH. (1) an inactive market, with few securities being bought and sold. (2) of a particular security, a market in which there is a very limited supply.

national accounts budget (U.S.A.) *see* budget (2).

national advertising *see under* advertising.

national bank (U.S.A.) *see* banking system.

national brand *see under* brand.

national budget *see* budget (2).

national capital *see under* capital.

national debt FIN. the total amount of money borrowed by the central government of a country on which it has to pay interest. In Britain, the Bank of England manages the national debt under the general control of the Treasury. *Syn.* public funds; (U.S.A.) public debt.

deadweight debt that part of the British national debt that represents money borrowed by the

government to fight two world wars which can now be considered as unproductive, because there is nothing left to be seen of the things on which the money was spent. Cf. productive *or* living debt.

external debt that part of the British national debt which consists of money borrowed mainly in the U.S.A. and Canada after the Second World War.

fixed debt *see* funded debt *below*.

floating debt that part of the British national debt that consists mainly of short-term Treasury bills.

funded debt that part of the British national debt which consists of loans to the government on which there is no fixed date for repayment, e.g. Consols, war loans. The lender has no claim to receive his principal back at any time, but has a right to receive interest for ever on the amount lent, and this right may be sold. Cf. unfunded debt; (U.S.A.) fixed debt. *Syn.* permanent debt.

internal debt that part of the British national debt which is represented by money borrowed within Britain, as opposed to external debt.

living debt *see* productive debt *below*.

permanent debt *see* funded debt *above*.

productive debt that part of the British national debt that represents money borrowed by the government and spent on productive national assets such as schools, hospitals, houses, roads and towns, loans to state-owned industries, etc. *Syn.* living debt; reproductive debt. Cf. deadweight debt.

reproductive debt *see* productive debt *above*.

unfunded debt that part of the British national debt which consists mainly of short-term loans to the government, e.g. Treasury bills, internal loans that are dated (have a fixed date for repayment) and external debt such as loans by foreign countries. Cf. funded debt.

national dividend *see* national income.

National Economic Development Council ('Neddy') ECON. & FIN. an organization set up by the British Government in 1962 to advise the government and industry on how the rate of economic growth can be increased. The Council has over 20 subcommittees called *Economic Development Committees* (E.D.C.s) and popularly known as 'Little Neddies' that examine and advise particular industries on how to become more efficient. *Abbr.* N.E.D.C.

National Enterprise Board (N.E.B.) IND. & FIN. a government organization set up in Britain in 1975 to give help to industries in need of financial help from the State, and to extend and manage state investment in industrial and commercial enterprises. Its activities are closely controlled by the Secretary of State for Industry.

National Giro see under Giro.

National Health Service (N.H.S.) in Britain, a government service begun in 1948 that allows all persons free medical treatment by practising doctors and in hospitals and, at charges much below cost, by dentists, opticians, etc. The cost is met partly from these charges and from national insurance contributions, but mainly from general taxation.

national income ECON. THEORY the total of all money incomes earned or gained by all members of the community. See gross national product.

National Income and Expenditure in Britain, official statistics published in an annual book of reference. See Central Statistical Office.

national insurance INSCE. & FIN. in Britain, a state insurance scheme administered by the Department of Health and Social Security (D.H.S.S.) by which every employer, employee and self-employed person makes weekly payments called *contributions* to provide insurance against accidents, sickness and unemployment, a pension on retirement, and other benefits, e.g. for widows and disabled persons. *Syn.* social insurance.

nationalism, economic see self-sufficiency.

nationalization IND. & FIN. the act of bringing land, industries, trade, etc. under the control and ownership of the nation.
to nationalize v. to change from private to state control and ownership. *Nationalized industries*, industries that are state owned and controlled.

national product see gross national product; net national product.

National Savings Bank FIN. & BKG. in Britain, the former Post Office Savings Bank, run by the government (still through post offices) to serve small savers. Deposits in ordinary accounts receive a low rate of interest which is tax free up to a certain amount each year. Deposits in investment accounts receive a much higher (but taxable) rate of interest. Cf. trustee savings banks.

national savings securities FIN. a group of British government securities meant for small investors. They consist of: *national savings certificates* which, if held for several years, give the investor a tax-free interest; *British savings bonds*, on which interest is paid half-yearly; and *premium savings bonds*, on which no interest is paid but investors have a chance to win tax-free prizes.

national savings stock register FIN. in Britain, a list of government stocks that can be bought from post offices. The service is intended to help small investors, the main advantage being that the interest is paid in full, i.e. without deduction of income tax. Formerly called the Post Office register.

national wealth see national capital *under* capital.

nation, most favoured see under most.

native language see mother tongue.

natural harbour see harbour.

naturalization LAW the process of law by which a person may become a full citizen of another country: *He is a British citizen by naturalization*, he was a foreigner but has been given British citizenship.

natural monopoly see under monopoly.

natural person see under person.

natural resources wealth supplied by Nature, such as mineral deposits, water for crops and for power, soil, forests and animals.

Nauru (Naoero) a small island republic in the Pacific Ocean, pop. 8,000 approx. (1973); language, English; currency unit, the Australian dollar, divided into 100 cents. Member, (British) Commonwealth.

naut. nautical.

nautical SHIPG. relating to ships and the sea, esp. to the science of navigation: *A nautical chart*, a map of the sea areas intended for use by seamen. *Abbr.* naut.

nautical assessor see assessor (3).

nautical mile see under mile.

nav. naval; navigation; navigator.

naval architect see under architect.

navig. navigation; navigator.

navigable SHIPG. that may be used, sailed through, by ships or boats; said of a river, canal or narrow or shallow areas of sea. *A navigable river*.

navigate SHIPG. & TRANSPT. (1) to direct the course of a ship or aircraft; to find one's way. (2) to travel across the seas in a ship or aircraft.

navigating bridge deck see deck.

navigation SHIPG. & TRANSPT. (1) the science of navigating, of directing the course of a ship (*marine navigation*) or aircraft (*air* or *aerial navigation*). *Abbr.* nav.; navig. (2) a canal.

navigation, accident of see marine accident *under* accident.

navigator a person qualified in the science of navigating ships or aircraft. *Abbr.* nav.; navig.

navvy IND. originally, an unskilled worker employed in digging canals, but now any person employed on heavy work such as building roads and railways.

navy SHIPG. the entire group of warships of a country, and the officers and men that serve in them and in their harbours and bases on land.
merchant navy see mercantile marine.

N.B. North Britain (Scotland); New Brunswick, Canada; nota bene (*Latin*, note well).

N.C. North Carolina, U.S.A.

N/C. no charge; new charter.

N.C.B. no-claim bonus; National Coal Board.

N.C.R. no carbon required.

N.C.V. no commercial value.

N.D. North Dakota, U.S.A.; Newfoundland, Canada; non-delivery.

n.d. non-delivery; no date; not dated.

N.E. North-East; no effects.

n.e. not exceeding.

N/E new edition; not entered.

Near East the countries of the eastern Mediterranean Sea. *Syn.* Levant.

near money *see under* money.

Neb., Nebr. Nebraska, U.S.A.

N.E.B. National Enterprise Board.

necessaries LAW things needed to support life, esp. the life of a dependant, such as food, clothing and shelter. *Syn.* necessities.

necessary (*colloq.*) *The necessary*, money, cash.

necessity, agent of *see under* agent.

necessity, flag of *see* flag of convenience.

N.E.D.C. National Economic Development Council.

'Neddy' a popular name for the National Economic Development Council (N.E.D.C.).

need, in case of *see under* case.

needful (1) what is needed: *To do the needful*, to do what is necessary. (2) (*colloq.*) the money needed for a particular purpose.

neg. negative; negligence.

negative covenant *see* covenant.

negative easement *see* easement.

negative income effect *see* Giffen's paradox.

neglected STK. EXCH. of a security, receiving no attention: *Chemicals were neglected*, there were very few deals in chemical shares.

negligence (1) LAW neglect to perform a duty. In law, where there is a duty to take care, the omission to do something which a reasonable man in normal conditions would do, or the doing of something which a reasonable, wise and careful man would not do. An employer who fails to provide a safe system of work for his employees is negligent. *Syn.* (Scotland) quasi-delict. *Abbr.* neg.

contributory negligence where an injured person's own carelessness helped to cause an accident, the court may reduce the damages according to the proportion of blame resting with each party.

(2) TRANSPT. & INSCE. (loss caused by) the careless failure of the shipper to pack and protect the goods properly or to tell the carriers that special care was needed. This is one of the *excepted perils* or risks not covered by the insurance policy and for which the carriers are not liable.

negligent (1) neglectful; failing to take care: *He is negligent in his duties/responsibilities/work*. (2) caused by or connected with carelessness: *A negligent act*.

negligent collision MAR. INSCE. a collision that could have been avoided if more care had been taken or if more skill had been employed. *Opp.* accidental collision.

negotiability BKG. & FIN. (1) the quality of being negotiable. (2) the ease or speed with which an instrument can be negotiated.

negotiable BKG. of a document, esp. an instrument, able to be negotiated, i.e. transferred by one person to another either by delivery (handing it over) as with a bank-note, or by endorsement (signing it on the back). Cf. 'not negotiable' (*see* crossed cheque *under* cheque).

negotiable cheque *see under* cheque.

negotiable instrument BKG. an instrument (formal document) the right to receive payment of which may be transferred (passed on) by one person to another. Negotiable instruments include: bank-notes, bearer share-certificates, bills of exchange, certain cheques, debentures payable to bearer, promissory notes, share warrants payable to bearer, Treasury bills. Cf. non-negotiable instrument.

negotiate (1) COM. to discuss formally for the purpose of arranging a business deal; to bargain formally: *To negotiate a contract/order/ prices*. (2) FIN. to reach an arrangement about money: *To negotiate a loan/mortgage/wage rates*. (3) BKG. to discount (sell at a discount) a bill of exchange, cheque or promissory note, or to transfer ownership of any of these to another party. *See* negotiable instrument; authority to negotiate.

negotiation COM. the act or process of negotiating, of bargaining over business deals.

negotiations *pl.* formal discussions on any kind of business with the aim of reaching an arrangement acceptable to all those taking part, such as *pay negotiations* between an employer and a trade union, or *trade negotiations* between one country and another.

neighbourhood unit in modern town planning a place that is part of a town but which is a relatively self-contained unit, having its own shopping centre, a post office, a school, a library, and perh. a health centre and branches of banks, building societies, etc.

nem. con. (*Latin*: nemine contradicente) no one disagreeing; words used in minutes (records) of the decisions made at a meeting. A motion is said to be carried *nem. con.* when no one has spoken or voted against it. *Syn.* nem. dis.: nemine dissentiente.

nem. dis. *see* nem. con.

Neo-Classical School (of economic thought) *see* Cambridge School.

neo-colonialism ECON. the new relationship that has grown between the advanced and the less-developed countries since the Second World War, a period during which most colonial countries have gained their independence. They are now connected by informal economic and other ties to the advanced countries on whom they were formerly dependent. Cf. colonialism.

Nepal a constitutional monarchy (kingdom) in southern Asia, to the north of India, pop. 12.8 million approx. (1976); capital, Katmandu, pop. 150,000; language, Nepali; currency unit, the Nepalese rupee (N.Re., *pl.* Rs.), divided into 100 paise, *sing.* paisa.

nest-egg FIN. (*colloq.*) (1) money saved for future spending, esp. in case of urgent or unforeseen need. (2) any reserve of money not allocated for a particular purpose.

net *or* **nett** COM. the exact amount after all allowances and reductions, such as discounts and rebates, have been deducted; an amount actually payable; an amount that will not qualify for any discount or other deduction: *Net price*, a price on which no discount will be allowed. *Terms net cash*, payment of the full amount stated is expected in cash, no credit or discount being allowed.

net annual value *see* annual value.

net assets *see under* assets.

Net Book Agreement COM. in Britain, a book-trade agreement made in 1901 and still in force, that publishers will supply certain books, called net books, at trade prices on the understanding that booksellers will not sell them to the public, including schools, libraries and other institutions in Britain, at less than the net published price fixed by the publisher from time to time. The purpose was to stop the price cutting that was at one time ruining the book trade. Net books are usu. school, college and reference books. *See also* resale price maintenance.

Netherlands, The a constitutional monarchy (kingdom) in western Europe, pop. 14 million approx. (1975); capitals, Amsterdam and The Hague; language, Dutch; currency unit, the guilder, divided into 100 cents. *Syn.* Holland.

net income *see under* income.

net interest *see* gross interest *under* interest.

net investment *see under* investment.

net loss *see under* loss.

net margin COM. the net profit made by a retailer on the sale of a commodity or article. It is the difference between the gross profit and the retailer's selling expenses, and is usu. expressed as a percentage of sales. *See* margin (5). Cf. gross margin.

net national product ECON. THEORY the amount of the gross national product after making an allowance for: changes in the value of stocks of goods owing to changes in the value of money; and capital consumption, i.e. the amount of capital goods used up in the course of production. *Abbr.* N.N.P.

net output *see under* output.

net personalty *see under* personal estate.

net present value *see* discounted cash flow.

net price *see under* price.

net proceeds *see under* proceeds.

net profit *see under* profit.

net receipts ACCTS. & FIN. the total amount of money received after making an allowance for expenses. Cf. gross receipts.

net register tonnage *see under* tonnage.

net rental FIN. the amount of rent received by the owner of property after deducting expenses such as general rates, water rates, insurance, and repairs.

net reproduction rate *see under* reproduction rate.

net sales ACCTS. gross sales reduced by amounts allowed to customers as credits for goods returned, goods over-invoiced, etc.

nett net.

netting-down COM. & FIN. the calculation of the net equivalent of a gross amount, by simply deducting a proportionate part or percentage. *Opp.* grossing-up.

net ton *see* short ton *under* ton.

net wage *see under* wage.

net weight *see under* weight.

network analysis *see* critical path analysis.

net worth ACCTS. & FIN. of a business, the difference between total assets and total liabilities. It represents the capital owned by the business. *Syn.* owners' equity; surplus.

tangible net worth net worth calculated without including any intangible assets, such as goodwill.

neutral *n.* in a war, a country that is not fighting on either side: *Ireland remained a neutral during the war. See* contraband of war *under* contraband.

adj. relating to a neutral country: *A neutral ship/flag/port. N.* neutrality, the state of being neutral.

Nev. Nevada, U.S.A.

never-never (system) COM. & FIN. (*colloq.*) the hire-purchase system: *To buy something on the never-never*, to pay for something by instalments.

New Deal ECON. HIST. a series of economic laws introduced between 1933 and 1939 by the U.S. Government under Franklin D. Roosevelt to rebuild the American economy after the severe depression of 1928–32. A very large programme of public works, esp. the building of dams and electric power-stations, relieved unemployment; financial help was given to farmers and to the smaller units of industry and commerce; and a general reorganization of the nation's financial system, labour laws and housing programmes, put the whole economy on a firmer basis.

New Economics *see* Keynesian Economics.

new impression *see* edition; reprint.

new issue market STK. EXCH. the part of the capital market that is concerned with new issues of shares. *See* issue of securities; issuing-house.

news agency an organization that gathers news from its reporters, correspondents and other contacts and sells it to newspapers, radio and television concerns and to individual subscribers such as offices, stock and commodity exchanges, and government departments. Cf. newsagent.

newsagent COM. in Britain, a shopkeeper who sells newspapers, magazines and books, usu. along with other kinds of goods, such as sweets, tobacco, stationery, toys, and simple medicines. Cf. news agency.

new share see under share.

newspaper circulation see under circulation.

news-stand COM. a stall in a street or other public place, at which newspapers are sold.

New York Stock Exchange STK. EXCH. the largest stock exchange in the U.S.A., started in 1792. The members consist of partners in firms, and officers of stock corporations; they are divided into brokerage or commission houses who buy and sell securities for the public; and floor traders and specialists who buy for themselves and sell through the brokerage and commission houses to the public. The N.Y. Stock Exchange has very strict rules for admitting corporations to a quotation; they must be enterprises of national importance, must possess large assets, and must be able to make big profits.

New Zealand a parliamentary democracy in the south-west Pacific, pop. 3 million approx. (1973); capital, Wellington, pop. 141,000 approx.; largest city, Auckland, pop. 800,000 approx.; languages, English and Maori; currency unit, the New Zealand dollar (NZ$), divided into 100 cents. Member, (British) Commonwealth; Colombo Plan.

next business MAN. at formal meetings, a motion 'that this meeting proceed with (or to) the next business', if approved by the votes of a majority of those present, is a reasonable way of putting an end to discussion that has lasted too long.

N/F (on a dishonoured cheque) no funds.

N.F., Nfd. Newfoundland, Canada.

ngultrum the standard currency unit of Bhutan, divided into 2 tikchung or 100 Indian paise.

ngwee the fractional currency unit of Zambia. 100 ngwee = 1 kwacha.

N.H. New Hampshire, U.S.A.

N.H.I. national health insurance.

N.H.S. National Health Service.

N.I. Northern Ireland; national insurance.

NIC Nicaragua's international vehicle-registration letters.

Nicaragua a republic in Central America, pop. 2 million approx. (1974); capital, Managua, pop. 300,000 approx.; language, Spanish; currency unit, the córdoba, divided into 100 centavos. Member, O.A.S.; O.C.A.S.

nickel FIN. (1) a hard metal, white like silver, used in alloys, esp. with copper (cupro-nickel), for making coins. (2) in U.S.A., a small coin worth five cents. (3) (colloq.) any coin of little value.

nicker (colloq.) one pound.

NIG Nigeria's international vehicle-registration letters.

Niger a republic in western Africa, pop. 4.5 million approx. (1974); capital, Niamey, pop. 60,000 approx.; languages, French, Hausa and Arabic; currency unit, the C.F.A. franc (CFA Fr.), divided into 100 centimes. Member, O.A.U.; O.C.A.M.M.

Nigeria a republic in West Africa, pop. 80 million approx. (1973); capital, Lagos, pop. 1 million approx.; languages, English, pidgin and tribal; currency unit, the naira, divided into 100 kobo. Member, (British) Commonwealth; O.A.U.

night safe BKG. a service provided by most banks that makes it possible for customers, by previous arrangement, to deposit cash with the bank after banking hours. The service is of special use to shopkeepers, who thus avoid having to keep large sums of money overnight.

nil nothing.

Nippon Kaiji Kyokai see Japanese Marine Corporation.

N.J. New Jersey, U.S.A.

NL the Netherlands' international vehicle-registration letters.

N. Lat. north latitude.

N.M. New Mexico, U.S.A.

n.m. nautical miles.

N/m. no mark(s) (on bill of lading).

N.N.P. net national product.

No. number. See also Nos.

N.O., N/o. no orders.

'no account' BKG. words written or stamped by a bank on a cheque that it is returning unpaid because the drawer has no account with that bank. Cf. 'no funds'.

'no advice' BKG. words written or stamped by a bank on a domiciled bill of exchange when the bank has received no advice or orders from the acceptor to pay, and therefore returns the bill unpaid. Syn. 'no orders'. Abbr. N/A.; N/a.

no carbon required (paper) a writing or typing paper that has been treated with chemicals so that it transfers an impression from the back of one sheet on to the front of the next sheet, thus giving a copy and making carbon paper unnecessary. It is much used for forms that have to be made in several copies. Abbr. N.C.R.

no-claim discount see under discount.

nod (colloq.) On the nod, on credit; to be paid for later. Syn. (colloq.) on tick.

nodal point a point where roads, railways, waterways and sea and air routes meet or cross, thus forming a place with strong advantages for the development of trade, industry and travel.

'no effects' see 'no funds'.

'no funds' BKG. words sometimes written or stamped by a bank on a cheque that is being returned unpaid because there are no funds in the drawer's account from which to pay it. This wording has been replaced in Britain by the words 'refer to drawer'. *Abbr.* N.F. *Syn.* 'no effects'.

no-liability company see under company.

nom. nominal.

nominal accounts see accounts, n. pl.

nominal assets see fictitious assets under assets.

nominal capital see authorized capital.

nominal coupon see nominal interest under interest.

nominal damages see under damages, n. pl.

nominal interest see under interest.

nominal ledger see under ledger.

nominal partner see under partner.

nominal price STK. EXCH. (1) a price (for a security) given by a jobber only as a rough guide, not a price at which he is willing to buy or sell. (2) the par value of a security.

nominal value see par value.

nominal wages see under wages.

nominal yield see under yield.

nominate (1) to propose a person by name for election to an office or for appointment to a post: *Mr John Smith has been nominated for election to the board of directors*, his name has been proposed as a person to be elected. *I nominate Mrs Mary Jones for appointment to the post of sales manager*, I put forward her name for this post. (2) STK. EXCH. & BKG. to appoint a person (called a nominee) or a company (a nominee company) to act as agent or representative in place of another person or organization whose name is to be kept secret.

nominee (1) a person who has been nominated (proposed by name) for election to an office or for appointment to a post. (2) STK. EXCH. a person or organization, such as a bank, appointed to act in place of another as holder of securities, in order that the name of the real owner shall be kept a secret. (3) INSCE. in an annuity policy, the person on whose life the insurance is based. (4) LAW in a lease of property, the person named as the lessee or tenant.

nominee company BKG. a company specially formed by a bank for the purpose of holding stocks and shares which have been given as security for advances made by the bank.

nominee director see under director.

non- (*Latin*, not) a negative *prefix*. (1) (usu. before a noun) not included in a particular group or class: *A non-member. A non-resident.* (2) (before an adj. or adv.) not; the opposite of: *Non-essential details. A non-contributory pension.* (3) (before a verbal noun) failure or re-

fusal: *Non-acceptance*, failure or refusal to accept. *Non-payment. Non-delivery.*

non-acceptance BKG. & COM. of a bill of exchange, failure by the person on whom the bill is drawn (the drawee) to accept it on presentation. *See* dishonour; protest.

non-assented stock see under stock.

non-business days BKG. & FIN. in Britain, certain days in the year that are not counted when the time for doing any act is limited to less than three days. These days are, broadly, Saturdays, Sundays, Good Friday, Christmas Day (25 December), New Year's Day (1 January), bank holidays and any special day ordered by the Crown to be a non-business day. All other days are business days. *See* bank holidays.

non-clearers see clearing banks.

non-contributory pension scheme one in which the employee does not contribute, since the employer bears the whole cost of financing the pension. Cf. contributory pension scheme.

non-cumulative preference share see under share.

non-durables see consumer non-durables.

non-executive director see under director.

non-feasance LAW failure to do an act that ought by law to be done. A person who leaves a restaurant without paying for his meal is guilty of non-feasance because he failed in his legal duty to pay before leaving. Cf. misfeasance.

non-forfeiture period INSCE. a length of time following non-payment of premiums on a life insurance policy during which the insurer allows the insured person to choose whether to surrender the policy or to have it made into a paid-up policy. If at the end of the period the premiums are still unpaid, the policy lapses (comes to an end). If the insured dies during this time, the insurers must pay the difference between the sum insured and the amount of the unpaid premiums.

non-insurable risk see uninsurable risk under risk (3).

non-joinder LAW failure to include in an action a person who ought to be a party to it.

non-marketable securities see under securities.

non-monetary investment see under investment.

non-negotiable instrument BKG. any instrument (formal document) the right to receive payment of which cannot by law or custom be transferred (passed on) by one person to another. Such instruments consist mainly of bills of exchange, including cheques, that are payable to a named payee only or that bear any restrictive endorsement; that are marked 'not negotiable' or 'not transferable'; or that are overdue. Cf. negotiable instrument.

non-participating share see under share.

non-physical money see substitute money under money.

non-price competition *see under* competition.

non-profit policy *see* without-profits policy *under* insurance policy.

non-recoverable *see* irrecoverable.

non-resident FIN. & BKG. in Britain, persons and organizations who are regarded by the exchange control authorities as living permanently outside the scheduled territories (the United Kingdom, the Channel Islands, the Isle of Man, the Republic of Ireland, and Gibraltar); and by the inland revenue authorities as living permanently outside the United Kingdom (only England, Wales, Scotland and Northern Ireland).

non-state socialism *see under* socialism.

nonsuit LAW *n.* (1) a decision by a judge against a plaintiff who has failed to produce sufficient evidence, or has no good reason in law for bringing the action, or has shown unreasonable delay in carrying on the action. (2) the stopping of a court action by the plaintiff after the trial has begun.
v. to order that the plaintiff has failed in his action.

non-trading partnership *see under* partnership.

non-voting share *see under* share.

'no orders' *see* 'no advice'.

n.o.p. not otherwise provided.

no-par-value share *see under* share.

Norf. Norfolk, England.

noria *see* sakia.

normal price *see under* price.

normal profit *see under* profit.

Norske Veritas SHIPG. the Norwegian ship-classification society. Cf. Lloyd's Register of Shipping. *See* classification societies.

Northants. Northamptonshire, England.

Northd. Northumberland, England.

North Korea a people's republic in eastern Asia, pop. 15 million approx. (1973); capital, Pyongyang, pop. 1.5 million; language, Korean; currency unit, the won, divided into 100 jon.

Norway a constitutional monarchy (kingdom) in northern Europe, pop. 4 million approx. (1975); capital, Oslo, pop. 500,000 approx.; language, Norwegian; currency unit, the krone or crown, *pl.* kroner, divided into 100 örer, *sing.* ore. *Abbr.* kr. Member, O.E.C.D.; E.F.T.A.

Nos. numbers: used in lists to refer to single articles, not dozens or any other unit such as those of volume or weight.

nostro account BKG. (*Italian*, our account) the account of a bank with its agent or correspondent in a foreign country and recorded in the currency of that country. The expression means 'our account with you in the currency of your country'. Cf. loro account; vostro account.

notarial LAW of or relating to a notary: *A notarial act*, an act that must by law be done by a not-

ary. *A notarial deed*, one drawn up by a notary. *A notarial ticket, see* noting.

notary LAW a public official, usu. a solicitor, who performs various duties with regard to legal documents, such as witnessing signatures, attending to persons making solemn declarations, noting (recording the dishonouring of) bills of exchange, etc. In Britain he is called a *notary-public. Abbr.* N.P. *Adj.* notarial.

notebook (1) a book in which notes are written. (2) a book in which details of promissory notes are recorded.

note-case a small case, usu. of leather, for banknotes and other personal papers carried by a man in a pocket of his clothing. *Syn.* billfold (U.S.A.); wallet; pocket-book.

note issue *see* currency circulation; fiduciary note issue.

note of hand *see* promissory note.

notes in circulation *see* currency circulation.

notice LAW information given formally in advance; a formal warning: *To give the shareholders notice of a general meeting of the company. To give an employee notice of dismissal/ of termination (ending) of his services. To give notice of dishonour of a bill of exchange. To serve notice on someone*, to hand a written document containing the notice to the person concerned, or to send it to him by registered post.

notice, distringas *see under* distringas.

notice of abandonment *see* abandonment (1).

notice of dishonour *see under* dishonour (1).

notify to give formal notice to, to inform somebody: *You must notify the police and your insurers that your money has been stolen. N.* notification.

noting LAW & BKG. the proving of the non-acceptance or non-payment of a bill of exchange when it becomes due. This is done by a notary appointed by the holder of the bill. The notary presents it again to the drawee for acceptance, or to the acceptor for payment. If the bill remains neither accepted nor paid, the notary notes it by giving it a special mark, adding his signature, the date and the amount of his charges, and by fixing to it a ticket, called a *notarial ticket* recording the reason that he has been given for non-acceptance or non-payment. All details are also recorded in his register. The noted bill is returned to the holder.

not in order BKG. words written or stamped by a bank on a cheque which is being returned unpaid because it contains a mistake, e.g. the words and figures do not agree.

notional income *see under* income.

notional price ECON. *see* impute.

notional rent ACCTS. *see* impute.

not negotiable *see* crossed cheque *under* cheque.

not provided for BKG. words written or stamped by a bank on a cheque returned unpaid because the drawer has not arranged to have enough money in his account to cover the amount. British banks now prefer to use the words *refer to drawer*. *Abbr.* n.p.f.

not sufficient (funds) BKG. words written or stamped by a bank on a cheque returned unpaid because there is insufficient in the drawer's account to cover the amount of the cheque. British banks now prefer to use the words *refer to drawer*. *Abbr.* n.s.; n.s.f.

Notts. Nottinghamshire, England.

novation LAW the replacing of an old contract by a new one, or of one debtor by another. It usu. happens when a contract between two parties is replaced by a new contract between three or more parties, the new parties being the persons who have taken over the duties and responsibilities of one of the old parties.

novelties *pl.* COM. small attractive or decorative articles, often intended as gifts, but usu. of little use or value, such as toys, cheap jewellery, and ornaments for the home or office. *Sing.* novelty.

N.P. notary-public.

n/p. net proceeds.

Np, np neap (tides).

n.p. net personalty; non-participating.

n.p.f. not provided for.

n.p. or d. no place or date.

nr. near.

N.R. no risk.

N.R.R. net reproduction rate.

N.R.T., n.r.t. net register tonnage.

N.S. Nova Scotia, Canada.

n.s. not specified; not sufficient (funds).

n.s.f. not sufficient funds.

N.S.W. New South Wales, Australia.

N.T. Northern Territory, Australia.

n.t. net terms.

Nt. wt. net weight.

nude contract *see under* contract.

nudum pactum (*Latin*, a ńude contract) *see* nude contract *under* contract.

nuisance LAW an inconvenience which interferes directly with the ordinary comfort of human beings.

common nuisance *see* public nuisance *below*.

private nuisance the unreasonable use of one's land to the harm of one's neighbour, or the wrongful allowing of harmful things to escape into a neighbour's land. Such nuisance may give good reason for an action in the courts for damages or for a court order to stop the nuisance. It is not a crime but a tort (a civil wrong).

public nuisance any act or omission which interferes with the safety, comfort, interests or rights of the public is a crime, and may be dealt with in the criminal courts. A person suffering special damage more serious than that suffered by the general public can bring a civil action in the courts. *Syn.* common nuisance.

null having no effect, no power: *The law has been declared null and void*, declared to have no force.

nullity LAW something that is declared by law as having never existed, such as an illegal contract, or a marriage illegally performed. *Syn.* void.

number *see* opposite number. *Also* No. *Abbr.* No.

numeraire FIN. & ECON. a French word used of money considered as a measure of value.

numerical filing *see under* filing system.

numismatic *adj.* of, relating to, coins and coinage.

numismatics *n.* the collecting and study of coins. *Also* numismatology.

numismatist *n.* a person interested in, or trained in, numismatics.

nummary of, relating to, dealing with, coins and money. *Syn.* nummulary.

nummular coin-shaped.

nummulary *see* nummary.

nurse (1) to take special care of, e.g. a child or sick person. (2) MAN. *To nurse a business*, to manage it well, esp. by making it grow and become profitable after it has been making losses. (3) COM. *To nurse stocks*, to keep stocks unsold in the expectation of higher prices. (4) BKG. *To nurse an account*, to help a customer whose debt is overdue by giving him time to pay what he owes, esp. when the market value of the security he has given will not cover the amount of his debt.

nursery (garden) AGR. a business in which plants are grown and sold. The owner or manager is called a *nurseryman*.

N.V. Norske Veritas.

N.W. North-West.

n.wt. net weight.

N.W.T. North West Territories, Canada.

N.Y. New York (State), U.S.A.

N.Y.C. New York City, U.S.A.

N.Z. New Zealand.

NZ$ New Zealand dollar.

O

O. Ohio, U.S.A.

o.a. overall (measurement).

o/a. on account of.

O. & M. organization and method(s).

O.A.P., o.a.p. old age pension(er) in Britain (now retirement pension(er)).

O.A.S. Organization of American States.

oath LAW a solemn declaration sworn in the name of God, promising to tell the truth as a witness in court or when signing certain documents, such as an affidavit. *To take an oath. To swear an oath. To give evidence on/under oath. To break/keep/be true to one's oath.* Cf. affirmation.

O.A.U. Organization of African Unity.

O.B. ordinary business (life insurance).

o/b. on or before (followed by a date).

obiter dictum LAW (*Latin*, said by the way, in passing) an opinion or remark on a legal question expressed by a judge in the course of giving his judgment, often while explaining the reasons for his decision; such remarks are not essential to his judgment and are not binding on future judges. *Pl.* obiter dicta.

objects (of a company) LAW the purposes for which the company has been formed, including the classes of goods or services in which by law it has power to deal. These objects are stated, usu. in much detail, in the *objects clause* of the company's Memorandum of Association, and its powers are limited to those given in this clause.

obligation (1) any duty, promise or agreement that is morally or legally binding: *To be under an obligation to*, to owe a duty to. *A moral obligation*, a duty arising from a sense of right and wrong, not from force of law, such as one's duty to help a friend, to entertain a traveller, to repay a kindness. (2) LAW (*a*) *A legal obligation*, any duty or agreement that has the force of law, such as a contract. (*b*) the formal document recording such an agreement, such as a bond. (3) the relation between debtor and creditor: *To meet/fulfil one's obligations*, to pay one's debts. (4) COM. *Without obligation*, without binding oneself (to buy a thing or to accept a deal).

implied obligation a duty or liability that is not expressed in a particular contract but which the law accepts as being in existence.

obligatory *adj.* morally or legally binding; that must be done; carrying an obligation: *Your attendance at the meeting is obligatory*, you must attend. *Syn.* compulsory. *Adv.* obligatorily.

oblige (1) to force, command, a person to do something: *Lack of demand obliges us to reduce production. You are not obliged to work after 5 o'clock.* (2) to owe a moral duty to: *I am much obliged to you for your kindness*, I thank you for being so kind. *I do not wish to become obliged to them by accepting their gifts/hospitality.* (3) to help, to do a favour for, somebody: *Please oblige me by giving me change for a five-pound note. He is very obliging*, he is very helpful. *Always try to oblige a customer*, try to help him.

obligee *see* bond, *n.*

obligor *see* bond, *n.*

obsolescence (1) becoming out of date. (2) ACCTS. the loss in value of an asset, such as a machine, when it becomes out of date, i.e. the owner would find it profitable to replace it by a newer and more efficient article.

planned obsolescence the replacement of goods, not because they are worn out, but because the owners have been persuaded to buy new goods by the pressure from advertisers wishing to expand their markets.

obsolete COM. & IND. no longer used; of a kind that is not now made or no longer in demand: *Obsolete machinery*, machinery that has been or ought to be replaced by more modern and more efficient kinds. *Obsolete stocks*, stocks of goods that are unsaleable because they are no longer in demand.

o/c. overcharge.

O.C.A.M.M. Organisation Commune Africaine, Malgache et Mauritienne (the African, Malagasy and Mauritian Common Organization).

Oc.B/L. ocean bill of lading.

occupancy TOUR. the degree, expressed as a percentage of the total, to which beds or rooms in a hotel are occupied (hired) by guests. Thus if a hotel has 100 rooms of which 85 were occupied by guests on a particular night, there was 85% occupancy. This is also known as the *occupancy ratio* or *occupancy rate*.

occupant a person who occupies (lives in or works in), esp. a house or room or office; the owner or tenant who lives in a house. *Syn.* occupier.

occupation (1) the kind of regular work that a person does to earn his living; his main profession, trade, business or situation as employee. *His occupation is that of lawyer/merchant/grocer/clerk. She is a dressmaker by occupation. Gainful occupation*, regular, paid work. *See also* occupations, *pl.* (2) having possession and control of land and buildings and the right to use them. (3) (*a*) the action of one country in seizing and controlling land belonging to another country. (*b*) the period during which the seizure and control lasts.

occupational of, having to do with, an occupation (one's trade or profession): *An occupational disease*, an illness caused by the work that one does.

occupational hazard a possible cause of harm, in the course of one's work, such as an illness from poisonous substances, dust, excessive heat; or injury from accidents with machines or from severe weather.

occupational lease *see under* lease.

occupational medicine *see* industrial medicine.

occupational pension *see under* pension.

occupational psychology *see* industrial psychology.

occupations *pl.* IND. & COM. kinds of work done in different industries, professions, trades and businesses.

commercial occupations the work of buying and of selling, both raw materials to producers and finished products to the users or consumers. *See* commerce.

constructional occupations *see* manufacturing occupations *below*.

extractive occupations the work of obtaining raw materials from the earth and the sea, such as all forms of agriculture, forestry, fishing, mining and quarrying, hydro-electric power, mineral oil and natural gas. *Syn.* primary occupations.

manufacturing occupations the work of making raw materials into finished products of all kinds. They include the constructional occupations such as building houses, bridges and roads. *Syn.* secondary occupations.

primary occupations *see* extractive occupations *above*.

secondary occupations *see* manufacturing occupations *above*.

service occupations the work of performing personal services of a skilled or semi-skilled nature, such as that of architects, lawyers, doctors, hairdressers and tailors.

occupier *see* occupant.

occupy (1) to live in, work in, or have possession of, usu. a space or place such as land and buildings or parts of buildings such as rooms, shops, flats, offices: *We occupy a flat on the ground floor. All our rooms are occupied. The new computer occupies less space than the old.* (2) to hold, to fill (a post). *Mr White will occupy the position/post of chief executive.*

ocean bill of lading *see under* bill of lading.

ocean-going SHIPG. of a ship, built to cross the oceans, far from land. *Syn.* sea-going.

Oceania the ocean area of the Pacific, lying between Asia and America and containing Australia, New Zealand and the Pacific Islands. It may be divided into four main regions: Melanesia, Micronesia, Polynesia and Australasia (Australia and New Zealand).

oceanic *see* maritime.

ocean terminal *see* terminal.

octroi TAXN. (1) a local tax on food and household articles brought into an area, such as a town or city governed by a local authority. Most countries have abolished the octroi as a means of raising taxes because of the high cost of collection. (2) the place where this tax is collected, and the officials who collect it. *Pron.* ok-trwa.

O/d, o/d on demand; overdraft; on deck.

odd (1) unusual; different from the normal or regular: *Odd sizes*, sizes e.g. of clothes, shoes, least often demanded. (2) incomplete; not in whole numbers or complete quantities: *Twenty pounds-odd*, some pence more than £20. *I have only a few odd pence*, the exact number is unimportant but is not enough to make up one

pound. (3) in a set of values, any value that cannot wholly be divided by 2, i.e. 1, 3, 5, etc.

odd-job (man) *see* job, *n*. (1).

odd lot STK. EXCH. an irregular and usu. small quantity of shares or stock, e.g. 67 shares or £67 of stock. Because dealers prefer to trade in round lots (regular units) e.g. of 100 shares or £100 of stock, odd lots are often more difficult to sell and therefore tend to have a lower price than round lots.

oddment COM. an article or commodity that is being sold cheaply because it is part of an incomplete set or because the quantity is unusually small.

odds *pl.* the chance or probability (of a certain thing happening): *The odds are against a good harvest after a dry summer*, the harvest will probably not be good. *The odds are in favour of a successful deal*, the deal will probably be a success.

odds and ends various bits and pieces left over or parts of incomplete sets.

odd time INSCE. the period from the date of a new insurance contract to the next quarter-day.

O.E.C.D. Organization for Economic Cooperation and Development (formerly O.E.E.C.).

O.E.E.C. Organization for European Economic Co-operation (now O.E.C.D.).

off. official.

off STK. EXCH. of prices, lower, falling. Cf. on.

off-board market *see* over-the-counter market *under* market.

offender a person who offends, breaks, the law: a criminal: *A first offender*, a person who is found guilty of an offence for the first time. *A juvenile offender*, see juvenile, *adj.*

offer *n.* (1) some thing or price that is offered: *An offer of services. A special offer*, an article offered for sale at a reduced price. *A firm offer*, an offer that is fixed, that the offeror will not change. *On offer* (of goods), for sale at a stated price. *Under offer*, esp. of property in Britain of which a sale is being discussed with a possible buyer. *Open to offer*, inviting offers. (2) LAW a clear proposal by one party (the offeror) to another party (the offeree) to do business. If the offer is unconditionally accepted, a bargain has been struck (made) and a binding contract can exist between the two parties. So long as the offer is not accepted it can be withdrawn (taken back, ended) by the offeror. The mere act of showing goods for sale, as in a shop, or of advertising them, is not considered in law to be an offer, but an *invitation to make an offer* for the goods, or an *invitation to treat* (to discuss how a bargain can be agreed).

offer and acceptance *see* offer (2).

offer(ed) price *see under* price.

offeree LAW a person receiving an offer.

offer for sale STK. EXCH. (1) an invitation by an issuing-house to the public to buy a new issue of shares. (2) the document containing the invitation and details of the company in which the shares are being offered.

offer of amends LAW an offer to pay an amount of money as compensation for a wrong said to have been done.

offeror LAW a person who makes an offer.

off-hire clause see breakdown clause.

office (1) a position of trust, responsibility and usu. of some importance in the administration and management of an organization. See office-bearer. (2) a building or room in which business is done, esp. one in which business papers are dealt with, or from which a concern is managed. (3) INSCE. an insurance company, e.g. a life office, a fire office.

booking office see under booking.

box-office see under box.

branch office see branch.

enquiry office an office where one can make enquiries and obtain information. Also inquiry office.

head office see under head.

loan office see under loan.

post office see under post.

registered office in Britain, of a company, an office that every company must by law have, to which notices, letters and other documents may be sent, and the full address of which is formally registered (recorded) with the Registrar of Companies.

register office in Britain, a government office (popularly called a registry office) where births, marriages and deaths are officially recorded in a register by an official called a registrar, and where civil marriages are performed.

registry office see register office above.

office accommodation rooms for use as offices.

office-bearer a person who has been appointed or elected to be an officer of an organization; a person who holds office.

office copier any machine or instrument for making copies of plans, documents, etc. in an office.

office copy (1) of a letter or other document, a copy intended to be kept in the office, usu. in a file. Syn. file copy. (2) LAW an official copy of a formal document, such as a power of attorney or a court order, made, stamped and sealed by a government officer who certifies it to be a true copy.

office hours the hours during which an office is open for business: Our office hours are from 9 a.m. to 5 p.m.

office junior see junior (3).

office machinery see under machinery.

office manager see under manager.

Office of Fair Trading COM. & LAW in Britain, a central body responsible for the laws protecting the rights of consumers; the Trading Standards Departments of local authorities are mainly responsible for the enforcement of such legislation. Abbr. O.F.T.

officer a person who holds office, who is in a position of trust and responsibility.

company officer see under company.

customs officer an officer of the customs service. See Customs.

ship's officer the master (captain) of a merchant ship and any of the other persons appointed to command members of the crew. See also mate.

Official Import and Export List see under Import and Export List.

official language see under language.

Official List see Stock Exchange Daily Official List.

official quotation see application for quotation.

official rate (of exchange) see under exchange rate.

official receiver LAW a government officer of a bankruptcy court whose duty is to receive and take care of the property of a bankrupt person, and also of a company that is being wound up. His duties normally end when a trustee in bankruptcy or a liquidator has been appointed. Abbr. O.R.

official referee see under referee.

official strike see under strike.

official support FIN. in Britain, action taken by the Bank of England to buy sterling in the foreign-exchange market or gilt-edged securities on the Stock Exchange and money market whenever it is considered necessary to support, i.e. to keep at a reasonable level, the sterling rate of exchange or the market price of gilt-edged securities.

officiate to perform the duties and carry out the responsibilities of an office. See office (1).

off-licence COM. (1) in Britain, a licence to sell strong drink on condition that it is consumed away from the premises in which it is sold. (2) a shop or other premises so licensed.

offload to unload.

offpeak IND. & TRANSPT. relating to those periods of the day or night when a service or supply is less used than at other periods: Offpeak rail and bus services. Offpeak fare, see under fare. Offpeak electricity rates, see offpeak tariff under tariff. Cf. peak.

offset see lithography.

O.F.T. Office of Fair Trading.

O.G.L. open general licence.

ohm the SI unit of electrical resistance. Sign: Ω.

O.H.M.S. On Her Majesty's Service; but On His Majesty's Service if the monarch is a king, not a queen.

oil (colloq.) n. excessive praise; bribery.
 v. to cheat.

oil-field an area where mineral oil (petroleum) is obtained from below the earth's surface, usu. by means of oil-wells.

oilman COM. (1) a shopkeeper who sells oil and, sometimes, other fuels, hardware, etc. (2) in U.S.A., an operator of an oil-well.

oil rig see drilling rig.

oil tanker see tanker (1).

Okla. Oklahoma, U.S.A.

old age pension see under pension.

Old Bailey LAW in England and Wales, the popular name for the Central Criminal Court in the City of London.

old-fashioned see under fashion.

Old Lady of Threadneedle Street BKG. & FIN. a popular name for the Bank of England.

old money see fresh money under money.

old share see new share under share.

oligarchy (1) a system of government in which ruling power is held by a few persons, usu. all from one class or group. (2) a country having such a system of government. (3) the persons (oligarchs) who hold the ruling power in such a system.

oligopoly ECON. THEORY a market in which there are only a few sellers. Cf. duopoly; monopoly.

oligopsony ECON. THEORY a market in which there are only a few buyers. Cf. duopsony; monopsony.

Oman a sultanate (country ruled by a sultan) in the eastern part of the Arabian peninsula, pop. 800,000 approx. (1975); capital, Muscat, pop. 30,000 approx.; language, Arabic; currency unit, the rial Omani (R.O.), divided into 1000 baizas. Member, Arab League.

Ombudsman see Parliamentary Commissioner.

omission, error of see error.

omnibus n. a bus.
  adj. relating to, containing, many things together at one time: An omnibus agreement/clause/resolution, one covering many subjects.

on STK. & COMMOD. EXCH. of prices, higher, rising, putting on: Tin on £112.50 to £6980 a metric ton.

on account see account, n. (2c).

on allotment see allotment money under allotment (1).

on application see application money.

on approval see approval (2).

on berth, on the berth see berth (1).

on-board bill of lading see shipped bill of lading under bill of lading.

O.N.C. Ordinary National Certificate.

oncost see fixed cost under cost.

one-man business see sole proprietor under proprietor.

one-man company STK. EXCH. (colloq.) in Britain, a private company that is entirely controlled by one man, the other shareholder necessary by law being no more than a nominee.

onerous contract see under contract.

on-line COMP. ready for immediate use for a particular purpose, such as a certain calculation or a presentation of information in a certain form, without needing to make special preparations.

o.n.o. or near offer: Car for sale, £500 o.n.o.

onshore ashore, not off the shore.

Ont. Ontario, Canada.

on tap COM. ready for immediate use, esp. for sale; ready for sale from present stocks.

onus of proof see burden of proof.

%, o/o per cent (sign).

°/oo, o/oo per thousand (sign); per mille.

o.o. on order.

oodles (colloq.) large amounts, esp. of money: There is/are oodles of cash/bank-notes in his safe. He has oodles of money, he is very rich.

O.P. open policy; out of print.

O.P.E.C. Organization of Petroleum Exporting Countries.

open account see credit account.

open-cast mining IND. the extraction of minerals from the earth by workings that are open to the sky, not under the ground. Cf. quarrying.

open charter see under charter, n. (3).

open cheque see under cheque.

open contract see under contract.

open cover INSCE. a general arrangement by which the insured agrees to have all consignments insured by a particular insurer at an agreed rate and under one policy, each consignment being declared to the insurer at the time of dispatch. See floating insurance under insurance, classes and kinds of.

open credit BKG. see clean credit under credit (3).

open-door policy the practice of a country of allowing the products of all countries to be imported on the same terms, giving no country an advantage over the others.

opened (cheque) see crossed cheque under cheque.

open-ended LAW of a contract or arrangement, that can be made to fit changed situations; not having fixed limits: An open-ended mortgage one for which there is no fixed repayment date.

open-end fund see mutual fund.

open-end trust (U.S.A.) STK. EXCH. a unit trust Cf. closed-end trust.

open-field system AGR. & ECON. HIST. the feudal system of agriculture by which part of the land of the lord of the manor consisted of a number of open fields; each field was divided into strips, and each of the lord's peasants was allowed to cultivate a number of strips scattered about in different fields so that good and bad land was fairly shared.

open general licence COM. an import licence for goods on which there are no import restriction (limiting controls). Abbr. O.G.L.

open indent see under indent, n.

opening STK. EXCH. the start of business for the

day: *The opening price* of a security is the market price early in the morning of the particular day. Cf. closing.

opening balance *see under* balance, *n.* (1).

opening stock ACCTS. the value of stocks of materials and finished products at the beginning of the accounting period, as compared with the closing stock. *See* closing accounts.

open insurance *see* floating insurance *under* insurance, classes and kinds of.

open market *see under* market.

open-market policy FIN. a method used by the Bank of England to control the level of interest rates by influencing conditions in the money market. It does this by buying and selling bills and securities in the open market, thus reducing or increasing the funds àvailable in the market, according to the needs of the time. *Syn.* open-market operations.

open-plan of offices, arranged on a plan which avoids having permanent inside walls, leaving large undivided spaces in which workers can see each other and be seen by supervisors. If a large space needs to be divided, this is done by using office furniture or low movable partitions (thin, light walls).

open policy MAR. INSCE. a floating insurance policy on a marine risk. *See* insurance, classes and kinds of.

open pricing *see under* pricing.

open shop IND. REL. a factory or other industrial or business concern where the employer is free to employ persons who are not members of a trade union. Cf. closed shop.

operate (1) to cause to work: *To operate the machine*, to control and use it, to make it work. *To operate a factory*, to run, manage it as a business. (2) to have, to be, to produce, an effect: *These rules do not operate in Scotland*, they have no effect in Scotland. *The exchange rate operates against us*, has an unfavourable effect on our business. (3) (*with* on) to perform a medical operation (the opening or removing of a diseased part of the body).

operating assets *see under* assets.

operating cost *see* operating expenses (2).

operating expenses (1) COM. & ACCTS. the expenses of running a business, such as salaries and wages, rent, rates, telephones, postages, advertising and distribution, but not including direct costs of factory labour, materials, and other manufacturing costs. *Syn.* overheads. (2) TRANSPT. the cost of running a transport service, usu. expressed as a unit cost per mile. *Syn.* operating cost.

operating profit *see under* profit.

operating statement ACCTS. & FIN. a statement of operating expenses.

operational research the use of scientific methods, esp. mathematics, to solve industrial, financial and commercial problems, esp. to help businessmen to make sensible decisions on present and future actions. *Syn.* (U.S.A.) operations research. *Abbr.* O.R.

operative IND. a person employed in industrial work, usu. in a factory: *Cotton-mill operatives*, workers in a cotton mill. *Syn.* factory-hand. Cf. operator.

to be operative *adj.* to be in operation, to be effective: *These rules are no longer operative*, they no longer have any force.

operative mistake LAW in a contract, a mistake that is so serious that it makes the whole contract void.

operator (1) IND. a person employed to operate (control and use) a machine or apparatus: *A telephone/telex/teleprinter/switchboard/radio operator. A keyboard operator* in a printing works using Linotype and Monotype machines. (2) an owner of a business such as a transport service, a coal-mine, that requires a government licence to operate. (3) STK. EXCH. a person who deals in stocks and shares. (4) a dealer who makes large deals in risky shares, a speculator. (5) (*colloq.*) a slightly dishonest person who is too clever to be discovered: *A shady operator*, a person whose honesty is doubtful. Cf. operative.

opinion MAN. professional advice.

banker's opinion *see under* banker's.

counsel's opinion a written statement by a leading barrister on a legal problem on which he has been asked to give his views and also to advise on what action should be taken.

opinion, public *see under* public.

opportunity cost *see under* cost.

opposite number a person in another organization who is in a position corresponding to one's own. *Syn.* counterpart.

optimum the best; the highest in quality; the most favourable. Cf. maximum.

option (1) STK. & COMMOD. EXCH. a contract by which one party, the *giver* or *holder*, gives a small sum of money, the *premium* or *option money*, to the other party, the *taker*, for the right to buy from, or sell to, him a certain quantity of a stated security or commodity during an agreed period, usu. three, six or nine months, at an agreed price, the *striking price*; this price remains fixed during the entire period of the option and allows the giver, who is usu. a speculator, to limit his losses and increase his gains according to movements in the market price during the period. *To acquire/ buy/purchase/sell/abandon an option. To leave one's options open*, to reserve one's right to choose, to decide, what to do. *Syn.* (U.S.A.) privilege.

call-of-more option an option that gives the buyer the right to buy double the stated quantity of securities if he so wishes. Cf. put-of-more option. *Syn.* buyer's option to double.

call option an option to buy, so named because the giver or holder of the call option has the right to call on the taker to sell the security or commodity at the fixed price agreed. Cf. put option.

day-to-day option an option for a period of only one day, but renewable from one day to the next if both parties agree.

double option an option that gives a right both to buy and to sell, at the wish of the giver or holder; it is therefore sometimes called a *put and call option*. Cf. single option. *Syn.* (U.S.A.) spread; straddle. *Abbr.* P.A.C.

employee stock option *see* stock option *below*.

put and call option (P.A.C.) *see* double option *above*.

put-of-more option an option that gives the seller the right to sell double the stated quantity of securities if he so wishes. Cf. call-of-more option. *Syn.* seller's option to double.

put option an option to sell, so named because the giver or holder of the put option has the right to put for sale the security or commodity which the taker has agreed to buy at the fixed price agreed. Cf. call option.

single option an option that carries a right either to buy or to sell, but not both. Cf. double option.

stock option an option issued by a large company to its executive employees giving them the right to buy stock or shares in the company at a specially favourable price. Such options are usu. not transferable to other persons. *Syn.* employee stock option.

traded option an option that can be bought and sold in the traded option market. In Britain, this market began in London in 1978 and deals in options on the stock or shares of a very limited number of companies. It is similar to the market that exists in Chicago.

(2) INSCE. dividend option, *see under* dividend.

optional left to choice; that may be done or need not be done, according to one's choice: *Optional extras*, extra things that can be supplied such as a radio with a new car, but do not have to be accepted if the buyer does not wish. *Optional dress*, on an invitation or notice, stating that one may wear what one wishes. *Optional meals* (in a hotel), meals that can be supplied at extra cost but do not have to be taken.

option(al) bond *see under* bond, *n.*

option contract *see under* contract.

option dealer STK. EXCH. in Britain, a stockbroker or stockjobber who is registered with the Stock Exchange authorities as a dealer in options. A stockbroker dealing in options may not deal with the public direct, but only through another stockbroker.

option dealing STK. & COMMOD. EXCH. buying the right to deal in a security during a fixed period at a fixed price (*see* option). This practice is much used by speculators as a safety measure to reduce risk of loss if market prices change in an unfavourable direction.

option money *see* option (1).

option mortgage *see under* mortgage.

option to double STK. & COMMOD. EXCH. on some exchanges, the name given to a put-of-more option (seller's option to double) and to a call-of-more option (buyer's option to double).

option to purchase (1) LAW a right given in a contract to buy property at any time before a certain date if the holder of the right so wishes. During this time the other party (the offeror) is bound by the contract not to withdraw his offer or sell the property to anybody else. (2) STK. EXCH. *Option to purchase shares*, a right given by a company to its shareholders to buy shares in the company at a favourable price, or to certain employees to receive shares free. *See also* option (1).

opulence riches, wealth: *A millionaire is a man of opulence*, he possesses great wealth. *Syn.* affluence. *Adj.* opulent.

O.R. owner's risk; operational research; operations research; official receiver.

ord. ordinary (shares).

order *n.* (1) a command, a direction from someone of authority to do something: *The chairman ordered the troublemaker to leave the hall. By order*, by command of the proper authority such as a local government authority. (2) methodical arrangement according to a desired relation of one thing to another: *Alphabetical/numerical/chronological order. To put documents in order. Out of order*, (*a*) not in the right order; (*b*) (of a machine) not working. (3) BKG. a direction to a bank to pay money to a certain person, or to the directions given by that person. *See* banker's order.

or order on an instrument, such as a cheque or bill of exchange, a shortened form of *or to his/their order*.

to order on an instrument, a shortened form of *in obedience to the order of*.

(4) COM. & IND. (*a*) a direction to a supplier to supply goods: *I enclose an order for 100 tons of paper*. (*b*) goods ordered or supplied: *Have you sent my order?* the goods I ordered from you. *To execute an order*, to supply the goods ordered.

cash order an order that is supplied against payment of cash before or at the time of delivery, no credit being given.

journey order *see under* journey.

landing order *see* warehousing entry *under* customs entry.

mail order (house) *see under* mail.

on order *The goods you want are on order*, we have ordered them from our supplier but we have not yet received them. *Abbr.* o.o.; o/o.

purchase order a document containing a formal offer from an intending buyer to buy from a supplier the goods listed, in the quantities and at the approximate prices stated in the order. A contract comes into existence as soon as the supplier sends the buyer a formal acknowledgment.

shipping order (*colloq.*) any large order.

to order only *We make goods to order only*, we do not keep stocks but we are willing to have the goods you want specially made for you, or to obtain them for you from another supplier. *Syn.* bespoke. *Abbr.* T.O.O.

transfer order *see under* transfer.

unexecuted order an order that has yet to be supplied.

(5) LAW a direction by a court of law, commanding a certain person or persons to act in a certain way: *A court order*. *See* garnishee order; judge's order; charging order; receiving order. (6) STK. EXCH. a direction from a client to a stockbroker to buy or sell securities.

limit order *see under* limit (1).

market order STK. EXCH. an order from a client to a stockbroker to buy or sell a security at the market price.

order bill of lading *see under* bill of lading.

order-book IND. a book in which all orders to supply goods are recorded as soon as they are received in the factory or shop. *A long/large order-book*, many orders to be supplied.

order cheque *see under* cheque.

order clerk IND. a person employed in the office of a factory to receive orders for goods and to see that they are correctly supplied.

order, money *see* money order.

order of business MAN. the methodical arrangement of matters to be discussed and voted on at a meeting, esp. of a company, club, association or similar organization. They should be dealt with in this order: (1) Apologies for absence; (2) Reading and confirmation of the minutes of the last meeting; (3) Matters arising from the minutes; (4) Correspondence; (5) Presentation and adoption of reports and accounts; (6) Election of officers; (7) Special business; (8) General discussion; (9) Any other business. *See also* point of order.

order of the day a programme of the matters to be discussed at a meeting, esp. of a law-making authority, usu. printed on an *order paper*. Cf. order of business.

order-picking *see* picking.

order, point of *see* point of order.

order, postal *see under* postal.

order-servicing *see under* servicing.

orders not to pay *see* stopped cheque *under* cheque. .

orders, standing *see under* standing.

ordinary account *see* National Savings Bank.

ordinary business INSCE. any kind of life insurance business that is not industrial business. *Abbr.* O.B.

ordinary capital *see under* capital.

ordinary creditor *see* general creditor *under* creditor.

ordinary damages *see* general damages *under* damages.

ordinary debt *see* unsecured debt *under* debt.

ordinary dividend *see under* dividend.

ordinary interest *see* simple interest *under* interest.

Ordinary National Certificate (O.N.C.) IND. & COM. in Britain, a certificate given to students who have completed a two-year part-time course, usu. in a commercial or technical subject, at one of the higher education institutions. Cf. Higher National Certificate, Ordinary National Diploma (O.N.D.), Higher National Diploma (H.N.D.).

ordinary partner *see* acting partner *under* partner.

ordinary partnership *see* general partnership *under* partnership.

ordinary resolution *see* resolution.

ordinary share *see under* share.

ordinary stock *see under* stock.

Ordnance Survey (O.S.) in Britain, the government organization responsible for producing maps of England, Scotland and Wales.

Ore., Oreg. Oregon, U.S.A.

öre the fractional currency unit of Denmark and Norway (one-hundredth part of a krone), and also of Sweden (one-hundredth part of a krona). *Pl.* örer.

Organisation Commune Africaine, Malgache et Mauritienne (O.C.A.M.M.) the African, Malagasy and Mauritian Common Organization, an association of largely French-speaking countries of Africa set up in 1965 to push forward economic and social development and improve political co-operation among its members, which include: Cameroon, Central African Republic, Chad, Congo, Dahomey, Gabon, Ivory Coast, Malagasy Republic, Mauritius, Niger, Rwanda, Senegal, Togo, and Upper Volta.

organization (1) the act of organizing, of arranging for people to work together for a common purpose: *A general manager is responsible for the organization of all parts of the business*. (2) MAN. that part of the work of management that consists of planning the structure of the concern and deciding how the work shall be organized, how responsibilities shall be distributed among the managers and supervisors, and how the effort of all employees can be made fully effective. (3) ECON. THEORY sometimes considered to be one of the factors of production, more usu. called enterprise, the organizing ability of a businessman and his willingness to bear risks. (4) the state of being organized; an orderly arrangement: *Where there is good organization there is high efficiency. Lack of organization is bad for morale and for profits.* (5) any organized group of persons working together in a systematic manner for a common purpose, such as a company, association, club, unit of government, or trade union.

organization and method(s) MAN. work-study in an office, i.e. applied to administration rather than production. *Abbr.* O. & M.

organization chart *see under* chart.

Organization for Economic Co-operation and Development (O.E.C.D.) ECON. an international association formed by members of O.E.E.C. in 1960 to replace O.E.E.C. and to work for the highest possible economic growth and employment and for a rising standard of living in its member countries; this was to be done by removing hindrances to international trade and to movements of capital. O.E.C.D. also co-ordinates economic aid to developing countries. It has over 20 members including all members of the E.E.C., the U.S.A., Canada, Japan, Australia, Austria, Finland, Iceland, Norway, Portugal, Sweden, Switzerland, and Turkey.

Organization for European Economic Co-operation (O.E.E.C.) *see* Marshall (Aid) Plan; Organization for Economic Co-operation and Development.

Organization of African Unity (O.A.U.) an association formed in 1963 to rid Africa of colonial rule and to give financial and military help to movements fighting for this cause. It has acted as mediator in disputes between some of its members, and has done much to develop a sense of co-operation between African states. All independent countries in Africa are members of O.A.U. except South Africa.

Organization of American States (O.A.S.) an association of all the independent countries of North and South America except Cuba and Canada. It was formed in 1948 with political and economic aims that included economic co-operation.

Organization of Central American States (O.C.A.S.) an association set up in 1951 by Costa Rica, Guatemala, Honduras, Nicaragua and El Salvador to encourage economic, political and military co-operation.

Organization of Petroleum Exporting Countries (O.P.E.C.) an association set up in 1961 of most of the countries that export a large part of their petroleum production; they combined together mainly to fix standard prices and, if necessary, to limit output. In 1973 O.P.E.C. suddenly began to use its strong bargaining power by raising the world price of petroleum so that by the end of the year 1974 the price had trebled in most importing countries. It has since been increased many times. Among its members are: Abu Dhabi, Indonesia, Iran, Iraq, Kuwait, Libya, Qatar, Saudi Arabia, and Venezuela.

organization, table of *see* organization chart *under* chart.

organized labour IND. REL. workers who have organized themselves in trade unions to use the power of collective bargaining in dealing with employers' organizations and the government.

organized market *see under* market.

organizer a person who organizes people or things, who gets them working together for a common purpose.

Orient the East, all the countries of Asia lying east of the Mediterranean Sea, but esp. the Indian subcontinent, Sri Lanka and the Far East.

original bill *see under* bill of exchange.

original entry *see* books of first entry.

original invoice *see under* invoice.

originating summons *see under* summons.

origin, certificate of *see under* certificate.

Ors. others.

O.S. Ordnance Survey; outsize.

O/s outstanding; out of stock.

Östmark *see* D.D.R. Mark.

Ottawa Conference ECON. HIST. *see* imperial preference.

ouguiya the standard currency unit of Mauritania, divided into 5 khoums.

ounce (oz) a unit, usu. of weight but also of volume, in general use in Britain, U.S.A. and some other English-speaking countries: one-sixteenth of a pound avoirdupois (28.3495 g); one-twelfth of a pound troy (31.1035 g); in liquid measure, the fluid ounce (fl. oz.) one-twentieth of a pint in Britain (28.4131 cm^3), but one-sixteenth of a pint in U.S.A. (29.5727 cm^3).

outbargain COM. to succeed in making a better bargain than another person; to defeat someone in the process of bargaining.

outbid to bid more (than another bidder); to make the highest bid. *He outbid me at the auction,* he bid higher than I and so he won the bidding.

outbound *see* bound (1).

'out' clearing BKG. cheques, bills of exchange, etc. sent by a bank for clearing at the clearing house. Cf. 'in' clearing.

outfit (1) a set of things needed for a particular purpose, esp. tools and clothes. (2) (*colloq.*) any group of people working together, such as a company or a team of workers. *Syn.* set-up.

outfitter COM. a shopkeeper who sells clothes: *A gentlemen's outfitter,* one selling men's clothes.

outgoing invoice *see* sale(s) invoice *under* invoice.

outgoings FIN. money going out, spent or being spent; expenses, as opposed to income, receipts. *Syn.* outlay.

outlay FIN. money spent or being spent: *Production outlay*, money spent on materials and labour to produce goods, or for buying finished goods, for sale as a regular business activity. *Advertising outlay*, money spent on advertising. *Syn.* expenditure.

outlay account (U.S.A.) *see* appropriation account.

outlay tax *see* indirect tax *under* tax.

outlet COM. a place from which goods are sold.
    captive outlet a shop or other business, such as a public house, that is allowed to use a building on condition that it sells goods obtained only from the owners of the building. *Syn.* tied house. Cf. free house.
    retail outlet a shop selling goods to the public.

outlook STK. EXCH. a view of the future; what is expected to happen: *The market outlook. A bearish outlook*, one that is unfavourable, with prices expected to fall. *A bullish outlook*, one that is favourable, with prices expected to rise.

out of date *see under* date.

out-of-date cheque *see* stale cheque *under* cheque.

out of order (1) not in the proper order of a methodical arrangement: *The papers in this file are out of order*, not filed in the order in which they should be. (2) MAN. at a meeting, not according to the rules governing the way the meeting must be conducted (carried on, held); for example, improper behaviour such as the use of bad language is out of order and must be stopped by the chairman. *See* point of order; order of business. (3) of a machine, equipment, etc. not working, needing repair.

out of pocket *see under* pocket.

out-of-pocket expenses *see under* expenses.

out of print *see under* print.

out of stock COM. & IND. having no stock left; unable to supply from stock. *Abbr.* o.s.; o/s.

out of work unemployed.

outport SHIPG. (1) a seaport serving a chief port because, being on the sea, it is easier for large ships to use. Tilbury is the outport of London; Avonmouth is the outport of Bristol. *Also* out port. (2) among British shippers, any British port except London. (3) a relatively small port at which no customs officers are permanently based.

output ECON. THEORY the total value of all goods produced and services performed by a producer, an industry or a country. *Syn.* product; outturn.
    gross output of a single producer, firm, industry or country, the total value of the goods and services produced, including the cost of materials and services bought from other producers or industries. Cf. net output.
    net domestic output the total of all the net outputs in an economy.
    net output the difference between the gross output and the total cost of the materials and services required to produce the commodity or service. It is the value added by the producer or the industry in the course of manufacture. The net output of an industry shows its importance in relation to other industries. Cf. gross output.

output tax *see* value added tax *under* tax.

output unit COMP. part of an electronic computer that is used to put the processed data (information) from the central processor on to magnetic tape, punched tape or cards, or on to paper in the form of a print-out. Cf. input unit.

outsell COM. to sell more than (somebody else): *We are outselling our rivals*, we are selling more than they are. *They are being outsold.*

outside broker STK. EXCH. a stockbroker who is not a member of any stock exchange. He is allowed to invite the public to buy securities from him, and he acts as a middleman between the public and members of the stock exchanges. Cf. outside dealer.

outside dealer STK. EXCH. a trader who is not a member of any stock exchange but is licensed to deal in (buy and sell) stocks and shares. He usu. buys large lots of securities on the stock exchange at his own cost and sells them in smaller lots to the public. Cf. outside broker.

outside director *see under* director.

outsize COM. of clothes, very large in size; made for a very large person. *Abbr.* O.S.

outstanding ACCTS. unpaid; remaining unpaid: *An outstanding account/debt*, one that is overdue for payment. *An amount outstanding*, an amount that continues to exist, or to be owed. *Orders outstanding*, orders that have yet to be supplied. Cf. arrears.

outturn (1) *see* output. (2) MAR. INSCE. the weight of cargo unloaded from a ship.

outvote to defeat in voting; to get more votes than the other side gets.

outward SHIPG. going out, as opposed to coming in: *Outward cargo*, cargo being exported. *Outward bill of lading*, *see under* bill of lading. *Outward clearance* or *clearance outward*, *see* clearance (2). *Opp.* inward; homeward.

outward bound *see* bound (1).

outwork IND. work given to persons to do in their own homes or workshops, usu. paid at piece-work rates.
    outworker *n.* a person who does outwork.

over applied for *see* oversubscribed.

overbid *v.* COM. (1) to bid a higher amount, to outbid, somebody. (2) to bid too much for a thing.
    n. a higher bid.

overboard SHIPG. over the ship's side: *Cargo thrown or lost overboard. Man overboard!* a cry made when somebody (man or woman) has fallen from the ship into the sea. *See also* free overboard.

overbook TRANSPT. & TOUR. to book more places (on a passenger vehicle or in a hotel) than can actually be provided, resulting in some people suffering the inconvenience of being transferred to other services or hotels.

overbuy (1) to buy more than one needs or more than one can pay for. (2) STK. EXCH. to buy stocks and shares on margin beyond one's ability to deposit money or investments as security with the stockbroker, as can happen when a fall in market prices reduces the value of the security deposit.

overcapacity see capacity (1).

overcapitalized (1) STK. EXCH. of a company, having more issued capital than can be profitably employed in the business. The result is that the company cannot earn enough profit to pay an acceptable rate of dividend to its shareholders. *Opp.* undercapitalized. (2) ACCTS. of a company, having an issued capital greater than the value of its net assets.

overcarry SHIPG. to carry goods beyond the port to which they have been consigned. If the shipowners find it impossible to land cargo at that port, they may unload it at another port. *See also* back freight *under* freight.

overcharge n. COM. & ACCTS. a charge that is above what it ought to be, either because too high a price has been charged by mistake, e.g. in invoicing, or because an unjustly high price has been demanded. If the overcharge is due to a mistake in invoicing, the customer is sent a credit note in order to put the account right. *Abbr.* o/c. *Opp.* undercharge.
v. to charge a price that is too high.

overdraft see bank overdraft.

overdraw BKG. to cause a debit balance to be recorded in one's account with a bank, usu. by drawing cheques for a total greater than the amount one has deposited with the bank. *To be overdrawn*, to have a bank account that shows a debit balance. *See* bank overdraft.

overdue (1) ACCTS. & FIN. past the time when due for payment, late in being paid: *An overdue account/instalment. The rent is overdue. Syn.* in arrear. (2) TRANSPT. & SHIPG. very late in arriving: *The ship/plane is overdue.*

overdue bill see under bill of exchange.

overdue cheque see under cheque.

over-employment see full employment.

over-entry certificate see under customs entry.

overextended FIN. of a business, owing far more money than the value of current assets.

over-full employment see full employment.

overhead cost see under cost.

overhead expenses see under expenses.

overhead price see under price.

overheads FIN. & ACCTS. the expenses of running a business, esp. those fixed costs that cannot be related to particular units of goods produced or goods sold, such as rent, rates and management salaries. *Syn.* overhead expenses; overhead cost; overhead charges; fixed costs; fixed charges; establishment charges; burden; oncost.

factory overheads see factory expenses.

overissue STK. EXCH. the issue of stock or shares in excess of the amount authorized in the Memorandum of Association of the company.

overloaded economy ECON. an economy in which demand is greater than supply but prices are, by strict government controls, prevented from rising. The condition is sometimes called *repressed inflation* (inflation held down by controls).

overpopulation ECON. the state of an economy in which there are too many people for the existing resources to support without lowering the standard of living. Cf. underpopulation.

overproduction ECON. the production of more goods than can be sold at a profitable price.

overrider see overriding commission *under* commission.

overriding commission see under commission.

overseas agent an agent who lives and carries on business in a country other than the country of his principal. Such agents are usu. given an exclusive agency for an agreed area, country or group of countries. The expression is often used in a general sense and may include an importer who is not an agent but an independent merchant buying and selling at his own risk. *Syn.* foreign agent.

overseas banks see foreign banks.

overseas company see under company.

overseas investment see foreign investment *under* investment.

overseas trade see international trade.

overseer MAN. a person employed in seeing that other persons do their work properly.

oversell COM. to agree to sell more of a product than can be delivered. *To be oversold*, to be bound by contract to do something, such as to deliver goods or securities, that one cannot do. *An oversold position*, an inability to deliver securities or commodities that one has promised to deliver on a fixed date.

over ship's rail SHIPG. words sometimes appearing in a bill-of-lading contract, meaning that the shipowner's responsibility for cargo begins at the moment that the goods pass over the ship's rail when being loaded, and ends when they pass over the ship's rail when being unloaded. Cf. under ship's derrick.

overside delivery SHIPG. the unloading of cargo over the side of the ship into lighters. *See also* free overside.

overside port see barge port *under* port.

oversold see oversell.

overstock v. to stock too much (of an article or commodity). *Overstocking*, ordering for stock more than is needed.

overstocks *n. pl.* excessive stocks that need to be reduced in order to release capital for more profitable use.

oversubscribed STK. EXCH. of a new issue of a security, the number of units applied for exceeds the number offered. *Syn.* fully subscribed; over applied for. *N.* oversubscription.

overt LAW open; that can clearly be seen: *An overt act,* an act that is openly, not secretly, done. *Market overt, see under* market.

over-the-counter market *see under* market.

overtime IND. (1) time worked in excess of an agreed number of working hours per day or per week: *He has worked ten hours' overtime this week,* he has worked the normal working week and a further ten hours' overtime. (2) the payment made to workers for extra hours worked beyond an agreed number of hours per day or per week; extra money paid for working overtime. Overtime is usu. paid at higher rates per hour than the ordinary working rate, called the *basic rate.* Thus, *time and a quarter* is basic rate + 25%; *time and a half* is basic rate + 50%; *double time* is twice basic rate.

overtime ban *see under* ban.

overtrading FIN. & MAN. trading beyond the normal limits set by the working capital of the business such as holding unnecessarily large stocks, or investing in assets that the business cannot afford to buy. Such action causes a continual lack of ready money needed to pay creditors and to meet the normal overhead expenses.

overvalued currency FIN. & ECON. a currency that, because of government controls, has a higher rate of exchange in relation to another currency than it would have if the normal economic forces of supply and demand were operating. If these forces were working freely they would bring a state of equilibrium (natural balance) based on the relative purchasing power of the two countries.

o.v.n.o. or very near offer.

own brand COM. & IND. a brand of goods, usu. in the grocery trade, bearing the private brand mark of a large retailer. It may be made specially for him or he may buy the goods unmarked directly from the manufacturer of a nationally advertised brand. The two articles are usu. exactly alike, but the own-brand article can be sold more cheaply because it does not have to bear the heavy cost of national advertising. *Syn.* house brand; dealer's brand; private brand.

owner-manager *see* sole proprietor *under* proprietor; managing owner.

owner-occupier a person who lives in a house that he owns.

owner's equity *see* net worth.

ownership, certificate of *see* certificate of registry *under* registry.

ownership LAW the right to hold a thing entirely as one's own, including complete and permanent control over it. Cf. possession.

absolute ownership the right to hold and enjoy a thing completely and for ever, including power to control, change, destroy or transfer it to others. *Syn.* complete ownership.

beneficial ownership a form of restricted ownership, being the right only to enjoy the use of a thing, without having power to change, destroy or transfer it to others.

common ownership *see* ownership in common.

complete ownership *see* absolute ownership *above.*

co-ownership *see* joint ownership *under* joint; *also* co-ownership of industry.

joint ownership *see under* joint.

private ownership ownership by private persons or groups of persons, not by the State.

public ownership ownership by the State.

restricted ownership ownership that is in some way limited, such as enjoyment only for one's lifetime (a life tenancy) or enjoyment shared with other persons (joint ownership, co-ownership).

ownership in common LAW of land, land owned together by two or more persons, no one person holding the rights in any part of the property. An owner may leave his rights to anyone in his will and the heir becomes an owner in common with the others. *See* joint ownership. *Syn.* tenancy in common.

owner's risk TRANSPT. in Britain, of goods carried by railway, at the risk of the owner, who will usu. have arranged separately for the goods to be insured while being carried. The carrier is, however, responsible if loss is caused by wilful misconduct (wrongful acts done on purpose) by the carrier's employees. Since the carrier has no risk to bear, his charges are lower for carrying goods sent at owner's risk than for those sent at carrier's risk. *Abbr.* O.R.; o.r.; O/R.

owner's risk clause MAR. INSCE. in a marine insurance policy, a condition that if the owners of the ship become responsible for damage caused by a collision, the insurers have to pay an agreed amount per ton of registered tonnage. Cf. running down clause.

Oxon. Oxfordshire, England; Oxford (City and University).

oz. ounce, ounces.

oz. T ounce (troy).

P

P Portugal's international vehicle-registration letter.

p penny, pence.

p. page (*pl.* pp. pages); per; pint; peseta; peso; post (after).

PA Panama's international vehicle-registration letters.

Pa. Pennsylvania, U.S.A.

P/A particular average; power of attorney.

P.A. particular average; personal assistant; public accountant (U.S.A.); power of attorney.

P/A. power of attorney.

p.a. per annum; press agent.

pa'anga the standard currency unit of Tonga, divided into 100 cents. *Syn.* Tongan dollar. *Also* palanga.

P. & L. profit and loss.

P.A.B.X. private automatic branch exchange.

Pac. Pacific.

P.A.C. (1) put and call (option). (2) GOVT. Public Accounts Committee.

Pacific Islands, Trust Territory of the a group of over 2000 islands in the north-west Pacific Ocean, of which only about 100 are inhabited (have people living permanently on them). The Territory is administered by the U.S.A. for the United Nations. Total pop. 15,000 approx. (1974); capital, Saipan, pop. 8000 approx. The islands are in three main groups, the Caroline Is., the Mariana Is., and the Marshall Is. Languages, English and various Micronesian. Currency unit, the U.S. dollar, divided into 100 cents.

Pacific Standard Time a time-zone in North America, eight hours behind Greenwich Mean Time and one hour behind Mountain Time. *Abbr.* P.S.T.

pack *n.* (1) a load, esp. one wrapped and arranged for carrying on the back by man or animal. *Syn.* burden. (2) COM. a container with something in it: *A pack of cigarettes/sweets. Syn.* packet. *Abbr.* pk. (3) AGR. & IND. a measure of weight used in the wool trade: a pack of wool = 240 lb. (108.86 kg).

package (1) IND. & COM. the wrapping or container in which goods are put after they have been manufactured. A parcel. *Abbr.* pkg.; pk.; pkge. (2) a combination or group of several things taken or treated together.

package deal (1) an offer consisting of several parts or conditions, all of which must be accepted or the whole refused. (2) an agreement that covers a number of different matters.

packaged goods COM. goods supplied in wrappers or containers ready for sale to the consumer, not loose.

package insurance *see* blanket insurance *under* insurance, classes and kinds of.

packaging IND. & COM. (1) the work of putting goods into the wrappers or containers in which they will be sold to the public. (2) the designing and planning of these wrappers and containers, with the aim of giving the goods an attractive

appearance and of making sure that they reach the consumer in good condition.

display packaging *see* display.

pack-animal TRANSPT. an animal used for carrying goods contained in packs on its back, esp. in places where there are no roads fit for vehicles: *A pack-horse, pack-mule. Pack train*, a line of pack-animals.

packer IND. & COM. a person employed to pack goods, either to protect them while being carried from place to place, or to make them attractive to the consumer.

packers *pl.* business organizations that perform a service for manufacturers by putting their goods into wrappers or containers.

export packers packers specially skilled in packing goods for shipment overseas.

packet (1) a small parcel or pack of something in a wrapper or container: *A packet of cigarettes/envelopes. A postal packet*, a small parcel sent by post. *An air packet*, a small parcel sent by airmail. *See* wage packet; pay packet. (2) a packet-boat. (3) (*colloq.*) a large amount of money: *This watch cost a packet*, it was very dear. *He ran into a packet of debt*, he accumulated many debts.

packet-boat SHIPG. a fast ship carrying mails, passengers, and parcels of goods. *Syn.* mailboat.

packet-port SHIPG. a port used mainly by packet-boats and ferry-boats.

packing COM. & IND. the covering given to goods to protect them from damage and theft while being carried from one place to another.

packing-case COM. & IND. a strong wooden box to contain and protect goods while being carried from place to place.

packing list COM. & IND. a list of the articles contained in a particular package or container, such as a packing-case, so that the contents can be checked on arrival. *Syn.* packing slip; packing sheet.

packing station IND. & AGR. a factory where goods, esp. foodstuffs, are packed for sale in shops or for shipment abroad. *Syn.* (U.S.A.) packing house; packers.

packman an old name for a pedlar.

pact a solemn agreement between two or more persons, organizations or countries. *Syn.* compact; treaty.

paddy AGR. rice, esp. when growing as a plant in a *paddy-field*, or the grain before the husk (outer covering) is removed.

paecottah *see* shaduf.

page *v.* TOUR. to try to find a person by calling his name, as is done by a page-boy in a hotel: *Please page Mr Smith; he is wanted on the 'phone.*

page-boy TOUR. a boy employed in a hotel to carry messages and to do other light work. *Also* a page.

paid bill *see under* bill of exchange.

paid cheque *see* cancelled cheque *under* cheque.

paid secretary of an association, society or club, a secretary who receives a salary or fee for his services, as opposed to an honorary (unpaid) secretary.

paid share *see* partly-paid share *under* share.

paid-up capital *see under* capital.

paid-up insurance *see under* insurance, classes and kinds of.

paisa in India & Pakistan, the fractional unit of currency and coinage, one-hundredth of a rupee. *Pl.* paise (India); paisa (Pakistan). *Also* pice.

PAK Pakistan's international vehicle-registration letters.

Pakeha a New Zealander of European origin.

Pakistan a federal republic in south Asia, pop. 70 million approx. (1975); capital, Islamabad, pop. 250,000 approx.; languages, Urdu and English; currency unit, the Pakistan rupee (Pak Re., *pl.* Rs.), divided into 100 paise or paisa (*sing.* paisa). Member, R.C.D.; Colombo Plan.

palanga *see* pa'anga.

Palantype the makers' name for a machine worked by touching keys on a keyboard with the fingers, for recording on a band of paper the actual words of speech while they are being spoken. The machine produces notes in the form of signs that can easily be read and written or typed as an exact record of what has been said, e.g. during a trial in a court of law.

Palgrave Sir Robert (1827–1919), English economist, editor of *The Economist* (from 1877 to 1883) and the writer of a well-known *Dictionary of Political Economy* (1894).

pallet TRANSPT. a strong, flat, wooden board or metal plate with spaces underneath, used for lifting and moving loads esp. by means of a fork-lift truck or pallet truck.

palm-grease *see* grease.

palm off (*colloq.*) to persuade somebody to buy something worthless; to sell deceitfully: *I was palmed off with a clock that does not keep good time. They tried to palm off valueless shares on him.*

palm-oil *see* grease.

pamphlet *see* brochure.

Panama a republic in Central America, pop. 1.6 million approx. (1973); capital, Panama City, pop. 420,000 approx.; languages, Spanish and English; currency unit, the balboa, divided into 100 centesimi (*sing.* centesimo). Member, O.A.S.

Panama Canal SHIPG. a ship-canal 51 miles long through the Isthmus of Panama, connecting the Atlantic and Pacific Oceans and able to take large ocean-going vessels.

panic FIN. & ECON. at a time of business crisis and lack of confidence, a sudden and very great public fear of a financial crash of prices on the stock exchanges and money markets; this fear causes people to rush to sell securities, driving prices even lower, to draw money out of banks, and to do other things that greatly disturb the economy.

'Panlibhonco' *see* flag of convenience.

paper (1) *On paper* (*a*) recorded in writing: *Please put the details on paper*, write them down as a record. (*b*) in theory but not in practice: *He should, on paper, make a profit, but if prices fall he will make a loss. The idea appears good on paper but it will not work in practice.* (*c*) still being planned or designed: *The new model exists only on paper. See* paper profit *under* profit. (2) FIN. & BKG. negotiable instruments, such as bills of exchange, and promissory notes, considered collectively.

commercial paper *see under* commercial.

commodity paper *see under* commodity.

financial paper *see under* financial.

fine paper *see under* fine.

first-class paper *see* fine paper *under* fine.

trade paper *see* trade bill *under* bill of exchange.

paper bail part of a typewriter, consisting of a hinged bar with two rubber rollers that hold the paper down on the cylinder of the machine.

paper, carbon *see* carbon paper.

paper credit FIN. & BKG. documents that consist of promises to pay money on demand or at some future date which can therefore be used in place of money.

paper currency *see under* currency.

paper-cylinder *see* platen.

paper-feed part of a typewriter which guides the paper round the platen or roller. *See* carriage (4).

paper, financial *see* financial paper.

paper loss *see under* loss.

paper, manifold *see* manifold.

paper measure standard units of quantity used for paper:

24 sheets = 1 quire
20 quires = 1 ream
480 sheets = 1 ream (stationer's)
484 − 516 sheets = 1 ream (printer's)
500 sheets = 1 long ream (U.S.A.).

paper mill *see* mill.

paper money *see under* money.

paper profit *see under* profit.

paper punch *see* punch.

papers, ship's *see* ship's papers.

paper standard *see under* standard.

paper title *see under* title.

Papua New Guinea an independent parliamentary state in the south-western Pacific, being the eastern half of the island of New Guinea, pop. 2.8 million approx. (1975); capital, Port Moresby, pop. 70,000 approx.; languages, English, pidgin and tribal; currency unit, the kina, divided into 100 toeas. Member, (British) Commonwealth.

par. paragraph.

par (1) equal in value; on the same level: *On a par with*. (2) STK. EXCH. of bonds, stocks, shares, etc., the nominal or face value, i.e. the sum at which they were issued. If the face value of a security is £100, then £100 is its *par value* or *par price* or *issue par* or *nominal par*. If the security can be bought for this sum, the price is *at par*; if it can be bought for a lower sum, its price is *below par* or *at a discount*; and if a larger sum has to be paid, its price is *above par* or *at a premium*. In the U.S.A. some securities are issued without a nominal or face value and are called *no-par-value* securities. (3) FIN. the relative value of the standard currency units of two countries, called the *par of exchange* or *par rate of exchange* or *par exchange rate*. It is the rate of exchange *at par*, i.e. without either premium or discount, and lies somewhere between the buying rate and the selling rate current in the market. *See also* mint par of exchange.

para. paragraph.

para a fractional unit of the currency of Turkey. 1 kurus = 40 para. 1 lira = 100 kurus.

paragraph one of the divisions of a letter, report or other document. It is a series of sentences dealing with a particular point or process of thought. Each paragraph should begin on a separate line, to let the reader know that a change of subject-matter, line of thought or argument is taking place. *Abbr.* par.; para.

Paraguay a republic in South America, pop. 2.6 million approx. (1973); capital, Asunción, pop. 450,000 approx.; language, Spanish; currency unit, the guarani, divided into 100 centimos. Member, O.A.S.

parallel (of latitude) *see* latitude.

parallel rate (of exchange) *see under* exchange rate.

parallel standard *see under* standard.

parameter in mathematics, a quantity that is fixed, that is not variable. Thus in a business, the top management may fix parameters, i.e. amounts of money, within which managers must limit the expenses of their departments.

parcel *n.* (1) a quantity of goods wrapped in paper or other material to make a package for carriage or storage. Cf. package. (2) a quantity or group of things put together to form a single unit for a particular purpose: *A parcel of shares*, a group of shares of a size suitable for selling in the market. *A shipment parcel*, a shipment of goods going together as a unit. *A parcel of bills of exchange*, a group of mixed bills having a common maturity date and therefore likely to be easily sold in the market. (3) a particular piece or plot of land, as opposed to other pieces or plots.

v. (1) to divide into parts or shares: *To parcel out*, to distribute parts to a number of persons. (2) to make (goods) up into packages, to package.

parcel post *see under* post.

parcels office TRANSPT. an office in or near a railway station where goods packed in parcels are received for carriage by passenger train or parcels train, and where parcels may be collected on arrival.

parent company *see under* company.

Pareto Vilfredo (1848–1923), Italian economist and sociologist, Professor of Political Economy at Lausanne, Switzerland. His application of mathematics to economic analysis led to his *Cours d'Économie Politique* (1896–7) which dealt in detail with the distribution of incomes and wealth. In his *Manuale d'Economia Politica* (1906) he introduced the concept (idea) of indifference curves as tools of analysis.

par exchange rate *see* par (3).

pari passu STK. EXCH. (*Latin*, by equal steps) ranking equally. Thus, an issue of new shares ranking *pari passu* with existing shares means that holders of both the new and the old have exactly equal rights for payment of dividends and, if the company is wound up, for repayment of capital.

Paris Bourse *see* bourse.

Paris Club *see* Group of Ten.

parish in Britain, originally a district having a church, but also now the smallest unit in the system of local government. It consists of an elected parish council with very limited powers and mainly responsible for presenting to the higher local authority, the district council, the views of the electors on matters of local interest.

park *n.* an enclosed area of land with grass and trees used for rest or amusement. *See also* industrial park.

v. to deposit, to leave temporarily, as in a car park (*see under* car).

Parkinson's Law MAN. a set of ideas put forward by C. Northcote Parkinson, English writer, in a half-amusing but half-serious way, relating to the administration of companies and other organizations: firstly, that work expands to fill the time available to do it, i.e. employees and managers will find or make unnecessary work if allowed to do so; and secondly, that expenditure rises to meet income, i.e. if expenses are not strictly controlled, money will be spent on unnecessary things.

Parliament the law-making body of the United Kingdom, of Great Britain and Northern Ireland. It consists of the House of Lords and the House of Commons.

Parliamentary Commissioner for Administration in Britain, an officer of Parliament responsible for examining complaints of maladministration by government departments. These complaints are passed to him by Members of Parliament who receive them from the public. *Syn.* Ombudsman.

par of exchange *see* par (3).

parol LAW of a contract, by word of mouth; oral; unwritten. *See* parol contract, simple contract *under* contract.

Parquet STK. EXCH. in the Paris Bourse, the body of official stockbrokers. Cf. Coulisse.

par rate of exchange *see* par (3).

parsimony *n.* the fault of taking too much care in the use of money. *Adj.* parsimonious.

part delivery *see* part order.

part-exchange *see under* exchange, *n.* (1).

partial acceptance *see under* acceptance (4).

partial analysis ECON. THEORY a branch of economic theory that studies the working of a relatively small part of the economy, without taking into account influences from outside. Cf. aggregate analysis. *Syn.* particular equilibrium analysis.

partial equilibrium *see* particular equilibrium *under* equilibrium.

partial loss MAR. INSCE. a loss of part of the thing or goods insured, not the whole. *See* average (4). *Abbr.* P/L; P.L.

participate *v.* to have a share in; to take or play a part in: *To participate in the management of the business and in its profits. N.* participation; participant. *See* employee participation.

participating bond *see* profit-sharing bond *under* bond, *n.*

participating insurance *see* mutual insurance *under* insurance, classes and kinds of.

participating preference share *see under* share.

participating preferred stock *see under* stock.

particular average *see under* average (4).

particular equilibrium *see under* equilibrium.

particular lien *see under* lien.

particulars detailed facts; full information: *Please give me full particulars of your new product. Syn.* details.

partition (1) division into parts or shares: *The partition of property among heirs.* (2) separation of parts: *The partition of India and Pakistan.* (3) a thing that separates, such as a light wall separating one office from another.

partly-paid share *see under* share.

partner LAW one of two or more persons who have joined together as an unincorporated (unregistered) association to carry on business for the purpose of making a profit. A member of a partnership. *Syn.* a co-partner; an associate.

acting partner one who takes an active part in the work of the firm. Cf. dormant/secret/silent/sleeping partner. *Syn.* active partner; general partner; ordinary partner; working partner.

active partner *see* acting partner *above.*

dormant partner *see* sleeping partner *below.*

general partner *see* acting partner *above.*

junior partner one who is lower in rank and importance than the other partner(s) in the firm. Cf. senior partner.

limited partner *see* limited partnership *under* partnership.

managing partner a partner who has been appointed by all the other partners to manage the everyday affairs of the firm.

nominal partner a partner in name only; a person who only lends his name to a partnership, usu. for reward. He is not a legal partner, takes no part in the management of the firm and has no right to a share in its profits.

ordinary partner *see* acting partner *above.*

senior partner one of the partners who are the highest in rank and importance in a partnership firm. Cf. junior partner.

silent partner *see* sleeping partner *below.*

sleeping partner one who only invests money in a partnership business. He has the right to a share in the profits but takes no active part in the management of the firm. *Syn.* dormant partner; silent partner.

special partner a partner who, in certain conditions, can be held liable only for a special amount.

working partner *see* acting partner *above.*

partnership LAW an unincorporated (unregistered) association of two or more persons carrying on business together for the purpose of making a profit. In England and Wales, a partnership is not a separate legal person (but in Scotland it is). Contracts made with the partnership are made with the partners themselves. The partners share in the profits in agreed proportions, they do not draw salaries, nor get interest on their capital. *Syn.* a firm; a co-partnership.

commandite partnership in France, a form of partnership roughly equivalent to a limited partnership in Britain. The partners are called commanditaires.

general partnership one which is not a limited partnership, i.e. the members do not enjoy limited liability. *Syn.* ordinary partnership.

illegal partnership one formed for an illegal purpose and therefore void (of no effect in law) from the beginning.

limited partnership a form of partnership, sometimes found in the professions, consisting of one or more *general partners* having unlimited liability and one or more *limited partners* whose liability is limited to the amount of capital they have promised to provide; but the limited partners may not share in the management of the partnership. Such firms must register with the Registrar of Companies.

non-trading partnership one which does not depend on the buying and selling of goods and is usu. an association of professional people such as doctors, lawyers and accountants. Partnerships of farmers and innkeepers have been held by the courts to be non-trading partnerships. *Syn.* professional partnership.

ordinary partnership *see* general partnership *above*.

professional partnership *see* non-trading partnership *above*.

trading partnership one which depends on the buying and selling of goods. Cf. non-trading partnership.

partnership accounts ACCTS. the accounts of a partnership; they are different from those of a sole trader (single owner of a business) only in having separate capital, drawings and current accounts for each partner, and a profit and loss appropriation account showing how the net profit of the firm is shared among the partners.

Partnership, Articles of *see* deed of partnership.

partnership deed *see* deed of partnership.

partnership policy *see under* insurance policy.

part order COM. & IND. an order supplied only in part; less than the whole order, with the balance either already supplied, or to be supplied later, or not to be supplied at all. *Syn.* part delivery.

part owner SHIPG. one of several holders of shares in a ship.

part paid *see* partly-paid share *under* share; *also* partly-paid stock *under* stock.

part performance *see under* performance.

part-time job *see* job.

party *n.* (1) a person, esp. one who is concerned in some action or matter being discussed: *I do not know the party you referred to.* (2) a group of people meeting for a common purpose such as (*a*) amusement: *A dinner/card/cocktail party*; or (*b*) to examine and report on a particular subject: *A working party. See also* Dutch party *under* Dutch. (3) LAW the person or each of a group of persons who form one side or the other in an agreement: *The contracting parties. The parties to the agreement*; or in a disagreement: *The opposing parties. The parties to the dispute*; or in a lawsuit: *Parties in/to the suit.* (4) LAW any person who signs a legal document. (5) TOUR. a group of people travelling together.

party wall LAW a wall dividing two buildings. If the buildings belong to different owners, each party owns the half of the wall on his side but also has the right to receive the benefit of support given by the other half.

par value (1) STK. EXCH. the price or value fixed by the organization issuing a security and printed on the stock or share certificate. If the market price is at par, a £1 share, if fully paid up, can be bought or sold in the market for £1. *Syn.* nominal value; nominal price; face value. (2) BKG. *see* par of exchange.

par voie télégraphique *French*, by telegraph. *Abbr.* p.v.t.

pass. passenger.

pass *n.* (1) a document giving the holder the right to pass, to enter or leave property freely, or to travel free of charge on buses, trains, etc.: *An official/entry/railway/gate pass.* (2) a trick, deceit (*see* passing off).

v. (1) to authorize, approve, adopt: *To pass a law/motion/resolution/judgment/sentence.* (2) to go by, let go by, without seeing or acting: *To pass a dividend*, to decide to pay no dividend. (3) (*colloq.*) *To pass round the hat*, to collect money as a present for somebody or because he is in serious need.

passage (1) SHIPG. a voyage from one port to another or through a particular piece of narrow water: *We had a rough passage from Suez to Bombay.*

on passage of a ship, still at sea, not yet having reached the port to which she is going. *Syn.* on voyage.

passage money money paid to and received by a carrier for the carriage of passengers. (2) LAW a right of way, esp. over water that is privately owned: *A right of passage.*

pass-book (1) BKG. a book, either bound or in loose sheets called pass sheets, containing a written or typed record of all debits and credits made in a customer's current or deposit account. It is held by the customer who, from time to time, hands it to the bank to be brought up to date. The pass-book has been almost entirely replaced by the computerized bank statement. *Syn.* bank book. *Abbr.* P.B. (current pass-book); D.P.B. (deposit pass-book). (2) FIN. a book recording payments made into and out of a building society account. (3) COM. a book sometimes supplied to a customer by a trader or shopkeeper, in which are recorded details of goods sold to the customer on credit.

passenger (1) TRANSPT. & SHIPG. a person who travels in a ship, plane, train, bus, car or other means of transport who is not the driver, pilot or other member of the crew: *The passengers and crew of a ship. A passenger ship/liner/vessel/plane/train*, one that is used mainly for carrying passengers rather than cargo or goods. *Passenger accommodation*, the space in a ship or plane reserved for use by passengers. *A fare-paying passenger. Abbr.* pass. (2) (*colloq.*) one of a group of workers who does less than his share of the work; an ineffective worker.

passenger list *see under* list.

passenger manifest *see under* manifest.

passing off LAW pretending that the product that one is selling is the product of another person. Thus, if a seller misleads buyers by selling goods bearing the name, mark or label of another producer, the injured party can bring an action against him in the courts.

passive balance (of trade) ECON. an unfavourable balance. *Opp.* active balance; favourable balance.

passive bond *see under* bond, *n.*

passport TOUR. & TRANSPT. an official document, usu. in the form of a book, issued by the government of a country to a person belonging to that country, allowing him to enter his country and to leave it to visit certain foreign countries. The holder uses this document when abroad to prove who he is, and to obtain the help and protection, if needed, of representatives of his government in foreign countries.

pass sheet *see* pass-book (1).

past consideration *see under* consideration.

past-due bill *see* overdue bill *under* bill of exchange.

pasture AGR. grassland on which cattle are raised; grassland used for grazing, not for making hay. *Syn.* grazing.

patent LAW in Britain, a special right given by the Crown to an inventor to be the only person to make and sell, or to authorize others to make and sell, a newly-invented machine or process. In law, the life of a patent is 16 years, but in certain cases this can be extended by five or ten years. *To take out a patent*, to patent.

v. to obtain a patent for a new machine or process.

patent agent LAW a professional person, trained in the law relating to patents and trade-marks and registered with the government. He acts for persons such as inventors in the highly complicated process of obtaining a patent for a new invention.

patentee LAW a person to whom a patent has been officially granted or in whose name a patent is officially registered.

patent medicine IND. a medicine, the composition of which is protected by a patent.

Patent Office LAW in Britain, the government office that receives and examines applications for patents, controls the granting of patents and attends to the registration of patents and trade-marks.

patrimony LAW money and real property that has passed by inheritance from father to son to grandson to great-grandson, and so on.

patron (1) COM. a regular supporter, esp. a person who supports a retail business by buying regularly from it rather than from others. (2) a person who helps a poorer but deserving person, or some charity, with money.

patronage COM. the regular support given by a patron to a business such as a shop or hotel.

patronize *v.* (1) to act as a patron, as a regular customer: *He patronizes the restaurant at the corner of the street.* (2) to treat a person as being of lower rank or importance than oneself: *An employer should not be patronizing towards his workers.*

pattern COM. a sample, esp. of a cloth or carpet, to show quality, colour and design.

pauper a very poor person, esp. a person who needs or receives support from the community.

pauperism the state of being a pauper. Continual poverty.

pawn *n.* LAW (1) an article of personal property deposited as security for a loan. *See* pawnbroker. (2) the state of being deposited as security: *Goods in pawn*, goods that have been deposited as security. *Syn.* gage; pledge.

v. to deposit, as security for a loan, personal property on the condition that if the loan is not paid within a certain time (in Britain, six months) the pawnee (lender) has the right to sell the good(s) pawned and from the money thus obtained to keep enough to cover the amount of the loan and any interest due; any balance remaining must be paid to the pawnor. *Syn.* pledge; (*colloq.*) pop. *See also* spout.

pawnbroker COM. & LAW one who lends money on the security of personal property such as jewellery, clothes, etc. The way he runs his business and the rate of interest he may charge are strictly controlled by law in Britain. His occupation is *pawnbroking*; his place of business is a *pawnshop*; he is the *pawnee*; he gives a *pawn ticket* to the *pawnor* (*or pawner*) for each *pawn* (article pledged). *Syn.* (*colloq.*) uncle.

pawnee LAW a person, such as a moneylender or pawnbroker, who takes personal property as security for a loan. If the debt is over £2 and is not repaid within six months, the pawnee may sell the property, take back the amount of the loan and give any balance to the pawnor. *Syn.* pledgee.

pawnor LAW a person who pawns, i.e. deposits personal property as security for a loan of money from the pawnee, usu. a pawnbroker. *Also* pawner. *Syn.* pledgor.

pawnshop *see* pawnbroker; spout.

pay *v.* (1) to give money for something: *To pay for a meal before leaving the restaurant. To pay one's way*, to pay one's share of expenses. *The business pays its way*, it covers its costs. *To pay through the nose*, to pay too high a price. *To pay on the nail*, *see* nail. (2) to settle a debt by giving money or performing some duty. *He has paid all that he owed. This bill is due to be paid today. You may pay by instalments.* (3) to produce a profit: *It pays to advertise. Publishing is a paying business.*

n. money earned by, or given to, an employee as wages or salary in return for his services. *I draw my pay weekly on Thursdays. His pay is higher than hers. See* free pay.

payable FIN. & ACCTS. (1) due to be paid: *This bill of exchange is payable three months from now. See also* account payable; bills payable. (2) that must or will be paid: *Interest is payable quarterly. See* account payable. (3) profitable:

A payable gold-mine, one that pays, or can be made to pay, a profit.

pay as you earn TAXN. in Britain, the popular name for a method of collecting income tax, by which an employer must by law deduct income tax from each employee's wages or salary, and must pay this tax to the government once a month. *Abbr.* P.A.Y.E.

pay cash BKG. words written by the drawer on a cheque which has already been crossed, in order to 'open' the crossing and to tell the paying bank to pay the payee in cash. This is done usu. where the payee has no bank account into which he could pay a crossed cheque.

pay day (1) the day on which an employee is paid. In Britain, each Thursday or Friday in the case of employees paid weekly wages; or the last Thursday or Friday in the month, or the last day in the month, in the case of employees paid a monthly salary. (2) STK. EXCH. Pay Day *see* Account Day.

P.A.Y.E. pay as you earn.

payee BKG. the person or organization whose name appears in a cheque or bill of exchange as being the person to whom, or to whose order, payment is to be made. *Account payee only, see under* account.

deceased payee a payee who is dead. A cheque or bill of exchange bearing the name of such a person may be paid after it has been endorsed by his legal representative such as his executor or administrator.

fictitious payee in a cheque or bill of exchange, a payee who although named, clearly does not and never did exist, or is somebody to whom the drawer clearly did not intend it to be paid, such as Sherlock Holmes. In such cases, payment may be made to bearer. Cf. impersonal payee *below*.

impersonal payee on a cheque, a payee who is clearly not a person or group of persons, e.g. 'wages or order'. A cheque bearing such a direction is not payable to bearer but may be paid if properly endorsed by the drawer in favour of a person. Cf. fictitious payee *above*.

payer BKG. a person who pays, esp. one who pays a bill of exchange or promissory note. *Also* payor.

pay freeze *see under* freeze.

paying bank(er) BKG. one on whom a cheque or bill of exchange has been drawn, and who pays it.

paying guest a person living in a private house or guest-house who, in return for payment, is provided with one or more rooms and with meals. Cf. lodger.

paying-in book BKG. a book of paying-in slips.

paying-in slip BKG. in Britain, the printed form used by a customer of a bank when paying cash, cheques, etc. to the bank for credit to his account. The form contains a list of the more usual items paid in, such as the various notes and coins in use, cheques, postal orders, etc. The form has a counterfoil which is stamped and initialled by the bank teller and handed to the customer as a receipt. *Syn.* credit voucher; credit slip; deposit slip (U.S.A.).

payload TRANSPT. of the total load that a vehicle can carry, that part that earns money, such as passengers and goods carried in return for fares and freight. *Also* pay load.

paymaster FIN. an official responsible for paying government employees their salaries, wages, or pensions.

payment (1) the act of paying: *The payment of wages/debts/taxes/rates must not be delayed.* (2) the money paid: *We have received payment of your bill. You agree to repay this loan by weekly payments of £10. Down payment, see* down (2). *Abbr.* pt.

payment after delivery *see* payment terms.

payment bill *see under* bill of exchange.

payment countermanded *see* stopped cheque *under* cheque.

payment for honour *see* payment supra protest.

payment in due course BKG. payment of a bill of exchange when it becomes due, i.e. at maturity.

payment in kind FIN. payment that is made or received, not in money, but in goods or services. *See* income in kind.

payment on account *see* account (2c).

payment on invoice/receipt of goods/statement *see* payment terms.

payments, balance of *see* balance of payments.

payments, preferential *see under* preferential.

payment stopped *see* stopped cheque *under* cheque.

payment supra protest BKG. the act of a person, other than the debtor, who pays a dishonoured bill of exchange after it has been protested, in order to protect the honour of the debtor. In paying it he must arrange for a notary to draw up and attest (witness) a formal document called a *notarial act of honour* which must state for whose honour the bill has been paid; this document must be fastened to the protest. *Syn.* payment for honour.

payment terms COM. the conditions agreed between buyer and seller concerning the method of payment for the goods; these conditions are usu. demanded or proposed by the seller and either they are accepted by the buyer when placing or confirming his order, or different terms are arranged by negotiation. The main methods used are: cash (or payment) with order; cash (or payment) on delivery; prompt cash; payment after delivery; payment on invoice or statement; monthly or quarterly account; open account; mail or cable transfer; bill of exchange; documents against cash, or against payment, or against acceptance; letter of credit; acceptance credit; banker's authority to negotiate.

documents against payment *see* cash against documents.

payment after delivery payment for a credit sale at an agreed number of days after delivery. Often, when a cash discount is offered, the seller will state on the invoice: *7 days 2%, 14 days 1%, 28 days net*, being days after delivery. A credit sale on open account is payable within a fixed credit period.

payment on delivery (P.O.D.) *see* cash on delivery.

payment on invoice payment which is due to be made as soon as the buyer receives an invoice, which may be before the goods are sent off, or at the same time, or soon after they are delivered. This method of payment is used esp. for a single sale, i.e. when there is no regular trading arrangement between buyer and seller such as would cause the seller to open an account in his ledgers in the buyer's name. Cf. payment on statement.

payment on receipt of goods *see* cash on delivery.

payment on statement payment which is due to be made when the buyer receives a statement of account or at an agreed later date. This method of payment is used when the seller has an account in his ledgers in the buyer's name. Cf. payment on invoice.

payment with order *see* cash with order.

payor *see* payer.

pay-packet FIN. (1) an envelope containing an employee's wages when paid in cash, together with a pay-slip stating how the amount paid has been calculated. (2) the amount earned by an employee as wages: *The average weekly pay-packet of a skilled industrial worker is £100.*

pay-roll ACCTS. & MAN. (1) a complete and permanent list of employees at a particular date, with details of the amounts paid, or to be paid, to each employee, and how these amounts are calculated. It may be divided into a *weekly pay-roll* and a *monthly pay-roll*, according to whether employees are paid a weekly wage or a monthly salary. *Syn.* wages sheet. (2) the total amount paid to employees as wages and salaries: *The weekly pay-roll of the company is £50,000.* (3) the cash needed to pay the wages of all employees who are paid in cash: *A pay-roll robbery*, a theft of cash intended to pay such employees. (4) the total number of persons employed by an organization: *The society has a pay-roll of 400.*

pay-roll clerk *see* wages clerk.

pay-roll tax TAXN. a tax on employers of a fixed amount weekly or monthly for each person employed. The purpose is usu. to make employers use labour more effectively.

pay-slip ACCTS. & MAN. a paper given to each employee each time he is paid, showing how the amount paid has been calculated.

P.B. pass-book.

P.B.X. private branch exchange.

P.C. postcard; police constable.

P/C prices current; petty cash; per cent.

p.c. per cent.

pc., pce. piece.

P.C.B. petty cash book.

pcs. pieces; prices.

Pd., pd. paid; passed.

P.D. port due.

p.d. per diem (per day).

PE Peru's international vehicle-registration letters.

P/E, p/e price-earnings (ratio).

peak (1) the pointed top; the highest point, e.g. of a mountain. (2) IND. the time of day or year when something is at its highest level: *Peak demand*, (a) the time when the demand for e.g. electricity, gas, travel are greatest. (b) the size of the demand at this time. *Opp.* off-peak. (3) STK. & COMMOD. EXCH. of prices, the highest point reached: *Prices are believed to be at their peak*, prices are expected to fall from now on.

peasant one of a class of persons, formerly on the continent of Europe, and in many developing countries, who own or rent, and cultivate, small farms, or are employed as agricultural workers.

peck in corn and dry measure, 2 gallons or 8 pints or a quarter of a bushel. 1 pk. = 9.092 litres.

peculation *see* embezzlement.

pecuniary relating to, consisting of, money: *He gives his services for no pecuniary reward*, he receives no money for his work. *To make a pecuniary gain*, to receive money. *To suffer a pecuniary loss*, to lose money. *To have a pecuniary interest in a business/contract/venture*, to have invested money in it. *Syn.* monetary.

peddle COM. to carry small articles from house to house selling them usu. very cheaply. Cf. to hawk.

peddler *see* pedlar.

pedestrian a person who is walking, esp. in a street or road.

pedlar COM. a person who peddles. *Also* (U.S.A.) pedler, peddler.

pedler *see* pedlar.

peg COM. & ECON. to keep unchanged: *To peg prices/wages*, by government action, to prevent them rising, esp. in a period of inflation. *Pegged rates of exchange*, rates held steady by the buying and selling of gold or foreign currencies in the foreign-exchange markets.

P.E.I. Prince Edward Island, Canada.

pelf money, wealth, riches, esp. in the sense of being something bad or dishonourable. Cf. filthy lucre.

Pen. peninsula.

penalty LAW (1) a punishment, esp. a payment of money, for breaking a law. *Syn.* fine. (2) an agreed sum of money to be paid as a punishment by the party who is guilty of breaking a contract. In Britain, a penalty for breach of contract will not be supported by the courts. Cf. damages.

penalty bond *see under* bond, *n*.

penalty clause LAW in a contract, a clause stating a sum of money (the penalty) that must be paid as a punishment by any party who is guilty of failing to perform his part of the contract. (But *see* penalty (2).)

pence *pl. of* penny, esp. in expressing a value: *The railway charges fifty pence a day for parking a car in the station car park.* But when separate penny coins are meant, the *pl.* form *pennies* is used: *The boy collected a box full of pennies. Abbr.* p.

pence rate *see* exchange rate.

pending (1) remaining undecided; not yet settled or completed: *Pending papers,* or *papers pending,* letters, bills, etc. waiting to be dealt with. *Pending tray/file,* a tray/file in which pending papers are kept. (2) while waiting: *Pending your instructions,* while we are waiting for you to instruct us. *Pending arrival of the ship the goods are to be stored at the port.*

Penn. Pennsylvania, U.S.A.

penni the fractional currency unit of Finland. *Pl.* pennia. 100 pennia = 1 markka (*pl.* markkaa) or Finnish mark.

penniless without a penny; having no money.

penny (1) the fractional currency unit of the United Kingdom and the Irish Republic, one-hundredth part of a pound. *Abbr.* p. *Pl.* pennies *or* pence (for explanation of which to use, *see* pence). (2) a popular name for the one-cent coin of Canada and the U.S.A. (3) any small sum of money: *The old lady was left without a penny,* without any money. *To buy in penny numbers,* in small lots, little by little. *See also* penny-pincher.

earnest-penny *see under* earnest.

penny-wise careful with money; inclined to save money rather than spend it.

(4) (*colloq.*) *Pretty penny,* a large amount of money: *He earns/spends a pretty penny on racing.*

-penny *suffix* in adjectives relating to price, such as *twopenny* (*pron.* tupni), *threepenny* (*pron.* threpni), *fourpenny* (*pron.* forpni), and so on. *A tenpenny bus fare/parking charge/bar of chocolate.*

penny-pincher a person who is too careful with money, or is inclined to save money rather than spend it, and will not give it away. *Syn.* pinchpenny.

pennyweight a small measure of weight in the troy system, one-twentieth part of an ounce

troy, and consisting of 24 grains = 1.5552 g. *Abbr.* dwt.; pwt. *See table on page 479.*

pennyworth COM. as much as can be bought for a penny; a very small quantity of something. *Also* penn'orth.

pension *n.* (1) a regular weekly or monthly payment, usu. of a fixed sum of money, made to a person in return for his past services, starting from the time he retires from regular full-time work, and continuing until he dies. (2) a similar payment to a disabled person or to a widow.

contributory pension *see* contributory pension scheme.

disablement pension *see under* disablement.

indexed pension one that is increased from time to time in proportion to increases in the cost-of-living index.

non-contributory pension *see* non-contributory pension scheme.

occupational pension a retirement pension that arises from, or relates to, past service with one or more employers under a pension scheme, as opposed to a state retirement pension payable under the national insurance scheme.

old age pension in Britain, the former name for the state retirement pension paid by the government to men usu. at age 65, and to women at age 60. *Abbr.* O.A.P. The expression is still in common use for a state retirement pension, *see below.*

retirement pension one that starts when an employee retires from regular work, and continues until his death. It may be the pension paid by the State under the British national insurance scheme (formerly called the old age pension); or it may be an occupational pension, *see above.*

top-hat pension *see under* top-hat.

widow's pension one that is paid to a woman from the time she becomes a widow and continues until her death. It is usu. of a smaller amount than the pension her husband would have received when he was alive.

(3) TOUR. on the continent of Europe, esp. in France, a small hotel or boarding house where the charge includes a room and meals. *Pron.* pon-syon.

pensionable service *see under* service.

pensioner a person who receives a pension.

pension fund INSCE. & STK. EXCH. a fund (stock of money) set aside by employers, and often by their employees as well, each making regular contributions, for the special purpose of providing retirement pensions and widow's pensions for their employees. In Britain, many pension funds work closely with insurance companies and investment trusts; together these have become very large buyers and sellers of securities on the Stock Exchange, and buyers of non-monetary assets such as works of art and real property, in which to invest the capital accumulating in the pension funds.

pension schemes see national insurance; contributory pension scheme; non-contributory pension scheme.

People's Bank dollar a popular name in the West for the yuan, the standard currency unit of China, divided into 10 chiao or 100 fen. *Also* renminbi; reminibi; ranminbi.

peppercorn rent a very small rent such as £1 per year, demanded by the owner of a property to show that there is a relationship of landlord and tenant, thus making it clear that he remains the legal owner.

p/e.r., P/E.r., P.E.R., p.e.r. price-earnings ratio.

per by: *Per bearer/passenger train/goods train/carrier/steamer. Abbr.* p.

per an., per ann. per annum.

per annum (*Latin*, by the year) yearly; for each year. *Abbr.* p.a.

per capita (correctly, *Latin*: per caput, by each head) for each person in the population. *Per capita income, see under* income.

per cent (*Latin*: per centum, by the hundred) for, or in, every hundred. *Three per cent of the population*, three persons in every hundred. *Interest at three per cent*, at the rate of £3 for every £100 invested or borrowed. *Sign*: %. *Abbr.* p.c.; P/C.

percentage (1) a rate per cent (per hundred): *To calculate the percentage of overhead costs to total sales.* (2) a commission of the selling price: *He is paid a percentage on the orders he gets for the firm.* (3) an allowance: *A printer is allowed a small percentage of paper for spoilage.* (4) (*colloq.*) a profit or gain: *We make a good percentage on our own brand of soap.* (5) generally, a proportion: *A large/high/good/low/small percentage of debtors pay their bills promptly.*

percentage profit see under profit.

perch in British linear measure, a length of 5.5 yds. or 16.5 ft, equal to 5.029 m. *Abbr.* p. *Syn.* rod; pole.
square perch 30.25 sq. yds. or 272. 25 sq. ft equal to 25.29 m², esp. of brickwork.

per contra (*Latin*, to the other side) to the opposite side (of an account). *A per contra entry or An entry per contra*, in book-keeping, a balancing entry, such as a debit to balance a credit, or a credit to balance a debit.

per diem (*Latin*, by the day) for each day. *Abbr.* p.d.

perfect competition see pure competition *under* competition.

perfect entry see under customs entry.

perfecting the sight see bill of sight.

perfect market see under market.

perfect monopoly see pure monopoly *under* monopoly.

perfect ream see ream.

performance LAW the act of carrying out the duties contained in a contract. The contract is discharged (completed and ended) once these duties have been performed.

part performance a guiding rule in law that one party to an unwritten or informal contract cannot avoid performing his part by saying that the agreement lacked formality, if the other party has performed his part, wholly or partly, in the belief that both parties had firmly intended to do what they agreed to do.

specific performance, decree of a court order commanding a party who has broken a contract to do what he had bound himself to do.

performance bond see bond, *n*.

performance guarantee see *under* guarantee, export.

performing rights LAW the legal rights held by the owner of the copyright in a literary or musical work or a play, to control and license public performances, including the right to charge fees.

peril INSCE. & MAR. INSCE. an event which may cause a loss; serious danger; risk: *To be in peril*, to be in great danger. *Perils of the sea*, storm, fog, shipwreck or any other cause of danger to ships and their cargoes, such as collision.

excepted perils see *under* excepted.

imminent peril a situation of great danger, when an event, such as shipwreck, is likely to happen at any moment, causing a loss.

period bill see usance bill *under* bill of exchange.

period cost see fixed cost *under* cost.

periodical a magazine or other publication that appears at regular intervals: *A weekly/fortnightly/monthly/quarterly periodical.*

perishables TRANSPT. goods, esp. foodstuffs such as meat, eggs, butter, fish and fruit, that will go bad unless they are delivered quickly or are carried or kept in cold storage: *A cargo of perishables.*

perjury LAW the offence by a witness or an interpreter of making an untrue statement on oath or affirmation, knowing it to be untrue or not believing it to be true.

perk see perquisite.

perm. permanent.

permafrost AGR. land on which the soil is frozen throughout the year.

permanent assets see fixed assets *under* assets.

permanent debt see *under* national debt.

permanent health policy see *under* insurance policy.

permanent income see *under* income.

per mensem (*Latin*, by the month) for, or in, every month.

per mille (*Latin*, by the thousand) for, or in, every thousand. *Abbr.* per mil.

permission to deal STK. EXCH. in Britain, formal permission of the Stock Exchange authorities for a new issue of shares to be dealt in by its members. This permission must be applied for within three days of the publication of a prospectus, and if the permission is not given within three weeks, any allotment of shares is void (has no effect) and any money received from persons applying for shares must be returned.

permit *n.* written permission, from a person or organization in authority, allowing a named person to do something or to go somewhere. *Syn.* licence. *Pron.* pérmit.

customs permit a document given by a customs officer allowing goods on which import duty has been paid to be moved away.

excise permit a document given by an excise officer allowing goods on which excise duty has been paid to be moved away.

export permit *see* export licence.

import permit *see* import licence.

residential *or* **residence permit** official permission in writing allowing a particular person to reside (live permanently) in a place, esp. a country.

work permit official permission given to a foreigner to stay and to work as an employee, usu. given for a limited period only.

perpetual annuity FIN. & STK. EXCH. an annuity that is payable for a period of time that has no fixed end, such as the annuity paid by the British Government in connection with its debt to the Bank of England, or the interest on an undated government security. Such an annuity is not made under an insurance contract.

perpetual bond *see* annuity bond *under* bond, *n.*

perpetual debenture *see* irredeemable debenture *under* debenture.

perpetual inventory *see under* inventory.

perpetuity LAW (1) a period of time that has no limit, that goes on for ever. (2) a property the ownership of which cannot ever be transferred by the owner. In many countries such arrangements are limited by law to the life of the present owner(s) and a further 21 years. (3) STK. EXCH. & FIN. a perpetual annuity.

per pro. per procurationem.

per procurationem (*Latin*, by procuration) (signing) for and with the authority of: *Per pro. Wood & Co., W. Jones;* or *Wood & Co., per pro. W. Jones.* In both examples W. Jones is signing for and with the authority of Wood & Co. A person who is formally authorized to sign documents for somebody else, e.g. a firm, is said to sign *per procurationem*; and the person or firm giving him this authority accepts responsibility for documents so signed. *Abbr.* p.p.; p. pro.; per pro.

perquisite something gained by an employee in a particular post over and above his salary or wages. *Also* perk (*colloq.*). Cf. fringe benefit; bonus.

person LAW in law, a single human being or a corporation (an artificial group of people who together are given an imaginary existence as a single being) having rights and owing duties.

artificial person *see under* artificial.

fictitious person *see* artificial person *under* artificial.

legal person *see under* legal.

natural person any single human being, whether man, woman or child.

personal accident policy *see under* insurance policy.

personal accounts *see* accounts, *n. pl.*

personal allowance TAXN. in Britain, a standard amount of income, which may be changed from time to time by the government, on which the taxpayer pays no income tax. The amount is smaller for an unmarried taxpayer than for a married one. *Syn.* personal relief.

personal assets *see* assets (2).

personal assistant *see under* assistant.

personal call a long-distance telephone call obtained by the operator who, at an extra charge, connects the caller to a named person and not to anybody else.

personal cheque *see under* cheque.

personal credit *see under* credit (6).

personal effects movable goods that are private property, such as clothes, books, jewellery, ornaments and private papers. *Syn.* personal property.

personal estate LAW movable property consisting of money, furniture, and other chattels, cattle, shares, ships, leasehold property, etc. *Syn.* personalty; personal property.

personal income *see under* income.

personal investment *see* financial investment *under* investment.

personality (1) existence as a person, either as a natural human being or as an artificial corporation. *See* person. (2) a person's nature as shown by the different qualities that together make up his character: *He has the right personality for this difficult post,* the right nature and qualities. (3) a well-known person: *A television/sporting/theatrical personality.*

personalized cheque *see under* cheque.

personal ledger *see under* ledger.

personal loan *see under* loan, *n.*

personal property *see under* property.

personal relief *see* personal allowance.

personal representative LAW a person appointed either as executor or administrator to settle the affairs and personal estate of a deceased person (one who has died). If the deceased has made a will, his personal representative will be the executor appointed in the will; and there may be several joint executors. If the deceased has died without making a will, or if after careful search no will has been found, the court will appoint one or more administrators to deal with the estate. *See* executor; administrator. *Abbr.* P.R.

personal saving *see under* saving.

personal sector ECON. in a mixed economy, that part of the economy that is owned and operated by private persons, and private businesses of all kinds that are not limited companies. Cf. corporate sector; private sector; public sector.

personal security FIN. & BKG. a written guarantee by a person who becomes guarantor or surety for the amount of a loan made by a lender, such as a bank, to another person. Thus a loan made on personal security differs from a loan made against deposit of impersonal securities such as stock and share certificates and title-deeds relating to property. *See* guarantee (2); guarantor.

personal selling *see under* selling.

personal share *see* registered share *under* share.

personalty *see* personal estate.

person, legal *see* legal person.

personnel MAN. the entire body of persons employed by an organization, as opposed to matériel.

personnel management MAN. the organizing and training of people at work with the object of getting each employee to make the biggest possible contribution to the success of the organization, and to be happy in his work.

personnel manager *see under* manager.

persuasive advertising *see* advertising.

perte totale MAR. INSCE. *French*, total loss. *Abbr.* P.T.

Peru a republic on the west coast of South America, pop. 16 million approx. (1975); capital, Lima, pop. 2.5 million approx.; languages, Spanish and Quechua; currency unit, the sol (*pl.* soles), divided into 100 centavos. Member, O.A.S.; L.A.F.T.A.

peseta the currency unit of Spain, divided into 100 centimos. *Abbr.* p.

peseta Guineana the standard currency unit of Equatorial Guinea, divided into 100 centimos. *Also* ekpwele.

pesewa the fractional currency unit of Ghana. 100 pesewas = 1 cedi.

peso the standard currency unit of a number of Spanish-speaking countries: Argentina, Bolivia, Colombia, Cuba, the Dominican Republic, Mexico, the Philippines and Uruguay. In all these countries the peso is subdivided into 100 centavos except in Uruguay, where it is subdivided into 100 centésimos. *Abbr.* p.

petit average *see* petty average.

petite vitesse TRANSPT. (*French*, low speed) in Europe, by ordinary goods train or slow train, as distinguished from grande vitesse (G.V.), fast goods train. *Abbr.* P.V.

petition (1) LAW in Britain, a formal request in writing to the Crown or to a public official for judicial action to set right a wrong or (*b*) for a court order commanding obedience to a judicial decision. (2) a humble request, addressed to somebody in authority, begging for a favour.

petition in bankruptcy *see under* bankruptcy.

petitioning creditor *see* petition in bankruptcy *under* bankruptcy.

petrodollars FIN. accumulations of U.S.A. dollars that have been deposited with banks and other financial concerns in the developed countries by members of the Organization of Petroleum Exporting Countries (O.P.E.C.) who, after the increase in oil prices in 1973, have very great amounts of money that they cannot immediately spend.

petties ACCTS. small items of petty cash expenses grouped together and entered in the books as a single total because they are too small to be worth entering separately.

petty average SHIPG. charges and expenses paid by the master during the voyage of a ship, such as pilotage, port charges. *Also* petit average. Cf. general average; particular average.

petty cash ACCTS. a sum of money kept in the office of a business, usu. in a strong *cash box* or *petty cash box*, from which are paid those small expenses that cannot be settled by cheque. A *petty cash account* is kept, usu. by a junior cashier called a *petty cashier*, in a *petty cash book*. *See* imprest system. *Abbr.* P/C.

Petty Sir William (1623–87), English statistician and economist, Member of Parliament, a founder of the Royal Society, and regarded by some as the founder of political economy because he introduced method and 'political arithmetick' into the study of money, foreign exchanges, taxation and employment. His writings, esp. *Treatise of Taxes and Contributions* (1662), *Essays in Political Arithmetick* (1672) and *Quantulamcunque, a Treatise Concerning Money* led the way to the classical economics of the eighteenth and nineteenth centuries.

pfennig the fractional currency unit of West Germany. 100 pfennigs = 1 Deutsche Mark.

Philippines a republic consisting of a group of islands in south-east Asia, pop. 41 million approx. (1973); capital, Manila, pop. 550,000 approx.; languages, Pilipino, Spanish and English; currency unit, the peso, divided into 100 centavos. Member, Colombo Plan, A.S.E.A.N.

phone (*colloq.*) telephone. *See also* freephone.

phone-box (*colloq.*) a public telephone box. *See* call-box.

photocopier a machine that makes photocopies.

photocopy *n.* a photographic copy of a letter, drawing, etc.

photolitho offset *see* lithography.

phut COM. (*colloq.*) *To go phut*, to collapse; to become insolvent. Of a person, to go bankrupt; of a company, to go into liquidation.

physical depreciation *see* depreciation.

physical deterioration *see under* deterioration.

physical geography the study of the natural shape and qualities of the earth's surface and surrounding atmosphere. *Syn.* physiography.

physical inventory *see* physical stocktaking *under* stocktaking.

physical stocktaking *see under* stocktaking.

Physiocrats ECON. HIST. a group of eighteenth-century French economists led by Quesnay, who considered that wealth came only from land and that economic activity should be kept entirely free from government control. *Syn.* les économistes.

physiography *see* physical geography.

PI Philippine Islands. The international vehicle-registration letters of the Philippines.

piastre the fractional currency unit of Lebanon: 100 piastres = 1 Lebanese pound (L£1); and of Turkey: 1 piastre or kurus = 40 para. 100 piastres or kurus = 1 Turkish lira.

pica a form and size of type used on some typewriters, having ten letters or spaces to one inch, each letter being 12 points (0.167 in.) high. Cf. elite.

pice *see* paisa.

picket IND. REL. in an industrial dispute, a group of employees (sometimes with hired supporters and organized by a trade union) who gather at the entrance to a factory, shop or office-building to persuade other employees not to do any work, suppliers not to deliver any materials, and customers not to buy or take away any finished products. By this action, called *picketing*, the employees forming the picket, called *picketers*, hope to force the management to agree to their demands. *Syn.* strike-picket.

picking COM. & IND. in a warehouse, the process, known also as *order-picking*, of collecting together all the things that are listed in an order before they are packed and dispatched to the customer. Picking is usually done from a *picking-list* or from a copy of the invoice.

pickpocket a thief who steals from people's pockets and handbags, usu. in places where there are crowds.

pick up *v.* COM. (*colloq.*) (1) to find by chance and buy, usu. very cheaply: *I picked this book up cheaply in a junk shop.* (2) to earn or obtain with difficulty: *He picks up a modest living selling waste paper. Please try to pick up some orders during your travels.* (3) STK. EXCH. of stock and share prices, to rise again: *After an early fall, industrials picked up rapidly before the close.* (4) to buy as many as possible of a particular security to force the market price to rise. (5) TRANSPT. to take passengers or goods into or on to a vehicle and to carry them: *A taxi picked him up at the corner. Opp.* to set down. (6) (*colloq.*) to find by chance a means of transport: *I picked up a passing taxi.*

pico- the *prefix* used in the metric system of SI units to mean one million millionth (10^{-12}): 1 farad = 1,000,000,000,000 picofarads.

pictogram (1) MAN. a diagram in which representations are shown by arranging various pictures of things such as men, animals, trees, boxes or factory chimneys in groups, (2) MAN. & TOUR. also used to indicate the services available in a locality using symbols, e.g. for car parking, information, toilets, etc.

pidgin a language with little grammar and few words, based on European languages, esp. English, French or German, and used between peoples who have no common language. It is not the mother tongue of any group, but is useful as a limited means of expression. Pidgin English has been made one of the official languages of the Solomon Islands and Papua New Guinea, and various forms of it are much used throughout the Far East and south-east Asia.

piece (1) FIN. a coin, usu. of stated value: *A fivepenny/tenpenny piece.* (2) COM. & IND. one single article, not a pair or a dozen or a gross: *Our stock of this article is 50 pieces. Please supply 18 pieces by return post. Abbr.* pc.; pce. *Pl.* pcs.

by the piece (*a*) (supplied or sold) as single articles, *see* piece-goods. (*b*) a single job of work, *see* piece-work.

piece-goods (1) textile goods, esp. silk, linen or cotton cloth, made and sold in standard lengths (pieces) that are convenient, e.g. for making clothes, as opposed to cloth supplied in bolts (rolls) containing many metres. (2) in U.S.A., pieces of cloth of any length desired by the customer and cut from the bolt. *Syn.* yard-goods.

piece market COM. the market, esp. overseas, for piece-goods.

piece rates *see* piece-work.

piece-work IND. a method of paying a worker wages based on the results of his work, i.e. according to the number of articles or pieces produced in a given time by him or by a group of workers of which he is a member. Cf. time-work. *Syn.* piece rates.

pie chart *or* **diagram** *see under* chart.

pier SHIPG. & TOUR. a long wall, road or other structure built out into the water from the shore to serve (*a*) as a landing-place for ships and boats; (*b*) as a breakwater enclosing a harbour; (*c*) as a place of amusement at a seaside town. *Syn.* jetty.

pierage SHIPG. charges that have to be paid by shipowners for the use of a pier. *Syn.* pier dues.

pier dues *see* pierage.

pigeon-hole *n.* a small division of a large box, each division being marked by a letter of the alphabet and formerly much used for storing letters and other papers. *See also* docket.

v. to put a proposal, a plan, on one side; to delay taking action in the hope, or with the intention, that action need never be taken: *The board have pigeon-holed our scheme for rebuilding the factory/having a workers' canteen.*

Pigou Arthur Cecil (1877–1959), English economist. He followed the great Alfred Marshall as Professor of Political Economy at Cambridge and led the Cambridge economists in carrying forward Marshall's work. He was particularly concerned with welfare economics, and his writings, of which the most important is *The Economics of Welfare* (1920), dealt with national income and output, and with employment, regarding which his views were much criticized by Keynes. *See* Cambridge School; Pigou effect.

Pigou effect ECON. THEORY a concept (idea) put forward by A.C. Pigou in 1944 about the effect on the real value of wealth made by changes in the price-level. He argued that if wages and prices are left free from control by government, there will in the long run always be a return to full employment; falling prices will cause increased consumption, money savings will then be used for increased spending, and the resulting check to falling prices will move the economy towards full employment. Keynes strongly opposed Pigou's views on this subject.

pilfer TRANSPT. to steal small things of little value, esp. from broken packages of goods, in a warehouse or while being transported from one place to another.

pilferage INSCE. loss caused by stealing goods being transported from seller to buyer, esp. when packages break open. *Syn.* petty theft in transit.

pillage originally, to rob violently of money and valuable things in time of war, but also, figuratively, (*a*) to obtain valuable things by cheating and to keep them illegally, (*b*) to charge excessively high prices.

pilot (1) SHIPG. a guide, esp. an officer qualified and authorized to bring ships through difficult or dangerous waters: *A sea/river/harbour pilot.* (2) TRANSPT. an officer qualified to take the controls of an aircraft.

pilotage SHIPG. the charge made for the services of a pilot. *Syn.* pilot dues.

pilot scheme IND. a small trial business or manufacturing activity made to get experience before investing in a larger scheme.

pin *see* cask.

pinch *v.* (*colloq.*) (1) to steal. (2) to be short of money or some other necessary thing: *I am rather pinched (for money) now, but I shall pay you next month. We are too pinched for time to be sure of catching that train.* (3) to catch, to arrest somebody, or to be caught or arrested: *The police pinched the thief. Be careful you don't get pinched.*

n. a difficult situation: *To feel the pinch,* to be short of money. *At a pinch,* in an emergency, if absolutely necessary.

pinchpenny *see* penny-pincher.
pin-money *see under* money.
pint a measure of volume used for both liquid and non-liquid substances, one-eighth of a gallon. *See* corn and dry measure; liquid measure. *Abbr.* p.; pt.

pioneer (1) a person who is one of the first to settle in a new country. (2) a person who is ahead of others in scientific research or some new activity. *See, e.g.,* Rochdale pioneers.

pipe a large barrel used in the wine trade, and varying in volume. The common English pipe holds about 185 U.K. gal. (841 l); smaller pipes from 92 to 126 gal. (418 to 573 l). *See* cask. *Syn.* butt.

piracy (1) LAW & SHIPG. robbery at sea. (2) LAW infringement of copyrights, called *literary piracy.*

pirate *n.* (1) LAW & SHIPG. a person, esp. one of a group who attack and rob a ship. (2) a person who infringes copyright, called a *literary pirate.* *v.* to publish and sell copyright material such as a book or artistic work without the permission of the owner of the copyright.

pit (1) IND. a hole in the ground, but esp. a coalmine. (2) STK. & COMMOD. EXCH. in U.S.A., an area of the floor of the exchange building where a particular commodity or kind of security is dealt in.

pitch (1) COM. a place in a street or market where a trader regularly places his stall or where a pedlar carries on his business. (2) STK. EXCH. the place in the Stock Exchange where a jobber carries on his dealings, and can usu. be found.

Pitman Sir Isaac (1813–97), inventor in 1837 of a system of shorthand based entirely on the sounds of speech.

pittance a very small amount of money or food, esp. when referring to a wage or allowance: *She works for a pittance because she cannot find a better job.*

pix ADVTG. (*colloq.*) pictures, esp. those used in advertisements, and advertising material of any kind.

pk. peck.
Pk. park.
pkg. packing; package.
pkge. package.
PL Poland's international vehicle-registration letters.
Pl. place; pole (measure).
P/L, P.L. partial loss.
P.L.A. Port of London Authority.
p.l.a. passengers' luggage in advance.
placing INSCE. (1) the act of making an insurance contract with an insurer or reinsurer. (2) the resulting insurance itself.

placings STK. EXCH. a way of issuing shares in a private company that is about to become a public company, by which the broker or issuing-house handling the issue places the shares with the public, i.e. finds from among his or their clients a small number of wealthy persons or organizations such as institutional investors (insurance companies, pension funds, etc.) who are willing to buy large numbers of the new shares. Cf. introduction.

plagiarism imitating somebody else's ideas or writings and pretending they are one's own.

plaint LAW (1) the cause of a plaintiff's complaint against the defendant. (2) in a lawsuit, a detailed statement made to the court by the plaintiff, giving the cause of his complaint, and requesting a remedy for the wrong done by the defendant. Cf. plea.

plaintiff LAW a person who brings an action against somebody in a court of law. Cf. defendant. *Abbr.* plf.; plff.; pltf.

plane TRANSPT. an aeroplane. *See* aircraft; airline.

planned economy *see* command economy.

planned obsolescence *see under* obsolescence.

planning the preparation of plans for future action and the control of the organizations responsible for carrying out these plans.

corporate planning MAN. the work of top management of deciding the main objectives (aims) of an organization, esp. a group of companies, and the preparation of detailed future plans telling managers how to gain these objectives. Such plans usu. lay down standards to be aimed at in such matters as capital investment, output, sales, and levels of profit, for each unit of the company or group of companies.

economic planning ECON. & IND. the direction and control of the economy by the government of a country according to a national economic plan. *Syn.* state planning.

planning permission LAW & IND. in Britain, permission that must be obtained from a local government authority to build on land or otherwise develop it, e.g. by changing the use to which it is put.

plant IND. (1) any apparatus needed by an industrial business to carry on its trade, i.e. machinery, tools, special buildings: *A water-filtering plant; a central-heating plant.* (2) a complete system of buildings, machinery and apparatus for a particular production process: *A chemical plant. Syn.* installation.

plantation AGR. (1) woodland or forest planted by Man. (2) a farm, usu. large, in a tropical country, and employing many workers, on which coffee, tea, sugar, cotton, tobacco, rubber and some other crops are grown.

Plantation House COMMOD. EXCH. a popular name for the London Commodity Exchange, which is partly in a building of this name in Mincing Lane, in the City of London.

plantations STK. EXCH. the stocks and shares of companies owning and operating plantations of coffee, tea, rubber, tobacco, etc.

planter AGR. a person owning or managing a plantation.

plant factor *see* capacity (1).

plant utilization IND. the time during which plant is in actual use for production, compared with the time it could be, but is not being, used. Cf. downtime. *See* capacity factor *under* capacity.

platform (1) a part of a floor that has been raised higher than the rest of the floor, as in a hall or theatre, for the use of speakers or actors. (2) TRANSPT. in a railway station, a raised area between or along the tracks for use by persons entering or leaving trains.

platen in a typewriter and some other office machines, the roller which receives and holds the paper while it is being typed or printed upon. *Syn.* paper-cylinder.

platform ticket *see under* ticket.

playing the market(s) STK. EXCH. buying and selling securities with the aim of making a quick capital profit without regard to the long-term possibilities of gain, or to investment income. *Syn.* speculating.

plea LAW (1) in a criminal case, a statement by the accused person saying that he is guilty or not guilty of the offence with which he is charged; or that he claims that the court has no jurisdiction (legal power) to try him; or that he has already been tried for the same offence and found not guilty. (2) in a civil action, formerly the document containing the defendant's reply to the plaint; but in Britain this has now been replaced by a document called a statement of defence.

plead LAW to make a plea; to answer a charge or accusation in court: *To plead guilty/not guilty. He is unable to plead because of insanity. He refused to plead.*

pleader LAW (1) an advocate. (2) a lawyer who prepares pleadings.

pleadings LAW in a lawsuit, statements by plaintiff and defendant giving only the material facts in the case; pleadings must not state the law, or the evidence that will be used to prove the facts.

pledge *n.* LAW & FIN. any article delivered by a borrower (the *pledgor* or *pledger*) to a lender (the *pledgee*) as security for a debt. The ownership remains with the borrower, but the lender has possession, usu. until the debt is repaid. *See* pawnbroker; pawnee. *Syn.* pawn.

a pledge any thing held as security for a debt.

v. (1) deliver as security for a debt: *He pledged his gold watch for £20.* (2) to give a solemn promise: *I am pledged to secrecy. He pledged his honour/word.*

to pledge someone's credit to contract a debt payable by another person, e.g. a wife usu. has the right to pledge her husband's credit, i.e. to buy necessary goods which he will pay for later.

pledgee LAW a person who accepts personal property as security for a loan of money. Cf. pledgor. *Syn.* pawnee.

pledger *see* pledgor.

pledgor LAW a person who deposits personal property as a pledge, i.e. as security for a loan of money from a pledgee or pawnee. *Also* pledger. *Syn.* pawnee; pawnor.

plf., plff. plaintiff.

Plimsoll line/mark *see* load-line.

plot *n.* a small area of land, usu. clearly marked by posts or fences to separate it from other land nearby: *A building plot*, one suitable for building houses, etc. *A vacant plot*, one that is empty, that has no buildings on it. Cf. parcel. *v.* to mark information on a map.

plough back FIN. to use some of the profit of a business to buy useful assets or to finance the expansion of the business, instead of paying the profit to the owners or shareholders. *Syn.* self-finance.

pltf. plaintiff.

plummet STK. EXCH. of prices, to fall suddenly and very steeply: *Industrials plummeted on news of the transport strike. Syn.* plunge.

plunder *v.* to rob on a very wide scale, such as by an army in a captured country, or by a group of thieves stealing from wrecked ships. *n.* the things taken in plundering; any object taken by theft or deception.

plunge *v.* STK. EXCH. (1) to buy and sell large quantities of securities without proper thought for the effect on market prices. To speculate recklessly. (2) of prices, to fall very suddenly and steeply. *Syn.* plummet.

plus (1) added to; increased by: *5 plus 3 equals 8*, written 5 + 3 = 8 in mathematics. *Opp.* minus. (2) the plus sign: +. *Opp.* the minus sign: −.

plutocracy government of a country by persons belonging to the wealthy class or having the power of wealth. Such persons are called *plutocrats*.

pluvius insurance INSCE. a policy of insurance against loss of income caused by rain, storm or other bad weather conditions.

ply (1) COM. to practise a trade or craft: *He plies the trade of grocer*, he carries on business as a grocer. (2) TRANSPT. to make regular journeys between one place and another: *A ship plying between Beirut and Alexandria. A bus plying between Delhi and Agra.* (3) *To ply for hire*, to wait or look for persons in the streets who will hire one's vehicle, such as one's taxi.

pm., Pm. premium.

p.m. (*Latin:* post meridiem) after noon.

P.M.B.X. private manual branch exchange.

p.m.h. per man hour.

P/N, P.N. promissory note.

P.O. post office; postal order.

P.O.B., P.O. Box post office box.

p.o.c. port of call.

pocket *n.* (1) a bag in a garment, used for carrying small personal things and money. *A coat/trouser pocket.* (2) an envelope with the opening on the shorter side. (3) (U.S.A.) a woman's handbag or purse. (4) money, esp. in relation to gaining or losing or spending: *To be in pocket*, to have gained a profit or surplus after a deal. *To be out of pocket*, to have made a loss, to be poorer, after a deal. *To put one's hand in one's pocket*, to pay out, give, spend money. *Out-of-pocket expenses, see under* expenses. *v.* to put into one's pocket, to gain: *To pocket a sum of money*, to put it in one's pocket; to take possession of it.

pocket-book *see* note-case.

pocket-calculator an electronic calculating machine small enough to fit into a pocket and to be carried everywhere.

pocket-money *see under* money.

P.O.D. pay(ment) on delivery.

point (1) BKG. in the foreign-exchange market, the fourth and last number after the decimal point of a rate of exchange calculated in U.S. dollars: *The pound gained four points against the dollar, moving from 1.9886 to 1.9890. Abbr.* pt. (2) STK. EXCH. the sum of money that is agreed by members as the smallest unit used in stating the price of a stock or share. In London, the smallest unit, or point, for stocks is 1/64 of a pound, or about 1½p. For shares, the smallest unit, or point, is a fraction of a penny, e.g. ¼p if the price is below £10, and a fraction of a pound, e.g. £⅛ if the price is £10 or over. (3) a measuring unit for type bodies in printing.

point, gold *see under* gold.

point of order an urgent matter, brought to the attention of the chairman by a person present at a meeting, concerning a possible breach of the rules under which the meeting is being held, such as the lack of a quorum (minimum number). Such matters may be raised at any time during a discussion, i.e. without notice; and the chairman must decide immediately whether they have any force. *See* out of order (2); order of business.

point of sale COM. & ADVTG. the place where the consumer actually buys an article or commodity, usu. a shop, but it may be a mail-order house, market stall or, in the case of door-to-door selling, his own doorstep. *See also* point-of-sale advertising *under* advertising.

point system (of wage-payments) *see* Bedaux system.

poisha the fractional currency unit of Bangladesh, 100 poisha = 1 taka.

Poland a people's republic in eastern Europe, pop. 34 million approx. (1974); capital, Warsaw, pop. 1.5 million approx.; language, Polish; currency unit, the zloty, divided into 100 groszy. Member, COMECON.

pole see perch.

police court see magistrate's court.

policy a general course of action, planned and determined in advance by the top management, and adopted as a guiding rule for all concerned in controlling the activities of a business or other organization: *Our policy is to overcome competition and to double our share of the market in the next five years. We must adopt a more cautious policy towards bad debts by introducing stricter credit control.*

policy holder INSCE. usu. the person named in an insurance policy as being the insured person, but sometimes the person who pays the premiums and possesses the right to claim under the policy.

policy of insurance see insurance policy.

political economy ECON. the branch of the social sciences from which the subject of economics was developed in the twentieth century. An old-fashioned synonym for economics.

poll at a meeting of the members (shareholders) of a company, a method of voting which takes account of each share owned by each voting member and whether the vote is given for or against the motion or resolution. Cf. show of hands.

poll tax see capitation tax *under* tax.

Polski Rejestr SHIPG. the Polish organization for surveying and classifying ships. See classification society.

Pommie (*colloq.*) in Australia and New Zealand, an Englishman. *Also* Pommy; Pom.

pontoon SHIPG. & TRANSPT. a floating structure used either as a landing-place by ships and boats, or as one of the supports for a floating bridge, called a *pontoon bridge*.

pony (*colloq.*) twenty-five pounds (£25).

pool (1) SHIPG. a place in a river where the water is deep: *The Pool of London*, the part of the River Thames below London Bridge but above Tower Bridge. (2) COM. & IND. an association of producers, and sometimes importers, who agree to share between them the output needed to meet the market demand at a certain fixed price. The money received from sales is paid into a common fund and then paid out to the members in agreed proportions. (3) MAN. in large offices, a number of typists working together to give a central secretarial service to all those employees who need it. *Also* typing pool. (4) FIN. the main reserve fund (accumulation of money) of the International Monetary Fund, into which are paid the contributions of member countries, in return for which they receive drawing rights.

poop SHIPG. a deck above the main deck at the stern end of a ship. *Also* poop deck.

pop. population.

pop (*colloq.*) to pawn.

population census see under census.

population, working see under working.

p.o.r. port of refuge.

port (1) a town with a harbour where ships can shelter and where there are arrangements for loading and unloading. *Abbr.* pt. See also harbour.

autonomous port a port that is controlled by an independent public organization usu. called a *port trust*, e.g. the Calcutta Port Trust, or a *port authority*, e.g. the Port of London Authority.

barge port a port where ships cannot tie up to a wharf so have to use barges or other small craft for loading and unloading. *Also* barging port. *Syn.* cartage port; craft port; overside port; surf port.

craft port see barge port *above*.

discharge port see lading.

domestic port a port that serves a large and thickly-populated area behind it, called its *hinterland*, handling goods brought into or sent out of this area. Cf. entrepôt port.

entrepôt port see entrepôt.

estuarine port see under estuarine.

free port a port that is entirely free of customs duties. In the port and in the area around it, called a *free zone*, importers, exporters and manufacturers have the special advantage of free entry for goods that will soon be exported, i.e. entrepôt trade. Examples are: Bremen, Bremerhaven, Copenhagen, Gdansk, Hamburg, New York City, Rotterdam, Salina City, Shannon, Singapore, Stockholm. *Also* freeport. *Syn.* free trade zone; foreign trade zone.

home port see port of registry *under* registry.

inland port a port that is far from, and usu. connected with, the sea by a large river or canal, such as Manchester. Many inland ports serve a system of inland waterways.

lading port see under lading.

outport see under out.

overside port see barge port *above*.

packet port see under packet.

quay port one where goods are unloaded from the ship on to a quay.

safe port one in which a ship is safe from the dangers of the sea and from political interference.

seaport usu. a large port on or near the sea, and able to accept large ocean-going ships, with arrangements for loading and unloading all types of goods and, in many cases, passengers.

surf port see barge port *above*.

treaty port one of many ports in the Far East, esp. in China and Japan, that were by treaty (formal agreement between two countries) opened from 1842 to traders of western coun-

tries such as Britain, France, Germany and the U.S.A. Although Japan ended the arrangement in 1899, most of the treaty ports in the other countries continued until the Second World War. Canton and Shanghai are examples of treaty ports that became very large industrial and commercial cities.
(2) the left-hand side of a ship when facing forward. *Syn.* larboard. *Opp.* starboard.

portable that can easily be carried: *A portable typewriter*, one in a case with a handle so that it can easily and safely be carried on journeys.

portage TRANSPT. a place where goods, and sometimes small river-boats, are carried over the land from one river to another.

port area the area of land controlled by a port authority.

port authority *see* autonomous port *under* port.

port bill of lading *see under* bill of lading.

port charges SHIPG. charges that have to be paid to a port authority by owners of ships using the port. *Syn.* port dues.

port dues *see* port charges.

porter (1) TRANSPT. a person who, for hire, carries goods such as parcels or luggage in a railway-station, etc. (2) TOUR. in a hotel, an employee, often called a *hall porter*, who serves as doorkeeper and also performs various services, such as attending to guests' letters, newspapers and messages, and calling taxis. Many hotels also employ a *night porter* who is present all night, a *luggage porter* and an *outside porter*, who carries luggage to or from the railway station or airline office. (3) SHIPG. *see* master porter.

porterage TRANSPT. the cost of hiring porters to carry goods by hand or by hand-cart.

portfolio (1) a large flat case or cover for carrying or storing large documents, drawings, photographs, etc. (2) STK. EXCH. the entire collection of investments belonging to an investor or held by a financial organization such as a bank, pension fund or investment trust.

portmanteau TRANSPT. a traveller's box or bag for carrying clothes. *Syn.* trunk.

port of call SHIPG. a port where ships regularly stop to get fuel, stores and repairs, and possibly also to load and unload cargo and passengers. *Abbr.* p.o.c.

Port of London Authority (P.L.A.) SHIPG. & TRANSPT. the public organization responsible for owning and managing the port of London, one of the largest in the world. It controls all the larger docks and warehouses from Teddington, the upper limit of tidal water, down the River Thames to Tilbury, the deep-water dock system near the river-mouth.

port of refuge SHIPG. a port that is not a ship's regular port of call but in which the vessel has taken shelter.

port of registry *see under* registry.

port payé *see* carriage paid.

port trust *see* autonomous port *under* port.

Portugal a republic in south-west Europe, pop. 10 million approx. (1973); capital, Lisbon, pop. 1.6 million approx.; language, Portuguese; currency unit, the Portuguese escudo. divided into 100 centavos. Member. O.E.C.D.; E.F.T.A.

Portuguese Guinea *see* Guinea-Bissau.

position STK. EXCH. *see* bear position; bull position.

positive covenant *see* covenant.

positive easement *see* easement.

possession (1) any material object that is possessed: *My house/watch/motor car is my most precious possession*, the most valuable thing that I own.
  possessions *pl.* property; wealth: *In her will, she left all her possessions to her son.*
(2) the act or state of possessing, of holding, using and controlling: *He got possession of the company by buying all the shares. To take possession of a home*, to move into, to occupy it as owner or tenant. *The deeds are in my possession*, I hold them in my control. (3) LAW the state of having the right to use and enjoy a thing such as a house, whether by right of ownership or not. *Possession is nine-tenths (or nine points) of the law*, the law tends to regard the person in possession as the owner unless somebody else has a better claim to ownership.
  constructive possession possession to which one has a clear legal right, as opposed to actual possession not supported by proof of such a right.
  immediate possession (*a*) possession reserved for oneself. (*b*) of a house for sale, ready for immediate occupation.
  incorporeal possession possession of a legal right, such as a patent or copyright, not of a material object such as a house or a motor car.
  mediate possession possession held and reserved for somebody other than oneself.
  vacant possession of a house for sale, ready for occupation now or by a date to be agreed.

possessory lien *see under* lien.

post *n.* (1) MAN. a position of employment; a job: *He has been appointed to the post of sales manager. He is looking for a new post with better pay.* (2) COM. a small trading centre, usu. in a place that is far from other commercial centres and is in a foreign land: *A trading post.* (3) a service run by, or under the control of, the government, for carrying letters, packets and parcels, and, in some countries, for telephone, telegraph and other public services. *See* Post Office. *Syn.* mail.
  letter post *see* first-class mail, second-class mail *under* mail.
  parcel post a postal service that carries and delivers parcels of limited size and weight. *Abbr.*

P.P. A *C.F. parcel* is one on which a compensation fee has been paid; if the contents are lost or damaged, the Post Office will pay compensation to the sender up to the market value of the article if lost, or the loss of value if damaged. *See also* registered post *under* registered.

v. (1) ADVTG. to put up (a poster, bill, notice on a hoarding, bill-board, etc.); to make known to the public. *Also* to post up. (2) ACCTS. in book-keeping (*a*) to record in the ledgers the entries made in the books of prime entry; (*b*) to set off, transfer, an entry from one account to another. (3) to send through the postal service, either by putting letters, etc. into a post-box or pillar-box or by handing letters, packets or parcels into a post office. *Syn.* (U.S.A.) to mail. (4) to station an employee at a place: *He was posted to Bombay.* (5) STK. EXCH. to make known to the public, esp. news about profit or loss: *Standard Oil jumped higher after posting sharply increased earnings*, the price of these shares suddenly rose after the company had announced (made known) that it had made much higher profits.

postage book *see* post book.

postage stamp *see under* stamp.

postal clerk MAN. an office employee working in a post room.

postal franking machine *see* franking machine.

Postal Giro *see* National Giro *under* Giro.

postal order FIN. a method of making small payments by post. Postal orders, in certain fixed values, can be obtained at most post offices in Britain. The value of the order may be increased to some small extent by adding postage stamps. The sender buys the postal order, paying a small extra fee, and sends it to the payee, who can obtain cash for it at almost any post office in Britain and certain other countries, unless the order is crossed like a cheque, when it will be paid only through a bank. A postal order is not negotiable. *Abbr.* P.O. Cf. money order.

post book ACCTS. an account book in which a record is kept of postage paid on letters, packets, parcels, etc. *Syn.* postage book.

postcode a code consisting of numbers or letters, or both, written after the address on a letter or postal packet to make possible rapid machine sorting at each stage of the journey. In Britain the postcode consists of letters and numbers, e.g. SG10 6BP, and states enough of the address to get the packets through to the delivery postman himself; he then has only to put the packets into delivery order before delivering them. In countries using postcodes consisting entirely of numbers, the postcode aims only to get the letter to the distant town, not through to the delivery postman. *Syn.* (U.S.A.) zipcode.

post-date BKG. & COM. to give a date to a cheque

or other document later than that on which it is drawn, written or signed, usu. to make it take effect from the later date. A bank will not pay a post-dated cheque before the date written on it.

post-dated cheque *see* post-date.

post entry *see under* customs entry.

poster ADVTG. a large advertisement or notice posted (put up) in a public place. *Syn.* (esp. U.S.A.) bill.

poste restante in many countries, a special service provided by the Post Office by which letters and packets addressed to a named person *poste restante* at a certain place are held at the post office there until the addressee comes to collect them. In U.S.A. the service is called *general delivery*.

post free COM. in price quotations, esp. in selling by direct supply, postage is included in the price quoted and will be paid by the seller; no extra charge for postage: *Our price is £3.50 per pair post free*, each pair will be delivered by post without your having to pay anything for postage. *Syn.* post paid.

posting ACCTS. the work of making entries in books of account, mainly from books of prime entry, e.g. items in the journal have to be posted, or entered in their proper accounts in the ledger. *See* post, *v.* (2).

posting error a mistake made in posting figures. Cf. casting error.

posting, certificate of *see* certificate of posting.

postmark the mark stamped or printed on letters, postal packets and parcels by the Post Office. This mark serves to cancel the postage stamps (so that they cannot be used again) and to show the place, date and hour or posting.

postmaster the officer in charge of a post office. *Fem.* postmistress. A sub-postmaster is a person who is an agent of the Post Office for the operation of a sub-post office.

postmistress a female postmaster.

post-nuptial settlement *see under* settlement.

post obit bond *see under* bond.

Post Office TRANSPT. a government department or state-owned corporation that is responsible for running the postal services of a country. *Abbr.* P.O.

post office box a numbered box or other container in a post office in which mail for a particular person or organization is kept until called for. Cf. box number. *Abbr.* P.O.B.; P.O. Box.

Post Office Guide a book published once a year by the British Post Office giving details of its services and charges and stating its rules and procedures.

Post Office register *see* national savings stock register.

Post Office Savings Bank *see* National Savings Bank.

post paid *see* post free.

post-postscript a further postscript written after the first. *Abbr.* PPS.

post room MAN. in an office, a room where incoming letters and parcels are received, opened, sorted and distributed to the various departments; and where outgoing letters and parcels are weighed, stamped and posted. Some post rooms also have arrangements for packing parcels. *Syn.* mail room.

post rules LAW in Britain, under the law of contract, rules concerning the making and acceptance of offers by post. An offer and a withdrawal or cancellation of an offer do not take effect until actually received by the offeree. An acceptance of an offer is effective as soon as it has been posted.

postscript words added, usu. at the bottom, to a letter after it has been written or typed. *Abbr.* PS., *pl.* PSS. *See also* post-postscript.

potential *adj.* possible, as compared with actual: *Young Mr Smith is a potential director. A potential danger/market.*
n. possibility of becoming, developing into, something or somebody greater or better: *The business is showing great potential*, has excellent possibilities for growth in the future. *Egypt's industrial potential*, possibility of developing its industries in the future.

pottle COM. (1) a small container usu. of folded or twisted paper or leaves, in which small fruit, nuts and similar foodstuffs are sold, esp. in shops and street markets in developing countries. (2) in liquid measure, 2 quarts.

pound (1) a measure of weight, *see* avoirdupois; troy weight. *Abbr.* lb. (2) FIN. the name of the standard currency unit of the following countries: Cyprus, Dominica, Egypt, Gibraltar, Irish Republic, Lebanon, Malta, Sudan, Syria and the United Kingdom of Great Britain and Northern Ireland. *See* these for more details. *Sign*: £.

poundage FIN. (1) in Britain, (an unofficial name for) the fee charged by the Post Office, of so much per pound of value, for issuing postal orders and money orders. (2) any tax or commission based on the pound weight or pound of value.

pound/cost averaging STK. EXCH. accumulating capital by regularly investing equal amounts of money in the same security. In this way, the average cost of the security is always lower than the average of the prices paid (except when the prices remain unchanged). For example, an investor invests £20 each month in a particular share. In the first month the price is £2.00 per share, so his £20 buys him 10 shares. In the second month the price is £1.00, so he gets 20 shares. In the third month the price is £0.80, so he gets 25 shares, giving a total of 55 shares for his outlay of £60, an average cost of

£1.09 per share. But the average of the prices paid (£2.00, £1.00, £0.80 = £3.80 ÷ 3) is £1.27 per share. The average *cost* has been reduced because the number of shares bought varies with the price paid, fewer being obtained when the price is high than when it is low.

pound-foolish neglecting to take care of large sums of money as a result of too much attention to small ones.

poverty ECON. a serious lack of wealth; the state of the poorest members of a community; a condition of having too little money, too few of the goods essential for the current standard of living, such as food, shelter, clothing, and of the opportunities for social development, such as education, medical care and employment.

poverty trap ECON. the condition of a person with a low income who has no encouragement to work harder, such as a low-paid worker receiving state welfare benefits which will be reduced by one pound for each further pound that he earns by e.g. working overtime. He can only escape from this trap if he can manage to earn so much more that his extra income is greater than his loss of benefits.

power (1) IND. any kind of force used for doing work, such as water power, wind power, steam power, electric power, nuclear power, and also manpower. (2) LAW legal ability to act, to decide for oneself one's relations with other persons, such as the ability to make a contract.

general power power held by a person arising out of an office or position that he holds, such as the power of a trustee, executor, administrator or solicitor.

private power power given by one person to another for a private, not a public, purpose.

public power power held from the State by a government official or agent, or a member of the judiciary.

special power limited power given or held for a special purpose, such as a power of sale, or by power of attorney.

power of attorney LAW a formal document made under seal by a person called the donor or grantor, authorizing another person called the donee or attorney to act for him, in all respects as if he were the donor, in regard to the matters stated in the document. *Abbr.* P.A.; P/A. *Syn.* letter of attorney.

general power of attorney one which relates to any matter that concerns the donor.

special power of attorney one that limits the attorney's powers to certain matters, or to perform some particular act, clearly stated in the document, such as to sell property, to sign cheques, or to receive money.

power of sale LAW the power held by one person to sell property owned by another person and to use the money to obtain repayment of a debt owed by the other person. A mortgagee has legal power to sell a mortgaged property. if the mortgage debt is not paid when due.

p.p. per procurationem; per procuration.

pp. pages.

P.P. parcel post.

ppd. prepaid.

p.pro per procurationem; per procuration.

PPS. post-postscript; Parliamentary or principal private secretary.

pr. pair.

P.R. personal representative; public relations.

practice *n.* (1) the business organization of a professional person such as a doctor, dentist, lawyer or architect, including the clients he serves. *Dr Smith and Dr Jones have bought a practice. They are in practice together.* (2) actual performance rather than thought or planning: *The idea looked good on paper but proved useless in practice.* (3) repeated exercise of some activity in order to gain a skill: *To become good at shorthand needs much practice. Practice makes perfect.* (4) a way of doing business: *A dishonest practice. You are guilty of sharp practice,* of behaviour that is not illegal but is unfair, morally dishonest. *Syn.* (U.S.A.) practise.

practise *v.* (1) to carry out, to perform, repeatedly or regularly, esp. a skill or profession: *To practise medicine/dentistry/law/accountancy.* (2) to make a habit of doing: *To practise economy,* to be economical always. (3) to obtain a skill by doing something, e.g. an exercise, repeatedly: *She is practising her shorthand and typing. Syn.* to exercise; (U.S.A.) practice.

pratique *see* certificate of pratique.

pre- *prefix,* before; in advance: *Pre-war; pre-judged; pre-arrange.*

preamble LAW a statement at the beginning of a speech, law or deed, of the reason why it is made and the intentions of the person(s) making it.

precaution care taken to prevent a loss or danger: *To take precautions against theft/fraud/fire.*

precedent an example that may be followed as a guide when taking later action in the same conditions: *There is no precedent in this company for electing a woman to the board. To create/ establish/set a precedent,* to do something, esp. to make a decision, that will be followed (used as an example) for future decisions.

precept FIN. & ACCTS. an order from a person in authority, directing the payment of money.

precinct in Britain, an enclosed area set aside for shops, where the public may walk about in safety because vehicles are not allowed to enter: *A shopping/pedestrian precinct.* In U.S.A., an administrative district of a city. Cf. ward.

précis a short restatement of the contents of a longer document. *Syn.* summary. *Pron.* praysi.

pre-date *see* ante-date.

predecease to die before (somebody): *The husband predeceased his wife,* he died before she did.

predecessor (1) a person who formerly held a particular office or owned a particular business that is now held or owned by somebody else: *Mr White is a better manager/grocer than his predecessor. My predecessor taught me my job.* Cf. successor. (2) a thing that has been replaced by another thing: *We prefer this machine to its predecessor.*

pre-emption (1) a right to preference over all other persons to have or to do something. (2) LAW the right of the State to buy property for public use before all other buyers. *Syn.* pre-emptive right.

pref., Pref. preference or preferred (stock, share).

preference (1) the act of preferring one person or thing to another: *Banks show a preference for short-term loans over (rather than) long-term.* (2) a person or thing preferred: *Our preference for the chairmanship is Mr Brown.* (3) the giving of some special advantage to a country or group of countries in international trade, rather than to others, esp. an import duty which favours one group of suppliers rather than another.

Commonwealth preference the practice which was agreed by countries who were members of the (British) Commonwealth of Nations of giving more favourable treatment to imports from other members of the Commonwealth, esp. in regard to import duties. This system ceased in Britain when the E.E.C. tariff was applied in full in 1977.

Community preference the rule that members of the European Economic Community (E.E.C.) should give more favourable treatment in their markets to imports from other member countries, esp. in regard to agricultural products.

preference capital *see under* capital.

preference dividend *see under* dividend.

preference, fraudulent *see under* fraudulent.

preference share *see under* share.

preference stock *see under* stock.

preferential (1) showing or giving preference: *Preferential terms,* terms such as those between companies in the same group, that are more favourable than those given to other customers. (2) receiving or having a claim to preference, such as preferential creditors.

preferential creditor *see* preferential payments.

preferential debt *see under* debt.

preferential duty TAX an import duty at a specially low rate on goods from a country that is being favoured, usu. because it is a member of the same group of countries. *See* Commonwealth preference and Community preference *under* preference.

preferential payments LAW & FIN. in distributing the estate of a bankrupt or the assets of a company in liquidation, those payments that must by law be made in preference to all others. *See* preferential debt *under* debt. If there are insufficient assets to meet the preferential debts in full, the preferential creditors rank equally with one another and receive payments reduced in an equal proportion. *Syn.* (U.S.A.) preferred payments.

preferred STK. EXCH. in Britain, of stocks and shares, having a greater claim than the holders of ordinary stock or shares to receive payment of interest or dividend when the company fails to earn profits large enough to pay both. *Syn.* preference.

preferred creditor *see* preferential creditor; preferential payments.

preferred debt *see* preferential debt *under* debt.

preferred share *see* preferred ordinary share *under* share.

preferred stock *see under* stock.

prejudice (1) an unfavourable opinion that is unfair because it is not according to reason: *A good manager never shows prejudice against a member of his staff.* (2) LAW harm to one's interests: *We must avoid doing anything to the prejudice of our claim.*

prejudice, without *see* without prejudice.

preliminary enquiries *see* enquiries before contract.

preliminary expenses *see* formation expenses *under* formation.

Premier *see* Prime Minister.

premises *n. pl.* (1) a building, esp. a house, and the land on which it is built. (2) LAW the property to which a conveyance relates.

premium *adj.* COM. of specially good quality and therefore sold at a higher price: *Premium grade petrol.*
n. (1) STK. EXCH. the amount which is paid for a stock or share over and above its nominal or face value. *At a premium*, at a price higher than the face value of the security. *See* par. *Opp.* discount. (2) BKG. the amount by which the market rate of exchange of a particular currency is above the par rate. *See* dollar premium. (3) ADVTG. *see* deal (4). (4) a sum of money formerly paid by an apprentice or articled clerk to a master or professional man as payment for his articles. (5) LAW a sum of money paid on a lease, usu. in advance of signature and over and above the rent. Cf. key money. (6) INSCE. the money paid by the insured to the insurers in return for insurance cover or benefits payable under the conditions in an insurance policy. *Abbr.* pm.; Pm.

additional premium an extra sum of money that the insurer has to pay when a contract of insurance is changed while it is still in force in order to cover increased risk or benefits.

annual premium the usual frequency of payment of premiums on insurance contracts, being the sum required to pay for one year's cover.

deferred premium an insurance premium that is paid by instalments. *See* deferred account.

deposit premium (*a*) an insurance premium paid only in part while the policy is drawn up, the amount being adjusted later. (*b*) any premium which is adjusted periodically.

extra premium an extra, or further, charge for insurance added during the period covered by the policy.

first premium on a new contract of insurance, the sum needed to give cover during the first period, usu. until the next quarter-day, after which a renewal premium is charged, usu. annually.

renewal premium the sum payable for a further period of one year's insurance cover.

return premium a sum paid back by the insurance company to the insured when a contract of insurance is stopped or changed. *Syn.* rebate.

unearned premium a sum paid back by the insurance company to the insured when the property has not been at risk, and the insurer could not have been liable to make good any loss.

premium bond *see* premium savings bond.

premium bonus *see under* bonus (2).

premium income INSCE. the total income received by an insurance organization from premiums on insurance policies during a given period.

premium pay *see* incentive bonus *under* bonus (2).

premium savings bond FIN. a form of savings bond issued by the British Government through the Post Office in units of £1, each with a different number. No interest is paid, but the bonds can be cashed at any time at full face value. Each bond has an equal chance of winning tax-free prizes, of from £25 up to very large sums of money, in lotteries in which numbers are chosen by chance by E.R.N.I.E., an electronic computer.

prepaid paid in advance: *Postage must be prepaid*, paid before posting. *A prepaid reply card*, a stamped postcard that can be used by an addressee for his reply to a message, without his having to bear the cost of postage. *See also* freight prepaid. *Abbr.* ppd.

pres. presumed.

Pres. president.

present *v.* BKG. & FIN. to produce and show formally, esp. a cheque or promissory note for payment, or a bill of exchange for acceptance or payment. The act of presenting is called *presentation* or *presentment*. *Pron.* prezént.
n. a gift. *Pron.* prézent.

presentation BKG. & FIN. the act of presenting a bill of exchange, promissory note, etc. *See* present, *v. Syn.* presentment.

presentment *see* presentation.

present value FIN. & BKG. (1) *of a bill of exchange*, the capital sum of money that would, if lent at a given rate of interest for a given time, accumulate to produce the amount of the bill. (2) *of an annuity*, the capital amount which, if invested at compound interest now, would allow a number of equal amounts to be paid out at fixed intervals. (3) *of an investment, see* discounted cash flow. *Syn.* present worth.

present worth *see* present value.

president MAN. the chief executive officer of a company in U.S.A., the equivalent of the chairman of the board of directors in Britain.

Press, The the newspapers and magazines of a country collectively: *The freedom/liberty of the Press*, the right freely to print news and opinions of public interest.

press agency *see* news agency.

press agent a person employed to do the publicity work of a business, i.e. to get its products and services known to the public. *Syn.* publicist. *Abbr.* p.a.

press conference a meeting to which news reporters are invited to hear a statement about a happening.

pressing COM. urgent: *Pressing orders*, orders that must be supplied as soon as possible. *Pressing payments*, payments that the creditors are demanding.

prestige a state of importance and power because of one's good reputation. *Prestige symbol*, an object owned or used by a person who wishes to tell others how important and powerful he is. *Prestige good*, an economic good that is demanded in spite of its high price, because to be able to buy it shows one's importance and wealth.

presume to take, accept as true; to suppose: *This parcel is presumed to contain diamonds*, it is supposed or believed to contain diamonds, but it is not certain that it does. *The ship/aircraft is presumed lost*, believed to be lost.

presumption LAW the acceptance of a belief or statement based on facts or experience as true, until it is proved not to be true: *The presumption of innocence is that the accused is innocent until he is proved guilty. Presumption of death*, formal authority to act as though a person who has disappeared is dead, so that his estate may be distributed according to the law.

pre-tax STK. EXCH. & ACCTS. (1) of profits, before income or company tax is deducted: *The chairman reported a pre-tax profit of about £1 million*. (2) of income, total receipts and earnings before deducting tax: *He has a pre-tax income of £15,000 a year*.

pretences *see* false pretences.

prête-nom BKG. & FIN. (*French*, a person who lends his name) a false name applied, e.g. to a bank account, to hide the true name of the depositor. *Syn.* dummy. *See* nominate (2); nominee (2).

prev. previous (to).

prevailing current, existing widely or most of the time: *The prevailing wind is westerly*, it blows from the west for most of the year. *Prevailing prices*, prices now current in the market. *The prevailing boom/depression/slump*.

preventive preventing something from existing or happening: *A customs preventive officer*, one whose responsibility it is to stop illegal imports and exports. *Preventive measures against accident/fire/theft/fraud*, planned ways of avoiding these from happening.

price *v.* to fix a price (of something): *We have priced our new product at £5. It is priced at £5. You have priced it too high/low. We are in danger of pricing ourselves out of the market*, by fixing our price so high there is a risk that few people will buy our product.

n. (1) ECON. THEORY the rate at which a commodity can be exchanged for another commodity or for money. The exchange value of an economic good. (2) COM. the amount of money for which an article or commodity can be bought and sold. (3) STK. EXCH. a value for a security quoted by a jobber at two levels, the lower or bid price, at which he is willing to buy, and the higher or offer(ed) price at which he is willing to sell. Thus: 150p, 153p. The difference is the *jobber's turn*.

actual price on the Stock Exchange, the price at which a bargain is made by a jobber, whether as buyer or as seller.

administered price ECON. THEORY a price fixed by the producer of a product at a level that controls the quantity that is bought in the market, rather than allowing the price to be determined by supply and demand. Administered prices are usu. found in a market in which there are few sellers, i.e. oligopoly.

asking price the price at which a seller is willing to sell. *Syn.* (U.S.A.) ask; ask price. *Also* asked price.

average price the arithmetic average of the current prices of a commodity. Cf. normal price.

bargain price *see* bargain.

basis price the price for the article without any extras. Cf. overhead price *below. Syn.* base price; basis rate; basic price.

best price on the Stock Exchange, the price that is the best that the stockbroker can arrange, i.e. the lowest possible price when buying, and the highest possible when selling.

bid price *see under* bid.

buying price *see* bid price.

cash price *see under* cash.

catalogue price *see* list price *below*.

ceiling price the highest price that can be obtained in the market, or is allowed by law.

close price on the Stock Exchange, a situation where there is little difference between the bid and the offer(ed) price. Cf. wide price.

closing price see closing.

common price a price fixed under a common pricing agreement. See common pricing.

competitive price see competitive.

cost price (a) the price paid by a merchant for the goods he buys for resale. (b) a price that represents the bare cost of production, without anything added for profit.

cut price a price that is unusually low, and well below that of most competitors.

delivered price see under delivered.

differential price(s) see under differential.

dirt cheap price see knock-out price below.

equilibrium price ECON. THEORY the market price of a commodity at which the amount demanded equals the amount supplied, i.e. demand and supply are balanced, or in equilibrium.

factor price ECON. THEORY the price of the factors of production. See gross national product.

fall-back price see reserve price (c) below.

firm price see firm, adj. (3).

fixed price see maximum price; minimum price below. Also see resale price maintenance.

forward price see under forward.

full-cost price one which includes the cost of production and a satisfactory profit.

guaranteed price(s) see under guaranteed.

guide price under the Common Agricultural Policy of the E.E.C. the price fixed by the European Commission as being a fair average price to the farmer producing certain kinds of meat.

hire-purchase price see under hire-purchase; also cash price.

in-bond price see in bond under in.

intervention price see under intervention.

invoice price the cost price of an article as shown on the supplier's invoice.

issue price see under issue.

'just price' in medieval times, roughly between AD 500 and AD 1500, before the economic laws of supply and demand had been understood, the customary price, i.e. the usual price, of a commodity or service. The European thinkers and writers of those days believed that it was wrong for a trader to raise his price in times of scarcity and equally wrong for buyers to offer lower prices when there was an excess of supply.

knock-out price (colloq.) a very low price. Syn. dirt cheap price.

list price (a) the retail price, i.e. the price paid by the consumer as fixed or recommended by the manufacturer or wholesaler and shown in his price-list. (b) the supplier's invoice price before any discount has been deducted (taken off). Many retailers also issue price-lists for the use of their customers and staff. Syn. catalogue price.

loaded price a price that is made unfairly high by having an excessive amount added for some small extra advantage, or for packing and delivery, or in time of a scarcity.

loco price see loco.

making-up price on the Stock Exchange, the price at which securities not paid for by Settling Day are carried forward to the next Settlement.

marked price COM. the price marked on goods sold in shops. In some countries retailers are forbidden by law to raise the price once the goods have been marked.

market price (a) the price (of an article or commodity) that is current in the market. See also middle (market) price below. (b) ECON. THEORY the equilibrium price.

maximum price a price of a commodity that has been fixed by the government at a level lower than the equilibrium price; it is illegal for dealers to buy and sell above the fixed price. Prices are usu. fixed when a government is concerned to keep prices down in a period of inflation. Unless the government can meet the excess demand from stocks held for this purpose, it must either ration existing supplies or accept the existence of a black market. Cf. minimum price. Syn. fixed price.

mean price see middle (market) price below. See also mean price under mean.

middle (market) price on the Stock Exchange, a price half-way between the bid price and the offer(ed) price. Syn. mean price.

minimum price a price of a commodity that has been fixed by the government at a level higher than the equilibrium price; it is illegal for dealers to buy and sell in the market below this price. Such prices are usu. fixed by a government to support the incomes of producers. Any excess supply is bought by the government from the producers and is sold elsewhere, destroyed or stored to meet a future excess demand. Cf. maximum price.

monopoly price the price current in a market under monopoly conditions, i.e. in which one supplier, or group of suppliers acting together, can control the market price.

net price a price on which no discount will be allowed.

nominal price see under nominal.

normal price in economic theory, the price (of an article or commodity) that one may reasonably expect to find under the conditions of demand and supply existing in the market, both in the short run and in the long run. It is the price towards which actual prices will tend to move.

offer(ed) price (a) STK. EXCH. the price at which

a willing seller will sell. Cf. bid price. *Syn.* ask(ing) price; selling price; (U.S.A.) offering price. (*b*) FIN. of unit trusts, the price at which the management company is willing to sell units. Cf. bid price *under* bid (2). The offer(ed) price includes the initial service and other charges that the buyer must bear.

opening price *see* opening.

overhead price the amount that must be added to the basis price to cover the charge for extras.

published price the retail price of a book, magazine or newspaper that has been fixed by the publisher for sale within the country. *See also* Net Book Agreement.

purchase price the price that has to be paid to buy something. The expression is used esp. in regard to buying land and buildings, a share in a business or some other asset costing a relatively large sum of money.

recommended (retail) price the price that the manufacturer of a product advises or urges retailers to charge when selling to the consumer. *Abbr.* R.P.; R.R.P.; M.R.P. (manufacturers' recommended price).

reserve price (*a*) at an auction, the lowest price that the seller is willing to accept for the article being auctioned. The article will be sold only to the highest bidder above the reserve price, and not to any bidder below it. *Syn.* (U.S.A.) upset price. (*b*) any price below which the seller will not sell. (*c*) under the Common Agricultural Policy of the E.E.C., the price fixed by the European Commission for fruit and vegetables. If necessary, subsidies are paid to make sure that each commodity is sold at its reserve price. *Syn.* fall-back price.

retail price the price paid by the consumer. Cf. wholesale price.

sale price (*a*) the amount of money that a buyer has to pay. *Syn.* consideration for sale. (*b*) a specially reduced price charged by a retailer during a sale in his shop. *See* sale (4).

selling price *see* offer(ed) price *above.*

shadow price ECON. THEORY the true marginal value of a good, which may be different from the market price.

sluice-gate price under the Common Agricultural Policy of the E.E.C., the price fixed quarterly by the European Commission for pig-meat, eggs and poultry. Levies (import duties) have to be paid if such goods are imported below the sluice-gate price.

split price *see* differential price *under* differential.

spot price in commodity markets, the price for spot (immediate) delivery. Cf. forward price. *Syn.* loco price; warehouse price.

street price *see* after-hours price *under* after-hours dealings. In U.S.A., a price for a security being bought or sold other than through a stock exchange.

supply price (*a*) the cost of producing an entirely new asset, as opposed to the market price of an existing asset. (*b*) the lowest price that a supplier will accept for a given quantity.

support price under the Common Agricultural Policy of the E.E.C., the price at which the authorities will enter the market as buyers to prevent a further fall in price.

target price under the Common Agricultural Policy of the E.E.C., the price of a commodity that is fixed from time to time by the European Commission. The target price is not intended to be a guaranteed price but rather an average price that will be fair to the producer.

threshold price under the Common Agricultural Policy of the E.E.C., the lowest price at which an imported farm commodity, esp. cereals, may be sold within the community. The C.A.P. authorities fix threshold prices from time to time and keep them at or near the target price by charging an import levy equal to the difference between the landed cost of a commodity and its threshold price.

trade price *see* wholesale price *below.*

upset price *see* reserve price (*a*) *above.*

wholesale price the price paid by a retailer to a wholesaler. Cf. retail price. *Syn.* trade price.

wide price on the Stock Exchange, a situation where there is a larger difference between the bid and the offer(ed) prices than is normal. Cf. close price.

price bulletin *see* price(s) current.

price-ceiling *see* ceiling.

price control ECON. in time of war or of serious inflation, rules made by the government to prevent consumer prices rising higher than the maximum fixed from time to time for each controlled commodity.

price cutting COM. selling at prices that are much lower than those at which most other suppliers are selling; the purpose may be to increase profits by attracting custom and increasing turnover to a point where bulk buying is possible and where the higher sales revenue more than covers the lower rate of profit per unit sold, or to force competitors to lower their prices and hope to drive them out of business. *See* price war.

price discrimination *see* discrimination.

price-earnings ratio STK. EXCH. the present market price of an ordinary share divided by the company's net earnings (distributable profits) per share usu. after tax. Thus e.g. a p.e.r. of 12 means that in buying a share one is paying a price equal to 12 times the current year's earnings per share. This ratio is much used as a guide when comparing share prices, esp. by investors looking for capital appreciation rather than for dividend income. Cf. dividend-price ratio. *Abbr.* p.e.r.; P.E.R.; p/e ratio; P/E ratio; P/e ratio.

price effect ECON. THEORY the result of a change in the price-level while the consumer's money income remains unchanged. After rearranging his purchases he will find that his real income, measured in goods or services, not in money, will have changed for the better or the worse according to whether the price-level has fallen or risen. *See* income effect; substitution effect.

price-fixing *see* resale price maintenance.

price-floor *see under* floor.

price fluctuations *see* fluctuations.

price freeze *see under* freeze.

price index *see under* index number(s); *also* international price index.

price leadership ECON. THEORY the practice by a group of producers of fixing the price of their product at the price charged by one leading member of the group; and whenever the *price leader* changes his price, the others follow. This practice is found esp. under a system of oligopoly (when there are few sellers).

priceless very valuable; of so high a value that no price can be put on it: *He is a rich old man who can spend millions buying priceless antiques.*

price-level ECON. the average of all prices in a country at a particular time. It is usu. calculated as a price index and is used to compare the average at one time with the average at other times. *Syn.* general level of prices.

price-list *see under* list.

price maintenance *see* resale price maintenance.

price ring *see* ring.

price(s) current COM. a printed price-list of articles and commodities, published regularly, usu. in large commercial centres, and used by dealers in quoting prices. *Abbr.* P/C. *Syn.* price bulletin.

price sticker *see under* sticker.

price support IND. & AGR. the help given by the government of a country to its industries, esp. primary industries such as agriculture, by paying support payments, also called deficiency payments or subsidies, to producers, if market prices fall below the support price. *See* support price *under* price; *also* Common Agricultural Policy.

price-tag COM. a mark or label placed on an article to show the price to the consumer.

price terms *see* quotations.

price theory ECON. THEORY the branch of economics that studies the price system, and esp. the things that influence the fixing of prices under different market conditions.

price war COM. a market situation in which all suppliers are competing to gain a larger share of the market by cutting prices, often without thought for the results. It may happen that, although one supplier may get a short-term advantage by cutting his prices, if the rest follow, all suppliers will suffer and the weakest may go bankrupt. To avoid this danger, most suppliers fix their prices at a reasonable level and refuse to reduce them further.

pricey (*colloq.*) expensive, dear.

pricing *see* double pricing.

prima facie (*Latin*, at first sight) (1) on the face of it. (2) LAW *A prima-facie case*, a criminal case that at first hearing appears to have sufficient evidence to justify a trial in a higher court. *Prima-facie evidence*, evidence that will be accepted in a court of law as being true unless it can be proved untrue.

primage SHIPG. & COM. a small payment, usu. 10%, made to shippers for taking extra care in loading or unloading a ship. *Syn.* (*colloq.*) hat money.

primage duty *see under* duty.

primary industry *see under* industry.

primary production *see under* production.

prime bill *see under* bill of exchange.

prime cost *see under* cost.

prime entry (1) ACCTS. *see* books of first entry. (2) COM. & TAXN. *see under* customs entry.

Prime Minister the chief minister in the government of certain countries. *Syn.* Premier.

prime rate BKG. the rate of interest at which British and American banks lend money to their largest and most creditworthy customers. *Syn.* fine rate; blue-chip rate.

primeurs AGR. & COM. early fruits and vegetables, usu. grown for export to colder regions.

principal *n.* (1) LAW & COM. a person who authorizes another person to be his agent or broker. The person for whom an agent or broker acts: *I am acting for my principals, Davies and Co. of Cardiff. Our relationship is that of principal and agent. Syn.* donor; grantor. (2) BKG. & FIN. money lent at interest, esp. the amount of the loan, not the interest paid on it.

adj. chief, highest in rank, most important: *The principal officer of a company*, the head of the company. *The principal activity of the business is cleaning carpets.*

principal debtor *see under* debtor.

principle (1) a guiding rule of behaviour or morality: *A manager must adopt the principles of honesty and fair play.* (2) the basic truths on which other truths rest: *The principles of economics*, the basic facts of economic theory given in a textbook. Cf. Acceleration Principle.

print printed matter; any matter, esp. a document, that has been printed, not handwritten or typewritten.

in print of a published book, can still be bought from the publishers.

out of print can no longer be bought from the publishers because all stocks have been sold and no reprint is planned.

small print (*colloq.*) in a printed document

such as a hire-purchase agreement, matter containing conditions printed in such small type and expressed in such difficult language that the customer cannot easily read or understand it and therefore does not understand his liabilities.

printer's ream *see* ream.

print-out COMP. processed data (information) from the output unit of a computer, presented in the form of readable printed matter on paper.

prior charge STK. EXCH. & ACCTS. any security, such as a debenture, loan stock or preference shares, that ranks before ordinary stock or shares for payment of interest or dividend, and, if the company is wound up, for repayment of capital.

priority (1) STK. EXCH. & FIN. the right of certain creditors and stockholders and shareholders to have their claims paid before the claims of others: *Preference dividends have priority over ordinary dividends.* (2) the state of being, the right to be, first in position or time: *Give this matter priority,* deal with it before all other matters. *A priority telegram,* one that receives urgent attention, being sent before all others.

prior preferred stock *see under* stock.

private arrangement *see* deed of arrangement.

private bank BKG. (1) a bank owned and operated by one person or a number of persons in partnership, not by a joint-stock banking company. In Britain, no banking partnership is allowed by law to have more than 20 partners, and the liability of each is unlimited. (2) in Britain and Europe, a popular name for any bank of which the share capital is owned by private persons or institutions and not by the State. (3) a bank that is not a member of a clearing house.

private brand *see* own brand.

private carrier *see under* carrier.

private company *see* private limited company *under* company.

private enterprise *see under* enterprise.

private health policy *see under* insurance policy.

private international law LAW *see under* international law.

private investment *see under* investment.

private law LAW that branch of the law that controls relations between one citizen and another. It includes the law of property, of contracts and of torts. Cf. public law.

private limited company *see under* company.

private nuisance *see under* nuisance.

private placing *see under* placing.

private power *see under* power.

private property *see under* property.

private right of way *see* right of way.

private sale *see under* sale.

private secretary *see under* secretary.

private sector ECON. in a mixed economy, that part of the economy that is owned and operated by private enterprise, not by government departments or public corporations. Cf. public sector; corporate sector; personal sector.

private treaty *see under* treaty.

private trust *see under* trust.

privilege (1) LAW a special right to some advantage not given to other persons or given only to very few, such as the right to freedom from arrest of Members of Parliament (called *parliamentary privilege*) and of ambassadors (called *diplomatic privilege*). (2) STK. EXCH. mainly U.S.A., an option.

privileged debt *see* preferential debt *under* debt.

privilege leave *see* annual leave *under* leave.

Privy Council LAW in Britain, a group of distinguished persons appointed formerly to advise the Crown in matters of government. Now it is mainly important for its *Judicial Committee,* a court of judges that hears and decides appeals from certain countries that are dominions and dependencies of the Crown and from certain courts and some professional organizations in Britain that hold judicial powers under the State.

Privy Purse FIN. in Britain, money allowed by Parliament to the monarch for personal expenses.

prize bounty *see under* bounty.

prize money *see under* money.

P.R.O. public relations officer; Public Records Office.

Pr. O. press officer.

pro. a professional, esp. in sport; a person who is paid to play games or to train people in sporting activity: *A golf/cricket pro.*

pro (*Latin,* for) (1) a point or argument in favour of (a proposal, motion, etc.).

pros and cons *pl.* (*with* con, against): *We must consider/weigh the pros and cons,* we must examine the arguments for and against.

(2) a person who is in favour of a proposal, motion, etc. (3) MAN. a short form of per pro. (per procurationem) used by a person signing a letter in place of another person, and with his authority.

probate LAW in Britain, an official document issued by the Probate Division of the High Court to the executor who has been appointed in the will of a dead person. The document states that the will has been *proved,* i.e. officially accepted as true and effective, that it has been registered (recorded) and that the executor has power to settle the affairs of the dead person according to law and to the wishes expressed in the will.

probity *see* integrity.

proc. procuration(em).

procedure the steps to be taken or the method to be followed in doing some particular thing, such as carrying out an industrial process, holding a business meeting, or bringing an action in the courts. *See* accounting procedure.

proceed (1) SHIPG. to go forward, esp. to begin a voyage: *To proceed to sea*, to sail from port. (2) LAW to bring an action in the courts against somebody: *We shall proceed against you if you do not pay within 30 days.* (3) COM. *see* proceeds, *pl.*

proceedings LAW legal action: *To start/institute proceedings to obtain a court order.*

proceeds *pl.* FIN. the sum of money received from a business deal, esp. the sale of an asset: *I have sold my house and have invested the proceeds in gilt-edged securities. The sale proceeds, after deducting our commission, amount to £5000. The proceeds of a bill of exchange.*
gross proceeds the total proceeds before deducting expenses, charges and commission.
net proceeds the amount of the total proceeds that remains after deducting all expenses, charges and commission. *See* account sales. *Syn.* (U.S.A.) avail.

process LAW (1) a formal document issued by a court of law, such as a writ or summons, as the first step in a lawsuit. *See* service of process. (2) the entire business, at all stages, of a lawsuit. (3) the lawsuit itself. *See also* abuse of process.

process-server LAW an official of a court of law who is responsible for formally presenting a writ or summons to the person to whom it is addressed. *See* service of process. *Syn.* bailiff.

procuration LAW taking care of the affairs of another person in his absence or when he is unable to attend to them himself. *Abbr.* p.; pro.; proc. *See* per procurationem.

procuration fee FIN. a payment made to a person for his services in arranging or negotiating a loan.

Procurator-fiscal LAW in Scotland, a public official who acts as the public prosecutor of a district. He takes legal action in the lower courts against persons who break the criminal law, and enquires into sudden or suspicious deaths.

procure to use special means or effort to obtain or buy: *The difficulty of procuring spare parts for an obsolete machine.*

procurement officer *see* materials buyer.

produce *n.* AGR. & COM. any commodity that is produced by agricultural industry, such as tea, coffee, sugar, corn and other grains, wool, cotton, and rubber. *Pron.* próduce.
v. to make, to manufacture, to bring into existence, to cause to grow, economic goods: things that are useful, scarce and have a price. *Pron.* prodúce.

produce broker *see* commodity broker; import broker.

produce exchange COMMOD. EXCH. any commodity exchange other than one dealing in metals.

produce market *see under* market.

producer a person who produces (manufactures, grows or extracts from the earth) commodities for sale. *Cf.* middleman; consumer.

producers' co-operative *see under* co-operative.

producer('s) goods *see* capital goods *under* goods (7).

producer's surplus ECON. THEORY the difference between the market price that a producer receives for his product and the lower price he would have been willing to accept as just enough to cover his costs of production and to give a normal profit. This surplus is an economic profit, an extra profit as reward for organizing the factors of production. *Also* producer surplus. *Syn.* employer's surplus.

product (1) a thing that is made, manufactured, brought into existence. *Pron.* próduct.
by-product *see under* by.
end-product *see under* end.
(2) the quantity obtained by multiplying two or more numbers together.

product abandonment COM. giving up, discontinuing, the production and marketing of an article.

product advertising *see under* advertising.

product differentiation *see* differentiation.

production (1) ECON. THEORY the making, bringing into existence, of useful goods and services which are scarce and have a price. (2) the act or process of producing; manufacturing. (3) the entire amount produced: *The production of coal in Britain is over 120 million tons per year.*
batch production *see under* batch.
direct production ECON. THEORY the simple and least effective system of production, by which a person satisfies all his wants by his own efforts and skills, not having or using the advantages of specialization or the division of labour. *Cf.* indirect production. *Syn.* self-sufficiency.
indirect production ECON. THEORY production using the advantages of specialization and the division of labour. *Cf.* direct production.
jobbing (shop) production *see under* jobbing.
primary production ECON. THEORY those activities that provide Man with the gifts of Nature, such as all forms of agriculture, forestry, fruit-growing, fishing and hunting, and mining.
secondary production ECON. THEORY the manufacturing of finished products from raw materials, and the building of houses, public buildings, factories, roads, ports, etc.
tertiary production ECON. THEORY the performing of services such as banking, insurance, transport and trade (commercial services), and the work done by the professions and service industries and trades.

production bonus *see under* bonus.

production census *see under* census.

production control *see under* control.

production cost *see under* cost.

production, factors of *see* factors of production.

production goods *see* capital goods *under* goods.

production manager *see* works manager *under* manager.

production, mass *see under* mass.

productive (1) AGR. of land, able to produce crops. (2) FIN. producing an income, such as interest or dividend: *A productive investment*. (3) ECON. producing goods and services that have a value or price: *The productive resources of a country*, the means of producing goods and services that a country possesses.

productive assets *see* active assets *under* assets.

productive debt *see under* national debt.

productive expenditure *see under* expenditure.

productivity ECON. & IND. the relation between the output or amount produced in a given period and one unit of the factors of production employed in producing that output. Thus, the *productivity of labour* is the average amount of goods produced by one worker employed in making the goods; the *productivity of land* is the gain from cultivating or letting one acre of it; and the *productivity of capital* is the income earned by investing a given amount of money, such as £100.

marginal productivity the addition to his total output that a producer will obtain from adding one more unit of a factor of production, such as another worker. *See also* Diminishing Returns, Law of.

productivity agreement IND. REL. an agreement between a trade union and an employer by which increased wages are paid for increased productivity.

productivity bonus *see under* bonus.

Productivity, Law of Diminishing Marginal *see* Diminishing Returns, Law of.

product research *see under* research.

profession (1) service as a practising member of a group or class of persons who, after a long period of study, have obtained special qualifications in a branch of learning or science. Originally one of the three *learned professions*: law, medicine and theology; but nowadays any of a number of others including teaching and the arts (the liberal professions) and various departments of science, such as architecture, engineering, and accountancy. *He is a lawyer/ doctor by profession. To exercise a profession.* (2) a group or class of persons practising such service: *The legal/medical/dental profession.*

professional indemnity policy *see under* insurance policy.

professional partnership *see* non-trading partnership *under* partnership.

professional services *see under* services.

proficiency the state of being proficient: *Proficiency pay*, extra pay for showing special skill.

proficient well skilled in doing something: *He is a proficient worker*.

profit *v.* (1) to make a profit or gain of any kind: *He profited to the extent of £2000*. (2) to take advantage: *We must profit by the financial difficulties of our competitors*.

n. (1) the amount by which the price received is greater than the cost; the difference between business income and expenses. *Opp.* loss; deficit. *Syn.* surplus. (2) ECON. THEORY the difference between the price received for a product and the amounts paid as rewards to the factors of production: to land as rent, to labour as wages and salaries, and to capital as interest. What remains is profit or loss depending on whether the amount received is greater than the amounts paid. Profit has been variously described by economists as reward for the businessman's enterprise in accepting the risks and uncertainties of business, and as a payment for skilled management.

attributable profit a profit that is regarded as belonging to, or coming from, a particular source, such as a division or department of an organization, or a particular period, or a particular contract or order.

book profit *see under* book.

capital profit a profit received from selling a fixed asset. Cf. income profit.

casual profit *see* casual (1).

distributable profit *see under* distributable.

excess profit *see* super-profit *below*.

gross profit in a business, the amount by which, in a given period, the value of sales is greater than the cost of goods sold, without taking note of any expenses for selling, distribution or administration. It is represented by a credit balance in the trading account. *Abbr.* G.P. or g.p. Cf. net profit. *See also* percentage profit *below*. *Syn.* trading profit.

income profit any profit that is not a capital profit.

monopoly profit in economic theory, the above-normal profit that a firm is able to earn when it is in a position of monopoly. The size of this profit is a measure of the strength of the monopoly. *Syn.* supernormal profit.

net profit in a business, the operating profit after allowing for payment of income tax.

normal profit in economic theory, a part of pure profit, being the amount of profit that is just high enough to persuade an entrepreneur to continue production. It is an opportunity cost, since it must be at least equal to the income that the entrepreneur could obtain if he invested his money in some other way.

operating profit in a business, the amount by which the gross profit is greater than the operating expenses or overheads. It is represented by a credit balance in the profit and loss account.

paper profit a profit that has been earned but has not been realized, i.e. has not been made in cash. Thus the value of a security may rise and show a paper profit, but this profit will be realized in the form of cash only if it is sold. Cf. paper loss; realized profit.

percentage profit the profit expressed as a percentage of sales. *Syn.* profit margin.

pure profit in economic theory, the profit that an entrepreneur expects to receive for bearing uncertainty, i.e. as reward for the risks he is taking. Cf. normal profit. *Syn.* economic profit.

realized profit profit or gain actually made on the sale of an asset, such as an investment. Cf. paper profit.

retained profit profit that has not been distributed or shared out among the shareholders, but has been retained, i.e. kept to allow the company to finance new investment without having to borrow money. *Syn.* undistributed profit.

supernormal profit *see* monopoly profit *above.*

super-profit in economic theory, any profit earned by an entrepreneur over and above normal profit. *Syn.* excess profit; surplus profit.

surplus profit *see* super-profit *above.*

trading profit *see* gross profit *above.*

undistributed profit *see* retained profit *above.*

windfall profit a profit that is not expected. Such profits are usu. caused by a sudden fall in the value of money (e.g. in a time of inflation) resulting in the market value of a product rising faster than the cost of production.

profitability FIN. the power of a business to earn profits, or the degree to which a business is profitable, esp. as compared with another business.

profitable (1) FIN. paying a profit: *A profitable business.* Producing an income: *A profitable investment.* (2) worth doing, useful: *A profitable piece of research.*

profit and loss account ACCTS. an accounting summary which is prepared for the purpose of calculating the net profit of the business before taxation, i.e. the gross profit (carried from the trading account) plus non-trading credits such as interest and discounts received, less the expenses of selling and of administering the business. *Syn.* gain and loss account; (U.S.A.) profit and loss statement. *Abbr.* P. & L. a/c.

profit and loss appropriation account *see* appropriation account.

profit and loss on consignment account *see* consignment account.

profit à prendre LAW a right to take something from another person's land, such as the right to collect firewood, to graze cattle, to catch fish and to hunt animals. Cf. easement.

profiteer COM. a trader who makes excessive profits by charging unreasonably high prices

when there is a shortage of a commodity at a time of national emergency, such as war or famine.

v. to be a profiteer: *If you continue to profiteer you will lose all your customers.*

profitgraph *see* break-even chart *under* break-even analysis.

profit margin *see under* margin (3).

profit motive ECON. the natural desire in human beings for wealth; the aim, that is believed and accepted by economists as being that of every entrepreneur, of making as much profit as possible.

profits INSCE. the amount by which a life insurance fund is greater than the total of its liabilities. These profits are shared among the holders of with-profits policies, usu. by adding a reversionary bonus to the sum insured when it is paid out. *See* with-profits policy *under* insurance policy.

profit sharing MAN. an arrangement between the owners of a business and its employees by which an agreed share of the profit is paid to each employee over and above his wages or salary.

profit-sharing bond *see under* bond, *n.*

profits policy *see* consequential loss policy *under* insurance policy.

profits tax *see* corporation tax *under* tax.

profit taking STK. EXCH. (1) selling securities now in order to make a profit while one can, because there are signs that the market price will fall. (2) selling by speculators of securities that have recently risen in price, to take the opportunity of making a quick profit.

pro-forma invoice *see under* invoice.

program *n.* COMP. a series of steps to be performed by the computer to solve a given problem.

v. to prepare a program for use in a computer.

programmer COMP. a person qualified to plan the order of the steps that a computer must take to solve a particular problem. Some programmers also produce the detailed directions, called coding, that tell the computer what it is to do at each step, using a machine language that the computer understands. Cf. systems analyst.

programming language *see* machine language *under* language.

progress chart *see under* chart.

progress chaser IND. in the office of a factory, a person who is responsible for recording the progress of the work being done and for seeing that it is completed within the time set by a production programme.

progress control *see under* control.

progression *see* arithmetic(al) progression; geometric(al) progression; harmonic(al) progression.

progressive tax *see under* tax.

progress payment IND. a payment, made under

a contract, to the builders of a ship, house, road, etc. when each stage of the building has been completed.

progress report *see under* report.

prohibit to forbid: *Prohibited imports/exports*, goods of which the import or export is forbidden by law. Such goods are known as *prohibited goods* or *prohibited articles*.

prohibition (1) the act of prohibiting, of forbidding. (2) LAW a law or order of a court forbidding a lower court or a minister or a government department from wrongly using the powers they hold from the State, such as acting against the rules of natural justice. (3) a law such as existed in the U.S.A. from 1919 to 1933 and now exists in some other countries, forbidding the manufacture and sale of strong drink except for use as medicine.

prohibitive tending to prohibit or forbid: *Prohibitive cost/price/expense*, so high as to forbid the spending of so much money. *Rail fares are becoming prohibitive*, are being raised so high that one cannot afford to pay them.

project a carefully-prepared plan, esp. one for a new product or for a new business activity: *A development project*, a plan for developing, improving, enlarging a part of a business or industry.

projected (1) planned for the future: *A projected new road/motorway*. (2) expected, estimated, judging from present information: *The projected population of Cairo is seven million in five years time*.

proletarian a member of the proletariat.

proletariat ECON. in a Marxist theory, the social class that consists of workers who, not themselves possessing any means of production, must sell the only saleable thing that they do possess, i.e. their ability to work, receiving in return a wage; and who, in a capitalist industrial economy, have no choice other than to work for capitalists. *See* class struggle; dictatorship of the proletariat.

promisee LAW a person to whom a promise is made. Cf. promiser.

promiser a person who makes a promise. Cf. promisee.

promissory note FIN. a formal document, in writing, containing an unconditional promise, signed by the person making the note, to pay a certain sum of money to, or to the order of, a certain named person, or to the bearer of the document. Ordinary promissory notes are widely used in the U.S.A. banking system but are now seldom used in Britain. There are certain special kinds of promissory note in use in most countries, such as the bank-note, which unlike other promissory notes, can be issued again and again. *See also* collateral note; installment note (U.S.A.); judgment note. Cf. I.O.U. *Syn.* note of hand. *Abbr.* P/N; P.N.

promoter *see* company promoter.

promotion (1) ADVTG. & COM. activities aimed to increase the demand for a product.

sales promotion the work of selling a product by all useful methods such as: powerful advertising; personal persuasion of possible customers by visit, phone or letter; exhibitions, displays and demonstrations; competitions for prizes; free samples; trading stamps, etc. (2) STK. EXCH. company promotion, the work of forming a new company. *See* company promoter. (3) MAN. an increase in the rank and responsibility of an employee: *We have given Mr Smith promotion to the grade of sales supervisor*. *Syn.* advancement.

promotional budget FIN. & ADVTG. an account of the probable cost of carrying out an advertising plan to promote (increase) the sales of a product.

promotion expenses *see* formation expenses.

promotion money *see under* money.

prompt COM. an agreement between a merchant and an importer by which the importer is allowed a period of time before he has to pay for a consignment of goods. A note called a *prompt note* is sent to the importer to remind him shortly before the date when payment becomes due.

prompt cash *see under* cash.

Prompt Day COMMOD. EXCH. the day payment is due for goods bought at a commodity-exchange auction sale. This day may be only two weeks after a wool auction or as long as three months after a tea sale. *Syn.* Settling Day.

proof of debt LAW a document completed and signed by a creditor who makes a claim against the estate of a bankrupt person. It is in the form of an affidavit verifying (declaring the truth of) the debt, and is delivered to the official receiver or to a trustee if one has been appointed.

proof of title LAW proof by the person selling land that he has the title, i.e. the right of ownership of that land, usu. contained in documents called *title-deeds*.

proof spirit a mixture of alcohol and water of a standard strength, measured by a specific gravity at 60°F. of 0.9198 in Britain, and of 0.9335 in U.S.A.

Prop. proprietor.

propensity ECON. THEORY the natural tendency or willingness in human beings to act in certain ways when faced with certain economic conditions, as pointed out by Keynes in his *General Theory of Employment, Interest and Money* (1936).

propensity to consume the relation between the size of consumers' incomes and the amount they spend on consumption goods. Keynes showed that when income increases or de-

creases, spending on consumption goods will increase or decrease too, but not usu. in proportion to the increase or decrease in income.
propensity to import the relation between changes in the national income and changes in spending on imports. In Britain, in the past, an increase or decrease in the national income has resulted in less than proportionate increase or decrease in imports, but in the U.S.A. the opposite has been true.
propensity to invest the willingness of private producers (not public authorities) to invest in capital goods. This willingness is determined mainly by profitability of the investment in capital goods as compared with current rates of interest. The lower the interest rates are, the higher the amount that will be invested in capital goods.
propensity to save the willingness of consumers to hold back from spending under certain conditions, thus enlarging that part of income that is not consumed but is saved.
propertied possessing much property, esp. land.
property LAW (1) any thing that has value and can be owned, including things having substance such as land, houses, furniture, money, jewels, and mere rights such as a right to receive money, a copyright, a patent. (2) a right of ownership: *Who has the property in the land/copyright/goods?*
freehold property land that is owned absolutely, i.e. free of payment or duty to other persons. Cf. leasehold property; real property.
immovable property *see* real property *below*.
industrial property patents, industrial designs and trade-marks.
leasehold property land and buildings held on lease, i.e. with the right to possess and use them for a stated period in return for payment of a premium or rent. Cf. freehold property. *Syn.* chattel real.
movable property *see under* movable.
personal property LAW any property other than real property. It consists of chattels real (leaseholds) and chattels personal, also called pure personalty.
private property land belonging to a private owner, not to the public or to the State.
public property land and buildings that are owned by the State or by local government authorities for public use, such as parks, public gardens and playing-fields, hospitals, schools, museums and other public buildings.
real property LAW freehold land and certain rights over land belonging to others. All other property, including leasehold land, is personal property. *Syn.* immovable property; real estate.
property and liability insurance (U.S.A.) *see* casualty insurance *under* insurance, classes and kinds of.

property bond *see under* bond, *n.*
property company COM. & STK. EXCH. a company that buys and sells land and buildings and lets property on lease as its main business activity.
property development building, or rebuilding, shops, houses, offices, etc. on land in such a way as to improve greatly the usefulness of the land and its value as an investment.
property register LAW in Britain, a record of the exact details of a property that has a registered title. See Land Registry.
property tax *see under* tax.
proportion, the BKG. the relation between the total of the Bank of England's cash reserve of notes and coin, and the Bank's liabilities to the public in the form of deposits, expressed as a percentage. *See* bank return.
proportional tax *see under* tax.
proposal INSCE. a printed form filled in and handed to an insurer by a *proposer*, a person intending to effect an insurance. The form gives the insurer the information he needs so that he can decide whether to accept the proposed insurance, and if so, what rate of premium to charge. The form is usu. a list of questions with spaces for writing the answers.
proposer (1) INSCE. *see* proposal. (2) MAN. at a formal meeting, the person who formally puts a motion to the meeting. He has the right to speak first in any discussion of that motion and to speak again at the end, immediately before a vote is taken. *See also* seconder.
proposition (1) a proposed plan, esp. for a business venture that needs to be considered: *This scheme is not a workable/economic/financial proposition, it will not be profitable. A good business proposition.* (2) a business offer: *A proposition for the supply of 1000 tons of coal per month.*
proprietary *adj.* of or relating to a proprietor (owner).
n. a group or association of proprietors. *Abbr.* pty.
proprietary company *see under* company.
proprietary insurance *see under* insurance, classes and kinds of.
proprietary product IND. & COM. a product that is produced and sold by the proprietor (owner) of a right, such as a patent for a medicine, that prevents other producers from making or selling the product. *A proprietary brand/formula/medicine.*
proprietary rights LAW rights of ownership, esp. in landed property and patent, trade-mark, brand name and similar commercial rights.
proprietor (1) the owner of land and buildings. (2) the owner of a business, esp. of a hotel, restaurant, or newspaper. (3) the owner of a copyright, patent or other legal right such as a brand name or trade-mark.
registered proprietor *see under* registered.

sole proprietor the one and only owner of a business. He provides all the capital, bears all the risk, and in return receives all the profits. Such a concern is called a *one-man business*, although the proprietor may employ a number of people. *Syn.* owner-manager. *Abbr.* prop.

proprietorship register LAW in Britain, a record of the registered owner of a property, his name, address, and the price at which he bought the property. *See* Land Registry.

pro rata (*Latin*, in proportion) at a certain rate: *Profits are divided among members pro rata to the number of shares they hold*, in proportion to their relative shareholding, or at a certain rate per share.

pro rata condition *see* average clause.

pros and cons *see* pro.

prosecute LAW (1) to cause a person to be charged with a criminal offence in a court of law. (2) to direct a case against a person being tried in a court of law by being a prosecutor.

prosecution LAW (1) the act and process of prosecuting a person. (2) the lawyers or other court officers responsible for stating the case against the accused person at a trial. (3) the authority that prosecutes, usu. the State or Crown on behalf of the public.

prospect *n.* (1) something that may be expected: *There is a prospect of a large order from Saudi Arabia. We see little prospect of making a profit this year. A prospect of finding oil.* (2) COM. (*colloq.*) a possible customer; a prospective buyer. *Pron.* próspect.
v. to search/explore a region for minerals: *They are prospecting for oil/gold in the desert. Pron.* prospéct.

prospective expected in the future; probable: *A prospective member of the board/of Parliament. A prospective buyer. Prospective yield*, *see under* yield.

prospector a person who explores a region, searching for gold, oil or other minerals.

prospects *pl.* (1) FIN. & COM. expectations; the future outlook: *The business prospects are good/poor/bad.* (2) MAN. expectations of success: *That young manager has good prospects*, he is expected to be very successful in his job.

prospectus (1) INSCE. a printed paper, sometimes part of a proposal form, giving information about the kinds of cover obtainable from the insurers, and the premium rates of each. (2) STK. EXCH. a document inviting the public to buy shares, stock or debentures in a public company. (3) ADVTG. a leaflet or other printed paper giving information about a product or service, such as a book, a hotel, a school.

prosper to grow; to become rich; to be successful: *The company has prospered under his chairmanship. Syn.* thrive.
prosperous *adj.* successful; having good fortune: *A prosperous business/year/man.*

prosperity a state of being rich, of having good fortune and success, esp. in financial matters.

prostitute a person who, in return for money, is willing to join in immoral behaviour.

protected bear *see* covered bear.

protected imports *see under* imports.

protection (1) ECON. action by a government to protect its producers against competition from foreign producers, by forbidding imports of certain goods or by placing protective import duties on such goods. *See* anti-dumping. (2) INSCE. insurance cover. (3) (*colloq.*) money paid by a shopkeeper, club owner or other businessman to avoid being attacked by criminals.

protection and indemnity club MAR. INSCE. an association of shipowners who form a fund of money to pay for losses against which the members cannot insure in the marine insurance market.

protective duty/tariff *see under* duty.

pro tem (*Latin*: pro tempore) for the present (time); temporarily: *We are working here pro tem because our new offices are not yet ready.*

protest *n.* (1) BKG. & LAW a formal declaration in writing made by a notary, or other person lawfully acting as notary, attesting (witnessing and recording) the dishonour of a bill of exchange or promissory note. This is a legal step taken by the notary after noting the bill or promissory note. *See* noting; acceptance supra protest. (2) LAW expressed unwillingness: *A payment under protest*, a payment made unwillingly by a person who states that he is not bound to pay and that he intends to claim the return of the money. *Pron.* prótest.
v. BKG. & LAW to make a solemn declaration that a bill of exchange or promissory note has been dishonoured. *See* noting. *Pron.* protést.

protest, captain's *see under* captain.

provide against/for FIN. & ACCTS. to arrange in advance, esp. for money to be ready for a particular purpose, such as for buying a new machine to replace an existing machine when it wears out. *To provide for depreciation/income tax/bad and doubtful debts. Syn.* to make provision against/for.

provided that LAW on condition that; on the understanding that.

provident fund FIN. & MAN. a fund set up by a government or a private organization and administered by trustees for the benefit of all the employees of the organization. The purpose of the fund is to make the employee save some of his current income for the future, and to make the employer provide for the employee after his retirement. As a condition of his contract of employment, a percentage (often 6¼%) of the employee's pay, and a similar or larger sum as a contribution by the employer, are paid, usu. monthly, into the employee's account with the fund during the whole of the employee's service. The trustees invest the money. During this time the employee may borrow from the fund, repaying the loan by instalments kept back from his pay. When the employee leaves his service, he has the right to receive the whole of the amount standing to the credit of his account with the fund, usu. with interest. In some countries provident fund schemes are preferred to pension schemes.

provident society *see* industrial and provident society.

province (1) an important administrative or historical division, or a natural region, of a country. (2) those parts of a country other than the area in which the capital city lies: *Prices in London tend to be higher than in the provinces. We are opening branches in the provinces.*
provincial *adj. The provincial cities/branches.*

proving a debt *see* proof of debt.

proving a will *see* probate.

provision (1) FIN. & ACCTS. (*a*) the act of providing (by setting aside money from profits) for the replacement of assets and for the reduction in their value, for bad and doubtful debts and for other liabilities that cannot be determined with accuracy. (*See* provide against/for.) (*b*) the amount of money required for this. Cf. reserve. (2) LAW a proviso. (3) a clause (in a law) that deals with a particular matter: *There is a provision in the Act for punishing habitual offenders.*
provisions *pl.* COM. stocks or supplies of food; groceries: *A provision dealer/merchant*, one dealing in foods such as butter, cheese, eggs and fruit.

provisional invoice *see under* invoice.

proviso (1) LAW a clause in a contract or deed that introduces a condition. Such clauses usu. begin with the words *provided always that.* (2) INSCE. *see* clause (2).

prox. proximo. *See* date.

proximate cause LAW & INSCE. the immediate cause of an event or chain of events. Cf. remote cause.

proximo *see* date.

proxy STK. EXCH. & MAN. (1) a written authority from a shareholder in a company giving power to another person to attend and vote on his behalf at a company meeting. (2) the person thus given power.
general proxy one that gives the proxy power to act at a number of meetings of the company.
special proxy one that gives power to the proxy to act at one particular meeting only.

PS. postscript, *pl.* PSS.

P.S.T. Pacific Standard Time (U.S.A.).

P.S.V. public-service vehicle.

psychology *see* industrial psychology.

Pt. point; port.

pt. part; payment; pint.

P.T. (*French*: perte totale) total loss.

p.t. part time.

Pte. Private (limited company).

PTM Malaysia's international vehicle-registration letters.

P.T.O. please turn over.

Pty. Proprietary (company).

p.u. paid up.

pub (*colloq.*) public house.

pub. public; published; publisher.

public *adj.* (1) of or relating to, all the people: *The public good*, the good of the people as a whole. *In the public interest*, for the benefit of everybody. (2) of or relating to the State, esp. as representative of the people: *A public official/building/highway. Abbr.* pub. (3) STK. EXCH. *to go public*, to change from being a private to a public limited company.
n. (1) the people who made up the community or nation: *The British public.* (2) a class or group of people having a common quality or interest: *The reading/theatre-going/sporting public. In public*, with members of the public present. *Opp.* in private.

public account BKG. a bank account for public money such as those of collectors of taxes, government departments and local government authorities.

public accountant *see* certified accountant.

Public Accounts Committee FIN. in Britain, a committee of the House of Commons that is responsible for checking that public money is being properly spent. With the help of the Audit Office, the committee examines cases of waste and inefficiency by government departments and its reports to the House of Commons are made known to the public. *Abbr.* P.A.C.

publican COM. an innkeeper, esp. a person who owns or manages a public house. He is sometimes also called the landlord.

public analyst IND. a person skilled in chemical analysis who provides a service to the public by checking the composition of materials and products.

publication (1) the act of making public, of publishing. (2) a published book, magazine or newspaper.

publication advertising *see under* advertising.

public carrier *see under* carrier.

public company *see* public limited company *under* company.

public corporation IND. & COM. (1) in Britain, a state-owned organization that manages a nationalized industry, such as British Airways, the British Gas Corporation, the Central Electricity Generating Board and the National Coal Board; or a public service, such as the Post Office and the British Broadcasting Corporation. (2) in U.S.A., any corporation (company) in which the government owns a controlling interest.

public debt *see* national debt.

public deposits FIN. & BKG. in the Bank of England return, the balances of the accounts at the Bank of England of British government departments.

public enterprise *see under* enterprise.

public examination LAW in Britain, a public meeting which a debtor who has been declared bankrupt must attend and at which he may be questioned by his creditors and by the official receiver or trustee concerning the causes of his bankruptcy and the details given in his statement of affairs.

public expenditure *see under* expenditure.

public finance FIN. & ECON. THEORY the study of how central and local government authorities obtain and spend public money, and of the effect of these activities on the economy as a whole. The subject includes the examination of tax systems, the management of the monetary system and the national debt, the allocation of funds between the public and private sectors, and the general growth of economic activity.

public funds *see* national debt.

public house COM. & TOUR. in Britain, an inn; a building with rooms called bars where adult members of the public can buy drinks and simple meals, and can sometimes obtain lodgings. *Abbr.* (*colloq.*) pub.

public investment *see under* investment.

public issue *see under* issue of securities.

publicist *see* press agent.

publicity ADVTG. (1) the business of attracting public attention and of encouraging general feelings of goodwill towards a product or service in order to sell it: *Miss Robinson is in charge of publicity. She is the Publicity Manager and head of the Publicity Department which produces our publicity material. Our rivals employ a publicity agent who runs a publicity bureau.* (2) public notice: *The reviews are giving the book valuable publicity. The publicity in the press has increased sales tenfold.* Cf. public relations.

publicize ADVTG. to advertise; to make known to the public.

public law LAW that branch of the law that controls relations between a private citizen and the State. It includes criminal law and constitutional law. Cf. private law.

public liability policy *see under* insurance policy.

public limited company *see under* company.

public monopoly *see under* monopoly.

public nuisance *see under* nuisance.

public opinion the opinion that most people in a community hold on a certain subject; the balance of opinion of a wide section of the public.

public ownership ownership by the State.

public power *see under* power.

public property *see under* property.

Public Prosecutions, Director of *see under* Director.

Public Prosecutor *see* Director of Public Prosecutions.

public relations ADVTG. the business of forming and preserving in the eyes of the public an attractive image of a person or organization. Cf. publicity. *Abbr.* P.R.

public sale *see* auction.

public sector ECON. in a mixed economy, that part of the economy that is owned and operated by government authorities and public corporations. Cf. corporate sector; personal sector; private sector.

public servant any person who is in the service of the government. If he serves the central government he is called, in Britain, a *Civil Servant*; and if he serves a local government authority he is known as a *local government officer* or *local government employee*.

public-service vehicle TRANSPT. any road vehicle that is licensed to carry passengers for reward, such as a taxi, bus or motor coach. *Abbr.* P.S.V.

public trust *see* charitable trust.

public trustee LAW in Britain, an official of the State whom any member of the public may appoint as executor, administrator or trustee of estates, as guardian of infants, and as trustee of a variety of other trusts. The main advantage of using his services is that his office is a corporation sole and he is therefore a trustee who will never become too ill to work, and will never go abroad, or die.

public utilities IND. industrial organizations that provide the public with essential goods and services such as electricity, gas, water, transport by bus, rail and air. Such industries are usu. monopolies and, in many countries, are under state ownership or control.

public utility company *see under* company.

public utility services *see* supply services *under* services.

public warehouse *see under* warehouse.

public works ECON. & FIN. the building of roads, schools, hospitals and other works on a large scale by governments; an attempt to provide useful work in periods of high unemployment, when private investment is usu. too low to have any real effect on employment.

publish COM. (1) to make known, to issue to the public, esp. by printing copies for sale, a book, magazine, newspaper, report, map, accounts, etc. *Published* (*company*) *accounts/balance sheet*, those that have been printed and circulated, esp. to the company's shareholders. (2) to place on sale on a certain day, called publication day, a book, magazine, etc. *Abbr.* pub.

published price *see under* price.

publisher COM. & IND. (1) a person or organization carrying on a business of publishing books, magazines, etc. (2) in U.S.A., the owner of a newspaper. *Abbr.* pub.; pubr.

publishing COM. & IND. the business of a publisher, also called a publishing house. Cf. publication.

publishing agreement LAW a contract between a publisher and one or more authors (writers of books) for the publication of a book or series of books.

pubn. publication.

pubr. publisher.

Puerto Rico an independent island state in the Caribbean, in association with the U.S.A., pop. 3 million approx. (1975); capital, San Juan, pop. 500,000 approx.; languages, Spanish and English; currency unit, the U.S. dollar (US$), divided into 100 cents. Former name, Porto Rico.

puff ADVTG. (*colloq.*) advertisement, esp. praise of a product or service in a newspaper or magazine article.

pugri, pugree *see* key money.

puisne mortgage *see under* mortgage.

pukka in India and Pakistan, real; true; of good quality; made to last: *A pukka road*, one with a hard surface. *A pukka house*, a well-built house, made to last a long time. *Opp.* kutcha.

pula the standard currency unit of Botswana, divided into 100 cents.

puli the fractional currency unit of Afghanistan. 100 puli = 1 Afghani.

pull (*colloq.*) personal influence, esp. when used to obtain some advantage or favour: *Mr Smith has some pull in the ministry/with the council.*

pull-in, pull-up a safe stopping-place for road vehicles.

to pull in money to earn money quickly.

Pullman car *see under* car.

pump-priming *see* deficit financing.

punch an instrument used in offices for making neat holes in paper, card, etc. Also called a paper-punch or letter-punch.

punched-card system COMP. a method of feeding information into a computer by using cards in which small holes are punched in various combinations or patterns by a punched-card operator. The holes cause small electric currents to operate the input section of the computer. A similar system is in use, using *punched paper tape* instead of cards.

punched paper tape *see* punched-card system.

puncheon a large barrel holding various amounts of liquid, from 72 to about 112 gal. (327 to 509 l).

punt a popular name for the Irish pound (£).

punter (1) a person who lives by betting on the results of horse races. A professional gambler. (2) STK. EXCH. a person who gambles in securities in the hope of making quick profits.

pur. purchase.

purchase *v.* to buy; to get, obtain, in exchange for money or other valuable goods.
n. (1) the act of purchasing, of buying. (2) a thing bought.
purchases *pl.* those goods that a business buys with the intention of selling by way of trade, not goods bought for use by the business. *Abbr.* pur.

purchase money *see under* money.

purchase order *see under* order.

purchase price *see under* price.

purchaser a buyer.

purchases account ACCTS. the account in the purchases (or bought) ledger into which are posted, on the debit side, periodical totals of entries in the purchases day book.

purchases book ACCTS. a book of prime entry, being that section of the day book in which a listing is made daily of all goods bought on credit by the business. Each entry is posted as a credit to the supplier's account in the purchases (or bought) ledger, and totals are posted periodically to the debit side of the purchases account in that ledger. Cf. sales book. *Syn.* purchases day book; bought book; bought day book; purchases journal; bought journal.

purchases day book *see* purchases book.

purchase(s) invoice *see under* invoice.

purchases journal *see* purchases book.

purchases ledger *see under* ledger.

purchases returns book ACCTS. a book of first entry, in which a listing is made of goods returned to the suppliers. Each entry is debited in the account of the supplier, and totals are posted periodically to the credit of the purchases returns account. *Syn.* purchases returns journal; returns outwards book.

purchase tax *see under* tax.

purchase, years' *see* years' purchase.

purchasing MAN. & IND. the work of buying the materials needed to manufacture the products of a business and the goods needed to operate it. *Syn.* procurement.

purchasing agent *see* buying agent.

purchasing officer *see* materials buyer.

purchasing power ECON. (1) of persons, the public, having the money to buy goods and services. *Syn.* spending power. (2) of money, the amount of goods and services that money can buy at a given time. This power varies in the opposite direction to changes in the level of prices, i.e. when prices rise, the purchasing power of money falls. *Syn.* buying power.

purchasing power parity ECON. THEORY the theory (not accepted by some economists) put forward by Gustav Cassel in 1916 that the rate of exchange between two currencies which are not both on a metallic standard is related to the degree of purchasing power of each currency in its own country.

pure competition see under competition.

pure economics see economic theory.

pure interest see gross interest under interest.

pure profit see under profit.

purloin to steal, esp. things of little value that the thief wants to keep for his own use: *Somebody has purloined my pen.* Cf. abstract; embezzle.

purse (1) a small bag, usu. of leather, for carrying money in a pocket or handbag. (2) the sum of money in such a bag, esp. when given as a prize or gift. *To hold the purse-strings*, to have control of expenditure, esp. in a family. *Purse-proud*, excessively proud of one's wealth. (3) in U.S.A., a woman's handbag.

Purse, Privy see under Privy.

purser SHIPG. in a large ship, an officer responsible for looking after money and keeping the accounts. In a passenger-carrying vessel he is responsible also for the care and comfort of the passengers.

pursuer LAW in Scotland, a plaintiff.

purvey COM. to provide for sale food, drink and other consumable goods needed by households.

purveyor (1) COM. a person who owns a grocery business, usu. on a large scale. (2) a person who provides news by word of mouth.

push v. (1) COM. to press, urge, people to buy a product. *See* share-pushing. (2) to peddle drugs. (3) (*colloq.*) *To be pushed*, to be short of money or time or materials.
n. (*colloq.*) (1) dismissal: *To get the push*, to be dismissed from employment. *To give someone the push*, to dismiss him. *Syn.* boot; kick; sack. (2) determination, energy, esp. in business.

put option see under option.

put-through deal STK. EXCH. a large deal between a buyer and a seller, through a jobber, at an agreed price that is well below the current market price. In Britain such deals are not allowed by the rules of the Exchange and are usu. kept secret.

P.V. (*French*: petite vitesse) low speed; by ordinary goods train.

p.v.t. (*French*: par voie télégraphique) by telegraph.

p.w. per week.

pwt. pennyweight.

P.X. private exchange.

PY Paraguay's international vehicle-registration letters.

pya the fractional currency unit of Burma. *Pl.* pyas. 100 pyas = 1 kyat.

pyramiding (1) FIN. & STK. EXCH. taking financial advantage of the relatively small amount of capital needed by those who hold the power of controlling a group of companies. This is because one needs only just over half the voting shares to control the holding company which, in turn, needs to own only just over half the voting shares in all its subsidiary companies to

be in control of them. (2) TAXN. the placing of a tax on an article or commodity at an early stage in its manufacture, with the result that the tax becomes part of the basis on which, at the next stage, more tax is payable, and so on.

Q

qanat AGR. a man-made underground water channel orig. in ancient Persia (Iran) but still found widely in Morocco, Cyprus and other Mediterranean and Arabian countries. *Syn.* (Oman) falaj.

Qatar an independent Arab sheikhdom on the east coast of the Arabian peninsula, pop. 170,000 approx. (1973); capital, Doha, pop. 95,000 approx.; languages, Arabic and English; currency unit, the Qatar/Dubai riyal or ryal, divided into 100 dirhams. Member, Arab League. *Also* Katar.

Q.B. Queen's Bench.

Q.C. Queen's Counsel.

qindar the fractional currency unit of Albania. 100 qindars = 1 lek. *Also* qintar; quintar.

Qlty. quality.

qr. quarter; quire.

qt. quart.

qto. quarto.

qtr. quarter.

quad., quadr., quadrupl. quadruplicate.

quadratic mean an average arrived at by adding together the squares of all the individual quantities, dividing by the number of quantities and taking the square root of the result. *Example*: to find the quadratic mean of 3, 5, 7, the squares, $3^2 + 5^2 + 7^2 = 9 + 25 + 49 = 83$. Then divide by 3 (the number of quantities) $83/3 = 27.667$ of which the sq. root is 5.26. The quadratic mean is higher than the arithmetic mean (5.0) the geometric mean (4.75) and the harmonic mean (4.44).

quadruplicate a fourth copy: *In quadruplicate*, four copies exactly the same, *or* an original document with three (carbon) copies. Cf. duplicate, triplicate, etc. *Abbr.* quad.; quadr.; quadrupl.

qualification share see under share.

qualified acceptance see under acceptance (5).

qualified endorsement see under endorsement.

quality control see under control.

quality, merchantable see merchantable (2).

quango (*colloq.*) a group of persons some of whom are not Civil Servants but who are appointed by a government minister and are given powers for the use of which they are not directly responsible to Parliament. The word quango, of U.S.A. origin, is a short form of quasi-autonomous non-governmental organization. *Example*: the Price Commission.

quantity discount *see under* discount.

Quantity Equation *see* Fisher Equation.

quantity index *see under* index number(s).

quantity rebate *see* quantity discount *under* discount.

quantity surveyor IND. a person skilled in calculating the probable cost of materials and labour needed for a new building. *See* bill of quantities.

Quantity Theory of Money ECON. THEORY the basic concept (idea) of the classical economists that the general level of prices is related to the quantity of money; that if the quantity of money in an economy is increased, money becomes less scarce, its value falls and prices rise. Irving Fisher argued that although this is true in theory, the position is much more complicated in practice, because other influences are affected by a rise in the quantity of money, such as the velocity (speed) of circulation of money and the total volume of goods and services; and these too have an influence on the general level of prices. *See* Fisher Equation.

quantum FIN. a particular quantity or amount, esp. a value expressed as an amount of money, not as a proportion or percentage of a larger amount: *The quantum of net profit was £1 million, or 20% of turnover. The quantum of interest due is £2000, being that earned on £20,000 at 10%.*

quantum meruit LAW (*Latin*, as much as he deserved) (1) a sum sufficient to reward a supplier of goods or services ordered by another party when no price or charge was agreed before the order was placed. (2) a sum sufficient to reward a party for the work he had done under a contract before it was breached by another party.

quarantine SHIPG. (1) the isolation (separation) by order of the health authorities, of a ship and all persons on board her, to prevent the spread of infectious disease. (2) the period of this isolation. *See* pratique; clean ship.

quarry IND. a place where stone is dug or cut from the surface of the ground.

quart in corn and dry measure, and in liquid measure, two pints or a quarter of an imperial gallon = 1.136 litre. *Abbr.* qt.

quarter (1) FIN. in U.S.A. and Canada, a coin of value 25 cents, i.e. a quarter of a dollar. (2) LAW a period of 13 weeks or a quarter of a year. *See* quarter-day. (3) a weight of 28 lb. (12.70 kg) or a quarter of a hundredweight. (4) a length of 9 inches (0.229 m) or a quarter of a yard. (5) a volume, esp. of corn, of 8 bushels or 64 gallons (290.94 l). *Abbr.* qr.; qtr. (6) SHIPG. the side of a ship between her middle and her stern: *On the port quarter*, in a direction to the left and behind the ship. *Quarter-deck*, a deck sometimes reserved for officers, usu. part of the upper deck near the stern.

quarterage FIN. any regular payment made quarterly (four times a year), such as some rents, pensions, allowances and interest.

quarter-day LAW in Britain, one of the four days in the year on which quarterly payments become due, esp. for rent, and when tenancies begin and end. The days are: in England and Wales, Lady Day (25 March), Midsummer (24 June), Michaelmas (29 September), and Christmas (25 December); in Scotland, Candlemas (2 February), Whitsun (15 May), Lammas (1 August), and Martinmas (11 November). *Syn.* term days.

quarterly *adj.* (1) happening four times a year, i.e. once a quarter or every 13 weeks. *See* quarter-day. (2) ACCTS. *Quarterly accounts/balance/audit*, made or made up to the end of a quarter.
n. a magazine, journal, etc. published once every quarter, or four times a year.

quartiles in a set of variables arranged in increasing or decreasing order of value, the value of the variable that is midway between the median (the value in the middle of the order) and the highest variable (*upper quartile*) or between the median and the lowest variable (*lower quartile*). *See* median. Cf. mode.

quarto (1) a size of writing paper 10 in. × 8 in. (254 mm × 203 mm). (2) any sheet of paper folded twice to give four leaves, or a book of this size. *Abbr.* 4to.; qto.

quash LAW of a decision by a court of law, to refuse, to cancel, to make of no effect: *The Court of Appeal quashed the conviction and the prisoner was set free.*

quasi- *prefix*, (*Latin*, as if it were) apparently, but not really, or not wholly, so: *Quasi-judicial act*, an act seeming to be that of a judge but in fact made by a person or organization not part of the judiciary.

quasi-contract *see under* contract.

quasi-delict LAW in Scotland, a civil wrong or harm resulting from failure to perform a legal duty to take care. *Syn.* negligence.

quasi-money *see* near money *under* money.

quasi-rent *see under* rent.

quay SHIPG. a place in a port, harbour, river or dock basin where ships can tie up to the shore to load and unload cargo. *Syn.* dockside; quayside; berth; wharf. *Pron.* kee.

quayage SHIPG. the charge made by port authorities for the use of quays. *Syn.* quay dues. *Pron.* keyij.

quay port *see under* port.

Que. Quebec, Canada.

Queen's Bench *see* Court of Queen's Bench.

Queen's Counsel LAW in Britain, a barrister who has been appointed by the Lord Chancellor to take precedence over other barristers, i.e. to become a *leader* at the bar. Cf. junior (1). *Abbr.* Q.C.

queen's enemies INSCE. & TRANSPT. (loss by) enemy action, one of the *excepted perils* which are stated in ordinary insurance policies and contracts of carriage as risks not covered by the policy and for which the carriers are not liable. *See also* enemy.

queen's shilling *see* king's shilling.

queen's warehouse *see under* warehouse.

queer street FIN. (*colloq.*) a state of financial difficulty: *To be in queer street*, to be in financial trouble, known to be in debt and probably about to be made bankrupt.

query (1) a question; an enquiry. (2) an uncertainty or doubt: *I will pay the invoice when my query on it has been settled*, when my question about the correctness of some part of the invoice has been cleared. *Abbr.* qy.; Qy.

questionable (1) of doubtful honesty or morality: *Questionable practices/deals/transactions*. (2) doubtful, uncertain: *It is questionable whether we shall make a profit on this contract*.

questionnaire a printed list of questions used esp. in consumer research to obtain information about opinions, tastes and habits of the public.

quetzal the standard currency unit of Guatemala, divided into 100 centavos. *Pl.* quetzales.

quick asset ratio *see* acid ratio test.

quick assets *see under* assets, *pl.*

quick money *see under* money.

quid FIN. (*colloq.*) one pound (£1): *I paid him five quid for it*, I paid him five pounds. *To be quids in*, to make a good profit on a deal. *Pl.* quid *or* quids.

quid pro quo (*Latin*, something for something) something given in return for something received. *Syn.* consideration; compensation.

quiet STK. EXCH. of market conditions, inactive, with little business being done.

quietus FIN. release from a debt or other liability; a receipt. *To obtain one's quietus*, to be discharged from an obligation. *To give quietus*, to release (someone) from a debt or duty. *Pron.* kwy-ee-tus.

quinquennium a period of five years.
    quinquennial *adj. A quinquennial valuation/grant*.

quint. quintuplicate.

quintal a measure of weight. (*a*) in Britain, a hundredweight, 112 lb; (*b*) in U.S.A. and the Liverpool grain trade, 100 lb; (*c*) in the metric system, 100 kg or 220.46 lb.

quintar *see* qindar.

quintuplicate a fifth copy: *In quintuplicate*, five copies exactly the same, or an original and four (carbon) copies. Cf. duplicate, triplicate, etc. *Abbr.* quint.

quire a measure of quantity of paper, usu. 24 sheets, or one-twentieth part of a ream of 480 sheets. *See* ream. *Abbr.* qr.

quittance *see* acquittance.

quorum MAN. at a meeting of an organization, the least number of members that must be present if the business is to be legally transacted (dealt with). The number is fixed and included in the charter, articles or other governing rules of the organization. If there are not sufficient members present, the meeting must be adjourned to another day.

quot. quotation.

quota COM. (1) a share or portion: *A quota agreement*, when members of a cartel agree to the share of the market that each member shall have. (2) a limit placed by a government on the amount of imports or exports of a particular article or commodity. The government first decides the total amount for a given period, and then gives licences to importers or exporters up to this amount.

quotation (1) COM. a statement of the current price and conditions upon which a supplier is willing to sell, or upon which services may be performed: *A quotation for supply of goods/rate of exchange. See* estimate; account terms. *Abbr.* quot. (2) INSCE. a statement of the premium for which an insurer is willing to accept a proposal of insurance. (3) STK. EXCH. *see* application for quotation; admission to quotation; Quotations Committee. *Syn.* official quotation.

Quotations Committee of the (London) Stock Exchange STK. EXCH. a committee of the Council of the Stock Exchange that examines all applications by limited companies for their shares or stock to be officially quoted and dealt in by members of the Exchange. *See* application for quotation.

quote *v.* COM. to give or make a quotation. *N.* a quotation.

quoted securities *see* listed securities *under* listed.

quoted share *see under* share.

Qy., qy. query.

R

R Romania's international vehicle-registration letter.

R. River; return (ticket, fare).

RA Argentina's international vehicle-registration letters.

R/A. refer to acceptor (bills of exchange).

r. & c.c. riot and civil commotion.

R. & D. research and development.

Rachmanism COM. the practice of some cruel and greedy landlords, of charging excessive rents for their properties and of using immoral and unlawful methods to drive their tenants away so that the properties can be let at higher rents.

racial discrimination *see under* discrimination.

racket COM. an organized plot to obtain money (*a*) from traders by threats of violence (*see* protection); (*b*) from the public by dishonest trading. *Syn.* ramp.

racketeer a person who organizes a racket.

rack-rent *see under* rent.

rack-renter (1) a person who lets land on lease in return for rack-rent. (2) a person who holds or uses land in return for payment of rack-rent.

radiogram a message sent by radio. A radio telegram. Cf. telegram; cable.

radio telegram *see under* telegram.

raffle a lottery for prizes that are usu. attractive goods, not sums of money.

rag trade COM. & IND. (*colloq.*) the activity of designing, manufacturing and selling clothes, esp. for women and children. *Syn.* the clothing trade.

rail *n.* TRANSPT. the railway as a form of transport: *Goods carried by rail. The journey is quicker by rail than by road. British Rail*, the system operated by British Railways. *Syn.* railway; (U.S.A.) railroad.
adj. relating to railways: *Rail travel/traffic*.

railcar *see under* car.

railhead TRANSPT. the place at which a railway line ends, esp. the furthest point from a port or from a commercial or industrial area. From this point, goods and passengers have to be carried by other means of transport, such as by road, river or canal.

railman a man who works on a railway. *Syn.* railwayman.

railroad (U.S.A.) TRANSPT. a railway. *Railroad track*, a railway line or track.

railroad bill of lading *see under* bill of lading.

railroad car *see under* car.

rails STK. EXCH. (*colloq.*) stocks and shares of railway companies.

railway advice TRANSPT. a document sent by a railway advising (informing) the consignee that goods have arrived at the local railway station and asking him to remove them.

railway carriage *see* carriage (3).

railway gauge *see* gauge (3).

railwayman *see* railman.

railway stocks/shares *see* rails.

raise *v.* FIN. (1) to arrange, to organize, esp. the obtaining of money: *To raise a loan/mortgage*. (*colloq.*) *To raise the wind*, to obtain money needed quickly. (2) to collect money: *To raise a tax/subscriptions/funds*.
n. (mainly U.S.A.) (1) an increase of wages or salary. (2) the amount of this increase. *Syn.* rise.

rake-off (*colloq.*) (1) a share of the profit or of the amount received in a business deal. (2) a secret, perh. unlawful, commission.

rally *v.* STK. & COMMOD. EXCH. of prices in the market, to regain strength, to improve: *Prices fell early but rallied later. The market rallied.*
n. an improvement: *An early rally was followed by dull trading.*

ramifications *n. pl.* COM. & IND. the branches or other organized units that are parts or subdivisions of a larger organization, esp. when spread over a wide area or over a large number of different activities: *A company with worldwide ramifications*, one having branches, agents, etc. all over the world. *The ramifications of the group include all kinds of groceries, soft drinks, and household cleaners.*

ramp *see* racket.

ranch *n.* AGR. a large farm with a wide area of grazing land on which cattle, horses and sheep are bred, esp. in Australia and N. America. *Syn.* (S. America) rancho; (New Zealand) station.
v. to own or to work on a ranch.

rancher AGR. (1) a worker on a ranch. (2) the owner of a ranch.

rand the standard currency unit of the Republic of South Africa, divided into 100 cents.

range COM. (1) a set of different articles of the same class, from which a choice can be made: *We stock a good range of woodworker's tools. They make a wide range of patterns/colours/ qualities.* (2) a line of shops, stalls, etc. esp. in a market. (3) the limits between which things vary: *A range of prices from £1 to £10.* (4) AGR. an area of wild grassland where animals may be put to graze: *The country provides plentiful range for cattle.* (5) *Free-range, see under* free.

rank *v.* FIN. & LAW to have a place in a set order fixed by law: *Preference shares rank for dividend before ordinary shares. Secured creditors rank for payment before unsecured creditors.*

ransom FIN. a price demanded or paid to obtain the release of a person held as prisoner, or of a valuable object that has been stolen. *To hold to ransom*, to hold a person or thing until the money demanded for his or its release has been paid. *A king's ransom*, a very high price, or a very large amount of money.

rarity ECON. the state of being few in numbers.

Ras al-Khaimah *see* United Arab Emirates.

ratable *see* rateable.

ratal TAXN. the rateable value, the amount on which rates (local taxes) are based in Britain. Cf. rental. *See* annual value.

rate (1) INSCE. the amounts charged by an insurer for different kinds of risk. The amount is usu. expressed as a percentage, e.g. a rate of £1.50 per cent, i.e. £1.50 for every £100 of the sum for which the goods, property, etc. are insured.
average rate the average of several rates for different kinds of risk.
short-period rate a rate for an insurance contract lasting less than a year.

(2) COM. & IND. the price of a unit of a commodity or service: *We enclose a list of our rates for supplying building materials/servicing boilers. A rate scale*, a fixed scale of charges. *A rate card*, a printed card listing these charges. *The rate of pay for a fitter is £2 per hour*, also called *the rate for the job* or *the going rate*. (3) TAXN. a payment based on a scale of charges, such as for a public water supply and sewerage, called a water rate, which is based on the rateable value of the property concerned. *See also* rates, *pl.*

rateable TAXN. in Britain, of buildings, etc., on which rates (local taxes) have to be paid. *Also* (U.S.A.) ratable.

rateable value *see* annual value.

rate-deficiency grant *see under* grant.

rate of exchange *see* exchange rate.

rate of interest *see* interest rate.

ratepayer TAXN. in Britain, the person or organization liable to pay rates (local taxes) on property, usu. the householder. Cf. taxpayer.

rates *n. pl.* TAXN. in Britain, local taxes payable to a local government authority, based on the annual or rateable value of properties, to pay for local public services. The amount payable on a property each year is calculated by multiplying the rateable value by the rate-poundage fixed annually by the rating authority at so many pence in the pound (of rateable value). The local authorities also receive grants from the central government. The charges for water supply and sewerage, called a *water rate*, are collected separately by the local water authority. *Syn.* municipal taxes; local taxes.

rates rebate *see* rates relief.

rates relief TAXN. a reduction of local authority rates (local taxes on property) for ratepayers who have low incomes. *Syn.* rates rebate.

rate-support grant *see under* grant.

ratify LAW to approve and adopt a contract; to give one's formal agreement to a document or arrangement, esp. when made by an agent or representative. *N.* ratification.

ratio the relation between two quantities expressed as the number of times one is greater than the other. The proportion between one quantity and another. Thus, if at a meeting 66 people vote in favour of a motion and 33 vote against, the ratio is 2 to 1, or 2:1, in favour. *Other examples: see* advances ratio; dividend-price ratio; price-earnings ratio.

ration an allowance, usu. fixed by authority, which each person may buy, esp. of food, clothing, fuel or other essential commodities, usu. in time of war or other national emergency.

rationalization MAN. & IND. a planned reorganization of an industry to improve its efficiency, usu. by horizontal and vertical combination of manufacturing units, by closing factories that make a loss, increasing the output of those that are profitable, and generally by reducing administrative costs. *See* combination.

RC Taiwan's international vehicle-registration letters.

RCA the Central African Republic's international vehicle-registration letters.

RCB Congo (Brazzaville)'s international vehicle-registration letters.

R.C.D. Regional Co-operation for Development.

RCH Chile's international vehicle-registration letters.

Rd. Road.

r.d. running days.

R/D (on a dishonoured cheque) refer to drawer.

Rds. roads (anchorage).

Re. rupee (*pl.* Rs).

re with reference to; in the case/matter of.

re- *prefix*, (1) again; repeating: *reappoint*, to appoint again; *rebuild*, to build again; *re-cover*, to cover again. (2) back: *recover*, to get back; *retrace*, to trace back.

reach SHIPG. a straight stretch of a river.

react STK. & COMMOD. EXCH. of market prices, to move in an opposite direction: *Markets reacted sharply to rumours of devaluation*, prices, which had been rising, fell after the rumours became known.

readable (1) that can easily be read and understood. (2) in plain language, not in code.

readership circulation *see under* circulation.

readership survey *see under* survey.

ready cash *see* cash, *n.* (1).

ready-made COM. & FIN. mainly of clothes and footwear, supplied ready to wear, not made to measure.

ready market *see under* market.

ready money *see under* money.

ready-money crop *see* cash crop.

ready reckoner a book of tables for use when making calculations of quantities and money.

ready sales *see under* sales.

ready, the (*colloq.*) ready money; cash in notes and coins.

real accounts *see* accounts, *n. pl.*

real assets *see* assets (2).

real capital *see under* capital.

real chattel *see* chattel real *under* chattel.

real cost *see* opportunity cost *under* cost.

real damages *see under* damages, *n. pl.*

reale a fractional currency unit of the Dominican Republic. 8 reales *or* 100 centavos = 1 peso.

real estate LAW & COM. an interest in land and buildings, esp. freehold property. *Syn.* real property; immovable property; realty.

real estate tax *see* property tax *under* tax.

real income *see under* income.

real investment *see under* investment.

realizable FIN. of investments, assets, etc., able to be sold quickly for cash. *Opp.* unrealizable.

realizable assets *see* quick assets *under* assets.

realization FIN. the sale of assets for cash, e.g. when a partnership is dissolved (brought to an end).

realization account ACCTS. a special account prepared on the dissolution (ending) of a partnership, to which amounts received from the realization of assets are credited, and the book value of the assets and the realization expenses are debited. The final balance of the account will show whether there has been a profit or a loss on realization.

realization concept ACCTS. the basic idea in accounting, that profit is regarded as made at the time when a sale takes place, i.e. when goods or services pass to the customer, not when the order is received, nor when a contract is signed, nor when the customer actually pays.

realize FIN. to sell assets for cash. *Syn.* to liquidate.

realized profit *see under* profit.

real money *see under* money.

real property *see under* property.

real securities *see under* securities.

realtor (U.S.A.) *see* estate agent.

realty *see* real property *under* property.

real value *see under* value.

real wage *see under* wage.

ream a standard measure of paper, 500 sheets, called a long ream in U.S.A. Formerly a *stationer's ream* or *mill ream* was 480 sheets or 20 quires of 24 sheets each; a *printer's ream*, also called a *perfect ream*, was 516 sheets (21½ quires to allow for wastage). *Abbr.* Rm.

reasonable moderate, not excessive: *Reasonable prices. A reasonable rate of interest.*

reassure *see* reinsure.

rebate (1) COM. an allowance of money in reduction of an amount to be paid, etc.; a discount: *A rebate for prompt payment. A rebate of tax. An export rebate.* Cf. refund. *See* aggregated rebates. *Syn.* discount (from a price); abatement (of tax); deduction.

quantity rebate *see* quantity discount *under* discount.

(2) BKG. a discount or reduction allowed on a bill of exchange which is paid before maturity (the date it becomes due for payment). (3) INSCE. *see* return premium *under* premium.

rebuttal LAW disproving, esp. of evidence given in a court of law.

recd., rec'd. received.

recede STK. & COMMOD. EXCH. of market prices, to fall, to move back or lower.

receipt *n.* (1) the act of receiving something: *To acknowledge receipt of a parcel/letter/cheque.* (2) COM. & ACCTS. a formal acknowledgment that money due has been paid or that goods have been received. A receipt for money is usu. in these words: *Received from Mr XYZ the sum of twenty-five pounds sixteen pence.* It

is signed and dated by the person receiving the money or by a person authorized to act for him. A copy of the receipt or a note of its contents is kept as an accounts voucher (record).

dock receipt *see under* dock.

mate's receipt *see under* mate.

trust receipt BKG. a signed document given to a bank by an importer who has accepted a D/P (documents-against-payment) bill of exchange but is not able to pay at the time the goods arrive. The document acknowledges receipt of the shipping documents and promises that the importer will pay the amount of the bill and the bank's charges when the goods have been sold. The bank meanwhile pays the exporter. Such an arrangement will only be possible where the bank can trust the importer to pay when the goods have been sold.

wharfinger's receipt SHIPG. & TRANSPT. a receipt given by a wharfinger (a person who owns or manages a wharf) to a carrier for goods delivered to a warehouse to be loaded into a ship. *Syn.* dock receipt.

to receipt a bill *v.* to write or stamp 'paid' on it, and to sign and date it.

receipts *pl.* FIN. money received: *Receipts from the sale of old machinery amounted to £1000. The receipts exceeded the expenses, leaving a surplus.*

receipts and payments account ACCTS. an account prepared by a small non-trading organization that does not own any assets, such as a club or society, the purpose of the account being to show only the cash position. The account is a summary of the cash book. *Syn.* income and expenditure account.

receivable FIN. & ACCTS. due to be received, as opposed to payable. *See* account receivable; bills receivable.

received bill of lading *see under* bill of lading.

receiver (1) a person who receives something. *Syn.* recipient. (2) an instrument that receives signals, etc.: *A telephone/radio receiver.* (3) LAW an officer appointed by the court in cases of disagreement about ownership, to act for other persons in receiving and taking charge of income from rents and profits and in protecting property while the claims of the parties are heard and settled. Receivers are also appointed, usu. by the courts: to realize assets when a partnership is dissolved (ended); in bankruptcy cases; when a mortgagee uses a power of sale; to manage the affairs of a person who is too ill mentally to manage them himself; and in certain other cases. *See also* official receiver. (4) LAW a person who receives stolen property. *Syn.* fence.

receiving note SHIPG. a note from a shipper to the master of a ship asking him to receive certain stated goods on board.

receiving order *see* petition in bankruptcy *under* bankruptcy.

reception (1) in a hotel or office, a place just inside the entrance where guests and visitors are received by a person called *a receptionist*. (2) a formal social gathering, usu. to receive or welcome somebody.

recession ECON. a temporary reduction in business activity, not as severe as a depression. *Opp.* boom. *See* trade cycle *under* cycle.

recipient a person who receives something.

reciprocal given equally to each other by two persons, organizations or countries: *A reciprocal trade agreement between Egypt and India. Reciprocal aid*, aid given in return for help received. *Reciprocal insurance, see* mutual insurance *under* insurance, classes and kinds of. *N.* reciprocity.

reciprocity COM. in foreign trade, agreement between two countries to charge specially low rates of duty on imports of each other's goods. *Syn.* fair trade.

reckless careless; not caring about the possible results of hasty action: *Reckless trading*, buying goods hastily without thinking whether they will be sold at a profit. *Reckless spending*, spending money now without caring about future needs.

reckon *v.* (1) to count; to calculate; to work out: *We reckon the cost of materials at £5 per article. Interest is reckoned from the date payment was due. Syn.* (U.S.A.) to figure out. (2) to settle a debt.

reckoning *n.* an account; a bill for an amount to be paid, esp. in a hotel, restaurant or shop.

reckoner *see* ready reckoner.

reclaim *v.* AGR. & IND. to make useless land usable: *To reclaim land from the sea/a marsh.* **reclamation** *n.* (*a*) the act of reclaiming land. (*b*) land that has been reclaimed, esp. from the sea. *A reclamation project/scheme.*

recognizance LAW a solemn promise made in a court of law, binding the person making the promise, *the recognizor*, and another person in whose interest it is made, *the recognizee*, to perform a stated act, such as to appear before the court, or before another court, when called upon to do so. If the promise is broken, an agreed sum of money has to be paid: *Enter into recognizances.*

recommended price *see under* price.

recompense *n.* (1) a payment as reward for some service. (2) a repayment in compensation for a loss. Cf. reimbursement. *V.* to recompense.

reconcile *v.* ACCTS. to bring into agreement, such as when two accounts that should agree do not. *See* reconciliation statement *under* statement; bank reconciliation statement *under* bank.

reconstruction the rebuilding of the industry, commerce, and social services of an economy that has been destroyed or severely damaged by war or some great natural misfortune, such as an earthquake.

Reconstruction and Development, International Bank for *see under* International.

reconstruction (of a company) STK. EXCH. & MAN. the changing of the capital structure of a limited company, esp. a company that is having financial difficulties. The change may be done: (*a*) by a merger or amalgamation with another company; (*b*) by forming a new company to receive the assets of the old company, for which the shareholders receive in exchange shares in the new company; (c) by a scheme of arrangement (*see under* scheme). *Syn.* reorganization.

recorded delivery in Britain, a service provided by the Post Office by which the sender of an inland letter or postal packet is given proof of its safe delivery to the addressee, and a small sum is paid in compensation if it is lost or damaged in the post. This service is cheaper than registered post.

recoup FIN. & COM. (1) to regain; to get back: *To recoup one's losses.* (2) to repay somebody his expenses (*see* reimburse). *N.* recoupment.

recourse (1) BKG. the right of the payee or holder of a bill of exchange that is dishonoured at its maturity to demand payment from the other parties, such as the drawer or an endorser, unless these parties have written the words *without recourse* or *sans recours* against their signatures. (2) FIN. a source of help; a person or place from which help can be obtained: *The company had recourse to the capital market*, obtained financial help from the capital market.

recover *v.* (1) FIN. to get back; to regain: *To recover one's expenses/costs/money. Syn.* recoup. (2) LAW to obtain payment under judgment of a court: *To recover damages and costs.* (3) STK. & COMMOD. EXCH. of market prices, to improve, to become higher again: *Prices recovered on publication of better trade figures.*

recoverable that can be recovered, got back, esp. of freight and other expenses. *Opp.* irrecoverable; non-recoverable; unrecoverable.

recovery (1) INSCE. any money which reduces the amount of a loss, such as salvage, the finding of lost or stolen goods, etc. (2) ECON. *see* trade cycle *under* cycle. (3) LAW the right to obtain payment or possession of property under a judgment of a court of law: *Recovery proceedings*, steps taken to obtain payment of a debt by bringing a lawsuit against the debtor.

rectify ACCTS. to put right: *We have found and rectified the errors/mistakes in the cash book. A rectified invoice*, one that is correct and replaces an earlier invoice containing a mistake. *Syn.* to correct; to adjust.

recto (1) the front of a document. (2) the right-hand page of a book. Cf. verso.

recuperate STK. EXCH. of market prices, to recover; to become higher: *Shares fell sharply before noon but recuperated towards the close.*

recurrent *or* **recurring costs** *see* variable costs *under* costs.

red. redeemable.

red BKG. (*colloq.*) *In the red*, of a bank customer's current account, overdrawn, i.e. having a debit balance (formerly written or typed in red ink in the account).

redeem (1) STK. EXCH. to repay or pay off, esp. loan stock, debentures and preference shares or stock. (2) FIN. to recover property that has been pledged or mortgaged as security for a loan, by repaying the loan. *To redeem a mortgage. Syn.* to amortize. (3) generally, to do something that one has bound oneself to do: *To redeem a promise. See* redemption.

redeemable bond *see* callable bond *under* bond, *n.*

redeemable debenture *see under* debenture.

redeemable goods FIN. goods that are in pawn, and can be redeemed (recovered) only when the loan for which they were left as security has been repaid.

redeemable preference share *see under* share.

redeemable stock *see under* stock.

redemption (1) FIN. & STK. EXCH. the act or process of redeeming, of paying off a loan. (2) BKG. the act of a note-issuing bank in giving cash in exchange for its bank-notes. (3) LAW the right of a mortgagor to recover mortgaged property on repayment of the loan and any interest due. *Syn.* equity of redemption.

redemption date *see under* date.

redemption, equity of *see under* equity.

redemption yield *see under* yield.

redevelopment COM. & IND. the rebuilding or improvement of private or commercial properties (houses, shops and offices) in the older parts of towns. *See also* property development.

redirect to readdress, esp. mail for somebody who has moved to another address. *Syn.* to forward.

rediscounting BKG. the discounting of a bill of exchange or promissory note that has already been discounted for another holder.

redistribution (of incomes and wealth) TAXN. the practice of governments of some countries of introducing taxes, such as a gifts tax, a capital gains tax and higher-rate taxes on investment income, that will cause wealth, and therefore incomes, to be more evenly distributed. In this way a greater part of the national income will be received by a greater proportion of the people.

re-draft a foreign bill of exchange, drawn by the holder of a dishonoured bill, for a sum equal to the amount of the dishonoured bill and the expenses of protest, etc. Cf. renewed bill.

red tape *see under* tape.

reduced *see* reduction of capital.

reducing balance method ACCTS. a way of providing for the depreciation of an asset by writing off each year a fixed percentage of its value the previous year, so that its book value will be equal to its scrap value at the end of its useful life. This method is usual for motor vehicles. *See* depreciation methods. *Syn.* reducing instalment system.

reducing instalment system *see* reducing balance method.

reduction of capital STK. EXCH. the act of a limited company in reducing its capital. To be effective, the reduction must be allowed by the Articles, be approved by a special resolution of the members (shareholders), and be confirmed by the court, which may order that the words *and reduced* shall be added to the company's name for a stated period, thus: *T. Smith and Company, Limited and Reduced.*

redundancy MAN. & IND. REL. of an employee, the state of being no longer needed by his employer. An employee whose job ceases to exist because there is no work for him. In Britain, such employees receive compensation called *redundancy payment* based on pay and length of service. They are helped by the government to find work in the same occupation, or to be trained for work in a different occupation.

reefer SHIPG. a refrigerated ship.

re-entry visa *see under* visa.

re-examination *see under* examination.

re-exchange BKG. the amount that the holder of a dishonoured foreign bill of exchange may by law recover from the drawer or from an endorser. The sum is calculated by taking the current market cost of a sight bill for the original amount and adding interest, the cost of the protest, commission, postage and any other expenses resulting from the dishonour.

re-exports COM. goods that have been imported and then exported in the same form, i.e. not put through any manufacturing or finishing process. *See* entrepôt.

Ref., ref. reference; refrigerated ship.

referee (1) BKG. a person or organization named in a bill of exchange as a *referee in case of need*, from whom the holder may demand payment if the bill is dishonoured. *See* case of need. (2) MAN. a person named by an applicant for a job as someone who will, if asked, support the applicant's character and qualifications. *Syn.* reference. (3) LAW an arbitrator. (4) LAW a person appointed by the parties in a dispute to settle differences between arbitrators. He is called a *special referee* or *umpire*. (5) LAW an official of a court of law, called an *official referee*, who reports on, and sometimes decides, matters about which he has special knowledge and is better able to decide than a judge and jury.

reference (1) at the top of a business letter, a note, usu. consisting of the initials of the persons signing and typing the letter, thus: AG/MJ. Sometimes the reference consists of the initials of a department and a file number, thus: SD/2539. Persons answering the letter, or referring to it, are expected to quote the reference so that the papers can easily be found in the files. (2) COM. persons or firms named by a customer asking a supplier for credit, from whom the supplier can get information about the business reputation of the customer. *Trade references* are members of the customer's own trade. *A banker's reference* is the customer's own bank. *See also* referee (2); character (1).

refer to drawer BKG. a note or answer written or stamped by the drawer's bank on a cheque that the bank will not honour. This is usu. because: there is not a sufficient credit balance in the drawer's account; or because the cheque has been stopped by the drawer; or because the amount in words and figures on the cheque do not agree; or because there is a garnishee order against the drawer; or because the drawer has been made bankrupt. The words mean that the payee should ask the drawer to pay or to explain why the cheque is not being honoured. *Abbr.* R/D.

refinancing FIN. & STK. EXCH. repaying loan capital, such as bonds or debentures, by fresh borrowing, usu. at a lower rate of interest. *Syn.* refunding.

reflate ECON. to adopt a policy of reflation of the economy.

reflation ECON. action by a government aimed to reduce excessive unemployment after a period of deflation, by encouraging a controlled increase in the supply of money to increase demand, but without going so far as to cause inflation.

reform *v.* to change the shape of something for the better; to improve, esp. a system that is unfair or inefficient: *To reform the company laws to protect the interests of investors.*

reformer a person who believes in and works for reform.

refrigerated warehouse *see* cold store.

refugee capital *see* hot money *under* money.

refuge, port of *see under* port.

refund *v.* to repay; to give back money: *We shall refund you your expenses. To refund a debt.* *n.* a repayment of money: *The railway will give you a refund of freight if the goods are lost.*

refundable repayable: *A refundable deposit.*

refund annuity *see under* insurance policy.

refunding *see* refinancing.

refunding bond *see under* bond, *n.*

reg. registration.

reg., regd. registered.

region *n.* (1) a large area of the earth's surface having some special quality or character: *A desert region. The natural/climatic/polar/equatorial regions of the earth.* (2) the area round a certain place: *The London region,* or in a part of a country: *The northern region of Nigeria.* (3) a division of an organization, such as the *Eastern Region* of British Rail.

regional *adj.* relating to a region or regions: *Regional transport services,* the services within a region, or between one region and another. *Regional geography,* the study of the geography of special regions of the earth.

Regional Co-operation for Development (R.C.D.) an association of countries in south-central Asia, Iran, Pakistan and Turkey, for economic, technical and cultural co-operation.

register *n.* a document, usu. in the form of a book, in which are recorded important lists of persons, places, things, events, etc.

cash register *see under* cash.

charges register *see under* charges.

company register *see* register of companies.

hotel register a book kept usu. in the entrance-hall of a hotel, in which the name, address and room-number of each visitor staying in the hotel are recorded. *See also* check in *under* check, *v.*

Lloyd's Register *see under* Lloyd's.

property register *see under* property.

proprietorship register *see under* proprietorship.

shareholders' register *see* register of members.

ship's register *see* certificate of registry *under* registry.

transfer register a register in which are recorded all transfers of a limited company's shares, also called *transfer book(s)*. These books are usu. closed for a number of days each year before the annual general meeting; no transfers of shares are registered during this period.
v. to record in a register.

registered bond *see under* bond, *n.*

registered capital *see* authorized capital.

registered coupon bond *see under* bond, *n.*

registered debenture *see under* debenture.

registered design *see under* design.

registered office *see under* office.

registered post in Britain, a service provided by the Post Office for transporting and delivering valuable or important letters and packets. In return for an extra charge for insurance and a registration fee, very special care is taken to see that they are safely carried and delivered only on signature of a receipt by the addressee. Compensation is paid to the sender in case of loss.

registered proprietor the owner of a property the title of which is recorded in a proprietorship register at the Land Registry.

registered share *see under* share.

registered stock *see under* stock.

registered title see under title.

register of charges LAW a register which has by law to be kept at the registered office of a limited liability company. In it are recorded all charges which relate to the company's assets. See charges on assets. Cf. charges register.

register of debenture-holders LAW & STK. EXCH. a book that must be kept by every limited company, giving details of its debenture-holders and their holdings.

register of directors LAW & STK. EXCH. in Britain, a register or book that every company must by law keep, showing the name, address, nationality and occupation of all the directors and managers of the company. A copy must be sent to the Registrar of Companies, who must be told of all changes made in the register.

register of directors' shareholdings LAW & STK. EXCH. in Britain, a book that every limited company must keep, showing the number of shares (or stock) and debentures of the company and its subsidiaries and holding company held by each of its directors; and details of all such shares and debentures bought or sold by the directors.

register office see under office.

register of members LAW & STK. EXCH. in Britain, a book that every limited company must keep, showing the shares held by each member (shareholder), distinguishing each share by its number, or the amount of stock held by each member, and the amount paid, or agreed to be considered as paid on the shares or stock of each member; also the date each person was entered in the register as a member, and the date he ceased to be a member. The register must be open, for at least two hours each day, to be examined by a member free of charge, and by any other person on payment of a small charge. It may be closed for not more than 30 days in each year if notice is given by advertisement in a newspaper circulating in the district in which the company's registered office is situated. Syn. share register; shareholders' register.

register of transfers see transfer register under register.

register ton see vessel ton under ton.

register tonnage see under tonnage of ships.

registrar (1) in Britain, an official responsible for keeping a register, esp. in a university. (2) one who keeps official records of births, deaths and marriages at a local office of the Registrar-General. (3) in a company, an employee who is in charge of the work of recording all transfers of the company's shares in the transfer register.

Registrar-General of Shipping SHIPG. in Britain, the public official responsible for registering ships. All British sea-going ships over 15 tons must by law be registered with him.

Registrar in Bankruptcy LAW in Britain, an official of the Bankruptcy Court who holds a public examination of the debtor and, if no composition or scheme of arrangement has been arranged, declares him bankrupt. See bankruptcy.

Registrar of Companies LAW in Britain, a government official who is responsible for the registration of limited companies and for keeping detailed records about them. He issues a Certificate of Incorporation to each new company as an acknowledgment that all necessary formalities have been properly completed.

Registrar of Friendly Societies see friendly society.

Registro Italiano Navale SHIPG. the Italian ship-classification society. Cf. Lloyd's Register of Shipping. Abbr. R.I.

registry a place, esp. an office, where a register is kept, where continuous and detailed records are collected and are usu. open for the public to examine, such as the Land Registry.

central registry a section in most government offices where files are kept and their movements between offices are recorded.

Land Charges Registry see under Land Charges.

Land Registry see under Land.

registry, certificate of SHIPG. an important document which the master of a ship must always carry and show when asked. It proves that the ship has been registered in a certain country and gives certain details about the ship such as her number, the name of her owner(s), her home port, her registered tonnage, the number of passengers she may carry, etc. Syn. certificate of ownership; ship's register.

registry office see register office under office.

registry, port of SHIPG. the port at which a ship is registered and where her owners can be found. All ships above a certain size must show the name of their port of registry on the stern of the vessel. Syn. home port.

regrating see forestalling.

regressive supply see under supply.

regressive tax see under tax.

regret, letter of see letter of regret.

regular adj. (1) COM. of goods, of normal size; of ordinary or moderate quality. This is our regular size of handkerchief, the size that most people buy. (2) of persons, keeping set times: He is very regular in his attendance, he is punctual and seldom absent. (3) A regular member, a full member, not an associate or other kind of member. (4) MAN. happening at fixed times: A regular meeting. A regular delivery of fuel-oil. **regular** n. (colloq.) a regular customer, one who frequently comes to buy.

regulation n. control and management: The regulation of traffic in the city centre. The regulation of trade between two countries.

regulations *n. pl.* (1) MAN. rules having the force of authority, esp. in relation to the control and management of an organization: *Staff regulations*, rules of behaviour to be followed by the employees. *Building regulations*, government rules for house-builders. *Fire regulations*, rules to be followed if there is a fire. *Quarantine regulations*, see quarantine. (2) LAW in the European Economic Community, a proposal made by the European Commission to the Council of Ministers and approved by that Council, becomes part of the statute law of all the members of the Community. (3) in Britain, one of the rules made by a government department under powers given to it by Parliament and having the force of law, such as the Motor Vehicles (Construction and Use) Regulations made by the Department of the Environment.

regulatory tax *see under* tax.

Reichsmark the (former) standard currency unit of Germany from 1924 to 1948, when it was replaced by the Deutsche Mark. *Abbr.* RM.

reimburse FIN. to repay a person who has spent money as one's agent or employee: *To reimburse a representative (for) his travelling expenses. N.* reimbursement.

reimport COM. to bring back into a country an article or commodity that has earlier been exported from the same country, such as a motor car being reimported after temporary export.

reinstate (1) to put back; to replace in a former position. (2) IND. REL. to give a dismissed worker his job back. (3) LAW to put back part of a document that has been cut out: *To reinstate a clause in a form of agreement.* (4) INSCE. *see* reinstatement.

reinstatement INSCE. (1) the replacing by the insurers of a thing lost by a thing of the same kind, quality and condition, so that the insured is neither richer nor poorer as a result of the loss. *See* indemnity; reinstatement policy *under* insurance policy. (2) the bringing into force again of a policy which, following a loss, has not been in force for some time.

reinsurance *see under* insurance, classes and kinds of.

reinsure INSCE. as an insurer, to share a risk with another insurer by transferring part of it to him, the premium also being shared in proportion. *See* reinsurance *under* insurance, classes and kinds of.

reinsured INSCE. an insurer who has reinsured a risk, i.e. has arranged with one or more other insurers to share any loss that may arise.

reinsurer INSCE. an insurer who accepts a reinsurance, i.e. who agrees to bear a fixed part of a loss insured by another insurer.

reject *v.* COM. & IND. (1) to refuse to take; to send back or throw away (goods) as unacceptable. *Rejected goods.* (2) to decide against, e.g. a

request; a motion at a meeting; an applicant for a job; a proposal, plan or idea. *Pron.* rejéct.
n. an article being sold cheap because it is imperfect. *Pron.* reeject. *Syn.* seconds, *pl.*

relapse STK. & COMMOD. EXCH. of market prices, to slip back, to return to a former low level: *Shares relapsed for lack of buyers of any kind.*

related company *see* affiliate company *under* affiliate.

relations, public *see* public relations.

release *see* freight release.

relief *see* tax relief.

remainder (1) LAW the interest of a person who will become the legal owner of an estate in land when the present life-tenant dies. (2) COM. in the book-publishing trade, what remains of the publisher's stock of a book after the main sale has ended and sales are slow; at this stage copies of the book are sometimes sold at a greatly reduced price; they are *remaindered*.

remainderman LAW a person who has the right to a remainder. Cf. a reversioner.

remand LAW a court order adjourning the hearing of a criminal case to a later date and directing that until then the accused person shall be held in prison (*remanded in custody*) or set free but on bail (*remanded on bail*).

remedy LAW a legal means of setting right a wrong, such as the bringing of a lawsuit by the injured party.

remisier *see* half-commission man.

remission (1) BKG. & FIN. the act of remitting, of making a remittance. (2) LAW release from prison (being set free) before the end of the sentence (period ordered by the court to be spent in prison). Remission is given usu. for good behaviour while in prison. (3) an official pardon. (4) TAX a repayment to the taxpayer by the tax authorities, of tax that he has overpaid. *Syn.* refund.

remittance (1) BKG. & FIN. a sum of money sent (remitted) from one place to another. (*The remitter* is the person sending the money; *the remittee* is the person to whom it is sent.) *To send/make a remittance.* (2) BKG. parcels of coins, notes, cheques, bills, etc. sent from one banking office to another.

immigrant remittance(s) *see under* immigrant.

remittance man (1) a man living abroad on money which he receives from his home country. (2) a person who is paid to keep away from his home country.

remittance slip ACCTS. & COM. a small printed form sent out blank with an invoice and intended to be sent back with the remittance by the person paying the invoice. When filled in by the payer, the slip tells the person receiving the money where it has come from and which invoice it relates to.

remote cause LAW & INSCE. a distant cause; a

cause which is not an immediate cause. Cf. proximate cause.

removal (1) TRANSPT. the act of moving the contents of a home, office, factory, etc. from one place to another.

removals *pl.* the business of making such moves.

(2) MAN. dismissal from office: *The members voted for the removal of the officers.*

removal bond *see under* bond, *n.*

removal expenses *see under* expenses.

removal van TRANSPT. a lorry specially designed, with a high roof and low floor, for transporting furniture.

remunerate FIN. & MAN. to pay (somebody) money for his services; to reward for work: *He is well remunerated for his responsibilities,* he is well paid. *The job is badly remunerated,* the pay is low.

remuneration FIN. & MAN. (1) money paid for services, not for goods. *Auditors' remuneration,* the fee paid by a business to the accountant(s) appointed to audit the accounts. (2) salary or wages: *We are increasing your remuneration by 10%.*

remunerative FIN. & MAN. profitable; that earns, brings in, a satisfactory income: *A remunerative business/job/occupation/hobby.*

render (1) to give; to perform: *To render a service/services/aid/assistance. Services rendered,* past, not future services. (2) ACCTS. to prepare and send out: *We render monthly statements by post. Account rendered,* a reference to an account that has been sent earlier. *N.* rendering; rendition.

rendu *see* franco.

renew (1) to extend the time for which an existing instrument, contract, etc. is to be effective: *To renew a bill of exchange/promissory note/insurance policy/lease/agency agreement/ licence.* (2) to make alive or effective again: *To renew one's business contacts. Let us renew public interest in our product by advertising it widely.*

renewal notice INSCE. a notice, often in the form of an invoice, sent by an insurance company to the insured, inviting him to renew the contract, i.e. to continue it, usu. for one year, by paying the renewal premium.

renewal premium *see under* premium.

renewed bill *see under* bill of exchange.

renounce to give up formally: *He renounced his claim to a share in the profits. N.* renunciation.

rent (1) ECON. money paid for the use of land considered as a factor of production; the price of, or the income received from, land. (2) FIN. the sum of money received by the owner of property in land and buildings as a periodic payment from an occupier or tenant. (3) (*colloq.*) any periodic payment charged for the use of a good.

chief-rent *see under* chief.

contractual rent the periodic payment for the hiring and use for a limited period of an asset such as land, buildings and machines.

dead rent *see under* dead.

differential rent a rent that is higher than normal because it includes a payment for some special advantage. *See* fertility rent; situation rent *below.*

economic rent in economic theory, an extra amount earned by a factor of production over and above what is needed to keep that factor from being moved to some other use. Note that the factor of production is not necessarily land, but can be any of the other factors such as labour and capital. *See* rack-rent.

fertility rent the extra rent that has to be paid for land that is more fertile than other land. A form of differential rent.

ground rent rent paid to a ground landlord by a holder of property that has been leased to him on condition that he builds a house or other buildings on it. Cf. chief-rent.

implicit rent ECON. THEORY the amount of rent that the owner of a piece of land could get if he let it to a tenant instead of using it for himself. It is the sacrifice he is making by not letting the land.

peppercorn rent *see under* peppercorn.

quasi-rent ECON. THEORY the extra payment that has to be made for the use of a factor of production, other than land, that is for the time being and in the short term abnormally scarce, such as the short-run surplus earned by a new and highly efficient machine.

rack-rent (*a*) the full annual rent that could be got for a property if it were let on lease, as opposed to ground rent. *Syn.* gross value. *See* annual value. (*b*) COM. an excessively high rent.

royalty rent in mining leases, either a percentage of the profits of the mine or a sum of so much for each ton of output from the mine. Cf. dead rent.

scarcity rent when the supply of land is fixed, i.e. all of it is taken, the extra rent that has to be paid for it because it is scarce. Cf. differential rent.

situation rent the extra rent that is obtained from land that is better situated than other land. A form of differential rent.

rental *n.* (1) (*a*) the amount, in money, of the rent for a particular property or part of a property. (*b*) the total sum of all rents received from the property. (2) the charge payable for hiring goods: *Television rental,* rent paid for hiring a television set.

adj. relating to rent: *Rental income/value.*

rent-charge *see* chief-rent.

rent control LAW in Britain, rights given by law to tenants, esp. of unfurnished property below a certain rateable value held by the tenant before 1956, preventing the landlord from raising the rent beyond a certain amount; and giving the tenant of such property security to stay and continue living in the property during his lifetime. *See also* rent regulation.

rente FIN. the income from *rentes*: *100 francs of rente*, an annual income of 100 francs for ever. *See* rentes, *pl. Pron.* ront.

renter LAW a person who, because he pays the rent for a property, has the right to use and enjoy it.

rentes FIN. the perpetual government bonds of a number of countries in Europe, esp. of France, roughly equivalent to Consols in Britain. *Pron.* ront.

rent freeze *see under* freeze.

rentier FIN. a member of that class of society that lives on income from *rentes* (fixed-interest government and other securities) and on rent received from land. *Pron.* rontyay.

rent officers *see* rent regulation.

rent regulation LAW in Britain, a system for deciding, by officials called *rent officers*, what shall be a fair rent for a property that is not let at a controlled rent, if the landlord and tenant do not agree.

rent restriction ECON. action by a government to limit rents of houses and flats to levels below those that would exist in a free market. Cf. rent regulation; rent control.

rent-roll FIN. a document listing details of the rents received from the properties owned by a person or organization.

renunciation, letter of *see under* letter.

reorganization bond *see* adjustment bond *under* bond, *n.*

reorganization (of a company) *see* reconstruction.

Rep. representative.

rep. representing; representative; report.

repairing lease *see under* lease.

reparation (1) putting right a wrong: *To make reparation for injury/loss/damage.* (2) the money required to do this. *Syn.* restitution.

repatriation (1) bringing or sending a foreign person back to his own country. (2) FIN. the sale and bringing back of capital invested in foreign countries for investment in the home country.

repeal *v.* to end the force or effect of: *To repeal a law/tax/order. Syn.* revoke; annul; rescind. *n.* the act of repealing: *The repeal of the Corn Laws.*

repeat COM. (*colloq.*) a repeat order, i.e. one that is similar to an order placed earlier.

replacement (1) a person or thing that replaces another: *A replacement for an employee who has left. A replacement engine/motor for a vehicle.* (2) the act or process of replacing: *We demand the replacement of the damaged goods.*

replacement cost *see under* cost.

replenish to fill again; to refill: *To replenish stocks of raw materials/finished goods*, to replace what has been used up or sold. *N.* replenishment.

replevin LAW the right of a person who claims that his goods have been wrongfully distrained (taken from him in settlement of a debt), to recover possession of them on condition that he signs a bond, called a *replevin bond*, promising to give them back if a court of law decides that he is not the legal owner.

reply coupons *see* international postal reply coupons.

reply, right of at a formal meeting, the right of the mover or proposer (but not the seconder) of an original motion to reply once, and only once, after all other persons have spoken on the motion.

répondez s'il vous plaît (R.S.V.P.) (*French,* please reply) usu. written in the abbreviated form at the bottom of an invitation, to show that the sender expects the addressee to reply, stating whether or not he accepts the invitation. It is considered to be bad manners not to reply.

report an account by one or more persons, called reporters, giving information to others about some subject or happening of interest, such as the business activities of a company, a trial in a court of law, financial dealings, negotiations with trade unions, a journey, an accident. *Syn.* account. *Abbr.* rep.

auditor's report *see under* auditor's.

chairman's report *see* directors' report *under* directors'.

company report *see* directors' report *under* directors'.

directors' report *see under* directors'.

market report *see under* market.

progress report a report on progress made, on what has been done until now.

situation report a report on the present situation or state of affairs in regard to a particular subject or problem, such as conditions in a foreign market, or the state of negotiations for a contract. *Abbr.* sitrep.

reporter (1) a person who, alone or as one of a group, prepares a report. (2) a person who gathers news and writes on it in the newspapers.

re-present to present (a document) again, esp. a cheque, bill of exchange or promissory note that was not honoured when presented earlier.

represent (1) to act for or in place of; to take another person's place: *A barrister represents his client in court*, acts for his client. *An agent represents his principal.* (2) to state, to express in words, facts or opinions intended to influence others: *He represented to the customer that the goods were of good quality.*

representation (1) the act of representing another person or organization, esp. as agent or commercial traveller. *We have the Ford representation in this town*, we are the Ford agents here. (2) the state of being represented: *We have no representation in India*, we have no agent there. *Our trade union is asking for representation on the board of directors*, asking for one of its members to represent it as a director on the board.

representation, false *see* fraud.

representative (1) a person who represents another person or others: *A travelling/overseas/foreign/sales/trade/representative. Abbr.* (*colloq.*) Rep., rep., a commercial traveller. (2) LAW *see* personal representative *under* personal.

representative money *see under* money.

representative, personal *see under* personal.

repressed inflation *see* suppressed inflation *under* inflation.

reprint a new printing of matter printed before. A new impression of a book, report, etc. without any changes. If there are a few, relatively unimportant corrections, it is called a *reprint with corrections. See* edition.

repro. reproduction.

reproduction of documents *see* facsimile.

reproduction rate the rate at which the population of a country replaces itself. It can be measured by relating the number of children born in a given period to a particular group of the population with the number of persons of that group who die in the same period. It may also be based on the number of children born per thousand women of child-bearing age, called the *maternal net reproduction rate*; or it can be based on the number of children born per thousand of the productive male population, called the *paternal net reproduction rate*.

reproductive debt *see* productive debt *under* national debt.

republic a system of government in which the ruling authority and the head of state, called a president, are elected by the vote of the people. *Adj.* republican.

repudiate LAW & FIN. to refuse to pay a debt or to honour a contract or other agreement, esp. in the case of governments that refuse to be bound by the promises of earlier governments that have been overthrown. *N.* repudiation.

request note SHIPG. & COM. a document given by the customs authorities at a port allowing the master of a ship to land a cargo of perishables before the ship has cleared customs.

require (1) to need: *We require larger offices/a loan/a works manager.* (2) to demand; to call on in a commanding manner: *You are required to attend the court*, you must be present. *We require payment in seven days.*

requirement that which is required, needed: *A*

knowledge of mathematics is an essential requirement in a computer analyst.

requirements *pl.* needs: *Your machines do not meet our requirements*, do not do what we need them to do.

requisition (1) (*a*) an official document demanding something such as a property or vehicle needed for use by the government. (*b*) the act of taking over such properties (*see* requisitioning). (2) COM. & IND. a written demand, esp. for the supply of materials from a store (a *materials requisition*) or from a shop (a *purchase requisition*) or from an office (*see* cheque requisition).

requisitioning LAW the taking possession of property (but not of its ownership) without the agreement of the owner, by a government organization under powers given by Parliament. These powers are used normally only in times of grave national danger such as a war. When the danger is over and the property is no longer needed by the government, it is *de-requisitioned*, i.e. possession is handed back to the owner. Cf. compulsory purchase; pre-emption.

resale price maintenance (R.P.M.) COM. any binding agreement between manufacturers or wholesalers and retailers not to sell goods below certain prices usu. fixed by the manufacturer. One object is to stop cut-throat or unfair competition and to keep prices at a level that will be fair to all parties. In Britain, such agreements are forbidden by law, except in a very few cases where R.P.M. can be shown to be in the public interest, the Net Book Agreement, for example. In U.S.A., such agreements are allowed and are called *fair-trade agreements. See* restrictive trade practices. *Syn.* price-fixing; price maintenance.

rescind *see* repeal.

research IND. & MAN. the use of scientific methods in searching for new or improved products, processes, and methods, esp. of curing and preventing diseases (medical research). A *research scientist*, a person highly qualified in science who is studying a problem to discover new facts, usu. in a *research laboratory*, with other *research workers*, also called *researchers*.

advertising research the choice of the most effective ways of advertising a particular product and the analysis of the results.

applied research the use of the findings of basic research to extend human knowledge of problems in a particular industry or public service such as health or education.

basic research the study of the most general problems affecting all branches of knowledge, such as the use of nuclear energy. Cf. applied research. *Syn.* pure research.

consumer research finding out the wants, tastes and habits of consumers, their incomes and possessions. This research is carried out by consumer surveys and market tests.

market research see under market.

media research see media analysis.

motivational research see under motivational.

operational research see under operational.

product research finding out consumers' wishes and judgments on a product and on its packaging.

pure research see basic research above.

research and development (R. & D.) two closely related activities in modern industry, by which new products and processes are being continually developed, esp. by engineers, designers and applied scientists, from the results of research by scientists such as physicists, chemists and biologists.

reservation TRANSPT. & TOUR. the reserving of places for future use by travellers, visitors, etc. of hotel rooms, seats in vehicles such as trains, buses, planes, and theatres; also of space for cargo: To make reservations on the night train to Glasgow. Syn. booking.

reserve capital see uncalled capital under capital.

reserve currency see under currency.

reserved market see restricted market under market.

reserve fund ACCTS. the accumulated profits of a business that have not been distributed as dividends, but ploughed back into it by buying useful assets and by financing its expansion.

reserve price see under price.

reserve ratio see cash ratio.

reserves ACCTS. & FIN. in a business, amounts set aside from profits to meet contingencies (unexpected future expenditure) or for future investment. Reserves are of two main kinds: revenue reserves, which a company is free to form and, if the money is found later to be no longer needed to be kept in reserve, to distribute as dividend; and capital reserves which, by law, may never be used for distribution as dividend except in certain cases and only then by authority of a court. Cf. provision.

capital redemption reserve (fund) see under capital redemption.

capital reserve an amount that must by law be kept as a reserve and which may not be distributed as dividends payable in cash. Examples: a capital redemption reserve fund, a share premium account, and a revaluation reserve. See above; also revenue reserve below. Syn. undistributable reserve.

emergency reserve see emergency.

extraordinary reserve a reserve formed to meet an expense or loss that may arise outside the ordinary course of business, such as the closing of a foreign market following a violent change of government.

general reserve a revenue reserve, i.e. built up

from undistributed profits, intended to be used to meet the increasing cost of running the business and the resulting need for more and more working capital, esp. in a time of inflation.

gold reserves originally the stock of gold coin and bullion (gold bars) held by a note-issuing bank in a country on the gold standard, when its notes could be freely converted into (exchanged for) gold on demand. Since notes are now no longer convertible into gold, a country's gold reserves are held mainly for the purpose of making international payments. In Britain these reserves form part of the government's exchange equalization account at the Bank of England.

hidden reserve a reserve that does not appear in the balance sheet, because it is hidden by an undervaluation of the assets or an overvaluation of the liabilities of the company. Such reserves are against the law. Syn. inner reserve; secret reserve. Opp. visible reserve.

inner reserve see hidden reserve above.

revaluation reserve a reserve into which is put any surplus arising from the revaluation and sale of assets.

revenue reserve a reserve that may be formed voluntarily by the directors of a company and, if no longer required to be kept in reserve, may be distributed as dividend. Cf. capital reserve.

secret reserve see hidden reserve above.

undistributable reserve see capital reserve above.

visible reserve the opposite of a hidden reserve; a reserve that is clearly shown in a balance sheet.

Reserve, The BKG. the cash in the form of notes and coin held in the Banking Department of the Bank of England to supply demands from depositors, mainly the joint-stock banks, who keep their surplus balances with the Bank of England.

reservoir AGR. & IND. a large container or artificial lake built to store water for supply to industry, agriculture and private homes.

re-shipment see trans-shipment.

reside to live (in a certain place) continuously; to make one's home (in a certain place): He works in London but resides in Cambridge.

residence (1) the house or place in which a person or family resides, makes its home, esp. a large or important-looking house. (2) the act of residing. (3) the length of time that one has resided in a place: After five years' residence in this country you may apply for citizenship. A residence permit, one allowing a person to reside permanently in a country. To take up residence, to go to a place intending to live there permanently.

residual unemployment see under unemployment.

residuary estate see residue.

residuary legacy *see under* legacy.

residuary legatee *see* legatee; residuary legacy *under* legacy.

residue LAW that which is left of the estate of a dead person after paying all debts, expenses, legacies and other claims. *Syn.* residuary estate.

resolution a decision, expressed in words in a form that is ready for discussion at a formal meeting, such as a meeting of shareholders of a company. In Britain, an *ordinary resolution* is one that needs to be passed by only a simple majority. An *extraordinary* resolution needs to be passed by 75% or more of the voters. A *special resolution* is an extraordinary resolution that can only be passed at a meeting of which 21 clear days' notice has been given. Cf. motion.

resolve to decide; to determine: *Resolved that*, words introducing a resolution passed at a formal meeting such as a meeting of the shareholders of a company, meaning that the meeting made a firm decision on the matter.

resort TOUR. a place, usu. a town, where people go to enjoy a holiday: *A seaside/summer resort.*

resources (1) ECON. collectively, things provided by Nature or accumulated by Man that can be used as means of satisfying wants, esp. the stock of such things in a country: *India has very large mineral and manpower resources. New Zealand's main resources are good agricultural land, forests and water power. We must rely on our own resources*, we must not expect help from others.

natural resources *see under* natural.

(2) FIN. the stocks of money and wealth that an organization possesses or can manage to use: *The financial resources of the City of London/the joint-stock banks. The cost of a new factory is beyond our cash resources*, so we must borrow some of the money. *The project is within our resources*, we have the money to pay for it.

respectable bill (of exchange) *see* fine trade bill.

respondent LAW the party who has to respond to (answer or defend) an appeal, summons or petition brought against him in a court of law.

respondentia BKG. & SHIPG. a formal document by which the master of a ship gives the cargo as security for a loan made to him in a foreign port to pay for essential repairs to the ship. Cf. bottomry bond.

Rest BKG. a heading appearing as a liability in the weekly return of the Bank of England; it is the reserve fund of the Bank itself, being the excess of its assets over its liabilities. The Bank's profits are paid into it and dividends to its proprietors are paid out of it.

rest BKG. & FIN. the time at which one period ends and the next begins in calculating the interest on a loan payable quarterly, half-yearly or annually: *Interest on your loan is charged at 11% per annum with half-yearly rests.*

restaurant-car *see* dining-car.

restaurateur COM. a person who keeps a restaurant. *Also* restauranteur; restauranter.

rest-house TOUR. a house, usu. run by the government, where travellers, esp. in India, Pakistan and Bangladesh, may lodge for a short time. *See also* dak-bungalow.

restitution (1) the act of restoring, giving back, something to its owner, such as stolen property: *The judge ordered the restitution of the diamonds to the plaintiff.* (2) the act of making good, of paying compensation to somebody for personal injury or loss or damage to property. *To make restitution. Syn.* reparation. (3) FIN. *see* export restitution.

restraint LAW the unreasonable prevention of a person, who is a party to a contract, from enjoying his freedom of action in earning a living or carrying on business as he wishes. In Britain, U.S.A. and many other countries, the courts will not support any contract that contains conditions *in restraint of trade*, such as a promise by an employee not to compete with his employer after leaving his service.

restrict to limit; to keep or hold within certain limits: *The membership of a private company is restricted to 50*, there may be no more than 50 members. *We must restrict our expenses/outlay/ production/output/borrowing until we can raise more capital. N.* restriction.

restricted (1) STK. EXCH. of market conditions, a small amount of business being done: *Dealings were restricted all day.* (2) TRANSPT. *A restricted train service on Sundays and bank holidays*, a reduced service on these days.

restricted-hour tariff *see* off-peak tariff *under* tariff.

restricted market *see under* market.

restricted ownership *see under* ownership.

restrictions on trade *see* trade restrictions.

restrictive covenant *see* covenant.

restrictive endorsement *see under* endorsement.

restrictive trade practices LAW & COM. agreements between buyers and sellers that interfere with or prevent free competition, esp. by fixing prices and other conditions of payment. Such agreements are examined and controlled in Britain by the *Restrictive Practices Court*, which will allow an agreement to continue only if it is in the public interest. *See* resale price maintenance.

resulting trust *see* constructive trust *under* trust.

results ACCTS. & STK. EXCH. the outcome of the year's (or half-year's) trading, called *trading results* or *company results*, expressed as an amount of profit or loss made during the period.

resume to begin again after a break or pause: *To resume negotiations/dealings/relations. We have resumed occupation of the building. Let us resume our discussions after the holidays. He resumed his powers when he was re-elected to the board.*

ret. return.

retail *n.* COM. the sale of goods to consumers, to the general public, esp. in shops, markets and by direct-mail trading. Cf. wholesale.
adj. selling to the public: *A retail shop/store/dealer/trader. The retail trade*, as compared with the wholesale trade.

retail co-operative *see* consumers' co-operative *under* co-operative.

retail distributive society *see* consumers' co-operative *under* co-operative.

retailers COM. traders who usu. buy their supplies in relatively small quantities from wholesalers and sell them to consumers in shops and markets. The large stores, esp. chain-stores and direct-mail houses, usu. buy in bulk from manufacturers and importers as well as wholesalers, but may themselves also be manufacturers.

retail outlet *see* outlet.

retail price *see under* price.

Retail Prices, Index of *see under* Index.

retail sale *see under* sale.

retained profit *see under* profit.

retainer LAW (1) (*a*) in Britain, an arrangement between a member of the public and a solicitor or a barrister to represent him in a lawsuit or a criminal trial. (*b*) the fee paid for this service. (2) the right of an executor of a will to receive payment of a debt due to him from the estate of the dead person before all other claims on the estate are paid.

retd. returned; retired.

retention money *see under* money.

retire *v.* (1) BKG. to pay the amount of a bill of exchange or promissory note on or before the date it is due. *Syn.* to take up. (2) FIN. to withdraw (notes and coins) from circulation. (3) MAN. to withdraw from regular or active work, esp. on reaching retirement age. (4) of a director or other elected officer, to reach the end of the term of office: *A retiring director who offers himself for re-election.* (5) to cause an employee to stop regular work and become a pensioner. *N.* retirement; retiral.

retired bill *see under* bill of exchange.

retirement annuity *see under* insurance policy.

retirement pension *see under* pension.

retour sans frais BKG. *see* sans frais.

retour sans protêt BKG. (*French*, return without protesting) words written by an endorser of a foreign bill of exchange or a promissory note, meaning that if the bill or note is dishonoured, it must be returned without being protested. *Syn.* retour sans frais.

retrench to reduce greatly the expenses of running a business; to economize. *N.* retrenchment.

retrieve to get back or bring back; to recover something that was lost: *To retrieve one's losses/reputation/fortunes.*

return (1) FIN. the gain from an investment, either as income or yield or as profit on the sale of the investment: *A financial return. A return on outlay. The return on capital invested/employed.* (2) LAW & MAN. *see* annual return *under* annual. (3) TAXN. in Britain, a statement which every taxpayer must by law make once a year, stating his (and usu. his wife's) income during the past tax year, and claiming allowances from taxable income: *A tax return.* (4) TRANSPT. & TOUR. a return ticket: *A second-class return to London. Abbr.* ret.; rtn.; R.

returnable (1) COM. & IND. that can or should be returned to the owner, esp. of containers, to be used again. Cf. returned empty. (2) LAW of a writ, that must first be served on the person to whom it is directed and that must then be reported to the court by a certain time and date as having been duly served: *The writ is returnable by noon on 8 November.*

returned cheque *see under* cheque.

returned empty IND. & COM. an empty container or wagon that is returned to its owner to be used again.

Returned Letter Office in Britain, a department of the Post Office which deals with letters which for any reason cannot be delivered normally and are if possible returned to the sender. *Syn.* Dead Letter Office (D.L.O.). *Abbr.* R.L.O.

return fare *see under* fare.

return freight *see* carriage inwards.

return load *see under* load; *also* back load.

return on capital FIN. & ACCTS. the rate of income received from capital, esp. the proportion that the profits of a business bear to its total issued capital or to the capital employed in the business. The return is usu. expressed as a percentage per annum: *A return of 11% p.a. Syn.* dividend yield; earnings yield; return on investment.

return on investment *see* return on capital.

return premium *see under* premium.

returns (1) ECON. the profit or yield per unit of output, esp. when compared with the cost per unit. (2) the advantages to be got from large-scale production. (3) COM. goods returned by a customer to the supplier, usu. because they are faulty.

returns inwards account *see* sales returns account.

returns inwards book *see* sales returns book.

Returns, Law of Marginal *see* Diminishing Returns, Law of.

returns outwards book *see* purchases returns book.

return ticket see under ticket.

Réunion an island in the Indian Ocean that is an overseas territory of France, pop. 500,000 approx. (1975); capital, St-Denis, pop. 100,000 approx.; language, French; currency unit, the French franc, divided into 100 centimes.

Rev. a/c. revenue account.

revalorization of currency FIN. in a country whose currency has suffered a severe devaluation, the act of the government in replacing its standard currency unit by a new unit equal to perhaps 100 of the old. For example, in 1959 the French Government revalorized the franc, so that 1 new franc was equal to 100 old francs. Cf. revaluation of currency.

revaluation of assets ACCTS. & MAN. the fixing of a new value on fixed assets and long-term investments. If the result is an increase in the value of assets in the balance sheet, the amount of the increase is placed in a revaluation reserve.

revaluation of currency FIN. the act of the government of a country in increasing the value of its currency in units of gold, silver or the currencies of other countries. The effect is to make imports cheaper but exports become dearer in foreign markets. Revaluation is usu. carried out when the country has a continuous balance-of-payments surplus and a currency that is undervalued abroad. Cf. revalorization. Opp. devaluation.

revaluation reserve see under reserves.

Revd. Reverend.

revenue FIN. & ACCTS. (1) money received in the form of cash, cheques, etc. during a particular period. (2) in public finance, the income received by the State from taxation.

Revenue see Board of Inland Revenue.

revenue accounts ACCTS. in book-keeping, those accounts in which revenues (money received or coming into the business) are recorded, such as a commissions received account. The total of all the revenue accounts is the income of the business. Cf. expense accounts. Abbr. Rev. a/c.

revenue expenditure see under expenditure.

revenue, marginal see under marginal.

revenue reserve see under reserves.

revenue tariff see under tariff.

revenue tax see under tax.

Reverend a title of respect given to a clergyman, a minister of religion. Abbr. Revd.

reversal of entries ACCTS. an error in book-keeping that is not uncovered by a trial balance, being due to a credit entry having been debited and the corresponding debit entry having been credited.

reverse takeover STK. EXCH. (1) the buying of a public company by a private company. (2) the buying by a smaller company of a larger one.

reversion LAW a right to possess land, or to receive the income from that land, at some future fixed date, when the lease under which it is at present let will end. Cf. remainder. Syn. reversionary interest.

reversionary annuity see under insurance policy.

reversionary bonus see under bonus (3).

reversionary interest see reversion.

reversioner LAW the person to whom a leased property will revert (be returned). Cf. remainderman.

review LAW in Scotland, an appeal to a higher court.

revival see trade cycle under cycle.

revocable letter of credit see under letter of credit.

revoke see repeal.

Revolution, Industrial see under Industrial.

revolving credit see under credit.

revolving fund FIN. a stock or accumulation of money from which loans are made and into which repayments of those same loans, with interest, are paid, so that the amount of the fund is kept up and its money can be lent and re-lent indefinitely.

reward (1) a gift of money or goods for services performed, or for excellent work or behaviour, or for an act of bravery. (2) money offered for information leading to the arrest of a criminal or to the recovery of lost or stolen goods. (3) payment for services generally.

rework IND. & ACCTS. the cost of materials and labour lost through bad workmanship.

RH Haiti's international vehicle-registration letters.

Rhodesia see Zimbabwe.

RI Indonesia's international vehicle-registration letters.

R.I. Registro Italiano (Navale); Rhode Island, U.S.A.

R.I., R/I reinsurance.

rial the standard currency unit of (a) Iran, divided into 100 dinars and (b) the Sultanate of Oman, the rial Omani (RO), divided into 1000 baizas. Cf. riyal; riel; ryal.

Ricardo David (1772–1823), English economist. He was drawn by the works of Adam Smith to the study of political economy. A successful businessman, he was made famous from 1809 by his newspaper articles. In 1813 he became a Member of Parliament. With James Mill, he was one of the first of the Classical School of economists who attempted to explain the basic ideas of economic theory. In his main book, Principles of Political Economy and Taxation (1817), his discussion of wages, rent and the Labour Theory of Value had an important influence upon the thinking of the later economists, esp. Karl Marx, Thomas Malthus, J.S. Mill and A. Marshall.

rider LAW (1) an addition to a document or to a law. (2) an opinion attached to a legal decision but not strictly part of it: *The jury found the accused (person) guilty but added a rider recommending mercy.* (3) MAR. INSCE. a clause added to a marine policy; an endorsement. (4) BKG. & COM. *see* allonge.

riel the standard currency unit of Kampuchea (Khmer Republic), divided into 100 sen. Cf. rial; riyal; ryal.

rig *see* drilling rig.

rigging the market STK. EXCH. obtaining temporary control of the market for a particular security by buying, or obtaining options to buy, large quantities; this causes an apparent scarcity which forces up the price. *See* manipulate.

right LAW an interest which is supported by the law, and which it is the duty of other persons to respect. A just claim.

right of action LAW the right to bring an action in a court of law against a wrongdoer. Businessmen such as bankers who deal with large sums of money are careful to see that they have a clear right of action against a defaulter.

right of entry LAW (1) the right of a person to enter on land to take or retake possession of it. (2) the right of a landlord to enter his property to obtain his rent. A condition of this right is that the entry must always be effected peacefully, i.e. without violence.

right of way LAW the right held by law to pass across land belonging to another person.

private right of way either a right held by custom, or an easement, to be enjoyed by one person or jointly by very few persons and their licensees.

public right of way also called a highway, which can be used by all for the purpose of passage. Some rights of way are limited to certain uses only, such as a footway (footpath).

rights *see* cum rights *under* cum.

rights issue *see under* issue of securities.

rights letter STK. EXCH. a document addressed by a company to one of its existing shareholders by name, offering him part of a new issue of shares at a specially low price. If the shareholder wishes, he can sell his rights letter in the *rights market* of the Stock Exchange, instead of accepting the offer. *See* rights issue *under* issue of securities.

rights market *see* rights letter.

rights, performing *see* performing rights.

right to strike LAW & IND. REL. the right of workers to withhold their services, i.e. to stop work, without being dismissed if there are good reasons for using this means to persuade their employers to improve wages and working conditions.

Riksbank BKG. the central bank of Sweden.

ring COM. & IND. a combination of manufacturers or dealers who agree among themselves to control market prices and conditions for their own advantage. In many countries such combinations are illegal unless they are in the public interest. *See* restrictive practices; bidders' ring. *Syn.* price ring; string.

riot LAW a disturbance of the peace by at least three persons who are helping each other in a common purpose and who intend to use violence against any person who opposes them. Cf. civil commotion.

riot and civil commotion INSCE. a risk that is usu. not covered by commercial or householder's policies unless a special extension to the policy is arranged, to give protection against malicious damage caused by rioters and other law-breakers. *Syn.* riot risk. *Abbr.* r. & c.c.

rioter a person who takes part in a riot.

riot risk *see* riot and civil commotion.

rise *n.* (1) a movement upwards: *A rise in price(s)*. (2) an increase in quantity: *A rise in output/productivity*. (3) an increase in pay: *He has received a pay-rise of £200 a year.* *Syn.* (U.S.A.) a raise.
v. to move upwards: *Prices are rising. A rising market*, one in which demand and prices are tending to increase.

risk INSCE. (1) something that may happen. (2) the chance of loss, esp. of something covered by insurance: *He is young and healthy and therefore a good risk. An old and rusty ship is a bad risk. There is a high risk of fire in a timber yard.* (3) a person or thing insured.

catastrophe risk *see* catastrophe.

insurable risk one that can be clearly described or calculated because it is one of a kind that is so regularly met that most businessmen insure against it, such as fire, theft, accident. Cf. uninsurable risk *below*.

riot risk *see* riot and civil commotion.

uninsurable risk one that cannot be clearly described or calculated and is not often met, so that no insurer will insure. *See* incalculable.

risk capital *see under* capital.

risk, carrier's *see* carrier's risk.

risk, company's *see* company's risk.

risk, owner's *see* owner's risk.

rival IND. & COM. a competitor in business.

rival demand *see* competitive demand *under* demand; *also* alternate demand *under* alternate.

river basin *see* basin (2).

river bill of lading *see* inland waterways b/l *under* bill of lading.

river dues SHIPG. charges that have to be paid to a waterways authority by owners of ships and boats using the river. *Syn.* river charges.

riyal the standard currency unit of Qatar and Dubai, the Qatar/Dubai riyal, divided into 100 dirhams. *Also* of Saudi Arabia, the Saudi riyal, divided into 100 halalah. *Also* of Yemen (San'a), the Yemeni riyal, divided into 40 buqshah. *Also* rial; ryal. Cf. riel.

RL Lebanon's international vehicle-registration letters.

R.L.O. Returned Letter Office.

Rly., rly. railway.

RM Malagasy Republic's international vehicle-registration letters.

Rm. ream; room.

RM. Reichsmark.

R.M. royal mail.

RMB reminibi *or* renminbi *or* ranminbi.

RMM Mali's international vehicle-registration letters.

RNR Zambia's international vehicle-registration letters.

RNY Malawi's international vehicle-registration letters.

RO rial Omani.

R.O. receiving order; receiving office; record(s) office.

road charges FIN. in Britain, charges payable to the local government authority by owners of houses along a road that is being permanently made for the first time. The charge is usu. based on the frontage of each property and is intended to cover the cost of making the road and pavements and putting in main services, such as drains, sewers, water, gas, electricity and street-lighting.

roads SHIPG. *see* roadstead.

roadstead SHIPG. a place where ships may safely lie at anchor, usu. outside a port. A sheltered anchorage. *The ship is at present lying in Brest roadstead. Syn.* roads. *Abbr.* Rds.

roaring (*colloq.*) highly successful: *His shop is doing a roaring trade in electrical goods. It is a roaring success.*

roaring forties SHIPG. the belt of latitude between 40°S. and 50°S., where strong winds blow at sea from the west all the year. *Syn.* brave west winds.

robber economy ECON. one that extracts materials from Nature without taking steps to see that what has been taken is replaced, e.g. by the growth of new forests. Minerals, such as coal, oil and metal ores, taken from the ground cannot be replaced, so should be used carefully, not wastefully.

Robertson Sir Dennis Holme (1890–1963), English economist, professor at the London School of Economics (1930–44) and Cambridge University (1944–57). His studies and writings, which were mainly on monetary theory and on the trade cycle, had much influence on the other economists of his day, including J.M. Keynes.

Robinson Joan Violet (1903–   ), English economist, professor at Cambridge University (1965–71). A critic of the neo-classical economists and of laissez-faire, her main contribution to modern economics has been the concept (idea) of imperfect competition, explained in her book, *Economics of Imperfect Competition* (1933).

Rochdale pioneers ECON. a group of 28 English weavers (cloth-workers) who, in 1844, started the first co-operative shop in Rochdale, Lancashire, and thus began the co-operative movement.

rock-bottom price COM. one which is the lowest possible: *I have quoted you a rock-bottom price. See* bottom.

rocket (1) STK. EXCH. to rise suddenly and very steeply: *Prices rocketed on the news of an election.* (2) COM. of sales, to increase sharply.

rocks, on the FIN. (*colloq.*) in great financial difficulty; in a hopeless financial situation.

rocky FIN. (*colloq.*) financially unsatisfactory.

rod *see* perch.

R.O.I. return on investment.

rolling stock TRANSPT. (1) on the railways, carriages and wagons that have no power to move themselves, but need an engine or locomotive to move them. Cf. hauling stock. (2) more generally, all rail vehicles, including engines and wagons, etc.

roll-on ship *see* roll-on ferry *under* ferry.

Romania a communist republic in eastern Europe, pop. 21 million approx. (1975); capital, Bucharest, pop. 1.5 million approx.; language, Romanian; currency unit, the leu (*pl.* lei), divided into 100 bani. Member, COMECON. *Also* Roumania, Rumania.

rood in England, an old measure of land, one quarter of an acre = 1210 sq. yds. = 0.101171 hectare.

rook to cheat; to obtain money by fraud.

roomer *see* lodger.

rooms lodgings; apartments (Britain): *Rooms with attendance*, lodgings in a private house, the owner or occupier of which provides cleaning service and (sometimes) cooks and serves meals in the guests' rooms.

assembly rooms a building containing rooms or halls that can be hired by the public for meetings and entertainments.

room service TOUR. in a hotel, the serving of food and drink, and the provision of laundry and cleaning services for clothes in rooms used by guests.

Room, The *see* Lloyd's Room.

root of title *see under* title.

ropeway TRANSPT. a long, endless rope supported on posts, usu. across difficult country, on which loads of raw materials, goods and sometimes passengers, are carried in hanging containers clear of the ground. *Syn.* cableway.

rotation a succession of events in a regular order.

rotation of crops *or* **crop rotation** growing a different crop on the same land during each of three or four years to keep the soil fertile; sometimes nothing is grown on the land during one of these years. *See* fallow.

rotation of directors in Britain, a system adopted in the Articles of most companies by which one-third of the directors for the time being retire from office. The directors to retire in a particular year are those who have been longest in office since their last election. A retiring director may be re-elected.

rouble the standard currency unit of the Soviet Union, divided into 100 copecks *or* kopecks. *Also* ruble.

Roumania *see* Romania.

round *adj.* (1) TOUR. & TRANSPT. there and back: *Round trip*, a journey from one place to another and back; a return trip. *Round-trip ticket* (U.S.A.), a return ticket. (2) STK. EXCH. acceptable; convenient: *A round lot of shares*, a simple quantity, usu. 100 shares, that investors are willing to buy. Cf. odd lot. (3) BKG. & FIN. *A round sum*, a sum made up to the next 10, 100, 1000, etc., avoiding too many numbers.

n. COM. (1) a regular daily course taken by a delivery man such as a milkman delivering milk to private homes: *A milk/bread round*.

rounds *pl.* of a family doctor visiting sick persons in hospital or in their own homes: *The doctor is doing his rounds*.

(2) a series of discussions, conferences or negotiations, esp. between different countries searching for the answer to a particular international problem, e.g. the Kennedy Round.

round dealing honest dealing.

round figures ACCTS. & MAN. approximate; guessed; estimated: *In round figures*, roughly, the figure given usu. ending in one or more noughts (zeros): *We have sold* 996 tons, or in round figures 1000 tons. Cf. even; odd. *Syn.* round numbers.

rounding bringing a value to the nearest (or next) higher whole number or to a round figure, such as a figure or quantity to the nearest (or next) 10, 100, 1000, etc., or a price to the nearest pound.

round numbers *see* round figures.

round-trip ticket *see* round, *adj.* (1).

roup *see* auction.

route *n.* (1) a way or course planned or taken to get from one place to another or others: *To travel by the shortest/cheapest/fastest route*. (2) a regular course taken by a transport service: *Our shop is on a bus route. The east coast rail route to Scotland. See also* trade route.

routine *n.* (1) a regular way of working; a fixed order for doing things: *Office routine*, the way the work is regularly done in the office. (2) COMP. directions given to a computer that cause it to perform a routine or common operation step by step, and sometimes to continue with a limited series of operations. A small program.

adj. regular, not changing: *Routine duties*,

those that have to be performed regularly, as opposed to special duties that have to be done whenever the need arises. *Routine inspection*.

routing order TRANSPT. directions to a carrier about the way he is to send a consignment, such as *Southampton/Cherbourg*.

roving wandering; moving about: *A roving salesman*, one who travels about looking for business. *A roving commission*, (a) a job that needs much travel, or (b) one that is not clearly defined but allows much freedom of action.

royal charter *see* charter, *n.* (1).

Royal Mint *see* mint.

royalty FIN. & LAW (1) money paid to the owner of a mine or other land for the right to extract minerals from it, usu. at an agreed rate per ton extracted. (2) money paid to the owner of a copyright for permission to publish copyright material, and to the owner of a patent for permission to use a patented design, usu. at an agreed percentage of the selling price of the product. (3) money paid by a publisher to an author, composer, etc.

royalty rent *see under* rent.

R.P. return (of) premium; reply paid.

R/P. reprint; reprinting.

R.P.M. resale price maintenance.

r.p.m. revolutions per minute.

Rs. rupees (*sing.* Re.).

RSM San Marino's international vehicle-registration letters.

R.S.O. railway sub-office.

RSR Zimbabwe's (formerly Rhodesia's) international vehicle-registration letters.

R.S.V.P. (*French*) répondez s'il vous plaît.

R.T.B.A. rate to be agreed.

rtn. return.

Rtng. returning.

RU Rwanda's international vehicle-registration letters.

rubber-neck (U.S.A.) TOUR. a tourist who is keen to see all the sights everywhere. Cf. globe-trotter.

rubber stamp *see under* stamp.

rubbers STK. EXCH. stocks and shares in companies producing rubber.

ruble *see* rouble.

rule of law LAW a basic principle of justice in English law, that all men are equal in regard to the law, including the government and its officials; that no one can be punished except by order of a court of law; and that every citizen has the right to personal freedom, and freedom of speech, of meeting and of association.

rule, working to *see under* working.

ruling *adj.* current: *At the price ruling at the time of delivery*.

n. a decision or order made by a person or organization in authority: *The chairman made/ gave a ruling that the question was in order. We await a ruling from the court*.

Rumania *see* Romania.
rummage SHIPG. & TAXN. a careful search of a ship by customs officers. *Syn.* rummaging.
rummage sale COM. *see* jumble sale *under* sale.
rumour a report or story that is of doubtful truth or accuracy, usu. spread by word of mouth: *Rumours of a devaluation caused nervousness in the commodity markets. Also* (U.S.A.) rumor.
run *v.* (1) COM. to manage, to administer, to operate, esp. a business or other organization: *The office manager runs the office; his wife runs a hairdressing business. A well-run company/household*, one that is made to work efficiently. (2) SHIPG. & TRANSPT. to make regular journeys (or voyages): *The vessel runs between England and Egypt. A bus runs every hour/once an hour to the station.* *n.* (1) COM. a rush by customers to buy an article or commodity: *The bakers' strike has caused a run on bread.* (2) SHIPG. a voyage: *The vessel is now on her run to Bombay.* (3) SHIPG. the distance travelled by a ship in one day: *The ship's/day's run was 300 miles yesterday.* (4) BKG. *see* run on a bank.
runaway inflation *see* hyper-inflation *under* hyper.
run down (1) SHIPG. to run into, collide with, a ship from behind: *Our ship was run down by a tanker.* (2) COM. & IND. to reduce the activities of a part or the whole of a business or factory usu. before closing it completely: *We are running down our business in Edinburgh before moving it to Glasgow.* (3) to reduce, esp. stocks of materials or finished goods, in order to improve the cash position of a business or before closing it down.
running broker *see* bill-broker.
running costs *see* overhead costs *under* costs.
running days SHIPG. in a charter-party, days that follow each other without a break, i.e. including Saturdays, Sundays and holidays. *Abbr.* r.d.
running-down clause MAR. INSCE. the same as an *owner's risk clause* except that the insurers will have to pay only a part of the amount of damages payable by the owners.
run on a bank BKG. a sudden rush by many of the customers and depositors of a bank to take the money out of their accounts because they fear that the bank may soon be unable to honour its debts.
run out COM. & IND. to be or become finished: *Our stocks of envelopes have run out. We have run out of stock*, we have no stock left.
runway TRANSPT. a long strip of flat ground with a strong, hard surface on which planes can land and take off (fly away).
rupee the standard currency unit of: India (Re. *pl.* Rs.), Pakistan (Pak Re.), the Maldives (MRe.). and Nepal (NRe.), all divided into

100 paisa *or* paise; also of Mauritius (MauRe.), Sri Lanka (SLRe.) and the Seychelles (SRe.), all divided into 100 cents.
rupiah the standard currency unit of Indonesia, divided into 100 sen.
Russia *see* Union of Soviet Socialist Republics (U.S.S.R.).
R.V. rateable value.
Rw Fr. Rwanda franc.
Rwanda a republic in east-central Africa, pop. 4 million approx. (1975); capital, Kigali, pop. 60,000 approx.; languages, Kinyarwanda, Swahili and French; currency unit, the Rwanda franc (Rw Fr.), divided into 100 centimes. Member, O.A.U.; O.C.A.M.M.; Associate, E.E.C.
ryal *see* riyal.
RYC in reply to your cable.
ryot AGR. in the Indian subcontinent, a small farmer, either owning his own land or farming government land.

S

S summer loading (on load-line); Sweden's international vehicle-registration letter.
s. steamer; shilling.
S. South.
$ dollar (the dollar mark).
S.A. Société Anonyme, the French equivalent of a limited company; like the English *abbr.* Ltd., always placed after the name of the company.
S/A. subject to acceptance.
S.A.A.F.A. Special Arab Assistance Fund for Africa.
sabbatical leave *see under* leave.
sack *n.* (1) a large bag, made of paper, jute-fibre, plastic, etc. for holding loose materials such as grain, flour, coal. (2) a variable unit of measure based on the amount that a sack can hold: a sack of flour, 280 lb (127 kg); of wool, 364 lb (165 kg). 12 sacks of wool = 1 last or 4368 lb (1981 kg). *Abbr.* sk. (3) (*colloq.*) dismissal: *To give someone the sack*, to dismiss him. *To get the sack*, to be dismissed from a job. *Syn.* boot; kick; push.
sacrifice *see* equality of sacrifice.
s.a.e. stamped addressed envelope.
safe a fireproof steel box or cupboard with very strong locks, for keeping money and valuable articles. *See* safe custody; safe-deposit; night safe.
safe custody BKG. in Britain, a service performed by most commercial banks for their customers, in taking charge and carefully guarding the safety of deed-boxes and packets of documents, esp. bearer bonds, by keeping them in locked strong-rooms. Cf. safe-deposit. *Syn.* safe-keeping.

safe-deposit BKG. a building with special strong-rooms, usu. under ground, containing small safes which are hired out to customers for the storing of valuable articles such as jewellery, money, bonds, etc. The customer keeps the key but can go to his safe only during banking hours. Cf. safe custody.

safe port see under port.

safety see industrial safety; industrial medicine.

safety stock see buffer stock.

sag STK. & COMMOD. EXCH. of market conditions, a lowering of prices: *Prices sagged all day. A sagging market for industrials.*

sailing card SHIPG. a printed card given by ship-brokers to their clients listing the ships that they will be loading in the coming weeks, and giving such details as the ports at which the ships will be calling, the types of cargo that they will be carrying, and probable dates of sailing and arrival. Cf. sailings list *under* list (2).

sailings list see under list (2).

sakia AGR. an ancient Arab method of providing water for irrigation by means of large water-wheels and raised channels. Some sakias are still in operation, esp. in Syria. *Syn.* noria.

salable see saleable.

salami see key money.

salaried staff MAN. employees who are paid a salary, as opposed to those paid a wage.

salary MAN. a regular monthly payment to an employee doing administrative work, esp. in an office, or carrying managerial responsibility. In Britain, salaries are expressed as an amount for a whole year, e.g. £6000 p.a., but in many countries they are expressed as a monthly figure, e.g. £500 p.m. Salaries are not closely related to the actual number of hours worked or the quantity of goods produced by the employee. Cf. wage; pay; remuneration. *Syn.* stipend.

salary scale MAN. a table showing the rates of salary paid by an employer to employees at various levels (called grades) of rank, responsibility, skill and length of service. The scale may also show the increments (regular annual increases) that an employee will receive while he remains in the same grade.

sale (1) LAW sale of goods, *see* sale contract; contract to sell. (2) ACCTS. *see* sales, *pl.* (3) COM. (*a*) the exchange of goods for money; the act of selling: *Our main business is the sale of houses. For sale*, offered for sale: *This shop/business/house is for sale*, the owner wants to sell it. *On sale*, can be bought: *Newspapers are on sale everywhere. See also* sale or return; sales, *pl.* (*b*) a particular deal in which something is sold: *On average our shop makes a sale every three minutes.* (4) in a shop, the selling of goods at specially reduced prices for a limited period to get rid of goods remaining in stock. *See* end-of-season sale *below*. (5) the selling of goods or property in public. *See* auction.

auction sale see auction.

bargain sale see under bargain.

bring-and-buy sale see under bring.

cash sale see under cash.

clearance sale see under clearance.

closing-down sale a clearance sale at specially reduced prices of the entire stock of a shop that is closing down, i.e. about to stop trading.

conditional sale a sale made under a contract that gives the seller the right to remain the owner of the goods or property until payment has been completed by the buyer. *Examples*: a sale on consignment, on sale or return, on approval, and by instalments. Cf. firm sale *below*.

credit sale see under credit.

direct sale see under direct.

end-of-season sale a clearance sale in which stocks of goods, esp. clothing, left unsold in a shop at the end of a season are sold at reduced prices to clear space for the new season's stock. In Britain, many such sales take place in January and July. Cf. clearance sale; closing-down sale.

firm sale (*a*) a sale at a fixed or agreed price. (*b*) a sale that is settled and is not conditional. Cf. conditional sale *above*.

forced sale a sale that takes place by order of a court of law, as opposed to a *voluntary sale*. *Syn.* winding-up sale.

hire-purchase sale a sale made under a hire-purchase agreement.

jumble sale a sale of second-hand unwanted articles, usu. organized to raise money for charity. *Syn.* rummage sale.

private sale a sale that is agreed privately by the seller and the buyer. Cf. public *or* auction sale.

public sale an auction sale. *See* auction.

ready sale a sale that is easy to make: *There is a ready sale for rare postage stamps/new potatoes.*

retail sale a sale to a consumer, as opposed to wholesale.

rummage sale see jumble sale *above*.

short sale see selling short.

trade sale see under trade.

voluntary sale a sale made with the willing agreement of the owner of the goods being sold. *Opp.* forced sale.

white sale a sale of linen.

winding-up sale see forced sale *above*.

saleable that can easily be sold. *Also* (U.S.A.) salable.

saleage IND. & COM. that part of the total production of a commodity that is of saleable quality: *The saleage of coal mined in Britain in 1970 was 140 million tons*, that part of the total tonnage was saleable, the rest being of unsaleable quality.

sale and lease back COM. an arrangement by which the present owner, usu. a company, sells an asset, such as a building or machinery, to a buyer for an agreed sum on the condition that the asset is immediately leased (hired) back to the seller at a fixed rent for an agreed period. The seller is thus able to get an immediate supply of cash for use in his business, and may also save some tax; and the buyer finds a satisfactory investment for his money.

sale as seen COM. a sale made without any guarantee by the seller regarding the condition of the goods sold, or of their fitness for any particular purpose.

sale, bill of *see* bill of sale.

sale by description COM. a sale made under the agreed condition that the goods must correspond closely with the description of them given by the seller. Cf. sale by sample.

sale by sample COM. a sale made under the agreed condition that the quality of the bulk of the goods must be at least as good as the quality of the sample. Cf. sale by description.

sale charges MAR. INSCE. the expenses paid in selling goods that have arrived damaged. *Syn.* sale fees.

sale contract LAW & COM. a contract for the sale of goods in which the seller agrees to transfer the ownership of the goods to the buyer, who agrees to accept them and to pay a sum of money called the price. The ownership of the goods usu. passes when the agreement is made or signed. If it is agreed that the ownership is not to pass until a later date, the contract becomes an *agreement to sell* or a *contract to sell*.

sale fees *see* sale charges.

sale of goods LAW the branch of English law that deals with the rights of the buyer and seller of any article or commodity other than land and buildings, money, and certain rights such as copyright and patent rights.

sale of work COM. a sale of articles made or given by the members of a society or club in order to collect money. Cf. bring-and-buy sale.

sale on approval *see under* approval.

sale or return LAW & COM. an agreement that allows the buyer of goods to return them to the seller within a stated time, or if no time has been fixed, then within a reasonable time. At the end of this time, the buyer must give the seller an account of his sales and must pay for any goods that he has not returned. *Abbr.* S.o.R.; S/R.

sale, point of *see under* point.

sale, power of *see under* power.

sale price *see under* price.

sale proceeds *see* proceeds.

sale ring COM. (1) at an auction sale, a ring of buyers round the auctioneer. (2) an enclosure in a market in which animals are shown before being sold.

sale room COM. a room where articles are sold by auction. *See also* commercial sale rooms.

sales (1) COM. & IND. the value of goods sold by a commercial organization in a given period. *See also* sale, *sing.* (2) ACCTS. the value received from selling only those goods that were manufactured and bought with the intention of being resold at a profit in the normal course of business; thus receipts from the sale of assets are not considered to be sales and are not so entered in the account books.

export sales the value of goods sold to buyers in other countries. Cf. home sales.

gross sales *see under* gross.

home sales the value of sales made to customers in the home country, not sales of goods exported.

impulse sales *see* impulse buyer.

net sales *see under* net.

ready sales sales that are easily made, because the product is always in demand.

sales account ACCTS. in book-keeping, a ledger account into which are posted on the credit side periodical totals of entries in the sales day book.

sales agent *see* selling agent.

sales analysis *see* analysis.

sales apathy *see* sales resistance.

sales book *see* sales day book.

sales budget MAN. & ACCTS. an account of the probable future sales during a series of equal periods, e.g. weekly, monthly, quarterly, made as the first step in the whole budgeting process, since it shows the main source of revenue of the business.

salesclerk (U.S.A.) COM. a salesman or saleswoman.

sales, cost of *see* cost of goods sold.

sales day book ACCTS. in book-keeping, that section of the day book in which are recorded daily all sales of goods on credit. Each entry is posted from this book to the debit side of the ledger account of the customer concerned. Periodical totals are posted to the credit side of the sales account in the ledger. Cf. purchases day book. *Syn.* sold day book; sales journal.

sales drive *see* drive.

sales finance company *see* commercial credit company.

sales forecast *see* forecast.

salesgirl a saleswoman.

sale(s) invoice *see under* invoice.

sales journal *see* sales day book.

saleslady a saleswoman.

sales ledger *see under* ledger.

sales letter ADVTG. a letter sent to possible customers for the purpose of interesting them in a product, or to remind them of its existence, or to suggest a personal visit to discuss the product.

sales literature ADVTG. any printed material

produced by a manufacturer or importer that is intended to increase sales. Literature includes catalogues, brochures, prospectuses, etc.

salesman a man employed to sell goods: *A motor-car salesman*, one who sells motor cars. *A door-to-door salesman*, one who goes from house to house to sell goods such as books, brushes and other things needed in the home. *Syn.* canvasser; drummer (U.S.A.). *Fem.* saleswoman; salesgirl; saleslady.

travelling salesman *see* commercial traveller.

sales manager *See under* manager.

salesmanship COM. special skill in being able to persuade the public, or a particular person, to buy the goods one is wanting to sell. *High-pressure salesmanship*, *see* hard selling. The main methods used are persuasive talk, clever advertising and attractive presentation of the product itself.

sales-mix ACCTS. & MAN. in a business selling various types of product, the proportion that the sales of each type bears to the total sales of the business. From the rate of gross profit earned by each type, it is possible to calculate its contribution to the total gross profit and to compare its profitability with that of the other types.

sales opposition *see* sales resistance.

sales outlet *see* outlet.

sales promotion *see under* promotion.

sales resistance COM. (1) a general lack of interest by the public in buying a product, also called *sales apathy*. (2) unwillingness to be persuaded to buy a product that is not essential, also called *sales opposition*.

sales returns account ACCTS. a ledger account into which are posted on the debit side periodical totals of entries in the sales returns book. *Syn.* returns inwards account.

sales returns book ACCTS. a book of prime entry in which details are entered of goods returned by customers. Each entry is posted to the credit side of the particular customer's ledger account. Periodical totals are posted to the debit side of the sales returns account. *Syn.* sales returns journal; returns inwards book.

salesroom *see* commercial sale rooms.

sales tax *see under* tax.

saleswoman a woman employed to sell goods usu. in a shop. *Syn.* salesgirl; saleslady.

Salop. Shropshire, England.

salt *n.* (*colloq.*) money.
v. to preserve for storing: *To salt away money*, to store it away for the future.

salutation *see* greeting.

Salvador *see* El Salvador.

salvage INSCE. (1) the act of saving goods from loss, e.g. by fire or shipwreck: *A salvage company/tug/vessel*. (2) the reward given or paid to persons who save goods, vehicles, etc. from loss, and esp. ships in danger of, or after, ship-

wreck: *Salvage charges*, based on the value of property saved. (3) the goods or property saved from loss, also called *salved goods/property*.

salvor INSCE. one who organizes or takes part in the salvage of goods, and esp. of a ship at sea.

salvor's lien the right of a salvor to hold the property he has saved until his claim for a salvage award (payment) has been settled.

sample (1) COM. an example, usu. given free, of an article or commodity being offered for sale, so that possible buyers can examine and test it. *See* dealer aids. (2) COMMOD. EXCH. a small part taken from a large quantity (the bulk) of a commodity being sold, such as tea, coffee or wool, and used as an example to show possible buyers the qualities of the bulk. *See* sale by sample. (3) QUAL. CONT. *see* acceptance sampling *under* acceptance (2). (4) ECON. THEORY in statistical enquiry, a small group chosen from a larger group for special study. To give satisfactory results, a sample should be both representative and random. *See* sampling.

random sample one for which every item in the whole group had an equal chance of being selected.

representative sample one composed of different items in the same proportions as in the whole group.

sample fair *see* fair, *n.* (2).

sampler a person employed to take, test, and report on samples of commodities, esp. raw materials for industry.

sampling ECON. THEORY a method of statistical enquiry in which only a carefully chosen part, called a *sample*, of the whole group of items is studied, and the results then applied to the whole group. In this way, the extent of the field of enquiry is greatly reduced: for example, to obtain the average age of the population at a certain date, one does not need to find the age of every person in the population, but only to study a representative and random sample. *See* sample.

sanction LAW a penalty or punishment for breaking the law.

sanctions, economic LAW & ECON. in international law, action taken, usu. by a group of countries, against another country, by refusing to trade with it; the intention is to force it to carry out some legal duty it owes under international law.

sandwich course IND. in Britain, a course of study, usu. for the Higher National Diploma (H.N.D.), Higher Diploma (H.D.) or a technological degree taken by a student who spends part of his working time as a trainee in an industrial organization such as a factory, and the other part studying at an institution of higher education.

sandwich man ADVTG. a man employed to walk

about a town carrying in front of, and behind, him boards bearing advertisement posters.

San Marino the smallest republic in the world, in eastern Italy, pop. 20,000 approx. (1973); capital, San Marino, pop. 5000 approx.; language, Italian; currency unit, the Italian lira (*pl.* lire), divided into 100 centesimi. In customs union with Italy.

sans frais BKG. (*French*, without expense) incur no expenses. Words sometimes written by the endorser of a bill of exchange, warning that he will not be personally liable to pay any expenses in connection with the bill. *Also* retour sans frais.

sans recours BKG. the French equivalent, sometimes used in English, of *without recourse. See* recourse.

São Tomé and Principe Islands a republic off west-central Africa, pop. 80,000 approx. (1975); capital, São Tomé, pop. 10,000 approx.; languages, Portuguese and tribal; currency unit, the Portuguese escudo, divided into 100 centavos.

s.a.p.l. sailed as per list (i.e. Lloyd's List).

Sask. Saskatchewan, Canada.

satang the fractional currency unit of Thailand. 100 satang = 1 baht.

satellite office COM. & MAN. a small branch office at some distance from, but controlled and managed by, a more important office of the same organization.

satellite town ECON. a small country town at some distance from, but depending on, a more important town for its economic life.

Satiable Wants, Law of *see* Law of Diminishing Utility.

satisfaction *see* utility; *also* accord and satisfaction.

Satisfaction, Memorandum· of *see under* Memorandum.

satyagraha IND. REL. in India, non-violent resistance used as a means of influencing others to see one's view: *The workers committed satyagraha by shutting the manager in his office.* Cf. sit-in; strike.

Saudi Arabia an Arab kingdom in south-west Asia, pop. 9 million approx. (1975); capital, Riyadh, pop. 300,000 approx.; language, Arabic; currency unit, the Saudi riyal or ryal, divided into 100 halalah. Member, Arab League.

S. Aus., S. Austr. South Australia.

s.a.v. stock at valuation.

save as you earn BKG. & FIN. in Britain, the popular name for a government scheme for organizing small savings. It consists of a contract between the government department for national savings and a private depositor who agrees to save a fixed regular sum every month. This sum may be paid by banker's order, by deduction from wages or salary, or in cash at post offices. After five years, depositors

receive a tax-free bonus, but deposits left for a further two years receive another such bonus. A similar savings scheme is operated by the Trustee Savings Bank and some building societies. *Abbr.* S.A.Y.E.

save, propensity to *see under* propensity.

saving (1) LAW an exception; as *adj.* in *a saving clause*, in an agreement, a clause stating that in certain conditions the whole or some part of the agreement shall have no force in law. (2) ECON. THEORY the difference in the economy as a whole between income and expenditure on consumer goods. The situation in an economy when total income is greater than total consumption. Cf. hoarding. *Opp.* spending; dissaving. (3) MAN. & IND. money and materials saved by economical working. (4) FIN. money, esp. profits, saved and put aside for future use, not spent or distributed.

compulsory saving amounts spent by governments when voluntary saving by private persons and businesses is insufficient for the growth of the economy. It is a form of forced saving.

corporate saving that part of the profits of companies that is not distributed as dividends but is held and later used to buy capital goods needed to expand business.

forced saving a reduction in the amount spent on consumer goods, caused by increased taxation or higher prices. *Syn.* forced frugality; compulsory saving.

involuntary saving unintended saving, such as money locked up in an increase in a producer's stock of finished goods, caused by reduced demand. Cf. voluntary saving.

personal saving saving by private persons for later personal spending or for investment to produce personal income.

voluntary saving in the economy as a whole, personal saving added to saving by companies in the form of undistributed profits and money set aside for depreciation. Cf. involuntary saving.

savings FIN. & BKG. sums of money saved, not spent but put aside for future use and in the meanwhile invested or held as cash.

savings account *see under* bank account.

savings bank BKG. a special kind of banking organization that has been set up to encourage saving by members of the public and to organize the pool of small savings. In Britain, there are the trustee savings banks and the National Savings Bank; and in the U.S.A., the mutual savings banks and the stock savings banks. *See these below.*

mutual savings bank in the U.S.A., a co-operative savings bank, owned by its depositors and run as a co-operative society. Many mutual banks offer personal loans, administer trust funds and provide a safe-deposit service. Cf. stock savings bank.

National Savings Bank *see under* National.

stock savings bank in the U.S.A., one of a number of privately-owned banks that specialize in receiving and investing deposits from small savers. These banks usu. provide a cheque-paying service and make loans. Cf. mutual savings bank.

trustee savings banks in Britain, non-profit-making organizations managed by trustees acting for savers under rules laid down by Parliament. Current accounts earn interest and are guaranteed by the government. Cheque-paying arrangements and personal banking services are provided, such as the payment of standing orders, the storing of valuables in safe custody, and the buying and selling of government securities. *Abbr.* T.S.B.

savings bond FIN. (1) in Britain, a savings security guaranteed by the government. *See* national savings securities; *see also* premium savings bond. (2) in the U.S.A., U.S. savings bonds, which mature in eight or ten years and are not transferable, can be bought up to a limited amount for each investor.

savings certificate *see* national savings securities.

sawbuck (*colloq.*) a U.S. ten-dollar note.

Say Jean-Baptiste (1767–1832), French economist, Professor of Industrial Economy, 1819–31, and of Political Economy, 1831–2, one of the classical economists and a founder of the doctrine of free trade. His *Traité d'Économie Politique* (1803) was the first popular book in French on the principles of the subject. In it he developed the idea, known as *Say's Law of Markets*, that it is production which creates markets for goods; that supply always creates its own demand; and that general overproduction is impossible. This view was accepted by most economists until, in the 1930s, J.M. Keynes strongly criticized it as having no relation to modern economic conditions.

S.A.Y.E. save as you earn.

sc. scruple.

s/c self-contained; *French*: son compte, (on) his account.

s.c. self-contained; salvage charges.

S.C. South Carolina, U.S.A.

scab *see* blackleg (1).

scale *see* diseconomies of scale; economies of scale.

scale fee FIN. & LAW a fee based on a standard scale of charges rather than on the amount of work actually done in a particular case: *A solicitor charges a scale fee for the conveyance of a house.*

scalp *v.* STK. EXCH. (*colloq.*) to buy and sell securities in small quantities and usu. at low prices, to make small but quick profits. *n.* the small profit so made.

Scandinavia a region of northern Europe consisting of Norway, Sweden and Denmark; Finland, Iceland and the Faeroe Islands may be included.

scarce currency *see under* currency.

scarce goods ECON. THEORY goods the supply of which is insufficient to satisfy the demand; they therefore have a price, as opposed to free goods, which are freely obtainable and bear no price.

scarcity ECON. the state of being scarce, of being insufficient to satisfy the demand: *A scarcity of labour/land/capital/raw materials.* Cf. rarity. *Syn.* dearth.

scarcity rent *see under* rent.

scarcity value *see under* value.

Sch. schilling.

sch. schooner.

schedule (1) a list, esp. one listing future events or operations and their times; a timetable: *To/on schedule*, at the time fixed. *Behind/ahead of schedule*. (2) LAW a list added to an Act of Parliament or other law or to any formal document such as a deed, agreement, or insurance policy. A schedule acts as a record of matters affected by the main document, which may be varied or added to from time to time. (3) TAXN. *see* schedules, tax.

scheduled flight *see* flight (3).

scheduled territories FIN. & BKG. in regard to British exchange control (when in force), the United Kingdom, including the Channel Islands and the Isle of Man, and also the Republic of Ireland.

schedules, tax TAXN. the six classes, lettered A to F, into which incomes are divided under British income-tax law:

Schedule A income from the ownership of land, such as rents and premiums on leases.

Schedule B income from woodlands that are grown as a business.

Schedule C income from gilt-edged securities and some foreign loans paid in Britain.

Schedule D income from trades, professions, interest and annual payments received, such as annuities.

Schedule E income from employment: wages, salaries, directors' fees.

Schedule F income from company dividends and other distributions.

scheme a plan or arrangement; any orderly system or design that has been worked out in detail and perh. proposed or adopted officially or formally. *See* pension scheme; scheme of composition *under* composition.

scheme of arrangement *see* scheme of composition *under* composition.

scheme of composition *see under* composition.

schilling the standard currency unit of Austria, divided into 100 groschen. Cf. shilling. *Abbr.* Sch.

schooner SHIPG. a fast sailing ship, usu. with two

masts and sails set lengthwise, not across the ship. *Abbr.* sch.

Schumpeter Joseph Alois (1883–1950), Austrian economist, Professor of Economics at Czernowitz, Graz, Bonn and, from 1932 until his death in 1950, at Harvard. He was a very active writer in many fields of economics, esp. on the working of the capitalist system and the trade cycle.

S.C.I.T. Special Commissioners of Income Tax.

scoop (1) COM. (*colloq.*) a large gain, such as the profit from a highly successful business venture. (2) (*colloq.*) the publication by a newspaper of a news story before any others publish it.

score (1) a set of 20, a unit used esp. in agriculture: *A score of animals.* (2) a weight of 20 or 21 lb, used for weighing pigs and cattle.

Scottish Agricultural Securities Corporation Ltd. *see* Agricultural Mortgage Corporation.

scrap *n.* IND. material that has been thrown away as useless by its owner but still having some value if fit for recovery and reuse: *An old ship sold as/for scrap. A scrap yard*, a place where old things are broken up and where scrap materials are sorted and stored. *Scrap metal/paper.* See scrap value *under* value.
v. to throw away or sell as scrap: *The owners have decided to scrap the vessel.*

screw *n.* (1) SHIPG. a ship's propeller. (2) (*colloq.*) wages or salary: *He gets a good screw.*
v. to cheat, obtain money by dishonesty or threats of violence.

scrip STK. EXCH. (1) a temporary certificate or receipt given to an investor who has paid the first instalment of the price of government bonds or debentures in a company. (2) any certificate relating to bonds and debentures. *See* bearer scrip *under* bearer; deferred interest certificate. *Also* script.

scripholder a person who owns scrip.

scrip issue *see under* issue of securities.

script (1) handwriting. The system of letters used in writing a particular language: *The Arabic script. Hindi is written in the Devnagri script, English in the Roman script.* (2) a short word for manuscript and typescript. (3) a document containing words to be spoken in a speech, play, film or broadcast. (4) STK. EXCH. *see* scrip.

scripts *pl.* answer-papers written by students at an examination.

scrivener (1) originally a writer, a copier of documents. (2) FIN. a person who, for a fee or commission, places his clients' money as loans to trustworthy borrowers.

scruple a small measure of weight, 20 grains or one twenty-fourth of an ounce troy = 1.296 g. *Abbr.* sc.

scrutineer a person appointed to examine and count the votes cast in a poll. *Syn.* teller.

scuttling SHIPG. causing a ship to sink by letting her fill with water. If this is done for an unlawful purpose, it is barratry.

S.C.W.S. Scottish Co-operative Wholesale Society.

SD Swaziland's international vehicle-registration letters.

S.D. sea damaged; short delivery; South Dakota, U.S.A.

s.d. short delivery; sine die.

sd. signed; sailed.

S.D.R. special drawing rights.

S.E. South-East; Stock Exchange.

S/E. Stock Exchange.

sea-captain SHIPG. the master of a merchant ship.

sea-chart *see* chart (1).

seafarer SHIPG. (1) a sailor. (2) a traveller by sea.

seafaring continually sailing the sea: *A seafaring man*, a seafarer. *A seafaring nation*, having many ships and sailors; doing much trade by sea.

sea-going *see* ocean-going.

sea insurance *see* marine insurance *under* insurance, classes and kinds of.

seal *n.* LAW (1) a common seal, *see under* common. (2) on a deed, a small paper disc, usu. red, stuck near the signature as a solemn mark expressing agreement by the person signing. *See also* locus sigilli.
v. (1) to fix a seal (on a document). (2) to close, e.g. an envelope or parcel, in such a way that it must be torn or broken open.

seal, company *see* common seal.

sealed-bid tender COM. *see under* tender.

sea mail *see under* mail.

seaman's lien *see under* lien.

sea mile *see under* mile.

seaport *see under* port.

seaplane TRANSPT. a plane fitted with floats instead of wheels, so that it can land on water.

search warrant *see under* warrant.

season TOUR. a time of the year when more people are touring or travelling than at other times: *The tourist season. See also* high-season fare *under* fare; dead season.

seasonal unemployment *see under* unemployment.

season ticket *see under* ticket.

seaway SHIPG. an inland waterway that is sufficiently wide and deep for ocean-going ships, such as the St. Lawrence Seaway. Cf. ship-canal.

seaworthy SHIPG. & MAR. INSCE. of a ship, properly equipped and manned, and in a reasonably safe condition to make a sea voyage. *Opp.* unseaworthy. *N.* seaworthiness.

sec. section; second; secretary; secretarial.

S.E.C. Securities and Exchange Commission.

second (1) the basic SI unit of time, one-sixtieth part of a minute of time. (2) one-sixtieth part of a minute of arc (angle). *Sign:* ". *Abbr.* sec.

secondary bank *see* finance house.

secondary industry *see under* industry.

secondary occupations *see under* occupations.

secondary production *see under* production.

second-class mail *see under* mail.

second-class paper BKG. & FIN. bills of exchange, cheques, and promissory notes drawn on, or accepted, endorsed or guaranteed by, persons whose commercial reputation is not of the highest class. Cf. fine paper.

seconder at a formal meeting, a person who seconds, i.e. supports personally, a motion proposed by somebody else. *Every motion must have a proposer and a seconder.*

second-half *adj.* STK. EXCH. & ACCTS. relating to the second half of the financial year: *Second-half profits showed a great improvement over the first-half.*

second-hand *adj.* COM. of goods, not new; already used; having had one or more owners already. *The second-hand car market,* that in which used cars are bought and sold. *A second-hand clothes dealer/bookseller/furniture shop.* *adv. We bought this machine second hand.*

second language *see under* language.

second mortgage *see under* mortgage.

second of exchange *see* bill (of exchange) in a set.

second-rate not of the best quality; of relatively poor standard: *We refuse to buy second-rate goods,* we will only buy goods of the best quality. Cf. first-rate.

seconds COM. & IND. goods of second-rate quality; goods that are below standard and are sold at a cheap price. *Syn.* rejects.

second via BKG. & COM. a second of exchange. *See* bill (of exchange) in a set. *Also* secundia via.

secretariat (1) the main offices of a large government or other administrative organization: *The U.N. Secretariat is in New York.* (2) the officials and staff collectively, usu. with a Secretary-General at their head, who carry out the secretarial work of such an organization: *He joined the secretariat of the state government.*

secretary (1) a person who deals with paperwork, writes or types letters, keeps records, and makes arrangements. *Abbr.* sec.; Secy. (2) a person who is the head of a government department: *The Secretary of State for Industry; the Foreign Secretary.*

company secretary *see under* company.

honorary secretary *see* honorary.

paid secretary *see under* paid.

personal secretary *see* private secretary *below.*

private secretary an employee in an office who helps an official or executive with his paperwork and other duties, taking dictation, typing letters and reports, keeping files, dealing with telephone calls, making arrangements for travel and entertainment, and receiving visitors. *Syn.* personal secretary; personal assistant.

Secretary-General the highest executive officer of a large international organization, and the person in charge of its secretariat: *The Secretary-General of the U.N.*

secret commission *see* bribe.

secret partner *see under* partner.

secret reserve *see* hidden reserve *under* reserve.

sector ECON. one of the parts into which a thing may be divided, esp. in economics, the divisions of the economy. *See* corporate sector; personal sector; private sector; public sector.

sector chart *see* pie chart *under* chart.

secular trend ECON. THEORY in the study of the trade cycle, the long-term tendency shown by the average course of economic activity during several trade cycles.

secundia via BKG. a second of exchange. *See* bill (of exchange) in a set. *Syn.* second via.

secure *adj.* safe; not in danger: *A secure investment,* one that is not in danger of being lost. *A secure job,* one that is safe, from which the holder is not likely to be dismissed. *To feel secure,* to have no worries about the future, esp. about finances. *Opp.* insecure.

v. (1) to make sure of obtaining: *I secured the job against much competition. He managed to secure a loan from a friend. We have secured you a seat on the plane.* (2) to make safe financially: *To secure a loan,* to make the loan safe for the lender by pledging or mortgaging property with him as security.

secured creditor *see under* creditor.

secured debenture *see under* debenture.

secured debt *see under* debt.

secured loan *see under* loan.

securities STK. EXCH. investments generally, and esp. stocks, shares and bonds which are bought as investments. Formerly the word had a narrower meaning: debts or claims the payment of which is in some way secured; but this meaning is seldom used in modern business language.

bearer securities *see under* bearer.

dated securities *see under* dated.

fixed-interest securities *see under* fixed.

gilt-edged securities *see under* gilt-edged.

government securities *see under* government.

listed securities *see under* listed.

long-dated securities *see* longs.

marketable securities any securities that can be bought or sold on a stock exchange, esp. those that can easily and quickly be sold. Cf. non-marketable securities *below.*

medium-dated securities *see* mediums.

national savings securities *see under* national savings.

negotiable securities *see* negotiable instruments.

non-marketable securities in Britain, government securities that cannot be bought on the

Stock Exchange, mainly those forming part of the national debt that consist of savings bonds, national savings certificates, premium bonds, terminable annuities, tax reserve certificates. Cf. marketable securities *above*.

non-negotiable securities *see* non-negotiable instruments.

quoted securities *see* listed securities *under* listed.

real securities mortgages of real property, i.e. land and buildings.

short-dated securities *see* shorts.

sterling securities *see under* sterling.

trustee securities in Britain, certain authorized securities, called narrower-range investments, in which, by law, a trustee must invest at least half of the total value of the trust moneys, otherwise he may become personally responsible for bearing any loss that may be suffered by the trust. The other half may be invested in wider-range investments. *See* trustee investments. The trustee securities are: savings bonds; national savings certificates; deposits in the National Savings Bank and the trustee savings banks; fixed interest securities issued by the local or other governments of the U.K., Northern Ireland and the Isle of Man; Treasury bills; certain overseas securities of commonwealth countries; debentures of U.K. companies; certain building society deposits; and certain mortgages and rent charges on land. *Syn.* legal investments.

undated securities *see* undated stock *under* stock.

unlimited securities *see* unlisted securities *under* unlisted.

unlisted securities *see under* unlisted.

Securities and Exchange Commission (S.E.C.) STK. EXCH. in the U.S.A., the commission that controls and administers the activities of stock exchanges and other markets in which securities are bought and sold, its main purpose being to protect investors from fraud. *See* commission (2).

securities, issue of *see under* issue.

securities market *see* Stock Exchange; *also* kerb market *under* kerb.

security (1) MAN. & IND. REL. freedom from the danger of losing one's job without good reason and compensation: *Security of employment*. *See also* social security. (2) LAW in Britain, the right called *security of tenure* of a tenant to continue to use or to live in leased property after the end of the lease or after being given notice to leave by the landlord, esp. in the case of short leases, furnished lettings, agricultural holdings and business premises. (3) FIN. & BKG. something valuable given to a lender by a borrower to support his intention to repay a loan, such as: the title-deeds of a house; government or commercial bonds; debentures; stocks and shares; life insurance policies; documents of title to goods; or a guarantee by a third party. If the loan is not repaid, the lender has the right to recover the amount of the loan, any interest due, and his expenses, by selling the security for cash.

collateral security *see under* collateral.

dead security *see under* dead.

government security of a loan or bond, the quality of being guaranteed by the government; i.e. that payment of principal and interest will be paid by the government if the issuing organization does not or cannot pay when due.

heritable security *see* heritable bond *under* bond, *n.*

personal security *see under* personal.

security capital *see under* capital.

security guard FIN. & BKG. a person employed to guard money and valuable documents, articles, etc. esp. while being transported from one place to another. In Britain, such guards do not carry guns.

security market *see* Stock Exchange; *also* kerb market *under* kerb.

Secy. Secretary.

seen *see* sale as seen.

see-safe COM. (1) an agreement to sell goods on sale or return. *See* sale or return. (2) a variation of (1) by which the customer pays for the goods when they are supplied, but has the right to return for credit any remaining unsold at the end of an agreed period. In this way, the supplier sees his customer safe, i.e. makes sure that the customer is not left with goods he cannot sell.

seigniorage FIN. the profit made by a government from the manufacture or issuing of coins. It is the difference between the face value of the coins and the actual cost (brassage or mintage) of making them. *Also* seignorage.

selected *see* choice.

self BKG. on cheques, a direction to the paying bank to pay to oneself, i.e. to the drawer of the cheque, thus: *Pay self*, means 'pay me'. If the drawer is not a single person but an association, partnership, company or other organization, the direction to the bank is put in the plural, thus: *Pay selves*, meaning 'pay us'. Such cheques are called self-cheques.

self-assessment *see under* assessment (2).

self-balancing ledgers ACCTS. in book-keeping, ledgers that have a control account which proves them correct.

self-contained of a house or flat, having its own kitchen, bathroom and lavatory, and a private entrance, so that none of these has to be shared with others. *Abbr.* s/c; s.c.

self-dependent *see* self-sufficient.

self-employed person COM. & IND. a person who works for himself, who is not employed by anyone else, such as the owner of a small business, a craftsman, artist, writer or jobbing gardener.

self-finance *see* plough back.

self-help LAW (1) the right of a private person suffering from a nuisance caused by another person, to enter that other person's land to put an end to the nuisance. (2) his right to put a trespasser off his own land.

self-insurance INSCE. the accumulation of a fund of money as a reserve to provide for possible losses in the future that could easily have been insured with an insurance company. It is considered to be an unwise method of insurance because the loss may arise before the fund is big enough to meet it. *Syn.* own insurance.

self-liquidating FIN. & BKG. of a loan, esp. a bank advance, repayable, with interest, in a short time out of the money received by the borrower from the sale of the product for which he needed the loan, such as a loan to a farmer to support him with money until after the harvest; or to a builder until he has completed and sold a new house.

self-made of a person, one who has succeeded in life through his own efforts, although he began with no advantages such as education, money or family influence: *A self-made man.*

self-service COM. a method of selling goods, esp. in shops, stores and supermarkets, where customers choose and take from the shelves the goods they wish to buy, paying for them when leaving.

self-sufficient *adj.* ECON. of a country, able to produce all the goods and commodities that it needs, without buying them from other countries. *Syn.* self-dependent. *N.* self-sufficiency. Cf. autarky; economic nationalism.

sell *v.* COM. (1) to exchange something for money: *I will sell you my watch for £10. He sold his house for £30,000.* *Opp.* to buy. (2) to deal in by way of trade: *We sell typewriters/ fresh fruit/sports goods,* we keep them for sale. *To sell insurance,* to arrange insurance contracts: *To sell out,* to come to the end of one's stock: *We have sold out of tickets; the tickets are/have sold out. To sell off,* to get rid of one's stock at a reduced price: *They sell off their old stock every January. To sell up* (*a*) to sell one's business; (*b*) to sell one's entire stock before closing the business; (*c*) to seize a debtor's property to pay his debts. (3) to cause, influence, people to buy: *Good advertising sells a product. See* hard selling; soft selling. *See* undersell. (4) (*colloq.*) to persuade someone of the value of something: *He sold the idea to them.* (5) to be in demand; to be bought: *This book sells well in Egypt; it sells mainly to students. To sell like hot cakes,* to be bought by the public in large numbers.

n. (*colloq.*) (1) a disappointment; something that proves to be not what one was told it would be; sometimes, a swindle (dishonest deception): *What a sell!* (2) hard sell; soft sell, *see* hard selling; soft selling.

a sell-out a show for which all tickets have been sold.

sell, contract to *see* sale contract.

seller (1) a person who sells something. *Syn.* vendor. (2) as *suffix,* -seller, to a commodity, a dealer in that particular commodity: *A bookseller, a printseller.* (3) a thing that is easily sold: *The novel was a best-seller,* it had a very large sale, better than that of (most) other novels.

seller's lien *see* vendor's lien *under* lien.

sellers' market *see under* market.

sellers' monopoly *see under* monopoly.

seller's option to double *see* put-of-more option *under* option.

sellers over STK. & COMMOD. EXCH. of market conditions, when there is an excess of sellers over buyers, or when there are no buyers at all: *There were sellers over in the market,* there were few buyers. Cf. buyers over.

selling finding a buyer; offering to sell; persuading people to buy.

direct selling *see* direct sale/selling.

distress selling *see under* distress.

forced selling STK. EXCH. an unwilling sale of shares by a shareholder who is forced to obtain cash to pay his debts.

hard selling *see under* hard.

inertia selling *see under* inertia.

personal selling the work of persons specially employed to keep in direct touch with customers by means of personal conversations, visits, phone calls and letters. Employees doing such work include shop assistants, commercial travellers and representatives, salesmen and saleswomen.

selling agent COM. one who sells goods for his principal. Cf. buying agent. *Syn.* sales agent.

selling costs COM. & IND. that part of the distributive costs that relates to advertising and display, salaries and commissions paid to salesmen, and after-sales service.

selling expenses *see under* expenses.

selling out STK. EXCH. action taken by an official broker of the Stock Exchange in selling securities that have not been paid for by the buyer by the due date. Cf. buying in.

selling price *see* offer(ed) price *under* price.

selling short STK. & COMMOD. EXCH. the action of a seller in promising to deliver at an agreed price, and at a fixed future date, a security or commodity which he does not yet possess but which he expects to obtain at a lower price before he has to deliver it. *Syn.* short sale.

selves *see* self.

semi- *prefix,* half; partly: *Semi-skilled labour; semi-finished goods,* goods that are only partly manufactured. *Semi-durable goods,* consumer goods that may be expected to last only a few years, such as household china and glass, and some kinds of clothing. *Semi-annual*, happening every half-year, or twice in each year. Similarly *semi-monthly, semi-weekly*.

semi-detached *see* detached.

Sen. Senior.

sen the fractional currency unit of Indonesia. 100 sen = 1 rupiah. *Also* of Japan. 100 sen = 1 yen. *Also* of Kampuchea (Khmer Republic). 100 sen = 1 riel.

Senate *see* Congress.

sender *see* consignor.

Senegal a republic in West Africa, pop. 4 million approx. (1973); capital, Dakar, pop. 700,000 approx.; languages, French and tribal; currency unit, the C.F.A. franc (CFA Fr.), divided into 100 centimes. Member, French Community; O.C.A.M.M.; Associate, E.E.C.

Senior after a name, the elder: *Thomas Jones Senior*, the father of Thomas Jones Junior. Cf. Junior. *Abbr.* Sen.; Sr.

Senior Nassau William (1790–1864), English classical economist, the first Professor of Political Economy at Oxford (1825). His main work, *An Outline of the Science of Political Economy*, gave the first explanation of the modern theory of capital. He is considered to be one of the earliest teachers of pure economics.

senior executive *see under* executive.

seniority MAN. & IND. REL. the state of being higher in rank, in age, or in length of service, than other employees in the same organization.

senior partner *see under* partner.

sensitive STK. EXCH. quickly and strongly affected by some outside influence: *Equities sensitive to Wall Street*, securities (on the London Stock Exchange) that go up and down in price according to whether American investors are buying or selling international stocks and shares.

sentence LAW the punishment ordered by a court of law for a criminal offence, usu. a fine or a period of imprisonment.

Sepon *see* Talisman.

sequestration LAW (1) the seizing and holding of property by order of a court of law, while a claim to ownership of the property is being settled by the court; or while the estate of a bankrupt is being divided among his creditors. (2) in Scotland, a bankruptcy.

sequestrator *n.* the person appointed by the court to hold property seized by order of the court.

serang (1) SHIPG. in India, the captain of a small ship. (2) a man in charge of a group of workers, esp. in loading or unloading a ship; a foreman.

serf ECON. HIST. a villein. *See* feudal system.

serfdom ECON. HIST. the social and economic condition of the serfs or villeins under the ancient feudal system in Europe, which bound them to perform services for the lord of the manor. *See* feudal system.

serial number the number given to a unit in a series: *The serial number of a bond*, the number, written or printed on the bond, that distinguishes it from all other bonds of the same issue.

servant (1) a person who serves (works for) another person for pay; an employee, esp. (*a*) a person who performs household duties in a private house, hotel or boarding house: *A domestic/general servant. A maidservant. A manservant*; (*b*) a person who works for the State: *A Civil/government/public servant*. (2) LAW a person who is bound by a contract of service to work for another person. *See* Master and Servant.

service *n.* (1) the act of being helpful or useful: *To be of service to the community. To have a spirit of service. We are at your service*, ready to help you. (2) (*a*) a regular supplying of something helpful to the community and in public demand: *A bus/train/boat/air service. A private taxi/car-hire service*. (*b*) a public organization controlling and operating such help: *The Fire Service. The National Health Service. The armed services*. (3) the art of serving somebody, esp. as an employee: *He has left/joined/ retired from the company's service. She is in service*, employed as a domestic servant. (4) (usu. *pl.*) the work done by an employee, consultant, adviser, or helper of any kind: *We shall pay you for your services. We need the services of a solicitor*. (5) the length of time that an employee serves the same employer: *He retired after 40 years' service with the bank*. (6) LAW the serving of a writ or summons. *See* service of process. (7) the care of guests in hotels, the serving of food and drink in restaurants, and the attention to the needs of customers in shops: *The food was good but the service was bad. Expensive shops often give the worst service*. (8) COM. & IND. the regular repairing of machines: *An after-sales service*. (9) ECON. THEORY *see* services, *pl*.

after-sales service *see under* after.

door-to-door service *see under* door-to-door.

pensionable service the number of years of an employee's service that count when calculating the amount of his pension when he retires.

v. (1) IND. of machines, to put or keep in good working order. (2) FIN. to pay the interest on a debt.

service agreement (1) LAW & MAN. the legal document containing a contract of service between an employer and an employee. In many cases it means the same as a service contract. (2) *see* after-sales service.

service charge (1) in a hotel or restaurant, a charge sometimes added to a bill, usu. 10% or 15%, to pay for the service given in waiting on the guest or customer. If such a charge is made, it is not usu. considered necessary to give any tip or gratuity, because, by agreement, the money collected from the charge is divided among the staff as an addition to their pay. (2) a handling charge, *see under* handling. (3) FIN. a fee paid, or charge made, to a person or organization for services in arranging a loan. (4) a charge made by the managers of a block of flats or offices to each of the occupiers to cover the cost of common services, i.e. the services needed for the common parts of the building. The charge may pay for local government rates, and the cost of the supply services: water, electricity, gas, telephones, cleaning, repairs and upkeep of the premises, and the management fees.

service contract LAW & MAN. a contract of service by which a company agrees to employ a director, manager or high executive for a stated period and for a stated salary or other payments. In Britain, service contracts must by law be shown to all members of the company (i.e. shareholders) if requested by any of them.

service, contract of *see* contract of service.

service flat a flat (U.S.A., apartment), the rent for which includes the cost of providing domestic service for cleaning, etc.

service industry *see* tertiary industry *under* industry.

serviceman a person who is a member of the armed forces of a country, i.e. the Army, Navy or Air Force.

ex-serviceman a former member of these forces.

service occupations *see under* occupations.

service of process LAW the formal delivery of a writ or summons to the person or organization to whom it is addressed, i.e. the defendant.

personal service delivery by a person authorized by the court to serve writs and summonses. This may be done at any time except on Sundays.

substituted service if ordered by the court, service by post; or personally on some person such as a solicitor, who will tell the defendant of the existence of the writ or summons; or by advertisement in newspapers. *See* acceptance of service *under* acceptance (1).

service road a road in a town, other than a main road, giving access for vehicles serving, esp. delivering goods to, shops, hotels, etc. without hindering traffic on the main roads.

services ECON. THEORY that class of economic goods that consists, not of commodities but of the work of human beings in the form of physical labour, skilled knowledge and advice, and organizing and commercial ability. These forms of work are scarce and command a price. *See* services to trade; service occupations *under* occupations; tertiary industry *under* industry.

commercial services *see under* commercial.

consumer services those services that are used widely by consumers in their daily life, such as: hairdressers; cleaners; repairers of household machines, electrical apparatus, houses and vehicles; plumbers; gardeners; all of whom are paid for their labour rather than for any article or commodity that they supply.

direct services *see under* direct.

industrial services *see under* industrial.

professional services the highly skilled services of members of the professions, such as accountants, architects, doctors, lawyers.

public utility services *see* supply services *below*.

supply services the public utility services supplying water, electricity, gas, telephones, etc. to the consumer in private houses, and commercial and industrial properties.

services, contract of *see* contract of services.

service station COM. & TRANSPT. a petrol-filling station, usu. with limited arrangements for servicing motor vehicles and for effecting small repairs.

services to trade ECON. those economic activities, such as banking, insurance and transport, that help traders by making their work easier and by reducing risks.

servicing (1) FIN. of debts, the payment of the interest due. (2) IND. of machines, the work of putting and keeping them in good working order. (3) COM. of orders, the work of gathering the goods together and of preparing the documents needed to supply and dispatch goods ordered by a customer.

servitude LAW a right possessed by one person to use the land of another for certain purposes, or to prevent such use. The right may be an easement or a profit à prendre.

servo-control *see* servo-mechanism.

servo-mechanism IND. an electronic or mechanical apparatus which controls machinery automatically. *Syn.* servo-control.

session (1) STK. EXCH. a working day on the Stock Exchange: *Share prices fell steadily throughout the session.* (2) (*a*) a formal meeting of an organization, esp. a law-making body or court. (*b*) a time, esp. a part of a year, during which such meetings take place: *Parliament will be in session again next month.*

set *see* bill (of exchange) in a set.

setback (1) STK. EXCH. a fall in prices after a period when they were rising: *After an early setback, prices advanced steadily.* (2) a small reduction in business activity after a period of increase.

set of bills *see* bill (of exchange) in a set.

set-off LAW & ACCTS. the balancing of one debt against another, or of a gain against a loss.

setting-up cost IND. the cost of changing a machine or group of machines between the end of the production of one product and the beginning of the next, esp. the cost of set-up time or idle time, during which the machine(s) and the persons working on them produce nothing.

settle (1) to pay (a bill, debt, charge, etc.). (2) LAW *To settle out of court*, of a lawsuit, to come to an agreement before the case is decided in court. (3) LAW *To settle land*, to make a legal settlement of land or other property in favour of somebody. *See* settlement (4). (4) LAW *To settle an estate*, to complete the division of the estate of a dead or bankrupt person among the persons having the legal right to it.

settled land LAW land that is held and administered by one or more trustees under a settlement.

settlement (1) FIN. the act of settling, of paying (a bill, debt, charge, etc.). (2) IND. REL. the ending of an industrial dispute by the parties reaching agreement. (3) STK. EXCH. *see* Account, The; Account Day. (4) LAW a document, in the form of a deed or a will, setting up a trust, by which the settlor or donor appoints one or more persons to be trustees to hold and administer land or other property, such as money or investments, in the trust for the benefit of one or more persons called beneficiaries. *See* trust instrument.

ante-nuptial settlement a settlement made before marriage.

marriage settlement a settlement made, usu. but not always before a marriage, limiting the use and enjoyment of property in trust and making special provision for the wife and children of the marriage. Such a settlement is not a voluntary settlement because marriage is, in law, itself a valuable consideration.

post-nuptial settlement a settlement made after marriage. Cf. ante-nuptial settlement *above*.

voluntary settlement a settlement that brings the settlor no valuable consideration, such as one made by a father out of love and affection for his daughter. Cf. marriage settlement *above*.

Settlement Day *see* Account Day.

settlement discount *see* cash discount; settlement terms *under* term.

settlement terms *see under* term, *n*.

settler (1) a person who settles, goes to live permanently, in a new or distant country. (2) LAW a settlor.

Settling Day (1) STK. EXCH. *see* Account Day. (2) COMMOD. EXCH. *see* Prompt Day.

settlor LAW a person who settles land or other property on somebody, under a settlement or trust deed. *See* settlement (4); *also* settler. *Syn.* donor. *Also* settler.

several LAW separate. *See* joint and several.

severance pay MAN. & IND. REL. money paid by an employer to an employee as compensation for loss of employment when the employee's services are brought to an end through no fault on his part. Cf. redundancy pay.

Seychelles an island republic in the Indian Ocean off East Africa, pop. 55,000 (1975); capital, Victoria, pop. 14,000 approx.; languages, English, French and Creole; currency unit, the Seychelles rupee (S Re., *pl.* Rs.), divided into 100 cents.

SF Finland's international vehicle-registration letters.

S/Fee survey fee.

SFr. Swiss franc.

S.G. ship and goods.

s.g. specific gravity.

sgd. signed.

SGP Singapore's international vehicle-registration letters.

sh. shilling.

shadow price *see under* price.

shaduf AGR. an ancient apparatus worked by hand for lifting water into channels to irrigate the land, still much used in Egypt and some other Arab countries, and in India, where it is called a denkli or paecottah. *Also* shadoof; shadouf.

shady (*colloq.*) of doubtful honesty, therefore not to be trusted. *A shady company/customer/financier. A shady deal/transaction*, one made by or with a shady person and therefore probably dishonest.

shaikh *see* sheikh.

shake-up MAN. & STK. EXCH. a complete change in the organization of a business, esp. the directors of a company, or in its capital structure: *A capital shake-up, see* reconstruction; reorganization.

shaky financially unsatisfactory.

sham *see* bogus.

share STK. EXCH. a particular separate part or portion into which the capital of a company is divided, thus, e.g. a company may have a capital of £1 million divided into two million shares of 50p each. Ownership of a share gives the owner, called a member or a shareholder, the right to receive a share in the profits of the company and to share in its management. The main classes of shares are: ordinary shares; deferred shares; preference shares and founders' shares; but there are many variations of these. Shares can be bought and sold on a stock exchange in lots or parcels according to their price. In a limited liability company, the liability of the shareholders is limited to the amount of their shares in the company. *See* limited liability company *under* company. In the U.S.A., although the capital of a stock corporation, the equivalent of a company, is divided into shares, they are called *stock* and their holders are called *stockholders*. *See* stock.

'A' share a class of ordinary share. *See* multiple voting share *below*.

amusement share *see under* amusement.

'B' share a class of ordinary share. *See* multiple voting share *below*.

bearer share a share that is issued to bearer, i.e. to no named person. It can be transferred (passed on) to another person simply by delivery (handing it over). It is not registered in the books of the company as belonging to any named person. Such shares are unusual in Britain. Cf. registered share.

bogus share *see under* bogus.

bonus share *see under* bonus.

cash share one of a number of shares issued for cash, as distinguished from shares issued for consideration other than cash. *See* vendors' share *below*; cash capital.

commercial share *see* commercials.

common share *see* ordinary share.

cumulative preference share a class of preference share on which the dividend accumulates at a fixed rate if not paid every year. *See* cumulative dividend *under* dividend. Cf. non-cumulative preference share *below*. *Abbr.* cum. pref.

deferred ordinary share the usual kind of deferred share (*see below*). *Abbr.* D.O.

deferred share (*a*) a special class of share on which a dividend can be paid only after all other kinds of share such as preference, ordinary and preferred ordinary shares have been paid. Deferred shares are usu. held by founders, promoters, vendors or managers and are sometimes named accordingly. Such shares often receive a very large proportion of the profits remaining after the ordinary shareholders have been paid an agreed rate of dividend. (*b*) another form of deferred share is that which receives little or no dividend at first, but after an agreed time will receive the same rate of dividend as the ordinary shares.

directors' share *see* qualification share *below*.

equity share an ordinary share. *See also* equity of a company.

excess share one of a number of shares in a rights issue not bought by the existing shareholders. Some companies offer to sell these excess shares to other members (existing shareholders).

forfeited share a share that has been given up because the shareholder to whom it was allotted, and who has paid part of its value, has not kept his promise to pay the balance when called by the company.

founders' share a class of deferred share that is sometimes issued to the founders of the company (the persons who first formed it). *See* deferred share (*a*) *above*.

fully-paid share a share of which the full face or nominal value has been paid up. Cf. partly-paid share *below*. *Abbr.* f.p.

growth share *see under* growth.

industrial share *see* industrials.

irredeemable preference share a preference share that the company issuing it has no right to redeem (to buy back).

junior share *see* ordinary share *below*.

management share a deferred share intended for the managers of a company as a means of increasing their interest in the success of the company. *Syn.* managers' share.

managers' share *see* management share *above*.

marked share a share of which the share certificate bears a mark or record that rights offered on the share have been taken up (exercised).

multiple voting share one of two kinds of ordinary share that a company may issue, usu. called 'A' shares and 'B' shares. 'A' shares may carry only limited voting rights, or even none at all; they are usu. issued to the public. 'B' shares carry full voting rights and are usu. reserved for issue to the original owners as a means of keeping control of the company in their hands. *See* non-voting share *below*.

new share one of a number issued in exchange for old shares in a fixed proportion, e.g. of one new share for three old shares. Cf. old share.

non-cumulative preference share a class of preference share on which the dividend does not accumulate if not paid every year. Cf. cumulative preference share *above*.

non-participating share a preference share that carries no right to any share in the profits, but only to a fixed rate of dividend. Cf. participating share *below*.

non-voting share a class of share the holder of which does not have a legal right to a vote at a general meeting of the company. Preference shares are usu. non-voting. Some ordinary shares, usu. called 'A' shares, are also non-voting. *See* multiple voting share *above*. *Syn.* voteless share.

no-par-value share a kind of share sometimes issued by limited liability companies in the U.S.A., Canada and Belgium, that have no nominal or par value. Such shares are not allowed by law in Britain and many other countries. Dividends on no-par-value shares are not given as a percentage of the nominal value, but as a fixed amount of money per share.

old share *see* new share *above*.

ordinary share the largest class of share, the owners of which have the right to share in the profits of the company after the preference shares have been paid their dividend but before the deferred shares. Ordinary shares may be preferred ordinary shares or deferred ordinary shares. Ordinary shareholders carry most of the risks: if profits are low, they get little or no dividend, but if profits are high, they may get a much higher return than do the holders of other classes of capital. *Syn.* common share; equity share; junior share.

paid share *see* partly-paid share *below*. *Also* fully-paid share *above*.

participating preference share a class of preference share the holder of which receives not only the fixed dividend but also the right to a limited participation (share) in the profits remaining after the ordinary shares and the deferred shares have received an agreed percentage.

partly-paid share a share of which the face or nominal value has been only partly paid up. Nowadays in Britain, issues of partly-paid up shares are made only in the case of rights issues, to allow shareholders to pay for the new shares by instalments over several months. Cf. fully-paid share *above*. *Syn.* paid share.

personal share *see* registered share *below*.

preference share a share that receives a fixed rate of dividend that must be paid before any dividend is paid on ordinary shares or deferred shares. Preference shares may be: cumulative preference shares; non-cumulative preference shares; participating preference shares; participating cumulative preference shares; participating non-cumulative preference shares; redeemable preference shares.

preferred ordinary share a class of ordinary share the holders of which have the right to be paid a dividend of at least an agreed amount before the deferred ordinary shares. Not to be confused with a preference share.

qualification share one of a number of shares in a company which a person must hold to qualify for election as a director of that company, if this is provided in its Articles of Association. *Syn.* directors' (qualification) share.

quoted share a share in a company for which an official quotation has been granted by the Stock Exchange. Cf. unquoted share.

redeemable preference share a preference share that the company has the right to redeem (to buy back), at any time it may decide.

registered share a share that is registered in the books of the company in the name of the owner. Cf. bearer share. *Syn.* personal share.

split share a share that is being, or has been, split or divided into a number of new shares, e.g. a share of nominal value £1.00 into four new shares of 25p. The purpose is to make the shares more easily saleable on the Stock Exchange.

subscription share a share in a building society that is, by arrangement, bought by regular instalments. Such shares receive the highest rate of interest of all building society shares.

unquoted share a share that has not been granted an official quotation by the Stock Exchange. Such shares are usu. those of private limited companies or of foreign companies.

vendors' share a class of shares so named because they have been issued instead of cash to the persons who sold the business when it was formed into a company. They may be ordinary shares or deferred shares, as may be agreed with the vendors at the time.

voteless share *see* non-voting share *above*.

voting share a share that gives its holder the right to a vote at general meetings of the company. *See* multiple voting share *above*. *Opp.* voteless share.

share allotment form *see* allotment letter *under* allotment.

sharebroker *see* stockbroker.

share capital *see* capital (2).

share certificate STK. EXCH. a legal document issued by a company to a member shareholder stating the class, quantity and serial numbers of the shares that he holds. It is usu. signed by two directors and the company secretary and stamped with the common seal of the company. *See also* balance certificate; fractional certificate. Cf. share warrant.

sharecropper (U.S.A.) AGR. a small tenant farmer who pays as rent, not money, but a share of the crop.

share exchange *see* exchange of shares.

share-hawking *see* share-pushing.

shareholder STK. EXCH. a member of a limited company and therefore a holder of one or more shares in that company. Cf. stockholder.

minority shareholder *see* minority interests.

shareholders' register *see* register of members.

share indexes *see under* Financial Times; Dow-Jones; Standard & Poor.

share of the market *see* market share; market-sharing.

share option *see* option.

share premium *see* premium, *n.* (1).

share-pushing STK. EXCH. dishonest dealing by some outside brokers, called *share-pushers* or *share-hawkers*, in stocks and shares which prove to be worthless. *Syn.* share-hawking. Cf. bucket shop.

share register *see* register of members.

shares, exchange of *see* exchange of shares.

shares, flotation of *see* flotation.

shares, issue of *see* issue of securities.

shares, lien on *see* lien on shares.

shares, option to purchase *see* option to purchase (2).

share transfer *see* transfer of shares or stock.

share warrant *see under* warrant.

sharing the market *see* market-sharing.

Sharjah *see* United Arab Emirates.

shark (*colloq.*) a greedy person who obtains money from people by trickery or threats. A cheat.

sharp(er) a cheat, esp. at card games: *A card-sharp(er)*.

sharp practice clever but dishonourable behaviour, though not illegal, esp. in business matters.

S/H.E. Sundays and holidays excepted.

shed SHIPG. a building in a port area where goods are stored before being loaded into, or after being unloaded from, a ship.

sheikh in Arabic, a title of respect; an Arab chief, esp. the head of a family or the ruler of a tribe. A prince or king of a territory in Arab lands. *Also* shaikh; shaykh; sheik; sheykh.

sheikhdom the office of a sheikh; the territory governed by a sheikh. *Also* shaikhdom; shaykhdom; sheikdom.

shekel the standard currency unit of the State of Israel, divided into 100 new agorot.

shelf-life COM. of goods kept on the shelves of a shop, the probable length of time from manufacture that the commodity may be expected to remain in a good and saleable condition, after which it will begin to go bad: *Tinned/canned foods have a shelf-life of several years; the shelf-life of foods in plastic packs is a few weeks.*

shell company *see under* company.

shell out (*colloq.*) to pay out money, esp. unwillingly. *Syn.* fork out.

SHEX Sundays and holidays excepted.

sheykh *see* sheikh.

shift *v.* TAXN. to pass on a liability to pay an indirect tax, usu. from seller to buyer.

n. IND. a group of employees working together during an agreed period of hours in a factory that is on shift-working, i.e. operating two periods called the *day shift* and the *night shift*; or three periods, usu. called *morning shift*, *afternoon shift* and *night shift*. Such employees are doing *shift-work*.

shilling (1) the standard currency unit of Kenya (KSh.), of Tanzania (TSh.), of Uganda (USh.), and of Somalia, each divided into 100 cents. (2) a former fractional currency unit of the United Kingdom, the Irish Republic, and a number of former British dominions, colonies and dependencies; 20*s*. (or 20/-) = £1; 12*d*. (pence) = 1*s*. (or 1/-). Cf. schilling (Austria). *See also* king's shilling.

ship *n.* SHIPG. any boat large and strong enough to sail the open sea.

v. to cause to be transported by sea (in U.S.A. also by rail, road and air). *Shipping*, the business of carrying goods and passengers by sea: *We specialize in shipping machinery to South America.* In U.S.A., also by other means of transport: *To ship goods by rail/sea/air/road.*

cargo ship *see* cargo boat. *Syn.* freighter.

clean ship *see under* clean.

coasting ship *see* coaster.

container ship *see under* container.

dry ship *see* general ship *below.*

general ship a cargo vessel that has not been chartered, and is therefore free to carry the goods of any shipper under bills of lading.

General ships are sometimes called dry ships, to distinguish them from tankers.

heavy-lift ship *see under* heavy lift.

merchant ship *see under* merchant.

motor ship *see* motor vessel. *Abbr.* M.S.

training ship *see under* training.

tramp ship a cargo ship that accepts any cargo it can get and will carry any goods to any port to which shippers have cargo to send. It works to no fixed programme. Cf. liner. *Also* tramp steamer; trampship; tramp.

ship agent SHIPG. a person or firm whose work is to represent shipowners in distant ports in arranging the loading and unloading of ships, the employment of crews, the supply of stores and fuel, the making of repairs, and the handling of customs and port health formalities. Ship agents do not usu. concern themselves with the work of finding cargoes. Cf. shipping agent; ship-broker.

ship bill of sale *see* bill of sale (2).

shipboard SHIPG. *On shipboard*, on board a ship. *See* board.

ship-broker SHIPG. a broker who acts as agent for shipowners and shipping companies, arranging bill-of-lading contracts, charter-parties and insurance; finding cargoes and, in some cases, passengers; and receiving for his services a commission calculated as a percentage of the business he gets for his principals. Cf. ship agent.

shipbuilders' policy *see under* insurance policy.

shipbuilding IND. & SHIPG. that part of the heavy engineering industry that is concerned with designing and building new ships and with repairing existing vessels.

ship-canal *see under* canal.

ship chandler SHIPG. & COM. a shopkeeper who sells the many articles needed by ships such as ropes, tools, metal goods, food and drink. *Also* ship's chandler.

shipload (1) SHIPG. the amount of passengers and cargo that a particular ship can carry when full, or is now actually carrying. (2) any large quantity of a commodity: *We sell timber by the shipload*, in large quantities.

shipmaster SHIPG. the master or captain of a merchant ship.

shipment SHIPG. (1) the act of putting goods on a ship: *These goods are ready for shipment. Abbr.* shipt. (2) the carriage of goods by ship, not by other means of transport: *Shipment is the cheapest form of transport.* (3) a quantity or collection of goods being carried together by ship: *The spare parts will be included in your shipment of machines aboard s.s. Mary Jones. Syn.* consignment.

shipment policy *see under* insurance policy.

shipowner SHIPG. in Britain, one of the persons registered as the owner of one or more of the 64 shares into which the property in a British ship is by law divided. He must be a British subject, and the ship must have a British port as its port of registry. *See also* managing owner. A shipowner may also be a corporation, such as a limited company with its principal place of business within British territory. *Abbr.* S/O.

shipowner's lien *see* carrier's lien *under* carrier's.

shipped bill of lading *see under* bill of lading.

shipper(s) SHIPG. & COM. a commercial organization that sends goods to a foreign country by ship. Shippers first make arrangements with a shipping company, or with a ship-broker or ship agent, to reserve cargo space in advance for a consignment on a particular ship. The shippers and the shipping company then sign a bill-of-lading contract for the carriage of the consignment. *See also* export merchant *under* export.

shipping SHIPG. (1) ships collectively, esp. the ships of a country: *The gross tonnage of Britain's merchant shipping was about 150 million.* (2) the movement of ships at sea: *The English Channel is crowded with shipping.*

merchant shipping cargo and passenger vessels collectively. *See also* ship, *v.*

Shipping, American Bureau of *see under* American.

shipping (and forwarding) agent COM. a business organization which will do the work of preparing shipping documents, arrange for shipping space and insurance and deal with customs formalities, in return for a fee. Some shipping agents are also forwarding agents, organizing the collection, carriage and delivery of goods between ports and the premises of merchants and manufacturers. Cf. ship agent. *Syn.* forwarder.

shipping articles *see* articles of agreement.

shipping bill SHIPG. a customs form giving a detailed description of goods to be removed from a bonded warehouse for re-export.

shipping card *see* sailing card.

shipping-commissioner *see* shipping-master.

shipping company SHIPG. a company that owns and operates one or more ships. A shipowner.

shipping conference SHIPG. an association of owners of liners sailing along the same route, who combine together to fix standard freight rates. *Syn.* shipping ring. *See* conference lines *under* conference.

shipping documents BKG. & COM. certain documents which, under the system known as *documents for collection*, are sent by an exporter's bank to the bank's branch or agent in the importer's country, who delivers them to the importer when he pays or accepts a bill of exchange. The shipping documents consist of: commercial export invoice; bill of lading; forwarder's receipt; consignment note; insurance

policy; insurance certificate; and, if necessary, certificate of origin, consular invoice, weight certificate, sanitary certificate, letter of hypothecation, export licence(s). Most if not all these documents are needed by the importer to obtain delivery of the goods, to clear them through customs and to claim on insurance if they are lost or damaged. *Syn.* export documents.

Shipping Federation SHIPG. in Britain, an organization formed by shipowners to deal with the training and supply of ships' crews and to control their conditions of work and pay.

shipping instructions COM. & SHIPG. a document prepared by an exporter and sent through his shipping and forwarding agent to the shipowners giving them directions and detailed information concerning the consignment.

shipping-master SHIPG. a port official responsible for seeing that arrangements for employing the crews of merchant ships are carried out according to law. Cf. master. *Syn.* (U.S.A.) shipping-commissioner.

shipping note COM. & SHIPG. a document prepared by the shipowners giving the superintendent (official in charge) of the docks details of the cargo to be carried. A duplicate copy is signed by the superintendent as a receipt for the goods.

shipping order (*colloq.*) any large order.

shipping space SHIPG. space for cargo in the hold of a ship: *To book/reserve shipping space for a consignment of goods.*

shipping specification SHIPG. & COM. a form that must by law be sent to the Customs giving full details of goods being exported.

shipping ton *see* freight ton *under* ton.

ship's articles *see* articles of agreement.

ship's certificate *see* certificate of registry *under* registry.

ship's chandler *see under* ship chandler.

ship's clearance *see under* clearance.

ship's company SHIPG. the entire crew of a ship, i.e. all the persons who are employed to work on the ship when at sea, including officers but not passengers.

ship's husband SHIPG. a person, usu. one of the joint owners of a ship, who has been appointed by the other owners to manage its affairs and to control its use.

ship's inventory *see under* inventory.

ship's log *see* log.

ship's manifest *see* manifest.

ship's papers SHIPG. certain documents that every ship, esp. a British ship, must always have ready for official examination. They are: the certificate of registry; the bill of health; the log book(s); the articles and muster roll; the charter-party if under charter; bills of lading, invoices and the manifest relating to the cargo; the passenger manifest if carrying passengers.

ship's protest *see* captain's protest *under* captain.

ship's rail SHIPG. the side of a ship.
  at ship's rail *see under* ship's derrick.
  over ship's rail *see under* over.

ship's register *see* certificate of registry *under* registry.

ship's report SHIPG. a report that must be made by the master of a ship to the port authorities on arrival at the port, giving details of the ship, its cargo and passengers.

ship's stores *see under* stores.

ship surveyor *see* Lloyd's surveyor.

shipt. shipment.

shipwreck SHIPG. (1) the loss of a ship by destruction at sea. (2) the wrecked ship itself.

shipyard a place in a harbour or port where ships are built or repaired, usu. with at least one dry dock, special cranes, and workshops for manufacturing parts made of steel, aluminium, copper and wood.

shop *n.* (1) a building or part of a building, open regularly to the public, where goods are kept and sold to consumers; a retail business. (2) sometimes also a place where wholesale trading is done, more often called a depot or warehouse. (3) a place where services are offered or arranged for the public, such as a *barber's shop*, a *shoe-repair shop*. (4) IND. a place where things are manufactured or repaired: *A workshop*; *a machine shop*; *a repair shop*.
  bucket shop *see under* bucket.
  closed shop *see under* closed.
  duty-free shop *see under* duty-free.
  junk shop *see* junk (2).
  lock-up shop *see* lock-up.
  machine shop *see under* machine.
  mobile shop *see under* mobile.
  multiple shop *see* chain-store.
  open shop *see under* open.
  tied shop *see under* tied.
  to set up shop to open a new business.
  to talk shop to discuss work or business matters when off duty.
  union shop *see under* union.
  v. to buy things in shops. *To shop around*, to look around the shops to find which is the cheapest.

shop assistant a person employed to serve customers and to help generally in a shop. *Syn.* (U.S.A.) salesclerk, *pron.* clurk.

shop floor *see under* floor.

shopkeeper a person who owns or manages a shop.

shop-lifter LAW & COM. a thief who steals goods from shops while pretending to be a customer.

shopper a person who shops, who goes to shops to buy things.

shopping centre a group of shops of different kinds, often outside the centre of a town and planned and built as a whole.

shop-soiled COM. of goods, made dirty or having a worn appearance from having been shown or used in a shop, and therefore no longer saleable at the full price of perfect goods. *Syn.* part-worn; shop-worn.

shop steward IND. REL. in a factory, workshop or office, an employee who is a trade-union official and is responsible for representing the other employees with whom he works, in negotiations with their employer.

shop window a window of a shop, usu. on a street, in which are shown some of the goods that are for sale in the shop, usu. arranged to attract the public to come in and buy. *Syn.* show window.

shortage (1) a lack or scarcity of something: *A shortage of labour/energy. Syn.* dearth. (2) some part that is missing: *A shortage of two cases in a consignment of 20 from Hong Kong*, of the 20, two cases have failed to arrive. *A shortage in delivery.*

short bill *see under* bill of exchange.

short-change *see* fluff.

short covering STK. EXCH. the act of a stockjobber, short of stock, who buys a security in order to keep his promise to deliver. *See* selling short; short of stock.

short-dated securities *see* shorts.

short delivery TRANSPT. & COM. a delivery from which, on arrival, some goods are missing. *Abbr.* s.d.; S.D.

shorthand a very quick method of writing down speech (words spoken), based on signs that represent sounds. The shorthand signs are then read by a typist, usu. the same person who wrote them down. *Syn.* stenography. A *shorthand-typist*, a person who can write down speech in shorthand and can also type it. *Syn.* stenographer; steno-typist.

short lease *see under* lease.

short of stock STK. EXCH. of a stockjobber, unable to buy a quantity of a particular stock or share that he has sold short, i.e. has promised to deliver at an agreed price. *See* selling short; short covering.

short rate *see under* exchange rate.

short run the distinction between the short run and the long run was first made by Alfred Marshall in connection with a change in demand. In the *short run* the supply of a commodity often cannot be varied and a change in demand will affect the price, sometimes strongly. In the *long run* the change in demand will be balanced by a change in supply and a new equilibrium price will be reached. *Syn.* short period. *See* long run.

shorts STK. EXCH. in Britain, gilt-edged and other fixed-interest securities repayable in less than five years from the present time. Cf. mediums; longs.

short sale *see* selling short.

short shipment SHIPG. that part of a shipment of goods that has not been loaded because the ship was full. Such goods are said to be 'left out' or 'shut out'.

short-term gain TAXN. a capital gain made in selling an asset within 12 months of buying it, which may attract a special rate of tax.

short-time working IND. of a factory or industry, working fewer hours than normal because a temporary lack of orders or a shortage of materials makes it necessary to reduce output.

short ton a measurement of weight commonly used in U.S.A., of 2000 lb (907 kg), as compared with the *long ton* commonly used in Britain, of 2240 lb (1016 kg), and the *metric ton* or *tonne* of 2204.6 lb. *Syn.* net ton; American ton; U.S. ton. *Abbr.* s.t.

shove (*colloq.*) *see* sack; boot.

show business IND. & COM. the business of entertaining the public, esp. by performances in theatres, on television, in films, etc. *Also* (*colloq.*) show biz.

showcard ADVTG. a printed card shown in a shop to draw attention to a product being offered for sale. Such cards are usu. supplied as display material by the manufacturer of the product. *See* dealer aids.

show-case ADVTG. & COM. a piece of furniture in a shop, consisting of a case with glass sides and top, in which goods are shown but cannot be handled by customers.

show of hands *see* hands, show of.

showroom COM. a room in which goods are placed on show for customers to see. Showrooms are usu. kept by wholesalers, but some retailers also call their shops showrooms, such as *carpet showrooms*, *motor-car showrooms*.

show window *see* shop window.

s.h.p. shaft horse-power (of a ship's engines).

shpg. shipping.

shunter (1) STK. EXCH. a stockbroker who buys and sells securities in both the London and the other stock exchanges in Britain. (2) TRANSPT. a road transport vehicle that carries goods short distances, delivers them, and returns empty to its depot. Cf. trunker.

shunting (U.S.A.) *see* arbitrage (2).

shut down IND. to stop production; to close a factory, usu. temporarily.

shut-down cost *see* prime cost *under* cost.

shut for dividend STK. EXCH. of a company's share transfer books, closed temporarily while the documents for the payment of dividends are prepared.

shut out SHIPG. not shipped; not loaded on the ship: *The consignment was shut out because it arrived at the docks too late. See* short shipment. *Syn.* short shipped.

shyster (1) (*colloq.*) a clever but dishonest person who earns money by mean tricks. (2) LAW (U.S.A. *colloq.*) an unprofessional lawyer who uses unfair and dishonest means to win his cases.

S.I. Shetland Isles, Scotland.

SI Système International *see* SI system of units.

s.i. sum insured.

Siam *see* Thailand.

sick leave *see under* leave.

sickness benefit INSCE. in Britain, an allowance of money paid to a person who is unable to work because of sickness, under a private health-insurance policy or the national insurance scheme.

siding TRANSPT. a short branch of a railway line, for wagons that are being loaded or unloaded, or being stored when not in use.

Sierra Leone a republic in West Africa, pop. 3 million approx. (1975); capital, Freetown, pop. 200,000 approx.; languages, English, pidgin English and tribal; currency unit, the leone, divided into 100 cents. Member, (British) Commonwealth; O.A.U.

sight BKG. in relation to a bill of exchange, the time the bill is first seen by the person responsible for paying it./

at sight of a bill of exchange, payable when presented to the debtor: *A bill payable at sight is called a sight bill.* Cf. usance bill.

after sight of a bill of exchange, payable on a date that is a stated number of days, usu. 30, 60, 90 or 120 days, after the bill is first presented to the debtor. Such a bill is called a usance bill. Cf. sight bill.

sight bill *see under* bill of exchange; *also* sight.

sight, bill of *see* bill of sight.

sight draft *see* sight bill *under* bill of exchange.

sight entry *see* bill of sight.

sight rate (of exchange) *see* short rate *under* exchange rate.

signatory LAW (1) one who has signed a document, esp. a country that has signed a treaty. *Britain is one of the signatories of the International Copyright Convention. Syn.* signer. (2) one of the persons who take part in forming a new limited company by signing the Memorandum and Articles of Association, so becoming the first members of the company.

signature the name of a person or firm signed (written personally) at the end of a letter or other document, so making its contents binding on the person signing it or the firm.

specimen signature BKG. a sample of a person's usual signature, given to a bank when a current account is first opened, and held in the bank's signature book or card index, so that the staff can recognize it and can check that the signature on a cheque really is that of the customer.

signature stamp *see under* stamp.

significance, marginal *see* marginal utility.

sign on MAN. (1) to accept employment, esp. by signing a contract of service. (2) to give a person a job, to agree to hire a worker's services.

silage AGR. food for farm animals that has been specially prepared and is stored in a silo. *Maize grown for silage. Also* ensilage.

silent partner *see* sleeping partner *under* partner.

silk-screen process a method of printing designs in colour on to paper, card, etc. by using stencils made of thin cloth, formerly silk. This process is relatively cheap for printing small quantities of notices, posters, etc.

silo AGR. a special cylindrical airtight structure for making and storing silage (food for farm animals), or for storing grain.

silver FIN. & BKG. coins made of silver, or of an alloy containing silver, or of cupro-nickel, a metal looking like silver. That form of the currency that is not paper money or copper.

silver certificates (U.S.A.) FIN. paper money still used by the U.S. Treasury, that can be exchanged for silver.

silver standard FIN. a monetary system that formerly existed in many countries, under which the value of the standard unit of the currency was by law made equal to a fixed weight of silver of a stated fineness; the coinage was largely made of silver; bank-notes were freely exchanged for silver on demand; and silver could be freely imported or exported.

sily *see* syli.

simple bonus *see under* bonus (3).

simple contract *see under* contract.

simple interest *see under* interest.

sincerely truly, faithfully: *Yours sincerely*, the closing words of a personal letter and of an informal business letter when the writer and the person to whom he is writing are on friendly, but not very close, terms.

sinecure an office or job that carries a good salary but demands little or no work.

sine die (*Latin*, without a day) without a fixed date; indefinitely. *See* adjournment sine die. *Abbr.* s.d.

Singapore an island republic in south-east Asia, pop. 2.3 million approx. (1975); capital, Singapore, pop. 2 million approx.; languages, Chinese, Malay, Tamil and English; currency unit, the Singapore dollar (Sing$), divided into 100 cents. Member, (British) Commonwealth; A.S.E.A.N.

single bond *see under* bond, *n.*

single cost *see under* cost.

single entry ACCTS. a simple system of book-keeping not now used except by small businesses, by which each transaction (business deal) is recorded by only one entry. Cf. double entry.

single fare *see under* fare.

single liability *see under* liability.

single option *see under* option.

single-premium policy *see under* insurance policy.

single ticket *see under* ticket.

single-use goods *see* consumer non-durables.

sinking fund FIN. & ACCTS. money set aside by annual instalments for a special purpose, such as to repay a debt, or to replace an asset, e.g. a lease of property, at a known future date. *See* amortize.

sinking fund policy *see* capital redemption policy *under* insurance policy.

sister company *see under* company.

sister ships MAR. INSCE. two or more ships belonging to the same owners. *A sister-ship clause* is usu. included in marine insurance contracts making special arrangements for arbitration if the ship collides with another ship belonging to the same owners, because the owners cannot bring a lawsuit for damages against themselves.

SI system of units (SI) a system of units based on six primary or basic metric units: the metre (m) for length, the kilogram (kg) for mass, the second (s) for time, the ampere (A) for electric current, the kelvin (K) for temperature, and the candela (cd) for luminous intensity (strength of light). Other SI units, such as the square metre (m^2) for area, are derived (developed) from these. There are also multiples (many times) such as the kilometre (km), and subdivisions such as the centimetre (cm). *See* international system of units; International Bureau of Weights and Measures.

sit. situation; sitting-room.

sit-down strike *see under* strike.

site the ground or area of land where something is placed: *The site of a house, factory, town. A building site*, the piece of land on which a building is being built.

sitrep. *see* situation report *under* report.

sits. vac. situations vacant.

situation (1) a position, esp. in relation to the surroundings: *The best situation for an office is near a railway station and on a bus route. The house has a fine situation on the bank of a river.* (2) FIN. a general state of affairs: *The economic situation does not encourage new investment. We are in a difficult financial situation.* (3) MAN. a position in employment; a job: *A well-paid situation in the sales department. Syn.* post.

situations vacant *pl.* in classified advertisements, a heading in which employers offer jobs that need to be filled. *Abbr.* sits. vac.

situations wanted *pl.* in classified advertisements, a heading in which people offer their services to employers.

situation rent *see under* rent.

situation report *see under* report.

sk. sack.

skin (*colloq.*) *see* fleece.

skint (*colloq.*) having no money; penniless.

skipper (1) SHIPG. the captain of a ship, esp. of a small merchant vessel. (2) (*colloq.*) a popular title for any person in charge of a team or group of workers.

slate club *see* loan club.

slaughter-house *see* abattoir.

slave a human being considered as a piece of property or merchandize. The master of a private slave has complete rights of ownership over the slave and his family and over the product of their labour, for which no wages are paid. Cf. serf, villein.

slavery (1) an economic and social system that recognizes legal rights of absolute ownership of human beings and of the product of their labour. (2) the condition of being a slave, of being bound to work for, and in all things obey, a master, who is the absolute owner of the slave's body and can buy and sell him for money in the slave market. Cf. serfdom.

slave trade ECON. HIST. the trade that existed in the seventeenth, eighteenth and nineteenth centuries in African negroes, millions of whom were taken by force from their homes in West Africa, transported under cruel conditions to the European colonies in North and South America, and sold as slaves, mainly to owners of plantations. Strong public feeling in Europe early in the nineteenth century, esp. in Britain, resulted in this inhuman trade being stopped after the American Civil War (1861–5). Complete abolition was introduced in the International Slavery Convention of the League of Nations in 1926; this work is continuing under the United Nations against the small trade in slaves that still exists in some parts of the world.

sld. sailed.

sleeper TRANSPT. (1) (a compartment in) a railway sleeping-car. (2) a train consisting entirely of sleeping-cars: *Please book me a berth on the night sleeper to Glasgow.*

sleeping-car TRANSPT. a special railway coach in which there are beds for passengers to sleep in during long night journeys. *See* sleeper.

sleeping partner *see under* partner.

sliding scale a scale of values that is planned to vary in accord with movements in some other value, such as a scale of wages that varies with the cost of living, or with the employer's profits.

sliding trend STK. EXCH. a severe fall in market prices; a collapse of prices.

slip, slipway *see* camber (2).

slogan ADVTG. a clever, easily remembered and often repeated saying, used in making a product better known by the public, or to remind the public about something, e.g. *Bread for energy. Stop, look and listen,* before crossing the road.

slot-machine COM. a machine for selling small articles esp. food, sweets, cigarettes, etc. The buyer obtains delivery of the goods by putting

a coin into a slot or special hole in the machine. Cf. automat. *Syn.* vending machine.

slot-meter a coin meter. *See* meter.

slow assets *see under* assets.

slow-down *see* go-slow.

sluice-gate price *see under* price.

slump *n.* ECON. *see* depression.

v. STK. & COMMOD. EXCH. to fall suddenly: *Today prices slumped after reaching high levels yesterday.*

slush (*colloq.*) false bank-notes.

slush fund COM. (*colloq.*) money set aside for making secret payments (bribes) to persons who, in return, will use their influence in getting favoured treatment for the maker of the secret payment. *Syn.* slush money.

slush money *see* slush fund.

smacker (*colloq.*) in Britain, a pound note; in U.S.A., a dollar.

small ads ADVTG. small (classified) advertisements. *See under* advertisement.

smallholding AGR. & LAW (1) a small farm. (2) in English law, a holding of agricultural land more than one acre but not more than 50 acres in extent, or having a rental value of not more than £150 per annum.

small print *see under* print.

smash *v.* FIN. (1) to ruin (somebody) financially. (2) to be financially ruined. (3) to become bankrupt.

n. a financial failure; bankruptcy or liquidation. *Syn.* crash.

SME Surinam's international vehicle-registration letters.

Smith Adam (1723–90), Scottish economist and philosopher, and founder of the Classical School. He studied at Glasgow (1737–40) and Oxford (1740–3) and became Professor of Logic (1751), then of Moral Philosophy (1752–63) at Glasgow. In 1759 he published *The Theory of Moral Sentiments*, about human nature. After travels on the continent (1764–6), he lived in Scotland and in London and wrote the most famous of all books on economics, *An Inquiry into the Nature and Causes of the Wealth of Nations*, published in 1776. He was the first to explain the advantages of specialization, or division of labour, which greatly increased the efficiency of labour, made men dependent on each other, and resulted in the setting-up of markets and a system of prices, with money as the medium of exchange. He argued that value was related to labour costs (*see* Labour Theory of Value); that Man's natural self-interest in a free and competitive economy would, if not interfered with by the State, result in an efficient economic system that would have the force to grow; that the State should concern itself only with public order, national defence and certain essential services, such as roads (*see* laissez-faire).

Adam Smith's teachings and writings had a very great influence on the political and economic policies of his times, esp. on the ending of mercantilist controls and the behaviour of the businessmen who led the Industrial Revolution.

smuggle to import or export goods secretly and illegally, esp. if customs duty is not paid or such imports are forbidden by law, e.g. drugs.

SN Senegal's international vehicle-registration letters.

S/N shipping note.

Snake FIN. formerly, *Snake in a/the Tunnel*, as a first step towards a European monetary system (E.M.S.), an arrangement among member countries of the European Economic Community (E.E.C.) by which the internal exchange rates between their currencies are allowed to vary only within quite small limits, like the movements of a snake in a narrow tunnel. Attempts to maintain the arrangement have not been very successful because one or two E.E.C. currencies always seem to be in difficulty.

snap check MAN. a sudden check, made without warning, to see that work is being properly done, or that there is no dishonesty among the employees doing the work. *Syn.* spot check.

snap up COM. to seize or buy eagerly: *To snap up a bargain/all the remaining stock.*

sneak-thief (1) a thief who steals small things. (2) a thief who enters and leaves a building by an open door without breaking in or out.

snide (*colloq.*) (1) false coin. (2) a person of bad character, unworthy of all respect. (3) of a remark, unkind, intended to be funny but also to hurt someone's feelings.

snip (*colloq.*) a bargain: *It's a snip at £5.*

S/O shipowner.

s.o. seller's option.

soar STK. & COMMOD. EXCH. of prices, to rise very high: *Prices soared on news of record profits.*

Soc. society.

social accounting ECON. & FIN. a system of making a set of accounts from government statistics, to show the income and expenditure of the various sectors of the national economy of a country, e.g. government sector, producers' sector and personal sector.

Social Credit ECON. a movement for economic reform started in Canada by Major C.H. Douglas, whose Social Credit Party was elected to govern Alberta in 1935. He argued that depressions are caused by a shortage of purchasing power; that this is because there is never enough money in the economy to buy all the goods produced, since not all the money spent on costs of production is used for consumption. He claimed that to relieve this shortage the government should increase purchasing power by extensive programmes of public

works, subsidies on consumer goods, and personal credits to private citizens to increase their spending. Most economists say that there is a fallacy (a basic error of reasoning) in Douglas's argument: all the money spent on costs of production is in the end paid in wages and salaries that are in turn spent on consumption; but the movement still has its followers.

social insurance INSCE. any system of state insurance for workers. *See* national insurance.

socialism a form of social organization in which the means of production are owned and managed by the State for the good of the whole community; all economic activity is directed by a central planning authority in place of a capitalist economy based on free enterprise, free markets and the profit motive. There are various degrees of socialism, the most advanced being communism, but all aim to produce a classless society, to redistribute incomes and wealth in order to get rid of poverty, and to give equal opportunities to all. *See also* Marx, Karl.

guild socialism *see under* guild.

non-state socialism an economic system under which industry would be controlled by those workers actually employed in an industry, and at all levels of responsibility; the shareholders would have no part in controlling industrial companies.

social security FIN. any government scheme for paying allowances such as sickness, maternity and unemployment benefits and retirement pensions, esp. if paid entirely out of taxation. If the cost is met wholly or partly from contributions paid by employees and employers to the State, the scheme is usu. called national insurance.

social security tax *see under* tax.

society (1) the general organization of any large group of people living together under a system of laws and accepted standards of behaviour: *Modern American/European/Indian society demands freedom from want. A dishonest person is not accepted in society. Well-organized society.* (2) an association of persons with common aims or interests: *A horticultural society*, one that brings together people interested in horticulture (gardening). *Abbr.* Soc.

affiliated societies *see under* affiliated.

approved society *see* friendly society.

benefit society *see* benefit club, etc. *under* benefit.

building society *see under* building.

co-operative society *see* co-operative.

friendly society *see under* friendly.

industrial and provident society *see under* industrial.

provident society *see* industrial and provident society *under* industrial.

socio-economic ECON. social and economic:

The socio-economic conditions in China, the conditions under which people live and work.

soft currency *see under* currency.

soft goods COM. & IND. (1) cloth of all kinds, for sale as material rather than made into articles such as clothes or curtains, (2) *see* consumer non-durables.

soft money *see under* money.

soft selling ADVTG. the use of quiet and hardly noticeable methods of advertising and selling a product. *Opp.* hard selling. *N. (colloq.)* a soft sell.

software COMP. the automatic programming methods and the materials and equipment used in operating a computer, as opposed to hardware, i.e. the computer itself.

soiled COM. of goods, dirty, esp. *shop-soiled*, made dirty or slightly worn by handling in a shop. *Syn.* shop-worn.

sol the standard currency unit of Peru, divided into 100 centavos. *Pl.* soles.

sola BKG. (*Latin*, sole) one and only; a bill of exchange of which only one document is issued, that being the original itself, there being no other copies. Sola is a short form of: sola of exchange; sole of exchange; sola bill. Cf. bill (of exchange) in a set.

sold *v.* (1) *past tense and past participle of* sell: *To be sold*, for sale. *Sold out*, of supplies or stocks, all have been sold and none remain. *Sold off*, got rid of at a reduced price. *See* sell. (2) *(colloq.)* cheated: *After paying the money I found I had been sold, because the goods were useless.*

sold day book *see* sales day book.

sold note STK. EXCH. a note to his client from a stockbroker who has carried out his client's order to sell a security. The note records full details of the particular deal. *See* contract note. *Opp.* bought note.

sole being the only one of a kind: *The sole owner of a business. A sole agent*, an agent who, by agreement, is his principal's one and only agent in a particular place *(see* exclusive sales agreement). *Sole rights*, rights that nobody else has.

sole bill *see* sola.

sole of exchange *see* sola.

sole proprietor *see under* proprietor.

sole trader *see under* trader.

solicit COM. to ask for, esp. by expressing a desire for something and inviting or urging that it be given: *To solicit orders/business/trade/subscriptions by advertising*, etc. *To solicit alms*, to beg for charity. Cf. unsolicited.

solicitor LAW a lawyer, esp. in England, who, after a period of training in a law office and after passing the examinations of the Law Society, has been made an officer of the Supreme Court. He thus becomes a member of that branch of the legal profession that is alone

qualified to be a legal adviser to clients, to act for them in cases in the civil and criminal courts, to represent them personally in the lower courts, and to prepare cases for barristers in the higher courts. Solicitors attend to a variety of other legal matters such as preparing wills, administering estates and trusts, conveyancing (transferring ownership of) land and buildings, forming companies, and drawing up contracts and other legal documents. Cf. barrister-at-law.

solicitor's lien LAW the right of a solicitor to keep in his possession documents which he holds in his position as solicitor until his fees have been paid.

solid measure *see* cubic or solid measure.

Solomon Islands a small independent parliamentary state, formerly a British protectorate, in the western Pacific Ocean, pop. 200,000 approx. (1977); capital, Honiara, pop. 15,000 approx.; languages, English and pidgin English; currency unit, the Australian dollar (A$), divided into 100 cents. Member, (British) Commonwealth.

solvency LAW & FIN. ability to pay one's debts in full when due; the state of being solvent. Cf. insolvency. *Syn.* solvability. *See also* acid test ratio.

solvent (1) LAW & FIN. able to pay one's debts in full when they are due for payment. Cf. insolvent. *Syn.* solvable. (2) ACCTS. of a business, having an excess of assets over liabilities.

Som. Somerset(shire), England.

Somalia an Arab republic in eastern Africa, pop. 3 million approx. (1975); capital, Mogadishu, 200,000 approx.; language, Somali; currency unit, the Somali shilling, divided into 100 cents. Member, Arab League; O.A.U.; Associate, E.E.C.

S.o.R. (on) sale or return.

sorter an employee in the Post Office who sorts letters.

sorting machine ACCTS. a machine that automatically sorts, e.g. punched cards into a certain order.

S.O.S. a call for help by a person in trouble, or a group of persons in very great danger of death. It is understood in all languages. *The sinking ship sent out an S.O.S. An S.O.S. message. Also* SOS.

source a place of origin, from which something comes or can be obtained: *My job is my main source of income*, how I get most of my income. *A source of supply of raw materials.*

South Africa a republic in southern Africa, pop. 23 million approx. (1975); capitals: administrative, Pretoria, pop. 500,000 approx., legislative, Cape Town, pop. 650,000 approx.; languages, Afrikaans, English and tribal; currency unit, the rand (R), divided into 100 cents.

South Korea a republic in eastern Asia, pop. 34 million approx. (1975); capital, Seoul, pop. 5.5 million approx.; language, Korean; currency unit, the won or hwan, divided into 100 chon.

South Sea Bubble ECON. HIST. a shameful event in 1720 concerning the South Sea Company based in London. People rushed madly to buy its shares, expecting it to make high profits from its newly-gained monopoly of trade with the South Sea Islands in the Pacific, given in return for taking responsibility for part of the British national debt. Encouraged by the king and the government, the directors dishonestly and foolishly used the company's capital to buy its own shares in the market, thus causing the price to go even higher. At last the public lost confidence and the crash came. Some had made great fortunes, but thousands were ruined. For over a century after this the formation of joint-stock companies was stopped by law. *See* bubble.

South West Africa *see* Namibia.

South Yemen *see* Yemen (Aden).

sov. sovereign.

sovereign (1) a king or queen (*see* monarch). (2) FIN. a gold coin, formerly the standard of the British coinage, equal to £1, but nowadays minted only for the gold reserve of the Bank of England and for use in certain areas in the Middle East. It is not legal tender in Britain. *Abbr.* sov.

Soviet Union *see* Union of Soviet Socialist Republics.

S.P. supra protest.

spa TOUR. a place where there is a spring of water that is taken as medicine for certain diseases, esp. such a place that has become a resort. *Syn.* watering place.

space-bar on a typewriter, a key in the form of a horizontal bar which, when pressed, causes the carriage to move forward one space.

Spain a monarchy (kingdom) in south-western Europe, pop. 35 million approx. (1975); capital, Madrid, pop. 3 million approx.; language, Spanish; currency unit, the peseta, divided into 100 centimos. Member, O.E.C.D.; expected to join E.E.C.

spare (part) an extra part of a machine kept ready to replace the part at present in use if it should fail.

spec. (*colloq.*) speculation, esp. in phrase *on spec.*, as a speculation/gamble.

special acceptance *see* qualified acceptance *under* acceptance.

special agent *see* agent.

Special Arab Assistance Fund for Africa (S.A.A.F.A.) *see* Arab Bank for Economic Development in Africa. *Also known as* the Arab Loan Fund for Africa.

special bonus *see under* bonus (3).

special buyer FIN. & STK. EXCH. in Britain, a member of a firm of discount brokers appointed and directed by the Bank of England to buy and sell Treasury bills and certain other first-class securities to the commercial banks and to the public as a means of controlling the monetary system. Cf. Government Broker.

Special Commissioners of Income Tax LAW & TAXN. in Britain, a judicial tribunal of officials appointed by the Treasury to decide appeals against assessments of certain classes of taxes on incomes.

special crossing *see* crossed cheque *under* cheque.

special damages *see under* damages, *n. pl.*

special delivery in Britain, a service performed by the Post Office, by which an urgent letter or packet is carried as first-class mail but receives favoured treatment and fast delivery, if necessary by special messenger. An extra fee is charged for this service. *Syn.* express (letter) delivery.

special deposits BKG. in Britain, deposits, usu. of very large sums, that must be made by commercial banks with the Bank of England when directed by the government, usu. as a means of controlling the money supply by limiting the amount of credit that the banks can give to their customers.

Special Drawing Rights (S.D.R.) *see under* Drawing Rights.

special endorsement/indorsement BKG. *see under* endorsement.

specialist a person who specializes: *A medical specialist*, a doctor who specializes in diseases and injuries of a particular kind, such as *an eye/heart/cancer specialist. A specialist in company law/management accounting/factory design*.

speciality a subject or activity in which one specializes, esp. in which one becomes well known: *Sports clothing is the speciality of that shop. Wedding cakes are our speciality. Also* (esp. U.S.A.) specialty.

specialization *see* division of labour.

specialize COM. & IND. to limit one's business activities to a particular kind of product or service: *Some furniture-manufacturers specialize in making beds, others in making chairs. We specialize in bridge-building/road construction/ animal foods*.

special offer *see under* offer.

special partner *see under* partner.

special power *see under* power; power of attorney.

special referee *see under* referee.

special resolution *see* resolution.

special survey *see under* survey.

specialty *see* speciality.

specialty contract *see under* contract.

specialty debt *see under* debt.

specie FIN. money in the form of coins, not bullion or bank-notes.

specie point see gold point.

specific capital see under capital.

specific duty see under duty.

specific grant see block grant under grant.

specific gravity the ratio of the density of a substance to that of water. *Abbr.* sp.gr.

specific legacy see under legacy.

specific performance see under performance.

specific tax see under tax.

specification (1) LAW under the law of patents, a very detailed written statement giving a description of the special character and method of operation of a new invention. (2) IND. any detailed description of the form and content of an article or commodity, or the process by which something is produced: *These goods are not to specification*, they are not as described.

specification, customs, see customs specification.

specification, job see under job.

specimen (1) COM. a sample: *A publisher sends specimen copies of his books to teachers.* (2) BKG. specimen signature, *see under* signature.

speculate (1) COM. to take risks in business, esp. to invest money in a risky business deal in the hope of making a big profit: *To speculate in land*, to buy land when prices are low, with the intention of selling it later when prices are higher, aiming to make a capital gain rather than merely to receive an income in the form of rent. Cf. gamble. *N.* speculation. (2) STK. EXCH. (*a*) to buy a security, not as an investment, but with the intention of selling it, if possible at a profit, during the present account period, i.e. before the security bought has to be paid for. (*b*) to buy gilt-edged securities when they are cheap, because interest rates are high, with the intention of selling them when they become dearer, i.e. when interest rates have fallen. (3) COMMOD. EXCH. to risk making a loss (*a*) in buying a commodity in the hope of making a large profit by selling it later when the price has risen or (*b*) in selling a commodity forward, i.e. for delivery at some future date, with the hope of buying it at a lower price before the delivery date.

speculation (1) the act of speculating. The use of capital to buy something in the hope of making a profit from a change in the market price. (2) the practice of buying goods on credit in the hope of selling them at a profit before having to pay for them. (3) any business deal or venture that is highly risky. (4) STK. & COMMOD. EXCH. dealing in futures, the practice of selling a security or commodity forward, i.e. contracting to deliver at a certain price on a fixed future date, with the hope of buying it at a lower price before the delivery date. *See* playing the market.

speculative relating to or concerned with speculation: *A speculative builder*, a house-builder who builds houses as a speculation, i.e. he uses his capital to buy the land, materials and labour in the hope or expectation that he will sell the finished houses at a profit.

speculative investment see under investment.

speculative market see under market.

speculator a person who speculates, esp. a person who buys in the expectation of making a profit from a change in the market price in the future.

spending, discretionary see under discretionary.

spending money see under money.

spending-power see purchasing power (1).

spendthrift a person who spends money carelessly and wastefully, without attempting to balance his income and his expenditure.

sp. gr. specific gravity.

spiral see inflationary spiral.

spirit, proof see under proof.

spiv (*colloq.*) a socially undesirable person who avoids honest work and likes to show how he can live a life of ease by making small business deals of doubtful legality, such as trading in the black market in time of war.

split capital STK. EXCH. a form of capital structure adopted esp. by investment trust companies, by which the capital consists of two kinds of shares, *capital shares* and *income shares*, with different rights. Income shareholders receive all the income during the life of the trust fund, but at the end get no share in the capital appreciation of the investments, being repaid only the nominal value of their shares. Capital shareholders receive no income, but when the trust fund is wound up, get a share of the capital gain, and repayment of the nominal value of their shares.

split price see differential price under differential.

split share see under share.

split the difference to reach agreement by halving the difference between the price asked and the price offered.

spoiling the market STK. & COMMOD. EXCH. causing the market price of a security or commodity to rise or fall suddenly by buying or selling an excessively large quantity at one time instead of spreading the deals over a period. *See* line (5).

spondulicks (U.S.A. *colloq.*) money. *Also* spondulics; spondulix.

sponge (*colloq.*) to live at somebody else's expense; to borrow habitually. Cf. cadge.

sponger *n.* a lazy person who prefers to be kept by others rather than to work for his living. An habitual borrower. Cf. bloodsucker.

sponsor *n.* a person who makes himself responsible for somebody or something: *A pro-*

gramme sponsor, on commercial radio and television, a company that pays the cost of a programme so as to get its name before the public. *v.* to become a sponsor, e.g. to support another person's application for a job or a loan, or to make a business venture.

spontaneous combustion INSCE. a tendency of certain substances, e.g. oily rags, to catch fire by themselves, without any outside cause, thus being a source of danger to insured goods and property.

spot cash *see under* cash.

spot check *see* snap check.

spot delivery COM. immediate delivery.

spot exchange FIN. & BKG. foreign currency bought or sold for immediate delivery. Cf. forward exchange.

spot goods COM. goods ready for immediate delivery.

spot market *see* cash market *under* market; *also* foreign-exchange market.

spot price *see under* price.

spot rate *see under* exchange rate.

spout (*colloq.*) a pawnbroker's shop.

up the spout (*a*) of a thing, in pawn; (*b*) of a person, in financial difficulties, ruined.

spread *n.* (1) COM. the difference between the cost price and the selling price, i.e. the margin of profit or mark-up. (2) STK. EXCH. the difference between a seller's asking (or offer) price and a buyer's bid price. (3) STK. EXCH. the range of different classes of securities contained in a portfolio of investments: *A wide/ broad spread of over 200 investments, from gilt-edged to mining shares*, thus reducing risks. (4) STK. & COMMOD. EXCH. the difference between the prices for spot delivery and future delivery. (5) STK. EXCH. in U.S.A., a put and call option in which there are two different prices, one for the put and another for the call. (6) INSCE. *see* spreading the risk.

spreading the risk INSCE. the basic idea of reinsurance, by which the insurer reduces his chance of serious loss by bearing only part of any one insurance contract himself, passing the rest to others, so that the risk is spread over, and shared by, a number of insurers in agreed proportions. *Syn.* reinsurance.

spree a period of freedom and enjoyment, esp. a time of uncontrolled spending: *A buying/ spending/shopping spree.*

spurt STK. & COMMOD. EXCH. of market prices, a sudden jump upwards: *Chemicals put on a spurt after days of quiet trading.*

spying *see* industrial spying.

Sq. square (open space in a town).

sq. square (measure).

squander to waste time, money or valuable goods, esp. to use up materials wastefully. *To squander a fortune*, to spend it wastefully.

square *adj.* fair; honest: *A square deal*, one that

is fair to both parties. *Square treatment*, fair and honest behaviour esp. by an employer towards his employees.

square pegs in round holes persons wrongly chosen for the work that they have to do.

n. (1) an open space, usu. having four straight sides, in a town. *Abbr.* Sq. (2) an area of 100 sq. ft (of flooring, roofing, etc.).

v. (1) to settle, esp. to pay one's debts: *We have squared all our accounts*, paid all our debts. *To square up with somebody*, to balance accounts and to pay or receive what one party owes to the other. (2) (*colloq.*) to bribe.

square measure measurement of area, i.e. of length multiplied by breadth. *See also* surveyor's square measure. *See table on page 476.*

Square Mile, The the City of London. *See* City, The.

squatter LAW a person who occupies land or buildings without permission from the owner and without paying rent. *See* squatter's title *under* title.

squeeze (1) FIN. controls by the government, usu. in times of inflation, as a means of limiting the quantity of money in the economy: *An income/pay squeeze*, a limit placed on the amount by which employers may increase the salaries or wages of their employees. *A dividend/profit squeeze*, a limit on the amount by which companies may increase the dividends they pay to their shareholders. *Syn.* monetary control; restraint.

credit squeeze *see under* credit.

(2) STK. EXCH. *Bear squeeze*, action by buyers of a particular security to force bears to deliver the shares that they have contracted to deliver at the agreed price on the due date; this the bears can only do by buying in the market at a loss.

Sr. Senior.

S/R. (on) sale or return.

S.R. & C.C. strikes, riot and civil commotion.

Sri Lanka formerly Ceylon, an island republic in the Indian Ocean, pop. 14 million approx. (1975); capital, Colombo, pop. 550,000 approx.; languages, Sinhala, Tamil and English; currency unit, Sri Lanka rupee (SLRe., *pl.* SLRs.), divided into 100 cents. Member, Colombo Plan; (British) Commonwealth.

S/S, S.S. steamship.

s.s. steamship.

St. street; saint; strait.

s.t. steam trawler; short ton.

S.T. Standard Time; Summer Time; spring tide.

Stabex *see* Lomé Convention.

stabilization ECON. action by a government to prevent or reduce large fluctuations (movements up and down) in the general level of prices, production, unemployment, and the value of the currency on the foreign-exchange markets. *See* stabilizers.

stabilization fund FIN. money set aside by a government, usu. in an account with the central bank of the country, for use in buying and selling gold and foreign currencies in order to prevent large upward and downward swings in the value of the country's own currency. In Britain, the Exchange Equalization Account.

stabilize to make, or cause to be, steady; to protect against changes: *To stabilize the currency. To stabilize a ship by loading her with ballast.*

stabilized bond see indexed bond *under* bond, *n.*

stabilizers (1) ECON. THEORY those economic influences that, in a free economy, have a tendency to reduce wide swings in the level of prices, incomes, production and employment. For example, if unemployment rises the government spends more on unemployment benefit and training schemes, which puts more money into the economy, increasing incomes and reducing unemployment. Other economic stabilizers are progressive income tax, interest rates, and government spending. (2) SHIPG. movable wing-like plates fitted under the water to the sides of a ship to reduce rolling movements in a rough sea.

staff *n.* MAN. (1) the employees collectively of a business or other organization: *The teaching staff* of a school, college, etc., as opposed to the pupils or students. (2) the managers of a business and their close helpers, esp. office workers such as secretaries, clerks, typists, designers, and certain outside workers such as salesmen, as opposed to factory and other industrial workers who actually produce goods. *v.* to provide with a staff of workers: *His job is to staff the new branch office*, to employ the workers needed to operate the new office.

field staff see under field.

salaried staff see under salaried.

staff restaurant see canteen.

Staffs. Staffordshire, England.

stag *n.* STK. EXCH. a speculator who applies for an allotment of shares in a new issue with the intention of selling them at a profit as quickly as possible. If the issue is oversubscribed, the market price when dealings begin on the stock exchange will probably be higher than the issue price, and the speculator will make a profit. But if the issue is undersubscribed, he will not be able to sell the shares at a profit, because the market price will be below the issue price. *v.* to apply for a new issue of shares, only in the hope of selling them at a profit, not to hold them as an investment. *To stag in new issues*, to speculate in new issues.

stage (1) TRANSPT. & TOUR. a stopping place on a journey: *Bus routes are divided into stages. Fare stage*, a part of a bus route on which the amount of a fare is calculated. *Stagecoach*, in former times, a horse-carriage travelling reg-

ularly by stages along a certain route. (2) SHIPG. a place where ships can load or unload cargo or passengers: *A landing stage*. (3) in a theatre, the raised area on which the actors perform. *See* platform. (4) actors collectively; the profession of acting, performing plays, etc. for the public.

stagger to spread holidays, working hours, meal times, etc. in such a way that fewer employees are away from work at the same time, or so that the inconvenience of rush-hour traffic, queueing in canteens, etc. is reduced: *Staggered holidays/lunch hours/working hours.*

stagnant (1) STK. & COMMOD. EXCH. of market conditions, inactive; dull; with little or no business being done. (2) COM. of trading conditions, inactive: *Business is stagnant, there being no buyers.*

stagnation see trade cycle *under* cycle.

staircase chart see bar chart *under* chart.

stake (1) a sum of money, called stake-money, that is risked on the result of a future race or fight. (2) COM. & FIN. money raised in a business venture: *We have a large stake in the new company*, we have risked a large sum on shares in the new company.

stakeholder LAW a person, such as an estate agent or a solicitor, who holds a sum of money deposited by the buyer in a transfer of ownership of land and buildings. The deposit will be paid to the seller only if the buyer agrees, or returned to the buyer only if the seller agrees.

stale cheque see under cheque.

stall see booth; stand.

stallage FIN. & COM. rent paid to a local government authority for the right to put up a stall or booth in a market-place, etc.

stamp *n.* (1) an instrument for printing or pressing a mark, esp. on documents, covers, etc.: *A date/rubber/signature stamp*. (2) a small piece of printed paper, gummed on the back, bought in advance for a certain sum, and stuck on a document, envelope or cover, etc. to show that a tax or price has been paid: *A postage/revenue/trading stamp*. *v.* to mark something with a stamp: *To stamp a letter/packet/parcel. A stamped envelope.*

adhesive stamp a stamp printed on gummed paper, intended to be stuck on to a document, envelope or cover, etc. Cf. impressed stamp.

appropriated stamp an adhesive stamp that bears on it a word or words naming the particular class of instrument on which it may be used, such as a broker's contract note; it may not be used on any other class of document.

date-stamp an instrument used for printing by hand the date on a document, envelope or cover, with an arrangement for changing the date as necessary.

impressed stamp a stamp that is pressed permanently into the paper of a document, cover, etc., as opposed to an adhesive stamp, which is stuck on with gum and can easily be removed.

postage stamp a small piece of paper, printed in colour with a value and gummed on the back, that can be bought at post offices to stick on letters, packets, parcels, etc. to show that the postal charges have been paid.

revenue stamp (a) a small piece of paper similar to a postage stamp but sold at government offices for sticking on documents to show that taxes have been paid. (b) an official mark that is pressed into the paper of a document usu. to show that taxes have been paid.

rubber stamp (a) an instrument, usu. of rubber with a wooden handle, for printing by hand an official mark or some words on to a document, such as a cheque or passport. (b) the mark or words so printed. (c) a person esp. an official or an organization, who authorizes or agrees to some activity automatically, without giving it proper attention.

signature stamp a rubber stamp for printing a copy of a person's signature on a document.

trading stamp a small piece of printed paper similar to a postage stamp, bearing a value and given by traders to their customers as a means of allowing a discount on the amount they spend. The customer collects the stamps in a special book which, when full, he can exchange for money or for goods at a special shop kept by the organization that sells the stamps to the traders.

stamp duty see under duty.

stamping machine MAN. a machine used in offices and warehouses for sticking postage stamps on to letters and packets. See also franking machine.

stamp note SHIPG. a document signed by a customs officer allowing goods to be loaded into a ship.

stamp pad MAN. a pad kept wet with ink, used for inking rubber or hand stamps.

stand (1) a temporary structure on which goods are shown at an exhibition or trade fair; or on which goods are shown for sale in a market or at a fair-ground. Syn. stall. (2) a frame of shelves, hooks, etc. for showing goods for sale in a shop, often supplied free of cost by a manufacturer to encourage the shopkeeper to stock his products. See dealer aids. Syn. rack. (3) COM. a small shop, esp. of a movable or temporary nature: A news-stand. (4) TRANSPT. a place where public service vehicles regularly stop or wait: A bus/cab/taxi stand. (5) LAW in a court of law, esp. in U.S.A., the witness box: The witness took the stand, went into the witness box.

standard adj. (1) usual; ordinary; not special: Goods of standard quality/size/weight. We stock all standard sizes of clothing. (2) of average size, weight or quality: Standard eggs/petrol. Abbr. std.

n. (1) a model or basis for comparison; a test for measuring; a pattern to be followed. (2) a degree of quality that is needed or desired for a certain purpose: The appearance of this article is not up to standard. We buy goods only of the highest standard. (3) SHIPG. a unit for measuring cargoes of timber: 165 cu. ft. (4) ECON. & FIN. a system, called a monetary standard, by which the value of the main currency unit of a country is fixed by the government as a certain weight of precious metal (esp. of gold); or as a certain number of units of the currency of another country; or as a variation of these.

automatic standard see under automatic.

bimetallic standard a monetary system having both gold and silver as standard metals. See bimetallism.

commodity standard a monetary system in which the main unit of the currency can be exchanged for a fixed quantity of a commodity other than gold and silver, such as cotton, tobacco or coffee. See commodity money.

double standard see parallel standard below.

fiat standard a monetary system in which the value of the main unit of currency is not fixed as an amount of gold, silver or other commodity, but as an amount of fiat money, i.e. money having a value only because it has been made legal tender by order of the government.

gold bullion standard see under gold standard.

gold exchange standard see under gold standard.

gold standard see under gold.

paper standard any monetary standard in which the par value of the main monetary unit is fixed, not as a certain weight of gold, silver or a commodity, but as a fixed number of units of some other currency.

parallel standard a monetary system having coins of more than one precious metal, with no fixed value of one metal in relation to the other(s). Syn. double standard.

tariff standard a monetary system in which certain foreign coins and notes are made legal tender and circulate at fixed values in relation to each other.

standard agreement LAW & COM. a printed form of agreement or contract that a contractor regularly uses in his business dealings with his customers.

Standard & Poor's 500 Stock Index STK. EXCH. in U.S.A., an index number of 425 American industrial companies and 75 railway and public utility concerns.

standard coinage see under coinage.

standard costs IND. & ACCTS. the planned costs, carefully estimated in advance of production, to show what the goods should cost if the plans are followed and if the estimates are correct. Later, as a form of management control, the standard costs are compared with the actual costs and any variations are studied and, if necessary, acted upon.

standard fire policy *see under* policy of insurance.

standard gauge *see under* gauge.

standardization IND. (1) a process of reducing the number of different articles produced, their various sizes, qualities, colours, patterns, etc. in order to simplify production by getting rid of unnecessary variety; also to obtain the economies of scale that result from increasing the quantities of the fewer varieties that are being produced; and generally to reduce the unit cost of production. (2) the existence of, or the process of introducing, a generally accepted system of standards for producers to follow in regard to the quality, size, weight, safety, etc. of their products. *See* British Standards Institution.

standard mark IND. in Britain, one of the marks put on new silver articles by the government assay office (*see under* assay). It shows the fineness of the silver used, which must be at least 925 parts pure silver in 1000 parts, called sterling silver.

standard money *see under* money.

standard of living (1) in a general sense, the degree to which a person or group of persons and their families, or a community, are able to satisfy their wants. The standard is low if they can buy only the barest necessities, as in many developing countries; it is high if they can buy all the food, clothing, housing and comforts that they desire, as in many advanced countries. A reasonable standard is one that is good enough for health and well-being, including food, clothing, medical care and education. (2) ECON. THEORY the amount of goods and services that a person can buy with the money that he earns, i.e. the real value of his income. This depends on the value of goods and services produced per head of the population; and living standards can increase only if output and productivity rise. *Syn.* living standard; (U.S.A.) level of living.

standard rate TAXN. of income tax in Britain, the rate of tax payable on all income above a certain level determined by the taxpayer's allowances. Extra rates, called *higher rate tax*, are payable on higher incomes. A further charge called the *investment-income surcharge* is payable, in addition to the standard and the higher rate, on unearned or investment income above a certain level. *Syn.* basic rate.

Standard Time the time adopted officially by the government of a country, usu. the local time of a certain meridian (a north-south line) passing through the middle of the country (or a region of a very large country). This meridian is chosen because it is a convenient number of hours or half-hours ahead of, or behind, Greenwich Mean Time. *See* time-zones. *Abbr.* S.T.

standard-time system IND. a system by which an industrial worker is paid according to the number of units of work that he performs, each unit being expressed as a fixed or standard period of time. If he finishes the work in less than the standard time, he is able to complete more units per day or per week, and his pay is increased accordingly. If he takes longer than the standard time to finish a unit of work, he will complete fewer units and will earn correspondingly less.

standby arrangements FIN. arrangements that members of the International Monetary Fund (I.M.F.) are able to make with the Fund, for which purpose reserves are· kept ready for use when necessary, esp. in an emergency such as when a country has temporary difficulty with its balance of payments. Such standby credits are extra to the amount of each country's Drawing Rights and may be further increased under the General Arrangements to Borrow (G.A.B.) provided by the Group of Ten. *Syn.* standby agreement.

standing credit BKG. an arrangement between a customer and his bank by which the customer may enjoy the convenience of cashing cheques, up to a certain value, at another named branch of his bank, or at a particular branch of another bank.

standing, financial *see under* financial.

standing order BKG. *see* banker's order.

standing orders MAN. & LAW a set of rules permanently adopted by an organization, governing the manner in which its meetings shall be held and managed, such as the appointment, powers and duties of the chairman, officers and committees, the order of business, the holding of discussion, and the system of voting.

standstill agreement FIN. an agreement between two countries, one of which cannot pay a debt due to the other, by which the debtor country is given a fixed extension of time to pay.

staple *adj.* COM. & IND. of commodities, products, etc., leading; most important: *The staple crop of Egypt is cotton. The staple food in Sri Lanka is rice.*
n. (1) the staple crop itself. (2) a metal fastening for joining papers together. *A stapling machine*, an instrument for fastening papers by means of a staple, also called a stapler.

starboard SHIPG. the right-hand side of a ship when facing forward. *Opp.* port; larboard.

stash (*colloq.*) to store up, esp. money: *He has a lot of money stashed away in a savings bank.*

state MAN. a short form of the word *statement*, used for any regular report, return, set of figures, etc. sent by a branch or department to the management of an organization: *A manning state*, a report on the number of workers present or absent on a certain date.

state banks (U.S.A.) *see* banking system.

state capitalism ECON. a socialist economic system in which capital, representing the means of production, is largely owned by the State, but the use and management of that capital and the direction of commerce and industry are mainly left to private businessmen working under the close control of the State. *See* capitalism.

state enterprise *see under* enterprise.

statement (1) LAW spoken or written words that state a fact or give views: *A signed statement*, a formal document signed by the person writing it, giving facts. *A sworn statement*, one made under oath or affirmation. (2) ACCTS. an amount of money owed or owing, received or paid: *A statement of expenses/of receipts and expenditure. See* statement of account.

bank statement *see under* bank.

completion statement *see under* completion.

financial statement *see under* financial.

operating statement *see under* operating.

reconciliation statement in book-keeping, a statement which explains the disagreement between two related accounts. *See also* bank reconciliation statement *under* bank.

statement in lieu of prospectus STK. EXCH. in Britain, a document similar to, but instead of, a prospectus, that must be sent to the Registrar of Companies by a public company that intends to make a new issue of shares. It must be sent to the Registrar at least three days before any shares are allotted to the public.

statement of account ACCTS. a financial document sent regularly, usu. monthly, by a seller to a buyer for whom he has a ledger account. The statement lists: on one side the number and date of all invoices sent; on the other side details of payments received from, and credit notes issued to, the buyer during the period; and at the end gives the balance in the account. The statement is a demand for payment of the balance without further notice, unless a period of credit has been agreed.

statement of affairs (1) LAW & ACCTS. a financial statement, similar to a balance sheet, setting out the assets and liabilities at a certain date, of a bankrupt debtor or of a company in liquidation. (2) ACCTS. any list of assets and liabilities, to take the place of a balance sheet where accounting records are incomplete.

statement of claim LAW in a High Court action, a document in which the plaintiff states the facts on which he bases his case against the defendant and the remedy which he claims is his by right.

statement, payment on *see under* payment.

state planning *see* economic planning *under* planning.

stateroom SHIPG. a private room or cabin in the passenger accommodation of a ship.

statesman a person who takes a leading part in the governing of a country.

States, the (*colloq.*) the United States of America: *He has gone on a visit to the States.*

state tax *see under* tax.

state, welfare *see* welfare state.

static economics ECON. THEORY a branch of economic science that examines certain basic situations in an economy, without taking note of any changes that may happen with the passing of time. Cf. dynamic economics.

stationer's ream *see* ream.

station manager *see under* manager.

stationmaster TRANSPT. an official in charge of one or more railway stations. Cf. station manager.

statism *see* command economy.

statist *see* statistician. *The Statist*, an important British statistical journal that calculates and publishes an index of wholesale prices.

statistic (1) a single number or value, esp. one calculated by examining a sample. (2) any number in a group of statistics. *See* statistics, *pl.*

Statistical Office *see* Central Statistical Office.

statistician a person who has special knowledge of, and training in, the science of statistics. *Syn.* statist.

statistics (1) a branch of mathematical science which deals with the collection, classification and use of facts in the form of numbers. (2) numbers that are, or can be, collected or calculated and presented in such a way that they show useful facts. *Trade/population/vital statistics.*

statistical *adj.* relating to, or containing, statistics: *Statistical information. The Statistical Year Book. Central Statistical Office (C.S.O.).*

status enquiry agency *see* credit agency.

statute-barred *see* limitation.

statute law LAW the written law made by a statute, i.e. the laws passed by the legislature or highest law-making body of a country. Cf. common law; case law; equity; special law; civil law.

statute mile *see under* mile.

Statute of Labourers *see under* Labourers.

statutory LAW that must be done as commanded by the law.

statutory books (of a company) LAW & MAN. in Britain, the five books of record that must by law be kept by every limited company: the register of members; the register of directors; the register of directors' shareholdings; the register of charges; and the minute book (of directors' meetings).

statutory company *see under* company.

statutory instruments *see* delegated legislation.

statutory meeting *see under* company meeting.

statutory report *see* statutory meeting *under* company meeting.

statutory rights LAW & COM. in the sale of goods, the rights given by the law of the country to the buyer to e.g. return to the seller any goods that are not of merchantable quality (not fit to be sold) or are not as described by the seller, on condition that the buyer was not told at the time of the sale that the goods were being sold 'without warranty'.

statutory tenant *see under* tenant.

stay of execution LAW the postponement, by a judge, of the putting into effect of an order of a court of law.

stay of proceedings LAW the stopping, by a court of law, of proceedings in a lawsuit, either permanently, such as when the action is an abuse of process, or temporarily, when there is a good reason to order a delay. *See* abuse of process.

std. standard; started.

S.T.D. subscriber trunk dialling.

steady STK. EXCH. of market conditions, prices are neither rising nor falling.

steamboat *see* steamship.

steamer *see* steamship.

    mail steamer a fast ship carrying mails. *Abbr.* m.s.; M.S.

steamship SHIPG. a vessel driven by one or more steam engines. Cf. sailing ship/vessel; motor vessel. *Abbr.* S.S.; s.s.; S/S. *Syn.* steamboat; steamer.

steep (*colloq.*) of a price, extremely high.

steerage SHIPG. a space in a ship where passengers paying the cheapest fares are accommodated: *To travel steerage. Steerage class.*

stem SHIPG. the front part of a ship: *From stem to stern*, the whole length of the ship.

stencil a sheet of thin waxed paper which, when written or typed upon, is used in an office duplicator for printing documents, or in an addressing machine for printing addresses.

stenographer a person whose work is to write down in shorthand words dictated by another person.

stenotyping machine *see* Palantype.

steno-typist *see under* typist.

ster. sterling.

stere a unit of volume used for measuring timber, being one cubic metre (m³) equal to 1.307954 cu. yd. or 35.3147 cu. ft.

sterling FIN. the name given to the British pound, as opposed to the pound of certain other countries, *see* pound (2). *The pound sterling*, British money generally. *Abbr.* stg.; ster.

sterling area FIN. the former name for the scheduled territories (*see under* scheduled). *Syn.* sterling bloc.

sterling balances FIN. (1) balances that were kept in London by member countries of the sterling area. (2) balances in the form of Treasury bills, short-dated gilt-edged securities and bank deposits, kept in London by foreign governments, banks, investors and businessmen.

sterling bloc *see* sterling area.

sterling bond *see under* bond.

sterling, external *see* external account.

sterling security FIN. & STK. EXCH. a security of which both capital *and* interest or dividends are payable in sterling currency or in the currency of another country in the scheduled territories.

sterling silver *see* standard mark.

stern SHIPG. the back end of a ship. Cf. stem; bows. *See also* astern.

stevedore SHIPG. (1) a worker who loads and unloads ships. Cf. docker. (2) a contractor who takes responsibility for loading and unloading ships.

steward (1) AGR. a person employed to manage a farm or a large estate. *Syn.* land agent. (2) SHIPG. & TRANSPT. a man who serves food and drink to passengers and attends to their comfort on a ship or plane. *Fem.* stewardess. (3) IND. REL. shop steward, *see under* shop.

stewardess SHIPG. & TRANSPT. a female steward on board a ship or plane.

stg. sterling.

sticker (1) ADVTG. a printed advertisement in the form of a label that can be easily stuck where it can be seen by many, such as a *window sticker*. (2) COM. a small label, esp. one with a price written or stamped on it, stuck on goods sold in shops: *Price sticker*. (3) *An airmail sticker*, a small printed label provided by the Post Office for sticking on airmail letters and packets.

stick-up (*colloq.*) an armed robbery; a hold-up.

stiff of a price, a condition, unusually severe; excessive. *He is demanding a stiff price for his flat. I find your conditions unreasonably stiff.* Cf. steep.

stiffening SHIPG. ballast or heavy cargo put into the bottom of a ship to make her steady.

sting COM. (*colloq.*) *with* for (1) to charge a person too high a price for something: *The jeweller stung him for £700 for a ring worth £300.* (2) to cheat somebody: *I was stung for £50 for this useless watch.*

stipend *n.* a salary, a fixed regular payment for services, esp. one paid to a magistrate, clergyman, or teacher.

    stipendiary *adj.* working for, receiving a stipend: *A stipendiary magistrate*, a qualified lawyer employed as a full-time magistrate, as opposed to unpaid Justices of the Peace.

stk. stock.

stock *v. To stock something*, to keep it usu. in stock; to be able to supply from stock, i.e. without having to get it specially. *To be stocked*, to have a stock: *We are well stocked with coal.*

    n. (1) AGR. livestock. *See also* dead stock (1).

(2) COM. & IND. a store of goods for sale: *We have a large stock of men's clothes. The company has too much money tied up in stock.*
to take stock to count it, *see* stocktaking. *Syn.* inventory.
(3) a store of raw materials for use in industry, esp. *pl. Stocks of coal/chemicals/steel.*
buffer stock *see under* buffer.
closing stock *see under* closing.
dead stock *see under* dead.
opening stock *see under* opening.
safety stock *see* buffer stock *under* buffer.
(4) STK. EXCH. in Britain, a portion of the capital of a company that has converted its fully-paid shares into units, usu. of £100 nominal value. *See* capital stock *below.* (5) STK. EXCH. a portion of those debts of a company that consist of money lent to it. *See* loan stock *below; also* debenture stock *under* debenture. (6) STK. EXCH. a fixed-interest security issued by the government of a country or by a local government authority. *See* gilt-edged stock; corporation stock *below; also* Treasury stock.
assented stock a capital stock, the holders of which have assented (agreed) to give up their holding in return for a quantity of some other security. *See* take-over bid. *Opp.* non-assented stock.
barometer stock *see under* barometer; *also* business barometer.
capital stock (*a*) the capital of a company that has been subscribed by its members. (*b*) in Britain, the capital of a company that has converted its shares into units, usu. of £100 nominal value. The capital of a company must always first be issued in the form of shares, each of which has a nominal or face value that cannot be divided into smaller units. If all its shares are fully paid, a company may convert them into capital stock, which may be divided and sold in any smaller amounts, such as £25 or £33⅓ of stock. The capital stockholders have the right to be paid a dividend out of the net profits of the company.
commercial stock *see* commercials.
corporation stock fixed-interest stock issued by British local government authorities, usu. repayable over a stated period after a fixed number of years. *Syn.* local government stock.
debenture stock *see under* debenture.
dollar stock *see under* dollar.
gilt-edged stock fixed-interest securities issued by the British Government. *See* gilt-edged securities.
government stock *see* government securities.
growth stock *see* growth share *or* stock.
guaranteed stock *see under* guaranteed.
income stock *see under* income.
industrial stock *see* industrials.
inscribed stock in Britain, a form of government security for which no stock certificates

are issued; instead, a document called a certificate of inscription can be obtained, stating that the holder's name has been inscribed (recorded) at the Bank of England, but this is not a certificate of title. Such stock is now rare.
irredeemable stock *see* annuity bond *under* bond, *n.*
loan stock a portion of those debts of a company that consist of money lent to it as a simple loan, not secured on some part of the company's assets. Holders of loan stock receive a fixed rate of interest. If the company is wound up, the holders of loan stock have the right to be repaid before the holders of capital stock. Cf. debenture stock. *Syn.* unsecured stock.
local government stock *see* corporation stock *above.*
money stock (*a*) any gilt-edged or other fixed-interest security that is to be repaid at a fixed date in the very near future. (*b*) the capital stock of a finance house, hire-purchase company, bank, insurance company, or investment trust company, all of which are traders in money.
motor stock *see* motors.
non-assented stock a capital stock, the holders of which have not assented (agreed) to give up their holding in return for some other security, and prefer to receive payment in cash.
ordinary stock capital stock that has been converted from ordinary shares and therefore has a claim to receive a dividend out of the net profits of the company after the fixed dividends on any preference stock has been paid.
participating preferred stock (U.S.A.) preferred stock, the holders of which have the right to a share in the profits if they exceed a certain figure.
personal stock *see* registered stock *below.*
preferred stock (U.S.A.) capital stock, the holders of which have a right to be paid a dividend at a fixed rate before the holders of common (or ordinary) stock, and to be repaid out of the company's assets before the common stockholders if the company is wound up.
prior preferred stock (U.S.A.) preferred stock, the holders of which have a first claim to payment of dividend or interest and to repayment of capital, before the claims of the preferred and common stockholders.
redeemable stock a fixed-interest security, such as a government, debenture or preference stock, that can be repaid at some stated time, called the redemption date, or at the wish of the issuing authority or company.
registered stock stock registered in the name of the owner in the stock register of the company. Cf. bearer stock. *Syn.* personal stock.
tap stock (*a*) any stock that can always be bought in the market because there are always some sellers. (*b*) British government securities

that are sold by various government departments as soon as the market prices of the securities reach a certain level. They are called *short taps* if they are short-dated, i.e. repayable in less than 5 years; or *medium taps* if medium-dated, repayable in 5 to 15 years; or *long taps* if long-dated, repayable in over 15 years.

undated stock *see* annuity bond *under* bond, *n*.

unified stock *see* consolidated bond *under* bond, *n*.

unsecured stock *see* loan stock *above*.

(7) TRANSPT. railway vehicles. *See* hauling stock; rolling stock.

stock book COM. & IND. a book in which, esp. in a small business, a continuous record is kept of the amount of stock held at any one time of each article or commodity dealt in by the business. The stock book will show details of the opening stock, stock received and issued and, at the end of an accounting period, the closing stock. In a larger business, the stock book is replaced by stock cards or other records, produced perh. by a computer.

stockbreeder AGR. a farmer who breeds and raises livestock.

stockbroker STK. EXCH. a broker who is employed by his clients to buy and sell stocks and shares in return for commission called brokerage. Brokers collect orders from members of the public and act for them in dealing with jobbers. Brokers form one of the two classes of members of the London Stock Exchange, the other being jobbers. A stockbroker who is not a member of any stock exchange is called an *outside broker*. *Syn.* share broker. (*French:* agent de change.)

stockbroker's clerk *see* authorized clerk.

stock certificate STK. EXCH. a large document, similar to a share certificate, issued by a company whose shares have been converted into stock, or which has issued debenture stock, declaring that the holder is the registered owner of a stated amount of stock in the company. *See also* stock certificate to bearer. *Syn.* (U.S.A.) stock warrant.

stock certificate to bearer STK. EXCH. a stock certificate that does not record the name of the stockholder but gives the bearer the right to hold a stated amount of stock in the company or issuing authority. Ownership can be transferred by simple delivery (passing on) of the certificate.

stock check *see* check (4).

stock cheque BKG. & STK. EXCH. the name given to a special kind of demand draft (bill of exchange) used by a stockbroker in one country as a means of paying for securities bought from a stockbroker in another country. *Syn.* stock draft.

stock control *see under* control.

stock exchange STK. EXCH. an organized market where securities are bought and sold under fixed rules. In Britain, the stock exchanges in London, Birmingham, Liverpool, York, Glasgow and Belfast form a single organization called *The Stock Exchange*, governed by a council in London. The members of the exchange consist of two kinds of firm: stockbrokers and stockjobbers. In U.S.A., the New York Stock Exchange is the largest. There are in addition the American Stock Exchange, also in New York, and a number of regional exchanges in Chicago, Boston and San Francisco, and one covering Philadelphia, Baltimore and Washington. *Abbr.* S.E.; S/E.

Stock Exchange Compensation Fund *see* Compensation Fund.

Stock Exchange Daily Official List STK. EXCH. a list published in London by the Council of the Stock Exchange at the end of each day's trading, giving details of price, etc. of all officially-quoted securities earlier that afternoon. Popularly called the Official List.

Stock Exchange quotation *see* application for quotation.

stockholder STK. EXCH. (1) a person who holds stock in a company, (esp. U.S.A.). (2) a shareholder.

Stockholm Convention *see* European Free Trade Association.

stock-in-trade COM. & IND. the stock of merchandise, i.e. goods intended for sale in the regular course of trade, held by a business at a given time. The value of the stock-in-trade at the end of the accounting year is included as an asset in the balance sheet. *Syn.* trading stock.

stock, issue of *see* issue of securities.

stockist COM. in Britain, a dealer who, in return for an extra discount and perh. other special buying terms, contracts to keep stocks of a particular manufacturer's products always at an agreed minimum level. Cf. distributor.

stockjobber *see under* jobber.

stock list *see under* list.

stockman (1) AGR. a man employed to look after livestock on a farm or in a stockyard. (2) IND. in U.S.A., a stock-keeper or storeman, a man employed to look after stocks of goods.

stock market (1) STK. EXCH. *see under* market. (2) AGR. & COM. a market where livestock are bought and sold.

stock option *see under* option.

stockpile *n*. (1) IND. a planned accumulation of stocks of raw materials, etc. made in expectation of a future shortage or before an increase in production. (2) a planned accumulation by a government of stocks of strategic raw materials and food in case of war, called a *strategic stockpile*.

v. to accumulate stocks for such a purpose. *Syn.* forward buying.

stock, railway see hauling stock; rolling stock.

stock receipt see certificate of inscription.

stock-rooms see commercial sale rooms.

stock savings bank see under savings bank.

stock size COM. & IND. (1) a size, esp. of clothing, that is regularly kept in stock by dealers: We sell only stock sizes. (2) the size of a person who can wear ready-made clothing without having it changed: She is a stock size.

Stocks, The STK. EXCH. in Britain, a popular name for perpetual annuities, or that part of the national debt that consists of stocks which have no fixed date for redemption (repayment) but on which the government is bound to pay the interest for ever. Example: Consols. See funded debt under national debt.

stocktaking MAN. & ACCTS. the business practice of listing, counting and checking every asset held in stock in a warehouse, store or shop. usu. at the end of each financial year. This stock list or inventory is used as the basis for the stock valuation. Syn. inventory.

continuous stocktaking in some large organizations, the practice of spreading the work of stocktaking continuously over the whole year instead of doing it all at the end of the year. Syn. perpetual inventory; continuous inventory.

physical stocktaking a careful check by counting and measuring the actual quantity of all goods held in stock at a certain time, as opposed to theoretical figures reached by calculation from the stock records. Syn. physical inventory.

stock transfer see under transfer.

stock-turn MAN. & ACCTS. the ratio of the average value of stock held by a business to the annual sales turnover. If the value of the stock is £10,000, and if the turnover is £30,000, a ratio of 1:3, it means that on average at any one time the business has ⅓ of a year, or four months' stock, in hand unsold. This ratio, or stock-turn, shows whether the business is over-stocking or is keeping too little stock. A fishmonger will tend to have a low stock-turn, e.g. 1:200 or lower, because he sells his entire stock almost daily; but a publisher of books may have a stock-turn of 1:2 or higher; because he has to print his books in editions which may take many months to sell. Also stock turnover.

stock valuation see under valuation.

stock warrant see stock certificate.

stockyard AGR. an enclosure for keeping cattle, sheep, pigs, etc. temporarily, usu. near a market or slaughter-house.

stone a customary unit of weight used in Britain, of various values from 8 to 24 lb according to the thing weighed, e.g. of human beings and animals, 14 lb (6.3503 kg); of meat, sugar and spices, 8 lb (3.6287 kg). Pl. stone. He weighs 12 stone: 168 lb (76.2035 kg).

stony-broke (colloq.) see broke, adj.

stop v. BKG. see countermand (1).

n. TRANSPT. a place where public-service road vehicles stop regularly to set down and to pick up passengers: A bus/coach stop.

stop loss STK. EXCH. a direction given to a stockbroker to sell a security if its market price falls below a stated value.

stop order see stopped cheque under cheque.

stop over v. TOUR. to stop for a short time at a place while making a longer journey: My ticket allows me to stop over in Beirut.

stopover n. I wish to make a stopover in Delhi.

stoppage (1) IND. REL. a stopping of work in a factory, etc. because of a strike: There have been five stoppages of work in that steelworks this year. (2) MAN. & ACCTS. money kept back by an employer from an employee's pay, usu. to cover agreed repayment of a loan. Syn. deduction (from pay).

stoppage in transitu LAW & COM. the right of a seller to stop, if he can, the delivery of goods while they are still in transit (in the course of being carried) if he hears that the buyer of the goods is unable to pay for them because he is insolvent.

stop payment see stopped cheque under cheque.

stopped cheque see under cheque.

storage (1) the act of storing goods: We specialize in the storage of furniture. (2) space for storing goods: They are looking for storage for their paper stocks. Fruit must be kept in cold storage. (3) a charge made for storing goods. Syn. warehousing.

storage unit COMP. see memory.

store (1) a shop where goods are kept for sale to consumers: A clothing/grocery/hardware/drug/general/store. (2) a large retail shop selling a wide variety of goods: A department(al)/chain-/co-operative store. (3) a wholesale shop selling goods to retailers: A cash-and-carry store.

cash-and-carry store see cash and carry.

chain-store see under chain.

department store a large retail shop with several or many departments, each having its own manager and staff and selling a different kind of goods, the whole being under a central control. Syn. departmental store.

drive-in/drive-up store see under drive-up.

drug store see drugstore.

general store see under general.

multiple store see chain-store.

self-service store see self-service.

store, bill of see bill of store.

store cattle AGR. cattle kept by a farmer for fattening and for sale as meat. Cf. milch cattle.

storekeeper (1) a person in charge of a store of goods. (2) (U.S.A.) a shopkeeper. Cf. storeman.

storeman COM. a man employed in a store-room of a factory or shop, to receive and issue stores and to keep the stock in a clean and orderly state. Cf. storekeeper.

stores *pl.* (1) supplies of food, drink, etc. stored for use when needed. (2) in a factory or workshop, a place where materials, tools, etc. are kept and issued when needed for use in production. (3) a store-room.

ship's stores the stock of food, drink and other consumable goods needed by the passengers and crew of a ship during the voyage, and not part of the cargo.

stores, bill of *see* bill of stores.

stotinka the fractional currency unit of Bulgaria. *Pl.* stotinki. 100 stotinki = 1 lev, *pl.* leva.

stow SHIPG. to pack, arrange, cargo in the hold of a ship in a safe and economical manner.

stowage SHIPG. (1) the act of stowing. (2) space for stowing goods. (3) the goods stowed. (4) the charge made, or wages paid, for stowing cargo.

stowage plan SHIPG. a carefully-prepared plan of a ship showing where each class of cargo is to be stowed.

stowaway SHIPG. a person found hiding aboard a ship or plane to avoid paying the fare.

Str. steamer; street.

straddle (U.S.A.) STK. & COMMOD. EXCH. a kind of double option that allows the price of the put and of the call to be the same, usu. the market price. Cf. spread. *See* double option *under* option.

straight of a person's character, honest; truthful; to be safely trusted, esp. in business dealings. *Opp.* crooked.

straight bill of lading *see under* bill of lading.

straight line method (of depreciation) *see under* depreciation methods.

strait *see* channel (2).

Straits dollar FIN. the standard currency unit of the former Straits Settlements, replaced in 1964 by the Malaysian dollar and the Singapore dollar.

stranded TRANSPT. of travellers, left (*a*) without any means of transport; (*b*) without money to pay for the journey home.

stranding SHIPG. the driving of a ship on to the ground, where it is held (stranded) for a considerable time. Cf. grounding. *Voluntary stranding*, an act of stranding done for the purpose of saving a ship from sinking.

strd. stranded.

streamline MAN. to make simpler, less complicated, a system or process by getting rid of any part that offers resistance to speedy production, or that slows the flow of work.

streetcar *see* tramcar *under* car.

street dealings *see* after-hours dealings.

street market *see under* market.

street price *see under* price.

Street, The (U.S.A.) a popular name for Wall Street in New York City, the main financial centre of the U.S.A. Cf. The City (of London).

street-trader *see* hawker.

strict liability LAW a citizen's liability to pay damages to someone who is harmed by an accidental happening, even where there is no question of wrongful intention or of negligence by the person liable. *Examples*: damage caused by an escape of water or some other substance from a man-made storage container; damage done by animals escaping. *Syn.* absolute liability. Cf. vicarious liability.

strike *n.* (1) IND. a discovery of gold, oil or other mineral. (2) a stroke of luck: *A lucky strike.* (3) IND. REL. an organized refusal to work by a group of employees, usu. in an attempt to force their employer to give higher wages or better working conditions. *Syn.* industrial action; direct action; withdrawal of labour/services. Cf. lock-out.

general strike an official strike on a very large scale, with members of all or most of the trade unions obeying the call of their union not to work. *Syn.* (Indian subcontinent) bandh.

lightning strike a strike of workers who stop work suddenly and without giving any warning or notice. Cf. wildcat strike.

official strike one which takes place on the directions of a trade union. Cf. unofficial strike.

sit-down strike one in which the employees come to their place of employment but refuse to do any work or to go home.

sympathetic strike a strike by a group of workers who are not in disagreement with their own employer(s) but are striking to give support to another group of workers who are going, or have gone, on strike.

token strike a strike of workers that lasts only a few hours, usu. as a warning to the employer that more serious action may follow if the workers' demands are not met.

unofficial strike a strike of workers who stop work against or without the directions of their trade union. Cf. official strike.

wildcat strike a strike of workers who stop in contravention of agreement and without being directed to strike by their trade union. Cf. lightning strike.

v. to stop work; to go on strike.

strike action IND. REL. another name for a strike, as opposed to the other forms of industrial action such as a go-slow, an overtime ban, or a work-to-rule.

strikebound SHIPG. & TRANSPT. unable to operate a service or an organization because of a strike. *The port is strikebound until tomorrow.*

strikebreaker IND. REL. (1) an employee who refuses to obey the direction of his trade union to go on strike, and who continues to work for his employer. (2) a person who attempts to make a strike fail. *Syn.* blackleg; fink (U.S.A.); scab.

strike pay IND. REL. an allowance that some trade unions pay to their members while they are on strike.

striker IND. REL. an employee who strikes, goes on strike, against his employer.

string see ring.

stripping see asset-stripping; dividend-stripping.

strong STK. EXCH. of market conditions, prices rising because the demand is great and supplies are lacking. *Opp.* weak.

strong-room BKG. a room in a bank, safe-deposit company, etc. built of very strong fire-proof materials and fitted with special locks to prevent thieves from stealing the money, valuable documents, etc. stored in the room.

structural unemployment see under unemployment.

stub see counterfoil.

study see feasibility study; job study.

stuffing ADVTG. & ACCTS. the work of putting advertising or accounts material into envelopes for posting.

stumer (*colloq.*) (1) a dishonoured cheque. (2) a cheat.

stump up (*colloq.*) to pay money, usu. unwillingly.

stunt ADVTG. a way of attracting public attention by means of an unusual show, or a show of great skill or daring, such as a plane writing a name or message in the sky with smoke.

style LAW an officially-recognized name or title: *A company trading under the style of John Baker Ltd.*

SU Soviet Union, the international vehicle-registration letters of the U.S.S.R. (Soviet Russia).

sub. subscription; substitute; subvention; subsidy; sub-editor; submarine.

sub- *prefix*, under; below: *A sub-basement*, one that has been built under another basement. *A sub-branch*, one that is under the management of a more important branch.

sub-agent MAN. a person who works for, is employed by, or represents, an agent.

subber (*colloq.*) a sub-contractor.

subbing (*colloq.*) sub-editing.

subcommittee MAN. a small group of persons who are members of a committee and have been appointed to form a smaller committee to do some special part of the work of the main committee. Thus, the management committee of a society may appoint an entertainments subcommittee to look after detailed matters relating to the amusement of the society's members generally.

subcontinent see under continent.

sub-contract *n.* LAW a contract in which one party, the sub-contractor, agrees to provide materials or services needed by the other party to perform another contract, to which the sub-contractor is not a party.

v. to sign, enter into, a sub-contract, either as the party giving it or accepting to perform it.

sub-contracting see disintegration.

sub-contractor LAW a person who is one of the parties to a sub-contract. *Syn.* (*colloq.*) subber.

sub-edit to correct, rewrite and generally prepare matter to be printed, esp. in a newspaper. *Syn.* (*colloq.*) to sub.

sub-editor an assistant editor. *Syn.* (*colloq.*) sub.

subject filing see under filing system.

subject to (1) LAW dependent upon; on condition that: *An offer subject to contract*, one that is made or accepted in the course of negotiation; it does not become binding until a final contract is signed. In buying a house, an offer or acceptance may be *subject to survey*, i.e. binding only if a surveyor's report is favourable. (2) INSCE. *Subject to average*, a condition in many fire insurance policies, that if the insured value of the property is less than its real value, the insured person becomes his own insurer for the uninsured part of the real value.

sub judice LAW (*Latin*, under a judge) now in the course of being considered or tried in a court of law, and therefore a matter that is still not decided. In Britain and some other, esp. English-speaking, countries, nobody is allowed by law to publish any comment on a question that is sub judice, i.e. being tried in the courts.

sub-lease see under-lease under lease.

sub-lessor LAW a tenant who sub-lets a property under a sub-lease to a sub-tenant. *Also* under-lessor.

sub-let LAW to let property under a sub-lease to a sub-tenant. *Also* sublet. *Syn.* under-let.

subliminal advertising ADVTG. a special method of advertising that causes a person to receive information about a product unconsciously; this may take the form, e.g. of flashing a name or a picture on a screen for a small fraction of a second, too short a time for the viewer to be conscious of it, but long enough for his mind to receive and store it.

submarginal land ECON. & AGR. land that is so unproductive that it is not worth the labour and expense of cultivating it at current prices.

submit (1) to yield; to give way: *We must submit to the decision of the court. I submit to your terms. To submit to arbitration.* (2) to put forward, send, for consideration or decision by a person or persons in authority: *He submitted a paper/report/request/scheme/plan to the board.* (3) to suggest; to argue: *Counsel submitted that the accused was telling lies.*

submission *n.* the act of submitting.

sub-mortgage see under mortgage.

subpoena LAW (*Latin*, under penalty) an order by a court of law commanding a named person to attend the court to give evidence as a witness. In a magistrates' court it is called a wit-ness summons.

subrogation INSCE. & LAW the legal right of an insurer to receive any money obtained by the insured as a result of his making use of his rights against third parties; this reduces the cost of the loss to the insurer and prevents the insured from obtaining more than his full indemnity. Sometimes the conditions of the policy give the insurer the right to bring a legal action against a third party who is liable for any loss suffered by the insured.

subscribe (1) LAW to sign one's name, usu. at the end of a document, to show one's agreement with it, or to promise to perform some act stated in it. *To subscribe (to) a Memorandum of Association.* (2) COM. *with* to, to pay money for the right to receive regularly for a certain period a commodity, such as copies of a periodical (magazine), or a service, such as the use of a telephone; or to enjoy membership of a club or society. (3) in the book trade, to promise in advance to buy a stated number of copies of a book when it is published. (4) to give money away: *To subscribe to charities.* (5) STK. EXCH. usu. *with* for, to apply for shares in a limited company: *He subscribed for 1000 shares in a new issue.* (6) INSCE. as an underwriter, to accept a stated share of the risk in an insurance contract in return for a share of the premium.

subscribed capital *see under* capital; *also* authorized capital.

subscribed fully *see* oversubscribed.

subscriber (1) a person who subscribes, e.g. to a magazine, club or society, or who pays for the use of a telephone connection. (2) STK. EXCH. a person who has agreed to become one of the first members of a limited company by signing the company's Memorandum of Association. *See* Declaration of Association.

subscriber capital *see* subscribed capital *under* capital; authorized capital *under* authorized.

subscribers to the Memorandum *see* Declaration of Association.

subscriber trunk dialling (S.T.D.) a telephone system that allows a subscriber to dial the number when making a trunk (long-distance) call, instead of asking an operator to do so.

subscription an amount paid by a subscriber.

subscription share *see under* share.

subshare STK. EXCH. a portion of a share in a foreign company. In Britain, a share cannot be divided.

subsidiary ranking lower in importance than something else: *Subsidiary earnings/income,* less than, but extra to, what is received from a main source. *Subsidiary occupation,* one that is less important than one's main job.

subsidiary books of account *see* books of first entry.

subsidiary company *see under* company.

subsidize FIN. & ECON. to give a subsidy to a person or an organization.

subsidy FIN. & ECON. money given by a government to certain producers, such as farmers, to help them to produce without loss to themselves, and yet at a low price, goods and services needed by the public. Possible subsidies include food subsidies and housing subsidies, export subsidies to encourage foreign trade, and employment subsidies to prevent unemployment. Cf. subvention.

subsistence ECON. (1) the bare cost of keeping alive. (2) a supply of goods that is just enough to cover the basic necessities of life, i.e. food, clothing and shelter.

subsistence allowance MAN. money, usu. a fixed sum per day, paid to an employee over and above his wages or salary to cover his living expenses, such as food and lodging, while he is away from home travelling for his employer. *Syn.* daily allowance; subsistence money.

subsistence crop AGR. one grown mainly for consumption by the farmer, as distinguished from one grown mainly for sale in order to bring in money. Cf. cash crop.

subsistence farming AGR. farming that produces only enough crops, etc. to meet the needs of the farmer and his family, leaving little or nothing for him to sell, as opposed to commercial farming. *Also* subsistence agriculture.

Subsistence Theory of Wages ECON. THEORY a view expressed by the early economists, esp. the Physiocrats in the eighteenth century, that by a natural law wages were never higher than at a level just sufficient to allow the workers to exist; for if wages rose higher than this subsistence level, the population would increase, and by competing for work, would force wages down to below that level. This theory is not considered useful today. *Syn.* Iron Law of Wages; Minimum-of-Existence Theory of Wages.

substance (1) of paper, the weight in grams of a square metre, thus: 70 g.s.m. or 70 g/m^2. (2) wealth, property: *A man of substance.*

substantial important; fairly large in quantity, size or value: *Britain exports a substantial tonnage of butter. A substantial sum of money. A substantial business.*

substantial damages *see* general damages *under* damages, *n. pl.*

substantive law LAW that part of the law that relates to rights and duties, as opposed to adjective law, which deals with practice and procedure.

substitute *n.* (1) a thing that replaces, or can be used in place of, something else: *Margarine is a substitute for butter. Tea is a substitute for cof-*

fee. (2) a person who replaces, takes the place of, somebody else: *A substitute driver.*

v. to replace a person or thing by another.

substituted service *see under* service of process.

substitute money *see under* money.

substitution ECON. THEORY the act of substituting one thing for another. *See* differentiation.

substitution effect ECON. THEORY the effect on the behaviour of a consumer when the price of a particular good changes. If the price falls, and the prices of other, similar, goods used up till now by the consumer remain the same, the effect will be that he will substitute the cheaper good for the now relatively dearer goods; he will rearrange his purchases to suit the new relative prices. Cf. income effect; price effect.

substitution, elasticity of *see under* elasticity.

Substitution, Law of ECON. THEORY the rule that in both production and consumption, the utility of the marginal unit is, in the long run, equal to its cost or price. The producer can choose in what ways he will combine the factors of production, and he will use such an amount of each factor that the value of the marginal revenue on each of them will be equal to its price. If the value of the marginal revenue on one factor is greater than the price, he will benefit by substituting more of that factor (because it is more profitable) for some of the other less profitable factors. Similarly, the consumer will keep rearranging the things on which he spends his money, substituting one commodity for another so that, in the long run, the marginal utility of each of the commodities he buys will tend to equal its price. *Syn.* Law of Equi-Marginal Returns.

sub-subsidiary company *see under* company.

sub-tenant LAW a tenant under a sub-lease, who rents property from a person who is himself a tenant of the landlord.

subtract to take one quantity from another; to take a smaller amount from a larger or from the whole amount: *To calculate a net income, take the gross income and subtract income tax. Syn.* to deduct. *Opp.* to add.

sub-unit FIN. a unit trust share-unit.

suburb the outer areas of a town, where many of the people who work in the town have their homes. *Adj.* suburban.

subvention FIN. & ECON. money given usu. by a private person or organization, but sometimes by a government, to bring help or relief to a person or group of persons performing some activity that deserves support for the good of the public, esp. in education and the arts and sciences. Cf. subsidy.

subway TRANSPT. (1) in U.S.A., an underground railway. (2) in Britain, an underground passage reserved for pedestrians (people walking) crossing a busy road.

succession *see* intestate succession *under* intestate. *Also see* testate succession *under* testate.

successor MAN. (1) one who comes after, who follows somebody in time: *Mr Black was a better manager than his successor, Mr White. Mr White is successor to Mr Black.* (2) a new owner who has replaced a former owner of a business, information that is sometimes given in a shop sign, or a letterhead, or in an advertisement: *John Jackson, Grocer, Successor to Thomas Brown.* If the new owner is a firm, i.e. *pl.*: *Jackson & Co., Grocers, Successors to Thomas Brown.* Cf. predecessor.

sucker (*colloq.*) a foolish person who is easily deceived and cheated of his money.

sucre the standard currency unit of Ecuador, divided into 100 centavos.

Sudan, The a republic in north-east Africa, pop. 18 million approx. (1975); capital, Khartoum, pop. 200,000 approx.; languages, Arabic, English and tribal; currency unit, the Sudanese pound (Sud £), divided into 100 piastres or 1000 millièmes. Member, O.A.U.; Arab League.

sue LAW to bring a lawsuit or other legal action against somebody in a civil court. *To sue for the recovery of a debt/for non-payment of rent/for breach of contract/for infringement of copyright.*

Suez Canal SHIPG. a ship-canal, 100 miles (160 km) long, across the isthmus of Suez between the Mediterranean Sea and the Red Sea.

Suff. Suffolk, England.

sufferance *see* bill of sufferance; baggage declaration.

sufferance, tenant at *see under* tenant.

sufferance wharf *see under* wharf.

sufficiency a state of being, or having, enough: *Britain has a sufficiency of milk products. Egypt lacks a sufficiency of paper.*

sufficient *adj.* enough.

suit LAW (1) the act of suing. (2) any civil action in a court of law: *A lawsuit.*

suitcase a light box for travellers' clothes, etc. with locks and a handle for carrying. *Syn.* valise.

suite TOUR. in a hotel, a set of connected rooms together forming a single unit, usu. consisting of a sitting/dining room, one or more bedrooms, dressing room(s), etc. *En suite* (of rooms and furniture) in a set; forming a connected series.

suli *see* syli.

sultanate a country ruled by a sultan (Muslim ruler).

sum (1) an amount, esp. of money. (2) a total of numbers added together. (3) a calculation.

lump sum *see under* lump.

round sum *see* round.

sum assured *see* sum insured.

SUMED IND. a large oil pipeline connecting the

Gulf of Suez to the Mediterranean. *Pron.* Soo-med.

sum insured INSCE. the most that an insurer will have to pay or that an insured can claim, under an insurance contract. In life insurance, the amount of money that the insurance company contracts to pay; the limit of the insurer's liability. *Syn.* sum assured. *Abbr.* s.i.

summary a short form of a longer document, giving only the important points: *A summary (of a) report. See also* accounting summary. *Syn.* précis.

summary book ACCTS. a simple form of cash book kept by clubs, societies and other non-profitmaking organizations, in which members' subscriptions received, and amounts paid as expenses, are recorded. *See* club accounts.

Summer Time *see* Daylight Saving Time *under* time.

summons *n.* LAW (1) in Britain, an order made by a magistrates' court commanding a named person to attend the court at a stated time and date. *Pl.* summonses. (2) in the High Court, a way of obtaining a decision on a matter of legal procedure from a judge in chambers before the trial itself begins.

originating summons a way of starting legal proceedings where the facts are not disputed but there is a need for a decision on the meaning of a law, contract, will or other document. *Cf.* writ.

to summon *or* **to summons** *v.* to issue or serve (deliver) a summons to a person to appear in court. *To take out a summons,* to apply for, cause, a summons to be issued.

witness summons *see* subpoena.

writ of summons *see* writ.

sumptuary law LAW a law or series of laws (*a*) putting limits on certain kinds of personal spending, e.g. on food, esp. in times of financial trouble; (*b*) forbidding the sale of certain commodities in the interests of public health or morality.

sumptuary tax *see under* tax.

sundries (1) COM. & ACCTS. various small things collectively; sundry articles. (2) TRANSPT. various small consignments, such as parcels and bicycles, carried by freight trains.

sundries account ACCTS. an account in the sales ledger or purchases ledger, or both, for recording dealings with occasional customers and suppliers for whom separate accounts are not necessary. *Also* sundry account.

sundries file *see under* file.

sundriesman COM. a trader who specializes in selling various small things required by a particular industry or occupation: *An artist's sundriesman,* one who sells paints, brushes, oils, and other materials needed by artists. *A printer's sundriesman.*

sundry various.

sundry debtor *see under* debtor.

sunk costs *see* fixed costs *under* costs.

sunspot theory *see* trade cycle theories *under* cycle.

superannuate MAN. to let or make an employee retire from service and then receive a pension; to pension off.

superannuation MAN. (1) the state or condition of being superannuated. (2) the pension or other payment received by a person who has been superannuated.

supercargo SHIPG. an officer on a merchant ship who is responsible for the safety of the cargo being transported and for the general profitabilty of the voyage.

superhighway (U.S.A.) in Britain, a motorway. *Syn.* (U.S.A.) expressway; freeway.

superintend to direct the work of others; to manage the operation of an organization.

superintendent (1) MAN. a person who superintends; one who is placed in charge of other persons, esp. a group of workers. (2) SHIPG. a person paid by the owners of a ship to direct the work of repairing it. *Marine superintendent,* an official responsible for the management of a shipping company's business at a large port or group of ports.

supermarket COM. a large self-service shop or store selling a wide variety of goods that are in much demand by consumers, esp. food and drink, and household cleaning and other materials. *Cf.* hypermarket.

supernormal profit *see under* profit.

super-profit *see under* profit.

superscription the part of a business letter that consists of the name and address of the person or organization to whom the letter is being sent.

supertanker SHIPG. a very large tanker (ship for carrying liquids in bulk. esp. oil).

supervise to have the responsibility for seeing that the work of others is properly done.

supervision MAN. (1) the act of supervising. (2) the condition of being supervised: *Mistakes are usu. due to bad supervision. This employee can be trusted to work without supervision.*

supervisor MAN. a person who supervises, esp. one who is given some authority, such as a telephone supervisor, who is in charge of a number of operators.

supplementary added; extra; additional.

supplementary allowance INSCE. in Britain, an extra amount of money paid weekly by the State under the national insurance scheme to bring unemployment benefit up to a standard level related to the current cost of living. *Syn.* supplementary benefit.

supplementary benefit *see* supplementary allowance.

supplementary costs *see* fixed costs *under* costs.

supplementary invoice *see under* invoice.

supplementary pension INSCE. in Britain, an extra amount of money paid weekly by the State under the national insurance scheme to bring a widow's pension or a retirement pension up to a standard level related to the current cost of living. The amount paid depends on the person's income and his/her rent and rates and, in some cases, the cost of heating his/her home.

supplement, family income INSCE. in Britain, under the national insurance scheme, an extra amount, paid as a weekly allowance by the State, to any worker whose income is less than a standard amount related to the number of children in his family and to the current cost of living. *Abbr.* F.I.S.

supplier COM. & IND. a person or organization who supplies goods, esp. regularly and for payment: *A publisher's main suppliers are paper merchants, printers and binders*.

supplier credit *see* trade credit *under* credit (4).

supplier's monopoly *see* commercial monopoly *under* monopoly.

supply ECON. THEORY the amount of an economic good that will be offered for sale in the market at a certain price and time; or at each of a series or range of prices at a certain time. Normally, the higher the price, the greater the supply, except where the supply is fixed or is regressive, *see below*.

aggregate supply the total supply of all goods and services coming on to the market at a given time. *See* aggregate supply curve *under* aggregate demand and supply curves; *also* aggregate supply price.

competitive supply the situation where the factors of production, esp. land and labour, are limited, and where producers of two or more commodities are competing for the use of those factors. If more of the factors are used for one commodity there will be less for the other or others, and the supply of these will fall.

complementary supply the supply of two or more commodities that are the result of the same production process, such as corn and straw, mutton and wool, where one commodity cannot be produced without producing the other. Cf. by-product. *Syn.* joint supply.

composite supply (*a*) the total supply of a commodity that comes from two or more sources or processes, such as natural rubber and artificial (synthetic) rubber, beet-sugar and cane-sugar. (*b*) the total supply of two or more commodities that can satisfy one kind of demand, such as butter and margarine, apples and pears, etc., i.e. goods that are near substitutes for each other.

excess supply a situation in which, at a certain price, the amount of a particular product demanded by buyers is less than the amount supplied by the industry. If the price is a full-cost price, i.e. one that includes a satisfactory profit, producers may reduce the price temporarily to encourage demand while they arrange to reduce their output; but in the long run the price is likely to return to and stay at the full-cost level, with the output just high enough to satisfy the demand. But *see also* Say's Law of Markets *under* Say, Jean-Baptiste.

fixed supply a situation in which, in the short run, an increase in price will not result in an increase in supply because stocks have all been sold and output cannot immediately be increased.

joint supply *see* complementary supply *above*.

regressive supply an unusual situation in which a fall in the market price results in an increase in the supply coming on to the market; for example, frightened farmers may sell their stocks rather than risk a further fall in price. Similarly, a rise in the price may result in a reduced supply, as in the labour market when an increase in wages sometimes results in a reduction in the supply of labour because some workers decide not to work so hard.

Supply and Demand, Laws of ECON. THEORY the natural tendencies that normally cause supply and demand to vary with price, and price to vary with supply and demand. Stated very simply, these tendencies are: (*a*) if, at a given price, supply exceeds demand, the price tends to fall, and if demand exceeds supply, the price tends to rise; (*b*) an increase in price tends to reduce demand and to increase supply, and a fall in price tends to increase demand and to reduce supply; (*c*) a state of market equilibrium (balance) will tend to be reached, in which the supply equals the demand at an equilibrium price. There are a number of exceptions, but these happen usu. in the short run.

supply, elasticity of *see under* elasticity.

supply price *see under* price.

supply services *see under* services.

support STK. EXCH. willingness to buy: *Newspaper shares found support*, there were many buyers for these shares. (2) FIN. official buying of a currency to keep its rate of exchange from falling: *There were signs of support for the pound*. *See* official support *under* official.

support price *see under* price; *also* Common Agricultural Policy.

suppress (1) to cause to discontinue; to bring to an end: *The bus/rail service has been suppressed*, stopped, discontinued. *What can we do to suppress competition?*, how can we get rid of, overcome it. (2) *To suppress a document/report/plan*, to prevent it from being published. (3) to hold back; to control: *To suppress inflation*, *see* suppressed inflation *under* inflation.

supra protest *see* payment supra protest; *also* acceptance supra protest *under* acceptance.

Supreme Court LAW in U.S.A., the highest court in the federal judicial system, the last court of appeal, and the court that decides questions relating to the constitution.

Supreme Court of Judicature LAW in Britain, the highest court for civil cases next below the House of Lords. It consists of the High Court of Justice and the Court of Appeal.

surcharge *n.* (1) TAXN. an extra charge, over and above another charge. *See* investment income surcharge *under* investment; import surcharge *under* import. (2) ACCTS. & MAN. to make a person who has spent public money, or his company's money, without proper authority become personally liable to repay it.

surety LAW & BKG. a guarantor. *Syn.* (Scotland) a cautioner.

surety bond *see under* bond, *n.*

suretyship *see* guaranty.

surface mail *see under* mail.

surface transport *see under* transport.

surf port *see* barge port *under* port.

surgeon a doctor who specializes in treating disease, injury and wrong growth by operating on the body. Cf. family doctor or general practitioner.

surgery (1) the art and practice of a surgeon. (2) a room or set of rooms where people come to be treated by a family doctor or dental surgeon. Cf. consulting room(s).

Surinam a republic in the north of South America, formerly Dutch Guiana, pop. 450,000 approx. (1975); capital Paramaribo, pop. 150,000 approx.; languages, Surinamese, Dutch, pidgin English and Hindi; currency unit, the Surinam guilder, divided into 100 cents.

surname a person's family name, as opposed to his Christian or first name. For example, Mr John Smith's surname or family name is Smith; John is his Christian or first name.

surplus (1) an excess, esp. over that which is needed or owed. (2) ECON. an excess of supply; an amount over and above what is demanded: *A surplus of wheat/butter.* (3) INSCE. the amount by which an insurer's assets exceed his liabilities. (4) ACCTS. the net worth of a business. (5) the excess of income over expenditure. (6) in the British nationalized industries, the equivalent of profit.

budget surplus *see* surplus budget *under* budget.

consumer's surplus *see under* consumer's.

employer's surplus *see* producer's surplus.

external surplus a favourable balance of payments.

producer's surplus *see under* producer's.

surplus capacity *see* capacity (1).

surplus profit *see* super-profit *under* profit.

surplus value *see* consumer's surplus.

surrender INSCE. the act of giving up, of discontinuing a policy of insurance before it has run its agreed time.

surrender value in life insurance, the amount of cash which a policy holder will receive if he surrenders his policy to the insurance company for cancellation. The amount will usu. be equal to, or less than, the total of the premiums he has paid. *Syn.* cash surrender (value); loan value. *Abbr.* s.v.

surrender rule BKG. & FIN. a rule of the British government exchange control, no longer in force, that investors who sold foreign securities that were bought with investment currency with a dollar premium must exchange 25% of the sale proceeds into sterling at the official rate. The investors thus had to surrender, or give up, and lose, part of the dollar premium.

survey (1) a general viewing and description of the whole of a system or organization: *An economic survey of British industry/world trade.* (2) the work of collecting information about the people's tastes and opinions from a sample of the population in order to plan how to advertise, distribute and sell a product: *A market/opinion survey.* (3) a close examination and detailed report on the condition of a particular thing such as a ship, plane, cargo, mine, factory: *A special survey,* of a ship, every four years, *see below.* (4) the measurement of the shape of the earth's surface and the preparation of maps and plans of areas of land: *A geodetic/aerial/cadastral survey.* (5) an official organization responsible for making and publishing a country's maps: *The Ordnance Survey. The Survey of India.*

aerial *or* **air survey** the making of maps of areas of the earth's surface from photographs taken from a plane flying at a great height. Aerial surveys are used in some countries to show how land is being used, what crops are being grown, the extent of floods, etc.

cadastral survey a survey that records in the form of a map, or set of maps, the boundaries and ownership of land.

consumer survey *see* consumer research *under* research.

geodetic survey the measurement and mapping of large areas of the earth's surface.

geophysical survey *see* geophysical surveying.

marine insurance survey an examination and report on the condition of a ship's cargo by a surveyor, made at the insurer's request, to decide liability if a claim is made under the insurance contract. *See* special survey *below.*

market survey *see* market research.

Ordnance Survey *see under* Ordnance.

readership survey a survey using a sample of the population to find out what newspapers and magazines are most read by different age groups, occupations and income groups.

special survey a complete and detailed examination of the condition of a ship. British ships have to receive such a survey every four years by Lloyd's surveyors. The class of the ship for insurance purposes is based on the results of this survey.

surveying *see* geophysical surveying.

surveyor (1) a supervisor, a person placed in charge and given responsibility for seeing that work is properly done, such as a surveyor of customs. (2) a person with special skill and knowledge and employed to make close examinations of things such as ships and their cargoes, planes, buildings and industrial machinery and to report on their condition: *A ship/insurance surveyor*. (3) a person skilled in measuring land and in making maps and plans: *A land/cartographic surveyor*.

customs surveyor *see* surveyor of customs.

engineer surveyor *see* Lloyd's surveyor *under* Lloyd's.

insurance surveyor in fire and accident insurance, a person with special knowledge employed by an insurance company to examine and report on a proposed risk.

Lloyd's surveyor *see under* Lloyd's.

marine surveyor *see* Lloyd's surveyor.

ship surveyor *see* Lloyd's surveyor.

surveyor of customs TAXN. the officer in charge of a custom house or customs warehouse.

surveyor's chain *see* chain.

surveyor's measure a measure of land: 1 link = 7.92 in. or 20.117 cm. *See table on page 476.*

survivor policy *see* contingent *or* survivorship policy *under* insurance policy.

survivorship annuity *see under* insurance policy.

suspected bill of health *see under* bill of health.

suspense account ACCTS. a temporary account that is brought into existence whenever necessary, to which are posted e.g. balances that are needed to make the trial balance agree; or in which can be recorded deals which are at present undecided. Such deals are said to be *in suspense*, in an undecided state.

s.v. sailing vessel; surrender value.

S.W. South-West.

swadeshi ECON. HIST. made in India, as distinguished from foreign or imported. A movement started in Bengal in 1905 to encourage the sale and use of home-made goods as part of the fight for home rule.

swag (*colloq.*) stolen property; goods stolen in a robbery.

swag-shop (*a*) a shop in which stolen goods are sold. (*b*) a shop selling cheap goods of low quality.

swap *see* swop.

Swaziland a small monarchy in southern Africa, pop. 500,000 approx. (1977); capital, Mbabane, pop. 15,000 approx.; languages, Siswati

and English; currency unit, the South African rand and the local lilangeni, *pl.* emalangeni. Member, (British) Commonwealth; O.A.U.

sweated labour IND. REL. (1) industrial workers who work very long hours in bad conditions for very low wages. (2) any group of workers whose employers take advantage of their lack of collective bargaining-power.

sweating *see* debasement of coinage.

Sweden a constitutional monarchy (kingdom) in northern Europe, pop. 8 million approx. (1975); capital, Stockholm, pop. 750,000 approx.; language, Swedish; currency unit, the Swedish krona or crown, *pl.* kronor, *abbr.* kr., divided into 100 örer, *sing.* öre. Member, O.E.C.D.; E.F.T.A.

sweep *see* sweepstake.

sweepstake a form of lottery in which the prizewinners are decided partly by chance and partly by the results of a sporting event such as a horse-race. *Colloq.* sweep.

sweeten to bribe.

swindle to defraud; to cheat.

swindler a person who obtains money or goods by deceiving people. *Syn.* cheat; fraud; trickster.

Swiss franc the standard currency unit of Switzerland, divided into 100 centimes. *Abbr.* SFr.

switchboard part of the apparatus of a telephone system that consists of a board on which are fixed many switches for connecting telephone lines. A *manual switchboard* is one controlled by hand by a telephone operator; there are also *automatic switchboards*.

switching (1) STK. EXCH. to go longer, *see* longer. (2) to change one's investments from one class of security to another, such as from fixed-interest securities to equity shares.

Switzerland a federal republic in western Europe, pop. 6.5 million approx. (1975); capital, Berne, pop. 270,000 approx.; languages, French, German, Italian and Romansch; currency unit, the Swiss franc (SFr.), divided into 100 centimes. Member, O.E.C.D.; E.F.T.A.

swop (1) COM. to barter; to accept a commodity as payment for another instead of money. *Also* swap; scorse. (2) FIN. to exchange one foreign currency for another foreign currency. (3) STK. EXCH. to exchange one security for another.

SX Sundays excepted.

Sx. Sussex, England.

SY the international vehicle-registration letters of the Seychelles.

Sy. Surrey, England; supply.

S.Y. steam yacht.

Syd. Sydney, Australia.

syli the standard currency unit of Guinea, divided into 100 cauris. *Also* suli; sily.

sympathetic strike *see under* strike.

syndic a person appointed by an organization such as a university to manage its business affairs.

syndicalism ECON. & IND. a proposed economic system not unlike communism, under which the workers, grouped into trade unions, would control and manage all industry.

syndicate (1) MAN. an association or joint venture in which several business concerns share their special knowledge and influence, and co-operate in some particular way, such as placing a new issue of shares, or planning the Channel Tunnel. (2) COM. a joint selling organization. *See* cartel. (3) INSCE. a group of Lloyd's underwriters working together as a unit, but each bearing personal responsibility for any liability which he accepts. Each syndicate tends to deal only in one particular class of insurance, other than life insurance. According to Lloyd's rules all premiums received are paid into a trust fund out of which claims are settled. *See* Lloyd's; Lloyd's underwriter; marine syndicate.

synonym a word having the same meaning as another. Another name for something. *Opp.* antonym. *Abbr.* Syn.

SYR Syria's international vehicle-registration letters.

Syria an Arab republic in south-west Asia on the eastern shore of the Mediterranean Sea, pop. 7 million approx. (1975); capital, Damascus, pop. 850,000 approx.; languages, Arabic, French and Aramaic; currency unit, the Syrian pound (S£), divided into 100 piastres. Member, Arab League.

system, monetary *see* monetary system.

systems analyst (1) COMP. a person with special skill and knowledge of computers, who is employed to manage the work of planning and installing a computer system in an office or factory, and to supervise the work of the programmers and other persons operating the system. (2) someone who applies techniques such as operational research and mathematical models to the problem of balancing costs and benefits in places where market analysis cannot be used, e.g. in public services such as hospitals.

sz. size.

T

T tropical loading (on load-line); Thailand's international vehicle-registration letter.

T., t. ton(s); tare.

T.A. travelling allowance.

TAB on a typewriter, *see* tabulator.

Table A LAW & STK. EXCH. in Britain, a model set of Articles of Association included in the Com-

panies Act 1948, for a company limited by shares. Most companies adopt these model Articles, but with changes. *See* Articles of Association.

table of organization (T.O.) *see* organization chart *under* chart.

tabulating machine ACCTS. & MAN. a machine that prepares tabulations from a mass of data fed into it in the form of punched cards. Such machines have been largely replaced by electronic computers.

tabulation MAN. & ACCTS. (1) an orderly and systematic presentation of numerical data in such a form as to make clear a particular problem. (2) any table of figures for recording and comparing information: *A tabulation statement.*

tabulator on a typewriter, a key marked TAB which, when pressed and held down, allows the carriage to move to a desired position. The tabulator is much used for typing tables of figures. *See* tabulation.

tachograph TRANSPT. an instrument, fitted to a road or rail vehicle, that records, on a paper marked with a time-scale, the starts, stops, speeds and distances travelled during a particular day or week or on a particular journey. *Syn.* tachometer.

tachometer *see* tachograph.

tack LAW in Scotland, a lease or tenancy of land.

tackle SHIPG. (1) any system of ropes and pulleys for working a ship, esp. for lifting or lowering anchors, loads of cargo, etc. (2) any machinery for doing this. *See* apparel and tackle; appurtenances.

tael FIN. (1) a Chinese unit of weight: 1.33 oz. avoirdupois = 37.6 g. (2) the value of this weight of silver, formerly much used in the Far East as a money of account.

tag a label, esp. one showing a price: *A price-tag.*

Taiwan an island republic in eastern Asia, pop. 15 million approx. (1972); capital, Taipei, pop. 1.7 million approx.; language, Mandarin Chinese; currency unit, the Taiwan dollar (T$), divided into 100 cents. *Also* Formosa.

taka the standard currency unit of Bangladesh, divided into 100 poisha.

take-home foods COM. foods sold freshly cooked and packed, ready for the customer to take away to eat in his home. Cf. in-hand foods.

take-home pay FIN. the amount of money that a worker actually receives from his employer; the sum that is left out of the worker's total pay after deductions have been made for income tax, state insurance contributions, union dues, etc.

take in (1) to give shelter or accommodation to: *To take in lodgers.* (2) to deceive; to cheat: *I was taken in by his clever salesmanship.* (3) STK. EXCH. to charge backwardation. Cf. give on. *N.* taker in.

takers in *pl.* brokers who borrow stock from other brokers. Cf. givers on.

take over (1) to accept responsibility for: *He took over my debts.* (2) to gain control of: *To take over a company/business.*

takeover STK. EXCH. the act or process of gaining control of a company by making its shareholders a general offer, called a *takeover bid*, usu. with a time-limit for acceptance, to buy, at a stated price that is higher than the market price, all the shares, or at least enough of them to give a controlling interest in the company. If the holders of 90% of the shares accept, the bidding company has the legal right to buy the remaining 10% at the same price. In most countries the authorities keep strict control of takeovers to protect the interests of shareholders. In Britain all takeovers must be according to rules in *The City Code on Takeovers and Mergers*, and an official panel of the London Stock Exchange watches and advises on the application of the *Code*. *Also* take-over.

taker (of an option) *see* option (1).

take up *see* retire (1).

takings *pl.* COM. the cash received, esp. in a shop, post office, etc.: *The day's takings*, the total of the cash taken, i.e. received from sales, during the day.

tala the standard currency unit of Western Samoa, divided into 100 cents. *Also* the Western Samoan dollar.

tale COM. a number, as opposed to a quantity expressed by weight or volume. *To reckon livestock by tale*, to express the quantity by the number of animals, not by their weight.

tale quale *see* tel quel rate *under* exchange rate. *Pron.* tahli kwahli.

Talisman STK. EXCH. in the London Stock Exchange, a centralized system for settling amounts due by members to each other, by which sellers transfer stock to a Stock Exchange nominee company called Sepon, and from this central pool buyers in turn receive their stock. Sepon keeps separate accounts for each jobber.

tally *n.* SHIPG. a list of goods loaded or unloaded as cargo. *Syn.* cargo list.
v. to agree with; to be correct according to: *Your list tallies with mine. These figures do not tally*, do not agree with each other.

tallyclerk SHIPG. a person employed to check cargo being loaded or unloaded against a tally or cargo list.

tallyman COM. a shopkeeper or travelling trader who sells goods, usu. cheap or of poor quality, and accepts payment by instalments. *Fem.* tallywoman.

tally-roll ACCTS. the rolled strip of paper on which an adding machine records each entry separately and the total value at the end.

tallyshop COM. a shop kept by a tallyman.

tally trade COM. (*colloq.*) the system of trading adopted by tallymen and tallyshops, accepting payment by instalments.

talon STK. EXCH. a printed slip, issued with certain bearer bonds, that the holder of the bond can exchange for a new sheet of coupons when the earlier coupons have been used up.

tambala the fractional currency unit of Malawi. 100 tambala = 1 kwacha.

tampering with the market STK. EXCH. operations by dealers aimed at affecting the course of market prices, resulting in more frequent and more violent swings upwards and downwards than would otherwise take place.

tangible assets *see under* assets.

tangible net worth *see under* net worth.

tank a large container for water, fuel or other liquids.

tanker (1) SHIPG. a ship specially planned and built to carry liquid cargo in bulk, i.e. in large storage tanks. Most of the world's tankers are used for carrying petroleum products but some special tankers carry wine, sugar products, and liquid gases. (2) TRANSPT. a vehicle specially planned and built to carry liquids in bulk by road or rail: *A petrol tanker.*

Tanzania a republic in eastern Africa, pop. 15 million approx. (1975); capital, Dar es Salaam, pop. 350,000 approx.; languages, English, Arabic and tribal; currency unit, the Tanzanian shilling (TSh.), divided into 100 cents. Member, O.A.U.; (British) Commonwealth; E.A.C.

tape *n.* (1) a narrow ribbon. (2) a message recorded on magnetic tape.

magnetic tape plastic or metal tape coated with a substance such as iron oxide that is affected by magnetism, used in a tape recorder to record sounds, or to store information in binary form in a computer.

red tape (*a*) pink or red cotton tape formerly used by clerks in government offices for tying bundles of documents. (*b*) (*colloq.*) excessive formality and paperwork.
v. to record a message or computer-information on magnetic tape.

tape recorder an instrument for recording sound or computer-information on magnetic tape.

tap issue FIN. a special issue of government bills or securities direct to a government organization, such as the Bank of England, without using the money market or the Stock Exchange.

tap stock *see under* stock.

tar (*colloq.*) a sailor. *Also* Jack Tar; jack tar.

tare (1) TRANSPT. the unladen weight of a lorry or railway wagon; this weight is usu. painted on the side of the vehicle so that the weight of its load can be found by weighing the vehicle when loaded and then deducting the tare. *Syn.* (U.S.A.) dead weight. (2) COM. & IND. the weight of a container or any other object or material in which goods are packed, such as drums, cases, bags, or wrapping paper. Tare is deducted from the gross weight to arrive at the net weight of the goods.

target price *see under* price.

tariff (1) any scale of prices or charges, or of rates of tax. (2) TOUR. (*a*) in a restaurant, a bill of fare; a menu. (*b*) in a hotel, a scale of charges for rooms and service, esp. a printed or typed list of these. (3) TRANSPT. a table of rates charged by a transport company for carrying various classes of goods and passengers: *A freight/passenger tariff.* (4) INSCE. an agreed scale of insurance premiums charged by all members of a group of insurers, called *tariff companies*; insurers who are not members and who are free to charge any rate they wish are called *non-tariff companies*. (5) IND. in the gas and electricity supply industries, a system of charging different classes of users. *See* two-part tariff; off-peak tariff *below*. (6) TAXN. (*a*) a synonym for a customs duty. *See* duty (3). (*b*) a printed list of the rates of customs duties.

tariffs *pl.* a system of customs duties.

ad valorem tariff an ad valorem duty, *see* ad valorem.

compound tariff a combination of ad valorem duty and specific duty, used in one of two ways: the charging of only one of these duties, that which is the higher in amount; or the charging of both duties on the same goods at the same time.

discriminating tariff *see* multiple tariff *below*.

multiple tariff a customs duty with variable rates depending on the country of origin of the goods. *Syn.* discriminating tariff.

off-peak tariff a specially low rate charged for electricity supplied during certain fixed hours, used mainly for heating private homes. *See* off-peak. *Syn.* restricted-hour tariff; time-of-day tariff.

protective tariff a protective customs duty. *See* protective duty *under* duty.

restricted-hour tariff *see* off-peak tariff *above*.

revenue tariff a customs duty that is intended to bring in revenue, as opposed to a protective duty.

time-of-day tariff *see* off-peak tariff *above*.

two-part tariff a method of charging consumers for electricity or gas, by which the charge consists of two parts: a fixed charge that has to be paid whether or not there has been any consumption; and a charge that varies with the amount consumed.

tariff company *see* tariff (4).

tariff standard *see under* standard.

Tas. Tasmania, Australia.

task bonus *see under* bonus.

task system of pay IND. a method of paying a worker an agreed sum for each job completed in an agreed standard time. If he completes it in less time, he will produce more jobs in a day and earn a higher total pay; but if he takes more than the standard time, he earns less. This system is little different from piece-work. *Syn.* task wages.

tax *n.* TAXN. a payment of money legally demanded by a government authority to meet public expenses.

ad valorem tax *see* ad valorem.

capital tax that class of tax that is charged on capital, as opposed to taxes charged on income (income tax) and on expenditure (expenditure tax). In Britain, capital taxes are the capital gains tax and the capital transfer tax.

capital gains tax (*a*) in Britain, a capital tax charged on a gain resulting from the sale of an asset by a private taxpayer. The gain is the increase in capital value, or the difference between the original cost and the selling price. The tax is not charged on the gain made from the sale of a person's home, car, personal possessions sold for less than a certain sum, certain gilt-edged securities, etc. Capital losses and selling expenses can be set against capital gains. Gains by companies are treated differently, being classed as profits and liable to corporation tax. *Abbr.* C.G.T. (*b*) in U.S.A., a gain from the sale of a capital asset is treated as income and liable to income tax, but at a lower rate than that charged on normal income.

capital transfer tax *see under* capital transfer.

capitation tax a tax formerly charged on every person in a country or in a group, at the same amount per person. In England, the Peasants' Revolt of 1381 was mainly directed against a tax on every person in the population. In U.S.A. in the late nineteenth century a poll tax or capitation tax on those exercising their right to vote in elections was used as a political tool to prevent the poorer people, who could not afford to pay the tax, from voting. *Syn.* poll tax; head tax.

consumption tax *see under* consumption.

corporation tax in Britain, a tax on the profits of limited companies. It is charged on the whole of the net trading profits of a company, whether they are paid as dividends or kept as reserves. This tax replaces the former *profits tax* and *company income tax. Advance corporation tax* (A.C.T.), the amount of tax paid by a company on the amount of profit distributed as dividend, charged at a rate equal to basic-rate income tax. *See* tax credit.

death tax (U.S.A.) *see* estate tax *below*.

degressive tax (*a*) a tax charged at a decreasing rate on incomes below a certain level. (*b*) a progressive tax that is charged at a decreasing rate as the income increases above certain levels.

direct tax *see under* direct.

discriminatory tax one charged on some industries in order to make it easier for other industries to compete in the market, such as a tax on natural gas supplies to help the electricity, coal and oil industries to compete for customers.

estate tax (U.S.A.) a tax on the value of property of any kind possessed by a person at his death. *Syn.* death tax; (Britain) estate duties; capital transfer tax.

excess-profits tax a tax charged usu. in time of war or other national emergency, on the excess of business profits over the average of profits earned during a standard period when conditions were normal.

excise tax *see* excise (2).

expenditure tax *see under* expenditure.

federal tax in U.S.A., a tax, either direct or indirect, that must be paid to the U.S. Internal Revenue Service or to the Bureau of Customs. Federal taxes include federal income tax, estate tax, gift tax, social security tax, excise tax, and customs duty. Cf. state tax; local tax.

gift tax *see* capital transfer tax *under* capital transfer.

head tax *see* capitation tax *above*.

hidden tax any indirect tax which is included in the price of goods or services and which the consumer does not realize he is paying.

higher rate tax *see* income tax *under* income.

income tax *see under* income; *also* income-tax schedules.

indirect tax a tax that is not paid by the taxpayer direct to the government, but is collected by suppliers, shopkeepers, stores, etc., e.g. value added tax (V.A.T.) and excise duties. Cf. direct tax. *Syn.* outlay tax; expenditure tax; consumption tax.

inheritance tax a tax charged on the value of property transferred at death to an heir. The rate of tax charged usu. depends on the amount inherited and on the closeness of the relationship of the heir to the dead person, being low if the heir is a close relation such as the wife or a child.

input tax *see* value added tax *below*.

land tax in Britain, tax formerly charged on the ownership of land, but now abolished. In many other countries, land is taxed. *See* property tax *below*.

local tax a tax payable to the local government authority by occupiers of land and buildings to pay for part of the cost of local public services, such as education, public health services, street lighting and cleaning; the other part of the cost is covered by grants from higher or central government authorities. In Britain, such local taxes are called rates. *Syn.* municipal tax.

luxury tax a special indirect tax on luxuries, i.e. on articles or services that are expensive and not really necessary for normal living, such as a tax on jewellery and non-essential goods.

multiple sales tax *see* sales tax (*b*) *below*.

municipal tax *see* local tax *above*; *also* rates.

outlay tax *see* indirect tax *above*.

output tax *see* value added tax *below*.

pay-roll tax *see under* pay-roll.

poll tax *see* capitation tax *above*.

profits tax *see* corporation tax *above*.

progressive tax a tax, such as income tax, that is charged at an increasing rate as the taxable income increases. Cf. degressive tax. *Opp.* regressive tax.

property tax a tax charged on the value of real property, i.e. land and buildings. In some countries it is also charged on other forms of property such as jewellery, furniture and investments. Cf. wealth tax.

proportional tax a tax that is charged at a rate that does not change as the taxable amount increases. Cf. progressive tax; regressive tax.

purchase tax an ad valorem tax on the wholesale price of certain non-essential goods, paid by the consumer to the retailer, who pays it to the government. In Britain, the purchase tax introduced in 1940 in time of war has been replaced by the value added tax (V.A.T.). *Abbr.* P.T. Cf. sales tax.

real estate tax *see* property tax *above*.

regressive tax a tax that is charged at a reducing rate as the taxable amount increases. *Opp.* progressive tax.

regulatory tax a tax used by the government as a means of regulating (controlling) some economic activity rather than raising money, such as a high tax on petrol to make people use less.

revenue tax a tax charged mainly for the purpose of raising revenue rather than to control the economy or to reduce inequalities of wealth and income.

sales tax (*a*) a tax charged as a percentage of the retail price of goods or of the price charged to the public for services. It is usu. a general tax on a wide range of commodities and services, both essential and non-essential. Cf. purchase tax. (*b*) a tax charged not only on retail prices but also on the prices charged by manufacturers and wholesalers, called a *multiple sales tax*, or *turnover tax*. The disadvantage of this tax is that the value taxed at each stage includes the tax paid at earlier stages. Value added tax avoids this form of multiple taxation. *Syn.* transactions tax.

social security tax in U.S.A., the equivalent of the British national insurance contributions, paid by employer and employee and by the self-employed, to provide social security benefits to unemployed, sick, disabled and other groups of persons unable to work, and retirement pensions in old age.

specific tax a tax at a rate based on a certain quantity of a commodity, such as the petrol tax of so much a gallon or litre, as opposed to an ad valorem tax, based on value.

state tax in U.S.A., a tax that must be paid to the government of one of the states, such as income tax, estate tax, inheritance tax, sales tax, property tax and certain licence fees. Cf. federal tax; local tax.

sumptuary tax a tax on costly non-essential goods, intended to reduce spending on such things. *Syn.* luxury tax.

transactions tax *see* sales tax (*b*) *above*.

turnover tax *see* sales tax (*b*) *above*.

value added tax (V.A.T.), an indirect tax, being a form of general sales tax, charged as a percentage of the selling price of an article or commodity. It is added to the invoice as *output tax* at each stage of production and distribution, from manufacturer to wholesaler and to retailer. At each stage, the taxable person must account to the government for the output tax but is allowed to set against it the *input tax*, i.e. tax charged to him by his suppliers. A system of V.A.T. exists in all the E.E.C. countries; in Britain it replaced the former purchase tax in 1966–7.

wealth tax a tax on the value of personal net assets above a certain limit. Cf. property tax.

v. to demand payment of a tax; to make something liable to a tax: *To tax a person according to his income. To tax luxuries more heavily.*

taxable income *see under* income.

tax assessment *see under* assessment.

tax assessor TAXN. in the U.S.A., the equivalent of an inspector of taxes in Britain.

taxation (1) the act or process of taxing somebody or something: *The use of taxation to control the economy.* (2) money paid to the government as taxes: *Reduced taxation means more money for private spending.* (3) LAW *Taxation of costs*, the process of deciding, by an officer of the court called the taxing officer, what the legal costs in a lawsuit amount to, and the share to be borne by each of the parties to the action. Legal costs include court fees, solicitors' fees and witnesses' expenses.

direct taxation the charging of direct taxes, *see* tax.

indirect taxation the charging of indirect taxes, *see* tax.

multiple taxation the taxing of a person by two or more government authorities demanding the same kind of tax, such as federal income tax and the state income tax in the U.S.A. *Syn.* dual taxation.

tax avoidance TAXN. action taken to avoid having to pay tax unnecessarily, using means that are not illegal. Cf. tax evasion.

tax base TAXN. the amount of income, capital gain, or value of property or goods on which a tax is liable to be paid. For income tax it is the taxable income.

tax collector TAXN. *see* collector of taxes *under* collector.

tax commissioners *see* Commissioners of Inland Revenue.

tax consultant TAXN. a professional adviser on tax matters.

tax credit TAXN. in Britain, a credit given to a shareholder for his share of the advance corporation tax paid by a company on the amount it distributes as dividends. The shareholder thus receives the dividend that has been declared, and at the same time is given by the company a document showing the amount of his tax credit. This document relieves him from paying basic-rate income tax on the dividend. If his total income is so low that he is not liable to pay any income tax, he can claim payment of the amount of the tax credit from the tax authority. If his income is high enough he will have to pay higher-rate tax and investment income surcharge on the dividend. *Syn.* (U.S.A.) tax offset.

tax efficiency TAXN. the ability of a taxpayer to invest his capital in such a way that the amount of tax payable on the income from it is kept as small as possible.

tax evasion *see* evasion.

tax disc *see under* token.

tax exemption TAXN. freedom from payment of taxes, usu. allowed by law to non-profitmaking organizations working for the public good, such as charities, religious associations, clubs and societies.

tax-free allowance *see* allowance (5).

tax-free income *see under* income.

tax holiday TAXN. & IND. a stated period of years during which, in some countries, a producer who sets up a new industrial unit, or expands his existing unit to increase his exports, enjoys the advantage of paying no tax on part or the whole of his profits. This freedom from tax is given as a means of attracting new industries, or of encouraging existing industries to export more goods.

tax impact *see* impact (3).

tax incidence *see* incidence.

tax inspector *see* inspector of taxes.

tax levy *see* levy.

tax offset *see* tax credit.

taxpayer TAXN. any person or organization liable by law to pay a tax or taxes. In Britain, where local taxes are called rates, a person who pays, or is liable to pay, local taxes is called a rate-payer.

tax relief TAXN. in Britain, a tax-free amount allowed in calculating a taxpayer's taxable income, e.g. interest on loans for housing, and life insurance premiums.

double income-tax relief *see under* double.

export-tax relief relief from income tax and company tax on profits made on exports, such as exists in Ireland, New Zealand, etc.

tax return *see* return (3).

tax schedules *see* Schedules A to E.
tax shifting *see* shift, *v*.
tax token *see under* token.
tax voucher *see* dividend warrant.
tax year *see under* year.
T.B. trial balance; Treasury bill.
t.b.a. to be advised; to be agreed.
T.C. traveller's cheque.
TD the international vehicle-registration letters of Trinidad and Tobago.
technical IND. having to do with the scientific methods used in industry, esp. in manufacturing processes: *A report written in technical language. He is studying chemical engineering/computer science/paper technology in a technical college.*
technical aid *see* foreign aid.
technical efficiency *see under* efficiency.
technical position STK. EXCH. of a particular security, the current trend of the market, whether the security is much in demand or is being steadily sold.
technocracy (1) a system of government in which ruling power is held by a few persons from a class or group highly trained in science and technology. (2) the persons (technocrats) who hold the ruling power in such a system.
technological unemployment *see under* unemployment.
technology IND. the study and use of scientific methods in industry, esp. the application of chemistry, physics and engineering to manufacturing processes.
tel., Tel. telegram; telegraph; telephone.
tele- *prefix* meaning distant: *Telegraphy*, writing at a distance. *Television*, a method of broadcasting pictures and sound over a distance.
telegram a message sent by telegraph, esp. along wires. *See* cable.
radio telegram a message sent by radio.
telegraphic address an abbreviated form of the name and address of a business, registered with the Post Office, printed as part of the business letterhead and intended to save money, and to reduce mistakes, when customers, etc. send telegrams and cables to the business.
telegraph(ic) money order *see under* money order.
telegraphic transfer (T.T.) BKG. (1) a quick way of sending money by cabled bank transfer to a person in another country. The payee can be paid either in cash or by credit to his bank account. The sender bears the cost of the cable unless he directs that this is to be borne by the payee. (2) *Telegraphic transfer rate, see* T.T. rate *under* exchange rate.
telephone box *see* call-box.
telephone exchange a central building where connections to telephone lines are made by means of switching apparatus. A *private*

branch exchange (P.B.X.) is an apparatus used in an office, hotel, etc. for switching calls to a number of instruments in the building. An *exchange line* is one from a P.B.X. to the central telephone exchange, and is sometimes called an *outside line*.
telephone kiosk *see* call-box.
teleprinter an apparatus for sending and receiving typewritten messages over long distances by telegraph. The message is typed on a keyboard, similar to that of a typewriter, at the sender's end of the line, and it appears as a typewritten document at the distant end. *See also* telex.
television advertising *see* advertising media.
telex (1) an international system for sending and receiving messages by teleprinter, using telegraph lines connected by automatic exchanges similar to those of a telephone system. (2) a message sent or received by telex.
teller (1) MAN. a person appointed at a meeting to count votes. *Syn*. scrutineer. (2) BKG. *see* cashier (3).
tel quel rate *see under* exchange rate.
temp. temporary; temperature.
temp (*colloq*.) a temporary worker, esp. a typist.
temporary annuity *see under* insurance policy.
temporary money *see under* money.
temporary policy *see* term policy *under* insurance policy.
tenancy LAW (1) the right of a person or organization to hold certain land or buildings under a lease, *see* lessee; or following the ending of a lease, *see* tenant at sufferance; or merely at the will of the landlord, *see* tenant at will; or under a settlement, *see* tenant for life. (2) a popular word for a lease.
tenancy in common *see* ownership in common.
tenant LAW a person or organization having the right to hold certain land or buildings, usu. under a lease or settlement. *See* tenancy; landlord and tenant. *Syn*. lessee; nominee.
joint tenant *see* joint ownership.
life tenant *see* tenant for life.
statutory tenant in Britain, a tenant whose tenancy is protected by a law that gives him the right to remain in the property even after his tenancy agreement with the landlord has come to an end.
sub-tenant *see* sub-tenant.
yearly tenant *see* tenant from year to year.
tenant at sufferance LAW a tenant who continues to hold land or buildings after the ending of the lease by which he originally came into possession of the property, and without the agreement of the landlord.
tenant at will LAW a tenant who holds land under a lease that gives both lessor and lessee the right to end the tenancy at any time on giving an agreed period of notice.
tenant-farmer AGR. a farmer who holds the land

he farms as a tenant under a lease, paying rent, not as a landowner.

tenant for life LAW a person who owns an interest in land or buildings only for his lifetime, i.e. a life interest. *Syn.* life tenant.

tenant for years LAW a person who holds land or buildings under a lease for a stated number of years, as opposed to a tenant at will, whose lease may be ended by the lessor at any time on giving an agreed period of notice. Cf. tenant from year to year.

tenant from year to year LAW a person who holds land or buildings under a lease that can be ended only by six month's notice ending at the period of the year when the lease originally began. *Syn.* yearly tenancy. Cf. tenant for years.

tender *n.* (1) LAW & FIN. an offer by a debtor of an exact amount of money in coin or notes needed to settle a debt in a strictly legal manner. *See* legal tender. (2) COM. a written offer by a supplier to supply certain goods and services at a stated price, usu. in competition with other tenderers: *To submit a tender for a public works contract. We have won/have been allotted/awarded a tender*, our tender has been accepted.

sealed-bid tender a system by which suppliers are invited, usu. by advertisements, to submit tenders for supplying certain stated goods or services. Each tenderer puts his bid in a sealed envelope so that none of the other tenderers knows what price he has quoted. At a certain time and place, all the envelopes are opened and the contract is given to the tenderer who quotes the lowest price if he is judged able to perform the contract satisfactorily. (3) STK. EXCH. *see* issue by tender. (4) SHIPG. a boat or small ship used for carrying passengers, goods, fuel, etc. from shore to larger vessels. *v.* (1) COM. to make an offer in competition with others in the form of a tender. *See* tendering. (2) FIN. to offer money, esp. in coin or notes or both, in payment of a debt: *To tender a five-pound note.* (3) MAN. to offer, esp. a formal document, such as a letter of resignation: *To tender one's resignation. He tendered his apologies/thanks.*

tenderer COM. a person or organization making a tender.

tender guarantee *see* guarantee (5).

tendering COM. the act or practice of making offers in the form of tenders.

collusive tendering *see under* collusive.

dummy tendering *see* collusive tendering *under* collusive.

level tendering *see* collusive tendering *under* collusive; *also* common pricing.

tender issue BKG. & FIN. in Britain, an issue of Treasury bills (*see* finance bill (*b*) *under* bill of exchange) made by the Bank of England once each week when it invites tenders from financial institutions other than the clearing banks, mainly from discount houses which supply the banks. The size of the issue can be varied and provides the government with a useful means of controlling the amount of bank credit.

tender, legal *see under* legal.

tenement (1) LAW real property, i.e. land and buildings, held by one owner. (2) LAW a house. (3) COM. a house, called a *tenement house*, consisting of a number of flats that are let usu. to families with low incomes.

Ten, Group of *see* Group of Ten.

Tenn. Tennessee, U.S.A.

tenner FIN. (*colloq.*) a ten-pound note; a ten-dollar note.

tenor BKG. the length of time for a bill of exchange or promissory note to reach maturity, i.e. to become due for payment. This time is always stated in the bill or note, e.g. *Three months after date pay to me or pay to my order,* etc. *Syn.* term.

tenure (1) LAW the conditions under which land and buildings are held or occupied; the arrangement existing between a landlord and his tenant. *See* security of tenure *under* security (2). (2) MAN. the holding of a position: *During his tenure of office*, while he held office.

term *v.* to give a name to, to call, to describe something or somebody: *His dealings can be termed criminal.*

n. (1) a word or group of words that expresses a specialized idea: *A financial/stock exchange/insurance/accounting/technical term.* (2) a fixed or agreed period of time: *In the long/short term*, over a long or short period. (3) LAW the time during which a legal right may be enjoyed: *The term of a lease/patent/copyright.* (4) a period of punishment: *A term of imprisonment.* (5) BKG. the length of time that may pass before payment or repayment: *The term of a bill of exchange/promissory note/loan. Syn.* tenor. (6) INSCE. the time for which an insurance contract is to last, esp. if less than a year.

terms *pl.* (*a*) rules or conditions: *The terms of a contract/agreement. Terms of service*, the rights and duties agreed by both parties in a contract of service. *Terms of supply/payment*, the conditions regarding prices, discounts and payment under which goods are supplied. *The terms of an offer. See* trade terms *below. To come to terms*, to reach agreement about prices, etc. *To dictate terms, see* dictate. (*b*) personal relations: *The management is on good/bad terms with the staff/trade union.*

payment terms *see under* payment.

settlement terms a scale of discounts allowed by a supplier which a customer may ˙deduct from the value of an invoice if it is settled within certain periods after its date, e.g. *30 days 5%, 60 days 2½%, 60–90 days net.*

trade terms a scale of discounts allowed by a wholesale supplier to retailers in a particular trade. *Please supply at best trade terms*, customary words used by a retailer when ordering goods from a wholesaler, meaning 'please supply at lowest prices and highest discounts'. *Syn.* terms to the trade.

term days *see* quarter-day.

terminable annuity *see* annuity insurance *under* insurance, classes and kinds of.

terminal TRANSPT. (1) a station at the end of a railway or bus route. *Syn.* terminus. (2) the office of an airline, usu. in the centre of a town, where passengers may board a coach which takes them to the airport, and where arriving passengers are brought by coach. (3) a building, called an *ocean terminal*, in a port where large passenger liners call to load and unload.

terminal bonus *see under* bonus (3).

terminal market *see under* market.

terminate *v.* to end; to put an end to; to come to an end: *To terminate somebody's employment/ services. The lease has terminated.*

termination *n.* an end, an ending: *The termination of an offer.*

terminus TRANSPT. a railway or bus station at the end of a line or route. *Pl.* termini.

term loan *see under* loan.

term of acceptance *see under* acceptance (4).

term policy *see under* insurance policy.

term sight bill *see* time bill *under* bill of exchange.

terms of trade ECON. THEORY in international trade, the relation between the prices of a country's imports and exports. It is usu. expressed as an index of terms of trade, calculated by using index numbers of the prices of a chosen group of imports and another group of exports, as follows:

$$\frac{\text{index of terms}}{\text{of trade}} = \frac{\text{index of export prices}}{\text{index of import prices.}}$$

If the index of terms of trade is greater than unity (i.e. one) it is favourable because imports have become cheaper relatively to exports. If the index is less than unity, the opposite is true, i.e. it is unfavourable.

terms, preferential *see* preferential.

terms to the trade *see* trade terms *under* term.

Terr. terrace.

terrace (1) AGR. a strip or area of formerly sloping ground that has been made level, esp. for growing rice and other crops under irrigation. (2) any level area in front of a house or hotel built on a slope. (3) a row of houses usu. joined to each other along a street.

territorial waters LAW & SHIPG. that part of the sea within three miles of the shore (in some countries up to 15 miles) over which a country has full jurisdiction under international law.

tertiary industry *see under* industry.

tertiary production *see under* production.

testament *see* will.

testamentary trust *see under* trust.

testate LAW (of a dead person) having left a will.

testate succession LAW succeeding to, becoming the owner of, property under the provisions of the will of a person who has died.

testator LAW the person who makes a will. *Fem.* testatrix.

testatrix *see* testator.

test case LAW a lawsuit brought in the courts to obtain a legal decision that will apply equally to other, similar, cases, thus making further legal actions unnecessary.

testimonial (1) MAN. a written declaration about a person's character and ability, by a person qualified to judge his fitness to perform certain work or to hold a position of responsibility. Cf. character (1); reference (2). *Syn.* recommendation. (2) a letter praising the qualities of a product, such as a medicine: *An unsolicited testimonial*, one written by a person without being asked.

testimony LAW spoken evidence given in court by a witness under oath or affirmation.

testing the market *see* market research.

Tex. Texas, U.S.A.

textiles (1) IND. & COM. cloth of all kinds. (2) STK. EXCH. the stock or shares of companies manufacturing or selling textiles.

TF SHIPG. on a load-line, a mark showing the level to which a ship may safely be loaded in tropical fresh water.

TG Togo's international vehicle-registration letters.

Thailand a constitutional monarchy (kingdom) in south-east Asia, pop. 40 million approx. (1975); capital, Bangkok, pop. 1 million approx.; language, Thai; currency unit, the baht, divided into 100 satang. Member, A.S.E.A.N.; Colombo Plan.

theft LAW the act of stealing. In Britain, a person is guilty of theft if he dishonestly takes possession of, and treats as his own, property belonging to another person with the intention of permanently preventing him from using it. *See* pilferage. *Syn.* larceny.

theft insurance *see under* insurance, classes and kinds of.

theory *n.* (1) an idea, based on reasoning, that attempts to explain certain facts: *The Keynesian theory of the trade cycle*, J.M. Keynes's explanation of the trade cycle. (2) the basic truths and methods of a science or of any human activity, as opposed to its practice: *Economic theory analyses the forces of supply and demand, while applied economics deals with the practical problems of markets in actual life.*

theoretical *adj.* of or relating to theory, not practice.

therm IND. a unit of heat; in Britain, used as a basis of charging for the supply of gas for heating, cooking, etc. 1 therm = 100,000 British thermal units (B.T.U.s).

thin market see narrow market *under* narrow.

third market see *under* market.

Third of Exchange BKG. & COM. the third part of a set of bills. *See* bill (of exchange) in a set.

third party INSCE. in insurance, a party who is not one of the parties who make a contract but who is intended to benefit under the contract if he suffers loss or injury as the result of some negligent act of the insured. The first and second parties to an insurance contract are the insurer and the insured; a third party is a person to whom a legal liability is owed. *Abbr.* T.P.

Thirty-Share Index see Financial Times Industrial Ordinary Share Index.

three-column accounts ACCTS. accounts in the style used by most accounting machinery; each account has three columns, headed debits, credits and balance. Cf. two-sided accounts.

threshold (1) a doorway or entrance. (2) a point at which one enters a system or class, e.g. of taxpayers: *A tax threshold*, the level of income at which a person's liability to tax begins.

threshold insurance policy see child's deferred policy *under* insurance policy.

threshold price see *under* price.

thrift *n.* (1) the personal quality of being careful to avoid waste and to spend money wisely. (2) a habitual desire to save goods or money for the future. *Opp.* wastefulness. *Syn.* economy. *Adj.* thrifty.

thrive COM. to be successful; to grow in profitability or wealth: *The business is thriving*, is in a very profitable state. *Syn.* prosper.

thro' through.

through bill of lading see *under* bill of lading.

throughput (1) IND. the amount of raw material that a factory can process in a stated time: *Our copper refinery has a throughput of 1000 tons of ore a day*. (2) COMP. the amount of data that a computer can process in a stated time.

tick (1) a mark, thus √, used when checking lists, etc. to show correctness or action completed. *Syn.* (U.S.A.) check. (2) COM. *(colloq.)* credit: *They bought their opening stock on tick*, on credit, to be paid for later. *You may buy/ have goods on tick until the end of the month*, you may take them now and pay at the end of the month. *Syn.* on the nod.

ticket (1) a printed slip of paper or card, usu. given in exchange for money, showing that the holder has the right to a service of some kind: *A bus/coach/rail/steamer/air ticket. Tickets for the theatre/cinema/circus. An admission ticket. A complimentary ticket*, one given free of charge. (2) COM. a label or notice, such as a price-ticket. (3) STK. EXCH. *see* name-ticket; Name Day. (4) *(colloq.)* a certificate or qualification: *He has a draughtsman's ticket*, he is a

qualified draughtsman. *A master's ticket*, the qualification necessary to anyone who takes command of a merchant ship, i.e. a master's certificate.

circular ticket a ticket that allows a traveller, esp. a tourist, to visit a number of places on a roughly circular route, starting and finishing at the same place. Cf. return ticket; round-trip ticket.

excursion ticket a ticket that allows a traveller to make a short pleasure trip at reduced cost. *See* excursion.

platform ticket a ticket bought by a member of the public who is not a traveller but wishes only to go on to the platform in a railway station.

return ticket a ticket that allows a traveller to travel from one place to another and, within a certain time, to return to his starting place. *Syn.* (U.S.A.) round-trip ticket. Cf. single ticket.

round-trip ticket see round, *adj.* (1); return ticket *above*.

season ticket a railway ticket that allows a traveller to make a stated journey as often as he wishes during a certain period, such as a week, a month, a quarter, a half-year, or a year; the rate is reduced according to the length of the period.

single ticket a ticket that allows a traveller to travel once only from one place to another. Cf. return ticket.

time ticket see time recorder.

ticket agency TRANSPT. & TOUR. the office or shop of an agent who sells theatre and travel tickets in return for a commission on the value of his sales and, in some cases, a small fee for making reservations.

ticket collector TRANSPT. a railway official who examines travellers' tickets before a train leaves, and collects their tickets when they complete their journey.

Ticket Day see Name Day.

ticket office see booking office.

ticket tout see *under* tout.

ticket-writer COM. a skilled writer of showcards, notices, price tags etc. for use esp. in shops.

tidal basin see *under* basin (1).

tied house (1) an inn or public house which is tied, i.e. bound by a formal agreement, to buy all its supplies from a particular supplier, who is usu. also the owner of the building. (2) a house or cottage, in which the owner of a farm allows an employee and his family to live only so long as the worker continues to be employed on the farm.

tied shop a shop or other business such as a petrol filling-station of which the owner is tied, i.e. bound by formal agreement, to sell only the products of a particular supplier, who is often also the owner of the land and buildings occupied by the business.

tight money *see* dear money.

tikchung the fractional currency unit of Bhutan. 2 tikchung = 1 ngultrum or 100 Indian paise.

till *n.* COM. (1) a box or drawer with divisions, in which a shopkeeper or cashier keeps money, esp. notes, coins and cheques. (2) a cash register. *To run away with the till*, to steal one's employer's money. *Caught with his hand/ fingers in the till*, caught in the act of stealing. *He could not keep his hand/fingers out of the till*, he was continually stealing small sums from his employer. *To ring (up) the till*, to make money, esp. by selling things in a shop. *Till money*, money taken in the course of a day's trading.

v. AGR. to cultivate land, esp. to prepare the soil before sowing seeds.

tillage AGR. (1) the act or practice of tilling the soil. (2) land that is tilled, as opposed to pasturage.

timber AGR. & IND. (1) land used for growing trees: *Land under timber*, planted with trees. (2) any growing trees that are intended for use as building material or other manufactures. *To fell timber*, to cut down trees. (3) wood prepared for building and other manufactures, sawn into beams and boards. *Syn.* (U.S.A. and Canada) lumber. (4) a straight or curved beam of wood, esp. if part of a building or a ship.

timber yard *see under* yard.

time (1) the relation between events that happen before or after each other; the quantity measured by a clock: *Past/present/future time*. (2) a length of time; a period during which something lasts. (3) a moment or point in time: *What time is it? Now is the time to sell. The time by the clock/the sun.* (4) frequency of happening: *Interest is paid four times a year. Trains leave every ten minutes or six times an hour.* (5) a relationship in numbers: *Profits amount to four times the dividend.* **Daylight Saving Time** time that, in some countries, is the result of putting all clocks one hour ahead of (i.e. later than) Standard Time, esp. during the summer, to add one more hour of daylight to the normal working day. *Syn.* Summer Time. *Abbr.* D.S.T.

down time *see* downtime *under* down.

local time *see under* local.

lost time *see* downtime *under* down.

Standard Time *see under* Standard.

Summer Time *see* Daylight Saving Time *above*. *Abbr.* S.T.

time and a quarter/half *see* overtime.

time (and motion) study IND. the practice of watching and recording the movements made by a worker in doing his work, esp. in a factory, to see how his efficiency can be improved, such as by giving him better tools, more comfortable conditions, and special training. Cf. ergonomics.

time bargain *see under* bargain (4).

time-barred *see* limitation.

time bill *see under* bill of exchange.

time charter *see under* charter, *n.* (3).

time deposit *see under* deposit (4).

time draft *see* time bill *under* bill of exchange.

time-keeping bonus *see under* bonus.

time-lag ECON. THEORY the delay that takes place before the effect of some action is seen, e.g. between the introduction of a monetary control, such as a change in the minimum lending rate or bank rate, and the desired effect, in this case, a change in the amount of money in circulation; or the time needed for supply to increase to meet a rise in demand.

time loan *see under* loan.

time-of-day tariff *see* off-peak tariff *under* tariff.

time policy *see under* insurance policy.

time preference ECON. THEORY a tendency of people to prefer not to save but to enjoy their money by spending it on consumption goods when interest rates are low, and to be more willing to save, i.e. to lend it, when interest rates are high. This idea is the basis of Böhm-Bawerk's Time-Preference Theory of Interest.

time recorder IND. a recording clock used in factories to record on a card, called a *time ticket*, the time of a worker's arrival and the time he leaves. *See* clock, *v.*

time-saving bonus *see under* bonus.

time-sharing COMP. an arrangement by which a number of users in different places may use the same computer by means of telephone or telex lines.

time sheet MAN. a printed form on which the hours worked by an employee are recorded for use in calculating his weekly wage.

time ticket *see* time recorder.

time wage(s) *see* time-work.

time-work IND. in the payment of wages, the system of paying a worker according to the number of hours he works, as opposed to piecework. *Syn.* time wage(s).

time-zone one of the 24 zones into which, by international agreement, the earth is divided. Each zone is of 15° of longitude or one hour of time. The time in each zone is the Standard Time kept on sea and land in that zone and is always a convenient number of hours or half-hours ahead of, or behind, Greenwich Mean Time. *See* Daylight Saving Time *under* time.

tin (*colloq.*) money.

tip (1) a gift of a small sum of money as a reward for personal service. (2) information given privately. (3) personal advice or warning.

title LAW (1) a legal right to ownership of a thing of value, esp. land and buildings and merchandise. (2) a formal document proving ownership, such as the title-deeds of a house or the bill of lading of a consignment of merchandise.

absolute title see under absolute.

abstract of title see under abstract.

defective title a title (to ownership of land) which is not registered with the Land Registry and does not entirely satisfy the condition of being a good title, i.e. that it must prove that for the past 30 years each owner has had a good legal right to ownership. There is, therefore, a risk that another person can claim to be the owner.

document of title see under document.

marketable title a title to land which will satisfy a buyer that the seller is the only legal owner and so has legal power to sell it. Cf. defective title above. See title-deeds under deed.

paper title a document that proves the holder's legal right to the ownership of land or to money or securities.

proof of title see under title.

registered title the right of ownership of a property that has been registered at the Land Registry, which means that the right is guaranteed by the State.

root of title one of the documents making up the title-deeds, by which the seller begins his abstract of title by proving ownership from a date at least 30 years ago to the present day. This document is not required for sales of properties with titles registered at a Land Registry.

squatter's title in Britain, a title to land that has come into existence by the mere fact that a person, called a squatter, has entered upon, and for 12 years has occupied (squatted on), the land without paying rent and without the original owner's permission.

title absolute see absolute title.

title-deeds see under deed.

title policy see defective-title policy under insurance policy.

T.L., t.l., T/L total loss.

T.M. ton mile.

T.M.O. telegraph(ic) money order.

TN Tunisia's international vehicle-registration letters.

T.O. table of organization.

To ACCTS. an abbr. of Dr to or Debtor to, meaning a debit entry in book-keeping: To goods £5, goods to a value of £5 have been invoiced and this amount is now debited to the customer's ledger account. Cf. By, used to show credit entries.

tobaccos STK. EXCH. stocks and shares of companies growing and selling tobacco.

tod an English measure of weight, usu. of wool, equal to 2 stones or 28 lb (12.70 kg).

toea see kina.

Togo a republic in West Africa, pop. 2 million approx. (1975); capital, Lomé, pop. 100,000 approx.; languages, French, Dagomba, Ewe and Mina; currency unit, the C.F.A. franc (CFA Fr.), divided into 100 centimes. Member, O.A.U.; O.C.A.M.M.; Associate, E.E.C.

token (1) a sign or mark, see e.g. tax token below. (2) a receipt for a stated sum of money, made in the form of an attractive card intended to be given as a gift. The card is exchanged in a shop by the person to whom it has been given for goods up to the stated value. See gift token; book token below. (3) a piece of metal or plastic, similar to a coin, given free for use in exchange e.g. for a meal in a canteen, or sold for money for use in a slot machine.

book token a gift token that can be used only in exchange for books in a bookshop.

gift token see under gift.

tax token in Britain, a receipt for tax paid for a licence giving the right to use a motor vehicle on the road. The receipt is in the form of a printed label which must be stuck in the front window of the vehicle as a sign to the authorities that the tax has been paid. Syn. tax disc.

token coin see token money; also token coinage under coinage.

token money FIN. coins, the legal value of which, as units of currency, is greater than the value of the metal in them. In Britain they are made of bronze (½p, 1p and 2p) and cupro-nickel (5p, 10p and 50p). Syn. token coin. See token coinage under coinage.

token payment COM. & FIN. a payment of a small part of an amount owed, to show that the debtor acknowledges the debt and binds himself to pay it. See earnest.

token strike see under strike.

to let relating to buildings, offered for letting.

toll (1) TRANSPT. & FIN. a payment demanded, usu. by a government authority, for some right, such as to pass along a road or canal, across a bridge, or through a tunnel; or to use a ferry. (2) SHIPG. a charge made by a dock company for providing transport to move goods in the dock area.

toll bridge see under bridge.

Tolpuddle Martyrs ECON. HIST. six low-paid farm workers from the village of Tolpuddle in Dorset who in 1834 were sentenced to seven years punishment in Australia for combining to form a trade union. They were greatly admired by many for their courage, and after much popular outcry they were pardoned and brought back to England after serving four years of their sentence. Syn. Dorchester Labourers.

ton (1) a unit of measurement of weight of varying values, see below esp. long ton; short ton; metric ton. (2) a unit of measurement of volume of varying values, see below esp. measurement ton; vessel ton. (3) (colloq.) a sum of one hundred pounds (£100). (4) (colloq.) a speed of 100 miles per hour.

American ton see short ton below.

avoirdupois ton *see* long ton *below.*

British ton *see* long ton *below.*

cargo ton *see* freight ton *below.*

displacement ton *see* displacement tonnage *under* tonnage.

English ton *see* long ton *below.*

freight ton a basic unit for charging freight on cargo either by weight or by measurement. When the cargo is heavy but takes little space, such as steel bars, the unit used is the ton of weight, either the imperial ton of 2240 lb (1016 kg), or the metric ton *or* tonne (1000 kg) (2205 lb). If the cargo is light but takes up much space, such as wood pulp, the unit used is the *shipping* or *measurement ton* based on the volume of water displaced by a ton weight, 40 cu. ft (1.132 cu. m (m^3)).

gross ton *see* long ton *below.*

imperial ton *see* long ton *below.*

long ton the avoirdupois ton of 2240 lb (1016.05 kg) in common use in Britain. *Syn.* imperial ton; U.K. ton; British ton; English ton; weight ton; gross ton.

measurement ton usu. 40 cu. ft. *See* freight ton *above.*

metric ton *or* **tonne** 1000 kg (2204.62 lb avoirdupois).

net ton *see* short ton *below.*

register ton *see* vessel ton *below.*

shipping ton *see* freight ton *above.*

short ton 2000 lb avoirdupois (907.18 kg), in common use in U.S.A. *Syn.* U.S. ton; net ton; American ton. *Abbr.* s.t.

U.K. ton *see* long ton *above.*

U.S. ton *see* short ton *above.*

vessel ton 100 cu. ft (2.83 cu. m), used for calculating the gross tonnage of a ship on which pilotage, dry-dock and other dues are based. *Syn.* volumetric ton; register ton.

volumetric ton *see* vessel ton *above.*

weight ton *see* long ton *above.*

Tonga an independent island kingdom in the south-west Pacific Ocean, pop. 100,000 approx. (1975); capital, Nuku'alofa, pop. 16,000 approx.; languages, Polynesian and English; currency unit, the palanga or Tongan dollar, divided into 100 cents. Member, (British) Commonwealth. Also called the Friendly Islands.

ton mile TRANSPT. a unit of measurement of goods transported, one ton of goods moved one mile. *Abbr.* T.M. The metric equivalent is the *tonne kilometre.*

tonnage SHIPG. (1) the total weight of all the ships belonging (*a*) to a particular country, or (*b*) to a given class of ship, e.g. tanker tonnage. *Also* tunnage. (2) the carrying-capacity or volume of a ship, expressed in tons, but in varying ways. *See below.*

cargo tonnage a method of expressing the cubic capacity of a ship *either* as a weight ton (2240 lb in Britain, 2000 lb in U.S.A.) *or* as a measurement ton, usu. 40 cu. ft.

deadweight tonnage the number of tons (of 2240 lb) of cargo, stores and fuel that a ship can carry when floating at load-line level. *Syn.* deadweight carrying-capacity. Cf. lightweight tonnage. *Abbr.* d.w.t.

displacement tonnage the weight in tons of water which a ship displaces (pushes aside) when floating, thus being the actual weight of the ship and everything in her. It is used as a measure of size, esp. of warships. One displacement ton is the weight of 35 cu. ft (0.99109 m^3) of water.

gross register tonnage a measure in tons of the capacity (volume of space) of a ship below the upper deck, calculated in cubic feet and divided by 100. Cf. net register tonnage. *Syn.* register tonnage; gross tonnage. *Abbr.* g.r.t.; gro.t.; G.R.T.

lightweight tonnage the weight of the hull, machinery and equipment of a ship, without any cargo, fuel or stores. Cf. deadweight tonnage.

net register tonnage the gross register tonnage after allowing for space used up by machinery, fuel, stores and living accommodation for crew and passengers. The gross and net register tonnages are recorded on the ship's certificate of registration. Most charges, such as port and harbour dues, light and buoyage dues, towage, etc. are based on net register tonnage. Cf. gross register tonnage. *Syn.* register tonnage; net tonnage. *Abbr.* n.r.t.; N.R.T.

register tonnage the tonnage of a ship as recorded in her certificate of registration which shows both her gross and her net register tonnages.

under-deck tonnage a measure of the capacity (volume of space) of a ship below the main deck, calculated in cubic feet and divided by 100. Cf. gross register tonnage.

tonnage deck *see under* deck.

tonnage dues SHIPG. charges based usu. on the net register tonnage of a ship, payable by a shipowner for the services provided when a ship enters or leaves a port or passes through a canal.

tonnage slip SHIPG. a note giving details of tonnage dues payable by a ship and forming one of the papers which have to be cleared by Customs before the ship can leave port.

tonne the metric ton, 1000 kg (2204.62 lb avoirdupois or 0.984 long ton).

tonneau the former name of the tonne.

tonne kilometre TRANSPT. a unit of measurement of goods transported: one tonne of goods moved one kilometre. Cf. ton mile.

tons burden *see* burden (3).

T.O.O. to order only.

tool *see* machine-tool.

top-hat pension MAN. an extra pension over and above a normal pension, provided for the high employees, esp. the chief managers and directors of a company. Usu. the employee gives up part of his salary; for example, he may give up £1000 a year salary to buy an extra pension on retirement of perh. £1500 a year. The amount of pension bought will depend on his age.

top-hat policy INSCE. & MAN. an endowment policy on the life of a highly-paid employee to provide him with an extra pension on retirement.

top management *see under* management.

tort LAW (1) a failure to perform a general duty which every citizen owes to his fellow citizens, such as to avoid causing them personal harm or damaging their property. (2) any civil wrong except one relating to a contract.

tortfeasor LAW a person who commits a tort, i.e. does a civil wrong or fails to perform a civil duty. When two or more persons are concerned in a tort, they are called *joint tort-feasors*.

toss-up (1) a way of deciding a question by chance, by throwing a coin into the air to see which side is uppermost when it has fallen. (2) an even chance, one way or the other; a doubtful venture, because of the uncertain result.

tot. total.

tot ACCTS. (*colloq.*) to total, esp. a column of figures; to add (figures) up or together: *You must tot up your expenses at the end of each day. Syn.* to cast.

total account *see* control account.

total cost *see under* cost.

total distribution *see* final dividend *under* dividend (5).

totalizator an apparatus on a race-course for recording in detail the amount of money placed as bets on a horse or dog race, and for calculating, after the race has been run, the amount of money to be paid to those persons who have made winning bets. *Also* the tote.

total loss INSCE. a loss in which the goods or articles insured are completely destroyed or are so badly damaged as to be beyond repair. *See* average (4). *Abbr.* T.L.; t.l.; T/L.
actual total loss *see under* actual.
constructive total loss *see under* constructive.

tote *see* totalizator.

totting COM. sorting through household waste and selling anything that can be saved.

touch *v.* (*colloq.*) to borrow or beg money from somebody by persuasion: *He touched me for a fiver*, he persuaded me to give him, or to lend him, £5. *Syn.* to cadge.
n. (1) a person from whom it is easy to borrow or beg money: *A soft touch.* (2) the money thus obtained.

touch at SHIPG. to stop at; to call at: *The ship will touch at Malta on its way from Marseilles to Port Said.*

touched bill of health *see under* bill of health.

tourism TOUR. the occupation or industry of organizing tours and holidays and providing services for tourists, esp. of making arrangements for their transport, accommodation, meals and safety.

tourist TOUR. a person who tours, makes tours, travels, esp. if he does so for pleasure, and in a country other than his own.

tourist class TOUR. second class, usu. in a plane or ship.

tourist visa *see under* visa.

tout *n.* COM. (1) a person who goes about asking strangers to buy, usu. something that is scarce and that commands a high price. (2) a travelling salesman who uses excessive persuasion or annoying methods to sell his goods.
a ticket tout a tout who buys tickets early for a show in a theatre, or for a sporting event, and sells them at a big profit to late buyers.
v. (1) to go about selling, usu. using excessive or dishonest persuasion. (2) to act as a tout.

tow SHIPG. & TRANSPT. to pull a vehicle along by means of a rope or chain (a *tow-rope* or *tow-line*). *To be on/in/under tow*, in the process of being towed.

towage SHIPG. (1) the act of towing or of being towed. (2) the charge paid by a shipowner for his ship to be towed.

tower SHIPG. a person or organization specializing in the work of towing ships.

township (1) a small town. (2) in North America and Australia, an area of land containing a number of towns and villages under the same local authority. (3) in South Africa, a town or part of a town reserved for black Africans to live in.

t. & p. theft and pilferage.

T.P. third party.

t.q., t/q, T.Q. tel quel (rate of exchange).

TR Turkey's international vehicle-registration letters.

T.R. tons registered.

tractor AGR. & TRANSPT. a motor vehicle specially made for use in pulling another vehicle, such as a trailer, or farm machinery, such as a plough.

trade *n.* (1) the business of buying and selling goods for money, or of exchanging goods for goods: *Britain is increasing her trade with the Arab world. The balance of trade. Trade is booming*, is very good. *To engage in trade. Barter is trade without using money. In the course of trade. Syn.* commerce. (2) the persons and organizations carrying on business in the same kind of commodity: *The book/clothing/grocery trade. The slave trade.* (3) IND. an occupation or employment needing a high degree of skill, esp. with the hands; a craft: *The trade of boilermaker/plumber/carpenter.*

barter trade *see* barter.

bilateral trade trade between two or more countries which have agreed that each country shall balance the import and export trade that it does with each other country. *See* bilateral trade agreements. Cf. multilateral trade.

domestic trade trade between a buyer and a seller who are both in the same country, as opposed to foreign trade. *Syn.* home trade.

entrepôt trade trade that is based on re-exporting. *See* entrepôt. *Syn.* transit trade.

export trade selling goods to customers in foreign countries.

external trade (*a*) trade with foreign countries. *Syn.* foreign trade; international trade. (*b*) *see* external trade *under* external.

fair trade *see under* fair.

foreign trade *see* international trade.

free trade *see under* free.

home trade (*a*) COM. trade within one country, as opposed to foreign trade. (*b*) SHIPG. voyages made by ships to ports within a certain area round the British Isles, including ports in the United Kingdom and Ireland, and all continental ports between Brest in France, and the River Elbe in Germany. *A home-trade ship*.

import trade buying goods from suppliers in foreign countries.

international trade *see under* international.

multilateral trade trade between countries which have agreed that there shall be perfect freedom of trade between them, with no quotas, customs duties, exchange controls or other hindrances. Cf. bilateral trade.

overseas trade *see* international trade.

rag trade *see under* rag.

retail trade *see under* retail.

slave trade *see under* slave.

tramp trade SHIPG. tramp ships collectively, as opposed to liners.

transit trade entrepôt trade.

triangular trade a situation where three countries keep a balance of trade between themselves.

trilateral trade *see* triangular trade *above*.

wholesale trade trade between one trader and another trader, not between a trader and a consumer.

v. to buy and sell, or exchange goods for goods. *See also* trading.

trade acceptance *see* trade bill *under* bill of exchange.

trade agreement *see* commercial treaty; bilateral trade agreement; multilateral trade agreement.

trade association MAN. an association of producers and dealers in the same trade, formed for the purpose of protecting and developing the interests of its members, and to represent them, e.g. in negotiations with the government, or with trade unions, or with other trade associations. *See* employers' organizations. *Syn.* trading association; trade organization.

trade balance *see* balance of trade.

trade barrier *see* barrier to trade *under* barrier; *also* trade restrictions.

trade bill *see under* bill of exchange.

trade, chamber of *see* chamber of trade.

trade commissioner COM. an important official in charge of a department of a British High Commission (*see* High Commissioner), whose main duty is to help British businessmen to trade with the country in which he is stationed. He reports on trading conditions, currency and tax laws, import and export licensing, competition, opportunities for tendering for contracts, the chances of setting up new industries, and on all matters affecting trade with Britain.

trade counter COM. a department of a wholesaler's office or warehouse where retail traders may buy goods over the counter.

trade cycle *see under* cycle.

trade debtor *see under* debtor.

trade deficit *see* trade gap; balance of payments deficit *under* deficit.

Trade, Department of in Britain, an important government department with a minister at its head, responsible for administering Britain's commerce and overseas trade.

trade description COM. & LAW a description of merchandise for the purpose of attracting buyers. In Britain it is an offence to make a false or misleading description of goods offered for sale.

trade directory *see* classified directory *under* directory.

trade discount *see under* discount.

trade discrimination *see* discrimination.

trade dispute *see* dispute.

traded option (market) *see* traded option *under* option.

trade fair *see* fair, *n.* (2).

trade fluctuations *see* fluctuations; trade cycle *under* cycle.

trade gap ECON. & FIN. an excess of visible imports over visible exports of a country. *Syn.* trade deficit.

trade in *v.* COM. to give something in part-exchange. *See* exchange, *n.* (1).

trade-in COM. *n.* goods given in part-exchange.
trade-in value *adj.* the amount which a supplier will allow a buyer for an article given in part-exchange.

trade, international *see under* international.

trade investment ACCTS. & FIN. words used in accounting, esp. in a balance sheet, for an investment by one company in the shares of another company in the same trade, perh. even in the same group, for the purpose of increasing or helping the business of the investing company.

trade-mark LAW & COM. a special mark that is

placed on a particular brand of article or commodity to distinguish it from similar goods sold by other producers. In Britain, new trademarks must first be approved by a government department and, if approved, they are registered at the Patent Office. A *registered trademark* becomes the property of the person or organization in whose name it is registered, and no other producer may use it without the owner's permission. If the trade-mark consists only of a name, it is called a *registered tradename. Also* trademark; tradename.

trade mission COM. a group of officials and businessmen sent by a government to a foreign country to discuss an agreement to increase trade between the two countries.

trade-name *see* trade-mark.

trade negotiations *see under* negotiations.

trade organization *see* trade association.

trade paper *see* trade bill *under* bill of exchange. Cf. bank paper.

trade price *see under* price.

trade protection society *see* debt collection agency.

trader (1) COM. a person whose occupation is to buy and sell goods with his own money and for his own profit; a merchant. (2) SHIPG. a merchant ship, esp. a tramp ship.

free-trader *see under* free.

sole trader a trader who owns his own business, manages its affairs, provides the capital, and bears all the risk.

street-trader *see* hawker.

trade reference *see* reference (2).

trade representative COM. a commercial traveller.

trade restrictions COM. & FIN. (1) various forms of bars to freedom, esp. of international trade, such as: the prohibition (forbidding) of imports and exports of certain goods; the placing of quotas limiting amounts that may be imported or exported; tariffs (customs duties) and exchange controls limiting the movement of money. (2) government action limiting production, consumption, credit, prices, wages, investment, etc.

trade route COM. & TRANSPT. a route on land or sea along which much merchandise is regularly transported: *The Suez Canal is on the trade route to India.*

trade sale COM. a sale made to somebody in the same trade as the seller, not to a consumer.

tradesman (1) COM. a shopkeeper, esp. one who delivers goods to private houses. (2) IND. a craftsman; a man who has a special skill with his hands, esp. in the army, navy or air force.

tradespeople COM. shopkeepers collectively, and their families. *Syn.* tradesfolk.

Trades Union Congress (T.U.C.) IND. REL. the central policy-making organization to which most British trade unions are affiliated. It acts as the representative of the workers in negotiating with the government and with the Confederation of British Industry (C.B.I.). The T.U.C. also sometimes settles disputes between its member unions.

trade terms COM. (1) the expressions and abbreviations used in foreign-trade contracts, such as f.o.b. *See* Incoterms. (2) the discount and payment terms normally allowed by a wholesaler to retailers. *See under* term.

trade union IND. REL. an association of employees who have permanently combined to improve their wages, hours and conditions of employment by means of collective bargaining. It also performs other activities in the interest of its members. *Syn.* (U.S.A.) labor union. *Abbr.* T.U.

company union *see under* company.

craft union a trade union, usu. a small union of skilled workers. Cf. industrial union.

general union *see* industrial union *below*.

house union *see* company union.

industrial union a trade union whose members all work in the same industry. Such unions tend to be large and to have a high proportion of unskilled workers. Cf. craft union. *Syn.* general union.

labor union (U.S.A.) a trade union.

trade union contributions IND. REL. the money that a member of a trade union regularly pays to his union; by agreement, the sum is often deducted by the employer from wages or salary and is paid to the union after each pay day. *Syn.* union dues.

trade unionism IND. REL. (1) the system of organizing employees into trade unions. (2) a movement that supports this system.

trade unionist IND. REL. a member of a trade union.

trade winds SHIPG. winds that blow steadily in the same direction for most of the year over the oceans, in a belt about 30° north and south of the equator; they blow from the north-east in the northern hemisphere and from the south-east in the southern hemisphere.

trading STK. EXCH. (1) the business of buying and selling securities. (2) the amount of business done in a certain period: *Trading was active/ dull throughout the day.*

insider trading *see under* insider.

instalment trading *see under* instalment.

trading account ACCTS. an accounting summary prepared for the purpose of calculating the gross profit of a business, i.e. the amount by which the value of sales is greater than the cost of goods sold. The balance in the trading account is carried to the profit and loss account. Sometimes it happens that the cost of the goods sold is greater than the value of sales, resulting in a gross loss.

trading association *see* trade association.

trading capital *see under* capital.

trading currency *see under* currency.

trading estate *see* estate (3).

Trading, Office of Fair *see under* Office.

trading partnership *see under* partnership.

trading stamp *see under* stamp.

Trading Standards Department *see under* Office of Fair Trading.

trading station *see* factory (2).

trading stock *see* stock-in-trade.

traffic (1) the transport of passengers and goods by railway, road, water or air: *Railway goods traffic, passenger coach traffic.* (2) the movement of people, vehicles, shipping, planes, etc. in a place or between places: *Heavy lorry traffic on the motorway. Increasing air traffic at London airport. Traffic in the Suez Canal/Straits of Dover. A traffic accident.* (3) COM. the buying and selling of goods, esp. trade in forbidden commodities: *Traffic in drugs/arms/slaves.*
v. to trade, esp. to buy, sell and transport articles or commodities forbidden by law: *To traffic in arms/drugs. Past tense,* trafficked; *present participle,* trafficking.

traffic census *see under* census.

traffic lights TRANSPT. electric lights, coloured green, amber (yellow) and red, that automatically control traffic at crossroads and pedestrian crossings.

traffic warden TRANSPT. in Britain, an official who controls road traffic, esp. the parking of vehicles, in the streets of a town.

trailer (1) TRANSPT. a road vehicle intended to be drawn by another road vehicle. Cf. tractor. (2) (U.S.A.) a caravan. (3) ADVTG. a very short piece of film, shown to advertise the film it comes from.

trailer park (U.S.A.) *see* caravan site.

train *v.* (1) to teach somebody a skill, occupation or profession: *His job is to train apprentices/engineers/computer programmers. A trained nurse/mechanic.* (2) with as, to be taught, to learn, a skill, etc.: *I trained as a pilot/teacher.*
n. TRANSPT. (1) a connected string of railway wagons or carriages pulled by a locomotive. (2) a string of pack-animals or carts carrying goods: *A baggage/supply/mule/ox train.*
down train a train travelling in a direction away from the capital of the country. *Opp.* up train.
express train a fast passenger or goods train.
freight train a goods train.
goods train *see* goods (3).
mail train a very fast passenger train that regularly carries mail over long distances.
passenger train *see* passenger.
up train a train travelling in a direction towards the capital of the country. *Opp.* down train.

trainee MAN. a person, esp. an employee, who is being trained to do work that needs some special knowledge or skill. *An industrial/executive/graduate trainee. A trainee editor/book-keeper.*

train ferry *see under* ferry.

training the act or process of training or of being trained: *Management training.*

training board IND. & MAN. in Britain, a government organization set up in each important industry to supervise and administer the training of workers, including managers, in the industry. Each board has power to collect money, called a *training levy*, from the employers in the industry, and to spend it on training courses provided by the board itself or by certain specially-chosen firms. The boards consist of representatives of the employers and of trade unions, and include some educationists, and each board has its own staff of paid officials and clerks. *Abbr.* T.B.

training ship SHIPG. a special ship used for training boys to be seamen.

train mile TRANSPT. a unit of measurement of railway traffic: the movement of one train along one mile. The total of train miles run by a railway is a measure of its size, and the profit per train mile is a measure of its profitability or efficiency. *Also* train kilometre.

tram *see* tramcar *under* car.

tramcar *see under* car.

tramp (1) a homeless person, esp. one who prefers to wander alone from place to place, sometimes doing a little work but usu. very poor. *Syn.* vagrant; (U.S.A.) a prostitute. (2) SHIPG. a tramp ship, *see under* ship.

tramp trade *see under* trade.

tramway *see* tramcar *under* car.

tranche FIN. (*French,* slice) (1) a part of a sum of money, such as a loan or payment, e.g. the *gold tranche,* that part of a country's I.M.F. quota that had once to be paid in gold. (2) an instalment.

trans- a *prefix* meaning across, beyond, over: *The Trans-Siberian Railway,* the railway that crosses Siberia. *A transatlantic liner/flight/cable,* one that crosses the Atlantic Ocean. Similarly, *transpacific; transcontinental; trans-Europe.*

transact (1) to attend to; to settle: *Business to be transacted at a meeting.* (2) to negotiate; to reach agreement on: *To transact a sale/purchase/bargain/loan.* (3) to deal (in business) with; to do (business) with: *We transact business with many foreign governments.* (4) to manage, deal with, business matters: *Solicitors transact affairs/business for their clients.*

transaction (1) COM. the act or process of transacting business affairs: *Banks are open for the transaction of business from 09.30 hrs. to 15.30 hrs. from Mondays to Fridays.* (2) BKG. a single entry crediting or debiting a customer's account: *Bank charges are based partly on the number of transactions made in a month.* (3) ACCTS. a single business deal, esp. a sale or purchase, by the business. Every invoice received or issued represents a transaction that must be entered in the account books.

bear transaction STK. EXCH. a deal by a bear, i.e. a dealer who, expecting prices to fall, promises to deliver at a fixed price on a future date securities which he does not at present possess but which he hopes to buy at a lower price before that date. Cf. bull transaction *below.*

bogus transaction *see under* bogus.

bull transaction STK. EXCH. a deal by a bull, i.e. a dealer who, expecting prices to rise, promises to accept delivery at a fixed price on a future date, of securities which he hopes to sell at a profit before he has to pay for them. Cf. bear transaction *above.*

Transactions Equation *see* Fisher Equation.

transactions tax *see* sales tax (*b*) *under* tax.

transcontainer *see under* container.

transcribe *v.* (1) to make a written copy: *To transcribe a report.* (2) to write down what has been said by a speaker: *To transcribe a speech.*

transcript *n.* a copy; a written record of what has been spoken.

transcription *n.* the act of transcribing; a transcript.

transfer *n.* (1) LAW (*a*) the passing of a right of ownership from one person or organization to another, by an intentional act by a transferor as a sale or gift, or as a result of the operation of law, such as bankruptcy or intestacy. (*b*) a document recording or authorizing such a change of ownership. (2) STK. EXCH. *see* transfer of securities. (3) TRANSPT. a planned change from one passenger vehicle or route to another. *Transfer passengers*, passengers changing at an airport from one airline or route to another. Cf. transit passengers. *Transfer ticket*, a ticket issued on one bus or railway route which allows a passenger to change, at some point on his journey, to another route without further payment. (4) BKG. the movement of money from one person or group of persons to another, or from one place or country to another. (5) IND. a means of applying lettering or designs to a product by heating, wetting, rubbing or pressing on it a paper or plastic surface on which the design has been previously printed.

airmail transfer BKG. *see* mail transfer *below.*

bank transfer BKG. *see under* bank.

blank transfer STK. EXCH. *see under* blank.

cable transfer BKG. *see* telegraphic transfer.

certificate of transfer STK. EXCH. *see* transfer certificate.

certified transfer STK. EXCH. a transfer for which a company has issued a certificate of transfer.

deed of transfer STK. EXCH. *see under* deed.

instrument of transfer STK. EXCH. *see* deed of transfer.

mail transfer BKG. a bank transfer made by mail, esp. airmail, as opposed to a telegraphic or cable transfer. *Abbr.* M.T.

stock transfer STK. EXCH. in Britain, a form approved by law for making transfers of stocks and shares as simple as possible. The form need give only the name and address of the transferee and needs to be signed only by the transferor. Cf. deed of transfer.

telegraphic transfer BKG. *see under* telegraphic. *v.* to pass from one person, place, state or condition to another. *Smith transferred his shares to Jones. We are transferring our business from Cairo to Alexandria.*

transferable able to be transferred from one person to another, or from one place to another. *Not transferable*, printed on a railway ticket, means that it may be used only by the person to whom it is issued, and that that person must not transfer it for use by another person.

transferable bond *see under* bond, *n.*

transfer cases storage cases, made of paper or cardboard, into which old records or papers not often referred to are transferred from the current filing system. *Also* transfer files; transfer boxes.

transfer certificate STK. EXCH. a document issued by a company declaring that a transfer of ownership of some of its stock or shares has been registered in the company's books. Transfer certificates are issued only by those companies that do not issue fresh stock or share certificates when a transfer takes place. The transfer certificate must be kept by the new owner (the transferee) with the original certificate.

transfer deed *see* deed of transfer.

transfer duty TAXN. & STK. EXCH. in Britain, the duty that must be paid to the government on all transfers of securities except on gilt-edged stocks, new issues, and debentures. It is payable by the buyer of the securities, in addition to the contract stamp and the broker's commission, and must be paid to a government stamp office within 30 days of the date of the transfer. When paid, the stamp office impresses a stamp on the transfer document. *See* transfer stamp. *Syn.* stamp duty.

transfer earnings *see* opportunity cost *under* cost.

transferee (1) a person or organization to whom something, e.g. property or a right, is transferred. (2) a person who is transferred from one place or job to another.

transfer fee STK. EXCH. a small fee which a company, under its Articles of Association, may charge for registering a transfer of stock or shares. It is so small that most companies do not trouble to collect it.

transfer income *see under* income.

transfer of securities STK. EXCH. (1) the passing of the rights of ownership of stock and shares from one person or organization to another. (2) the legal and administrative formalities needed to make a transfer effective. In Britain, formerly, all transfers were deeds made under seal, but since 1963 a simpler method is usu. adopted, called the stock transfer form, which needs to be signed only by the transferor.

transferor LAW a person who transfers, i.e. gives, to another person some right or property. Cf. transferee.

transfer order BKG. & COM. an order signed by a bank to a warehouse-keeper to transfer goods held in the bank's name to a stated customer's name.

transfer payments see transfer income under income.

transfer receipt STK. EXCH. a receipt given by a company when a stock or share transfer is sent to it for registration. The receipt is later exchanged for a new share certificate which may take some time to prepare.

transfer register see under register.

transfer stamp TAXN. & STK. EXCH. in Britain, the impressed stamp applied by the government stamp office on the document relating to a transfer of securities, acknowledging payment of the stamp duty. See transfer duty.

tranship see trans-ship.

transhumance AGR. the seasonal moving of sheep, cattle, etc. between summer and winter feeding grounds.

transient TOUR. passing through; staying only for a short time: A transient visitor/guest.

transire SHIPG. a document signed by a customs officer allowing a coasting ship (one not visiting foreign ports) to load her cargo and to leave port. The document is handed by the master of the ship to the Customs at the port of arrival to prove that the cargo has come from a home port, not a foreign port.

transit (Latin, it passes across or through) a passing; a state of movement from one place to another: Goods in transit, goods in the course of being carried from one place to another. Sea/air transit, a journey by sea or air.

transit entry see under customs entry.

transitory income see under income.

transit shed a shed in which goods in transit are stored.

transit trade see entrepôt trade under trade; also entrepôt.

transitu see stoppage in transitu.

transit visa see under visa.

translation bureau a business that offers a service for translating documents from one language to another.

translator a person who translates, usu. written matter, but sometimes spoken, from one language into another. Cf. interpreter.

transmit v. (1) to send or pass something from one person, thing or place to another: To transmit a message/information/mail. Syn. to convey. (2) to send out by signals, to broadcast by radio, etc.

transmitter n. an apparatus for transmitting by radio.

transmission (a) the act of transmitting. (b) matter that is transmitted or broadcast.

transport n. TRANSPT. (1) the act of carrying persons or goods from one place to another: Transport is the life-blood of commerce. Transport by air/sea/rail/road. The best method/ means of transport. A system of transport. Surface transport, on the ground or on the sea, as opposed to air transport. (2) vehicles and other means generally, for carrying persons or things: Motor transport, road vehicles. Also (esp. U.S.A.) transportation. Pron. tránsport. (3) SHIPG. a ship for carrying soldiers and their equipment, vehicles, etc.: A troop transport. v. to carry persons or goods from one place to another. Pron. transpórt.

transportation see transport (2).

transport café a cheap restaurant on a main road where the customers are mostly drivers of goods vehicles travelling long distances.

transporter TRANSPT. a large vehicle used for transporting other vehicles: A car transporter.

trans-ship (1) SHIPG. to unload goods from one ship and load them at the same port into another. (2) TRANSPT. esp. in U.S.A., to unload goods from one vehicle and load them on to another. Also transship; tranship.

trans-shipment SHIPG. the act of unloading goods from one ship and loading them at the same port on to another vessel. Also transshipment; transhipment. Syn. re-shipment. Abbr. T/S.

trans-shipment note see bond note.

travel to move from place to place as a salesman to obtain orders: To travel in men's clothing/ sports goods/groceries.

travel agency COM. & TRANSPT. a business that sells tickets for journeys by land, sea or air, arranges package holidays, hotel accommodation, insurance, visas, etc. in return for a commission, booking-fees and other charges.

travel agent COM. the owner or manager of a travel agency.

traveler (U.S.A.) see traveller.

traveller a person who is travelling, or who frequently travels, from place to place. See commercial traveller. Also (U.S.A.) traveler.

traveller's cheque see under cheque.

traveller's letter of credit see under letter of credit.

traveller's policy see under insurance policy.

travelling expenses see under expenses.

travelling salesman see commercial traveller.

trawler SHIPG. a fishing vessel that uses a trawl, a

net in the shape of a long bag with an open mouth, that is pulled along the bottom of the sea. Cf. drifter.

Treas. Treasury.

treas. treasurer.

treasurer an officer of an association, club, society or company who is responsible for taking care of money. *Abbr.* treas.

honorary treasurer an unpaid treasurer. *Abbr.* Hon. Treas.

treasure trove LAW in Britain, money and objects made of precious metals found hidden in a private house or buried in the earth. Such objects belong by law to the crown and, when found, must be reported to a coroner. If they are of historical interest they are sent to the British Museum, which pays the finder some part of their value.

Treasury FIN. in Britain, the government department responsible for the finances of the country, the management of its monetary system, and the carrying out of the government's economic policy. The Prime Minister, as First Lord of the Treasury, is its nominal chief, but in practice its real head is the Chancellor of the Exchequer. *Abbr.* Treas.

Treasury bill FIN. in Britain, a bill similar in some ways to a commercial bill of exchange, issued by the Bank of England on the authority of the Treasury, promising to pay a stated person a fixed sum of money on a certain date, usu. three months from the day of issue. Treasury bills bear no interest and are therefore tendered for at a discount. They are bought by the discount market in units varying from £5000 to £100,000. *Syn.* finance bill.

Treasury bond *see under* bond, *n.*

Treasury directive *see* directive.

Treasury note *see* currency note.

Treasury stock FIN. & STK. EXCH. (1) long-dated stock issued by the British Government, such as Treasury 13¼%, 1997 stock. (2) in U.S.A. (*a*) stock of a corporation that has been bought back from the stockholders and is held for re-issue at some future time. (*b*) stock that, although authorized for issue, has not been issued.

Treasury warrant *see under* warrant.

treat *v.* (1) to entertain a person or persons at one's own expense: *He treated us to a meal. Let me treat you to a drink/an ice-cream.* (2) COM. to discuss how a bargain can be agreed: *We are treating with a possible buyer. Syn.* to bargain; to negotiate.
n. (*colloq.*) a special pleasure such as a good meal or entertainment.

invitation to treat *see* offer (2).

treaty (1) bargaining; an agreement reached by bargaining. (2) any formal agreement between two or more countries.

commercial treaty a formal agreement between

two or more countries relating to trade between them. *Syn.* treaty of commerce.

private treaty any contract not made by auction; a contract reached by personal bargaining between the parties. *For sale by private treaty*, of land, being offered for sale but not by auction.

treaty port *see under* port.

Tree. trustee.

trend *n.* a tendency; a general direction: *The trend of events is favourable to investment. Market trends. To buck the trend, see* buck. *Secular trend, see under* secular.
v. to move in a general direction; to show a tendency: *Fashions are trending towards brighter colours.*

trendy (*colloq.*) highly fashionable; in advance of the present fashion.

trespass LAW an unlawful act that causes harm to others. *Trespass to land* is unlawful interference with the legal possession and enjoyment of land, such as wrongfully entering upon it and remaining on it or depositing things on it without permission. *Trespass to the person* consists of acts of assault (personal violence) and wrongful imprisonment. *Trespass to goods* is wrongful removal of, or interference with, the property of another, such as conversion and detinue. Remedies for trespass are a court order for damages, or to return property illegally held, or to stop the trespass from continuing.

trespasser LAW a person who is guilty of trespass to land. Force may, in Britain, be used to a reasonable degree to prevent a trespasser from entering, or from remaining on, land.

trial balance ACCTS. a means of checking the correctness of a set of account books. All the debit balances are put in one column and all the credit balances in another. If the totals do not agree, a mistake has been made in adding, copying out, or posting. If the columns agree, the books can be considered free of this kind of mistake; but some mistakes are not uncovered by a trial balance. *See* compensating errors; reversal of entries; posting error *under* error.

trials *see* acceptance trials *under* acceptance (2).

triangular trade *see under* trade.

tribal of or relating to a tribe: *A tribal language/custom/area.*

tribunals LAW in Britain, groups of specially-chosen persons given power by Parliament to decide appeals from the public against decisions made by officials under delegated powers (*see* delegated legislation), esp. where the citizen cannot appeal to the courts. There are also a number of private tribunals controlling the activities of members of some professions such as the Law Society for solicitors, and the General Medical Council for doctors. *See also* administrative tribunals.

trilateral trade see triangular trade *under* trade.

trim SHIPG. & TRANSPT. to attend to the balance of a ship or plane by seeing that its load is properly distributed and safely stowed (packed) so that it cannot move about.

Trinidad and Tobago an independent island state in the eastern Caribbean Sea, pop. 1.1 million approx. (1975); capital, Port of Spain, pop. 100,000 approx.; languages, English, Hindi, Spanish and French; currency unit, the Trinidad and Tobago dollar (TT$), divided into 100 cents. Member, (British) Commonwealth; O.A.S.

Trinity House SHIPG. in Britain, an ancient organization that is responsible for aids to navigation around the coasts of the British Isles. Trinity House looks after matters relating to lighthouses, lightships, buoys, beacons, pilot services and lifeboats. Most of its income comes from the light-dues paid by ships using the harbours in British waters.

triplicate book a book usu. of blank forms, similar to a duplicate book but with the forms in sets of three. See duplicate book.

trlr. trawler.

trolley-bus TRANSPT. an electric public-service vehicle similar to a motor bus but receiving its power from overhead wires. Cf. trolley-car (U.S.A.).

trolley-car (U.S.A.) any electric streetcar, including a tramcar. Cf. trolley-bus.

tropic each of two parallels of latitude at 23° 28′ N. (the Tropic of Cancer) and at 23° 28′ S. (the Tropic of Capricorn) which form the limits of the hot belt of the earth called the tropics. In this belt, the sun shines from exactly overhead at midday on at least two days in the year. **tropical** adj. of or relating to the tropics.

trouble shooter COM. & IND. a person employed specially to discover and remedy the causes of trouble, such as inefficiency and delays, in production, distribution and accounting.

trough see trade cycle *under* cycle.

trove see treasure trove.

trover see conversion.

troy weight an ancient system of weights used (now rarely) in Britain and North America, etc. for precious metals. See table on page 479.

trs. transfer; transpose; trustees.

truck n. COM. (1) dealing, esp. in trade: *European merchants had truck with the Chinese in the thirteenth century.* (2) goods exchanged for other goods, not for money. Syn. barter goods. (3) AGR. the produce of a market garden, esp. fruit and vegetables grown for sale as food for human beings. (4) TRANSPT. any vehicle on wheels for carrying goods, such as a *railway truck* (an open goods wagon), and an *industrial truck* (a fork-lift truck). In U.S.A., a lorry. (5) LAW the payment of wages in goods. See truck system.

v. COM. (1) to have dealings with, esp. in trading. (2) to trade by exchanging commodities. Syn. to barter. (3) to pay one's employees in goods. See truck system. (4) TRANSPT. (U.S.A.) to carry by truck. See trucking.

truckage TRANSPT. (1) the carriage of goods by truck. (2) the charge made for such carriage.

truck farm see truck (3); market garden.

trucking (U.S.A.) (1) TRANSPT. the business of carrying goods by truck. Syn. road haulage. (2) AGR. market gardening.

truck system LAW & ECON. HIST. in Britain, the unfair practice of employers during the eighteenth and nineteenth centuries of paying their employees part of their wages in kind or in tokens which could be exchanged for goods only in a shop owned by the employer. This was usu. to the great disadvantage of the employee. The system was made illegal by a series of Truck Acts beginning in 1831, which commanded that the whole of an employee's wages must be paid in cash, or by cheque or money order, or into his bank account, without any deductions unless they were authorized by law or by agreement with the employee. It is illegal for an employer to control how the employee will spend any part of his earnings.

true discount BKG. & FIN. an amount representing interest for a fixed period, rather than a discount. It is the amount that would be earned at a given rate of interest on a certain sum invested now to bring it up to a known sum payable at the end of a stated period. For example, £100 will be needed to settle a debt due one year from now, and the current rate of interest is 5%. £1 invested at 5% will, in one year, become £1.05. £100 divided by £1.05 is £95.2381. This is the sum that, if invested now at 5% will become £100 a year from now (£95.2381 × 1.05 = £100). The true interest is the difference: 100 − 95.2381 = 4.7619%. Cf. banker's discount.

true investment see *under* investment.

true yield see *under* yield.

trunk adj. of or relating to a main way along which persons or things move: *A trunk road,* a main road for use by vehicles travelling long distances. *A trunk call,* a long-distance telephone call, using a *trunk line,* a telephone line between exchanges a long distance apart. **trunks** pl. (colloq.) that part of the telephone system that deals with trunk calls; a trunk telephone exchange: *Give me/put me through to/connect me to trunks.* See also subscriber trunk dialling. Syn. (U.S.A.) long distance.

trunker TRANSPT. a long-distance road vehicle used in trunking. Cf. shunter.

trunking TRANSPT. for the transport of goods, the running of long-distance road services connecting a number of distribution depots, each serving a local area with collection and delivery.

truss *see* hay and straw measure.

trust *n.* (1) faith in a person's honesty and ability: *He enjoys our trust*, we have faith in him, we trust him. *Mutual trust*, a relationship between persons who trust each other. (2) STK. EXCH. an investment trust company, *see under* company. (3) ECON. & STK. EXCH. in U.S.A., a monopolistic combination of business corporations carried out by transferring the shares to a trust in return for trust certificates. This system gave the trustees very great commercial and industrial power, and was made illegal under the Sherman Anti-Trust Act of 1890 and later laws. (4) a general, often disrespectful, name for any large business organization which is so big that it is in a position of partial or total monopoly. (5) LAW a formal responsibility, usu. expressed in a document called a *trust deed* or *trust instrument*, placed on one or more persons called trustees, to take charge of and to manage land, money or other property for the benefit of a person or object called the *beneficiary*, of whom there may be several. The person causing the trust to be formed is called the *donor* or *settlor* or, in the case of a will, the *testator*. *To create a trust*, to cause a trust to exist, to form it. *To hold money, etc. in/on trust*. *To accept a trust*, to agree to become a trustee. *Syn.* a use (an ancient meaning).

active trust *see under* active.

charitable trust *see under* charitable.

closed-end trust (U.S.A.) an investment trust company.

constructive trust a trust that exists by the operation of the law of equity, not by any planned intention of the parties, such as when a mortgagee uses his power of sale and sells the property at a surplus he becomes a trustee under a constructive trust for the amount of the surplus. He must in fairness pass the surplus to the mortgagor. *Syn.* implied trust; resulting trust.

debenture trust a trust, formed by a company under a trust deed, by which the trustees are responsible for holding certain of the company's assets that are the security for an issue of debenture stock. In Britain it is usual not to appoint private trustees for this purpose, but to use the services of a professional trustee organization such as a bank.

discretionary trust *see under* discretionary.

executed trust a trust formed by a person in his will, to which the testator transfers property on his death, with clear directions about how it is to be used. Cf. executory trust.

executory trust a trust formed under a will, in which the testator gives only an outline of his intentions as a guide to the trustees. Cf. executed trust.

expressed trust a trust that has been formed by clearly stated words, esp. in a document, as opposed to a constructive or implied trust.

fixed trust a unit investment trust that must invest its funds in a fixed class or range of securities, such as in plantations, or oils; the managers have no power to buy any security not included in the fixed class or range. While this guards the members against mismanagement, it greatly limits the managers' freedom. Cf. flexible trust.

flexible trust a unit investment trust that is run by managers who have power to sell any security held and to buy any other security, usu. within certain stated limits. Cf. fixed trust. *Syn.* (U.S.A.) general management trust.

general management trust *see* flexible trust *above*.

horizontal trust a combination of businesses that are carrying out the same stage of the production process. Cf. vertical trust.

implied trust *see* constructive trust *above*.

inter vivos trust a trust formed by a person so that it becomes effective during his lifetime, as opposed to a trust formed by a will. Cf. testamentary trust.

investment trust an investment company. *See under* company.

open-end trust (U.S.A.) a unit trust.

private trust a trust set up for the benefit of a named person or persons, as opposed to a charitable or public trust.

public trust *see* charitable trust.

resulting trust *see* constructive trust *above*.

testamentary trust a trust that has been set up under the provisions of the will of a dead person.

unit trust *see under* unit.

vertical trust a combination of businesses that are carrying out all stages of production of a class of product. Cf. horizontal trust.

v. (1) to have faith in somebody or something: *We trust our cashier completely. They cannot be trusted to keep a bargain.* (2) to hope, expect: *We trust that you have received our quotation. I trust that you will reply immediately.*

trust, breach of *see* breach of trust.

trust company *see under* company.

trust corporation LAW in Britain, the Public Trustee, the Treasury Solicitor, the Official Solicitor, and certain persons appointed specially by a court of law; also certain persons otherwise qualified by law to act as custodian trustees.

trust deed LAW a formal document, made under seal, by a donor, creating a trust, appointing one or more trustees, stating the purposes and conditions under which the trust is to be administered, transferring certain clearly defined land and other property or money to them to hold and manage for the benefit of a clearly identified beneficiary or beneficiaries or charitable objects. There is a variety of forms of trust deed, such as: a deed of arrangement, made by an insolvent debtor; a deed of covenant; a deed of gift; a deed of assignment; a debenture deed.

trustee LAW (1) a person who has entered into a binding promise to hold and administer, honestly and wisely, land, money or other property for the benefit of some other person or persons, or for some particular object allowed by law. For this purpose, the trustee is made the legal owner of the property. *Syn.* feoffee to uses (an ancient form now seldom found). (2) a person may also find that he is a trustee without intending to become one, such as when a trust is considered to exist by operation of the law. *See* constructive trust *under* trust.

bare trustee *see under* bare.

constructive trustee a person who is held by law to be a trustee under a constructive trust.

custodian trustee a trustee who has the duty of holding and taking care of trust property, such as the securities in the trust fund of a unit trust, but without having any duty to manage it. In Britain he may be the Public Trustee or any large banking or insurance company or other body corporate that qualifies to act as a custodian trustee under the law. *See* trust corporation.

Public Trustee *see under* Public.

trustee for sale LAW a trustee appointed under a trust for sale.

trustee in bankruptcy LAW a person who, as an officer of a bankruptcy court, is given power to take possession of a bankrupt's property and to hold it in trust for the creditors, to sell it and to share the money out among the creditors according to the law. *See* bankrupt; bankruptcy. *Syn.* assignee in bankruptcy.

trustee investments LAW in Britain, investments in which a trustee may by law invest trust funds. These may be the investments stated in the trust deed, but if the deed does not state any, he must invest at least half the trust funds in *narrower-range investments.* (*See* trustee securities *under* securities.) The other half may be invested in *wider-range investments,* such as ordinary shares and preference shares of profitable quoted companies registered in Britain; shares in certain building societies; and unit trusts. *See* trustee status.

trustee savings banks *see under* savings bank.

trustee securities *see under* securities.

trustee status LAW & STK. EXCH. in Britain, a special set of qualities that shares or debentures in companies must by law possess if they are to be bought as trustee investments. A commercial stock or share or debenture has trustee status if it is in a company that has been incorporated in Britain with a paid-up share capital of at least £1 million and has paid a dividend on all classes of its shares for at least five years.

trust for sale LAW a trust that binds the trus-

tee(s) to sell land or other property immediately and to give the sale proceeds to the beneficiary. Such a trust arises, e.g. from a will, an intestacy, a bankruptcy or a liquidation.

trust fund LAW the assets including property of any kind, held in trust by a trustee for the beneficiary of the trust.

trust instrument LAW a formal document, such as a will or deed, placing land in trust for a named person or persons. Such land is called settled land. *See* settlement (4). *Syn.* settlement.

trust receipt *see under* receipt.

Trust Territory *see* Pacific Islands.

trust unit FIN. a share in a unit trust.

trustworthy fit to be trusted; able to be depended upon: *He is one of our most trustworthy employees/customers/suppliers,* *we know that we can always trust him, that he deserves our trust. A trustworthy source of news/information,* a source that tells the truth.

t.s. twin screw; turbine ship.

TS. typescript.

T/S trans-shipment.

T.S.B. trustee savings bank(s).

TSS. typescripts.

TT, T.T. telegraphic transfer.

T.T. rate *see under* exchange rate.

T.U. trade union.

tube TRANSPT. an underground railway. *Syn.* (U.S.A.) subway.

tube-well AGR. & IND. a metal pipe sunk deep into the ground, up which water is pumped to the surface for irrigating crops and for supplying homes and factories. Cf. artesian well.

T.U.C. Trades Union Congress.

tug SHIPG. (1) a small, very powerful ship specially built for towing (pulling along) other, usu. much larger, ships. *Syn.* tugboat. (2) any vessel that is being used for towing another vessel.

tugrik the standard currency unit of the Mongolian Republic, divided into 100 möngös.

tun a very large barrel; for wine, 252 gallons; for beer, 216 gallons.

Tunisia a republic in North Africa, on the Mediterranean Sea, pop. 5.7 million approx. (1975); capital, Tunis, pop. 500,000 approx.; languages, Arabic and French; currency unit, the Tunisian dinar, divided into 1000 millimes. Member, O.A.U.; Arab League.

tunnage *see* tonnage.

tuppence (*colloq.*) twopence, i.e. two pence.

tuppenny-ha'penny (*colloq.*) of very little value.

turf accountant *see* bookmaker.

Turf, The horse-racing as a sport.

Turkey a republic in western Asia, pop. 39 million approx. (1975); capital, Ankara, pop. 2.5 million approx.; language, Turkish; currency unit, the Turkish lira, *pl.* lire, divided into 100 kurus or 4000 para. Member, Council of Europe; Associate, E.E.C.

turn *see* jobber's turn.

turnover ACCTS. (1) the total value of business done during a given period, usu. the total annual sales. (2) the rate at which the stock of goods is turned over, i.e. sold in the course of trade. *See* stock-turn. (3) the number of times that a stock of goods or of money is replaced in a given period.

capital turnover *see under* capital.

investment turnover *see* capital turnover *under* capital.

turnover ratio ACCTS. the ratio between total sales of a business in a given period, usu. a year, and the value of its fixed assets.

turnover tax *see* sales tax (*b*) *under* tax.

turnpike TRANSPT. (1) a bar or gate across a road, where a toll is paid. *Syn.* toll gate. (2) a road on which tolls are charged. (3) in U.S.A., a motorway on which tolls are charged.

turn-round TRANSPT. & SHIPG. the unloading, cleaning, refuelling, reloading and completion of formalities of a ship, road vehicle or railway train before it can start on another voyage or journey: *Liners must make a quick turn-round if they are to be profitable.*

TV television.

'tween deck SHIPG. space for stowing cargo between the decks of a ship, as opposed to space in her holds. *A 'tween deck ship, a 'tween decker,* a ship with a deck below the main deck.

twin-bedded TOUR. of a hotel room, with two single beds. Cf. double-bedded.

twin-berth clause *see* berth clause.

twin-screw SHIPG. of a ship, having two screws or propellers. *Abbr.* t.s.

twister (1) a cheat; a clever but dishonest person. (2) (U.S.A.) a wind-storm.

two-part tariff *see under* tariff.

two-sided accounts ACCTS. accounts in the form usually adopted when they are written by hand in account books; each account has a left-hand or debit side, and a right-hand or credit side. Cf. three-column accounts.

typescript work that has been produced on a typewriter, esp. material for a printer to set up in type. *Abbr.* TS., *pl.* TSS.

typist a person skilled in operating a typewriter.

copy-typist *see under* copy.

invoice-typist a typist specially skilled in the typing of the many different kinds of invoice forms, credit notes and any work consisting mostly of figures.

shorthand-typist *see* steno-typist *below.*

steno-typist a typist who is also able to write speech in shorthand. *Syn.* shorthand-typist.

U

U Uruguay's international vehicle-registration letter.

uberrimae fidei *see* utmost good faith.

u/c. undercharge; upper-case.

Uganda a republic in eastern Africa, pop. 12 million approx. (1975); capital, Kampala, pop. 350,000 approx.; languages, English, Kiswahili and tribal; currency unit, the Ugandan shilling (USh.), divided into 100 cents. Member, (British) Commonwealth; O.A.U.

U.K. United Kingdom (of Great Britain and Northern Ireland).

U.K. ton *see* long ton *under* ton.

ullage COM. (1) the amount by which the actual contents of a barrel or other vessel containing liquid falls short of the full measure, owing to loss by evaporation (drying up) or by leakage (escaping). (2) the actual contents of a container at the time of importation; this is the basis on which a specific duty is calculated by the Customs.

ult. ultimo.

ultimo *see* date.

ultra vires LAW (*Latin,* beyond the powers) in excess of the powers held under the law. Where, e.g. a company contracts to do something that is not included in the list of objects authorized in its Memorandum of Association, that contract is ultra vires, i.e. beyond the company's legal powers, and is void.

u/m undermentioned.

Umm al-Qaiwain *see* United Arab Emirates.

umpire *see* referee (3).

U.N. United Nations (Organization).

un- *prefix,* not: *Unaccompanied,* not accompanied. *Unclaimed/undistributed/unidentified/unpaid.* Cf. uni-, *prefix.*

unanimous of one mind; in full agreement: *The motion was carried by the unanimous vote of the members of the company,* all voted in favour of the motion. *The board was unanimous in refusing the offer. Adv.* unanimously. *Pron.* youn-.

unavoidable costs *see* fixed costs *under* costs.

unbalanced budget *see under* budget.

uncalled capital *see under* capital.

uncertainty (1) ECON. THEORY business risks that are borne by the entrepreneur. (2) INSCE. a risk that cannot be insured against because its probability cannot be measured, such as the risk that a business will make a loss. (3) LAW in a legal document, a lack of certainty in a description or a direction; a failure to describe a gift clearly in a will or trust deed may make the gift *void for uncertainty.*

uncle (*colloq.*) a pawnbroker.

unclean bill of lading *see* dirty bill of lading *under* bill of lading.

unconfirmed letter of credit see under letter of credit.

unconvertible see inconvertible currency under currency.

uncrossed (cheque) see crossed cheque under cheque.

U.N.C.T.A.D. United Nations Conference on Trade and Development.

uncustomed goods TAXN. (1) goods that are not liable to customs duty. (2) goods on which customs duty is payable but has not been paid.

undated securities see undated stock under stock.

undated stock see annuity bond under bond, n.; also irredeemables.

under bond see bond, n.

undercapitalized STK. EXCH. of a business, esp. a company, having not enough share-capital to support the amount of trading activity. Cf. overcapitalized.

undercharge ACCTS. a charge that is below what it ought to be, usu. because the customer has, by mistake, been charged too little on the invoice. To put the accounts right, the customer is sent a debit note for the amount not charged. Opp. overcharge. Abbr. u/c.

Underconsumption Theory ECON. THEORY a theory held by some of the classical economists, that trade depressions are caused by a lack of spending by the public, either because of low wages or because of excessive saving, with the result that business activity is reduced and prices and profits tend to fall.

under-deck tonnage see under tonnage.

under-developed countries ECON. countries that possess natural resources but are economically backward, esp. countries in which the income per head of the population is low when compared with that of the developed countries. Under-developed countries tend to lack the capital and the enterprise needed for the advancement of industry; there are often not enough schools and technical training institutions, resulting in a lack of skilled labour, much unemployment and underemployment, and a dependence on subsistence farming. Various agencies of the United Nations are doing much to help these countries to raise the income per head of their populations. Syn. developing countries; emerging countries; less-developed countries.

under-employment ECON. (1) having too little work to do; a state in which a person, such as a subsistence farmer, has some work but too little to keep him busy for the full working day. He therefore tends to be poor. Cf. unemployment. (2) a state in which there is some unemployment in an economy, i.e. there is not full employment.

underground TRANSPT. in Britain, esp. in London, an electric railway system that runs in tun-

nels under a large city. Syn. (Britain) tube; (U.S.A.) subway.

under-insurance see under insurance, classes and kinds of.

under-lease see under lease.

under-let see sub-let.

under-manager see under manager.

under-mentioned mentioned below, later in this document: The ship will call at the under-mentioned ports. Abbr. u/m. Also undermentioned. Syn. below-mentioned.

under offer see offer.

underpopulation ECON. a state of an economy which has too small a population to supply the number of workers needed to make the best use of its resources. Cf. overpopulation.

under protest see protest (2).

undersell COM. to sell goods more cheaply than one's competitors: We undersell all other suppliers, we sell our goods more cheaply than anybody else. We are never undersold, nobody ever sells more cheaply than we do.

under ship's derrick SHIPG. words sometimes appearing in a bill of lading contract, meaning that the shipowner's responsibility ends when the goods have been placed in such a position on board the ship at the named port that the consignee or his agent can have them unloaded, using the ship's derrick(s) or other unloading equipment suited to the nature of the goods. Cf. over ship's rail. Syn. at ship's rail.

undertake (1) to take upon oneself, esp. a duty or responsibility: To undertake the reorganization of the company. To undertake a sole agency/trusteeship/guardianship. (2) to agree to do; to promise: He undertook to work better in future. (3) to begin to do; to cause to be done: We are undertaking an extensive modernization of our factory.

undertaker (1) ECON. an entrepreneur. (2) COM. a person who arranges funerals. (3) IND. a public utility company. Syn. undertaking.

undertaking LAW (1) a firm promise: The insurers paid him £10,000 on his giving a signed undertaking that he would make no further claim upon them. (2) a solemn promise made to a court of law during legal proceedings by one of the parties to the action or by his lawyer. A promise so made has the force of a court order. (3) COM. & IND. any business enterprise, esp. a public utility: An electricity undertaking.

undertone STK. & COMMOD. EXCH. the current feeling that influences the actions of buyers and sellers in the market: The market undertone was caution. The undertone of the market is more confident than it was last week.

undervalued currency FIN. & ECON. a currency that, because of government controls, has a lower rate of exchange in relation to another currency than it would have if the normal economic forces of supply and demand were operating. Cf. overvalued currency.

underwrite (1) FIN. to agree to pay the cost of making or doing something: *The ministry has underwritten the cost of his research work. Syn.* to finance. (2) COM. to guarantee a person against commercial loss: *The council has agreed to underwrite the publication of the book*, will bear any loss that the publishers may suffer. (3) INSCE. to accept liability for loss under a contract of insurance.

underwriter INSCE. (1) in an insurance company, a person highly skilled in insurance business who has power to accept risks for the company and to fix rates and conditions of insurance contracts. *Syn.* underwriting agent. (2) a member of the Corporation of Lloyd's who, either singly or as one of a syndicate, accepts insurance contracts. *See* Lloyd's underwriter. (3) a general expression for any person who sells insurance or offers to advise people on insurance business. (4) MAR. INSCE. a person or firm that accepts marine insurance contracts. *A marine underwriter.* (5) STK. EXCH. a person or organization who, for an agreed commission, enters an agreement to buy any part of a new issue of shares that is not bought by the public.

Underwriters, Institute of London *see under* Institute.

underwriting agent *see* underwriter (1).

undischarged bankrupt *see under* bankrupt.

undistributable reserve *see* capital reserve *under* reserves.

undistributed profit *see* retained profit *under* profit.

undue debt FIN. a debt that is not yet due for payment.

undue influence LAW unfair influence that has been put on a person to press him to enter into a contract. The person so influenced has the right to declare the contract void if he wishes.

unearned income *see under* income.

unearned increment ACCTS. & TAXN. an increase in the value of land and buildings as the result of natural causes, of increased demand or of inflation, not because of improvements made by the owner.

unearned premium *see under* premium.

unemployable of a person, unfit for employment; not worth employing because of low efficiency, laziness or disability.

unemployed *adj.* (1) of persons, having no employment; unable to obtain employment: *He has been unemployed for over a year. Syn.* out of work. (2) of money, capital, assets, not being used to earn income; idle.

n. unemployed persons generally: *He was dismissed from his job and joined the ranks/army of the unemployed. A scheme for retraining the unemployed.*

unemployment (1) the state of being unem-

ployed; of being unable to obtain paid work. (2) the number of persons that are unemployed in a country: *There is an increase in unemployment this month.*

casual unemployment that kind of unemployment which exists where workers are employed only irregularly and for short periods whenever they are needed, such as in the building trade. This leaves many workers unemployed between periods of casual employment. *See* casual labour.

disguised unemployment *see* hidden unemployment *below.*

frictional unemployment unemployment that is usu. temporary, because workers are changing jobs, or because demand and supply are temporarily out of balance.

hidden unemployment unemployment which is known to exist but which is not taken into account in government statistics. For example, some employers may temporarily be paying workers who are on short time or are completely idle, but for whom there will soon be a full day's work; and some workers, from fear of being unemployed, may be making the work last longer. *Syn.* disguised unemployment.

involuntary unemployment the kind of unemployment that exists where total demand is large enough to provide work for every person who wants a job, but where employers fail to employ more workers, either because they do not realize the size of the total demand or because they are slow to take advantage of it. Cf. voluntary unemployment *below.*

residual unemployment that kind of unemployment which exists among persons who are of such low efficiency, from laziness or some form of disability, that they are not worth employing.

seasonal unemployment that form of unemployment which exists in those trades or occupations where the amount of work and the number of jobs depend on the seasons, such as in hotels and catering, esp. at the seaside or in winter-sports centres, and in some kinds of agricultural work.

structural unemployment unemployment caused by the changing structure of the economy, such as an industry that is getting smaller or perhaps dying, because of a reduction in demand for the product.

technological unemployment unemployment that results from changes in methods of production.

voluntary unemployment that form of unemployment which exists because some persons do not wish to work, perhaps because they cannot find a job that is well enough paid. Cf. involuntary unemployment *above.*

unemployment benefit INSCE. an allowance paid by the government to persons who cannot earn because they are unemployed. *See* national insurance. *Colloq.* dole.

unenforceable contract *see under* contract.

U.N.E.S.C.O. United Nations Educational, Scientific and Cultural Organization.

unexecuted order *see under* order.

unfair competition *see* anti-dumping.

unfunded debt *see under* national debt.

uni- *prefix*, one; single: *Uniform*, having one form. *Unilateral*, concerning only one side. *Unilingual*, using, knowing, only one language. Cf. un-, *prefix*. *Pron.* youni-.

unified bond *see* consolidated bond *under* bond, *n.*

unified stock *see* consolidated bond *under* bond, *n.*

unilateral contract *see under* contract.

unincorporated association LAW & MAN. an association that does not need to be registered or incorporated. Such an association has not a single legal personality. *See* incorporation. If the association is formed for business purposes it is called a partnership and the size of its membership is limited by law; but if it is formed for an object other than profit, such as a club or society, there is no limit to the number of members. *Pron.* un-in-.

uninsurable risk *see under* risk.

union *see* trade union.

unionism *see* trade unionism.

Union of Soviet Socialist Republics a federal union of 15 republics in eastern Europe and northern Asia, pop. 255 million approx. (1975); capital, Moscow, pop. 7 million approx.; languages, Russian and local; currency unit, the rouble *or* ruble, divided into 100 copecks *or* kopecks. Member, COMECON. *Syn.* Soviet Russia. *Abbr.* U.S.S.R. *Pron.* youn-.

union shop *see* closed shop.

unissued capital *see under* capital.

unit banking BKG. a banking system in which a bank is not allowed to open branches; this system is quite common in the U.S.A. but in Britain each bank has many branches.

unit cost *see* average cost *under* cost.

United Arab Emirates a federal union of seven emirates on the Arabian Peninsula in southwest Asia, pop. 200,000 approx. (1975); capital, Abu Dhabi, pop. 50,000 approx.; language, Arabic; currency unit, the U.A.E. dirham, divided into 100 fils; *also* the Bahrain dinar, divided into 1000 fils, and the Qatar/Dubai riyal, divided into 100 dirhams. The member emirates are Abu Dhabi (pop. approx. 50,000), Ajman (5000), Dubai (65,000), Fujairah (15,000), Ras al-Khaimah (25,000), Sharjah (40,000), Umm al-Qaiwain (5000). Member, Arab League. *Abbr.* U.A.E.

United Kingdom of Great Britain and Northern Ireland an island monarchy (kingdom) in north-western Europe, population 56 million approx. (1975); capital, London, pop. 12.6 million approx.; language, English; currency unit, the pound sterling (£), divided into 100 pence, *sing.* penny (p). Member, E.E.C.; (British) Commonwealth; O.E.C.D.; Colombo Plan. *Abbr.* U.K. The United Kingdom consists of the main island of *Great Britain* comprising England, Wales and Scotland, including the Orkney Is., the Shetland Is., and the Hebrides or Western Isles; and *Northern Ireland*, the northern part of the island of Ireland. The Channel Is. and the Isle of Man have separate governments and are not part of the United Kingdom. *Pron.* youn-.

United Nations (U.N.) an international association formed in 1945 of which nearly all the countries of the world are now members. In signing the U.N. Charter, each member promises to work for peace and friendship among nations, and to help the economic and social progress of the world. The U.N. consists of six main organs (departments): the General Assembly; the Security Council; the Economic and Social Council; the Trusteeship Council; the International Court of Justice (at the Hague); and the U.N. Secretariat in New York. The U.N. also has a number of special agencies, of which the following are of particular importance to trade and finance: the International Monetary Fund (I.M.F.) in Washington; the World Bank; the U.N. Conference on Trade and Development (U.N.C.T.A.D.); the Food and Agriculture Organization (F.A.O.) in Rome; the International Labour Office (I.L.O.) in Geneva; and the International Finance Corporation (I.F.C.). *Pron.* youn-.

United Nations Conference on Trade and Development (U.N.C.T.A.D.) a permanent organization set up by the United Nations in 1964 to encourage international trade, esp. by helping the developing countries to increase their exports and to finance their export industries in years when world prices for their products are low. *Pron.* youn-.

United States of America a federal republic in North America, consisting of 50 states, pop. 215 million approx. (1975); capital, Washington, pop. 2.6 million approx.; language, English; currency unit, the U.S. dollar (US$), divided into 100 cents. Member, O.A.S.; O.E.C.D.; Colombo Plan. *Pron.* youn-.

unit fraud FIN. a type of share-pushing, in which a dishonest person buys some land and divides it into a number of plots (sections) each producing some kind of produce, usu. fruit or grain. Each plot is represented by a unit, which is sold to the public, the buyer being told that, when the produce is sold, he will receive his share of the profits from his plot. He finds later that many more units have been sold than there are plots.

unitized handling TRANSPT. the transport of goods by container.

unit load *see under* load.

unit, monetary *see* monetary unit.

unit of account (1) a unit of money considered as a measure of value, esp. for accounting purposes, rather than as a means of payment or as a store of wealth. (2) the standard currency unit of a country. *See* account, money of. (3) in the European Economic Community (E.E.C.) an artificial currency unit used for fixing farm prices, for calculating the E.E.C. budget and for certain trade agreements with countries which are not members of the E.E.C.

unit trust FIN. in Britain, an organization that collects money from subscribers, called unit-holders, usu. small investors, and invests it in securities for their benefit. The securities bought are held, usu. by an important bank or insurance company, acting as custodian trustees under a trust deed that must be approved by the government. The work of investment and administration is carried out by a professional investment management company, called the managers, in return for certain charges controlled by the government. The managers buy the securities, divide them into units of equal value, and offer these units to the public at an offer price. Each unit-holder becomes the owner of a fraction of all the securities held in the trust fund. After deducting the trustees' and managers' charges, the net income received as dividends from the securities is distributed to the unit-holders, usu. every six months. The managers will, at any time, buy back units from the public at a bid price, a little below the offer price. Unlike an investment trust, a unit trust is not a company, and trust units are not traded on the Stock Exchange.

Universal Postal Union originally set up in 1875, but now a special agency of the U.N. that co-ordinates and controls postal services throughout the world. *Abbr.* U.P.U. *Pron.* youn-.

unladen TRANSPT. without a load. *Unladen weight*, the weight (of a vehicle) when not loaded. *Opp.* laden.

unlimited company *see under* company.

unlimited liability *see under* liability.

unlimited securities *see* unlisted securities.

unliquidated damages *see* damages at large.

unlisted market *see* over-the-counter market *under* market.

unlisted securities STK. EXCH. in Britain, securities that are not included in the Official List of securities dealt in by members of the Stock Exchange. Cf. listed securities. *Syn.* unlimited securities; unquoted securities.

U.N.O. United Nations Organization (the U.N.).

unofficial rate (of exchange) *see under* exchange rate.

unofficial strike *see under* strike.

unquoted securities *see* unlisted securities.

unquoted share *see under* share.

unrecoverable *see* irrecoverable.

unsecured creditor *see under* creditor.

unsecured debenture *see* naked debenture *under* debenture.

unsecured debt *see under* debt.

unsecured loan *see under* loan.

unsecured stock *see* loan stock *under* stock.

unship SHIPG. to unload cargo and to disembark passengers from a ship.

unsolds COM. (1) goods supplied to a retailer but unsold and therefore, by custom or agreement, returnable to the supplier for credit, such as newspapers that remain unsold by a newsagent and are returned to the publishers. (2) any goods returned to a supplier who has supplied them on sale or return.

unsolicited ADVTG. not requested; not asked for: *Unsolicited letter*, a letter that somebody has freely written, usu. praising a product, without being asked. *See* unsolicited testimonial *under* testimonial.

unvalued policy INSCE. an insurance policy that states the total sum insured but leaves the insurable value of different parts of the insured objects to be decided if and when a claim arises. Cf. valued policy.

update (1) to bring up to date: *To update the sales figures every month*. (2) COMP. to make changes in the information stored in the data file of a computer.

upkeep (1) the process of keeping something, esp. a building, roads, or machinery, in good order. (2) the cost of doing this. *Syn.* maintenance.

up-market COM. of a shop or store, a tendency to supply what is wanted by buyers in the richer sections of the market: *That dress shop has become up-market*, is selling dearer goods of higher quality than before. *Opp.* down-market.

upper deck *see* deck.

Upper Volta a republic in West Africa, pop. 6 million approx. (1975); capital, Ouagadougou, pop. 100,000 approx.; languages, French and tribal; currency unit, the C.F.A. franc (CFA Fr.), divided into 100 centimes. Member, O.A.U.; O.C.A.M.M.; Associate, E.E.C. *Also* Voltaic Republic.

upset price *see* reserve price (*a*) *under* price.

uptime *or* **up time** COMP. the time that a computer is free from mechanical trouble, i.e. is fit to operate or actually operates, expressed as a percentage of the time that it has been planned to operate. Cf. downtime.

up to date *see under* date.

uptown warehouse *see under* warehouse.

up train see under train.

U.P.U. Universal Postal Union.

Uruguay a republic in South America, pop. 3 million approx.; capital, Montevideo, pop. 1.5 million approx.; language, Spanish; currency unit, the peso, divided into 100 centesimos.

U.S. United States (of America).

US$ United States dollar.

U/S useless; unserviceable.

USA the international vehicle-registration letters of the U.S.A.

U.S.A. United States of America.

usage (1) custom; common practice or behaviour: *The usages of the port of Alexandria.* (2) treatment in use: *Typewriters are not made to bear rough usage.*

usance (1) BKG. & COM. the usual period at which, by custom, foreign bills of exchange are drawn between two countries, e.g. in London, bills on Paris are usu. drawn at three months' date, on Bombay at 30 days' sight, and so on. *To draw a bill at usance*, at the period usual for bills drawn on the particular country. *At double usance*, at twice the usual period. (2) the rate of interest (a meaning now little used). (3) ECON. any income or advantage received in money or goods by the owner of wealth.

usance bill see under bill of exchange.

use LAW (1) the legal right of a person to enjoy the benefit of possessing property without interference by other persons. *Syn.* user. (2) a trust. *A feoffee to uses*, a trustee.

use and occupancy policy see consequential loss policy *under* insurance policy.

user see use (1).

U.S.S.R. Union of Soviet Socialist Republics.

U.S. ton see short ton *under* ton.

usufruct LAW the legal right to enjoy during one's lifetime the benefits of using property belonging to another person, on condition that it is given back to the owner in its original state, allowances being made for normal wear and tear.

usufructuary LAW a person who has been given a usufruct.

usurer FIN. a person who lends money at an excessively high rate of interest, esp. a rate higher than that allowed by law.

usurious adj. *A usurious rate of interest.*

usury n. (a) the lending of money at excessive rates of interest. (b) the amount received in such interest.

Ut. Utah, U.S.A.

utilitarianism see Bentham, Jeremy.

utility (1) usefulness. (2) ECON. THEORY the amount of satisfaction that a consumer receives from a commodity or service. *See* marginal utility; Diminishing Utility, Law of. *Opp.* disutility. (3) IND. one of the services, called *public utilities*, that supply the public with electricity, gas, water, transport, etc.

Utility, Law of Diminishing see under Diminishing.

utilization (1) the degree to which something is used: *In market gardening there is a high utilization of land. See* plant utilization. (2) the purpose for which something, esp. land, is used: *The Land Utilization Survey*, a survey of Britain that records on maps the use to which the land is put.

utilized capacity see capacity (1).

utmost good faith INSCE. & LAW a basic rule of insurance law, that a person making a proposal for insurance is legally bound to give the insurers all facts and information which might affect their assessment of the risks to be insured. No essential facts must be kept back. The insurers, by the same legal rule, are legally bound not to mislead the insured, e.g. by putting conditions into the contract that are unfair or have not been seen by or discussed with the insured. *See* disclosure (1). *Syn.* uberrimae fidei.

utter LAW to put into circulation, to publish, with the intention of deceiving: *To utter forged cheques/counterfeit money. See* passing off.

U/w. underwriter.

V

V the Vatican City's international vehicle-registration letter; volt.

v. versus.

Va. Virginia, U.S.A.

V.A. value analysis.

vac. vacation, vacant.

vacancy (1) an empty place, e.g. hotel room. (2) a post that needs to be filled by a new employee.

casual vacancy see under casual.

vacancy rate (1) COM. in the property market, the proportion of properties that are at any one time unlet, usu. expressed as a percentage: *The 5% vacancy rate in the City is the lowest for three years.* (2) the proportion of hotel rooms unlet. *Opp.* occupancy rate.

vacant empty; unfilled, esp. (a) of posts, jobs, that need to be filled by new employees: *Situations vacant*; (b) of rooms in a hotel, cabins in a ship, seats in a vehicle, etc., unoccupied, not in use. *Abbr.* vac.

vacant possession see under possession (3).

vacation (1) a holiday, usu. lasting several weeks, esp. in a college or university. *A vacation job*, temporary employment for a student during the vacation. *Abbr.* vac. (2) LAW in Britain, certain fixed periods of the year when the law courts are closed to ordinary cases. During these periods urgent matters are dealt with by vacation judges.

vagabond see vagrant.

vagrant an idle, homeless person, who wanders from place to place, perh. begging or stealing or otherwise making trouble. *Syn.* vagabond; tramp.

valid LAW (1) legally effective; in good order and having force at the present time: *A valid passport/driving licence/tax token/ticket.* (2) that will be supported by a court of law: *A valid will/receipt.* (3) that is binding on a person or persons: *A valid contract.*

valid contract see *under* contract.

validate LAW (1) to make valid. (2) to confirm the effectiveness or legality of: *I can validate his order*, I can confirm it.

validity the state of being valid: *The validity of this ticket has expired*, it is no longer valid.

valise see suitcase.

valorization FIN. the fixing by artificial means of a value or price, esp. of a commodity or a currency, and the action needed to keep that value or price in force in the market. Cf. revalorization.

valuable (1) that can be valued, given a value, esp. in units of money. (2) that has some or much value in units of money: *A valuable work of art/asset.* See also valuables, *pl.* (3) that has value in use, regardless of price: *Good judgment is a valuable quality in a manager. The telephone is a valuable aid to a busy merchant.*

valuable consideration see *under* consideration.

valuables *pl.* things, esp. personal property, having some or much value in units of money if sold in the market: *He has a house full of valuables*, full of things of much value.

valuation (1) the act or process of fixing or estimating the value of something. (2) the value so fixed or estimated, expressed in units of money. (3) ACCTS. (*a*) the process of arriving at the probable present value of the assets of a business. (*b*) the value so arrived at. This value is needed in preparing the balance sheet. (4) TAXN. the value of real property, i.e. of land and buildings, fixed by the central government valuation officer, on which a local government authority bases the amount of the rates payable on the property. See quinquennial valuation *below*. (5) the value of the estate of a person who has died. See probate valuation *below*.

inventory valuation see stock valuation *below*.

probate valuation in Britain, the fixing of the value of the assets of a person who has died, to arrive at the value of his estate, on which capital transfer tax (C.T.T.) is payable. Stocks and shares are valued for probate at the lower quoted price on the date of death, plus a quarter of the difference between that price and the higher quoted price. Thus stock quoted at 96–98 will be valued at 96½ for C.T.T. *Syn.* valuation for probate.

quinquennial valuation in Britain, a valuation of real property, i.e. land and buildings, made usu. every five years, to provide a basis on which the rates (taxes paid to the local government authority) are charged. The valuation is made by a valuation officer in the service of the central government and is called the rateable value.

stock valuation the fixing of the value of the stock of a business at the end of the accounting year, to provide the figure needed in preparing the balance sheet. In a company, the directors are responsible for fixing this value, and usu. base it on cost or market value, whichever is the lower. *Syn.* inventory valuation. See also current cost accounting.

value *n.* (1) the quality of being useful, of satisfying Man's wants; or of being desirable for his enjoyment or happiness. Usefulness; utility; desirability. (2) ECON. THEORY the amount of satisfaction that is obtained from an article, commodity or service. See value in use. (3) ECON. THEORY the amount that can be obtained for something by exchanging it for money or goods. See value in exchange. (4) COM. what an article or commodity is worth: *Good value for money*, well worth the price.

added value see value added.

annual value see *under* annual.

assets value see *under* assets.

book value see *under* book.

capital value see *under* capital.

capitalized value see capital value *under* capital.

exchange value see value in exchange.

existing-use value a value of land and buildings based on the price obtainable in the open market for use for the same purpose as that for which it is at present being used, rather than the price that could be obtained if it was used for some other purpose.

face value the value printed on a financial document such as a bank-note, stock or share certificate, postal or money order. See par value. Cf. market value.

future value the value in the future of a present sum of money if invested at compound interest. $F = P \times (1 + r)^n$ where F is the future value, P the present sum, r the interest on £1 for one year, and n the number of years. For example, £100 invested at 8% per annum for 5 years will produce a future value F of £100 × $(1 + 0.08)^5 = 100 \times 1.08^5 = £146.93$.

gross value see *under* gross.

intrinsic value see *under* intrinsic.

loan value see surrender value *under* surrender.

market value see *under* market.

nominal value see par value.

no par value see no-par-value share *under* share.

par value see *under* par.

present value see *under* present.

rateable value *see* annual value *under* annual.

real value the amount of goods and services that a given sum of money can buy at a particular time. A comparison of this amount at various times provides a means of measuring inflation.

scarcity value a value that is high because the demand is large but the supply is small and is not easily increased.

scrap value the value of an article as scrap, i.e. as waste material if fit for recovery, such as scrap metal for remelting, or scrap paper for pulping.

surplus value *see* consumer's surplus.

surrender value *see under* surrender.

trade-in value *see* trade-in.

use value *see* value in use.

v. to set a value on, to estimate, or fix the value of, something. *To value a house at £25,000. To value the stock of a business.*

value added ECON. THEORY the value that is added to a product by a particular producer or during a particular stage in the process of production or distribution. It is the difference between the producer's sales and the amount that he has paid to his suppliers, i.e. it is the increase in value of the product as the result of the manufacturing and marketing operations performed on it.

value added tax *see under* tax.

value analysis IND. the science of studying a product in very great detail to find out in what ways it can be altered so as to reduce its cost of production without lowering its quality or saleability. Cf. value engineering. *Abbr.* V.A.

valued policy *see* agreed-value insurance *under* insurance, classes and kinds of.

value engineering IND. the practice of making a very detailed scientific study of each stage in the manufacture of a product, to see what changes can be made to the process and machinery to reduce the cost of production without lowering the quality and saleability of the product. Cf. value analysis.

value index *see under* index number(s).

value in exchange ECON. THEORY the value of an article or commodity considered in relation to the price that can be obtained in exchange for it, either in units of money or in quantities of goods. Cf. value in use.

value in use ECON. THEORY the value of an article or commodity considered only in relation to its usefulness to Man, not to its price, or value in exchange. Cf. value in exchange.

value of money ECON. the quantity of goods and services that money will buy at a certain time; the buying power of a given sum of money. *See* purchasing power (2).

valuer COM. a professional person who, for a fee, gives advice on the market value of property of any kind. *Syn.* (U.S.A.) appraiser.

value received BKG. words used in a bill of exchange to show that the bill is a means of payment for goods supplied or services performed, to the value of the bill, and that it is not a means of transferring, e.g. a gift of money.

Value, Theories of *see* Labour Theory of Value; Cost of Production Theory of Value; Marginal Theory of Value.

van TRANSPT. (1) an enclosed motor vehicle for carrying goods, esp. furniture, parcels and small goods, by road. *A motor van.* (2) an enclosed railway wagon for goods and luggage. *A guard's van,* a van in which the guard of a train rides, usu. with a space for parcels and luggage. (3) a lift-van, *see* container.

van ship *see* container ship *under* container.

variable annuity *see under* insurance policy.

variable budget FIN. & ACCTS. a budget that is not fixed, but can be varied from time to time if desired. *Syn.* flexible budget.

variable cost *see* direct cost *under* cost.

variable expenses *see under* expenses.

variable levy *see* import levy *under* levy.

Variable Proportions, Law of *see* Diminishing Returns, Law of.

variance FIN. & MAN. in budgetary control, an amount by which a budgeted cost differs from the actual cost. Large variances draw attention to the need for explanation and, possibly, for stricter control of expenditure.

Varityper an electric typewriter with a range of various type-faces and type-sizes, and a system for making all lines of equal length.

V.A.T. *or* v.a.t. value added tax.

vatman TAXN. (*colloq.*) in Britain, a tax official responsible for collecting value added tax (V.A.T.).

vault *see* bonded vaults.

Veblen Thorsten Bunde (1857–1929), American economist who became a professor at Chicago University (1892) and is known as the founder of institutional economics. His best-known books are: *The Theory of the Leisure Class: an Economic Study of Institutions* (1899), and *The Theory of Business Enterprise* (1904). He attacked the world of business finance and the social behaviour of the rich, originating the expressions 'conspicuous consumption', i.e. buying things only for show, and 'pecuniary emulation', i.e. matching one's standard of living with that of one's neighbours.

vegetable *n.* AGR. a plant, esp. one grown for food. *Abbr.* veg.

adj. relating to plants: *Vegetable oils,* oils obtained from plants, not from animals or minerals.

vegetable parchment COM. & IND. a special kind of paper for wrapping butter, fish and other greasy or wet commodities.

vegetarian a person who eats only foods prepared from vegetables.

vegetation (1) the plants collectively that grow in a place or area. (2) plants generally.

vehicle TRANSPT. any means of travel or transport, esp. a carriage that moves on wheels. *Syn.* conveyance.

vehicle ferry *see* auto ferry *under* ferry.

velocity of circulation ECON. THEORY of money, the speed at which money is passed from person to person in an economy. It is the average number of times that a unit of money is used in a given period, and can be roughly calculated by dividing the total spent in that period by the amount in circulation, including bank deposits; but this does not include cash dealings, which are most difficult to measure. The velocity of circulation has an important influence on the value of money, but it is difficult to calculate in practice.

vendee LAW a person to whom something is sold. Cf. vendor.

vender *see* vendor.

vending machine *see* slot-machine; automat.

vendor LAW a person who sells something, esp. the seller of a house or business. *Also* vender.

vendor's lien *see under* lien.

vendors' share *see under* share.

vendue COM. (U.S.A.) a public auction.

Venezuela a republic in the north of South America, pop. 12 million approx. (1975); capital, Caracas, pop. 2 million approx.; language, Spanish; currency unit, the bolivar, divided into 100 centimos. Member, O.A.S.; L.A.F.T.A.

venture *n.* COM. a business, or a business deal, in which there is some degree of risk, which is accepted in the expectation of making a profit: *To start a new venture*, to open a new business. *A commercial venture*, a deal made in the usual course of business. *A joint venture, see under* joint. *Syn.* enterprise; speculation; adventure. *v.* to risk money in business in the expectation of making a profit.

verbal, expressed in spoken words rather than in writing: *A verbal offer/order/request. Syn.* oral.

verbatim (*Latin*, in the same words) repeating exactly the same words: *A verbatim report* of a speech, etc., giving the exact words used by the speaker.

verification of assets ACCTS. the work of an auditor in checking the existence and the value of the assets of a business.

verify to check the existence, correctness or truth of something, such as facts, accounts, a statement, the contents of a list or a parcel. *Syn.* to confirm.

Veritas *see* Bureau Veritas.

verso 1. the back of a document. 2. a left-hand page in a book. Cf. recto.

versus LAW (*Latin*, against) a formal way of showing which party is bringing a lawsuit against the other or others: *Jones versus Smith*,

Jones is suing Smith. Usu. abbreviated in use to v. *or* vs.

vertical combination *see* vertical integration *under* integration.

vertical expansion *see* expansion (2).

vertical integration *see under* integration.

vertical suspension filing *see under* filing system.

vessel SHIPG. a ship or large boat.

motor vessel *see under* motor.

vessel ton *see under* ton.

vest LAW to give legal power: *To vest a local government authority with power to hold public land. To vest property in a trustee.*

vested interests persons or groups of persons who hold a commanding position in the economy because they have strong powers and rights over property, finance and business, which they are unwilling to lose.

vesting date LAW the date on which a new law comes into force and on which certain organizations such as government departments, local government authorities and public corporations receive their new legal powers.

vet. veterinary surgeon.

veterinary surgeon AGR. a professional person who treats the diseases of domestic and farm animals. *Syn.* (U.S.A.) veterinarian. *Abbr.* vet.

vexatious action *see* abuse of process.

via (*Latin*, by way of) (1) (*a*) by a particular route passing through one or more stated places: *To travel to Glasgow via London.* (*b*) by a particular means of communication: *A message via radio-telephone.* (2) BKG. a copy of a bill of exchange in a set, the equivalent of a First of Exchange (*First via* or *1st via*), Second of Exchange (*Second via* or *2nd via*), etc.

Vic. Victoria, Australia.

vicarious liability LAW a responsibility that arises when a person authorizes another person (gives him permission and power) to do something for him which wrongs someone else; then both may be liable jointly as tortfeasors (persons who do a civil wrong). Cf. strict liability.

vice- *prefix meaning* in place of; next in importance to: *The vice-chairman,* a person who acts in place of the chairman, when necessary, and who is next in importance to him. *Vice-president, Vice-Consul. Syn.* deputy.

vice *see* inherent vice.

vice propre *see* inherent vice.

victimization the act of an employer in unfairly choosing certain of his employees for unkind treatment or dismissal because he personally dislikes them or because they make trouble for him, esp. during an industrial dispute or strike. *See* constructive dismissal.

victual *v.* COM. (1) to supply, or provide with, victuals, i.e. food. (2) to obtain victuals. *Pron.* vitl.

victuals *n. pl.* food, usu. ready for eating. *Pron.* vitlz.

victualler (1) COM. a supplier of victuals, i.e. food. *Licensed victualler, see under* licensed. *Pron.* vitler. (2) SHIPG. a ship that carries supplies of food, etc. for a group of ships. *Syn.* supply-ship; store-ship.

victualling bill SHIPG. a document prepared by the master of a ship declaring to the Customs details of all goods taken on board from a bonded warehouse or under drawback, to be used as ship's stores on the coming voyage. *Syn.* bill of victualling.

Vietnam a republic in south-east Asia, pop. 23 million approx. (1973); capital, Hanoi, pop. 900,000 approx.; language, Vietnamese; currency unit, the dong, divided into 10 hao or 100 xu.

villein ECON. HIST. under the feudal system in Europe, one of a class of agricultural workers who were bound to do a certain amount of work for the lord of the manor, and in return were allowed to cultivate for their own profit some strips of their lord's land. *See* feudal system. *Syn.* serf.

V.I.P. very important person.

visa TRANSPT. & TOUR. an endorsement made on a document, esp. a passport, by the representative of a foreign country, usu. a Consul, to show that the document has been checked and is in order, and allowing the holder to enter the country for a certain purpose and to stay for a stated period. *Also* visé.

entry visa a visa that allows a foreign person to enter a country and to stay there for a stated period or permanently, usu. with freedom to obtain employment or to carry on business. A *permanent entry visa* allows the holder to stay permanently.

re-entry visa a visa that allows the holder of an entry visa, who has temporarily left the country, to re-enter it. A *multiple re-entry visa* allows the holder to re-enter any number of times during the period of his entry visa.

tourist visa a visa that allows a traveller to enter a country for a stated period as a tourist or private visitor, on condition that he does not obtain employment or carry on a business.

transit visa a visa that allows a traveller to make only a short stop while passing through the country, not to stay in it.

visible *adj.* that can be seen; open to view, not hidden.

visibles *n. pl.* ECON. imports and exports of goods, as compared with invisible items of trade such as payments for services.

visible balance *see* balance of payments; balance of trade.

visible exports *see under* exports, *pl.*

visible imports *see under* imports, *pl.*

visible reserve *see under* reserves.

visiting card *see* calling card.

visual control board MAN. a method of showing very clearly by means of movable markers on a board or wall, a summary of important facts, such as the progress of work on a contract or in production, and the movement of stores or stocks.

vital statistics ECON. THEORY statistics that relate to the lives of human beings, such as, of population, births, deaths, occupations, age groups, diseases, accidents and education.

VN Vietnam's international vehicle-registration letters.

vocation a trade, profession or occupation; the kind of work that one does for a living. *Adj.* vocational.

vocational training training in a trade or occupation, esp. a course of training in a vocational school.

vogue *see* fashion (2).

void LAW of no legal effect, considered as having no legal existence and therefore not recognized by the courts. Thus, a contract to perform an illegal act is void; it will not be supported by a court of law and is therefore not legally binding. *Cf.* voidable.

voidable LAW of an agreement (1) that can be declared void; (2) that can be avoided by a refusal to be bound by it. *Cf.* void.

voidable contract *see under* contract.

void contract *see under* contract.

vol. volume.

volt the SI unit of electric potential, i.e. the pressure of an electric current. *Abbr.* V.

Voltaic Republic *see* Upper Volta.

volume (1) the space occupied by something, expressed in cubic units of measurement, such as cubic metres (m^3) or cubic feet (cu. ft). *See* cubic or solid measure *table on page 477.* (2) a total amount or quantity. *The volume of trade between two countries. The volume of business/production/output.* (3) a bound book, esp. one of a set or series of several such books.

volume business COM. trading only in very large quantities of goods, usu. at wholesale.

volume index *see* quantity index *under* index number(s).

volume of trade ECON. the total amount of goods bought for money in a given period.

volumetric ton *see* vessel ton *under* ton.

voluntary done or made willingly, by choice, without being forced: *A voluntary payment/contribution/donation. Opp.* compulsory; obligatory.

voluntary absentee *see* absentee.

voluntary contributor *see under* contributor.

voluntary liquidation *see* winding-up.

voluntary sale *see under* sale.

voluntary saving *see under* saving.

voluntary settlement *see under* settlement.

voluntary stranding *see* stranding.

voluntary unemployment *see under* unemployment.

voluntary winding-up *see under* winding-up.

vostro account BKG. (*Italian*, your account) the account of a bank with an agent or correspondent in a foreign country and recorded in the currency of the bank's own country. The expression means 'your account with us in the currency of our country'. Cf. loro account; nostro account.

vote *v.* to make a formal expression of one's choice or wish, such as in electing a person to an office, or in choosing the winner of a competition, or in deciding for or against a proposal. Voting may be organized in various ways: by voice, each voter calling Aye (yes) or Nay (no); by a show of hands; by a poll; by ballot; or by division, the voters being separated into groups. In each case the votes for and the votes against are counted and the decision is that for which the greatest number of votes were given. *To vote for or against.*
n. (1) the act of expressing a choice or wish by voting: *To take a vote of the members.* (2) a right to vote: *Each share carries a vote.*

casting vote *see under* casting.

voteless share *see* non-voting share *under* share.

voting share *see under* share.

voucher (1) ACCTS. a receipt for money paid. (2) any document that proves or supports an entry in the accounts, e.g. a petty-cash voucher.

gift voucher *see* gift token.

luncheon voucher *see* luncheon.

tax voucher *see* dividend warrant.

vouching ACCTS. the responsibility of an auditor in carefully checking all vouchers and other documents, such as invoices, that prove or support the accuracy of entries in the accounts and that provide authority, esp. for payments made by the business.

voyage SHIPG. a journey made by a ship, from the moment she sails from one port to the moment she enters another port. *Syn.* passage.

voyage charter *see under* charter.

voyage policy *see under* insurance policy.

V.P.P. value payable post (India).

vs. versus.

Vt. Vermont, U.S.A.

W

W winter loading (on load-line); watt.

W. West.

W.A. with average.

WAG Gambia's international vehicle-registration letters.

wage *sing.* (1) money paid for human work. (2) the price paid for work, based on hourly, daily,

weekly or piece-work rates: *The daily wage of a temporary worker is £10. He receives a wage of £50 a week. See also* wages, *pl.*

basic wage the amount on which the wages earned by a worker are calculated. *See* basic wage rate.

gross wage the total amount earned during a period, including bonuses, overtime and any special payments, before any deductions are made. Cf. net wage.

guaranteed wage an agreement between employers and trade unions by which workers in an industry are guaranteed (promised) a minimum amount of wages each week, whether or not there is work for them to do.

incentive wage any system of wages in which the earnings of the worker vary according to his output, or productivity, such as piece-work, or a bonus system.

living wage *see* living.

minimum wage *see under* minimum.

net wage the gross wage reduced by all deductions, such as for P.A.Y.E., income tax, national insurance contributions, pension fund contributions and union dues.

piece wage *see* piece-work.

time wage *see* time-work.

wage-ceiling *see under* ceiling.

wage differential *see* differential pay.

wage drift MAN. & IND. REL. the difference between the basic wage or wage-rate and the total earnings of a worker, including any bonus and overtime payments.

wage-earner IND. & COM. a person who works for a wage, as opposed to a person who is paid a salary. *Syn.* (U.S.A.) wageworker.

wage freeze *see under* freeze.

Wage-Fund Theory *see* Wages-Fund Theory.

wage-packet (1) the envelope in which a worker is given his wages on pay day, usu. weekly. (2) a general expression for the amount of money people actually receive in wages after deductions. *See* take-home pay.

wage-price spiral *see* inflationary spiral.

wager *see* bet.

wagering contract *see under* contract.

wager policy INSCE. an insurance policy in which one of the parties has no insurable interest. Such a policy is a wagering contract and will not be held by a court of law to be binding on the insurer. Cf. aleatory insurance.

wages *pl.* (1) regular income from employment, usu. paid weekly in an envelope, but perh. daily for casual or temporary workers. (2) the earnings of weekly-paid employees who work with their hands or do the simpler jobs in an office, as opposed to monthly salaries earned by supervisors and managers. (3) ECON. THEORY the price or reward of labour considered as one of the factors of production. Cf. rent; interest. (4) income from all forms of employment, including the salaries, commission, etc. of supervisors and managers.

fair wages the rates of wages ruling in a particular trade in the area where the work is done. *See* fair wages clause.

money wages the amount of actual money received or paid as wages, as opposed to the real wages (i.e. the amount of goods and services that money wages will buy).

nominal wages money wages, not real wages.

real wages the amount of goods and services that can be bought with a worker's money wages.

wages clerk MAN. a clerk employed in an office to deal with the complicated work of paying the employees their wages or salaries and of keeping detailed records of such payments. *Syn.* pay-roll clerk.

wages floor *see under* floor.

Wages-Fund Theory ECON. THEORY a view held by a number of classical economists in the early nineteenth century, that since wages must be paid before the product is sold, the money must come out of a fund of the national capital, called the wages fund. It was thought that the size of the fund was fixed by the amount of the national capital, and it followed that the average wage was therefore determined by the number of workers in the population; there could be a general increase in wages only if there were fewer workers or if profits were reduced. Since the population was then increasing, wages ought, by this reasoning, to have fallen to around subsistence level, but this was clearly not happening. The theory was proved to be basically false because there is no fixed wages fund.

Wages, Iron Law of *see* Subsistence Theory of Wages.

Wages, Marginal Productivity Theory of *see under* Marginal.

Wages, Minimum of Existence Theory of *see* Subsistence Theory of Wages.

wages of management ECON. THEORY in a business enterprise, that part of the total profit that can be considered as being due to the owner or entrepreneur for his work in managing the enterprise. They are the wages that he could command if he hired his services as manager to another enterprise of a similar size and nature. *Syn.* earnings of management.

wages sheet *see* pay-roll (1).

Wages, Subsistence Theory of *see under* Subsistence.

Wages Theory ECON. THEORY that branch of economics that attempts to explain what influences determine the general level of wages, and why wages vary in different industries and places. The three main wage theories are: the Subsistence Theory; the Wages-Fund Theory; and the Marginal Productivity Theory.

wageworker *see* wage-earner.

waggon *see* wagon.

wagon *n.* TRANSPT. (1) any large road vehicle with four wheels, usu. drawn by horses, for carrying large or heavy loads of goods. (2) a railway goods-vehicle, esp. an open truck or a closed van. *Also* waggon.
v. to travel by wagon; to move goods by wagon.

wagonage TRANSPT. (1) the carriage of goods by wagon. (2) the charge made for this.

wagon-lit TRANSPT. & TOUR. on the continent of Europe, a railway sleeping-car. *Pl.* wagons-lits. *Pron.* vagon-lee.

waiter (1) COM. a man who serves people with meals at table, esp. in a restaurant or hotel. *Fem.* waitress. (2) STK. EXCH. an attendant in uniform, employed by the Stock Exchange to carry messages, papers, etc. about the House.

waitress COM. a female waiter.

waive LAW to give up one's legal rights in a matter; to hold back from pressing a right or claim. *He waived his* (*right to a*) *commission on the profits.*

waiver LAW the act of waiving, of giving up a right or not pressing a claim. *See* discharge of contract.

WAL Sierra Leone's international vehicle-registration letters.

wallet (1) a note-case. *Syn.* (U.S.A.) a billfold. (2) an envelope that opens on the longer side. Cf. pocket.

Wall Street STK. EXCH. a popular name for the New York Stock Exchange, which is situated in Wall Street in New York. The expression sometimes includes also the various financial institutions such as banks and the money market which are grouped in and around Wall Street. The expression is the American equivalent of 'The City', meaning the City of London. *Syn.* The Street.

Walras Marie-Esprit Léon (1834–1910), French economist and reformer, Professor of Political Economy at Lausanne, in Switzerland. He was one of the first to use mathematics in economic analysis, developing (independently of Jevons and Menger) a marginal utility theory of value. His greatest contribution to economics was his analysis of the automatic tendency in the economy towards a state of general equilibrium. His chief book was *Éléments d'Économie Politique Pure* (*Elements of Pure Economics*) (1874–7).

WAN Nigeria's international vehicle-registration letters.

want ECON. THEORY a desire for a commodity or service to satisfy a human need or wish. Only those wants are of interest to the economist that are satisfied by spending purchasing power, and it is these wants that are the basis of effective demand.

ward (1) LAW in Britain, an infant in the care and protection of a guardian. Such a person is *in ward: A child in ward.*
ward of court *see* ward in chancery *under* Chancery.
(2) one of the districts into which a town or city is divided for administrative purposes, such as electing councillors.
warden a person having responsibility for keeping or managing some place or organization such as a port, a college, or a hostel. Cf. warder. *See also* traffic warden.
warder a person employed to guard prisoners in a prison. Cf. warden. *Fem.* wardress.
ware COM. formerly goods for sale as merchandise; now combined with another word: *Hardware, stoneware, silverware, kitchenware,* things used in a house, home, restaurant, etc.
wares *pl.* articles for sale, esp. if carried by a travelling seller such as a hawker or pedlar.
warehouse COM. & IND. (1) a room or building for storing wares, i.e. goods intended for sale as merchandise. (2) any place where other goods, not necessarily intended for sale, may be stored, such as a furniture warehouse. *Syn.* depot; store; stores; godown.
bonded warehouse *see under* bonded.
customs warehouse *see* bonded warehouse.
queen's warehouse in Britain, a warehouse belonging to, or approved by, the government, in which crown property is stored, as well as privately-owned goods such as passengers' baggage, and ships' stores.
uptown warehouse a bonded warehouse that is some distance away from the port area of a seaport.
warehouse-keeper COM. a person responsible for the safe keeping of goods in a warehouse. He is in the position of a bailee, and must take good care of them. He has a lien on the goods for the price of their storage.
warehouse-keeper's order COM. & TAXN. a formal order signed by a customs officer to a warehouse-keeper authorizing the release of bonded goods usu. to a licensed carman or lighterman for removal to a ship for re-export. The order usu. takes the form of a slip joined to a bond warrant. *Syn.* warehouseman's order.
warehouse-keeper's receipt COM. a signed receipt declaring that the goods stated in it are held in a public warehouse. It is a document of title but is not negotiable. *Syn.* warehouse receipt; warehouse-keeper's certificate; (U.S.A.) non-negotiable warehouse receipt.
warehouseman (1) a man employed in a warehouse. (2) a person in charge of a warehouse, *see* warehouse-keeper.
warehouse price *see* spot price *under* price.
warehouse receipt *see* warehouse-keeper's receipt.

warehouse warrant *see* bond warrant; dock warrant.
warehousing COM. & IND. a charge made for storing goods in a warehouse, usu. based on the amount of floor space or cubic space taken. *Syn.* storage (charge).
warehousing entry *see under* customs entry.
Warks. Warwickshire, England.
warrant *n.* (1) a formal document that gives somebody legal authority to do something: *A dividend warrant,* an authority to a bank to pay a dividend. (2) COM. a receipt for goods stored in a public warehouse. (3) LAW a document signed by a magistrate authorizing an officer of the court or the police to arrest a person, or to make a search of a named place, or to seize property that may have been stolen or unlawfully hidden, etc.
bond warrant *see under* bond.
deferred interest warrant *see* deferred interest certificate.
deposit warrant *see* dock warrant.
distress warrant a document authorizing an officer of the court to seize goods to obtain payment of rent, rates, taxes in arrear, or unpaid fines.
dividend warrant *see under* dividend.
dock warrant *see under* dock.
duplicate warrant *see* entry for free goods *under* customs entry.
general warrant a warrant for the arrest of any person or persons suspected of a crime, without the name of any person being given in the warrant.
interest warrant a warrant, or order to a banker, to pay a stated sum as interest on government stock or on debentures and similar securities. Cf. dividend warrant; deferred interest warrant.
search warrant a legal authority given by a magistrate to the police to search a place for property that may have been stolen, or may have been hidden by a bankrupt to avoid having to give it to his creditors.
share warrant STK. EXCH. a legal document, issued by a company to a member shareholder, declaring that the bearer of the document has the right to a stated number of fully-paid shares in the company. The name of the member to whom the warrant is issued is not mentioned. The document is a negotiable instrument.
stock warrant *see* stock certificate.
Treasury warrant in Britain, an order issued by the Treasury for the payment of money owing by the Exchequer.
warehouse warrant *see* bond warrant; dock warrant.
wharfinger's warrant *see* dock warrant.
v. (1) to assure or promise firmly. (2) to guarantee.

warranted COM. & IND. guaranteed by the manufacturers: *Warranted 18 carat gold. Warranted free from impurities. Abbr.* wd.; w/d.; Wtd.

warrant of attachment LAW a court order authorizing property to be seized. *See* attachment (2).

warrant of attorney LAW a document signed by a debtor authorizing his solicitor (the attorney) to appear in court and to allow judgment to be made against the debtor. A person lending money sometimes demands such a document as security, on the condition that it will be used only if the debtor fails to repay the loan by the agreed date.

warrantee a person to whom a warranty is given.

warrantor a person who gives a warranty. *Also* warranter.

warranty (1) LAW in a contract, a promise or binding statement which is not essential to the main purpose of the contract, so that a failure to honour a warranty does not cause the contract to be ended but may give the other party good reason to claim damages for breach of warranty. Cf. condition. (2) INSCE. a statement made by the insured declaring that facts given by him are true and that the insurance contract may be void if any of these facts prove to be untrue. (3) COM. a promise or statement by the seller to the buyer concerning the quality of goods or their fitness for a particular purpose. *Without warranty*, the goods are being sold on the condition that the seller has no responsibility for any faults or imperfections in the goods, and that the buyer has no right to return them or to claim damages or any other remedy.

express warranty one that is clearly stated in the contract document, e.g. that certain things will or will not be done, such as that an insured ship will not sail certain seas in winter, or will not carry certain kinds of cargo.

implied warranty, one that is not written in the contract document but which both parties understand to be included in the agreement, and feel bound by, e.g. that the purpose of the contract is allowed by law.

Wash. Washington, U.S.A.

washeteria *see* launderette.

wastage (1) loss by wasting. (2) an amount wasted. (3) the act of wasting, of being wasteful.

waste (1) LAW neglect of, or damage to, leased property by the tenant. (2) ECON. failure by an entrepreneur to use resources in such a way as to produce the greatest possible satisfaction of wants; waste would not have happened if the entrepreneur had used his resources more wisely. (3) IND. useless material that is produced in the course of a manufacturing process. *See* waste product. (4) in mining, rock dug from a mine but having no mineral content. *Syn.* spoil.

waste product IND. a substance produced in the course of a manufacturing process and regarded by the manufacturer as useless for his purposes, but of value to other users, e.g. cotton-waste to cleaners and mechanics.

wasting assets *see under* assets.

watch SHIPG. (1) one of the two-hour or four-hour periods of duty kept (worked) by sailors at sea. (2) the group of sailors who keep watch during the same period.

water (1) SHIPG. the times of high and low tide, *see* high water; low water. (2) COM. (*colloq.*) *To be in deep water*, in financial trouble. (3) COM. (*colloq.*) *To spend money like water*, to spend freely, wastefully.

waters *pl.* an area of water, esp. at sea. *In British/French waters. In coastal/inshore waters*, sea areas near the coast. *See* territorial waters.

waterage TRANSPT. (1) the carriage and delivery of goods by barge or boat, esp. on waterways such as rivers and canals. (2) the charge made for this.

watered stock STK. EXCH. (1) shares in a company that has raised its issued capital to a figure much greater than the value of its tangible assets. (2) shares in a company that has increased its issued capital by making only book entries, without obtaining any additional capital in the form of money. (3) loan stock in a company that has increased the amount of its loan capital without making proper provision for paying the additional interest.

watering-place TOUR. (1) a seaside resort. (2) a place where people go to drink the local water to cure an illness. *Syn.* spa.

water-line SHIPG. the level of the water along the side of a floating ship. *See* load-line.

water power IND. the force of moving or falling water used to drive machinery. *See* hydroelectric power.

waterways *see* inland waterways.

watt (W) the SI unit of power, being one joule per second. 745.70 W = 1 horsepower (hp).

W. Aus., W. Austr. Western Australia.

way-bill TRANSPT. in inland road, rail and air transport, a document that is both a receipt for goods and a record of the existence of a contract of carriage. The carrier makes three copies, keeps one, gives one to the consignor, and gives the third to the consignee when the goods are delivered. It is not a bill of lading and is not negotiable. *Also* waybill. *Syn.* consignment note. *Abbr.* W.B.

way-leave LAW (1) a right of way to walk or drive over land belonging to another person. (2) (*a*) permission to place things in, on or over another person's land, such as drains, waterpipes, telephone, telegraph and electric power lines, roads, railways, ropeways. (*b*) the money paid for such permission.

ways and means FIN. (1) the organization and money needed to carry out a planned object: *Let us discuss the ways and means of building a village hall.* (2) methods and laws for raising money for the purposes of government.

Committee of Ways and Means in Britain, a committee of the House of Commons that controls the country's finances, esp. the ways in which the government obtains its money. The committee considers in great detail, before they are passed by Parliament, all taxes that need to be renewed annually, or that are being increased or otherwise changed. It also authorizes payments to be made out of the Consolidated Fund.

ways-and-means advances FIN. short-term loans by the Bank of England, and sometimes also by government departments, to the Treasury to meet temporary gaps in the receipt of revenue by the Exchequer.

W.B. way-bill.

w.c. without charge.

WD Dominica's international vehicle-registration letters.

wd., w/d. warranted.

W.D. War Department.

weak STK. EXCH. of market conditions, prices falling because demand is small and supplies are plentiful. *Opp.* strong.

wealth ECON. (1) a stock of goods that are useful, scarce, and can be exchanged for a money price. *See also* accession; redistribution. (2) the state of being rich, of having a great store of valuable possessions: *He is a man of wealth*, he is rich. *Developed countries ought to share their wealth with the less developed. Opp.* poverty. *Syn.* affluence; riches.

national wealth *see* national capital *under* capital.

wealthy *adj.* rich, affluent.

Wealth of Nations *see* Smith, Adam.

wealth, redistribution of *see* redistribution.

wealth tax *see under* tax.

wear COM. & IND. goods for wearing; now usu. combined with another word: *Men's/women's/children's wear. Footwear*, boots and shoes, socks and stockings. *Underwear*, underclothes. *Winter/summer/sports/beach/evening/night wear.*

wear and tear ACCTS. & MAN. the reduction in the value of buildings, machinery and other capital assets caused by ordinary use and the passing of time.

weather insurance *see under* insurance, classes and kinds of; *also* pluvius insurance.

weather side SHIPG. the windward side of a ship. *Opp.* lee side.

weather theory *see* trade cycle theories *under* cycle.

Weekly Earnings, Index of *see under* Index.

weekly return *see* bank return.

weighbridge TRANSPT. a machine for weighing vehicles and their loads.

weight (1) the quality of heaviness caused by gravity (the pull of the earth). (2) the measure of how heavy something is: *The weight of the parcel is 10 kg.* (3) any system of units for measuring and expressing heaviness: *Avoirdupois weight; troy weight.* (4) a unit of weight: *A pound; a kilogram.* (5) a metal object made to an exact weight, for use as a standard when weighing articles, commodities or substances generally. (6) (*fig.*) a great amount of worry: *You have taken a weight off my mind.*

dead weight *see under* dead. *See also* dead-weight.

gross weight the full weight of a package before taking off any allowance for packing, etc. Cf. net weight. *Abbr.* gr. wt.

net weight the actual weight of the goods, without packing or any kind of container. Cf. gross weight. *Abbr.* Nt. wt.; n. wt.

weighted average in statistical calculations, an arithmetical mean that gives each item its proper weight or importance. The weighted average is calculated by first multiplying each item by a weight according to its importance relative to the other items, then totalling these products and dividing by the total of the weights. For example, an investor buys three parcels of shares: 600 shares at 50p, 100 at 45p, 300 at 40p. To find the weighted average price, he uses as weights the number of shares bought at each price: $600 \times 50, 100 \times 45, 300 \times 40 = 30000 + 4500 + 12000 = 46500$. The total of the weights is $600 + 100 + 300 = 1000$. The weighted average price is $\frac{46500}{1000} = 46.5\text{p}$. By comparison, the simple (unweighted) average price is $50 + 45 + 40 = \frac{135}{3} = 45\text{p}$. By weighting, proper importance is given to the greater number of shares bought at the highest price.

weighted index *see under* index number(s).

weighting in the calculation of averages, esp. those needed for index numbers, the method of giving a higher value to items that are judged more important than others so that their price or cost movements have a bigger effect on the index number. *See* weighted average; index number(s).

weight note COM. & TRANSPT. a document given by a dock company or authority stating the exact weight, size and other details of a consignment of imported goods at the time it is unloaded from the ship.

weights and measures *see* avoirdupois weight; corn and dry measure; cubic or solid measure; hay and straw measure; linear measure; paper measure; square measure; surveyor's measure; troy weight; *also tables on pages 475–80.*

Weights and Measures, International Bureau of *see under* International.

weight ton *see* long ton *under* ton.

welfare ECON. a condition of general happiness and well-being, when Man enjoys good health, comfortable living, rewarding work, personal freedom and security from unemployment.

welfare economics *see under* economics.

welfare state a name given to a social system in which the government is responsible for looking after the welfare of the people, esp. in matters of social security, education, health and housing.

well off having enough money to live comfortably; fairly, but not very, rich: *They have two cars and a boat so they must be well off. Syn.* well to do; comfortably off.

well to do *see* well off.

welsh v. (*colloq.*) (1) of a bookmaker, to cheat by leaving without paying what he owes to persons who have bets placed with him. (2) generally, to go away without paying one's debts. *N.* welsher.

West End an important district in the middle of London, in which there are many good shops, theatres, hotels and offices, and expensive houses and flats.

West(ern) European Time (W.E.T.) a name sometimes given to Greenwich Mean Time (G.M.T.) to distinguish it from East(ern) European Time (E.E.T.), which is two hours ahead of G.M.T., and Central European Time, which is one hour ahead of G.M.T.

Western Samoa an independent island state in the south-west Pacific Ocean, pop. 160,000 approx. (1975); capital, Apia, pop. 35,000 approx.; languages, English and Samoan; currency unit, the tala or Western Samoan dollar, divided into 100 cents.

West Germany *see under* Germany, Federal Republic of.

W.E.T. West(ern) European Time.

wet dock SHIPG. a dock in which the water is kept continuously at the same level by means of locks or gates. This makes it possible for ships to load and unload cargoes at any time. Cf. dry dock.

wet goods COM. goods that are of a liquid nature and are packed in bottles or barrels. Cf. dry goods.

wey AGR. in Britain, (*a*) a measure of corn, *see* corn and dry measure *table on page 477*. (*b*) a measure of wool, 6½ tods of 28 lb or 182 lb (82.554 kg). 2 weys = 1 sack of wool, 364 lb (165.108 kg).

Wf. wharf.

W.F.T.U. World Federation of Trade Unions.

WG Granada's international vehicle-registration letters.

wharf SHIPG. a quay provided with sheds (buildings for storing goods) and other essential ser-

vices including Customs, water and fuel supplies, telephones, cranes, railway and road arrangements, etc. *See* quay. *Pl.* wharves *or* wharfs. *Abbr.* Wf.; Whf. *Pron.* worf, worvz.

sufferance wharf a place in a port where the customs authorities allow ships to load and unload dutiable goods under a bill of sufferance.

wharfage SHIPG. (1) the payment that a shipowner has to make for using a wharf. (2) the charge for storing goods at a wharf. *Syn.* wharf dues.

wharf dues *see* wharfage.

wharfinger SHIPG. a person or organization that owns or manages a wharf. *Pron.* worfinjer.

wharfinger's receipt *see under* receipt.

wharfinger's warrant *see* dock warrant.

wheeler-dealer COM. a popular name for a clever, forceful businessman who is too ready to use unfair means to get what he wants in his dealings with others.

wherewithal the money and other things needed for making or doing something: *He has not the wherewithal to start his own business,* he has not the necessary amount of capital.

Whf. wharf.

white coal IND. moving or falling water, when used as a means of power to drive machinery. Hydro-electric power.

white-collar workers IND. office workers (in reference to their clean working clothes). Cf. blue-collar workers. *Syn.* black-coated workers, blackcoats.

white goods (U.S.A.) white household fabrics like sheets, towels, etc. and equipment such as refrigerators, washing machines.

Whitehall (1) a street in central London in which there are many government offices. (2) the British Government or its policy. Cf. White House.

White House (1) the official residence of the President of the United States of America. (2) the American Government or its policy. Cf. Whitehall.

white paper (1) LAW an official report of the British Government on a matter of public interest, esp. one being considered by Parliament. (2) BKG. *see* fine paper.

white sale *see under* sale.

Whitsun *see* quarter-day.

whizz-kid a bright young person with a quick and inventive mind, who becomes highly successful, esp. in business.

W.H.O. World Health Organization.

whole-life policy *see under* insurance policy.

wholesale COM. the sale of goods in large quantities, esp. to retailers or jobbers, not to consumers: *To buy and sell by wholesale,* in large quantities, on a large scale, not in small amounts. Cf. retail.

wholesale co-operative *see under* co-operative.

wholesale price *see under* price.

wholesaler COM. a person or company dealing only in large quantities of goods, buying in bulk from producers, manufacturers, importers and other wholesalers, and selling in smaller quantities to shopkeepers. Cf. retailer. *Syn.* merchant.

wholesale trade *see under* trade.

wide price *see under* price.

wider-range investments *see* trustee investments.

widow's pension *see under* pension.

wife's earned income allowance TAXN. in Britain, a married taxpayer whose wife earns an income will be allowed a certain amount of her earnings free of tax, in addition to the married man's personal allowance.

wildcat COM. & MAN. of a business, managed irresponsibly, taking unreasonable risks without providing for the possibility of loss: *A wildcat enterprise/scheme.*

wildcat strike *see under* strike.

will LAW a formal document in which a person states how and by whom he wishes his possessions to be distributed after his death. The person making the will is called the *testator*; any person appointed by him to administer his affairs after his death is called an *executor*, or if female, an *executrix*; the possessions left by the testator form his *estate*; and the person or persons receiving gifts of property of any kind under the will are *heirs, legatees* and *beneficiaries. Syn.* testament.

will, tenant at *see under* tenant.

Wilts. Wiltshire, England.

Winchester bushel *see* bushel.

windfall FIN. (1) money or property received or gained unexpectedly; a piece of good fortune: *A windfall gift/legacy.* (2) a financial result that was not foreseen: *A windfall profit/loss,* due usu. to an unexpected change in prices. *See* windfall profit *under* profit.

winding-up LAW & STK. EXCH. the process of bringing to an end the existence of a company or a partnership, and the settling of its affairs, i.e. the sale of its assets, the payment of its debts, and the division of any surplus among the members. *Syn.* liquidation.

compulsory winding-up *see under* compulsory.

voluntary winding-up (*a*) of a partnership, the ending of the firm by agreement between the partners. (*b*) of a company, the ending of the company by agreement between the members, usu. without the supervision of the court; or by the creditors acting together as a group, usu. with, but sometimes without, the supervision of the court. *See* liquidation; liquidator. *Syn.* voluntary liquidation.

winding-up sale *see* forced sale *under* sale.

windjammer SHIPG. a sailing ship.

window-dressing (1) COM. the act of making a show of goods in a shop window to attract customers. (2) FIN. the unfair practice of making a business matter look attractive by hiding its faults and difficulties.

window-shopping COM. the practice of some members of the public who find it amusing to look at goods in shop windows but do not buy anything.

wind up LAW & STK. EXCH. to close; to bring to an end the existence of a partnership or company. *See* winding-up.

windward SHIPG. of a ship, on or towards the side that is facing the wind. *Syn.* weather side. *Opp.* leeward; lee side.

W.I.P. work(s) in progress.

wire *n.* (*colloq.*) a telegram.
  v. (*colloq.*) to send a telegram.

wireless radio: *A wireless message,* a message sent by radio.

Wis. Wisconsin, U.S.A.

with average MAR. INSCE. words on a marine insurance policy that covers all particular average losses, to show that a special rate of premium is payable because the risk borne by the underwriter is higher than for a policy that does not cover average losses. *See* average (4). *Abbr.* W.A.

withdraw *v.* BKG. to take out, to draw out, esp. money deposited in a bank. *Opp.* to deposit.

withdrawal *n.* (1) the act of withdrawing money from a bank account. (2) an amount of money so withdrawn. *Opp.* deposit.

without engagement COM. words used by a seller when making a quotation to supply goods, esp. for export, meaning that the prices quoted are not binding on the seller and are liable to change without notice.

without prejudice LAW without harming any existing right or claim; words which may appear at the top of a document, such as a solicitor's letter, when the writer wishes to make it clear that he is not to be considered finally bound by the contents of the document, e.g. an offer to settle a disagreement. The words may also mean that the writer is agreeing to do something on this occasion, e.g. pay a claim, but that he is not to be considered bound to do the same on similar occasions in future. A letter headed *without prejudice* cannot be used in such a way as to harm the interests of either party to a negotiation or a disagreement.

without-profits policy *see under* insurance policy.

without recourse *see under* recourse.

with rights *see* cum rights *under* cum.

witness summons *see* subpoena.

Wk., wk. week.

WL St Lucia's international vehicle-registration letters.

W/M weight or measurement.

WNA winter North Atlantic loading (on load-line).

w/o without.

w.o. wireless operator; written order.

w.o.b. washed overboard.

w.o.c. without compensation.

w.o.g. with other goods.

won the standard currency unit of South Korea, divided into 100 chon. *Also* hwan.

Worcs. Worcestershire, a former county in England, now part of the new county of Hereford and Worcester.

words and figures do not agree BKG. & LAW a note written or stamped on a cheque or other document or instrument of payment. Some bankers pay the lower amount; others pay the amount stated in words; and others refuse payment, and refer the payee to the drawer. *See* amounts differ.

work-day *see* working day.

worker participation *see* co-ownership.

working account *see* trading account.

working capital *see under* capital.

working class that part of the population that consists mainly of labourers and other workers who work with their hands, as opposed to the middle and professional classes who work mainly with their brains.
working-class adj. *He comes from a working-class home.*

working couple a man and his wife who are employed to work together in domestic service, the man usu. as a butler or a valet, the woman as a cook or a maid.

working day (1) the hours during which work is done, e.g. in an office or factory. (2) a day on which people work, as opposed to a holiday. *Syn.* work-day.

working expenses *see* overhead expenses *under* expenses.

working man/woman a person who works, esp. with his or her hands.

working partner *see* acting partner *under* partner.

working population ECON. the number of persons in a country who have a job at a given time.

work in process (U.S.A.) *see* work(s) in progress.

work(s) in progress ACCTS. the value of goods in the course of manufacture, i.e. of goods only partly completed, at the end of the accounting year. *Syn.* (U.S.A.) work in process; goods in progress. *Abbr.* W.I.P.

work load *see under* load (2).

workman (1) a man who works, esp. with his hands. (2) a worker who is skilled in one of the industrial arts such as carpentry, metal work, plumbing and painting. A skilled tradesman.

workmanlike IND. done with skill: *A workmanlike piece of furniture*, well made.

workmanship IND. (1) the skill of a specialized workman. (2) the quality of the work done in making something: *Shoes of excellent/poor workmanship.*

work measurement MAN. & IND. the process of measuring and calculating the time taken by a qualified worker to do a certain job of work to a fixed standard or quality. Cf. work study.

workmen's compensation *see under* compensation.

work permit *see under* permit.

works pl. IND. a factory or workshop.

work, sale of *see* sale of work.

works manager *see under* manager.

work study *see* method study.

work-to-rule IND. REL. a means used by employees of putting pressure on their employer by refusing to work overtime, by working slowly, and by keeping strictly to the factory's rules or other rules.

World Bank *see* International Bank for Reconstruction and Development.

World Federation of Trade Unions (W.F.T.U.) IND. REL. an international labour organization, with its offices in Prague, Czechoslovakia, to which belong the national labour federations mainly of the communist countries of Eastern Europe led by the U.S.S.R. Cf. International Confederation of Free Trade Unions.

World Health Organization (W.H.O.) a special agency of the United Nations, with its offices in Geneva. Its purpose is to improve the health of the peoples of the world, to control diseases by training workers, by giving guidance to governments and by collecting and spreading useful information on health problems.

world language *see under* language.

world money *see under* money.

worn coinage *see* debasement of coinage.

worth adj. (1) having an amount of value in exchange: *This article is worth £5/a fortune/its weight in gold. One share in Company A is worth three shares in Company B. She is not worth her keep*, her services are not worth the cost of her wages. (2) of relative value: *Your plan is worth studying. The ship is not worth repairing. The journey is not worth the trouble and expense of making it.*
n. (1) quality; excellence: *A man of worth. A jewel of the highest worth.* (2) value measured in units of money: *We give good money's worth*, good value for your money. (3) the value of the assets or capital of a business.

money's worth *see* money.

net worth *see under* net.

present worth *see* present value.

total worth *see* assets value.

worthless having no value or worth: *A worthless cheque*, a cheque that is returned unpaid. *A worthless venture*, an unprofitable enterprise.

worth while adv. profitable, rewarding: *The work would not be worth while*, not worth the time spent on it.

worthwhile *adj.* worth the time or trouble needed: *A worthwhile journey.*

W.P., w.p. without prejudice; weather permitting.

W.P.A. with particular average.

W.R. warehouse receipt.

wrapping light materials used for covering and packing goods, esp. paper, cardboard, cloth, sacking, plastics.

gift-wrapping *see under* gift.

wreck (1) SHIPG. a ship that has been abandoned (left with nobody on board) at sea and has been driven on shore or has sunk to the bottom. (2) MAR. INSCE. an insured thing, esp. a ship, that is so badly damaged that it can no longer be used for its intended purpose.

wreckage TRANSPT. & SHIPG. (1) goods driven on shore from a wrecked ship. (2) broken pieces of a wrecked ship or aircraft. Cf. flotsam; jetsam.

writ LAW in Britain, a document issued by an official of a court of law in the name of the monarch, commanding the person to whom it is addressed to do, or to stop doing, some stated act. A *writ of summons* is a writ issued by the High Court at the request of a plaintiff as the first step in a lawsuit; it commands the defendant to appear before the court and to give an answer to the claim, unless he decides to admit it. A *writ of execution* is a writ issued for the purpose of putting into effect a judgment of the court by forcing the defendant to pay or to perform what the court has commanded; it is usu. addressed to one of the court's officers, ordering him to do some act, such as to seize some stated property.

service of writs *see* service of process.

write (1) INSCE. to underwrite insurance business, i.e. to accept liability under an insurance contract: *He has written £1 million of insurance this month*, he has made insurance contracts for this amount. (2) COMP. to introduce or feed new information into the storage section of a computer.

write back *v.* ACCTS. to take action which is the opposite to writing off or writing down; this becomes necessary when an asset which has been written off is unexpectedly found not to be valueless, such as when a debt which was taken as bad is, after all, paid. *N.* a write-back. *See* write off; write down.

write down *v.* ACCTS. to reduce, but not wholly to wipe out, the book value of an asset. *N.* a write-down. *See* write off; write back.

write off *v.* (1) ACCTS. to reduce to nothing the book value of an asset that has become valueless, such as an unfortunate investment, a lease that has come to an end, or machinery that is worn out. Bad debts are written off by debiting them to a bad debts account, the balance of which will later be debited to the profit and loss account as a reduction of the profit. *See* write down; write back. (2) MAN. to abandon, to treat as useless, a plan or project.

a write-off *n.* an amount written off; a thing abandoned.

writer (1) LAW in Scotland, a writer to the signet, a lawyer similar to a solicitor in England. *Abbr.* W.S. (2) INSCE. an underwriter of insurance risks. (3) MAN. a clerk employed in an office. (4) SHIPG. a clerk employed on board ship.

wrong LAW an unjust act, esp. an act that harms, offends or interferes with a right. If it offends the right of a private person it is a *private wrong* or *tort*; if it offends a public right it is a *public wrong* or *crime against the community*.

wrongful LAW that which is wrong; that offends the law; unlawful.

wrongful dismissal MAN. & LAW the act of dismissing an employee for a reason that is not admissible or serious enough to deserve such treatment.

WS Western Samoa's international vehicle-registration letters.

W.S. writer to the signet.

wt. weight.

Wtd. warranted.

WV St Vincent's international vehicle-registration letters.

W. Va. West Virginia, U.S.A.

W/W warehouse warrant.

Wy., Wyo. Wyoming, U.S.A.

X

x ex, excluding.

x.a. ex all, excluding all benefits.

x.b. ex bonus, excluding bonus shares.

x.c. ex cap, excluding capitalization.

x.cp. ex coupon, excluding coupon.

x.d., ex dist., x.dist. ex distribution, excluding distribution.

x.d., ex div., x.div. ex dividend, excluding dividend.

Xerox process a quick method of making copies of documents, drawings, etc., by xerography.

x.in. ex interest, excluding interest.

x. new ex new, excluding new share issue.

x.r. ex rights, excluding rights.

xs. excess.

xu a fractional currency unit of Vietnam. 100 xu or 10 hao = 1 dong.

Y

Y. yuan.

Y/A. York-Antwerp (Rules).

yacht SHIPG. a privately-owned boat or small ship used for pleasure such as racing or cruising, not for commerce. *Pron.* yot.

yachting TOUR. (1) the sport of sailing a yacht. (2) the practice of travelling or touring by yacht. *Pron.* yotting.

yachtsman SHIPG. & TOUR. a person who sails or owns a yacht. *Pron.* yotsman.

Yankee (1) a person from New England, U.S.A. (2) a person from any of the northern states of the U.S.A. (3) a popular word for any citizen of the U.S.A. *Abbr.* Yank.

Yankees STK. EXCH. stocks and shares in companies in the U.S.A.

Y.A.R. York-Antwerp Rules.

yard (1) a common measure of length in Britain, U.S.A. and some other English-speaking countries, equal to 0.9144 metres and consisting of 3 feet or 36 inches. *See* linear measure *table on page 475. Abbr.* yd. (2) enclosed ground near or around a building, or where some special activity takes place: *A railway marshalling yard*, a special area with many railway lines where carriages and wagons are made up into trains. *See also* shipyard.

junk yard *see* junk.

timber yard a place where timber is stored and sold.

yard-goods *see* piece-goods.

yardstick (1) a stick of wood 1 yard long, usu. marked in 36 divisions of 1 inch each, used esp. for measuring cloth. (2) (*fig.*) a standard, a model, or example with which other things can be compared or measured.

Y/A Rules York–Antwerp Rules.

YD Yemeni dinar.

yd. yard.

year a period of 365/366 days reckoned by the sun, *see* calendar year *below*; or of 354 days reckoned by the moon, *see* lunar year *below*.

accounting year the period of 12 months covered by the annual accounts of an organization. *See* accounting period.

calendar year the year of 12 months or 365 or 366 days from 1 January to 31 December. *See* calendar.

financial year *see under* financial.

fiscal year *see under* fiscal. *Syn.* tax year.

leap year a calendar year coming every fourth year, containing 366 days, the extra day being put at the end of February.

lunar year a period of about 354 days, consisting of 12 lunar months each of about 29½ days, reckoned by the moon.

sabbatical year *see* sabbatical leave *under* leave.

tax year in Britain, the government financial year, from 6 April in one year to 5 April in the next year. *Syn.* fiscal year.

yearbook a book, giving information on a subject or group of subjects, published once every year: *The Stock Exchange Yearbook.*

yearling bonds (yearlings) *see* local (authority) loans.

yearly tenancy *see* tenant from year to year.

years' purchase FIN. the value of a property or a business calculated by multiplying the annual income from rent or profits by a certain number of years, the number of years being related to the degree of risk in getting the future income. Thus the value of a house let at a rent of £1000 a year at 8 years' purchase is £8000, giving a yield of 10% or $12\frac{1}{2}\%$. The value of a business giving an average annual profit of £5000 at 3 years' purchase is £15,000, giving a yield of 10% or $33\frac{1}{3}\%$, which is high because of the future risks in a business.

years, tenant for *see under* tenant.

year to year, tenant from *see under* tenant.

Yellow Pages (*colloq.*) classified telephone directories which list businesses according to the goods or services they supply.

Yemen (Aden) *or* **South Yemen** a people's republic in the Arabian peninsula in south-west Asia, pop. 1.6 million approx. (1975); capital, Madinet al-Shaab, pop. 10,000 approx.; chief city, Aden, pop. 250,000; language, Arabic; currency unit, the South Yemeni dinar (YD), divided into 1000 fils. Member, Arab League.

Yemen(San'a) *or* **Northern Yemen** a republic in the Arabian peninsula in south-west Asia, pop. 6.5 million approx. (1975); capital, San'a, pop. 145,000 approx.; language, Arabic; currency unit, the Yemeni riyal, divided into 100 fils. Member, Arab League.

yen the standard currency unit of Japan, subdivided into 100 sen.

yield (1) that which is produced, esp. the produce of the soil or from work. (2) the amount of useful materials obtained from natural resources, such as water from springs, wells and rivers; minerals from mines; timber from forests; and fish from the sea. (3) STK. EXCH. the income received by an investor from a security, usu. expressed as a percentage of the money invested or of the current price of the security.

current yield of an investment, the income expressed as a percentage of its present market price.

dividend yield the gross income (i.e. before deduction of income tax) that a shareholder receives for each £100 that he has invested in a particular share.

earnings yield of a company, the proportion of the total profits available for distribution to the total value of the ordinary shares at the present market price.

flat yield the rate of interest earned by a fixed-interest security expressed as a percentage of the amount invested, no account being taken of any gain or loss arising on redemption. Cf. redemption yield. Thus the flat yield on £100 invested in 6% stock priced at £75 is $\frac{100}{75} \times 6 =$ 8%. *Syn.* flat rate.

gross yield the percentage return on an investment before income tax is paid.

nominal yield the rate of interest stated on the bond document of a fixed-interest security. The nominal yield of a 5% bond is £5 per £100 of its nominal value. Cf. true yield.

prospective yield the income expected from an investment.

redemption yield on a fixed-interest security, the current yield added to the capital profit that will be made on redemption (repayment) expressed as a percentage of the current market price of the security. If there will be a capital loss on redemption, this must be deducted from the current yield before calculating the percentage. The *net redemption yield* is the redemption yield calculated after deducting income tax payable on the current yield. *Syn.* yield to redemption.

true yield the annual income from a security expressed as a percentage of the current market price of the security. It may be calculated by the formula: yield per cent = $\frac{\text{nominal value}}{\text{market price}}$ × dividend per cent.

yield method *see* discounted cash flow.

yield to redemption *see* redemption yield *under* yield.

York-Antwerp Rules SHIPG. & MAR. INSCE. a set of rules made and accepted internationally by shipowners, underwriters, merchants and lawyers, relating to the adjustment (sharing) of general average losses. *See under* average (4).

Yorks. Yorkshire, England.

young person LAW in Britain, a person aged over 14 and under 17. Such persons cannot be punished by being sent to prison, but are sent for training at a Borstal school or at a detention centre or remand home.

youth employment officer in Britain, a local government official given the responsibility in a certain area to find jobs for boys and girls leaving school.

Yr. your.

yr. year.

Yrs. yours.

yt. yacht.

YU Yugoslavia's international vehicle-registration letters.

yuan the standard currency unit of China, divided into 10 chiao or 100 fen. *Syn.* Chinese People's Bank dollar. *Abbr.* Y.

Yugoslavia a federal socialist republic in eastern Europe, pop. 22 million approx. (1975); capital, Belgrade, pop. 1.2 million approx.; languages, Serbo-Croat, Macedonian, Slovenian and Albanian; currency unit, the Yugoslav dinar, divided into 100 paras. Associate member, O.E.C.D.; COMECON. *Also* Jugoslavia.

YV Venezuela's international vehicle-registration letters.

Z

ZA South Africa's international vehicle-registration letters.

Zaïre a republic in central Africa, pop. 24.5 million approx. (1975); capital, Kinshasa, pop. 1.5 million approx.; languages, French and tribal; currency unit, the zaïre, divided into 100 makuta. Member, O.A.U.; O.C.A.M.M.; Associate, E.E.C.

zaïre the standard currency unit of Zaïre, divided into 100 makuta.

Zambia a republic in central Africa, pop. 4.5 million approx. (1975); capital, Lusaka, pop. 250,000 approx.; languages, English and tribal; currency unit, the kwacha, divided into 100 ngwee. Member, (British) Commonwealth; O.A.U.

zemindar in India, a landowner charged with a duty of collecting land tax from tenant farmers and paying it to the government.

Zimbabwe (formerly Rhodesia) a self-governing country in southern Africa, pop. 6 million approx.; capital, Salisbury, pop. 450,000 approx.; languages, English, Afrikaans, Shona and Sindebele; currency unit, the Zimbabwean dollar, divided into 100 cents.

zipcode (U.S.A.) *see* postcode.

zloty the standard currency unit of Poland, divided into 100 groszy.

Zürich *see* Gnomes of Zürich.

Useful information

Metric prefixes

The metric system is built up by adding PREFIXES which are the same for every kind of measure.

The British system, unlike the metric one, is not built up in 10's: 1 lb = 16 oz = 7000 grains.

	abbreviation	*factor*
tera-	T	10^{12}
giga-	G	10^{9}
mega-	M	10^{6}
kilo-	k	10^{3}
hecto-	h	10^{2}
deca-	da	10^{1}
deci-	d	10^{-1}
centi-	c	10^{-2}
milli-	m	10^{-3}
micro-	μ	10^{-6}
nano-	n	10^{-9}
pico-	p	10^{-12}
femto-	f	10^{-15}
atto-	a	10^{-18}

Linear measure

metric

metric units			*British equivalent*
		1 millimetre (mm)	0.0394 in.
10 mm	=	1 centimetre (cm)	0.3937 in.
10 cm	=	1 decimetre (dm)	3.937 in.
10 dm	=	1 metre (m)	39.370 in.
10 m	=	1 decametre (dam)	10.94 yds.
10 dam	=	1 hectometre (hm)	109.4 yds.
10 hm	=	1 kilometre (km)	0.621 m.

British

British units						*metric equivalent*
		1 inch (in.)				25.4 m
12 in.	=	1 foot (ft.)				0.305 m
3 ft.	=	1 yard (yd.)				0.914 m
2 yds.	=	6 ft.	=	1 fathom (fm.)		1.829 m
5.5 yds.	=	16.5 ft.	=	1 rod, pole or perch		5.029 m
4 perch	=	22 yds.	=	66 ft.	= 1 chain	20.12 m
10 chain	=	220 yds.	=	660 ft.	= 1 furlong (fur.)	0.201 km
8 fur.	=	1760 yds.	=	5280 ft.	= 1 (statute) mile (m.)	1.609 km
1 U.K. nautical mile*	=	6080 ft.				1.853 km
1 international nautical mile (naut.m.)						1.852 km

Note: nautical speed is usually measured in *knots*:
1 knot = 1 nautical mile per hour.

Square measure

metric

metric units		British equivalent
	1 square millimetre (mm²)	0.0016 sq. in.
100 mm²	= 1 square centimetre (cm²)	0.1550 sq. in.
100 cm²	= 1 square decimetre (dm²)	15.5000 sq. in.
100 dm²	= 1 square metre (m²)	10.7639 sq. ft.
		(= 1.1959 sq. yds.)
100 m²	= 1 square decametre (dam²)	1076.3910 sq. ft.
100 dam²	= 1 square hectometre (hm²)*	0.0039 sq. m.
100 hm²	= 1 square kilometre (km²)	0.3861 sq. m.

British

British units		metric equivalent
	1 square inch (sq. in.)	6.4516 cm²
144 sq. in.	= 1 square foot (sq. ft.)	0.0929 m²
9 sq. ft.	= 1 square yard (sq. yd.)	0.8361 m²
30¼ sq. yds.	= 1 square perch	25.29 m²
40 sq. perch	= 1 rood	0.1012 ha
4 roods or 4840 sq. yds.	= 1 acre	0.4047 ha
640 acres	= 1 square mile (sq. m.)	2.5900 km²
100 sq. ft.	= 1 square	9.2903 m²
272¼ sq. ft.	= 1 rod of brickwork	25.2928 m²

*Note: The square hectometre is also known as a *hectare* (ha).
The hectare can be sub-divided into *ares:*

metric units			British units
100 m²	= 1 are		119.59 sq. yds.
1000 m²	= 10 ares	= 1 dekare	1195.9 sq. yds.
10 000 m²	= 100 ares	= 1 hectare	2.471 acres

Surveyor's measure

Surveyor's linear units		equivalents British	metric
	1 link	7.92 in.	20.117 cm
25 links	= 1 pole	5.50 yds.	5.029 m
100 links	= 1 chain	22 yds.	20.12 m
10 chains	= 1 furlong (fur.)	220 yds.	0.201 km
80 chains	= 8 fur.	1 mile (m.)	1.609 km

Surveyor's square units		equivalents British	metric
100 × 100 links or 10,000 sq. links			
	= 1 sq. chain	484 sq. yds.	404.7 m²
4 × 4 poles or 16 sq. poles	= 1 sq. chain		
22 × 22 yds. or 484 sq. yds.	= 1 sq. chain		
100,000 sq. links or 10 sq. chains	= 1 acre	4840 sq. yds.	0.4047 ha

Cubic or solid measure

metric

metric units		British equivalent
1000 cubic millimetres (mm³)		
= 1 cubic centimetre (cm³)		0.0610 cu. in.
1000 cubic centimetres (cm³)		
= 1 cubic decimetre (dm³)		610 cu. in.
1000 cubic decimetres (dm³)		
= 1 cubic metre (m³)		35.3147 cu. ft.

The *stere* is also used, in particular as a unit of measurement for timber:

1 cubic metre	= 1 stere	35.3147 cu. ft.
10 decisteres	= 1 stere	35.3147 cu. ft.
10 steres	= 1 decastere	353.1467 cu. ft.
		(= 13.0795 cu. yds.)

British

British units		metric equivalent
	1 cubic inch (cu. in.)	16.39 cm³
1728 cu. in.	= 1 cubic foot (cu. ft.)	0.0283 m³
27 cu. ft. or 1 load of earth	= 1 cubic yard (cu. yd.)	0.7646 m³
1 ton of shipping	= 40 cu. ft.	1.1327 m³
1 register ton of shipping	= 100 cu. ft.	2.8317 m³

Corn and dry measure

British and U.S. units

		metric equivalent British	U.S.
	1 pint (pt.)	0.568 l	0.550 l
2 pints	= 1 quart (qt.)	1.136 l	1.101 l
4 qt. or 8 pt.	= 1 gallon (gal.)	4.546 l	4.405 l
2 gal. or 16 pt.	= 1 peck (pk.)	9.092 l	8.810 l
4 pk. or 8 gal.	= 1 bushel (bu.)	36.37 l	35.24 l
2 bu. or 16 gal.	= 1 strike	72.74 l	70.48 l
4 bu. or 32 gal.	= 1 coomb	145.47 l	140.95 l
8 bu. or 64 gal.	= 1 quarter (qr.)	290.94 l	281.90 l
36 bu. or 288 gal.	= 1 chaldron*	1309.25 l	1268.57 l
40 bu. or 5 qrs. or 320 gal.	= 1 wey or load	1454.72 l	1409.52 l
2 weys or 80 bu. or 640 gal.	= 1 last	2909.44 l	2819.04 l

U.S. and British equivalents

U.S.	British
1 pint	0.9689 pt.
1 bushel	0.9689 bu.

*Note: the chaldron is now used only for coals.

Liquid measure

metric

metric units		British	U.S.
10 millilitres (ml)	= 1 centilitre (cl)	0.0176 pt.	0.0211 pt.
10 cl	= 1 decilitre (dl)	0.176 pt.	0.211 pt.
10 dl	= 1 litre (l)*	1.76 pt.	2.11 pt.
		(= 0.22 gal.)	(= 0.264 gal.)
10 l	= 1 decalitre (dal)	2.20 gal.	2.64 gal.
10 dal	= 1 hectolitre (hl)	22.0 gal.	26.4 gal.
10 hl	= 1 kilolitre (kl)	220.0 gal.	264.0 gal.

British and U.S.

British and U.S. units		metric equivalent British	metric equivalent U.S.
	1 minim (min.)	0.059 cm^3	0.062 cm^3
60 min.	= 1 fluid dram (fl. dr.)	3.552 cm^3	2.957 cm^3
8 fl. dr.	= 1 fluid ounce (fl. oz.)	28.413 cm^3	29.573 cm^3
5 fl. oz.	= 1 gill British	142.065 cm^3	
4 fl. oz.	= 1 gill U.S.A.		118.291 cm^3
4 gills	= 1 pint (pt.)	568.261 cm^3	473.163 cm^3
2 pt.	= 1 quart (qt.)	1.136 l	0.946 l
4 qt.	= 1 gallon (gal.)	4.546 l	3.785 l

U.S. and British equivalents

U.S.	British
1 fluid ounce	1.0408 fl. oz.
1 pint	0.8327 pt.
1 gallon	0.8327 gal.

*Note: 1 litre is equal in capacity to 1 cubic decimetre (1 dm^2).

Measurement of mass or weight

metric

		avoirdupois equivalent
	1 milligram (mg)	0.015 gr.
10 mg	= 1 centigram (cg)	0.154 gr.
10 cg	= 1 decigram (dg)	1.543 gr.
10 dg	= 1 gram (g)	15.43 gr. = 0.035 oz.
10 g	= 1 decagram (dag)	0.353 oz.
10 dag	= 1 hectogram (hg)	3.527 oz.
10 hg	= 1 kilogram (kg)	2.205 lb.
1000 kg	= 1 tonne (metric ton)	0.984 (long) ton = 2204.62 lb.

avoirdupois

		metric equivalent
	1 grain (gr.)	64.8 mg
	1 dram (dr.)	1.772 g
16 drams	= 1 ounce (oz.)	28.3495 g
16 oz. (= 7000 gr.)	= 1 pound (lb.)	0.4536 kg
14 lb.	= 1 stone	6.3503 kg
28 lb.	= 1 quarter (qr.)	12.7006 kg
4 qrs. or 112 lb.	= 1 hundredweight (cwt.)	50.8024 kg
20 cwt.	= 1 ton (U.K. or long ton)*	1.01605 tonnes

*Note: in the U.S.A. the *short* hundredweight and *short* ton are more common:

		metric equivalent
100 lb.	= 1 short hundredweight	45.36 kg
2000 lb.	= 1 short ton	0.9072 tonnes

Troy weight

British		metric equivalent
	1 grain	0.065 g
4 grains	= 1 carat of golf or silver	0.2592 g
6 carats	= 1 pennyweight (dwt.)	1.5552 g
20 dwt.	= 1 ounce (oz.)	31.1035 g
12 oz.	= 1 pound (lb.)	373.242 g
25 lb.	= 1 quarter (qr.)	9.331 kg
100 lb.	= 1 hundredweight (cwt.)	37.324 kg
20 cwt.	= 1 ton of gold or silver	746.48 kg

Note: the grain troy is the same as the grain avoirdupois, but the pound troy contains 5760 grains, the pound avoirdupois 7000 grains. Jewels are not weighed by this measure.

Circular measure

metric

metric units		*British equivalent*
	1 microradian (μ rad)	0.206 seconds
1000 μ rad	= 1 milliradian (m rad)	3.437 minutes
1000 m rad	= 1 radian (rad)	57.296 degrees
		= 180/π degrees

British

British units		*metric equivalent*
	1 second	4.860 μ rad
60 seconds	= 1 minute	0.2909 μ rad
60 minutes	= 1 degree	17.45 μ rad
		= π/180 rad
45 degrees	= 1 oxtant	π/4 rad
60 degrees	= 1 sextant	π/3 rad
90 degrees	= 1 quadrant or 1 right angle	π/2 rad
360 degrees	= 1 circle or 1 circumference	2 π rad
1 grade or gon	= 1/100th of a right angle	π/200 rad

Temperature

Equations for conversion

$$°\text{Fahrenheit} = (\tfrac{9}{5} \times x\,°\text{C}) + 32$$
$$°\text{Centigrade} = \tfrac{5}{9} \times (x\,°\text{F} - 32)$$
$$°\text{Kelvin} = x\,°\text{C} + 273.15$$

Some equivalents

	Centigrade	Fahrenheit
Normal temperature of the human body	36.9°C	98.4°F
Freezing point	0°C	32°F
Boiling point	100°C	212°F

Table of equivalents

Fahrenheit	Centigrade	Centigrade	Fahrenheit
100°C	212°F	30°C	86°F
90°C	194°F	20°C	68°F
80°C	176°F	10°C	50°F
70°C	158°F	0°C	32°F
60°C	140°F	−10°C	14°F
50°C	122°F	−20°C	4°F
40°C	104°F	−30°C	−22°F

Paper measures

International standard sizes*

designation	metric size mm	British equivalent inches
A0	841 × 1189	33.11 × 46.81
A1	594 × 841	23.39 × 33.11
A2	420 × 594	16.54 × 23.39
A3	297 × 420	11.69 × 16.54
A4	210 × 297	8.27 × 11.69
A5	148 × 210	5.83 × 8.27
A6	105 × 148	4.13 × 5.83
A7	74 × 105	2.91 × 4.13
A8	52 × 74	2.05 × 2.91
A9	37 × 52	1.46 × 2.05
A10	26 × 37	1.02 × 1.46

book page sizes – metric and British

designation		trimmed 8vo page size mm	inches
Crown	metric	186 × 123	$7^3/8 \times 4^7/8$
	British	184 × 124	$7^1/4 \times 4^7/8$
Large Crown	metric	198 × 129	$7^3/4 \times 5^1/8$
	British	197 × 130	$7^3/4 \times 5^1/8$
Demy	metric	216 × 138	$8^1/2 \times 5^3/8$
	British	216 × 140	$8^1/2 \times 5^1/2$
Royal	metric	234 × 156	$9^1/4 \times 6^1/8$
	British	248 × 156	$9^3/4 \times 6^1/8$
A5	metric	210 × 148	$8^1/4 \times 5^7/8$

paper quantities

traditional		modern standard†
24 sheets	= 1 quire	25 sheets
20 quires (480 sheets)	= 1 ream	⎰
516 sheets	= 1 printer's ream	⎱ 500 sheets

*Note: standard international paper sizes have now largely replaced the traditional British paper sizes.

†Note: the change to metrication in the paper trade has led to standard paper quantities based on subdivisions of 1,000.

Chemical symbols

symbol	element	atomic number	symbol	element	atomic number
Ac	actinium	89	Mn	manganese	25
Ag	silver	47	Mo	molybdenum	42
Al	aluminium	13	N	nitrogen	7
Am	americium	95	Na	sodium	11
Ar	argon	18	Nb	niobium	41
As	arsenic	33	Nd	neodymium	60
At	astatine	85	Ne	neon	10
Au	gold	79	Ni	nickel	28
B	boron	5	No	nobelium	102
Ba	barium	56	Np	neptunium	93
Be	beryllium	4	O	oxygen	8
Bi	bismuth	83	Os	osmium	76
Bk	berkelium	97	P	phosphorus	15
Br	bromine	35	Pa	protactinium	91
C	carbon	6	Pb	lead	82
Ca	calcium	20	Pd	palladium	46
Cd	cadmium	48	Pm	promethium	61
Ce	cerium	58	Po	polonium	84
Cf	californium	98	Pr	praseodymium	59
Cl	chlorine	17	Pt	platinum	78
Cm	curium	96	Pu	plutonium	94
Co	cobalt	27	Ra	radium	88
Cr	chromium	24	Rb	rubidium	37
Cs	caesium	55	Re	rhenium	75
Cu	copper	29	Rf	rutherfordium	104
Dy	dysprosium	66	Rh	rhodium	45
Er	erbium	68	Rn	radon	86
Es	einsteinium	99	Ru	ruthenium	44
Eu	europium	63	S	sulphur	16
F	fluorine	9	Sb	antimony	51
Fe	iron	26	Sc	scandium	21
Fm	fermium	100	Se	selenium	34
Fr	francium	87	Si	silicon	14
Ga	gallium	31	Sm	samarium	62
Gd	gadolinium	64	Sn	tin	50
Ge	germanium	32	Sr	strontium	38
H	hydrogen	1	Ta	tantalum	73
He	helium	2	Tb	terbium	65
Hf	hafnium	72	Tc	technetium	43
Hg	mercury	80	Te	tellurium	52
Hn	hahnium	105	Th	thorium	90
Ho	holmium	67	Ti	titanium	22
I	iodine	53	Tl	thallium	81
In	indium	49	Tm	thulium	69
Ir	iridium	77	U	uranium	92
K	potassium	19	V	vanadium	23
Kr	krypton	36	W	tungsten	74
La	lanthanum	57	Xe	xenon	54
Li	lithium	3	Y	yttrium	39
Lr	lawrencium	103	Yb	ytterbium	70
Lu	lutetium	71	Zn	zinc	30
Md	mendelevium	101	Zr	zirconium	40
Mg	magnesium	12			

Countries of the world

This chart shows the countries of the world with
their adjectives, languages and currencies. The
languages given for each country are the main
languages used in business; in many cases, however,
other local and regional languages may also be
widely spoken and used.

country	adjective	language	currency
AFGHANISTAN	Afghan (*person, sing.*: Afghanistani; *people*: Afghans)	Pashto, Farsi	afghani (Af) = 100 puli
ALBANIA	Albanian	Albanian	lek (Lk) = 100 qindars/qintars
ALGERIA	Algerian	Arabic, French	Algerian dinar (AD) = 100 centimes
ANDORRA	Andorran	Catalan	French franc (Fr) = 100 centimes (Spanish pesetas also widely used)
ANGOLA	Angolan	Portuguese	kwanza (Kw) = 100 cents
ANTIGUA	Antiguan	English	East Caribbean dollar (ECar$) = 100 cents
ARGENTINA	Argentinian	Spanish	Argentine peso (Ar P) = 100 centavos
AUSTRALIA	Australian	English	Australian dollar (A$) = 100 cents
AUSTRIA	Austrian	German	Schilling (Sch) = 100 groschen
BAHAMAS	Bahamian	English	Bahamian dollar (Ba$) = 100 cents
BAHRAIN	Bahraini	Arabic	Bahraini dinar (BD) = 1000 fils
BANGLADESH	Bangladesh (*person sing.*: Bangladeshi)	Bengali	taka (Tk) = 100 poisha
BARBADOS	Barbadian	English	Barbados dollar (Bds$) = 100 cents
BELGIUM	Belgian	Flemish, French	Belgian franc (Bf) = 100 centimes
BELIZE	Belizean	English	Belize dollar (B$) = 100 cents
BENIN	Beninese	French	C.F.A. franc (CFA Fr) = 100 centimes

country	adjective	language	currency
BERMUDA	Bermudan	English	Bermuda dollar (Bda$) = 100 cents
BHUTAN	Bhutani	Bhutanese, Dzongkha	ngultrum (N) = 2 tikchung/100 Indian paise
BOLIVIA	Bolivian	Spanish	Bolivian peso (B$) = 100 centavos
BOTSWANA	Botswanan (*person sing.*: Motswana, Batswana; *pl.*: Batswana; *people*: Batswana)	Tswana, English	pula (Pu) = 100 cents
BRAZIL	Brazilian	Portuguese	cruzeiro (Cr) = 100 centavos
BRUNEI	Bruneian	Malay	Brunei dollar (Br$) = 100 cents
BULGARIA	Bulgarian	Bulgarian	lev (*pl.* leva) (Lv) = 100 stotinki
BURMA	Burmese	Burmese	kyat (Kt) = 100 pyas
BURUNDI	Burundian	French	Burundi franc (Bur Fr) = 100 centimes
CAMEROON	Cameroonian	English, French	C.F.A. franc (CFA Fr) = 100 centimes
CANADA	Canadian	English, French	Canadian dollar (Can $) = 100 cents
CAPE VERDE ISLANDS	Cape Verdean	Portuguese	Cape Verde escudo (CV Esc) = 100 centavos
CAYMAN ISLANDS	Cayman Island (*person sing.*: Cayman Islander)	English	Cayman Island dollar (Cay I $) = 100 cents
CENTRAL AFRICAN REPUBLIC		French, Sango	C.F.A. franc (CFA Fr) = 100 centimes
CHAD	Chadian	French	C.F.A. franc (CFA Fr) = 100 centimes
CHILE	Chilean	Spanish	Chilean peso (Ch$) = 100 centavos
CHINA	Chinese	Mandarin Chinese	yuan (Y)/Chinese People's Bank dollar = 10 chiao (jiao)/100 fen
COLOMBIA	Colombian	Spanish	Colombian peso (Col$) = 100 centavos
CONGO	Congolese	French	C.F.A. franc (CFA Fr) = 100 centimes
COSTA RICA	Costa Rican	Spanish	Costa Rican colón (CR ₡) = 100 centimos

country	adjective	language	currency
CUBA	Cuban	Spanish	Cuban peso (Cub$) = 100 centavos
CYPRUS	Cypriot	Greek, Turkish	Cyprus pound (C£) = 1000 mils
CZECHOSLOVAKIA	Czech (*person sing.*: Czech or Czechoslovak)	Czech, Slovak	koruna (*pl.* koruny) (Kčs) crown = 100 haleru
DAHOMEY *see* Benin			
DENMARK	Danish (*person sing.*: Dane)	Danish	krone (*pl.* kroner) (D Kr) = 100 örer
DJIBOUTI	Djibouti	French, Arabic	Djibouti franc (Dj Fr) = 100 centimes
DOMINICA	Dominican	English	East Caribbean dollar (ECar$) = 100 ¢ents
DOMINICAN REPUBLIC	Dominican	Spanish	Dominican Republic peso (DR$) = 8 reals/100 centavos
ECUADOR	Ecuadorian	Spanish	sucre (Su) = 100 centavos
EGYPT	Egyptian	Arabic	Egyptian pound (E£) = 100 piastres/ 1000 millièmes
EL SALVADOR	Salvadorian	Spanish	El Salvador colón (ES ₡) = 100 centavos
EQUATORIAL GUINEA	Equatorial Guinean (*person sing.*: Bantu) (*people*: Bantu)	Spanish	ekpwele/peseta Guineana (E) = 100 céntimos
ETHIOPIA	Ethiopian	Amharic	birr (Br) = 100 cents
FALKLAND ISLANDS	Falkland Island (*person sing.*: Falkland Islander)	English	Falkland Islands pound (FI£) = 100 pence
FIJI	Fijian	English	Fiji dollar (F$) = 100 cents
FINLAND	Finnish (*person sing.*: Finn)	Finnish, Swedish	Finnish mark/markka (*pl.* markkaa) (F Mk) = 100 pennia
FRANCE	French (*person sing.*: Frenchman; *fem.*: Frenchwoman; *pl.*: Frenchmen; *people*: French)	French	French franc (Fr/F/Frs) = 100 centimes
FRENCH GUIANA	Guianan	French	French franc (Fr/F/Frs) = 100 centimes
GABON	Gabonese	French	C.F.A. franc (CFA Fr) = 100 centimes

country	adjective	language	currency
THE GAMBIA	Gambian	English	dalasi (Di) = 100 butut
GERMANY, DEMOCRATIC REPUBLIC OF	East German	German	DDR Mark/Ostmark (M) = 100 pfennig
GERMANY, FEDERAL REPUBLIC OF	West German	German	Deutsche Mark (DM) = 100 pfennig
GHANA	Ghanaian	English	cedi (¢) = 100 pesewas
GIBRALTAR	Gibraltarian	English	Gibraltar pound (Gib£) = 100 pence
GREECE	Greek	Greek	drachma (Dr) = 100 lepta
GRENADA	Grenadian	English	East Caribbean dollar (ECar$) = 100 cents
GUATEMALA	Guatamalan	Spanish	quetzal (Q) = 100 centavos
GUINEA	Guinean	French	syli/suli/sily (Sy) = 100 cauris
GUINEA-BISSAU		Portuguese, Guinea creole	Guinea-Bissau peso (GB P) = 100 centavos
GUYANA	Guyanese	English	Guyana dollar (Guy$) = 100 cents
HAITI	Haitian	French	gourde (Gde) = 100 centimes
HONDURAS	Honduran	Spanish	lempira (La) = 100 centavos
HONG KONG		English	Hong Kong dollar (HK$) = 100 cents
HUNGARY	Hungarian	Magyar	forint (Ft) = 100 filler
ICELAND	Icelandic (*person sing.*: Icelander)	Icelandic	Icelandic króna (*pl.* kronur) (I Kr) = 100 aurar
INDIA	Indian	Hindi, English	Indian rupee (Re; *pl.* Rs) = 100 paise
INDONESIA	Indonesian	Indonesian, Bahasa	rupiah (Rp) = 100 sen
IRAN	Iranian	Farsi, Persian	rial (Rl) = 100 dinars
IRAQ	Iraqi	Arabic	Iraqi dinar (ID) = 1000 fils
IRELAND (ÉIRE)	Irish (*person sing.*: Irishman; *fem.*: Irishwoman; *pl.*: Irishmen; *people*: Irish)	Irish, English	Irish pound (£)/punt = 100 pence

country	adjective	language	currency
ISRAEL	Israeli	Hebrew, Arabic	shekel (IS) = 100 new agorot
ITALY	Italian	Italian	lira (*pl.* lire) (L) = 100 centesimi
IVORY COAST	Ivorian	French	C.F.A. franc (CFA Fr) = 100 centimes
JAMAICA	Jamaican	English	Jamaican dollar (Jam$) = 100 cents
JAPAN	Japanese	Japanese	yen (Y) = 100 sen
JORDAN	Jordanian	Arabic	Jordanian dinar (JD) = 1000 fils
KAMPUCHEA (CAMBODIA)	Kampuchean, Cambodian	Khmer (Cambodian)	riel (C Rl) = 100 sen
KENYA	Kenyan	English, Swahili	Kenyan shilling (KSh) = 100 cents
KOREA, NORTH	North Korean	Korean	North Korean won (NK W) = 100 jon
KOREA, SOUTH	South Korean	Korean	South Korean won/hwan (Sk W) = 100 chon
KUWAIT	Kuwaiti	Arabic	Kuwaiti dinar (KD) = 1000 fils
LAOS	Laotian	Lao	kip pot po (Kp) = 100 at
LEBANON	Lebanese	Arabic	Lebanese pound (L£) = 100 piastres
LESOTHO	Sesotho (*person sing.*: Mosotho; *pl.*: Basotho; *people*: Basotho)	Sesotho, English	loti (*pl.* maloti) (L) = 100 lisente
LIBERIA	Liberian	English	Liberian dollar (L$) = 100 cents
LIBYA	Libya	Arabic	Libyan dinar (LD) = 1000 dirhams
LIECHTENSTEIN	Liechtenstein (*person sing.*: Liechtensteiner)	German	Swiss franc (S Fr) = 100 centimes
LUXEMBURG	Luxemburg (*person sing.*: Luxemburger)	French, German	Luxemburg franc (L Fr) = 100 centimes
MALAGASY REPUBLIC	(*person sing.*: Malagasy citizen)	French	Malagasy franc (Mal Fr) = 100 centimes
MALAWI	Malawian	English	Malawi kwacha (Mk) = 100 tambala
MALAYSIA	Malaysian	Malay	ringgit/Malaysian dollar (M$) = 100 cents

country	adjective	language	currency
MALDIVES	Maldivian	Divehi	Maldivian rupee (MvRe) = 100 paise
MALI	Malian	French	Mali franc (M Fr) = 100 centimes
MALTA	Maltese	Maltese	Maltese pound (M£) = 100 cents/1000 mils
MAURITANIA	Mauritanian	Arabic, French	ouguiya (U) = 5 khoums
MAURITIUS	Mauritian	English	Mauritius rupee (Mau Rs) = 100 cents
MEXICO	Mexican	Spanish	Mexican peso (Mex$) = 100 centavos
MONACO	Monegasque	French	French franc (Fr/F/Frs) = 100 centimes
MONGOLIAN REPUBLIC	Mongolian	Khalka, Mongolian	tugrik (Tug) = 100 möngös
MOROCCO	Moroccan	Arabic, French	dirham (Dh) = 100 centimes/ Moroccan francs
MOZAMBIQUE	Mozambiquean	Portuguese	metical (*pl.* meticais) (M) = 100 centavos
NAMIBIA	Namibian	Afrikaans, English	South African rand (R) = 100 cents
NAURU (NAOERO)	Nauruan	Nauruan	Australian dollar (A$) = 100 cents
NEPAL	Nepalese	Nepali	Nepalese rupee (N Re) = 100 paise
THE NETHERLANDS	Dutch (*person sing.*: Dutchman; *fem.*: Dutchwoman; *pl.*: Dutchmen; *people*: Dutch)	Dutch	guilder (gulden/florin) (Gld/Fl) = 100 cents
NEW ZEALAND	New Zealand, Maori (*person sing.*: New Zealander)	English	New Zealand dollar (NZ$) = 100 cents
NICARAGUA	Nicaraguan	Spanish	códoba (C) = 100 centavos
NIGER	Nigerien	French	C.F.A. franc (CFA Fr) = 100 centimes
NIGERIA	Nigerian	English	naira (N̶) = 100 kobo
NORWAY	Norwegian	Norwegian	krone (*pl.* kroner)/crown (N Kr) = 100 örer
OMAN	Omani	Arabic	rial Omani (RO) = 1000 baizas

country	adjective	language	currency
PAKISTAN	Pakistani	Bengali, Urdu, English	Pakistan rupee (Pak Re) = 100 paise
PANAMA	Panamanian	Spanish	balboa (Ba) = 100 centésimos
PAPUA NEW GUINEA	Papuan	Papuan, English	kina (Ka) = 100 toea
PARAGUAY	Paraguayan	Spanish	guarani (G) = 100 centimos
PERU	Peruvian	Spanish	sol (S) = 100 centavos
PHILIPPINES	Philippine (*person sing.*: Filipino; *pl.*: Filipinos)	Pilipino, English	Philippine peso (PP) = 100 centavos
POLAND	Polish	Polish	zloty (Zl) = 100 groszy
PORTUGAL	Portuguese	Portuguese	Portuguese escudo (Esc) = 100 centavos
PUERTO RICO	Puerto Rican	Spanish, English	United States dollar (US$) = 100 cents
QATAR	Qatari	Arabic	Qatar riyal (QR)/Dubai riyal = 100 dirhams
ROMANIA	Romanian	Romanian	leu (*pl.* lei) = 100 bani
RWANDA	Rwandan	Kinyarwanda, French	Rwanda franc (Rw Fr) = 100 centimes
SAN MARINO	San Marinese	Italian	Italian lira (*pl.* lire) (L) = 100 centesimi
SAUDI ARABIA	Saudi Arabian (*person sing.*: Saudi, Saudi Arabian)	Arabic	Saudi riyal (SA R) = 100 halalah
SENEGAL	Senegalese	French	C.F.A. franc (CFA Fr) = 100 centimes
SEYCHELLES	Seychellois	English, French, Creole	Seychelles rupee (S Re) = 100 cents
SIERRA LEONE	Sierra Leonean	English	leone (Le) = 100 cents
SINGAPORE	Singaporean	Malay, Chinese, Tamil, English	Singapore dollar (Sing$) = 100 cents
SOMALIA	Somali	Somali	Somali shilling (So Sh) = 100 cents
SOUTH AFRICA	South African	Afrikaans, English	South African rand (R) = 100 cents

country	adjective	language	currency
SPAIN	Spanish (*person sing.*: Spaniard)	Spanish	peseta (Pa) = 100 centimos
SRI LANKA	Sri Lankan	Sinhala, Tamil	Sri Lanka rupee (SL Re) = 100 cents
SUDAN	Sudanese	Arabic	Sudanese pound (Sud£) = 100 piastres/ 1000 millièmes
SURINAM	Surinamese	Dutch	Surinam guilder (S Gld) = 100 cents
SWAZILAND	Swazi	Siswati, English	lilangeni (*pl.* emalangeni) (Li) South African rand (R)
SWEDEN	Swedish (*person sing.*: Swede)	Swedish	Swedish krona (*pl.* kronor)/ crown (S Kr) = 100 örer
SWITZERLAND	Swiss	German, French, Italian	Swiss franc (SFr) = 100 centimes
SYRIA	Syrian	Arabic	Syrian pound (S£) = 100 piastres
TAIWAN	Taiwanese	Chinese	Taiwan dollar (T$) = 100 cents
TANZANIA	Tanzanian	Swahili, English	Tanzanian shilling (TSh) = 100 cents
THAILAND	Thai	Thai	baht (Bt) = 100 satang
TOGO	Togolese	French	C.F.A. franc (CFA Fr) = 100 centimes
TRINIDAD AND TOBAGO	Trinidadian, Tobagan	English	Trinidad and Tobago dollar (TT$) = 100 cents
TUNISIA	Tunisian	Arabic	Tunisian dinar (TD) = 1000 millimes
TURKEY	Turkish (*person sing.*: Turk)	Turkish	Turkish lira (*pl.* lire) (TL) = 100 kurus
UGANDA	Ugandan	Swahili, English	Ugandan shilling (USh) = 100 cents
UNITED ARAB EMIRATES		Arabic	U.A.E. dirhams (UAE Dh) = 100 fils
UNITED KINGDOM OF GREAT BRITAIN AND NORTHERN IRELAND	British	English	pound sterling (£) = 100 pence
UNION OF SOVIET SOCIALIST REPUBLICS	Soviet, Russian	Russian	rouble (ruble) (Rub) = 100 copecks (kopecks)

country	adjective	language	currency
UNITED STATES OF AMERICA	American	English	dollar (US$) = 100 cents
UPPER VOLTA	Voltaic (*person sing.*: Voltain)	French	C.F.A. franc (CFA Fr) = 100 centimes
URUGUAY	Uruguayan	Spanish	Uruguayan new peso (UN$) = 100 centésimos
VENEZUELA	Venezuelan	Spanish	bolivar (B) = 100 céntimos
VIETNAM	Vietnamese	Vietnamese	dong (D) = 10 hao/100 xu
WESTERN SAMOA	Samoan	English, Samoan	tala/Western Samoan dollar (WS$) = 100 cents/sene
YEMEN (ADEN)/ SOUTH YEMEN	Yemeni	Arabic	South Yemeni dinar (YD) = 1000 fils
YEMEN (SAN'A)/ NORTHERN YEMEN	Yemeni	Arabic	Yemeni riyal (YR) = 100 fils
YUGOSLAVIA	Yugoslavian (*person sing.*: Yugoslav)	Serbo-Croat, Slovenian, Macedonian	Yugoslav dinar (Yu D) = 100 paras
ZAÏRE	Zaïrean	French	Zaïre (Z) = 100 makuta
ZAMBIA	Zambian	English	kwacha (K) = 100 ngwee
ZIMBABWE	Zimbabwean	English	Zimbabwean dollar (Z$) = 100 cents

International time differences

In the table the time in each country is given relative to Greenwich Mean Time (GMT). The abbreviations used are as follows:

a 3 hr. = 3 hours ahead of GMT
b 3 hr. = 3 hours behind GMT
GMT = same as GMT

An asterisk (*) indicates that the country in question operates Summer Time or Daylight Saving Time during a certain period of the year, thereby altering the stated relationship to the GMT standard for that period.

country	time	country	time
Afghanistan	*a* 4½ hr.	France	*a* 1 hr.*
Albania	*a* 1 hr.*	French Guiana	*b* 3 hr.
Algeria	*a* 1 hr.*	Gabon	*a* 1 hr.
Andorra	*a* 1 hr.	The Gambia	GMT
Angola	*a* 1 hr.	Germany,	
Antigua	*b* 4 hr.	Democratic	
Argentina	*b* 3 hr.	Republic of	*a* 1 hr.
Australia	*a* 8–10 hr.*	Germany,	
Austria	*a* 1 hr.	Federal	
Bahamas	*b* 5 hr.	Republic of	*a* 1 hr.
Bahrain	*a* 3 hr.	Ghana	GMT
Bangladesh	*a* 6 hr.	Gibraltar	*a* 1 hr.
Barbados	*b* 4 hr.	Greece	*a* 2 hr.*
Belgium	*a* 1 hr.	Grenada	*b* 4 hr.
Belize	*b* 6 hr.	Guatemala	*b* 6 hr.
Benin	*a* 1 hr.	Guinea	GMT
Bermuda	*b* 4 hr.	Guinea-Bissau	GMT
Bhutan	*a* 5½ hr.	Guyana	*b* 3 hr.
Bolivia	*b* 4 hr.	Haiti	*b* 5 hr.
Botswana	*a* 2 hr.	Honduras	*b* 6 hr.
Brazil	*b* 3 hr.	Hong Kong	*a* 8 hr.
Brunei	*a* 8 hr.	Hungary	*a* 1 hr.
Bulgaria	*a* 2 hr.	Iceland	GMT
Burma	*a* 6½ hr.	India	*a* 5½ hr.
Burundi	*a* 2 hr.	Indonesia	*a* 7–9 hr.
Cameroon	*a* 1 hr.	Iran	*a* 3½ hr.
Canada	*b* 3½–8 hr.*	Iraq	*a* 3 hr.
Cape Verde Islands	*b* 1 hr.	Ireland	GMT*
Cayman Islands	*b* 5 hr.	Israel	*a* 2 hr.
Central African		Italy	*a* 1 hr.*
Republic	*a* 1 hr.	Ivory Coast	GMT
Chad	*a* 1 hr.	Jamaica	*b* 5 hr.
Chile	*b* 4 hr.	Japan	*a* 9 hr.
China	*a* 6–8 hr.	Jordan	*a* 2 hr.*
Colombia	*b* 5 hr.	Kampuchea	*a* 7 hr.
Congo	*a* 1 hr.	Kenya	*a* 3 hr.
Costa Rica	*b* 6 hr.	Korea, North	*a* 9 hr.
Cuba	*b* 5 hr.	Korea, South	*a* 9 hr.
Cyprus	*a* 2 hr.*	Kuwait	*a* 3 hr.
Czechoslovakia	*a* 1 hr.	Laos	*a* 7 hr.
Denmark	*a* 1 hr.	Lebanon	*a* 2 hr.*
Djibouti	*a* 3 hr.	Lesotho	*a* 2 hr.
Dominica	*b* 4 hr.	Liberia	GMT
Dominican Republic	*b* 5 hr.	Libya	*a* 2 hr.
Ecuador	*b* 5 hr.	Liechtenstein	*a* 1 hr.
Egypt	*a* 2 hr.	Luxemburg	*a* 1 hr.*
El Salvador	*b* 6 hr.	Malagasy Republic	*a* 3 hr.
Equatorial Guinea	*a* 1 hr.	Malawi	*a* 2 hr.
Ethiopia	*a* 3 hr.	Malaysia	*a* 7½–8 hr.
Falkland Islands	*b* 3–4 hr.	Maldives	*a* 5 hr.
Fiji	*a* 12 hr.	Mali	GMT
Finland	*a* 2 hr.	Malta	*a* 1 hr.

International time differences *(continued)*

country	time	country	time
Mauritania	GMT	Singapore	a 7½ hr.
Mauritius	a 4 hr.	Somalia	a 3 hr.
Mexico	b 6–7 hr.*	South Africa	a 2 hr.
Monaco	a 1 hr.*	Spain	a 1 hr.*
Mongolian Republic	a 8 hr.	Sri Lanka	a 5½ hr.
Morocco	GMT	Sudan	a 2 hr.
Mozambique	a 2 hr.	Surinam	b 3½ hr.
Namibia	a 2 hr.	Swaziland	a 2 hr.
Nauru	a 11½ hr.	Sweden	a 1 hr.
Nepal	a 5 hr. 40 min.	Switzerland	a 1 hr.
The Netherlands	a 1 hr.*	Syria	a 2 hr.*
New Zealand	a 12 hr.*	Taiwan	a 8 hr.
Nicaragua	b 6 hr.	Tanzania	a 3 hr.
Niger	a 1 hr.	Thailand	a 7 hr.
Nigeria	a 1 hr.	Togo	GMT
Norway	a 1 hr.	Trinidad & Tobago	b 4 hr.
Oman	a 4 hr.	Tunisia	a 1 hr.
Pakistan	a 5 hr.	Turkey	a 2 hr.*
Panama	b 5 hr.	Uganda	a 3 hr.
Papua New Guinea	a 10 hr.	United Arab Emirates	a 4 hr.
Paraguay	b 4 hr.	U.K.	GMT*
Peru	b 5 hr.	U.S.A.	b 5–9 hr.*
Philippines	a 8 hr.	U.S.S.R.	a 3–13 hr.
Poland	a 1 hr.*	Upper Volta	GMT
Portugal	GMT*	Uruguay	b 3 hr.
Puerto Rico	b 4 hr.	Venezuela	b 4½ hr.
Qatar	a 3 hr.	Vietnam	a 7 hr.
Romania	a 2 hr.	Western Samoa	a 11 hr.
Rwanda	a 2 hr.	Yemen, North	a 3 hr.
San Marino	a 1 hr.	Yemen, South	a 3 hr.
Saudi Arabia	a 3 hr.	Yugoslavia	a 1 hr.
Senegal	GMT	Zaïre	a 1–2 hr.
Seychelles	a 4 hr.	Zambia	a 2 hr.
Sierra Leone	GMT	Zimbabwe	a 2 hr.